FINAL SOLUTION

Also by David Cesarani

Arthur Koestler:
The Homeless Mind

Justice Delayed:
How Britain Became a Refuge for Nazi War Criminals

Eichmann:
His Life and Crimes

Major Farran's Hat:
Murder, Scandal and Britain's War Against Jewish Terrorism 1945–1948

DAVID CESARANI

FINAL SOLUTION

THE FATE OF THE JEWS 1933–1949

St. Martin's Press
New York

www.stmartins.com

The acknowledgements on pages xvii and 1014 constitute an extension of this copyright page.

Map artwork by ML Design

Library of Congress Cataloging-in-Publication Data

Names: Cesarani, David, author.
Title: Final solution : the fate of the Jews 1933–1949 / David Cesarani.
Description: First U.S. Edition. | New York : St. Martin's Press, 2016.
Identifiers: LCCN 2016033310| ISBN 9781250000835 (hardcover) |
    ISBN 9781250037961 (e-book)
Subjects: LCSH: Holocaust, Jewish (1939–1945) | World War, 1939–1945—Jews. | Holocaust,
    Jewish (1939–1945)—Causes. | BISAC: HISTORY / Holocaust.
Classification: LCC D804.3 .C434 2016 | DDC 940.53/18—dc23
LC record available at https://lccn.loc.gov/2016033310

Our books may be purchased in bulk for promotional, educational, or business use. Please contact your local bookseller or the Macmillan Corporate and Premium Sales Department at 1-800-221-7945, extension 5442, or by e-mail at MacmillanSpecialMarkets@macmillan.com.

First published in Great Britain by Macmillan, an imprint of Pan Macmillan

First U.S. Edition: November 2016

10 9 8 7 6 5 4 3 2 1

CONTENTS

Maps

1. Central Europe, September 1940

SWEDEN

DENMARK

Copenhagen

North
Sea

UNITED
KINGDOM

NETHERLANDS

Amsterdam

London

Hamburg
Neuengamme

Ravensbrück
Sachsenhausen
Berlin

GERMANY

Leipzig

Dresden

Antwerp

Brussels

BELGIUM

Cologne

Buchenwald

Prague

PROT
BOHE

LUX.

Frankfurt-am-Main

Flossenbürg

Drancy

Paris

Nuremberg

FRANCE

Baden-Baden

Mauthausen

Dachau

Munich

Linz

Salzburg

AUSTRIA

Berne

Vichy

Lyons

UNOCCUPIED
ZONE

Milan

Venice

Adriatic
Sea

Gurs

Genoa

ITALY

Le Vernet

Les Milles

Rivesaltes

Marseilles

Ligurian
Sea

SPAIN

0   100   200   300 miles

0   100   200   300   400   500 kilometres

Rome

LATVIA

Riga

Baltic States to USSR, 1940

⊗ Shauli

LITHUANIA

Baltic Sea

THE CORRIDOR

Danzig

Königsberg

EAST PRUSSIA

Kaunus ⊗

⊗ Vilnius

Minsk

USSR

Poznan

General Government

⊗ Warsaw

Lodz ⊗

⊗ Piotrków

Lublin

⊗ 🗼

to USSR, 1939

Kiev

Breslau

Nisko ⊗

P O L A N D

Bedzin ⊗

⊗ Cracow

Lwow

ECTORATE OF MIA & MORAVIA

SLOVAKIA

to Hungary, 1939

Bratislava

Vienna

Awarded to Hungary from Slovakia, 1938

Awarded to Hungary from Romania, 1940

to USSR, 1940

Budapest

H U N G A R Y

R O M A N I A

Belgrade

Bucharest ●

YUGOSLAVIA

to Bulgaria, 1940

Black Sea

Germany, March 1938

Germany, September 1940

Other international boundaries, 1940

Other international boundaries obsolete by 1940

Other boundaries

Concentration Camp

Internment camp

Transit or other camp

⊗ Ghetto/city

2. The Limit of German Occupation of Europe, December 1941

Legend:

— Limit of German occupation, 5 December 1941

- - - Army Group boundaries

—— Reichskommissariats established in the territory of the USSR

------ Internal German boundaries

- - - International boundaries

—— Greater Germany

☠ Death camp

⚱ Concentration or transit camp

⊗ Ghetto/city

☠ Killing site

NORWAY

Oslo

Stockholm

SWEDEN

DENMARK

Copenhagen

Baltic

Danzig

North Sea

UNITED KINGDOM

London

Westerbork

Amsterdam

NETHERLANDS

Vught

Malines/Mechelen

Brussels

BELGIUM

Compiègne

Drancy

Paris

Pithiviers

FRANCE

Natzweiler

Strasbourg

Hamburg

Neuengamme

Ravensbrück

Sachsenhausen

Berlin

Bergen-Belsen

GERMANY

Posen

Dora-Mittelbau (Nordhausen)

Leipzig

Buchenwald

Frankfurt-am-Main

Theresienstadt

Katowice

Prague

Ostrava

Flossenberg

PROTECTORATE OF BOHEMIA & MORAVIA

Dachau

Munich

Linz

Mauthausen

Vienna

Zurich

Salzburg

SWITZERLAND

Bratislava

Lyons

UNOCCUPIED ZONE– UNTIL NOVEMBER 1942

Milan

San Sebba

Zagreb

Venice

Trieste

Campo di Fossoli

CROATIA

ITALY

Marseilles

Leningrad

SOVIET UNION

Tallinn

ARMY GROUP
NORTH

Riga–Bikernieki Forest
⊗ ☠

REICHSKOMMISSARIAT
OSTLAND

Shauli ⊗   Daugavpils ⊗

Kaunus–Ninth Fort
⊗ ☠

ARMY GROUP
CENTRE

Königsberg

⊗ ☠
Vilnius–Ponary   ☠
                Minsk ☠

Stutthof

⊗ Grodno

Bialystok ⊗

BIALYSTOK

Treblinka ☠

☠
Chelmno   ⊗ Warsaw

⊗ Lodz   Sobibor ☠

GENERAL
GOVERNMENT   ⊗ Lublin
                ☠ Majdanek

REICHSKOMMISSARIAT

Babi Yar
☠
☠ Kiev

ARMY GROUP
SOUTH

Auschwitz-
Birkenau ☠
       ⊗ Cracow

Nisko ●   ☠ Belzec
        ● Lwow

Kamenets-Podolski
☠
                ☠
SLOVAKIA   TRANSNISTRIA
                ☠
                    ☠
Cernauti ●   ☠
                    ☠   Bogdanovka
                  ☠ ⊗ ☠
Iasi ☠   Chisenau
                ☠ Odessa

UKRAINE

Budapest ●

HUNGARY

ROMANIA

Black Sea

Belgrade ●

SERBIA

0   100   200   300 miles

0   100   200   300   400   500 kilometres

ROMANIA
Bucharest

Belgrade

SERBIA

CROATIA

MONTENEGRO

Sofia

BULGARIA

ALBANIA (ITALIAN)

Tirana

Skopje

MACEDONIA

THRACE

Adriatic Sea

Naples

ITALY

Salonica ⊗

to Albania

Aegean Sea

Messina

Athens ⊗

GREECE

Mediterranean

CRETE

Benghazi

Tobruk

LIBYA (ITALIAN)

0   100   200   300 miles

0   100   200   300   400   500 kilometres

3. The Eastern Mediterranean in the Second World War

German occupation zone	
Italian occupation until July 1943 then German occupation until 1944	
Annexed by Bulgaria	
Bulgarian occupation until September 1943 then German occupation until 1944	
••••••• Obsolete frontier of Greece	
— — — International frontiers, 1943	
British Internment camps	
⊗ Ghetto	

Black Sea

Istanbul

Ankara

T U R K E Y

Alexandretta

DODECANESE
(ITALIAN)

CYPRUS
(BRITISH)

Caraolos

Dekhilia

SYRIA

LEBANON

Beirut

a n   S e a

Haifa

Athlit

Tel Aviv

Jerusalem

PALESTINE
(BR. MANDATE)

TRANSJORDAN
(BR. MANDATE)

SAUDI
ARABIA

Alexandria

El Alamein

E G Y P T

Cairo

List of Illustrations

Section One

1. Hitler and Hindenburg shake hands at 'The Day of Potsdam' on 21 March 1933.
2. A stormtrooper enforces the boycott of Jewish shops, 1 April 1933.
3. 'Hyenas are never decent, therefore neither are the Jews. Jews, get out!'
4. A sign on the outskirts of a German village declaring that 'Jews are our misfortune.'
5. Jews made to clean pavements in Vienna on 13 March 1938.
6. The mass arrest of Jewish men in Oldenburg, 9 November 1938.
7. The Horovitz Synagogue on Frankfurt's Bornestrasse in flames during the pogrom of 9–10 November 1938.
8. The aftermath of 'Kristallnacht' in Magdeburg.
9. Medical examination of Jewish refugee children in the Netherlands, autumn 1938.
10. Jewish refugee girls from Germany being inspected by a British policeman, autumn 1938.
11. Raymond-Raoul Lambert.
12. Norbert Troller.
13. Philip Mechanicus.
14. Ruth Maier.
15. Abraham Krouwer, Abraham Asscher and David Cohen.
16. Victor Klemperer.
17. Philipp Manes.
18. Hélène Berr.
19. Mary Berg.
20. Adam Czerniaków.

Section Two

Section Three

Acknowledgements

1–10, 17, 22–28, 32, 34, 38–43, 46, 48: courtesy of the Wiener Library, London

11: Yad Vashem

12: courtesy of the Leo Baeck Institute

13 and 15: Collection Jewish Historical Museum, Amsterdam

14: © Erling T. Hofmo/NTB scanpix

16: © Aufbau-Verlag/ullstein bild via Getty Images

18: Mémorial de la Shoah/Coll. Mariette Job

19: United States Holocaust Memorial Museum, courtesy of Mary Berg

20: Adam Czerniakow. / Forum / Bridgeman Images

21, 30 and 47: United States Holocaust Memorial Museum

29: sourced from the YIVO Institute

31: © Paul Popper/Popperfoto/Getty Images

33: United States Holocaust Memorial Museum, courtesy of Trudi Gidan

35: © akg-images / Bildarchiv Pisarek

36: Keystone-France\Gamma-Rapho via Getty Images

37: © Roger-Viollet/REX Shutterstock

44: © Mondadori Portfolio via Getty Images

45: © Jewish Historical Institute

Acknowledgements

First and foremost I would like to thank my agent, Peter Robinson, without whose unstinting support and friendship this book would neither have been started nor completed. Georgina Morley has been a patient and understanding editor, whose suggestions made the finished product shorter and better. I must also thank Nicole Foster for copy editing, Nicholas Blake for overseeing production, and Martin Lubikowski for the maps.

The book has benefited from the staff and resources of the three great libraries and archives that cover its subject. At the United States Holocaust Memorial Museum in Washington, DC, I would like to thank Paul Shapiro, the director of the Centre for Advanced Holocaust Studies, Suzanne Brown-Fleming, Jürgen Matthäus, and Martin Dean. During visits to the Centre, often unannounced and informal, Jürgen and Martin have generously given their time to discuss my work, answer questions, and offer suggestions. I am especially grateful to Jürgen, who shared with me the fruits of a major USHMM archival find, the diary of Alfred Rosenberg, before it was published. During a sabbatical at the USHMM I was able to meet Jeffrey Herf when he was completing his book about the place of the Jew and anti-Semitism in Nazi wartime propaganda. Jeffrey is both an ally and a stimulating colleague. At Yad Vashem in Jerusalem I was fortunate to have been able to spend time with David Bankier, head of the International Institute for Holocaust Research, before his untimely death. Dan Michmann, the current director of the Institute, has been a constant source of information and a challenging critic of my ideas. Rob Rozett, director of the Library, read an early version of the manuscript and made many wise comments, often drawing my attention to new publications in the field. David Silberklang, editor of *Yad Vashem Studies*, commissioned me to write a number of reviews and other pieces that have helped clarify my thinking on historiography; his editorial comments have always been valuable. Rob and David are also dear friends and have welcomed me, and my family, into their homes many times. One of the compensations for working on such grim material for so long is that over this time our families have come to know one another and our friendships have deepened. Thanks to my visits to Yad Vashem and also my involvement with the International Holocaust Remembrance Alliance (formerly the Task Force for International Cooperation on Holocaust Remembrance, Education and Research) I have also had the opportunity to discuss aspects of my work with Yehuda Bauer, whose fund of knowledge and insight is peerless. The Wiener Library in London has been an indispensable, local resource and I would like to thank its director, Ben Barkow, and the head librarian, Kat Hübschmann, for their hospitality and unfailing assistance. Needless to say, all three institutions would not function without many members of staff, too numerous to list: I would just like to say a big Thank You to all of them.

Aspects of this research have been presented in lectures and I would like to thank the organizers of these events and acknowledge the feedback they garnered. In 2011 as the Wilkenfeld Family Lecturer in Holocaust Education at the Sidney Jewish Museum I benefited from the advice and insight of my host, Konrad Kwiet. The following year, Milton Shain, director of the Kaplan Centre for Jewish Studies, University of Cape Town, invited me to an unusual gathering at the city's wonderful Jewish Museum at which 'Holocaust historians' were invited to reflect on the autobiographical dimension of their work. Over the course of several days I enjoyed the company and conversation of Steven Aschheim, Doris Bergen, Christopher Browning, Richard J. Evans, Robert Erikson, Steven T. Katz, Michael Marrus, Antony Polonsky, and Karl Schleunes. Despite having met each other on various occasions in different circumstances, this was a particularly fruitful and reflective encounter. In 2014 I was invited to deliver the Raul Hilberg Memorial Lecture at the University of Burlington, Vermont. Francis Nicosia and Jonathan Heuner were perfect hosts, but they also made valuable observations on my paper attempting to bring together the history of the war and the fate of the Jews. Jerold D. Jacobson, who generously supports the lecture series, proved an incisive critic as well as a jolly dinner companion. Jacques Fredj, director of the Mémorial de la Shoah in Paris, has invited me to address audiences there on several occasions, which has also given me the opportunity to use the resources of the centre's library and archive. Our post-lecture conversations at a restaurant around the corner are always a highlight of these visits. In 2015, Guri Schwarz enticed me to a conference on remembrance of the Holocaust held at the new Memoriale della Shoah in Milan. This gave me the chance to explore the bleak, subterranean freight yard from which over a thousand Italian Jews were deported. The participants in the conference included Tal Bruttmann, whose path-breaking research earlier led me to revision the plight of Jews during the last phase of the German occupation of France. A few months later, at the invitation of Antony Polonsky, I attended a three-day conference to mark the opening of the permanent exhibition of Polin – the new museum of Polish Jewish history in Warsaw. The conference heard from a cadre of Polish historians who, since 1990, have transformed the way we understand the fate of Polish Jews. The fruits of their research pepper the footnotes of this book. In this connection I would like to acknowledge the impact of publications and presentations by Jan T. Gross and Jan Grabowski, whom I had occasion to meet during their visits to London and elsewhere. Their pioneering and courageous work has had a huge influence on my approach to the subject. Finally, I would like to thank Stephen Feinberg, recently retired from the US Holocaust Memorial Museum, for inveigling me into educational events in Washington, Kaunus, and Budapest. Steve has been a superb sparring partner for many years and, once again, it mitigates the darkness of the subject to know that through it I became friends with him and his no less feisty partner, Patt Moser.

Over the duration of this book I have participated in numerous conferences where I have had the opportunity to hear the latest findings delivered by doctoral students as well as veterans in the field. In particular I would like to mention the tri-annual conference series *Beyond Camps and Forced Labour*, which is jointly organized by Suzanne Bardgett, the Imperial War Museum, London; Johannes-Dieter Steinert, Wolverhampton University; Jessica Reinisch, Birkbeck, University of London; and the Centre for Holocaust Research at Royal Holloway, University of London. The gatherings that have taken place every three years at the Imperial War Museum since 2003 have provided a showcase for new research on the experience of Jews and other victims of Nazi persecution during and in the aftermath of the war. Much of this work has since been published and found its way into the footnotes and bibliography of this book. I have been fortunate to attend successive *Lessons and Legacies* conferences organized by the Holocaust Educational Foun-

dation, Chicago. I would like to thank Theodore Zev Weiss, who inspired
this unique, bi-annual gathering of scholars, for urging me to attend
and participate. To do so was to enter an extraordinary community of
researchers who were both supportive and challenging. It would be
impossible to mention all those involved in the conferences and the sessions, but I would like to mention Wendy Lower, Mark Roseman, Omer
Bartov, and Gershon Greenberg, with whom I have enjoyed memorable
conversations that sharpened my thinking. The Kagan Fellowship
scheme of the Conference for Material Claims against Germany Inc. –
named in honour of the late Saul Kagan, a doughty fighter for the rights
of survivors, whom I was privileged to meet several times – has supported the doctoral research of dozens of young scholars from around
the world. As a member of the fellowship committee I was invited to
attend the annual workshops for the award holders, held in either
Washington or Jerusalem, and mentor the fellows – but I consistently
learned more from them than I could ever have imparted in return. The
fellows are too numerous to mention individually but the scheme has
already led to the completion of many fine theses and a small shelfload
of books, some of which are cited in this work.

At this point I would like to acknowledge what I have learned from
the doctoral students whom I have been lucky enough to supervise at
Royal Holloway, University of London: Salvatore Garau, who worked on
early fascism; Daniel Tilles, who researched fascist anti-Semitism and
Jewish responses in 1930s Britain; Katarzyna Person, who studied
assimilated, Polonized Jews and converts in the Warsaw ghetto; Russell
Wallis, who shed light on British public and governmental responses to
the persecution of German Jews; Yoav Heller, who explored the fate of
Jewish twins in Birkenau and the role of their protector, Zvi Spiegel;
Rachel Century, who probed the beliefs and functions of women who
provided secretarial support to the German army, SS, and occupation
authorities; Dorota Mas, currently working on Nazi elite schools; and
Rachel Pistol, examining the internment of 'enemy aliens' in the USA
and Britain. I am delighted and proud that Salvatore Garau, Daniel
Tilles, Katarzyna Person, and Russell Wallis, have already published
monographs based on their doctoral research; more books are to follow.
Katarzyna read an early version of the manuscript and saved me from
numerous howlers concerning Polish Jewry. During my visit to Warsaw
in May 2015, Katarzyna took me to Treblinka so that I could explore
the site. While Katarzyna did the guiding, her mother kindly did the

driving. We were accompanied by Suzanne Bardgett and it was a sobering, instructive, and deeply moving experience.

These students were drawn to Royal Holloway partly by the outstanding MA in Holocaust Studies and the activities of the Centre for
Holocaust Research. The Centre boasts a unique concentration of
expertise in the subject and since I joined it in 2004 I have learned a
great deal from my colleagues, past and present. So I would like to
thank Peter Longerich, Dan Stone, Bob Eaglestone, and Barry Langford,
who combine academic excellence with collegiality to an extent that is
all too rare in universities these days. I am privileged to hold a research
chair at Royal Holloway, and would also like to express my gratitude to
a succession of superb departmental heads – Justin Champion, Sara
Ansari, and Jonathan Phillips – who have supported my work (both
academic and extra-mural) and tenaciously defended the highest values
of a research-led History Department. My colleague Rudolf Muhs read
sections of the manuscript and helped me to sort out tricky questions of
title and rank in Nazi Germany as well as offering sensitive advice on
how to present the crisis of German Jews after 1933. Over the years,
Rudolf and Daniel Beer have made the long car journey from Royal
Holloway to north-west London both enlightening and enjoyable.

From 1999 to 2001, I was involved in the creation of a Holocaust
memorial day for the UK and served for six years as a trustee for the
Holocaust Memorial Day Trust. Throughout this period, and subsequently in various roles, I have taken part in numerous discussions
about both the past and how best to commemorate it. I cannot list all
those who have enriched my thinking in these debates, but I must single
out Ben Helfgott, a survivor of the Piotrków ghetto and numerous
camps, who is the honorary president of the HMD Trust as well as
long-serving chair of the '45 Aid Society. Thanks to the Trust, on 27
January every year since 2001 I have been able to join Ben, mingling
with survivors and former refugees, hearing their stories and learning
from their experiences. Ben has been a constant source of inspiration as
well as a crucial 'reality check'. No less important, his children became
family friends and his grandchildren the school-friends of my children.
For many years I have also been a historical consultant to the Holocaust
Educational Trust, which published my first attempt at a brief history of
the Holocaust. HET gave me the opportunity to test out my ideas on
generations of young people enrolled in its Ambassador programme
and made possible a key visit to Bergen-Belsen on the seventieth

anniversary of the liberation of the camp. I would like to thank Karen Pollock, HET director, for embracing me in its work, and Andy Pearce, Alex Maws, and Martin Winstone for making me think harder about history and memory.

I have participated in many radio, television, and film documentaries, but a few must be mentioned as specially informative, intellectually challenging, and rewarding. Thanks to Adam Kemp of Aeon Productions, who produced *Death Camp Treblinka: Survivors' Stories* for the BBC in 2012, I was able to meet and interview Kalman Tiegman and Samuel Willenberg, the last survivors of the uprising in Treblinka, as well as Samuel's equally redoubtable wife, Ada. It was a privilege to be associated with the restoration of Sidney Bernstein's uncompleted 1945 film *German Concentration Camps. Factual Survey*, conducted by a team at the Imperial War Museum under the meticulous direction of Toby Haggith, from whom I learned as much about the liberation of Belsen as about the film that British cameramen made of it. The story of that film is at the core of *Night Will Fall*, a Spring Films/BFI production, for which André Singer interviewed me in the grounds of Buchenwald on a cold and windy morning – an educational experience in itself. As the historical consultant for *Jusqu'au dernier. La destruction des Juifs d'Europe* (broadcast in the UK as *Annihilation*), directed by William Karel and Blanche Finger for Zadig Production, under the benign supervision of Paul Rozenberg, I was able to test some of the ideas that made their way into this book, although the documentary series itself offers a variety of perspectives by leading experts. In 2011, I contributed to a French TV documentary on Adolf Eichmann. The filming took place in the apartment of Annette Wieviorka, with whom I have collaborated on several conferences and who has always offered bracing perspectives on the fate of Jewish people in France as well as wider questions on the history and memory of the Jewish catastrophe. Lastly, I must thank Richard Overy, who was my tutor in modern European history at Queens' College in the late 1970s. Richard gave me a solid grounding in the historian's craft and we have been exchanging ideas and arguing with one another about history and politics ever since. Richard may be partially responsible for my becoming a historian but neither he nor anyone mentioned above is responsible for the content of this book: the errors and the opinions are all my own.

In the closing stages of this book, I joined Rabbi Jonathan Wittenberg and his son Amos on a research trip to Lublin, Ostrov-Lubelski,

Lubartov, Majdanek and Belzec. Jonathan, the rabbi of the New North London Synagogue and senior rabbi to the Masorti Movement, is an old friend from university days who officiated at my marriage to Dawn Waterman and blessed my children, Daniel and Hannah. He has shared with me his passion for understanding and chronicling the tragic history of Europe's Jews and provided endless wisdom and guidance on every aspect of life. On Friday nights and Shabbat lunches, his wife, Nicola Solomons, the CEO of the Society of Authors, has nourished me with advice on the book trade and bowls of her delicious home-made soup. They know well how all-consuming it can be to write a book and this one has taken far too much time away from those I love most, Dawn, Daniel, and Hannah. It is for them, all the same.

Over several decades I have become acquainted with many former refugees from Nazi Germany and survivors of the 'final solution', some of whom I got to know well or stayed in touch with for extended periods. I did not always appreciate the significance of what they were telling me about those times, but in the course of writing this book my thoughts were frequently interrupted by recollections of what they said. I cannot know whether they would have agreed with all or any of this book, but it has been enriched by hearing of their experiences and listening to their reflections. It is dedicated to their memory: Joseph 'Joey' Burmanis, Ernst Fraenkel, Hugo Grynn, Yisrael Gutman, Trudi Levi, Yogi Maier, Roman Halter, Hans Jackson, Stephen Roth, and Kalman Tiegman.

David Cesarani, 2015

Publisher's Note

David Cesarani died while *Final Solution* was still in preparation. The publishers are deeply grateful to Professor Richard J. Evans and Andras Bereznay for their assistance and care in completing the text and maps for publication.

Introduction

The Holocaust has never been so ubiquitous. It has never been studied so extensively, taught so widely, or taken with such frequency as a subject for novels and films. On 1 November 2005, the General Assembly of the United Nations adopted 27 January as International Holocaust Remembrance Day so that it is now commemorated almost universally, held up as the global benchmark for evil, as the ultimate violation of human rights and crimes against humanity. The seventieth anniversary of the liberation of Auschwitz and the concentration camps was marked with ceremonies attended by heads of state and church leaders alongside the frail, shrinking band of survivors.[1]

However there is a yawning gulf between popular understanding of this history and current scholarship on the subject. This is hardly surprising given that most people acquire their knowledge of the Nazi past and the fate of the Jews through novels, films, or earnest but ill-informed lessons at school, which frequently rely on novels for young adults or their filmic versions. Misconceptions are reinforced by the edited and instrumentalized versions purveyed by campaigning bodies and the constellation of organizations devoted to education and commemoration. Although these efforts are made in good faith, they are subordinate to extraneous agendas, be it the desire to cultivate an inclusive national identity or the laudable determination to combat anti-Semitism, racism, homophobia and other forms of political, religious or ethnic intolerance. Some lazily draw on an outdated body of research, while others utilize state-of-the-art research but downplay inconvenient aspects of the newer findings.[2]

It is easier to arrange one-day visits to Auschwitz-Birkenau, where an estimated 960,000 Jews were murdered, than to Treblinka, where some 860,000 Jews were killed in a shorter space of time, let alone to the broadly dispersed but omnipresent killing fields of Belarus and Ukraine, where around one and half million Jews were shot to death.

Conscientious educators preparing and accompanying the flying visits to Auschwitz and Birkenau strive to frame the concentration and extermination camp within the larger history of the genocide inflicted on the Jews, but the emotional charge that imprints the historical data on the mind is inevitably shaped by physically witnessing this one site. Notwithstanding the intense preparation, the other locations where most Jews suffered, died, and were done to death remain distant. As a result the customary narrative is lopsided. The emphasis on deportations to death camps, particularly from western Europe and particularly to Auschwitz, overshadows the benighted experience of Jews in Polish ghettos. Yet the number of Jews incarcerated in the ghettos of Warsaw and Lodz in 1940–1 exceeds the combined Jewish populations in France, Belgium and the Netherlands at the same time. More Jews died in Warsaw than were deported from France to the killing sites of eastern Europe. More Jews were shot within walking distance of their homes in Kiev on 29–30 September 1941 than were forced to endure the horrendous five-day journey in box-cars from transit camps in Belgium to death camps in Poland. Yet one of the most typical Holocaust memorials is a freight car mounted on a segment of rail track.[3]

The use of survivor testimony routinely trumps the dissemination of scholarship. Survivors may only be able to illuminate a tiny corner of the sprawling historical tragedy from their own experience, but they were there, so their every word is highly charged. However, the use of survivor testimony in educational and commemorative settings swerves comprehension in the direction of a small cadre whose experiences are unrepresentative.

It is trite to remark that as survivors they are atypical of what the majority of Jews endured under Nazi rule. More pertinently, the passage of time dictates that they could only have experienced the Nazi years as children, teenagers or young adults. They observed the dilemmas of adults and can report on how things were for their mothers, fathers, grandparents and older relatives, but they cannot testify to what it felt like to be a middle-aged person confronted by persecution and unnatural death. They can only offer an echo of what it meant to lose homes and businesses, the painfully acquired achievements of a lifetime or several generations. Young people were largely insulated from, or took no direct part in, the internecine struggles that typified life in Jewish communities under ruthless pressure to divide one from another: those fit to work from those unfit, those with resources from those with none, those with contacts amongst the authorities from those bereft of patronage. They witnessed but did not feel the emotions of adults trying to protect children and loved ones, the despair and rage that accompanied helplessness and, ultimately, loss.

On the contrary, what survivors offer is a wonderful example of how youthful traumas can be overcome. They show how it is possible to rebuild in one generation what was mercilessly destroyed in the previous one. Inspiring testimony such as this inevitably carries a redemptive message. No matter how unpleasant or unvarnished the content, the age of the speaker, and the courage they show in recalling horrendous times bestows on them a heroic aura. They are envoys from a fearful distant past, bearing a message of hope – that survival and recuperation is possible whatever the odds against them.[4]

Commemorative events, especially those with survivors present, are naturally constructed to avoid sensitive and conflicted subjects. They steer around phenomena like the corruption of life in the ghettos and the moral degradation of camp inmates. They skirt awkward questions of forced cooperation with the German authorities or acts of premeditated revenge. They maintain a discreet silence over instances of voluntary infanticide, sexual exploitation amongst the Jews, rape and even cannibalism. Yet all these things occurred at times in ghettos, camps, urban hideouts and forest sanctuaries. Educational programmes have more latitude and ambition when confronting such touchy issues, but since they are designed to inoculate against racism, the emphasis is on the crimes of the Germans, their allies and accomplices or the indifference of 'bystanders'. To dwell on the terrible things that Jews did to Jews would be tantamount to 'blaming the victims', a variety of prejudicial thinking that 'Holocaust education' is itself supposed to expunge. Ironically, these are the very areas currently being explored by responsible, conscientious researchers.[5]

The nomenclature is itself increasingly self-defeating. The Holocaust, capitalized here to signify the cultural construction rather than the historical events to which it is assumed to refer, has come to imply a unitary event characterized by systematic procedures and a uniformity of experience. But newer histories point to the nuances between different countries, regions, districts, and even adjacent villages. They are more sensitized to variations over time, breaking it down into locales and segments, each with distinctive characteristics that could accentuate the chances of life or death. Certain historians argue that a number of overlapping genocides raged within The Holocaust. Romania, for example, embarked on murderous ethnic cleansing against local Jews to suit a national agenda that was distinctive from, and even cut across, German aspirations. Perspectives on the catastrophe are changing, yet this is barely reflected in the reproduction of an agreed but ageing narrative.[6]

This book grew out of a concern about the discord between, on the one side, evocations of The Holocaust in popular culture, education and its commemoration and, on the other, the revelations by researchers in many disciplines, operating within and outside an academic framework. The divergence has become acute since the 1990s, thanks to the vastly increased volume of research that followed the end of the Cold War and the opening of archives in eastern Europe. Access to these new archives facilitated individual scholarship and enabled teams to investigate Jewish slave labour and the fate of Jewish property and assets. Over a dozen countries organized historical commissions to deal with accusations about their wartime record. Their example was followed by financial institutions and industrial corporations. The result was a flood of weighty reports, scholarly articles, and monographs, not to mention accounts by journalists, politicians and activists. Around the turn of the century, historians including Michael Burleigh, Ian Kershaw, Peter Longerich, Christopher Browning, Richard Evans and Saul Friedländer wove this new material into fresh narratives of Hitler's life, the Third Reich, and the destruction of the Jews. They were outstanding works of synthesis and original insight. While several enjoyed healthy sales world-wide, others had little impact beyond the circle of aficionados.[7]

A number of TV documentaries distilled the new work, although the richness of the original research and some of its shocking implications remained locked away in detailed monographs. There were also several shorter histories that necessarily required analysis, generalization and the recital of bare facts, with the effect that something quintessentially bloody became metaphorically bloodless.[8] Moreover, in his two-volume history of the persecution and extermination of the Jews, Saul Friedländer raised the bar for all historians tackling the subject. Friedländer set out to construct an 'integrated history' that encompassed the perspectives, actions and reactions of the Jews, those who tormented them, and those who observed the unfolding horrors either close-up or from a distance. By drawing on a multitude of contemporary sources he attempted to recover the contingency of events and the chaotic experience of Jews caught up in them, not knowing why things were happening or how they would end.⁹

This account too strives for an 'integrated history', but the focus is primarily and unapologetically on the Jews. It also sets out to challenge the traditional concepts and periodization that have until now framed constructions of The Holocaust.

The reappraisal begins with the term itself, a term that arguably is well past its sell-by date. This is not due to the politicization of the word and arguments over what it means, although these are certainly good enough reasons to retire it. To some historians the appellation connotes the Nazi persecution and mass murder of Jews and other victims of the lethal racial-biological policies implemented by the National Socialist regime. It is commonly taken to also embrace the deliberate mass death of over three million Red Army personnel taken prisoner of war in the wake of the German invasion of the USSR in 1941. Other historians point to the plans adumbrated by certain Nazi officials for the destruction or deliberate starvation of Polish and Russian populations to suggest that they were in part, and potentially in whole, victims of The Holocaust. Many Jewish historians insist that the term be limited to the Jewish victims of specifically anti-Semitic measures. In Israel the word Shoah is preferred because, as a Hebrew word, it automatically tends to refer to Jews only. In this respect it echoes the Yiddish terminology favoured by many survivor-historians immediately after 1945, such as 'churban', although they also made free use of the Yiddish equivalent of words such as catastrophe and destruction. However, Yiddish authors wrote unselfconsciously while those who use Shoah do so deliberately to denote a Jewish event. Since the word is both Judeocentric and embodied in the official Israeli memorial day Yom ha-Shoah, such usage is frequently taken to indicate a supposedly 'Zionist' version, in which Jew-hatred is ineradicable, genocide was inevitable, and the only security for Jews lies in statehood.¹⁰

This ideological dispute over meaning is not, however, the real problem. Rather, the ubiquity of a standardized version under the rubric of The Holocaust in popular culture and education has created a received wisdom about what it was. The expectations conjured up by the word are then often confirmed and reinforced by the rituals of commemoration.

In this standardized version, to which I have myself contributed, The Holocaust was the outcome of racist and anti-Semitic policies that were implemented in Germany by the Nazis and then imposed on countries they conquered or adopted by the allies they made. It unfolded in stages. First the Jews of Germany were subjected to discrimination and exclusion from 1933 to 1938. Persecution intended to encourage emigration intensified into forced migration from Germany and Austria in 1938–9. With the coming of war the German authorities began expelling Jews from the Greater Reich and areas they conquered. Throughout 1939–40 Jews in German-occupied Poland were concentrated in ghettos, forced to live under appalling conditions. The physical annihilation of Jewish communities began with the invasion of Russia in 1941, followed by the deportation of Jews from all over Europe to death camps in Poland from 1941 to 1944. It ended with death marches during the last months of Hitler's Reich. Along the way, the Jews were demonized and dehumanized in propaganda and forced to resemble the reviled image of 'the Jew' in centuries-old stereotypes as well as more modern prejudicial representations.

It has become an article of faith that The Holocaust involved the systematic use of state power, modern bureaucratic methods, scientific thinking, and killing methods adapted from industrial production systems. For example, the website of the Holocaust Memorial Day Trust (of which I was a trustee for several years), responsible for overseeing the annual commemorative and educational activities in Britain around the 27 January anniversary of the liberation of Auschwitz, states that 'Between 1941 and 1945, the Nazis attempted to annihilate all of Europe's Jews. This systematic and planned attempt to murder European Jewry is known as the Holocaust.' The interlocking set of assumptions inherent in the nomenclature is so potent that it is almost impossible to begin a historical work, a novel or a film bearing the label 'Holocaust' without anticipating how it will pan out, a phenomenon that Michael André Bernstein labelled 'backshadowing'.[11]

This reassessment challenges these widely accepted preconceptions. It starts by showing that the Nazi Party did not come to power because of anti-Semitism. Of course it was an anti-Semitic party, but it had few concrete ideas about what to do with the German Jews if it took office. During its first years in government, Judenpolitik – anti-Jewish policy and measures – was marked by improvisation and muddle. There is a paradox here. Adolf Hitler and the core of Nazi true-believers were convinced that 'the Jews' were the enemy within and that they were at war with 'international Jewry', yet the strength of this often adumbrated conviction did not express itself clearly or directly in practice. By contrast, Hitler was unwavering in the pursuit of his oft-stated goal to restore German power. Economic and social policy was determined by this objective as much as it guided diplomacy and the policy of rearmament. Even racial policy was so intertwined with Hitler's belligerency that it is hard to say what came first: war and conquest to provide the basis for a healthy Volk or a healthy Volk capable of sustaining war and conquest? The key to understanding the paradox lies in the phantasm of the 'Jewish enemy'. Hitler and his acolytes believed that to succeed they had to break the 'power' of the Jews in Germany and intimidate world Jewry. Sanctions against German Jews were not just intended to ruin them and drive them out of Germany, they were a threatening gesture to 'international Jewry'. Once the Third Reich was actually at war, the Jews were perceived as both hostages and combatants. Hence diplomacy, military preparations, and waging war were functions of the struggle with Jewry. Policy was perpetually informed by the fantasy of the 'Jewish enemy' even if particular measures were not explicitly anti-Jewish.[12]

Unlike most previous narratives, this account contests whether Nazi anti-Jewish policy was systematic, consistent or even premeditated. Throughout the 1970s and 1980s historians argued whether Hitler always intended to destroy the Jews of Europe or whether the genocide emerged 'bit by bit' as a by-product of other processes. Whereas the one school argued that Nazi policy was driven by a Judeophobic obsession tempered by shrewd opportunism, the other maintained that anti-Jewish policy was sharpened by competition between competing elites and agencies in the Third Reich, a process of 'cumulative radicalization'. In the 1990s a consensus developed that instated ideology and anti-Semitism at the heart of the Nazi project while acknowledging that in practice anti-Jewish policy might not develop in a linear fashion due to competing priorities from other sectors of society or the economy, institutional rivalries, and the perennial issue of feuding personalities. However, even this middle way – exemplified in the work of the German historian Peter Longerich – reads into Nazi policymaking a purposefulness that it lacked. While it is possible to locate programmatic statements from key players, particularly in the SS, there was no overall, centralized, coherent policy or practice until late 1938. While there may have been a broad anti-Semitic consensus within the Nazi movement and throughout the institutions of government, and even if policy tended in one direction towards ever-harsher measures, this does not mean that one thing led to another logically, necessarily, or even deliberately.[13]

History is replete with examples of unintended consequences and contingency. This is the 'cock-up theory' of history or the Cleopatra's nose version. Could it be that what happened in the past was the result of chance occurrences, such as the seductive beauty of a queen? It may seem offensive to think about the Jewish fate in this way, but the alternative is to assume that events could not have had any other outcome – which has implications for how we regard the behaviour of the Germans, their accomplices, the Jews, and those who observed the dire situation. It also runs against the grain of what historians have revealed about the central mission of Hitler and the Third Reich: making war.

Recent work by military historians has exposed the Reich's erratic preparations for war, the good fortune it enjoyed from 1938 to 1941, and the inadequacy of its response when the tide of war turned thereafter. New campaign studies demonstrate that German victories in 1940–1 were not the inevitable result of greater resources, industrial efficiency, superior arms, and better military leadership. The operational doctrine of the German army and its tactical accomplishments were more advanced than the forces it engaged and, in some areas, it enjoyed a technological edge. Overall, however, the German armed forces achieved decisive victories mainly thanks to the mistakes of their opponents. No one was more surprised by the speed and totality of the German triumph in France in 1940 than the Germans themselves.[14]

What has this to do with the fate of the Jews? Well, since war was Hitler's overweening preoccupation and the raison d'être of the Nazi state, if we have to reconsider the inevitability of German military victories in 1939–42, then surely it is appropriate to re-examine the apparently inexorable progress of anti-Jewish policies.

The German way of warfare and the campaigns of the Second World War suggest more than a different way of thinking about the Third Reich. Until quite recently, historians of the war tended to ignore the fate of the Jews or at best included it as a subset of Nazi occupation policies. Conversely, Holocaust historians treated the war merely as the reason why more Jews fell under Nazi domination, while the prolonged fighting gave the Nazis more time to kill them and delayed the moment of liberation for the remnant. Typically, the German invasion of the

Soviet Union in June 1941 was the only point at which Holocaust historians deemed the course of the war to intersect with the unfolding of Nazi anti-Jewish policies. Since the earliest histories of the 'Final Solution' it has been held that Hitler invaded the USSR in order to obtain 'living space' and to destroy the Bolshevik regime that he conflated with the menace of 'Jewish power'. Hence the mass murder of male Jews on Soviet territory was an integral part of the invasion plan, which soon escalated into the massacre of entire communities and, eventually, morphed into a European-wide programme of annihilation.[15]

Holocaust historians felt under little obligation to pay attention to the progress of arms on the German side because they believed that Nazi anti-Semitism and racial policy trumped military imperatives. They maintained that the slaughter of Jews in Poland and Russia deprived the Nazis of a valuable labour resource, while the use of trains to send Jews from the four corners of Europe to death camps in Poland diverted valuable rolling stock from the war effort. In fact, both these notions are incorrect. Although Jews did provide skills and labour in some places for a time, they were never indispensable and hardly contributed to essential aspects of the Nazi war machine. The Germans and their allies were desperately short of locomotives and rolling stock by 1941, but the number of special trains used to carry Jews was a minute proportion of the total volume of rail traffic and the army always had priority. The deportation of Jews was routinely stopped to ensure that supplies flowed to the front but no military action was ever suspended to ensure that the shipment of Jews to the gas chambers continued without interruption. When the shortage of labour in the Reich became acute, the Jews were perceived as a valuable resource. The Germans occupied Hungary in March 1944 partly to get their hands on Jewish labour; military exigencies drove anti-Jewish policy, not the other way round.[16]

This reappraisal will show that by ignoring the war, Holocaust historians have missed the single most important thing that determined the fate of the Jews – more important even than Hitler's anti-Semitism. Hatred of the Jews was essential to his self-identity, but Hitler also saw himself as a warrior. He regarded the outbreak of the Great War in 1914 as the turning point in his life and he was shaped by his experience of the trenches. Germany's defeat in 1918 so scarred him that in his messianic quest to restore Germany's power he was fanatically committed to avoiding any repeat of the conditions that engendered the country's collapse. These fixations guided his personal direction of the war, which became increasingly heavy handed from mid-1941 onwards.[17]

Since he blamed the Jews for Germany's downfall, once the Fatherland was again at war Hitler presided over a regime that monitored Jewish activity closely, removed Jews from any function in society or the economy in which they could sabotage the war effort or poison morale, limited the resources they consumed, expelled them from German living space, and, when that was not possible, liquidated them. He made strategic and even tactical decisions in the light of how he believed the Jews were assaulting Germany. His global strategy, such as it was, cannot be disentangled from his world view. In effect he was fighting two wars at the same time, although in his warped perception they were actually the same.[18]

Hitler's conduct of this dual war is not the only reason that military matters demand closer attention. Although his personal interventions were crucial, he did not shape Germany's military traditions. Regardless of the Führer's meddling, the German way of warfare had catastrophic implications for the Jews of Europe.

The strategic and operational doctrines that were developed in the era of Frederick the Great were passed from one generation of Prussian generals to another until they were encoded in the DNA of Hitler's Wehrmacht. Germany was a medium-sized economic and military power, occupying an unfavourable geo-strategic location in the middle of Europe, surrounded by potential enemies but without easily defensible natural borders. Consequently, in the event of an inter-state conflict it was necessary to assemble a powerful army, concentrate it against the main enemy, and combine manoeuvre with overwhelming force to knock them out as quickly as possible. Campaigns had to be rapid and decisive because the country could not sustain large armies in the field for a long drawn-out conflict. To achieve the knock-out blow, the Prussian tradition dictated the encirclement and total destruction of the strongest enemy units. The general staff otherwise paid little attention to strategic issues. If the German armies were operationally successful, strategic issues would sort themselves out: there was simply no alternative to victory. If Germany failed to achieve a decisive outcome in the opening campaign it would have enemies on all sides that were better supplied and able to fight a war of attrition. This was what happened in 1914 when, indeed, the generals had no answer.[19]

Hitler and his martial advisers absorbed the lesson that there was no point holding back military assets if the country would be doomed in a long war, and that it was necessary to be absolutely ruthless in order to secure victory in the shortest possible time. But from the start of hostilities in 1939 they were confounded. Instead of isolating and fighting Poland, they found themselves confronted with a war on two fronts. Although it was relatively straightforward to defeat the Polish armies, in the west they faced two imperial powers with vastly greater resources. Hitler was lucky in his enemies, though, and more by luck than judgement scored an astonishing victory in the spring and summer of 1940. This success turned out to be an illusion. Britain, with her massive imperial hinterland, refused to surrender and Germany lacked the means to finish her off. Hitler proposed to solve his strategic dilemma by invading Russia, thereby denying Britain the hope of assistance from the last major land power on the continent. The German army then prepared for an assault modelled on the successful campaign in the west, popularly known as the 'blitzkrieg'. Yet the conditions in western Europe conducive to that style of warfare simply did not obtain in eastern Europe. Furthermore, the planning by the German general staff was astonishingly slapdash. The result was a military disaster in the autumn and winter of 1941 that condemned Germany to a war it could never win.[20]

The Jews paid the price for German military failure. The preferred solution to the 'Jewish question' from 1939 to 1941 was a combination of forced emigration and expulsion. As the Germans conquered one country after another they hoped to exploit their territories or possessions as a dumping ground for unwanted Jews: first a corner of occupied Poland, then French-controlled Madagascar, and finally the land beyond the Urals. After Operation Barbarossa foundered, the Siberian solution remained a mirage. Germany's defeat in Russia in 1941 not only removed the option of ejecting millions of Jews from areas under German control, it had a domino effect across the continent. Plunging morale at home led the Nazi leaders to step up actions against the German Jews. Party bosses clamoured for Jews to be deported, freeing up apartments for bombed-out German families. To make room for 'Reich Jews' in ghettos in the east, local Nazi rulers prepared to massacre the Polish Jews packed within their confines. Jewish civilians in occupied Russia were perceived as a security threat from the inception of Operation Barbarossa, but as the military position worsened and

German supply lines were plagued by Russian marauders Jews became prime targets for pacification operations. Finally, military failure created a resource crisis for the German army and the home front. There was not enough food for both the men under arms and the civilian population. The shortfall was met in part by depriving the populations in occupied Europe of food and fuel. Given Nazi racial predilections, the peoples of Poland and the USSR were condemned to the most drastic reductions in food supply; but the Jews were subjected to a policy that amounted to forced starvation.[21]

Hitler had repeatedly threatened that if Germany found itself in a world conflict, the Jews would be punished. With the German declaration of war on the United States on 11 December 1941, the war became global. Jews ceased to be hostages whose lives were held as a guarantee of American non-intervention; instead, they became culprits who deserved sanguinary retribution. Ultimately, the course of the war rather than decisions within the framework of anti-Jewish policy triggered the descent into a Europe-wide genocide.[22]

The German way of war sheds light on the fate of the Jews in other important respects. Historians have long argued over the balance between decision-making at the centre of the Nazi regime and the actions of satraps at its periphery. Did the Führer initiate measures or react to prompts from his entourage? Did central agencies in Berlin formulate solutions to the 'Jewish problem' or did they respond to pressure from below? There has been a similar debate about the role of middle-level officials and experts. The stereotypical depiction of mindless drones obeying orders has been replaced by investigation into how much autonomy they had. Ian Kershaw has suggested that Hitler set broad policy goals through the expression of wishes and left it up to his subordinates to make them a reality. Since success was judged in terms of realizing the aspirations of the leader, at all levels of the regime personnel 'worked towards' the Führer. Moreover, individuals competed to devise the speediest, most thoroughgoing means to gratify the leadership.[23]

The notion of 'working towards the Führer' resembles the German military doctrine of Auftragstaktik, according to which superior officers issued broad objectives to their subordinates and left it to them to use their initiative and familiarity with local conditions to fulfil the goal. It is hardly surprising that the ethos of Auftragstaktik pervaded the ranks of the Nazi Party and its agencies. Hitler was made by his time in the army. He surrounded himself with men who had years of military service under their belt. Younger Nazis who regretted missing out on the Great War adopted a martial approach to life and work. They rejected democratic processes and consensual decision-making in favour of charismatic leadership, individual toughness, goal-oriented conceptions, and decisive gestures. The men who framed and carried out anti-Jewish policy repeatedly followed this behaviour pattern. The Nazi system did not operate either by simple delegation or 'working towards the Führer'; rather, it gave junior operatives scope for interpreting broad orders for the attainment of objectives in the light of operational and tactical conditions.[24]

When SS officers commenced planning and implementing the genocidal assault on Europe's Jews in the course of 1942, they did so using quasi-military concepts. The aim was to annihilate the Jews in one campaign by the application of overwhelming force. However, it was dogged by the same limitations that were simultaneously hampering the operations of the Wehrmacht: ambition was brought up short by lack of resources. Having failed to exterminate Europe's Jews in 'one blow' they faced evasion, concealment and resistance. Apart from a few exceptional cases, Jews were never again to prove such an easy target. This reappraisal shows how during 1943 and 1944 the Germans fought their war against the Jews under the same exigencies that they fought the Allies: with overstretched manpower and unreliable allies, dependent on fanatical but erratic auxiliaries motivated by plunder rather than ideological convergence. Conversely, it pays greater heed to forms of Jewish self-defence, including flight, the construction of hiding places, camouflage (or 'passing' as an 'Aryan'), and armed confrontations.

One of the major themes to emerge from research since the 1990s is the extent to which despoliation and economic exploitation underpinned the anti-Jewish policy of the Nazis, their allies and collaborators. For the Germans, the confiscation of Jewish wealth was an important supplementary source of funding for the voracious war economy. The expropriation of Jewish homes, furniture, furnishings, household articles and clothing supplied the needs of poor Germans and families whose own residences had been destroyed by bombing. State-run theft helped to pay for the construction of a more egalitarian society, albeit one that limited material benefits to the racially chosen. Later, it helped to stave off popular discontent and buy the complaisance of the Volk even when the war turned sour. However, by widening the circle of those who benefited from persecution and genocide, recent research has called into question the notion of 'bystanders' as passive onlookers whose culpability was limited to a sin of omission.[25]

The distribution of loot amongst Germany's collaborators strengthened their attachment to the Third Reich. By encouraging local populations to plunder their Jewish neighbours, the Germans inveigled them into complicity with persecution and genocide. Throughout occupied Europe, the Germans succeeded in transforming the Jews into 'fair game'. By putting a price on the head of Jewish fugitives and creating opportunities for exploiting those in hiding, they transmuted Jews into commodities, an economic resource to be exploited by populations living in straitened, uncertain times. Greed not anti-Semitism motivated many people to align themselves with the German occupiers. Jew-hatred became as much a justification for despoliation as a motive. Those who enriched themselves at the cost of the Jews became committed to an anti-Jewish stance regardless of their previous intentions or feelings about Jewish people. The steady intensification of anti-Jewish feeling during the war was undoubtedly a product of German propaganda, but it was also a consequence of German-orchestrated plunder. Fear of restitution played a role in the hostility directed at Jewish survivors by people liberated from German rule while in possession of purloined Jewish property. Inverting the traditional narratives that begin with the origins of modern anti-Semitism, this one suggests that avarice engendered prejudice. Looking for the roots of Jew-hatred in religious traditions, culture and ideology overlooks the most powerful and rapid device for generating antipathy: the guilty feelings that accompany ill-gotten gains.[26]

Perhaps the most distressing aspect of the latest research is the light it throws on the rape of Jewish women and the sexual exploitation of Jews in ghettos and camps, in hiding and on the run. Early reports by survivors tended to be quite frank about sexual relationships and abuse. As time passed, however, this facet of Jewish life under the Nazis became veiled in silence. Eventually researchers stopped even looking for or asking about it. A myth developed according to which Nazi doctrines of racial hygiene, the ban on sexual contacts between Jews and Aryans, had actually forestalled the mass rape of Jewish women. Now, thanks to a new generation of women historians, greater interest in immediate post-war testimony, and increased awareness of rape in wartime, that reticence has been put aside. Innovative research shows that German racial inhibitions were patchy at best and, in any case, did not extend to Germany's allies in the field. And sometimes Jews preyed upon Jews. Sex, however, was not always violent and forced. It may appear to be in the worst possible taste to dwell on sexuality during a genocide, but consensual sexual relations offered comfort and escapism. Many diarists remark on their own love affairs or observe the frenzied coupling of others, in the bleakest circumstances. As this account will show, as long as life went on so did love and lust.[27]

In order to avoid lengthy digressions I have dispensed with discussions of what previous historians wrote and why they were either pioneers or erroneous. However, readers can use the endnotes to locate my sources and I have indicated where there are significant divergences between these interpretations and my own. I have also limited the exegesis of Nazi decision-making, summarizing what seems to be the historical consensus as to why the Jews suffered as they did at the hands of others. The source material and secondary literature is international and vast, but for the sake of manageability and ease of access I have restricted my references mainly to English-language texts.

This book deals with the fate of the Jews, not of 'other victims' of Nazi political repression and racial-biological policies. Several other groups endured social exclusion, incarceration in concentration camps, and mass murder. However, the rationale for the persecution of these groups differed radically from the intentions that underlay anti-Jewish policy. Even though homosexual men and women, Germans of African descent, and the severely mentally and physically disabled were all disparaged in Nazi racial thinking, and depicted as a threat to the strength and purity of the Volk, only the Jews were characterized as an implacable, powerful, global enemy that had to be fought at every turn and finally eliminated. When Hitler reiterated his determination to avert a collapse similar to that which brought down Germany in 1918, he referred to the danger posed by Jews rather than any other element of society.[28]

What follows is a chronological narrative and apart from sections where I analyse particular questions or themes, the analysis is implicit in the structure. I have tried to give the reader a sense of the contingent and chaotic course of what we know as history, but what was experienced at the time as a bewildering present and an uncertain future. In order to capture this sensation, I have drawn on letters, diaries, reports and documents from the time. I have used post-war testimony sparingly and, as far as possible, used statements composed not too long after the events they describe.

Finally, a word about periodization. The story begins conventionally enough in 1933, with a glance back to Hitler's career and the antecedents of the Third Reich. But it concludes with a brief epilogue covering the years 1945 to 1949. I have chosen to end in this way rather than to offer readers the customary coda hinging on the liberation of the camps and the end of the war in Europe on 8 May 1945 because this is not how Jews saw the diminution of their travails. Thousands of Jews were freed from Nazi domination nearly a year *before* the war ended; amongst them were the first to chronicle the catastrophe and to collect records concerning the fate of the Jews, without knowing how or when the war would end. Thousands of Jews who were released from Nazi captivity once Germany was defeated did not enjoy complete freedom for months or years afterwards. Instead, they were penned into camps for 'Displaced Persons'. Jews continued to die of wounds, disease and malnutrition in huge numbers for weeks *after* their murderous Nazi guards were removed. Thousands more who attempted to reach Palestine ran into the Royal Navy blockade mounted to prevent Jews entering the territory, which was administered by Britain under a mandate from the League of Nations. They ended up behind barbed wire in detention camps at Athlit, near Haifa, and on Cyprus. In 1947 the British were holding more Jews behind barbed wire than the Germans had been in 1937.

For the Jews, as against the Allied armies and the peoples of Europe liberated from Nazi rule, the end of the war did not mark an end to death or suffering. To the mass of survivors in refugee camps, 8 May 1945 heralded the opening of a liminal period during which they began the task of rebuilding their lives and reconstructing their communities without any certainty about where they would ultimately be able to settle. Jewish citizens who were fortunate to emerge into freedom in their own countries faced an uphill battle to recover their rights, property, assets, and even children, who had been placed with Christian families or handed into the custody of convent schools. The struggle for restitution and reparation was carried forward alongside efforts to achieve justice against the Nazi criminals and their collaborators. Yet political circumstances were frequently uncongenial to a full or adequate judicial reckoning. In this sense The Holocaust did not end when the guns fell silent. The neat conclusion implied by the term is as much in need of reappraisal as the implied uniformity of experience that its promiscuous use confers on the fate of the Jews.[29]

PROLOGUE

What to make of Hitler and the Nazis?

Adolf Hitler was sworn in as Chancellor of the German Republic at 11.30 a.m. on 30 January 1933. The brief ceremony took place in the office of the German President, Field Marshal Paul von Hindenburg, on the second floor of the Reich Chancellery. In contrast to the political odyssey that had brought him to this point, Hitler did not have far to travel to get there. Since the previous February he had been staying at a plush hotel nearby. His presence was well known to Berliners and despite the cold weather for several days an atmosphere of expectancy drew people to the scene. Three days earlier, Chancellor Kurt von Schleicher had resigned after just a few weeks in office. There was confusion over who would replace him. Would it be Franz von Papen, his immediate predecessor, whom he had toppled? Or would it be Adolf Hitler, who led the largest party in the Reichstag (the German parliament)? Hitler was a relative newcomer to national politics who had never held high office; indeed, his entire career had so far amounted to very little. Certainly he commanded the biggest phalanx of Reichstag deputies, but was it credible that this outsider, only recently a marginal and derided figure, could assume the helm of state?[1]

The French Ambassador, André François-Poncet, observed developments. Hitler 'had settled at the Kaiserhof Hotel, his usual residence in the capital, a few steps from the Chancellery and from the Palace of the President. A considerable throng filled the square, watching the comings and goings whenever Hitler appeared.' What they could not see was the peculiar sequence of events unfolding in the presidential suite.[2]

Hindenburg had sworn in the new minister of defence, Werner von Blomberg, even before Hitler. Speed was essential because Schleicher had combined control of the army with the chancellorship and had not surrendered the former role. There were rumours that he was planning a coup. Hindenburg and his political advisers had to deprive him of his last power base and, crucially, ensure that the new government directed the armed forces. Hitler arrived later, using a back route. He was accompanied by his retinue, including the only two members of his party who would serve in the cabinet with him. Other ministers-to-be, from various parties, arrived individually, gathering in a ground-floor office in the Reich Chancellery before being taken upstairs to meet President Hindenburg for their formal swearing-in just after quarter past eleven in the morning. The whole process had the feel of a last-minute improvisation.[3]

By midday special editions of the Berlin newspapers were carrying news of Hitler's appointment, detailing the new coalition government. At nightfall the victors held a torchlight parade through central Berlin, converging on the Brandenburg Gate in the heart of the government district. First came thousands of brown-uniformed men of the Nazi Party militia, the Sturmabteilung (SA, storm troop units). They were followed by members of the Stahlhelm (the steel helmets), a paramilitary association of war veterans that was allied with the Nazis. They marched past the presidential palace, where Hindenburg watched from one window, Hitler from another. François-Poncet was also watching. 'In massive columns, flanked by bands that played martial airs to the muffled beat of their big drums, they emerged from the depth of the Tiergarten [a park] and passed under the triumphal arch of the Brandenburg Gate. The torches they brandished formed a river of fire, a river with hastening, unquenchable waves, a river sweeping with a sovereign rush over the very heart of the city. From these brown-shirted, booted men, as they marched by in perfect discipline and alignment, their well-pitched voices bawling warlike songs, there rose an enthusiasm and dynamism that were extraordinary.' Events had moved so rapidly during the day that no one had thought to film the parade. Rather like Mussolini's fabled 'March on Rome', which had inspired Hitler in his abortive bid for power a decade earlier, it had to be restaged the next day for the benefit of newsreel cameras.[4]

But what did the change of government signify? As a condition for accepting the chancellorship Hitler insisted that Hindenburg dissolve the Reichstag and call new elections. This could reinforce the NSDAP, which was already the biggest party in parliament, and give him an even stronger mandate. However, he conceded the demands from Hindenburg's advisers to preserve the conservative complexion of the outgoing cabinet and limit the number of Nazi Party ministers to two. This pair were 'old fighters' who had been side by side with Hitler since the early days of the movement. Wilhelm Frick was appointed Reich minister of the interior while Hermann Göring became a minister without portfolio. Göring was also made interior minister of Prussia, which meant that he controlled the police force of the largest state in Germany. Yet they were outnumbered eight to three by the non-Nazi members of the government. As his reward for orchestrating the downfall of Schleicher and to ensure that Hitler was held in rein, Papen, the Catholic conservative who served as chancellor in 1932, was vice chancellor. The foreign minister, Baron Konstantin von Neurath, the postmaster general, and minister of transport, Paul von Eltz-Rübenach, and the defence minister, Blomberg, were also familiar faces. They were old-fashioned conservatives. The post of minister for commerce and agriculture went to Alfred Hugenberg, a press baron who led the right-wing German National People's Party, with which the Nazis were loosely allied. Franz Seldte, the Stahlhelm leader, assumed responsibility for labour affairs. The minister for justice, Franz Gürtner, and Lutz Schwerin von Krosigk, minister of finance, were also traditional conservatives. To outward appearances, then, little had changed except that Germany at last seemed to have a government that rested securely on the dominant faction in the Reichstag.[5]

It was difficult even for diplomats and seasoned political observers to figure out what might happen next. One who had a better claim than most to sharp analysis was Leopold Schwarzschild. Since 1922 he had edited *Das Tage-Buch*, one of Germany's most respected periodicals, which boasted a galaxy of political commentators as well as cultural stars. Schwarzschild's acute antennae were sensitized by his own background. He came from a Jewish family that had dwelled in the German lands for hundreds of years and become totally assimilated into German life. Schwarzschild had studied politics, economics and history at university before serving in the German army during the Great War. He welcomed the overthrow of the Kaiser following Germany's defeat and the creation of the German Republic (known as the Weimar Republic after the town where the new constitution was promulgated). In every issue of his magazine he championed the values enshrined in the new republic: democracy, equality, individual freedom. Yet he greeted the appointment of a sworn enemy of parliamentary democracy as chancellor with caution rather than foreboding. In an article published on

4 February 1933, Schwarzschild noted that prior to entering office Hitler's political strength was ebbing. In the last parliamentary elections, in
November 1932, the Nazi Party had *lost* two million votes. The Nazis
might stage victory parades, but the victory was a myth. They had not
won power, it was given to them. 'Hitler was already a defeated man
when victory was gifted to him. His play for power had already failed
when he was offered the opportunity to gain it by the back door. It
wasn't a march on Berlin that brought the German Mussolini to power,
but a piece of chicanery by the camarilla of Prussian Junkers and West-
phalian industrialists.'[6]

Schwarzschild spotted that the clique advising President Hindenburg saved the Nazi Party, 'which was threatened with bankruptcy,
which was tearing itself apart with factionalism and mutiny, and which
was bound automatically to revert to being a harmless, petit-bourgeois
anti-semitic party as soon as an upturn in the economy drained off the
support which desperation had driven to Hitler'. He believed that the
party was still doomed and predicted that the left-leaning element
would revolt against an alliance with conservatives. Meanwhile, the fortunes of democrats, the socialists, and the working classes might revive.
In any case, he regarded these elements as 'strong enough to prevent
extreme excesses on the part of the new regime'. If Hitler failed to provide food and jobs for the masses he would quickly be turfed out of
power.[7]

A similar prognosis was transmitted to the Foreign Office in
London by the British Ambassador, Sir Horace Rumbold. He had
arrived in Berlin in October 1928 as the culmination of an exemplary
diplomatic career. From the moment the Nazis made their electoral
breakthrough in September 1930 Rumbold sent back a stream of incisive dispatches dissecting their programme and Hitler's performance.
While Rumbold had some sympathy for National Socialist aspirations,
and certainly shared their dislike of Jews, he clearly saw the limit of
their appeal. When the Nazi Party gained 37 per cent of the vote in the
parliamentary elections of July 1932, winning 230 seats in the Reichstag,
he did not share the widespread belief that final success was imminent
and inevitable. Instead, he reported to the Foreign Office that Hitler
'seems now to have exhausted his reserves'. On 27 January 1933, Rumbold had dinner with Otto Meissner, President Hindenburg's chief of
staff and one of the 'camarilla' that plotted Schleicher's downfall. Rumbold relayed to London Meissner's conviction that 'Hitler had shown

signs of late of moderation and had realized that his policy of negation was leading nowhere'. Instead of demanding complete power, he was now willing to share it. The soothing conclusion was that 'a government under Hitler which included a proportion of ministers who were not Nazis would be unable to embark on dangerous experiments'.[8]

Georges Simenon, the Belgian journalist and crime writer, put things more pithily. He was staying in the Kaiserhof while covering the German political drama for the journal *Voilà*. On at least one occasion he found himself sharing the elevator with Hitler and frequently overheard conversations amongst his entourage as well as groups of politicians passing through the hotel lobby. Hitler, they said, was 'Papen's man . . . Hugenberg's man . . . He is a puppet.'[9]

German Jews made their own assessment of 'the Hitler experiment'. The *CV-Zeitung*, the journal of the Centralverein, the central association of German Jews (a representative body that also carried out Jewish defence work), had long kept an eye on Hitler and the Nazi Party. In the last issue before Hitler's appointment it, too, noted the crisis in his ranks. After he was installed at the Chancellery it reflected the general uncertainty about Hitler's prospects. Had he 'triumphed or been tamed'? Would his government last any longer than its predecessors? The fact that it was the legitimate authority obligated Jews to moderate their opposition; but the editors were convinced that 'no one will dare to touch our constitutional rights'.[10]

Der Israelit, the newspaper of Orthodox Jews, expressed a cautious optimism. Now Hitler was in government he would be held in check by his coalition partners and President Hindenburg. Leadership of a front-rank nation would, by itself, oblige him to act responsibly. It might actually be worse for the Jews if the new government failed, unleashing the search for a scapegoat. If it held on without being able to achieve anything, though, it might launch a 'cold pogrom' as a safety valve for popular discontent. Much would then depend on how the civil service and the police behaved; would they adhere to the old standards now they were commanded by the Nazis? There was also the danger of fresh elections strengthening the far right and threatening the constitutional order, with its checks and balances. 'Only time will reveal whether these questions are justified.'[11]

German Zionists showed little anxiety at the turn of events. Zionist leaders like Robert Weltsch, editor of the Zionist weekly *Jüdische Rundschau*, had consistently drawn attention to the dangers of anti-Semitism because it validated their ideological position that Jewish life in the diaspora was untenable. Notwithstanding his professional pessimism, though, even Weltsch could not conceal astonishment at how things in Germany had turned out. 'Overnight the event that no-one wanted to believe would happen has become fact; Hitler is Chancellor of the German Reich.'[12]

Although he was no Jewish nationalist (and frequently compared Zionists to Nazis), the Austrian writer and journalist Joseph Roth sensed the worst. From his hotel room in Paris he wrote to his friend Stefan Zweig, the bestselling author, 'we are headed for a new war. I wouldn't give a heller [coin of little value] for our prospects. The barbarians have taken over. Do not deceive yourself. Hell reigns.'[13]

Yet that was not how it seemed to Jews across Germany. A few years later, Ernst Marcus, a Jewish lawyer then living in Breslau, recalled that 30 January 1933 was 'relatively calm. Broad circles of the middle class, including us and our Jewish friends, believed that things "will not be so bad"'. His wife was so relaxed that she went on holiday to Bavaria. In Hamburg, at first it seemed to Jews as if nothing changed at all. On 6 February, Jewish ex-servicemen held their annual memorial ceremony in the presence of city and federal representatives. They were doubtless reassured when state senator Curt Platen used the occasion to condemn anti-Jewish prejudice.[14]

For Jews, as for the rest of the population, the month following the advent of Hitler was a period of transition. The government had altered but almost everything else remained the same. There were certainly incidents of abuse and violence against Jews, usually perpetrated by gangs of SA men swaggering around the streets of towns and cities, enjoying their new legitimacy. But such assaults had been common before 1933 and notwithstanding the new chancellor they remained illegal. While the country plunged into another election, punctuated by violence and political drama, Jews entered a 'twilight period', during which they tried to comprehend the implications of what was happening around them and formulate appropriate responses. That involved thinking fast about their community's history, their identity, and their options, as well as evaluating Hitler's career and the possible trajectory of the Nazi Party. What seemed obvious a few months or years later, and what has acquired the aura of inevitability in most personal or historical accounts since 1945, was not at all self-evident at the time.[15]

The Jews of Germany

The self-identifying Jewish population of the German Republic numbered roughly 525,000 of whom about 100,000 were recent immigrants from eastern Europe, universally (and derisively) known as Ostjuden. Most German-born Jews traced their roots back centuries and were well integrated into German society. Outside a few islands of modern Orthodoxy, the practice of Judaism was heavily diluted. Every December the typical German Jewish family lit candles to celebrate the Jewish festival of Chanukkah *and* had a Christmas tree at home. Rates of intermarriage for men reached 25 per cent, while 16 per cent of Jewish women married out of the faith. The children in these mixed marriages were almost invariably raised as Christians. At an individual level, whether they were members of the Jewish community or declined to associate with it, German Jews were barely distinguishable from other Germans.[16]

Yet there were certain demographic, geographic, social and economic discrepancies that enabled Judeophobes to single them out. Whereas half the German population lived in small towns and villages, over two thirds of German Jews lived in cities. A third of the entire Jewish population (144,000) was concentrated in Berlin, where they made up 4 per cent of the capital's inhabitants. Within Berlin, as within other cities, there were certain residential districts that were densely populated by Jews. Often these were the most prosperous parts of town. The average Jewish household income was three times that of the average Gentile family. Although there was a significant stratum of poor Jews, which placed a heavy burden on Jewish welfare bodies and drained wealth from the better-off, the majority of Jews were comfortably middle class.[17]

As well as being geographically concentrated, Jews favoured a rather narrow range of occupations. Three quarters earned their living from trade, commerce, finance and the professions as against only one quarter of the non-Jewish population. While nearly a third of Germans worked on the land, barely 2 per cent of Jews were farmers. However, 25 per cent of wholesalers in the agricultural sector were Jewish. The Jewish grain merchant and cattle dealer was ubiquitous in rural areas such as Hesse. Jews were even more numerous in the textile and clothing sectors. They owned 40 per cent of wholesale textile firms and fully two thirds of wholesale and retail clothing outlets. Berlin's fashion district was virtually a Jewish district. Although department stores accounted for a relatively modest slice of the retail sector, nearly 80 per cent of turnover came from emporiums that were Jewish-owned, such as Hertie, KaDeWe and Wertheim, retail palaces that loomed over city-centre thoroughfares. Jews dominated the publishing industry: two houses, Ullstein and Mosse, were pacesetters for the production of books, magazines and newspapers. Non-Jews were also likely to meet Jews in key professional roles. Jews supplied 11 per cent of Germany's doctors, 13 per cent of attorneys and 16 per cent of lawyers. These proportions were not evenly spread across the country, though. There was massive bunching in the big cities where most Jews lived, notably Berlin, Frankfurt-am-Main, Hamburg, and Breslau.[18]

The most concentrated and visible segment of the Jewish population were the Ostjuden. They comprised a quarter of Berlin's Jewish inhabitants and actually outnumbered German-born Jews in Leipzig and Dresden. Ostjuden lacked German citizenship, spoke Yiddish and were religiously Orthodox, although their children rapidly assimilated into German society. By contrast to the German Jews, they were to be found in the more run-down inner-city districts, like the Scheunenviertel in Berlin. Large numbers were self-employed in artisanal trades or manual labour. Ironically, the success of the department stores made it ever harder for these Jewish shopkeepers, cobblers and tailors to make a living. They were hard hit by the Depression and often depended on relief from Jewish charities. This endeared them even less to German Jews, who blamed them for rising levels of anti-Jewish feeling. In the wake of the Great War, German federal and state authorities had tried to stop Jews entering the country across the eastern border. The Prussian authorities rounded up and deported some 4,000 Jewish illegal immigrants between 1918 and 1921. These measures were a continuation of long-established practices to check unwanted immigration from the east, but the attacks on Ostjuden acquired added venom after the Russian Revolution. Conservative and nationalist Germans had for a long time falsely accused the eastern Jews of importing crime, vice and disease; to that list was added the contagion of revolutionary ideas.[19]

The Jews who confronted Nazi anti-Semitism, especially those active in politics or in anti-defamation organizations, were hardly naive or ignorant about the challenge they faced. The oldest members of the com-

munity could recall a time when Jews were not even equal citizens. Max
Liebermann, head of the Prussian Academy of Arts and Germany's most
esteemed living painter, was born in 1847, a year before the revolutions
that made Jews citizens in several German states. Full equality only came
with the completion of German unification in 1870. Emancipation, the
achievement of civic equality, was no sooner won than it was under
threat. A deep depression in trade and agricultural prices in the early
and mid-1870s fomented discontent amongst Germany's small businessmen, artisans and farmers. Their discomfort was aggravated by the
emergence of organized labour and the mass-based Social Democratic
Party (Sozialdemokratische Partei Deutschlands, or SPD). The SPD
espoused hard-core Marxist doctrines, deepened the antagonism
between workers and employers, and preached the elimination of private
property. So where could the 'little man' turn? During the 1880s, a crop
of middle-class political agitators found they could win an audience
amongst farmers, shop owners and small manufacturers by blaming
Jewish bankers for the slump and attacking Jewish middlemen in the
rural economy. Other agitators who wanted to deflect workers away
from Marxism preached varieties of Christian Socialism that usually
boiled down to using Jews as a scapegoat for economic and social ills.[20]

For a while in the 1890s a number of avowedly anti-Semitic parties
achieved success in state elections and also managed to get deputies into
the Reichstag. The right-wing German Conservative Party was so
alarmed that it threw the antisemites a bone by including in its 1892
programme a reference to curbing the 'decomposing Jewish influence in
our national life'. This only gave respectability to the anti-Semites. They
won over 340,000 votes in the 1893 Reichstag elections and gained
sixteen deputies. Yet, while the Conservatives toyed with anti-Jewish
slogans, they condemned 'excesses'. The German state never succumbed
to the sort of anti-Jewish frenzy that gripped French institutions during
the Dreyfus affair. The 1893 national elections marked the high-water
mark for the anti-Semitic movement; from then on their parties splintered and foundered. By 1912, they attracted just 130,000 votes and
elected only six deputies.[21]

The failure of political anti-Semitism did not signify a waning
of anti-Jewish prejudice. If anything, the controversies stoked by the
anti-Semites made people more 'Jew conscious'. Amongst conservative-
minded Germans who were uneasy with rapid urbanization and mass
culture it became a nostrum that Jews, who seemed to have benefited

disproportionately from these developments, had too much influence in culture, society and the economy. Liberals disparaged religious prejudice and racism, but precisely for these reasons expressed bemusement that Jews did not intermarry and clung to their 'clannish' ways. Nationalists tended to see Jews as irredeemably alien, incapable of genuine loyalty to the Reich. Racial anti-Semites, known as völkisch because of their belief in the existence of a racially distinctive German people or folk, argued that Jews were unassimilable and constituted a threat to the German people. And, all the while, traditional forms of religious prejudice against Jews and Judaism persisted amongst churchgoing Catholics and Protestants. They thought of Germany as a Christian state. If so, how could Jews belong in it? The Social Democrats scorned such beliefs and were the most consistent opponents of anti-Semitism, but some were not averse to identifying Jews with capitalism and exploitation of the working class. Even as the Reichstag proved barren ground for anti-Semites seeking to revoke Jewish emancipation and segregate Jews by law, anti-Semitism spread as a 'cultural code', an attitudinal marker separating Jews from non-Jews.[22]

However, if Jews in 1933 could recall the sordid history of prejudice they also had an inspiring model of Jewish defence. Forty years earlier German Jews had formed the Centralverein deutscher Staatsbürger jüdischen Glaubens (the central association of German citizens of the Jewish faith) to combat the lies propagated by anti-Semites and oppose them when they stood for election. Over the next two decades, the CV proved quite effective: suing rabble rousers for defamation, funding candidates pledged to contest anti-Semitism, producing voluminous amounts of educational material about Judaism and Jewish life, and coordinating the activity of sympathetic non-Jews ashamed of prejudice within their communities. The CV also fostered a sense of Jewish pride and German patriotism, asserting the synthesis of Jewish and German identity.[23]

To patriotic German Jews the outbreak of war in 1914 offered the chance to demonstrate their love for the Fatherland. The Kaiser announced a truce in civic conflicts and declared that Germany recognized no confessional divide. Jews responded enthusiastically. The number that served in the armed forces was approximately their proportion of the population as a whole. Others, like the industrialist Walther Rathenau and the scientist Fritz Haber, made a huge contribution to the German war effort. Sadly, when German success on the battlefield faltered the army looked for someone to blame. In 1916, the Prussian War Ministry, possibly egged on by völkisch-minded generals in the high command, demanded an inquiry into the number and status of Jews in the military. The results of the census, known crudely as the Judenzählung (the Jew-count), were never made public but suspicion lingered that Jews had shirked their duty. Although 12,000 Jews died in combat while thousands more were maimed (again in proportion to their numbers in the population), the war did more to divide than unite Jews and non-Jews.[24]

The disastrous impact of the Great War

The way the war ended and its aftermath were a disastrous turning point in Jewish–Gentile relations. Despite massive territorial gains in the east, the German high command was unable to achieve a decisive victory on the western front. Instead, the British naval blockade led to ever worse food shortages and civilian unrest at home, while the entry of the United States on the Allied side tipped the military balance. By August 1918, the German army was being pushed back inexorably. Civilian morale began to crack, resulting in food riots and demonstrations calling for peace. This unrest was led by the Independent Socialists, militants who broke with the SPD over its support for the war. Several of their leaders, like Rosa Luxemburg, were Jewish. Mutinies broke out amongst sailors and soldiers inspired by the example of the Bolshevik Revolution. It did not escape the notice of conservatives that many leading Bolsheviks were of Jewish origin too, and that one of the most prominent, Leon Trotsky, was calling for revolution in Germany. In September the army told the Kaiser that the war was lost, but the efforts of the civilian leadership to wind down the conflict and preserve the fabric of the old order were swept away by revolutionary unrest. Germany was forced to sue for peace and on 9 November 1918 the deputy leader of the socialist party in the Reichstag, Philipp Scheidemann, announced that Germany was now a republic. A national assembly was elected to meet in Weimar and draw up a constitution. Its guiding light was Hugo Preuss, a politician of Jewish origin. To monarchists and everyone else who mourned the end of the German Empire, it looked as if it was overthrown by Jewish subversives. Many in the armed forces felt this even more keenly. Germany had capitulated before the Allied forces actually reached German territory and the front line was never broken. To those who could not accept that the army failed in the test of arms, the only explanation for defeat was treachery.[25]

Over the next few weeks socialist politicians, led by the new chancellor, Friedrich Ebert, struggled to prevent the upheaval running to extremes. Ebert promised the army that the socialists would head off a Bolshevik-style revolution if the army put its troops at the disposal of Germany's new republican rulers. His moderation led to a definitive split in the left, with the formation in December of the German Communist Party (KPD). Many of its leading lights, notably Luxemburg, were Jewish. While Berlin descended into chaos, a left-wing government took power in Bavaria, led by the Jewish journalist Kurt Eisner. It lurched further and further leftward until a Soviet state was proclaimed. Several 'commissars' of Red Bavaria, including Ernst Toller, Gustav Landauer, and Eugen Leviné, were Jewish-born. In order to shore up the federal government, Ebert and his colleagues had recourse not only to the army but to volunteer units of officers and NCOs who had no possibility of a career in the shrunken peace-time army but could not adapt to civilian life. The embittered and battle-hardened men who filled these units, known as Freikorps, were fanatically anti-Bolshevik and usually anti-Semitic. They were responsible for a wave of murders, assassinations and savage campaigns to repress working-class insurrections. They also fought on Germany's eastern border in the Baltic and against the Poles. In the minds of the Freikorps and outraged nationalists, the 'November criminals' who betrayed Germany, the Bolsheviks, the Jews, and the Poles were all cut from the same cloth.[26]

The Versailles Treaty, accepted by the German National Assembly under duress in June 1919, deprived Germany of territory including Alsace-Lorraine and Silesia. It forced Germany to accept guilt for starting the Great War and imposed a huge burden of reparations. The humiliating terms of the treaty outraged the population and in years to come every single German politician, from the left to the right, pledged to revise it. To republicans the treaty was like a curse. The birth of parliamentary democracy was forever associated with defeat and dishonour. The memory of chaos and a feeling of national shame tainted the constitution promulgated at Weimar, overshadowing its democratic and progressive spirit. The Weimar Republic gave its Jewish citizens equal rights and protection by the courts, but to the far-right and anti-Semites this only served to damn it.[27]

The years between 1919 and 1923 were horrendous for Germans, with German Jews suffering as much from political instability and economic turmoil as everyone else. During 1920 the government in Berlin faced a coup attempt from the right and the left, as well as workers' uprisings in the Ruhr industrial area. Communist-inspired unrest persisted throughout 1921, culminating in the 'Marsh action' in Saxony. Meanwhile, the government courted disaster with the Allied powers by resisting the payment of reparations. The German economy simply could not generate the kind of sums the French, especially, were demanding and in November 1922 the government announced it was defaulting. The French responded by sending troops to occupy the Ruhr and oversee confiscation of what they felt was due to them. In reply, the government in Berlin called on the population to engage in passive resistance and printed money to pay striking workers. The result was runaway inflation that turned the life savings of millions of Germans into worthless paper. While some smart businessmen profited from the hyperinflation, for ordinary Germans it was a catastrophe. They knew that politicians had allowed them to become innocent victims of the financial crisis; their belief in traditional values, the virtues of parliamentary democracy, law and order never recovered. Large clusters of angry citizens crystallized in associations that rejected the republic. They cultivated a sense of themselves as a wronged and victimized people, a Volk at odds with its own state; and sometimes they nurtured murderous fantasies of revenge.[28]

There was, however, a singular dimension to the Jewish experience: during these troubled years anti-Semitism metastasized. Anti-Semitic groups moved from the margins of German society into the mainstream. One of the first symptoms of this development was the formation of the Deutschvölkischer Schutz- und Trutzbund (German People's Defence and Protection League) in February 1919. Intended as a rallying point for anti-Semitic groups, the league dedicated itself to bringing down the Weimar Republic and fighting the alleged influence of the Jews, who it blamed for Germany's defeat. Its membership reached 180,000 by 1923, whereupon it was banned by the government because of its constant incitement to violence. Millions joined associations that represented Germans who had left the areas awarded to Poland by the Versailles Treaty or devoted themselves to securing their return. The Verein für Deutsche im Ausland and the Deutscher Ostbund each boasted a million members. As a corollary to campaigning on behalf of the ethnic Germans marooned in Poland these associations spewed hate towards the eastern Jews who had settled in Germany. The composition of the Reichstag in the first years of the republic reflected these currents. The Deutschnationale Volkspartei (DNVP, German National People's Party), launched in 1918, brought together the old conservative and nationalist parties in opposition to the Weimar Republic. The DNVP was unthinkingly, unsystematically anti-Semitic. In the 1924 Reichstag elections, at the peak of its popularity, the party won 21 per cent of the vote. For these völkisch groups and parties, anti-Semitism was as much about contempt for the Weimar Republic, its constitution and laws as it was about dislike of Jews. Attacking the Jews verbally or physically became a trial of strength with those who upheld the 'November constitution'.[29]

Most shockingly for German Jews, hateful thoughts and violent speech turned into physical assaults and murder. Jewish politicians were the favoured targets of right-wing assassins. Rosa Luxemburg, a leading figure in the German Communist Party, Kurt Eisner, premier of Bavaria, and, most prominently, Walther Rathenau, the foreign minister, fell to the bullets of killers who were celebrated as heroes in right-wing, völkisch circles. When the Freikorps suppressed the Soviet regime in Bavaria they tortured and shot Jewish activists who fell into their hands. In November 1923, at the height of the hyperinflation, when a loaf of bread cost 200,000 million Reichsmarks, a food riot in central Berlin turned into a pogrom. Thousands of hungry, resentful Berliners invaded the Scheunenviertel, where they smashed and looted Jewish shops for several hours. There were attacks on Ostjuden in other cities, too. Members of the most visible and vulnerable segment of the Jewish population were 'the first real victims of a brutalised German anti-semitism'.[30]

Then, almost as suddenly as it had come, the hyperinflation disappeared. The new chancellor, Gustav Stresemann, ended the practice of printing money to cover the deficit and stopped subsidizing resistance in the Ruhr. Stresemann introduced a new currency, the Rentenmark, pegged to the dollar, and, instead of trying to prove that reparations were unfeasible, resumed negotiations with the Allies. The following year, Stresemann, now serving as foreign minister, concluded a practical reparations plan. By August 1924, the nightmare had ended.[31]

German Jews did not observe these developments passively. The Centralverein engaged in vigorous anti-defamation work, distributing

50,000 handbills and 10,000 pamphlets on one day alone. Its membership soared as Jewish citizens threw themselves into the task of defending the good name of their community. Jewish ex-servicemen were particularly energetic. The Reichsbund jüdischer Frontsoldaten (Reich association of Jewish combat veterans, RjF) organized Jewish veterans across the country to ensure that the sacrifice made by Jews in the trenches was not overlooked. They fiercely contested efforts to traduce the loyalty of Jews to the Fatherland and drew on ties of comradeship forged in the ranks to bring non-Jews into the struggle against anti-Semitism. The Jüdischer Abwehr Dienst (Jewish defence service) provided physical security in times of tension. During the Scheunenviertel riots members of the Reichsbund jüdischer Frontsoldaten, took up weapons and patrolled the streets. Rather less heroically, communal leaders enjoined Jewish citizens to avoid 'provocation' by ostentatious behaviour or involvement with political extremism. For some nationalist Jews, like Max Naumann, this self-policing took the form of relentlessly criticizing the Ostjuden. 'Whoever comes from "half Asia" is a dangerous guest', he opined. Naumann suggested that German Jews should show their commitment to Germanness by demanding the expulsion of Jewish immigrants.[32]

In January 1933, then, German Jews were neither naive nor passive spectators of events. Their assessments of the 'experiment' with Hitler were not made just on the strength of recent events, the products of short-sightedness or momentary delusion. The conviction that Hitler had been appointed at a moment of weakness and might fall at any time rested on knowledge about the trajectory of his 'rise' and his curious career. He was placed in the context of previous political instability and waves of anti-Semitism, their ebb and flow. This awareness applied also to the range of Nazi policies, not least their attitude towards and plans for the Jews. So what did Germans, Jews and non-Jews, and the rest of the world know about Adolf Hitler and the Nazis?

Who was Adolf Hitler and what did he want?

Adolf Hitler only became a national political figure in the late 1920s and did not represent a significant political force until September 1930. Until then, only professional students of politics bothered to pay him much attention. Jews, like Alfred Wiener and Hans Reichmann, who were involved in anti-defamation work for the Centralverein naturally monitored the Nazis and reported on their activities. From the party's inception its members were infamous for their extreme hatred of Jews and willingness to extend verbal violence to physical assault. But most Jews, like most other Germans in areas where the Nazi Party was weak or absent, knew little about it or its leader. The majority scrambled for information after the party had made its first big parliamentary gains in 1930. Consequently, Hitler was in the public eye for a mere two years before he became chancellor and during that time he behaved with consummate moderation. His rhetoric was toned down, he chose positive themes for his speeches, and his public attacks on the Jews diminished to vanishing point.[33]

Furthermore, Hitler and his propaganda machine carefully controlled his image. His autobiography and statement of political beliefs, Mein Kampf, was a key text. In the first part, which is essentially biographical, Hitler depicts himself as a man of humble origins who experienced hardship and poverty in his youth. He describes his political awakening, when he perceived the malign influence of socialism and the Jews, and summarizes what he learned as an autodidact in those years. Hitler reiterates his belief in the centrality of blood and race to human history and his adhesion to the guiding principles of Social Darwinism and eugenics. The vividly written passages about the years he spent in the army portray him as an ordinary front-line soldier who shared the discomforts and made the same sacrifices as millions of others. He repeats the widespread belief that Germany was stabbed in the back in 1918 and blames Jews for the defeat, but rather more unusually suggests that if a few thousand had been killed by poison gas Germany might not have lost the war. The biographical section of Mein Kampf concludes with his entry into politics after the war and the foundation of the Nazi Party. The second part covers the early history of the party and Hitler's leading role, commingled with explanations of its philosophy, its aspirations, and practical thoughts on organization, propaganda and tactics.[34]

However, Mein Kampf was published in 1925–6 (originally, the first and second parts appeared separately). A great deal had changed between then and January 1933. Hitler now presented himself as more moderate than his tract suggested, as a responsible politician. He had second thoughts about publishing a further volume in 1928 precisely because he realized that his words might hang around his neck like a political albatross. So, a perusal of *Mein Kampf* gave the reader in 1933 a sense of who Hitler was and the intensity of his hostility to Jews, but how reliable was it as a guide to his current thinking or future action? In October 1930, Sir Horace Rumbold summed up the Nazi programme as 'striving for a greater, better, cleaner and less corrupt Germany'. His successor, Sir Eric Phipps, doubted that Hitler would adhere to positions 'expressed with such incredible violence in a work written in a Bavarian prison ten years ago'. Both men believed that Hitler was consistent about the Jews although they were equally convinced that in general he had moderated his views. Hence, Hitler's early life and career were not necessarily predictors of what he would do once he was in a position of power. In any case, as historians have shown, the Hitler depicted in *Mein Kampf* or the hagiographies published by the party or his friends bore little relationship to the facts of his life.[35]

Hitler was born in 1889 in a small town close to the border between the Austro-Hungarian Empire and Imperial Germany, but grew up in Linz. His father, a customs official, died when Adolf was fourteen years old. His mother supported his ambitions to become an artist and in 1907 he applied unsuccessfully to the Academy of Fine Arts in Vienna, the year his mother died. Hitler returned to Vienna, spending half a decade as an impecunious, aspiring artist. He sold paintings to Jewish art dealers and according to the available evidence he had no inhibitions about interacting with them. Nor is there any record of him voicing anti-Jewish sentiments. There were signs, though, of his hatred for Marxism.[36]

In 1913 he moved to Munich, a cosmopolitan city with a flourishing artistic milieu. For a little over a year he sold his paintings and enjoyed cafe society. The outbreak of war changed the course of his life. In Vienna, Hitler had become a fervent German nationalist. He also read a great deal of popular Social Darwinist literature that extolled struggle as a way of life. According to these tracts the struggle between nations and 'races' found its supreme expression in war. Combat was also the testing ground for an individual's worthiness to live. Hitler felt invigorated by the prospect and enrolled in the 16th Bavarian Reserve Infantry Regiment. This was a poor-quality unit filled with over-age reservists, few of whom were as enthusiastic as him. Hitler served as a regimental dispatch runner, a job that involved considerable risk. He displayed genuine valour and was awarded the Iron Cross, second class and first class (the latter thanks to the recommendation of a Jewish officer).

Despite the image he later fostered, though, Hitler was not really one of the lads. He was quartered with the regimental staff well back from the front line and was a bit of a loner. In October 1918 he was temporarily blinded by a British gas attack near Ypres and evacuated to a military hospital. He learned of Germany's capitulation while he was still recovering from his wounds: the news came as a terrific shock. Having been insulated from the crumbling morale of the ordinary infantrymen he was only too ready to believe the myth that the army had suffered a 'stab in the back', that Germany was brought down by subversion, by enemies within.[37]

Hitler remained in the army for two more years, based in Munich. He showed no inclination to quit even when his unit came under the authority of the short-lived revolutionary regime in Bavaria. Throughout this period he operated as a field agent for military intelligence, collecting evidence on radical and rebellious groups. To assist his work he was given training as an education officer, took courses in politics at Munich University, and was briefed about the range of subversive ideologies. His mentors were right-wing army officers – extreme nationalists who were anti-Marxist and anti-Semitic. Under their tutelage Hitler began to write and speak about the Jews as a dangerous 'race' who were enemies of the German people. Sent by the army to infiltrate the right-wing, anti-Semitic German Workers' Party (Deutsche Arbeiterpartei, DAP), he ended up joining it. In February 1920 he participated in drafting the party's twenty-five-point programme and renaming it the National Socialist German Workers' Party (Nationalsozialistische Deutsche Arbeiterpartei, NSDAP) to distinguish it from Marxist groups. Thanks to the army, Hitler discovered a talent for oratory and propaganda. His ability to draw and hold large audiences on the beer-hall circuit propelled him to ascendancy over his party comrades. He left the military and began to live as a professional political agitator, circulating in the far-right, racist and nationalist milieu in Munich that thrived on the bitterness of defeat and economic disruption.[38]

The Nazis, as the National Socialists quickly became known, were just one of several völkisch groups in Bavaria. Hitler was only distinguished by his extremism, his energy, his oratorical skills and his messianic self-belief. By July 1921 he had established the principle that he alone could lead the party and decide policy: the Führerprinzip. His experience in the trenches and his memory of a Germany united by a patriotic and self-sacrificing ethos guided him throughout his political journey. Under his direction the party took on a paramilitary hue. It acquired its own militia in October 1921 when an ex-army captain, Ernst Röhm, set up the Sturmabteilung (SA) to protect Nazi meetings from disruption. The storm troops took their name and inspiration from the assault units that led German attacks on the western front. Violence of language and the readiness to use force set the Nazis apart from the völkisch pack and attracted others to their ranks. A year later, Julius Streicher led his völkisch group into the NSDAP. Streicher, a Nuremberg teacher with a strong war record, was a pathological anti-Semite. He founded a paper, *Der Stürmer*, to promote National Socialism and disseminate a particularly vicious and sex-obsessed brand of Jew-hatred. By early 1923, NSDAP membership had risen from 20,000 to 55,000. Hitler had now gathered around himself a core of loyal and effective acolytes. They included Hermann Göring, a former fighter ace; Rudolf Hess, a veteran of the trenches and the Freikorps; Alfred Rosenberg, an ethnic German from Estonia who had trained as an engineer but had a gift for writing; and Max Amann, previously the NCO commanding Hitler's section in the 16th Bavarian Infantry. These men had complete faith in his political vision and offered him virtually unconditional obedience; they would remain his closest, most trusted lieutenants.[39]

It looked as if the tide was running their way. The French occupation of the Ruhr, hyperinflation, and communist activity in several German states energized the far right. Munich was a snakepit of anti-republican plotters. Alarmed by what they perceived as the drift to the left, Bavarian state officials planned to topple the government in Berlin and restore order. Hitler was now cooperating with several völkisch groups and in October 1923 it looked like a coalition comprising the Bavarian government, the NSDAP and other parties would march on Berlin to suppress parliamentary democracy, much as Mussolini had marched on Rome the year before. At the last minute, however, the Bavarian leadership pulled back. Hitler, desperate to keep up the momentum, hoped he could bounce them into action by staging his own coup in Munich. He made his move on the night of 8 November 1923, but by that time the army high command in Berlin had rallied to the central government and there was little chance that the Bavarian ministers would risk a showdown. Despite being joined by General Ludendorff, a hero of the Great War, the Nazis found themselves more or less alone. Undaunted, the next morning Hitler led his followers towards the Bavarian Defence Ministry; but when the insurgents reached the Odeonsplatz in central Munich the police opened fire. Several National Socialists were shot dead, Göring was badly wounded, and Hitler injured his arm when he was pulled to the ground. The putsch dissolved and within the next few hours the leading conspirators were rounded up. In February 1924 Hitler stood trial alongside Ludendorff – who was only too happy to let the ex-corporal take credit for the abortive coup. Hitler used the proceedings to set out his beliefs with skill and passion, winning the sympathy of the right-wing judges. He was sentenced to five years in Landsberg fortress, but before he left the court the judges indicated that they hoped he would serve even less time. Hitler emerged from the trial as a martyr and hero.[40]

The press coverage of the trial enhanced Hitler's status in far-right circles. His centrality was underlined by the factionalism that tore apart the NSDAP in his absence, although the far right as a whole went into decline thanks to the stability that finally settled over Germany. Hitler filled his time in prison writing and dictating *Mein Kampf* to Rudolf Hess, his personal assistant. When he emerged in 1925 he had a fully formed ideology and an ever-stronger sense of mission, but power seemed a distant goal. He was not allowed to speak in public until 1927, in some German states not until 1928. Yet these were hardly wasted, wilderness years. During the late 1920s the Nazi Party perfected the techniques and the appeal that would attract more and more Germans to its ranks.[41]

In February 1925 Hitler relaunched the NSDAP. He renounced the strategy of the coup and pledged to follow a parliamentary course. This did not mean eschewing violence or abandoning his determination to bring down the republic. Anti-Semitism remained at the core of the party's ideology, crucial for both its internal coherence and its external operations. However, the NSDAP was not merely a negative force. It put down roots in local communities, offering help to hard-pressed citizens. Unlike the parliamentary parties of the right that became increasingly remote from ordinary people, the Nazis paid attention to interest groups and regional questions. Above all, they offered a positive social vision. Hitler promised to restore the sense of unity and purpose that had animated the nation in 1914–18; he painted a future of social harmony, equality and mutual respect. While he was always vague about detailed policy, he was able to mobilize the idealism of young people especially, and groups that felt left out of politics. Women and new voters were drawn in by the Nazis' concern for ordinary folk, their willingness to address the plight of the homeless and the unemployed, distressed farmers, struggling small businessmen and underpaid civil servants. Because the parties of the left, the SPD and KPD, spoke the language of class and threatened those with property, the NSDAP was able to channel the discontent of the large middle class – and a fair number of disgruntled workers, too. It imitated the Marxist parties in terms of its relentless search for new members, ceaselessly building a mass base, and the discipline of those who joined its ranks.[42]

Activism and violence were essential to the party's message. Parades and rallies, accompanied by banners and bands, allowed the Nazis to occupy the streets symbolically. In small towns and villages, particularly on key days in the Nazi and the national calendar, large numbers of SA men and party members would virtually take over the public spaces. At the same time as speakers denounced the 'November criminals', the Weimar Republic, the Versailles Treaty, reparations, and 'the Jews' who were responsible for all these ills, the brown-shirted militia presented a physical challenge to the constitution and the law. When they insulted Jews or damaged Jewish-owned property they issued a challenge to the republic. If the police force intervened it placed the forces of law and order on the side of a despised republic and an unloved minority. Violence also illustrated in the most brutal terms who was a part of the nation and who was an outsider. By forcing an identification of interests between the republic and the victims of intimidation, the Nazis suggested that both were opposed to the true Germans, the people of the racial-national community, the Volksgemeinschaft, that were as yet excluded from power.[43]

Still, the party remained a 'fringe irritant'. In the parliamentary elections of 1928 the Nazis received just 2.6 per cent of the vote and won only twelve seats. Membership stood at around 130,000. Hitler gained some valuable publicity and a new degree of respectability by joining forces with Alfred Hugenberg and the DNVP in opposition to a new deal for reparations, the Young Plan, but the NSDAP was very much the junior partner. The paramilitary Stahlhelm was far larger than the SA and while it indirectly reinforced the Nazi message the effect was masked as long as it supported the DNVP and was loyal to Hindenburg (whom it did much to elect as President of the republic in the national election of 1925). On the tenth anniversary of the Weimar Constitution, Leopold Schwarzschild sounded a celebratory note. It was undeniable that 35 per cent of voters still chose parties that wanted the republic to fail: 'But there are welcome signs that the position of the individual is being strengthened, and more than elsewhere. We have fewer regulations, fewer prohibitions, but also greater guarantees of personal liberty than almost any other country on this ravaged continent.'[44]

Hitler's bumpy road to power

Within just a few weeks such optimism wilted under the effect of the Wall Street Crash. In 1929 the German economy was already in trouble, out of balance and unable to generate enough jobs to match the growing population. When American banks started calling in loans made to German financial institutions and enterprises they tipped Germany into a catastrophic deflationary spiral. Banks stopped advancing credit and demanded repayment of loans they had made; businesses responded by laying off workers and cutting wages. When they could not release sufficient capital that way, they went bankrupt. As spending power was reduced, industry and agriculture that depended on domestic consumption suffered accordingly. Tax revenue plummeted while welfare expenditure soared. The state and federal governments now made deep cuts too, throwing more out of work and inflicting short time or reduced wages on the large public sector.[45]

The political system could not cope. In March 1930 the 'Grand Coalition' government of Social Democrats, German Democrats, German People's Party, and the Catholic Centre Party collapsed over an increase of the social contributions. Now the weaknesses of the Weimar Constitution came into play. The constitution granted considerable power to the president, but the ageing Hindenburg was increasingly manipulated by men in his entourage and the army leadership with whom they were closely connected. At their suggestion Hindenburg appointed the Catholic Centre politician Heinrich Brüning as chancellor. Brüning had no significant support in parliament. Knowing that he could not secure legislation to balance the budget he fell back on Article 48 of the constitution that allowed the president to rule by decree with the consent of the Reichstag. Intended as an emergency clause, Article 48 became the routine basis of governance. In July 1930, Brüning sought to break the opposition of the left-wing parties by calling elections. The result, declared on 14 September, was a 'political earthquake'. The middle-class parties collapsed while both the extreme left and the far right gained tremendously. The NSDAP achieved 18.3 per cent of the vote, winning 107 seats. They were now the second largest party after the socialists. Brüning, who brought this result on his own head by a disastrous miscalculation, was kept in power by the president, the SPD, and the Centre Party, which preferred him to the alternatives.[46]

A month after the results were declared, the Jewish socialite and gossip columnist Bella Fromm noted 'a touch of panic in certain quarters. Should we leave Germany and wait outside and see what happens?' Fromm grew up in a well-off assimilated family in Bavaria but straitened financial times forced her to take up journalism. As a writer for the liberal Ullstein press, she thought the Nazis were 'noisy roughnecks'. She was dismayed that conservative newspapers treated Hitler's electoral breakthrough with gravity, even more so when establishment figures like Hjalmar Schacht, the president of the Reichsbank, suggested giving the Nazis a chance in government. Fromm probably composed her 'diary' after she had emigrated from Germany to the USA in 1938, but she nevertheless captured the confusion evoked by the unfamiliar political landscape.[47]

The Nazis had succeeded thanks to a clever and well-organized campaign that built on their previous steady, if unspectacular, success at the grass roots and in local elections. Their message was simple and attractive. Parliamentary democracy had brought nothing but conflict and misery; only Hitler could unite the country; only the NSDAP could thwart the rise of the communists. Hitler barely mentioned Jews in his major speeches, although to many Germans his attacks on Marxism and his criticism of modern society were understood as coded references to Jewish influence. If anything, it was the idealism and sincerity which the Nazis projected that brought Germans to acceptance of anti-Semitism rather than the other way round.[48]

Indeed, Hitler reiterated his commitment to achieving power by peaceful and legitimate means. He sought to reassure the international press that the Nazis 'had nothing against decent Jews'. His minions, on the other hand, paid little heed to these tactical declarations. The day that the new parliament assembled, 13 October 1930, Nazi gangs vandalized the Wertheim and Teitz department stores in Berlin and attacked Jewish shops along the Kurfürstendamm, the main shopping street of central Berlin. Jubilant Nazis installed themselves in towns and villages across Germany, signifying their presence with banners, flags and parades. Wherever they gained a foothold they incited local people to cease buying from Jewish shops or dealing with Jews. On the eve of the Jewish New Year, 12 September 1931, 1,000 storm troopers again rioted along the Kurfürstendamm, assaulting anyone who they thought looked Jewish. Similar violence took place in Nuremberg and Würzburg. The police could barely cope with organized violence on this scale.[49]

During 1931, Brüning pursued a dangerous game of using the economic crisis to force the British, French and Americans to cancel, or at least lighten, the burden of reparations. Threats to suspend the repayment of foreign debt only increased the flight of capital from Germany. Although Brüning eventually managed to get reparations suspended this did nothing to ameliorate the disastrous situation: unemployment continued to climb. By the end of the year one fifth of the workforce was unemployed. There were 600,000 jobless in Berlin alone.[50]

The Nazi Party now became a 'catch-all party of discontent', stacking up votes in a series of state elections. Mainstream politicians and figures from business and industry, men like Hjalmar Schacht and the steel magnate Fritz Thyssen, sought meetings with Hitler to explore how serious he was about the 'socialist' elements of the party programme. Early in 1932, Fromm observed that 'Society slowly gets accustomed to the originally plebeian National Socialist movement. People from the upper crust are turning to Hitler.' Not that it was a smooth run for the Nazi leadership. The swelling ranks of the SA were chafing at the bit to seize power. Hitler was forced to replace their leadership and recall Ernst Röhm (who had gone to South America in pursuit of other opportunities) to bring them into line. He also faced a scandal when his girlfriend, Geli Raubal, who was also his half-niece, committed suicide in his Munich apartment.[51]

In a bid to keep up the political momentum, Hitler and his advisers considered whether he should run as a candidate against Hindenburg, whose presidential term was coming to an end. There was a danger that in so doing Hitler would appear anti-patriotic, plus there was the minor problem that he was not even a German citizen. To get around the latter, NSDAP officials in Braunschweig appointed him as a government councillor, a post that brought with it German citizenship. In March 1932, Hitler launched himself into another election, posing as the youthful alternative to the respected field marshal.[52]

The campaign was brilliantly conducted by Joseph Goebbels, a journalist whom Hitler had appointed party boss of Berlin in 1926. Goebbels came from a humble Catholic background in the Rhineland and had put himself through university with the help of Catholic charities. Due to a deformity of the right foot he had not served in the war, but he was a pugnacious intellectual with a belligerent world view. As a youth he was drawn to conservative völkisch ideas that he spiced with a hatred of capitalism and the bourgeoisie. Thanks to coverage of the putsch trial he discovered Hitler and came to regard him as a messianic figure. Goebbels began writing for the völkisch press and in 1925 published 'The National Socialist's Little ABC'. Soon he had become one of the party's most effective speakers and propagandists. For a while his association with the left wing of National Socialism hindered his progress, but after Goebbels abandoned it Hitler posted him to Berlin with a mission to win over the capital's working-class population. Goebbels was well suited to the challenge and over the following years honed his propaganda techniques. He played on themes of sacrifice and redemption, used ceremony and invented rituals, and latched on to the possibilities of modern media. In particular he saw the utility of film and radio. His genius for publicity coalesced in his orchestration of Hitler's bid in 1932 to become head of state.[53]

In the first round Hitler won 30.1 per cent of the vote, as against 49.6 per cent for Hindenburg, and thereby forced a second poll. To emphasize Hitler's youth and dynamism, as against the staid, ancient field marshal, Goebbels, by now the party's propaganda chief, arranged for Hitler to fly from city to city addressing mass rallies. Between 22 March and 9 April, the leader spoke twenty-three times before mass audiences in twenty-one locations, directly reaching one million people with his message. Even more people saw newsreel reports of 'Hitler over Germany'. The result revealed that Hindenburg had scored 52 per cent of the vote, while Hitler had pushed his share up to 36.8 per cent. The doddering president had become the last refuge for defenders of the Weimar Republic, while Hitler was on the way to co-opting the entire völkisch-nationalist electorate.[54]

Even so, Jews and supporters of the republic did not see this as cause for alarm. Schwarzschild actually argued that it was time to 'let him have a go', reasoning that the longer Hitler was kept out of power the more his support would accumulate, until the Nazis received enough votes to form a government independently of other parties. Since the economy was bound to deteriorate, it made sense to let the

Nazi Party take office while its vote hovered below 40 per cent. Crucially, Schwarzschild added that 'As long as the democratic mechanism continues to function, even the maximum extension of Hitlerism will always remain within a limit which will mean that the slightest counter current will send it tumbling back into a minority.' In April 1932 it seemed perfectly credible to argue, 'Let him govern, but with the proviso that no change can be made to the constitutional framework.'[55]

No sooner was the presidential race over than campaigning began in a slew of elections for state legislatures. In an attempt to curb the violence that now routinely accompanied electioneering and to peg back the National Socialists, Carl Severing, the Prussian minister of the interior, ordered raids on party headquarters, while Wilhelm Groener, the interior minister, banned the SA and the SS. The fightback came too late. The Nazis won 36 per cent of the vote in Prussia, 32 per cent in Bavaria and a remarkable 40 per cent in Anhalt. They were able to form administrations in Oldenburg, Mecklenburg-Schwerin and Thuringia. In such circumstances it was increasingly difficult to treat them as pariahs. But the resistance to Nazism was also being undermined from within.[56]

At the same time as Brüning was getting tough with the Nazis, Kurt von Schleicher, a former general staff officer who headed the liaison office between the army and Hindenburg's office, began exploring ways to bring them into government. He lined up Franz von Papen, an old friend who was an ex-diplomat and Catholic politician, as the man to lead an administration open to the National Socialists. Then he persuaded men in the president's circle that the plan was viable. Unable to secure a governing majority in the Reichstag and deserted by Hindenburg, Brüning resigned on 30 May 1932.[57]

Schleicher had discussed the transition in several secret meetings with Hitler and his advisers. In return for their compliance, Hitler and Goebbels demanded the unbanning of the SA and the SS plus fresh parliamentary elections. They were convinced that if they could push up their vote they could demand the right to form a government on their own. Schleicher's plan misfired. Papen was made chancellor and began to construct a cabinet, but the dissolution of parliament and the announcement of elections unleashed a fresh tide of violence. The SA and SS were permitted back onto the streets and resumed battle with the Social Democratic Party militia and the communists. On one day alone, eighteen people were killed in the northern port city of Altona.

Regardless of the chaos, Papen and Schleicher ploughed on with their agenda to form a right-wing regime. On 20 July 1932 they deposed the SPD government in Prussia, appointing commissioners in its place. Ten days later the elections gave the NSDAP 37.4 per cent of the vote, netting it 230 seats in the Reichstag.[58]

In accordance with his grand manoeuvre, Schleicher, who was now army minister, met Hitler to induce him into joining the government under Papen. But with 230 Reichstag delegates in his pocket Hitler felt emboldened to demand nothing less than the chancellorship. Schleicher was prepared to swallow that, but Hindenburg refused to contemplate a 'Bohemian corporal' serving as chancellor. On 13 August, Hindenburg met privately with Hitler and asked him to enter government as a junior partner. Hitler refused, demanding instead 'full powers'. Hindenburg was equally implacable, so the talks ended. The presidential palace subsequently issued a statement implying that Hitler was power-hungry and put party before country. This rebuff left the Nazis looking bad and, indeed, they were in a sticky position. The party was short of funds after the succession of costly election campaigns; its activists were exhausted; and the SA was losing patience with the democratic route to power. There were rumblings of discontent with the party leadership. For the first time, the Nazi vote dipped in local elections. Meanwhile, Schleicher and Papen intended to dissolve the Reichstag, postpone elections until they could ensure a favourable outcome, and rule by decree as a 'presidential cabinet'. In a chaotic session of the Reichstag, however, Papen was stampeded into a dissolution without obtaining a postponement. The elections had little chance of breaking the deadlock, but were potentially disastrous for the cash-strapped, battle-weary NSDAP. In the national ballot on 6 November 1932, the Nazis lost 2 million votes, 34 Reichstag seats, and saw their share of the poll fall to 33.1 per cent. To many it seemed that the republic had been saved.[59]

Instead, thanks to the machinations of Papen, Schleicher, and the coterie around the president, it lurched into another crisis. Following the elections Papen resigned but Hindenburg asked him to form a new government. The president again requested Hitler to serve under Papen, and Hitler again refused – this time to the alarm of his entourage and the despair of his followers. But none of the other parties could be induced to support Papen either. Schleicher now lost patience with his friend and convinced himself that with the backing of the army he could do better. He persuaded Hindenburg to withdraw his support for the chancellor, compelling Papen to resign for a second time. The next day, 3 December 1932, Schleicher assumed the chancellorship. Although he lacked any parliamentary or party base, Schleicher had a vision of an authoritarian regime that could win popular support through measures to benefit the working class. He opened talks with trade unionists and, after Hitler spurned his advances, courted the left wing of the Nazi Party, led by Gregor Strasser. When Strasser responded favourably it looked as if the Nazi Party was going to implode. Party workers and supporters were fed up with fighting campaigns that led nowhere; they could not understand why their leader shied away from high office. Hitler had to move nimbly to quell this unrest and crush the 'Strasserites'. Even so, his prospects looked bleak.[60]

At the turn of the year, Leopold Schwarzschild detected 'a break in the clouds'. He believed that a fascist takeover had been averted. There were signs of economic recovery while 'the political tide has changed direction and lost some of its violence'. The nationalist camp was falling apart, the Nazis were crumbling, and Schleicher was beginning to improve things for ordinary people.[61]

Schwarzschild did not know that the embittered Papen was conspiring to bring down Schleicher and put Hitler in his place. On 4 January 1933 the two men met secretly in Cologne and agreed to seek a change of government without new elections. News of the conclave leaked out and immediately boosted Hitler's standing. The Nazi Party received another fillip when it won nearly 40 per cent of the vote in the state of Lippe. Even though it was a tiny electorate and the Nazis had poured in resources, the victory gave the impression that they were on the march again. The success strengthened Hitler sufficiently to face down dissent amongst senior party men who warned that he could not play a waiting game much longer. According to an internal report the party was going to haemorrhage support unless it achieved a decisive success.[62]

At this juncture Joachim von Ribbentrop, a well-connected wine merchant from the Rhineland with a military and diplomatic background, who had been attracted to Hitler's cause, offered to act as an intermediary between Hitler and Papen. While Schleicher tried vainly to shore up his position, Hitler bargained with Papen over the shape of a new cabinet. Initially the talks went badly because Hitler insisted on the chancellorship. Fortunately for him, Oskar von Hindenburg, the president's son, disliked Schleicher even more than the prospect of a government led by Adolf Hitler. Oskar von Hindenburg and Hindenburg's chief of staff, Otto Meissner, joined the discussions and helped steer them towards the formation of a cabinet with Hitler as chancellor and Papen as his deputy – on the assumption that the president and the vice chancellor could contain Hitler. A few days later Papen proposed this solution to Hindenburg. The old man baulked yet again, but he was equally unwilling to let Schleicher call fresh elections before the Reichstag reconvened and, inevitably, voted down his government. In desperation Schleicher intimated that the army might have to take control, raising the prospect of civil war. The previous day, 15,000 SA men had smashed their way into the headquarters of the Communist Party before marching to hear Hitler address them at a rally. As they marched they shouted, 'We shit on the Jew republic . . . We shit on freedom'. Things were spiralling out of control and the army was not even certain that it could keep the contesting sides apart. Finally, Schleicher ran out of options. On 28 January he told the cabinet that he would seek permission to dissolve the Reichstag, put off elections indefinitely, and govern in the interim as a 'presidential cabinet'. If Hindenburg refused, he would resign. Although Hindenburg had previously permitted the constitution to be bent, this time he stood on principle and refused to let Schleicher sidestep the legislature and rule by decree: he was fed up with the chancellor and his advisers were worried by several of Schleicher's pro-labour measures. Ironically, one of the last of these was a massive public works scheme worth RM500 million that would eventually put two million Germans back to work, but under Hitler.[63]

With Schleicher's resignation it remained for Papen to persuade Hindenburg to swallow Hitler's appointment as chancellor and construct a new government in such a way as to reassure the field marshal that the Nazi Party would not run rampant. The prospect of a 'nationalist front' induced Franz Seldte, leader of the Stahlhelm, to join, while Papen gained the adhesion of Hugenberg by offering two important ministries to the DNVP. The choice of two traditional conservatives, Werner von Blomberg and Konstantin von Neurath, as respectively army minister and foreign minister, further placated Hindenburg. Hitler asked for just two portfolios. Wilhelm Frick, a lawyer and former civil servant, got the Interior Ministry. Hermann Göring, who had been president of the Reichstag since July 1932 as a reflection of the Nazi ascendancy, joined as a minister without portfolio and Prussian minister of the interior. Papen himself took the role of commissioner for

Prussia as well as vice chancellor, which, on paper, put him in a strong position. When a conservative Prussian aristocrat who knew Papen expressed alarm at the prospect of Hitler in power, Papen told him to calm down. 'You're mistaken. We've hired him.'[64]

Judgements and misjudgements in January 1933

Contemporary assessments of Nazism varied widely and this variation is itself telling. No one in January 1933 could accurately assess the nature of the new regime, let alone how it would develop in the future or what it would deliver. Of course many Jews were now fully apprised of the Nazi Party's rabid attitude towards the Jewish people and felt a sense of foreboding. Three weeks prior to the Nazis entering the national government the *Jüdische Rundschau* reflected that things had come to a sorry pass when Jews were relieved that a right-wing government led by the head of the army had managed to keep Hitler out of the Chancellery. Even that relief evaporated at the end of the month.[65]

However, other Jews saw nothing ominous in Hitler's rise. In September 1930 Siegmund Warburg, a well-connected and well-informed member of the Hamburg banking dynasty, asserted to his Swedish father-in-law that 'Once they are in government they will immediately become, first, more sensible and, secondly, once again less popular.' After all, there were precedents for this transformation: 'Our Social Democrats were also once irresponsible demagogues and have today nearly all become bourgeois and willing to compromise.' Warburg was not alone amongst the Jewish elite of Weimar Germany. During the course of 1932, Rudolf Hilferding, a leading SPD politician, Hans Schäffer, the managing director of the Ullstein publishing concern, the banker Oscar Wassermann, and Warburg's colleague Carl Melchior all advocated giving the Nazis a stab at government. Like Schwarzschild they were convinced that power would tame rather than inflame the Nazis and that Hitler was as likely to fail as to succeed.[66]

These Jews were not gullible or prey to wishful thinking derived from a pitiful desire to be accepted as Germans. Walther Karsch, a fearless opponent of fascism who wrote for the radical weekly *Die Weltbühne*, opined in September 1930 that 'Anyone who believes that these people will now make a serious attempt to implement their anti-semitic ideas may be reassured. There is absolutely no reason to start applying for passports and packing your bags. In order to get back at the Jews there would need to be a change to the constitution. Where is the necessary two thirds majority?' To Karsch, 'anti-semitism is no more than an advertising slogan'.[67]

Proximity to events did not necessarily alter perceptions. The young Joachim Fest, growing up in a Catholic household in Berlin dominated by his anti-Nazi father, later remarked that 'the continuation of the familiar blurred any sense of a break'. Curt Riess, a Jewish journalist working for a left-liberal newspaper, remembered sub-editing a head-line announcing that Hitler had become chancellor 'without the slightest feeling, without any concern that it might affect me'. Yet a few weeks later he was an exile in Paris and in 1941 made his way to New York, where he published numerous anti-Nazi tracts.[68]

Experienced diplomats reached diametrically opposed conclusions about Hitler, based on their own observations and soundings amongst knowledgeable Germans. Without any caveat Sir Horace Rumbold transmitted to the Foreign Office Papen's belief that 'a government under Hitler including a proportion of ministers who were not Nazis would be unable to embark on dangerous experiments'. A week later he echoed the line advanced by the German foreign minister, Neurath, that 'The Hitler experiment had to be made sometime or other.' When he met Hitler for the first time, Rumbold found him 'simple and un-affected' although his words and actions were 'more calculated to appeal to the mob than to the critical faculty'.[69]

Yet the American James G. McDonald saw the Nazis in a different light. McDonald was a tall, blond Midwesterner who had gained a PhD in political science at Harvard and won notice in Germany for his cri-tique of Allied atrocity propaganda during the Great War. Between 1919 and 1933 he was chairman of the American organization supporting the League of Nations which metamorphosed into the Foreign Policy Asso-ciation (FPA). It was as a representative of the FPA that he travelled to Germany in autumn 1932 and met with Ernst 'Putzi' Hanfstaengl, Hitler's American-educated publicist. Hanfstaengl got McDonald into a key rally at the Berlin Sportpalast on 1 September 1932 at which Hitler steadied the nerve of his followers. The next day he lunched with Hanf-staengl and asked him about Hitler and the Jewish question. In a report to the FPA he wrote that 'Immediately his eyes lighted up, took on a fanatical look, and he launched into a tirade against the Jews. He would not admit that any Jew could be a good patriot in Germany.' To McDonald, 'It was clear that he and, I presume, many of the Nazis really believe all these charges against the Jews.'[70]

Ordinary Germans greeted the new government in myriad ways depending on their political orientation, their religious affiliation, where they lived, whether they had jobs or not and a host of other variables. Many embraced National Socialism out of youthful idealism, a longing for change, and in a frenzy of hope rather than hate. Luise Solmitz, a Hamburg housewife, was married to a war veteran who had converted from Judaism to Protestantism. They were conservatively minded and fervent German nationalists who had supported the DNVP through its years of stagnation. In her diary on 30 January 1933 she expressed the relief and optimism of millions of others who were not Nazis: 'Hitler Chancellor! And what a government! A government we hardly dared to dream of last July. Hitler, Hugenberg, Seldte, Papen!! On every one of them rest my hopes for Germany. National Socialist vitality, German national prudence, the party independent *Stahlhelm* and the never to be forgotten Papen . . .'[71]

Melita Maschmann was one of those who watched the Nazi victory parade that evening in central Berlin. Aged fifteen she was taken to see history in the making by her anti-Semitic and pro-Nazi parents. Melita was enraptured by the spectacle and what she believed it portended. 'For hours the columns marched by. Again and again amongst them we saw groups of boys and girls scarcely older than ourselves.' At one point a spectator was assaulted but this did not deter her. 'The horror it inspired in me was almost imperceptibly spiced with an intoxicating joy . . . I wanted to escape from my childish, narrow life and I wanted to attach myself to something that was great and fundamental.' National Socialism promised that 'people of all classes would live together like brothers and sisters'.[72]

Hitler's route to power was paved by idealism, the desire for strong communities, and love of Germany. For some Germans anti-Semitism helped to define the nation and the community, with Jews embodying everything that was false, corrupt, alien and wrong. But Hitler was not made Chancellor of Germany because of anti-Semitism. It was obviously central to his world view and it was essential to the core activists of the Nazi Party, yet on 30 January 1933 this gave no indication of what lay in store for the Jews of Germany.

PART ONE

THE FIRST YEAR

1933

Protest and boycott

Hitler's priority on taking office was to make good his promise to repair the economy and restore national unity. Terminating parliamentary democracy was both a means to this end and a fundamental Nazi objective. Hitler did little that appeared immediately relevant to Germany's Jews *as Jews*. The drastic restrictions on individual rights and the extension of police powers seemed more to do with political warfare. In those first heady weeks there was nothing to suggest that the state posed a threat to innocent citizens who belonged to an innocuous religious minority.[1]

At the inaugural meeting of the new cabinet Hitler obtained agreement to hold fresh elections on 5 March 1933. The coalition would seek an absolute majority in order to pass legislation suspending parliamentary government. The election campaign then got under way with the customary marches, rallies and raucous propaganda. As usual, 'electioneering' led to street violence. The SA and SS targeted communist and socialist bases; the leftists defended themselves. Now, however, the National Socialists were in government and the SPD was compelled to act with circumspection in case it provoked a crackdown. On 22 February, Göring enrolled 50,000 men of the SA, SS and Stahlhelm as 'auxiliary policemen' in Prussia. François-Poncet noted sardonically that the government had 'entrusted the maintenance of order to the very forces that were disrupting order'.[2]

The odds in the one-sided electoral contest were tipped further when an arson attack on the Reichstag building gifted the government a pretext to take even more power into its hands. The fire was started on the night of 27 February by Marinus van der Lubbe, a demented Dutch ex-communist. It is not clear if the Nazis were implicated, but Göring didn't hesitate to claim that the blaze presaged a communist putsch. He ordered the police to round up KPD leaders and thousands of rank and file. The next day President Hindenburg issued an emergency decree suspending civil rights, permitting the police to make arrests, search houses and confiscate property without a warrant. The security forces were empowered to take people into 'protective custody' in anticipation of a crime being committed by or against them. For good measure the Nazi interior minister William Frick slipped into the decree a clause extending the writ of central government throughout the individual states, laying the foundations for an unprecedented centralization of power in Germany.[3]

Terror gripped the left. Anyone who had once challenged the Nazis, particularly if they were Jewish, felt vulnerable. The SA set up makeshift detention centres in derelict factories, the basements of office blocks, and disused army barracks. These sites were dignified with the technical term 'Konzentrationslager' (concentration camp). Unsupervised by the regular police or the judicial authorities, they became a byword for brutality.[4]

The aspiring English novelist Christopher Isherwood captured the mood in the weeks before the March election. 'Every evening, I sit in the big half-empty artists, café by the Memorial Church, where the Jews and left-wing intellectuals bend their heads together over the marble tables, speaking in low scared voices. Almost every evening, the SA men come into the café . . . Sometimes they have come to make an arrest. One evening a Jewish writer, who was present, ran into the telephone-box to ring up the Police. The Nazis dragged him out, and he was taken away. Nobody moved a finger. You could have heard a pin drop, till they were gone.'[5]

The decapitation of the KPD and harassment of SPD party workers created a distinctly uneven playing field. The Nazi campaign also bene-fited from an inrush of funds from industrialists and big business, keen to be on the winning side. Despite this massive effort the NSDAP only managed to push its share of the vote up to 43.9 per cent. To cross the 50 per cent threshold the National Socialists had to continue in coali-tion with Hugenberg's DNVP. While frustrating, the continuation of a government with conservative ministers had the virtue of lending the Nazis an air of respectability. The leadership strove to reinforce this impression with the ceremony to mark the opening of the new Reichs-tag. It was held on 21 March at the garrison church in Potsdam, rich in imperial history. Newsreels showed Hitler, clad in a cutaway coat, alongside the president and members of the old royal family. It was a gloriously sunny spring day, but it marked the eclipse of democracy in Germany.[6]

At the first session of the parliament, held in Berlin's Kroll Opera House, the Nazis bullied through an Enabling Act that allowed the government to make laws without the consent of the Reichstag or the president. The two-thirds majority to amend the constitution was attained by excluding the KPD delegates and twisting the arms of the Catholic Centre Party. Only the ninety-four socialist delegates bravely stood their ground. Leopold Schwarzschild marvelled at the speed and ease with which the National Socialists brushed aside the constitutional safeguards protecting individual rights. As a National Socialist tsunami toppled mayors, local government officials, police commissioners, and any office holder considered inimical to the 'national revolution' he reflected, 'History is brutally unsentimental.'[7]

During the election campaign, SA violence had been directed towards political opponents. Afterwards, party activists turned on the Jews. From early March a rash of local boycotts spread across the country. Unauthorized picketing and marking of Jewish-owned stores and shops was often accompanied by thuggery, especially if the proprietors objected. These incidents were not centrally planned or coordinated, but they stemmed from the well-honed Nazi practice of using intimidation to drive a wedge between Jews and non-Jews, signifying who was a secure member of the Volksgemeinschaft and who was a vulnerable outsider. But whereas anti-Jewish violence and stigmatization before 1933 had represented an assault on the law and the republic, the fact that the law was now enforced in the name of Adolf Hitler created unforeseen complications. It was one thing to defy the state when it was the creature of the 'November criminals'; it was quite another when it was the vehicle for the 'national revolution'. To muddy the waters further, many state and municipal authorities, as well as private organizations, began taking measures against Jews. These were often justified as a response to 'spontaneous' and 'popular' anger directed at the Jewish population. SA men who triggered such 'self-cleansing' actions then felt empowered to seek fresh targets. Within days of enjoying electoral legitimacy and constitutional sanction, the Nazi leaders found themselves presiding over a spiral of discrimination and violence. It resulted in friction between party activists and the police, threatened to undermine the new regime's authority as the guardian of law and order,

compromised its image as responsible politicians and triggered an international backlash.[8]

In Berlin, the day after the election, SA men worked their way down
the Kurfürstendamm picking on anyone who looked Jewish to them.
The correspondent for the *Manchester Guardian* reported that 'many
Jews were beaten by the Brown Shirts until their heads and faces flowed
with blood. Many collapsed helplessly and were left lying in the streets
until they were picked up by friends or pedestrians and brought to the
hospital'. On 7 March the old synagogue in central Königsberg was set
on fire and, two days after that, Jewish-owned stores. East Prussia soon
became notorious for persistent and widespread anti-Jewish activity. In
Gollnow, near Stettin, the owner of a department store complained to
the mayor when a storm unit demonstrated outside his establishment.
The mayor at first advised him to close, but when the proprietor refused
to oblige he sent the police to keep order. At night the SA returned and
defaced the building anyway.[9]

On 11 March storm troopers invaded Jewish-owned department
stores and shops in the centre of Breslau, forcing them to close. An SA
detachment barged into the court buildings and compelled Jewish
lawyers and judges to suspend business. The disturbances continued
until the police intervened 'forcefully' to restore order. The siege of the
courthouse went on for three days and only ended when a senior judge
agreed to limit the number of Jewish lawyers to seventeen. In a country
that prided itself on being a Rechtsstaat, a state of law, the violation of
judicial premises and the harassment of the judiciary was tantamount
to desecration, not to say contempt of court. But it was a deliberately
symbolic act, indicating that the law applied to, and could only be
administered by, Germans for Germans. The SA were inciting Germany's new rulers to articulate this shift and to validate it. As the
final settlement in Breslau indicates, the naturally conservative and
rightward-leaning judiciary found it relatively easy to accommodate to
Nazi conceptions.[10]

Over 27–29 March disturbances occurred in cities across the Ruhr.
In Bochum Nazi rowdies smashed the display windows of thirteen
shops while in Dortmund shots were fired into the establishment of a
Jewish merchant. A hundred Jews were taken into 'protective custody'
by the SA. The local rabbi and five other Jews were forced to parade
through the street in Oberhausen. A Jewish court official and several
Jewish men were later treated to 'protective custody' by Brownshirts.[11]

Once they were transferred to the SA detention centres, Jewish men were in extreme danger and suffered disproportionately compared to internees from other backgrounds, mostly political prisoners. Rabbis and Orthodox Jews, who were distinctive because of their beards, were singled out for brutal treatment. In what would become a trademark practice, many had their beards crudely shorn. If they were held over Jewish holy days, the SA (who, like the SS, had a spiteful familiarity with the Jewish ritual calendar) made a practice of inflicting particular humiliations, displaying a hatred of Judaism as much as of Jews. KPD members with Jewish names were also selected for especially rough handling. SA men delighted in tormenting Jewish lawyers who were placed in their hands, relishing the fate of those like Hans Litten who had prosecuted Nazis or engaged in anti-defamation work. In Dachau, of approximately one hundred political prisoners who were dead by May 1933, a dozen were Jewish.[12]

Thanks to diplomatic dispatches, the coverage by foreign correspondents, and private communications (including stories told by returning visitors), foreign governments and the public in other countries were kept abreast of these grim developments. The plethora of information that reached the British Embassy in Berlin from consuls around Germany caused Sir Horace Rumbold to warn the Foreign Office that a 'massacre' of Jews was on the cards. In a private letter to her family in England, Lady Rumbold noted 'All sorts of terrorising of Jews and socialists . . . It is hateful and uncivilised.' Over this period the *New York Times*, the *Chicago Times*, the *Los Angeles Times*, the *Atlanta Constitution* and the *Washington Post* carried 455 articles and editorials on Hitler and the Jews (half in the *New York Times* alone). Two hundred local newspapers in the USA printed 2,600 pieces on events in Germany.[13]

The reaction was swift and sharp. In the USA and Britain the extensive coverage of events led to outrage in Jewish communities. Within days of Hitler taking power, 4,000 Jewish war veterans took to the streets in New York carrying banners decrying Nazi atrocities. Jews on both sides of the Atlantic demanded that their governments intervene or at least condemn what was happening. In the course of March Jewish leaders conferred repeatedly and a head of steam built up for a boycott of German goods and services.[14]

However, the American Jewish leadership was at odds over what steps to take. The differences of approach reflected deep rifts in the

Jewish population. The assimilated and well-off section that stemmed largely from the German Jewish immigration of the mid-nineteenth century tended to favour quiet diplomacy with State Department officials and politicians. This tactic was routinely used by the 'uptown' American Jewish Committee (AJC). The more recent and more numerous immigrants from eastern Europe, who were predominantly lower-middle and working class, tended to respond viscerally and noisily to news of Jewish suffering. Many were enrolled in trade unions and socialist organizations; a significant portion were Zionists. The American Jewish Congress represented this section of the population and was consistently more activist and vocal. But the clamour alarmed the patricians of the AJC. On 20 March a deputation led by Cyrus Adler, AJC president, called on the US administration to 'make proper representations' to the German authorities. At the same time, it condemned 'boycotts, parades, mass meetings and other similar demonstrations'. This injunction reflected their instinctive discretion and reluctance to legitimize the politics of the Jewish masses; it was also a calculated response to pleas from German Jews *not* to launch attacks on the Nazi-led coalition.[15]

Their discretion was of no avail. The American Jewish Congress, led by the charismatic Rabbi Stephen Wise, went ahead with a mass rally in Madison Square Gardens. When the doors opened on 27 March, 20,000 Jews filled the auditorium, leaving 35,000 milling around outside. They heard anti-Nazi speeches from Senator Robert Wagner, former presidential contender Al Smith, the president of the American Federation of Labor, the mayor of New York, and two bishops. On the same day 10,000 Jews marched through Brooklyn, with roughly the same number rallying in Chicago and Los Angeles. Six thousand Jews demonstrated in Baltimore, 3,000 in Newark and Washington, and 2,500 in Atlantic City. It was estimated that a million people had rallied against the Nazis, making it one of the largest demonstrations of its kind in US history.[16]

When the AJC asked Wise not to go ahead, he replied that if mainstream Jewish organizations refused to organize protest events their place would be taken by 'Socialist Jewish meetings, Communist Jewish meetings'. His comment offers an insight into the triple bind in which American Jews found themselves. They were under pressure from German Jews not to act, while the Jewish street clamoured for action. Behind-the-scenes lobbying failed to meet these popular demands and left the way open for radicals who would confirm prejudices about Jews on both sides of the Atlantic. Whatever they did was liable to backfire on them or on the German Jews.

Calls for a boycott of Germany posed even more acute dilemmas. During March, a self-made millionaire and communal activist, Samuel Untermyer, put himself at the head of a spontaneous movement to persuade Jews and non-Jews to desist from purchasing goods originating from Germany. When both the AJC and Wise leaned on Untermyer he retorted that 'The Hitlerite Party is bent on the extermination of the Jews in Germany, or upon driving them out of the country.' By October 1933 the American Jewish Congress buckled to pressure from its constituents and declared support for the boycott. It was joined by Hadassah, the largest mass-membership Zionist organization in North America.[17]

A similar dynamic unfolded in Britain, where letters calling for a boycott poured into the London *Jewish Chronicle*. The editor, Jack Rich, took up the cause in a leading article on 24 March. 'If, as seems evident . . . there is a strong longing to institute a boycott of German goods and services, by all means let it be done. Let Jews, here and in every land, borrow from the Germans their weapon of the boycott and turn it against them.' The *JC* was influential at the best of times; this issue sold out completely.[18]

As in America, the established Jewish leadership presided over a socially stratified and ideologically fissured community. Neville Laski, the president of the Board of Deputies of British Jews, was a lawyer from Manchester. He led a body that was elected mainly by synagogue members, but broadly articulated popular feeling amongst the Jews who had immigrated to England from Russia and Poland around the turn of the century. Leonard Montefiore, president of the Anglo-Jewish Association (AJA), was more of a patrician, who spoke for the wealthier and highly assimilated section of the Jewish population. Laski temperamentally sided with the more reticent Montefiore and tended to discount what his members were saying. At a meeting with Robert Hankey, permanent undersecretary at the Foreign Office, on 21 March, they deprecated noisy demonstrations, while Hankey warned strongly against giving any official sanction to a boycott.[19]

And as in the United States the caution of the official Jewish leadership did nothing to inhibit the wider expression of opinion. The boycott movement spread like a bush fire through the East End of London, where 100,000 Jews lived. Signs appeared in shop windows announcing that the owners did not deal with German suppliers. On Friday 24 March, after businesses closed early for the Sabbath, thousands of Jews marched from the East End to the German Embassy. The following Sunday there were angry exchanges at an emergency conference, called by the English Zionist Federation, when Laski refused to place the Board of Deputies at the head of the boycott movement or organize a protest rally. His admonition that it would antagonize the Germans and make life difficult for 'moderates' like Papen was met with derision. Delegates found it harder to dismiss the pleas of German Jews. Laski and Montefiore succeeded in winning time to arrange a decorous mass meeting to be addressed primarily by non-Jewish figures.[20]

Diplomats in Washington and Whitehall felt the heat of Jewish indignation. In his private journal J. P. Moffat, chief of the Western Division in the US State Department, recorded the pressure. 'The situation concerning the Jews in Germany is causing the utmost alarm to the race here. There have been a series of meetings held far and wide over the country and a huge one is scheduled for Monday next. The reports reaching the Jews here from their co-religionists who have left Germany are alarming to a degree.' Importantly, though, Moffat went on to express his professional scepticism. 'Thus far, nothing we have received from the Embassy tends to bear this out. We drew up a telegram, however, telling the Embassy it was important for us to have the exact facts and requesting them to telegraph a full report after consultation by telephone if necessary with the consulates in the principal cities.'[21]

The press coverage and Jewish lobbying propelled diplomats into formal interventions with German ambassadors and the German Foreign Office. In March 1933, Horace Rumbold alerted the German foreign minister, Neurath, to the adverse impact of persistent anti-Jewish attacks. Neurath reassured him that German Jews had nothing to fear; on the contrary, it was the Germans who felt put upon.[22]

To the Nazis, the overseas campaign against them was proof that 'the Jews' were an international force. The diplomatic initiatives on their behalf in Washington and London, however mild, were taken as evidence that Jews controlled the governments there. The protest wave also played into the German people's sense of being victims of international aggression. It enabled Hitler and the Nazis to whip up rage against 'the Jews' and at the same time pose as the defenders of vulnerable, wounded Germany. The Nazis then satisfied the feelings of rage by punishing world Jewry through inflicting suffering on their German brethren.

They used the threat of further retribution to deter future interventions. German Jews thus became hostages, held against the good behaviour of 'international Jewry'.

In fact, close scrutiny of the Jewish response in February and March 1933 would have revealed only division and dissonance. There was no chorus of 'international Jewry'. However, the very multiplication of efforts to stage protests and organize boycotts, amplified by rivalry between competing Jewish organizations and leaders, created a cacophony that impressed Germans abroad and at home. Nazi believers in the *Protocols of the Elders of Zion* misread Jewish pluralism and weakness as a sign of unity and strength. If anything, these early weeks of turbulence in foreign opinion and diplomatic circles served to harden Nazi preconceptions.

A week after the March election, Hitler attempted to rein in the violence against political opponents and Jews, explicitly forbidding Einzelaktionen (unauthorized individual actions). Although the *CV-Zeitung* publicized his announcement it did nothing to assuage the din of foreign protest, not least because the prohibition did little to prevent states and municipalities from amending regulations to the detriment of Jews – for instance by banning 'shechita', the slaughter of livestock according to Jewish religious law. As adverse press coverage and diplomatic interventions continued, François-Poncet noted the effect with his usual sarcasm: 'nothing exasperated the Nazis so much as to find themselves blamed abroad'.[23]

The regime responded to what it perceived as a barrage from world Jewry by going onto the offensive. On 26 March, Göring summoned German Jewish leaders and instructed them to persuade the Jews in London and New York to call off the boycott and cut out the 'atrocity propaganda'. Kurt Blumenfeld, president of the German Zionist Federation, and Julius Brodnitz, chairman of the Centralverein, duly cabled the American Jewish Committee: 'We protest categorically against holding Monday meeting, radio and other demonstrations. We unequivocally demand energetic effort to obtain an end to demonstrations hostile to Germany.' A delegation flew to London to convey the same message to Laski and his colleagues.[24]

To add force to the message, Hitler gave his approval for an official nationwide boycott of Jewish shops, businesses and professionals unless 'world Jewry' backed off. After meeting the leader in Berchtesgaden, Hitler's rural retreat in Bavaria, Goebbels confided to his diary, 'He has pondered the whole matter fully and has come to a decision ... We shall make headway against the foreign lies only if we get our hands on their originators or at least beneficiaries, those Jews living in Germany who have thus far remained unmolested. We must, therefore, proceed to a large-scale boycott of all Jewish businesses in Germany. Perhaps the foreign Jews will think better of the matter when their racial comrades in Germany begin to get it in the neck.' Goebbels then sent out an order for party branches to carry it out. 'We are going to take our revenge. The Jews in America and England are trying to injure us. We shall know how to deal with their brothers in Germany.' [25]

When Hitler informed the cabinet that he had sanctioned the boycott, some ministers were uneasy. Neurath, in particular, was 'perturbed about the Jewish boycott' which he considered would be 'disastrous for Germany's foreign prestige'. At the last minute, with Hitler's consent, the German Foreign Office offered to call off the boycott if foreign governments agreed to stop 'atrocity propaganda'. In London, Lord Reading and Lord Samuel, two Jewish peers, received this proposal from the German Ambassador and passed it on to the Foreign Office, where it was considered a satisfactory outcome to the trial of strength. The US Secretary of State Cordell Hull likewise got the offer and responded in conciliatory terms. Drawing on Moffat's research he averred that 'many of the accusations of terror and atrocities which have reached this country have been exaggerated'. By the time these diplomatic exchanges had been concluded it was too late to cancel the boycott outright, but it was curtailed to one day, Saturday 1 April. [26]

In Nazi thinking, the boycott was a rational response to an adversarial situation, the first foreign policy crisis they faced in office. But few diplomats or politicians at the time could grasp this. George Messersmith, consul at the American Embassy in Berlin and in most respects an incisive analyst, was convinced that the foreign protests were just an excuse for the boycott. He believed that the Nazis thereby showed their disdain for world opinion. In characteristically pungent language he reported to Washington that 'reason is in reality absent from the majority of the leaders of the National Socialist movement. They have no comprehension of the outside world and its reactions. They have further than that a complete disregard of what the outside world thinks.' [27]

Messersmith was wrong. It was precisely because the Nazis did care about overseas opinion that they mooted and then abbreviated the boycott. More recent analysis that depicts the boycott as a device to channel

SA energies or a means to impose control over a chaotic situation is equally wide of the mark. The reality – as the Nazis saw it – was a show-down between them and international Jewry. The foreign boycott was proof of Jewish solidarity, proof that they manipulated governments, and proof that they were a dominant economic force. Because the boy-cott was an economic weapon it proved that the Jews were a financial world power. This meant that if the Jews could use the power of money to attack the Germans, they might also be forced to use it to save their own people. At a formative stage in Nazi policy-making the boycott verified, according to their world view, the association of Jews with international finance and indicated that if one section of world Jewry was squeezed painfully, another section could be forced to pay for its relief from pressure. Equally, if Jews were threatened in one place they could make a government somewhere else react. From this point onward these principles assumed an *a priori* status in Nazi thinking.[28]

In Dresden, Victor Klemperer, an academic with a distinguished war record, saw this all too clearly. Klemperer was born into a Jewish family but had converted to Protestantism and was a fervent nationalist. He paid scrupulous attention to the language of Nazi pronouncements so as to tease out their true meaning. On 27 March he wrote, 'The gov-ernment is in hot water. "Atrocity propaganda" from abroad because of its Jewish campaign. It is constantly issuing official denials, there are no pogroms, and has Jewish associations issue refutations. But it openly threatens to proceed against the German Jews if mischief-making by "World Jewry" does not stop.' As the mood darkened and violence intensified he feared a pogrom. The day the boycott was announced he declared, 'We are hostages.'[29]

It did no good when James McDonald, who had arrived from the USA on 29 March, tried to explain to Putzi Hanfstaengl that the agita-tion in the USA was not instigated by Jews and nor was there unanimity amongst them. 'Indeed', he told Hitler's foreign press liaison man over dinner at Horcher's restaurant, 'powerful conservative Jews in New York, like Warburg and the American Jewish Committee, had opposed the Jewish agitation'. According to Hanfstaengl, though, Hitler had pro-claimed 'we are not afraid of international Jewry. The Jews must be crushed. Their fellows abroad played into our hands.' After McDonald protested that most German Jews were patriots, Hanfstaengl retorted, 'we cannot trust them. They are not, they cannot be Germans.' Mc-Donald got much the same response from Hjalmar Schacht, the former liberal and now president of the Reichsbank. 'Yes, not all Jews are unpatriotic, but why should those . . . in the East End of London dictate to us. We do not attack Jews as we do socialists and communists. Anyhow, after a week or two, nothing more will be heard of it.'[30]

The days running up to the boycott saw violence against Jews reach an unprecedented pitch. Bella Fromm noted 'the baiting of Jews continues incessantly. It has become accepted practice for Jewish victims to be dragged from their beds before dawn and taken away.' In Straubing, a small city in Lower Bavaria, a Jewish shop owner named Otto Selz was abducted from his home at dawn by men in 'dark uniforms' (probably SS), and driven away. His body was found later in a wood. In Bad Kissingen a rabbi and local councillor were taken into 'protective custody'. In Düsseldorf the windows of Jewish-owned shops were smashed. In Cologne, sixty Jewish lawyers were obstructed while going about their work and detained for several hours.[31]

Messersmith cabled the State Department on the eve of the boycott: 'The anti-Jewish movement . . . has reached an intensity and a diffusion of action which was not contemplated even by its most fantastic proponents, and there is real reason to believe now that the movement is beyond control and may have a bloody climax.'[32]

The leading members of the Jewish community in Germany were in a quandary. On the one hand, it protested that German Jews could not be held accountable for foreign opinion and denounced the 'atrocity' stories. On the other, it informed its constituents that the fight against defamation had to continue – albeit as a domestic matter. When McDonald met with Siegmund Warburg and Carl Melchior they told him 'their people were considering a public statement signed by a hundred prominent Jews pleading for the rest of the world to leave the problem to Germany'. In this spirit, Jewish war veterans addressed a public letter to President Hindenburg seeking the abatement of the boycott. But Victor Klemperer noted that the night before, the SA were already taking up position outside Jewish premises. Protests were 'hopeless'.[33]

When morning arrived on 1 April 1933 a peculiar atmosphere hung over the shopping precincts of German cities and village high streets. Large numbers of Jewish shopkeepers opted not to open up for business. For Orthodox Jews this was normal for the Sabbath in any case. A few displayed notices expressing solidarity with Germans against foreign 'atrocity propaganda'. Klemperer went into Dresden and found storm troopers standing outside Jewish shops with placards reading

'Whoever buys from the Jew supports the foreign boycott and destroys the German economy'. People walked down the streets, gawping. Willy Cohn, a history teacher in Breslau, got 'the impression that decent Christian circles are increasingly keeping their distance from such events'. Yet an eve of boycott appeal by local Jewish leaders to Cardinal Bertram of Breslau was met by silence. While there was no Church protest, there was mercifully little violence; the Nazi police chief Edmund Heines had demanded 'calm and order'.[34]

The American consul in Leipzig, Ralph Busser, reported to the US Embassy that the local SA were straining at the leash prior to the boycott. On the day itself pickets and placards were accompanied by 'numerous acts of violence'. Storm troopers 'raided the Kaufhaus Brühl, one of the largest department stores in Leipzig, drove out the customers and expelled or arrested the Jewish shop assistants'. In the fur district Jews were forced to parade wearing insulting placards. Polish Jews were arrested and made to scrub slogans off walls. 'In fairness to the German people', he added, 'it must be said that the boycott was unpopular with the working-class movement and the more intelligent section of the population.'[35]

From exile a few years later, Edwin Landau vividly recalled that day in his home town of Deutsch-Krone in West Prussia. A decorated veteran of the Great War, he was the chairman of the Jewish community and proprietor of a plumbing business. 'I couldn't believe my eyes. I simply could not imagine that something like this was possible in the twentieth century. Things like this only happened in the middle ages.' But there they were: two young Brownshirts outside the entrance to his shop. The sight collapsed his self-identity as a German. 'And we young Jews had once stood in the trenches for this people in the cold and rain and spilled our blood to defend our nation.' Boiling with rage and shame he went home, put on his medals, and walked back into town. Although some old customers passed by his premises with smirks on their faces, others, particularly Catholics, quite deliberately came in as a gesture of solidarity. One, an official of the DNVP, was later sacked for the handshake he gave Landau. After a while, Edwin shut up shop and went to the synagogue where he found an entire community in grief and shock.[36]

In Hamburg, Henrietta Necheles-Magnus, a doctor, arrived at the entrance of her practice to find it patrolled by two SA men with a sign bearing a yellow circle. Once inside her first task was to console her non-Jewish receptionist. 'We are so ashamed of our fellow countrymen,' she wept. Necheles-Magnus noted that the Jewish war widow who ran the grocery across the road did brisker trade than usual. Then patients started to arrive bearing flowers and gifts to show what they thought about the boycott. It started to rain and the storm troopers looked increasingly despondent, taunted by burly dock workers who patronized the clinic. 'All in all, the boycott was unpopular,' she remembered from her new home in America seven years later. Luise Solmitz had the same impression. She felt 'ashamed in front of shops with daubs of paint and before every Jew . . . The mood of the people appeared depressed, unhappy, most really cannot support this.'[37]

James McDonald in Berlin derived a more chilling lesson. He walked to the Wertheim department store, where he found SA men lined up in front of the entrances. They had plastered the display windows with signs showing a yellow circle on a black background. The employment of a medieval symbol shocked him. 'No doubt the boycott was effective,' he wrote. 'It showed that Jewish trade could be completely stifled. No hand was raised against the SA. But the boycott is only the outward sign of an equally destructive discrimination against all Jews.' By chance, Lady Rumbold tried to enter Wertheim's at roughly the same time. Her way was blocked and she gave up. She reported in the language typical of her class that all down the Kurfürstendamm 'in front of each Jew shop were two or three Nazis standing blocking the door'. She was mortified when obstructive Brownshirts upset her small son. 'It was utterly cruel and Hunnish and the whole thing, just doing down a heap of defenceless people.'[38]

Summing up from his diplomatic perch, Messersmith considered the day had been a failure. 'The heart of the SA men was no longer in the boycott as it had been so emasculated by restraining measures which had been issued the night before. It seems as though they felt that if the boycott was to last only a day and to be conducted in so orderly and restrained manner that it was not really worth-while at all.' It was 'not generally popular with the German people'. However, he added, 'There is no indication that the feeling against the Jews has in any sense died down, but merely that popular opinion does not approve of a means which even the man in the street realises may be destructive of the internal economic life and seriously affect Germany's foreign trade.'[39]

Messersmith's sanguine conclusion missed one point of the operation and its consequences. The mere fact that he, a US diplomat, was taking such an interest in German Jews chimed with Nazi anti-Semitism. It did not matter for the moment if ordinary Germans were ambivalent: the NSDAP was still drawing the lines between 'them' and 'us', demonstrating that 'they' were now fair game. If the population baulked at certain activities because they hindered economic recovery this only made the continuity of Jewish life conditional on economic necessity. Prudence offered Jews some leverage in the short term, but the converse was that it rendered them expendable at the point at which their utility was exhausted.[40]

The 'national revolution'

The boycott was only one thread of what the Nazis dubbed the 'national revolution'. In a report to the State Department a month later, Messersmith observed that the NSDAP had already gained control over the levers of power in Germany. In his eyes the takeover was a genuine popular insurgency. 'The masses are for the moment the dictator in Germany and the party leaders are merely their spokesman', he told Washington. By contrast, his colleague in Munich, Consul General Charles Hathaway, noted the silence and obedience of the population: the 'abundant arrests have done their work'. These divergent perceptions reflect the bewildering pace at which the National Socialists consolidated their grip, liquidating first opponents and then rivals until they had created a one-party state. They engineered the complete centralization of power and the regulation of culture until, almost in the blink of an eye, they presided triumphantly over a totalitarian state. Throughout the process they appealed to and seemed to evoke a genuine tide of popular feeling. The alacrity with which swathes of society voluntarily aligned with the Nazis, sometimes pre-empting administrative fiats, defied simple notions of the takeover being exclusively either a top-down coup or a bottom-up revolution.[41]

One of the most important measures to impose Nazi control was the Law for the Restoration of the Professional Civil Service, promulgated on 7 April 1933. It authorized the dismissal of officials deemed politically unreliable, especially those with a record of socialist political activity. Paragraph III stipulated the enforced retirement of 'non-Aryan' officials, with the exception of those who were combat veterans or who

lost fathers or sons in the Great War. As well as facilitating the removal
of many Jews (though far fewer than the Nazis anticipated), the law set
in motion the Nazification of the most crucial instrument of state power
alongside the security forces. A parallel process was set in train in the
judiciary, rippled through local and municipal government and spread
from the army into the private sector. As the 'Aryan paragraph' was
voluntarily adopted across the spectrum of civil society Jews were asked
to leave or were expelled from sports clubs, recreational associations,
professional networks, and cultural organizations.[42]

Jews were not, for the present, the chief concern of the regime. The
government organized a spectacular show for the celebration of labour
on 1 May, appropriating the mantle of the left, then the next day sent
the police to arrest the trade unions' leadership. The following week
the SPD was struck; the party was finally banned on 21 June. By the
summer, 100,000 political prisoners had been held, mostly for short
periods, beaten and terrorized, in the concentration camps. Around 600
prisoners died. It was, in the words of historian Richard J. Evans, a 'massive, brutal, murderous assault' on political opposition. The message for
Hitler's coalition partners and the centrist parties was stark. Hugenberg
was prevailed upon to merge the DNVP into the NSDAP, while the
Stahlhelm was absorbed into the SA. The Catholic hierarchy agreed to
dissolve the Centre Party, which defended the interests of Catholics, in
return for a concordat between the Third Reich and the Vatican that
guaranteed the rights of the Catholic community. By July 1933, Hitler
was able to proclaim that the NSDAP was the only legal party in Germany; the party was the state.[43]

There were few protests against this transformation but there was
unease about the brutishness that accompanied it, especially the grisly
stories emanating from the 'wild' concentration camps. Occasional
assaults on foreigners further damaged Germany's image abroad and
provoked the question: who was in charge? On 6 July, Hitler used an
address to newly installed Nazi state governors to announce an end to
the 'national revolution'. Next month, Göring terminated the auxiliary
police role of the SA. The semi-official detention centres they had run
were shut down and Himmler, police chief in Bavaria, moved to tighten
SS control of the remaining authorized sites. He installed Theodor Eicke
as commandant of Dachau concentration camp with instructions to
draw up a disciplinary code covering both the guards and the remaining prisoners. Over half were released (although 37,000 political

prisoners were incarcerated in state prisons). As a quid pro quo for this concession camp inmates were removed from the jurisdiction of the Ministry of Justice.[44]

Although the political opposition was broken, there was no let-up to surveillance of 'unreliable elements'. In September, Göring established an independent political police in Prussia, the Geheime Staatspolizei, better known as the Gestapo. It soon attained a scary reputation for assiduous investigation and merciless torture of suspects. In fact, the Gestapo was a relatively small organization and lacked sufficient personnel to initiate inquiries on a large scale. It relied more on informers and denunciations by letter. That it acquired a fearsome record for locating and eliminating dissidents was more a testimony to the support National Socialism enjoyed in the population than it was a tribute to the effectiveness of the police state. With little difficulty the entire police force was brought under the command of party men. The definition of crime and the nature of policing itself were transformed by the Law against Dangerous Habitual Criminals. Criminality was now deemed a genetic disorder. Since lawbreaking was an inherited tendency there was no point in attempting to deter or re-educate 'habitual' criminals. The law mandated that after three convictions a felon would go to prison, no matter what the crimes happened to be.[45]

Under Nazi guidance, the Ministry of Education quickly produced new textbooks that embodied National Socialist ideas. The teaching profession, which already had a large cadre of NSDAP members, was purged and the residue subjected to a mixture of re-education and blandishments. Within three years practically every teacher in the Reich was a Nazi Party member. Indoctrination was not confined to the schoolroom. The whole nation was put through a learning experience. Its chief instructor was Goebbels, who was appointed to run the new Ministry of Propaganda and Popular Enlightenment on 13 March 1933. Goebbels set himself the task of convincing Germans that they were part of the Volksgemeinschaft, the racial-people's community. His mission began by establishing control over the cultural sector and creative industries, purging them of political opponents and Jews. The keystone of his project was the Reich Chamber of Culture, established by law on 22 September. Every cultural organization was required to join and to police its membership. At the behest of Goebbels a succession of laws led to the dismissal of Jews from orchestras, opera companies, art galleries, theatres, radio and the film industry. In October, legislation was passed barring Jews from working as editors for newspapers.[46]

The most dramatic and symbolic moment in the 'cleansing' of German culture was the burning of books by authors considered anti-German, Marxist or Jewish. The literary auto-da-fé was held on 10 May. Instigated by Nazi students, the pyres were constructed in squares outside universities, which was convenient for students carrying stacks of books from libraries to the bonfires. When Stefan Zweig complained that his works were blacklisted by mistake, possibly the result of confusion with the communist Arnold Zweig, his acerbic friend Joseph Roth put him right. 'They confuse you not because your name is Zweig, but because you are a Jew . . .' Ironically, while Roth urged Stefan Zweig to accept his fate as a Jewish author, Robert Weltsch in the Zionist *Jüdische Rundschau* contested the inclusion of books by assimilated authors such as Stefan Zweig with no 'Jewish' theme. 'We refuse to designate literature as Jewish based on the negative criteria of being "not German".' At this stage the preservation of internal distinctions was more important to some Jews than the danger posed by the externally imposed myth of homogeneity.[47]

Millions of Germans who disliked modernist culture found this vandalism deeply satisfying. They also applauded measures designed to bolster traditional sectors of the economy, improve the welfare of ordinary families, and strengthen the health of the people. In July 1933, Hugenberg realized that the conservatives had been sidelined, and resigned from the cabinet. He was replaced as minister of agriculture by Walther Daré, a Nazi thinker with a background in economics. Long a champion of the peasantry, a cause that lay close to Hitler's heart, Daré passed a law to protect the tenure of farmers and prevent their holdings from undergoing fragmentation. The government also acted to prevent the growth of chain stores and department stores, restricting their ability to undercut small shopkeepers by offering hefty discounts. The regime paid careful attention to the morale of industrial workers, too, aware that they were essential to economic recovery and a potentially threatening source of discontent. In November 1933, the Kraft Durch Freude (Strength Through Joy) organization was set up to offer cheap foreign holidays, cruises, tours and recreation to deserving German workers. To further compound the impression of a nation in which every man and woman was valued, united by a common spirit of self-sacrifice, the Nazis passed legislation to expand their annual pre-Christmas collection in aid of the needy, Winterhilfe (winter relief), into a national drive. Contributions were effectively obligatory.[48]

The most far-reaching measures to mould the German people into a racially aware, biologically robust and homogenous community, a true Volksgemeinschaft, were the eugenic laws. On 14 July 1933, the Reich interior minister, Wilhelm Frick, issued the Law for the Prevention of Hereditarily Diseased Progeny. It established Hereditary Health Courts consisting of doctors, psychiatrists and social workers who were empowered to order the compulsory sterilization of individuals deemed mentally or physically disabled and liable to pass on their disability if they had children. It was the most radical expression of the Nazis' utopian project to create a Volk that was biologically pure and perfect according to their racist vision. Subsequent legislation would deny state secondary schooling to the congenitally disabled, prohibit marriage to a person believed to carry a hereditary illness, and ease the divorce of one partner from a spouse unable to conceive. These negative eugenic measures were accompanied by pro-natalist social engineering. Laws were passed to prohibit contraception and abortion. Tax breaks and cheap loans were given to newly married couples. Childbirth was rewarded with grants and perks. While heterosexuality and marriage were vaunted, the police were encouraged to employ existing laws against homosexuality with greater vigour. Although relatively few men were sent to prison for homosexual acts, centres of gay life were repressed while thousands of gay men were arrested and cautioned.[49]

The headline-grabbing policy initiatives to bring about the national renewal cascaded through society, proliferating into a multitude of individual choices. In each case a German had to decide whether to opt in or to opt out, with their previously held convictions and affiliations weighing against the powerful urge to share in a great idealistic project. Behind this emotional tug-of-war was knowledge that nonconformity could result in terrible punishment. Crucially, Germans were not being asked to hate Jews; they were being asked to love other Germans.[50]

The choices in question were superficially tiny: whether to give the Adolf Hitler greeting or to persist with traditional salutations, whether to wear a party badge, whether to don a uniform, whether to participate in celebrations such as Adolf Hitler's birthday or attend the rituals marking the anniversary of the November putsch. In addition to voluntary choices, Germans found themselves increasingly directed into activity that tacitly aligned them with the regime. Work could be interrupted by mandatory listening to a Hitler speech on the radio or attendance at a Nazi factory cell meeting. Every tenement had a 'block leader' and a discussion forum. Recreational activity was channelled through the Strength Through Joy organization. Shopping became an assertion of identity, not just because of the campaign to avoid Jewish shops. Products were increasingly labelled and advertised as 'Germanic', healthy for the Volk. Goebbels inveighed against the wearing of French-designed clothes for women and called for an authentically German style of couture. Life-cycle events turned into an affirmation of racial allegiance. It was necessary to prove one's Aryan status and racial health to obtain a marriage certificate. The birth of a full-limbed healthy child was joyful in itself, but it also allowed the parents to anticipate financial benefits and free schooling.[51]

From childhood, young German boys and girls experienced the thrill of belonging to the Volksgemeinschaft and were impregnated with its values by teachers, youth leaders, labour service officers, university professors and military trainers. It began with the Deutsches Jungvolk for children aged 10–13 years; it was continued into the Hitlerjugend (Hitler Youth) for boys up to 18 and the Bund deutscher Mädel (Associ-ation of German Girls). Then came Reich Labour Service for six months, followed by two years in the armed forces. Young people had a natural affinity to National Socialist ideals of equality, integration, par-ticipation and self-sacrifice. They instinctively shared the spirit of revolt against bourgeois norms and the restrictive life of the traditional family. To ensure they got the message, youths passed through a succession of camps where they were sequestered from their families and lived according to the new values. There were 2,000 summer camps for the Jungvolk, Hitler Youth and the BDM, sweeping up 600,000 youths each year. Nearly half a million teenagers went through labour service and army barracks. At each stage they received indoctrination in National Socialism. Equally important was the lifestyle and the values exempli-fied by each collective activity. There were, of course, no Jews.[52]

Yet it would be a mistake to equate Nazi values with hatred. What gave them such force was their capacity to evoke feelings of love and belonging. Melita Maschmann recalled that 'No catchword has ever fascinated me quite as much as that of the Volksgemeinschaft.' It gener-ated a 'magical glow'. 'What first drew young people to National Socialism was not hatred', she later wrote, 'but love of Germany. It was in the service of this love that they wished to make themselves tough, swift, and hard.'[53]

For older members of the population the same effect was achieved by the constant atmosphere of struggle and emergency. Leopold Schwarzschild observed that 'It is not the armaments that are the priority at the moment, but the nation's psychology, whose pressure gauge is constantly kept at the level of an army camp about to march off to war.' There was the battle for jobs and the battle for food production. Everyone was drawn into the campaigns to economize and to help the needy. Increasingly, adults who were too old for military service were obliged to participate in civil defence exercises. The measures for racial hygiene required the creation of a vast new bureaucracy and the assignment of manifold tasks to university professors, teachers, civil servants, municipal officials, doctors, nurses, psychiatrists and social workers. They were employed to determine the racial status of individuals and, having resolved who belonged to the Volk, to police its conduct and defend its boundaries. All these executors of racial-biological policies had to be selected and trained. Party membership was virtually obligatory for anyone who wanted advancement. So, 215,000 teachers out of 300,000 in the entire profession attended two-weekly 'retreats' at which they were familiarized with National Socialist ideology and policy, and how to apply it. A network of research institutes was created to provide intellectual and scientific underpinning for Nazi eugenic, racial and anti-Jewish policies, and to cloak them in respectability.[54]

In the pithy formula of the historian Peter Fritzsche, 'Race defined the new realities of the Third Reich.' This reality was less questioned with each year that passed, more firmly entrenched with each generation graduating from the learning machine that the Third Reich became. The dictatorship was driven by young people; from the Nazi leadership, which was predominantly in its forties, downwards. As the number of young adults for whom National Socialism provided a basic value system increased, they filled more and more official positions at all levels of the state and in social organizations. Membership in the SA peaked at nearly three million in 1934. At its height, during the war, the SS embraced 800,000 men who, with their spouses, equated to over 1 per cent of the entire German population. Six million Germans passed through the Reich Labour Service and seven million served in the German armed forces. For these millions, 'the Nazi conscience' was the natural and normative reflex of moral choice. While the majority of the population remained formally unaffiliated, they too were enmeshed in a system that fostered the internalization of Nazi values. When the Nazi Party succeeded in delivering political stability, social order, and prosperity its values were accepted with sincerity and gratitude.[55]

Judenpolitik was crucial to the construction of the Volksgemeinschaft. As historians now appreciate, anti-Jewish measures were not simply the fulfilment of goals long held by anti-Semites or even the expression of hatred towards Jews. While for Nazis like Streicher anti-Semitism was an end in itself, for others it was instrumental. Personal feelings hardly mattered. The exclusion of Jews defined the Aryans. Anti-Jewish propaganda and actions helped to control public opinion. What was permitted or prohibited helped to 'reshape the public domain'. Racial policy gave the state licence to intrude into ever more private and personal realms. It 'made possible the almost complete elimination of a private sphere'. Soon all policy was examined in the light of race and framed with the Jews in mind.[56]

Yet the Third Reich was a dysfunctional regime; its fragmented leadership was constantly trying to accomplish a great deal in a short time with limited resources. Personalities and policies tugged in opposite directions, cut across one another or just ran out of steam. It is possible in retrospect to over-interpret the instrumentality and coherence of Judenpolitik. Ascribing a clear sense of purpose to Nazi policy-makers, in turn has the effect of making the German Jews look like misty-eyed fools. In fact, the 'victims' have something important to tell historians. At the time Judenpolitik didn't appear coherent or purposeful because it wasn't; it was improvised, unplanned and, hence, unpredictable. The Nazis may have been able to draw upon a history of anti-Semitic thinking and civil servants may even have had draft legislation for discriminatory measures in their filing cabinets, but what emerged was confused, contradictory, half-baked and usually temporary.[57]

The first anti-Jewish laws

The government followed up the orchestrated indignation of 1 April 1933 with a succession of laws directed at the exclusion of Jews from areas of German life that the Nazis considered sensitive and where a Jewish presence had always been considered irksome. On 7 April, Jews

were forbidden from entering the legal profession. Jews who were qualified and practising were untouched, but those still studying found the
ground removed from under them. On 22 April, Jewish doctors and
dentists were barred from practising within the state sector. Three days
later, the Law Against the Overcrowding of German Schools imposed a
1.5 per cent quota on the admission of Jews to schools and universities
and a 5 per cent limit to the total allowed. On 14 July, legislation was
passed to denaturalize Jews who had entered Germany after November
1918. Despite the readiness of the Interior Ministry to nullify the citizenship of everyone Jewish, Hitler limited the blow to Ostjuden. The creation of the Reich Chamber of Culture and laws to exclude political
opponents and Jews from work in the press or radio added to the roster
of Jewish unemployed. However, these measures were comparatively
mild, especially when the exemptions were taken into account. Sacked
civil servants even enjoyed a reasonable pay-off and retained a proportion of their pension.[58]

The relative temperance of anti-Jewish legislation contrasted with
the unrestrained abuse, discrimination and violence emanating from
the SA and the Nazi Party ranks. In April 1933, Annemarie Schwarzenbach wrote to her friend Klaus Mann, author and son of Thomas Mann,
that 'in spite of all Hitler's appeals and admonitions, individual actions,
of the worst sort, take place every day'. Disorder reached the point at
which central government could no longer remain passive and the
regime redoubled its efforts to end anti-Jewish activity that threatened
to disrupt the economy. On 7 July, Rudolf Hess, the deputy Führer, prohibited actions against department stores. Three days later, Wilhelm
Frick, the interior minister, issued a circular forbidding unauthorized
individual actions. Three weeks after his previous communiqué, Hess
issued a specific injunction against party members getting involved in
such affairs. At the start of September, the Reich Economic Ministry
circulated instructions that there were to be no blacklists of Jewish businesses or people doing business with Jews; that Jewish businesses were
not to be denied the right to advertise; that signs and pickets outside
Jewish shops or stores were to be removed.[59]

Yet these edicts were more often honoured in the breach. The result
was wide regional variations and further uncertainty. Franconia (northern Bavaria), where Julius Streicher wielded the greatest influence, was a
particular hot spot. Here local NSDAP branches and SA detachments
bridled against the restraints imposed by Berlin. In Neustadt an der

Aisch, north-west of Nuremberg, a public meeting condemned the
Economics Ministry for seeking to prevent boycotts and the 'occasional
excesses'. Municipalities dominated by Nazis used their local competence to exclude Jews from public amenities. An early ordinance
forbade Jews access to public swimming baths, a spiteful gesture that
reflected Streicher's pathological aversion to Jews and the widespread
desire to prevent any physical contact with Aryans. There was also
intermittent violence. In Aschaffenburg, SS men went on the rampage,
abducting and beating Jewish men, while the boycott was revived in
Würzburg and a synagogue in Miltenberg was vandalized. The district
head office of the National Socialist Company Cell Organization
(Nationalsozialistische Betriebszellenorganisation, NSBO) was then
sharply admonished to rein in the boycotters. In October 1933, police
clashed with SA and SS units that attacked Jewish bookshops with, they
claimed, the authority of Julius Streicher.[60]

The contrast between Berlin and Bavaria was graphically revealed to
Martha Dodd, the daughter of the newly arrived American Ambassador, when she went on a road trip to the south in the company of the
journalist Quentin Reynolds. As they approached one town after
another they encountered banners strung across the main road proclaiming that Jews were not wanted there. The atmosphere was febrile.
In Nuremberg they saw SA men force a woman to walk through the
streets with a placard strung around her neck reading 'I have offered
myself to a Jew'. Reynolds decided not to report the incident because
'there had been so many atrocity stories lately that people were no
longer interested in them'.[61]

Such humiliations were not confined to Streicher's realm. From the
outset Nazi rule unleashed a wave of sexual abuse and gendered
violence, usually masked by the pretence of interdicting physical contact between Jews and Aryans. At the same time as National Socialism
denounced the libertinism attributed to the Weimar Republic and advocated a new form of puritanism, it fostered a prurient interest in sexual
activity through the policing of personal relationships. The permission
to pry, expose, and discuss sex was a welcome relief; it was also a legitimate way to indulge in salacious talk and misogynistic violence.

During that first long, hot summer of National Socialism Jewish
men and non-Jewish women who defied the new line between Aryans
and non-Aryans were subject to public pillory. The Gestapo office in the
government district of Kassel reported that 'a number of Jews who had

intimate relations with German girls were brought in recent days to police headquarters by the population, assisted by the SS'. Before they were hauled in 'the Jews in question were paraded publicly through the streets. This was accompanied by repeated spontaneous anti-semitic demonstrations by the agitated crowd.' In Hamburg, Kurt Rosenberg, a lawyer who was sacked due to the Aryan paragraph, watched a German girl and a Jewish man paraded through Cuxhaven. He noted in his diary that she bore a cardboard notice inscribed 'I am a pig because I took up with a Jew'.[62]

Couples in mixed marriages also came under hostile scrutiny, especially in small places where they were denied the anonymity people enjoyed in the big city. Lilli Jahn was in her early thirties, a qualified doctor, married to a non-Jew who she had met while they were medical students. After her marriage to Ernst Jahn in 1926 they moved to Immenhausen, in Hesse, where he obtained a practice. When she was not having children and raising them Lilli assisted Ernst in the clinic. They prospered and lived happily until 1933. The town was under an SPD mayor and council until March when the SA evicted the left-wingers. Somehow the local Nazis knew that Lilli was Jewish and on 1 April organized a boycott of the practice. In anguish she wrote to friends, 'We've had a shocking time of it! Can you imagine how I'm feeling? Can you understand how heavy hearted I am and how bitterly hurtful it all is . . . Just imagine, they also boycotted Amadé [her pet name for Ernst] because he has a Jewish wife! I can't find the words to tell you how profoundly shocked I was. And, of course, we are now very fearful. Will there be other repercussions on us?' Ernst Jahn stood by his wife, who was pregnant with their third child, but she stopped practising so as not to 'give offence'.[63]

When autumn arrived, relations between party yahoos and the state authorities grew more strained. The upturn in the economy, partly thanks to the pay packets of men employed on public works schemes, meant that the Christmas season got under way strongly. Jewish-owned shops and stores benefited along with suppliers and wholesalers. NSDAP members making their Yuletide purchases were offended to find the window displays in Jewish-owned businesses decorated with Christmas trees and religious symbols. Worse, the shops were full of customers. The result was another wave of actions aimed at Jewish-run retail outlets. Raymond Geist, in the American Embassy, reported that 'The revival of anti-Jewish propaganda has intimidated Jews in many towns and it is reported that they avoid showing themselves in the streets during the day as much as possible and lock themselves in their houses at night.' This was not what Schacht or Schmitt, the economics minister, wanted to hear. In mid-December, the Reich Economics Ministry sent around instructions that under no circumstances should shopping be disrupted.[64]

Jewish responses

These contradictions and fluctuations help to explain the divergent Jewish responses to persecution during 1933. At the most extreme point on the spectrum, dozens of Jews took their own lives out of despair. Around 37,000 German Jews emigrated, most to adjacent countries. The vast majority stayed. Some remained because they believed, like lots of other Germans, that Hitler could not last long. Those who were less hopeful that the government would fall believed they could adapt to life under Hitler. These pessimists could reassure themselves that however bad it was in Germany, it was worse for Jews in Poland and far worse to be a refugee anywhere. Jewish perceptions also varied according to class, occupation, age, gender, and where they lived. In some regions, such as Streicher's domain or East Prussia, there was constant anti-Jewish agitation. Elsewhere, Jews enjoyed relative calm. The Jewish population of the big cities was more lightly affected than Jews in small towns and villages. Individual Jews could pass unnoticed in the urban conurbations and the authorities were more capable of preventing violence or disorder. In rural communities the few Jews were well known, at the mercy of officials and local SA men who could do almost what they pleased.[65]

The twilight period between Hitler's appointment as chancellor and the elections was particularly fluid. Left-wing Jews were naturally apprehensive. Jewish shopkeepers who were exposed to events on the street felt distinctly vulnerable. Wealthy, conservative, nationalistic Jews who moved in more decorous circles wondered whether they might not be able to share in the national revolution. On the same day that the Reichstag went up in flames Siegmund Warburg began a diary in which to record 'the huge political upheavals of the last few weeks'. He found them 'especially moving for a Jewish German and above all for one such as myself, who feels his entire being to be so inextricably rooted in Germandom'.[66]

Listening to Hitler's eve of poll speech on the radio, Warburg thought the oratory was 'clearly idealistic, powerfully proactive, delivered with authentic inspiration'. Intimidation alone could not explain the seven and a half million votes cast for the NSDAP; the result was a tribute to the 'idealistic forces which above all have brought it about'. National Socialism represented the struggle between dynamic youth and sluggish bureaucracy. The Nazis deployed a 'decisive analysis' and showed a 'self-sacrificing will to fight'. Despite the anti-Semitism of the movement, he considered the 'prospects are good'. The new regime offered opportunities for like-minded German Jews. 'Perhaps the coming man is now precisely this type among both Aryan and Jewish Germans – a Jewish German of this type can therefore rightly say that he would be a Nazi if it weren't for the Nazis' anti-Semitism.' He suspected that such Jew-hatred was symptomatic of the Nazis' arriviste status; it would pass.[67]

A week later, the new Nazi incumbents in Hamburg's city hall obliged Siegmund's older cousin, Max Warburg, to resign from his position with the finance department. Siegmund now felt more dubious about how the wind was blowing. 'We have fascism, but the big question remains whether it will be a good German fascism, in other words a fascism that wants to be orderly and just, akin to the Italian, or a fascism closer to that of Moscow, a fascism which leads to arbitrariness, and communism, to brutality and ignorance.'[68]

Nor was there a uniform reaction to the boycott. In a front-page article in *Jüdische Rundschau*, Robert Weltsch urged Jews to respond to discrimination by glorying in their heritage. Entitled 'Wear the Yellow Star With Pride' the piece was intended to evoke Jewish triumphs over past waves of discrimination rather than express meek acceptance of persecution. The RjF, led by the decorated ex-army captain Leo Löwenstein, believed in constructive engagement with the regime. When it won concessions for combat veterans the entire Jewish population saw this as an example of how best to reply to Nazi persecution. The Jüdischer Frauenbund, however, spurned engagement and withdrew from the League of German Women, expressing its alienation from Germany. Nationalist Jews formed the Verband nationaldeutscher Juden (the Association of German National Jews) and sought to prove their loyalty to Germany by denouncing both Zionism and Ostjuden.

These ultra-patriotic German Jews declared that 'Anyone who leaves and goes abroad is a traitor.' Orthodox Jews wrote to Hitler seeking reassurance that Germany did not wish for their destruction. They got no reply.[69]

There were reasons to be hopeful. The boycott had provoked moving gestures of solidarity. It was, in itself, a response to international protest, signifying that the Jews of Germany were not alone. Moreover, a succession of pronouncements from the Reich Chancellery, the Ministry of the Interior, and the Ministry of Economics indicated that the regime put the maintenance of stable, calm trading conditions above the implementation of demands to expel Jews from economic life. Hence, Victor Klemperer interpreted the cancellation of the boycott as a 'wild turnaround' and a sign that the regime had capitulated to resistance at home and external pressure. 'I have the impression of swiftly approaching catastrophe,' he wrote excitedly. To many Jews it did not seem possible for the conservatives to remain in government with the Nazis or 'put up with the National Socialist dictatorship much longer'. Edwin Landau and his friends agreed that Hitler would last a year at the most. 'We believed that the outside world could not tolerate such behaviour in the twentieth century.'[70]

It was no simple matter for Jews to evaluate the significance of the anti-Jewish measures. Nor was it easier to determine how non-Jews felt. History and previous experience offered little guidance to the unprecedented situation. The Jewish population was familiar with religious antagonism; there was nothing new about prejudice and discrimination. True, the German state had never sanctioned nationwide quotas or sought to restrict Jewish economic activity; but the boycott had lasted only one day, while there were anti-Jewish quotas in other countries where Jewish life continued without detriment. The inconsistent application of the Aryan paragraph gave hope that not all Jews would be excluded from society and the economy. Finally, the behaviour of the president, Hindenburg, provided substantial reassurance.

Out of loyalty and gratitude to the Jews who had served under him in the Great War, Hindenburg responded to protests by the association of Jewish ex-servicemen against the treatment meted out to its members. On 4 April, he wrote to the chancellor that 'Recently, a whole series of cases has been reported to me in which judges, lawyers, and officials of the Judiciary who are disabled war veterans and whose record in office is flawless have been forcibly sent on leave, and are later to be dismissed for the sole reason that they are of Jewish descent.' Hindenburg informed Hitler that 'It is quite intolerable for me person- ally . . . that Jewish officials who were disabled in the war should suffer such treatment.' He asked the chancellor to inquire into the matter and find 'some uniform arrangement' for all branches of the public service. Unless there was a specific case against them, 'As far as my own feelings are concerned, officials, judges, teachers and lawyers who are war inva- lids, fought at the front, are sons of war dead, or themselves lost sons in the war, should remain in their positions.' He concluded resoundingly, 'If they were worthy of fighting for Germany and bleeding for Germany, then they must also be considered worthy of continuing to serve the Fatherland in their professions.' Hitler replied the next day, sniffily pointing out that Jews had been conscripted like other Germans, but promising to accommodate the president's reservations in forthcoming legislation to 'remove the solution of these questions from arbitrary action'. The exemptions that Hindenburg specified were embodied in the 7 April legislation, greatly softening the blow. Furthermore, there were still many non-Nazi officials holding posts in ministries and town halls who were willing to interpret the new regulations helpfully and who behaved towards Jews with old-fashioned courtesy.[71]

When the government revoked the naturalization of Ostjuden who had settled in Germany since November 1918, it reinforced the impres- sion that anti-Jewish measures were targeted rather than aimed universally at all Jews. It was hard to discern the distinction between expressions of a familiar nationalism and the construction of the Volks- gemeinschaft on the basis of a racial identity. It took time to grasp that nation and race were now considered coterminous and that the Jews were aliens in Germany despite what their passports said or what their war record demonstrated.

Despite the boomerang effect of the foreign protests, continued overseas pressure began to tell on the regime. This was largely because of the linkage made between Germany's image abroad and exports. Victor Klemperer, whose position at the university was saved by Hin- denburg's intervention on behalf of Jewish war veterans, even speculated that the reaction against the anti-Jewish measures would bring down the government. 'The fate of the Hitler movement will undoubtedly be decided by the Jewish business,' he wrote on 25 April. 'I do not under- stand why they have made this point of their programme so central. It will sink them.'[72]

Continuing foreign protests

Although he was not a diplomat James McDonald was chairman of the Foreign Policy Association and the Germans knew he was well connected, so when he spoke up for the Jews he was taken seriously. A week after the boycott, Hanfstaengl got him an interview with Hitler at which McDonald broached the Jewish issue. A few days later, Messersmith raised the question with Göring, telling him it was damaging Germany in the United States. Hitler got the same message from Sir Horace Rumbold. The British foreign secretary, Sir John Simon, instructed him to inform the chancellor that the 'oppressive policy' towards the Jews had cost Germany a great deal of sympathy in Britain. Hitler did not take this well and responded as he had to McDonald, insisting that at a time of national crisis Jews had to suffer like the rest. Rumbold concluded that 'he is a fanatic on the subject'.[73]

A second wave of protests underscored the point made by diplomats. On 10 May 1933, 100,000 Jews marched through New York condemning National Socialism and demanding a popular boycott. Similar demonstrations were held in other cities: in Chicago the number was 50,000, in Philadephia it was 20,000, and in Cleveland 10,000. Letters and telegrams poured into the White House appealing for the administration to act. President Roosevelt remained silent, but the Germans noticed a drop-off in trade with the US that they could ill afford. In London the Board of Deputies of British Jews finally convened a protest rally on 27 June 1933. It was addressed by mainly non-Jewish figures, including the Archbishop of Canterbury. The following month East End Jewish organizations, including the left-wing Workers' Circle, trade unions and Zionist groups operating under the umbrella United Jewish Protest Committee, organized an anti-Nazi rally in Hyde Park. It was attended by 50,000 Jews, many of whom had processed from the East End with banners proclaiming 'Restore the Rights of Jews in Germany'. In September the boycott was institutionalized under the supervision of the Jewish Representative Council for the Boycott of German Goods and Services. The council, chaired by the industrialist Lord Melchett, embraced dozens of trade unions, friendly societies, synagogues and Zionist groups with an estimated 170,000 members.[74]

The arrival of William E. Dodd, the new US Ambassador to Germany, was a further, forceful reminder that the persecution of the Jews was noted abroad. Dodd, a historian who had received his doctorate from Leipzig University in 1904, was a life-long Democrat, a devout Baptist, and a dyed-in-the-wool liberal on matters of religious liberty and personal freedom. Roosevelt selected him personally and briefed him in the White House before his departure. According to Dodd's diary (which may have been embellished by his daughter after his death), the president told him that 'The German authorities are treating the Jews shamefully and the Jews in this country are greatly excited.' It was not a governmental matter and the ambassador could not make an official intervention unless the anti-Jewish measures touched a US citizen; but 'whatever we can do to moderate the general persecution by unofficial and personal influence ought to be done'. Dodd also had a lengthy meeting with American Jewish leaders, including Stephen Wise. He had barely disembarked at Hamburg on 13 July 1933, when a journalist from the *Israelitisches Familienblatt* asked him if he was going to intercede on behalf of the Jews. Despite a suitably diplomatic reply, the paper carried the story that Dodd had come on a mission to rectify the wrongs done to the Jews. One of his first tasks on entering the US Embassy the next day was to correct the report. But it was true to the spirit of the man if not his official role.[75]

Dodd raised the mistreatment of Jews at his first meeting with Bernhard von Bülow, undersecretary at the German Foreign Office. Bulow admitted that 'the hostility of the Jews in the US did much harm'. The following month, Dodd tackled Neurath on the subject. He insisted that 'You cannot expect world opinion of your conduct to moderate as long as eminent leaders like Hitler and Goebbels announce from platforms, as in Nuremberg, that all Jews must be wiped off the earth.' According to Dodd, the foreign minister was 'embarrassed as on one or two previous occasions. He did not promise any reform much as he seemed to lament the facts.' However, Dodd refrained from embarrassing Hitler when he finally met the chancellor in October. There was hardly any need to; by this time he had gained a reputation in Berlin as a friend of the Jewish people. This did nothing to help them. By reminding the Germans that he cared about the Jews without actually being able to do anything positive, Dodd squandered his authority. More seriously, he added to the impression that Jews controlled the White House.[76]

The new British Ambassador, Sir Eric Phipps, did not make the same mistake. He barely mentioned the Jews in his exchanges with officials on the Wilhelmstrasse. This did not mean he was unaware of or unconcerned about anti-Semitism. Phipps made a careful study of *Mein Kampf* and concluded that Hitler was consistent in his attitude towards the Jews. However, he doubted that Hitler would adhere to positions 'expressed with such incredible violence in a work written in a Bavarian prison ten years ago'. Like Dodd, Phipps was convinced from the moment he met Hitler that the chancellor was intent on rearming Germany and reversing the Versailles Treaty by force of arms if necessary. His chief objective during his years as ambassador in Berlin was to impress on the British Foreign Office the need to contain Hitler.[77]

Jews in Germany and sympathetic foreign diplomats in Berlin hoped that the conservatives in the cabinet would persuade Hitler to wind down the anti-Jewish campaign. They believed that the economy would supply them with the necessary leverage and therefore pinned their hopes on the non-Nazi minister for economics, Kurt Schmitt, and the president of the Reichsbank, Hjalmar Schacht. They were not entirely disappointed. Schacht had met Jewish leaders when he visited New York in May 1933, shortly after his reappointment to the Reichsbank. At that time he intimated to McDonald his conviction that the persecution of the Jews was 'a mistake'. When they met again in August, in Berlin, Schacht was less emollient. Nevertheless, in September the Reich Economics Ministry issued instructions to government officials, municipal officers, magistrates and members of the NSDAP to refrain from boycotts of Jewish-owned enterprises or any other interruption to the conduct of business, such as refusal to list Jews as suppliers, denying Jews the right to advertise goods or services, or intimidating customers. Defiance would be treated as 'offences against the Führer principle' and constitute 'economic sabotage'. The instructions were published in the *CV-Zeitung* on 11 October 1933.[78]

The insistence that Jews should be allowed to carry on their business was seen as a vital breakthrough and buoyed up hopes that the Jewish population would get by. In fact, the pledge that Jews could carry on business unmolested was more than an economic life-line: it gave them legal traction. When unauthorized actions occurred, especially in small communities, Jews were able to fight back. The Centralverein collated information about breaches of the rules and prodded central government into asserting its prerogative, often to the annoyance of local authorities, Nazi organizations and SA men.[79]

The primacy accorded to economic growth indicated that the regime was not united with regard to Judenpolitik, that there was tension between the party and the state. It was evident that opinion was divided even within the party, and it was not clear which faction was uppermost at any moment or which would win in the long run. No single minister or department was responsible for dealing with the Jews and there was no single party office with a brief to devise and implement Judenpolitik. In these confused circumstances, the Jews were able to play off one agency against the other; they rallied and bounced back.[80]

The Jewish leadership realized that individual initiatives were no substitute for a unified front and could even be a liability. In September 1933 a constellation of prominent Jews joined together to form the Reichsvertretung der deutschen Juden (RV, the Reich Representation of German Jews). It was the first centralized, representative body of German Jews including all sections of the community except the pro-Nazi Verband nationaldeutscher Juden (VndJ) and the Orthodox, who did not wish to rub shoulders with reform or liberal Jews and traditionally pursued their own interests in splendid isolation. The RV was intended first and foremost to mediate between the government and the Jewish population. But it also coordinated responses to the problems caused by the anti-Jewish laws and acted as the address for foreign aid. Its Education Committee promoted the development of Jewish schools. Most importantly, it worked with (and subsequently absorbed) the Zentralausschuss für Hilfe und Aufbau (Central Committee for Assistance and Reconstruction, ZAHA). Jews were still eligible for state assistance, but it was parsimonious and constantly squeezed by new regulations. ZAHA provided supplementary relief to Jewish families that were already hard-hit by the Depression. The Advice Service for Economic Assistance gave emergency aid to newly unemployed Jewish workers in the form of grants and loans. In the winter of 1933–4, some 30,000 Jews in Berlin were in receipt of welfare from Jewish sources. For those who gave up on Germany the Hilfsverein der Deutschen Juden advised about emigration. The Palestine Office of the RV handled enquiries specifically about the Jewish national home as a destination.[81]

Needless to say, it took a while for these agencies to get up and running. In the early months the situation was chaotic and precarious.

Alexander Szanto, a Hungarian-born but naturalized German Jew, who became chairman of the Economic Assistance Service in Berlin, recalled that 'thousands of Nazi victims turned to the gemeinde [Jewish community organizations] for help. Its offices were swamped by a flood of confused and desperate people.' In the first months, 'people virtually stormed the building from morning to night'. Szanto's staff did not just provide help to tide over those dismissed from jobs. It was their motto that 'no position in public, and particularly economic life, should be abandoned without a struggle. This tactic proved successful in numerous cases and saved the livelihood of many coreligionists.' Where they could not keep a Jew in a job they insisted on a decent redundancy payment that would enable the former employee to set up independently. For the first few years, 'many Jewish merchants and tradesmen really were prosperous enough to cover their financial obligations alongside the cost of living'. Jewish businesses absorbed a high proportion of the Jewish unemployed, partly thanks to the Jewish Labour Exchange. In Breslau, the career advice office helped 2,300 Jews.[82]

Jewish children felt the impact of Nazi persecution no less than adults and in some respects even sooner. Around 117,000 attended state schools from primary level to gymnasia. The Law Against the Overcrowding of German Schools made it impossible for many to find places at the start of the 1933 school year while thousands were withdrawn by parents unhappy at the abrasive effect of Nazi rituals and ideological teaching. Existing Jewish schools expanded to absorb the new intake and those moved out of the state system, but since there were hardly enough places a crash programme of school building was set in motion. Many of the new establishments were located in less than ideal premises and often the teachers were hastily retrained academics or men and women sacked from other jobs. But the Jewish schools provided a safe and sympathetic environment, while the educational experts working for the RV produced thoughtful teaching guidelines and curricula adapted to the new circumstances. They attempted to bolster the children's sense of self-worth by extensively teaching about Judaism and Jewish history. A great deal of time was devoted to Palestine, which was increasingly seen as the most desirable place for young Jews to grow up.[83]

The promise of a new life in Palestine brought the claims of the Zionist movement to the fore. Previously a marginal element in German Jewish life, Zionism now seemed a lot more interesting and relevant.

Membership of the German Zionist Federation (Zionistische Vereini-gung für Deutschland, ZvfD) leapt. Young Jews applied in large numbers to go on agricultural training courses, 'hachshara', that would qualify them for permits to settle in the Jewish national home. The attractions of Palestine were greatly enhanced in August 1933 when the German Zionist Federation concluded an agreement with the Reich Economics Ministry that enabled Jews moving there to take with them £1,000 in foreign currency and to sell German goods in Palestine to the value of RM50,000 that they had paid for prior to their departure. This unusual arrangement, known as the Ha'avara, or transfer, agreement, had grown out of the Hanotea scheme, devised by a private business-man, Sam Cohen, who imported agricultural machinery and other products from Germany into Palestine. The Economics Ministry and the Reichsbank were happy to cooperate because the scheme boosted exports, broke the boycott of German goods, and assisted the emigra-tion of Jews while minimizing the drain on foreign currency reserves. Indeed, the device was so successful that Cohen was elbowed aside by the Anglo-Palestine Bank, the financial arm of the world Zionist move-ment. The Bank and the ZvfD, with the assistance of the Warburg banking house, concluded the Ha'avara agreement with the German government to set up trusts in Germany and Palestine to handle, respectively, the purchase and sale of the manufactured items.[84]

With this agreement in hand, German Zionists took minimal in-terest in the defence of Jewish rights in the Third Reich. In their eyes, the success of National Socialism vindicated their prognostications about the illusion of emancipation. However, emigration in general was anathema to nationalistic German Jews and Zionism remained a heresy. No matter how vehemently the VndJ or the RjF denounced the rising interest in both, it was symptomatic of economic despair and the crisis of German Jewish identity.[85]

This predicament was accentuated by the dismissal of Jews from the creative industries. Jews were told that they could not share in or even perform the classics of German drama, opera and music. They were to be confined to 'Jewish culture'. In April 1933, Kurt Baumann, sacked from his position as an assistant theatre and opera director, realized that the 175,000 Jews in Berlin ought to be able to support theatre, opera and concert performances on their own. He gathered other Jews who had been made unemployed and formed a Jewish cultural association to perform specifically for Jewish audiences. Baumann persuaded Kurt

Singer, former director of the Municipal Opera, to lead the venture. The CV agreed to support it, largely to provide work for Jewish artists who had not been able to find work abroad and partly to raise morale. From exile in America a few years later Baumann recalled, 'For us in those days it was much more important to provide the Jewish public in Germany, which had once stood at the forefront of German cultural life, with a home for as long as possible.' The CV obtained permission from the authorities and in October 1933, the Kulturbund Deutscher Juden (German Jewish Cultural League, later the Jüdischer Kulturbund, JKB) was launched in Berlin. Baumann was uncertain how the Jewish population would respond to Jewish-only events, but the performances sold out. The Kulturbund rapidly spread to other Jewish centres. Its programmes attracted large audiences, giving work to hundreds of unemployed Jewish artists, performers and musicians. Inevitably, the repertoire fostered a keen sense of Jewish difference. The experience of attending a concert of music by a Jewish composer, performed by a Jewish orchestra with a Jewish conductor, to a Jewish audience was reassuring to some Jews and fortified their sense of identity. To others, it was a deplorable sign that Jews were slipping back into the ghetto.[86]

After a law was passed annulling contracts between Jewish authors and Aryan publishers, Joseph Roth pleaded with Stefan Zweig to recognize that his career as a German writer was over: 'Germany is dead. For us it is dead . . . It was a dream. Please see that, won't you!' But it was hard to accept the passing of a hard-won and long-cherished identity. Victor Klemperer was scathing about Jews who accepted that they were no longer entitled to think of themselves as Germans. 'Especially repugnant to us', he wrote, 'is the behaviour of some Jews. They are beginning to submit inwardly and to regard the new ghetto situation atavistically as a legal condition which has to be accepted.'[87]

After nearly a year of life under National Socialism the November 1933 plebiscite to approve Germany's withdrawal from the League of Nations cruelly forced German Jews to confront their identity. The Nazi Party treated the plebiscite as if there were a genuine contest. Hitler's speeches were broadcast in public; SA men put up posters and flags exhorting the population to vote. Jews were harassed in the traditional manner. But should the Jews vote and, if so, how? Dr Rudolf Löwenstein in Soest, Westphalia, was representative of many Jews when he wrote to the CV urging it to take a positive stand on the poll. 'Come what may, we feel that we are bound to our German Fatherland. We feel most painfully all the exclusionary laws that the Reich government has issued against us and that the ruling party enforces with even greater rigour. All of that, however, has to take a backseat in the interest of the nation's fight against foreign defamation and oppression.' German Jews resented the humiliations Germany suffered at the hands of the international community just as much as Aryans. So, 'in this moment we stand with pride, confidence and without qualification behind the leadership of the new German Reich, behind the chancellor Adolf Hitler'. The *CV-Zeitung* eventually published an article recommending that German Jews vote 'Yes' in the plebiscite even though it was in effect an endorsement of the Third Reich. Some Jews, like Willy Rosenfeld, were disgusted. 'Is it your duty as representatives of German Jewry to support these hateful measures?' Victor Klemperer voted 'No'; his wife left her ballot paper blank.[88]

By the end of 1933, the police reported that Jewish associational activity had picked up strongly and that Jews felt more secure economically. Jewish veterans' groups were flourishing and so were branches of the Zionist federation. Jewish cultural and sports associations were booming. The police HQ in Nuremberg-Fürth was somewhat startled by the transition from anxiety to confidence, 'in full awareness of the security they have been guaranteed'. To the indignation of the police, CV agents were amassing evidence of boycotting, newspapers that refused to take advertisements from Jews, the exclusion of Jews from markets, and signage announcing that Jews were not welcome or would not be served. They were optimistic that 'there will soon be a return to normal conditions'.[89]

The stabilization of Jewish life was reflected in the steep decline in the number of Jews leaving the country and the rising number of those returning. These fluctuations had a serious effect on foreign perceptions of the refugee crisis. Just as Jewish protests against Nazism peaked early, leaving behind an impression of Jewish power and unity that was increasingly at odds with reality, the effort to assist refugees was intense, frantic and expensive, only to peter out at the point at which it was really needed.

The first refugees

The wave of terror and anti-Jewish violence of spring 1933, followed by the boycott and the sacking of Jewish employees, produced the first great wave of Jewish emigration from the Third Reich. That year, about 37,000 Jews sought temporary refuge or new homes outside Germany. Many of these fugitives were politically active and as fearful of political repression as much as anti-Semitism. A large proportion were young men who had not fought in the Great War and who were made unemployed in the wave of dismissals from the state sector. The majority moved no further than neighbouring countries – France, Netherlands, Austria, Czechoslovakia – in the hope that conditions would soon change, allowing them to return. Approximately 8,900–9,500 Jews entered France, nearly 4,000 went to the Netherlands, about 5,000 crossed into Switzerland, and some 300–400 arrived each month in Britain. They were only one tributary feeding the river of émigrés, numbering 60,000–65,000, that flowed out of the Third Reich, including communists, socialists, artists and intellectuals. To citizens in the receiving countries it was not easy to distinguish fleeing Marxist intellectuals like Berthold Brecht from sacked Jewish doctors; consequently, the number of Jews seemed larger than it really was. Although the volume of emigrants fell to 23,000 in 1934 and hundreds returned (1,200–1,500 from the Netherlands alone), the initial impact had severe consequences.[90]

Few had sufficient resources to live independently and most had to look for work in countries already burdened with high unemployment. Initially, the refugees were greeted with sympathy. The newspapers were full of atrocity stories and many of the émigrés were distinguished figures from the arts and sciences who had been dismissed from university posts or purged from the cultural scene. Jewish communities outside Germany rallied to their aid. In France the Jewish community pledged to the government that it would not allow the new arrivals to become a burden on the public purse. Although this had no effect on the administration of the immigration rules, the French government signalled that it would uphold traditions of asylum and made it relatively easy for German Jews to obtain entry visas or cross the border pleading sanctuary. France had long welcomed foreign workers to bolster its depleted population and anti-German feeling made the refugees' cause temporarily popular. It did not take long for the mood to change.[91]

Foreign workers were less needed when unemployment was climbing. Professional groups, such as doctors and dentists, lobbied hard to exclude German competitors. French consuls warned the Foreign Ministry of a danger that France would be flooded with communists and disreputable elements fleeing Nazi justice. In December 1933, Senator Henry Bérenger, chairman of the foreign affairs committee of the Senate, announced that France would act as 'a way station for refugees, but not as a dumping ground'. The new year saw a tightening of immigration controls: now applicants would have to obtain visas and, once in France, would only be allowed to work if they had a work permit. The French police were ordered to hunt down illegal immigrants and deport them. Over 1934–5, the spectacle of police raiding bars and cafes frequented by foreigners or entering workshops demanding to see employment papers became a common sight. It became official French policy to prevent foreigners from settling in France and to encourage the emigration of those already arrived.[92]

As hostility to the inundation mounted along with the cost of supporting the newcomers, the French Jews became less accommodating. HICEM, the Paris-based aid organization that brought together the Hebrew Immigrant Aid Society of New York with the Jewish Colonisation Association, actually started assisting the repatriation of German Jews. The Zentralausschuss für Hilfe und Aufbau in Berlin warned that Jews should not leave unless they had arranged a means of subsistence.[93]

The reaction was felt most strongly in France, which bore the brunt of the initial wave. Just as the anti-German boycott movement divided American and British Jews, the treatment of refugees became a bone of contention between different sections of the French Jewish population. Jacques Helbronner, a vice president of the Consistoire, the central representative body of the French Jews, lobbied against unrestricted entry. Despite being a member of the executive of the National Committee to Aid German Refugees, he hated Germans and believed that as a French Jew he could best demonstrate his patriotism by casting aspersions on his German co-religionists. Helbronner was abetted by Robert de Rothschild, a key figure in fund-raising efforts who also chaired the National Committee to assist refugees, and Louis Oungre, the director of the Jewish Colonisation Association, which historically played a leading role in helping Jewish refugees settle in new lands. Raymond-Raoul Lambert, a war veteran and former civil servant, championed the refugees within the national committee, but made little headway. Polish Jews in France who were usually sensitive to immigration issues failed to mobilize on behalf of German Jews, who, they recalled, had been so snobbish towards Ostjuden. Lambert was even unable to prevent the committee that supposedly existed to succour refugees closing a makeshift camp in a disused army barracks at the Porte d'Orleans.[94]

The situation of most German and German Jewish refugees in France was miserable. Unable to work legally, they lived off whatever cash they had been able to bring with them, until it ran out. Some 2,000, mainly Polish or stateless Jews, ended up living in the old barracks donated by the French authorities. Conditions were rudimentary and the food was poor. James McDonald, who visited the site, described them as 'pitiful'. In mid-1933, nearly 6,000 Jews relied on payments from the Jewish community, which were costing it $225,000 per month. If the American Jewish Joint Distribution Committee (AJJDC), the main American Jewish overseas aid organization, had not come to its rescue, the French committee would have gone broke.[95]

Joseph Roth had always lived out of a suitcase. However, his Austrian nationality and modest fame gave him a degree of security that the refugees lacked. In 1935 he joined the Paris Hilfskomitee, which doled out aid to German exiles. In a letter to Stefan Zweig he described their miserable existence: 'valuable people, queuing every day for a work card, a piece of paper, a free meal, a paltry sum to appease the hotelkeeper – only for a short time'.[96]

Conditions in Britain were much better, thanks in part to the unified efforts of the Jewish community, and in part to the stringent restrictions on the number of Jews admitted permanently. On 5 April 1933, the British home secretary, Sir John Gilmour, met a delegation from the Anglo-Jewish community who asked for the lifting of immigration controls to enable Jews seeking escape from Germany to find refuge quickly. The delegation promised that the community would use its own resources to guarantee that German Jews who reached the UK would not become a burden on the public purse. When the cabinet met the following day it discussed the danger of a mass influx and set up a special committee to consider the options. The Cabinet Committee on Refugees met once and resolved that controls on the entry of aliens would not be changed. The only concession it made was to relax the rules in the case of distinguished individuals seeking asylum. It did however accept the pledge by the Jewish community to guarantee that Jewish immigrants from Germany would be financially supported. This arrangement placed the onus of screening potential refugees on the

Jewish Refugees Committee (later renamed the German Jewish Aid Committee, which sounded less alarming) and restricted the number that could be helped according to the funds at their disposal.[97]

Around the same time, President Roosevelt proposed relaxing visa controls on Jews hoping to emigrate to the USA. The suggestion was promptly squashed by the State Department, which pointed to high levels of domestic unemployment, and Congressional hostility to any amendment of the immigration rules. Although the quota for immigrants from Germany was 25,557, only 1,919 Germans arrived in 1933, mostly Jews. In early September 1933, Wilbur J. Carr, director of the Consular Service, transmitted instructions to US consuls in Germany stating that no preference was to be given to Jews who applied for an entry visa: 'the admission of such aliens into the United States is governed by the existing laws in the same manner as in the case of aliens of other classes'. Carr stipulated that the word 'refugee' was not to be used lest it be construed as interference in the internal affairs of another country.[98]

Jews in the United States hoped that the League of Nations could alleviate the plight of the refugees. Partly at the suggestion of New York Jews, in September 1933 James McDonald travelled to Europe to collect information for the Foreign Policy Association and lobby the League to extend assistance to Jewish refugees through the establishment of a High Commission for Refugees. While he was in Europe he met Jewish leaders to canvass support for the idea. He found their attitude disappointing. Few saw any need for a concerted international effort and fewer still were prepared to donate significant sums to fund it. The British Jewish leaders, he reported to Felix Warburg, were 'not yet . . . willing to face the realities of the situation'. In Paris, Robert de Rothschild told him that 'even French Jews think of the German refugee Jews as Germans rather than Jews, as Boches, former hated enemies and possible enemies of the future . . . the French Jews are French first and Jews second'. McDonald also encountered the bitter divisions between Zionists and non-Zionists. Chaim Weizmann, president of the World Zionist Organization, mocked the 'well to do Jews in the West [who] completely failed to sense the realities of the situation'. He disparaged the German Jewish leadership as 'the worst form of assimilationists, as persons who cringed and whimpered when the test came'. Weizmann condemned spending money to maintain Jews in Germany or European countries of refuge. He insisted that there could be only one permanent solution to the Jewish refugee problem: Palestine. Neville Laski, president of the Board of Deputies and a non-Zionist, sneered that 'Weizmann [who was born in Russia] was not really an Englishman.'[99]

McDonald was successful in persuading the member states of the League to establish a High Commission for Refugees, but it was gravely weakened by German insistence that the office should be semi-detached from the League and work only with refugees outside Germany. It was not to receive any League funding. Nevertheless, leading American Jews, including Felix Warburg, Samuel Untermyer and Stephen Wise, thought it was worth running with the scheme and proposed that McDonald should become the first High Commissioner. In November 1933 he travelled to Geneva to accept the post. He soon discovered he had been handed a poisoned chalice. British cooperation was vital, but the Foreign Office, which was responsible for maintaining tranquillity between Jews and Arabs in Palestine, insisted on playing down the role of Palestine in any solution to the refugee crisis lest an influx of Jews trigger Arab unrest. Because the new organization would be separate from the League, McDonald had to set up a governing body and advisory council that would give it international standing. This made it prey to the whim of governments who appointed representatives guaranteed not to accept any burden on their own country. The French cynically placed Senator Bérenger on the governing body and arranged the secondment of Jacques Helbronner to the advisory council. Because it had no budget from the League, McDonald had to raise money, which placed him at the mercy of the refugee aid organizations, each of which had its own agenda, and wealthy members of various Jewish communities. He found himself sucked into Jewish communal politics and personal feuds, while his efforts to meet with the German government were consistently rebuffed. Modest proposals to provide emigrating Jews with simple documentation were waved aside by junior Foreign Ministry officials. McDonald could not get near Schacht to ask for a relaxation of the foreign currency controls that prevented Jews leaving with more than a small proportion of their wealth. But his greatest frustration was the inability of Jewish organizations and personalities to agree on a plan of action or provide sufficient funds even to run his office. After a stormy meeting of the High Commission's governing body in December 1933, McDonald raged to his diary, 'I almost feel as if I wished each half of the Jews would destroy the other half. They are impossible.'[100]

At the start of 1934, J. P. Moffat, at the State Department, noted in his journal that 'McDonald, the High Commissioner, has had immense difficulty in steering a course between the rival Jewish factions . . . has not succeeded in making contact with the German Government either on the question of travel documents or the question of Jewish property in Germany.' Indeed, McDonald spent more time with President Roosevelt than with the president of the Reichsbank. Not that this did much good either. Roosevelt took a strong interest in McDonald's work and welcomed the High Commissioner at the White House whenever he was back in the United States; but when McDonald requested modest funding for his office, Roosevelt was unable to get the State Department to make a grant of just $10,000. McDonald was under no illusions about the increasing futility of his work. When the governing body of the High Commission met there was no consensus on where Jewish refugees could be settled or how they could be helped. The bodies represented on the advisory council disagreed over whether to fund schemes in Germany for the vocational retraining of potential émigrés and quarrelled over whether to use funds to maintain Jews where they were or move them on. McDonald's grand plan for a corporation to negotiate with the German government to liquidate the entire refugee problem in one go, using funds from world Jewry and the proceeds from selling Jewish assets in Germany, was regarded as wildly over-ambitious by some and by others as a reckless invitation to the Nazis to expel the German Jews. Like many potential emigrants, it got nowhere.[101]

PART TWO

JUDENPOLITIK

1934–1938

'No end in sight'

A year after Hitler was appointed as chancellor, Victor Klemperer wondered, 'Has Germany really become so completely and fundamentally different, has its soul changed so completely that this will endure?' He was not alone in questioning whether Hitler would last. Joseph Roth advised Stefan Zweig that 'Hitler's situation was never so bad as now. The foreign powers are watching him like a hawk, and he's almost lost his only friend, which is Italy.' Leopold Schwarzschild concurred that the regime was surrounded by discontent on all sides although 'the bayonet and systematic terror [are] an excellent basis . . . for remaining in power for a long while'.[1]

The many Jews who doubted the viability of the regime were not engaging in wishful thinking. Their estimations were based on everyday experience and the intelligence they were able to gather about domestic politics, the economy, and international relations. Similar prognoses also abounded within the diplomatic community.

Sir Eric Phipps considered that Hitler faced 'real difficulties with his own extremists, with the Catholic and Protestant Churches, with the economic and financial situation'. There was tension between radicals in the National Socialist movement, notably the SA, who wanted to resuscitate the 'national revolution', and the government. The army was particularly alarmed by SA pretensions to supplant the military. Within the government, ministers were at loggerheads over security and economic policy. Göring and Himmler were jousting for control of the police. Robert Ley, head of the Deutsche Arbeitsfront (DAF, the German Labour Front), was contesting control of the economy with Hjalmar Schacht and the ailing Kurt Schmitt. The regime's patronage of a Nazi Christian movement, not to mention anti-religious pronouncements by Walther Daré and Alfred Rosenberg, had generated conflict

with the Church. Meddling in the affairs of Austria had alienated the
government in Vienna, annoyed Mussolini, and incurred international
disapproval. The continued weakness of the economy posed the most
serious challenge to the regime. Despite investment in public works
schemes unemployment stubbornly hovered around the three million
mark. Those in work saw their purchasing power continue to fall and
there were periodic shortages of staple foods. Poor exports led to a
chronic balance of trade deficit and a foreign currency crisis. This
meant that by late summer it was not possible to make up for a bad
harvest with imports.[2]

Ambassador Dodd reported to Washington that 'Evidences of dissatisfaction continue to reach me from various quarters.' Ferdinand von
Bredow, who had served in Schleicher's cabinet, told Bella Fromm that
'at Wilhelmstrasse they are hopeful for the speedy finish of the National
Socialist government. The bosses of the party are continually knifing
each other. When that has gone far enough, they think, the whole
structure will topple.' When Goebbels launched a campaign against
'grumblers', Klemperer reckoned it was a tacit admission of anti-
government feeling. He commented witheringly, 'There is desperation
behind the whole speech, a last attempt at a diversion . . . The whole
system is on its last legs.'[3]

The crisis came to a head in mid-June when the vice-chancellor,
Papen, gave an address at Marburg University in which he criticized the
national revolution. Having finally woken up to Hitler's totalizing ambitions, Papen was attempting to rally the conservatives and all those
who resented or feared the hegemony of the NSDAP. Dodd excitedly
reported that after the speech Papen was 'mobbed'. Although this
belated turnaround was not connected with the simmering conflict that
ranged the army and the state against the SA, Hitler and his inner circle
resolved to settle matters with both the SA and the vice-chancellor at
the same time.[4]

On 30 June 1934, the police and SS acting under the personal direction of Hitler, Göring and Himmler moved against the SA. Ernst Röhm
was arrested on the pretext that he was planning a coup and shot a few
days later in a Munich prison cell. Dozens of other SA leaders were executed or imprisoned. Hitler's erstwhile rival for leadership of the Nazi
movement, Gregor Strasser, was assassinated. In Berlin, SS men gunned
down Kurt von Schleicher (and his wife) at his home and killed Edgar
Junge, who had written Papen's Marburg speech. Other conservatives,

including several Catholic activists, against whom the Nazis harboured a grudge were murdered. Subsequently Hitler addressed the Reichstag and in a stunning gesture took personal responsibility for the massacre that became known as the 'Night of the Long Knives'.[5]

International opinion was shocked as much by the admission as by the bloodletting. To Phipps the events confirmed his conviction that Hitler was 'unbalanced' and surrounded by dangerous men; it was a 'mad regime'. All the same, he shrewdly divined that Hitler must have felt confident to 'dismiss some of President von Hindenburg's old comrades in arms in this offhand fashion'. Dodd wondered if he ought to resign the ambassadorship. He was convinced he could never achieve anything while Hitler, Göring and Goebbels were in power and refused to attend the Reichstag session to hear Hitler justify himself. 'I have a sense of horror when I look at the man,' he told Phipps. Like many Jewish onlookers, Joseph Roth predicted some months later that 'Hitler won't last more than another year and a half'.[6]

As it turned out, the 'Night of the Long Knives' strengthened Hitler and helped to entrench the police state. The army now felt indebted to Hitler for neutralizing the threat posed by the SA, while the public was relieved that a source of disorder had been eliminated. In preparation for the strike Göring placed Heinrich Himmler in charge of the Prussian political police, effectively giving him control of the Gestapo throughout Germany. Himmler, who was just thirty-four years old, was the son of a teacher who became a tutor to the Bavarian royal family. His family were strict Catholics and utterly respectable. He was just old enough to serve in the army in the First World War, but did not see action. While studying agronomy at university after the war he began to move in right-wing, völkisch circles and from notes he kept it is possible to see how (like Goebbels) he adopted an anti-Semitic world view from a purely cerebral standpoint. He was involved in the 1923 putsch as a member of a right-wing militia allied to the Nazis and joined the NSDAP soon afterwards. Initially he worked for Gregor Strasser, but in 1926 Hitler chose him to run the party's national propaganda operation. For two years he was deputy head of Hitler's paramilitary escort, the Schutzstaffel or SS, a role he combined with running a poultry farm. In January 1929 he was promoted to Reichsführer of the SS, at which time it was still a small and relatively unimportant organization with about 1,400 members. But Himmler was a workaholic with a genius for organization and a vision of what he wanted the SS to become. Within

three years he had built it into an elite formation of 10,000 men selected
for their ideological commitment to National Socialism and conformity
to his ideal of 'Aryan' manhood. He was also a skilled political operator
and soon withdrew the SS from subservience to the SA, establishing it
as a virtually autonomous fiefdom. By the time of the showdown with
the SA, he had expanded the SS to 100,000 and it was rewarded with
independent status. Thanks to the roles he now held in the police,
Himmler could set about making the SS the core of the Nazi police
state. Himmler appointed Reinhard Heydrich, head of the Gestapo in
Bavaria, to run the Berlin head office. Since Heydrich was also head of
the Sicherheitsdienst (SD), the security service of the SS, this represented a decisive aggregation of power for both the SS and the SD.[7]

Luck also came to Hitler's aid. A month after the purge, President
Hindenburg died. Without waiting for any constitutional sanction
Hitler combined the chancellorship with the functions of head of state.
All members of the army were immediately required to swear an oath of
allegiance to the Führer. Hitler's assumption of the presidency was later
given popular sanction by a plebiscite and retrospectively authorized by
a law passed through the Reichstag. As Klemperer noted, it was a 'complete coup d'état'. Phipps reported to London, that 'no change of regime
here must be expected for some time to come'. The people might face a
hard winter, but the Nazis were firmly in the saddle. Moreover, 'large
numbers of Germans regard Hitler with a species of mystic adoration'.
Dodd could only take comfort from expressions of discontent amongst
'the more thinking classes'. Klemperer now reflected miserably, 'there is
no end in sight'.[8]

Until then German Jews could see how deeply the regime was pre-
occupied with its own entrails. They noted a dramatic falling off of
anti-Jewish activity, at least at the summit of the state and the party.
Between December 1933 and mid-1935, there was no major legislation
on Jewish matters. Whereas in 1933 Berlin Jews had to cope with eighty
ordinances, the number fell to fifteen in 1934 and just two for the first
six months of 1935. Hitler made hardly any public reference to the
'Jewish question' over this period. Goebbels occasionally related the
parlous state of Germany's exports to the Jewish boycott, but he did
not engineer a sustained campaign in the Nazi-controlled media. Only
Streicher's *Der Stürmer* maintained a barrage of anti-Semitic propaganda. The issue on 1 May 1934 was particularly striking because it
disseminated the medieval myth that Jews were responsible for the

murder of Christian children to use their blood for religious rituals. However, while Streicher's incitement led to spikes in local violence there was no concerted, nationwide action. The 'cold pogrom' against the Jews was sustained by party members on their own initiative and to their bewilderment these activists often found themselves in conflict with the state authorities.[9]

Historians have consequently treated 1934 as a 'relatively quiet year' or a 'brief respite' in which Jews had the 'illusion' of stability. The reality was more complex, as Jews at the time appreciated. There was no uniform policy emanating from Berlin and no uniform picture across the country. Individual, unauthorized actions continued, although they frequently incurred censure from central government. The Jews seized on these inconsistencies and used them to their advantage. Meanwhile, Nazi activists were perplexed and increasingly resentful. The rest of the population, when they took notice, were bemused at the sometimes ludicrous contradictions. This shambles was the matrix for subsequent policy initiatives. Having allowed hurriedly conceived, partially thought-out policies to create a situation that satisfied no one and caused much restlessness amongst loyal party comrades, the Nazi leadership had to figure a way out. This was becoming a familiar pattern.[10]

Hjalmar Schacht and Judenpolitik

At the start of the year, the Reich Interior Ministry issued a decree forbidding unauthorized interference with Jewish businesses. The directive gave teeth to previous instructions intended to prevent boycotting or blacklisting. However, Kurt Schmitt was hardly a forceful personality and was increasingly enfeebled by ill health. When Schacht replaced him as acting minister for economics in July 1934, the protection of the economy gained a more powerful champion. Not that Schacht needed to work hard on Hitler; the foreign currency crisis was ample cause to demand that the party rein in the elements continuing to hinder Jews from going about their business. In the latter half of the year he again called on Frick and Göring, who controlled the police, to ensure that Jews were not molested.[11]

Schacht's appointment gave a fillip to the Jews who regarded him as their most plausible defender in the government. He had been a founder member of the Deutsche Demokratische Partei in 1919 alongside the

Jewish politicians Walther Rathenau and Hugo Preuss, Albert Einstein, and the publisher Rudolf Mosse. During the 1920s, the DDP attracted over half of the Jewish vote in Reichstag elections. Even though Schacht had travelled to the right over the intervening years it was hard to believe that he could have abnegated his principles entirely. Unfortunately, the DDP was always in thrall to nationalism and its intellectual inspiration came from Friedrich Naumann, who championed a form of 'völkisch liberalism'. By 1930, the party was ideologically hollowed out. To survive as an electoral force it allied with the anti-Semitic Jungdeutsche Orden to form the Deutsche Staatspartei. This new party avoided any expression of support for the Jews. Thus by the time he entered Hitler's coalition, Schacht was a liberal and a democrat in memory only. He never fought for Jewish rights as such and never sought to frustrate Nazi policy on the Jews. He did nothing to stop the dismissals of Jews from their jobs in April 1933 and unhesitatingly implemented the Aryan paragraph in the Reichsbank. Nor was he averse to the transfer of Jewish enterprises into Aryan hands; he just wanted it to be conducted in a businesslike fashion. Even so, his insistence on the priority of economic goals, his sensitivity to Anglo-Saxon opinion, and his aversion to disorder, acted as a significant counterweight to the ideologues within the regime.[12]

External pressure or the perception of external pressure continued to ameliorate anti-Jewish policy, too. When James McDonald visited the Foreign Office in February 1934 to discuss ways to alleviate the Jewish refugee crisis, Hans Dieckhoff, an official specializing in US and British affairs, went out of his way to reassure him that 'there would be a general moderation'. Dieckhoff 'cited the announcement by interior minister William Frick to the heads of the states that they should not go beyond the letter of the law in anti-Jewish discrimination'. Neurath, whom he saw later, said he wanted to liquidate the refugee problem partly to avoid giving fodder to anti-German propagandists. McDonald ultimately emerged from these meetings empty handed and gloomier about the prospect for German Jews, but his interlocutors on the Wilhelmstrasse understood their encounters very differently. Significantly, so did some German Jews. Otto Hirsch, a member of the Reichsvertretung executive, told McDonald, that Hitler was trapped 'by the beasts in his party'. If foreign pressure was maintained on the regime, the economic and military leadership would convey the appropriate message to him.[13]

Ambassador Dodd continued to signal his disdain for the regime's anti-Jewish policies. In February his son and daughter organized an embassy ball and invited the Jewish-born violinist Fritz Kreisler to entertain the guests. Kreisler would not otherwise have been allowed to perform in front of a non-Jewish audience. He was invited back twice during 1934. Dodd also had the satisfaction of explaining to irate German diplomats the reasons behind the unceasing anti-Nazi protests and the boycott of German goods in the US. In March, the American Jewish Congress and the American Federation of Labor organized a mock trial of Nazi Germany. The witnesses for the prosecution included the former governor of New York Al Smith and mayor Fiorello LaGuardia, whose mother was Jewish. Dodd was summoned to Neurath's office to hear an official complaint against the planned spectacle. The foreign minister demanded that he cable Washington to call the event off. Instead, the ambassador gave Neurath a lecture about freedom of expression and added that 'the Jewish policy of Hitler would bring further trouble if not changed'. Shortly after this encounter, Dodd had an audience with Hitler himself. According to his diary, he cautioned the Führer about the effect of Nazi propaganda in the United States. When Hitler claimed that it was 'all Jewish lies' Dodd bluntly explained the state of play in New York. Hitler responded angrily that 'if the agitation continued in the outside world he would make the end of all the Jews in Germany'.[14]

Dodd again met with American Jewish leaders while he was home on leave during the spring. When they impressed on him their determination to maintain the boycott of Germany he attempted to deflate their protests by claiming that the condition of Jews in Germany was somewhat eased; but he confirmed that the Nazi leadership did make a link between foreign opinion and the fate of German Jews. He left it up to them to decide how to proceed. Back in Berlin, though, he pointedly informed Dieckhoff of this latest round of talks with Jewish representatives and at his next meeting with Neurath, Dodd claimed credit for cooling Jewish tempers. Neurath reciprocated by confiding that he, Schacht and Schmitt had together prevailed upon Goebbels to hold anti-Jewish propaganda in check. When the drain on Germany's gold reserves forced the government to announce a moratorium on debt repayments, Dodd did not hesitate to attribute the country's abysmal trade performance to its standing in overseas opinion. He warned Göring himself that as long as the government persecuted the Jews it would be harder to remove barriers to German exports.[15]

Dodd was not taken in by blandishments from Wilhelmstrasse officials that the persecution was being fundamentally modified. He repeatedly noted the discrepancy between the assurances he was given and practical actions. Nevertheless, external considerations in combination with internal dilemmas did cause the German elite to think twice. In May, Phipps told London that 'The party leaders realise that in this [relations between the army and the SA] and in other questions of foreign policy . . . and the Jews, the interests of the country and those of the Party tend to conflict.' There was friction over 'the policy to be adopted towards the Jews in view of the foreign trade slump'. Two months later, Raymond Geist informed the State Department that 'it is the feeling here that the German government wishes for the time being to maintain an armistice with respect to the Jewish question owing to the pressure of other problems'.[16]

So, even if Nazi leaders reacted to outside pressure for the wrong reasons it did lead to some relief for Germany's Jews. The sensitivity to foreign opinion and considerations of overseas trade help to explain the regime's sporadic efforts to curb anti-Jewish boycotts and prevent unauthorized acts of discrimination. These exhortations were a psychological boost to German Jews and, more importantly, gave them tools to work with locally or when dealing with central agencies. The result was a strange situation in which some Jews suffered persecution while others prospered. Conversely, Nazi activists who wanted to carry out party policy found themselves hampered by the police and the Gestapo.

Rechtsschutz – Jewish self-defence

Having reeled in shock from successive blows over the previous year, the Jewish population rallied. The Centralverein adopted a policy of Rechtsschutz: using the law to defend the ability of Jews to earn a living. Through its network of branches, the CV collected evidence that official decrees were being violated and passed it on to the Reich Economics Ministry. East Prussia, under Gauleiter Erich Koch, was notorious in this respect. Hans Reichmann, based at the CV central office, replied to a plea from the East Prussia branch, 'What you say about the contradiction between orders from government agencies and those from other functionaries who are not authorised to give them is correct. Ninety per cent of our current work is consumed with this problem.' Reichmann redoubled his efforts to use every lever and loophole to secure the conditions in which Jews could make a living.[17]

The practice of Rechtsschutz, which as Reichmann indicated was always gruelling, became harder after Himmler assumed control of the Gestapo across Germany and stepped up its role in Jewish affairs. The Gestapo ordered the CV to cease monitoring and reporting anti-Jewish activity, but to confine itself to the collection of strictly economic data. In any case, the CV could not do much about legalized discrimination or invisible boycotts. When local authorities fell under Nazi control they routinely terminated business with Jewish suppliers of good and services. The Nazi women's organization encouraged its members not to purchase from Jewish shops.[18]

Dauntless Jews acted on their own initiative. In Hamburg Max Eichholz successfully sued an SS man for calling him 'a dirty Jew'. A decorated war veteran and a lawyer with a long record of public service, Eichholz also went to court to forestall the application of the Aryan paragraph to a civic association that he ran. Other efforts were more quixotic. Heinrich Herz, a plumber from Hamborn am Rhein, wrote to Hitler complaining that despite the numerous ordinances from the Ministry of the Interior he was losing customers due to a local boycott. 'Just as you have battled for years to achieve your goals, Herr respected Reich Chancellor, so I would like to lead the battle of my coreligionists.' Hertz got no reply and eventually Eichholz had to accept defeat.[19]

The CV took up the cases of Jews who were dismissed from their jobs. When there was proof that the law had been breached they went to the labour court and often succeeded in getting the victim reinstated. However, with each challenge, the courts set about closing the successfully exploited loophole. In March 1934, for example, a labour court ruled that if clients or customers did not want to interact with a Jewish employee, that constituted sufficient 'economic' grounds for dismissal. Nazi workers insisted that they were unable to operate alongside Jews, forcing employers to dismiss them. In a survey for the Paris office of the AJJDC, David Schweizer remarked that 'Outwardly Berlin presented during my recent stay there a normal appearance.' But on closer inspection, 'while one can observe a Jewish department store crowded as usual with non-Jews and Jews alike, one can observe in the very next department store the total absence of a single Jewish employee.'[20]

To cope with the mounting number of Jews thrown out of work, the RV labour exchange helped the Jewish unemployed to find jobs.

Increasingly this meant encouraging Jewish enterprises to hire Jewish staff. A burgeoning Jewish economic sector emerged in which Jewish enterprises took on displaced Jewish workers to provide goods and services for an exclusively Jewish clientele. Vocational retraining grew ever more important to help the newly unemployed find a live-lihood and also to compensate for the exclusion of Jews from state-run training establishments. Some were directed towards emigration, mainly to Palestine, but the CV and the RjF continued to treat emigra-tion as a form of surrender.[21]

During 1934, the predominant view was that Jews could manage to live and even prosper in the main German cities. During a trip to the races in Hamburg, Sir Eric Phipps noticed 'several prominent Jewish race-owners, such as Herr von Weinberg and Baron Oppenheim' in the same enclosure as Nazi and government dignitaries. In Breslau, the Jewish community set about expensive renovations on the New Synagogue and planned to build a second old people's home. The com-munities had 'substantial resources' at their disposal to care for those in need.[22]

The emigration panic subsided so noticeably that the governmental partners and Jewish sponsors of the High Commission for Refugees began to wonder if it had any point. Wealthy British Jews who ran the Central British Fund for German Jewry debated whether an appeal would be necessary for the following year. Thousands of dispirited Jews were returning to the Reich and James McDonald was forced to admit that 'even within Germany the Jews were better off than as refugees'. He now began to contemplate winding up the High Commission unless it got stronger backing from the League. However, at a meeting in July the League's Secretary-General, Joseph Avenol, asserted that sympathy for the Jews had 'substantially died down during the past twelve months'. Conversely, anti-Semitism had grown and it would be a mistake to seek more powers for the High Commission in case this aggravated things. When the governing body met in London in November, the British-appointed chairman Sir Robert Cecil declared that 'We are accomplishing nothing.' There was tepid consent that it should be dismantled.[23]

McDonald did not share the confidence of Jewish leaders in London and New York. He observed at the start of the year that in small towns 'the situation was again becoming critical'. He complained to James Rosenberg, 'How, under these circumstances, Jews of intelligence dare plan as though the worst is over, is beyond my comprehension.' Rural and small-town Jews were not emigrating: they were moving to the cities where they might become a burden on the *Gemeinde* but would not fall within the purview of the international Jewish aid agencies.[24]

McDonald heard about the plight of rural Jews from Wilfred Israel, a German Jew living in England whose family owned one of the largest department stores in Berlin. 'Israel sees signs of group evacuation by Jews from the smaller towns. This is a new development.' The British consul general in Frankfurt, Robert Smallbones, made the same point to Phipps. 'In some of the larger towns . . . even the SA and SS men in uniform do not hesitate to visit Jewish shops. Generally, it can be said that the smaller the town the greater the handicap under which they are. The village Jew is therefore in a particularly difficult position.' Raymond Geist sent a similar message to Washington. The situation of the Jews in Germany, he wrote, 'appears for the present in the larger cities to be fairly satisfactory. The business of Jewish merchants in Berlin and other large centres of Germany is in a satisfactory position. In the smaller towns, however, the anti-Jewish boycott is going on strongly.' Franconia and Hesse were particularly bad. When Ambassador Dodd made a road trip through southern Germany in the autumn, he saw evidence of an unremitting 'cold pogrom'. 'All through this region, we have seen signs as we drove into the towns which read: "Keine Juden erwünscht" . . . "Juden sind unser Unglück".'[25]

Reports from regional officials and police offices to the Gestapo headquarters in Berlin remarked on the returning self-confidence within large Jewish urban communities. Police offices recorded that significant numbers of Jews were re-entering the Reich. In October, the Gestapo for the Berlin region observed the reflux of Polish Jews who found more opportunities for work there than abroad. The Nazi chief of police in Berlin, Count Wolf-Heinrich von Helldorf, treated the strengthening of Jewish associational life as an affront and could not fathom why it was tolerated. 'The aggressive behaviour of the Jews that has been in evidence for some time is becoming ever more pronounced.' According to him, 'very large segments of the population do not comprehend why the authorities are exercising such restraint in dealing with this aggressive behaviour'.[26]

Letters addressed to Hitler reflected the bemusement of Nazi supporters. They also show how individuals cynically used anti-Semitic feeling and policy as instruments to obtain personal benefit. Richard Fichte, from Chemnitz, complained that bulk buyers of glassware got

better deals from suppliers than small businessmen like him. This benefited the Jewish-owned department stores. 'From this it seems that in
the Third Reich Jews can still buy considerably more cheaply than businessmen of German blood.' Jakob Falkenstein, a leader of the farmers'
association, wrote to the Führer to protest that Jewish cattle dealers in
his hometown of Huttenfeld in Hesse still dominated the livestock
market where 'even the Storm Battalion Reserve does business with
Jews'. Elizabeth Barth, a widow from Chemnitz, was indignant that she
got a smaller pension than a Jewish woman who had married her
ex-husband. 'It is presumably not in accordance with the policy of
National Socialism', she railed, 'that in our sacred Third Reich a Jewish
woman is given such an advantage over an honest German woman.'[27]

As the year went on, a crescendo of reports arrived at the Gestapo
Head Office in Berlin (Gestapa) testifying to irritation amongst the
rank and file of the party and, allegedly, amongst the populace when
the practice of inflicting misery on Jews ran up against the protective
mantle of the authorities. The Jewish affairs department of the Gestapo
headquarters, Referat Judentum II 1 B 2, reported that 'Broad segments
of the population are bewildered by these decrees by state and local
bodies. When they learn of such ordinances, their trust in the idea of
National Socialism is shaken. The Gestapa has thus called the attention
of the competent offices in the national government and the Party to
these cases and requested that these deficiencies be eliminated.' There
was a danger of ill-feeling and violence if nothing was done to curb the
'self-assurance, aplomb, and purposeful activity of the Jews'. This would
have the effect of 'placing the police in the unpleasant position of
having to protect the Jews and their property against the incensed
population.'[28]

The Stapostelle (Gestapo office) in the Kassel government district
was similarly perplexed at how to deal with a spasm of anti-Jewish
propaganda incited by NSDAP branches, which led to vandalism and
the hanging of signs across the streets. 'To date, the Stapostelle has
always taken action against such signs placed at the entrance to localities in order to prevent provision of potential material for use by foreign
propaganda.' But now it found itself in conflict with the party locally, a
predicament that was complicated by the inconsistencies between one
area and another. 'The authority of the state is compromised and damaged if something is to be prohibited here that is permitted and
tolerated in neighbouring districts.' The police appealed for a steer from

central government. 'A clear and unmistakable statement by the competent central authorities on this question would appear to be necessary.'[29]

In some places friction between the party and the state drifted into
absurdity. On the night of 28–29 October 1934, the synagogue in
Schöllkrippen, Lower Franconia, was plundered and silver items stolen
along with Torah scrolls. The police investigated and quickly arrested
two SA men. Although the Brownshirts were later released, there was
much anger among the local division of the SA. In Hanau, a town in the
Kassel government district, police stopped SA men from singing
anti-Jewish songs in front of Jewish enterprises. Similar incidents
occurred all over Germany as Christmas approached and 'storm detachments' resorted to the customary harassment of Jewish-owned shops. In
Braunschweig, capital of the free state of Brunswick, a series of inflam-
matory speeches by Streicher led to confrontations between party
members and the police. The Interior Ministry of Brunswick assured
Berlin that it would implement the relevant ordinances, but continued
that 'it cannot be the will of the Reich government for these to be
enforced in a form where a contingent of uniformed police resort to
force against an angered German crowd whose point of view can be
based on the fundamental principles of the NSDAP.' Just before
Christmas, a military police squad in Frankfurt-am-Main came danger-
ously close to an armed fracas with members of the Nazi traders'
association (Nationalsozialistische Handwerks-, Handels-, und Gewerbe-
Organisation, NS-HAGO), SA and SS personnel, who were blocking
access to Jewish businesses. The military police protested that 'the attitude of the Gau leadership [in permitting the boycott action] remains
incomprehensible.'[30]

The Nazi authorities were keenly aware of the discrepancy between
the city and the countryside. The Gestapo office for the Cologne government district informed Berlin that 'In the small towns, the boycott
against Jewish shops is more effective than in metropolitan areas,
because it is easier to keep tabs on who is shopping at a Jew's store.' Yet
even here the picture varied. Victor Klemperer impishly charted the
ways that people evaded supervision in their own community. 'In
Falkenstein one is not allowed to buy from the "Jew". And so people in
Falkenstein travel to the Jew in Auerbach. And the Auerbachers buy
from the Falkenstein Jew.' It was a frequent refrain by police officials
that the rural population, especially in Catholic areas, seemed impervious to the National Socialist message. The Gestapo office in the

Koblenz government district regretted that 'the rural population shows less understanding of the Jewish Question and continues, now as before, to have very active business dealings with Jewish traders. This holds true even for some members of the Party.' Raymond Geist relayed intelligence reaching him that 'the Catholic population in many of these places [in Franconia and Hesse] is openly making purchases from Jewish stores in a veritable spirit of bravado.'[31]

Thus, after two years the impact of National Socialist rule on the Jews was patchy, and responses to anti-Jewish measures varied across Germany as well as between town and country. According to a recent re-evaluation by the historians Jürgen Matthäus and Mark Roseman, at the start of 1935 German Jews actually had 'good reason' to believe 'that they were winning the fight and helping to eradicate disturbances from the streets'. Nazi officials sounded increasingly peevish as they confronted this resilience. The state minister for Hesse wrote in his summation of political affairs, 'Jews who now believe that they have suffered economic damage report this directly to the Reich Economics Ministry in Berlin. In any event, unfortunately once again, the Jew is rather optimistic about his future in Germany.' For Nazi true believers, the sight of Jews going about their daily business was a form of aggression. Worse still, Jewish protests were putting the authorities in the position of appearing to be 'Jew-friendly'.[32]

Throughout autumn 1934 and into 1935 the regime continued to act with diffidence. In addition to concern about the economy, the government was on its best behaviour in advance of a crucial vote in the Saarland. Since 1919, the Saar basin had been administered by France under a mandate from the League of Nations. The mandate was due to expire in January 1935 and the population given the opportunity to vote on whether to return to German sovereignty, join France, or remain under the League. The Saar was a mainly Catholic region with a large concentration of industry and mines. Catholics and workers were the two constituencies that had proven least susceptible to National Socialism before 1933 and which continued to manifest signs of resistance. Anti-fascists hoped that it would be possible to mobilize them against returning to Germany and converted the vote into a referendum on Nazism. This placed the Jewish leadership of the Centralverein in a quandary. League of Nations stewardship offered some protection for Jews in the Saar and there were rumours that the CV was warning of a Jewish exodus if the Third Reich took control. Fearful of appearing disloyal to Germany the CV felt it had to reject these charges, but it could hardly advocate a Yes vote. Finally, on a nearly immaculate turn-out, over 90 per cent of Saarlanders who voted opted for union with the Third Reich. Victor Klemperer was staggered by the scale of both the turnout and the majority. Nazi celebrations plunged him into gloom: 'Today the man seems ineradicable again.'[33]

Hitler followed up the Saarland triumph by ordering the reintro-duction of conscription. Expansion of the army and rearmament were a direct violation of the Versailles Treaty. Britain and France protested and held talks with Italy, supposedly to signify their determination to contain German ambitions. In reality the response was feeble. A few months later, Germany signed a naval agreement with Britain that allowed the German surface fleet to be enlarged. These accomplish-ments were wildly popular not just with the German armed forces but with the entire population. Klemperer lamented that Hitler's foreign policy success 'consolidates his position very greatly'.[34]

Other German Jews grieved that they were not able to share them. Following the reintroduction of military service on 16 March, the Deutscher Vortrupp (German Vanguard), a right-wing association of German Jews led by Hans-Joachim Schoeps, publicized the willingness of its members to serve in the army. Their patriotism was allowed to froth until further provisions, added on 21 May, explicitly excluded non-Aryans. For mixed-race Jews like Freddy Solmitz, in Hamburg, this was another blow to his identity. In her journal his non-Jewish wife spelled out their distress: 'The terrible thing for us is that they want to take away our claim to be part of the German volk and Fatherland and we have no ideal to put in that place.'[35]

The inconsistencies of Judenpolitik

With the regime riding high on a wave of foreign policy triumphs, those within the Nazi leadership who wanted to pursue tougher measures against the Jews were given a freer hand. In April 1934, Himmler had been appointed head of the Gestapo in Prussia, effectively completing the unification of the political police under the mantle of the SS. He brought Heydrich, head of the SD, with him. It was a fundamental prin-ciple of the SS that the Jews were enemies of the German people. But

Heydrich and the intellectuals like Werner Best whom he recruited to the SD translated this enmity into practical policy, steering the Gestapo towards the enforcement of racial doctrine and tackling the Jewish threat.[36]

The Gestapo Head Office in Berlin began producing regular reports on the Jewish community. The first stated, 'in keeping with his inner attitude, [the Jew] will always be an enemy of the National Socialist state. There can be no reconciliation between his liberalistic international world view and the conceptual world of National Socialism.' The political police devoted more resources to monitoring Jewish organizations, compiling card-catalogues of Jewish institutions and personalities. Gestapo and police officials were encouraged to spy on Jewish activity in their districts.[37]

These reports show the emergence of a Gestapo line on how best to deal with the Jewish enemy. In the short term, the influence of Jews on society and the economy should be drastically curbed; in the long term, the Jews should be encouraged to leave Germany completely. Surveying the conflict between Zionists and German nationalists in the Reichsvertretung, the Gestapa noted that 'The efforts of the Gestapo are oriented to promoting Zionism as much as possible and lending support to its efforts to further emigration.' It concluded with satisfaction that the Zionists had gained the upper hand over the CV and Jewish veterans so that 'In place of a rushed and poorly prepared emigration in 1933, we now have well-regulated emigration whose sole destination is Palestine.'[38]

The lines between the state political police and the party's political police became increasingly blurred. An early SD memorandum noted the division between religious Jews, assimilationists (or national-German Jews) and Zionists, and warned that if national-German Jews succeeded in fortifying the resolve of German Jews to hang on in Germany, 'We will perhaps have to recognise the Jews as a minority, and then they will be on our hands for the rest of eternity.' To avoid this the SD argued that it was necessary to make Jewish life in Germany so uncomfortable that the Jews would want to leave. The authorities had to weaken the national-German Jews and eliminate sources of support and sympathy for them in the surrounding population. Conversely, the SD favoured the Zionists and promoted their activity.[39]

However, until 1935 the SD had only a minor interest in Jewish affairs and no specific department dealing with the Jews. Its main activity was collecting intelligence on political opponents at home and abroad. With Heydrich elevated to control over the Gestapo, he saw an opportunity for the SD to expand its influence by offering intelligence and guidance on Jewish affairs. He recruited Edler von Mildenstein to build up a Jewish department and develop a distinctive set of policies for combating the Jewish enemy. Mildenstein, a trained engineer and talented writer, had visited Palestine and written articles for the SS magazine, *Das Schwarze Korps*, about the Jewish settlements there. He believed that Jews were aliens in Germany but saw little point in just suppressing them. Instead, they should be assisted to emigrate to their own homeland. To this end, the agencies of the party and the state should work with Zionist organizations rather than frustrate their operation.[40]

In the course of staffing his new bureau Mildenstein recruited Adolf Eichmann, a twenty-nine-year-old SS corporal who had recently transferred from a clerical job in an SS office at Dachau concentration camp to the SD Head Office in Berlin. Eichmann was German-born although he grew up in Austria. He joined the Austrian NSDAP and SS in April 1932, but when the party was suppressed two years later he crossed into Germany. He had applied to the Sicherheitsdienst, thinking it would offer exciting work, only to find it was an under-resourced organization collecting information on enemies of the party and the Reich. Mildenstein rescued him from a tedious job and taught him about Jewish history and Zionism. After Mildenstein departed, Eichmann became the SD's specialist on Jewish emigration and the Zionist movement.[41]

To Heydrich and his experts on Jewish affairs, the Judenreferenten, it was obvious that Jews would not emigrate if they felt they had a future in Germany, if life was comfortable, and as long as Jewish organizations promoted the belief that Jews were Germans. SD surveillance revealed the need for stricter measures to exclude the Jews from the economy, undermine the basis for Jewish life, and make them feel as if they had no place in the country. With the encouragement of the SD, the Gestapo began to place obstacles in the way of the CV's continued resistance to anti-Jewish measures aimed at driving Jews out of the economy.[42]

With suspicious uniformity, reports by Gestapo officers on the state of public opinion now emphasized discontent at the sight of Jewish cultural life flourishing, Jews prospering, and émigrés returning. Police and state officials began to clamour for legislation to regulate relations between Jews and Aryans, to put the Jews in their place. Gestapo agents in the Berlin district decried Jewish behaviour: 'They cannot and do not want to comprehend that they are only aliens in the Third Reich. Their intent is to steal slowly their way back once again into the Volksgemein- schaft.' It was 'simply incomprehensible to the people, who are thinking ever more along racial lines, that the state does not act to put an end to such actions by the introduction of draconian legislation'. The district governor of Koblenz noted that buoyant sales in Jewish shops suggested a 're-conquest of the economy'. Renewed picketing was causing clashes between the party and the police but 'These could be avoided if there were a uniform approach in the Jewish Question by the movement and the state authorities.' The county commissioner in the small town of Fritzlar-Humberg in Kassel stated that it 'would be desirable if basic agreements could be worked out between the central government and the Party over how the Jewish Question should be dealt with'.[43]

The stress created by these contradictions became ever more appar- ent. On 11 April 1935, the deputy Führer, Rudolf Hess, sent a circular to party members prohibiting 'individual actions' while at the same time reiterating a 1934 ban on party members having contact with Jews. Foreign correspondents could not help noticing the incongruities. During an Easter break with his wife at Bad Saarow, William Shirer saw the spa town to the south-east of Berlin 'mainly filled with Jews and we are a little surprised to find so many of them still prospering and apparently unafraid'. Shirer thought they were 'unduly optimistic'. Out in the countryside, things looked different. When Virginia Woolf drove through Germany in the course of a summer holiday with her Jewish husband, Leonard, she was struck by the sight of 'Banners stretched across the street' proclaiming '"The Jew is our enemy" "there is no place for the Jews"'. In southern Germany she found the atmosphere more relaxed but even here 'every village had a painted sign, "Die Juden sind hier unwunscht"' [Jews not wanted here]. Diplomats who followed these erratic developments debated the wisdom of further intervention. When Dodd broached the matter to Phipps during one of their walks in the Tiergarten, his colleague advised him 'it can do no good . . . Hitler is fanatical on the subject.'[44]

Tension was ratcheted up by a campaign against Rassenschande, race defilement, in *Der Stürmer*. Streicher's lurid tales of swarthy Jewish men seducing innocent Aryan maidens triggered a blast of vitriol and violence against Jews and their non-Jewish partners. In December 1934 a special issue on the alleged abuse of Christian children set off inci- dents across Germany. In Bad Neustadt, for example, the gendarmerie reported that the home of a Jewish cattle dealer was daubed with 'Pig Jew defiler of young girls'. Streicher outdid himself with a special issue in April 1935 devoted to 'ritual murder', a toxic mixture of child abuse, torture and religion. The tempo of incidents accelerated and for the first time the police involved themselves in regulating sexual relations. The Gestapo in Berlin started collecting evidence on Aryan women who 'give themselves to Jews and have intimate relations with them'. The absence of any legal basis for such intrusions was reflected in the tortured prose of one police report: 'To the extent that there was a sufficient legal basis for action, the Jews involved were taken into protective custody.' Gestapo officers in Königsberg registered the paradoxical situation in which action was taken without either legal sanction or public understanding of the issue. 'In East Prussia the number of cases where Jews sexually abused Aryan girls is also on the rise, though it must be said that the girls surrender to this without much thought.'[45]

The police were mendaciously generating a scandal that had not previously existed, creating the need for legal action to address it. After picking up seventy-two persons in one month, the Berlin force concluded, 'Despite enlightenment in the National Socialist press, the race-defiling activity of the Jews has assumed proportions that necessitate giving greater attention to their activity.' The authorities fostered the impression of broad public support, although their own evidence suggests that the publicity surrounding the apprehension of Jews for alleged race defilement was as much a part of educating the Volksgemeinschaft about racialized boundaries as it was a response to public abhorrence of race-mixing. In Breslau, in July 1935, twenty Jews and non-Jews were sent to concentration camps for alleged Rassenschande. The action was accompanied by cheers from thousands of citizens although only 'after race defilement of Aryan women by Jews has finally been presented to the public in a very clear and unambiguous light'. The effect was contagious. By early September the police office in Minden was reporting that 'large segments of the population have been seized by a certain kind of race-defilement psychosis. They seem to sense race-defilement everywhere . . .'[46]

Boycotts and violence also surged. In one report after another, local and police officials posed as reluctant agents of law and order struggling to enforce unpopular edicts that ran counter to their National Socialist consciences and the people's rage. The district governor of Wiesbaden boasted that he had kept 'defensive measures' by the people within the 'confines of the law'. In Berlin the police blamed the 'provocative behaviour of the Jews' for 'a strong anti-semitic wave'. Apparently, Berliners now regarded Jews as 'fair game in every respect' and there had been many 'outrageous events' leading to awkward clashes between demonstrators and police. The positive side of this was that the 'population is clearly having its eyes opened ever wider'. Officials in Münster did not disguise the self-fulfilling nature of these practices. 'As in most places in the Reich, locally here in the district in recent weeks the Jewish Problem has once again become a focus of general concern. Everywhere the propaganda against Jews and most especially against business persons, has been intensified.'[47]

The calculated nature of the disturbances was transparent to outside observers. Samuel Honaker, the US consul-general in Stuttgart, reported that the riots and boycotting in his city had 'come as no surprise . . . The way was carefully prepared by a series of developments which tended to direct the attention of the people towards the alleged harmful influence of the Jews. Newspaper propaganda against the Jews grew in volume and in variety, gradually undermining the resistance of various elements of the population.' Honaker discerned that the young 'seem especially to have been infected by the anti-semitic agitation'. Some people disapproved, but 'there is much doubt as to whether the attitude of this element will prevail in the long run and as to whether the situation may not develop along dangerous lines'.[48]

In rural areas incidents of physical abuse and vandalism multiplied. The county commissioner in Hünfeld, a small agricultural town in Hesse, explained that 'the perpetrators think that they are protected from any sanctions under the law'. In Wiesbaden, parents demanded the removal of the remaining Jewish teachers and refused to let their children be taught by them. During the hot summer weeks when people repaired to the public swimming baths, Hitler Youth chased Jews out of any facilities from which they were not already banned. Yet none of this was legal. The contradictions of policy led to ever more insistent demands for a resolution of the gulf between activism and what the law permitted. The Cologne Gestapo complained that 'The events of the past two months have shown that in future, it is necessary to have absolutely clear instructions from the central authorities regarding what *is permissible* in *the framework of anti-Jewish propaganda and what is not permitted*'. If nothing was done, the Cologne political police warned, the authority of the state would be eroded.[49]

The anti-Semitic wave culminated in a week of disturbances along the Kurfürstendamm in Berlin on 22–28 July 1935. Jewish shops and ice-cream vendors were attacked, while SA and SS men in civilian clothes manhandled passers-by. When police intervened they were barracked by mobs shouting 'Jew lackeys' until NSDAP and SA officials were called in to quell the uproar. Writing in America in 1940, Martin Gumpert recaptured the events over those sultry, terrifying days. He had been director of a dermatological hospital until he was dismissed in 1933, but stayed on because he thought of himself as totally German. That is, until he witnessed the Kurfürstendamm rampage. 'I saw a man with a golden Nazi Party badge kicking an old Jewish woman. An old man was struck down and hauled away. A young man with a pince-nez on his nose ran panic-stricken across the street, a howling mob in pursuit.' The reaction of onlookers was sobering. 'A much larger crowd stood on the sidewalks and watched. They didn't say a word. The expression on their faces alternated between curious amusement and revulsion.' There was worse. 'The most appalling sight was the police . . . [they] sat expressionless in their cars and did nothing when someone called for help or collapsed onto the pavement.' The next day, Gumpert decided he could not allow his daughter to grow up in 'this lunatic atmosphere' and resolved to leave Germany.[50]

Jews detected the changed mood. Protests against the 'ritual murder' issue of *Der Stürmer* were brushed aside. Instead, the graphic front page was displayed in the streets in the special cabinets for wall newspapers. Victor Klemperer observed anti-Jewish slogans appearing all over town. A few weeks later he was finally dismissed from his job. 'The Jewbaiting and the pogrom atmosphere grow day by day,' he wrote. By August the level of incitement had reached such a pitch that 'we expect to be beaten to death at any moment'. More young people were participating in the outrages, often in organized groups of Hitler Youth wearing their uniforms. In Bad Kissingen, a spa town in northern Bavaria, James McDonald was shocked to see children as young as nine attacking Jews. Jewish families in the town were afraid to go out at night and shopkeepers would not serve them. The police were increasingly passive or held back. When perpetrators were apprehended and put on trial, they received derisory punishments.[51]

It was also evident that the state's attitude was shifting. Since the early months of the regime, NSDAP branches and some marriage registrars had expressed concern about the legal obligation to perform ceremonies uniting Jews with non-Jews. However, no action had been taken. Then, in May 1935, the law that established the Wehrmacht forbade marriage between serving personnel and non-Aryans. At around the same time, the Interior Ministry issued advice to registrars not to carry out mixed marriages.[52]

Zionists saw the pressure towards segregation as fulfilment of their assertion that Jews were a separate nation with no place in Germany, and that it was time for the Jews to leave. But the Centralverein continued to urge calm. 'No one should be criticised for deciding to emigrate when conditions force them to do. But to argue that emigration and the liquidation of everything that pertains to German Jewry is the only solution would be out of line with the current situation.' When hints emanating from the regime suggested that a dramatic move to curtail Jewish citizenship was in the offing the CV put on a brave face, suggesting that any legislation would only recognize the existing state of affairs. By August, the Reichsvertretung was almost pleading for a law: 'Otherwise there will be no limit to the competition to be the most anti-semitic.'[53]

The government eventually acted in mid-1935. Yet its decision was not the straightforward expression of a long-held desire by the Nazi elite (or the rank and file) to fulfil cherished ambitions derived from either a traditional obsession with Jews as sexual predators or the more recent pseudo-scientific dogmas about Jews polluting German blood. There were other, more short-term and pragmatic considerations. The Nazi leadership continued to face a difficult economic situation: unemployment remained high while the direction of funds into rearmament was beginning to cause inflation. The SA had lost a leader in July 1934 and had yet to find a role; its members were chafing at the bit for some kind of action. Above all, the inconsistencies of government policy and party doctrine were insupportable. The army required clarification of who was mixed race in order to work out how many conscripts it could expect and who would be excluded from military service. Heydrich and the SD were calling for a radical separation of Jews from Aryans. In a memorandum for the Reich Chancellery in July he argued that uncoordinated boycotts and scattered violence would not accomplish anything. It was imperative to pass laws making it clear that Jews stood outside the racial community and to police this divide. To drive home his point Heydrich attributed the recent unrest to 'the previously inconsistent approach against Judaism'. The people demanded 'more severe measures'. Finally, Schacht had been personally embarrassed by the chaos and was determined to end the free-for-all. In early August, the NSDAP in Arnswalde named a senior Reichsbank official seen shopping at a Jewish-owned establishment, accusing him of treason. Schacht was informed and ordered the removal of the placard listing his errant subordinate and its replacement by a declaration of his innocence. When the local party refused to comply, he petulantly shut down the Arnswalde branch of the state bank. Clearly, the muddle over Judenpolitik was becoming intolerable.[54]

Race laws

On 20 August 1935, Schacht convened an inter-ministerial conference at the Reichsbank in an attempt to end the confusion and resolve the tension between the party and the state authorities. It was attended by Wilhelm Frick, the interior minister; Franz Gürtner, the justice minister, Bernhard von Bülow, the permanent secretary at the Foreign Ministry, and Adolph Wagner, the Bavarian interior minister and Gauleiter of Munich, who was also speaking for the Nazi Party. Schacht opened by reviewing the 'serious damage to the German economy produced by the exaggeration and excesses of the anti-semitic propaganda'. He pointed out that the drift into lawlessness 'was among other things putting the economic basis of rearmament at risk'. The DAF, which controlled the Nazi shop-floor cells (the NS-HAGO), and Streicher were particularly to blame for this state of affairs. The party programme had to be enacted, but legally. Frick concurred and cited a draft directive to the state governors to prevent disorder. Gürtner warned that no one would obey the law if some people thought it was possible to defy the state. Bülow adverted to the effect on Germany's image abroad and cast a glance forward to the upcoming Olympics. However, while Wagner made obeisance to the need for law and order, he maintained that the turmoil stemmed from the divergence between party doctrine on the Jewish question and the way the state handled it. He insisted that the government had to take account of the 'anti-semitic mood' of the population and take steps urgently to eliminate Jews from the economy. The gathering ended with agreement that the situation could not be allowed to continue, but without any consensus on how this was to be achieved – other than a shared belief that there had to be a legal fix.[55]

During August, Himmler, Hess, Frick, and even Streicher put their names to directives intended to curb the tumult. The excesses were finally brought under control, but there were ominous signs of what lay ahead when the Interior Ministry banned the conduct of mixed marriages. Raymond Geist warned James McDonald that 'The Jews were being fed to the lions to distract attention from the economic situation.' New laws were 'imminent' and they would serve 'further to differentiate the Jews from the mass of Germans and to disadvantage them in new ways'. Ambassador Dodd feared segregation. The British consul in Frankfurt-am-Main wrote to Sir Samuel Hoare, the foreign secretary, 'The Jew, both as a private individual and as a businessman, is at present an outlaw, subject to any arbitrary treatment the local Nazi Boss may decree, and often even to the whim of the individual SA man. There are indications, however, that this state of lawlessness will not last much longer.' However, he concluded, 'even if the campaign against the Jews is to be legally regularised, it will only be systematised rather than abated'.[56]

Hitler now made a personal intervention. As so often, the trigger was an event that seemed to show the world Jewish conspiracy at work against Germany, though by any objective appraisal it was a minor diplomatic incident. On 26 July, anti-fascist dockworkers in New York boarded the liner *Bremen* as it was about to set sail and ripped down the swastika flag that flew alongside the revived imperial colours. To Hitler this was a Jewish-inspired assault on the National Socialist movement. He resolved to use the forthcoming party rally at Nuremberg on 9–15 September to retaliate and at the same moment settle the direction of Judenpolitik. He ordered a special session of the Reichstag to convene in Nuremberg on the last day of the rally, to pass a law making the swastika the national flag and prohibiting Jews from using it. During the rally, possibly as a result of lobbying by hardliners, Hitler and the Nazi leadership decided that they would also use the session to enact laws to forbid marriages between Jews and Aryans and create a legal barrier against race defilement.[57]

The new race laws were drafted in a hurry by a civil servant from the Ministry of the Interior, Bernhard Lösener, who was summoned at short notice from Berlin. However, laws to separate Jews from Aryans had been under consideration for some time and there was no shortage of suggestions for marking or segregating Jews. The problem was that Hitler wanted to give the party faithful something spectacular but, at

the same time, did not want to do anything that would inspire an international boycott of the forthcoming Winter Olympics in Garmisch
Partenkirchen in February 1936 or the summer Olympics in Berlin the
following August. He therefore requested options offering legislation of
varying degrees of harshness that spread the racial net more or less
capaciously.[58]

Hitler opened the party rally with an attack on Jewish Bolshevism
that clearly presaged some concrete blow. On the last day, 15 September
1935, he delivered. A new law would forbid marriages between Jews and
Aryans; prohibit sexual relations between Jews and Aryans; and prevent
Jews from employing young Aryan women as domestic servants. Jews
would be banned from displaying the German national flag although
they could fly 'the Jewish colours'. Hitler also unveiled a Reich Citizenship Law that he had solicited at midnight from weary Interior Ministry
civil servants and which had only been typed up in the early hours
of that morning. The law restricted citizenship to persons who were of
'German or kindred blood', who had proven that they merited such
status. Jews were reduced to subjects of the Reich, with civic obligations
and certain legal protection but no political rights. In his speech, Hitler
explicitly related the passage of the laws to 'international unrest' and
Jewish opposition to German interests. He asserted that the government
was meeting this challenge head-on by legal means and warned that
random acts of revenge by party zealots were no longer acceptable. On
the contrary, he anticipated that with the new legislation in force 'the
German people may find a tolerable relation towards the Jewish people'.
Yet he added a threat: 'Should this hope not be fulfilled and the Jewish
agitation both within Germany and in the international sphere should
continue, then the position must be examined afresh.' In a later address
to party leaders, Hitler maintained that the Jews were being 'offered
opportunities of living in their own national life in all areas' and reiterated his order to the party to avoid all individual actions against Jews.[59]

In fact, the Nuremberg Laws actually created more dilemmas for
the regime. The legislation did nothing to regulate the economic relations between Jews and Aryans that were a running sore with party
activists, who fumed at the sight of Jewish-owned shops heaving with
customers or farmers trading with Jewish cattle dealers. They did not
tackle specific situations such as access to municipal swimming baths or
the display of anti-Jewish banners at the entrance to villages. The laws
were silent on the vexed question of whether Jews were entitled to

welfare payments. Worse, they did not define who was a Jew, leaving those who were deemed mixed-race under the Aryan paragraph no more enlightened about their situation, even though much more was now at stake. The Nuremberg Laws were a typical Hitlerian attempt to get out of a mess by taking a radical step, in effect a gamble, without thinking through the consequences.

Months of meetings by civil servants ensued before a definition of Jewishness was finalized. The work was led by Dr Wilhelm Stuckart and Dr Hans Globke from the Interior Ministry. In the end, they had to settle for an amalgam of pseudo-scientific racial thinking and old-fashioned religion. On 15 November 1935 the first of several supplementary regulations defined a person as a 'full Jew' if they had three or four Jewish grandparents. It did not matter if the grandparents were converts to Christianity: Jewish blood was thicker than the water of the baptismal font. A person would also be regarded as a full Jew if they had only two Jewish grandparents, but married a Jew and joined a Jewish community. In such cases, known as Geltungsjuden, or 'Jews by definition', religious affiliation and choice was as much a factor as the inexorable influence of blood. Conversely, if a person with two Jewish grandparents was not a member of a Jewish community and married to an Aryan, they would be considered of mixed race, Mischlinge of the first degree; just one Jewish grandparent placed them in the category of Mischlinge of the second degree.[60]

However, because of disagreement between party representatives and state agencies the precise rights and obligations of the Mischlinge remained unresolved. The Interior Ministry and the Wehrmacht wanted Mischlinge of the first and second degrees treated as citizens. Frick worried that otherwise a large number of Aryans married to Mischlinge would feel alienated from the state; the army feared that it would lose hundreds of thousands of potential conscripts. By contrast, racial warriors speaking for the party wanted to exclude all classes of Mischlinge from Aryan society and prevent them marrying other than their own kind. Their proposals for extensive discrimination against Mischlinge of all types were stymied, but the hardliners were able to limit a Mischling's marriage choices. On the grounds that the 'bad blood' should be contained, Mischlinge of the first degree were permitted to marry only Jews or other Mischlinge, while the 'good blood' in the Mischlinge second degree was retained for the Volk by forbidding marriage to other than Aryans. There was little disagreement, though, on the second supplementary decree to the Nuremberg Laws. This enabled the dismissal of all Jews remaining in state employment. As a sop to sentimental feelings towards war veterans and disabled ex-servicemen, they were allowed to keep their pensions.[61]

The British Ambassador, Sir Eric Phipps, found the discomfort the regime brought on itself as a result of the Nuremberg Laws faintly amusing. 'The difficulty of giving effect to the Nuremberg resolutions regarding the status of the Jews continues to give Hitler sleepless nights', he wryly observed. In a more serious vein Phipps accurately perceived that the Nazi leadership preferred to avoid endangering foreign trade or the Olympics rather than go to extremes in tying up loose ends.[62]

But to the African American intellectual and civil rights activist W. E. B. DuBois, the Nuremberg Laws were no joke. DuBois visited Germany between July and December 1935 and witnessed the first steps towards segregation. On his return to the USA the founder of the National Association for the Advancement of Colored People wrote in the *Pittsburgh Courier*, an African American journal, that the 'campaign of racial prejudice' against Jews in Germany 'surpasses in vindictive cruelty and public insult anything I have ever seen; and I have seen much'. It was the greatest tragedy of modern times, 'an attack on civilisation'. As evidence, DuBois cited cases of 'Jews jailed for sexual relations with German women; a marriage disallowed because a Jewish person witnessed it; Masons excluded from office, because Jews are Masons; advertisements excluding Jews; the total disenfranchisement of all Jews; deprivation of civil rights and inability to remain or become German citizens; limited rights of education, and narrowly limited right to work in trades and professions and the civil service; the threat of boycott, loss of work and even mob violence for any German who trades with a Jew; and, above all, the continued circulation of Julius Streicher's *Der Stürmer*, the most shameless, lying advocate of race hate in the world, not excluding Florida.'[63]

Living under the race laws

Thanks to his own experience of racism, W. E. B. DuBois captured the painful new world of Jews in Germany. Paradoxically, though, their first response was one of relief. The Nuremberg Laws held out the promise of stability and an end to random abuse. While Jews lost their political rights, the economic rights of those still in trade and business were not affected. And as long as the majority of Jews were allowed to continue earning a living they could support those who were less fortunate. With help from Jews abroad they could maintain Jewish welfare services, schools and, crucially, assist the young to emigrate. On the other hand, the Jewish leadership of all stripes recognized that while the Jews in Germany could survive, there was no longer a normal or desirable future for the young.[64]

In its formal response, published in the Jewish press, the Reichsvertretung described the race laws as 'the heaviest blow for the Jews of Germany'. It seized on Hitler's declaration that the laws 'must create a basis on which a tolerable relationship becomes possible between the German and the Jewish people' and averred that it too would work towards that end. This did not entail meekly accepting second-class status though: 'a precondition for such a tolerable relationship is the hope that the Jews and Jewish communities of Germany will be enabled to keep a moral and economic means of existence by the halting of defamation and boycott'. However, the Reichsvertretung did not regard the new status quo as adamantine any more than Hitler did; both parties were wary of future developments. For the time being, then, the Jews had little choice but to make the best of what was offered. Consequently, the Reichsvertretung shouldered the task of organizing the community to function as a self-contained minority. It would provide educational services to the young, with the emphasis on equipping them for emigration. It would continue to offer a full cultural life for Jews in Germany, thereby also employing those who could no longer find work in the cultural sector. It would continue to care for the sick, the needy and the elderly. But the Jewish leadership stated bluntly that in order to fund this activity it would fight to protect every job and enterprise in the Jewish sector. It would also use its resources and the assets of the community to support large-scale emigration. For the first time, the heads of all the Jewish organizations agreed that they had to make emigration a communal priority. There was still no unanimity about where Jews should go, but the Reichsvertretung emphasized the role of Palestine and stated that education for the young would pay special attention to the prerequisites of life in the Jewish national home.[65]

As the new emphasis on emigration and Palestine suggests, the Nuremberg Laws had a shattering effect on the self-image of Jews who had always considered themselves to be Germans first and only. By contrast, Zionist and Orthodox Jews like Willy Cohn applauded the recognition of Jews as a minority and the establishment of separate spheres along religious and racial lines. Cohn had sat by his radio at home in Breslau on the evening of 15 September listening to Hitler's address. As a Zionist he welcomed 'racial separation', while 'from a Jewish point of view' he unhesitatingly approved the ban on mixed marriages. He was actually struck by the moderate tone the Führer adopted towards the Jews and seized on the phrase 'tolerable relationship' despite realizing that 'much was left unclear'. When he went out to buy the Zionist newspaper the *Jüdische Rundschau* a few days later, Cohn sensed that the Nuremberg initiative had exerted 'a certain calming effect on German–Jewish relations'.[66]

To Jews at the other end of the spectrum of Jewish identity, the institutionalization of a racial definition was appalling. Luise Solmitz, married to a baptized Jew, had a totally opposite reaction. 'Today our civil rights were cut to pieces', she wailed in her journal. Her husband Freddy was deemed a full Jew and the regulations meant that their daughter Gisela was now a Mischling of the first degree. Gisela would not be permitted to marry a German, and who knew what other avenues of life would be closed to her? 'Our child is an outcast, excluded, despised, decreed worthless . . . No career, no future, no marriage.' The family had to dismiss their maid, which meant more housework for Luise. The prohibition on flying the national colours was a cruel restriction on Freddy, who had fought and bled for Germany. From this point he felt he was 'Here only on sufferance . . . a foreigner in the Fatherland'. The couple clung to each other for support and consoled themselves that suicide was always an option. 'On days like this', Luise wrote, 'you get an inkling of what comfort this final possibility offers.' But for the moment the family redoubled their efforts to hold on. Indeed, once the supplementary decrees were published Luise and Freddy spotted openings they could exploit on Gisela's behalf. A Mischling of her status could marry a German, with Hitler's permission, they thought. And because Freddy was a wounded war veteran, he kept his pension and the family could retain their maid.[67]

The distress suffered by the Solmitz family typified the experience of thousands of Jews in mixed marriages or of mixed parentage who now entered the world of Nazi racial bureaucrats to contest the identity ascribed to them and manipulate the tendentious Nuremberg categories. Freddy's request that his daughter be exempted was turned down.

But 4,000 out of 52,000 appeals to the Reichssippenamt (Reich Kinship Office) resulted in full or partial Jews gaining a more benign classification, usually by proving that their paternity was not what it appeared.[68]

For Lilli Jahn, in Immenhausen, the race laws completed her isolation and transformed her into a dead weight on her husband's career. Ernst was barred from the National Socialist medical association and most of his colleagues would only communicate with him by phone. As her sister Elsa wrote from England, after visiting her in Germany, 'It seems to be the German government policy to gradually cut the ground from under the feet of all Jews, non-Aryans, and people related to Jews by marriage, thereby prompting them to the leave the country.'[69]

After he was sacked, Victor Klemperer considered emigration and contacted a number of organizations offering to place academics abroad. Nothing came of this but Palestine offered little attraction as an alternative. In the wake of Nuremberg he asked himself, 'Where do I belong? To the "Jewish nation" decrees Hitler. And *I* feel the Jewish nation ... is a comedy and am nothing but a German or a European.' The majority of Jews lay somewhere between these poles. Dr Leo Baeck, a member of the leadership group in the Reichsvertretung and in effect the Chief Rabbi of Jews in Germany, sought to comfort them with a special prayer he composed for Yom Kippur, the Jewish Day of Atonement, in October 1935. He reminded Jews that they had brought the world monotheism, the Ten Commandments, and the prophets of social justice. 'Our history is the history of spiritual greatness, spiritual dignity. We turn to it when attack and insult are directed against us.'[70]

Jews could also console themselves that, as Klemperer observed, 'the Jew baiting has subsided for a few weeks'. But the remission was short-lived and localized. Reports of individual actions continued to flow into the headquarters of the Centralverein (as a consequence of the Reich Citizenship Law now renamed the Central Association of Jews in Germany, rather than an association of *German* Jews). Worse, Germans were interpreting the race laws as giving them licence to refuse any contact with Jews. Signs began to appear in shops in East Prussia stating that Jews would not be served; inns and hotels refused accommodation to Jewish travellers. As one CV official noted, this was hardly an example of 'tolerable relations'. The community in Bielefeld warned worshippers in advance of the Yom Kippur services that they should not hang around outside the synagogue or walk in conspicuous groups.[71]

Once the full implications of the Nuremberg Laws were digested, the Jewish leadership in Germany and outside accepted the need to evacuate young Jews and resettle them in countries that offered normal prospects for education, careers and marriage. The Centralverein broadened its internal educational programme beyond fortifying Jewish identity and, by implication, the resolve to stay in Germany, and started providing courses on how to prepare for emigration. It even held meetings explaining the practicalities of moving to Palestine. All the same, the antipathy between assimilation-minded Jews and Zionists did not evaporate. The Reichsvertretung set up a training farm on an estate at Gross-Breesen, near Breslau, to offer instruction in agronomy and domestic science to young men and women. Gross-Breesen was very similar to the training camps run by the Zionist organization but it was deliberately non-ideological and intended to make its graduates eligible for settlement anywhere in the world that workers were needed on the land.[72]

The Jewish world reacts to the race laws

In New York to meet Jewish leaders, James McDonald sought to dispel any hopes that the Nuremberg Laws were a harbinger of 'stability', warning instead that they supplied the 'basis for the development of a wide range of anti-Jewish attacks'. He told Felix Warburg bluntly that there was 'no future for the Jews in Germany'. Likewise, Bernard Kahn, reporting on the situation for the AJJDC, counselled its European executive that Nuremberg did not supply any credible foundation for Jewish continuity: 'fear, insecurity, nervous unrest are characteristics that describe the conditions of the Jews in Germany today'. There was a danger that Jews would flee en masse into neighbouring countries. Raymond Geist alerted the State Department that 'The new Jewish laws and the indications of the expropriation of Jews have resulted in a panic-like movement among these people who are seeking every possible means to leave the country'.[73]

Unfortunately, just when it was most needed the High Commission for Refugees was rendered impotent. In February 1935, McDonald had decided it was achieving little except to create the illusion that the international community was doing something. He informed the League of Nations that he intended to resign at the end of the year and left it up to the secretariat to decide whether to wind up the office or appoint a successor. In the interim, he made a three-month-long tour through South America, meeting politicians and officials in Brazil, Uruguay and Argentina in the hope of persuading them to permit the large-scale settlement of Jewish refugees. His terse summary of a meeting with President Vargas of Brazil was typical of these encounters: 'The talk went on and on, but not much that was new was added.'[74]

The final report of the High Commissioner estimated that 80,000 Germans, mainly Jews, had left the country between January 1933 and June 1935. Of these, 27,000 had gone to Palestine, 6,000 to the USA, and 3,000 to South America, and 18,000 had been 'repatriated' to countries in eastern and central Europe. The majority had found some degree of permanence. However, McDonald's team calculated that about 27,000 refugees were still adrift in the world, dependent on hand-outs from aid agencies. Some $10 million had been raised and spent on assisting this migration, of which American Jews had contributed $3 million while the much smaller British Jewish population had provided $2.5 million. This was a huge drain on the resources of two communities in countries still gripped by the Depression, yet relatively few Jews had been helped.[75]

Even as he was bidding farewell, McDonald had a sense of foreboding. In July 1935, he had written to Eleanor Roosevelt: 'It is my conviction that the party leaders in the Reich have set themselves a programme of forcing gradually the Jews from Germany by creating conditions there which make life unbearable.' The Nuremberg Laws fulfilled his prognostications but by then his course was set. He used his resignation statement to excoriate the League of Nations and the governments that had failed to intercede with Germany on behalf of the Jews. 'Without such response, the problems caused by the persecution of the Jews and the "Non-Aryans" will not be solved by philanthropic action, but will continue to constitute a danger to international peace and a source of injury to the legitimate interests of other States.'[76]

In private McDonald bemoaned the complacency of the Jewish diaspora, but at last that began to change. During January and February 1936, British and American Jewish leaders, in consultation with the Reichsvertretung, inaugurated a far-reaching programme for the systematic emigration and resettlement of Jews from Germany. The main aid agencies pooled their resources and expertise to form the Council for German Jewry (CGJ). The Council united Zionists and non-Zionists in a single, cross-community effort. It dedicated itself to settling Jews anywhere, but recognized the special role of Palestine. To this end it agreed to fund vocational training and the costs of migration for Jews in Germany as well as Jewish refugees in other countries. Fund-raising and the allocation of resources were intended to reflect these priorities. Zionist bodies suspended separate drives in return for a fixed percentage of the money raised by the Council; the allocations committee was divided 50:50 between Zionists and non-Zionists. This degree of co-operation was unprecedented and reflected a new sense of urgency. However, success would depend not only on exceptional levels of generosity from Jews around the British Commonwealth and across the North America; it needed the cooperation of German officials.[77]

Germans and Jews under the race laws

Nazi monitoring agencies gleefully registered the decline of the assimilationist organizations, the surge of interest in Zionism, and the redoubling of efforts to emigrate. The Gestapo office in Cologne commented on the 'disillusionment' of Jewish war veterans who 'did not expect that people would construct a ghetto for them'. Even these stalwarts of patriotism were now eager to learn more about emigration possibilities. Nevertheless, towards the end of the year the initial disorientation wore off and once again Jewish traders focused on the seasonal business opportunities. The Centralverein recorded optimism in Pomerania: 'The outlook among retail shop owners has become more confident. Sales have increased ... the atmosphere of panic and the urge to sell at any price have disappeared.' By late autumn there was a familiar, tetchy ring to dispatches reaching the SD Head Office in Berlin. The county commissioner in Melsungen, a small town south of Kassel in Hesse, expressed gratitude for the clarification of relations between Jews and Aryans, but wondered what to do about the enthusiastic individual who wanted to strike a blow at the Jews by himself. Should such an activist be penalized for 'unlawful' acts? The Gestapo in Breslau once again demanded guidance concerning the sticking of signs on Jewish-owned premises and boycotting.[78]

The population as a whole received the Nuremberg Laws with relief, if for very different reasons to the Jews. They too welcomed an end to bouts of violence, unseemly brawls between party members and police, and uncertainty over the correct relations with Jewish people in a commercial or business setting. According to the Gestapo, Berliners rejoiced that the laws 'finally cleared the air and brought clarity . . . In future and for all time to come, no interference is possible in the Völkisch affairs and concerns of the German nation.' The new laws were 'a great source of satisfaction'. The police office in the Minden government district relayed the 'particularly warm reception'. The Führer's speech 'finally made it crystal clear to all Party members and Volksgenossen [racial comrades] that the time for individual actions against Jews had passed'. Germans employed by Jews were especially relieved; their jobs and their consciences were now untroubled. By the onset of winter, Minden reported that 'interest in the Jewish Question has declined' and 'a certain calm has set in with regard to the Jewish Question'. The Gestapo in the Magdeburg district actually admitted that workers resented boycott actions since they prevented them buying at the cheapest prices. Workers who were suffering from low wages and facing food shortages were frankly uninterested in the race laws.[79]

The reaction of Catholics was modified by the heightened tension between the Church of Rome and the Third Reich. Several prominent Catholics had been killed during the 'Night of the Long Knives', while the dismissal of Papen appeared to leave Catholics unrepresented in government. The anti-Semitic wave that prefigured the race laws also overlapped with a drive against the Church by leading Nazi figures. Catholic clergy and laity were anyway predisposed to look askance at an act of state that contradicted religious imperatives, in this case conversion and the sanctity of marriage. Friction between the regime and the Catholic hierarchy engendered a degree of empathy and even solidarity with Jews, especially in rural areas.[80]

In May 1935, the NSDAP District Office in Eichstätt, a small town in Franconia, complained that 'it is still not possible to say that all Volksgenossen have recognised the importance of the Jewish Question. But that is probably due to the fact that the Church acts as a brake on this, quietly engaging in opposition'. On the eve of the 1935 Nazi Party rally, the state police office in Aachen observed that 'the Roman Catholic population sees the Jew as a human being, and only secondarily thinks of evaluating the matter from the standpoint of race policy . . . When it comes to the Jews the Catholic population is extremely tolerant. It resolutely rejects, insofar as the individual Jew is concerned, any and all measures'. Weeks after the race laws were passed, the population of the Catholic town Allenstein, in East Prussia, persisted in buying from Jews.

The local Gestapo official protested that 'a segment of the Catholic population maintains a friendly attitude towards Jews and shows little
understanding when it comes to the racial laws'. He conceded, 'one
cannot see visible signs of success of the anti-semitic efforts'.[81]

A similar dynamic was behind the stance of Protestants affiliated to
the breakaway Confessing Church. Beginning in April 1933, Pastor
Dietrich Bonhoeffer, based in Berlin, rallied Protestant churchmen
within the Evangelical Church who defended the principle and practice
of conversion. The dissidents also objected to efforts by the self-declared
German Christians, led by Nazi-appointed Reich Bishop Ludwig Müller,
to deJudaise the Bible. Eventually dissenting Protestants coalesced into
a rival ecclesiastical organization, the Confessing Church. In spite of
sharing fundamental assumptions about the Jews with the German
Christians and the regime, notably that Jews were alien and subversive,
the Confessing Church would not renounce the redemptive quality of
conversion or abandon existing non-Aryan Christians. Occasionally
this position resulted in the arrest of a pastor. The county commissioner in Gelnhausen informed Berlin in July 1935 that the pastor from
Aufengau was taken into protective custody, 'since he had called on the
Church congregation to pray for Jews in distress'. Robert Smallbones,
the British consul general in Frankfurt-am-Main, believed that 'there
are great numbers of Germans of all classes to whom this persecution is
abhorrent'. He thought that the Nazi campaign against the Old Testament and their attempts to deJudaise Christianity actually worked to
create sympathy for Jews.[82]

Towards the end of the year a querulous tone entered the surveillance reports more generally. In Magdeburg party activists received the
Nuremberg Laws as 'an act of liberation' that left them wanting more,
such as the registration and badging of Jewish-owned businesses. Once
again, there was a state of 'uncertainty'. Similar demands were heard
from Breslau at the start of 1936. In truth, violence and boycotting
never went away. Police officials in Trier admitted to the persistence of
violence against Jews despite contrary instructions to party members.
The Berlin police cast a jaundiced eye over Jews returning to bars and
cafes. The NSDAP Head Office for Municipal Policy began to cry out
for Jewish businesses to be marked officially. For this agency, at least,
the Nuremberg Laws had exerted 'a stimulating effect'. At the peak of
the Christmas season police officials in Baden and Arnsberg reported
disapprovingly that 'customers are flocking to Jewish shops'.[83]

The race laws had not had the anticipated educational effect on the German population. The County Commissioner's District Office in Bad Kissingen complained that 'there are still some persons who believe they have to protect the Jews'. Hamburg exporters continued to place their business interests above those of the Volksgemeinschaft. In September 1936, the Jewish desk at the head office of the SD concluded that the Nuremberg Laws had not been wholly effective: there were still relations between Jews and non-Jews, most especially in Catholic regions. Non-Aryan Christians, that is to say converts, often proved the porous element in the barrier between the populations.[84]

In the shade of the Berlin Olympics

1936, the year of the Berlin Olympics, has customarily been deemed another quiet period for Jews in Germany, a 'period of outward calm and a certain degree of legal security'. Hitler wanted to avoid giving any excuse to the international community to boycott the games, so the Nazi leadership 'soft-pedalled its anti-Jewish stance'. Obnoxious signs and banners were removed so as not to affront foreign visitors and *Der Stürmer* was not displayed in the streets. Richard Evans has described this phase as a sort of 'charm offensive'. Jewish or part-Jewish athletes, like the fencer Helen Mayer, were even allowed to compete in the games to forestall demonstrations by competitors from other nations.[85]

Yet 1936 was a decisive year in the development of Judenpolitik. Out of view, the tectonic plates of the Third Reich were shifting. A tussle commenced between the conservatives still in the government and the new Nazi elite that was elbowing its way into more powerful positions. Jews in Germany sensed these developments; in any case, the day-to-day experience of those in small towns and rural areas indicated that the restraints on the Nazi rank and file were mainly cosmetic. The 'cold pogrom' did not abate in the deep countryside and distant East Prussia, even if Jews in Berlin could once again stroll down the Kurfürstendamm, buy a copy of the *Jüdische Rundschau*, and drink coffee in a restaurant while observing foreign visitors bustle to and fro between the Hotel Adlon and the Olympic park.[86]

Nor were foreign correspondents fooled by the air of normality. William Shirer was reprimanded by the Foreign Press Department of the Propaganda Ministry after he revealed that before the opening of the Winter Games Nazi officials in Garmisch 'had pulled down all the signs saying that Jews were unwanted (they're all over Germany) and that the Olympic visitors would thus be spared any signs of the kind of treatment meted out to Jews in this country'. Bella Fromm, who was now writing for an Austrian newspaper, commented sarcastically that 'There's been a notable improvement in our streets. They've taken away the *Stürmer* showcases so as not to shock the Olympic visitors with the pornographic weekly.'[87]

Victor Klemperer was struck by the regime's unnaturally restrained reaction to the shooting of a senior Nazi in Switzerland. Wilhelm Gustloff, the founder and leader of the Swiss Nazi Party, was assassinated by a young Jew, David Frankfurter, on 4 February 1936, just two days before the opening of the Winter Games. But instead of unleashing a wave of revenge, Nazi Party headquarters immediately ordered party bosses and SA leaders to prevent anti-Jewish demonstrations and individual actions. The Nazi elite contented themselves with giving Gustloff a state funeral in Schwerin, his birthplace, at which Hitler delivered a eulogy blaming 'our Jewish foe' for his death. The Führer incorporated Gustloff into a litany of murder and sacrifice, culminating in the civil strife of 1918–19, and declared that the 'same power' stood behind each and every instance. For the moment, though, rhetoric stood in for deeds. In Aachen there was some vandalism and in Berlin the Jewish Cultural Association was ordered to suspend its programme as a punishment. But that was the extent of the official riposte. Klemperer predicted that 'They will turn on the hostages, on the German Jews later.'[88]

Jewish life in rural areas continued to deteriorate. Mark Wischnitzer, who worked for the Hilfsverein, told James McDonald that 'Jews in the smaller places are selling their businesses and property for what they can get, and some are fleeing to the larger cities, there anxiously searching for opportunities for emigration.' Robert Smallbones informed the British Embassy in Berlin in November 1935 that 'So far, the extremists have had it all their own way, and the position of the Jews is becoming quite unbearable.' One trader after another was being pressurized into liquidation. In some villages in Hesse Jews could not even buy bread because bakers refused to serve them. 'While "separate action" is officially discouraged it seems to be the intention to deprive Jews of the possibility of earning a living in a systematic manner.' A report for the World Jewish Congress in January 1936 contrasted the superficial calm with the malevolence seething below the surface. It was true assaults had 'all but ceased in recent weeks' thanks to the influx of foreign visitors, yet 'blackmail and threatening letters' proliferated. The Nuremberg Laws, with their promise of stability, masked unceasing pressure on Jews to give up their businesses. Nazis were using all sorts of legal devices and chicanery to drive Jews out of the economy.[89]

The rural Jewish population was in terminal crisis. Communities had shrunk by up to 40 per cent as young Jews left for the greater security and job prospects of the cities. Most had fallen below the critical mass necessary to survive. Half of those in Prussia numbered under fifty souls and they were often destitute. The dissolution of entire communities now figured more frequently in the reports that Nazi officials remitted to Berlin. The governor of the Koblenz district crowed that Jewish cattle dealers had been almost completely eliminated so rural Jews 'no longer believe in the possibility of continuing to remain in Germany, and expect that within about ten years there will no longer be any Jews'. The state police in Hanover reported that because wealthy Jews had left the villages and small towns the communities could not afford welfare or pay for teachers in the Jewish schools. While Jewish cattle traders were clinging on around Wiesbaden, there was a steady flight of the Jewish population to large urban centres, mainly Stuttgart. In Butzbach, Hesse, 'The Jews have been excluded almost completely from commerce, and most prefer to disappear gradually by going abroad.'[90]

Nazi activists continued to educate the Volksgenossen, their racial comrades, about the correct way to see the Jews. The language used in their reports to the Gestapo and SD indicate not just how they thought but how they expected the population to think. The district governor in Kassel spoke apologetically of continued Einzelaktionen, only to excuse them as the result of 'economic oppression at the hands of the Jews over the span of centuries'. The reports also give evidence of the dynamic between activists, party agencies, and the state. Kassel officials dutifully enforced order and banned 'individual actions', but complained that such actions derogated from the authority of the government and the image of the Führer. The county commissioner in Mayen, a small place west of Koblenz, moaned that Jews continued to have too much influence. 'The people involved are still so used to the individual Jew and do not see the facts: namely that on the stage of world politics, it is only the Jew with his international ideas and money that brings so much disorder to the world.' Local Nazi officials were building the Volks-gemeinschaft through the relentless, daily targeting of the Jewish population. Even the dead could play a role in educating the living. The district governor of Lower Bavaria and Upper Palatinate reported that the Christian burial of a baptized Jew in the town of Weiden led to the decision in future to treat deceased converts as Jews. The gendarmerie in Gunzenhausen, the scene of a murderous incident in April 1934, bragged that it was unthinkable for Germans any longer to attend the funeral of a Jew. The district governor of the Palatinate reported a fuss because some Catholics had the temerity to attend the burial of a Jewish neighbour. In Haigerloch in Bavaria, officials of the farmers' league photographed the funeral procession of a Jewish merchant so as to identify Aryans breaching the lines of the Volksgemeinschaft. It was feared they might pass them on to *Der Stürmer* for publication.[91]

The Jewish leadership in Germany did not accept these develop-ments passively, but their ability to resist was diminishing. Suspecting that a policy of Aryanization was being stealthily implemented with government knowledge and consent, in October 1935 the Centralverein challenged Schacht. 'Since the Nuremberg Laws Jewish entrepreneurs have been urged *very insistently* to sell off their businesses ... a great many rumours have promoted the idea that even the Reich Economic Ministry is reckoning on the complete exclusion of Jews from the German economy within a year'. The CV reminded Schacht of his earlier decrees against boycotts and the dismissal of Jewish staff, and asked for them to be reiterated. Otherwise the public would treat them as in abeyance. Its plea was ignored. Personal contacts were no more effective. In October 1935 the Israel family lost control of their depart-ment store and a Nazi official warned them that unless they sold it quickly they might not be able to sell it at all. Wilfred held out little hope for an intervention by the minister.[92]

Schacht's silence was deeply worrying. In mid-1935 he had con-tended with the racial hardliners and anti-Semites in the Nazi Party. After a speech criticizing unauthorized actions, the state police in Cologne reported 'numerous voices saying that the President of the Reichsbank, with his stated views on the problem of the economy and the Jewish Question, has achieved a splendid victory over the move-ment'. The relative moderation of the Nuremberg Laws was partly down to his restraining influence, abetted by Frick and civil servants in the

Interior Ministry. For a moment Schacht, like Papen in 1934, appeared to hold the banner of opposition aloft.[93]

Foreign diplomats, like German Jews, regarded him as a beacon of reason within the regime. Thanks to his fluent English and his command of issues concerning reparations and foreign trade he was a main interlocutor for the British and the Americans. Dodd, Phipps and McDonald routinely believed that they could influence the regime's Judenpolitik through him. That perception seemed to be confirmed by the contact that Schacht preserved with Jewish bankers and businessmen, notably Max Warburg. But after Nuremberg they detected a chill in his demeanour. It transpired that he was willing to accept the expulsion of Jews from society and, ultimately, their departure from Germany. To André François-Poncet, Schacht was a cynic and an opportunist. 'He was perfectly aware of Hitler's blunder in persecuting the Jews and rousing Anglo-Saxon opinion against the Nazi regime' but he 'never had enough courage or influence to prevent excesses'.[94]

Even so, in late 1935 Ambassador Dodd thought that Schacht was almost single-handedly holding back the Nazis who wanted to expropriate all Jewish property. He told James McDonald that the minister for economics had enjoyed 'a sort of victory' over the extremists at Nuremberg. But 'since the radicals' pressure never relaxes, the net result is always to leave the Jews worse off than before'. The much-respected correspondent for The Times, Norman Ebbutt, shared this view. In his opinion, 'whatever lull follows will be only temporary. Moreover, each new attack begins from where the last one left off. In this way, despite the efforts of Schacht, the radicals are able to register steady advances.' Max Warburg gave the same message to Dodd. He told the ambassador 'that he and Dr Schacht had not been able to do anything to relieve the Jewish situation'.[95]

Following a wide-ranging conversation, Phipps briefed London that Schacht's position was becoming increasingly anomalous. He told the minister that he 'followed with sympathy and with interest his efforts on behalf of the Jews'. Schacht replied 'with surprising frankness. He said that he had only a few days ago attacked the Führer on the subject, urging how essential it was that no special action or persecution of the Jews should be indulged in outside the recent legislation. Herr Hitler had given him assurances in this respect and he therefore hoped, though evidently without much conviction, that such action would cease.' Schacht added that 'anti-semitism was a cardinal principle of

Herr Hitler's policy . . . it was practically impossible for him to enforce moderation on all his subordinates'. In a fascinating anticipation of the notion that Nazis were 'working towards the Führer', Schacht recalled that one Gauleiter told his activists 'they would be interpreting his [the Führer's] true wishes if they continued their persecution of the Jews'. Phipps concluded waspishly that 'I need hardly add that Dr Schacht's solicitude for the Jews is inspired solely by financial and economic considerations in which humanitarianism plays no part.'[96]

Whatever his motives for preventing harsher action against the Jews, foreign diplomats correctly suspected that his power was waning and interpreted his slide as symptomatic of other less visible developments. Paradoxically, Schacht was a victim of the regime's success and his own contribution to it. No sooner were the Winter Olympics brought to a splendid conclusion than Hitler carried off his most daring foreign policy coup. On 7 March 1936, he sent 22,000 German soldiers into the Rhineland, which had been declared a demilitarized zone under the Versailles Treaty and the 1925 Locarno Treaty. Hitler had timed the operation exquisitely. The French government was in crisis, both the British and the French economies were mired in the Depression, and they had lost the support of Mussolini after condemning the Italian invasion of Abyssinia the previous October. While the French and the British blamed each other for not resisting the move, Hitler organized a plebiscite that proved he enjoyed near-unanimous support for the final repudiation of Versailles. As the nation rejoiced, Victor Klemperer reflected morosely, 'His position is secured for an indefinite period.'[97]

Hitler quickly built on the regime's soaring popularity and Germany's enhanced geo-strategic position. In the aftermath of the Olympics he composed a memorandum arguing that Germany had to prepare for war within four years. However, the Four-Year Plan went far beyond a statement of economic priorities. It was a declaration of Hitler's ideological goals and the clearest indication yet that he was determined to achieve them by force. It had profound implications for the Jews of Germany because it was the first policy directive that explicitly linked the Jews to Bolshevism in the context of a plan for waging war. The plan thereby tied the fate of the Jews to Germany's geo-strategic exigencies. And by proposing an alternative to Schacht's economic strategy it demoted his importance, diminishing whatever influence he cared to wield to soften anti-Jewish measures. Despite this, it has usually been treated as falling outside the history of Judenpolitik.[98]

The Four-Year Plan was a confession of Germany's economic weakness, in which the Jews were implicated. The economy was too small, unbalanced and weak to support an improved standard of living for the population and afford massive expenditure on rebuilding the armed forces. Ironically, recovery had aggravated the quandary. Unemployment had fallen to around one million and even though wages remained below pre-Depression levels, steady employment allowed workers to spend more. Consequently, imports had risen, leading to a balance of payments crisis. Germany was not exporting enough: demand in the world economy was feeble while productive resources were being diverted to manufacturing arms and munitions. To make matters worse, the armaments sector was sucking in expensive raw materials. Germany lacked the foreign currency reserves to pay for imported mineral oil and high-quality iron ore at the same time as importing foodstuffs such as animal fats, eggs and fodder. Efforts to improve agricultural productivity still left the country 15 per cent short of its food requirements. Thus the regime was faced with difficult choices. If it continued to rearm at breakneck speed, it would have to hold down living standards and restrict consumption. Yet the Nazis had come to power by promising better days. How could these goals be reconciled? Schacht had staved off the reckoning with a series of ingenious short-term measures. The government also promoted schemes to substitute synthetic foodstuffs and raw materials for imported varieties. However, by early 1936 Schacht had run out of tricks and Germany was running out of foreign currency. Shortages led to 'grumbling' in the population and armament factories had to slow or even stop production. But Schacht's recommendations to relax the tempo of rearmament and boost exports only served to irritate Hitler.[99]

On 4 September 1936, Göring read Hitler's memorandum to the cabinet. It began with the Führer's thoughts on politics and war. Politics was the struggle of nations for survival. The threat that Germany faced came from the east, from Bolshevism. Since the Russian Revolution, international Jewry had established itself in Russia and was poised to extend its conquest over other countries and ultimately the whole world. 'Since the beginning of the French Revolution the world has been drifting with increasing speed towards a new conflict, whose most extreme solution is named Bolshevism, but whose content and aim is only the removal of those strata of society which gave leadership to humanity up to the present, and their replacement by international

Jewry.' The victory of Bolshevism would mean victory for the Jews and the destruction of civilization. By virtue of its geo-political situation and the ideology of National Socialism, Germany stood in the way of this catastrophe. 'Germany will as always have to be regarded as the focus of the western world against the attacks of Bolshevism.' It was impossible to predict when the showdown would occur, but it was Germany's 'destiny' and failure would mean the 'annihilation of the German people'. To prevent this it was essential to enhance Germany's military: 'The extent of the military development of our resources cannot be too large, nor the pace too swift.' Unfortunately, Germany was unable to feed its population on its own and lacked sufficient raw materials for rearmament. The conundrum could only be solved in the long term by 'extending our living space [Lebensraum]'. In the short term, steps had to be taken to prepare Germany for achieving Lebensraum. Since Germany could not export enough to finance the arms build-up and it could not be slowed down, it was necessary to mobilize the whole of society and the economy. The memorandum stipulated the achievement of self-sufficiency in food as far as possible, substituting synthetic products for imported items, and limiting imports to essentials. Hitler threatened that if private industry was not prepared to accomplish these objectives, the state would take the lead. Finally, he demanded two new laws. The first would make economic sabotage punishable by death. The second made 'the whole of Jewry liable for all damages inflicted by individual specimens of this community of criminals upon the German economy and thus upon the German people'. His memorandum concluded, '(I) The German armed forces must be operational within four years (II) The German economy must be fit for war in four years'.[100]

The memorandum gives a startling insight into Hitler's thinking. He was above all a warrior. His years in the trenches were the formative experience in his life and his constant point of reference. His chief enemy was international Jewry. The Jews had caused Germany's defeat in 1918 and had succeeded in conquering Russia, from where they planned to take over the whole world. Only Germany, National Socialism, and he himself barred their path. However, even as Germany girded itself for war it had to watch the enemy within. The war against international Jewry could not be fought without suppressing the Jews in Germany. While de-emancipation satisfied the demands of old-fashioned anti-Semites, and reducing or eliminating the influence of the Jews met the demands of conservatives, Hitler envisaged something

very different. He was even thinking beyond the demands for segregation that emanated from racial anti-Semites, who saw the threat of Jews
expressed in terms of blood and miscegenation. Hitler believed that
Germany was at war with the Jews. The survival of Germany depended
upon military preparedness and, as a prerequisite of that, territorial
expansion. Lebensraum would necessitate war; war would necessitate
the ruthless suppression of the Jews. His thinking was apocalyptic and
his reasoning was circular; but it was entirely coherent.[102]

Foreign diplomats detected the shift in gear. Ambassador Dodd
noticed that the speeches by Hitler, Goebbels and Rosenberg at the 1936
Nuremberg party rally were even more belligerent than usual. They
referred to the outbreak of the Spanish Civil War and the election of a
left-wing Popular Front government in France, led by a Jew, Léon Blum,
as evidence of communist aggression and, behind it, the Jews. On 18
October 1936 a decree formally made Göring responsible for the
achievement of the Four-Year Plan, establishing his role as economic
supremo and sidelining Schacht. A few days later Phipps compared
Schacht to 'a skilled navigator who in a moment of pique joined a pirate
vessel, confident that he would reform the pirate captain and his crew'
only to find that he was 'compelled to engage in piracy'. He had 'succeeded in warding off the worst attacks of the Nazi extremists. There
has been no general confiscation of Jewish or other property'. But, by
implication, the weakening of Schacht's position spelled trouble for the
Jews.[102]

The other, not unrelated, realignment of the power structure within
the Third Reich during 1936 concerned the security apparatus. In June
1936, Himmler was appointed chief of the German police, uniting control of the Gestapo, the criminal police (Kriminalpolizei, Kripo), the
uniformed police (Ordnungspolizei, Orpo), the SD, and the SS. While
the uniformed police remained under the direction of Kurt Daluege, the
Gestapo and Kripo were amalgamated into the Sicherheitspolizei (Sipo,
security police), under Heydrich. The result was a transformation of the
way crime was regarded and the function of policing. Consolidation of
the security apparatus and its reorientation were also tightly bound to
the Four-Year Plan and preparations for war. German society had to be
purged of racially weak and degenerate elements. This included 'hereditary' criminals and those who would not conform to National Socialist
norms. Anyone with a criminal record was liable to be rounded up and
sent to a concentration camp. Beggars, tramps, those who refused to

work were also deemed 'asocial' and swept into the rapidly expanding concentration camp system. The Gypsies, too, fell victim to this blurring of policing, traditional prejudice and biological racism. Finally, Germans of mixed Black African and German parentage, the children of German colonial settlers, were subjected to compulsory sterilization along with the offspring of relationships between German woman and French colonial soldiers contracted during the French occupation of the Rhineland in 1922.[103]

However, none of these groups was considered as menacing as the Jews. They alone represented an international, global threat to the German people. They were regarded as the hidden force behind the new socialist government of Léon Blum in France and the Soviet-backed republican government in Spain. In a speech in June 1936, marking his appointment as chief of the German police, Himmler laid bare the nexus between the existence of the Jewish enemy and the creation of a unified security apparatus to defend the Volk: 'We must assume that this struggle will last for generations, for it is the age-old struggle between humans and sub-humans in its current new phase of the struggle between the Aryan peoples and Jewry and the organisational form Jewry has adopted of Bolshevism. I see my task as being to prepare the whole nation for this struggle by building up the police welded together with the order of the SS as the organisation to protect the Reich at home . . .'[104]

Preparations for the battle against international Jewry required intensified measures against the Jews. At the start of 1936, the SD Head Office was reorganized and liaison with the Gestapo improved. A thrusting young intellectual, Kurt Schröder, was appointed to head the SD Jewish bureau, Department II/112. These Jewish experts held a number of conferences during the year at which they briefed SD field officers tasked with observing and reporting on Jewish affairs. As well as keeping an eye on the Centralverein and the RjF, Heydrich proposed to the Interior Ministry that their activities should be curtailed or banned. His sweeping programme was rejected, but the Gestapo stepped up the harassment of the non-Zionist Jewish organizations. It also began to take an active part in pressurizing Jews to abandon their businesses. The Gestapo used the role it had been given by Göring to prevent foreign currency violations to investigate and threaten Jewish businessmen.[105]

Power over Jewish affairs was slipping away from the ministries that had formerly devised and implemented anti-Jewish measures. Perhaps sensing that they needed to wrest back their influence, on 29 September

1936, representatives of the Interior Ministry, the Finance Ministry and Rudolf Hess, the deputy Führer, met to discuss Judenpolitik. They agreed to the 'complete and total emigration' of the Jews and the use of law to limit Jewish economic activity to 'sustaining life'. However, they did not feel that the moment for such drastic action was opportune in view of the delicate state of the economy. Unlike the Sipo-SD apparatus, for them the primacy of economics still trumped ideology. By pulling back, they inadvertently left the way open for Himmler and Heydrich to make the running.[106]

The intensifying assault on German Jews

For most Germans the autumn of 1936 brought the year, framed by the reoccupation of the Rhineland and the Berlin Olympics, to a glorious conclusion. Despite periodic food shortages their living standards improved modestly thanks to sustained employment. The growth of the state bureaucracy in many sectors, including the security apparatus, offered opportunities for promotion and upward social mobility. But for Jews it was a time of growing anxiety. Kurt Rosenberg jotted in his diary, 'For weeks the Jews have been whispering into each other's ears that it will become even worse after the Olympics in August . . . long ago we lost the ability to take pleasure in small things and celebrations – because over everything hangs the eternal question, *Is it still worth it?*' As the games neared their end Victor Klemperer worried that 'an explosion is imminent, and naturally, they will first of all take things out on the Jews'.[107]

The rabidly anti-communist and anti-Jewish oratory at the Nuremberg rally in September 1936 sounded more than usually ominous to Mally Dienemann, the wife of the rabbi in Offenbach. After hearing one of the speeches on the radio she predicted that things would 'go downhill'. If there was to be a war 'it will start with the extinction of the Jews'. Victor Klemperer heard the same broadcast with its 'insane Jew baiting'. It 'beggars all imagination,' he wrote. Three weeks later, on his birthday, Klemperer was banned from the reading room of his local library. At the start of December the telephone in his home was removed in accordance with the latest anti-Jewish regulation. 'An almost symbolic act', he typed in his diary. Now they were 'Completely impoverished and completely isolated'. For Zionists and religious Jews like the Dienemanns it was possible to retreat into Jewish life and derive sustenance from Judaism or visions of a Jewish national future in Palestine. But to totally assimilated German Jews and converts like Klemperer there was, quite literally, nowhere to go.[108]

Until late 1936, sufficient Jews were in employment or in business, some doing quite well, to preserve the impression that German Jewry was holding its own. Sacked civil servants and other state employees, like Klemperer, still got their pensions. Jewish professionals, such as doctors, dentists and lawyers, could provide their services to other Jews. Lawyers could even appear in court. Thousands of Jewish children were still at state schools. However, towards the end of the year the Reichsvertretung found its resources strained to breaking point to alleviate the misery that enveloped the steadily increasing number deprived of jobs or the opportunity to make a living through trade. Had it not been for support from the Council for German Jewry during the winter of 1936–7, the local Jewish relief agencies would not have been able to cope.[109]

The increasing pressure took its toll on Jewish unity. Georg Kareski, a right-wing Zionist, believed that he was in a better position to deal with the German government than the mainstream leadership. At the start of 1937, the Reichsvertretung had to fight off a bid by Kareski and members of his Staatszionistische Partei to take over the executive. The Gestapo was disappointed by the resilience of the traditional leaders, but to Jews in Britain and the USA their steadiness was admirable. David Glick, a field officer for the AJJDC, reported to the New York headquarters that 'they are displaying a courage and a mentality that is absolutely magnificent . . . they refuse to go down as cowards or animals, but are maintaining to the last a spirit of brave and cultured men and women'.[110]

In January 1937, the SD Jewish office came up with proposals for a systematic campaign against the Jews in Germany intended to drive them out within the shortest time possible. The paper 'On the Jewish Problem', possibly authored by Adolf Eichmann, announced that 'the Jew is one of the most dangerous of all enemies, because he is elusive and never completely within reach'. The guiding concept of SD strategy was to achieve the deJewification of Germany by eliminating the economic basis for Jewish existence. The Jews would then be obliged to emigrate, although they would be steered to regions that were undeveloped and poor, where they could not regroup and pose a threat to the Third Reich. In a departure from earlier Judenpolitik, the paper suggested that reliance on Zionism alone might not suffice. The Jews in Germany had not felt under sufficient pressure to reconcile themselves to Zionism, while riots by Palestinian Arabs against Jewish immigration had acted as a deterrent. It was therefore imperative to exclude Jews from the economy, apply greater pressure on them, and exploit all available opportunities for emigration. This campaign had to be accompanied by consciousness-raising amongst the population to cut off sources of sympathy and succour: 'It is necessary to generate among the population a widespread attitude hostile to the Jews in order to create a basis for a sustained attack to effectively repel the enemy.' The use of military metaphors reveals the mentality of the SD personnel and their fantasy vision of the Jews as a powerful, dangerous foe. The paper also reveals their capacity for brutality and cynicism: 'The most effective way to deprive the Jews of a feeling of security is the wrath of the people, *as manifested in violence.*' Jews feared pogroms so violence was highly effective, even though it was illegal. Yet by virtue of recommending pogroms, the SD gave the lie to the existence of popular anger. Having intimated how Jews would thus be encouraged to emigrate, the paper sketched out technical means for speeding their departure. It proposed setting up a 'central office' to handle emigration and help Jews on their way.[111]

Over the course of 1937, elements of this programme were put into effect at the prompting of Heydrich and SD officers liaising with the Gestapo. Partly through its interventions in Jewish affairs, the SD, which was ostensibly just an intelligence-gathering organization, inched nearer to obtaining executive powers. The fearsome implications of this development are evident from the 'Guidelines on the Jewish Question' for SD officers drawn up by the latest head of the Jewish bureau, Dieter Wisliceny, a corpulent ex-theology student. 'The struggle against the Jews is from the outset a basic principle of National Socialism. The Jewish question is for National Socialism not only a religious or political question but a race question. Hence the possibility of any compromise is closed. The adversarial position of the NSDAP against the Jews runs through the whole Party programme. The Jew is for the National Socialist simply the enemy.' The Guidelines recalled that since May 1935, the SD had been formulating a systematic, research-based strategy for dealing with them. 'The solution of the Jewish question can only lie in the total deJewification of Germany' but the attainment of this goal was 'thinkable only through the Zionist emigration.'[112]

Reports compiled by the Jewish desk of the SD Head Office during 1937 showed discontent with the pace of Jewish emigration and frustration with the resilience of Jewish communities. In April 1937, the summary for the first quarter noted that 'the social situation of the Jews in general is so favourable that most prefer staying on in the country to emigrating'. The Arab uprising against British rule in Palestine had taken the shine off the Zionist message. Instead, the Centralverein and the RjF were experiencing a revival. The JKB, the Jewish cultural association, was 'slowly leading the Jews into an intellectual and cultural ghetto', but that was an ambiguous development since it offered Jews consolation and distraction from their woes. The SD also complained that Jews were getting support from Catholics, especially 'the rural population which opposes National Socialism'.[113]

Ever watchful for the machinations of international Jewry, the SD pounced on an anti-Nazi speech by New York mayor Fiorello LaGuardia in March 1937. As a reprisal the Gestapo dissolved the Jewish fraternal society B'nai Brith and imposed a two-month ban on all Centralverein and RjF meetings as well as any Jewish cultural activity. Only Zionist meetings were permitted. Ambassador Dodd made a formal protest to the German Foreign Ministry about the Nazi press attacks on LaGuardia, but ministry officials now seemed impervious to such démarches. In November, he noted wearily that in a speech Streicher had claimed 'the Jews govern the US, LaGuardia being their chief'. By now Dodd was inured to such rhetoric and had practically given up meeting with Nazi officials.[114]

In May, the protected status of Jews in Upper Silesia expired. This anomaly stemmed from the struggle between Poland and Germany for control of the province after the Great War. Under the terms of the 1922 Geneva Convention on Silesia the territory was partitioned and the national minorities in each portion had their rights guaranteed for fifteen years; they were even entitled to appeal to the League of Nations in case of alleged violations. After the Nazis attained power Upper Silesia became a thorn in their side because the area was immune to discriminatory laws and because the Jewish population was permitted to make submissions to the League. During 1933, the American Jewish Congress used this device to send half a dozen petitions to Geneva protesting against German treatment of the Jews. Anticipating the restoration of full German sovereignty, the SD directors assigned Adolf Eichmann to draw up plans for bringing the local Jews to heel in quick time. In addition to the immediate extension into the province of all the race laws and anti-Jewish regulations, Eichmann recommended the prompt arrest of Jewish communal leaders, a ban on assimilation-orientated Jewish organizations, registration of all Jews and, especially, a rapid appraisal of their businesses to prevent Jews appointing Aryans to run them, a procedure known as 'cloaking'. Heydrich and Franz Six, head of Department II of the SD Head Office and Eichmann's line manager, approved the plan. Eichmann was duly dispatched to Breslau and as soon as the German security forces were relieved of international inhibitions he accompanied the Gestapo on their mission against the Jewish population. It was the first time that an SD officer had translated ideas into concrete policies and gone into the field to see them implemented. Eichmann's mission provided a model for later actions.[115]

Throughout 1937, the SD Jewish experts maintained a critical eye on the exclusion of Jews from the economy and monitored the rate of Jewish emigration. In July a formal agreement with the Gestapo, the Funktionsbefehl, enhanced their influence on the conduct of Judenpolitik. And they were relentless. While noting with approval that county commissioners were refusing to renew permits for Jewish cattle dealers, one report cavilled 'Even though the "Aryanization" efforts are continuing now as before throughout the entire territory of the Reich, to the keen satisfaction of the broad public, and have retained their intensity, there is nonetheless still substantial Jewish influence on economic life.' It was not good enough that Orthodox Jews and Jewish veterans who once spurned the notion of leaving Germany were now discussing group emigration, 'If numerous Jews from the assimilationist camp nonetheless remain resolute in their will to remain in Germany, that is due in significant measure to the partial preferential treatment being accorded them by the authorities ... and the generally lackadaisical attitude shown by the general public towards the Jewish Question.'[116]

The SD's other preoccupation was emigration. Since the conclusion of the Ha'avara agreement in 1933, the Nazis had favoured Zionism and assisted Jewish migration to Palestine. In the first year of Nazi rule, 7,600 Jews had emigrated to the Jewish national home, a quarter of the total who left Germany. During 1934 the number rose to 9,800, close to a third of all emigrants. The rate peaked at around 8,600–8,700 over the next two years, but never exceeded more than 30 per cent of total Jewish emigration. More might have gone, but the number was limited by the British Mandatory authorities. The British calculated the optimum rate of Jewish settlement according to the economic absorptive capacity of the country and, crucially, political considerations. Since the anti-Jewish riots of 1921, whenever there were violent Arab protests the British reduced the volume of immigration. With the renewed outbreak of communal disturbances in 1936, the government halved the number of immigration permits.[117]

The German Foreign Office and the SD had both watched anxiously while the British responded to the Palestinian Arab uprising. Although the rebellion was effectively suppressed, the authorities concluded that the mandate was unworkable. In July 1937, a Royal Commission led by Lord Peel recommended that Palestine should be partitioned into Jewish and Arab states. The Peel report sounded alarm bells along the Wilhelmstrasse and in SD headquarters. If the Jews gained a state it would be eligible for membership of the League of Nations. They would then have a platform from which to attack Germany and defend Jews in other countries.[118]

During 1936 the SD Jewish experts had established contact with a member of the Jewish underground army in Palestine, the Haganah, who seemed to offer the possibility of increasing Jewish emigration. In October 1937, Herbert Hagen, the senior officer on the Jewish desk, and Adolf Eichmann, the expert on Zionism, travelled to Palestine to follow up this lead. They were also supposed to investigate the alleged role of the Haganah in the assassination of Wilhelm Gustloff. Both aspects of the enterprise were a failure. Hagen and Eichmann were thrown out of Palestine by the British authorities only a few hours after they disembarked at Haifa. Their efforts to meet with Jewish informants who might shed light on Gustloff's killing were fruitless. Nevertheless, the journey enhanced Eichmann's reputation as the SD's point man on Jewish questions. The report he penned subsequently with Hagen signified a serious policy shift. While Palestine would remain a major destination for Jewish emigration it would not be the only or most preferable one. Nor should the Third Reich do anything to strengthen the Jewish community of Palestine or assist the achievement of statehood.[119]

The fortunes of Zionists in Germany were thus closely tied to both British policy and Judenpolitik. Zionism had attracted only a small minority of German Jews before the 1930s, and during the first years of the Nazi regime those who were previously unconvinced retained the hope that they could live out their lives in their German homeland. Although Willy Cohn was suspended from his job as a schoolteacher in

Breslau, he resisted his wife's pleas to go abroad. In June 1933 he wrote in his diary, 'Trudi is always pushing for us to emigrate; I don't think that the prospects for leaving are very good for us, not with my background.' His thinking reflected the attitude of many other German Jews; 'for now one should wait to see how things develop'. At the age of forty-six, Cohn was reluctant to 'start all over again'. In Breslau 'I can do something, here I am someone, but whether I can make it down there remains to be seen.' Notwithstanding some dreadful rows with his wife he insisted on staying put: 'I have deep roots here.'[120]

In the wake of the Nuremberg Laws interest in emigration generally, and more specifically to Palestine, grew. The Gestapo reported an intensification of Zionist activity across the country. In Bavaria more young people started training programmes while in Düsseldorf the community started running evening classes in Hebrew. Erich Sonnemann, head of a non-Zionist youth group, wrote bitterly to the head of the movement that 'only two things remain: move towards Zionism where one does not stop being a human being at age 23 or buy oneself a rope!' Yet the attractiveness of Zionism depended upon the opportunities for emigration to Palestine and the perception that the Zionists enjoyed the patronage of the regime. As soon as there was trouble in Palestine, Jews turned to agencies that could find them new homes somewhere else and the assimilation-oriented Jews, especially the RjF, took delight in exposing the drawbacks of the Zionist remedy.[121]

By early 1937, Cohn had changed his mind. He travelled to Palestine with Trudi to visit his son Ernst (who had settled there in 1934) and see the country for himself. They landed at Haifa on the eve of Passover and spent six weeks on Kibbutz Givat Brenner, where Ernst lived, and exploring the country. However, they remained ambivalent about making the move. In any case, it was becoming harder and harder for Jews in Germany to get a Palestine permit, especially if like Willy Cohn they were middle-aged. The Zionist movement, which controlled the distribution of permits, favoured those who were capable of manual labour or work on the land, or brought capital with them. It also preferred those who had shown a commitment to the Zionist idea by joining Zionist organizations or parties. In January 1934, Weizmann shocked James McDonald by expressing disdain for the mass of European Jews who did not fall into such categories. He 'expressed his contempt for German Jews as a whole, his indifference to their fate, and for that matter, his indifference to the fate of millions of Jews elsewhere, just so long as a saving remnant

could be preserved in Palestine'. The diminishing opportunities for emigration to Palestine and the bias towards the young had dramatic
consequences. Jews like the Cohns who had bided their time now found
it had run out. A wave of suicides swept through the ranks of elderly
Zionists who realized their dream was thwarted.[122]

It was not only getting harder to move to Palestine. One country
after another erected barriers to the immigration of Jewish refugees.
Consequently, Jews were now prepared to settle in places that they
would formerly have scoffed at. The main emigration aid agency in Germany, the Hilfsverein, working with the JCA and HICEM, searched
restlessly for havens, interceding with governments to increase numbers
or prevent restrictions. In 1936, South Africa admitted about 2,500
German Jews, then slammed the door. Brazil accepted 1,000, then
reneged on its agreement with HICEM. Even if it was possible to find a
destination, it was becoming prohibitively costly to leave. Due to the
drain on Germany's foreign currency reserves, the Reichsbank lowered
the threshold on personal wealth that was liable to the 'flight tax' from
RM200 to RM50. Moreover, the valuation used 1933 as the benchmark.
In order to cover the amount that the authorities insisted on receiving,
prospective emigrants had to pay over such a large slice of what they
realized in the sale of their assets that little remained with which to
build a new life in another country. Furthermore, the exchange rate
available to those seeking to leave the country permanently was skewed
so that emigrants obtained half of what their Reichmarks were worth in
1933. By 1939, they could expect just 4 per cent of the foreign currency
that their money would once have purchased. Unsurprisingly, those
with substantial assets were inclined to hold on in the hope that they
could survive in Germany with what they had rather than take a
massive loss and have to start all over again with almost nothing.[123]

Despite the election of the Popular Front government in May 1936,
France maintained its restrictive immigration policy. However, the new
administration made a serious effort to alleviate the conditions of the
roughly 10,000 refugees still in the country and dependent on charity.
Most importantly it allowed more of them to work. In a further attempt
to liquidate the refugee problem, the colonial minister, Marius Moutet,
proposed settling at least some on the French colonial island of Madagascar. This idea quickly attracted the enthusiastic attention of the
Polish government, which was looking for places to send Jews considered surplus to the Polish economy. A joint Franco-Polish mission,

largely comprising Jewish experts, went so far as to investigate the possibilities offered by the island. Finally, in May 1938, a new minister for the colonies, Georges Mandel (who was himself Jewish), definitively rejected the plan as unworkable and undesirable.[124]

The only widening crack in the wall was opening into the USA. In US fiscal year 1935–6 the number of applicants receiving approval for an entry visa reached 25 per cent of the quota. In the following year, just under half of the available places were filled, a total of 10,815. This increase followed pressure on the State Department from the White House and lobbying by American Jewish organizations. However, the requirements for aspiring emigrants were so tough that only a fraction of applicants succeeded. Hopefuls had to pass a medical examination and show they possessed the means to support themselves or give proof that they had family in the States who would prevent them becoming a charge on the public purse. Consuls also insisted that emigrants had to buy their own ticket. This rule was intended to stop the importation of foreign labour, but took no account of the possibility that even respectable migrants would be so impoverished as to rely on relatives or contacts in the USA to pay their passage. Although consuls had a good deal of latitude in applying the rules, most stuck to the letter until they could no longer ignore the mayhem at their doorstep.[125]

In December 1937, the Reichsvertretung opened a central office for Jewish emigration that brought together all the relevant agencies under one roof. The accelerating effort to get young people out of Germany testified eloquently to the sense that the community as a whole had no future. Youth Aliyah, a Zionist organization, worked with the RV emigration section to send 12,000 unaccompanied children to Palestine between 1934 and 1939. Resources were poured into non-Zionist initiatives like the training farm at Gross-Breesen, although the scale of its achievements was pitifully small. In all, about 18,400 young people left Germany through such schemes. Jewish organizations also helped non-Aryan children to emigrate. The Paulusbund in Berlin, which looked after the interests of converts, joined with the British-based Inter-Aid Committee to provide education in Britain for 450 Christian children who had fallen foul of the Nuremberg Laws.[126]

The pressure was unrelenting. Directives to exclude Jews from the economy empowered local Nazis, municipal officials, and the Gestapo to deny them the right to carry on trading or intimidate them into closing down their businesses. Under the policy of Aryanization, enterprises

were transferred from Jewish ownership to Germans, often for a fraction of their true value. As the pace of Aryanization accelerated, even
Germans who had looked askance at the violation of property rights felt
compelled to join the gold rush or see rivals prosper. Jews who protested to the authorities against interference with their businesses were
now more likely to be sent to a concentration camp than to get a sympathetic hearing from the Reich Economics Ministry. Yet Jews denied a
licence to trade by the police continued to appeal to administrative
courts and, to the annoyance of the SD, sometimes succeeded.[127]

The result was the virtual collapse of Jewish economic activity outside a handful of large urban communities. The mayor of one small
town in Hesse boasted that 'There are now only just a few Jewish stores
left in Bad Nauheim, but these will disappear as time passes.' The county
commissioner in Gelnhausen, also in Hesse, rejoiced that the economic
influence of the Jews was 'totally extinct'. Aside from a few exceptions,
'commerce with Jews has ceased to exist'. Most of the Jews in the town
were poor and miserable. 'The Aryan population no longer gives them
any attention and they live withdrawn from society.' In other places,
especially with a Catholic population, Jewish traders clung on. The gendarmerie officer in Cham, in eastern Bavaria, reported that the Jews
were 'still enjoying their sales to the rural population. The farmers here
refuse to be enlightened, and they refuse to grasp the paramount aim.'
But the overall trend was all in one direction. As the SD office for the
north-east of Germany reported at the start of 1938, Jews were leaving
the countryside and moving to Berlin. The SD office for the south-east,
based in Breslau, recorded the final dissolution of several small communities. The SD division for the north-west reported that over the
previous year even wealthy Jews had left, 'since in the rural countryside
they have been stripped of almost any source of income'. Only in
Munich was there a reverse pattern. The Munich Gestapo bragged that
the anti-Jewish boycott was well enforced, accompanied by 'compulsion
to transfer businesses to Aryan hands'. Consequently, Jews were fleeing
into rural areas where the recalcitrant Catholic population offered some
degree of succour.[128]

Schacht had resisted just such an onslaught but his ability to impose
order on Aryanization and to prevent arbitrary or illegal acts had ebbed.
Of rather more concern to Schacht personally, he was losing the battle
against Göring for control of the economy. On 26 November 1937 he
tendered his resignation as Reich minister for economics. Hitler, who

now saw him as an obstruction, accepted his departure. Eight weeks later, he sacked Schacht from the presidency of the Reichsbank. To the French Ambassador, François-Poncet, the dismissal of Schacht was 'a warning impossible to disregard'. Schacht's departure sent a tremor of dread through the Jewish community. The Reichsvertretung warned that it would be impossible to maintain 'orderly emigration' unless Jews could continue to earn a living in Germany.[129]

Around the time of Schacht's resignation, Heydrich took stock. The SD Jewish desk estimated that there were 392,000 full Jews left in Germany, 412,000 if converts were included, plus 280,000 half and quarter Jews. Emigration was running at about 2,230 per month and some 107,000 Jews had already left. It was SD policy to achieve the 'total elimination of assimilationism and promotion of emigration'. To do this it was necessary to overcome the resistance of Jews and destroy the support for them amongst Catholics and the Confessing Church. The report took note of the debate for and against the creation of a Jewish state and expressed the SD's view that statehood would be regrettable 'since the Jews could then pursue the boycott of National Socialism more intensively utilizing diplomatic means'.[130]

Uncertainty over the future of Palestine did not cause the SD to falter for one moment in the application of pressure on the Jewish population. The Nazis were not Zionists in any conventional sense of the word: they did not care where Jews went when they left Germany, and treated Palestine as merely a dumping ground. If for any reason it ceased to be available they would force the Jews to go elsewhere. So the SD continued to up the tempo of anti-Jewish actions. Jews still able to practise in various professions, if only for Jewish clients, were now denied licences to work at all. Restaurants and inns were instructed no longer to serve Jews.[131]

The drift of policy was evident to foreign eyes. In April 1938, Pope Pius XI issued a papal encyclical, *Mit Brennender Sorge*, which condemned racism and race-based policies. The encyclical was chiefly intended to defend the prerogatives of the Roman Catholic Church in Germany and to register disquiet over policies of compulsory sterilization. It did not mention Jews explicitly, yet the restatement of Catholic principles in opposition to racial determinism threw a mantle of protection over converts. Jews took heart from the statement, while it emboldened Catholics.[132]

Ambassador Dodd noted in his diary that 'stricter observation and punishment of Jews is evident'. But he had virtually stopped trying to influence the policy-makers in Berlin. His isolation and powerlessness were increased when Sir Arthur Henderson replaced Phipps as British Ambassador. Henderson was an arch-appeaser and Dodd moaned to his diary that he 'seemed not to be aware of British–American opposition to the ruthless Nazi treatment of Catholics, Protestant and Jews'. This was unfair to Henderson insofar as he knew only too well how much Jews were suffering; he just did not think it weighed very heavily against the more serious business of keeping Hitler off the war-path. On 29 December, Dodd left Germany for the last time. He returned to the United States with a sense of relief to be away from Berlin and a grim presentiment about what the future would bring. The passenger ship carrying him homeward also carried a large contingent of refugees setting off for new lives in America.[133]

The Jews in Germany entered 1938 with a feeling of dread and growing helplessness. While the Vatican's critique of National Socialism had provided a lift to morale, the departure of Schacht was devastating. This was not because of any false notion that he had been their champion or protector. Rather, it was because his displacement confirmed that the radicals were in the driving seat and that the trend to squeeze Jews out of any economic niches left to them was a centrally mandated and driven policy. Even so, Jews continued to resist. The World Jewish Congress took advantage of the fact that the Free City of Danzig was now the last part of Germany under League of Nations control to submit a petition to prevent the extension of the Nuremberg Laws into the province. The NSDAP had enjoyed an absolute majority in the Free State of Danzig's legislature since June 1933, but final authority lay with a League-appointed commissioner and hundreds of Jews had moved from the Reich into the relative shelter of the port city. This precarious haven would survive a little longer.[134]

Within the Reich itself, Jews abandoned any hope that National Socialism was ephemeral or vulnerable to domestic opposition. Victor Klemperer catalogued the growing acceptance of Nazism with a mixture of fascination, disbelief and horror. He observed how the traditional prejudices of ordinary Germans formed a bridge to the regime and eased their acquiescence. In October 1936, the local librarian, Fräulein Roth, visited him after he was banned from using the facility. She was 'vehemently opposed to the Nazis' but conceded that some of their anti-Jewish measures were fine. She told him '"If they had expelled the Eastern Jews or had excluded Jews from the bench, <u>that</u> at least would have been comprehensible."' To her their offence was not that they abrogated the civil and human rights of innocent citizens; they just went too far. A year later and Klemperer detected how the idea of the Volksgemeinschaft had become common sense, bringing with it the exclusion of certain groups without the need for conscious hatred. He noted the case of a man who was no 'Jew-hater' but articulated National Socialist ideas unthinkingly. 'About the necessity of the community of the people, of distinct races; of the identity of the law and power, of the unquestionable superiority of the new German army . . . of the need to repel communism . . . the man is quite unaware of how much of a National Socialist he is . . . I said to myself once again, that Hitlerism is after all more deeply and firmly rooted in the nation and corresponds more to the German nature than I would like to admit.'[135]

This did not mean that the security of the regime was assured against external shocks. Klemperer continued to hope that Hitler would launch a rash foreign policy adventure, stumble and fall. But even if Hitlerism passed, Klemperer felt irremediably alienated from the German nation: 'my inner sense of belonging is gone'. He spoke for many others whose identity as German Jews had been smashed beyond repair.[136]

Jews lived in ever greater isolation from the rest of the population. Looking back from exile, Heinemann Stern, the principal of a Jewish school in Berlin and a member of the executive of the Centralverein, saw his world shrinking by degrees. He was used to taking an annual holiday at Bad Reinerz, a mountain resort in Silesia that had once been patronized by Felix Mendelssohn-Bartholdy. Stern liked to patronize a cafe that bore a plaque commemorating the composition of a much loved Mendelssohn song. But in 1937 he noticed that the plaque had gone. When he went to the toilet he found a sign saying 'No Jews'. The innkeeper explained that he had put the sign there rather than deter Jewish customers from entering at all, although that did not make Stern feel any less uncomfortable. 'Private relations – or, to be more precise, human relations in general – between us and our surroundings tore, loosened, vanished. The result was isolation, and in the end isolation is just another word for slow death.'[137]

The indignities and loneliness were most acute in rural areas. Hans Winterfeldt was born in the small town of Lippehne in Brandenburg and was seven years old in 1933. The first attempt at a boycott of his father's shop was ineffectual and business continued much as before. But by 1935 'it was impossible for us to spend much time in any public places'. For relief, each Christmas holiday Hans' parents sent him to the capital with a group organized by the RjF. He noticed that 'people didn't take the Nazis seriously in Berlin'. People there told him 'the Nazi regime would not be able to hold on much longer'. However, in 1937 his father saw no alternative to selling up and moving to Berlin, where he obtained a licence to work as a travelling salesman. In a tragi-comic footnote to this tale, some time after they arrived in Berlin his myopic grandmother got into trouble for sitting on a bench that was only for Aryans. She moved back to the village where she at least knew her way around.[138]

A steady number of Jews responded to social death by taking their own lives. Each instance of suicide was regarded as a victory by National Socialists. In May 1937, the mayor of Amt Altenrüthen reported with evident satisfaction that 'The Jew butcher Sally Pollack, resident here, committed suicide a few days ago by hanging himself.'[139]

Jewish women experienced the mounting pressure differently to men. As the wider world contracted, the domestic environment became more important as a place of comfort and consolation. Domestic Jewish rituals, such as celebrating the Sabbath, offered a chance for parents to make their children feel that being Jewish was not merely a disadvantage or a burden. Mothers had to offer support and affirmation to make up for the cold, if not hostile, atmosphere experienced by children still getting an education in state schools. They inevitably took the lion's share of this responsibility because their husbands were working or, increasingly, resided abroad.[140]

For single women there were special dangers. A friendly or intimate relationship with a non-Jew could result in charges of Rassenschande. Gerta Pfeffer, a textile designer working in a weaving mill in southern Germany, dreaded overtures from 'Aryan' men. Paradoxically, the passage of the Nuremberg Laws made her feel even more vulnerable. 'I was afraid to go home at night because I always feared encountering a group of unwanted admirers. By daylight they cursed me as a Jewess, and at night they wanted to kiss me. They were disgusting.' The threat of punishment for making sexual overtures towards an Ayran could be used to coerce a Jewish woman into intimate relations. She could deny that she had acted voluntarily and accuse the male of initiating the encounter, but he could always claim he did not know the woman he was hitting on was a Jew and blame her for instigating the liaison. Rosy Geiger-Kullman remembered that 'During the Hitler era I had the immense burden of rejecting brazen advances from SS and SA men. They often pestered me and asked for dates. Each time I answered: "I'm sorry that I can't accept, I'm married." If I had said I was a Jewess they would have turned the tables and insisted that I approached them.' Since neither party to such a coercive relationship would want it known about, it is impossible to know how many Jewish women were cornered in this way. The situation was made harder for Jewish women because the shelters in public places, particularly railway stations, that were once run by the League of Jewish Women were shut down when the League's activities were circumscribed.[141]

After the race laws were passed, the rate of denunciation for Rassenschande increased steadily. The annual number reported to the Würzburg Gestapo rose from three in 1934 to thirty-one in 1936, falling back to twenty-one in 1937 and twenty-eight in 1938. The dropping-off reflects the greater caution exercised by men and women and the effect of intimidation on relationships. Hans Kosterlitz, the managing director of a 'fixed price shop' in Uelzen, a small town in Lower Saxony, had to conduct his relationship with his girlfriend Trudi in secret. 'We were truly playing with fire, but we were blind with passion. We were attempting something that in our situation amounted to challenging destiny itself.' Hans passed up the chance to emigrate to Chile because of his love affair. Then, in 1935, a new employee in the shop began to pay attention to Trudi. He was in the SS and Hans found himself having to watch the courtship proceed under his nose without being able to do or say a thing. Finally Trudi ended his agony by taking up with the SS man. 'Her weak character was broken by the atmosphere in which she was living. As for me, I had rescued my freedom, but at what a price! ... I cursed Hitler and his bandits, who revelled in extortion, even when it touched on the most personal relations a man can ever know: love.' Hans soon emigrated to Italy and from there to Shanghai.[142]

The Nuremberg Laws empowered the authorities to inquire into what had once been the most private affairs of men and women and, by policing relationships, exert power. In October 1936, the District Office in Bad Brückenau, a spa town in northern Bavaria, became worried because of a large influx of Jews into two Jewish-owned hotels. Disturbed by the possibility that Jews might interfere with the young women employed in the two establishments, officials ordered the police to keep watch. Fortunately for the guests and the Jewish owners, 'Despite very strict surveillance, it was not possible to confirm that there was race defilement in the Jewish hotels.' The race laws made no distinction between business and pleasure. In Breslau four Jewish women of 'ill repute' were taken into custody and sent to a concentration camp. The Gestapo fumed that it was 'absolutely intolerable that these women should engage in sexual intercourse with Aryan males in exchange for money'. The chief public prosecutor in Mannheim expressed concern over the case of a Jewish madam who was running a bordello even though the prostitutes were all Aryan. There was, however, a danger that the public might think that the prostitutes were giving their services to Jewish men. In the Third Reich, love did not vanquish everything. In Karlsruhe, in 1936, a shoe-maker was sentenced to several years in prison for having sexual relations with his Jewish girlfriend. Almost as soon as he was released he resumed the relationship. Somehow the authorities were informed that 'he had sexual intercourse with her repeatedly'. He was re-arrested, tried, found guilty of Rassenschande a second time and sentenced to another lengthy prison term.[143]

PART THREE

POGROM

1938–1939

Austria

Victor Klemperer greeted 1938 with gloom. He briefly hoped that Schacht's ejection from government might presage an internal power struggle. Instead the regime celebrated its fifth anniversary with sublime self-confidence. 'I no longer really believe I shall live to see a change,' he sighed. Despite domestic success and stability he noticed that the Jewish question was being ramped up again; new regulations prevented Jews from working in a slew of professional occupations. A month later he listened to Hitler make a speech to the Reichstag that sounded like nothing less than 'a threat of war'.[1]

Hitler's belligerence and the heightened pressure on Jews were linked. To hard-core National Socialists the Jews were the enemy. It made no sense to fight international Jewry while leaving Jews in Germany free to sabotage the economy or poison morale. That was the mistake made in 1914–18. The means to destroy the basis for Jewish existence now converged with the ends set out by the Four-Year Plan. Denying Jews the opportunity to make a living would hamper their potential for economic destabilization and, ultimately, force them to leave. Starving Jewish enterprises of resources, as well as markets, would mean more raw materials to direct elsewhere. Soaking the Jews through draconian taxation would provide a welcome income stream for the Finance Ministry as it strained to pay for rearmament.

From this point, persecution of the Jews became ancillary to making war. Their fate would be determined more by Machtpolitik – the setting and achievement of geo-strategic goals by diplomacy or force of arms – than by Judenpolitik. To be sure, Hitler's Jew-hatred, shared by his inner circle and echoed by the Nazi Party, commingled with the aspiration to make Germany into a great power; but it was not a driving force in and of itself. Rather, Germany's economic exigencies, strategic priorities, military successes and setbacks would decisively influence how Jews were treated.

Hitler was approaching fifty and feeling anxious about his health. Would he have long enough to overturn the Versailles settlement and create an empire to sustain the German people in the coming struggle for global domination between Aryan civilization and international Jewry? In the memorandum for the Four-Year Plan he put Germany's civilian leadership on notice that he was preparing the country for war. On 5 November 1937 he met with the military leadership, ostensibly to settle competing claims between branches of the armed forces for the allocation of resources. The meeting was attended by General Werner von Blomberg, minister of war, Admiral Erich Raeder, commander of the navy, General Werner von Fritsch, commander-in-chief of the army, Göring, commander of the Luftwaffe, and Konstantin von Neurath, foreign minister. Typically for Hitler an initiative intended to solve a relatively limited practical problem actually ended up by going in a radically new direction, creating more dilemmas.[2]

Hitler reiterated his conviction that Germany could not solve its shortages of food and raw material through autarky or trade its way out of trouble. Salvation lay in the acquisition of a continental empire. To the question of how this could be achieved Hitler answered with brutal simplicity: 'Germany's problems could be solved only by the use of force.' Nor was this some vague, futuristic aspiration. The necessary steps had to be taken by 1943–5 because, by then, Germany's enemies would be too powerful and the German armed forces would have lost their manpower and technical edge. It might be possible, and necessary, to move even sooner if France collapsed or got into a war with Italy. In any eventuality, the immediate targets were Austria and Czechoslovakia. The 'annexation of Czechoslovakia and Austria would mean the acquisition of foodstuffs for 5–6 million people, on the assumption that the compulsory emigration of 2 million people from Czechoslovakia and a million from Austria was practicable'. It would also greatly strengthen Germany's geo-strategic position and release forces 'for other purposes'.[3]

Blomberg, Fritsch and Neurath were disconcerted by their Führer's game plan. In order to deal with a shortage of resources he was planning to take on Europe's strongest military land power ensconced behind the most elaborate fortifications ever seen, the Maginot Line. Not only was he planning to wage a war that was bound to consume the very resources it was supposed to secure, but even if it ended successfully it would still involve the forced displacement of millions of people in order to free up sufficient foodstuffs for the Volk. However, Hitler was determined not to allow the diffidence of his generals or diplomats to hold him up. In the new year he embarked on a cabinet reshuffle, sacking Blomberg and replacing Neurath with Joachim von Ribbentrop, who had run the Nazi Party office for foreign affairs and served as ambassador in London for a brief and inglorious year. Fritsch was removed a few weeks later on trumped-up charges of homosexual activity. The new cabinet that convened for the first (and last) time on 5 February 1938 also included Walther Funk, the freshly appointed Reich minister for economics, who was wholly subordinate to Göring's Office for the Four-Year Plan. The command structure of the army was reorganized and dozens of senior figures removed. A cadre of young officers who were more in tune with National Socialism were promoted to key staff and field positions.[4]

It was not long before Hitler made his move. Since becoming chancellor he had hankered after the unification of Austria with Germany and used the Austrian Nazi Party as a tool to this end. His meddling in 1934, before he had cleared the way with Italy, led to an embarrassing setback. But four years later Italy and Germany were allies: Germany had supported Italy after the invasion of Abyssinia provoked international condemnation, they had signed a formal pact to fight communism, and their troops fought side by side with Franco's forces in Spain. At a meeting with Göring in September 1937, Mussolini indicated his acquiescence should the Austrian NSDAP make another bid for power. On cue from Berlin the banned Austrian Nazis set out to render Austria ungovernable. As disorder spread, Hitler demanded to see the Austrian prime minister, Kurt Schuschnigg. They met on 12 February 1938 at Berchtesgaden, the Führer's lofty residence in the Bavarian Alps. In this intimidating spot Schuschnigg was told he must legalize the Austrian NSDAP, appoint its leader Arthur Seyss-Inquart as minister of the interior, and turn Austria into a vassal state of the Third Reich. Schuschnigg returned to Vienna, but instead of submitting he cast around for some device to deflect his slavering neighbour. He came up with a plan to hold a referendum that would enable Austrians (over the age of twenty-five) to express their view of whether the country should remain independent. When the dodge was announced on 9 March, with polling set to take place just four days later, Hitler was furious. He ordered the newly appointed commander-in-chief of the

army, General Walther von Brauchitsch, to prepare an invasion before
the vote could be held. While the Wehrmacht scrambled into action,
Hitler issued an ultimatum to Schuschnigg to call off the referendum
and resign in favour of Seyss-Inquart. During 11 March, as uniformed
Austrian SA and SS men took to the streets, Schuschnigg's resolve
collapsed. Seyss-Inquart took his place as chancellor and immediately
called in the German army to 'restore' order.[5]

Even before the first motorized units of the Wehrmacht, much
depleted by breakdowns, arrived in Vienna, the Austrian SA and SS had
taken control of the streets. A reign of terror descended on the city's
Jewish inhabitants that exceeded anything experienced by Jews in Germany. In the words of the playwright Carl Zuckmayer, 'That night all
hell broke loose. The netherworld had opened its portals and spewed
out its basest, most horrid, and filthiest spirits. The city changed into a
nightmare painting reminiscent of Hieronymous Bosch . . . What was
being unleashed here had nothing to do with the Machtergreifung, the
Nazi seizure of power in Germany, which at least externally seemed to
proceed legally and was witnessed by parts of the population with dis-
pleasure and skepticism or with simpleminded national idealism. What
was being unleashed here was the revolt of envy; malevolence; bitterness; blind, vicious vengefulness – all other voices were condemned to
silence.'[6]

Around 176,000 Jews lived in Austria's capital, comprising 90 per
cent of the country's Jewish population. Although Jews had dwelled in
Vienna for centuries, the bulk of the community had arived quite
recently. The first wave of migration came from the provinces of the
Austrian Empire, mainly Bohemia and Moravia, after 1867, when Jews
in Austria gained civil rights. The Great War and its aftermath saw a
second influx, mainly war refugees from the eastern borderlands of
the Austrian Empire, in particular Galicia. These Jews enjoyed spectacular social mobility. It was not unusual for Jewish men whose fathers
or grandfathers had pursued traditional Jewish occupations in the
countryside to become lawyers, physicians or writers. Jews dominated
the free professions: they constituted over two thirds of the capital's
lawyers and nearly half of all its doctors. Yet, while Vienna boasted a
large and sophisticated Jewish middle class (typified by Stefan Zweig
and Sigmund Freud), in the inner-city districts there was a substantial
concentration of less well-off Jewish craftsmen, shopkeepers and traders. A significant section of the community were Yiddish-speaking,

Orthodox Jews. Some 30 per cent of Viennese Jews were in receipt of welfare. In addition, thousands of German Jewish refugees had entered Austria over the previous five years, many of whom lived on aid from the Israelitische Kultusgemeinde (IKG), the central communal organization. While the leaders of the IKG had not harboured much affection for Chancellor Schuschnigg, his right-wing Catholic politics or his neo-fascist Fatherland Front, they nevertheless appreciated that he was a patriot and, more to the point, their only shield against Hitler. The IKG had made a generous donation to Schuschnigg's referendum fighting fund. The Austrian Nazis knew this and it was pay-back time.[7]

George Gedye, the Vienna correspondent for the *Daily Telegraph*, had a ringside view of the ensuing drama. From the window of his office he could see up and down Vienna's main shopping street and towards the alleys that led into the historic Jewish quarter. As soon as the appointment of Seyss-Inquart as chancellor was announced, he saw SA and SS men, along with hordes of Nazi Party members, now sporting the lapel badge that proclaimed their allegiance, invade the districts where Jews lived. They smashed up shops, ransacked apartments, and stole cars belonging to Jews. The permissive atmosphere was such that Nazi activists would not only steal cars from their Jewish owners, but demand 'petrol money' from them. Policemen just watched. William Shirer, now attached to American radio network CBS, was down on the Graben amongst the mob. He noticed that many police officers were already wearing makeshift swastika armbands. No one lifted a finger to stop the wanton destruction. 'Young toughs were heaving paving blocks into the windows of Jews' shops. The crowd roared with delight.' Gedye witnessed pillaging on an industrial scale. 'Outside a big Jewish store stood a string of lorries into which the storm troopers were pitching all kinds of millinery goods as they took them from the shop. Police stood by to see that they were not interfered with.'[8]

Hitler's triumphal entry into Vienna on the afternoon of 14 March and his speech on the Heldenplatz the following morning drew vast crowds onto the streets. Ruth Maier, a Jewish schoolgirl who had just turned eighteen, recalled the scenes in her diary. 'All the Austrians were celebrating and jumping about in excitement. Flags were hoisted, people hugged and kissed each other in sheer joy.' The obverse of this euphoria was an outpouring of hate for the capital's Jews. The presence of German troops made no difference. They were impressively well disciplined, but held aloof from the mayhem. Gedye recorded that 'day after day, Nazi storm troopers, surrounded by jostling crowds, jeering and laughing mobs of "golden Viennese hearts" dragged Jews from shops, offices and homes, men and women, put scrubbing brushes in their hands, splashed them well with acid, and made them go down on their hands and knees and scrub away for hours at the hapless task of removing Schuschnigg propaganda. All this I could watch from my office window overlooking the Graben.'[9]

The brutality inflicted on Vienna's Jews was not random and nor was it simply revenge for the support they had given to the deposed chancellor or their attachment to the Austrian Republic. Gedye noted a pattern of ritual degradation. The Austrian Nazis targeted well-dressed Jews, especially women. They were forced to engage in tasks that were socially as well as politically symbolic. SS men seized Jews and took groups, fifty at a time, to clean the latrines at the SS barracks. Crowds that gathered to watch Jews perform these labours jeered "'Work at last for the Jews'' . . . "We thank our Führer for finding work for the Jews." Where Jewish shops and stores were not wrecked, they were subjected to a throttling boycott. Aryans who purchased at the wrong place could find themselves pilloried. In organizing these displays, Austrian Nazis, many drawn from the lower middle classes and the unemployed, were venting years of envy towards the Jews who they perceived as the idle rich or business competitors. They relished the reversal of roles: now the Jews were the ones performing menial tasks. The crowds of Viennese Nazis were symbolically marking the end of a regime that had protected Jews, demonstrating the complete vulnerability of this minority. It was also a terrifying message to the remaining Austrian loyalists and the tens of thousands of working-class Viennese who had supported the labour movement.[10]

After a week of untrammelled violence and plunder Heydrich ordered the German security forces to impose order. Contrary to appearances at the time, and the common interpretation of historians subsequently, the explosion of anti-Semitism in Vienna was not the fulfilment of Nazi goals or even the culmination of the hatred Hitler claimed to have learned in the city three decades earlier. It was actually the result of the Germans *not* being in control. As events unfolded over the next week it became clear that the new management had not anticipated how the Austrian NSDAP would behave. Nor did they approve. The disgraceful scenes that were reported around the world fuelled 'atrocity propaganda', although this was not what bothered Heydrich or his masters in Berlin. The incoming Germans were alarmed that if the plunder continued there would be nothing left for them individually or for the Reich.[11]

Although Hitler had long dreamed about combining Austria and Germany, it was characteristic that he had given little thought to the practical details of how this was to be accomplished. Would Austria become part of a confederation or be absorbed into the Reich, and if the latter to what extent would it preserve its regional identity? The day after Hitler arrived in Vienna he announced to a frenzied crowd in the Heldenplatz that Austria would be annexed to the Reich. Initially the territory would be ruled from Berlin through a Reich Commissar. Josef Bürckel, who had overseen the reincorporation of the Saarland, was named to the post of Reich Commissar for the Reunification of Austria with the German Reich. Subsequently the Ostmark more or less disappeared as a distinct territorial unit, replaced in 1942 by the two Reich regions of the Alps and Danube. Before then the Austrians were given the chance to register their enthusiasm for annexation by voting in a plebiscite.[12]

The Reich security apparatus was quicker off the mark. For Himmler and Heydrich the occupation of Austria offered an opportunity to prove their worth and extend their powers. They were amongst the first Germans to arrive in Vienna on 12 March. Later, Heinrich Müller, head of the Gestapo, was brought in to set up a local office subordinate to Berlin. In due course, he handed over to Franz Stahlecker. The first task of the SD and the Sipo, security police, was to arrest political opponents. However, Heydrich soon realized that the greed and indiscipline of the local Nazis was almost as much of a liability to the Reich as deliberate opposition. On 17 March he advised Bürckel that unless the depredation and random violence was brought under control, the security police would start arresting Austrian NSDAP activists. Four days later the Interior Ministry in Berlin issued a similar call to Bürckel. The 'foreign domination' of the economy would be tackled through the law once the plebiscite and elections to the German Reichstag were held on 10 April.[13]

Imposing control from Berlin did not end the terror or thieving. It simply became better organized and more purposeful. Shirer lived with his heavily pregnant wife in a rented apartment next to the Rothschild Palais, home to the Viennese branch of the Rothschild family. The SS requisitioned the building to serve as their headquarters (Eichmann was given an office there). But no sooner were the guardians of order installed as his neighbours than Shirer saw SS officers 'carting up silver and other loot from the basement. One had a gold-framed picture under his arm.' Gedye chanced upon a vehicle park packed with cars that bore the SS sign hastily stencilled on their mudguards. The ritualized abuse of Jews continued. Two weeks after the occupation Shirer reported, 'On the streets today groups of Jews, with jeering storm troopers over them and taunting crowds around them on their hands and knees scrubbing the Schuschnigg signs off the sidewalks. Many Jews killed themselves. All sorts of reports of Nazi sadism.' Both Shirer and Gedye reported that at the Seitenstettengasse Synagogue, which also served as a community centre in the heart of the Jewish district, Orthodox Jews were forced to clean toilets while wearing tefillin (phylacteries), which were customarily donned for morning prayer.[14]

While his colleagues in the security police were hunting down political opponents, Adolf Eichmann was deputed to deal with the Jews. The template for his operation was the extension of Judenpolitik into Upper Silesia in May 1937. His immediate objectives were to arrest the Jewish leadership, suppress the assimilation-oriented communal organizations, seize their records and send the papers back to Berlin for analysis. His long-term goal was to implement the SD policy of engineering Jewish emigration. In this respect he found his work was hindered by the chaos that enveloped the Jewish population. Without leaders, official guidance, or institutions, Jews who wanted to emigrate were forced to scurry from one government and municipal office to the next with only a dim idea of what was needed to leave the country let alone any inkling of where they could go. They were forced to queue outside embassies and consulates for hours, presenting an inviting target for abuse and violence. If they managed to get into official buildings, Austrian officials often delighted in sending them away empty-handed. When Leo Lauterbach, a senior executive in the World Zionist Organization, visited Vienna in mid-April he found a situation 'characterised by confusion, uncertainty and a state of flux'. There seemed to be 'no established authority from whom the official policy could be reliably ascertained and whose intervention solicited'. This was the exact opposite of what the SD wanted to achieve.[15]

In a bid to re-establish order and get emigration moving Eichmann summoned the Jewish communal functionaries who were still at large and told them what the SD wanted. When the terrified Jews grasped that the security police were primarily interested in emigration they explained what was needed and sought their help to get communal agencies up and running again. Eichmann, in turn, realized that he could harness the willingness of Jewish officeholders to his own ends. He arranged for the release of key administrators from detention and interviewed several until he found the right type to do his bidding. Dr Josef Löwenherz, a member of the IKG executive, appealed to him as the kind of energetic, forceful personality needed to get things done. He gave Löwenherz a pencil and some paper and told him he had twenty-four hours to outline exactly what was required to enable the community to resume functioning. Then he sent him back to his cell. When they met the next day, Löwenherz handed Eichmann a list of essential offices and personnel. Eichmann then obtained the approval of Heydrich for the re-establishment of the IKG, the Palestine Office and the Zionist Association, all with the sole aim of assisting Jews to emigrate. Crucially, the Jewish organizations would operate under the supervision of the SD.[16]

Eichmann thereby achieved a dramatic accretion to the power of the Sipo-SD. He had been sent to Vienna with modest executive powers that extended little further than organizing the arrest of some Jews. But through the guise of furthering Jewish emigration he ended up controlling the destiny of the entire Jewish population. Probably without even realizing it he showed how Heydrich and the security apparatus could create a domain over which they ruled unchallenged simply by gaining the right to implement SD policy. The Jews may even have contributed to this forward leap by embracing cooperation with the SD, if only on the grounds that Eichmann seemed genuinely interested in establishing order and helping them to escape the madhouse that the Austrian Nazis had created.

The Anschluss led to another unforeseen development that was soon to have fateful consequences. Within Hitler's inner circle Göring had been the most bullish about taking over Austria, which he saw as a valuable source of raw materials, labour and financial assets. It was, therefore, infuriating to see the Austrian Nazis siphoning off Jewish wealth for personal gain, destroying the stock of Jewish enterprises, and appropriating businesses in an uncontrolled bonanza. By mid-April around 7,000 Jewish-owned enterprises had been 'Aryanized' by semi-official 'commissions' of local Nazis using the threat of a beating or imprisonment to get their way. Usually they acted on their own authority and were doing little more than putting a rival out of business or lining their own pockets by purchasing a commercial concern at a knock-down price and then selling it on for a rather more realistic one. This was intolerable to the Nazi leadership in Berlin.[17]

On 11 April, Göring met with Hans Fischböck, the minister for trade in the transitional government in Vienna, Walter Funk, the Reich economics minister, and other officials to review the incorporation of Austria into the German economy. When the question of Jewish-owned property came up for discussion the delegation from Vienna proposed to register all Jewish assets in the Ostmark. This amounted to taking out an option on everything that was left and sticking on it a notice saying 'Hands Off, Property of the Reich'. The idea appealed to Göring, who immediately resolved to apply a similar measure in Germany. On 13 April, Seyss-Inquart issued the 'Law Concerning the Appointment of Commissarial Administrators and Supervisory Personnel' with the intention of finally curbing the 'wild commissions'. Two weeks later Göring published a decree for the registration and disposal of Jewish assets in the whole of the Reich, explicitly empowering the Office of the Four-Year Plan to 'undertake measures in order to guarantee utilization of the registered property in the interest of the German economy'.[18]

Fischböck and his colleagues had unwittingly made a breakthrough in Judenpolitik and established a model that would be replicated again and again. Control of the German economy was already centralized in the hands of Göring and bureaucrats at the Office of the Four Year Plan, but as yet they lacked a coherent set of policies or tools for use against the Jews. There were no laws to enable Jewish enterprises to be taken over or dissolved; there was not even a definition of a 'Jewish enterprise'. Jewish-owned businesses might be driven to the wall or their proprietors forced to sell out, but this was most commonly the result of local action by NSDAP party bosses. Occasionally, Aryanization took the form of a hostile takeover by a financial institution or a corporation. The developments in Vienna opened Göring's eyes to the possibilities of comprehensive legislation to eliminate Jews from the economy in an orderly fashion, maximizing the benefits to the Reich and the preparations for war.[19]

Thus the occupation of Austria and the despoliation of the Austrian Jews was not a linear development of Nazi Judenpolitik. The one did not lead to the other. On the contrary, by accident Vienna turned into a laboratory for the implementation of radical new ideas that, once tried and tested, were imported back into Germany.

The following month, a Property Transfer Office was set up in Vienna to evaluate Jewish-owned firms officially and ensure that the change of ownership was legal even if it was nowhere near fair. By August, 23,000 concerns of various sizes had ceased to exist or been placed under new management. Great uncertainty still remained over the status of property that had been seized before the new legislation. That was only solved retrospectively in October and the authorities had to accept that they would get only a fraction of the total wealth robbed from Jews in the first chaotic weeks. The veneer of legality and subsequent claims that the new rulers had deliberately set out to rationalize the Jewish sector of the economy were, at best, ex-post-facto justifications for larceny and extortion.[20]

The sudden imposition on Austrian Jews of the accumulated German anti-Jewish legislation of half a decade also had unintended consequences. On 15 March all state officials wishing to remain in post were required to take an oath to Adolf Hitler. Jews were forbidden to swear allegiance to the Führer and were therefore dismissed. The Ministry of Justice summarily sacked all Jewish and half-Jewish judges and lawyers. There were no exceptions for those who had performed military service. Jews were no longer allowed to practise any form of law. The universities first announced that no Jews would be admitted, then expelled Jews who were already taking courses. All Jewish teaching staff were dismissed within the month. Jews were sacked from newspapers, theatres, orchestras and the opera houses. Since they had played a disproportionate part in Vienna's cultural life the effect was devastating. The same was true of their presence in the medical profession. Suddenly thousands of families had no breadwinner and Jewish men had no prospect of earning a living. When Eichmann permitted the resurrection of the IKG, Löwenherz stressed that it was essential to allow the community to organize welfare services. Bizarrely, at the same time as Eichmann collected a huge fine from the Viennese Jews as a punishment for supporting the Schuschnigg referendum, the German authorities had to lend the IKG 600,000–700,000 Reichsmarks to get its relief operation going. Soon the IKG was providing free meals to about 15,000 Jews every day. Less than 5 per cent of Jews of working age any longer had jobs.[21]

The impoverishment of the community threatened to work against emigration. In May, Eichmann gave the IKG and the Palestine Office a target of sending 20,000 Jews abroad. But few countries were prepared to accept penniless refugees. Before long, Bürckel and Fischböck realized that they faced the prospect of ruling a city with an immovable mass of destitute Jews. While Nazis puzzled over this dilemma, the IKG came up with a solution: Jews in Britain and America would fund their emigration. With Eichmann's agreement, Löwenherz arranged for the JDC and the Council for German Jewry to pay $50,000 per month into a special account. Only the IKG could access the account and the money could be used only for emigration costs. There was a further twist to the scheme. When rich Jews exchanged local currency for dollars, the rate of exchange was so skewed that the transaction generated extra income for the IKG. This revenue covered its running costs and augmented the funds needed to finance emigration by the poorest section of the Jewish population.[22]

However, obtaining the necessary papers to emigrate was still long drawn out and sometimes perilous. Jews had to sell property, settle all debts, clear any outstanding bills, pay municipal and state taxes, and get numerous documents to qualify for an exit visa. Officials were often unhelpful or malicious, turning Jews away or inventing obstacles. It was not unusual for a Jew to get a time-limited entry visa to another country only to see it elapse before he or she had completed the paperwork to leave. Whether Eichmann recognized that the entire process could be accelerated if the necessary offices were brought together under one roof or whether the initiative came from Jewish functionaries is not clear. But once again he ordered Löwenherz to draw up a plan. The result was the Zentralstelle für jüdische Auswanderung, the Central Office for Jewish Emigration. Eichmann submitted the proposal to Bürckel, who consulted with Berlin before agreeing.[23]

The Central Office for Jewish Emigration opened for business on 20 August 1938, with Stahlecker as the nominal head and Eichmann as the day-to-day manager. Superficially it was intended to expedite Jewish emigration, but its creation had more far-reaching implications. By subordinating all Jewish organizational activity to the furtherance of emigration and subordinating control of emigration to the Sipo-SD, Eichmann effectively gave the security apparatus a controlling interest in all Jewish matters. The Zentralstelle was a decisive step towards placing the fate of the Jews in the hands of the most radical element of the Nazi power structure. It also inaugurated the system by which the

Sipo-SD could dramatically expand its operations at no extra cost and with the minimum of additional manpower. The Jews did the work and the overheads were covered by money squeezed from them. The emigration office was, amongst other things, a ferociously efficient means of stripping Jews of their assets. As well as paying regular taxes, Jews applying to emigrate had to pay a flight tax and an 'atonement tax'; they had to liquidate their property and exchange their wealth for a relatively tiny proportion of its true value in the form of foreign currency. To the delight of Göring and the Finance Ministry, this foreign currency was not even coming out of Germany's own reserves: it was supplied by Jews abroad. Eichmann's enterprise was so successful that it was soon taken up as the model for the removal of the Jews from the Old Reich.[24]

The imposition of German rule over Austria was so sudden and brutal it gave Austrian Jews almost no time to adapt. Unlike Jews in Germany they were not able to equip institutions gradually to cope with the onslaught. Overnight all points of reference disappeared. Jewish children in school were suddenly ostracized. Philipp Flesch, a teacher in a state school, recalled that a teacher who had been dismissed for violent Nazi activism was brought directly from prison to be the school's new headmaster. Ruth Maier was forced to move to an overcrowded Jewish school to continue her education. It was run by Orthodox and Zionist Jews with whom she had nothing in common. Jewish ex-soldiers put on their medals when they ventured into the streets in the belief that decorations for valour would offer a degree of protection from the anti-Semitic mobs, only to be mocked and abused. An ex-officer who was blinded during the war found a chest full of ribbons of no avail when he appealed against the confiscation of his business. A Nazi official told him, 'you can shove that Habsburg stuff up your ass. Shove off, and don't come back . . .' Private property was no longer secure and the home no longer a sanctuary. Baruch Zuckerman, a representative of the World Jewish Congress who was based in Trieste, wrote to Nahum Goldmann that Jews were 'constantly taken out of their homes and forced to clean and scrape slogans from the walls and sidewalks'. The number of Jewish funerals rose from three or four per day to 140. Zuckerman drily informed Goldmann that 'suicides and heart failures are the majority'.[25]

As the world of Austrian Jews collapsed, hundreds succumbed to despair and took their own lives. George Gedye found this quiet surrender in the fragile privacy of their homes even worse than the assaults and humiliation that he witnessed outdoors. 'Much more terrifying was the acceptance of suicide as a perfectly normal and natural incident by every Jewish household. It is quite impossible to convey to anyone outside Austria in how matter-of-fact a way the Jews of Austria to-day refer to this way out of their agony.' His Jewish friends 'spoke to one of their intention to commit suicide with no more emotion than they had formerly talked of making an hour's journey by train'. Many of those arrested and sent to concentration camps died in custody, even though they were fit young men, and were cremated without ceremony. It was common to hear that a family received a curt note informing them that 'Your Jew is dead. Pick up the urn.'[26]

Reactions to the mayhem in Austria

Newspaper readers around the world were well informed about the grotesque scenes enacted on the streets of Vienna. Reporters like William Shirer went to great lengths to get the story out. Denied facilities to broadcast from local studios and distrustful of the prospects in Berlin, he flew to Amsterdam and thence to London, where it was nearly midnight when he finally transmitted his account of Austria's extinction. Descriptions of the atrocities agitated public opinion, but the governments of the democracies seemed at a loss for a response.[27]

However, it would be impossible to avoid the tidal wave of refugees set off by the Anschluss. The president of the Jewish Refugees Committee (JRC) in Britain warned the Home Office that it could not support an influx of Austrian Jews on top of those Jews it was already maintaining (although only 11,000 German Jews had entered and remained in England, many of whom came with assets). In view of the looming crisis the Cabinet Committee on Refugees convened for the first time since 1933. The Home Office, fearing that Jews would arrive from Austria posing as tourists and then seek to stay, recommended the imposition of visas. The committee, worried by high levels of anti-Semitism in Britain, agreed to this. As a result, British consuls in Austria were inundated with applications that they had to vet. Male applicants were scrutinized most closely. It was considered easier to screen women who were applying to come to Britain to work as domestic servants. Over half of those admitted, some 20,000 before September 1939, were female. To ease the burden on staff in its Aliens Department, the Home Office delegated the vetting of professionals to specialist refugee committees. Hundreds of doctors and psychiatrists reached the UK thanks to their efforts. Sigmund Freud, who arrived in London on 6 June, was the most famous refugee to reach Britain. It took Herculean efforts involving supporters from several countries to extract him and his family. Few Viennese Jews were fortunate to have such assistance. They were reduced to sending letters to relatives pleading for a financial guarantee or an offer of employment in an acceptable occupation, usually menial labour or domestic service.[28]

Only about 600–700 Austrian Jews were able to enter France. Since its election, the Popular Front government had struggled to reconcile humanitarian impulses with policy designed to appease workers and professionals who remained implacably opposed to immigration. While the police continued to deport fresh illegal immigrants, the government tried to make it easier for German Jews already in the country by getting them recognized refugee status and easing the procedures for naturalization. Nevertheless, most of the 8,000–10,000 German Jewish refugees continued to eke out a miserable existence, living in terror of a visit from the immigration police. At the time of the Anschluss, a centre-right government succeeded the Popular Front administration and tightened border controls even further.[29]

President Roosevelt was the only world leader to grasp the urgency of a coordinated, international response. But he was boxed in by Congress which reflected public opinion in its hostility to any relaxation on immigration controls. When he met his cabinet on 18 March he went as far as he believed was possible to offer a helping hand to 'political refugees'. The most immediate, practical step was to merge the immigration quotas for Germany (25,557) and Austria (1,413), allowing Austrians to take unused places on the German quota. Consular officials were also instructed to be more flexible regarding documentation and to take cognizance of the difficulties Jews faced in even reaching a consulate. Although many US diplomats continued to regard the importuning Viennese Jews as an irritant, the quota for the fiscal year 1939 (1 October 1938 to 30 September 1939) was the first to be entirely filled.[30]

If he could not prise open America's doors any further Roosevelt hoped that he might encourage other countries to be more generous and by acting in concert contribute towards solving the refugee problem. His cabinet backed his proposal to initiate an international conference to discuss the crisis. Two weeks after the German army crossed into Austria, Secretary of State Cordell Hull issued the invitations. George

Messersmith, now at the State Department, told Hull that in the mean-time he had warned American Jewish leaders to keep their heads down. With pro-German and isolationist voices growing ever stronger they needed little encouragement to pursue a policy of discretion.[31]

After several years working for the *New York Times*, James McDon-ald found himself drawn back into refugee work and returned to his self-appointed mission of shaking American Jews out of their compla-cency. Now his jeremiads rang true. At a meeting in New York in March 1938 he admonished the audience, 'The attitude of many people, who are otherwise presumably intelligent, is that to crush a Jew is no more unworthy or reprehensible than to step on vermin and crush the life out of such creatures. The war that the Nazis are waging is not a war against the Jews of Germany, but against all Jews, whose influence must be obliterated and who themselves should either be exterminated or driven out of all civilized lands. But if you think because you live in the United States you are immune you are very foolish.' In mid-May he was invited to the White House to learn about a committee being set up to follow through the results of the international conference, now scheduled to take place in July at Évian in France. Subsequently, McDonald was elected chairman of the Presidential Advisory Committee on Political Refugees and had a key role coordinating the efforts of pro-refugee groups and American Jewish relief agencies.[32]

'Only the complete destruction of Jewish life'

International disquiet over the treatment of Austrian Jews had little impact in Germany. Hitler's popularity soared in the wake of the Anschluss. Even those who thought of themselves as opponents of the regime, like Joachim Fest's father, could not suppress a surge of admira-tion. The fact that the Fests were Catholics and Hitler had brought Catholic Austria into the Reich amplified their ambivalence. 'Why does Hitler succeed?' Fest senior asked plaintively.[33]

The patriotic euphoria did not leave Jews untouched. Willy Cohn admitted, 'Perhaps we Jews in Germany should not join in this welling up of national emotion, but one does so nevertheless.' Victor Klemperer, on the other hand, was sickened. 'The last few weeks have been the most wretched of my life so far.' He reeled at the 'immense act of vio-lence' that accompanied the annexation and gasped at the 'defenceless trembling of England, France'. Klemperer could not believe that the nations of Europe would allow Germany to get away with such conduct. The more he was convinced that Hitler and anti-Semitism were rooted in the German people, the more he invested his hopes for change in some external shock, probably a war. In the meantime, he felt utterly adrift. 'How ... unbelievably I deceived myself my whole life long, when I imagined myself to belong to Germany, and how completely homeless I am.'[34]

The flag-waving was succeeded by another burst of anti-Semitism. As on previous occasions it was whipped up by Streicher and *Der Stürmer*. Since the marginalization of Schacht and the change of policy towards the Jewish sector of the economy there was no holding him back. In his Nuremberg stronghold the boycott was revived with a vengeance at the onset of the Christmas shopping season. Jewish shops were marked and vandalized; employees and customers alike were intimidated.[35]

The pusillanimous international response to the Anschluss and the imperative of gearing up for war gave Göring the impetus to accelerate the elimination of Jews from the German economy. The decree of 26 April 1938 for the registration and potential sequestration of Jewish property on behalf of the Four-Year Plan supplied the warrant the regime needed in order to press ahead. When Luise Solmitz and her husband learned that Jews who owned property, businesses and assets had to complete a four-page questionnaire and return it to the authorities they immediately suspected 'this means expropriation'. Freddy lodged an appeal on the grounds that he was a wounded combat veteran and got an exemption. Klemperer was not so fortunate. As the deadline approached he pored over the list of his meagre assets. 'What is the point of this inventory?' he wondered. From his observations, the British consul-general in Breslau had no doubts about its purpose. He reported that 'even the most tenacious, optimistic and stubborn among the Jews, of whom there have been quite a few in this district, have come to realise that only the complete and total destruction of Jewish life and enterprise will satisfy the National Socialist programme'.[36]

The 'inventory' was in itself an incitement to Aryanization. The SD Head Office purred with delight that since the order was promulgated, Jews were selling their assets in fear of imminent expropriation. Large corporations, trading houses, and banks that had formerly held aloof from the process now began to initiate the takeover of Jewish-owned enterprises. Some were driven by apprehension lest competitors pick off the juiciest businesses; others intended to get a fair deal for the Jewish proprietors, frequently people they had done business with for years. The casualties included over twenty private banks, one of which was M. M. Warburg. Max Warburg had finally given up any hope of amelioration from the regime and was no longer able to assist distressed Jewish clients. He emigrated to the United States.[37]

Between January and November 1938 nearly 800 firms changed hands, including 340 factories, of which the majority were producing leather goods or clothing. The Berlin fashion district ceased to exist, as almost every Jewish clothing manufacturer, wholesaler or retail outlet either closed down or entered new ownership. Almost 300 wholesalers were sold across Germany. The state economic agencies used the control of raw materials to strangle Jewish-owned factories, compelling the proprietors to shut or sell out. Jewish importers were denied access to foreign currency while firms dependent on overseas markets were prevented from accessing export credits. According to the Reichsvertretung, between 4,500 and 5,000 enterprises of all types were Aryanized over this period.[38]

A string of supplementary regulations to the Reich Citizenship Law prohibited Jews from practising medicine, law, and a host of other professions. A small proportion of Jews were allowed to continue working, but only to serve Jews and in a deliberately humiliating capacity. Of 3,152 Jewish physicians just 709 were licensed to treat Jewish patients; they were obliged to describe themselves as Krankenbehandler, carer for the sick. Of 1,753 Jewish lawyers, just 10 per cent were permitted to act for Jewish clients as legal consultants or Rechtskonsulenten. Jewish cattle traders were denied licences. Jews were no longer permitted to operate as travelling salesmen or pedlars. Since thousands of men who had been previously dismissed from work, forced to surrender their businesses, or lost their shops were now scraping a living by travelling from place to place selling from suitcases or their cars, this was a crippling blow.[39]

On top of the suppression of Jewish economic activity, the regime hacked away at the ligaments of communal existence. In March, the corporate status of Jewish communities was revoked. This meant that the Gemeinde was no longer exempt from taxation. Faced with heavy property taxes, many backdated, dozens of communities filed for bankruptcy. As a result, soup kitchens, schools, and old people's homes had to close, rendering Jewish life unviable in one town after another. Jewish families lost any remaining tax breaks or benefits, driving many into penury. But Jews who were forced to seek aid from the state were now required to work for it, cleaning the streets or performing other menial tasks assigned by the municipality.[40]

Local Nazi Party bosses, mayors, police chiefs and even council officials responded to the signals emanating from Berlin that it was open season on the Jews. In villages and towns across Germany, Jewish families were forced to abandon not just their livelihood but their homes. The district governor of Upper and Central Franconia reported that 'In Feuchtwangen, the last Jewish family left the town on 1 March 1938.' After 'the last Jewish-owned stores were transferred to Aryan ownership', the NSDAP District Leadership in Königshofen-Hofheim, in Franconia, exalted that 'In the year 1935, the Jews were still behaving like lords . . . Today the Jews have not only disappeared completely from public life, but Adolf Hitler Square is also "judenrein," and the former Jewish houses and stores all over Königshofen are now without exception in Aryan hands.'[41]

The regional offices of the Centralverein could only log the instances of expulsion and file away pathetic letters such as the one from 'Alfred' in Schopfloch, who informed the CV branch in Württemberg that 'on Friday we received the so-called expulsion order. The local head of the Nazi party literally said: If you Jews don't disappear soon, we'll make an awful mess.' Just what sort of a mess could be gauged from events in Aschaffenburg, near Munich, where even the district governor was concerned by the wanton vandalism against synagogues and private homes. In Böchingen in the Palatinate, explosive devices were used on the house of a Jewish resident. The gendarmerie in Hösbach reported that the homes of four Jewish cattle dealers were wrecked. With no hope of protection from the police or succour from cowed Jewish organizations, dozens of Jews made their exit through suicide. Each self-inflicted death was a triumph for Nazi officials determined to make their areas free of Jews one way or another and, therefore, worthy of record. Why else would the district governor of Lower Bavaria and Upper Palatinate go to the trouble of informing his superiors that 'A Jewish cattle dealer in Schwandorff killed himself by hanging'?[42]

In the tortured language that was typical of their expatiations, the SD Referenten, or experts, were pleased to note that 'As a result of these drastic measures, the last hope among Jews for remaining in Germany has disappeared, so that the desire for emigration has been significantly strengthened.' It was also evident to them that a burgeoning proportion of the Jewish population was impoverished and that communal support networks were collapsing. This raised the spectre of a mass of unemployed, indigent Jews unable to emigrate because they lacked the wherewithal. The SD was coming face to face with a new conundrum arising from Judenpolitik. A report for April–May reflected that 'given sufficient foreign currency, a substantive emigration can be achieved despite the growing difficulties in the major countries of immigration.' Unfortunately, German Jews were broke and it was dangerous to rely on financial aid from Jews abroad. Once again, the Nazis had painted themselves into a corner thanks to uncoordinated and poorly planned policy. For the SD the way out of this dilemma was to exert even greater pressure on the Jews.[43]

In mid-summer, joblessness in the Third Reich suddenly became a terrifying condition. With the economy at full stretch and a growing labour shortage, Himmler saw that the concentration camp population controlled by his SS was a potential gold mine. Prisoners could be forced to work for a pittance supplying raw materials such as granite for prestige construction projects. Or they could be hired out to industrial concerns, bringing income to the SS. In June 1938, on the orders of Heydrich, the criminal police (Kripo) began a systematic round-up of 10,000 men considered asocial or work-shy. These categories embraced men with a prior criminal record who had served a custodial sentence, the long-term unemployed, and the homeless. The Kripo dragnet swept beggars, vagrants and Gypsies into Buchenwald, Sachsenhausen and Dachau concentration camps. Amongst the internees were 2,600 Jews.[44]

The treatment meted out to the Jewish detainees was significantly different. To begin with the police were instructed to scoop up any Jews convicted of an offence, no matter how trivial. The number affected was larger than in any previous anti-Jewish action. On 15 June alone, 600 Jews were dispatched in one massive transport of 1,000 asocials from Berlin to Dachau. The inclusion of elderly Jewish men who were incapable of work suggested that there were other reasons for seizing them than to augment the workforce. Indeed, those who were able to emigrate were released, some quite quickly. The work-shy action was intended to spread terror through the Jewish population and jolt those who were still dithering over emigration. The stories that emerged from the camps with those who were released had the required effect. They told how Jewish prisoners were routinely abused and beaten, how they lived in overcrowded quarters and performed senseless labour in striped uniforms bearing a black triangle superimposed over a yellow one. Up to 200 were killed, died, or committed suicide. The pretext that the victims were criminals or social parasites was too flimsy to conceal the fact that the German government had ordered and carried out a mass arrest of Jews just because they were Jews. A fundamental line had been crossed. It was no longer sufficient for Jews to keep their head down and stay out of trouble: it was now a crime to be a Jew in Germany.[45]

Over the same period the security apparatus struck at the Jews in Austria. In the wake of the Anschluss dozens of Jews known for their political activity, journalists, and Jewish communal leaders were arrested and sent to Dachau. These focused arrests were followed by several round-ups that were indiscriminate except insofar as the victims were Jewish: the victims were seized off the streets and dragged out of cafes. The scale of the Judenaktion was unprecedented. Jews were assembled and dispatched in a series of big transports: 601 on 31 May, 595 on 3 June 1938. In all, 2,000 were seized, although this was actually less than the target of 5,000 set by the SD office in Vienna. Unlike Germany, where police guarded the trains carrying internees, the Austrian transports were guarded by SS men and were accompanied by unprecedented brutality. In one transport at least twelve Jews died en route to the camps. When they arrived they were subjected to a brutal induction, shoved into inadequate accommodation, and assigned back-breaking, pointless work. Heydrich appears to have stopped the mass arrests because of adverse foreign publicity and most of the men were released within twelve months so they could emigrate. As in the Old Reich, the round-ups were transparently an adjunct to the policy of forced emigration.[46]

During the summer, violence and intimidation escalated to heights unseen for years. On 16 June, SA and SS units alongside other Nazi Party organizations launched a Judenaktion in Berlin. Over the next fortnight, shops and offices belonging to Jews were picketed and marked. Hugh R. Wilson, an American diplomat, noted that the disturbances were 'significant as being the first attempt since 1933 to revive organised marking and picketing of Jewish shops'. He was struck by the sight of onlookers enjoying the spectacle and by the participation of Hitler Youth. The presence of high-spirited and ill-disciplined youngsters contributed to the extensive vandalism and looting, although the bland SD report merely mentioned that 'there was some destruction and plundering of Jewish shops, as well as physical assaults'.[47]

Bella Fromm and a friend took the risk of walking through downtown Berlin to see for themselves. 'The entire Kurfürstendamm was plastered with scrawls and cartoons. "Jew" was smeared all over the doors, windows, and walls ... It grew worse as we came to the part of town where poor little Jewish retail shops were to be found. The SA had created havoc ... Windows were smashed, and loot from the miserable little shops was strewn over the pavement and floating in the gutter.' The two women were inside a small jewellery shop when it was invaded by Hitler Youth armed with knives. While some of the youngsters wrecked the place one 'crouched in a corner of the window, putting dozens of rings on his fingers and stuffing his pockets with wrist watches and bracelets'.[48]

The outrages in Berlin were coldly calculated. They were designed to eviscerate any hope remaining to Jews in the capital, and throughout the Reich, that they might be able to continue living in Germany. They were also intended to send a message to the international community, which the Nazis believed took its orders from the Jews, that it had to make more of an effort to remove them.[49]

Following President Roosevelt's initiative, the international conference to address the refugee crisis assembled at the Hotel Royal in Évian-les-Bains between 6 and 14 July 1938. Roosevelt selected Myron Taylor, a Quaker steel magnate who was subsequently appointed the president's 'peace ambassador at the Holy See', to lead the delegation and chair the meetings. James McDonald, who went along as his adviser, warned in advance against 'exaggerated expectations'. He knew that the US quota was fixed and to avoid it being questioned the very invitation to the conference stated that participants would not be expected to admit more immigrants than their laws already permitted. The principal French delegate, the restriction-minded Henry Bérenger, opened the conference by proclaiming that France had already done much to solve the refugee problem and could do no more.[50]

Nor was Great Britain inclined to lead the way. The Foreign Office approached the conference almost with dread. Whitehall feared that any concession on immigration controls would encourage Poland and Romania to step up their efforts to force Jews out. Behind the suffering of Jews in Germany and Austria stood the spectre of four million impoverished Jews in eastern Europe facing boycotts, discrimination and intermittent violence. Stephen Wise, speaking on behalf of the World Jewish Congress, demanded that the international community face up to this challenge by rescuing German Jews while admonishing other states against persecuting their Jewish citizens. But it was in vain to expect the conference to sanction any form of interference in the internal affairs of sovereign powers. Nor could Wise wish away the global economic crisis, which had worsened after a period of recovery, or the intensification of anti-Jewish feeling. William Shirer, who reported on the conference, privately noted that 'The British, French, and Americans seem too anxious not to do anything to offend Hitler. It's an absurd situation. They want to appease the man who is responsible for their problem.'[51]

The only concrete outcome of the Évian Conference was the creation of the Intergovernmental Committee for Refugees. It resembled the League's High Commission for Refugees in that it had no funds and no powers, although its remit was broader and encompassed the Jews of Austria and eastern Europe. Unlike McDonald, George Rublee, the American appointed as its head, was authorized to negotiate with the Germans to allow Jews to emigrate and cajole other countries into letting them in.[52]

The Nazis seized on the desultory outcome of the Evian Conference as evidence that the Jews were unpopular everywhere. They derided expressions of sympathy for the plight of Jews in Germany emanating from countries that would not deign to offer Jews a refuge. At the same time, the regime maintained the pressure for emigration as if to persuade the democracies that they had no choice but to offer homes for the Jews. The SD Head Office reported that 'Along with the familiar measures through laws and ordinances, the steps taken by the police against the Jews especially in Berlin in the last few months are worthy of mention. The instructions from the head of the police in Berlin pursue the aim of rendering it so difficult for the Jews to stay on in Germany that despite the difficult financial situation new impetus will be given to their wish for emigration.' Writing in his diary on 24 July, Goebbels reported Hitler saying that in ten years the Jews would be driven out of Germany.[53]

Anti-Jewish measures in other countries

The reluctance of France, Britain and the USA to admit Jewish refugees was a response to both domestic pressure and anxiety about ominous developments in other countries with large Jewish populations. Across eastern and south-eastern Europe Jews were assailed as the quintessential aliens, potential agents of foreign influence. To observers in the west these anti-Jewish gestures resembled little more than a cynical bid to curry favour in Berlin. The spread of fascism added to the appearance of a homogenous anti-Semitic wave. Fascist parties certainly agreed on the need to reduce the alleged influence of Jews and appropriate their wealth for 'the people'. But the anti-Jewish policies that were put in place during 1938 in one country after another had their own aetiology and were essentially local initiatives.[54]

Romania had a Jewish population of around 757,000 out of a total population of 20 million. One third of the Jews resided in the Regat, the core of the country which had gained independence from the Ottoman Empire in the 1870s. From its inception, the men who led Romania saw the country as a Christian state and were ambivalent about including Jews in the nation as full citizens. They did so only under international duress. Romania was on the winning side in the Great War and was rewarded with extensive territories that held large Jewish communities, notably in Bessarabia, Bukovina and Transylvania. The Jews in these new regions were regarded with even greater suspicion. Economic and social friction added to religious and ethnic antagonism. Around half of the Jews in Romania were engaged in commerce and around 15 per cent in manufacturing; they dominated the bourgeoisie of Bucharest and comprised between 40 and 50 per cent of the urban dwellers in Bessarabia and Moldavia. Only a tiny fraction lived on the land. Although the majority of Jews were actually quite poor, Romanians noted their preponderance in the professions, in commerce, and the existence of a few fabulously wealthy families who controlled financial or industrial enterprises. Anti-Semitism pervaded intellectual life and cloaked baser antipathies with a veneer of respectability.[55]

Throughout the 1920s anti-Semitic parties demanded the reduction of alleged Jewish influence and the expropriation of Jewish wealth. The National Christian Party, led by Octavian Goga and Alexandru Cuza, advocated the 'Romanization' of the economy and revoking the citizenship of the inhabitants of regions bolted onto Romania in 1919. The fascist Iron Guard movement, founded in 1927, characterized the Jews as the enemy of the nation and sought to achieve similar goals – if necessary through violent revolution. In the mid-1930s the Romanian Front government adopted a policy of 'proportionality', limiting Jewish participation in the economy to their proportion of the population. Elections at the end of 1937 resulted in a minority government led by Goga and Cuza that lasted long enough to enact a 'review' of citizenship to determine whether Jews who had become Romanians in 1919 or who had been naturalized in old Romania before that date deserved legal equality. As a result, over 70,000 lost their civil rights, residence rights, and licences to work or trade. Other measures were pushed through for 'Romanization' of the economy and purges of the cultural sphere.[56]

One of the early victims of the anti-Jewish laws was Emil Dorian. Born in 1893 he had served as a medical officer in the Romanian army during the war and combined a medical practice with writing *belles lettres* and translating. On 14 January 1938 he reported curtly in his diary, 'I have been dismissed from my position with the state medical services because I am a Jew.' Disgusted by the pusillanimous response of the Jewish leadership, he formed a Jewish organization to oppose the review of citizenship.[57]

Although the anti-Jewish measures in Romania emerged from indigenous traditions and gratified local aspirations, the Goga-Cuza regime also used them to align the country with Nazi Germany even while Romania was formally allied to the western democracies. At first glance it looked as if increasing proximity to the Third Reich was driving the introduction of anti-Jewish laws in Hungary, too. But the fate of Hungarian Jewry was equally rooted in local conditions.

The Jewish population of Hungary numbered 444,567 in 1930, and comprised just over 5 per cent of the country's inhabitants. They were divided between a modernized, Neolog community and the Orthodox who formed about a third of the total. The two communities were quite distinct, with their own welfare structures and representation. Most Orthodox Jews lived in the regions or in the densely packed central districts of the capital where Yiddish-speaking Jews from Galicia had settled between the last decades of the nineteenth century and the Great War. Around the turn of the century, Jews had come to form over 10 per cent of the capital's inhabitants. They dominated segments of economic and cultural life, constituting 55 per cent of Hungary's lawyers, 40 per cent of its doctors, and 36 per cent of its journalists. Around 40 per cent of the country's commerce was in the hands of Jewish merchants, retailers and traders. Jews owned 70 per cent of the largest industrial concerns. Yet half the Jews in Budapest were too poor to pay taxes and the typical Orthodox communities in small towns and cities in the regions enjoyed quite modest lifestyles.[58]

Between 1867, when they achieved full civic equality, and the demise of the Austro-Hungarian Empire in 1918, the Jews played a leading role in the industrial, commercial and cultural development of the country. Many were honoured for their contribution, but success bred resentment. Anti-Semitic agitators cultivated a myth of Jewish wealth, claiming that Jews prevented genuine Magyars from benefiting: the country would be rich and happy if only the Jews were expropriated. These voices were marginal until economic slowdown and defeat in the Great War propelled them to the centre of politics. In 1918–19 revolution swept away the 'dual monarchy', culminating in a short-lived Hungarian Soviet republic. The leader of the communist regime, Béla Kun, was a Jew, as were several other of its leading lights. Even though the revolutionaries were unrepresentative of the Jews in Hungary, the Moscow-backed dictatorship led to the irreparable association of Jews with Bolshevism. Kun's regime collapsed after a Romanian invasion, and was followed by a 'White Terror', during which hundreds of Jews were killed in massacres and pogroms.[59]

In 1920, Admiral Miklós Horthy became regent, or head of state. Conservative-nationalist parties dominated the political scene. During his first year as regent the government introduced a numerus clausus (quota) limiting the number of Jews allowed into higher education. Right-wing agitators demanded more extreme restrictions. The main goals of the Hungarian National Independence Party, led by Gyula Gömbös, were recovering the territories lost by Hungary under the post-war treaties and reducing the alleged power of the Jews. The Arrow Cross movement, founded by Ferenc Szálasi, aimed at entirely eliminating Jewish influence from society and redistributing the fabled wealth of the Jewish population. Even respectable figures such as Béla Imrédy, president of the National Bank, contemplated legal measures to reduce the preponderance of Jews in finance, commerce and culture.[60]

In February 1938 the prime minister, Kálmán Darányi, announced that his government intended to reach a 'solution on systematic and legal lines' for Hungary's Jewish problem. Legislation to impose a 20 per cent quota on Jewish participation in the professions and the economy passed through the lower house of parliament with a big majority. Imrédy, who had meanwhile replaced Darányi as prime minister, piloted the anti-Jewish law through its final stage in the Upper House. The 'first Jewish law', as it became known, defined Jews by a mixture of religion and descent; tellingly it refused to recognize as Christians Jews who converted to Christianity after 1919, the year of the Soviet Republic. The Jewish population responded by lobbying, public appeals and declarations of loyalty. At this point they enjoyed support from Hungary's embattled liberal, cultural elite. However, a public protest signed by artists and intellectuals, including the composers Zoltán Kodály and Béla Bartók, achieved nothing. Hungarian Jews finally swallowed the law because it was infinitely less harsh than the treatment being meted out to Jews in neighbouring Austria and because they saw Imrédy as the only thing standing between them and the Arrow Cross fanatics.[61]

With Germany rampant, the Hungarian political leadership realized that the only hope of recovering the land lost in 1918 was through an alliance with the Third Reich. In November 1938, a second Jewish law was announced that was intended to signal alignment with Nazi anti-Jewish policy. The law, guided through parliament by Prime Minister Pál Teleki (who replaced Imrédy after it was revealed that he was part-Jewish), tightened the definition of a Jew and struck even more harshly at the economic basis of the Jewish population. Jews, now defined in racial terms, lost all their political rights. They were dismissed from state employment and prevented from practising in journalism, the arts and several professions. Licences to trade, essential to shopkeepers and market stall owners, were rescinded. The number of Jewish employees in private enterprises was limited. It is estimated that up to 70,000 Jews lost their jobs as a consequence, while 40,000 were deprived of permits to earn their living through commerce. In all, 200,000 Jews were affected and most were thrown onto the charity of the Jewish communities. The second Jewish law shattered the economic basis of Jewish life in Hungary while encouraging Jews to emigrate.[62]

The next country to introduce anti-Jewish legislation was Italy. A census in August 1938 revealed that there were 37,241 Italian Jewish citizens plus approximately 9,400 foreign Jews resident in the country, including refugees from Germany. Although Jews had dwelt in the Italian peninsula since antiquity, they never formed more than a tiny proportion of the overall population. Jews had enjoyed civic equality in Piedmont and Tuscany since the mid-nineteenth century and had become well integrated into the new Italian polity in the decades after unification, serving in government posts and the armed forces in numbers that reflected their intense patriotism. Overwhelmingly urban, middle class and comfortably off, a large proportion of the community had supported fascism since its early years. By 1938, 6,900 Jews were members of the Italian Fascist Party – nearly 30 per cent of the Jewish male population over twenty-one years of age.[63]

However, anti-Jewish currents persisted in Italian society and culture. As well as nurturing traditional religious odium towards the Jews, the hierarchy of the Catholic Church lumped Jews in with the secular liberal and left-wing opponents of the clergy. Vatican publications adopted the language of 'race' to differentiate the Jews and adverted to a malign 'Jewish power'. Italian fascism was a broad spectrum and the party contained elements that had always regarded the Jews as foreign, inclined towards radicalism, and out of place in a Christian country. Mussolini himself had a chequered record. Early in his political career he inveighed against 'the great Jewish bankers of London and New York, linked by race with Jews in Moscow as in Budapest who seek revenge against the Aryan race'. But under his leadership the Fascist Party never adopted an official anti-Jewish stance and, on the contrary, admitted Jews to its highest ranks. In the early 1930s Mussolini dismissed racial anti-Semitism as 'nonsense'. When James McDonald met him in May 1934, he expressed nothing but contempt for *Der Stürmer*.[64]

Mussolini's ambivalence gave way to hostility over the course of 1934–7. The prominence of Italian Jews in anti-fascist groups operating inside Italy and abroad annoyed him. He detected 'international Jewry' behind the campaign of sanctions against Italy that followed the conquest of Ethiopia in 1935–6. To escape diplomatic isolation and to solidify their shared interest in supporting General Franco in the Spanish Civil War, in November 1936 Mussolini formed the Rome–Berlin Axis with Hitler. At around this time, anti-Semitic articles began to appear with regularity in the fascist press. However, this was not the first expression of racist thinking and racial anti-Semitism in official quarters. Racism and race laws emerged organically in the Italian colonies in North Africa and were codified with the proclamation of the Italian Empire. In 1937 the categories of race were imported back into Italy and established as operating principles for new government agencies tasked with demographic monitoring of the Italian population.[65]

Count Galeazzo Ciano, the Italian foreign minister and Mussolini's son-in-law, reflected this vacillation in his diary. In early September 1937 he reported that Mussolini 'hurled abuse against America, country of blacks and Jews, disintegrating element of civilization'. Nations were liable to be 'destroyed by the acid of Jewish corruption'. Three months later, however, Ciano responded indignantly to criticism that Italy colluded with Germany in anti-Jewish measures. 'Neither do I believe it would be in our best interests to unleash an anti-semitic campaign in Italy. The problem does not exist here.' But Ciano then cynically observed that there were 'many other pretexts' for persecuting Jews.[66]

In February 1938 the Italian state began to move in just that direction, at first by innocuously requesting information about the number of Jews in ministries and universities. In April and May foreign-born Jews were sacked from government employment and the tempo of anti-Jewish propaganda was stepped up. Finally, in July 1938, Mussolini summoned experts to hammer out a statement on the 'problem of race'. According to Ciano, whose aggrandizement of his father-in-law makes him a less than reliable witness, 'He is studying measures where marriages of Italians are prohibited with people of other races, including the Jewish race.'[67]

For Mussolini, harsh anti-Jewish measures were intended to harden the Italians, especially the young, and promote the construction of the new, fascist man. He told Ciano that 'we must instil in our people a higher racial concept, which is indispensable to proceed with the colonisation of the Empire'. Italians, he believed, were going to have to take race seriously and toughen up.[68]

On 6 October 1938, the Fascist Grand Council published a declaration on race, setting out the basis for legislation. Its definition of a Jew was even stricter than that prevailing in Germany, with less flexibility for 'half' or 'quarter' Jews. The legislation that was promulgated at the end of the year deprived Jews of full civil rights, excluded them from swathes of economic activity, and banished them from cultural life. Foreign Jews were given a few months to leave the country or face internment. Mussolini encountered some dissent, but he was in no mood to compromise: 'Anti-semitism is now injected into the blood of Italians', he told his son-in-law. 'It will continue to circulate and develop on its own.' When King Victor Emmanuel objected to the penalization of Jews who had fought for Italy, Mussolini poured scorn on 'people with weak backs'. He personally insisted on the expulsion of Jews from the Fascist Party and dismissed calls from the Vatican to exempt converts. According to Ciano, 'The Duce rejected such a request which would transform the legislation into a confessional, rather than racial law'.[69]

Ordinary Italians took the message to heart. Officials applied the laws with zeal and Jews who sought to evade them faced denunciation. There was no lack of buyers for Jewish-owned businesses or properties. As in Nazi Germany, Jews were threatened with the prospect of becoming stateless paupers. In a bid to avert this, at the start of 1939 the United States Ambassador, William Phillips, delivered a letter from President Roosevelt to the Duce asking for Jews to be allowed to take enough assets from the country to enable them to emigrate and settle elsewhere. Phillips was left in no doubt that Mussolini was in deadly earnest. The envoy was 'impressed by his apparently genuine antagonism to the Jews'. There was, according to Mussolini, 'no room for the Jews in Europe, and eventually, he thought, they would all have to go'.[70]

Czechoslovakia and the Sudeten crisis

William Shirer had squeezed his coverage of the Évian Conference between trips to Prague to report on the international crisis provoked by Hitler's designs on Czechoslovakia. The occupation of Austria had placed Czechoslovakia in an unenviable strategic position, exactly as Hitler had hoped in his memorandum on the Four-Year Plan. He now used the ethnic Germans living in the Sudetenland, the region on the Czech–German border, in the same way that he had wielded the Austrian Nazis. For several years representation of the German-speaking minority had been monopolized by the Nazi-affiliated Sudeten German Party, led by Konrad Henlein. He routinely agitated for regional autonomy, incurring the wrath of the Prague government and spasmodic repression. Hitler, who often referred to the suffering of the Sudeten Germans, now took up their cause aggressively. In late March 1938, he instructed Henlein to demand autonomy for the region. Predictably, the campaign invited a crackdown by the Czech authorities that, in turn, gave Hitler the pretext for threatening action in defence of his fellow Germans across the border. On 20 May he ordered the

German army high command to prepare a plan for the 'lightning' conquest of Czechoslovakia. As rumours abounded that the German and Czech armies were mobilizing, the British and the French governments issued a warning that they would not stand by in the event of hostilities. This had the desired effect of making Göring and the army chief of staff General Ludwig Beck apply the brakes to Hitler's militancy. But Hitler was not to be deterred and in August Beck resigned. Meanwhile, the British lost their nerve and in a flurry of diplomatic exchanges over the following weeks indicated that they would not go to war to prevent the ethnic Germans gaining autonomy. Abandoned by its allies, the Czech government was obliged to concede Henlein's demands. However, this was no longer enough for Hitler. He believed he had a window of opportunity to conquer Czechoslovakia before British and French rearmament made it possible for them to pose a serious military threat to Germany's western frontier. Hitler told Henlein to up the stakes by demanding secession, and on 12 September, at the Nuremberg rally, threatened that if the Sudetenland was not granted self-determination there would be war.[71]

Military preparations were accompanied by a ferocious propaganda campaign. Germans were treated to endless stories of atrocities against their brothers and sisters who languished under the thumb of semi-civilized Slavs. There was, indeed, some skirmishing between Sudeten Germans and the Czech security forces. Fear and repression resulted in numbers of Volksdeutsche, ethnic Germans, crossing the border as refugees. The escalating belligerency and popular indignation in Germany discharged itself against the Jews. The Hitler Youth who smashed up the jeweller's shop while Bella Fromm looked on were screaming, 'To hell with the Jewish rabble! Room for the Sudeten Germans.' In Vienna, on the eve of the Jewish Day of Atonement, dozens of Jewish families were turfed out of their apartments by SA men to make way for Volksdeutsche refugees. Ruth Maier heard that they demanded bed linen and clothing from the very Jews they had displaced.[72]

As war loomed, German Jews were gripped by panic. On 23 July the government decreed that they had to obtain new identification papers. When they collected them they found a 'J' stamped on the front. This was intended to make it harder for Jews to evade detection inside Germany and to assist the border protection agencies of those countries reluctant to allow entry to Jews in case they applied for asylum or went underground as illegal immigrants. As an added humiliation, on 17 August,

the Interior Ministry required all Jews to adopt a 'Jewish' first name –
Israel for men and Sarah for women – and inscribe it on all their official
documents by January 1939. Now even the redoubtable Bella Fromm
gave up the fight to stay and joined the queues outside the American
Consulate General.[73]

Those who could not or would not make for the exit subsisted in a
state of permanent anxiety. When Victor Klemperer did not hear from
friends for several weeks he confessed 'the silence around me is frightening'. Freddy Solmitz was so distressed by the thought of having to
take a Jewish moniker that he wrote to Frick, the Reich minister for
the interior, asking for an exemption. His wife, Luise, confided to her
journal that 'There is nothing worse than being homeless in one's own
home ... It's a kind of war, and we find ourselves in it without any
defences, without weapons, without the remotest possibility of defending ourselves by legal means or protest'. In one of his last dispatches
from Berlin, André François-Poncet warned the French Foreign Office
that since the Anschluss anti-Semitism had attained a new ferocity.
Over the final days of his ambassadorship, as he walked through the
park between his residence and the embassy he observed, with disgust,
benches marked 'Only for Aryans' or 'Only for Jews'.[74]

The turbid atmosphere in the late summer and early autumn was
punctuated by countless incidents of violence against Jews. According
to the Jewish desk in the SD Head Office, 'Under the impress of events
abroad, the mood of animosity against the Jews in the population has
intensified.' An example of what this entailed in practice comes from the
SD branch in Wiesbaden, which reported that in Rauenthal two Jews
were dragged from their beds by 'the people' and whipped down the
road in their nightclothes. One may surmise that this couple included a
terrified, half-dressed woman.[75]

Synagogues, always the target of casual vandalism, were now the
objects of sustained, destructive fury. In Hanau, Nazi zealots bricked up
the door of the prayer house. When a member of the community tried
to remove the obstruction they had him arrested. The SD reported that
'Unfortunately, the proceedings ended with the acquittal of the Jew who
was however taken into protective custody'. In Nuremberg, Streicher
convened a mass rally at which he announced that the main temple in
the city would be demolished. A crowd of thousands watched Streicher
give the signal that started the work of destruction. In Kaiserslauten and
in Albersweiler, in the Palatinate, the municipality 'purchased' the syna-

gogue so that it could be knocked down. At the end of September, in Mellrichtstadt in central Franconia, a crowd entered the synagogue and wrecked it. After a rash of such incidents, the district governor of the Palatinate explained that 'The population desires the departure of the Jews from the villages, and seeks to avenge itself in this way for the insolent behaviour of the Jews during the critical period in September.'[76]

The Sudeten crisis reached its climax that month. After Hitler rattled the sabre at Nuremberg, Neville Chamberlain, the British prime minister, flew to Germany and met Hitler for one-to-one talks at Berchtesgaden. Chamberlain hoped that by meeting in private he could persuade Hitler to moderate his demands. Instead, Hitler sensed that the British prime minister was desperate to avoid war and reiterated his demand for secession of the Sudetenland. He was right. Instead of standing shoulder to shoulder with the Czechs, Chamberlain and the French government persuaded their erstwhile protégé to give the Germans what they wanted. Chamberlain returned to Germany on 21 September to convey Czech agreement to the surrender of the Sudetenland, but to his astonishment Hitler demanded even more. He insisted that the Czechs pull out their forces by 1 October, making way for German troops to occupy the region. Chamberlain flew back to London and consulted his cabinet. This time they withstood Hitler's bullying. For several days it looked like war was inevitable: the British Home Fleet put to sea and French forces began to mobilize. At the eleventh hour, Mussolini responded to British overtures and offered to mediate. On 29–30 September, Hitler, Mussolini, Chamberlain and the French prime minister, Édouard Daladier, convened in Munich. The two democratic powers signed away the Sudetenland, over the head of the Prague government, in return for promises from Hitler that Germany had no further territorial designs. As a last act, Chamberlain obtained Hitler's signature on a pledge of peace between the two countries.[77]

Europe collectively exhaled in relief, but Leopold Schwarzschild unflinchingly denounced the outcome as a terrible defeat for the democracies. Power had shifted fundamentally in favour of Germany. He was unsparing in his criticism of Chamberlain, who demonstrated an 'absolute lack of understanding of the nature and role of the man he is dealing with'. Hitler had broken every single pledge he had ever made. Indeed, Hitler was less than happy with the outcome. Although he obtained the Sudetenland without a shot being fired, he was denied the chance to conquer Czechoslovakia and fight Britain and France when he felt Germany was the stronger. His resentment would soon have catastrophic effects on the Jews in Germany and Austria.[78]

Jews like Victor Klemperer had pinned their hopes on a coup by the army high command to prevent a war, or a Franco-British victory. It seemed inconceivable that Hitler could succeed and when he did they were plunged into despair. 'And truly it is indeed an unimaginably huge success,' Klemperer wrote. 'Hitler is being acclaimed even more extravagantly than in the Austria business ... something tremendous really has been achieved. But *we* are now condemned to be negro slaves, to be literally pariahs until our end.' For the first time he contemplated suicide.[79]

Raymond Geist gave George Messersmith, who was now at the State Department, a vivid impression of the emigration psychosis that swept German Jews. 'During September we had to deal with thousands of desperate people, who stormed the Consulate General day after day. At times it seemed that we could not control the situation any longer; but we kept our heads and finally brought the applicants under control and now everything is going smoothly again.' There were 125,000 applications for 27,300 quota places, which meant that fresh applicants were doomed to wait three to four years before their number came up. 'This is a desperate situation for many, who are sure unless they can effect their emigration to the US, they cannot survive. We can only be sympathetic and kind; in most cases little practical help can be given.'[80]

Klemperer rued his failure to seek emigration earlier. He recalled the friends who had made it to safety and reflected bitterly, 'All these people have made new lives for themselves – but I have not succeeded in doing so, we have been left behind in disgrace and penury, in some degree buried alive . . .'[81]

Ruth Maier, in Vienna, set down the humiliations that Jews were now subjected to from anyone who had the good fortune to be an Aryan. One day in early October, she was in a queue outside the tax office in Porzellangasse: 'It was raining. We had been standing there in the rain, soaked to the bone and freezing cold, since seven o'clock that morning. A street sweeper appeared with his broom and bellowed at us, waved his hands in the air, shouted. He was foaming at the mouth: "If you don't go away you bastards, I'll drag you all away." How delighted he was, the street sweeper, that he could take out all his fury on us, the inferior race.'[82]

The Viennese Nazis hardly needed the encouragement provided by the anti-Semitic exhibition 'The Eternal Jew' which opened in the city. During October there were repeated invasions of Jewish residential districts, accompanied by the forcible eviction of Jews from their homes. On Sunday 16 October 1938, Ruth began her diary entry 'Pogroms!' She continued, 'The temple [synagogue] is being destroyed. They're cutting the beards off old men. They're bashing the women. They're smashing windows.' In the evening it started all over again in the narrow lanes of the Jewish quarter. 'It's gruesome . . . medieval . . . they want to murder me because I am a Jew.'[83]

This sort of frenzied, fanatical violence was exactly what Hitler wanted. He had been disappointed by the lack of enthusiasm for war during the Sudeten crisis. On 10 November he praised a gathering of 400 German journalists for their part in the psychological war against Czechoslovakia, overcoming the unreadiness of his own citizens. He complained that the succession of bloodless victories had induced a sense of complacency and softness. 'It was only out of necessity that for years I talked of peace,' he told them. 'But it was now necessary gradually to re-educate the German people psychologically, and to make it clear that there are things which *must* be achieved by force if peaceful means fail.' The people had to believe unquestioningly that they would triumph in any conflict and that the leadership was correct, notwithstanding defeats or mistakes.[84]

Hitler was implicitly referring back to the reasons for the German collapse in 1918, and signalling his determination that in the coming war the people would follow their leaders to victory or annihilation. In his vision, there was no room for squeamishness or humanitarian impulses. What better way to inure the population than by exposing them to violence and destruction in their own towns and cities? Repeated assaults on the Jews reinforced their sense of superiority and invulnerability. It taught them to quell compassion for those designated racial outsiders or the enemy. Of equal importance, it educated them in the importance of being on the right side of that distinction.[85]

Over the next weeks the regime instigated a wave of arrests, internments, deportations and expulsions. This was not an innovation. Since the Anschluss some 3,870 Jews had been expelled from the Burgenland, the border district of eastern Austria, into Hungary and Slovakia. 'A cleansing was undertaken of functionaries with foreign nationality in Jewish organizations, in order to prevent the formation of an intelligence network hostile to Germany'. However, the regime was about to make a quantum leap: targeting the 70,000 Polish Jews in the Reich. This step was triggered by the government in Warsaw, which had passed legislation enabling it to strip émigré Poles of their citizenship. Denaturalization would render the Polish Jews in Germany stateless and make it much harder for them to emigrate. In order to avoid being saddled with tens of thousands of despised Ostjuden, the Gestapo, possibly with encouragement from the Foreign Office, took steps to arrest and deport 17,000 Jews of Polish nationality in a nationwide operation commencing on 27 October 1938.[86]

Josef Broniatowski was a Polish-born Jew living in Plauen, a city in Saxony near the old Czech–German border. At 1 a.m. on the night of 28 October, police rang his doorbell and handed him a letter informing him that he was to be deported. He was taken to the local police station where he found seventy-five other Polish Jews, ranging in age from infants to grandfathers. The following day they were bussed to the city of Chemnitz and loaded onto a train that took them to Dresden. There they were added to a throng of Jews numbering about 8,000 who were entrained and transported to Beuthen. Over this period Josef was not given anything to eat or drink and was under constant SS and police guard. At eleven o'clock at night the train stopped in open countryside. They were taken out of the railway carriages and marched across open fields for two miles until they reached the waterlogged ditch that marked the German–Polish border. Some people collapsed and a few died during the trek. The SS guards 'stole everything the people had quickly packed'. The Jews were then forced to scramble across the barrier into Poland while the guards screamed at them. No sooner were they on Polish soil than Polish border troops chased them back. Shots were fired. By 8 a.m. the next morning, the bedraggled crowd was back on the German side of the ditch. The SS men herded them towards a regular crossing point, where Polish officials grudgingly allowed them through. Eventually they were transported to Katowice, where the local Jewish community received them with food and medical aid. Broniatowsk recalled that Polish miners who saw the wretched Jews arrive wept at the sight.[87]

In the wake of the round-up Mally Dienemann telephoned the families of Ostjuden she knew in Offenbach – only to find that almost all the menfolk were gone. She immediately set about assisting the wives and children left behind, while communal networks of Polish Jews in Leipzig and Dresden did what they could to alleviate the suffering of those deported and those remaining. The few Polish Jewish men not picked up appealed to the Polish consul for help, without success. Shortly afterwards fifty to sixty families, mainly women, children and the elderly, were transported to Beuthen and the border. They were given just fifteen minutes to pack.[88]

Of the 16,000–17,000 Polish Jews who were expelled, some ended up back in Germany, some were admitted to Poland, and some were trapped in no-man's-land for days enduring terrible weather until the outcome of negotiations between the Polish and German governments. Having initially refused entry to the deportees, the Polish authorities relented and allowed the majority across the border, where they were gathered into makeshift camps. The largest was at Zbaszyn, west of Posen. Here 6,000–7,000 wet, cold and starving Jews were quartered in a town with a population numbering less than that, including seven Jewish families. Hundreds sat and slept on the damp ground in stables and Polish army barracks provided by the authorities. Around 2,000–2,500 were taken into the homes of kindly Poles. The American Jewish Joint Distribution Committee rushed aid to the town, distributing food and dry clothes and even setting up a field hospital. The AJJDC also established a nursery for the 300–500 children. After several days, supplies and funds also began to arrive from the Jewish communities in Lodz and Cracow.[89]

The November pogrom

The mass expulsion of Polish Jews from Germany represented a dramatic escalation of anti-Jewish measures. But governments and the public in other countries scarcely had time to register the shockwave. On 7 November, an illegal Jewish immigrant in France, Herschel Grynszpan, walked into the German Embassy in Paris and shot a young official called Ernst vom Rath. Grynszpan had been born in Germany in 1921 but, like most Polish Jewish immigrants and their offspring, he had Polish nationality. When he was fifteen he illicitly entered France in search of education and work, but without the necessary papers he was at the mercy of officialdom. As French policy towards refugees became ever harsher, he was driven further into a marginal existence. On 3 November he received news that his mother and father, along with two younger siblings, were amongst the Polish Jews deported from the

Reich. His sister told him that they were stranded in Zbaszyn, homeless and miserable along with thousands of others. Grynszpan snapped. He obtained a gun and set off for the German Embassy, allegedly with the intention of assassinating the ambassador. Instead he fired at the first German he encountered, a humble third secretary. Grynszpan was soon disarmed and arrested by the French police while the wounded diplomat was rushed to hospital.[90]

Goebbels was informed of the shooting and immediately blew it out of all proportion, rather like his treatment of the Reichstag fire. The work of one deranged individual became the tip of a global Jewish conspiracy to engineer war between Germany and France. According to him, the Jews were aiming for the 'extermination' of National Socialism; but it was they who would be 'called to account'. In personal terms, if for no other reason, the assassination attempt was a gift to the minister for propaganda. Hitler was annoyed with him for conducting an affair with a Czech actress, Lída Baarová. Normally, Hitler cared little about his minions' peccadilloes but he was fond of Goebbels' wife and had no affection for Czechs of any kind. Goebbels saw the response to the Paris shooting as an opportunity to reaffirm his fealty and demonstrate his worth to the Führer by inflicting misery on the Jews, something that always pleased Hitler. The following day he ramped up the campaign. The German press hurled imprecations against warmongering Jewry while Rath was depicted as a flawless martyr. Hitler helped by promoting Rath so as to escalate the gravity of Grynszpan's crime and sent his personal doctor to the victim's bedside. The Berlin police chief, Count Helldorf, ordered Jews to surrender all weapons and the Gestapo punitively shut down the remaining Jewish newspapers published in the capital. During the evening sporadic anti-Jewish violence occurred, most seriously in Hesse.[91]

Throughout 8 November, as Rath lingered between life and death, the Nazi Party leadership assembled in Munich for the annual events to commemorate the heroes of the movement who fell in the abortive 1923 putsch. It was an unforeseen but combustible conjunction. In the evening Hitler delivered his traditional speech at the Bürgerbräukeller. He did not mention the latest martyr of the NSDAP, concentrating instead on the international scene and hinting that war with France and Britain was unavoidable. Yet the imminence of war (in Hitler's mind) is germane to understanding his actions over the next few hours. In contrast to the constraints he was under when Wilhelm Gustloff was killed, he no longer felt inhibited by diplomatic niceties or the fluctuations of international trade. Soon there would not be any trade at all, and what other countries thought of Germany would be immaterial. This time he could indulge his passion for revenge against the Jews.[92]

The next day was taken up with the commemorative ceremonies, but Hitler had time for several conversations with Göring and Goebbels. During the afternoon they were informed that Rath had died. They also learned that the news had triggered disturbances in Dessau, where Jewish shops were looted and the synagogue burned. That evening Hitler joined the party elite for the customary dinner in the Old Town Hall. Usually he made a speech there, too, but on this occasion he left early. Before departing he spoke in whispered tones to Goebbels. At 9.30 p.m., when Hitler was back at his apartment, Goebbels addressed the hundreds of Gauleiters, party bosses, SA officers and rank and file in the hall. By this time most of them had eaten well and drunk a lot. Everyone knew about Rath's passing and the atmosphere was heavy with alcohol fumes, cigarette smoke and vengefulness. In his diary Goebbels described his role: 'I go to the party reception in the Old Town Hall. A gigantic event. I describe the situation to the Führer. He decides: let the demonstrations continue. Withdraw the police. For once the Jews should feel the rage of the people. This is correct. I issue corresponding instructions to the police and the party. Then I speak briefly to the officials of the party. A storm of applause. They all rush to the telephones. Now the people shall act!'[93]

The inebriated, inflamed party men crowded around public telephones or hastened back to their hotel rooms to instruct their local branches and SA units. What ensued was not the spontaneous 'rage' of the people, but nor was it a well-planned, centrally executed operation, either. Hitler and Goebbels triggered a nationwide pogrom without any clear goals and no thought for the methods that were to be employed. According to the authoritative analysis by Alan Steinweis the operation was characterized by 'hasty and improvised organisation' that resulted in 'messiness and miscommunication'. The result was murder, rape, looting, destruction of property, and terror on an unprecedented scale. The extent of the desolation stunned the population and rocked the regime. Within days, the Nazi leadership responded with far-reaching decisions about Judenpolitik that arose from the November pogrom, but did not share the same roots. The onslaught against the Jews on 9–10 November 1938 was an exponentially aggravated continuation of the violence that had been erupting sporadically since the start of the year, but it led to a fundamental rupture in Nazi thinking. Afterwards, the regime would begin to employ new ways of dealing with the Jews in Germany and it would never again stage anti-Jewish violence on German streets. Instead, the violence would be exported or disguised.[94]

Contrary to what he wrote in his diary, Goebbels never sent instructions to the police. Although Himmler and Heydrich were in Munich, they only seem to have learned of Hitler's intentions during a meeting with the Leader before a midnight wreath-laying ceremony. The head of the Gestapo, Heinrich Müller, transmitted the first orders to the Gestapo at five minutes to midnight. As a preface he explained that the party was to carry out an action against synagogues. The task of the Gestapo was to seize Jewish communal archives from these buildings, presumably before they were burned to a cinder, and 'prepare the arrest' of 20,000–30,000 Jews, especially those who were wealthy. Heydrich added detail in a telex to the Sipo-SD issued at 1.20 a.m. The security police were to prevent looting and protect Aryan property. Elderly or infirm Jews were excluded from the round-ups that Müller had already ordained. Heydrich added that Jews taken into custody should not be mistreated. Also in the early hours, Himmler briefed SS leaders in Munich and told them to keep their men out of the affray. However, the lack of coordination meant that many SS personnel did join in and some committed theft or murder. Even before he knew about how much property was destroyed and the scenes of lawlessness, Himmler was livid. It was Vienna all over again. At three o'clock in the morning, he composed a memo recording his suspicion 'that Goebbels – in his hunger for power, long since evident to me, and his blockheadedness – has given the start signal for the action'. The uniformed police, commanded by Kurt Daluege, didn't get any orders until dawn, when they were instructed to prevent fires being set.[95]

By that time, around 1,000 synagogues and prayer rooms had been gutted or smashed up. In some places explosives were used to demolish the buildings. Approximately 7,500 shops, out of about 9,000 remaining in Jewish hands, had been wrecked. Display windows had been shattered, shop fittings ripped out, and stock looted or scattered in the streets outside. The authorities calculated that 39 million Reichsmarks' worth of property had been damaged. Over ninety Jews were killed and several women raped or abused. While it seemed well coordinated – the perception of Jews and onlookers at the time that is embodied in most historical accounts – it was in fact a disorderly, improvised, and chaotic episode. What made it so terrifying for the victims, and also for ordinary Germans, was the *lack* of control. The party leaders, SA men, security police, SS, and regular police all got instructions at different times, often saying different things. They got phone calls and teletype messages in the late evening or early hours when they were either drunk, half-asleep, or both. It was relatively easy to mobilize the party branches and SA because they had congregated for local commemorations of the 1923 putsch but, as in Munich, that entailed a hearty dinner and large quantities of beer. Whole units of the SS joined in, mostly in mufti or wearing coats over their uniforms, even though Himmler wanted them to stay clear. The SD were eventually roused from their slumbers to get documents from buildings that were often in flames. When the security police went to arrest Jews at their homes, they often found their quarry had been chased away by mobs or gone to ground to escape the pandemonium. It was, in this sense, a typical Nazi operation that gained coherence and purpose only in retrospect.[96]

In dozens of localities, the assault took the form of a 'degradation ritual' directed at Judaism as much as at Jews. Despite years of propaganda distinguishing racial anti-Semitism from Christian Jew-hatred, crowds enacted scenes that would have been familiar to a visitor from the Middle Ages. In Bensheim local Jews were forced to dance around the blazing synagogue. In Laupheim Jews were collected together, marched to the flaming building and forced to kneel in front of it. In Gailingen and Beuthen Jews were compelled to stand and watch as their synagogues burned. Torah scrolls and prayer books were removed and desecrated, torn apart or kicked around, often by youths. Rabbis were picked out in numerous towns, dragged to their synagogues and made to look on while the incendiaries went to work. In Vienna numerous rabbis had their beards cut off.[97]

Jews were systematically humiliated. In Gütersloh they were marched through the city streets in their nightclothes. In Neustadt and Emden, Jewish homes for the elderly were emptied of their frail residents, who were then paraded around in pyjamas. Jewish men in Düsseldorf were driven barefoot across ground covered in shards of glass. Age and infirmity offered no protection. As well as the old-age homes that were targeted, Jewish orphanages were invaded and ransacked in Dinslaken and Königsberg. The patients were herded out of the Jewish hospital in Nuremberg with such ferocity that several died.

Over 200 Jews arrested in Regensburg were marched through the streets on their way to Dachau concentation camp led by one man carrying a placard declaring 'Exodus of the Jews'.[98]

There was also a strong economic aspect to the pogrom. Looting was widespread, especially before Heydrich ordered the security police to prevent it. The SD in Bielefeld reported twenty-one robberies. In Wolfersheim and other places, rioters took care to destroy ledgers recording mortgages and debts owed to Jews. Extortion flourished under the guise of carrying out Aryanization and rendering localities Jew-free. In Munich, SA men went to the home of the art collector Paul Bernheimer and threatened him until he made out a cheque to the Hitler Youth. The NSDAP district officer in Garmisch-Partenkirchen reported that Jews in the winter resort 'submitted a declaration of their intent to leave the district immediately and never to return, and to give up their land and residential property by selling it to new owners'. By the afternoon of 10 November 'all Jews departed from the district'.[99]

Gender was no defence, either. The SD in Bielefeld reported that an eighty-four-year-old woman died after she 'fell down the stairs'. The wife of the rabbi in Mossbach was sentenced to four weeks in jail for trying to shield her husband and eighty-six-year-old father from Brownshirts who came to arrest them. Many women who later gave testimonies or wrote memoirs recalled the violation of domestic space by drunken, thuggish men. The invaders smashed up furniture, broke ornaments, shattered crockery, and used their daggers to slash furnishings, including pillows and mattresses. For these women the pogrom was represented less by broken glass and more by flying feathers. Their experiences wrench attention away from buildings and public places such as synagogues and shopping streets which are inanimate and impersonal, back to the most private spaces in which the victims were totally vulnerable, forced to stand in nightdresses and pyjamas with their children huddled around them while everything secure and familiar was disrupted and soiled.[100]

In more than a few places (the true extent will never be known) the rioters indulged in sexual violence. Four SA men were tried and expelled from the Nazi Party for rape and sexual assault. One abused a thirteen-year-old Jewish girl in Duisberg. In Lichtenfels a Jewish woman was found dead outside town; it is likely that she was raped and her body dumped. Uniformed SA men assaulted several other women in the town during the night. Two Austrian Brownshirts in Linz forced a

Jewish woman to undress and molested her in her own home. In Brigit-tenau, the inner-city district of Vienna that was heavily populated by poor Galician Jews, 200 women were forced to dance naked in a base-ment for the amusement of a Nazi gang. One woman who refused to provide sport for the onlookers was tied to a table while other women were compelled to spit on her.[101]

At least ninety Jews were murdered or died. This was not because homicide was intended. If that had been the case the casualty rate would have been astronomical. Rather, it was a symptom of the half-baked way the pogrom was initiated, the poor chain of command, and indiscipline. Indeed, historians know so much about the November pogrom because it was the subject of disciplinary proceedings by the Nazi Party. Although Jews were fair game, and the atmosphere was dis-tinctly permissive, there were no orders to kill anyone. Nor were there any instructions to wreck Jewish commercial premises. Since the spolia-tion in Vienna and the obsession with husbanding resources for the war effort, the regime had become intensely protective of Jewish-owned wealth to which it had staked a claim. Heydrich specifically instructed the security police to prevent looting.

Instead, the law had been breached on such a prolific scale and so blatantly that the authority of the state would be compromised if no action was taken against at least some of the miscreants. To preserve the notion that Germany was still a Rechtsstaat, a law-governed state, con-servative figures in the government, such as Johannes Popitz, the finance minister for Prussia, demanded that Göring punish those responsible. Göring deflected Popitz by asking him sarcastically, 'Do you want to punish the Führer?' But the public's unease was not so easily assuaged. Unlike the murderous rampage of 30 June–1 July 1934, which had a measure of support as the termination of a public nuisance, not to mention the just-credible accusation that the SA was planning a coup, the pogrom had no plausible defence. It was one thing to admit to ordering a revenge action against the Jews, but another to condone the killing of old ladies and the wholesale looting of private homes. Hence the Gestapo, police and public prosecutors initiated investigations and began to make arrests. However, Heydrich could not allow this to go too far. In many cases the offenders were let off if they handed over the loot. In more serious cases, jurisdiction over the investigations was switched from the Ministry of Justice to the party's own courts.

Eventually thirty men were arraigned before the highest tribunal of the party, in Munich, between December 1938 and February 1939.[102]

These trials brought to light the murder of a doctor and his wife in Lesum, a small town on the outskirts of Bremen in north Germany. The commander of the SA storm unit there had been dragged out of bed at 3 a.m. by an official from the town hall who told him that the commander of the SA in Bremen wanted to talk to him on the phone. The officer informed him that the SA had been instructed to get rid of the Jewish population; Lesum was his responsibility and he should jump to it. The Sturm leader collected his men and told them they had been ordered to dispatch the Jews. When asked by his unit what this meant he tried to get clarification from the Bremen HQ, but was left none the wiser. He assumed it was time to kill the Jewish inhabitants on their patch, yet when his men inquired if they should use clubs or pistols he was unable to say. In the end they armed themselves with their pistols and got as far as the home of one Jewish family, where they shot a seventy-eight-year-old doctor and his sixty-five-year-old wife. That was enough for the Brownshirts; they abandoned the escapade and headed off for a stiff drink.[103]

In Aschaffenburg, a small city in western Bavaria, men of an SS unit decided to kill two Jews in revenge for the death of Rath. Their victims were not chosen arbitrarily: both were known for their wealth, and local Nazis resented the fact that they were still there. The first was attacked in his home, the other seized and driven to the edge of town for administration of the coup de grâce. Unfortunately for the SS the execution-style killings were botched. Both victims survived multiple bullet wounds, although one died several days later in hospital. Not only had these SS men failed to get the correct instructions in time, but they were clearly also ill prepared for what they assumed to be their job on the night. In 1938 the average SA and SS man was not familiar with the mechanics of execution on a small, let alone a large scale.[104]

The incompetence of the pogromists did nothing to diminish the horror they inflicted. It possibly made things even worse, since Jews were confronted by 'a horde of drunken animals in uniform' whose actions could not be predicted, making it harder to palliate them if the chance arose. Their terror, and the anguish of the following weeks, was captured in hundreds of testimonies penned by refugees in 1939 and 1940. Within the Reich and outside, Jews knew that an epochal event had occurred, that crimes had been committed on a vast scale, and that history would one day judge the guilty even if justice did not catch up with them. The Central Information Office, set up in Amsterdam by Alfred Wiener to chronicle Nazi crimes (and later moved to London), obtained dozens of eyewitness reports from refugees while the events were still fresh in their memory. Another recording project was initiated by Edward Hartshorne, a young academic at Harvard University, working with the sociologist Gordon Allport. In 1939 they offered a prize for the best essay on 'My Life in Germany Before and After January 30, 1933'. Initially publicized in the *New York Times*, the competition elicited 155 responses in the USA, 31 from Britain, 20 from Palestine and 6 from Shanghai. The majority of the writers were Jews who had fled Berlin and Vienna after November 1938.[105]

Rudolf Bing, a lawyer and veteran of the Great War, was woken at three in the morning by a crowd outside his apartment. When he phoned the local police station to express his concern, he was asked 'Are you an Aryan?' When he said 'No,' the receiver at the other end was put down. Soon he heard cries and screams coming from his Jewish neighbours and when this was succeeded by hammering on his own door he decided to make a getaway. Thinking quickly, the sixty-year-old attorney tossed a mattress out of a back window and leapt onto it. For the rest of the night Bing hid in a garden shed. In the morning a compassionate family who lived nearby helped him. He later recalled: 'A deep feeling of depression and shame clearly gripped the public. For the first time, some of the population dared to show sympathy with us.' When he got back to his home he found that his office and the living rooms were all smashed to pieces; even his clothes had been slashed. A few months later, he emigrated to Palestine.[106]

Hugo Moses, aged forty-two, had worked for the Oppenheim bank. At 3 a.m., SA and SS men, 'blood-thirsty savages, brutal creatures', broke into his apartment. They wrecked the place, then left. In the morning uniformed policemen came to his home, surveyed the damage, and declared, 'It's a disgrace.' But in the evening, another officer arrived to arrest him. The officer did not hide his sympathy for Moses and he was relatively well treated while he was held in the police station. From there he was taken to a prison where he joined about 800 Jews. Conditions were poor, but no one was maltreated. He was released on 19 November. When he arrived home he found that German neighbours were helping his wife. They protested, 'This is worse than Russia,' and worried that their church might be the next target. But the pogrom had the required effect on Moses. 'Up to that point I would have found it very difficult to leave the old homeland and my parents' house ...' No longer. He obtained an affidavit from his wife's uncle in the USA and emigrated with his family.[107]

Luise Solmitz observed the pogrom in Hamburg through the eyes of a Christian married to a Jew. November 10 was 'a terrible day'. She went into the city to do shopping and saw crowds of people milling around, blocked roads, and the smashed windows of Jewish-owned stores. As she walked she heard 'An incessant rattling and clinking from the splintered windows on which glaziers were working. I've never heard such a clattering in all my life.' In the early evening the radio announced that the Führer had ordered a halt to the demonstrations, although new laws pertaining to the Jews would soon follow. 'This means our fate is relentlessly approaching doom', she wrote. 'I always thought, now we have reached the worst point. But now I see it was always just a prelude to the next thing. Now the end is near.' Two days later the Gestapo visited her husband Freddy, but Heydrich had already decided that elderly Jews and those with wounds from the trenches should be released from custody. So, on account of his war record, they left him alone.[108]

Children were not spared the frightfulness. Toni Lessler, a teacher at a Jewish school in the Grunewald neighbourhood of Berlin, recalled how distressed children arrived in the morning with stories that the temple in Fasanenstrasse was on fire. Shortly afterwards, another group arrived bearing news that the synagogue on Prinzregentstrasse was alight. Then tearful children trickled in from the neighbourhood saying that 'our little temple in Grunewald is burning and the fire-fighters are standing around without intervening'. It was impossible to accomplish anything with classes full of trembling children so they were sent home in groups, each accompanied by a teacher. The school remained closed for ten days and when it reopened the roll was much reduced. Many children had already left the country with their families; over ninety had fathers in concentration camps.[109]

The violence was, if anything, more pronounced in Vienna. Over forty synagogues were destroyed and twenty-seven Jews were beaten to death. Siegfried Merecki, a lawyer in his fifties whose family had migrated to the city from Galicia, watched the demolition of his synagogue, tears streaming down his face. 'Every little thing that was still inside was taken out and smashed ... The people seemed to have superhuman strength; their faces were distorted.' His apartment was raided by SA men and ruined. They cut up his clothing and then forced him to wear it on his journey to the local police station where he was abused and beaten. Whereas in the Old Reich, policemen tended to divide into decent older types and younger Nazified zealots, in Vienna they all seemed to take pleasure in tormenting Jews. Merecki was interrogated and repeatedly asked if he had sexual relations with Aryan women. When the police had finished, the Jews were shipped off to a riding school converted into a detention centre. After a few days he was released because he already had emigration papers. He was amongst the lucky ones.[110]

Ruth Maier was looking forward to celebrating her eighteenth birthday on 10 November. Her reveries about impending womanhood were interrupted by the news that Rath had been shot by 'a Polish Jew. My God!' Like other Viennese Jews she suspected what this could mean. 'No Jew goes outside. We're scared that they'll beat us up because a Polish Jew wanted to kill a German.' Her fears were soon realized. 'We've been attacked,' she wrote on the 11th. 'Yesterday was the most awful day of my life. Now I know what pogroms are. I know what human beings are capable of.' Ruth was at her Jewish school when warning came that trouble was brewing. The children were dismissed and she hurried home through streets that looked 'like an abattoir'. It was 'as if war had broken out'. She saw a lorry packed with Jews 'standing up like livestock on its way to the slaughterhouse! I'll never forget this sight – I must never forget it.' People stood and stared while crowds went about the work of destruction 'with desire and pleasure'. Unlike in the Old Reich, huge numbers of apartments were seized, nearly 2,000, and the Jewish occupants summarily evicted. Ruth saw Jews expelled from homes in the provinces arriving in Vienna. All their belongings were piled in 'removal lorries, massive and simple lorries full of bed linen, crates, rocking chairs, coffee mills – everything in a heap: a Jew's home, just a Jew's home.'[111]

Rather like the boycott of April 1933, the only other nationwide anti-Jewish action staged by the party, the November pogrom was ill thought out and counterproductive. It provoked the wrath of Göring and Himmler, neither of whom had been included in the planning, and resulted in a backlash at home and abroad.

Some of the anger displayed by members of Hitler's inner circle was synthetic, motivated by hostility for Goebbels and a desire to keep him in his box. Yet the pogrom also aroused the genuine annoyance of

Heydrich and the SD thinkers who despised attacks on the Jews that were not coordinated with the policy of emigration. Eichmann, in Vienna, was apoplectic when he arrived at the IKG offices in the early hours to find broken typewriters littering the courtyard. The membership files of the community were still in the blazing synagogue next door. To prevent their work being further disrupted he placed the Jewish workers at the Zentralstelle under his protection and stationed a guard outside the Rothschild Palais where the emigration office was located. 'This whole "Night of Broken Glass" was fully opposed to our wishes and our goal,' he later told an interviewer. 'Neither the SD nor the Gestapo had anything to do with it; on the contrary they were infuriated, because they had, in accordance with the instructions of the Reichsführer-SS [Himmler], through the most painstaking detailed work, built up organizations and offices which were ruthlessly attacked and shattered.' A report on the overall impact of the pogrom by the SD Head Office in January 1939 lamented that 'Valuable archival material and art treasures were destroyed as a result of the imprudence or ignorance of those involved.'[112]

On 10 November, Goebbels and Hitler met over lunch at the Osteria restaurant in Munich to take stock of their handiwork. By now they had information on the dimensions of the destruction, but they also had the first intimations that it was less than applauded by other members of the National Socialist hierarchy. They agreed to end the physical assaults immediately while promising to intensify the cold pogrom through legislation. Specifically, Hitler wanted to expropriate all Jewish businesses and impose a fine on the entire Jewish population as further atonement for the death of Rath. Goebbels wanted to make the Jews pay the clean-up costs, including the insurance bill. In the afternoon, the Deutsches Nachrichten Büro, the government news agency, announced 'A strict order . . . to the entire population to desist from all further demonstrations and actions against Jewry, regardless of what type. The definitive response to the Jewish assassination in Paris will be delivered to Jewry via the route of legislation and edicts.' Goebbels sent a special message to Gauleiters requiring that 'anti-Jewish actions be halted with the same speed with which they originated'. For good measure Rudolf Hess, Hitler's deputy, signalled all NSDAP branches that 'On the explicit order of the very highest authority setting fire to Jewish shops or similar actions may not occur under any circumstances.'[113]

The lacklustre popular response to the threat of war during the

Sudeten crisis and now the recoil from the pogrom may explain the speech that Hitler made to journalists later in the day regretting that Germans still lacked a warlike spirit. Goebbels not only had to rebut the atrocity stories that were all over the international media, but had to use the German press to justify the pogrom to his own people. A press conference at the Ministry of Propaganda on 17 November issued elaborate guidelines for articles to appear over the following days that would explain to the population the conspiratorial and parasitic nature of the Jews.[114]

Opinion reports collected by the SD offer a fine-grained impression of public reactions. Four days after Hitler ended the progrom, the SD sent out a questionnaire seeking data about Aryanization, criminal acts committed on the night, whether weapons were discovered, the amounts of valuables or cash seized, and the scale of insurance claims. Question 14 asked: 'How does the population view the operation. Impact on popular mood.' Respondents were asked to reply carefully and truthfully, 'without whitewashing'. Although it suited the SD to exaggerate the extent of public disquiet (especially concerning the ruination of property) in order to embarrass Goebbels, the feedback from their informants is corroborated by other contemporary sources.[115]

The city authorities in Minden reported that the action was 'expressly applauded by many' although the next day in the market square 'individuals here and there were especially reserved in their remarks'. Several weeks later the district governor added that there was 'an embarrassed silence, as if by common agreement regarding the operation ordered by the Party on 9–10 November'. He regretted that the local authorities had not been properly notified, otherwise senseless destruction, arson and 'anarchistic' behaviour could have been avoided. As a result, there was a mood of 'depression'. The mayor of Lemgo, in Westphalia, catalogued the devastation of the Jewish community. However, 'a portion' of the population could not understand why the synagogue was destroyed when 'the building could have been put to good use'. The mayor of Amt Borgentreich, a town in Westphalia, wrote that 'In many instances, the population had no understanding for the operation, or better, did not wish to understand it. The Jews were also the object of pity.' The inhabitants of Atteln, a rural community, had no objection to the arrest and removal of the Jews. 'In general', according to the mayor, 'the only thing the population took exception to was the material destruction.'[116]

The county commissioner in Halle, in Westphalia, gave a very detailed and totally detached account of the events based on reports from several locations. 'Generally', the mayor of Versmold stated, 'the population was noticeably quiet in its response.' They endorsed the idea of a reprisal but dissented from the 'destruction of public property of the German Volk'. In Brockhagen the small crowd that gathered to watch the house and stables of a Jewish cattle-dealer being consumed by flames stood in silence. In the small town of Werther, 'A large part of the population does not approve of this operation, most especially of the manner in which it was carried out.' The police there were angry that they had been alerted so late because initially they had tried to restrain the arsonists, only to be ignored. This had caused 'damage to the reputation and authority of the police'.[117]

Bielefeld's lord mayor discerned a 'definite understanding for the need to struggle against Jewry. It is likewise generally recognised as self-evident that if Jews are to be disposed of, extremely severe measures will have to be employed.' On the whole, there were few objections to the demolition of the synagogue. 'But the manner in which the Jewish shops, or the displays in Jewish shop windows were attacked – have generally not met with approval.' People were cynical about the claims of spontaneity. The Gestapo in this medium-sized industrial city confirmed that 'In general, the operation of 10 November 1938 has had a rather unfavourable impact on the public mood.'[118]

The rural population in the area around Koblenz manifested a blend of profiteering and pity. Many were 'engaged in large purchases of furniture and household goods from the Jews', presumably from those who were about to leave. Other peasants, who were influenced by the Churches, felt sympathy for them. The rural police in Muggendorf, a little town in Upper Franconia, likewise reported that the population was divided between those who felt the action was justified and a 'far larger' proportion who looked on it as 'improper and unwarranted'.[119]

Foreign observers confirm the divergent responses of the German population. Edwin Kemp, US consul general in Bremen, was quick to transmit the information that fifty Jews in the city had been arrested on the morning of 10 November and paraded along the street under SA guard. 'It was curious to note the lack of public enthusiasm at the spectacle. The parade was greeted with complete silence. The crowd viewing the broken shop windows also had nothing to say.' By contrast, when twenty-five Jewish community leaders in Stuttgart were led away, the US consul-general, Samuel Honaker, reported that 'bystanders cursed and shouted at them'. Honaker also observed that much of the damage to Jewish shops was caused by young men, often out of sight, in side streets off the main shopping avenues. 'These actions have caused a great part of the population to feel very uneasy and quietly to give expression to their lack of enthusiasm with such practices.' Only about 20 per cent of the people, by his estimate, were happy with the pogrom. Hugh Wilson, based at the embassy in Berlin, remarked that 'a surprising characteristic of the situation here is the intensity and scope among German citizens of a condemnation of the recent happenings against Jews'.[120]

The British consul in Frankfurt-am-Main, Robert Smallbones, identified several distinct phases to the pogrom there. It started with attempts to set fire to the city's three main synagogues. These were not terribly successful and the fires had to be reignited. Then the attack moved to shops and offices, whereupon there was widespread looting. Later, the Hitler Youth joined in and the onslaught spread to private residences, proceeding from the poorer Jewish neighbourhoods in the east end of the city towards the wealthier west end. By the time lorries drove up to collect the Jews arrested in the morning, 'a large crowd had gathered, which hurled abjective [sic] and abusive insults at every convoy as it arrived'. Smallbones also reported that Jewish refugees from small rural communities arrived in the city bearing tales of violence and destruction. In a later account sent to Sir George Ogilvie-Forbes, chargé d'affaires at the British Embassy, Smallbones groped for reasons why peace-loving Germans whom he generally admired could behave so awfully. 'The explanation of this outbreak of sadistic cruelty may be that sexual perversion, and in particular homosexuality, are very prevalent in Germany. It seems to me that mass sexual perversity may offer an explanation for this otherwise inexplicable outrage.'[121]

One report after another emphasized the unease of the Catholic population or its overt sympathy with the Jews. Catholics and Confessing Christians in Bielefeld 'cautiously criticised the burning of the synagogues' and some said 'the churches would be next in line'. The county commissioner for Höxter in Westphalia, with a population of around 30,000, recalled that the initial welcome for the arrest of the town's Jews evaporated when its inhabitants saw 'these more or less miserable looking individuals'. He contended that 'the population harboured no sympathy for this operation. The population was in a serious mood and depressed. There were clear signs here and there of pity.'

Catholic residents asked: would the church be next? Such reservations were not simply attributable to religious scruple. The 'preponderant majority' of the rural citizenry did not 'consider such an operation to be compatible with the reputation and dignity of the Germans'. The mayor of Bad Lippspringe, north of Paderborn, admitted frankly that 'The overwhelming proportion of the population failed to understand the operation against the Jews and condemned it, saying that such a thing should not be allowed to happen in a civilized society'. The county commissioner for the district of Paderborn stated bluntly that the Catholic population 'rejects the operation against the Jews. These circles, which are, as a matter of fundamental conviction, especially opposed to the National Socialist state due to their political-ecclesiastical ties, are particularly angered by the fact that the "houses of worship" of the Jews were set on fire.' They stubbornly treated the Jews as a religious group, not a race, and feared that other religions could suffer persecution. In a few places, clergymen were taken into custody for articulating sympathy for the Jews in the form of sermons or leading prayers for their welfare. Others got into trouble for insisting on the value and efficacy of baptism.[122]

The pogrom drew criticism from certain social groups for moral reasons. The SD District Office in Gotha, an industrial city in Thuringia, sent Berlin news of the 'immense satisfaction' felt by the population when over fifty Jews were arrested (of whom twenty-eight were sent to Buchenwald). Yet it noted expressions of sympathy from the 'better circles'. People in Ebermannstadt, a village in Upper Franconia, approved the fine on the Jews but not the destruction, 'because the consciousness of what is lawful began to waver'. The convoluted prose of the district officer adverted to popular outrage against the incidence of looting and 'selfish acts' such as the forced cancellation of debts owed to Jews and the transfer of property under duress. 'Such infractions of the established limits have transformed the purpose and value of the measures of retaliation into their very opposite.' In other words, citizens were appalled that some of the rioters used the occasion for their own benefit and were more interested in profit than principle. Honest folk, though not necessarily friendly to the Jews, wondered where the infringement of property rights would stop and how the law would be respected if it could be waived in the case of one, arbitrarily selected group. The president of the district court in Trier formulated the dilemma succinctly: 'The upshot of non-interference by the police is a new general feeling of insecurity regarding law and order. They say that what happened to the Jews can also happen at any time to other groups in the population, people who have made themselves the object of dislike because of some event or other.'[23]

The involvement of children and youths added to the discomfort of both the 'better circles' and more humble Germans who shared a prudent concern about the correct upbringing of the young. To the consternation of adults, in a number of places schoolchildren were released from classes on the morning of 10 November to spectate or to help tear down synagogues. In the usually tranquil spa town of Baden-Baden they were assembled to watch eighty Jewish men, who had been arrested by the SS earlier in the morning, paraded towards the synagogue where they were forced to sing the 'Horst Wessel' song. After the Jews were loaded onto trucks and driven off to Dachau, the synagogue was set on fire. In Großen-Linden, the main assault was delivered by 200 students who were transformed from budding scholars into a howling mob. The county commissioner of Halle reflected the disapproval of the role taken by youth, remarking that 'locally it is possible to discern an undeniable brutalization among young and certain other elements'.[124]

In its final overview, circulated on 7 December, the Jewish desk at the SD Head Office admitted that 'the civilian population participated only to a very limited extent'. No fewer than 14,000 Germans were made unemployed by the devastation of thirty-one department stores, thousands of smaller outlets, and numerous manufacturing concerns. The SD estimated the final cost of the damage at 990 million Reichsmarks. 'The attitude of the population to the actions, which initially was positive, changed fundamentally when the extent of the material damage inflicted became generally known.' They deplored the setback to the Four-Year Plan and feared the impact it would have on Germany's foreign relations. 'There was a particular condemnation by members of the armed forces of the methods against the Jews.' In Catholic areas the 'clear rejection of the entire operation' proved that 'internal political adversaries are exploiting this mood'.[125]

The November pogrom exposed deep fissures within the putative Volksgemeinschaft, between generations, between confessional groups, and between those with pre-Nazi political allegiances and those socialized under the Third Reich. One of the things that most appalled middle-aged conservative figures like the former German Ambassador to Rome, Ulrich von Hassell, was the involvement and enthusiasm of youth. On 25 November he confided to his diary, 'I am writing under the crushing emotions evoked by the vile persecution of the Jews … Not since the world war have we lost so much credit in the world.' Apart from his brazen fib that that the pogrom was spontaneous Goebbels was 'shameless enough to mobilise school classes'. Hassell feared that 'the lowest instincts have been aroused; and the effect, especially among the young, must have been bad'. Weeks later he visited Berlin and detected 'a deep sense of shame which has weighed heavily on all decent and thoughtful people since the hideous events of November. There is talk of little else.'[126]

Young people, by contrast, threw themselves into the pogrom when they had the chance and expressed few misgivings afterwards. Karl Fuchs was a twenty-one-year-old at the University of Würzburg where he was training to become a teacher. His father had joined the National Socialists as far back as 1923 and Karl was marinated in Nazi ideology. He joined the Hitler Youth, performed his Reich Labour Service, and had recently completed national service collecting the harvest. In a few months he would enter the army. He was the very incarnation of the Volksgemeinschaft. In a letter to his parents he recalled his part in the pogrom. 'My God, you should have been in Würzburg during this Jewish mess. I don't know if things were as hectic in Nuremberg but we made a clean sweep here. I can tell you that the authorities didn't miss one of those pig Jews. You should have seen the insolent behaviour of these Jews! Several times for instance, some of these old Jewish hags spat right in front of young girls! At any rate, it is significant that the whole world with the exception of old England, is turning against these scoundrels today. From now on, these Jewish gentlemen will think twice before firing on a German citizen abroad in order to hurt our entire nation. The people here were really upset.'[127]

Melita Maschmann, who was working in the press and propaganda office of the Bund deutscher Mädel in Frankfurt-an-der-Oder, attended a demonstration outside the town hall on 9 November. The next day she travelled to Berlin where she saw the shattered windows of Jewish stores and shops. 'I said to myself: The Jews are the enemies of the new Germany. Last night they had a taste of what this means. Let us hope that Western Jewry, which has resolved to hinder Germany's "new steps to greatness" will take the events of last night as a warning. If the Jews sow hatred against us all over the world, they must learn that we have hostages for them in our hands.' This was the Volksgemeinschaft in action.[128]

Jews into the concentration camps

The violence and robbery that typified the pogrom did not end after it was suspended. Rather, the terror moved to more discreet locations where it could be applied more precisely and according to a plan of sorts.

During the course of 10 November, the Gestapo and the security police attempted to carry out Hitler's orders, transmitted by Heydrich and Müller. The intention was to arrest and hold 30,000 Jews, mostly affluent, until they agreed to liquidate their businesses and emigrate. Heydrich carefully discounted Jews who were customarily spared the effect of anti-Jewish measures: men with distinguished war records or wartime wounds, plus the elderly and the sick. But the security police were unprepared and lacked sufficient strength to carry out this mission in one sweep. Nor did they have anywhere to hold the detainees. So it was necessary for the SA to help out, with the result that often Jews who were supposed to be excluded from the arrest category were taken away. The unfortunates were held in police cells, prisons, and make-shift detention centres such as cellars and empty buildings. Policemen and prison wardens were usually businesslike towards the Jews in their charge, but the inmates of temporary sites were guarded by ill-disciplined Brownshirts who used the opportunity to torture, humiliate and rob them. Philipp Flesch was arrested in Vienna and held with 2,000 other men in a cellar until he had an opportunity to show an SS officer his medal certificate proving that he had served in the trenches. He was then freed. Even as some men were being let out, others were being arrested. In Hamburg, many of the intended victims had gone into hiding when the pogrom started so the hunt for Jews went on for days.[129]

Those who were not immediately released were taken to railway stations and transported to Buchenwald, Dachau and Sachsenhausen concentration camps. There were no facilities to cope with them in the camps, either, so they were crammed into tents or improvised barracks. The overcrowding, lack of sanitation, inadequate food, and bad weather added misery to the systematic brutality of the SS-Totenkopf guards.

Almost all the survivors recalled the beating they received en route from the disembarkation point into the camp. This vicious induction was followed by the 'Appell' (roll call) that went on for hours despite the cold, rain or time of day. Such treatment was standard practice, but the Jewish men were utterly unprepared for what befell them. They were predominantly middle-aged and middle-class, transported from domestic calm into a hellish environment within a matter of hours.[130]

Around 11,000 Jews flowed into Dachau, transforming the camp population. The Jews were segregated and held in an area called the 'small camp' where conditions were far worse than in the long-established barracks. By February 1939, 187 had died. In Buchenwald the influx of just under 10,000 Jewish men was accommodated in a cluster of hastily erected tents labelled the Sonderlager, or special camp. The first arrivals were put to work building makeshift huts while further transports poured in. These primitive constructions had no floors and offered barely more protection against the elements than the tents they replaced. Cases of sickness soon multiplied, obliging the camp administration to convert the laundry into a hospital. It is estimated that 222 died in the special camp. Approximately 6,000 Jews were transported to Sachsenhausen, where about 100 perished. Overcrowding, malnutrition and exposure were responsible for the first epidemics to afflict the camp population. The massive inflow brought more than just disease; many new arrivals arrived with cash that they managed to keep in their possession or were sent money, tobacco and food. The sudden expansion of numbers, combined with the availability of money or goods for exchange, created a vibrant black market and stimulated corruption amongst the prisoners and the guards alike.[131]

However, the majority of Jewish men did not have to endure the camps for very long. Already on 16 November, Heydrich ordered the release of several categories. His instructions reflected both cynicism and public disquiet. Those with emigration papers, Jews who were ready to sell their businesses, and the lawyers needed to assist them were amongst the first to be let out. Elderly men and combat veterans followed suit. Finally, men over fifty years old and teenagers were released. By early 1939, only about 2,000 were left behind the wire. No matter how short the stay, though, the experience was traumatic and numbers of men never recovered from incarceration either physically or psychologically.[132]

Karl Schwabe, a forty-seven-year-old shopkeeper in Hanau, was arrested on 10 November and held with other Hanau Jews in a gymnasium. The elderly and ill were sent home following medical examinations by police doctors, but Karl was amongst those marched to the railway station. As they passed groups of spectators he noticed 'a few laughed, but sympathy and dismay could be seen on many faces'. Although the police who escorted them were friendly, once they arrived at Weimar the mood and tempo of events shifted dramatically. They were beaten from the trucks that unloaded them all the way until they were inside Buchenwald. The days that followed were marked by thirst, hunger, roll calls, and constant arbitrary violence. After ten days the SS started releasing men: the old, the young, decorated veterans. Food parcels and mineral water began to arrive in the camp; Karl got a package of clothing and a blanket from his wife. 'The days went by, and it was always the same thing. Dirt, diarrhoea, boredom and the constant waiting strained our nerves.' A month after his arrest, he was set free and driven back to the station in Weimar. There he was led to a room where Jewish women were serving coffee and white rolls. 'The coffee and rolls tasted unbelievably good. The friendliness with which they were given also did us good, and it was amazing how well the ladies worked together with the police.' After disposing of all their assets and paying the necessary taxes, Karl Schwabe, his wife and two children travelled to England and from there emigrated to America.[133]

Hans Reichmann, the doughty champion of Jewish interests, had been living from day to day in expectation of a visit from the Gestapo. For all the brutality of the welcome, when he finally arrived in Sachsenhausen he felt a kind of relief. The path had 'come to its pre-determined end'. Life settled into a routine of privation, abuse, pointless labour, and humiliation. During the moments of peace, in the packed barracks, the Jewish men comforted one another and discussed their situation. Each man knew that 'Outside our wives will be fighting to free us, but will they be able to do it on their own? The lawyers are here with us ...' Eventually Hans Reichmann's formidable wife Eva was able to extract him from the camp; in April 1939 they reached England.[134]

It was a period of extraordinary stress and anxiety for the women: wives, mothers, sisters and daughters raced against time to obtain the necessary papers to guarantee that fathers, husbands, brothers or sons could emigrate once released – if they lived that long. Hertha Nathorff's husband, a physician, was arrested on 10 November when he returned to his apartment from the Berlin clinic where he had been treating Jews injured during the night. Two days later she was at the American Consulate amidst a throng of women all trying to get entry visas for the USA that would qualify their husbands for release. 'Pale, aggrieved women from Berlin, Leipzig, Breslau all bore the same pain and they stood quietly, acting on behalf of their husbands and weeping in their hearts – a women's crusade.' It took a month for Hertha to get the necessary documents; her husband returned on 16 December. They emigrated to the United States early in 1939.[135]

Mally Dienemann, in Offenbach, went to the local police station with a medical certificate to show that her sixty-three-year-old husband, detained on 10 November, was unfit to remain in prison. She was told that only the Gestapo could approve his release. At dawn the next day she watched as her husband and other Jews were driven off in a bus: their destination was Buchenwald. Over the next days Mally pleaded with officials on behalf of her husband. Then she heard that prisoners were being freed if they had emigration certificates for Palestine, so she telegraphed her children, who were already there, and told them to get one for their father. But this was only the start of a different ordeal. 'And now a series of offices awaited me. The official emigration office in Frankfurt, the Gestapo, the police, the finance office, a petition to Buchenwald, a petition to the Gestapo in Darmstadt'. It took over a week to get the paperwork done. Rabbi Dienemann was reunited with Mally in Offenbach on 29 November. They emigrated to Palestine early the next year, but he never recovered from his incarceration. A few months after arriving in the Holy Land, Rabbi Dienemann died.[136]

A meeting at the Air Ministry

The detention of Jewish men in concentration camps was the fulfilment of SD Judenpolitik and marked a step-change in treatment of the Jewish question. Nationally coordinated and (more or less) carefully prepared actions covering the entire Jewish population, combining intimidation with legal measures, now came to the fore.[137] The accidental outcome of the November pogrom was a more coherent and strategic multi-agency approach, typified by greater centralization of planning and inter-ministerial conferences. This new era was marked by the first great 'conference' on Judenpolitik, convened by Göring in the imposing new Aviation Ministry building.

The conference on 12 November 1938 opened at eleven in the morning and lasted nearly four hours. It was chaired by Göring and attended by the major players in economic and domestic affairs: Goebbels; Frick, the minister for the interior, and his senior civil servant Wilhelm Stuckart; Gürtner, the justice minister; Funk, the minister for economics; Schwerin von Krosigk, the finance minister; Ernst Woermann, representing the foreign office; Kurt Daluege, head of the uniformed police; and Heydrich, chief of the Sipo-SD. Bürckel and Fischböck attended to speak for interests in the Ostmark and to provide their experience of implementing Judenpolitik in conditions less hamstrung by vested interests and legislative niceties. Representatives of the insurance industry were present, ex officio. Their spokesman was Eduard Hilgard, director of the Allianz company and head of the Reich Group of Insurers. With the addition of other ministerial delegates, assistants and experts there were around a hundred people in the room. All those present sensed that it was a momentous gathering, and if they had any doubts they were put right by Göring in his opening remarks.[138]

He began by announcing that Hitler had personally given him the task of bringing together all the different strands of Judenpolitik and coordinating them in one, concerted drive to settle the Jewish question, 'one way or another'. Göring then referred back to previous, failed attempts to formulate and push through policy to eliminate the Jews from the German economy. It was, he declared, essentially an economic question though it would need legal measures to achieve a solution and propaganda to explain why. The public needed to understand that rioting was no panacea. 'I have had enough of demonstrations! They don't harm the Jew, but me, who is the ultimate authority for co-ordinating the German economy ... It's insane to clean out and burn a Jewish warehouse then have a German insurance company make good the loss. And the goods which I need desperately ... are being burned ... I may as well burn the raw materials before they arrive.' Yet this was secondary: 'the fundamental idea in this programme of the elimination of the Jew from the German economy is first, the Jew being ejected from the economy transfers his property to the State.'[139]

Göring then outlined how he envisaged the takeover or closure of Jewish shops, stores, manufacturing enterprises and factories. Still smarting from the gold-rush in Vienna, he set out rough guidelines for a trustee office that would value Jewish concerns and arrange for their transfer to suitable owners at a reasonable price, while also trying to favour deserving and competent party members. Factories that were not necessary to the economy would be shut down; but every effort would be made to protect German employees. He also stipulated that the interests of foreign Jews would have to be respected, a gesture to the Foreign Office. Göring continued, saying that although they were to be deprived of their livelihoods Jews would not benefit directly from the sale of their property; they would be compensated with bonds that would generate enough income for them to live off.[140]

Funk was anxious whether Jewish-owned stores would be reopened. What would happen to their stock, much of which had not been paid for by the store-owner? What would happen to the employees? Instead of resolving these difficult matters, Göring got sidetracked into exchanges about the extent of the damage to synagogues – which provided an opportunity for Goebbels to jump in. He advocated the razing of surviving synagogue structures, obliterating any memory of their existence. With his peculiar astringency he then went on to propose measures for driving Jews out of the public sphere entirely. They should be banned from attending cinemas, theatres and concerts; limited to one, designated carriage on trains; and prohibited from all except a few places of open-air recreation such as resorts, beaches, woods and parks. Those specific sites, even park benches, should be marked as only for Jews and strictly segregated. Finally, he demanded the expulsion of those Jewish children remaining in the state school system.

At this point, Eduard Hilgard was called in to give a presentation on the insurance question. As the Allianz director was making his way through the crowded room, Göring mentioned that the regime had contemplated imposing an atonement fine on the Jews after the assassination of Gustloff. This time they would do it, but the tantalized audience had to wait for details. With Hilgard in position, Göring reverted to the subject at hand and explained the dilemma they had regarding insurance payments. What could the Jews claim? What measures could be taken to stop them benefiting? In a fascinating disquisition that has been overlooked by historians, Hilgard enumerated the different causes of damage. There had been fire, smashed glass, and theft. Jews were insured against fire and theft; but the plate glass was commonly insured by the building owner, usually Germans. When Göring heard this, he groaned: 'It doesn't make sense. We have no raw materials. It is all glass imported from foreign countries and has to be paid for in foreign currency! One could go nuts.'[141]

Hilgard then moved on to the matter of theft. Far from treating the pogrom as state-sanctioned vengeance on the Jews, he characterized it as an outbreak of mass criminality. Göring tried to reclassify the depredations as 'rioting' in the hope that this would deflect the insurance claim, but Hilgard would have none of it. As an example he cited the sacking of the Margraf jewellery store on Unter der Linden that resulted in losses amounting to RM1.7 million. Again, Göring was incensed. Addressing Daluege and Heydrich he commanded them to recover the stolen goods: 'You'll have to get me this jewellery through raids, staged on a tremendous scale!' Daluege responded that police investigations had already begun and 150 people had been arrested. Heydrich added that there had been 800 cases of looting across the Reich. Recovering the stolen property was no simple matter because much stock had been tossed into the street where it had been picked up. 'Even children have filled their pockets, just for fun.' In a telling confession, he told the meeting that in view of their bad behaviour the Hitler Youth would be held back from such actions in the future.

The embarrassment deepened when Hilgard moved on to the question of compensating foreign companies and citizens. There was no way to avoid this without compromising Germany's commercial standing in the world. Nor was there a way to avoid paying out to Jews if the claims were legitimate: otherwise trust in German insurance companies would evaporate. Since such an outcome was unpalatable the meeting digressed into a technical discussion of how insurance payments could be made without the Jews actually benefiting. It was eventually agreed that the claims would be met, but the payments would never reach the German Jewish claimants. As Heydrich put it, 'That way we'll save face.' However, while the Allianz director assumed that Göring would let the insurers recover the money they paid out, the head of the Four Year Plan arbitrarily announced that the state would confiscate it. Hilgard fumed at this blatant larceny, but he was unable to respond on the spot. Instead, he spent months bargaining with the regime to reduce the liability of the insurance companies.[142]

When Heydrich pointed out that the state would also lose sales taxes, taxes on property and taxes on income from 7,500 stores and shops, Göring could not conceal his exasperation: 'I wish you had killed 200 Jews, and not destroyed such values.' Heydrich did not disagree, but pointed out that only thirty-five Jews had died. It was of course far more across the Reich and in Austria, yet the death toll was not the real issue and he knew he was safe from Göring's ire: he had not started the pogrom.[143]

Göring became even more bad-tempered and abusive when discussion moved back to compensating foreign property owners. He was indignant that 'every dirty Polish Jew' who suffered damages had legal rights. After Woermann, presenting the Foreign Office point of view, warned that the United States might retaliate if foreign-born Jews were not properly compensated, Göring expostulated that German businessmen should sell up and get out of 'that country of scoundrels', that 'gangster state'.

Funk then wrenched the meeting back to the outstanding dilemma regarding the reopening of Jewish shops and department stores. Here Fischböck intervened with a detailed report on Austria. According to a carefully researched plan based on what the local economy required, 12,000–14,000 of the 17,000 Jewish-owned enterprises in Vienna were to be shut down, and only about 3,000 transferred to new owners. Fischböck explained how the scheme was designed to eliminate fraud and corruption, placing businesses in competent hands. At last, Göring heard something that pleased him. 'I have to say this proposal is grand. This way the whole affair would be wound up in Vienna, one of the Jewish capitals, so to speak, by Christmas or the end of the year.' Funk seized his chance and told the meeting that the Economics Ministry had prepared a law to achieve something similar in the Reich. From 1 January 1939, Jews would be forbidden to conduct any business. But Fischböck wasn't finished. He asked the meeting for its agreement to requisition thousands of apartments in Vienna owned by Jews and to expropriate their equities. The victims would be compensated in the form of a low interest payment on the notional debt accrued to the state through the purchase. That way the state would not actually have to pay more than a fraction of the true cost of the assets. Again, Göring liked the idea.

By now, several hours had passed. Perhaps sensing that the meeting was drawing to a close, Heydrich made a decisive intervention. 'In spite of the elimination of the Jews from economic life, the main problem, namely to kick the Jew out of Germany, remains. May I make a few proposals to that effect?' He then sketched the work of the Central Office for Emigration in Vienna, run by Eichmann, and bragged that it had secured the emigration of 50,000 Jews (he used the term 'eliminated') from Austria while over the same period only 19,000 had been 'eliminated' from the Old Reich. This caught Göring's attention: 'How is that possible?' Heydrich then explained how rich Jews were fleeced to pay for the emigration of 'the Jewish mob'. Göring retorted, 'Have you ever thought that this procedure may cost us so much in foreign currency that in the end we won't be able to hold out.' Having reassured him that the Jews could only take out a limited amount of foreign currency, Heydrich asked permission to set up a similar emigration office in the Old Reich. He envisaged an emigration rate of 8,000–10,000 Jews per year for eight to ten years. Even so, this would still leave behind a great mass of Jews who, because of the economic restrictions, would be unemployed and indigent. 'Therefore, I shall have to take steps to isolate the Jew so he won't enter into the normal German routine of life.' As a means to this end he proposed marking the Jews, including those who were foreign-born.

His suggestion sparked an exchange that reveals a great deal about Judenpolitik at this stage and illuminates the foundations on which later initiatives rested. Göring was alarmed that ghettos would result from what Heydrich was proposing. Heydrich was quick to correct this misapprehension: he agreed that closed ghettos were a bad idea because his police would not be able to monitor the Jews within. It was better that they should be surrounded by 'the watchful eyes of the whole population'. 'The Jew' would be barred from certain areas and limited to places where he could buy food and services from his own kind. Göring interjected, 'One moment. You cannot let him starve.' If Jews were allowed to have shops and businesses on certain streets they would be back to square one – a sort of ghetto. Ultimately, both Göring and Heydrich agreed, in effect, to residential segregation. Funk observed, as though the matter was settled, that it would involve overcrowding and starvation. Undeterred, Heydrich went on to enumerate numerous other restrictions he wanted to impose on Jews: the confiscation of driving licences and car ownership permits, prohibition from spas and resorts, ejection from hospitals and the creation of Jewish-only health services.

In the closing minutes, Göring recurred to the notion of a fine. When everyone assented, he started drafting the decree out loud: 'that German Jewry shall, as punishment for their abominable crimes etc., etc., have to make a contribution of one billion. That'll work. The swine won't commit another murder. Incidentally, I'd like to say again that I would not like to be a Jew in Germany.'

Bringing the meeting to an end, Göring warned that 'If, in the near future, the German Reich should come into conflict with foreign powers, it goes without saying that we in Germany should first of all let it come to a showdown with the Jews.' In other words, the Jews were hostages and if a conflict were to break out they would pay the price. However, foreign governments could lift the threat by helping to remove them. To this end Hitler was trying to induce other countries to assist the solution of the Jewish question. Göring specifically cited the 'Madagascar project', the suggestion made by the French government in 1937, and revived in 1938, to settle Jewish refugees on the island off the coast of east Africa. Thus in the dying moments of the conclave Göring previewed two of the main planks of future German policy towards the Jews, reiterating the fundamental nexus between foreign policy, war, and Judenpolitik.[144]

At 2.30 in the afternoon, the meeting dispersed. Presumably those of the participants who were not compelled to return to their offices, or other business, went off in search of a late lunch. They had accomplished a great deal: a plan for eliminating the Jews from the German economy that would be centralized and implemented under Göring's authority; agreement to establish a central emigration office for the Old Reich, under the management of the security police and SD, intended to emigrate 100,000 Jews in ten years; a neat solution to the problem of settling insurance claims in the wake of the November riots; and a massive fine to be levied on the German Jews to help pay for war preparations. The tone and style of the meeting was almost as important. The language was intemperate, callous, abusive and violent. Jews were discussed in terms of a problem and a danger that had to be dealt with ruthlessly. No one was inhibited by compassion or concern with civil or legal rights. Where necessary, decrees would bring the law into line with what they wanted to do to the Jewish population. Not even the conservatives still in the government, like Krosigk, objected to this. Ultimately, the Jews would be driven out of Germany and any that remained would be segregated, monitored and closely controlled. They were pawns in a geo-strategic game. Foreign powers were now expected to help solve the Jewish question, but if they chose not to do so the Jews would suffer. If war broke out, there would be a 'showdown'. The format of the meeting established a model for future discussion of ways to solve the Jewish question and fixed the personnel, more or less. Göring was now firmly in control of Jewish affairs; Heydrich was his executive arm. Other ministries and agencies were subordinate, although they would always be able to assert their prerogatives; otherwise they would have to butt their way in and justify a leading role. Judenpolitik had reached a turning point and it was not long before Jews felt the consequences.

The total exclusion of Jews from society and the economy

Before the day was out, Göring had promulgated the first Decree on the Exclusion of the Jews from German Economic Life. Jews were henceforth prohibited from earning a livelihood through selling goods or services wholesale, in fixed retail outlets, by mail order, at markets and fairs, or by peddling. Those still in employment were dismissed and they were forbidden to run firms. Other ministers hastened to pass similar ordinances concerning their domains; no one wanted to appear soft on the Jews. On the contrary, there was competition to show who could be the most punitive. Goebbels followed up his threats by prohibiting Jews from access to places of public entertainment. Heydrich revoked the driving licences held by Jews and, for good measure, invalidated their car ownership permits. The last Jewish children still attending state schools were told not to return to class. Jews were banned from all sporting and recreational activity. The surviving Jewish newspapers were suppressed and replaced by one gazette, the *Jüdisches Nachrichtenblatt*. Its function was primarily to inform Jews of official measures against them. A week later, the Decree on Public Welfare imposed on municipal and local welfare offices a uniform policy towards Jewish supplicants. It curtailed any remaining benefits to which Jews were entitled. A few thousand, including disabled war veterans, continued to receive state relief; but most of those who were now made unemployed or cut off from a living were thrown on the resources of Jewish aid agencies.[145]

At the start of December 1938, the Decree on the Utilization of Jewish Assets brought to the whole of the Greater Reich the methods pioneered in Austria to Aryanize Jewish businesses. It mandated the compulsory sale of Jewish-owned enterprises, the proceeds to be paid into special accounts that were controlled by the authorities. The decree also obligated Jews to move all their securities into blocked accounts. Thereafter they would need permission to realize even small portions of their assets in the form of shares or bonds. In an address to Gauleiters on 6 December, Göring made it absolutely clear that he would not

tolerate individual banditry or the senseless destruction of Jewish property. Only the ravenous German state would benefit from the wealth
accumulated by Jews through decades of hard work.[146]

The forced sale of Jewish businesses was more strictly regulated
than in Austria, but it triggered a bonanza nonetheless. Julius Lippert,
mayor of Berlin, reported a 'flood of inquiries' to the trustees appointed
to oversee the transfer process. He was in the happy position of being
able to gratify these supplicants, selecting worthy applicants with the
Reich economics minister. Their criteria were wide open to cronyism
and corruption: 'Preference should be given to long-time and deserving party members who had suffered an injury during the period of
struggle.' Next in line were party members with some commercial
experience who wished to go into business, Berliners displaced by
urban redevelopment, and, lastly, 'long-time employees of Jewish firms,
as long as these persons are not "Jew lackeys".' Lippert presided over
the liquidation or sale of 976 tailoring establishments, 364 furriers, 268
hat-makers and milliners, 181 shoe-makers, 114 watch-makers, and 49
gold- and silversmiths. Throughout Germany by April 1939, state-nom-
inated trustees had liquidated 15,000 of the 39,000 Jewish businesses in
existence a year before and were in the process of selling 17,000 to new,
Aryan owners.[147]

A further decree on 21 February 1939 commanded Jews to surrender jewellery and precious metals to the state in exchange for cash. The
order embraced items such as brooches, necklaces, candelabra, silverware and ritual objects often associated with the practice of Judaism and
celebrations of the life-cycle. Jews were required to take their valuables
to state pawnshops where the managers naturally paid out the lowest
conceivable amount and took no account of antiquity or rarity, let alone
sentimental values. In Breslau, an eighty-year-old Jewish man named
Leo Bernstein pleaded with the authorities to be allowed to keep two
sabbath candlesticks, a silver kiddush cup, and a few other items that he
and his wife had used annually on Jewish festivals over the course of
fifty years of married life. Abraham Ascher, the historian of Breslau
Jews, comments that 'the pawnshop did not generally honour such
requests'. Wedding rings were exempted.[148]

Jewish labour was also perceived as a potential resource for the
omnivorous war economy. At the end of 1938 Göring demanded plans
to mobilize Jews so as to free up German workers for the munitions
industry. It was taken for granted that this new labour force could not

be allowed to operate alongside Germans. Jewish workers were to be segregated and strictly monitored.[149]

Around the same time, and again following the 'Vienna model', city authorities across Germany began to compile registers of Jewish residences. The implications of this survey were realized at the end of April 1939 with the announcement of the Law on Renting to Jews. Under this legislation Jews lost any protection against eviction. Conversely, municipal authorities could order a Jewish home owner to rent space to another Jew or an entire Jewish family. The means were thus created to herd Jews together in apartment blocks or houses, often adjacent to one another or on the same street. They were known as Judenhauser, Jew-houses, and were a short step away from ghettos.[150]

Finally, after the German occupation of Bohemia and Moravia in March 1939, the bank accounts of Jews in what became the Protectorate were frozen and access to safety deposit boxes was controlled. A few months later this practice was extended into the Reich. The expropriation of the German and Austrian Jews was now total. Access to whatever wealth and property they retained was on the sufferance of Nazi officials and awaited confiscation whenever the regime desired.[151]

The intensification of anti-Jewish measures inevitably brought the status of Mischlinge into sharp relief. This offered an opportunity for Frick to exert his much-depleted authority in Jewish affairs. On 16 December 1938 he convened his own conference to determine the fate of part-Jews. Representatives of the party, the Finance Ministry, regional officials, Heydrich and the Berlin police chief attended. In imitation of Göring, Frick commenced by announcing that he had obtained Hitler's permission for a series of new contrivances. Having established his mandate, he explained that after due consideration Mischlinge were to be excluded from the hail of persecutory legislation: there were simply too many – estimated at 700,000 – to alienate. The main thrust of Judenpolitik was to be the forced emigration of the Jewish population; the Jews left behind would be concentrated in Jew-houses and subjected to compulsory labour. But the Führer had ruled out marking them or the creation of ghettos. Subsequently, Göring proclaimed a new category of 'privileged Jew' intended to cover Jews married to Aryans. The aim of this bewildering set of regulations was to preserve the offspring of mixed marriages for the German people and to insulate them, for the time being, from expropriation. Thus, a mixed-race couple with children who were being raised as Christians would be allowed to retain their home and pass on wealth to their offspring. But if the couple were childless they would be treated as Jews, could forfeit their property and be forced into a Jew-house. The same applied if they had opted to bring up their children in the Jewish faith. If an Aryan chose to divorce their spouse, the Jewish half of the couple lost his or her privileged status.[152]

Both Göring and Frick at their respective meetings emphasized that the regime prioritized systematic Jewish emigration. On 24 January 1939, Göring ordered Heydrich to establish a Jewish emigration office for the entire Reich modelled on the prototype in Vienna. With its creation, the Sipo-SD acquired unrivalled power over the fate of the Jews in Germany. Just as Eichmann had reshaped the IKG to serve as an instrument of emigration, at the same time as holding the Jewish population under his control, in February the Interior Ministry commenced the reconfiguration of the Reichsvertretung into the Reichsvereinigung der Juden in Deutschland. This wholly Nazi-appointed body was streamlined to facilitate emigration while maintaining the minimum level of services for the remaining Jews, such as education for the young, health care, relief for those with no means of support, and care for the elderly.[153]

Foreign reactions

While Göring and the German leadership were devising ever more inventive ways to extrude and exploit Jews, governments and citizens around the world looked on aghast. However, the international response did not translate into practical aid to the victims. Local anti-Semitism, domestic politics and diplomatic priorities negated the exercise of compassion. Furthermore, governments in western Europe were apprehensive lest German action, which had already inspired a spate of anti-Jewish legislation in Italy, Romania and Hungary, might engender a wave of expulsions. Any willingness to take in German Jewish refugees on German terms might be read as an invitation by other countries to rob their Jews and kick them out.

The British press reported the November pogrom in excruciating detail, eliciting editorials and letters that were universally damning. The *Daily Telegraph*, on 11 November, commented that 'Racial hatred and hysteria seems to have taken complete hold of otherwise decent people.' Even advocates of appeasement buckled. In *The Times* the following day the Archbishop of Canterbury, Cosmo Lang, wrote, 'there are times when the mere instincts of humanity make silence impossible. Would that the rulers of the Reich could realize that such excesses of hatred and malice put upon the friendship which we are ready to offer them an almost intolerable strain.' Prime Minister Neville Chamberlain, the arch appeaser, wrote to his sister Ida, 'I am horrified by the German behaviour to the Jews.' Though he viewed the events chiefly as a stumbling block to the improvement of Anglo-German relations, he could not conceal his dismay. 'It is clear that Nazi hatred will stick at nothing to find a pretext for their barbarities.'[154]

The British government came under considerable pressure to alleviate the plight of Jews attempting to flee the Reich. Eleanor Rathbone, an independent MP for the combined English universities, set up a Parliamentary Committee on Refugees to coordinate the efforts of members in all parties, including Victor Cazalet and Harold Nicolson, who were responding to considerable grass-roots concern. In cabinet on 14 November, the home secretary, Sir Samuel Hoare, warned that there were 'signs the House of Commons and the country might get out of hand'. Chamberlain himself received a deputation from the Council for German Jewry comprising Viscount Samuel, Lord Bearsted, Lionel de Rothschild, the Chief Rabbi and Chaim Weizmann, president of the World Zionist Organization. The Jewish leaders conceded at the outset that Britain could not open its doors to unlimited immigration but asked that it provide temporary refuge for German Jewish children. They also asked the prime minister to persuade dominion and colonial governments to offer settlement opportunities. Lionel de Rothschild spelled out the financial implications of evacuating the bulk of the German Jewish population and asked for the government to underwrite the £30 million he estimated it would cost. Chamberlain doubted that homes could be found for Jews in Britain or the empire, but promised to see what could be done.[155]

The pressure was not only domestic. At the next cabinet meeting, Lord Halifax, the foreign secretary, urged his colleagues to do something to mollify opinion in the United States, which was increasingly irritated by the restrictions Britain was imposing on Jewish immigration into Palestine. However, Hoare told them that British Jews were 'averse from allowing very large numbers of Jews to enter this country' and feared an 'anti-Jewish agitation'. Ministers concurred with the home secretary who told the House of Commons during a debate on the refugee crisis that there was an 'underlying current of suspicion and anxiety rightly or wrongly, about alien immigration on any big scale. It is a fact that below the surface there is the making of a definite anti-Jewish movement.'[156]

Nevertheless, Britain became the only country to ameliorate its immigration rules as a direct response to the unfolding tragedy. Whereas Jewish women applying for jobs as domestic servants had previously been obliged to go through the Ministry of Labour, the Home Office now took responsibility for processing applications and farmed it out to the Jewish refugee agencies. Soon 400 applicants a week were being churned through the system, enabling roughly 14,000 women to reach the UK. Speaking in the House of Commons on 21 November, Sir Samuel Hoare also announced that Britain would admit refugees awaiting migration elsewhere, training for emigration, and unaccompanied minors. Consequently, while only 11,000 German Jews had arrived in the period up to March 1938, in the following nineteen months around 50,000 German, Austrian and Czech Jews poured into the country. This included roughly 9,000 below the age of seventeen on special chartered trains known as the Kindertransport. The number was further swollen by the unofficial actions of British consuls and passport control officers. Frank Foley, who was actually a spy based in the British Embassy in Berlin, used his position as a PCO to issue visas to desperate Jews with only the flimsiest of guarantees from persons in the UK. He worked closely with Wilfred Israel who was struggling to secure the emigration of the remaining Jewish employees after the forced sale of his family's business.[157]

News of the November pogrom was a page one story in the *New York Times* for three days and received similar treatment in newspapers across America. At a press conference on 14 November, President Roosevelt declared: 'The news of the past couple of days from Germany has deeply shocked public opinion in the United States ... I myself could scarcely believe that such things could occur in a twentieth century civilization.' The president announced that he had instructed the State Department to recall the American Ambassador for consultations. But, he told reporters, there would be no change to the immigration quota. This did not preclude helpful gestures. At a subsequent cabinet meeting he seized on a proposal by Francis Perkins, the Secretary for Labor, to extend the stay of Germans who were already in the USA on temporary visas. He also urged the State Department to work energetically to encourage South American governments to make land available for Jewish settlement projects. Indeed, Roosevelt became almost obsessed with the notion of creating Jewish settlements in undeveloped parts of the world and summoned experts to the White House to review the possibilities. The president probably wanted to do more, but he was restrained by the State Department and chastened by his party's poor performance in the recent mid-term elections. There was no political risk in asking other countries to take Jewish refugees. He also tried to bounce the British into adopting a more generous approach to immigration into Palestine, which may have encouraged Chamberlain to give the green light to the child-rescue scheme. In cabinet, Lord Halifax, the foreign secretary, had thrown his weight behind it specifically because it would gratify the Americans.[158]

Like the president, US diplomats and State Department officials were pulled this way and that. On 5 December, Raymond Geist wrote privately to George Messersmith, 'The Jews of Germany are being condemned to death and their sentence will be slowly carried out, but probably too fast for the world to save them.' In reply, Messersmith cautioned against 'hysterical action'. J. P. Moffat, though not lacking sensitivity, was irritated by Jewish lobbying. He confided to his diary: 'The pressure from Jewish groups all over the country is growing to a point where before long it will begin to react very seriously against their own best interests.' He acknowledged that Jews were enduring a terrible time and admitted that any reasonable person would wish to help, but added menacingly, 'no one likes to be subjected to pressure of the sort they are exerting and the American public does not like pressure in favour of one particular population or group'.[159]

These cross-currents help explain the fate of an American bid to emulate the Kindertransport scheme. In February 1939, Robert Wagner, a Democratic senator for New York, and Edith Nourse Rogers, a Republican congresswoman, came up with the idea of circumventing the immigration quotas by passing special legislation to allow the entry of 20,000 German refugee children over a limited period. The Wagner–Rogers Bill garnered extensive support, but was just as vigorously opposed by the restrictionists. One cynical argument against the proposed measure was that it sanctioned the splitting up of families, which offended Christian values. More prosaically, the State Department baulked at the prospect of processing thousands of extra visas. With polls showing that over 80 per cent of Americans were against any liberalization of immigration controls, Roosevelt declined to give White House backing to the bill. By spring it had perished in committee.[160]

The French government, which was in the throes of negotiating a statement of Franco-German friendship, remained mute about the pogrom. The foreign minister, Georges Bonnet, actually accused French Jews of sabotaging good relations with Germany by harping on about the suffering of their co-religionists. The interior minister ordered the border police to turn away Jews even if they had a valid visa to enter France. As an alternative, Henry Bérenger, the principal French delegate at the Évian conference, breathed life back into the proposals to settle Jews in Madagascar. This time it was the Germans who took notice. In early December 1938, Ribbentrop sent a note to Hitler reporting that the French wanted to send 10,000 Jews to the island. The notion evidently appealed to the Nazi hierarchy since Hitler adverted to it in a speech a month later.[161]

In the *Neues Tagebuch*, Schwarzschild drew political as well as moral conclusions from the international reaction. He maintained that the cynicism and brutality with which Germany treated its Jews mirrored its conduct of foreign policy. Conversely, the failure of the international community to offer succour to the Jews (by evacuation if necessary) reflected its supine response to German aggression. Both were manifestations of moral enfeeblement. 'People have never understood the extent to which the method the Third Reich employed in the matter of the Jews was symptomatic of the method it employs in general, in all matters. A whole host of mistakes in foreign policy could have been avoided if people had been capable of relating the Nazis' procedure in the matter of the Jews to their procedures in general.' Schwarzschild marvelled that the USA, Russia and Europe with a combined population of 600 million could not absorb 600,000 Jews. He warned that it might soon be too late, in any case. 'Is it even certain today that the Nazi Reich, with its shortage of manpower, will be willing to let these people leave? Are their plans not heading in another direction, towards using them as slave labour, perhaps even, occasionally, as shooting targets?'[162]

Fleeing the Reich

In the months after the pogrom, the closure of the Centralverein and the detention of communal leaders left the terrified Jewish population of Germany and Austria directionless, with almost no institutional support or functioning networks. Acting individually, Jewish men and women struggled to find ways to escape by legal or illegal routes. As their choices narrowed they found themselves exploring ever more unlikely options.

Victor Klemperer had escaped the worst horrors of the pogrom because he was in hospital getting treatment for a bladder infection. Nevertheless he was arrested and briefly detained by the police after a search of his house revealed a weapon: his old wartime sabre. Once he was back home he was consumed by 'the struggle to emigrate'. He tried to get information about obtaining a visa for Cuba, which he heard was willing to accept German Jews, at a price. He even looked into the possibility of emigration to Rhodesia or Alaska.[163]

On 30 March 1939, Heinz Hesdörffer and his brother Ernst crossed the frontier into the Netherlands. Heinz was a bright sixteen-year-old, bespectacled but good-looking and full of charm. He was born in the spa town of Bad Kreuznach, where his father owned a sweet factory. The family, which was religious by German Jewish standards, lived well. As a result of anti-Semitic abuse Heinz was transferred to a Jewish school in Frankfurt-am-Main, where he lived with an aunt. During the November pogrom SA men wrecked the sweet factory and the business was wound up. His mother (his father had died) tried to get visas for emigration to the United States, but this proved impossible. Instead Ernst and his brother took advantage of a scheme under which 2,000 unaccompanied minors were admitted to the Netherlands into the care of the Jewish community. They were not allowed to work and had to live in a refugee camp, but at least they were safe.[164]

Thousands of others illicitly entered neighbouring countries, chiefly France. They saved themselves from Nazi persecution, but immediately faced other dangers. Their passports were stamped with a red 'J' that might as well have been the mark of Cain. It left them at the mercy of the local police, who were empowered to arrest and intern illegal immigrants. Without papers entitling them to work, these Jews were condemned to eke out what money they brought with them or risk taking a badly paid job in a workshop liable to be raided at any time by the immigration police.[165]

Ernest Heppner, like Heinz Hesdörffer, came from a religious Jewish family. He was born in 1921 in Breslau, where his father, a decorated war veteran, operated a factory making unleavened bread (matzoh) for the Passover festival. After the Nuremberg Laws Ernest was expelled from school. Nevertheless, his mother and father shared the view that 'anti-semitism was directed primarily towards the immigrants, the Polish Jews . . . German veterans and their families had nothing to fear.' The November pogrom ruined this illusion and ended any hope that things in Germany would improve. Although his father evaded arrest, Ernest's brother was sent to Buchenwald. He contemplated crossing into Poland illegally until he learned from the Hilfsverein der Juden in Deutschland that it was possible to enter Shanghai without any visa. While this seemed miraculously simple, the vista was hardly inviting. 'Shanghai, China. What we heard was not comforting: the Japanese, who were allies of the Nazis, had bombed and razed Chinese cities . . . there was a war raging in the coastal areas. There would be no way for us to make a living in Shanghai and no assurance that we would be able to survive there.' But such was their trepidation about the future of Jews in Germany that even this option now seemed attractive. At the last moment they were able to secure berths on a liner sailing from Genoa. Ernest's father hurriedly sold his factory and their apartment; his mother acquired the necessary papers. These included a new passport with the 'J' stamp. The Heppners discovered what this signified when British customs officials stopped them disembarking at Port Said, on the Suez Canal, to see the sights. Border police around the world understood that anyone carrying such a passport was probably a refugee and liable to become an illegal immigrant if given half the chance. They continued on the long journey to their distant and dubious haven.[166]

In Vienna the IKG, under the direction of Benjamin Murmelstein, assisted thousands of would-be emigrants each week. The staff swelled to over a thousand as paid workers and volunteers struggled to complete the paperwork and fund the emigration in the face of escalating German demands and extortion. Nearly 100,000 Austrian Jews, most from Vienna, departed in the eighteen months following the Anschluss – getting on for 50 per cent of the entire Jewish population. Priority was accorded to orphans and children whose fathers were in concentration camps. Zionist emissaries from Palestine, led by Moshe Agami and Ehud Avriel, assembled groups of young pioneers who were ready to attempt illegal emigration to Palestine in defiance of the British blockade. On the very margins of the emigration effort were the people smugglers. The most prominent and successful was Berthold Storfer, a Jewish-born Viennese businessman, who developed a close working relationship with the SD on the basis of their mutual desire to get Jews out of the country, by fair means or foul.[167]

In her diary, Ruth Maier logged the people she knew who 'secretly vanished' from Vienna, heading illicitly to Palestine, Bombay, Shanghai. Thanks to help from a former English teacher, she anticipated going to Britain to work as a domestic servant. While she waited for confirmation of the job and a visa, she observed the deteriorating scene. 'When I first saw "For Aryans Only" on the benches, or "No Jews" in the cafes, the broken windows, I could hardly believe it. Now I just pass by and scarcely notice.' She heard that two Jews committed suicide, leaving behind a note reading 'This is how you get over the border in 24 hours.' She also witnessed the night-time departure of the first Kindertransport from Hütteldorf Station on the outskirts of Vienna. 'The Jewish stewards lit up the platform with torches. Boys and girls with rucksacks and suitcases. Endless kisses. One more kiss, a final one. Next to me a woman was crying; not just discreetly to herself; she was wailing, groaning, sighing deeply. Her whole face was shaking . . . Small four year old children were screaming. Madness! They had to be carried away. And the mothers! The fathers of the young ones were in Dachau . . .' In January 1939, Ruth got a three-month permit to visit Norway, where an employee of a telegraph company, an active socialist, offered to guarantee her until she moved on to England.[168]

The Kindertransport that Ruth Maier watched was one of dozens that carried around 9,000 unaccompanied, mainly Jewish (and non-Aryan Christian) children from Berlin, Vienna and Prague to the Netherlands, where they transferred onto ferry boats that brought them to the United Kingdom. This operation was virtually the only successful attempt at the mass evacuation of Jews from Germany and the territory it controlled. Ironically, it was made possible by Britain's refusal to consider increasing Jewish immigration to Palestine.[169]

During the meeting at 10 Downing Street on 15 November, Weizmann asked Chamberlain to allow 10,000 Jewish children to enter Palestine under an established scheme run by Youth Aliyah. Chamberlain would not allow that, but his imagination was taken by the notion of evacuating thousands of imperilled youngsters. The next day he obtained cabinet consent to admit unaccompanied children under the age of seventeen into the UK on a temporary basis. Instead of requiring individual visas and guarantees, the refugee organization would receive block visas on condition that they select, place, maintain and supervise the children appropriately. The scheme was a genuine breakthrough, although it was deeply equivocal in spirit and implementation. The government was prepared to allow refuge for children, but not for adults who might enter the labour market. And, eventually, the young people would be expected to move on. As the historian Louise London comments, 'Admission saved the children's lives. Exclusion sealed the fate of many of their parents.'[170]

While the Kindertransport operation produced genuine heroes, it was marred by a slapdash approach. Wilfred Israel risked the unwanted attention of the Gestapo by returning to Germany to lay the organizational groundwork. The German Jewish youth worker Norbert Wollheim suspended his own emigration to begin assembling the children in Berlin. Although Viscount Samuel broadcast an appeal for funds on the BBC on 25 November, there was never enough money for guarantees and maintenance, nor were there sufficient Jewish homes once the influx began. The first train left Berlin on 1 December 1938, followed by one from Vienna a week later. A third centre was activated in Prague, initially to deal with Jews displaced from the Sudetenland and, later, imperilled Czech Jews. Once they reached England the children were housed in unused summer holiday camps near Harwich and Lowestoft. Those fortunate to have found a foster home went direct to Liverpool Street Station to meet their guardians. A far larger proportion were picked by kindly folk who visited the camps. During these visits the children were lined up for inspection, something they termed the 'cattle market'. Inevitably, the young, cute ones were taken first. Siblings were often sundered, to remain apart for years and, in some cases, never to meet again. The Refugee Children's Movement was criticized at the time for not paying sufficient attention to the children's cultural or religious backgrounds. There was no kosher food at the Dovercourt camp at Harwich. Jewish children from Orthodox backgrounds frequently ended up with non-Jewish families who did not have a clue about their needs.[171]

The effort in Prague was led by Nicholas Winton, a stockbroker, who aborted a skiing holiday at the request of a friend who was assisting Czech refugees. Winton came from a family with German Jewish origins, but practised Christianity. He saw no problem in cooperating with the Barbican Mission, a conversionist organization that was 'touting for business' in Prague. When the Mission offered to find homes for around a hundred Jewish children, as long as they could be baptized, he jumped at the opportunity. Such pragmatism outraged the Chief Rabbi who set up his own operation, the Chief Rabbi's Emergency Committee, under the management of his son-in-law Rabbi Solomon Schonfeld. This buccaneering enterprise succeeded in bringing to the UK a couple of hundred young Orthodox Jews, mainly from Poland, who would otherwise have been neglected by the RCM.[172]

Hitler makes a prophecy

On 30 January 1939, Hitler addressed the first Reichstag of the newly proclaimed Greater German Reich, including representatives from areas recently incorporated into the empire. His lengthy speech vaunted the Nazis' achievement in reuniting the German people. He attributed their rapid success to the turn away from parliamentary democracy and towards a system whose leaders expressed the unified will of the Volksgemeinschaft. Yet much work was still needed to make all Germans aware of their racial unity and create leaders who would put the interests of the Volk before intellectual, cultural or legal scruples. Such racial awareness and unity were essential ingredients for victory in the struggle facing Germany. This was the battle for economic self-sufficiency that, in turn, necessitated the acquisition of Lebensraum. In a version of his memorandum on the Four-Year Plan he explained why the German people could not permanently export their way out of food and raw material shortages. Ultimately, economic security required external security. Building up the armed forces diminished the productive capacity that could be used for generating exports but there was no alternative to rearmament. Hitler then attacked the democracies, Britain and the USA, for allegedly threatening war on Germany. He attributed their purported bellicosity to Jewish agitators and the Jewish-controlled press. The German people had to understand this dynamic and the need to fight back, just as in Germany 'we brought the Jewish world-enemy to its knees'. In his mind, conflict with the USA, especially, was already connected with a solution of the Jewish question.

Hitler ridiculed the hypocrisy of the democracies for condemning Germany's treatment of the Jews while refusing to accept Jewish immigrants. Once again harking back to the Great War, he refused to be lectured about humanity by the powers that had imposed suffering on the Germans after 1918. Germany was determined to remove the Jews;

other nations should play their part in resolving the issue. A solution to the Jewish question was a key to peace in Europe. The Jews, too, would have to play their part and adapt to constructive labour elsewhere in the world. Otherwise they 'will succumb to a crisis of unimaginable proportions'.

In the midst of his peroration Hitler made a pronouncement that he believed would be memorable: 'I was often a prophet in my life and was usually ridiculed for it. At the time of my struggle for power, it was chiefly the Jewish people who laughed at my prophecies that I would one day assume in Germany leadership of the state and the entire Volk, and would then, among other things, also bring the Jewish problem to a solution. I believe, however, that the Jews in Germany have already choked on the uproarious laughter of those days. I wish to be a prophet again today: should international financial Jewry in and outside of Europe succeed in plunging the nations once again into a world war, the result will not be the Bolshevization of the world and thus the victory of Jewry, but the annihilation of the Jewish race in Europe.' It was a transparent threat that the Jews would be punished if the democracies, which he believed did the bidding of world Jewry, went to war with Germany.

Yet this was neither the end nor the climax of his speech. Hitler went on to defend the National Socialist record on the treatment of religion. He maintained that Christianity flourished in the Reich and depicted Germany as the defender of civilization against Bolshevism. He also lauded Mussolini, Italy and the 'Japanese Volk' who stood with Germany in resisting Bolshevization. The threat to peace came only from the Jewish-controlled press. He again threatened reprisal against this alleged Jewish 'smear campaign' and averred that Germany only wanted peace with its neighbours, England and the United States.[173]

Hitler's menacing oration was prophetic but not programmatic. If it had any concrete application it was in the immediate here and now. As the historian Hans Mommsen has argued, Hitler could not really predict what might or might not occur in three or four years' time. Rather, he was making a 'rhetorical gesture designed to put pressure on the international community' to expedite the mass emigration of the remaining German and Austrian Jews. Klemperer, who listened on the radio, was left in no doubt: 'Hitler once again turned all his enemies into Jews and threatened the annihilation of the Jews in Europe if they were to bring about war against Germany.' Some days later he wistfully noted advertisements in the sole official Jewish publication, the *Jüdisches Nachrichtenblatt*, for emigration to Shanghai.[174]

At the start of 1939 there were roughly 200,000 Jews left in Germany and under 100,000 in Austria. Due to the skewed effect of emigration more than half of the German Jews were aged over forty-five and there was a preponderance of women. Almost all were without a livelihood. The better-off drew income in small, regulated amounts from sequestered assets. Most subsisted on welfare from the Jewish community which, itself, relied overwhelmingly on infusions of cash from the Council for Germany Jewry and AJJDC. Increasingly, they were forced out of their homes and into shared accommodation in Jew-houses. Although a few individuals managed to maintain social and business contacts, on the whole Jews were totally isolated. A 'sense of fatalism' gripped the communities and all but the most stubborn and wealthiest were fixated on emigration.[175]

A Nazi Party cell leader in Herne, in the Ruhr, explained the National Socialist thinking behind the eviction of Jews from their homes. First, Aryans with large families needed more spacious accommodation and Jews frequently possessed such apartments. Furthermore it was necessary for the realization of the Volksgemeinschaft: 'This means that the tenants should, among themselves, nurture the spirit of National Socialist community. But a house community can only be formed by German-thinking persons of Aryan descent. It is impossible to include individuals of Jewish origin.' Along with evictions and emigration, impoverishment increased the housing stock. The SD Head Office noted with satisfaction that 'As a result of their rapidly progressing pauperization, the Jews are conforming to the will of the lawmaker to restrict them to the smallest possible living space; several Jewish families are now often renting a larger apartment jointly, with each family occupying a single room.'[176]

In May 1939 the SD Head Office also took note of the first compulsory labour of unemployed and indigent Jews. A month later, 'The deployment of Jews as conscript labour, ordered due to the growing shortage of German workers, is now in high gear.' However, few of the Jews were young or fit for work. It was also necessary to segregate them, which required special arrangements for lockers and lunch. In view of the objections of German workers, the SD considered that labour camps for Jews would be preferable where they were needed for big projects in larger numbers.[177]

The regime also tightened the pressure on Aryan spouses in mixed marriages. This segment of the population bulked ever larger, since they were less willing to emigrate and hence stood out increasingly amongst the diminished Jewish population. On 6 July 1938 the marriage laws were amended to make it easier for someone to divorce a partner who was deemed unhealthy, incarcerated in a concentration camp, or without a livelihood. By now most Jewish men fell into one of the last two categories and the Gestapo made a point of harassing non-Jewish husbands or wives to encourage them to break their wedding vows. As Richard Evans observes, 'It took a good deal of courage, loyalty and love to maintain a mixed marriage in such circumstances.'[178]

Ominously for Lilli Jahn, at just this time her husband developed a wandering eye for other women. After a disastrous summer holiday in 1939, when the family were turned away from a hotel that would not admit Jews, Ernst began an affair with his locum. Lilli was now pregnant with their fifth child and was hardly able to compete with the attractions of this young, carefree woman.[179]

All but a small fraction of the Jews now existed in a state of penury. Klemperer was forced to surrender his wife's jewellery, and was thrown back on the meagre state pension he still received as an erstwhile state employee who was a war veteran. A British visitor to Breslau in June 1939, Michael Mitzman, wrote that the Jews there were 'absolutely poverty stricken'. Mitzman, an envoy for a refugee agency, recalled that the leaders of the community 'implored us to get their children out . . . I cannot describe the terror in the people's faces and their absolute despair at not knowing where to go and to whom to turn.' The situation there was typical: 150–200 wealthy Jews were able to draw income from blocked accounts; a handful of lawyers were allowed to serve other Jews; there were 40–50 doctors and 15 dentists tending the Jewish community; 50–100 people were employed in commercial enterprises, such as cobblers servicing a purely Jewish clientele; and no less than 1,360 worked for the Jewish community itself. While in some rural areas a few Germans stubbornly continued to trade with Jews, almost everywhere else Jewish economic life had come to a standstill. The SD office for the Upper Division East boasted that 'the Jewish Question has, for the first time since the takeover of power, reached a decisive phase in the report period. In regard to excluding the Jews from the various spheres of life, it has entered a final phase.'[180]

As the circumference of Jewish life constricted and living conditions deteriorated, with little hope of escape or alleviation, large numbers of elderly Jews opted to die by their own hands. Suicide was a consequence of despair, not a gesture of resistance. Often it testified to a sense of rejection by the Nazis, rather than a rejection of Nazism. On 28 November 1938, Hedwig Jastrow wrote, 'I am leaving this life as someone whose family has had German citizenship for over one hundred years and has always remained loyal to Germany . . . I don't want to live without a fatherland, without a homeland, without an apartment, without citizenship rights, ostracized and reviled.'[181]

Officials paid close attention to the suicide rate; to them it was a benchmark of success rather than failure. In mid-December 1938 the gendarmerie in Bad Reichenhall recorded the fate of a sixty-seven-year-old Jewish woman whose house had been adorned with anti-Jewish placards. She took an overdose of veronal, but the local Aryan doctor refused to treat her, and she died. The gendarmerie officer concluded, 'The cause for this act was a nervous breakdown as a consequence of the measures taken against her as a Jewess.' A few months later, the SD office for southern Germany remarked that the stream of anti-Jewish legislation did 'not allow the Jews to regain any equilibrium. One can note a definite hysteria spreading among Jewish women and men.' Amongst 'the most striking signs of a progressive proletarianization of the Jews' was 'the rising number of suicides'.[182]

The end of Czechoslovakia and occupation of Bohemia and Moravia

The misery spread to a further 87,000 Jews when German troops occupied Bohemia and Moravia. Hitler had never surrendered his ambition to take over the rich, industrial areas beyond the Sudetenland. As the shortage of labour and raw materials in Germany worsened, the prospect of seizing the Czech arms industry and stores of munitions became irresistible. Following German prompting, on 14 March 1939, Slovak nationalists declared independence and appealed for German aid against Czech countermeasures. The next day, the Czech president travelled by train to Berlin, where Hitler and Göring bullied him into signing a document calling on the Germans to secure order in what was left of the country, now re-named Czecho-Slovakia. Twenty-four hours later German troops marched in and the Czech lands were declared a Protectorate of the Greater Reich.[183]

They arrived in Prague on a wretched day, punctuated by flurries of snow and rain. Helga Weiss, a precocious nine-year-old who kept a diary, noticed the sad expressions on people in the frozen streets. When she returned from school in the afternoon she saw German military vehicles parked along the roads. 'In this way we came under the "protection" of the Third Reich, without knowing how or what from. We also got a new name. Instead of Czecho-Slovakia we were now called the Protectorate of Bohemia and Moravia.'[184]

The Protectorate was another curious Nazi improvisation, part annexation and part colonization. A puppet government under Emil Hácha was allowed to continue ruling Czechs according to Czech law, but under the overall supervision of a German Protector. The first post-holder was Neurath, the former foreign minister. At the same time as he was installed, German law was extended to the territory and enforced by the German security apparatus, the Gestapo and Sipo-SD. Ethnic Germans were treated as subjects of German law, able to lord it over Czechs. In short order the Germans plundered the country's gold reserves, while over the longer term the economy was geared to German needs.[185]

German aggression was now plainly revealed to the world. There were no suffering Volksdeutsche in Prague and no territorial claims arising from the Versailles Treaty to justify the occupation. In an article exposing German ambitions, Leopold Schwarzschild declared, 'We've finally got there.' The evisceration of Czecho-Slovakia dispelled any surviving illusions about Nazi aims and blew away Hitler's professed commitment to the peace of Europe. 'To subjugate everything, to have power over everything – that is their sole, their simple, undivided goal, like a beast in heat they will be satisfied with nothing less.' Now that the democracies knew what they were up against, he argued, they had to formulate a defensive strategy. President Roosevelt concurred. He responded by beginning the task of revising the Neutrality Act that prevented the US administration giving military aid to belligerents overseas. Sensing the hardening attitude of the major powers, Victor Klemperer again hoped that there would be some sort of international backlash that would lead to a change of regime.[186]

For the moment, though, the German occupation spelled ruin for Jews in the Protectorate. The Czech authorities under Hácha drafted anti-Jewish laws just days after the occupation, but the Germans took this over and the full panoply of measures were immediately applied. Aryanization swung into operation. According to the SD, 'The dissolving of Jewish business enterprises made many Jews jobless. In numerous localities it became necessary to set up collective work camps for Jews so as to keep them from becoming a burden for public welfare.' Helga Weiss experienced conditions worsen from one day to the next. Since the morning the Germans arrived, she wrote in her diary, there was 'not a calm day'. They could not keep up with the torrent of anti-Jewish ordinances. 'The worst of it has landed on us Jews . . . We can't help being Jews and nor can we help any of these other things. No one asks; they just feel they have to pour out their anger on someone.' She was excluded from her school and forced to begin studying with a group of Jewish girls taught by students who had been thrown out of university.[187]

One of the measures imposed on the Jews was a tax to fund emigration. The Germans wanted to strip Czech Jews of their wealth, but had no intention of being saddled with a mass of Jewish paupers unable to leave the country. They had learned this lesson in Vienna and in the wake of the November pogrom. So, Franz Stahlecker was transferred from Vienna to Prague to set up the Sipo-SD apparatus for the Protectorate and in April brought in Adolf Eichmann to establish a Central Jewish Emigration Office. Eichmann was accompanied by Hans Günther and Alois Brunner, two Austrians who he had recruited to his operation in Vienna. They were typical of the Austrian SS men who filled new posts in the expanding Nazi domain: hardened activists who felt it was their turn to get ahead after years of living marginal, semi-underground lives. Eichmann's men gathered officials of the Czech Jewish community, briefed them on their new tasks, and sent them to Vienna to learn the ropes from Murmelstein and the IKG. The new office ran in parallel to the Central Office for Jewish Emigration in Berlin, established on 27 February 1939 in response to an 'intensified pressure to emigrate'.[188]

In the autumn of 1938 the British government, smitten by guilt over the fate of its abandoned ally, offered help to Czechs displaced from the Sudetenland. Although 20,000 Jews were amongst those forced to leave, they were not specifically included in this aid package. While the Germans wanted to get rid of the Jewish population but prevent political opponents evading their clutches, the British government put in place measures to achieve the opposite. The sum of £4 million was advanced for the settlement in Britain of Czech political refugees and their families; if Jews were assisted it was because they were Social Democrats not because they were Jewish. Meanwhile, the refugee organizations in London were so strapped for cash coping with the flood from Germany and Austria that they felt unable to take on financial responsibility for yet more impoverished migrants. Consequently, the British authorities began to apply visa controls to Czechs applying to enter the UK, making it almost impossible for Jews without means of support to obtain entry. A few hundred reached Palestine, with British agreement, and just over 660 children were taken to England on children's transports.[189]

As the refugee crisis continued to mushroom, the Americans and the British pinned their hopes on George Rublee, director of the Intergovernmental Committee for Refugees. The Foreign Office and the State Department believed that Jewish refugees would stand a much better chance of settling outside Germany if they were allowed to take some wealth with them. Rublee was empowered to negotiate with the Germans on this score and both governments ardently wished him to reach some sort of deal with Berlin. In mid-December 1938 it looked as though the Nazis were willing to discuss terms, if only for their own convenience. Hjalmar Schacht agreed to meet Rublee during a visit to London on business for the Reichsbank. He proposed that 150,000 Jews would be enabled to emigrate over three years with some capital if world Jewry paid funds into a trust to finance their departure; the property of German Jewry would stand as collateral for this enormous loan. Rublee travelled to Berlin in January to continue the negotiations, only to discover that Schacht had been sacked. Instead, he found himself in discussion with Hermann Göring and a senior executive in the Office of the Four-Year Plan, Helmuth Wohlthat. Nevertheless, his Nazi interlocutors appeared to be in earnest. Apart from adding a sanctions-busting element to Schacht's proposal, they endorsed it. Rublee reported to London and Washington that a deal was in the making.[190]

In late April 1939, Sumner Welles submitted a memo to President Roosevelt outlining an agreement that would secure the orderly emigration of German Jewry. It was not to be. Jewish leaders in London and New York looked askance at a scheme that enjoined them to finance the liquidation of the German Jewish community. No less objectionable was the notion that Jews would be compelled to act as a corporate body, thus vindicating Nazi claims for the existence of international Jewry. When Myron Taylor, chair of the President's Advisory Committee on Political Refugees, met Jewish figures to discuss setting up a trust as the necessary instrument, they gave him the cold shoulder. Nor was Sir Herbert Emerson, the High Commissioner for Refugees, able to overcome their reluctance. Robert Pell, a State Department official who was in the thick of the negotiations, summed up the stalemate in a letter to Taylor on 15 May 1939: 'My candid impression is that our business is becoming a tug of war between the Government and our Jewish financial friends. The Governments are striving hard to shift the major part of the responsibility to Jewish finance and Jewish finance is working equally hard to leave it with the Governments.' To further complicate matters, Jewish opinion was divided. Zionist leaders like Stephen Wise refused to back the plan because it ignored Palestine as a settlement option. By June 1939 only $0.8 million had been raised, mostly by the AJJDC. Emerson and Wohlthat were scheduled to meet again in July, but international developments nullified their discussions.[191]

The impasse over Jewish refugees was highlighted by the saga of one ship carrying would-be emigrants from Germany to Cuba. On 13 May 1939, the *St Louis*, a liner in the Hamburg-America fleet, left Bremen bound for Havana with 937 passengers holding Cuban entry visas. The Jews on board were not aware that just a week earlier the Cuban government had cancelled the visas on the grounds that many were forged. When the vessel arrived off Havana a fortnight later all but twenty-nine of the passengers were denied the right to land. The ship's captain, Gustav Schröder, was unusually solicitous towards his human cargo. He sailed towards Florida and along the US coast while Jewish organizations lobbied the government to allow the refugees in. The State Department adamantly refused to breach the quota for immigrants from Germany and Roosevelt did nothing. Eventually, the *St Louis* returned to Europe where the IGCR had brokered an arrangement that allowed 288 passengers to enter the UK, 224 to go to France, 214 to Belgium and 181 to the Netherlands.[192]

After this debacle, shipping companies demanded that Jews purchase return tickets in case the refugee passengers were refused leave to land at their destinations. But while the experts in the SD acknowledged that emigration was getting harder and harder, they did not draw the conclusion that Jews should be allowed to keep some wealth in order to make themselves more appealing prospects as immigrants. Rather, they argued that it was essential to keep up the pressure on them and on the refugee agencies.[193]

For those who had found new homes, like Ruth Maier, life remained fraught. She had been welcomed into the Strøm family in Lillestrøm and was working hard to learn Norwegian even though she hoped, ultimately, to emigrate to England and train as a nurse. She agonized over the choice: 'I don't know what's better – to stay in Norway or to go to England.' At the same time as she was vacillating she bombarded her sister Judith, already in the UK, to get a visa for their mother who was stuck in Vienna. After the German occupation of Prague she sensed that war was impending and became ever more anxious, both for her mother and herself. 'Norway', she wrote in her diary, 'is only separated from Germany by a small stretch of water.' However, she had become infatuated with Arne Strøm, her guarantor, and began to hope that with his support she could pursue academic studies in Oslo. In April, Ruth's mother finally made it to London but Ruth's visa for the UK expired. Her choice was made, determined as much by her heart as her head. She wrote to her sister on 1 June 1939, 'there is something else apart from high-minded thoughts about socialism and Jewish persecution . . . your body'. Ruth met a boy, started smoking, indulged in sexual experiments, planned to attend a new school, and went on holiday. Doubts continued to plague her. She asked her sister, 'I don't want to be in Norway if there's a war. Do you think I should write to London about my visa?' If war broke out she could be of use in England as a nurse, but not where she was. 'After all, I have to help. Norway will remain neutral.'[194]

Jewish refugees scattered across the continent scanned newspapers apprehensively as spring turned to summer and Hitler gave signs of preparing for war against Poland. In January 1939, Germany had begun to press the Polish government to return the port city of Danzig to German sovereignty. The Poles reacted robustly and entered discussions with Britain about a defensive treaty designed to thwart German designs. In March, the German occupation of the Czech lands so shocked Neville Chamberlain and his colleagues that the government offered to guarantee the Polish border against German aggression. The gesture counted for little with Hitler who now harboured only contempt for British and French politicians. On 28 April he informed the Reichstag that Germany was renouncing its non-aggression treaty with Poland and tearing up the Anglo-German naval pact. Having earlier ordered the army high command to plan the invasion of Poland, he held a series of meetings in which he set out his objectives to the party and the military. Germany needed living space in order to survive. The only way to gain resources was by force and he intended to conquer territory and resources in eastern Europe, hopefully without triggering war with Britain and France. During the following months, the German Foreign Office worked overtime to conclude a series of diplomatic and trade agreements with the aim of isolating Poland and removing potential threats to Germany. The diplomatic offensive culminated in the conclusion of a non-aggression treaty with the Soviet Union on 24 August 1939.[195]

The outbreak of amity between Nazi Germany and the USSR was an astonishing turnaround for both regimes. Nazi propaganda suddenly stopped referring to the Jewish-Bolshevik enemy. Stalin ordered that German communists, including many Jews, who had found refuge in Moscow should be handed over to the Nazis, who he had once encouraged them to oppose. The public did not know that Ribbentrop and Molotov, the new Soviet Commissar for Foreign Affairs, had also concluded a secret agreement to divide Poland or that Germany had consented to the Soviet Union occupying the Baltic states and a strip of Romanian territory. Nevertheless it was as plain to the man on the street as it was to experienced diplomats that the treaty opened the way for a German assault on Poland. Furthermore, it made it possible for German forces to confront the British and the French, if necessary, without having to worry about a threat in their rear. Victor Klemperer, in Dresden, struggled to digest the implications of the 'incredible turn about'. In his eyes it posed 'Incalculable danger for all Jews here'. Ruth Maier wrote to her sister Judith setting out the advantages of being in a non-belligerent country now that war was all but inevitable. She hoped that Britain would emerge victorious but 'If Germany "wins" (strange word for mass murder) in the end, then at least we'll know where we are.'[196]

For several days diplomats in Paris, London and Rome tried to engineer a peaceful resolution to Germany's demands on Poland. But this time Hitler was not to be denied his war. On his orders the SS intelligence service created a casus belli by fabricating an attack by Polish militia against a German radio station on the border near Gleiwitz. In the light of this 'provocation', German forces crossed the Polish border on the morning of 1 September 1939. Hitler was rattled that Britain and

France continued to stand by their defensive alliance with Poland: he had not envisaged war in the west so soon. Gambling that it was actually a bluff he refused to heed a British ultimatum to desist from the invasion and, consequently, on 3 September the Third Reich found itself at war on two fronts.[197]

To Hitler, Germany was at war on a third front, too. In his mind the entire conflict could be reduced to an existential struggle between the Jews and the Germans, representing civilization. He told Nazi Party members, 'Our Jewish democratic global enemy has succeeded in placing the English people in a state of war with Germany . . . The year 1918 will not be repeated.' From this point, the fate of the Jews was locked into the course of the war.[198]

Yet Helga Weiss welcomed the invasion of Poland. 'No one was surprised. The way events turned out, we had to come to it. However horrid the prospect that this could lead to a world war, it's the only hope.' Strange as it may seem, Jews received news of the war with relief: it heralded a fundamental change in international opinion about the Third Reich. At last those who opposed Nazism, who were persecuted by the regime, had powerful allies. However, Victor Klemperer did not see it that way to begin with. As he contemplated their predicament, caught between warring titans, he considered that the time had come for him and his wife to take their own lives. But he steadied and they, too, decided to wait and see what war would bring. After all, Germany was now ranged against two powerful empires and no one could foretell the outcome. Klemperer was not being fanciful. Several senior German generals thought Hitler had taken leave of his senses and members of the conservative opposition believed that the regime was riding for a fall, giving them an opportunity to topple the Nazis.[199]

One way or another, war would determine the fate of the Jews. As Hitler made clear in his address to Nazi Party members, they were, in effect, enemy combatants. It was implicit that the Jews had to be treated as ruthlessly as any other enemy, no matter what guise they took. Hitler had already threatened that the German Jews would be held hostage against the good behaviour of their co-religionists in the USA who clamoured for America to declare war against Germany. If that came about he was unequivocal that they could expect a terrible retribution. Even if he had merely been trying to scare the democracies into evacuating the German Jews, he had conceived a potentially lethal scenario that hinged on geo-strategic developments. When Hitler warned that

'1918 will not be repeated' he was evoking the alleged Jewish treachery and subversion that had cost Germany the last war. Thus, not only were Jews the enemy, and hostages, they were also in the firing line lest things go wrong. Finally, Hitler had stressed time and time again that the war was being fought for food and raw materials to ensure the well-being of the Volk, while the Jews were to be squeezed and exploited mercilessly. Rationing had already been introduced in the Reich: it was hardly likely that in conditions of scarcity Jews would be well fed and cared for. If Hitler had not actually planned a war against the Jews, the Jews were now at the mercy of military developments. Strategy and tactics would be as influential as ideology and anti-Semitism in deciding their treatment. Judenpolitik and the politics of war commingled. However, since war was paramount, ultimately the fate of the Jews would rest on the clash of arms.

PART FOUR

WAR

1939–1941

The Polish campaign and Operation Tannenberg

The war that Germany found itself fighting in September 1939 was not the war that Hitler intended. He originally hoped to isolate Poland diplomatically and pick it off in much the same way that he had gobbled up Czechoslovakia. He simply did not believe that Britain and France would stand by their guarantee of Polish territorial integrity, a delusion encouraged by Ribbentrop, who thought he knew the English well after his stint as ambassador in London. When he received news that Britain had declared war, Hitler was thrown into a panic. Germany now faced enemies on two fronts, a predicament that all Germans dreaded and potentially a rerun of the First World War. According to Paul-Otto Schmidt, his translator, the blood drained from Hitler's face and he asked Ribbentrop, 'What now?' The Nazi leadership could only hope that the generals would deliver a speedy victory while the French and British took their time mobilizing for an assault on western Germany. With luck they would have enough time to switch the bulk of the German army from the east to the west before the French and the British were in a position to attack.[1]

At another level, the war was exactly as predicted. It was a continuation of the struggle with world Jewry, only now fought with different weapons. Hitler and the Nazi leadership were sure the Jews had brought about the diplomatic calamity that resulted in hostilities. The debacle was further proof that Germany was encircled and threatened with destruction; therefore the war was being fought to defend the German people, defeat the Jews and punish them for warmongering. This was a major theme of Goebbels' propaganda in the autumn of 1939. It explained not only Anglo-French belligerence but also America's tilt towards the Allies. When it was not labelling President Roosevelt a Jew, the Nazi-controlled press routinely referred to the 'Jewish Camarilla' that supposedly controlled policy-making in Washington. In early November 1939, William Shirer copied into his journal a typical statement from a Nazi publication along these lines: 'Behind all the enemies of the German ascendancy stand those who demand our encirclement – the oldest enemies of the German people, and of all healthy, rising nations – the Jews.' Of course this explanation was grotesquely contradicted by the non-aggression pact with the USSR, a country that was also supposed to be under Jewish control. Instead, propaganda against 'Jewish Bolshevism' gave way to a more appropriate trope. Shirer observed that in Hitler's end-of-year message to the German people, the Führer referred to the 'Jewish reactionary warmongers in the capitalist democracies' who started the war. A few days later Robert Ley explained to readers of *Der Angriff*, 'We know that this war is an ideological struggle against world Jewry. England is allied with the Jews against Germany . . . England is spiritually, politically, and economically at one with the Jews . . . For us England and the Jews remain the common enemy.'[2]

The fact that Jews were the enemy in what was now a real rather than a shadow war had immediate and grave ramifications. Within Germany they were potential spies and saboteurs. Wherever Jews were encountered on the battlefield or in occupied territory, they were regarded as actual or potential combatants. Jewish women and children were treated as part of the conspiracy against the German people: they were the biological matrix that produced Jews who were openly or secretly fighting the Germans and provided them with a support base for subversive activity. None could be trusted or spared the harshest treatment. However it ended, the result of the conflict was likely to be catastrophic for Jews whose fate placed them within reach of the Nazis. If the war went well, the Jews would face retribution for causing it; if it went badly, they would pay for German suffering.[3]

Nevertheless, despite the centrality of the Jewish threat to Nazi analysis of world-wide developments, the war was not launched by Hitler as primarily a war against the Jews, a war designed to eventuate in their annihilation. It quickly became apparent that anti-Jewish policy in Germany was laced with as many contradictions as before, paradoxes that were exported to newly conquered countries. For a while Jews were even able to exploit these disjunctions for their own salvation.[4]

Nor were anti-Jewish measures necessarily driven by anti-Jewish sentiment. The Third Reich at war faced inescapable geo-strategic and economic exigencies that required drastic expedients and stringent

sacrifices. In 1939 the German economy had been revved up to breaking point. Hitler pressed for every arm of the military to be expanded as
fast as possible, but the country lacked the financial reserves, resources
or labour to meet such demands. These chronic inadequacies were
aggravated by Hitler's bellicose stance: no one would lend money to
Germany while he courted a military confrontation with the most
powerful, richly endowed, and best-resourced countries in Europe.
German exports plummeted while imports soared to feed the resource-
hungry war industries. The resulting credit crisis was so severe that on
the eve of the conflagration the government was forced to cut back arms
production and introduce rationing of certain foods. Paradoxically, this
critical juncture only incited Hitler. Knowing that the German economy
had reached its maximum capacity for producing munitions while the
British and French had only recently started to build up their war
machines, Hitler reasoned that Germany might as well fight them now.
But this turned the war into a frightening gamble. It had to be won, and
won quickly. Germany lacked the economic reserves to sustain a long,
attritional conflict and could not survive a sustained blockade. If
imports were interdicted, key raw materials, fuel (notably mineral oil)
and essential foodstuffs for humans and livestock would run out after
only a few months.[5]

Even in the most optimistic scenario, Jews would meet the bill for
Hitler's recklessness and Germany's inferiority. They would soon be
allotted less food than the Aryan population; they would be stripped of
any remaining assets and usable items, including their homes; and they
would be compelled to work at minimal rates of pay, while paying the
maximum taxes. Wherever the German army conquered, Jews would
face even more severe forms of exploitation. The Jews would, quite literally, be forced to pay for the war. And they would eat less so that
Germans had full stomachs. Of course, it was not necessary for Jews to
be penalized in this way. The hardships of war could have been spread
evenly across the population in Germany and shared more fairly
throughout the nations they overwhelmed. However, German economic
and food policy was premised on Nazi racial-biological ideology. Within
the Reich there was a racial pecking order: only those members of the
Volksgemeinschaft fit to fight, work, and breed would be fed adequately.
Racial aliens would receive only enough nutrition to perform tasks for
the Volk and the war effort. The same principles were to be applied in
occupied countries, even more sharply where the Germans considered

the natives to be racially inferior to begin with. In every place the Jews were regarded as exploitable and expendable. Yet this policy cannot be reduced to racism alone. All the German leaders, civil and military, were seared by their experiences during the Great War. They were determined that civilian morale would not be eroded by hunger and that deprivation would never provide fuel for revolution. If they could agree that the Jews would go without, it was not because they all hated Jews in the same way for the same reasons. Pragmatists were quite able to work with fanatical adherents of racial-biological theory to square the circle of the Third Reich's geo-strategic and economic dilemmas.[6]

Furthermore, how the war was fought and by whom it was fought meant that it was going to have a disproportionate, disastrous impact on the Jews. Between 1935 and 1939 the German army had grown from 100,000 to 2.6 million men. The bulk of this growth was accounted for by conscripts aged 18–21. They had been schooled, socialized and polit-icized under the Third Reich, spending their formative years in the Hitler Youth and Reich Labour Service even before they received mili-tary training and ideological preparation in the armed forces. Even if they were not card-carrying Nazis, to a very great extent they perceived the world through the lens of Nazi propaganda. Furthermore, the army had absorbed 106,000 former SA men. These were hardened street fighters from the 'years of struggle', imbued with a crude hatred of Jews that was already routinely expressed through violence. On top of this, the army had recruited, enlisted or promoted about 85,000 officers. These, too, were mainly young men. Their training involved mastery of Nazi ideology and their advancement increasingly rested on a capacity for fanaticism as well as operational competence.[7]

The army that prepared to invade Poland was primed to blame the Jews for causing war in the first place. It was imbued with animosity towards Jews, with a particular asperity reserved for the Ostjuden or eastern Jews who had featured so largely in pre-war hate-literature. In the figure of the Ostjude anti-Jewish prejudice melded with anti-Polish prejudice. Young Germans had been filled with a spirit of revenge against the Poles who allegedly oppressed their countrymen in the lands taken away in 1918–19. Youths were taught to despise Polish society for its mediocre living standards and supposed cultural backwardness. This was a poisonous combination that lent itself to brutality even before the fighting men had experienced the shock of combat and the loss of comrades.[8]

The invasion of Poland was not going to be an ordinary military campaign, either. In a clandestine briefing of the senior military leadership at Berchtesgaden on 22 August, Hitler had summed up the goal as 'Annihilation of Poland'. In his record of the meeting the chief of the general staff, Franz Halder, noted, 'Means to this end. It does not matter what they are. The victor is never called upon to vindicate his actions.' Hitler demanded that the Wehrmacht should be 'Harsh and remorseless. We must steel ourselves against humanitarian reasoning.' After victory part of Poland would be incorporated into the Reich and the rest would become a protectorate; the country would cease to exist. On 17 October, Hitler declared: 'The Polish intelligentsia must be prevented from forming itself into a ruling class'. Poland was 'of use to us only as a reservoir of labour'.[9]

The liquidation of the Polish intelligentsia was assigned to the SS under the code name Operation Tannenberg. For this purpose Heydrich ordered the creation of four, then five, later seven Einsatzgruppen, or task forces, each subdivided into two to four Einsatzkommandos with 120 to 150 men to each subdivision. They were commanded by officers and men of the security police (Sipo, combining the Gestapo and the criminal police) and the SD. They were equipped with arrest lists totalling over 60,000 names and instructed to file regular reports to headquarters in Berlin charting their progress. A special unit under Udo von Woyrsch that deployed several battalions of order police (Orpo) was tasked with carrying out executions. Werner Best selected the senior personnel of these squads on the basis that they would act 'ruthlessly and harshly to achieve National Socialist aims'. In a series of meetings on 25, 26 and 29 August 1939, Heydrich and Best conferred with Eduard Wagner, quartermaster-general of the army, to demarcate the spheres of responsibility for security and pacification between the SS and the Wehrmacht.[10]

These coordination meetings were left until the last minute. Surprisingly, even less thought was given to handling the Jewish population. Jews were not the target of Operation Tannenberg. Despite the fact that they bulked so large in the Nazi imagination, and the fact that Poland had a Jewish population of 3 million, there is no surviving record of any conferences to determine policy on Jewish questions. Instead, as in so much else, policy was drawn up on the hoof. What later appeared to be the first stage of a carefully thought-out strategy of anti-Jewish measures was in fact a set of hasty improvisations. On the eve of the invasion, other than treating Jews as a special security threat, the Nazi leadership and its minions did not have a clue about how the huge Jewish population should be treated as a whole.[11]

Nevertheless, the SS and the army had together crossed a line of fundamental significance. Operation Tannenberg was conceived without any regard to human or civil rights, the Geneva Convention or the laws and usages of war. On the basis of ensuring immediate rear-area security and, in the longer term, defending the German people from threat, the SS proposed to arrest and execute tens of thousands of Poles on the thinnest of pretexts following the most rudimentary investigation and judgement (if any). It amounted to nothing less than a murderous expedition into occupied territory. As such, it was the first Nazi programme for mass murder and served as a template. The lessons learned by the SS in Poland would quickly lead to technical as well as operational refinements; but the basic tasks of the SS in wartime were laid down and, crucially, were accepted by the civil and military authorities in Germany.[12]

The Einsatzgruppen and the German army in Poland

The Polish campaign lasted little more than three weeks. The German armed forces were more numerous than the Polish defenders, better equipped and far better commanded. Although relatively few, the armoured and motorized units of the Wehrmacht caused disarray by rapidly breaking through the Polish main line of defence and striking into the rear of the Polish armies. The German air force, the Luftwaffe, outmatched the Poles in every respect (except courage) and established air superiority on the first day. German commanders were able to co-ordinate ground and air attacks with devastating ferocity; Polish communications and transport were fatally disrupted. Within three days, the German 4th Army had occupied the Polish Corridor and turned south-east, sweeping around Warsaw from the rear. Advanced elements of 4th Army reached the suburbs of the capital on 7 September. As the German 8th Army blasted its way into central Poland, the fast elements of 10th and 14th Armies burst out of Upper Silesia and Slovakia, swept through Galicia and swung north. A week later they met 4th and 3rd Armies, advancing south from East Prussia, and encircled the main concentration of Polish forces. Warsaw was now isolated.

On 17 September, the Red Army crashed through a thin screen of Polish frontier forces and advanced to the River Bug, the demarcation line agreed between Molotov and Ribbentrop. The Polish capital held out until 27 September under a pitiless artillery and aerial bombardment. By that time the government had evacuated and the Polish high command had fled to Romania. Scattered resistance continued until 5 October when the last Polish units put down their weapons.[13]

The Einsatzgruppen broke down into smaller operational detachments that followed the German combat formations. On their own initiative and sometimes at the request of local army commanders they rounded up and shot Polish irregulars, often hastily mobilized militia who were not issued with uniforms. They also executed alleged bandits and partisans handed over to them by regular army elements. SS detachments carried out reprisals for the killing of hundreds of ethnic Germans in the first days of the war, notably in Bydgoszcz. In just two massacres between 5 and 17 September, Einsatzgruppe IV and military police units, assisted by sundry army formations, shot 900 Poles. By the end of the pacification process around 1,200 people had been executed in Bydgoszcz, including almost the entire Jewish population of the town. Approximately 1,500 Poles were murdered by Einsatzgruppe IV and the unit led by Woyrsch in East Upper Silesia. In addition to the targeted killings, executions and reprisal shootings by the Sipo-SD units under SS command, the army itself executed no fewer than 16,000 Poles before the fighting stopped.[14]

Indeed, as the historian Alexander Rossino has shown, during the initial onslaught the army took thousands of hostages and killed many more Poles than the Einsatzgruppen. According to German army doctrine, campaigns had to be prosecuted with overwhelming force and the utmost violence. Any manifestation of civilian unrest or guerrilla warfare was to be met with ruthless countermeasures. It was permissible to take hostages to guard against partisan activity and in the event that frontline or rear echelon troops came under attack by non-uniformed fighters, they could be shot. Regular army units therefore seized hostages as soon as the invasion commenced. Thanks to the pervasive hostility towards Jews and the conflation of Jews with the enemy, a disproportionate number of hostages were Jewish. Young enlisted men and officers did not require brutalization to facilitate the killing of civilians or the humiliation, torture and killing of Jews; it came quite easily to them. Older reservists were just as capable of indulging in rape, pillage and murder.[15]

While the atrocities that army units committed against Jews were unmethodical, Einsatzgruppen, police and Waffen-SS units routinely focused their attention on Jewish communities. The Orpo battalions under Woyrsch caused havoc amongst the Jews of Katowice, Bedzin and Sosnowiec in south-western Poland. Jewish-owned property was wrecked and synagogues burned down. Jewish men were assaulted for no particular reason and dozens shot, sometimes on the alleged grounds that they were armed but more often because they posed some vague threat. During a rampage lasting several days 500 Jews were murdered in Bedzin, including women and children. In the Przemysl region, Einsatzgruppe I and men under Woyrsch conducted a series of massacres. In Dynow they forced a dozen Jews into the synagogue and set it on fire. Sixty more Jews were seized and shot in a forest outside the town. In Przemysl itself, Sipo-SD men pillaged Jewish homes and shops while hunting down rabbis and leading Jews. Most of them were shot at various sites. Between 500 and 600 Jewish men were murdered in and around the city. In Bialystok, in the north, Einsatzgruppe IV was responsible for looting the homes of Jews in the course of searching for arms. They also rounded up hundreds of Jewish men. Einsatzgruppe V, operating out of East Prussia, began assembling Jews and ordering them out of their towns. During at least one of these operations, Jews were shot. In Goworowo, artillery men belonging to a Waffen-SS armoured division joined with personnel from one of the army's secret field police detachments to mount a reprisal action. Fifty Jews were seized and brutally forced into the town's synagogue, which was then set alight. Another SS regiment, the Liebstandarte Adolf Hitler, slaughtered fifty Jews who had earlier been detained in Błonie under army orders.[16]

Several of these incidents elicited formal complaints by senior army officers. After the atrocities in Katowice and Bedzin, Lieutenant General Georg Brandt, who was responsible for rear-area security for Army Group South, demanded that the Army Group commander, General Gerd von Rundstedt, court-martial Woyrsch. The chief of staff of 14th Army, Brigadier General Eberhard von Mackensen, was so annoyed by the mayhem Woyrsch caused in Przemysl that he placed all SS and police units under army control. General List, commander of 14th Army, issued instructions for his officers to stop what appeared to be illegal acts by the Sipo-SD kommandos. Quartermaster-General Wagner later asked Heydrich to pull Woyrsch and his unit out of the area completely. General Georg von Küchler, commander of 3rd Army, in the north, was outraged by reports of security police driving Jews from their homes. When he heard that in Mława Jews were killed in the course of one of these actions, he ordered the nearest available army troops to disarm the Sipo-SD squads. He also demanded that General Werner Kempf discipline the men who perpetrated the outrage in Goworowo. Lieutenant General Lemelson, the commanding officer of the 29th Motorized Infantry Division, had the SS man who initiated the Błonie killings arrested. His order was subsequently confirmed by the head of 10th Army, General Walter von Reichenau.[17]

These objections were echoed and taken up by the most senior army officers in Berlin. Information about the atrocities had reached the capital within days of the campaign beginning. Halder noted in his journal on 10 September, 'SS artillery of the armoured corps herded Jews into a church and massacred them. Court martial sentences them to one year's penitentiary. Küchler has not confirmed the sentence, because more severe punishment is due.' He was concerned that these outrages were a gift to the 'English propaganda campaign on German atrocities'.[18]

Following a meeting with Heydrich, a week after the campaign opened, Admiral Wilhelm Canaris, the head of military intelligence, learned of Operation Tannenberg and the extra-judicial killings. He immediately protested in person to General Wilhelm Keitel, head of the armed forces high command. On 19 September, Wagner obtained a meeting with Heydrich to discuss the testy relations between the field army and the Einsatzgruppen. The chief of the security police and SD reiterated that the Einsatzgruppen had been given special tasks of the highest order. Thwarted in his effort to curb their activity generally, Wagner insisted that the relevant army authorities had to be alerted to specific operations. In terms that signify the friction was more of an irritant than anything else, Halder later summarized the topic of the exchange as 'Housekeeping: Jews, intelligentsia, clergy, nobility'. He reported that 'Army insists that "housekeeping" be deferred until the army has withdrawn and the country has been turned over to the civil administration. Early December.'[19]

The next day, General von Brauchitsch, commander-in-chief of the army, intervened directly with Hitler in an effort to bring Heydrich's security police under military jurisdiction. His only achievement was an agreement to greater consultation and coordination between the Einsatzgruppen and army units in their operational areas. Symbolically, though, he prohibited the military police, including the secret field police, from working with the Sipo-SD. The next day, Brauchitsch also met Heydrich, who was on a mission from Himmler to palliate the army high command. But Heydrich drew the line at placing his men under army law. To underline his desire that the SS should remain unfettered when carrying out missions that he deemed essential, at the end of the campaign Hitler ostentatiously pardoned every soldier and SS man who had successfully been prosecuted for war crimes by the army judicial authorities.[20]

Many of the objections raised by army personnel against SS and Sipo-SD activities were, in any case, practical rather than legal or moral. Brandt was concerned to enforce the army's responsibility for security matters and wanted to rein in the Einsatzgruppen rather than cancel their operations in toto. Mackensen was disturbed by the disruption they caused and the effect of looting on the morale of his troops. Officers at all levels were acutely aware that an overly permissive attitude towards plunder could result in the loss of discipline and the dissolution of entire units diverted by the opportunities for enrichment. List was worried that illegal acts were being committed on his turf, not the nature of the acts themselves. Only Küchler seems to have displayed moral anguish. Several of the complainants continued to work with the police formations in sweeps for partisans and pacification measures. List even recalled Einsatzgruppe I to his area of operations once he was assured that its murderous endeavours had been endorsed from on high. From senior commanders down to the rank and file, there was concurrence that the army, the SS and the Sipo-SD shared interests and common perceptions. The army valued the ruthless police work and effective countermeasures of the Sipo-SD while the average infantry-man did not see Poles or Jews that differently from the SS trooper. Given that the fate of the Jews would rest in the hands of the military for weeks to come, and in subsequent campaigns, this was a grim development.[21]

The Polish Jews

The 3 million Polish Jews formed about 10 per cent of the country's entire population, but were heavily concentrated in a few major cities and in small to medium-sized towns spread across Poland, with the largest proportion in the south and the east (which fell under Soviet rule). One tenth of Polish Jewry lived in Warsaw, with over 200,000 in Lodz, 60,000 in Lwow, nearly 60,000 in Cracow, and 40,000 in Lublin. They constituted 30 per cent of the inhabitants of these centres. Jews formed a similarly high proportion, often even comprising a majority of the residents in towns in rural districts. They dominated trade and commerce throughout the country and supplied a high proportion of the lawyers and doctors who served communities in the countryside and urban areas. While there was a wealthy elite of industrialists, merchants, bankers and professionals, the vast mass of Polish Jewry was extremely poor. Thirty per cent derived income from trade, which usually amounted to manning a market stall or peddling, and another third scrambled a living as craftsmen in overstocked occupations such as shoemaking. Almost 10 per cent had no jobs at all. In spite of this poverty, Polish Jewry supported an astonishingly rich and varied political, cultural and spiritual scene. The Jewish Socialist Bund and the Zionist parties flourished. Warsaw was the capital of a global linguistic empire, hosting dozens of Yiddish newspapers, journals, publishing houses, theatrical troupes and film companies. The most famous Talmudic academies were in Poland.[22]

Yet the vivacity of Yiddish culture and the numerical preponderance of Orthodox Jewry – including the manifold adherents of Hasidic sects with their distinctive side-curls and quarter-length gabardine jackets (kapotes or caftans) – did not mean that Jews were separated from their environment by language, religion or custom. In 1935 only 19 per cent of the 425,566 Jewish children of school age attended Jewish schools (which included secular schools run by the Bund or Zionists). The Jewish population was heavily Polonized at all social levels, especially the middle and upper classes. A generation of brilliantly gifted Jewish writers, poets, novelists and essayists dazzled Polish readers. This did not stop anti-Semitism, though. On the contrary, since the late nineteenth century the development of a Christian Polish middle class caused increasing friction with the Jewish communities. The rebirth of independent Poland in 1918–19 was accompanied by vicious pogroms. Throughout the interwar years nationalist parties campaigned for Polonization of the economy and encouraged a boycott of Jewish businesses. On the eve of the German assault, Polish Jewry was socially stratified, politically divided, economically stretched, and at odds with the Christian majority.[23]

Twenty-five years earlier, German troops invading the Russian

Empire were received by Polish Jews as a benign force. The Kaiser's men released them from a despotic regime that was responsible for anti-Jewish laws and pogroms. German Jewish soldiers, and rabbis attached to the German army, formed a bridge to the occupation authorities. In September 1939 things could not have been more different. German soldiers abused easily identifiable Orthodox Jews in the streets and looted Jewish-owned shops. When they needed hostages they made a beeline for the Jewish quarter. Private Grömmer of the 111th Mountain Artillery Regiment typifies the preconceptions that drove such behaviour. In an account of his campaign experience he described the Jews as 'beasts in human form. In their beards and caftans, with their devilish features, they make a dreadful impression on us. Anyone who was not a radical opponent of the Jews must become one here. In comparison with the Polish caftan-Jews, our own Jewish bloodsuckers are lambs.'[24]

Highly educated and humane Germans were just as prone to seeing Jews in the light of anti-Jewish stereotypes. Konrad Jarausch, a teacher and co-editor of a Protestant theological journal, was called up in 1939 and served as a sergeant in a reserve security division. On the way to manage a POW camp at the end of September 1939 he remarked in a letter to his wife that 'the Jews have filled the scene with their miserable seediness. How squalid and pathetic. How sordid they are in their wretched humanity.' Although Jarausch regarded the Jews as human, he could not help seeing them as anything other than dirty and furtive.[25]

United by a common dread of the Germans, and filled with a surge of patriotism, Jewish Poles and their Christian co-citizens initially worked and fought side by side to repel the invasion. In Warsaw on 1 September, Chaim Kaplan, the principal of a Hebrew school and frequent contributor to the Hebrew press, joined with other journalists to dig trenches. He knew exactly what was now at stake: 'Wherever Hitler's foot treads there is no hope for the Jewish people,' he wrote in his journal. Wladyslaw Szpilman, a concert pianist who worked for Polish Radio, left the studios to answer the call for volunteers who could handle a spade. 'On the first day an old Jew in kaftan and yarmulka was shovelling soil beside me. He dug with Biblical fervour . . . "I have a shop", he whispered.' Dawid Sierakowiak, a high school student in Lodz, signed up with an anti-aircraft unit. In the days before the attack he too excavated trenches. Excitedly he reported in his diary: 'All Jews (Hassids too), the old, and the young, women, like all other citizens (except for the Germans), volunteer in droves. The bloody Kraut won't pass!' He revelled in the sensation of solidarity, cheered like his fellow Poles by the belief that the English and French would soon come to Poland's aid.[26]

This euphoria waned as they heard news of one city after another falling to the Germans. Rabbi Shimon Huberband in Piotrków was amongst the first to witness the consequences. After the city was bombed on 2 September he and his family took flight to Sulejow. It was a tragic decision. The small town had few sturdy buildings with cellars; when it came under German aerial bombardment his entire family was wiped out. Huberband limped back to Piotrków to find the city gripped by terror: German soldiers had shot twenty Jews as soon as they arrived. Over the ensuing days, Poles escorted Germans to Jewish-owned businesses and helped them loot. So many Jews were beaten up on the streets that they dared not go out. In notes he made shortly after-wards, Huberband recorded that 'If a bearded Jew was caught, his life was in danger. They tore out his beard along with pieces of his flesh, or cut it off with a knife and bayonet.' The occupiers were particularly savage towards anything symbolic of Judaism. Germans smashed mezu-zot, the small cases affixed to the right-hand doorposts of Jewish homes and businesses containing words of scripture. 'Woe unto the Jew found with tefillin and religious books!' Jews caught wearing a tallit katan, a modified prayer shawl worn under the shirt, were 'beaten horribly and cruelly'. Unusually, he also heard that in a couple of cases the local German military authorities actually seized and returned stolen prop-erty to Jews, apologizing to the victims.[27]

On 9 September, Dawid Sierakowiak watched the Germans enter Lodz, Poland's largest industrial centre. While ethnic Germans (about 10 per cent of the population) turned out to cheer the troops, Jews were rounded up for forced labour. 'First signs of German occupation: they are seizing Jews to dig.' Jewish shops were pillaged on a daily basis. With calculated perversity, on the eve of the Jewish New Year (13 September), when most Jews gather to pray, the Germans closed the synagogue and forced Jews to open their businesses. To Sierakowiak it was 'the worst blow to the Jews here in centuries . . . To take away from a man his only consolation, his faith, to forbid his beloved, life-affirming religion is the most horrendous crime. Jews won't let Hitler get away with it. Our revenge will be terrible.'[28]

In Piotrków a week later the Germans marked the Jewish Day of

Atonement, Yom Kippur, with a combination of racial, religious and sexual abuse. Straining for words that would not offend religious modesty, Huberband wrote, 'Jews were forced to pull down their trousers and to beat and to whip a certain part of each other's bodies. They were forced to crawl on their stomachs while looking at a certain point.' This blend of traditional and modern antipathies, far removed from coldly scientific racism, was repeated elsewhere. Huberband heard that in one town Germans forced well-dressed Jewish women to cut the hair of bearded Jews and then eat it. They also forced shaven Jews to kiss Jewish girls. Despite the risks of attending a religious gathering, Huberband managed to observe the holy days between the New Year and Sukkot, the festival of tabernacles. His devotion was hardly isolated: rather, it exemplified the resistance of religious Jews in Poland to the assault on Judaism.[29]

As the German spearheads approached Warsaw, Kaplan observed well-off Jews, including much of the communal leadership, fleeing eastwards. 'The big shots have deserted us,' he wrote scornfully. After the besieged and battered city surrendered he watched the Germans march in. Unlike the hungry, dirty and downcast citizens, the soldiers looked healthy and smart. It did not take long, though, before they started helping themselves to Jewish property, stopping Jews in the street and stealing from them whatever items they fancied. Bearded Jews were a favourite target for robbery and battery; they were also the first to be grabbed off the street for forced labour, clearing away bomb damage. Polish bystanders laughed at this sight. Kaplan noticed that some Poles started helping the Germans to identify Jews and their belongings. 'The conquerors and the conquered find common cause in their hatred of Israel,' he noted bitterly.[30]

Helena Szereszewska lived in a modern house on a fine street in Warsaw. Her husband, Stanislaw, was the director of a distillery and they were thoroughly Polonized. This did not save them from depredations at the hands of the occupier. Within a few days of entering the capital, 'The Germans were now coming for our furniture almost every day. They had teams of Jews to carry the furniture downstairs and load it onto a lorry.' These teams were not volunteers. 'The Jews were rounded up on the street and it sometimes happened that people took their own furniture.'[31]

On 4 October in Lodz, Dawid Sierakowiak was impressed into labour. 'I have never been so humiliated in all my life,' he protested to his diary as he recalled the jeering onlookers. 'Only one response remains: revenge.' After a few days he was able to go back to school, but food and fuel began to run out and Jews were now prevented from shopping normally. Queuing at the few shops where they were permitted to make purchases was an invitation to casual violence from ethnic Germans or passing soldiers. The pillaging of Jewish homes and enterprises continued relentlessly. Eventually a German officer visited his family's apartment to check out the contents but left disappointed. Others struck a rich vein of plunder, emptying homes with impunity. 'Sometimes German officers bring trucks and load furniture, telling the owners to wait to be paid from heaven.' A few days later an ethnic German guided soldiers to his father's business and helped them strip it bare.[32]

A large part of the Polish intelligentsia was shocked by such instances of collaboration. In his daily record of the occupation, Zygmunt Klukowski, the superintendent of the county hospital in Zamość, coolly detailed the modus operandi of both the invaders and local opportunists. 'The usual routine went like this. A few German soldiers would enter the open store and, after taking some items for themselves, start throwing everything else out onto the street. There some people waited to grab what they could. These people are from the city and the neighbouring villages. They would take home their loot, and the soldiers would move on to the next store.' He observed that the German order police and the Sipo-SD men were far worse than the soldiers. But they were outdone by the militia raised from local ethnic Germans, the Selbstschutz. 'The Germans are treating the Jews very brutally. They cut their beards; sometimes they pull the hair out.' Once they sensed the permissive attitude of the new rulers, Poles joined in the violence. 'Sorry to say, some citizens are as equally brutal as the Germans are towards the Jews.'[33]

It was hardly surprising that under these circumstances many Jews initially welcomed the Soviet occupation of the eastern part of Poland. Kaplan wrote, 'When the news reached us that the Bolsheviks were coming closer to Warsaw, our joy was unlimited.' Thousands of mainly young Jews made for the Soviet zone. 'They looked upon the Bolsheviks as redeeming Messiahs.' This was not how most Poles saw it, least of all when the Soviet occupation authorities unleashed their own terror. But Kaplan saw a key difference. 'The Russians plunder one as a citizen, and as a man, while the Nazis plunder one as a Jew.' Even the Polish patriot

Zygmunt Klukowski was relieved when the Russians briefly occupied
Zamość. 'I have to admit, I like them better than Germans.'[34]

German plans for Poland

As the campaign wound down, Hitler and the Nazi leadership faced the
question of what to do with their victory. Beyond vague aspirations to
wipe out the Polish nation and reduce the population to virtual slavery
they had no concrete, detailed plans for the future of what had been
Poland. For a brief period, Hitler even entertained the idea of allowing
Poland to exist as an entity under German suzerainty. Then, around
26 September, in the course of settling the demarcation line between the
two powers, Stalin hinted that in addition to the occupation of eastern
Poland he had designs on the Baltic states. The prospect that substantial
numbers of ethnic Germans would fall under Russian rule in both
Poland (notably Volhynia in the south-east) and the Baltic jolted Hitler
into a snap decision to seek an exchange of population for land. Stalin
got the territory he wanted in the Baltic, while Hitler obtained the
right to evacuate ethnic Germans and bring them 'home to the Reich'.
Ribbentrop was dispatched to Moscow to confirm the deal while a programme and the machinery to implement it were hurriedly stitched
together.[35]

In conversation with confidants Hitler now declared that occupied
Poland would be divided into three zones or belts of land. The first strip,
consisting of the areas lost in 1918, was to be annexed to the Reich.
Poles and Jews would be cleared out and replaced by repatriated ethnic
Germans, Volksdeutsche. The second zone would be placed under some
sort of colonial regime and contain the bulk of the Polish population,
held in subjection as a pool of labour. At the very edge of the new im-
perium, there would be a 'Reich ghetto' to which the Jews of Germany
and Austria would be sent. It all sounded very tidy and logical but it was
actually another case of improvisation dressed up as policy. With little
idea of what they were getting into, Himmler and Heydrich immediately offered the services of the SS to realize Hitler's vision. The SS had
already established its expertise at getting rid of Jews and was acknowledged as the pace setter on matters of racial policy. So vetting ethnic
Germans and helping them to settle seemed a logical extension of its

remit. More to the point Himmler was desperate to expand the role of the SS in wartime and to extend his power into the occupied lands.[36]

In a victory speech before the Reichstag on 6 October, Hitler announced his intention to preside over 'a reordering of ethnographic relations, a resettlement of nationalities' in eastern and south-eastern Europe, where there were many settlements of ethnic Germans. His statement came in the course of a long justification for the war in which he claimed he was doing the world a favour by completing the reversal of the Versailles Treaty. The misguided and vengeful statesmen of 1919 had bequeathed numerous points of ethno-national friction to Europe; Poland was one cause of instability. But now Poland would cease to exist and the borders of the Reich would be redrawn to conform with the distribution of ethnic groups. In the course of disposing of Poland, Hitler also briefly mentioned 'an attempt to reach a solution and a settlement to the Jewish problem'.[37]

The next day, following the usual struggle between ministerial rivals, Himmler was appointed to the newly created post of Reichskommissar für die Festigung deutschen Volkstums (Reich Commissar for the Strengthening of Germandom) and charged with bringing ethnic Germans 'home to the Reich'. Now, in addition to clearing the annexed areas of Poles and Jews, Himmler's men had to find homes, farms and jobs for Volksdeutsche settlers in the east. Within a matter of hours and days, a project of colossal dimensions had been conjured up without giving any thought to the nuts and bolts, let alone the human dimension.[38]

It was characteristic of his impulsive style that when Hitler triggered this momentous and destabilizing project the division of the occupied territories and the establishment of a civil administration had barely been settled. Josef Wagner, Gauleiter of Silesia, temporarily assumed the running of East Upper Silesia, now restored to the Reich and attached to his Gau. Albert Forster, the Gauleiter of Danzig, was given control of the former Polish corridor through West Prussia plus the district of Zichenau. On 8 September, Hitler appointed Arthur Greiser, previously the president of the Danzig senate (and rival of Albert Forster), to head the civil administration in the other areas of western Poland due for incorporation into the Reich. For a while, however, he was nominally under the authority of the Nazi jurist Hans Frank, minister without portfolio, whom Hitler placed in overall charge of occupied Poland. On 12 October, Frank's domain was limited to the zone of central Poland, roughly equivalent to the second belt envisaged by Hitler, dubbed the General Government. Ten days later, Greiser was appointed Reichsstatthalter, governor, of the newly christened Reichsgau Posen (later renamed Reichsgau Wartheland and commonly referred to as Warthegau), that now included a prime chunk of what had been Frank's real estate, containing the industrial city of Lodz and surrounding districts.[39]

Each of the new rulers brought into his domain teams of administrators, usually on secondment from their original office. Ministries in the Reich assigned men to fill cognate positions in the east, usually mediocre or incompetent staffers whom they could afford to lose. A goodly share of posts went to opportunists and adventurers. The essential qualification was a strong track record as a National Socialist activist. Consequently, while they may have been corrupt and inefficient the administrations were filled with men who hated Jews and loathed Poles. At the same time, the security apparatus was extended eastwards. In late September 1939, Himmler created the Reichssicherheitshauptamt – the SS Head Office, usually abbreviated to RSHA – ostensibly to harmonize the activities of the SD, the Gestapo and the police. The RSHA, whose first head was Heydrich, actually did little more than add a layer of management on top of an already confused and overlapping array of agencies. But it added clout to his insistence that the Sipo-SD operate independently in the new areas. Soon 500–600 Sipo-SD men were based in occupied Poland. While technically under the Interior Ministry or the civilian authorities, the police forces were actually controlled by Himmler and Heydrich. In addition, Himmler assigned five Höhere SS- und Polizeiführer (HSSPF or Higher SS Police Leaders), to the new regions to oversee SS work and report personally to him. As if this was not enough cause for confusion, Himmler claimed further powers for himself and his subordinates in his capacity as Reich Commissar for the Strengthening of Germandom. Finally, Göring exercised sweeping authority over economic matters through the eastern projection of the Office of the Four-Year Plan. Within their respective domains and spheres of responsibility, Göring, Himmler, Gauleiter Forster, Reichsstatthalter Greiser and General Governor Frank pursued different policies towards the Poles. There was little uniformity or coordination.[40]

Remarkably, the treatment of Poland's Jews had not received much more consideration than the Polish question as a whole. Heydrich held briefing sessions with Einsatzgruppen leaders on 7 and 21 September, respectively one week and three weeks into the military campaign, at which he set forth his ideas. He also held meetings with Himmler on 14 and 21 September at which, amongst other things, they discussed anti-Jewish measures. To begin with, the SS leaders seemed to assume that anti-Jewish policy would continue along the lines obtaining in the Reich and as implemented in Austria and the Czech lands. Jews who were deemed a security risk would be arrested, imprisoned or executed; the Jewish population as a whole would be subjected to discriminatory laws and segregated; their property and assets would be seized for the Reich; where possible groups would be driven across the nearest border or obliged, under pressure, to emigrate. But the implementation of these measures depended in part on where the demarcation line between the Reich and the USSR would fall. Deporting Jews to the east, outside German territory, could not be undertaken until the SS knew where 'the east' would be.[41]

Heydrich gained the impression that Hitler envisaged the removal of the entire Jewish population from the Reich, including areas that were to be annexed to it, into some sort of reservation, possibly in the province of Galicia in southern Poland. Later that was amended to a 'Reich ghetto' in the Lublin area. Hitler certainly broached the subject with the army. Halder noted in his war diary on 20 September 1939, 'Ghetto plan exists in broad outline; details are not yet settled; economic needs are prime consideration.' Halder did not express a view one way or the other about the moral standing of such an outlandish suggestion; he merely reiterated the army's insistence that no major population movements should be undertaken until military operations had ceased. At this point it would only be appropriate to explore 'which population groups must be resettled and where'.[42]

At Gestapo headquarters in Berlin the next day, Heydrich inducted his field commanders into the fast-crystallizing policy. Because not all were able to attend he subsequently compiled a Schnellbrief, a summary for express distribution. Heydrich began by distinguishing between the 'final goal (which will require a lengthy period) and the stages leading to the fulfilment of the final goal (which can be carried out in short periods)'. The 'overall measures (i.e. the final goal)', were to be kept 'strictly secret'. This ultimate objective was never clearly explicated. But it would require 'the most thorough preparation in both the technical and the economic sense'. The first, immediate prerequisite was 'the concentration of the Jews from the countryside into the larger cities'. This was to be carried out rapidly according to a set of territorial priorities.

Danzig, West Prussia, Poznan, East Upper Silesia were to be 'cleared of Jews' or, if that was not possible, the number of concentration points was to be kept to a minimum. In the rest of the conquered land the number of places where Jews would be gathered should also be held down. The cities appointed to receive the Jews should be on rail junctions or located on railroad routes 'so as to facilitate subsequent measures'. Small communities of under 500 souls were to be dissolved and transferred to these larger ones.[43]

Heydrich mandated that 'In each Jewish community a Council of Elders is to be set up which, as far as possible, is to be composed of the remaining leading persons and rabbis'. Councils were to comprise up to twenty-four members, depending on the size of the community. Their members were to be made 'fully responsible, in the literal sense of the word' for the implementation of existing and future directives. 'In case of sabotage of such instructions, the Councils are to be warned that the most severe measures will be taken'. They were to carry out a census of the Jews in their area and then organize the evacuation of small communities to the cities. If asked why, 'The reason to be given for the concentration of the Jews in the cities is that the Jews have taken a decisive part in sniper attacks and plundering'. The councils were also given responsibility for housing Jews brought in from rural areas. Jews being moved to the cities would be allowed to bring with them whatever they could carry. They would be warned of the most severe penalties for not complying.

In the only paragraph that mentioned how the German authorities should manage the 'concentration of Jews' Heydrich proposed that the demands of policing and security 'will probably call for regulations which forbid their entry to certain quarters completely and that – with due regard for economic considerations – they may, for instance, not leave the ghetto, not leave their homes after a certain hour in the evening etc.'

All these measures were to be taken in the closest consultation with the army and the civilian regimes. Economic requirements had to be taken into account, too. 'For instance, for the time being it will scarcely be possible to avoid, here and there, leaving behind some trade Jews who are absolutely essential to the provisioning of troops, for lack of other possibilities'. In such cases 'the prompt Aryanization of these enterprises is to be planned'. Jewish-owned munitions factories and other essential industries, along with enterprises important to the Four-

Year Plan, had to be 'maintained for the time being'. Eventually they were also to be Aryanized 'and the move of the Jews completed later'. Heydrich's instructions took equal cognizance of the food situation in the occupied territories. Land farmed by Jews had to be handed over to neighbouring Germans 'or even Polish farmers' to ensure the harvest was brought in and crops planted for the next season. In the event of conflict between the security police and the civil administration Heydrich was to be informed at once so that he could reach a decision about what to do.

The last section of the Schnellbrief stipulated that the Einsatzgruppen commanders were to report continuously on the numbers of Jews in their operational zones and the pace of evacuations from the countryside to the cities. Heydrich wanted to know where the Jews were to be concentrated, when they would be transferred, details of their major economic enterprises and Aryanization proceedings. How many Jews worked in specific enterprises and could they be kept running without them? If not, how would they be replaced? No district was left untouched. To notify the relevant state agencies, and also to signify his authority in these matters, copies of the Schnellbrief were sent to the provisional civil authorities in the occupied territories, the army high command, the office of the Four-Year Plan, the Reich Interior Ministry and the Ministry of Food.[44]

Although the summary left the 'final goal' unstated, in this meeting on 21 September and at a later briefing at the RSHA on 29 September, Heydrich did elaborate on the eventual fate of the Jews. They were to be removed from the Reich and deported to a 'foreign Gau' (that is to say, a district under German control reserved for aliens) or forced over the demarcation line into Soviet territory. Hence, all the actions specified in the Schnellbrief were temporary and designed to culminate in the removal of the Jews within the next twelve months. Partly for this reason, Heydrich devoted little attention to details or definitions. Although the word ghetto was used, his summary never elaborated on what it meant. Rather than requiring the construction of enclosed Jewish districts, part of the message actually suggested that Jews would be allowed to wander anywhere in cities apart from specifically prohibited zones. The Jewish councils were made responsible for the enumeration, removal and rehousing of Jews from the countryside, but apart from that they had no other functions. The Schnellbrief shows that Heydrich was still obliged to pay obeisance to the civil authorities and the army, as well as the economic agencies of the Reich. Notwithstanding the affirmation of a coordinated multi-agency approach, there was no hint about how the Jewish communities would be supervised or maintained until the 'final goal' was attained or by whom.[45]

Eichmann and the Nisko project

Several of Heydrich's subordinates took these early aspirational state-ments to be policy guidelines, ignoring the caveats uttered by high-ranking officers such as Halder and the reservations included by Heydrich in the short summary. In mid-September, Adolf Eichmann (based in Vienna) and Franz Stahlecker (now commanding the Sipo-SD in Prague), discussed the removal of 300,000 Reich Jews to the reser-vation that had been mooted in Berlin. Heinrich Müller, head of the Gestapo, was closer to the epicentre of decision-making. On 6 October he ordered Eichmann to prepare the deportation of 70,000–80,000 Jews from the Protectorate and the districts annexed to Silesia. Eichmann wasted no time initiating practical steps in the cities initially designated for the operation: Katowice in East Upper Silesia and Ostrava in the Protectorate. Vienna was soon added to the list. The German authorities there and in Katowice were thrilled at the prospect of substantially diminishing their Jewish populations. Eichmann deputed his staff at the central emigration office in Vienna to handle the logistics. Theo Dannecker and Alois Brunner set about obtaining the necessary trains, while Rolf Günther briefed the hapless Jewish leaders in each place about what was expected of them. On 10 October, Josef Löwenherz, the head of the Jewish community in Vienna, was told to select over 1,000 able-bodied men and equip them with food, clothing and tools. They would prepare the way for the masses to follow. Similar instructions were issued in the other centres.[46]

However, with just a week to go before the transports were due to leave, Stahlecker and Eichmann still had no idea where the Jews would go. On 12 October they flew from Ostrava to Cracow to begin looking for a suitable reception area. Eichmann disliked flying, so the choice of transportation suggests the pressure they were under. Having spent three days scouting locations in the Lublin area, some still patrolled by Red Army units, they alighted on Nisko and Zarzecze, two villages on opposite sides of the River San. Both were on a railway line and close to unused marshy ground that stretched from the edge of town to the river bank. Satisfied that they had found the spot, Eichmann telexed the basic details to his officials. Twenty-four hours later he was back in Vienna, where he hastily briefed his aides before travelling to Ostrava to do the same there. The very next day, 916 Czech Jewish men clambered aboard a train with twenty-two passenger carriages and twenty-nine freight cars for the provisions and equipment – all paid for by local Jews. As if to underline the random nature of the enterprise, Eichmann agreed to a last-minute request by Arthur Nebe, head of the criminal police in Berlin, to add a few freight cars to take away unwanted Gypsies. A second trainload, with over 1,000 Jews, was dispatched from Vienna on 20 October. A third left from Katowice. Then things started to go wrong. The first train was held in a siding overnight and several men had to be removed due to sickness. No sooner had it arrived at Nisko than Rolf Günther got information from the SD Head Office that the initiative required central approval and the cooperation of other agencies. This admonition was quickly succeeded by an unequivocal order from Berlin to stop any more trains going east. Amidst the confusion Eichmann sent off two more trainloads, one from Vienna and one from Ostrava. A trainload also departed from Prague but was turned back due to floods. Little more than a week after its inauguration the plan foundered. Instead of 80,000 Jews, a mere 4,700 had been removed. Müller later explained to Eichmann that the army had priority on rail transport; it was more important to extract Polish POWs from the war zone than to dump Jews there. The high command also objected to the creation of a massive Jewish population adjacent to what might become the next front line.[47]

Although short-lived, the Nisko scheme was horrendous for the Jews caught up in it. At breakneck speed and considerable cost, the Jewish communities had obtained the materials for prefabricated huts, building tools and provisions for several weeks. When the first trainload arrived, Eichmann greeted them in person. He announced that they were there to begin constructing 'a new homeland' for the Jews. But there was no infrastructure, the ground was marshy, and there was no shelter for the workers. The SS and police guards had no interest in the project and after Eichmann had left they attempted to drive several groups across the demarcation line into the Soviet zone. As more Jews arrived, a few huts were erected and the camp took shape, but the men could not survive without help from the Jewish community in Lublin. The harsh winter weather decimated their ranks. Without any form of sustenance or work some made their way to the city or transferred to labour camps in East Upper Silesia. In April 1940 the camp was wound up and the 300 survivors were allowed to return home.[48]

The abortive Nisko venture came to be seen by historians as a policy departure, or at least an experiment that led to the perfection of techniques for the mass deportation of Jews. In fact, it was an attempt to continue on a larger scale the policy that had led to the expulsion of Polish Jews from Germany almost exactly a year earlier. The only new ingredient was in the nature of the destination: a peripheral territory under the control of the Reich. The men who hatched the scheme lazily assumed that this would obviate the problems experienced in October 1938. Instead, this brashly conceived 'territorial solution' was stymied by protests from the army. It was also cut short by Himmler, who was trying to cope with a far more pressing movement of population: the influx of Volksdeutsche and the expulsion of Poles whose farms and homes were required for their resettlement. The failure was an evil portent, but for Himmler and Heydrich rather than the Jews. It became the first in a catalogue of disasters that autumn which threatened to tarnish their careers and the reputation of the SS.[49]

In mid-October the first Volksdeutsche arrived in Danzig. Greiser was keen to receive them in his Gau because he presided over a province with 325,000 Germans and 4.9 million Poles. The number of Jews alone was roughly equal to the number of Germans. On his appointment as Reichsstatthalter he proclaimed that he would create a 'model Gau' that would be productive, modern, and thoroughly German. But he faced an uphill battle. The only way he could hope to realize his dream was by working with Himmler and utilizing the manpower and resources of the SS, even if that involved ceding a degree of sovereignty. Indeed, at first Greiser was almost a spectator to the upheavals in his own back yard.[50]

At the end of the month, Himmler issued guidelines for the purification of the incorporated territories. He entrusted Wilhelm Koppe, the HSSPF in Posen, with the mission to displace 1 million Poles and 300,000 Jews from Danzig-West Prussia and the Wartheland into the General Government within four months. Koppe delegated the job to Albert Rapp, who quickly revised the figure down to more manageable proportions. Ten days later he announced that the target was now just 200,000 Poles and 100,000 Jews. A little over two weeks later, Heydrich intervened. He limited the operation to the Warthegau and stipulated that the goal should be 80,000 Poles and Jews. Retaining, if only on paper, the intent to cleanse the new lands of their entire alien and hostile population, he chopped up the operation into stages. The opening phase was dubbed Nahplan, or short-term plan, 1.[51]

The entire process was haphazard. The security police set about identifying and registering Poles, often erroneously. On appointed days in particular districts thousands were given a few hours' notice that they had to leave. However, the SS lacked the personnel for an endeavour of this scope so that order police, ethnic German militia, the civil authorities, and even students at a Nazi leadership school were drafted in to help. Between 1 and 17 December eighty trains were sent out of the Gau carrying 87,833 Poles. When the transports arrived in the General Government the freezing, hungry refugees were deposited into the care of the local population. Chaos mounted in the districts where refugees piled up. Hundreds made their way back to their homesteads, in some cases with the intention of vandalizing the properties rather than see them taken over by strangers.[52]

About 10,000 Jews were included in this first wave, uprooted mainly from Posen, Kalisch and Lodz. The inclusion of Lodz in the Warthegau, with its Jewish population of approximately 200,000, posed a massive headache for Greiser and his officials. Could they be extracted without wrecking the local economy and where could they go? Only around 5,000–6,000 were forcibly located to the General Government before Nahplan 1 ended. Greiser and his advisers realized that Jews were not the priority when it came to settling Volksdeutsche: the incomers needed farms and manual employment whereas the Jews were urban dwellers and hardly any worked the land.[53]

It also became clear to Heydrich that things were not going well. Just before Christmas he brought in Adolf Eichmann to review the deportations and devise a more efficient system. Eichmann had already convened a meeting of the SD Referenten to discuss how to deal with the Reich Jews in the light of new opportunities in the east and the competing obligation to rid the annexed territories of undesirable populations. When the Jewish Department II/112 of the SD Head Office was transferred to the Gestapo and reclassified office IVD4 – with responsibility for emigration and evacuations – Polish policy and anti-Jewish policy became fatefully entangled.[54]

In the second phase, Nahplan 2, Heydrich envisaged the deportation of 600,000 Jews from the new portions of the Reich to a reservation in the General Government where they would be held as hostages against the good behaviour of the Americans. The operation would commence on 15 January 1940, assuming that the Transport Ministry provided trains sufficient for 5,000 deportees per day. This time the details were to be worked out in advance and coordinated between the necessary agencies. However, when Eichmann convened the first coordination meeting early in the new year he lowered the target to 350,000 Jews and now included Poles. A sudden flood of Volksdeutsche from Volhynia had revived the urgency of finding room on the land for incomers by evicting Polish farmers. Once again a revised programme had to be delayed. Due to the parlous condition of the Reichsbahn and the priority demands of the Wehrmacht, there wasn't enough available transport. Furthermore, Hans Frank had developed ambitions for making the General Government economically productive and resented his fiefdom being treated as a rubbish bin for unwanted populations. In the end, Nahplan 2 was shelved and an interim plan was set in motion to remove 40,000 Poles to make way for ethnic German settlers. Even this limited evacuation, conducted between 10 February and 15 March 1940, was a shambles. Despite the sweeping goals outlined by Heydrich, only a very small proportion were Jews.[55]

The Nazi leadership was reluctantly forced to concede the impossibility of achieving everything at once. A meeting of the key Gauleiters at Göring's private estate in mid-February voiced concern that uncontrolled resettlement was disrupting the economy in the areas whence Poles were being removed and where they were being deposited. Göring reiterated that the smooth production of munitions and food had to take priority over population movements. While everyone agreed that it was desirable to deport Jews from the incorporated territories to some kind of Jewish reservation in a corner of the General Government, Himmler was boxed in. Frank accepted his role, with the proviso that he was offering a temporary solution. Yet two comparatively minor expulsions of Jews, from Stettin on 12 February (the day of the meeting) and Schneidemühl a month later, were the straws that broke the camel's back. Frank declared that he could not tolerate further uncoordinated resettlements and, this time, Göring backed him up forcefully. On 23 March he told Himmler to desist from further removals of Jews to the General Government.[56]

Nahplan 2 was resurrected in March 1940 and continued in fits and starts until January 1941, by which time 143 transports had carried 133,508 Poles to the General Government. Only three trains were used to deport Polish Jews, chiefly from Posen. The majority of Jews in the incorporated territories ended up staying where they were. Apart from Stettin and Schneidemühl, as shocking as these expulsions were, the Jews of the Reich remained undisturbed. Himmler and Heydrich, along with Greiser and Frank, discovered that they had taken on objectives that actually frustrated one another. It was all very well to talk about clearing the Wartheland of Poles, but Poles were the labour force and farm evictions disrupted agricultural production. The settlement of 360,000 ethnic Germans created all sorts of challenges that would have strained the agencies of the Reich even had they not taken on other responsibilities. Removing Jews was ideologically satisfying, but did not materially assist the fulfilment of other goals. Moreover, Greiser and Frank discovered that the Jewish question, in the form it assumed in Poland, was more complicated than they thought.[57]

Anti-Jewish policy and Jewish responses in occupied Poland

While the Nazis wrestled with a knot of intertwined problems caused by their long-term population policies, the Jews had to cope with German rule in conquered Poland on a day-to-day basis. There was little consistency or uniformity to their experiences. At first they lived in a war zone, then under military rule, and finally under civilian authority. The treatment meted out to them varied in each phase and, confusingly, from one region to another. Jews had no way of knowing what caused this muddle, but they couldn't help noticing the barrage of orders and counter-orders transmitted down the chain of command, the unrealistic nature of many policy declarations, the dissonance between what Berlin decreed and what local rulers did, and the regional variations. German ordinances were all the more terrifying because they were so baffling. At the start of December 1939, Chaim Kaplan observed shrewdly, 'The liquidation of Polish Jewry is in full force, but it is not proceeding everywhere at a uniform rate. It is a mistake to think that the conqueror excels in logic and orderliness. We see quite the opposite of this. Everything that is done by those who carry out his exalted will bears the imprint of confusion and illogic. The Nazis are consistent and systematic only with regard to the

central concepts behind their actions – that is, the concept of authoritar-
ianism and harshness; and in relation to the Jews – the concept of
complete extermination and destruction.'[58]

Initially the army presided over the acts of violence, destruction and
despoliation. In addition to the thousands of Jews killed in security
actions or reprisals, 25,000 of the 60,000 Jewish soldiers in the Polish
army who became prisoners of war were dead by the following spring.
Several thousand were sent to Germany for forced labour, where they
were treated better than in the POW camps. After about a year some
were even repatriated to Poland. Meanwhile, army commanders were
the first to impose discrimination and segregation on Jewish communities. On 8 October 1939 the military authorities in Piotrków Trybunalski
decreed that the 15,000 Jews in the city were to be confined to a ghetto.
It was the first of its kind, but did not indicate a trend and was hardly a
model for what followed. Jews continued to live outside the Piotrków
ghetto even after the boundary was set. Although ghettos became the
iconic feature of German anti-Jewish policy in Poland they were established sporadically, over a long period, and rarely for the same reasons.
Regardless of the instructions issued by Heydrich only seven other
cities or towns had ghettos by the end of 1939.[59]

In the Wartheland, Greiser's aim was to eject the Jews as quickly as
possible, so he had no particular interest in setting up ghettos. It was
only towards the end of 1939, when it became apparent that the Jewish
population could not be deported within a few months, that Friedrich
Übelhör, the chief of the Kalisz district, first gave serious consideration
to means of segregating Jews from the German and Polish populations.[60]

As long as there was a prospect of a Jewish reservation in the Lublin
district Hans Frank showed even less interest in forming ghettos. On
4 November, the SS in Warsaw summoned the Jewish leadership and
informed them that the German authorities intended to create a ghetto
on a number of streets in the city. The Jews were appalled and refused to
accept the blow meekly. Adam Czerniaków, an engineer who had been
appointed by Warsaw's mayor to chair a committee representing its
Jewish population during the siege, led a delegation to General Karl von
Neumann-Neurode, military commander of the city. It turned out that
Neumann-Neurode had not been consulted about this momentous and
potentially disruptive move. The army put a stop to the plan and it
remained on the shelf for months until the civil authorities, in consulta-

tion with experts and the security police, came up with a more considered proposal. The Germans did however put up notices barring their troops from Jewish districts on the grounds that they were seething with infectious diseases. This was a dangerous precedent, but for the moment the 360,000 Jews counted in the census conducted at German insistence continued to live all over Warsaw. In Cracow, which he made his capital, Frank was content for the time being to designate the part where most Jews lived a 'Jewish residential district'.[61]

Despoliation on a small and large scale was more ubiquitous. Looting by German soldiers continued for months. In October, Michael Zylberberg, headmaster of a Jewish school in Warsaw, recorded that Germans were still 'breaking into homes and looting'. In Lodz the havoc all but prevented the young diarist Mary Berg from celebrating her fifteenth birthday on 10 October. Her father's art dealership was ransacked and paintings by Poussin and Delacroix carried away from their apartment. They were 'visited by German soldiers' again at the start of November. The Germans re-enacted the Reich pogrom of November 1938 by torching the city's synagogues at the same time as carrying on with their wild plundering. Dawid Sierakowiak exclaimed, 'There's something sick about the Germans. Yesterday they started horrible, chaotic looting.'[62]

Across the Warthegau and the General Government the civilian powers froze the bank accounts of Jews, emptied their safety deposit boxes, and confiscated the securities they owned. Göring's Central Trust Office East moved with alacrity to seize the homes, businesses and enterprises of Jews in the incorporated territories. Greiser, who was thereby cheated of the richest pickings, was reduced to pillaging their movable property and personal assets to fund his administration. Frank vigorously resisted Göring's ambition to achieve the same monopoly in the General Government and set up his own Trust Organization to expropriate and dispose of Jewish-owned property. By the end of the year Göring was forced to agree to a compromise whereby Frank became his plenipotentiary for economic matters. The Trust eventually sold off 3,600 businesses and 50,000 properties. It was also common practice to impose fines on Jewish communities, often accompanied by the taking of hostages. In Lodz the Germans levied a fine of 25 million zloty; in Warsaw it was just 1 million. Jewish councils desperately collected the money, often making up the amount with appeals for Jews to hand over foreign currency, gold rings and precious stones.[63]

Decrees by the military authorities, echoed and extended by the civilian rulers, forced Jews out of one livelihood after another. Jewish civil servants were immediately dismissed. The suppression of Jewish schools left thousands of teachers idle. Jews who worked for newspapers, publishers, theatres and concert orchestras were denied a livelihood. Chaim Kaplan estimated that the ban on Jews manufacturing or trading in textiles and leather affected about half of all the Jews employed in Warsaw. Soon 70,000–80,000 were unemployed.[64]

The Germans continued to seize Jews for forced labour. Army units, the SS and civilian agencies competed to obtain and keep Jewish workers. In the Lublin area the HSSPF Odilo Globocnik was quick to establish a monopoly on Jewish muscle power, thereby creating the basis for an economic empire of his own. In the rest of the General Government Frank's officials tussled with the Sipo-SD for control of this lucrative resource. Since the toil was accompanied by beatings and arbitrary killings many Jewish men preferred to flee into the Soviet sector and take their chances there.[65]

Women abducted for labour were frequently abused. Kaplan reported that in Lodz 'girls were compelled to clean a latrine – to remove the excrement and clean it. But they received no utensils. To their question "With what?" the Nazis replied: "With your blouses." The girls removed their blouses and cleaned the excrement with them. When the job was done they received their reward; the Nazis wrapped their faces in the blouses, filthy with excrement, and laughed uproariously.' Mary Berg heard that Germans (she did not identify whether they were soldiers, SS or local militia) gathered couples in a room and forced them to strip and dance naked. Two young girls she knew from school who were compelled to perform in this way returned to their homes bruised from the ensuing struggle. Berg did not elaborate on what had happened to them.[66]

Random kidnappings such as these terrified the Jewish population and were one of the first things that the newly appointed Jewish councils sought to ameliorate. Typically, although these institutions were supposed to be standardized they emerged chaotically and varied widely. Like his instruction to concentrate Jews, Heydrich's directive to establish a Judenrat, or Jewish council, in every community was hazy. He did not specify who was eligible or how members should be chosen. Sometimes the military authorities took the initiative, sometimes commanders of the Einsatzgruppen or Sipo-SD officers. In Radom, the

Einsatzgruppe chief plucked Jews from the street to serve on a council. Frequently, Jews offered their services to the occupiers in the hope of mitigating the looting and arbitrary forced labour. In most cases these individuals came from the ranks of pre-war communal activists or civic committees set up to deal with war damage and refugees, but in some they were opportunists with no qualifications except chutzpah. In late November 1939 Hans Frank issued his own decree stipulating the formation of Jewish councils in the General Government, requiring that they should be elected. Hardly any were. Jewish councils did not even have uniform titles. In East Upper Silesia they were known as the Council of Elders of the Jewish Religious Community.[67]

The composition of the councils was not only the consequence of an erratic appointments process. Flight and emigration, along with indiscriminate and targeted killings, decapitated many Jewish communities. Political activists, especially on the left, and members of the intelligentsia fled to Lithuania, the Soviet zone, or to Romania. Wealthy Jews, who typically presided over welfare and cultural organizations, had the means to escape or to emigrate. So the leadership pool was denuded even before the Germans began selecting men to establish or serve on Jewish councils. Nevertheless, almost everywhere local leaders were drawn from men who had held pre-war positions in communal organizations and frequently included members of the local rabbinate.[68]

In Warsaw the military authority agreed to the appointment of Adam Czerniaków as head of the Jewish community. Czerniaków was a chemical engineer with a wealth of experience in civic affairs. He had been selected by the capital's mayor as the chief representative of Warsaw Jews during the siege and already chaired a Jewish civic committee. After Hans Frank issued his own directive for the formation of a council, Czerniaków recruited two dozen representatives of the main welfare organizations, political parties and religious groups to serve alongside him. They were honourable men with years of public service between them. Unfortunately, several chose to escape abroad over the following months. These included Dr Henry Shoskes, Apolinary Hartglas and Shmuel Zygielbojm, who together had taken a courageous stand against the formation of a ghetto. As the council lost men of such standing and acquired the task of implementing ever harsher German decrees it steadily lost prestige and respect amongst ordinary Jews.[69]

One of the first tasks of the Warsaw Jewish council was to provide the Germans with a census of Jews in the city. The head count at the end of October 1939 revealed a Jewish population of approximately 360,000, although it grew daily due to the inflow of refugees and Jews expelled from the Warthegau. To prevent the chaotic and violent raids to seize Jews for work details the council organized labour battalions that could be provided to the Germans when they needed manpower. Soon the labour office of the Warsaw Judenrat was supplying the German rail-ways, garrison, municipal authorities and SS with 1,000 workers per day. In January 1940 the Germans ordered the council to register Jews aged 14–60 who were fit for work. Over 112,000 Jews were tallied (including converts), although only a fraction of them ever carried a pick or a shovel. The labourers were not remunerated by their employ-ers; instead, the Jewish council paid them a small sum, 3–4 zlotys per day, with which to maintain themselves and any dependants. It was a paltry amount, sufficient only to act as an inducement to refugees who had no other hope of employment. Better-off Jews preferred to buy their way out. Instead of rejecting such practices for the sake of equality, the Jewish council used the sale of exemptions to provide an urgently needed revenue stream. While the Germans blocked access to the bank accounts of community organizations as well as Jewish individuals, they expected Czerniaków to secure funds for a mammoth budget covering the cost of services provided by the Warsaw municipality, the wage bill for forced labour (which indirectly maintained tens of thousands of Jews), welfare, health, and emergency housing for refugees. It was an impossible task and even with money from overseas aid agencies Czer-niaków staggered from one financial crisis to another.[70]

The next most urgent priority of the councils was to house and feed refugees from the fighting, those bombed out of their homes, or families evicted from the incorporated territories. When the Germans started pushing Jews out of small rural settlements into larger towns or cities, the councils had to care for them as well. Overcrowding meant that the councils were soon compelled to take sanitation in hand, too. As more Jews were deprived of a livelihood or forced from their places of work, councils took up the task of providing emergency meals in communal canteens or soup kitchens. This obliged them to seek and manage food supplies. Gradually the councils also assumed responsibility for health services, welfare for the elderly and the young, and education.[71]

Aid from Jews in the USA was crucial to sustaining Jewish life in Poland. The American Jewish Joint Distribution Committee continued to send funds to Warsaw, where they were used locally or parcelled out to communities across the country. In the capital its local representatives worked with a central coordinating committee that brought some order to myriad overlapping and competing Jewish welfare organizations. The Coordinating Commission of Jewish Aid and Civil Society was set up in the early days of the war as a sub-section of a national relief effort. It was chaired by Michael Weichert, a lawyer and a well-known pre-war figure, and included representatives from the main welfare agencies, political parties and religious groups. Czerniaków met several times with Weichert to plead for increased funding. At the start of 1940, the Germans severed Jewish relief work from national and local Polish aid organizations. Weichert nevertheless continued to coordinate Jewish activity across the General Government while a separate Welfare Work Section in Warsaw provided the liaison between separate agencies. Its secretary was Emanuel Ringelblum, a schoolteacher better known as an historian and activist in the left-wing Zionist movement. In mid-1940 the Germans insisted that US aid had to be funnelled through Cracow, capital of the General Government. Thanks to the manipulated rate of exchange only about 20 per cent of the value of the money transferred to Poland actually reached the Jews. Most went into the coffers of Frank's administration.[72]

The yellow star, which like ghettoization became a signature of Nazi policy, was also introduced unevenly and Jewish reactions were far from uniform. Greiser's administration officially required Jews to wear a star made of yellow cloth on their outer garments from 11 November 1939. When he learned of the decree Dawid Sierakowiak railed in his diary, 'We are returning to the Middle Ages. The yellow patch once again becomes a part of Jewish dress.' Despite the latest indignity and a draconian curfew from 4 p.m. to 8 a.m., he was convinced 'we will live through this action to see a fine, shining future.'[73]

Frank did not ordain a similar measure in the General Government until a month later, when decrees required Jews to wear an armband printed with a blue Star of David and to mark all Jewish businesses. Wladyslaw Szpilman later recalled his indignation. 'So we are to be publicly branded as outcasts. Several centuries of humanitarian progress were to be cancelled out, and we were back in the Middle Ages.' In stark contrast, as an Orthodox Jew and a Zionist, Chaim Kaplan relished the edict. '[T]he conqueror is turning us into Jews whether we like it or not. Nobody is being discriminated against. The Nazis have marked us with the Jewish national colours, which are our pride.' He observed the difference between Warsaw and Lodz. 'The "yellow badge" of medieval days has been stuck to them, but as for me I shall wear my badge with personal satisfaction.' In a further echo of medieval antipathies, the Germans banned Jewish schooling and forbade worship in synagogues or use of ritual baths.[74]

Constant harassment and the fear of compulsory labour encouraged those who could to escape German rule and for the meantime the borders of German-occupied Poland remained relatively porous. About 350,000 Jews who fled eastward during the fighting inadvertently ended up in the Soviet zone. They were joined by a steady stream of fugitives, usually young men who preferred Russian rule. 'In tens of thousands our youths flee to this "Russian" territory from the inferno awaiting them under the rule of Nazism', Kaplan commented on 27 November 1939. At first they were welcomed as 'excellent material for Bolshevism' until the Soviets lost patience with the flood and closed the border. Still, many were willing to risk getting shot by Red Army patrols as against the danger of staying put. Yet not everyone found the Soviet system to their taste. Mary Berg's father went east, but then returned. Lots of young left-leaning Jewish men like Dawid Sierakowiak would have chosen socialism over Nazi tyranny, but felt bound to stay with their families. Meanwhile, those with the means and the necessary papers were still able to emigrate. Having taken part in the defence of Warsaw, Helena Szereszewska remarked that 'some people were leaving for Russia, others via Italy for Brazil, and some via Japan for the United States. And there were even some who managed to get to Palestine, via Wilno [Vilnius], Odessa and Constantinople.' Yitzhak Zuckerman, a youth worker in the left-wing Zionist movement HeHalutz Ha-Tsair, slipped into the Soviet zone and began to secretly organize groups of young Zionists for emigration to Palestine via Romania.[75]

Ghetto building in Lodz and variations elsewhere

During the first months of 1940 the persistence of dense Jewish populations under their charge drove the Germans to more drastic and often self-contradictory measures. On 10 December 1939, Übelhör informed Nazi Party representatives in Lodz, the municipal government, and the security police that 'Their immediate evacuation is not possible.' As a strictly temporary expedient Jews would be confined to a ghetto. 'The establishment of the ghetto is of course a transitional measure. I reserve to myself the decision at what point in time and with which means the ghetto and the city of Lodz will be cleansed of Jews. In any event, the final goal must be that we completely cauterize out this pestilential boil.'[76]

Übelhör's initial conception was a tightly constricted ghetto for those who could not work combined with guarded barracks scattered across the city for the essential Jewish labour. This was no more practicable than removing the entire Jewish population to the General Government. Instead, Greiser agreed to proposals by city officials to move all the city's Jewish residents into the slum districts of Baluty and the Old Town, where 60,000 Jews already lived. An outbreak of typhus supplied a pretext for designating the 'Jewish residential area' and establishing control points for entering and leaving. On 8 February 1940, the Lodz police president published an ordinance condemning about 100,000 Jews to leave their homes for the cramped, squalid Baluty district within thirty days. At first the relocation proceeded voluntarily, but it was too slow for the Germans so it was speeded up by police raids and shootings in which hundreds died. By early March most Jews were inside the assigned area and the Germans began sealing it off with fences and barbed wire. The Jews within were forbidden to leave on pain of death. When the last stretch was completed on 1 April 1940 the ghetto was hermetically closed to the outside world. To symbolize the Germanization of the city it was renamed Litzmannstadt.[77]

In the eyes of German urban planners, Lodz could only be turned into an ideal German city if the Jews were shunted out of sight and tightly contained. As a consequence of their racialized understanding of space and progress, 164,000 people were crammed into 4.13 square kilometres. The ghetto contained just over 48,000 residential rooms, creating a density of 3.5 persons per room. Most of the buildings were old and poorly built; 95 per cent of residences lacked running water or toilets. Only 49 apartments had a bathroom. The flip-side of modernization and Germanization was thrusting the Jews back into a bygone era of squalor and deprivation.[78]

The internal organization of the ghetto was equally slapdash. On 13 October 1939 the Germans had appointed the sixty-three-year-old Chaim Rumkowski as the Elder of the Jews. Rumkowski was not such a bad choice. Having failed at business he became the director of an admired orphanage and achieved much in the field of education and child welfare. An odour of scandal hung around him, but he was one of the few members of the pre-war elite who had stayed at their post. His mandate was sweeping: 'to carry out all measures of the German civil administration with regard to all persons belonging to the Jewish race'. He was commanded to dissolve the existing communal organizations, recruit a council and levy taxes on the Jewish population. Rumkowski picked over two dozen solid, experienced citizens to assist him, only for them to be arrested and shot or imprisoned within weeks. He and two others were the only survivors of the first Council of Elders. Its next incarnation was hardly distinguished. After the ghetto was sealed, the mayor of Lodz awarded him wide powers 'to maintain an orderly public life in the Jewish residential area'. Unfortunately this brought out the worst in his character. A vain, autocratic type at the best of times he now became dictatorial, convinced that he alone could save the Jewish community.[79]

Having said that, the task facing the Elder of the Jews required a man of enormous energy and inexhaustible self-belief. Rumkowski presided over a vast, impoverished population with no obvious means of sustenance. The ghetto contained three hospitals, four orphanages and thirty-two primary schools amongst other institutions, all of which required supply and maintenance. Thousands of people who scurried into the ghetto at the last moment, with shots ringing in their ears, lacked accommodation or means of support. How could the ghetto afford to pay teachers and doctors, or purchase provisions and medical supplies? On top of this expenditure, since October 1939 the Jewish council had been paying wages to 2,000–3,000 Jewish workers whose services were demanded by the Germans each day. The Germans cynically declared that the ghetto would manage on the basis of 'autarky', meaning that Jews would draw on their mythologized wealth to purchase what they needed. In fact, 'autarky' was a polite word for extortion and cannibalization. Rumkowski was forced to be ruthless and ingenious in order to generate sufficient revenue to obtain medicine, food, fuel and raw materials.[80]

Shortly after the ghetto was sealed, he wrote to the city mayor proposing that 8,000–10,000 skilled Jewish workers could be put to work for the benefit of the authorities if they were supplied with raw materials and paid a wage. He offered to establish an office to allocate work in the ghetto and undertook to deliver products that could be exchanged for cash or food. Rumkowski also asked for a loan: 'I hope that I and my co-workers in all this will succeed in obtaining a subvention from the authorities in order to carry out the budget in the ghetto.' He specifically mentioned the upkeep of an Order Service that he had been instructed to establish to police the ghetto's inhabitants and also funds to 'keep the poor and needy viable'. For the moment, though, the Germans scoffed at the thought of extending finance to Jews, in a ghetto, but they saw the point of putting Jews to work if it meant that the ghetto would pay for itself. In May, the first sewing workshop started to operate. Within four months the number of clothing workshops rose to seventeen. Around 40,000 Jews, out of 146,000, found work. Unfortunately, because the Germans refused to supply machinery to the ghetto, production was almost entirely manual, unskilled, and dogged by low productivity. This state of affairs was somewhat improved by the arrival of Hans Biebow, a businessman from Bremen, to run the Food and Economy Office of the German ghetto administration. Biebow was technically an employee of the municipality which, up to that time, had been responsible for supplying the ghetto with food in exchange for products and labour. Under him the office solicited orders for enterprises located inside the ghetto and exercised close supervision over all aspects of production and labour. As the ghetto became an accepted fact, his bureau evolved into a full-scale ghetto administration employing 400 staff. Biebow was not averse to profiting personally from contracts and soon identified his own interests with the fate of the ghetto.[81]

Although the Lodz ghetto became a model that other German officials in Poland would seek to emulate, it was never the fulfilment of a deliberate, long-term policy formulated by the Nazi leadership. Rather, it was a desperate expedient launched by local administrators in response to the failure of deportation plans and the impoverishment of the Jewish population which was, itself, the by-product of German measures. Stuck with a mass of unemployed, indigent, malnourished Jews the best solution that Greiser and Übelhör could come up with for the moment was pushing them behind a wall where they would be out of sight. It was a spectacular solution, yet it was not adopted throughout the Wartheland, anywhere in East Upper Silesia or as a rule in the General Government.[82]

In early April 1940, the thirteen-year-old David Rubinowitz travelled freely between the village of Krajno, where he lived with his family, and the city of Kielce, where his uncle had a house. David's father, an Orthodox Jew, owned a dairy and continued to run it almost untroubled by the new regime. Around the very time that the Kielce Jews were being bottled up in a ghetto, he wrote in his diary, 'I went into the woods with my brother to search for mushrooms.'[83]

Gerda Weissmann was fifteen when the Germans occupied Bielitz in East Upper Silesia. Her father had a stake in a factory producing furs and though he lost the business, his family managed to retain their large house on the edge of town. When Gerda's brother, aged nineteen years, was obliged to register for forced labour he made his way to the Russian zone, but the rest of the family stayed put. Like the other 90,000–100,000 Jews in the region, mainly concentrated in Katowice, Bedzin and Sosnowiec, they were not confined. Fritz Bracht, the Gauleiter of the newly created Gau of East Upper Silesia, preferred to exploit his Jews as a valuable labour resource. Instead of being uselessly penned up they were organized into labour units by Albrecht Schmelt and assigned to armaments plants, engineering works and textile factories.[84]

As the unusually harsh winter turned to spring, Jewish life in Warsaw assumed a new normality. The Judenrat became more elaborate, with over twenty departments assuming functions previously carried out by the municipality. A census conducted in February at the behest of the Germans revealed that it was now responsible for the fate of 395,000 Jews. Amongst its most pressing concerns was finding accommodation and food for the 40,000–50,000 Jews displaced into the ghetto from the western parts of the region or expelled from the annexed territories. On arrival they were given baths, quarantined and then quartered in hostels. Since the council could only manage to house a maximum of 17,000, soon they were forced to find places themselves or live on the streets. In order to earn something, even if only a pittance, hundreds volunteered for work in the labour battalions run by the Jewish council's labour office (and escorted by its own unarmed guards, the Order Service). Czerniaków had only limited access to funds and had to rely on endless improvisations to cover this burgeoning cost.[85]

The Judenrat instituted and managed an elaborate rationing system. The entire Jewish population was registered for ration cards, although only the poorest got them for free: others had to pay a tax. The card entitled the holder to purchase flour, bread, sugar (or a substitute), kasha (buckwheat porridge), jam, soap and matches. The official ration amounted to an average of 503 calories per day, falling to below 450 in April–June 1940. However, Jewish council officials and workers were awarded far more, respectively 1,665 and 1,229 calories per day.

Refugees got just 807 and those without work or means received even less. Consequently, Jews had to supplement the official ration with food obtained on the black market. This was plentiful, but expensive.[86]

Thousands of the unemployed jostled for work in strange, new occupations, such as the manufacture and distribution of armbands, translating German documents, queuing for ration cards or food parcels on behalf of someone else. They joined the already overcrowded trades in which Jews were permitted to serve other Jews, notably tailoring, shoemaking, hairdressing and photography. The majority became hawkers on the street.[87]

Relief organizations began to get a grip on the effects of unemployment and the influx of refugees. But welfare work exposed as much as it alleviated social divisions. Bodies funded by the AJJDC enjoyed a measure of autonomy and competed with each other for influence as well as posing as rivals to the Jewish council. Leadership positions were often taken by members of the pre-war intelligentsia, such as teachers, writers and actors, or left-wing activists. The Bund, guided by men like the veteran activist Bernard Goldstein, mounted its own relief effort and marshalled the employees in workshops and factories. Observing the proliferation of bodies, each with its own constituency, and the character of the men who managed them, Chaim Kaplan lamented, 'The Jew lacks community feeling and a sense of collective responsibility.' Rather than help the neediest first, they aided members of their own parties, unions, cultural circles, or families. Corruption was widespread. Refugees who arrived from the Wartheland with no means or connections were quite literally lost; unless they were fortunate enough to be housed and fed in a hostel they ended up on the streets, obtaining money for food by selling their possessions and, once these were gone, by begging.[88]

Few were as lucky as Mary Berg, who arrived in Warsaw at the end of 1939 with her family, money, and her mother's US passport. They were able to move into a two-room apartment and did not have to wear the Jewish armband. Mary's mother stuck one of her visiting cards on the door of their apartment to indicate that they were also immune to calls for forced labour. For the moment, they pinned their hopes on being able to emigrate.[89]

Cultural life sprang back into existence and schooling resumed, albeit covertly. There were approximately 48,000 children of school age in the Jewish population. Teachers from every one of the pre-war educational streams stealthily established gymnasia or religious schools. The kitchens set up to feed orphans and children of the poor also ran classes. Eventually, about 20 per cent of children received schooling. This resurgence was testimony to the resilience and optimism of the population. Yitzhak Zuckerman returned to Warsaw from the Russian sector in April 1940 to begin reorganizing Zionist youth. He turned an apartment into a social and educational centre that simultaneously dispensed free meals to young comrades displaced from other towns. Years later he explained that 'The idea was "iberlebn" [Yiddish: survival] – we'll get through this. We tried to solve the problems of reinforcing the spirit and education of the young, and so we cared about schools.' Shimon Huberband, now in Warsaw, observed the defiant attitude of religious Jews. Although the festival of Purim fell in the midst of Polish incursions into the Jewish neighbourhoods, Jews were not deterred from raucous celebrations. Every courtyard rang with recitations from the Book of Esther, during which Jews relished the downfall of their tormentors in a previous age. The following month Huberband noted that Passover was celebrated almost universally. Czerniaków was able to win permission for the manufacture of matzoh, unleavened bread, and there was no shortage of this or other foods. Kaplan recorded defiantly that 'The synagogues are closed but in every courtyard there is a holiday service, and cantors sing the prayers and hymns in their sweet voices. As to holiday provisions, without question even the poorest Jew does not lack for matzoh.'[90]

At the start of 1940, realizing that the Jews were not going anywhere for the time being, the Sipo-SD began to exploit their economic potential as a source of labour. The security police set up a string of camps at sites were workers were needed and started filling them with able-bodied Jewish men from the towns and cities. To Kaplan the system of forced labour was received as a 'catastrophe'. It spelled nothing less than 'complete annihilation.'[91]

Women continued to be the most vulnerable to abuse through forced labour. Class-, race- and gender-hatred merged in these acts. Ringelblum recorded that the Germans targeted 'women in fur coats. They're ordered to wash the pavements with their panties, then put them on again, wet.' Mary Berg remarked that women dared not go onto the streets for fear of being seized. 'Better-dressed Jewish women have been forced to scrub the Nazis' headquarters. They are ordered to remove their underclothes and use them as rags for the floors and windows. It goes without saying that often the tormentors use these occasions to have some fun of their own.' Doctrines of racial purity actually served to mask the frequent occurrence of rape. According to Ringelblum, women were abducted from cafes 'no one knows where to; it is said that about one hundred came back a few days later, some of them infected'. A month later he wrote that 'At Tlomacki Place three lords and masters ravished some women; screams resounded through the house. The Gestapo are concerned over the racial degradation ... but are afraid to report it.' Even if German men did not assault Jewish women directly they had other ways to abuse them. Berg recalled that German police entered a building to conduct a search for valuables and forced men and women to strip 'hoping to find concealed diamonds'. 'The women were kept naked for more than two hours while the Nazis put their revolvers to their breasts and private parts and threatened to shoot them all if they did not disgorge dollars or diamonds.' Ringelblum heard of a German soldier who went from house to house 'forcing men to have sexual relations with women in his presence'. Eventually he was arrested.[92]

The permissive atmosphere induced unscrupulous and criminal elements in the Polish population to grab what they could. Berg recorded that 'Polish hooligans' led Germans to the homes of well-off Jews and joined in the 'looting in broad daylight'. Appeals by Jews in the name of patriotism were useless. German propaganda drove the communities further apart and Jews were increasingly perceived as outside the Polish nation. For several days in late March 1940, gangs of Polish ruffians pillaged Jewish shops and assaulted Jews on the streets. Kaplan saw German influence behind the outbreak: 'The Jewish quarter has been abandoned to toughs and killers who were organised for this purpose by some invisible hand.' Military patrols stood idle while German army newsreel-teams filmed the riots. In several quarters the Bund mobilized 'slaughterhouse workers, transport workers, party members' in self-defence. Bernard Goldstein crowed that 'When pogromists appeared in these sections the following morning, they were surprised to find our comrades waiting for them. A bloody battle broke out immediately.' Poles clashed with Jews bearing iron pipes and brass knuckles, leading to casualties on both sides. Emanuel Ringelblum condemned the Polish intelligentsia, the Church and the underground for failing to dissociate themselves from such behaviour, even when it was clearly engineered by the occupier. Such incidents scared Jews into believing that maybe a ghetto would be safer.[93]

The Germans had not given up the idea of ghettoization. In January 1940 Ludwig Fischer, the Warsaw district governor, established a Resettlement Office and brought in experts to plan the removal of Jews from the city. They encountered endless difficulties. By now Jewish workers were performing valuable services for the occupiers. Relocating nearly 400,000 Jews to the outskirts would be hugely disruptive, while closing off inner-city areas would interrupt traffic and trade. Nevertheless, the fear of a typhus epidemic stemming from the Jewish inhabitants spurred them on. Cases began to multiply at the start of the year. As waves of undernourished refugees were jammed into poor housing with inadequate sanitation, the disease spread. On 27 March, when the epidemic reached its climax, Czerniaków was instructed to cordon off a large area encompassing the most densely populated Jewish wards. It was designated a 'Seuchensperrgebiet', a 'plague-quarantine area'. Czerniaków's arguments disputing the necessity for such a measure and the extent of the boundary were unavailing. Nor was he able to deflect the requirement that the Jewish council pay for the materials and labour that would be needed. Construction began at the start of April and went on fitfully for weeks while Czerniaków contested the demarcation of every street and house. On 10 May he wrote despondently in his journal, 'A ghetto in spite of everything'. Suddenly, however, the war took a dramatic turn. It seemed as though there were new prospects for removing Polish Jews, German Jews and potentially all the Jews in the German sphere of influence.[94]

War and persecution in the Reich

While war overturned the lives of Jews in Poland, for the Jews in Germany initially little changed. There were still around 240,000 Jewish inhabitants of the Greater Reich, with roughly 185,000 in Germany, of whom 30,000 were in Berlin. A third of them were aged over sixty, three-quarters had no jobs, and a quarter depended on welfare from the Jewish aid agencies. Nearly 11,000 Jewish children remained in the Reich. Those of school age were crammed into a small number of educational institutions. There were just two Jewish schools in Berlin for 3,000 pupils; Cologne, Frankfurt and Hamburg each had one school.

Few students stayed beyond their sixteenth birthday. Under wartime conditions the policy towards converts and non-Jews in mixed marriages created endless anomalies. According to the tenth supplement to the Reich Citizenship Law, establishing the Reichsvereinigung, even converts like Freddy Solmitz and their spouses now had to belong to the Jewish community. There were thousands of Jewish women who had husbands or sons in the German army. Conversely, there were soldiers fighting for the Reich who had a Jewish father labouring under discriminatory legislation. Yet, at the same time that Jews were being murdered in Poland by the Einsatzgruppen and army units, German Jews suffered nothing worse than a severe curfew. Ex-civil servants still got their pensions. Most Jews still lived in their own homes. Those who wanted to leave and who were fortunate enough to have somewhere to go were able to emigrate. Only Polish Jews in the Reich were subjected to arrest and imprisonment according to a decree by the chief of the Sipo-SD issued a week after the outbreak of war.[95]

However, this lull did not last long. The population greeted news of the war coolly and were soon obliged to cope with rationing, price inflation and higher taxes. In addition to the inconvenience of travelling during the blackout, ordinary Germans began to notice the shortage and declining quality of public transport. There was almost no petrol for private cars, and taxis began to disappear from city streets. Everyone dreaded bombing and with Britain and France in the war there was no confidence that the conflict would be either swift or successful. In this turbid atmosphere the Jews were the object of fears and fantasies amongst the population at large. The SD office in Worms reported that 'the population find it exceedingly unpleasant to observe that the Jews are shopping once more in all stores with their food ration cards; their comportment is marked by a striking air of security and confidence'. It did not matter that German Jews like Victor Klemperer were petrified by the thought of what lay in store for them whether Germany won or lost. While events hung in the balance Jews acted as a lightning conductor for popular emotions. Hence their fate depended not only on Nazi beliefs about the culpability of the world Jewish conspiracy against the Reich; as ordinary Germans experienced the vicissitudes of war, they projected their aspirations and anxieties onto the Jews.[96]

The authorities now began to subject Jews to a succession of restrictions. They were subjected to a curfew from 8 p.m. to 6 a.m. and only allowed to shop at certain times at specific retail outlets. They were ordered to hand over their radios; the delivery day was fixed for the Jewish Day of Atonement. Elderly and infirm Jews were evicted from care homes, such as the Jewish old-age home in Breslau, that the authorities coveted for other purposes. In order to free up individual apartments and houses, local authorities pressured Jews to move into Jew-houses. By the start of December, Victor Klemperer found himself limited to buying groceries in one shop and struggling to keep his home. 'The sadistic machine simply rolls over us,' he wrote in his diary.[97]

Although an unsuccessful assassination attempt on Hitler on 8 November 1939 led to a spasm of attacks on Jewish communities in Bavaria, paradoxically there were few outbreaks of violence connected with the war itself. Expulsion, assault and murder began at the Reich's eastern borders. Word of these actions soon filtered back into German society, though. The SD in Bad Kissingen reported 'animated discussion' about news that 'Jews, the whole lot of them, are being resettled in the territory between the San and Bug rivers around Lublin . . . These measures have been welcomed by members of the party and a large proportion of the Volksgenossen.' Klemperer did not remark on the deportation of Jews from Vienna to Nisko, but the eviction of the Stettin Jews to Lublin in March 1940 shook him. It triggered another, desperate attempt to secure emigration to the United States. The SD reported that terrified Jews in the eastern parts of the Reich were moving to Berlin, Breslau and Leipzig in response to the news.[98]

In April 1940, Klemperer finally lost his house. He and his wife had to move into a villa occupied by several Jewish families. Even though he was relieved to discover that it was a handsome, well-appointed building it still felt like a 'superior concentration camp'. He was oppressed by the 'lack of space, promiscuity, chaos' and 'never-ending washing-up'. Several of the residents treated him with undisguised contempt because he was a convert. Like other converts and Mischlinge, he felt caught between two worlds, neither of which wanted him. 'No one will help us. To the Jews I am an apostate . . .'[99]

All over Germany, Jews were disappearing. The mayor of Bad Nauheim boasted, 'A majority of Jews have sold their property . . . at the insistence of the Gestapo. Some have since left or found shelter in the Jewish Home for Men and Women. Recently, the number of Jews present in the town has declined substantially as Jews have moved away. Provision of food for the Jews is likewise handled by the Gestapo so that the Jewish element is no longer a notable presence in public transport

1. Hitler and Hindenburg shake hands at 'The Day of Potsdam' on 21 March 1933.

2. A stormtrooper enforces the boycott of Jewish shops, 1 April 1933.

3. 'Hyenas are never decent,
therefore neither are
the Jews. Jews, get out!'
An anti-Semitic poster in
a Berlin street, 1930s.

4. A sign on the outskirts of a
German village declaring that
'Jews are our misfortune.'

5. Jews made to clean pavements in Vienna on 13 March 1938.

6. The mass arrest of Jewish men in Oldenburg, 9 November 1938.

7. The Horovitz Synagogue on Frankfurt's Bornestrasse in flames during the pogrom of 9–10 November 1938, later known as 'Kristallnacht'.

8. The aftermath of 'Kristallnacht' in Magdeburg.

Photo courtesy of the Wiener Library, London

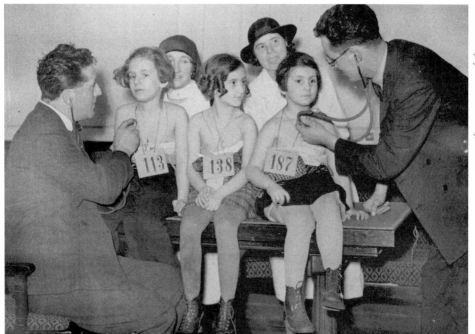

9. Medical examination of
Jewish refugee children in the
Netherlands, autumn 1938.

10. Jewish refugee girls from
Germany being inspected
by a British policeman,
autumn 1938.

Photo courtesy of the Wiener Library, London

11. *Above, left.* Raymond-Raoul Lambert: a French war veteran and leader of the Union générale des israélites de France (UGIF); he was arrested in Drancy and murdered in Auschwitz.

12. *Above, right.* Norbert Troller: a Czech war veteran and architect whose visual record of Theresienstadt was smuggled to the West; he survived Auschwitz and emigrated to the US.

13. *Below, left.* Philip Mechanicus: a Dutch journalist who recorded life in Westerbork, characterizing himself as 'an official reporter giving an account of a shipwreck'; he was murdered in Birkenau.

14. *Below, right.* Ruth Maier (right, with Gunvor Hofmo): a Viennese schoolgirl: she escaped to Norway but was deported to Auschwitz and murdered on arrival.

15. *Above, left.* (From left to right) Abraham Krouwer, Abraham Asscher and David Cohen: Asscher was a Dutch professor and Cohen the president of the Great Synagogue, who formed the Jewish Council of the Netherlands, the Joodse Raad; Cohen was sent to Westerbork and Theresienstadt and Asscher was sent to Westerbork and Bergen-Belsen; both survived the war but were accused of collaboration.

16. *Above, right.* Victor Klemperer: a Protestant Jew in Dresden who recorded daily life under the Nazis; he survived without imprisonment and escaped to the American zone in February 1945. Klemperer is seen here with his non-Jewish wife Eva in 1948.

17. *Below, left.* Philipp Manes: a German war veteran; he was deported to the Theresienstadt ghetto, and murdered with his wife in Birkenau.

18. *Below, right.* Hélène Berr: a student at the Sorbonne who refused to flee Paris; she was sent to Auschwitz-Birkenau on her twenty-third birthday and was murdered in Belsen on 14 April 1945, the day before it was liberated.

19. Mary Berg (on the left) with her friend Mickie Rubin: a schoolgirl from Lodz; she lived in the Warsaw Ghetto and in the Pawiak prison but was allowed to emigrate to the US in 1944, where she published her diary.

20. Adam Czerniaków: a Polish engineer; he was the head of the Jewish community in the Warsaw Ghetto, and committed suicide when the Germans ordered mass deportation to the east in 1943.

and in economic life. As a result of the new curfew laws, they are forced to remain more or less out of sight in the city.' The mayor of Schwandorf in eastern Bavaria reported that 'there are only three Jewish hags left here. They too will soon disappear.' The erasure of full Jews exposed Mischlinge to greater scrutiny. A showdown on this policy was looming in any case, partly because men who had fought in the army demanded the right to be able to marry whomsoever they chose. Consequently, in April 1940 the Nazi Party began to clamour for tighter controls on mixed-race Jews of the first degree. By the end of the year, most service men with a Jewish parent had been dismissed, notwithstanding their war record.[100]

Yet Jewish emigration continued. That this should be so was not self-evident to some in the SD and Gestapo. The SD office in Leipzig checked with headquarters whether the legal, orderly departure of Jews should still be promoted. Indeed, it remained official policy and the Emigration Consulting Office in Cologne reported brisk business as long as it was possible for Reich Jews to leave via Italy or Holland. The problem was not getting out, it was finding somewhere to go to. William Shirer heard that 248,000 Jews were on the waiting lists to enter the United States. Instead, Jews aimed for Shanghai or used the corrupt services of diplomats representing Honduras and Haiti. In Hamburg, Max Plaut, head of the local branch of the Reichsvereinigung, worked with the Gestapo officer responsible for Jewish affairs in the city to secure the legal and illegal departure of hundreds of Jews. Adolf Eichmann formed a working relationship with Berthold Storfer, who had put his business acumen at the disposal of the Viennese Jewish community after March 1938 and worked on numerous emigration projects. Two years later, Eichmann placed him in charge of organizing and financing illegal transports of Jews to Palestine. While the mainstream Zionist organizations operating clandestine emigration routes from neutral countries (notably Romania) still preferred to take only trained and ideologically motivated young pioneers, Storfer sent anyone who could pay. There was no love lost between them. Despite this discord and the British blockade, around 10,000 Jews reached Palestine between 1939 and 1940 in a variety of dubious craft. About 37,000 Jews reached the USA legally and 10,000 found refuge in other countries. Some 20,000, though, made it no further than Portugal or French North Africa where they were stuck awaiting the correct papers or funds to move on.[101]

Compulsory euthanasia

German Jews who were trapped in the Reich may have lived in miserable conditions, but apart from the relatively small numbers in the
concentration camps they were not in immediate danger of death. By
contrast, the sense of urgency and ruthlessness engendered by the war
had lethal consequences for certain members of the German racial
community. For several years the regime had been considering the
introduction of compulsory euthanasia; Hitler had discussed the matter
several times with medical advisers. Eliminating those with severe
physical and mental disabilities was a potential cost-saving measure,
would free up space that could be converted to the care of wounded soldiers, and in the long term could contribute to the creation of a
biologically pure, healthy Volk. Regardless of any alleged material benefits that might accrue from getting rid of those considered a 'burden' on
the state, war created the circumstances for implementing an ideologically driven policy that was close to the core of Nazi beliefs.[102]

In early 1939, Hitler's private office, the Führer Chancellery, received
a petition from a family begging for permission to terminate the life of a
cruelly deformed child. The plea prompted the reactivation of a secret
committee founded late in 1936 or early in 1937 to investigate the viability of euthanasia as a whole. As usual in the Third Reich there was an
extended period of planning, during which rival factions jockeyed for
control of a programme that personally interested the Führer. Initially,
the project operated out of Hitler's Chancellery. It had no legal basis and
was run covertly under the auspices of Philipp Bouhler, head of Hitler's
office. Viktor Brack, who was the liaison between the Führer Chancellery and the Health Ministry, developed the organization and recruited
the necessary personnel. Karl Brandt, Hitler's personal physician, mus-
cled his way into the business and effectively displaced Leonardo Conti,
who was head of the Nazi medical association and, more pertinently,
the Reich Health Ministry. The team then drew on the expertise of the
committee responsible for overseeing the compulsory sterilization of
those deemed to have severe hereditary mental or physical illnesses. On
18 August 1939, the committee required the compulsory registration of
severely malformed infants, but the scheme quickly evolved beyond the
'mercy killing' of children. Within a few weeks of the invasion of

Poland, special task forces, led by SS officers Herbert Lange and Kurt Eimann, massacred nearly 13,000 inmates of clinics and asylums in the areas annexed to East Prussia. In addition to mass murder by shooting, Lange used mobile gas chambers. These were removal vans converted so that bottled carbon monoxide could be piped into the cargo compartment inside which forty to fifty souls had been packed. The murders in Poland had a blowback effect in the Reich; by October, the compulsory euthanasia programme had been extended to adults and was too large to run from the Chancellery. It obtained premises in a villa that had been expropriated from its Jewish owner, overlooking the leafy Tiergarten. The address provided the code name for the now much-expanded operation: T-4. At around this time, Bouhler obtained from Hitler a signed authorization to give some legal cover to the operatives. It was a rare example of Hitler recording his explicit sanction for an otherwise illegal measure and gives a key insight into how his personal system of government worked, as well as how delegated authority enabled subordinates to establish elaborate undertakings without referring back to the Führer or involving him at any level of detail. No less important, the authorization was backdated to 1 September 1939, tying the murderous operation to the outbreak of war and thereby exemplifying the symbiosis between war and ruthless domestic policies that prevailed in Nazi minds.[103]

Using the pretext of economic necessity in time of war and operating under the cloak of a charitable foundation, the central office at Tiergarten 4 required asylums and sanatoria to register all adults incapable of work and report on their condition. Doctors chosen for their political reliability then processed the forms en masse, denoting those 'unworthy of life'. Meanwhile, Bouhler's men identified several clinics that could be adapted as killing centres and set up a transport company to ship the selected inmates to these locations for what was dubbed 'special treatment'. In addition to the specially recruited doctors and nurses, plus the stokers who manned the crematoria, the SD provided staff to deal with security matters. Initially, the disabled were murdered using injections of poison; in early 1940 the clinics were equipped with gas chambers. Between October 1939 and August 1941, over 70,000 men, women and children deemed 'unworthy of life' by the physicians and psychiatrists who were supposed to be caring for them were driven in grey buses (with blacked-out windows) to the clinics. On arrival they were undressed and led into airtight gas chambers that appeared to be innocuous shower rooms; bottled carbon monoxide was piped through false shower-heads until they were asphyxiated. The corpses were incinerated in crematoria on site, but not before gold teeth had been removed. This dental gold provided a handy bonus to the staff who were, in any case, paid above average wages for their secret work.[104]

The clandestine nature of the operation was impossible to sustain. People living in the vicinity of the clinics could not fail to notice the volume of inbound traffic, as compared with the absence of departures. Some noted a correlation between the arrival of the grey buses and the appearance not long afterwards of smoke from the clinic chimneys. The odour of burning flesh was itself a giveaway. Relatives and legal guardians began to receive death certificates giving unlikely reasons for the demise of loved ones or persons under their protection. The sheer number of these deaths was a cause for concern. Since many asylums from which inmates were taken were run by religious foundations, church leaders were drawn into the circle of concern. Yet, even after it was clear that the disabled were being killed, there were few public protests. In August 1940, the Protestant Bishop Theophile Wurm of Württemburg addressed a letter to Wilhelm Frick, minister of the interior, expressing his reservations about what was happening. His anxiety was echoed by Cardinal Adolf Bertram, leader of the Fulda conference of bishops, who contacted Hans Lammers, head of the Reich Chancellery. A few weeks later Cardinal Faulhaber of Munich expressed his objections to Franz Gürtner, the minister of justice. These private communications triggered apprehension within the regime, but nothing more. Officials examined the possibility of legislation to validate the programme, although no steps were actually taken and the killing went on for another year regardless of the flimsy legal basis on which it rested. It was finally stopped on Hitler's orders after Clemens August Graf von Galen, the Bishop of Münster, delivered a well-trailed sermon on 3 August 1941, roundly condemning the taking of life on such grounds. However, the T-4 action was not suspended primarily because of church protests. The invasion of Russia had temporarily stalled, casualties were high and morale on the home front was dented by shortages as well as increased bombing by the Royal Air Force. These considerations, rather than the moral indignation of church leaders, induced Hitler to call off the murder of the severely disabled.[105]

By this stage, compulsory euthanasia was an open secret in Germany and news of it had reached the outside world. On 21 September

1940, William Shirer recorded that an informant, designated as 'X' had 'told me a weird story. He says the Gestapo is now systematically bumping off the mentally deficient people of the Reich. The Nazis call them "mercy deaths". The following month, Paul Dutko, the United States vice-consul in Leipzig, sent the State Department a long dispatch headed 'Mysterious Deaths of Mental Patients from Leipzig Consular District and the Connections with the SS'. According to Dutko, people in the city were 'shocked beyond description' by rumours that people were taken to a clinic at Grafeneck that was run by the SS and done to death. Opinion held that the SS was out of control. By November 1940, Shirer had uncovered more or less the whole sordid episode and was also able to report pressure on the regime to curtail the killings.[106]

Although the so-called 'euthanasia campaign' did not centre on Jews, they were affected by it. Hundreds of Jewish inmates were taken from care homes to be killed. Even if they could show some capacity for work or economic value, for them there was no reprieve. Being Jewish was a more certain death sentence than being disabled. Max Plaut, in Hamburg, figured out what was going on because he was the guardian of someone slated for removal from an asylum, and the Reichsverein-igung did its utmost to get vulnerable Jews out of the targeted institu-tions. Even Victor Klemperer, stuck in a Judenhaus, got wind of T-4. On 2 November 1941 he noted in his diary how a visitor told him that Galen had 'preached publicly against the Gestapo and the killing of the mentally infirm'.[107]

In time, the techniques used to kill biological outcasts in the Reich would be applied to the racial enemy, the Jews. But there was no inher-ent or logical connection between T-4 and what came later. T-4 certainly honed techniques of mass murder and created a corps of experienced killers. Although the programme was suspended in August 1941, the use of gas vans and lethal gas chambers did not stop. Rather, the killing was transferred to the concentration camps under the designation 14f13. Just as inmates of sanatoria and asylums who were deemed unfit for work and hence 'unworthy of life' had been separated out and con-signed to the murderers, the prisoner population was culled to remove those estimated by SS medical staff to be useless for hard labour. Nor did Brandt desist from his homicidal activities. Instead, he launched an 'action' to clear space in asylums that could be used to replace hospitals damaged by bombing and accommodate the increasing number of civilians injured in air raids. It is thought that around 35,000 people were murdered under this 'wild euthanasia' programme. Brack, too, continued in his murderous ways: he would provide personnel who had served in T-4 and equipment to kill Jews. However, the continuity of personnel and methodology is not the same as cause and effect.[108]

Some historians, notably Robert Jay Lifton and Henry Friedlander, have seen the forced euthanasia programme as a crucial step towards the mass murder of Europe's Jews. Lifton described it as a 'medical bridge to genocide', while for Friedlander T-4 was 'Nazi Germany's first organised mass murder' and the 'opening act of Nazi genocide'. But the Germans crossed that line when they crossed the border into Poland on 1 September 1939, taking with them plans to target sections of the Polish population for mass execution. By the end of 1939, more Poles, including Polish Jews, had been shot to death in Poland than would die in the T-4 gas chambers over a comparable period. The Einsatzgruppen operations in Poland created the model for mass murder, not T-4. Operation Tannenberg, not compulsory euthanasia, was the bridge to genocide.[109]

Reactions to the persecution of Polish Jews

The unease that spread through the German population when confronted by evidence of mass killing within the Reich stands in contrast to the insouciance with which most Germans greeted information about the treatment of Poles and Jews in the occupied territories. Few German servicemen in Poland exhibited qualms about the humiliation, torture and murder of Jews. Despite being deeply religious, Konrad Jarausch expressed little indignation about the torching of a synagogue in Zgierz where he was based with his battalion. 'Last night here', he remarked matter-of-factly in a letter to a colleague in Germany, 'the Jewish synagogue was set on fire. Today the Jewish meeting house is in flames. In Lodz Jews and Poles have been strung up in the market places because they were putting up anti-German posters.' He was similarly neutral about the exploitation of Jewish forced labour and the menace of sexual abuse. A few days later he wrote home, 'It's amazingly clean in our quarters. Jewish girls and women have to scrub the barracks and clean the windows. Many come from good families. The comrades behaved themselves. The Nuremberg race laws can perhaps serve to protect Jewish women . . .' His bland commentary extended to the displacement of Jews from their homes. 'Since the Wolhynian Germans are to arrive over winter, the Jews are being driven out in large numbers. There's a concentration camp on the road between Lodz and Zgierz that holds almost 5,000 Jews of all ages. On the roads you can see trucks heading off. Of course all this doesn't occur without victims.'[110]

Jarausch accepted the results of brutal political decisions almost as if they were acts of nature. However, by comparison with other officers, he was a compassionate observer. He was moved by the sight of a dese-crated Jewish cemetery and commented on the clash between the SS spirit and the traditional Prussian, Christian values that he espoused. He also noted generational differences, as evidenced by attitudes towards a field service. 'The older comrades are generally tolerant . . . the younger ones felt entirely different about it – they expressed intoler-ance toward everything – the church, the Jews.'[111]

Melita Maschmann exemplified those 'younger ones'. In late 1939 she was assigned to the Warthegau, where she worked with ethnic German farmers collecting the harvest before taking up a post as head of the Hitler Youth press office in Posen. She interpreted everything in Poland according to National Socialist ideology, so what she saw con-firmed what she had been taught. When she observed Jews in the Kutno ghetto she 'fiercely suppressed any kind of metaphysical consideration'. A group of Jewish men reminded her of 'a flock of crows'. The fact that Jews were deprived of their livelihoods and stood around with nothing to do was translated into proof of the Jewish reluctance to engage in useful work. When she indulged the fashion for ghetto tourism and visited Lodz, she saw 'well-dressed women' in fur coats. Conversely, she felt a sense of connectedness with Volksdeutsche and relished her part in the mission to Germanize the east. It gave her a warm sense of belonging because 'release from the ego and simultaneous identity of myself with something greater than myself, the nation or the national community, created an inner attachment'. Her hatred of Jews was the obverse of her love for Germans.[112]

Ulrich von Hassell, the retired diplomat, stood at the opposite end of the generational spectrum. To him the invasion and occupation of Poland spelled disaster. He doubted whether Germany could win the war and was perturbed by reports reaching him about the behaviour of German soldiers. In his diary he confessed to 'the disgrace that has sul-lied the German name through the conduct of the war in Poland; namely, the brutal use of air power and the shocking bestialities of the SS, especially towards the Jews'. Admittedly Hassell was well connected, but his case demonstrates that if they wanted to, Germans could learn a great deal about the atrocities in Poland. 'When people use their revolvers to shoot down a group of Jews herded into a synagogue,' he added, 'one is filled with shame.' At the end of 1939, he commented grimly on the 'shameless actions in Poland, particularly by the SS' as well as the appalling conditions in 'the Jewish district'. Hassell knew about the eviction of Jews from Stettin to the 'Jewish reservation in Poland' almost as soon as it had taken place.[113]

The presence in Berlin of journalists from the USA and other neutral countries ensured that information about the goings on in Poland was transmitted to western Europe and across the Atlantic. Shirer's journal illustrates just how much was available to the curious. In mid-November 1939 he recorded that 'Frank, the Governor-General of occupied Poland today decreed that the Jewish ghetto in Warsaw henceforth must be shut off from the rest of the capital by barricades and placed under sharp police control. He says the Jews are "carriers of disease and germs".' An American who returned from Warsaw told him the German policy was 'simply to exterminate Polish Jews. They are being herded into eastern Poland and forced to live in unheated shacks and robbed of any opportunity of earning bread and butter. Several thousand Jews from the Reich have also been sent to eastern Poland to die.' This was an exaggeration, but the general trend was accurate. If anything, the outrage at early German measures blunted sensitivity to what came later; just as in 1933 the volume of news and the horror it aroused provoked a response that could not be sustained – even when things worsened. And they soon did. In the new year, Shirer noted 'The greatest organised mass migration since the exchange of populations between Greece and Turkey after the last war is now coming to an end in Poland.'[114]

The Times and the London Jewish Chronicle carried extensive coverage of anti-Jewish measures in German-occupied Poland. On 24 October 1939, The Times reported that three million Jews were destined for Lublin, a fate that 'would doom them to famine'. Readers learned within days about the deportations to Nisko. At the end of the year, The Times concluded that the reservation scheme 'envisages a place for gradual extermination'. News about the establishment of ghettos and the conditions in Warsaw and Lodz was accurately transmitted to the breakfast tables of newspaper readers in the UK. In March 1941, the Jewish Chronicle carried photographs of the Warsaw ghetto.[115]

But the main channel of information to western governments was the Polish government-in-exile, which had set up shop in France. The official exile leadership was routinely fed intelligence from across the country by its underground representatives, the Delegatura. All parties and factions were represented on the exile Polish National Council, including Polish Jews. Nevertheless, the two Jewish delegates, Henryk Rosmarin and Ignacy Schwarzbart, sometimes felt that they were there just to give the British and French the impression that the Poles were inclusive. In fact, many members of the Polish exile leadership – and not just adherents of the ethno-nationalist Endek party – were anti-Jewish. Their attitude was hardened by allegations that Jews had welcomed the Soviet invasion and were collaborating with the Red regime. A key report on conditions in Poland, carried to the west by the courier Jan Karski in February 1940, fortified this impression. After a gruelling journey Karski reached Angers in France, where he told Stanislaw Kot, the interior minister in the exile government, that most Poles believed the Jews had welcomed the Soviet occupier and were now colluding in the oppression of Polish patriots. Whatever the truth was or whatever the explanation for Jewish responses, so many Poles believed the Jews had behaved treacherously that the leadership in exile considered it would be unwise to make pro-Jewish gestures. Official publications aimed at western audiences or Allied governments stressed the appalling treatment of Poles and ignored what was happening to Jews. It was not until the government-in-exile relocated to London after the fall of France that it began to issue statements specifically addressing the Jewish plight.[116]

The Poles, though, were not the only government keen to play down the extent of Jewish suffering. For reasons connected with its Middle East policy the British government, too, was reluctant to highlight the fate of Jews in eastern Europe. In May 1939 the government issued a White Paper maintaining that it had fulfilled its obligations to establish a Jewish national home in Palestine. The entire population of the territory – 450,000 Jews and 1 million Arabs – would be given self-government in ten years' time. Jewish immigration would be limited to 75,000 for the first half of that period and there were stringent limitations on the amount of land that could be purchased for future Jewish settlement. These stipulations virtually guaranteed the emergence of an Arab state with a Jewish minority. The White Paper, approved by the House of Commons on 22 May 1939, was intended to appease Arab feeling in Palestine and the independent Arab governments across the region so as to minimize the need to commit British troops for peace-keeping purposes and prevent any threat to oil supplies. However, it alienated Jewish opinion in Palestine and outraged Zionist supporters across the world. They naturally summoned the spectre of Jewish refugees in Europe as a potent argument for increased immigration.[117]

The British government was not merely fighting a propaganda war: it used diplomatic tools and military assets to block the flow of Jews to the putative national home. The Foreign Office tracked the progress of refugees who were able to leave the Reich as they passed through Yugoslavia, Bulgaria and Romania to ports where Zionist organizations had secured boats to transport them onward to Palestine, and leaned heavily on national governments to obstruct their passage. Between October 1939 and March 1940 Jewish immigration to Palestine was suspended entirely on the grounds that illegal entrants had effectively filled the quota. From April to September 1940, the Palestine administration distributed 9,060 immigration certificates, of which only half were actually used since it was almost impossible to get them to those in greatest need. Thanks to British rather than Nazi policy, legal emigration to Palestine offered an infinitesimally small segment of the Jewish population subjected to German persecution a chance of escape.[118]

Whitehall was also apprehensive about pressure to allow Jewish refugees to enter the United Kingdom. On 25 September 1939, the Cabinet Committee on Refugees resolved that the defeat of Germany took priority over succour for fugitives from Nazi mistreatment. Only special cases would be allowed into the country; the mass of Jews fleeing Nazi rule were excluded. To actually reduce the numbers that had piled up in the UK during the last months of peace the government decided to offer funds to refugees for the purposes of on-migration. It was a helpful, if not a hospitable, gesture. As a separate measure, tribunals assessed the cases of over 74,000 refugees and foreign nationals who were now 'enemy aliens' to determine whether they had to be interned as a threat to security in the event of a national emergency. Of these, 64,244 mainly German and Austrian Jews were exempted from any restrictions. Nevertheless, wartime stringency did not prevent refugee aid organizations pleading for government assistance and a relaxation on immigration controls.[119]

The British government was sensitive to any publicity or official statements likely to increase public sympathy for Jews. On the eve of the war the Ministry of Information advised the BBC that 'no special propaganda addressed to Jews is necessary outside Palestine'. For the purposes of reporting to UK audiences and European service listeners, Jews were to be treated as citizens of the countries in which they lived. As part of the propaganda war against the Third Reich, in October 1939 the government issued a White Paper on the concentration camps that touched briefly on the vicious treatment of Jewish inmates. This collation of reports by consular officials and released prisoners charted the brutality of the camps in the late 1930s, but skirted any discussion of the anti-Jewish legislation that led to Jews, specifically, ending up in them. The unwillingness to pay special attention to the widening persecution of Jewish populations was underpinned by a deep-seated scepticism in Whitehall about the nature and truth of such reports. Although the Foreign Office was well supplied with information, senior officials tended to discount much of what landed on their desks. In April 1940, one civil servant minuted 'Jewish sources are always doubtful'. Rex Leeper, head of the Political Intelligence Department (later the director of the Political Warfare Executive), commented a few months later that 'as a general rule Jews are inclined to magnify their persecutions'.[120]

Similar prejudices coloured the perception of officials in the US State Department. Until the outbreak of war they had been at loggerheads with the White House over its marginally more generous policy towards Jews seeking asylum in America. However, with the coming of hostilities Roosevelt and the State Department concurred that national security was now the paramount concern. The president ordered the FBI to enhance its monitoring of refugees and immigrants in order to guard against an influx of spies. In April 1940, Roosevelt approved the transfer of responsibility for immigration and naturalization to the Justice Department. Visa controls were tightened and consular officials were instructed to assess whether admission of an aspiring immigrant 'would or might be contrary to the public safety'. The risk of racial persecution was not in itself a sufficient reason to be granted entry to America. Predictably, the number of Jews granted permits and arriving in the United States fell precipitously. With a presidential election looming in November 1940, Roosevelt was even less inclined to challenge isolationists and advocates of immigration restriction.[121]

American Jews, like Jews in Britain, did not lack for information

about their immiserated co-religionists in Germany and Poland. However, the nature and treatment of the news shifted perceptibly. The *New
York Times* transferred its European bureau to London and withdrew
most of its correspondents from the war-torn continent. Instead, it
relied on the wire services, notably AP's man Louis Lochner and UP's
Frederich Oeschsner, who remained in Berlin. Stories from occupied
Poland about the Jews rarely, if ever, made the front page in 1939–40.
To papers whose editorial line and political attachments meant that
they favoured isolation, anything that smacked of warmongering was
frowned upon. Reports of Nazi atrocities were reminiscent of the
atrocity propaganda foisted on the US by the Allies during the First
World War, and easily dismissed as sabre-rattling. Since much of the
news now came from wire services and drew on unofficial sources, it
lacked the authority of coverage by 'our own correspondent'. Ultimately,
the content came from a far-away place and frequently seemed quite
unbelievable.[122]

The security crisis engendered by the war made Jews in the Nazi
domain ever more vulnerable, but it simultaneously weakened the influence of Jews in the democracies. At just the moment the Nazis
believed they were girding their loins to fight the hydra of 'international
Jewry', Jews around the world were never more fragmented, powerless
and bemused. The councils of British Jews were divided between the
Orthodox and the non-Orthodox, the left and the right, Zionists and
anti-Zionists. It was hard to find an agreed policy to deal with the plight
of Jews in Germany and Poland while there were, anyway, pressing
demands closer to home. The cost of maintaining tens of thousands of
refugees week after week was staggering. One of the first tasks that the
British Jewish leadership set itself was persuading the government to
share some of this burden. By 1940, the taxpayer was contributing half
of the costs of care for refugees. But this generosity (soon to rise to
100 per cent) made it hard for British Jews to contest other aspects of
government policy.[123]

American Jews were even more unprepared for the scale of the
challenge. They were unused to confronting international issues of such
complexity and found it hard to agree a common approach. Their main
response was philanthropic: the AJJDC channelled $8.5 million to
Europe in 1939, although only a sixth of this was allotted to the hard-
pressed Jews of Poland. Nearly half was committed to supporting Jewish
refugees in various countries. The international Jewish relief agencies

met in Paris a few days before the war erupted but spent most of the meeting squabbling over how or whether to maintain a neutral stance towards Germany.[124]

The Jewish population of Palestine was fixated by its own travails, too. The Zionist leadership considered its first duty was to contest the White Paper and to maintain levels of immigration, illegally if need be. The events in Europe seemed distant, while communication with Jews in Poland became increasingly strained. To many it seemed that the main problem there was one of starvation, to which the answer was food parcels. It was regarded as a temporary affliction and less significant than the long-term fate of the Yishuv. Under the guidance of David Ben-Gurion, chairman of the Jewish Agency Executive, the quasi-government of Jewish Palestine, the Hebrew press focused on immigration, diplomatic issues, and the future. The day-to-day plight of Jews in Poland and the Reich receded into the distance.[125]

War in the west

Thanks to the inertia of the western allies, Hitler had avoided a war on two fronts but after the defeat of Poland he still confronted an alliance of two global empires. His first instinct was to attack in the west as early as possible, in November 1939, but his generals and bad weather held him back. The ensuing 'phoney war' was the butt of many jokes in Britain, but it was a period of anxiety in the Third Reich. The economy was strained to breaking point. The German railway system was barely able to cope with the demands of the military and the civilian sectors. Production of armaments could only be maintained at the expense of suppressing domestic consumption across the board, mobilizing women, and importing foreign labour. Daily life on the home front became a little bit harder with each passing month and with each dip in living standards public morale sagged. In October 1939, William Shirer noted the sale of rubberized footwear was limited; the following month clothing was rationed; in December coal ran short. Journeys by train were slow and uncomfortably crowded, making it all the more regrettable that soap was also in short supply. In March 1940, Shirer found it hard to get gasoline for his car and the next month the number of taxis allowed to operate in Berlin was halved. When the middle-aged writer and diarist Friedrich Reck-Malleczewan visited Munich he grumbled that his hotel was shabby and unheated, the restaurants were only open for a few hours and the meat they served was distinctly strange.[126]

Hitler knew that time was running out for the Reich. Since there was no point in husbanding resources for a long war he might as well throw everything he had into one enormous onslaught against the Anglo-French forces. When the assault began, Shirer commented perceptively that 'It is Hitler's bid for victory now or never. Apparently it was true that Germany could not outlast the economic war. So he struck while the armies still had supplies and his air force had a lead over the Allies. He seems to realize he is risking all.'[127]

The campaign in the west was triggered by a British naval incursion into Norwegian waters in February 1940. In an attempt to limit iron ore imports to Germany, the British next mined Norwegian sea lanes and landed troops at Trondheim. On 9 April, Hitler responded by launching an invasion of Norway and ordered the occupation of Denmark. The Danes capitulated within a day, but land battles in Norway and naval engagements continued for eight weeks until Allied troops were evacuated. These small-scale actions were a sideshow to the main offensive, which was unleashed on 10 May 1940. Originally, Hitler and his high command planned a conventional invasion through the Netherlands, Belgium and Luxemburg into northern France, during which they hoped to destroy the bulk of the British and French forces. But a copy of the plan, Case Yellow, fell into Allied hands. This gave impetus to a rethink that was already under way thanks to the efforts of General Erich von Manstein, chief of staff of one of the army groups assigned to the attack. Manstein proposed using the advance through the Netherlands and Belgium as a ruse to attract the main Allied forces while powerful German armoured columns pushed through the Ardennes, far to the south. The panzer divisions would cross the Meuse river, breach the French positions where the heavily fortified Maginot Line ended, and then strike into the rear of the Allied armies, threatening them with encirclement. Hitler, ever the inspired amateur strategist, had been toying with such a notion himself. When Manstein's so-called 'sickle-cut' version of Case Yellow was brought to his attention, he seized on it.[128]

Thanks largely to the conservatism of the Anglo-French military leadership, Manstein's plan worked perfectly. While the best of the British and French divisions rushed into Belgium, the heaviest concentration of German mobile forces wound through the Ardennes and on

13 May fought their way across the Meuse river into a sector defended by second-rate French divisions. By 15 May, the panzer divisions had opened a forty-mile gap in the French line and were moving towards the English Channel, severing lines of communication between Paris and the main Allied force. Five days later, German tank commanders found themselves gazing on the sea at Abbeville. The British Expeditionary Force, which had begun to withdraw south a few days earlier, was instructed to fall back on the coastal ports from where it could be evacuated. Between 26 May and 3 June, 338,226 men, British and French, were taken off the beaches and from the port of Dunkirk. Meanwhile, the German armies closed up to a line along the Somme and Aisne rivers and after a pause to regroup, attacked southwards. In just ten days the remainder of the French army was cut to pieces. The French government, now led by Marshal Pétain as prime minister, sued for an armistice. The formalities were concluded at Compiègne on 21 June 1940, in the same railway carriage in which the Germans had signed the document signifying their capitulation on 11 November 1918. Hitler was jubilant.[129]

This excursus into military history is essential for understanding not just the imminent fate of Jews in the newly conquered countries, but also the unfolding of Jewish policy in the Reich and occupied Poland. Furthermore, the reasons for German victory in the west and the false confidence it inspired in the Wehrmacht leadership are fundamental to grasping the reasons for German military failure in the east a year later, which was to have catastrophic consequences for the Jews in Russia and, ultimately, across Europe.

Unlike in Poland, the German armed forces and the SS in France were not assigned murderous tasks outside of combat. Although several units of the armed SS, the Waffen-SS, distinguished themselves in the ground fighting, Himmler and the security apparatus otherwise had little role in the campaign or the establishment of occupation regimes afterwards. There were no Einsatzgruppen and Heydrich kept himself busy flying missions for the Luftwaffe. Nevertheless, the campaign was not free of atrocities. Waffen-SS units massacred surrendered British army personnel at the Flanders villages of Le Paradis and Wormhoudt on 27–28 May 1940.[130]

At least 1,500 French colonial troops (and possibly as many as 3,000) were shot when captured or while in prisoner of war camps. Most of the victims were Tirailleurs Sénégalais. The German soldiers who encountered these Africans were predisposed to view them as uncivilized. The fact that some fought with knives and attacked Germans from the rear compounded the image of barbaric mercenaries: to German troops their assailants appeared to be savages who did not know how to fight like Europeans. After they surrendered, dozens were mown down by riflemen from panzer and infantry divisions as well as by Waffen-SS troopers. However, in a crucial distinction between the treatment of Black Africans as against Poles and Jews, the killing usually ended in the combat zone. General Halder noted in his war diary under the heading 'Coloured PWs' [prisoners of war], that they were 'to be put in special battalions, receive good treatment'. Black prisoners were not to be sent to the Reich for labour, preserving the principle of racial segregation, but were to be repatriated. The Germans never considered murdering them all and, on the contrary, were content for them to return home. Of course, this lenient policy came too late for the hundreds who were shot or bayoneted in cold blood in trenches and fields in northern France. Yet the fate of captured French colonial soldiers illustrates a fundamental difference between the perception of Jews and others inserted by the Germans into racially defined categories. The Jews were a powerful, dangerous, mortal enemy in a way that other racially differentiated groups were not.[131]

The war fought in the west in 1940 may not have been a race war, but the outcome had a dramatic impact on Nazi racial policy. Initially the treatment of the Jewish question was conditioned by the unexpectedness of the German victory. The defeat of France was not designed as 'blitzkrieg', or lightning war; no one was more surprised by the rapidity of the French collapse than Hitler and his generals. But this left them totally unprepared for what followed. Thus the immediate fate of the Jews hinged on the speed and the apparent totality of the victory; subsequently, it was shaped by the (erroneous) lessons that the Nazi elite drew from it. In 1940 the Germans planned for a long conflict and were caught unawares when it ended quickly, whereas in 1941 they planned for a brief struggle and were caught on the hop when it dragged out.[132]

The Nazi hierarchy had no plans for what to do with the countries they had conquered. Over the summer months, Hitler and his inner circle put in place a series of structures for occupation and governance that were shaped by short-term considerations. Denmark, which had barely resisted, was allowed to keep its entire system of government, police and civil service, which continued to run the country. Since it was a vital source of foodstuffs for the Reich, the Germans put a premium on continuity and stability. The Danes only had to put up with a small garrison and the German security apparatus was kept to a minimum. In Norway, where the Germans had faced tough opposition, government was placed in the hands of a Reichskommissar, Josef Terboven. For a while Terboven tried to co-opt Norwegian politicians into a collaborationist government, but he ended up appointing trusted Nazis from Germany or the local Nazi Party to run government ministries. Vidkun Quisling, the head of the Norwegian Nazi Party, which was very small, proved to be a liability and was kept at arm's length. Like the Norwegian king, the royal family of the Netherlands was evacuated to Britain along with the government. Hitler had ambitions to absorb the Dutch into the Reich so he appointed a civil administration under Arthur Seyss-Inquart, former Nazi governor of Austria. Seyss-Inquart, in turn, appointed German Nazis to oversee the key ministries of the government and gradually levered Dutch Nazis into positions of authority. Day-to-day governance was left in the hands of the Dutch civil service coordinated by a committee formed of the state secretaries, the official heads of each ministry. In contrast, Belgium was placed under military administration, much along the lines of 1914–18, on the grounds that the country would be the launch pad for an invasion of Britain and was, in any case, of strategic importance. Since the Belgian government had fled, daily affairs were left in the hands of civil servants answering to German military personnel.[133]

For political as well as geo-strategic reasons, occupation policy for France was different again and far more complicated. There was also an element of vindictiveness in the terms of the armistice treaty imposed on France. It compelled the French to reduce the size of their army to 100,000 men, leaving hundreds of thousands of POWs in German hands as a bargaining chip for future dealings. The country had to pay for the costs of the German occupation, with the franc valued at a ruinously low rate against the Reichsmark. As a result, German soldiers on leave stripped the shops of perfumes, soap, stockings, couture, and every sort of food along with wines and spirits and shipped them back to their families. The occupation was a form of organized state larceny. The strategic and highly industrialized regions of the north-east were sundered from France and placed under the military administration of Belgium. The rest of northern France and the entire coastal strip from the Pyrenees to the Belgian frontier was garrisoned and placed under a military administration headquartered in Paris. The demarcation line between the occupied zone and the 'Free Zone' was policed and used to control the flow of people as well as goods and foodstuffs. However, France was allowed to retain its government and was theoretically an independent state. Marshal Pétain chose the spa town of Vichy as the new seat of government and from here it claimed jurisdiction over the whole country. In practice, though, its rule was only untrammelled in the Free Zone. In the north, decrees and directives of the Vichy authorities were subject to approval by the German military administration, headed by General Otto von Stülpnagel. It was, nonetheless, intended as a benign occupation. Hitler hoped to win over the French to his new European order and obtain their willing military as well as economic cooperation. The Germans also wanted to achieve maximum cooperation so as to minimize the manpower needed for administration and security.[134]

The inconsistent pattern of German rule over what is sometimes, rather misleadingly, termed 'Hitler's empire', inflected the initiation and implementation of anti-Jewish measures. In general, the defeat of the democratic countries eroded faith in democracy itself, endowing Nazi parties and pro-German politicians with an aura of power. Not only was liberalism eroded as an ideology, but the emergency conditions fostered by defeat and occupation eroded the force of law. In France defeat fomented an upsurge of nationalist feeling, a reaction against the Third Republic and the principles of the 1789 revolution which it espoused. On 10 July 1940, the remaining members of the French National Assembly revoked the constitution of the Third Republic and gave virtually dictatorial powers to Marshal Pétain and his deputy (and designated successor) Pierre Laval. Pétain evoked the disillusionment with republican values when he proclaimed a 'national revolution' based on 'Travail. Famille. Patrie' ('Work. Family. Fatherland'). His regime set about purging the administration at all levels, from ministries to mayoralties, of anyone associated with the Popular Front. The Jewish prime minister from 1936–7, Léon Blum, was pilloried as the antithesis of the new regime. Anti-Semitism became a fundamental ingredient of the patriotic revival, shared between churchmen who envisaged a state re-founded on Catholic beliefs, conservatives who blamed the defeat on the decadence of modern culture, anti-communists and anti-socialists. Yet it took time for these passions to take the form of anti-Jewish policies. Everywhere the German occupiers proceeded cautiously. They had not prepared any measures against the Jews and were so busy setting up the occupation framework and ensuring that things got back to normal that the Jews were not the first priority. This was not true, however, for the specialists in Jewish policy in Berlin.[135]

'Treatment of the Alien Population in the East' and the Madagascar plan

On 25 May 1940, Heinrich Himmler submitted to Hitler a memorandum entitled 'Some Thoughts on the Treatment of the Alien Population in the East'. It contained his suggestions for the Germanization of annexed Poland. Himmler recommended that the indigenous population should be reorganized into ethnic categories, although no national consciousness should be permitted. Small minorities of all these peoples could be used to provide mayors and local police officials; Poles should receive only the most elementary education. They should be taught simple arithmetic and basic religious precepts such as 'God's commandment to be obedient to the Germans'. Children 'of our blood', opined Himmler, should be taken to the Reich where they would be raised as members of the Volk, whether their parents agreed or otherwise. The 'inferior remnant' would end up in the General Government, where it would provide a reservoir of cheap, unskilled labour. Some ethnic groups would simply disappear. Significantly, he mentioned, as an aside, that this would be the fate of the Jews. 'I hope to see the term "Jew" completely eliminated through the possibility of large-scale emigration of all Jews to Africa or to some colony.'[136]

Himmler may have been referring back to the idea of sending Jews to Madagascar, a notion that had been floating around since late 1938. Or he may have been reacting to the possibilities opening up thanks to the impending defeat of France. This prospect offered Germans the entire French overseas empire to dream about, including the island of Madagascar. Well before the armistice with France was concluded, Franz Rademacher, the head of the Jewish desk in the German Foreign Office, seized on the possibility of utilizing these territories as a destination for unwanted Jews. Early in July, he circulated a paper suggesting that the peace treaty to terminate the war should include a provision for sending the Jews to Madagascar. Rademacher opened with a flourish: 'The approaching victory gives Germany the possibility, and in my view also the duty, of solving the Jewish question in Europe. The desirable solution is: all Jews out of Europe.' He specified that 'In the Peace Treaty France must make the island of Madagascar available for the solution of the Jewish question' and resettle the 25,000 French citizens living there. The island would be transferred to German rule under a mandate that would prevent the Jews gaining any of the rights associated with statehood. Unlike Palestine, the island would not have a political or spiritual significance either. It would in effect be another version of the Lublin 'reservation' where the Jews 'will remain in German hands as a pledge for the future good behaviour of the members of their race in America'.[137]

Rademacher's initiative caught Heydrich and the RHSA off guard. Heydrich was immediately worried that the Foreign Office might grab the glory with its solution of the Jewish problem and become the main arm for carrying it out. So, on 24 June, he brusquely reminded the Wilhelmstrasse that the security apparatus, the RSHA, was in charge of Jewish matters. In a later version, dated 3 July, Rademacher added that the island would be governed by the German police forces, ultimately responsible to the Reichsführer-SS, Himmler. But this was not good enough for Heydrich. He wanted his own people to come up with a more detailed format that would bear the exclusive imprimatur of the RSHA. So he appointed Eichmann, the lead expert on Jewish affairs, to devise a rival proposal. Eichmann went to work with his customary diligence, digging up quantities of information on Madagascar and conditions in the tropics. By 15 August the RSHA scheme was ready for submission to Ribbentrop, the foreign minister. It envisaged sending four million Jews to the island using two ships a day, each carrying 1,500 people. Eichmann and his aide, Theo Dannecker, went into great detail about registering Jews and their property, expropriating their wealth, and using the proceeds to cover the cost of the project. The first waves would include 'pioneers' to create the infrastructure that would absorb the rest. It was like a parody of the Zionist enterprise in Palestine. But Eichmann did not permit any level of self-government to the Jews: the island would be little more than an open prison under SS management.[138]

Characteristically, Eichmann turned to Jewish leaders for much of the preliminary work. On 3 July, he instructed representatives of the Jewish organizations in Berlin, Vienna and Prague to prepare a memorandum outlining how Jewish populations could be mustered for shipment overseas. The Reichsvereinigung was shocked when it learned that the German authorities were giving serious consideration to such an outlandish idea. However, with customary stoicism they set about devising a framework for Jewish life on a remote and less than hospitable island. Word about Madagascar quickly spread through the Jewish communities in Germany and Austria. Victor Klemperer got wind of it from a friendly German woman who heard it mentioned in a radio programme. William Shirer figured out that the regime was thinking seriously about Africa when he heard that members of the SS were learning Swahili.[139]

Hans Frank was informed of the project by Hitler personally on 8 July 1940. He was thrilled at the thought, not least because the prospect of an imminent solution meant that Hitler agreed to suspend further deportations of Jews into his domain. A few days later Frank reported to his subordinates in Cracow, 'It is planned after the peace to transport the whole Jewish gang from the Reich, the General Government, and the Protectorate as soon as possible to some African or American colony. Madagascar, which France would have given up for this purpose, is what is foreseen . . . I shall try to arrange that the Jews from the General Government are also able to make use of this chance to build their own life for themselves in this territory.' The Madagascar project therefore had an immediate effect in Poland. Plans for the creation of a ghetto in Warsaw were suspended and thousands of Jews were spared the necessity to leave their homes and move to designated areas. Adam Czerniaków noted in his diary that the Sipo-SD officer Gerhard Mende, who supervised the Jewish council, 'declared that the war would be over in a month and that we would all leave for Madagascar'. Across Poland ghetto-building suddenly stopped.[140]

As rumours swept through the Nazi ranks, Gauleiters in the Reich could not contain their impatience. After Alsace and Lorraine were formally annexed to the Reich in July, the new rulers expelled over 24,000 French Jews into the unoccupied zone to await shipment to the Indian Ocean. They ended up in camps under Vichy French supervision. The Nazi Party bosses of Baden and the Saarpfalz followed suit in October, having obtained Hitler's approval to cleanse their precincts of Jews. To the horror of the Reichsvereinigung, 6,500 German Jews were given a day's notice to prepare for deportation into France. This was the first mass deportation of Jews from western Germany and the Reichsvereinigung felt compelled to react. Its leaders declared a fast while Otto

Hirsch addressed a formal protest to the authorities. The protest was as courageous as it was futile; Hirsch was arrested and sent to Mauthausen where he perished about four months later. The Vichy French authorities were not consulted in advance and remonstrated with the German Foreign Office about the imposition. Needless to say, the reproach had no effect. Without any interest in caring for the deportees, most of whom were old and in poor health, the French dumped them in a bleak internment camp at Gurs in south-west France. The number of inmates soared from 1,400 to 12,000 without the provision of any additional accommodation or facilities.[141]

But there was to be no 'Madagascar solution'. First of all, Hitler hoped to woo the French into joining the Axis and therefore left them in possession of their navy and their overseas possessions. Even if the Germans had taken Madagascar there was no way to reach it while Britain commanded the sea-lanes, but Hitler's ham-fisted offer of peace in a speech on 19 July got no response from London. Winston Churchill, prime minister since 10 May, had persuaded his colleagues that the only realistic policy for the survival of the country and the empire was to fight on.[142]

Britain's defiance placed the Germans in a quandary: they might possess the most powerful land force in Europe but there was no way they could use it to finish off the British, who were protected by the English Channel, the Royal Navy and the RAF. In mid-July, Hitler ordered the army high command to draw up plans for an invasion in August, Operation Sealion, but the Wehrmacht was ill-equipped for such an undertaking. Nor could the small German navy hope to protect the invasion force or its supply lines from attack by British naval units. The Luftwaffe might deter or drive back a naval assault, but its ability to shield the armada depended on achieving air superiority. Consequently, at the end of July, Hitler ordered Göring to break the RAF within two weeks. The air offensive failed – albeit narrowly. On 17 September 1940, Hitler postponed Sealion.[143]

For the moment, the fate of Europe's Jews had been decided on the battlefield, in the air and at sea. It was shaped less by anti-Semitism and prior anti-Jewish policy than by the geo-strategic framework in which Hitler and his confederates were operating. Had Britain capitulated and had Germany stripped France of its colonies, Jews might have been deported to Madagascar in the autumn of 1940. In which case, the German navy, the Kriegsmarine, would have been instrumental in realizing a vision first conceptualized by the Poles and the French in 1938. Instead, the Germans continued to fumble their way towards a solution according to their racial-biological precepts, but under circumstances they could not entirely control. In the interim, the suspension of plans to remove the Jews from Europe obliged the German occupation authorities, as well as their allies and collaborators, to frame and implement policies to deal with the 'Jewish question'.

Jews as 'enemy aliens': mass internment in Britain and France

The extension of the war had an impact on Jews beyond those who were directly caught up in the fighting, turned into refugees, or condemned to endure a period of foreign occupation. Overnight it turned refugees into 'enemy aliens'. In Britain and France steps were taken to register and, if necessary, intern enemy nationals along with others deemed a threat to security because of their political affiliations with the far right or the far left. Jewish refugees bore the brunt of these measures.

Approximately 64,000 refugees in Britain had been classified category 'C' by tribunals, meaning that although they were technically enemy nationals they were considered innocuous. The vast majority were Jews from Germany and Austria. German and Austrian nationals classed as 'A' were immediately arrested and imprisoned; most of them had Nazi connections or were Germans of military age. Category 'B' denoted people with political records that rendered them suspicious, including left-wing anti-fascists and communists; they were subject to restrictions. Until the German offensive against France most German and Austrian refugees were left alone. The Home Office, under Sir John Anderson, had no wish to repeat the mass internment of the Great War and saw no reason to apprehend people who had fled Nazism. Unfortunately, MI5 (the secret service) did not see things in quite the same way and regarded the refugee population as a potential nest of spies. The use of German parachute troops behind Dutch and Belgian lines increased their anxiety about allowing refugees to roam freely. How would it be possible to tell if they were bona fide fugitives or storm troopers in disguise? The rapid collapse of Dutch and Belgian resistance as well as the disarray of the French gave birth to the myth of a 'Fifth Column': German or pro-German elements that subverted the defenders from within. Consequently, pressure built up on the government to impose controls on enemy aliens.[144]

Winston Churchill was sensitive to the warnings issued by the intelligence community and wanted to show the population that his government meant business. On 11 May, the day after he was appointed prime minister, the cabinet agreed to remove enemy nationals from coastal zones and, the following day, to begin selective detention of men in category 'B'. The catastrophe at Dunkirk generated a panic and the War Office demanded wholesale internment of adult male Germans and Austrians regardless of whether they were Jewish or classed as refugees. With Churchill's backing the army chiefs of staff and the security services overcame the home secretary's reluctance to initiate mass internment. At a cabinet meeting on 27 May, in an atmosphere of crisis, there was near-unanimous agreement to round up everyone in category 'C'. The next day police began to arrest men aged 16–60, even if the tribunals had declared them refugees who were 'ready to assist this country rather than to assist the enemy'. Italy's entry into the war on 10 June added 10,000 Italians to the tally of 'enemy nationals' and heightened the sense that treachery was afoot. Churchill now issued instructions to 'collar the lot'. Within a month, 27,000 refugees were being held in makeshift detention centres in disused factories, racecourses, and hastily converted boarding houses on the Isle of Man. From 20 June, groups of internees were deported to camps in Canada and Australia. Over 7,300 ended up in barbed-wire encampments in remote locations, sundered from friends and family, uncertain of what the future held for them. Those detained in Britain were in the miserable position of being trapped behind barbed wire when a German invasion was expected at any moment.[145]

Tragically, on 1 July 1940, the SS *Arandora Star*, carrying over 1,200 internees (Italians and Germans) to Canada, was torpedoed in the Irish Sea and sank with the loss of over 700 lives. This disaster intensified criticism of the mass internment policy that had been building up amongst Members of Parliament and in sections of the press. The backlash was abetted by news about the SS *Dunera*, a transportation ship that reached Australia with nearly 2,300 refugees who had been robbed and abused by the British soldiers guarding them. After a period of hesitation, the Jewish leadership began to lobby Whitehall to modify its stance. It was tribute to the courage of these critics and the resilience of the democratic system that by autumn 1940 internment had been abandoned. Ever-increasing numbers of Jews were released if they had special skills or wished to enter the Pioneer Corps.[146]

Those stuck in the camps, 10,000 on the Isle of Man alone, made the best of their enforced idleness and engaged in an astonishing array of educational and cultural activities. Yet the improvised Viennese-style coffee houses, camp art, witty cyclostyled journals, erudite lectures and string quartets could only partly compensate for the ugly experience of arrest and detention for no good reason. For some German and Austrian Jews it was actually the second time that they had been incarcerated unjustly, although they, especially, recognized the difference between the malice that lay behind the Nazi concentration camps and the impromptu and usually good-natured confinement under the Union Flag. Nevertheless, it was an unpleasant, sombre episode in the midst of Britain's 'finest hour' that revealed the potential of xenophobia and anti-Semitism, especially when combined with security fears and military exigencies.[147]

The fate of Jews interned in France was incomparably grimmer. On 3 September 1939 the French authorities ordered all German and Austrian nationals to report at assembly centres. The decree immediately affected 13,000 German and 8,000 Austrian Jewish refugees. They were joined by individuals whom the police and secret service deemed subversive, mostly communists and anti-fascist activists like Arthur Koestler. After days of detention, and without any legal procedures, they were transported to internment camps in the south of the country. These camps, notably St Cyprien, Argelès-sur-Mer, Barcures, Gurs and Le Vernet, consisted of crude wooden barracks with the minimum of facilities surrounded by barbed-wire fences and watchtowers manned by gendarmes. In his searing account *Scum of the Earth*, written in 1941, Koestler recalled that Le Vernet was 'a mess of barbed wire and more barbed wire'. The huts sat on ground that was 'stony and dusty when dry; ankle deep in mud when it rained'. It was 'run with that mixture of ignominy, corruption, and *laisser-faire* so typical of the French administration' and guarded by men of the Garde Mobile who were 'the most reactionary and brutal force in France'.[148]

French Jews declined to assist the internees. Morris Troper, representing the AJJDC in Paris, reported that 'French Jewry was paralysed. Fearful lest any activity on their part on behalf of German refugees might be construed as consorting with enemy aliens, and further that it might provide a basis for antisemitic sentiment during a period when anything might happen, French Jewry disassociated itself completely from any activity on behalf of the refugees.' After a while, though, the Committee for the Assistance of Refugees led by Raymond-Raoul Lambert got aid to the internees and pressed for their release. By the end of the year about 8,000 had been discharged because they were old or sick, prepared to join the army (or the Foreign Legion), were valuable to the economy, or had papers to emigrate to the USA.[149]

Koestler was extracted from Le Vernet after a campaign coordinated by his wife, and returned to Paris in January 1940. But he was only at liberty for a few months. The German offensive triggered an even more ferocious wave of xenophobia and suspicion aimed at foreigners. During May 1940, 8,000 German refugees, including 5,000 who were Jewish, plus around 10,000 fugitives from Belgium and the Netherlands, were rounded up by police in Paris and held in converted sports halls, the Buffalo Stadium and the Vélodrome d'Hiver. The police came for Koestler a second time on 22 May and took him to the Buffalo Stadium, only on this occasion he refused to comply and escaped amidst the confusion. Like thousands of other Frenchmen and women he took to the roads and headed south, away from the Germans. He eventually made contact with American refugee workers who were assisting Jews and political fugitives to get out of France.[150]

The Jews under Vichy and under German occupation in France, Belgium and Holland

For weeks after the French capitulation it seemed to Jews in both the north and south as if nothing much had changed. The period of fighting and the chaotic stampede southwards had left the Jews divided roughly half-and-half between the two zones, with about 150,000 Jews in Paris of whom some 60,000 were foreign-born. One of them was the pioneer historian Léon Poliakov, who had arrived from Russia with his family after the Great War. Poliakov recalled in his memoirs that 'Life in Paris seemed normal. One was not even alarmed for the Jews. The Germans were "correct"; there were no massacres and no pogroms.' Indeed, the German military authorities took care to prevent anti-Jewish disturbances by either their own people or Frenchmen who blamed Jews for the calamity of defeat.[151]

To a Jew like Poliakov, who had already been uprooted by war and revolution, normality was a relative concept. Raymond-Raoul Lambert's family had lived in France for generations and the shambles left him groping for familiar reference points. Having served as a reserve officer with a unit of colonial troops until it disintegrated he made his way to Nîmes in the south. In early July he resumed writing in his journal to make sense of events, a habit he got into during his service in the trenches in 1914–18. 'After the past four weeks,' he wrote, 'which have seen unfold the most tragic events in our history, and for me the most terrible anxieties I have ever known, I am trying to recover my intellectual balance.' Lambert averred that to recover from the disaster France required a 'spiritual reformation'.[152]

The men of Vichy concurred that France was in dire need of spiritual reform but Lambert was shocked to discover that they identified him and his co-religionists as a main source of the rot. Within days of its establishment anti-Jewish edicts began to issue from the new regime. On the 13 July it was decreed that only men of French parentage could serve in government. A few days later, civil service posts and the right to practise medicine were restricted to those of French birth. On 22 July foreigners who had been naturalized since 1927 lost their French nationality. This regulation, which struck at approximately 6,000 Jews, was aimed particularly at Jewish refugees from Nazi Germany and Eastern and Central Europe. The following day, citizenship was rescinded from anyone foreign-born who had fled France; their property was seized by the state. Next month, the Marchandeau Law was revoked, an act of profound symbolic and practical significance. The law had been passed in 1881 to protect members of religious and racial groups from abuse in the press and became an icon of the liberal Third Republic. Now the way was cleared for unmitigated verbal assaults on Jews, who no longer had recourse to the law in their own defence. Finally, on 3 October 1940, the Vichy government promulgated a charter fixing the status and place of Jews in the new France, the Statut des Juifs. The statute defined who was a Jew more strictly than the Nuremberg Laws. It excluded Jews from public posts and a range of occupations in the professions and cultural life. Jews could serve in the army but were not permitted to obtain commissions. For good measure, on 7 October, Pétain's government repealed another iconic act of the Republic: the Crémieux Law. This legislation, passed in October 1870, had granted full citizenship to the Jews of Algeria. At a stroke, it deprived 117,000 Jews of their civil rights.[153]

This hail of decrees emanated mainly from the Ministry of Justice under Rafaël Alibert. They were not a response to German pressure or even prompting. On the contrary, until October 1940 interventions by the German military administration concerning Jewish matters were confined to 'unsystematic bursts of propaganda and border controls'. It was the Vichyites who treated the 'national revolution' as the perfect opportunity to roll back the advances made by Jews in France since the Dreyfus affair, if not the revolution of 1789. They were symbolically settling scores with the Popular Front government as well as the Dreyfusards and using the Jews to make a statement about the character of French renewal. The France of Vichy rejected parliamentary democracy, liberalism, modern culture, cosmopolitanism, and of course Marxism. Léon Blum, who was slated to stand trial for his alleged role in corrupting and weakening France, personified the evils wrought by Jews. An official statement in the Parisian newspaper *Le Temps* explained: 'The government in its task of national reconstruction has ... studied the problem of the Jews and of certain foreigners, who, having abused our hospitality, have contributed to a significant degree to the defeat. Although there are some notable exceptions ... the influence of the Jews has been undeniably corruptive and finally decaying. The government ... respects the individual Jew as well as his possessions. It will forbid him however to hold certain administrative responsibilities, authority in the national economy and education. Past experience has shown to all impartial minds that the Jews represent an individualistic tendency which leads to anarchy.' At another level, Laval saw anti-Semitism as a useful gesture of amity towards the Germans. His approach seems to have been coldly instrumental and, if anything, he regarded himself as a barrier to the progress of even more radical anti-Semitic elements in French society.[154]

The statute struck at the identity of French Jews and left them reeling. Lambert noted, 'So it is possible that within a few days I shall see my citizenship reduced, and that my sons, who are French by birth, culture, and faith, will find themselves brutally and cruelly cast out of the French community ... I cannot believe it. France is no longer France. I repeat to myself that Germany is in charge here, trying still to excuse this offence against an entire history ...' Nevertheless, he refused to contemplate emigration. In his journal he argued back and forth whether the indignities heaped upon the Jews were the result of external pressure or an expression of authentic French prejudices. 'The

Jews of France, even those who died for our country, have never been assimilated. Racism has become the law of the new state. What boundless disgrace! ... All my illusions are crumbling around me ... I shall never leave this country for which I risked my life, but can my sons live here if they are not allowed to choose freely what career to follow?' As an ex-officer with a keen sense of military affairs, Lambert speculated that the situation had two possible outcomes: an Anglo-American victory over Germany or a long night lasting for a hundred years during which the Jews would live as they had done in the Middle Ages.[155]

Yet the future historian Jacques Adler, a child of immigrants, remembered that daily life for Jews in Paris 'regained a normalcy reminiscent of the days before the exodus'. Some of the Jews who attempted to flee south returned to the capital. The synagogues were full for the high holy days. Cafes and communal life returned to normal. Money was raised for relief work and those out of work or homeless were helped. For months it seemed as if the worst was over.[156]

Paradoxically, things were worse for refugees in the Free Zone, and much worse for those in the internment camps. In May and June 1940, thousands of French and foreign-born Jews, like Léon Poliakov and Irène Némirovsky, took to the roads to escape the Germans. Foreign Jews often lacked papers but were more inclined to flee, whereas French Jews had the necessary documents but were more attached to their homes and homeland. It is estimated that around 20,000 managed to escape abroad legally or illegally by the time the Germans were able to seal the frontiers. Many remained stranded in the south, homeless and without any livelihood. Given the disorder afflicting the economy, unemployment and shortages, the presence of these outsiders was greatly resented by local people. They were also vulnerable to food controls since they lacked the permanent address and identification papers necessary to obtain ration cards.[157]

The number of internees was swollen by a decree of the Vichy regime on 4 October 1940 to detain all 'foreign-born nationals of Jewish race'. It was aggravated still further by the wave of expulsions from Baden-Württemberg. Although many foreign Jews evaded the Vichy edict, about 34,000 went into the camps. Conditions in Rivesaltes and Gurs were especially bad; during 1940–1 some 3,000 Jews died due to the poor conditions. Partly as a result of this high mortality, the Vichy authorities appointed a civilian inspector to report on the situation. His verdict was so damning that the authorities allowed in relief workers and inaugurated a policy of selective releases. Within a year only about 17,500 inmates remained, of whom 60 per cent were Jews. Thousands were released into labour battalions, while up to 12,000 were assisted to emigrate by Jewish and international aid agencies. HICEM was even permitted to maintain staff inside the internment camp at Les Milles, outside Marseilles, where the Vichy French authorities gathered those with a good chance of legal emigration. Of the 6,538 Reich Jews from Baden-Württemberg and 1,125 from the Saar-Palatinate shoved into the Free Zone on 22–23 October 1940, nearly 2,000 emigrated while almost 3,000 were let out to perform labour service. But 12 per cent died in Gurs. By the end of the year Jews in the north and the south had organized relief programmes, drawing heavily on money sent via the AJJDC, and in January 1941 set up a coordinating committee to rationalize the services provided by numerous Jewish bodies.[158]

In the north, the German occupation administration crystallized. It was a tangled skein of agencies, each with a claim to jurisdiction over aspects of Jewish affairs. The head of the military administration, the Militärbefehlshaber in Frankreich (MBF), was Otto von Stülpnagel. His chief of civil affairs was Werner Best, who arrived from the head office of the SS in Berlin. In August 1940, Ribbentrop appointed Otto Abetz Ambassador to France. His mission included a Jewish desk that was manned from April 1941 by Carl-Theo Zeitschel. Although the army insisted on retaining control of security matters, Heydrich succeeded in assigning a senior SS officer, Helmut Knochen, to run the small Sipo contingent. This was the Trojan horse for the insertion of Gestapo officers, led by Kurt Lischka and Herbert Hagen. Finally, Eichmann sent one of his closest co-workers, the ambitious and hyperactive Theo Dannecker, to set up a branch of office IVB4 of the RSHA responsible for Jewish affairs. Göring's economic office began pressing to take over Jewish enterprises while a special staff responsible to Alfred Rosenberg arrived to pillage the art collections of Jewish dealers and connoisseurs. Finally, an Armistice Commission dealt with matters arising from the peace agreement, notably the fate of German political émigrés in France.[159]

During the summer, a commission led by Dr Ernst Kundt, a German Embassy official, trawled through the internment camps looking for people wanted by the Gestapo. The Kundt Commission was not interested in the mass of German and Austrian refugees who were Jews. Indeed, the German Foreign Ministry was doing what it could to facilitate their emigration. However, there were huge obstacles to emigration. The Jews were frequently old and lacked funds. Most pertinently, they lacked destinations. By a supreme effort between July 1940 and May 1941 HICEM assisted 1,400 German Jews to emigrate. Admiral Darlan, who became de facto prime minister in December 1940, unilaterally removed 2,000–3,000 to North Africa.[160]

The MBF did not neglect the Jewish question. Its first measure was designed to prevent Jews who had fled to the south from returning to the occupied zone. In late September 1940, the MBF ordered a census of all Jews in the occupied zone combined with registration, including addresses and occupations. The identification papers of foreign and French Jews were marked 'Juif'. While the military rulers stopped the wild picketing and looting of Jewish-owned shops, they insisted that Jewish enterprises should be marked. The main interest of the military was securing Jewish economic assets for the Reich. On 18 October 1940, the MBF promulgated an ordinance for the expropriation of Jewish property in the occupied zone, to be accomplished by the end of the year. This step provoked panic in Vichy circles. The French were determined not to let the Germans walk off with the wealth of French Jews. In a great rush the regime established the Service de Controle des Administrateurs Provisoires (SCAP) to conduct its own 'Aryanization' programme in *both* zones. Within twelve months, 15,000 enterprises had been taken over and 2,800 French administrators appointed. For the Jewish owners expropriation spelled ruin and the danger of forced labour on the grounds that they were economically inactive.[161]

The relationship between the central offices in the Reich that were responsible for Jewish policy and the MBF was tortuous. Between August and November 1940, Berlin was working towards the deportation of Jews from the occupied zone to Madagascar. Abetz understood from Hitler that his intention towards the conquered countries was to 'transfer their Jewish citizens outside of Europe'. On arrival in Paris he told the MBF to prepare for expulsions and stop Jews leaving the occupied zone. Best was simultaneously pushing for the registration of Jews and their separation from the rest of society – as in the Reich. By autumn, when the promise of expulsion had evaporated, thought was turned to the longer-term management of Jewish affairs. It was at this point that the MBF introduced the ordinance of 27 September to survey and register all Jewish assets. At the same time, the SS personnel under Knochen began to agitate for a centralized Jewish representative body that would enable them to monitor and exploit the Jews on the model of the Reichsvereinigung and the Jewish councils in Poland. Early in 1941, Dannecker began to urge the Vichy authorities to create a single office to handle Jewish issues. In March 1941, Darlan caved in to Dannecker's relentless pressure and ordained the creation of the Commissariat-général aux questions juives (CGQJ). But Darlan then proceeded to place it under Xavier Vallat, a disabled war veteran who loathed Germans. The Vichy government wanted to placate the occupier and demonstrate concord on the Jewish question, but it had no intention of allowing the Germans to interfere in the destiny of French citizens even if they were Jewish and second-class.[162]

For the Vichy French, the fate of the Jews was a field of contested sovereignty and competition for assets. Early in April 1941, Best and Stülpnagel met with Vallat to brief him about German expectations. They demanded the expulsion of Jews from the occupied zone and the internment of 'undesirable' Jews. They also wanted to see the discriminatory laws that had been enacted in the Free Zone extended to the north. Vallat had no wish to see more Jews dumped in the south and palmed that demand aside. However, he was delighted at the prospect that the Germans would recognize Vichy legislation and proposed to draft a new raft of measures for application in both zones – a 'French' solution to the Jewish question. Ambition, avarice and aversion to German power thus gave birth to the second Statut des Juifs on 2 June 1941. This variant built in a harsh racial definition and a draconian set of exclusions that drove Jews out of almost every professional niche. It also mandated a census of Jews in the Free Zone, including details of property and wealth. To Jews this was a shocking departure since responsibility could not be laid at the feet of the occupier. Even though Vallat inserted a number of exclusions – for old French Jewish families, those who had served the nation with special distinction, veterans and the immediate family of men who died for France – the second statute 'pushed all Jews to the margins of French society'.[163]

Ironically, given the antipathy of the Vichy regime to foreign-born Jews, the cumulative impact of the anti-Jewish legislation was most severe on long-established French Jewish citizens. In Paris many were civil servants and professionals, owners of businesses and property. The first wave of exclusions barely touched the immigrants, who were left to practise their humble trades. For some, though, the blow was softened by severance pay and pensions. More than a few engaged in protracted wrangling to claim exemption; 215 Jewish civil servants kept their jobs until mid-1942. The extension of Aryanization to the unoccupied zone was equally devastating, but Jews adapted. They exploited loopholes to hang on to businesses or retain an income from them. Others found new jobs, sometimes with the help of Jewish aid agencies. In the north the semi-covert Amelot committee distributed welfare to the unemployed and the impoverished. In the south a similar role was performed by the Nîmes committee. Lambert, who was now working flat out for the relief effort in the south, still found time for his journal and continued to argue with himself over who was to blame for the increasingly parlous situation of Jews in France. He identified the influence of Germans, the corruption of the press, but also felt that Jews had to carry some of the burden for their own fate. 'Certain facts that unfortunately have seemed to justify modern racism,' he jotted down, included 'too many Jews in press, film, banks, politics and it must be said, their inborn exuberance'.[164]

In Belgium, the military administration was even more securely entrenched and successful in excluding SS influence than in occupied France. Baron Alexander von Falkenhausen was appointed head of the administration and made it his business to ensure maximum calm. For the first weeks of his rule he expected that Jews would be evacuated, so there was no urgent need for activity regarding the Jewish population. There were about 70,000–75,000 Jews in the country on the eve of the war but thousands fled into France and some escaped by ship to Britain. Of the 65,000 that remained, under 10 per cent were actually Belgian citizens. The vast majority were recent immigrants, mainly from Poland. Just over half of the Jews lived in Antwerp and of these, half were Polish. They made their living from small retail businesses and the crafts, notably clothing manufacture, making leatherwear, and the diamond trade. The balance of the population was mainly in Brussels where, again, about 50 per cent were of Polish origin. These eastern European Jews supported a dense network of cultural and welfare associations that enabled them to surmount the anti-Jewish measures that eventually arrived.[165]

On 28 October 1940 the military government published a Jewish statute that required Jews to register with the authorities and subjected them to the same discriminatory measures as in occupied France. By the end of the year Jews were driven out of public service, the professions and employment in the cultural sphere. Over the next eighteen months supplementary and additional edicts arrived at the rate of roughly one per month. Jews were confined to the cities of Brussels, Antwerp, Charleroi and Liège, where they were subjected to a curfew. Jewish children were excluded from the school system and Jews banned from places of sport and recreation. Falkenhausen also presided over a modest policy of Aryanization that mainly targeted small-scale enterprises. Nevertheless, for the mass of Jews in Belgium, who were well used to circumventing government edicts, things continued much as they had been.[166]

In the Netherlands there were approximately 140,000 Jews, of whom about a tenth were German Jewish refugees and 7,000 from other countries. Dutch Jews could point to a long and distinguished presence in Holland, which was one of the first European societies to give Jews freedom of religion and allow them to live and work as they pleased. Yet however much Jews had acculturated, they were still a distinctive element set apart by religion, occupations and geography. Nearly 60 per cent of Dutch Jews lived in Amsterdam, with 10 per cent each in The Hague and Rotterdam. The remaining 20 per cent were scattered across small towns and rural communities. Wherever they resided, Jews tended to cluster in certain districts and streets. They were also bunched in a few livelihoods, with an elite in banking and commerce, and a large working class making a precarious living in clothes-making, the wholesale and retail trades, and the diamond industry. Since the Dutch political system was organized along confessional and class lines Jews were largely absent from government and administration.[167]

The German occupation regime in the Netherlands was quite different to that in Belgium and France, with severe implications for the speed and character of anti-Jewish policy. Hitler ordered that the country be placed under a civil administration immediately after it was conquered and on 29 May 1940 appointed a Nazi die-hard, Arthur Seyss-Inquart, as his Reich Commissioner. Seyss-Inquart in turn appointed trusted Nazis to oversee the key areas of Dutch governance: Friedrich Wimmer for administration and justice; Hans Fischböck for the economy and finance; Hanns Rauter for security and policing; and Fritz Schmidt for propaganda and political affairs. Rauter had the status of a Higher Police and SS Leader (HSSPF) and as such also represented the interests of Himmler and RSHA. This team met weekly with Seyss-Inquart plus representatives of the German Foreign Office, the Sipo-SD, and intelligence services. In March 1941 the security police were placed under Wilhelm Härster, who also answered to Himmler and Heydrich. As a consequence of these arrangements there was no buffer between Berlin and the Nazi occupation bosses in The Hague and Amsterdam. Paradoxically, though, this made it harder for Eichmann's man in the Netherlands, Willi Zöpf, to make his presence felt. Anti-Jewish policies and the control of Jewish affairs flowed from the Central Office for Jewish Emigration, the Zentralstelle, set up under Härster's auspices. It was nominally managed by Willy Lages but actually run day-to-day by an SS captain, Ferdinand aus der Fünten.[168]

The Germans left routine administration to the top civil servants of each ministry, the general secretaries. They were coordinated by Karel Frederiks, the most senior of their number, who ran the Interior Ministry. Frederiks believed his mission was to preserve the existing personnel who conducted local government in the provinces, cities and towns, thereby blocking the advance of Dutch Nazis and resisting the imposition of German appointees. His other priorities were to safeguard public order, resuscitate the economy and ensure the supply of food. In order to achieve these goals he was prepared to reach many compro-mises with the Germans; he was certainly not prepared to jeopardize his authority or that of provincial governors and mayors for the sake of the small Jewish minority.[169]

The readiness of Dutch civil servants to defend the rights of Jewish citizens was further undermined by the apparently piecemeal way that the occupiers proceeded. On 2 July, on German orders, Jews were expelled from the air raid protection service. At the end of the month, *shechita* (the slaughter of cattle according to Jewish religious law) was banned. None of these measures seemed very oppressive. In late August, however, the Germans instructed Frederiks and his colleagues to require that all civil servants declare their 'Aryan' status. The general secretaries swallowed this, too. Only some university staff and church leaders objected to the requirement to attest whether one was an Aryan or not. They could see where this was leading. On 4 November 1940, Wimmer instructed the general secretaries to dismiss all civil servants who were non-Aryans. After an anguished debate the civil servants capitulated. In a token gesture of resistance they agreed only to suspend rather than sack Jews from public office. This merely delayed the final indignity until March 1941.[170]

Whether or not it was a premeditated strategy – and it is most likely a reflection of how unprepared the Germans were – their step-by-step approach left Dutch Jews with the feeling that little had altered and that things were not so bad. Then, at the start of 1941, the situation lurched suddenly and ominously. On 6 January, the Germans commanded the registration of all Jews in the Netherlands. This labour-intensive exercise was conducted through the Dutch civil service and enjoyed its full compliance. The census – which revealed 140,552 'full' Jews, 14,549 'half' Jews and 5,719 'quarter' Jews – served as the basis for the issuance of new ID cards stamped with a 'J'. The ability to identify Jews on the street enabled the Germans next to decree the exclusion of Jews from a range of occupations, sports and recreations. Jewish-owned businesses were marked.[171]

Within the Nazi regime there was a vigorous debate as to whether the Amsterdam Jews should be formally ghettoized and, a related question, how to eliminate Jewish traders from the sprawling open air market at the heart of Amsterdam. Both questions acquired a certain urgency due to persistent brawls between Jews and Dutch Nazis, and on occasion German soldiers, who barrelled into the market intent on mischief. On 12 February, Hans Böhmcker, the Nazi commissioner for Amsterdam and an advocate of ghettoization, dispatched Dutch police to seal the Jewish quarter on the pretext that it was a hazard to public order. During the day he also summoned the Chief Rabbis of the Ashkenazi and the Sephardi communities along with Abraham Asscher, the president of the Great Synagogue who was also the head of the main Dutch Jewish refugee relief organization. Bömcker explained the rationale for shutting off access to the Jewish areas of the city and told them to form a Jewish council, Joodse Raad, to serve as an interlocutor and executive for future measures. Asscher agreed to take on the task of forming the council but the two Chief Rabbis stepped down and several other nominees declined to serve. The sole representative of the Jewish workers also soon departed, leaving a group that consisted overwhelmingly of the Dutch Jewish bourgeoisie. Nevertheless, by the end of the day Asscher had assembled a credible team, co-directed by Professor David Cohen, who had been working side by side with him for several years on behalf of German refugees. The following morning the Joodse Raad held its first meeting and declared that it would have a 'predominantly executive and mediatory task, but could not bear responsibility for the orders it had to transmit, nor could it accept orders that were dishonourable to the Jews'. Asscher and Cohen introduced the council to Amsterdam Jews at a mass meeting that same evening. The Germans quickly abandoned the ill-considered effort to construct a ghetto, but the Jewish council remained.[172]

As if to underline the half-baked thinking that informed German decision-making and actions, Dutch Nazis continued to harass Jewish traders and young Jews continued to respond forcefully. On 19 February a brawl flared up in an ice-cream parlour out of which the Dutch Nazis came off the worst. This time the Germans responded with a large-scale raid on the Jewish district by Ordnungspolizei, during which they seized 400 predominantly young, male Jewish hostages. The German police conducted the operation in broad daylight and with a brutality that shocked the Jewish community and the city's inhabitants at large. Communist-led Dutch labour organizations, which had been restive for some time, were galvanized into bringing forward strike action, their indignation against the Germans bleeding into their economic demands. The strike spread across the city on 25 February, paralysing municipal services, the docks and the trams. Over the next two days German order police and SS units assailed the strikers, resulting in seven deaths and many more casualties. The strike was broken and despite the sacrifice it achieved nothing for the Jews. On 27 February, 389 hostages were deported to Buchenwald. Some time later 340 were transferred to Mauthausen. Within a few months all were dead.[173]

The general strike was a courageous act but it had tragic consequences. While sympathy for their Jewish compatriots did not diminish, ordinary Dutch people were chastened by the repression that active gestures invited. The fact that the unfortunate hostages were sent to concentration camps in Germany led to the impression that all subsequent deportations were directed to similar destinations. However bad they might be, it was believed that concentration camps were survivable. Hence the strike of February 1941 perversely influenced Dutch perceptions of the fate awaiting the Jews and, more importantly, their capacity to do anything that might avert it.[174]

German strategic dilemmas and Judenpolitik in occupied Poland

At its worst the experience of Jews living under German rule in western Europe bore no comparison to the horrors inflicted on the Jews in German-occupied Poland between June 1940 and June 1941. During the battle for France, Polish Jews followed the news closely, knowing that their future depended on the outcome. The mood in Warsaw rose and fell with each bulletin. 'Misery after the defeat of Norway', Emanuel Ringelblum jotted down. 'Our spirits have fallen.' When the Germans broke the French line on the Meuse he wrote, 'The population is enveloped in deep melancholy.' Disregarding his anger against the British over their handling of Palestine, Chaim Kaplan rejoiced that they locked horns with Germany. His glee soon turned to gloom: 'Every military victory of the Nazis ... casts us into melancholy.' The fall of Paris elicited 'weeping and wailing'. With his usual perspicacity Kaplan speculated that it might be better for the Jews if the Germans now finished off the war quickly. Italy's entry into the war was a blow to those who still had a chance to emigrate because it meant that Italian ports were closed to them. Mary Berg's mother made a desperate journey to Berlin to find a way out of Europe; it was too late.[175]

However, the increasingly appalling conditions under which Jews languished were not simply the result of racial anti-Semitism or an intended policy outcome. Rather, they were a consequence of the strategic impasse in which Hitler found himself in the autumn of 1940. Policy towards the Jews, such as it was, stemmed from a succession of failures to find a way to remove Jews either from German living space or the Reich's wider sphere of influence, failures that related directly to the course of the war and the 'unconscious incompetence' of the German military leadership.[176]

At the end of July 1940, Hitler called his most senior commanders together at the Berghof. The Leader still considered an invasion of Britain, but meanwhile he entertained various alternatives. The Mediterranean option involved the conquest of Gibraltar and a drive on the Suez Canal in cooperation with Mussolini's troops in Libya. Under blockade and cut off from the empire, Britain would then be forced to surrender. However, this plan required the compliance of Spain and the assistance of Vichy France, which still commanded significant naval assets. The continental option rested on Hitler's conviction that Britain was staying in the fight in the hope that America would enter the fray or that Russia would attack Germany. He believed that a victorious assault on the Soviet Union would remove that hope. It would also free Japan to turn on America, depriving the British of succour from across the Atlantic. There was general agreement that, one way or another, Germany would end up in a showdown with the USSR and the United States. Over the next four months, Hitler explored all these angles.[177]

He was frustrated at every turn. Franco was reluctant to commit Spain except at an impossibly exorbitant price: fuel, arms, weapons, and chunks of the French Empire in north and west Africa. Marshal Pétain was equally unwilling. Finally, Hitler travelled to Florence to confer with Mussolini, who had, in the meantime, launched an ill-judged invasion of Greece. Inadvertently this sucked Hitler into a version of the Mediterranean option, but without his full-blown commitment. Shortly afterwards, Vyacheslav Molotov, the Soviet foreign minister, arrived in Berlin for talks. It was a fraught visit, punctuated by a British air raid that reminded his German hosts of their dilemma: Britain was still at war with Germany and Germany was still in an awkward strategic position. In July 1940, Stalin had seized Bessarabia and northern Bukovina from Romania. Hitler was forced to concede this land-grab while he took on the British and the French. But it placed Soviet forces within striking distance of the Romanian oil fields at Ploesti, the only major source of mineral oil for the embattled Reich. By the autumn it seemed to Hitler that there was no alternative to confronting the Soviet Union. It was essential to push back the Red Army in order to protect the Ploesti oil region and, by defeating the USSR, remove Britain's last potential ally on the continent. Furthermore, success would leave the Third Reich in control of limitless natural resources that would render Germany invulnerable to blockade and fully up to wrestling with America.[178]

On 17 September 1940, Hitler postponed Operation Sealion; a month later the invasion was called off indefinitely. Instead, he instructed General Brauchitsch, commander-in-chief of the army, to prepare plans for an invasion of the Soviet Union to take place in May the following year. In Directive 21, issued on 18 December, Hitler announced his intention to 'crush the Soviet Union in a rapid campaign'. He had, of course, always anticipated a Manichaean struggle with Jewish Bolshevism. Victory would not only eliminate the greatest threat to the Volk, indeed to mankind, it would also offer huge territories in which to settle the German people. And it offered a solution to the pressing question of what to do with the Jews.[179]

Despite the secrecy attached to Operation Barbarossa, word of Hitler's broad intentions percolated throughout the Nazi hierarchy. During November, Eichmann was working on a memorandum for Himmler summing up progress towards solving the Jewish problem. In the final version, dated 4 December 1940, he mentioned 'the final solution of the Jewish question. Through resettlement of the Jews from the

European economic sphere of the German Volk to a territory as yet to be determined.' Theo Dannecker used a similar formula in a letter to Eichmann several weeks later and Eichmann repeated it at a meeting in the Reich Propaganda Ministry in March 1941. The precise location of the region 'to be determined' was hinted at in the record of a discussion that Heydrich had with Göring regarding areas of responsibility in the territories in the east that it was anticipated would soon fall under German control. Heydrich wanted to ensure that Alfred Rosenberg, who was designated to head a new ministry for the occupied eastern territories, was under no misunderstanding about who would be controlling Jewish affairs there.[180]

At the same time as these decisions were being taken in Berlin, Arthur Greiser and Hans Frank were adjusting policy in the expectation that Jews would soon be removed from their provinces. In June 1940, Frank had been led to believe that the Jews dumped in his backyard would soon be shipped off to Madagascar. For this reason he suspended efforts to create a ghetto in Warsaw: why bother if the Jews were on the way out? Unfortunately for him nothing came of the Madagascar pipedream and, worse, in early 1941 Heydrich proposed a scheme to displace 1 million Poles into the General Government. To Frank's relief, though, on 15 March 1941, Heinrich Müller, the head of the Gestapo, vetoed any further transports. This time the rationale was the anticipated removal of Jews to Siberia following the defeat of the Red Army. Between these dates, however, Greiser and Frank were forced to improvise ways to deal with the presence of huge, impoverished Jewish populations. These improvised measures had calamitous effects.[181]

At the end of July 1940, Greiser and the Higher SS Police Leader for the Wartheland, Wilhelm Koppe, met with Frank and the senior SS personnel in the General Government. Greiser sought Frank's agreement to let him deport the Lodz Jews to the General Government because 'it would be impossible to keep these Jews packed together in the ghetto over the winter'. Koppe added that 'the situation regarding the Jews in the Warthegau worsens day by day'. They had only agreed to establish the ghetto in Lodz on the assumption that the Jews would be swept into the aborted Lublin reservation. But Frank refused to help out. For a while it looked as though Madagascar would provide an alternative, but by September that too resembled little more than a mirage. In the absence of any possibility to expel the Jews from Litzmannstadt (Lodz), Greiser adopted the approach pioneered by Biebow. This involved an extraordinary U-turn. On 19 September, the German city government approved a loan of 3 million Reichsmarks to keep the ghetto afloat. Without this, Rumkowski would have been unable to feed his workers or obtain the raw materials his workshops needed. The loan created an entirely new nexus between the ghetto and the city, the Jews and the Germans. A month later Greiser and Übelhör signalled that Rumkowski could enlarge his workshops. He responded by creating a Central Bureau of Factories, devoted in part to scrounging equipment from Jewish communities that were being liquidated elsewhere in the Wartheland. During the course of the year production inside the ghetto broadened to underwear, furs, leather goods, wooden and metal items, brushes and electrical components. Although private contractors established firms in the ghetto, such as the Josef Neckermann Underwear and Clothing Factory, the bulk of orders came from the German army. By September 1941, the ghetto was producing 2.5 million items of clothing for the military.[182]

Over 5,000 Jews worked for the Jewish council, known as the Beirat. This sprawling organization had a multitude of agencies dealing with finance (including rent collection), food and fuel provision, rationing, the allocation of labour, welfare, education, policing and justice. It included a statistical and records bureau (also responsible from January 1941 for keeping a chronicle of events), a fire department and a post office. The housing department was responsible for running tenements and also finding accommodation for Jews displaced into Lodz from other towns and, later, Jews deported to the ghetto from western Europe. All these offices carried perks, most immediately the immunity to forced labour outside the ghetto. Beirat employees usually worked indoors in heated rooms and were assigned higher rations than other workers. Above all, employees of the Beirat had connections that offered them a degree of security and all sorts of opportunities for private enrichment at the expense of fellow Jews.[183]

One of the most important branches of the administration was the Order Service formed at the start of May 1940. Often called the ghetto police, the Order Service (OS) was intended to do what its name suggested rather than carry out the roles normally associated with a police force – that is, prevention and detection of crime. As Rumkowski explained: 'On the basis entrusted to me, I have established an Order Service Guard for the protection of the Jewish population and for the maintenance of calm and order.' Rumkowski called on the Jewish population 'to be strictly obedient to the Order Service and to obey their commands unconditionally. Acts of resistance and contravention will be punished.' He expected the Order Service men, who reached a maximum of 530 officers and other ranks, to 'behave calmly and politely towards the public'.[184]

Rumkowski set out to create an equal society inside the ghetto by regulating labour, income, rationing, housing and providing welfare services for everyone. He contrasted his regime with that in Warsaw where Adam Czerniaków presided over a laissez-faire system that, Rumkowski claimed, encouraged extremes of wealth and poverty, leading to high rates of mortality. In fact, due to incompetence and corruption, the Beirat manufactured inequality. Once word reached the ghetto about the atrocious conditions in the forced labour camps dotted across the Wartheland, only the most desperate men volunteered to meet the weekly and sometimes daily requisitions for workers. Around 40 per cent of men summoned simply failed to turn up while 10 per cent bought a substitute to take their place. The ability of rich or well-connected Jews to buy their way out of forced labour caused resentment and cast a shadow over the Beirat's reputation, but Rumkowski needed the revenue. The forced labourers were paid so badly that the Beirat expended RM1 million on subsidies for their dependants. Hence, only the poorest and most vulnerable marched out of the ghetto to toil on drainage projects, railways, road building and forestry. Few of the labour camps had medical facilities and rations were even worse than in the ghetto. Those who were injured or fell sick were often shot. Almost none of the 12,000 sent out to work ever returned. Eventually, Rumkowski deployed the Order Service to seize men for labour. He also used the manpower requisitions ruthlessly as a means to get rid of people he considered troublemakers.[185]

The provisioning system was equally open to manipulation and unfairness. In June 1940, Rumkowski introduced a ghetto currency (called 'mark-receipts') and prohibited use of the Reichsmark and Polish zlotys. The idea was to allow the Beirat to calibrate wages, rents and the cost of food to what the ghetto was earning as a whole and eliminate inequalities based on savings. In conjunction with control of the currency, the Beirat attempted to regulate the importation and consumption of food. For a period there was a mixed economy combining an official ration with a number of sanctioned food outlets under private ownership, at which people could purchase whatever they could

afford. Private restaurants co-existed alongside soup kitchens. Unfortunately, so many people lacked the means to purchase what they were
permitted under the rationing system that almost half the population
were eating less than their entitlement. Meanwhile, the cost of supplying free meals to the poor, to schools and hospitals was rocketing. At
the end of 1940, the Beirat took over the entire food supply and distribution network. Everyone now had to purchase ration cards *and* pay for
their food and meals. The Provisioning Department ended up controlling seventy public kitchens in tenements and workshops, plus over
a dozen private establishments. The Beirat expended more than RM16
million on food in 1940.[186]

But this was only half the story. The Germans ordained that in
terms of calories each Jew would be entitled to roughly what a prisoner
of war could expect. In reality, the delivery of food was erratic and the
quality was often poor. Inside the ghetto the Beirat established a nutritional hierarchy that penalized the non-working population. Senior
administrative workers and those employed by the Beirat in heavy tasks
such as waste removal, along with skilled workers, received the most.
Other Beirat employees, Order Service personnel, fire fighters and
factory workers were awarded a lesser basic ration but were entitled to
various supplements such as meat and sausage when they were available. Factory workers could also buy meals in their workplace. Children
got specially concocted cheap meals and those who were sick were prescribed restorative foods. The unemployed had to survive on the basic
ration. This amounted to around 1,000 calories per day. In optimal circumstances, those in work could hope to get about twice as much.
However, since a normal human being working during the day requires
approximately 3,000 calories to maintain their health and 2,400 is the
minimum needed to survive, even the most privileged in the community were starving.[187]

The consequence of overcrowding, poor sanitation and undernourishment was a soaring rate of mortality. According to the statistical
office, 6,197 inhabitants died in 1940, 11,378 in 1941 and 18,134 in
1942. The chief killers were dysentery, typhus and tuberculosis – all of
which were easily avoidable in normal times. They struck in seasonal
cycles. Dysentery was most severe in the summer and was aggravated
because the Germans made it difficult to remove faecal waste or contain
it safely. Even the Germans recognized this danger. Mayor Werner
Ventzki wrote to Übelhör in November 1941, 'The hygienic facilities in

the ghetto are as pitiful as one can only imagine . . . So if due to the density of the population an epidemic breaks out, it will be a danger not only for the ghetto population but to the city.' What the Germans most feared was typhus, the original pretext for the enclosure of the Jewish residential quarter. Typically typhus struck in the spring and raged until summer. It ravaged the most abject, the young and the old. Tuberculosis, which was related to malnutrition and overcrowding, was the next most predominant killer. Jews arriving from small communities and ghettos often brought diseases with them and were more prone to die than the indigenous population, which had better access to medical care and nutrition. German Jews sent to the ghetto, mostly elderly, had very poor life expectancy. Jews from Vienna and Prague managed better, partly thanks to their knowledge of Yiddish and their ability to find their way around faster. Isaiah Trunk, historian of the ghetto, estimated that overall between May 1940 and August 1944, 43,800 people died, when the normal mortality over this period ought not to have exceeded 5,100 souls. Ultimately one third of the ghetto population perished due to the conditions imposed by the Germans.[188]

The Beirat's health department struggled to improve hygiene and control epidemics. It ran several hospitals with up to 2,000 beds and nearly 200 doctors. But it was hamstrung by a terrible shortage of medicine and equipment. Rumkowski also tried to protect the most vulnerable through the establishment of special institutions: an orphanage, a home for the aged, and a summer camp in the less densely populated Marysin quarter where youngsters with TB could spend a couple of weeks inhaling relatively fresh air and enjoying sunshine.[189]

Poverty and relentless toil bore down on the health of the family as much as the welfare of individuals. Round-ups and deportations for forced labour had so skewed the gender balance in the ghetto that by the end of 1940 there were almost 50 per cent more women than men. Thousands of wives and mothers not only had to care for their families alone, they had to work to feed them. Absent fathers and working mothers meant that children were often left unsupervised during the day. Gangs of juveniles roamed the ghetto looking for food and getting up to mischief. Even when husbands and fathers remained in the ghetto they were very likely to be unemployed and unable to provide for their families. Youngsters lost respect for parents who could not house, clothe or feed them adequately; mealtimes became an ordeal of humiliation and helplessness that could tear families apart. Some young people chose to leave and forage for themselves, existing on the margins of legality. Unsurprisingly, the birth rate plummeted. Apart from the undesirability of bringing new life into such a ghastly place, men were frequently rendered impotent by exhaustion, malnutrition and illness while women ceased menstruating for the same reasons. The Jewish family was dying, too.[190]

Social solidarity in the ghetto all but collapsed as pre-war class formations and the ties that accompanied them evaporated. The bourgeoisie were stripped of their comforts and shared culture; Jewish workers were wrenched out of the secure employment on which collective action rested. A nouveau riche class appeared that inverted former class relations. In a crazy reversal of fortunes the residents and owners of slum properties in the Baluty district suddenly became property magnates, able to let rooms at exorbitant rates. The criminal element who knew the district intimately had the edge over the newcomers and the Order Service. Intellectuals and pre-war politicians found themselves marginalized; Rumkowski had no wish to debate policy with sensitive souls or men who felt they had to respond to popular feeling. During July 1940 Bund activists and members of Poale Zion (the labour Zionist Party) channelled unrest against the paucity of food supplies and the inadequate ration for those without means. On 10–11 August hundreds gathered in front of the Beirat shouting, 'We want bread, we're dying from hunger.' When the numbers grew too large for the Order Service to disperse them with rubber truncheons and batons, Rumkowski notified the Germans. A unit of order police with rifles made short work of the protest. Although Rumkowski publicly denounced the 'irresponsible elements that want to bring agitation into our life' a few days later he held private talks with workers' representatives and made significant concessions. He faced another strike wave in December 1940, this time by ghetto employees. Rumkowski now felt much stronger and denounced the strikers as 'criminals'. He had the leaders arrested and sent to labour camps.[191]

Rumkowski may have developed a dictatorial streak, but he took huge pride in Jewish education and for as long as possible defended schooling in the ghetto. During 1940 and 1941, the Jewish administration devoted significant resources to the education of children and vocational training. The ghetto maintained no less than forty-five elementary schools attended by 6,263 children, with two religious schools, one secular institution and a college for teaching crafts. Of the 7,336 children receiving full-time education, three-quarters got free meals. The schools also provided employment for teachers and instructors. Rumkowski encouraged them to foster a 'national spirit', using Yiddish as well as teaching Hebrew and Judaism. Dawid Sierakowiak was one of those who benefited from Rumkowski's commitment to education. While men were being registered for forced labour and sent out of the ghetto, he was attending the Zionist-run school in Marysin.[192]

Rumkowski also saw the value of cultural activity, as long as it was carefully regulated. Musical performances, dramatic productions, poetry readings sprang up spontaneously, often in connection with the soup kitchens, where they provided entertainment and a moment of escapism. The Bund supported a Yiddish cultural society that promoted lectures and concerts, until Rumkowski shut it down in March 1941 as part of his drive against political parties, dissidents and 'troublemakers'. Instead, the Beirat labour department mounted concerts and revues at the grandly named House of Culture. The influx of Jews from Germany, Austria and Czechoslovakia brought with it an accession of talented artists. In 1941 there were one hundred concerts. The Beirat employed artists to adorn official reports and statistical presentations. It also maintained a library: the most popular books were classics in Polish and German. The Polish translation of François Mauriac's life of Disraeli was one of the most frequently borrowed volumes.[193]

While he was not religious himself, Rumkowski defended Sabbath and festival observance and made immense efforts to ensure that there was appropriate food to celebrate the Jewish high holy days. The Beirat employed several rabbis, notably in the Cemetery Department, and maintained a rabbinical court comprised of ten distinguished local rabbis plus five who arrived with the Jews from western Europe. The Germans, however, targeted religious Jews and Jewish observance relentlessly. They routinely forced Jews to work on Yom Kippur, the holiest day of the Jewish ritual calendar, and after 1942 compelled them to observe Sunday as a day of rest. In addition to banning Kashrut, they forbade the wearing of beards, side-curls and traditional dress. Many religious Jews conformed to these prohibitions, but others resisted. A group of Orthodox Jews, called the B'nei Horeb, ran study circles and offered private lessons to children. One religious association campaigned, in vain, against the consumption of non-kosher food; another devoted itself to fixing mezuzot on the doorposts of homes and institutions. There was a society that offered free bread and coffee for Jews prepared to make the blessings and observe the rituals before eating.[194]

Only the most resolute could withstand the pressure to abandon tradition. The rabbinical court granted exemptions on the consumption of non-kosher food and relaxed the regulations concerning marriage to enable women whose husbands disappeared into the labour camps to remarry. Josef Zelkowicz, a Yiddish author who came from a Hassidic background, charted the decay of religiosity with an unflinching eye. In one story, he sketched the fate of a Hassidic rebbe whose followers gradually deserted him: 'when life became cruel and pitiless and the soul froze and atrophied inside the body, the Hassidim forgot about their rebbe . . . Instead of dreaming about "Torah", they dreamed about "flour".'[195]

Observers noted the dramatic erosion of moral standards in the ghetto: crime was endemic, almost always centred on foodstuffs. Those in the food supply chain practised fraud, adulterating and short-weighting the produce that passed though their hands. Gangs of youngsters and starving men raided shops, warehouses and wagons. There were murders for food. In one case a Hassid killed a thirteen-year-old girl to get her ration coupons. During the winter of 1940–1, Jews also stole combustible material, sallying out after nightfall to rip apart fences and entire wooden buildings to fuel stoves and cookers. Although extreme hunger was the chief motor of criminality, Zelkowicz attributed the pervasive moral degeneration to the brutish conditions of life. 'Grave crimes were committed in the ghetto. The gravest of them was the transformation of people who had worked for decades to main-tain their culture and ways, the fruits of millennia of efforts, into predatory beasts after half a year of life under inhuman conditions. Overnight they were stripped of every sense of morality and shame. Ghetto inhabitants pilfered and stole at every opportunity whether they needed the booty or not. Some rummaged in the trash like pigs for left-overs, which they ate there and then. Some starved and died, but others exploiting the opportunities available to them stole, pilfered, gorged themselves, and drank themselves silly.'[196]

The crime wave grew so severe that in January 1941 Rumkowski set up a summary court; after three months its chairman was arrested for corruption. The Order Service referred the most heinous offences, such as murder and rape, to the German criminal police, who maintained a post inside the ghetto. Lesser infractions were handled internally and could carry a custodial sentence; the Order Service maintained a prison for such malefactors. In March 1941 this establishment held 200 Jews on various charges, although many of them were 'troublemakers' who had crossed Rumkowski rather than felons. According to Zelkowicz the real law breakers escaped justice. 'Managers of the food shops had the very best victuals – meant for the entire population – sent to their homes with the mediation of their lackeys in the Kehilla [Beirat]. To make up the shortfall that their pilfering created, they cheated their "customers" on weights. The supervisors of the summary-justice courts left these pirates and thieves, who controlled the ghetto streets, untouched and unaccountable for their crimes.' Vice and promiscuity were equally rampant. The OS had a special unit to combat prostitution although it turned a blind eye to the prevalence of mistresses attached to members of the Beirat.[197]

The winter of 1940–1 was particularly cruel for the inhabitants of the ghetto. In January a group of pre-war writers, poets and academics began recording daily events for an official chronicle, collecting documents and conducting research. The first entry stated baldly: 'Today 52 people died in the ghetto. The principal cause of death was heart disease, followed by exhaustion from hunger and cold with tuberculosis in a third place.' Thefts continued but the Order Service itself was restive over wages, fuel and food supply. The authors of the chronicle wrote under the patronage of the Elder of the Ghetto and in danger of examination by the Germans, so they employed Aesopian techniques to disguise their real meaning. But the facts spoke for themselves. Over the next three days, for example, the fuel shortage worsened, food deliveries were erratic, there was a three-day 'backlog' for burials, and a starving mob attempted to loot a turnip wagon.[198]

In a desperate attempt to increase rations for the population as a whole, Rumkowski ordered a reduction of the allocation for skilled workers. The cut led to protests by militant carpentry workers that culminated in the occupation of the joinery workshops. After negotiations failed Rumkowski sent in the Order Service. The carpenters were locked out of their shops, condemning them to starvation, and the ringleaders arrested. At the end of the month the strike was broken. When food protests recurred in March 1941, the chronicle recorded: 'Chairman Rumkowski made it known that he is bringing the most rigorous of methods to bear against individuals who impede him in his work, the criminal element in particular; that is, malefactors and notorious criminals, and thieves of public property are being ousted from the ghetto and sent to do manual labour in Germany.'[199]

Throughout April, transports left Lodz for labour camps. Sierakowiak commented with relief that 'All the letters that arrive from those sent out for labour assure us about satiety there.' The ghetto inhabitants were not to know, but the deployment of Jewish labour was connected with the build-up of German forces in preparation for the assault on the Soviet Union. Ironically, the voracity of the German armed forces as they geared up for the invasion acted as a tonic on the ghetto economy: orders poured in. In May 1941 Greiser toured the factories with an entourage of officials and journalists. On 7 June the ghetto received an even more illustrious visitor: Himmler. The entire population was placed under curfew while the Reichsführer-SS went to the German ghetto administration in Baluty Square and then inspected a clothing enterprise. The new mayor of Litzmannstadt, Karl Marder, reflected that since the decision in the previous October not to dissolve the ghetto it had evolved into 'a significant element in the economic system'. German attitudes were transformed not just by the benefits that the ghetto brought to the Reich; one of Eichmann's men, based in Poznan, insinuated that 'Übelhör . . . does not favour the liquidation of the Lodz ghetto because it gives him an opportunity to earn a great deal of money.'[200]

Although more Jews gained employment the food situation remained dire throughout spring 1941. The ghetto was shocked by the case of a father who concealed the rotting body of his dead child in order to collect the infant's ration; but this was far from an isolated case. People driven to the edge by starvation, unable to sell anything or earn money, committed suicide by throwing themselves off the bridge that crossed the Aryans-only road bisecting the ghetto. By a supreme effort, Rumkowski secured flour to produce matzoh for the Passover festival although other basic foods were perilously short. Sierakowiak noted sardonically, 'Our holiday starvation will be identical to what we experienced every other day of the week.' He had secured a job in a warehouse, weighing out turnips, and was able to monitor the 'system of connections employed by the people doing the weighing to favour clerks and other parasites'. Things improved in early summer and Rumkowski was able to arrange an extra ration of bread for the festival of Shavuot. However, as the German army reached its maximum strength it sucked up supplies, leaving Poles and Jews with the scrapings. Quite literally: one shipment of flour consisted of the detritus swept off the floor of a flour mill. In August 1941, according to the chronicle, 'a freight car of meat arrived in the ghetto. It had been travelling for three days. The meat was covered with worms.' Ghetto food experts tried to salvage what they could, but only succeeded in triggering a wave of food poisoning. To Zelkowicz the apt symbol of the ghetto was not barbed wire or the yellow star: 'The symbol of the ghetto is the pot.' All people could think about was the ache in their stomachs and where they could find something to eat. The death rate soared again, overwhelming the cemetery department. 'Decent people bury their dogs with greater dignity than the people of the ghetto are buried', he despaired.[201]

Amidst this horror children continued to attend school. At the end of the final term, 700 high-school students sat their examinations. The soup kitchen for the intelligentsia managed to provide up to 1,000 meals per day, offering those 'who are today déclassé and pauperized . . . a clean and well-set table . . . and, finally, pleasant surroundings and good company'. Although the political opposition to Rumkowski was cowed by the arrests and deportations in March–April 1941, groups continued to meet covertly. Dawid Sierakowiak had begun reading Marx and Lenin and considered himself a communist; he attended a meeting of his 'union' and remarked that 'we've become a committed element of the political movement in the ghetto'. On May Day he joined a celebration at which a communist teacher 'pointed out the need to hold out and survive the ghetto. She spoke of being ready to act and fight.' A month later, two communist teachers were fired by Rumkowski, that 'sadist-moron'.[202]

Dawid was buoyed up by letters from a friend in Warsaw and by news about the war. The ghetto was not cut off from the outside world. Indeed, it had one of the busiest post offices in Poland. In March 1941 it handled a million letters and postcards, 135,000 parcels from the Reich, and over 14,000 from other countries. The parcels often contained food that supplied the ghetto's black economy. One of the major informal currencies was tobacco. That month smokers were gratified by the delivery of 1.5 million cigarettes. By mid-1941, when Germany launched Operation Barbarossa, Jews and Germans had developed a lopsided rapprochement underpinned by rational self-interest. In the short term the invasion would lead to an improvement in conditions in Warsaw as in Lodz.[203]

In the Warsaw ghetto

Warsaw Jewry avoided full ghettoization until November 1940. Indeed, the period from mid-May to mid-August was marked by vacillation and confusion amongst the city's German rulers. On 10 June work was completed on the barrier around the Jewish residential district, but at the start of July the SS officer who liaised with Czerniaków told him that the war would soon be over and that the Jews 'would all leave for Madagascar'. A fortnight later, Czerniaków heard that the Germans had abandoned the idea of a ghetto. In fact, German planners had returned to the notion of a closed Jewish quarter but had given up the idea of locating it on the city outskirts. During August they published details of the quarter where Jews would be permitted to live and sent a delegation to Lodz to see how it was done there. Czerniaków noted in mid-September, 'The project of the ghetto outside Warsaw has been abandoned. In its place the Sperrgebiet.' (This was the area previously demarcated off-limits to Germans and Poles on health grounds.) Waldemar Schön, the director of the Resettlement Office, reasoned that in addition to the necessity of separating Aryans from Jews, a closed residential district was essential for health reasons and to prevent Jews draining the city's food supply. In theory segregating the Jews would cut their access to the black market, depress prices and release food for the Polish population to consume.[204]

The proposed Jewish living area was significantly smaller than the quarantine zone and Czerniaków haggled over every street and building. On the eve of the holy day marking the Jewish New Year, 2 October 1940, Ludwig Fischer, the district governor, decreed that Jews had until the end of the month to move into the Jewish district; conversely, Poles had to relocate over the same period. He also issued instructions to Czerniaków to establish an Order Service. Nothing, though, could avoid the chaos that ensued when 138,000 Jews who were obliged to leave their homes moved in, while 113,000 Poles moved out. The disruption was so severe that the Germans agreed to extend the deadline by two weeks. On 16 November, the ghetto was sealed. From this point Jews would need permits to enter or exit through one of the twenty-two gates (later reduced to thirteen) that were guarded on the outside by German order police and Polish policemen. The German contingent consisted of one lieutenant and eighty-seven other ranks: from their point of view it

was an extraordinarily efficient use of manpower. When the ghetto was
finally severed from the outside world it covered 452 acres and was surrounded by 11 miles of wall. About 395,000 Jews were confined within,
an average of 128,000 per square kilometre. Because only 375 acres were
covered by residential buildings the density of population was actually
greater than this equation suggests, with 9.2 people per room. Thirty
per cent of Warsaw's population was jammed into less than 2.5 per cent
of the city's area. Yet the Germans constantly decanted more Jews
into the ghetto from surrounding districts and, eventually, deportees
from the Reich. They also periodically excised streets and blocks, reducing the availability of housing still further.[205]

In terms of numbers, the movement into the ghetto was roughly
equivalent to merging the Jewish population of the Netherlands into the
Jewish population of France. The population exchange was made even
more anarchic by the ghetto's shifting boundaries. Sometimes Jews had
to move two or three times because the building they went to was
re-zoned. Czerniaków was himself caught up in the confusion, spending several days looking for accommodation for himself and his wife.
Helena and Stanislaw Szereszewska made their move weeks earlier,
possibly anticipating the dénouement because Stanislaw was so well
connected. They located a three-room, bomb-damaged flat, which they
occupied along with their daughter, granddaughter, son-in-law, and his
mother and sister. Thanks to the wealth they managed to salvage they
had the services of a Polish maid for several months, and a Jewish maid
thereafter. The gas and electricity meters continued to be read by a
Polish municipal employee until June 1942. But the Szereszewska family
belonged to the aristocracy of the ghetto. Stanislaw ran the Welfare
Department of the Jewish council and went to work each day with
starched shirt and clean collar. Their youngest daughter and son-in-law
worked for the Jewish council, too; their niece was married to an Order
Service man. Less fortunate people repeatedly begged Helena to help
them get jobs. Mary Berg's family had the good fortune to find accommodation on Sienna Street, one of the best thoroughfares assigned to
the ghetto (although eventually it would be switched to the Aryan side).
Nevertheless, they too were joined by other family members and sub-let
a room.[206]

For most Jews the formation of the ghetto was a nightmare. Large
numbers clung to their homes until the last minute in the hope that the
edict would be suspended. When there was no miracle, Bernard Gold-

stein recalled, 'Everywhere there was wild panic, unashamed hysterical terror. People ran frantically through the streets, a deathly fear unmistakable in their grim, weary eyes. They searched desperately for any kind of conveyance to transport their belongings. The multitude filled the streets, a nation on the march. Long, long lines of little carts and all sorts of makeshift vehicles heaped with household possessions, wailing children, the old, the sick, the half dead, moved from all directions towards the ghetto, pulled or led by the stronger and healthier, who plodded along, tearful, despairing, bewildered.' In the precincts of the ghetto, 'the unfortunate hunted for living quarters, an apartment, a room, a corner of a room, anything. They searched the cellars, the hallways, the rubble of bombed-out buildings, for a place to lay their heads or shelter their children. They lay on the streets or roamed through the gutters, soaked by the rain, shivering from the cold, hungry, worn-out, helpless.'[207]

Jews watched the wall being completed and wondered what it would mean. Mary Berg heard some people express approval because the wall would insulate Jews from raids by Poles and Germans. Stanislaw Adler, a lawyer who had returned to Warsaw from Soviet-ruled eastern Poland, noticed that many Jews, fed up with assaults by Volksdeutsche, 'hoped for improved conditions once they were assembled in a closed quarter'. Chaim Kaplan, Zionist and champion of Orthodoxy, greeted the ghetto decree with satisfaction: 'They have segregated us as a separate ethnic group, and this separation has made us into a nation, living alone with all its cultural, literary and artistic attributes.' He changed his tune when he confronted the perils of extreme congestion. 'There is no filthier place capable of spreading contagious diseases, than a Jewish trolley on a single ride, where everyone is infected, where sick people sweat and slobber on you.' As he digested the implications he was gripped by apprehension. 'A closed ghetto means death by starvation in a concentration camp with inhuman living conditions.' The influx of people was stupefying: 'There is no room in the ghetto – not an empty crack, not an unoccupied hole.' The Jewish council tried to get a grip on the crisis, calling on house and building committees to supply information about any spare accommodation. However, rents soared and so did the cost of food. As soon as Jews were cut off from the free market, shortages occurred and prices rose. Kaplan's hopes for Jewish self-government had turned into a sick, disastrous parody. 'Polish Jewry', he lamented, 'has been destroyed.'[208]

The number of ghetto inhabitants fluctuated over the following year. Tens of thousands left (usually unwillingly) to perform forced labour and tens of thousands died. Meanwhile, 130,000 refugees were forced in. The ghetto reached its peak population of 445,000 in April 1941. Feeding, housing and finding employment for this mass of humanity was insuperable. Initially, the Germans had no interest in the ghetto developing any kind of economy to generate jobs and revenue. To the contrary, the forced relocation of population had produced mass unemployment by tearing artisans away from their ateliers, depriving them of raw materials, and cutting them off from their markets. The Jewish council desperately tried to reconstruct the Jewish economy inside the ghetto, scraping together or cannibalizing machinery to form workshops and recycling anything that could be used for raw material. German perceptions changed during 1940, partly due to the transfer of forces eastwards and the possibility of production for the military. Towards the end of the year the establishment of the Transferstelle under Alexander Palfinger and army demand for carpentry, brushes, and clothing began to exert a positive effect.[209]

With the preparations for Operation Barbarossa, the General Government became a vast military base area and transport hub. Suddenly Hans Frank, who as Governor-General of the Occupied Territories had responsibility for their well-being, could see value in the ghetto. In January 1941 he convened a meeting to explore ways to harness production to the war effort and increase output. The new policy resulted in a certain liberalization of the regime, allowing for the opening of synagogues and schools. The advent of Heinz Auerswald as commissioner for the Jewish district in May 1941 further transformed the district's economy. The Transferstelle was removed from the resettlement department and attached to the office of the new commissioner. Auerswald appointed Max Bischoff, who had gained experience in Lodz, to manage its operations in a commercial spirit. Under Bischoff, the Transferstelle was turned from a provisioning agency into an import/export business, seeking orders, purchasing raw materials, and handling financial transactions. The Germans actually set up a clearing bank, later utilizing a branch of the Polish Cooperative Bank. German entrepreneurs and businessmen gravitated to the Jewish district, many acting independently of the Transferstelle. Thirty factories were established inside the ghetto, with eighty-five smaller firms and no less than 1,900 businesses. However, throughout 1941 the ghetto failed to break even. It

cost the Jewish council 12.6 million zlotys per month to feed the inhabitants, but the most it earned monthly was 1.2 million zlotys. While
45,000 Jews were employed in productive enterprises this was only two
thirds of the number needed to generate sufficient revenue to cover the
council's expenditure. Furthermore, the Germans continued to exert a
stranglehold over the food supply. The result of the persistent shortfall
was a crippled Jewish council and a catastrophic nutritional deficit.[210]

Immediately following the announcement of the ghetto, Adam
Czerniaków summoned a meeting of the Jewish council and appointed
commissions to handle housing, the economy and establishment of the
Order Service. The council, housed at 26 Grzybowska Street, mutated
into a quasi-government, but with little money and limited authority. It
had twenty-six departments covering finance, labour, trade and production, provisioning, housing, welfare, health, education, internal policing,
sanitation and the postal service. Like Lodz, Warsaw was connected to
the outside world by mail. In May 1941, the postal service received
114,000 letters (including telegrams and money orders) and dispatched
29,000 postcards. That month 113,000 packages arrived, mostly food
parcels that provided sustenance for families and specialities that could
be sold to delicatessens. One peculiar feature of the ghetto was the
role played by the municipality, which continued to supply the Jews
with water, electricity and gas. The council had to negotiate separately
with Polish officials responsible for these services and hundreds of city
employees were given permits to move in and out. These meter-readers
and maintenance men frequently acted as couriers for information and
were a mainstay of smuggling. Czerniaków thus had to deal with a host
of Polish and German bureaucrats, but he was ultimately answerable to
the security police and the Jewish office of the Gestapo. While steering
between these agencies, with their conflicting priorities, he had to
manage the demand for forced labour, oversee the ghetto institutions
and raise funds.[211]

Czerniaków, who could not speak Yiddish and was not particularly
observant, favoured Polonized Jews and converts for senior roles in his
administration. At best, such men had useful connections on the outside, but beneath the patina of sophistication they were often incompetent and lacked empathy with the Jewish masses. Kaplan complained
that 'Strangers in our midst, foreign to our spirit, Sons of Ham who
trample on our heads, the president of the Judenrat and his advisers are
muscle men who were put on our backs by strangers. Most of them

are nincompoops no one knew in normal times. They were never elected and would not have dared dream of being elected Jewish representatives.' Kaplan derided Czerniaków personally: 'Who paid any attention to some unknown engineer, a nincompoop among nincompoops, who was an assimilationist not for ideological reasons but for utilitarian purposes.' Stanislaw Adler was rather more respectful. He viewed Czerniaków as 'a man of crystal clear character but weak convictions'. The council chairman could be indecisive and verbose and was 'easily impressed by people who were ready to undertake action even if they had questionable ethical standards'. Like Rumkowski, Czerniaków became less and less tolerant of debate and dissent. In April 1941 Ringelblum grumbled that 'The Jewish council has adopted the old Czarist slogan: "Keep quiet. Don't argue." No discussion is permitted at any of their meetings and certainly no questions.' Czerniakow was 'regarded as an idol. His edicts are not to be questioned: his word is command.' It smacked of the 'Führer principle'. Yet no one doubted the chairman's courage. In February 1940 he was offered an emigration certificate for Palestine, but chose to stay with his people. He had contempt for members of the elite who got out when they had the chance. More than once he was detained and beaten. And he was no youngster: Czerniaków went through one such ordeal just a few days before his sixtieth birthday.[212]

Yet conditions in the ghetto were not only attributable to German malice and the impossible economic situation; some of the suffering was self-imposed, the result of decisions made by Jews. In August 1940, the labour department was compelled to supply the Germans with 1,000 men per week; by November 30,000 were slaving for the Germans. The news that trickled back from camps in the Lublin area was so dismal that the council sent doctors and truckloads of food and clothing. Meanwhile, the welfare department had to maintain 70,000–80,000 dependants in the ghetto. To avoid alienating the rich and to cover this huge expenditure, Czerniaków allowed those with means to buy substitutes. So the rigours and brutality of the labour camps fell most heavily on the poor. Rather than impose a tax on personal wealth, he chose to use indirect taxes on consumables that everyone had to purchase regardless of their income. Again, this imposed the heaviest burden on those least able to afford it. Basic services such as waste removal were subcontracted to entrepreneurs who got rich through smuggling. Finally, he relied on voluntary payments by the well-off and self-taxation from the house and building committees to support welfare and health services. His laissez-faire approach was a recipe for confusion, corruption and inequity.[213]

When the Order Service was launched it claimed an exalted mission and was able to pick and choose from the cream of the ghetto, mainly lawyers and middle-class men. Many of its senior personnel, though, were Polonized Jews and several were refugees from Lodz. They knew the Order Service there but felt no particular bond with Warsovians. To run the service, Czerniaków selected Jozef Szerynski, an ex-colonel of the Polish police who brought experience and the promise of close cooperation with the Poles. But Szerynski was a Catholic convert and quickly earned the hatred of the ghetto. His force started with 1,000 patrolmen, plus an administrative organization of several hundred, reaching a peak of 2,500 in July 1942. Its first tasks were escorting labour columns to and from the ghetto, patrolling the streets to regulate vehicle traffic and pedestrians, and preventing petty crime. It also enforced sanitation regulations and quarantined buildings where typhus was detected. One unit kept order in the Jewish council building and another maintained a prison. Order Service men manned the ghetto gates, which handed them a key part in smuggling. Although the service was awarded good rations and had access to health care, its members did not receive pay. Inevitably, they started exploiting their activity to earn money. In addition to facilitating smuggling for a cut of the profits, they took bribes from men evading forced labour.[214]

When they first appeared on the street, the Order Service men caused Jewish hearts to beat faster. Mary Berg experienced 'a strange and utterly illogical feeling of satisfaction when I see a Jewish policeman at a crossing'. Even the usually sceptical Kaplan was charmed by the sight: 'The residents of the ghetto are beginning to think they are in Tel Aviv. Strong bona fide policemen from among our brothers, to whom you can speak in Yiddish! First of all it comes as a godsend to the street vendor. The fear of the Gentile police is gone from their faces. A Jewish policeman, a man of humane sensibilities – one of our own brothers would not turn over their baskets or trample their wares.' However, Stanislaw Adler, who joined up to avoid labour service, saw the force from the inside and quickly gained a different impression. Although he was asked to draw up a legal code governing the operation of the force he received no remuneration; he had to sell his belongings to survive. Adler saw other servicemen in the same position resort to partnerships with smuggling gangs, Poles and Jews, passing entire truckloads of contraband through the ghetto gates for a generous fee. This illicit activity 'badly demoralized the Order Service. Large and uncontrolled incomes allowed many to lead debauched and corrupted lives. Against a background of universal impoverishment and misery, this contemptible conduct resulted in a macabre effect and it helped to erect a barrier not only of loathing, but of absolute hatred between them and the rest of the population.' The rot started at the top: Czerniaków left Szerynski to run his department and Szerynski used this autonomy to appoint cronies. Since none of the department heads or district chiefs had an adequate budget, private initiative was at a premium, blending institutional priorities with personal gain. As decent men left the service they were replaced by opportunists and criminals.[215]

To complicate the administration of law and order, a separate anti-smuggling unit, the Office to Prevent Profiteering and Speculation, was set up by the German security police in late 1940. Dubbed 'The Thirteen' because it operated out of 13 Leszno Street, it consisted of 300–400 men under Abraham Gancwajch. They were mostly not from Warsaw and a fair number were recruited from the criminal fraternity. Gancwajch set out to undermine Czerniaków by setting up and funding a rival network of welfare agencies. A long power struggle ensued between his shady outfit and the Jewish council until the Gestapo tired of its creature and dissolved it in mid-1941. The Thirteen was reputed to include Gestapo agents, although according to Rabbi Huberband, from the first instance the ghetto was 'flooded with a huge number of informers, collaborators, blackmailers and thieves'. The porters who helped Jews to move in would frequently lead Germans to the homes and stashes of the wealthy. Carpenters who built hidden spaces to contain jewellery 'were well paid for such work. But in many cases they informed on the wealthy Jews.'[216]

Unemployment, inadequate rations, hunger and swarms of refugees led to begging, crime and even cannibalism. Of 173,000 inhabitants of working age only half had anything like a job: 50,000 worked in manufacturing, 18,000 eked out a living from commerce, mostly street trading, while 9,600 were employed by the Jewish council, including 3,000 in the Order Service. The Jewish council issued the population with ration cards to cover staple items: flour, sugar, potatoes, kasha, marmalade, bread, soap and matches. But unless they were destitute, ghetto residents had to pay a tax on their ration cards. In January 1941,

20 per cent were exempted from paying this impost, finally reaching 140,000 in October 1941. By this time 34 per cent of Jews in the ghetto were so poverty-stricken they could not even afford to purchase ration cards. The only way to survive was by getting supplementary meals or by purchasing food on the black market, which led to grotesque inequalities. Ultimately, this life-sapping deficiency stemmed from the Germans' refusal to supply the ghetto with anything like adequate provisions and the council's inability to purchase more through the Transferstelle. It was worsened by the uneven rate of food deliveries, which depended on the whim of the Germans, but it was aggravated by adulteration and cheating by the food handlers inside the ghetto.[217]

The paucity of rations forced Jews onto the black market, the motor that propelled smuggling. The chief conduits for contraband were municipal employees and labourers who went to and from the ghetto each day, specialist gangs and children. Workers employed outside the ghetto purchased produce and concealed it in their clothing when they returned. Sometimes gangs cooperating with Polish policemen and the Order Service at the gates were able to bring in wagons packed with foodstuffs. Youngsters were particularly adept at crawling through breaches in the fence and openings made in cellar walls enabling passage between the ghetto and the Aryan side. One of the main routes was via the cellars under the municipal courts. Leszno Street, which bordered the wall, was another prime smuggling location. Bags were tossed over, packages were hurled from the tram that passed through, and even livestock was brought in via the Jewish cemetery. It was estimated that illicit imports exceeded the amount legally admitted to the ghetto by a factor of forty. Over 80 per cent of provisions were the result of smuggling operations. The effect on Warsaw's economy was so pronounced that the Germans repeatedly tried to crack down, imposing the death sentence on smugglers. German order policemen routinely shot and killed Jews caught in the act or even those who strayed too close to the barrier.[218]

Adults who would have been conspicuous on the Aryan side arranged for children to cross over to obtain food. Kaplan noted that 'These children are clever, and they are sent by their parents to buy food cheaply. Usually they are successful in their mission, and bring home bargains.' Adler rhapsodized over the child smugglers, easily distinguished by the rents in their garments caused by the jagged apertures they passed through in the course of their risky business. 'Sole breadwinners of their families, they spend hours lying in wait in order to glide like an eel at the moment the gendarme wiped his nose or the policeman turned his back.' If they were captured they could expect a beating and were frequently lacerated with barbed wire.[219]

Poor nutrition, appalling overcrowding and abysmal sanitation combined to generate repeated epidemics and a phenomenal mortality. The main scourges were typhus, tuberculosis and oedema. Professor Ludwik Hirszfeld, a world-renowned expert on typhus who became chairman of the ghetto's Health Council, summed up the causes pithily: 'If you pack into a district 400,000 ragged paupers, take everything away from them, and give them nothing, then typhus is created. In this war, typhus is the work of the Germans. And history might even forgive medicine for this. For you cannot make German medicine responsible for political crimes. But it will not forgive the lie that responsibility for the epidemic which they themselves called forth, lay on the shoulders of the Jewish council.' Typhus was commonly imported by refugees and the worst phases of the disease coincided with major inflows, in January–May 1940 and January–March 1941. Lice flourished on filthy bodies encased in rancid clothing. There was not enough soap in the ghetto and what could be found was poor quality. Nor were there enough private or public baths. The sanitation teams sent to quarantine and disinfect houses were regularly bought off by tenants who feared the inconvenience and loss of income if they could not go to work. Para-doxically, there were more doctors per person inside the ghetto than outside but they lacked medicine and facilities. The ghetto had one large general hospital that ran an inoculation service and pharmacies, and boasted a single X-ray machine. At the height of the epidemics it was so packed with the sick (and dying) it did more to spread illness than con-tain it. There was also a well-equipped children's hospital. Self-employed doctors ran expensive private clinics and dispensaries, often supplied by smugglers. But nothing could alleviate the enormous death toll. In 1941 it reached 43,000, fully 10 per cent of the entire ghetto population. Mortality eventually levelled off in the autumn when the food supply and employment situation improved and the sanitation effort paid off. The other reason was tragic: the most vulnerable, particularly the old, the frail, and the very young, had already died.[220]

The Jewish council endeavoured within its limited power and resources to provide welfare for precisely these groups. The welfare department ran shelters and soup kitchens for refugees and subsidized the dependants of forced labourers. There was also an elaborate network of independent relief organizations operating under the umbrella of ZTOS, Jewish Self-Aid, which received funds from the AJJDC until November 1941. These organizations consciously arrayed themselves against the Jewish council, promoting a spirit of self-reliance as against paternalism and encouraging democratic participation. They worked closely with the spontaneously formed tenement and house committees that took charge of sanitation, organized childcare, and raised funds in their locale. Mary Berg entered public life by putting on a show in her building to raise money for refugees from Lodz. Bernard Goldstein and other Bundists tried to use the tenement committees to restore a semblance of social cohesion and collective action, turning courtyards into community centres and making them a platform for political work. But the money that trickled down from the AJJDC was 'a pebble thrown into a bottomless pit'.[221]

A range of charities focused on the plight of refugee children and orphans. The TOZ organization (Society for the Protection of Health) worked to improve hygiene and combat tuberculosis. It ran a clinic with an X-ray machine, day-care centres, and twenty-three soup kitchens for children, each one equipped with a doctor and trained nurses. CENTOS (Central Organization for the Care of Orphans) maintained the central refuge for street children, thirty other children's homes, and an orphanage directed by Poland's foremost child-care expert, Janusz Korczak. Michael Zylberberg remarked that to Korczak, keeping Jewish children fit and happy in his clean, bright and meticulously run establishment on Chlodna Street was a form of resistance. 'He regarded the struggle for life as a personal battle with the enemy.' Toporol, a society that offered agricultural training, marshalled youngsters to cultivate vegetables on the few patches of arable ground within the walls and supplied the produce to CENTOS. Another pre-war charity, ORT, provided vocational training that proved enormously important because it enabled youths to enter the workforce in skilled occupations such as leatherworking, carpentry and metallurgy. Mary Berg went to ORT classes to learn graphics and her sister was taught how to make children's clothing. There were about 48,000 children of school age in the ghetto, including 10,000 refugees. Until it was permitted in late 1941 schooling continued covertly on a limited scale, mainly for those who could afford to pay for private tuition singly or in groups. Kaplan, a teacher himself, boasted to his diary that 'Jewish children learn in secret. In back rooms, on long

benches near a table, little children sit and learn what its like to be
Marranos [secret Jews in the era of the Spanish Inquisition]. Teaching
went on at the homes for children and soup kitchens. Pre-war youth
movements and parties arranged clandestine gymnasia, including Dror,
where Yitzhak Zuckerman was a teacher, and Tarbut, the Hebrew-
oriented cultural organization. Religious Jews ran numerous classes and
one underground school for girls, Bet Yaakov. Sadly, most children got
their education on the streets, where they absorbed harsh lessons in
survival under awful circumstances.[222]

Illicit schooling and artistic creativity became means to fight the
dehumanizing effects of German policy and conditions in the ghetto.
Bernard Goldstein recollected that 'As a reaction to the campaign of
hatred and discrimination against the Jews, educational and cultural
activity took on a new importance. The ghetto days were marked by a
compulsion to build spiritual and moral defences – compensation for
our utter helplessness.' Kaplan, who was otherwise rather staid, welcomed the 'frivolity in the ghetto, in order to somewhat lessen its
sorrow . . . It is almost a mitzvah [good deed] to dance . . . Every dance
is a protest against our oppressors.' The council established a Central
Committee for Artists that registered nearly 300 actors, musicians and
singers. Professionals and amateurs, like Mary Berg, put on shows to
raise money for good causes. The ghetto supported a full symphony
orchestra that regularly played to packed houses at the Melody Palace.
There were several theatres, including the Eldorado and the Femina,
each catering for different kinds of audience. For those with spare cash
it was possible to see an operetta, a Yiddish melodrama or a classic
European play performed by professional actors every week. Stanislaw
Adler observed a 'craving for books' that was as intense as the distraction of card-games. Several privately run lending libraries did brisk
business, although borrowers had to be careful in case the volumes they
took out were lice-infested.[223]

Religious Jews, who formed a majority of the population, maintained the observance of tradition with an energy and fortitude that
many observers found inspiring. The Germans had long banned
shechita and until late 1941 forced the synagogues to stay closed. Collective prayer, monthly visits to the ritual bath, Sabbath and festival
observance all went on in secret. During the high holy days in October
1940, Chaim Kaplan ruefully confided to his journal, 'We have no
public worship, even on the high holy days. There is darkness in our

synagogues, for there are no worshippers – never before in our history, drenched in tears and in blood, did we have so cruel and barbaric an enemy.' Nevertheless, the believers were not intimidated. 'Secret minya-nim [prayer quorums] by the hundred throughout Warsaw organise services, and do not skip even the most difficult hymns in the liturgy. There is not even a shortage of sermons. Everything is done in accordance with the ancient customs of Israel.' He felt pride when Hassidim celebrated the festival of Sukkot with song and dance. Chanukkah was marked with even greater fervour since it evoked the struggle for freedom. The festival of Purim in March 1941 occasioned great merriment, which Kaplan shared with a group of like-minded Zionists at their soup kitchen. They made music, sang, read poetry and enjoyed the traditional cakes, hamentashen, with coffee. Individual Hassidic sects continued to cluster around their rebbe, studying when possible and worshipping as tradition prescribed. In February 1941, Ringelblum reported, 'In the prayer house of the hassidim from Braclaw on Nowo-lipie street there is a large sign: "Jews Never Despair!" The hassidim dance there with the same religious fervour as they did before the war.' The Jewish administration strained to ensure that there would be food appropriate for the festivals, particularly Passover. Ringelblum noted in April 1941 that 'Passover Seders complete with meat, kneidlech, wine were held at many of the refugee centres. For a brief moment the refugees were able to forget the sadness of their situation and their misery. The Seders were a source of spiritual strength to the exhausted and homeless refugees.'[224]

The concentration of Jews in one place had curious effects on religious observance. Shimon Huberband observed the fluctuations and adaptations of religiosity in the ghetto for the Oyneg Shabas project. He noticed that because there were no non-Jews in the ghetto it was impossible to find Gentiles to kindle a fire on the Sabbath. As a result, more Jews had recourse to the traditional Sabbath repast, cholent, a stew that was prepared before sundown on Friday and kept hot in a baker's oven to be consumed the next day. He noted, wryly perhaps, that when the Germans mandated observance of the Sabbath in 1941, the Order Service was given the job of enforcing rest and fining violators. This caused howls of protest from the genuinely observant who pointed out that it was futile to make unwilling Jews keep the Sabbath, especially if in the process the enforcers themselves violated it by levying fines or taking bribes.[225]

The strangest and saddest manifestation of faith was the community of about 5,000 non-Aryan Christians. Many of them lived on Sienna Street where, in December 1940, Mary Berg observed them taking delivery of Christmas trees smuggled into the ghetto. She was struck by the painful situation of their children. 'These Christian children, born of Jewish parents are now living through a double tragedy as compared with Jewish children. They feel entirely lost . . .' While she looked on them with a compassionate eye, Chaim Kaplan viewed their existence as 'a truly unique tragicomedy'. Czerniaków saw no problem appointing converts to the Jewish council, but the rabbis in the ghetto protested vehemently. They had no interest in the paradoxes of Nazi racial policy that forced converts back into a Jewish community they had chosen to leave. Michael Zylberberg captured the absurdity of their predicament: 'They suffered as Jews and finally died as Jews, unable to resolve the terrible dichotomy created by their religious and philosophical conflicts . . . For us it was an inevitable adjunct of our heritage; for them it was an additional burden, an unrelieved trauma.'[226]

Daily life in the ghetto was characterized by a lack of space and privacy, a constant hubbub, disgusting smells and distressing sights. While certain avenues such as Sienna and Chlodna were lined by handsome buildings inhabited by the well-off and privileged, more were dominated by rows of grim tenements that resembled ant-heaps. In September 1941, Ringelblum remarked that 'On Sienna Street, where the Jewish aristocracy lives – particularly the baptized Jews – fashion is in full swing again. Smartly dressed women promenade up and down . . .' By contrast, Edward Reicher, entering the ghetto for the first time in December 1940, was 'completely stricken' by the vista he encountered. 'Filthy, narrow, dark streets. Swarms of children, a huge tattered crowd. Leszno Street led straight to hell. There were market stalls along both sides, one after another, selling cheap, shoddy merchandise . . . Next to them were poorer traders whose tables were spread with spools, thread, ribbons, lace, pins, or nails . . . There were peddlers too, with all their wares on their back – bric-a-brac, clothes, often even dirty laundry. The sidewalks were dotted with hundreds, even thousands of beggars pleading for a piece of bread . . . Most were so weak that they could no longer sit up.' Because the tenements formed steep canyons, Kaplan observed that to catch sunlight 'mothers take up positions on the sidewalks with their children's cradles and they lean against the sides of buildings all along the street'. Where Bernard Goldstein lived, 'continual fights took place for access to the kitchen, the bath, the toilet, the right to use the gas or get a key to the entrance door. The privacy of family life, even of the bedroom, could not be preserved.'[227]

People became accustomed to the new occupational and social hierarchy, signified by the armbands of the Order Service, the Jewish council staff, welfare and health workers. Inequality defined the ghetto. Those who had managed to bring money and valuables with them could obtain practically anything that was available outside. Employees of the administration who took bribes (most of them), anyone connected with the food supply system, owners and managers of workshops, corrupt OS men, smugglers and criminals provided the clientele for smart clothes shops, delicatessens, restaurants and nightclubs. In private Czerniaków raged against 'The arrogant rich [who] talk back, each and every one of them, taking advantage of my good will.' He was appalled when he heard that his deputy and other council officials went to 'a party with caviar, smoked salmon and brandy'. But such indulgence was widespread. Ringelblum, who was a socialist, noted that 'A number of caviar shops have been set up.' Yet when 'appeals were made to the Warsaw rich to levy a tax on themselves for the benefit of the refugees, they replied "That won't help. The paupers will die out anyway."'[228]

In the spring of 1941, Mary Berg, who belonged to the golden youth of the ghetto, wrote gaily that 'new cafés and expensive grocery stores have appeared, where everything can be had. On Sienna Street and Leszno Street, women are seen in elegant coats and dresses fashioned by the best dressmakers.' For those who could afford it there was a 'beach' on a piece of open ground where 'For two zlotys one can bask in the sun for an entire day. Bathing suits are obligatory.' Berg patronized nightspots like the Café Sztuka where Wladsylaw Szpilman played. He recalled that 'Besides the concert room there was a bar where those who liked food and drink better than the arts could get fine wines and deliciously prepared cotelettes de volaille or boeuf Stroganoff. Both the concert room and the bar were nearly always full.' He also played at a rather less respectable establishment, Café Nowoczesna, where 'To the sound of popping champagne corks, tarts with gaudy make-up offered their services to our profiteers seated at laden tables.' He added caustically that 'No beggars were allowed outside the Nowoczesna. Fat doormen drove them away with cudgels.'[229]

Prostitution was a common sideline of waitresses in the restaurants. At Café Hirschfeld, Mary Berg saw 'the most expensive liqueurs, cognac, pickled fish, canned food, duck, chicken and goose. Here, the price of a dinner with drinks is from 100 to 200 zlotys. The café is the meeting place of the most important smugglers and their mistresses; here women sell themselves for a good meal.' It was not the only place in the ghetto where sex was for sale: the Britannia Hotel was notorious. According to Adler, who worked for the OS, 'Clandestine prostitution was carried on in the circles of dancers, barmaids, and waitresses; they drew their clientele from Jewish Gestapo men, collectors of spoils . . .' Ringelblum realized that women were selling sex in order to survive. 'Recently streetwalking has become notable,' he wrote in January 1941. 'Yesterday a very respectable-looking woman detained me. Necessity drives people to do anything.' Edward Reicher, who obtained a job as an inspector with the housing department, gained insights into the lengths to which poor women were driven. He documented the case of an eighteen-year-old girl whose family was starving. 'Prostitution was the only way out, but Yola had too much integrity.' So she became a smuggler, instead, using her looks to charm her way past the police at the gates. This only shifted her vulnerability to sexual exploitation from one location to another. One day, a Pole stopped her on the Aryan side and when she begged him to let her go replied, '"Oh no, you're too pretty for that. You can go afterwards."'[230]

Starvation eroded moral standards relentlessly. Adler remarked, 'How can one speak of moral behaviour in a concentration camp . . . Or of culture in a place where every day hundreds of human beings die in the street of hunger and disease?' Children who could no longer be fed were abandoned on the steps of the Order Service headquarters. Gangs started excavating bodies from the mass graves under cover of darkness in the hope of finding gold in the dentures of the deceased. Families would offer refuge to the terminally ill in order to strip them of their clothing and sell it once they were dead. There were cases of cannibalism. But the most prevalent manifestation of moral decay was the epidemic of theft, with Jews preying on each other mercilessly. Ringelblum recorded that 'The hunger is so great that the poor people are snatching bread from the equally poor bread vendors.' In his eyes, though, the greatest crime was the inequality of suffering. 'The rich boys are working on the police force, in the community organisations, or are registered with the sick fund as supposedly employed by various firms – but, most important, they can always buy their way out of work-camp duty.' By spring 1941 when the pool of volunteers for forced labour dried up, the Order Service began to press-gang those without work. In response, Jewish men vulnerable to apprehension hid or resisted. Their evasion led to a downward spiral of pursuit and violence. Between 19 and 21 April, the Order Service smashed their way into the homes of men requisitioned for labour and dragged them to the Germans. These were 'hideous days', Ringelblum lamented, 'and they will forever be remembered unto the Jewish council as a mark of shame'.[231]

The refugees who poured into the ghetto existed at the bottom of the social and economic scale. They were driven out of communities that had been plundered and wrecked over a period of months. Many had been penned in temporary ghettos where they had starved and fallen prey to typhus. Since the men had been taken for forced labour, the refugees were overwhelmingly the old, the very young, and female. Mary Berg recalled that 'All of them tell terrible tales of rape and mass executions.' They arrived 'ragged and barefoot, with the tragic eyes of those who are starving . . . They become charges of the community, which sets them up in so-called homes. There they die, sooner or later.' The Jewish administration bathed, quarantined and provided quarters for the refugees in hostels that rapidly became squalid slums. In April 1941 there were 17,000 of them. Michel Mazor recollected that 'They had no inkling that in a very short time, hunger, filth, deprivation, sickness, and a promiscuous lack of privacy would transform them into living corpses – emaciated or inordinately swollen – with only agony and death to follow. A terrible fatality hung over these people, and nothing in the life of the ghetto could defeat its implacable course.' Without jobs or possessions they were driven to beg on the streets, where thousands expired: in the summer they were stricken by dehydration and malnutrition, in the winter they froze to death.[232]

During the spring and summer of 1941, the conjunction of hunger, disease and the influx of refugees turned Warsaw into a city of death where the sudden extinction of life was an ordinary occurrence. Ringelblum registered the numbness that overcame the population: 'Almost daily, people are falling dead or unconscious in the middle of the street. It no longer makes a direct impression . . . Death lies in every street,' he wrote. 'The children are no longer afraid of death. In one courtyard, the children played the game of tickling a corpse.' Social structures could no longer cope. 'The mortality rate is so high that the house committees have to worry now as much about the dead as about the living'. Since it cost 15 zlotys to bury someone, corpses were hauled out of buildings and left on the pavements. It was then up to the OS to arrange for the cadavers to be taken to mass graves in the Jewish cemetery. These pits were shallow and covered with a meagre layer of sandy soil. As a result, 'On hot summer days, the stench from these mass graves is so strong you have to hold your nose when you pass.' Bernard Goldstein reported, 'sick children lay, half-dead, almost naked, swollen from hunger, with running sores, parchment-like skin, comatose eyes, breathing heavily with a rattle in their throats. The elders stood around them. Yellow and gaunt, whimpering in their weakness, "A piece of bread . . . A piece of bread . . ." The street [Leszno] was packed with people: death, death and more death; yet there was no end to the overcrowding. People elbowed their way through the noisy throngs, fearing to touch each other, for they might be touching typhus.' In some buildings where the last member of a family died the corpse would lie, rotting, until the smell alerted neighbours. Rats fed on decomposing bodies in houses where starvation and typhus had carried off all the residents. 'If things continue this way', Ringelblum wrote bitterly, 'the "Jewish Question" will soon be resolved very quickly in Warsaw.'[233]

Ringelblum did not know that at this very moment the Germans were, indeed, planning to resolve the 'Jewish Question', but not in Warsaw or Lodz or Lublin. The war was taking a fateful turn, entering a phase that would have shattering consequences for Jews across the continent.

PART FIVE

BARBAROSSA

1941

Planning for 'special tasks' in Russia

Hitler's invasion of the Soviet Union on 22 June 1941 was a turning point in the Second World War and came to be seen as 'a tragic turning point' in German anti-Jewish policy. According to the historian Martin Gilbert, 'a new policy was carried out, the systematic destruction of entire Jewish communities'. However, Hitler did not order the invasion primarily because of anti-Semitism, or even anti-Bolshevism (which amounted to much the same thing in his mind). The decision to invade stemmed from his strategic dilemma in mid-1940, and policy towards the Jewish population in the opening phase of the campaign was, if anything, a continuity of earlier practices. To be sure, the number of Jews murdered was far greater than in Poland in 1939 but the wave of targeted killings followed by anti-Jewish regulations and the formation of ghettos demonstrated a striking contiguity. When anti-Jewish measures lurched into a second, incomparably more destructive phase it was the result of a foundering military campaign. The contest of arms, more than a preconceived agenda for the treatment of the Jews, created the conditions for a murderous dynamic of unprecedented proportions and stupefying savagery. Both originated from the same German quandary: how to fight and win a war with limited resources against more powerful enemies.[1]

A year earlier, Germany appeared to be at the height of its power. Yet Britain refused to capitulate and the Reich found itself saddled with responsibility for sustaining the countries it had vanquished as well as supporting its allies. Thanks to the continuing British blockade and the inability of France, Belgium and the Netherlands (plus, later, Yugoslavia and Greece) to feed themselves, it was simply not feasible to sit tight. Before long German industry would run short of raw materials, the military would have to draw on stocks of fuel and lubricants, while famine would threaten Europe. The impending crisis was no secret: William Shirer was briefed to this effect by government officials. He reported that the German Foreign Office 'told us today [8 August 1940] that Germany declines all responsibility for any food shortages which may occur in the territories occupied by the German army'. The threat of dearth in the Reich raised the spectre of declining morale and the danger that 1918 could be repeated. This was no fantasy of the regime. In January 1941, Sydney Redecker, the US consul in Frankfurt-am-Main, told the State Department that the population was becoming depressed by the increasing hardships. The 'food situation in particular is a principal source of dissatisfaction'.[2]

The Soviet Union emerged as the key to unlocking this predicament. After Hitler conferred with his service chiefs at the Berghof on 31 July 1940, General Halder summarized the Führer's conclusions, 'with Russia smashed, Britain's last hope will be shattered. Germany would then be master of Europe and the Balkans.' Triumph would leave the Reich in possession of vast agricultural regions that could feed the German population and supply grain to Germany's clients; it would give German industry access to unlimited natural resources; and it would lead to control of the largest oil fields in Europe, putting Germany in a position to challenge the USA for global dominance. But the very factors that drove Hitler towards this expedient rendered it extremely problematic. The assault would consume enormous resources and could not be protracted, because the Reich lacked the wherewithal to sustain a campaign on such a titanic scale for more than a few months. In the short term, hostilities would make the supply situation much worse: it would disrupt the flow of grain, raw materials and mineral oil from Russia as agreed under the German-Soviet pact of August 1939. Victory would have to be swift.[3]

From the outset, the war against the Soviet Union was planned as a 'colonial war of extraction'. It might be more accurate to describe it as a smash and grab operation, since less attention was paid to establishing a long-term colonial regime than to stripping the territory of assets for the war effort and shipping the residue back to the Reich as quickly as possible. During the winter of 1940–41, Herbert Backe, State Secretary for Food and Agriculture and head of the Food Division of Göring's Four-Year Plan, drew up a memorandum on the Reich's food situation for 1941, predicting a significant shortfall due to a poor harvest. Around the same time, he also wrote a paper setting out the implications of a campaign against the USSR. Backe pointed out the enormous growth of home demand for grain and meat products in the USSR due to industrialization and the expansion of its cities. Consequently, the country's grain surplus had steadily declined. If Germany conquered the Soviet Union it would not be sufficient merely to extract this surplus, it would be necessary to 'suppress' local consumption. Furthermore, to feed the German army for the duration of the campaign and the occupation without causing severe shortages for the German population, the army would have to live off the land. Backe stated bluntly that 'the war can only continue if the entire Wehrmacht is fed from Russia in the third year of the war [1941]'. He foresaw that these simultaneous policies would lead to mass starvation and estimated that thirty million Russians would die as a result.[4]

Backe's nutritional prognosis, combined with contemporaneous reports on the supply and stockpiling of fuel, lubricants and crucial raw materials, had a dramatic effect on the military's thinking. In February 1941, General Thomas, head of the army's economic and armaments department, warned General Keitel, chief of the high command, that there were only adequate supplies to keep the army in the field, fully mobile and at maximum fighting capacity until September 1941 – at the outside. The following month, the army set up an Economic Staff East devoted to securing local resources in the context of a rapid, successful campaign; the staff did not anticipate feeding the Russian population or restoring production to Russian industry. On 2 May, Thomas met with the senior civil servants of the Reich ministries for food and the economy, plus other officials, to discuss exploitation of the land. During these discussions Backe reiterated his belief that to feed both the army and the home front it would be essential to strip the Soviet Union bare, even at the cost of 'tens of millions' of deaths. The military did not object to his proposal, although they diverged somewhat by emphasizing the desirability of reviving some industrial production to meet the army's immediate needs. Regardless of any differences of emphasis, on 23 May the army issued 'Economic and Political Guidelines for Operation Barbarossa' that stressed the need to limit food consumption locally so that the maximum could be diverted to the Wehrmacht. Furthermore, the guidelines required that Russia should be divided into a northern grain deficit zone and a southern grain surplus zone. The northern zone contained the majority of the cities and industrial centres, while the south comprised the rich arable lands of Ukraine.

The demarcation line was to be policed so that grain from the surplus zone would be exported solely to the Reich; by implication the cities of the north would starve. 'Many tens of millions of people in this country will become superfluous and will die or must emigrate to Siberia.'[5]

The projected onslaught was not only intended to denude the native inhabitants of the means to live. As planning reached its climax in spring 1941, Hitler, Himmler and the army refined the tools and the procedures to destroy both the military assets and political structures of the USSR.

The Wehrmacht intended to engage the bulk of the Soviet armies close to the border where they were deployed and annihilate them in a series of encirclement battles. Everything was going to be thrown into a fast-moving assault of overwhelming strength and ferocity designed to wipe out Soviet resistance in a matter of weeks. Halder noted in his journal prior to one high command conference, 'force must be used in its most brutal form'. Hitler injected the political dimension into the campaign at a briefing session with 250 of his generals on 30 March 1941. In his notes of the Führer's speech (which lasted two and a half hours), Halder included references to 'colonial tasks' and the 'clash of ideologies'. It was not going to be an ordinary war: with chilling clarity he jotted down, 'This is a war of extermination.'[6]

The task of uprooting and eliminating Bolshevism would fall to the regime's political soldiers: the security police-SD assisted by the order police and the Waffen-SS. To avoid the sort of clashes over jurisdiction that bedevilled Operation Tannenberg, on 13 March 1941 Heydrich commenced negotiations with the quartermaster-general of the army, Eduard Wagner. A fortnight later they concluded an agreement that formed the basis for instructions issued by the army high command to the troops as 'Orders for Special Areas in Connection with Directive 21 [Operation Barbarossa]'. The army leadership stipulated that the Reichs-führer-SS, Himmler, was to be entrusted with 'special tasks for the preparation of the political administration – tasks which will derive from the decisive struggle that will have to be carried out between the two opposing political systems. Within the framework of these tasks the RFSS will act independently and on his own responsibility.' Security police units would get logistical support from the army and liaise with its intelligence officers as well as the secret field police; but otherwise the special units of the Sipo-SD would be left to operate against the civilian population at will.[7]

Taking their cue from Hitler's characterization of the coming struggle, the army gave its personnel legal immunity for ruthless measures against civilians. The 'Decree on the Exercise of Military Jurisdiction' did away with the need to convene courts martial and empowered officers at battalion and regimental level to sanction the execution of individuals caught in acts of resistance or suspected of being involved in anti-German activity. They could also order collective punishments where specific individuals were not identified. In 'Guidelines for the Conduct of the Troops in Russia' the high command explained that the war was not to be fought within the usual parameters. No quarter was to be given or expected. 'Bolshevism is the deadly enemy of the National Socialist German people ... The struggle requires ruthless and energetic action against Bolshevik agitators, guerrillas, saboteurs, and Jews, and the total elimination of all active and passive resistance.' Finally, under the 'Guidelines for the Treatment of Political Commissars', issued on 6 June 1941, officers and men of the Wehrmacht were instructed to separate party officials attached to army units from other prisoners and shoot them immediately.[8]

Despite the habitual conflation of Jews with Bolsheviks, and awareness that 'Jewry is strongly represented in the USSR' (to quote the 'Guidelines for the Conduct of the Troops in Russia'), specific planning for the Jewish population was left late and remained vague. In Hitler's way of thinking the Jews were of course behind every development in the geo-strategic constellation. He saw the attack on Russia as a blow against the 'Jewish' blockade of Germany that was held in place by Jews acting behind the scenes in Washington, London and Moscow. When a coup in Yugoslavia toppled the pro-German regime in Belgrade in March 1941, leading to a treaty of friendship with the USSR, Hitler blamed the 'conspiracy of Anglo-Saxon warmongers and the Jewish men in power in the Moscow Bolshevik headquarters'. Nevertheless, Jewish policy across the continent remained in a 'holding pattern', typified by various blends of emigration, segregation, confinement and exploitation. The planning process for Operation Barbarossa did not produce any specific initiatives regarding the Jews.[9]

To Himmler and Heydrich, control of Jewish policy in the coming struggle was as much about extending their power, and compensating for the setbacks they had experienced after the western campaigns, as it was about the realization of any sweeping vision. Himmler was particularly keen to show Hitler that he was capable of implementing far-reaching settlement plans to colonize the Ukraine, unlike the stop-start disappointments that typified the ingathering of Volksdeutsche to Poland. The closer the invasion came, the grander became the fantasies about *Lebensraum*. For his part, Heydrich was determined to impose his role as pacifier and prevent the army wresting responsibility for security – as had occurred in France. For this reason he envisaged a campaign of unbridled terror, putting all other security agencies in the shade. Since security on the ground was a prerequisite for settlement, Himmler was happy to support him and throw his own units into the fray. However, apart from immediate security issues relating to the Jews, the larger policy seems to have been a continuation of practices in Poland: expulsion to a territory at the fringes of or just beyond the boundaries of National Socialist power. Hence, until days before the campaign opened, the Jews figured mainly in discussions about secur-ity, jurisdiction, and the possibility of exploiting the area beyond the Urals as a dumping ground for European Jewry. The only innovation was that the 'territorial solution' (expulsion) now built on the ambitions that crystallized at the time of the Madagascar episode for removing *all* Jews from *all* the parts of Europe under German domination.[10]

The 'special tasks' assigned to the SS were to be carried out, as in Poland, by task forces or Einsatzgruppen. During March and April, the head of personnel at the RSHA, Bruno Streckenbach, and Heydrich selected the men who would lead each Einsatzgruppe (EG) and the sub-units into which they would break down, the Einsatzkommando (EK) and Sonderkommando (SK). The senior officers were almost all drawn from the higher ranks of the SS Head Office, especially the department heads of the Sipo-SD and Kripo. Well over half of the commanders of Einsatzgruppen, Einsatzkommandos and Sonderkommandos were offi-cers of Sipo-SD, the ideological core of the SS. Many of the lower-ranking positions were filled by cadets from the Sipo leadership school, young men who were soaked in National Socialism. During April and June these cadres received briefing and training at improvised facilities in Pretzch, Düben and Bad Schmeidenburg in Lower Saxony. At the same time, the RSHA pulled together support staff and assigned the 9th Reserve Police Battalion and elements of 1st SS Infantry Brigade to provide the manpower and security that they would need.[11]

Each task force was roughly the size of a battalion with 600–1,000 men (and some women in the clerical and communication sections). The groups were entirely motorized and subdivided into elements that could vary in size from company strength to a platoon – which gave them the flexibility to respond quickly to opportunities or emergencies and to cover a lot of ground, quickly. However, the total force never exceeded 3,000 and it relied on the army for fuel, provisions and quarters. At crucial points they had to call on the army for manpower while at other difficult, and rather more serious, moments the army was prone to summon the Einsatzgruppen to reinforce endangered sectors of the front.[12]

Einsatzgruppe A, under SS-Colonel Dr Walter Stahlecker, was assigned the Baltic area, operating in the rear of Army Group North (comprising 18th Army, 4th Panzer Group, 16th Army). Einsatzgruppe B, led by SS-General Arthur Nebe, the head of the criminal police, had responsibility for Byelorussia and took under its wing the vanguard unit destined for the Soviet capital, the Vorkommando Moscow. It tucked itself behind Army Group Centre (9th Army, 3rd Panzer Group, 2nd Panzer Group, 4th Army). Einsatzgruppe C, commanded by SS-Brigadier General Dr Otto Rasch, followed in the wake of Army Group South (6th Army, 1st Panzer Group, 17th Army). Rasch, who had two doctorates and was addressed as Dr Dr Rasch, was borrowed from his post as commander of the Sipo-SD in Königsberg, where he had overseen the killing of the mentally ill in sanatoria across East Prussia. Rasch had to cover a vast area of north and central Ukraine, including much of the Pripet Marshes. Einsatzgruppe D was headed by SS-Colonel Professor Otto Ohlendorf, seconded from running the Inland Office of the SD. Ohlendorf, too, faced a daunting task as he was directed to operate across the southern Ukraine and down into the Crimean peninsula.[13]

At the temporary bases the officers were informed about the extensive nature of the undertaking. The Einsatzgruppen were expected to ensure rear-area security, seeking out and eliminating resistance. They also had to supply the RSHA with intelligence on the political situation, the mood of the people, and economic data. These situation reports, similar to the secret reports on the Reich that the SD had been compiling since the mid-1930s, were to be transmitted regularly to the head office of the Gestapo in the RSHA, where they would be analysed, digested and distributed. The reports were to include details of arrests and executions. Typically, Himmler added a further layer of senior officers who reported directly to him. These were the Higher SS Police Leaders. One HSSPF was appointed for each army group: Hans

Prutzmann in the north, Erich von dem Bach-Zelewski in the centre and Friedrich Jeckeln in the south. These men were to exercise a crucial command and control function as well as deploying substantial forces of their own to back up the Einsatzgruppen.[14]

The precise content of the briefings for senior commanders and their preparation is hard to reconstruct due to the lack of surviving contemporary documentation. However, it is almost certain that the Einsatzgruppen officers were instructed to seize and execute Jewish men credibly associated with Soviet power. This was the gist of an ill-tempered memorandum to the HSSPF that Heydrich circulated ten days into Operation Barbarossa, setting out guidelines for the activities of the security police and Einsatzgruppen. He explained that 'Owing to the fact that the Chief of the Order Police [Daluege] invited Higher SS Police Leaders to Berlin and commissioned them to take part in Operation Barbarossa without informing me of this in time [22 June] I was unfortunately not in a position also to provide them with basic instructions regarding the sphere of jurisdiction of the Security Police and SD.' He therefore set out 'the most important instructions given by me to the Einsatzgruppen and Kommandos of the Sipo-SD'. These included under the heading 'Executions': 'All the following are to be executed: Officials of the Comintern (together with professional Communist politicians in general; top and medium-level officials and radical lower-level officials of the Party, Central Committee and district and sub-district committees; People's Commissars; Jews in the Party and State employment, and other radical elements (saboteurs, propagandists, snipers, assassins, inciters etc.).' He added the qualification that they were to be killed insofar as they no longer had value as sources of information or 'for the economic reconstruction of the Occupied Territories'. The Einsatzgruppen were also to foster spontaneous actions against Jews. 'No steps will be taken to interfere with any purges that may be initiated by anti-Communist or anti-Jewish elements . . . On the contrary, these are to be secretly encouraged.' This was an invitation to unleash the sort of mayhem that characterized the occupation of Austria in 1938 and the depredations by Volksdeutsche in Poland in 1939, although it is noteworthy that Heydrich did *not* want the SS to be held responsible.[15]

Heydrich's hasty reminder about the functions of the Einsatzgruppen was intended to avoid any confusion about who was in charge of their activities and what those activities were to consist of. It is a striking indication of the haphazard preparations and the usual, bewildering chain of command. It is also significant because it underlines the paramount security role of the Einsatzgruppen: the murder of Jews was a subset of activities devoted to purging the occupied areas of communists, breaking the power of the Communist Party, and eradicating the leadership of Soviet society.

The Jews under Soviet rule

Just over three million Jews lived in the Soviet Union on the eve of Operation Barbarossa, representing about 1.8 per cent of the Soviet population. Although they bulked large in the Nazi imagination, the Jewish citizens of Stalin's Russia wielded little influence, had virtually no power, and were rapidly ceasing to be Jewish at all. Jews had lived on land ruled by the Russian Empire since the eighteenth century but for most of the time were confined to the region on its western borderlands, conquered from Poland, known as the Pale of Settlement. Forced by residential controls into hundreds of cities and small towns, shtetls, across the overcrowded and impoverished Pale, they endured state discrimination and periodic anti-Jewish violence. Nevertheless, Russian Jews were extraordinarily resilient and creative, giving birth to practically every major modern Jewish ideology.[16]

Under Lenin and Stalin they experienced a breathtaking social transformation. Prior to 1917 the Russian Jewish masses were Yiddish-speaking, religiously observant, and mainly earned a living from commerce and crafts. The abolition of residential, educational and occupational restrictions enabled Jews to move into the cities and benefit from both the huge expansion of the state sector and rapid industrialization. By the 1930s, the majority lived in cities and held white-collar jobs or worked in the professions: a quarter of a million Jews lived in Moscow, 224,000 in Kiev and 200,000 in Leningrad. Nearly 90 per cent of the entire Jewish population were urbanized and fully half congregated in just eleven cities. Still, around 290,000 laboured on the land in collective farms, mainly in southern Ukraine and the Crimea. In some districts they enjoyed local self-government. While religious observance had been suppressed since the revolution, Jews were recognized as a separate nationality and enjoyed extensive cultural autonomy during the 1920s. That ended with Stalin's ascendancy: the use of Yiddish was curbed and in the following decade a distinctive Russian Jewish identity began to ebb away as Jews became successfully integrated into Soviet society. Even so, anti-Jewish prejudice persisted. Although anti-Semitism was officially outlawed, it contributed to the gradual removal of Jews from positions of power in the Communist Party and state agencies. Once, Jews had played a disproportionate role in the leadership of the revolutionary movements and the early governance of the USSR, but by the late 1930s they were distinctive mainly by their absence.[17]

The total of Jews in the USSR was greatly increased as a result of Soviet expansion into territories that were historically areas of dense Jewish settlement. Under the Nazi–Soviet pact of August 1939, the Soviet Union had occupied eastern Poland and seven months later annexed Lithuania, Latvia and Estonia, as well as the eastern rim of Romania known as Bessarabia plus northern Bukovina (all previously part of the Russian Empire). This occupation did not just add to the numbers of Soviet Jewish citizens: it had a shattering effect on Jewish society in these regions and poisoned relations between Jews and non-Jews.

The Jewish population of eastern Poland, divided between west Byelorussia in the north and west Ukraine in the south, stood at 1,300,000 in the Polish census of 1931, although refugee movements meant that the actual number was probably closer to one and half million by June 1941. The largest concentration in the north was in Bialystok, a city with a well-developed textile industry and a long tradition of Jewish political activism. Its 42,000 Jewish inhabitants formed 42 per cent of the city's populace. Around 25,000 Jews lived in Grodno. The central region, known as Polesie, was the heartland of the old Pale of Settlement and contained up to half a million Jews, spread across numerous villages, towns, and small cities, like Pinsk and Slonim, with respectively 20,000 and 16,000 Jewish dwellers. A quarter of a million Jews lived in Volhynia, most of them in large towns. In Rovno, Lutsk and Kovel they comprised up to 40 per cent of the inhabitants with a maximum number of 25,000. There were many more smaller places, where Jews might comprise anywhere from 50–60 per cent of the total, although the absolute number ranged from just a few hundred to a few thousand. Jews were a vital element of commerce in these regions. A high proportion were also employed in crafts or small manufacturing. Over half a million Jews dwelled in the southernmost region, eastern Galicia. Approximately one fifth of them lived in the provincial capital Lwow, although this number grew to well over 200,000 due to the influx of refugees from German-occupied Poland. Lwow boasted a large, cosmopolitan Jewish middle class drawing its livelihood from the professions, commerce and manufacturing. A substantial slice of the community was made up of humble artisans and traders, mostly Yiddish-speaking and Orthodox. The countryside was dotted with towns and villages each containing a high ratio of Jewish inhabitants. These shtetl Jews, many of them farmers or part of the agricultural economy, were steeped in Orthodoxy and Hassidism in particular. Galicia had been part of the Austro-Hungarian Empire and Jews had enjoyed civic equality there since 1867. But Lwow and its surrounds was a cauldron of national and ethnic rivalries between Poles, Ukrainians and Jews.[18]

The Jewish inhabitants of Lithuania numbered approximately 147,000 before the war, but their ranks were swollen to over 240,000 by the incorporation of Vilnius after the Soviet annexation and the influx of refugees from Poland. The native Jewish population had a long and distinguished history, boasting several of the world's leading Talmudic academies. Jews were concentrated in the main cities of Kaunus and Vilnius, but there were hundreds of small rural communities, shtetls, across the country where Jewish people lived humble lives, mostly in strict adhesion to traditional Judaism. During the 1920s the Lithuanian Jews had enjoyed a measure of cultural autonomy that enabled Yiddish and Hebrew language schools to flourish, along with every variety of Jewish cultural and political life. Sadly, this expansive environment contracted in the 1930s due to the collapse of democracy and the development of an authoritarian regime. Right-wing nationalist movements that were pro-German and pro-Nazi gained strength in the years before the Soviet annexation, and after the imposition of Russian rule many leading nationalists fled to Germany, where they were nurtured by the Third Reich in preparation for a Russo-German conflict.[19]

A similar dynamic occurred in Latvia, which had roughly 95,000 Jewish citizens. They were concentrated in three cities, Riga, Liepaja and Daugavpils, where they were engaged mainly in business, manufacturing and the professions. There were also many smaller, rural communities in the Latvian countryside. During the 1920s, Jews had benefited from full civic equality and prospered. In 1934, however, a fascist coup curtailed the tolerant atmosphere and allowed nationalistic and anti-Semitic groups to mushroom. The leaders of these movements were pro-German and many escaped to the Third Reich when Soviet rule was imposed in 1940. The exiles worked with Nazi intelligence agencies and the military in anticipation of the time when Hitler and Stalin fell out. Estonia had a tiny Jewish population of 4,500 who lived almost entirely in the capital, Tallinn.[20]

In the Baltic states, across eastern Poland and in Bessarabia many Jews, especially veterans of the Communist Party and the young, acclaimed the Soviet occupation. Nachum Alport, in Slonim, recalled that the Jews 'welcomed the Red Army with joy and relief, as if they sensed an end to Polish anti-semitism. No more discrimination and demeaning of Jews . . . And, more important, no more danger of falling into the hands of the murderous Hitlerites.' Moty Stromer, a small businessman in Lwow, was elated: 'The Soviet government turned many Jews into human beings.' This may only have been the perspective of a few, youthful idealists, but such attitudes coloured the perception of Poles who were suddenly displaced from power and rendered liable to persecution. In fact, the Soviet security apparatus decapitated the Jewish communities, too, arresting office holders and liquidating political along with religious institutions. While some small traders and artisans benefited from Sovietization of the economy, Jewish factory owners and merchants were considered capitalists and saw their businesses nationalized. Professionals, too, suffered a major setback. One victim of the new communist order was Simon Wiesenthal, a young architect living in Lwow; he was interrogated by the Soviet secret police and deprived of his job and his apartment. Jews in the annexed areas of Poland joked that they had escaped a death sentence under the Germans only to face life imprisonment under the Soviets.[21]

A few attained positions in local government and the security apparatus, but the Soviet authorities were as loath to promote Jews in the new Soviet republics as in the old Soviet Union. Thousands who were considered capitalists or opponents of communism were arrested in the course of 1939–40. Up to 260,000 Jews who refused to accept Soviet citizenship in mid-1940 (including the bulk of Jewish refugees from Poland who had crossed into the Soviet-occupied areas) were deported to camps in Siberia and central Asia. Nevertheless, it remained a popular belief that Jews had relished Soviet rule and collaborated with the occupiers. It did not matter that, whether calculated in either absolute numerical or proportional terms, more Poles, Ukrainians, Lithuanians and Latvians had rallied to the Soviet regime. The facts did not stop right-wingers, abetted covertly by the Nazis, from sedulously fostering the myth that all Jews were communists and traitors. Consequently, as soon as Operation Barbarossa commenced and Soviet power began to rock, nationalist partisans, assisted by German special forces and Berlin-trained émigrés, launched insurrections that were aimed almost as equally against the Jews as against the Red Army.[22]

The Einsatzgruppen

At 0315 hours on 22 June, German artillery unleashed a furious bombardment of Soviet border positions as three air fleets of the Luftwaffe delivered a devastating blow to the Soviet air force while it was still on the ground. Then 3 million men, 3,600 armoured fighting vehicles, 600,000 halftracks, lorries and prime-movers, as well as 600,000 horses towing artillery and supply wagons plunged across the frontier. They were closely followed by the lead elements of the Einsatzgruppen, so closely in fact that Sipo-SD men were frequently caught up in the fighting to clear towns and cities in the path of the invaders. The course of the fighting determined where the Einsatzgruppen could operate and how long they would spend in any one place. It also influenced thinking in the Führer's headquarters about future policy on civil as well as military affairs. For these reasons the unfolding of the campaign, spatially and temporally, became critical for determining the fate of Soviet Jews.[23]

Army Group North advanced rapidly into Lithuania, spearheaded by special forces and aided by nationalist partisans. By early July, Wilhelm Ritter von Leeb's army group had overrun Lithuania and cleared southern Latvia up to Riga and the Dvina river. The armoured and motorized divisions of Army Group Centre smashed through the Soviet border defences and advanced nearly 400 miles in ten days. A series of pincer movements severed the Soviet armies concentrated in western Byelorussia from their command centres and cut off their supplies. On 28 June, Minsk fell, although it took another week to eliminate the huge pocket that stretched back to Bialystok containing 300,000 beleaguered Soviet troops. Meanwhile, the advance elements of the army group closed up to the land bridge between the Dniepr and Dvina rivers, the historic route to Moscow. Smolensk was captured on 15 July as the result of another pincer movement, although substantial Soviet forces were able to escape the envelopment. The exhausted German divisions were now encountering ever-stronger resistance and had to repel numerous powerful counter-attacks. Four days later Hitler ordered Army Group Centre to go onto the defensive.[24]

The mass execution of Jewish men began as soon as German troops crossed into Soviet-occupied Lithuania. In fact, the first costly skirmishes with Russian border guards provided the justification for the killing. As in Poland in September 1939, the military blamed their losses partly on unscrupulous tactics by the enemy and the use of francs-tireurs. Communists and Jewish civilians were automatically suspected of firing on German troops so they were immediately rounded up and condemned to the firing squad. The shooting of Jews in towns along the border also typifies the ad hoc nature of the operations, which drew on Einsatzgruppen personnel, regular army formations, police units and the civil authorities – in this case, customs officers from Tilsit. Local Lithuanians played their part, too, helping to identify suspects and soon taking part in the massacres. Ad hoc though they may have been, these scratch forces were effective: by 18 July, 3,302 Jews had been 'liquidated in the course of cleansing operations on the other side of the Soviet–Lithuanian border'. It was the murderous consensus across a spectrum of agencies that made such killing rates possible. The widely shared belief that Jews were the enemy, combined with the absence of significant resistance to that idea, made it possible to mobilize substantial numbers of men to seek out and destroy Jews on a staggeringly large scale.[25]

Meanwhile, the Einsatzkommando sub-units of Einsatzgruppe A sallied forth from Tilsit, crossed the frontier, and raced towards Kaunus, which they reached on 25 June. Sub-units moved into Leipaja, Yelvaga and Shauli by 27 June. During the first week of July, Stahlecker's headquarters entered Riga while Einsatzkommando 1b followed the army into Daugavpils. Even before German troops and security police arrived in these cites, Lithuanian nationalists organized in partisan groups fell on the Jewish inhabitants. Around 5,000 Jews were seized on the street or hauled out of their homes and murdered by members of the Lithuanian Activist Front and ethnic Germans. Kaunus, the pre-war capital of Lithuania and focal point of nationalist agitation, was the epicentre of the atrocities. Abraham Golub, a Hebrew educationalist, kept a diary throughout the occupation and recorded the shock felt by Jews who were suddenly exposed to the fury of local mobs. The Lithuanians 'did not conceal their joy at the outbreak of the war: they saw their place on the side of the Swastika and expressed this sentiment openly'. With the retreat of the Red Army and the collapse of Soviet power, 'The Jews are left behind as fair game; hunting them is not unprofitable . . . Slaughter the Jews and take their property – this was the first slogan of the restored Lithuanian rule.' Orthodox Jews, identified by their beards and clothing, were routinely humiliated; hundreds of yeshiva students and their rabbis were massacred in the Slobodka yeshiva. Long columns of men were marched from the city, leaving their homes wide open to invasion. 'Many Jews were murdered in their apartments. Robbery and looting followed. There were cases where women were raped at the very moment when looting and murder were in progress.' In one horrific episode, forty Jewish men were herded into the forecourt of a garage on Vitauskus Avenue and bludgeoned to death by Lithuanian patriots wielding iron poles. The incident took place in mid-afternoon and attracted crowds of spectators, including German servicemen who filmed and photographed the incident.[26]

Karl Jäger, the commander of Einsatzkommando 3, arrived to take charge of security and policing on 7 July. Since his kommando had less than 140 personnel he needed the local police and militia that Lithuanian politicians had called into being during the brief period when they thought the Germans would allow them independence. These auxiliaries, known as Schutzmannschaften, became essential to the implementation of anti-Jewish policy. Now acting under German direction, they carried out systematic round-ups, taking Jewish men to disused Tsarist-era fortresses on the edge of the city. The Seventh Fort and the Ninth Fort, bleak and forbidding structures honeycombed with subterranean chambers, were converted into prisons. In reality they were no more than holding pens: the forts were surrounded by deep earthworks that were convenient as both shooting sites and burial pits. Between 7 and 14 July, 5,000 Jewish men were executed there.[27]

Jews were stunned by the attitude of the local population. While a few courageous Lithuanians offered refuge to Jews, the vast majority in the city and the countryside either abetted the killers or remained passive. When a Jewish deputation managed to see the Lithuanian foreign minister in the short-lived provisional government to plead for his intercession, he replied that the Jewish response to the Soviet occupation revealed that 'we did not have a common path with the Jews and never will'. He concurred with the German plan for a ghetto: 'the Lithuanian and the Jew must be separated'.[28]

The German army had already ordered the marking of Jews with an armband adorned by the Star of David and subjected them to a curfew. On 10 July the military authorities issued orders for all Jews in Kaunus to move into the dilapidated suburb of Vilijampole where the wrecked Slobodka yeshiva was located. Ignoring Jewish protestations that the district lacked basic amenities or sufficient room, they were given until 15 August to transfer. Meanwhile, Jäger's security police, reinforced by Lithuanians (who continued to cooperate despite the dissolution of the Lithuanian provisional government in August), settled down to a routine of arrests and executions. The German actions were aimed primarily against Jewish men, more or less of military age. Although 740 Jewish women were among the victims, hundreds who had been taken to the Ninth Fort were subsequently released. By mid-August over 8,200 Jews had been shot at the forts.[29]

Vilnius, the capital of Lithuania, fell to the Germans on 30 June. The command element of Einsatzgruppe B arrived a few days later, then moved off and left the city in the hands of Einsatzkommando 9. It proved harder for the Germans stationed there to trigger 'self-cleansing' actions because a large proportion of the population was Polish. Nevertheless, within a short while Einsatzkommando 9, led by Alfred Filbert, was able to organize teams of Lithuanian Ordnungspolizei and with this additional resource was able to begin shooting 500 Jews daily. The atmosphere in the terrified city is captured in the diary of Herman Kruk, a middle-aged Jewish socialist and cultural organizer who had fled to Vilnius from Warsaw in October 1939. The day after the invasion started he resolved to stay and record what transpired: 'I leave myself to the mercy of God; I'm staying. And, right away, I make another decision: if I'm staying and I'm going to be a victim of fascism, I shall take pen in hand and write a chronicle of the city.' Notwithstanding his remarkable courage, Kruk was soon on the run, staying at a different house each night to evade the 'Lithuanian snatchers' in the Ipatinga Buris militia, who were searching for Jewish men. Kruk noticed that when Lithuanians tormented and beat up religious Jews the German soldiers in the vicinity watched, laughed and filmed the degradation ritual. Occasionally though, an indignant German would free a Jew from the mob. During early July, the military administration ordered the formation of a Jewish council and imposed the wearing of an armband with a Star of David. The Jewish council had to pay a huge 'fine' to the SS and also supply the military and the municipality with forced labour. Rumours started to trickle back to the cowed Jewish population that those who were arrested were being taken to the Ponary forest not far from the city and murdered.[30]

What happened to the men detained in Vilnius and then transported beyond the city limits was recorded in a wartime diary by Kazimierz Sakowicz, a forty-seven-year-old Pole who had moved to a cottage in the forest in 1939 after he was forced to give up work as a publisher. His home overlooked a large fenced-off area, close to the main road between Kaunus and Vilnius, that had been developed by the Red Army as a fuel depot. The Soviet engineers had only got as far as excavating a number of circular pits when they were chased away by the Germans. This was the place to which the Jews from Vilnius were brought in columns of several hundred at a time. On 11 July, Sakowicz noted 'the first day of executions. An oppressive overwhelming atmosphere. The shots quiet down after eight in the evening; later, there are no volleys, but rather individual shots . . . By the second day, July 12th, a Saturday, we already know what is going on . . .' At three in the afternoon he saw a line of 300 men, 'mainly intelligentsia, with suitcases, beautifully dressed' being marched into the site. An hour later the volleys began. The killers, who Sakowicz dubbed Shaulists (a local paramilitary association), were mainly young men acting under German command. From a window in the attic of his house he could observe Jews being shot in batches of ten. 'They took off their overcoats, caps, and shoes, but not their trousers.' That would alter within about ten days as a result of the changing behaviour of the Jewish men. When one column of 500 arrived on 23 July they resisted in various ways, most commonly by making a dash for the perimeter fence. As a result, the killers had to chase them and the operation fragmented. Sakowicz observed elliptically, 'They began to escape; shooting throughout the forest the whole night and during the morning. They were caught, shot, and finished off.' From then on the Jews were forced to strip to their underwear. That proved a major psychological obstacle to flight and had the added benefit of adding to the stock of clothing to be distributed and sold afterwards. He noted contemptuously, 'Brisk business in clothing . . . Shaulists with bulging knapsacks, with watches, money etc.'[31]

As German rule consolidated, murder spread across the Lithuanian countryside, engulfing one small Jewish community after another. Sometimes Lithuanians would take the initiative, at others they were triggered into action by the arrival of a German Sipo-SD contingent. Nesya Miselevich was living in Tauroggen, close to the border, when war broke out. She fled to Rosenay, where Germans and 'local fascists' were arresting men and women and putting them to forced labour. 'While they were working the women were subjected to all sorts of humiliations. The arrested men were first sent to do forced labour in the forests; there they were abused and tortured.' In mid-July she fled the town and made her way from village to hamlet, usually finding that the Jewish denizens had already been slaughtered. Eventually she ended up in a camp run by Lithuanians at Vyshvyany near Telshay, a town famous for its yeshiva. The Jews of Telshay had been plundered and then forced into the camp, which consisted of some barns and stables, without any sanitation. They were barely fed and were subject to random assaults. 'The bandits would burst into the camp by night, drag young women out, and have their way with them.' Since most of the men had already been shot, the women tried to defend themselves against these brutal incursions. After a few weeks, the female survivors were released.[32]

When the German 18th Army pushed up into Latvia and occupied Riga, the military authorities issued a slew of anti-Jewish orders. In the first weeks Jews were ordered to register and were marked, their property and assets were confiscated, they were subjected to a curfew, and finally ordered into a ghetto. As in Lithuania, the arrival of the German forces was pre-empted by local militants who started arbitrarily arresting Jews on the grounds that they were communist sympathizers. Within a matter of days these patriots were organized into auxiliary police units under the control of the Sipo-SD. The fluid situation was reflected in the reports transmitted by Einsatzgruppe A to Berlin. On 4 July it informed the Gestapo Head Office that 'Entire nationalist leadership of Riga deported or murdered [by the Soviets]. Pogroms have been started.' There was doubtless a connection between the recent deportations and the anti-Jewish violence that followed the departure of the Soviets, but it is not clear how far the assaults were spontaneous or engineered by the Germans. In any case, ideological motives would not explain the burning of synagogues, including the Elijas Street synagogue, which was set on fire after dozens of Jews from the neighbourhood had been forced inside. This suggests that the eruption of violence was as much an explosion of traditional Jew-hatred, aggravated by recent events, as it was a direct response to Soviet repression. Two weeks later, Einsatzgruppe A reflected that 'The Latvians, including their leading activists, have been, so far, absolutely passive in their anti-semitic attitudes, not daring to take action against Jews.' In this respect they were 'unlike the Lithuanians who had an active attitude, the Latvians are hesitatingly organising and forming a front against the Jews'. This reticence did not prevent the Germans from recruiting useful numbers of ex-Latvian army men and members of the AIZSARGI [Aizsargi organizacija] self-defence militia into auxiliary police companies. The most prominent was a 300-strong unit commanded by Victor Arajs, a former police lieutenant who led one of the anti-Soviet partisan groups that emerged on 22 June.[33]

The additional manpower made it possible for Stahlecker to initiate 'cleansing operations' in Riga and across occupied Latvia. Beginning in early July, Jewish men were systematically arrested by units of the German and Latvian Sipo-SD, taken to the police headquarters in Riga and imprisoned. After a few days they were trucked in groups of 200–400 to the Bikernieki woods a few miles outside town, where they were shot into pits. Max Kaufman was caught in one of these raids. In a postwar memoir he recalled that on 3 July, 'Armed Latvian youngsters pushed into my residence, plundered what they could find, and took my unwell son and me with them as they did the other Jewish residents of the house.' As the Jews trudged to the prefecture, volunteer Latvian militia assaulted them and chanted 'Jews, Bolsheviks'. The police building was 'full of Jews. From all sides came screams – the Latvians tortured their victims. Their sadism knew no limits. Old and sick people were brought into the courtyard, without their underwear, completely naked . . . Young women who were brought in were stripped naked and thrown into the cellar of the prefecture for the purposes of orgies.' A special room was set aside for holding Jewish girls, who would be raped at night then shot in the morning. Kaufman and his son were rescued from this nightmare by a neighbour, an ethnic German, who arranged for them to work at a German army facility. They were fortunate. The Einsatzgruppe informed Berlin that 'the arrested men are shot without ceremony and interred in previously prepared graves'. In addition to the 400 Jews slaughtered in the pogroms, 1,500 men were shot by Latvian security police and Einsatzkommando 2. Other mass shootings by Latvian units occurred in Daugavpils and Liepaja, where over 1,000 Jews were shot into pits dug in the sand dunes overlooking the Baltic Sea.[34]

While the northerly elements of Einsatzgruppe B passed through Vilnius, the bulk of its activity was further south. Here Nebe's men were pushing into an area of dense Jewish settlement. Separate Einsatzkommandos charged through Brest-Litovsk, Slonim and Baranovichi, converging on Minsk on 3–4 July. Einsatzkommando 8 passed through Bialystok then remained in Byelorussia, based in Minsk and later Mogilev. Several smaller sections were active in Bobriusk, Gomel and Roslavl. Einsatzkommando 9 operated in Grodno before moving eastward when Army Group Centre resumed its advance. The pause of several weeks from late July to early September and the evolving security situation were to have a dramatic effect on the nature of the Einsatzgruppen operations.[35]

As in the Baltic, the initial German advance was rapid and only about 5 per cent of the Jewish population was able to escape. Jews of military age mobilized into the Red Army were amongst them, although many never got further than depots or assembly areas before they were cut off by the German vanguard. Units of Einsatzgruppe B arrested hundreds of Jewish men – mainly those considered part of the Jewish leadership, professionals or those with a higher education – and executed them. The task was so great that they were assisted by other formations, notably police battalions, army security divisions and often by the regular army. Police Battalion 307 shot 5,000 Jews in Brest-Litovsk, including many women, while Police Battalion 309 accounted for up to 7,000 Jewish men in Bialystok during late June and early July. However, Nebe's Einsatzkommando 8 managed to kill 1,200 Jews in Slonim more or less unaided. In other centres, such as Baranovichi and Novogrudok, the number was in the low hundreds. Much depended on the available manpower and the duration of the stay by the Sipo-SD men who drove the killing process.[36]

German troops assaulted and humiliated Jews as they passed through one town after another, as if there was a seamless continuity between their behaviour in September 1939 and June 1941. In Radziwil, in eastern Poland, 'Soldiers ordered the Jews to bring out all the holy books of the Torahs from the synagogue and the prayer house and burn them. When the Jews refused, the Germans ordered them to unroll the Torahs and to douse them with kerosene and set them alight. They ordered Jews to sing and dance around the huge burning pile. Around the dancing Jews a jeering crowd was assembled that beat them freely.' These spectacles, exemplifying anti-Judaism as much as anti-Bolshevism, gave licence to local people once the front line moved on. When it seemed clear that the Soviets were gone for good pogroms swept across the region.[37]

The worst anti-Jewish riots in eastern Poland occurred in the province of Suwalki. In Radzilow, crowds of Poles forced Jews to desecrate their holy books, perform 'exercises', and beat them up. According to a post-war deposition, 'Around the tortured ones crowds of Polish men, women and children were standing and laughing at the miserable victims who were falling under the blows of the bandits . . . The only Polish doctor who was in town . . . refused medical assistance to people who had been beaten'. After days of such sport, on 6 July, Poles from the town and surrounding hamlets fell on the Jews with knives and axes and slew up to 1,000 men, women and children. In nearby Jedwabne a spate of murderous assaults culminated in a few hours of mayhem on 10 July, during which seventy Jews were 'butchered' by 'local hooligans' armed with axes and clubs studded with nails. The dead were buried in a pit into which Jews had previously been forced to consign a statue of Lenin. A survivor recalled that as the day wore on, 'Beards of old Jews were burned, newborn babies were killed at their mothers' breasts, people were beaten murderously and forced to sing and dance'. Finally, the surviving Jews, perhaps 800, were driven into a barn which was set alight. Their assailants came from all parts of Polish society, including professionals and members of the local authorities who had been restored to power by the Germans. They were incited by representatives of the new order, but the pogrom followed a time-honoured pattern in which religious antipathy was leavened with greed and opportunism.[38]

Having swept across the pre-1939 frontier between Poland and the USSR, the Germans occupied Minsk on 28–29 June. It was the first large Soviet city to fall into their hands and due to the successful German encirclement, which trapped 300,000 soldiers of the Red Army, few of its 75,000 Jewish inhabitants escaped. The Jewish communist Hersh Smolar, who compiled the first account of the occupation, conveyed an impression of what it was like in the early days. 'When the Germans appeared in town, people were robbed, raped and shot for no reason. Jews were subjected to particular harassment'. Soldiers went from house to house, driving away with truckloads of loot from humble Jewish abodes. But the Germans soon noticed a difference in relations between Jews and non-Jews in comparison to occupied Poland: there were no pogroms. Indeed, the military authorities reinforced the solidarity of the city's citizens by arresting many of the male population and imprisoning them along with tens of thousands of dejected, hungry POWs in the Drozdy camp. Approximately 2,000 Jewish men regarded as members of the 'intelligentsia' were taken from the camp and executed in the first days of

July, but this was only a fraction of the total who were shot or perished in the dreadful enclosure. Nevertheless, several thousand Jews were actually released. Even though the registration of the Jewish population, the order to fix a yellow patch on their outer clothing, and the creation of a ghetto set Jews apart, important links remained between them and the other inhabitants of the benighted city.[39]

The magnitude of the task that confronted the Germans in Byelorussia stimulated somewhat anxious reflections on their objectives. One month into the campaign, Einsatzgruppe B grumbled to Gestapo headquarters that 'A solution to the Jewish question during the war seems impossible in this area because of the tremendous number of Jews. It could only be achieved through deportations.' This message reveals once again the astounding lack of foresight and planning for the 'Jewish question', notwithstanding the importance it held for Nazi thinkers and leaders. It may only represent what Nebe and his staff thought, yet if the commanders of one Einsatzgruppe were confounded by the size and density of the Jewish population it suggests that others may have been similarly ill-prepared for what greeted them in the USSR. It is also significant to note that at this point the expulsion of the Jewish population was considered a desideratum, even if no one was quite sure how it was to be accomplished or to where. Nebe's headquarters reported that in the meantime Jewish councils had been set up, the Jews were registered, marked and subjected to forced labour; but the Germans were apprehensive about the prospect of erecting ghettos in Byelorussia due to the size of the Jewish population.[40]

Further south, separated from Einsatzgruppe B by the expanse of the Pripet Marshes, Einsatzgruppe C erupted into eastern Galicia and thence into Volhynia. On 30 June, after heavy fighting around Brody, German forces entered Lwow. Deportations by the Soviets had reduced the volume of Jewish refugees in the city and a significant number of Jews were able to flee thanks to the protracted battle. Nevertheless, about 160,000 Jews were still there. The advance elements of the army were accompanied by two battalions of special forces, codenamed 'Nightingale' or 'Nachtigall' and 'Roland', consisting of Ukrainian exiles with German officers. These Ukrainians had been recruited from the nationalist underground movement, the OUN, that had operated in independent Poland. After the Soviet annexation, OUN activists decamped to Berlin where they were nurtured by the Abwehr, German military intelligence. On their return to Ukraine they attempted to

establish a provisional government in conjunction with local nationalists. Also high on their agenda was settling scores with the Jews on
account of their alleged support for Soviet rule. Before they evacuated
the city, Soviet security forces had slain dozens of political prisoners in
the military gaol. The Germans hardly needed to turn this atrocity into
anti-Jewish propaganda: people jumped to their own conclusions. The
Einsatzgruppe reported that 'The population is greatly excited. 1,000
Jews have been forcefully gathered together.' Their work was made
easier thanks to a pastoral letter issued by the metropolitan archbishop,
Andrey Sheptytsky, welcoming the Germans and thanking them for liberating Ukrainians from Soviet tyranny. In a recap on 16 July, the
Einsatzgruppe explained that 'The prisons of Lvov were crammed with
the bodies of murdered Ukrainians . . . Maltreating them, the Lwow
inhabitants rounded up about 1,000 Jews and took them to the GPU
[Soviet secret police] prison.'[41]

According to a Polish observer, 'hundreds of Jews were removed
from the nearby houses, men, women, old people, youngsters, boys and
girls, children, all naked, after their clothes and underwear had been
plucked from them, bleeding, followed by blows and kicks into the
prison courtyard'. One Jewish witness testified that 'The local fascists,
accompanied by SS men, dragged Jews from their apartments and took
them away to the prisons and barracks of Lvov. At the entrance to the
assembly points clothes were ripped off and valuables and money were
confiscated. The fascists tormented and beat people until blood flowed
. . . Then these people were shot.' Edmund Kessler, a lawyer from an
assimilated Jewish family, kept a diary throughout the period. He noted
how the first hours of the occupation were relatively calm, distinguished
only by occasional assaults on religious Jews by German military police
and the sudden appearance of the Ukrainian national colours on badges
worn by locals. Then news of the prison massacre spread. 'A fanatic mob
orgy of bloodshed and pillage began, but even so it took place according
to a certain system. The orchestrators were the Germans. It is they who
decided when to begin the pogrom, when to stop it, how long to torture
the victims; whether until they lost consciousness or to slaughter them.'
For three days, Ukrainians organized into a militia seized Jews and
delivered them to the Germans. 'A furious search of Jewish homes com-
mences. The rioting, ransacking, and plundering grows in strength and
intensity. Beaten, whipped, and tortured, the inhabitants are dragged
into the streets. Hiding in the cellar or attic mostly does not help. Gangs

of Ukrainian children inspect the nooks and crannies of houses and apartments and point out hidden Jews.' In addition to the hundreds beaten or shot to death in the prison precincts, the German security police executed 7,000 'in retaliation for the atrocities'.[42]

A lesser bloodbath occurred in Tarnopol, where thousands of Ukrainians had been deported and murdered by the exiting Soviets. 'In retaliation', reported Einsatzkommando 4b, 'arrest of Jewish intelligentsia has begun, since they are responsible . . . The number is estimated at 1,000.' On 5 July, 'about 70 Jews were assembled by the Ukrainians and finished off with concentrated fire. 20 more were slain in the streets by Ukrainians and soldiers in retaliation for the murder of 3 soldiers who were found in prison.' The Sipo-SD reporter added that 'The German army demonstrates a gratifyingly good attitude towards Jews.' Similar eruptions occurred across the region. For example, some 300 Jews were killed by Ukrainian militia in Zlochow; in Dobromil, German security police and Ukrainian auxiliaries shot about 130 Jews before locals destroyed the ancient synagogue; while in Sambor, Ukrainian police killed fifty Jews.[43]

Pogroms spread across Volhynia, too, claiming the lives of perhaps 500 Jewish men and women. Peasants routinely plundered the homes of Jewish village dwellers, driving off the cattle of Jewish farmers. In numerous towns Ukrainian residents helped the Germans to locate Jews and guard them prior to mass shootings. Rape was common. From the commencement of the military administration, Jews were excluded from the economy, subjected to a curfew, and prevented from travelling. They were forced to wear distinguishing yellow patches on their outer garments. In the large towns, Jewish councils were set up and required to supply Jews for forced labour. Many Jewish communities were obliged to pay levies or special taxes to the Germans. Under the mantle of the army, contingents of Sipo-SD constantly executed Jews accused of being communists or suspected of anti-German activity: 2,000 in Lutsk, 3,000 in Ostrog, 1,075 in Dubno. An estimated 15,000 Jewish men perished in these first weeks. Frantic to evade the firing squads and forced labour, Jewish men ran to nearby forests or hid in their houses; but this tactic only exposed their womenfolk who had to either perform forced labour or forage for food.[44]

The southern wing of Einsatzgruppe C, comprising Einsatzkommandos 4a and 4b, pressed on to Zhitomir and Berdichev in the Soviet Ukraine. This huge region was home to about 1.5 million Jews and their fate hung on the progress of the campaign. Initially Army Group South encountered heavy resistance from strong Soviet forces and made relatively little progress. This gave Jews more time to flee or take advantage of the evacuation procedures put in place by the Soviet authorities. By the time the Einsatzkommando reached Zhitomir on 9 July most of the Jewish population had escaped. However, when the front stalled for several weeks in mid-July the pause gave the killing units time to sweep through towns and cities that had been briefly visited or bypassed. Several hundred Jewish men were shot in Zhitomir and over a thousand in Berdichev, many of them Jews who had fled to the town from other locations.[45]

The southern Ukraine, including Bessarabia, which the Soviets had annexed, the Black Sea coast and the Crimea, was assigned to Einsatzgruppe D, which had travelled all the way from Bratislava to its jumping-off point. Military operations along the Romanian–Soviet border opened several days later than further north and the advance of the German 11th Army and the Romanian armies was sluggish once they had sliced through Bessarabia and reached the Dniester river. Part of the Romanian leadership actually wanted to halt there and simply digest the recovered territory. Eventually, the Romanian army group was thrust forward in its role of protecting the right flank of Army Group South, taking it all the way to Odessa at the start of August. In the meantime, the Romanians commenced the expulsion of Jews from Bessarabia and northern Bukovina with a savagery that shocked even German observers.[46]

The Romanians

Romania embarked on the invasion of the USSR in alliance with Nazi Germany partly in the hope of recovering some of the land and prestige it had lost during the previous year. With the collapse of France, Romania was diplomatically isolated and at the mercy of more powerful neighbours. King Carol opted for the protection of Germany. He invited a Wehrmacht mission to Bucharest and to further demonstrate its realignment, the Romanian government declared that it would proceed to tackle the 'Jewish problem' in the country. However, German friendship came at a steep price. In June 1940, when Hitler wanted peace and quiet in the east, he acquiesced while Stalin compelled Romania to give up Bessarabia and northern Bukovina to the USSR. Two months later, Germany obliged the Romanian government to cede northern Transylvania to its more senior client, Hungary. In September, as the final indignity, the province of Dobruja was handed to the Bulgarians.[47]

The Romanians responded by looking for a scapegoat, the role traditionally performed by Jews. Romanian troops and police on their way out of Bessarabia and Bukovina attacked Jewish communities, killing an estimated 200 men and women. They also staged pogroms as they settled into the new border strip in Moldavia, claiming several hundred more innocent lives. On 9 August, King Carol's government promulgated a new statute on Jewish citizenship. It restricted full civil rights to Jews who had been settled in Romania prior to 1916 and veterans of the armed forces. Jews not in those categories were dismissed from government employment and forced to pay special taxes. Jews were also summarily evicted from border towns and sent to do forced labour. Emil Dorian reflected that the laws would prove 'especially harmful first to the poor and then to the middle class, the professionals. The wealthy Jews, the businessmen, and the industrialists will continue to do well for a while.' Nevertheless, he smarted at the imputation of disloyalty. 'Many gentiles do not understand the feeling of human degradation the Jew experiences now that he is a pariah in Romanian society.' He recalled a joke that the three categories to which Jews were assigned entailed three different greetings: '"Mr Kike", "Hey, you kike" and "Up yours, kike!"'[48]

King Carol sought to shore up his authority, and also please the Nazis, by bringing representatives of the Iron Guard into his government. However, none of these measures could salvage his popularity and he abdicated in October 1940, leaving power in the hands of the prime minister, Marshal Ion Antonescu. For several months Antonescu attempted to balance the need to appease the Germans against the disruptive antics of the rabidly anti-Semitic Iron Guard. Antonescu was anti-foreigner and anti-Bolshevik but he knew several wealthy Jewish businessmen and respected both their patriotism and their contribution to the economy. He therefore announced that Romania would seek an 'orderly' and an authentically Romanian solution to the Jewish question. The regime set about the legal expropriation of Jewish-owned land and imposed high taxes on Jewish enterprises. It set up commissions to nationalize Jewish firms, remove Jewish employees, and send unemployed Jews to forced labour. Such devices only tried the patience of the Iron Guard, who preferred boycotts and extortion. When Emil Dorian heard that they were entering government, he immediately feared 'a strict implementation of the programme to exterminate the Jews'. Wherever they held power in local or regional government guardists marked Jewish businesses, forced Jews to sell up, and extorted funds for their movement. They were so parasitical that Jews preferred to sell their enterprises to ethnic Germans or carpetbaggers from the Third Reich. In certain cases, the German legation ended up protecting Jewish-run concerns. Towards the end of 1940, Iron Guard violence in the provinces was spiralling out of control: entire Jewish communities were pillaged and driven out of their towns and villages. Dorian, who was now working in a Jewish school, witnessed the turmoil. 'The Jewish merchants are being systematically eliminated. Jewish stores are being expropriated. Very many Jews are led to Iron Guard police stations where they are beaten up. Hundreds of thousands of lei [Romanian money] taken from them . . .'[49]

The revolutionary, not to say chaotic and corrupt, shenanigans of the Iron Guard threatened to destabilize the country and provoked a showdown with Antonescu. The result was three days of confused street fighting that ended with the killing or imprisonment of the militants. In the process, law and order broke down in the capital and the Iron Guard rampaged against the city's Jews. Over one hundred were abducted to woodlands outside the city and murdered; more were attacked in their homes. Men were tortured and murdered, women raped. Emil Dorian struggled to describe the scenes. 'Shop after shop with shutters wrenched off their hinges, windows smashed, walls burned, rooms emptied – it is impossible to tell what had been there before. The mind cannot grasp how looting bands were able to wreak such utter destruction in so short a time . . . Jews were taken from their homes by Iron Guard bands and led to several spots in the city where they were slaughtered. On the road to Jilava dozens of corpses have been found . . . Before the victims were killed, their noses were smashed, their limbs broken, their tongues cut out, their eyes gouged.' Unlike the official Jewish leadership, Dorian did not feel much relief that the Iron Guard had been crushed. He observed German troops pouring into the country and pondered what would happen to the Jews when war came. With great acuity he understood that in the German mind the Jews would be held responsible.[50]

For the next six months, though, Jews had to endure nothing worse than laws for the expropriation of their property, including their homes, and further dismissals from work to make way for Romanians. They did not know that when Antonescu met with Hitler in Munich on 12 June 1941 the two dictators shared information about the forthcoming attack on Russia and the associated anti-Jewish policy. Romania was on the verge of regaining its lost possessions and Antonescu determined that the Jewish inhabitants, whom he regarded as aliens, would be scourged from them. He personally issued secret orders to this effect to the gendarmerie and special army units. The marshal later explained to his cabinet, 'I am all for the forced migration of the entire Jewish element of Bessarabia and Bukovina, which must be displaced across the border.' He thereby authorized a programme of population transfer that degenerated into a carnival of murder, rapine and sexual violence that interacted fatally with the mass executions of Jewish men that were simultaneously being carried out by the Germans.[51]

It began with a pogrom on 28–29 June in Iasi, a city that was actually in Moldavia, a Romanian province. Iasi had a Jewish population of 50,000, half the city's denizens, and with the opening of hostilities every one of them became a potential fifth columnist. The frenzy was apparently triggered by allegations that Jews were signalling to Soviet bombers during an air raid or spying for the Red Army. In fact, Antonescu had previously intimated that he wanted Iasi cleansed of Jews and communists. Within hours, police and men of the 'second section' of army intelligence had murdered 8,000 Jews in their homes, on the streets, or at the main police station. A further 4,530 were loaded into box-cars on two trains that were sent on a three-day journey to Calarisi, halfway to the Black Sea. The freight wagons were not supplied with food, water or sanitation and by the time the human cargo was released just over 1,000 men on the first and 818 on the second were still alive.[52]

As Romanian army units fought their way across Bukovina and Bessarabia, police and special units carried out massacres of Jewish men in all the main urban centres. These massacres were pre-planned. At a conference at Galati on the eve of the invasion, the inspector general of the gendarmerie, General Vasiliu, bluntly told his officers to 'cleanse the land' of Jews. Over the following weeks approximately 2,000 were shot in Cernauti, occupied on 5–6 July, and 10,000 in Chisenau, reached on 17 July. These figures dwarf the modest accomplishments of Einsatzkommando 10b which executed 682 and 551 Jews in these same cities as well as a few hundred more elsewhere. Over 10,000 Jews were massacred in the first weeks of Operation Barbarossa by Romanian police units and contingents of the security services, abetted by rehabilitated Iron Guard formations. Police and army cadets were drafted in, too. Nevertheless, the Romanians did not earn gratitude or admiration from their German partners. On the contrary, the Einsatzgruppen reports express persistent criticism of Romanian conduct. In Palesti, the Sipo-SD men complained, 'the Romanians content themselves with looting everything'. In Beltsi they were responsible for 'considerable excesses', probably referring to the murder of women and children, which was not then standard German practice. The greatest drawback of working with the Romanians was their sloppiness. 'The Romanians take action against the Jews without any preconceived plan. There would be nothing to criticise about the many executions of Jews had their technical preparations and their manner of execution not been inadequate. The Romanians leave the bodies of those who are executed where they fall, without burying them. The Einsatzkommando has required the Romanian police to be more orderly from that stand-point.'[53]

Following this first wave of killing, the Romanians began to organize the expulsion of the Jewish population. This was a forbidding task: there were 93,000 Jews in Bukovina, with over half in Cernauti alone, and over 200,000 in Bessarabia, 20 per cent of whom were in Chisenau. But Antonescu told officials setting out to govern the reconquered areas that they were to aim for 'complete ethnic liberation' and 'the removal or isolation of all Jews to labour camps'. Local officials in Dorohoi county in northern Moldavia and villages adjacent to the annexed territories actually jumped the gun and began expelling Jews even though these areas were not slated for clearance. In early to mid-July, columns of Jews started to wend eastwards, escorted by police, gendarmes and soldiers. As they left, their homes and property were seized by officials or looted by locals. En route the Jews were stripped of anything valuable, robbed by their guards or peasants standing by the wayside. About 25,000 were herded as far as the Dniester river, but only a portion crossed. The Germans did not want thousands of destitute, starving and sick Jews wandering in the rear of their armies. At least 8,000 were turned round and marched back.[54]

In a letter to a friend, penned in 1944, Rakhil Fradis-Milner recorded her experiences on one of these marches. Her hometown, Edineti, was occupied on 5 July. For the next three weeks 'savage terror reigned in the shtetl, during which eight hundred people were shot and numerous young girls, practically children, were raped, and this is even without mentioning the cruel beatings and the plundering.' On 28 July, 'the entire Jewish population was driven out of the shtetl'. Along with hundreds of Jews from other places they were 'driven out like cattle, struck with whips and rifle butts'. The journey went on 'from Bessarabia to Ukraine, back to Bessarabia, then back to Ukraine. The whole way was strewn with corpses.' Even the Einsatzgruppe staff took exception to the Romanians' relentless 'quest for plunder' and remarked censoriously that 'shootings and rape are frequent occurrences'.[55]

The Romanian plan for ejecting Jews from Bukovina and Bessarabia into the USSR ground to a halt, much as German plans for expelling Jews in 1939–40 had failed for lack of proper planning or coordination. Instead, the Jews of Cernauti and Chisenau, plus refugees from the surrounding areas, were confined in hastily demarcated ghettos, with about 50,000 and 11,000 respectively. Thousands of others were herded into camps located close to the Dniester: 26,000 at Vertujeni; 11,000 at Marculesti; 12,000 at Edineti; and 17,000 at Secureni. Conditions in these makeshift centres were dreadful. In Cernauti, Jews were marked and used for forced labour, repairing war damage. Women were employed in laundries and sorting looted clothing; they were frequently targets for rape. The German commandant of the city used Jewish labour to construct a bridge over the Prut river; many Jews fell off the structure and drowned. Meanwhile, the Romanian National Bank confiscated the cash Jews possessed (on the pretext of exchanging roubles for lei), leaving them without means to purchase food. Starvation and sickness were soon endemic. For the moment, the Romanian solution to its Jewish problem was stuck. In a short time, though, developments at the front line would open up new possibilities.[56]

German military progress in Russia and anti-Jewish measures

Despite the intensity of the fighting, persistent worries about the supply situation, and the unpleasant discovery that Soviet tanks were better, the mood in the army high command and at Hitler's headquarters after the successful conclusion of the frontier battles was jubilant. On 28 June, Christa Schroeder, Hitler's secretary, heard him say that in four weeks' time 'Moscow will be razed to the ground.' Having mentally bagged the Soviet capital, the Führer addressed the chief of the army general staff, Franz Halder, about future operations in theatres as distant as Afghanistan. A few days later even the normally cautious Halder was brimming with confidence. He wrote in his war diary that enemy forces had been destroyed to the west of the Dnieper–Dvina river line leaving nothing more than 'partial forces, not strong enough to hinder realization of German operational plans'. He believed it was not an over-statement to say that 'the Russian campaign has been won in the space of two weeks'. At the Führer HQ the talk was of German power extend-ing as far as the Nile and the Euphrates.[57]

Intoxicated with the prospect of imminent triumph, on 16 July 1941 Hitler met with Himmler, Göring, Rosenberg, Lammers, Bormann and Field Marshal Keitel, head of the army high command, to determine the civilian administration in the occupied territories and set out future policy. Alfred Rosenberg was formally installed as minister for the occupied eastern territories (the Ostministerium). Serving immediately under him were two Reichkommissars: Hinrich Lohse was appointed overlord of the Ostland, an artificial area encompassing the Baltic states and part of northern Byelorussia, and Erich Koch was placed in charge of the sprawling Reichskommissariat Ukraine. Reich governors were also selected to oversee the Bialystok district and east Galicia, which was bolted on to the General Government. The participants agreed to the speedy resettlement of the newly conquered land: in Hitler's pithy formulation they were going to 'first, dominate it, secondly administer it and, third, exploit it'. The east was going to be their 'Garden of Eden'. Moscow and Leningrad were to be 'razed'. Hitler had little patience for Rosenberg's proposal to treat the locals well. Göring's only interest in them was to ensure that the harvest was brought in and food shipped back to the Reich. Of course, this was subsequent to pacification of the territories. Hitler advised 'shooting anyone who even looks sideways at us'. Keitel, speaking for the army, pointed out that it was impossible to guard every installation, so the goal of security policy should be to instil fear. That would be Himmler's job: he was made supremo of all security matters.[58]

Security and resettlement had been Himmler's responsibility in Poland in 1939–40, and he learned the hard way that to succeed he needed complete autonomy and sufficient resources. The day before the meeting at the Führer headquarters he received the draft of a long-term plan for the east prepared by Dr Konrad Meyer, a professor of agron-omy who was also chief planning officer for Himmler's settlement organization, the RKfDV. The document, one of several versions known as Generalplan Ost (General Plan for the East), never got beyond uto-pian fantasies for settling Germans in the occupied lands, but it was clear about one thing: the Jews would be expelled to Siberia to make room for them. Having achieved freedom of action in all policing issues, which included determining the fate of the Jews, Himmler took steps to increase the forces at his disposal. Over the following days he assigned the SS Cavalry Brigade to Erich von dem Bach-Zelewski, the HSSPF for the area of Army Group Centre, and the 1st SS Brigade to Jeckeln, his Higher Police Leader in the south. Despite Hitler's leery attitude towards arming locals, Himmler also authorized raising more units of auxiliary policemen, Schutzpolizei or Schutzmannschaften. By the end of the year there were 32,000 auxiliaries in the Ostland and 14,000 in Ukraine. During 1942 the number of Schutzmannschaften would rise to a total of 300,000.[59] According to the record of the meet-ing on 16 July, the future of the Jews was not discussed. But the decisions were fateful nonetheless. In the best of circumstances there could be no place for Jews in a 'Garden of Eden' for the German Volk. When circumstances changed for the worst, the presence of Jews lurched from being an inconvenience to being a deadly menace.

The appearance of partisans in the occupied areas, combined with the temporary paralysis of the front line, caused jitters amongst the German leadership. Halder had noted the problem of scattered enemy forces in the rear of Army Group North as early as 28 June: cut-off Red Army personnel who declined to surrender burned and looted villages; some of them operated with tanks. Worryingly, the 'applica-tion of effective counter-measures' was 'frustrated by the expanse of the country and the limitation of our manpower resources'. Although these groups were often stragglers who raided German supply columns simply to survive, they disrupted provisioning and spread anxiety. Others coalesced around a genuine partisan mission and made contact with Soviet commanders. On 3 July, in his first public speech since the offensive opened, Stalin declared that 'Conditions in the occupied regions must be made unbearable for the enemy and all of his accom-plices.' Although his call for partisan warfare did not immediately lead to the organization and reinforcement of these groups, it created a degree of hysteria amongst the Germans, who automatically associated Jews with Bolsheviks and, hence, with partisans.[60]

Quite suddenly, the mood in the Führer headquarters and the high command changed. Hitler got worried about the concentration of Russian forces in Ukraine and around Kiev that menaced the southern flank of a potential advance on Moscow. He was also tempted to divert forces from Army Group Centre to reinforce the thrust towards Leningrad. Despite stunning operational successes, leading to the destruction of several Soviet armies and the capture of hundreds of thousands of prisoners, within a month of the first cannonade the strategic conception of Operation Barbarossa began to unravel.[61]

The roots of the July crisis went back to the planning stage. Despite the enormity of the commitment, the campaign had been approached in an astonishingly casual spirit. German intelligence on Russian military strength was poor and senior officers made up for lack of hard data with preconceptions that were based on little more than racist assumptions. It was assumed that the Red Army would shatter under the impact of the first blows, leaving the way clear for the Germans to advance on Moscow virtually unopposed. The high command believed that the defeat of France offered an operational blueprint for achieving such a rapid, crushing victory. Yet the conditions that made fast, mobile warfare possible in the west were absent in the east. The relatively small size of the theatre in western Europe made it possible to concentrate forces to achieve overwhelming superiority in the key sectors. The German armoured spearhead advancing from the Ardennes had to travel only 200 miles to reach the English Channel, along a superb road network, assisted by conveniently located petrol stations and a railroad system compatible with that of the Reich. In any case, the field of battle was close to the main supply centres in Germany. The opposite was the case in Russia. As German forces advanced they became more spread out. The railroad gauge was different, so the network had to be converted to take German locomotives and rolling stock. In the meantime, the motorized units and supply columns had to move along appalling roads that steadily deteriorated, especially in bad weather. The distances were forbidding: it was 600 miles from the start line to Moscow, yet even in France half the vehicles had suffered mechanical failure covering a third of that. Crucially, the German armed forces had limited manpower reserves and only stockpiled sufficient petrol and oil, spare parts for vehicles, and ammunition for a campaign running at full tilt for a few weeks. Instead of collapsing, though, the Red Army rallied after a succession of devastating setbacks. The Soviet system demonstrated an awesome capacity for 'force generation', raising new units faster than the Germans could pulverize them. Finally, the Germans had not foreseen the problem of stragglers and partisans operating in the forests and marshes in their rear. By the time Army Group Centre paused at the land bridge, combat casualties as well as wear and tear had reduced the strength of its armoured and motorized strike force by a third to a half. The supply situation was dire.[62]

The Wehrmacht's failure to deliver a knock-out blow to the Red Army exposed a fundamental rift between Hitler and his commanders. The generals wanted to launch an all-out assault on Moscow in the belief that capturing the capital would so disrupt Soviet command and control mechanisms that effective resistance would end. Hitler wanted to strike south to eliminate the threatening concentration of Soviet forces in the Kiev area and capture Ukraine, the fabled breadbasket of the USSR. He also wanted to strengthen the attack on Leningrad. This disagreement over priorities had been latent during the planning of Operation Barbarossa but Halder had sidestepped a confrontation with Hitler by blurring the objectives. Now it was in the open and after several rancorous encounters, Hitler got his way.[63]

During August one part of Army Group Centre's armour was diverted to the north while another part was sent southwards, cutting behind the bulge of Soviet forces around Kiev to link up with Army Group South. This manoeuvre, aided by poor Russian generalship, inflicted a disaster on the Red Army. Kiev was captured and 400,000 Russians went into captivity, leaving Ukraine open to the Germans. As spectacular as it was, though, the battle of Kiev was a pyrrhic victory. The distances travelled and the ferocity of the fighting further eroded the strength of German forces. When Hitler ordered the resumption of the advance on Moscow, on 30 September, German infantry divisions were at barely more than 50 per cent of their complement while the panzer divisions could field only 30–40 per cent of their fighting vehicles.[64]

Military failure had an impact on all aspects of German policy, long before the retreat from Moscow. As early as mid-August, the high command recognized that it had severely miscalculated. Halder lamely admitted, 'We have underestimated the Russian colossus.' By October Hitler accepted that the war would be prolonged into 1942, stretching the resources of the Reich and the morale of the Volk. Just two months after the euphoric leadership discussed razing Moscow and Leningrad to the ground, Backe met Göring to discuss food rationing over the coming year. Some members of Hitler's retinue even considered seeking a negotiated peace with Stalin. Meanwhile, captured Red Army soldiers were dying by the thousand every day because the Wehrmacht had not anticipated having to handle them for very long and did not intend to divert food supplies to feed captured Bolsheviks. Between summer 1941 and spring 1942, two million captured Russians would die of starvation, exposure and associated diseases.[65]

To add to the German nightmare, in the autumn Soviet partisans emerged as a potent force. They were now being equipped by airdrops and reinforced by officers and commissars who were parachuted in to lead them. One example of the damage they were doing was the delay that 'railway disruption' imposed on the transfer of the Spanish 'Blue' Division to the Leningrad front. Infuriated by such incidents, on 6 September 1941 Hitler issued a directive for dealing with the 'bandit war'. His orders to the army denied the partisans any legitimacy as a fighting force; they were criminals who had to be wiped out. A month later, Himmler sent out his own instructions for combating 'bandits'. He made explicit the connection with the Jewish population and echoed the call for their extermination.[66]

Army commanders issued blood-curdling imprecations against the Jews, inciting and legitimizing murderous actions against them. In a proclamation forbidding the army to utilize Jews for auxiliary services Keitel proclaimed that 'The struggle against Bolshevism demanded ruthless and energetic action, and first of all against the Jews as well, as the main bearers of Bolshevism.' In his order of the day on 10 November 1941, Field Marshal Walter von Reichenau, commander of 6th Army, declared that 'the soldier must have complete understanding for the necessity of the severe but just atonement of Jewish subhumanity. This has the further goal of nipping in the bud rebellions in the rear of the Wehrmacht which, as experience shows, are always plotted by the Jews.'[67]

The combined effect of these developments was to shift anti-Jewish policy in a new, even more murderous direction. This change was not the result of anti-Semitism alone or a logical outgrowth of existing practices, a process of radicalization. It certainly contained elements of continuity, but it was pre-eminently a response to the conjunctural crisis that gripped the civilian and military leadership of the Third Reich from late July 1941. Paradoxically, the utopian optimism of early July and the sober practicality of late July edged policy in the same direction: towards the total annihilation of the Jewish population in the occupied USSR. To Göring and Backe, Jews were a drain on food supplies, so measures that constricted or eliminated their consumption of resources were welcome. In pressing his claims to supremacy regarding security matters and clearing the undergrowth to enable the Garden of Eden to flower, Himmler had resolved to remove the Jews by the most radical means imaginable. For Heydrich, the destruction of Jewish populations would signal to the civil administration that their anti-Jewish policies were superseded and put the security forces at the vanguard of meeting Hitler's wishes. The army, strapped for supplies, hard pressed at the front and harassed in the rear, largely approved the liquidation of Jewish-Bolsheviks. Some officers dissented from the means that were employed, but few challenged the policy in principle.[68]

Himmler orchestrated this step-change in a series of visits to Einsatzgruppen commanders and Higher SS Police Leaders during late July and mid-August. He encouraged them to up the rate of executions and no longer to stop at Jewish men or those plausibly connected with the communist apparatus or anti-German activity. It was time to wipe out the Jews entirely. Although his instructions were delivered orally, they were echoed in a written order dated 1 August to the SS Cavalry Brigade, which was detailed to clean out partisans and resistance in the Pripet Marshes: 'All Jews must be shot. Jewish women to be herded into the marshes.' Hence, after each encounter with his field commanders the number of Jews murdered increased massively and now routinely included women and children. Whole communities were rounded up and slaughtered. In a parallel development, ghettos were created to contain the Jews and also to enable selections prior to the massacres. Skilled workers and their families were held back, temporarily, if a strong case could be made that they were servicing the army or the civil administration. These ghettos were mostly short-lived and the conditions in them were atrocious: they were barely supplied with food and the Germans made no effort to provide amenities. Despite Himmler's direct intervention, though, there was still little consistency in the application of the new policy. The extraordinary escalation in the rate of killing occurred mainly in Lithuania, Byelorussia and the Ukraine. Some ghettos created in June and July were purged of non-working Jews while others were relatively unscathed until later in the year, when they were hit for different reasons. Nor was the policy carefully coordinated with the German civilian authorities. There was constant friction between the SS executioners who answered to Himmler, and the Reich commissioners subordinate to Rosenberg. There was still no uniformity about anti-Jewish policy.[69]

In order to accomplish the task of eliminating hundreds of thousands of Jews and forming ghettos, Himmler drafted in fresh units and authorized the creation of many more. The assignment of the SS Cavalry Brigade and 1st SS Infantry Brigade added 19,000 men to the roster of killing units. Ohlendorf and Einsatzgruppe D were able to draw on newly formed Ukrainian auxiliary police formations as well as the Romanians. In the north, the Higher SS Police Leader Prützmann and Einsatzgruppe A could rely on the reservoir of Lithuanian and Latvian police battalions.[70]

By the end of the year, 12,000 officers and men of the order police, grouped in three police regiments (north, centre, and south, each comprising three battalions), were also engaged in anti-Jewish actions. Nine others partnered Wehrmacht infantry regiments in security divisions and each army group headquarters disposed of a regiment for rear-area duties. These men were mainly young conscripts who had been trained by the SS for policing duties in the occupied territories. Older men who served in reserve police battalions had been indoctrinated in their regular police service in the Reich and received further ideological training when they were inducted into the militarized police battalions. A third of the officers in the police battalions were members of the Nazi Party and up to a quarter were 'old fighters' from the SA.[71]

Killing innocent men, the elderly, women, children and babies appears to have presented few problems for most of the rank and file. They were predisposed to view the inhabitants of the east as virtually savages, the Jews even more so. Those who were ideologically honed saw themselves waging a racial war for the supremacy, if not the survival, of the German Volk. Almost all policemen, troops and those in the civilian echelons shared this outlook to some extent. The harder the fighting and the longer the campaign, the more Germans were inured to pangs of compassion; on the contrary, feelings of solidarity with their comrades and anxiety about the future of loved ones at home came to the fore. The real problems of food supply and raids by partisans offered proof that ruthless, merciless action was essential to prevent the situation deteriorating.[72]

While some historians argue that the Nazi leadership used the partisan menace to ease ordinary Germans into killing innocents, the evidence points in the opposite direction. On 10 August, Einsatzgruppe A requested advice from Berlin for the reason that 'Army Group Centre urgently demands a quick solution because of the difficult situation with the partisans.' It mentioned partisan attacks again on 15 and 22 August, including a strike against the vital Pskov–Luga highway. From mid-August, Einsatzgruppe B reported clashes with partisans along the Minsk–Moscow highway. This main artery for Army Group Centre passed through a chain of cities and towns with substantial Jewish populations. In Byelorussia and more widely it was a fatal coincidence that German lines of communication ran through areas of Jewish population, drawing attention constantly to the presence of an 'enemy' in close proximity to essential supply routes, transport hubs and depots.[73]

On 24 September 1941, the commander of the rear area of Army Group Centre invited officers who had experience of anti-partisan warfare to share their knowledge at a three-day conference in Mogilev. Most of the sixty participants were junior officers from security divisions but there were also personnel from infantry regiments. Amongst the speakers were Nebe, Bach-Zelewski and the commander of the SS Cavalry Brigade. A summary of the presentations and recommendations for anti-partisan warfare was later distributed and the commander of the German army, Brauchitsch, incorporated parts of the proceedings into the 'Guidelines for Fighting Partisans' issued a month later by the high command. In these guidelines, German soldiers were instructed to be absolutely merciless in dealing with the partisan threat.[74]

The fact that German anti-partisan operations in 1941 did not lead to many casualties amongst the security units does not mean that counter-insurgency was merely a cover for killing defenceless men, women and children. The point of guerrilla tactics is to avoid confrontations with superior enemy forces; Soviet partisans created havoc but were adept at evading German countermeasures. Conversely, the point of counter-insurgency is to deny the enemy civilian support by winning over the population or deterring it from aiding guerrillas. At its most brutal, as practised by the Germans, anti-partisan warfare involved removing or killing civilians suspected of abetting the enemy.

So the war on partisans was not just a pretext for mass murder or a device to engage ingénues in the unpleasant business of slaughtering Jews. Letters, diaries and interrogations of German soldiers and officers, policemen, and civilian officials show that it was a shared belief, a matter of common sense, that Jews were Bolsheviks and therefore nurtured the partisans. Jews may have been an imaginary enemy, but it was not irrational to think of them as a foe. On the day after the invasion started one corporal wrote, 'Now Jewry has declared war on us . . . All that are in bondage to the Jews stand in a fight against us. The Marxists fight shoulder to shoulder with high finance as before 1933 in Germany . . .' Corporal Paul Lenz put it bluntly, 'Only a Jew can be a Bolshevik.' In Russia, he continued, 'wherever one spits one finds a Jew'. German troops were convinced that Jews were behind the atrocities revealed when the Red Army retreated. A private, referring to the massacres in Lwow and Tarnopol, asserted, 'You see evidence of Jewish, Bolshevik cruelties which I can hardly believe possible.' Lance Corporal Paul Rubelt echoed this claim, 'Jews were for the most part the evil doers' in Lwow. A month into the campaign, a corporal wrote home, 'The great task that has placed us in battle against Bolshevism lies in the destruction of Judaism . . . When you see what the Jew has brought about here you can begin to understand why the Führer began this struggle with Judaism.' In October, a railroad inspector reacting to partisan raids casually mentioned that 'In case of attack numbers of people are picked out of the local population, especially Jews, and are shot there on the spot and their homes set on fire.'[75]

Karl Fuchs, who advanced into the USSR in a tank of the 25th Panzer Regiment, told his wife Madi that 'we are fighting for the existence of our entire people, of our Volk'. Russia was 'nothing but misery, poverty and depravity! That is Bolshevism.' And behind it all were the Jews. He wrote to his father that 'Everyone, even the last doubter, knows today that the battle against these sub-humans, who've been whipped into a frenzy by the Jews, was not only necessary but came in the nick of time.'[76]

Crucially, senior officers held in respect by their men confirmed such preconceptions and incited the rank and file to see Jews as a threat. On 20 November, Manstein issued an order of the day to 11th Army in the Crimea stating that 'Jewry constitutes the mediator between the enemy in the rear and the still fighting remnants of the Red Army and the Red leadership . . . The Jewish-Bolshevik system must be eradicated once and for all.' At roughly the same time Herman Hoth, commander of 17th Army in Ukraine, advised his troops that they were in a battle against an opposing spiritual conception 'whipped up by a small number of mostly Jewish intellectuals'. The battle 'can only end with the destruction of the other; a compromise is out of the question.'[77]

The new mission called for new techniques. Jeckeln figured out that it helped to maximize the use of the space in the burial pits if the Jews walked into them and lay down before being killed. This became known as the 'sardine packing' method. It also made it easier for officers to walk over the corpses to deliver a coup de grâce to those only wounded by the fusillade. Notwithstanding the increased efficiency of the killing, the experience of slaughtering women, children and babies was beginning to take a psychological toll on the killers. When Himmler observed a mass execution in Minsk in mid-August he was troubled by the potential effects on his officers and men. He was already getting word that some SS personnel were suffering nervous disorders as a result of constant involvement in killing operations and it seems that around this time he asked for research into other techniques for mass murder. After seeing a mass shooting, also in Minsk but probably in November 1941, Adolf Eichmann protested to colleagues in the SD in Lwow that 'Those men will either go mad or turn into sadists.' He repeated to Heinrich Müller, head of the Gestapo in Berlin, 'we're training our men to be sadists'.[78]

Mass murder and ghettoization in the occupied USSR

In Lithuania the first mass killing to include women and children occurred at Rokisis on 14–15 August, claiming 3,200 victims. Over the next two weeks the Einsatzkommandos and their Lithuanian assistants murdered 33,000 Jews across the country. Stasis at the front meant that the killing units had more time to comb through small towns and villages. Once the advance on Leningrad resumed, the growing anxiety about the shortage of food, supply difficulties and partisans in the rear of Army Group North added impetus to the massacres. The intensified slaughter was sustained for the rest of the year thanks to the plethora of Lithuanian auxiliaries who provided the firepower. Viktor Kutorga, a member of the Lithuanian underground, later published a brief account of these days in the hope of stirring the world's conscience. One entry on one community can stand for dozens of others: 'October 16. They did away with 900 Jews in Semelishki. There, in the ghetto, the "partisans" and the Germans particularly distinguished themselves by their savagery – they robbed, killed and raped women. The Jews worked every day in three shifts, day and night at the airfield – 1,200 men and

800 women from the ages of 17 to 55. When on any day these numbers did not reach their preliminary levels, the Germans would go through apartments in the ghetto and drag men and women out of their beds to work.' As this extract shows, Jews were not murdered if they could be exploited for labour. This only meant that a fraction of the communities survived for the time being. By December, the Germans and their Lithuanian collaborators had shot to death 133,000 Jewish men, women and children.[79]

Ghetto-building, exploitation of Jewish labour and mass murder were synchronized. In Lithuania, the Germans formed three ghettos: Kaunus, Vilnius and Shauli. The Jews of Kaunus moved into the designated area between 10 July and 15 August. During the last frantic days Abraham Golub saw 'Lithuanians simply throw Jewish residents out onto the streets and take for themselves "liberated" apartments.' Dr Elchanan Elkes, a much-respected physician who had been elected as 'Oberjude' (head Jew) of the community, negotiated tenaciously with the authorities over the extent of the ghetto, the food supply, and forced labour. Despite his courageous efforts the ghetto was shrunk and divided into two parts, one large and the other small. It soon became apparent that this bifurcation was intended to facilitate the policy of eliminating all Jews except those considered essential for the economy or the war effort. An Order Service was created at around the same time and from its inception Golub doubted that it would be a force for good.[80]

Meanwhile the slaughter at the Seventh Fort continued. The inclusion of women and the extensive employment of Lithuanians for guard duties alongside the shooting squads changed the procedure somewhat: mass rape as well as mass murder became routine. Golub reported that 'Night after night the Lithuanian henchmen would proceed to elect their victims: the young, the pretty. First they would rape them, then torture them, and finally murder them.' For the killers there was also good business to be done. Lithuanian police and militiamen took the clothes of the dead and sold them. Officials and opportunists stripped apartments vacated by Jews and disposed of the furniture and household goods. The Germans, though, reserved the real estate to themselves – and this was considerable. Jews owned nearly 40 per cent of the residential dwellings in Lithuania, a total of 35,600 units. Regardless of religion, racism or ideology, greed was a powerful incentive for both locals and carpetbaggers to eliminate the Jewish population.[81]

In early October, the boss of the ghetto, an SA captain called Fritz Jordan, gave the Jewish council 5,000 work certificates. This placed the Jewish leadership in a horrendous position since they guessed that non-possession of a certificate was tantamount to a death sentence. Three weeks later the SS sergeant responsible for Jewish affairs, Helmut Rauca, ordered the Jewish council to separate working from non-working Jews. Golub recorded the agonizing debate that ensued when the Jewish council sought rabbinical advice. Rabbi Shapira judged that 'communal leaders were bound to summon their courage, take the responsibility, and save as many lives as possible'. By virtue of this decision, Golub commented scathingly, the Jewish council thereby 'inadvertently became a collaborator with the oppressor'. Jews working for the German military, skilled workers and of course anyone connected with the Jewish council received the prized certificates. Rauca then summoned a roll call of the entire ghetto and divided those with work permits and their families from those without, sending 10,000 to the small ghetto and 17,000 back to their homes in the main ghetto. Next day, 29 October, some 9,000 Jews were taken to the Ninth Fort and murdered. The Order Service was directed to search the small ghetto for any recalcitrants. Thereafter the survivors were left alone, stunned and mournful.[82]

The ghetto in Vilnius was not set up until early September, after the inauguration of civilian rule in the Ostland. Herman Kruk watched as 29,000 Jews trundled their possessions into a district where 4,000 once dwelled. 'Christians came to help – friends, comrades, fellow workers. Others came to buy for almost nothing; others came like jackals – already waiting for the Jews' belongings.' From the start the ghetto was in two parts: ghetto 1 housed about 30,000 Jews, while 10,000 were immured in the lesser ghetto 2. The Germans appointed a Jewish council and ordered the creation of an Order Service, which took shape under Jacob Gens, an ex-Lithuanian army officer. The Jews in ghetto 1 were gradually issued with work certificates that they hoped would save them from the culling that occurred regularly. When the Jewish council made sure it got 400 permits for its employees there was outrage. Eventually about 12,000 Jews held the priceless documents. Almost immediately, the Germans began removing non-working Jews. The Order Service assisted, in the belief that work permits would be respected, although Jews in the large ghetto were targeted as well. The purges went on until the small ghetto was emptied and over 15,000 Jews had been sent to Ponary. A further effort to reduce the number of Jews in the main ghetto in November encountered passive resistance: thousands hid, with the result that German police and Lithuanian auxiliaries entered the ghetto and shot hundreds on the spot before rounding up over 1,000. By the end of the year only 15,000 'legal' Jews were left in the Vilnius ghetto, although probably a few thousand more survived in 'malinas' (hiding places) or bunkers.[83]

Kazimierz Sakowicz continued to observe the fate of those who made the short, one-way journey to Ponary. During August he counted 250–300 shot every day for seventeen days, except for Sunday, the day of rest. Throughout this time he spotted only one woman. In late August larger numbers of women began to appear. He heard one shooter, who he happened to know slightly, boast that 'stripped naked they looked very pretty'. The Germans, the man said enviously, held them for an hour before they were shot and '"contaminated the race with the Jewish women"'. The Lithuanians were somewhat placated because they were able to sell the women's silk stockings the next day. In early September the dejected columns included many more women plus children and babies. The Lithuanians now comprised almost the entire complement of one hundred guards and eighty shooters. 'They shot while they were drunk. Before the shooting they tormented the men and women horribly . . . The women were stripped to their underwear.' Sakowicz observed that the victims were forced to lie on top of the corpses already in the pits while the shooters walked back and forth over the bodies, firing into their heads. Children and babies were torn from their mothers and thrown onto the piles of dead and dying. Other Lithuanian guards 'took the little ones from their mothers and killed them with rifle butts'.[84]

The massacres were considered both a spectacle and a bonanza. Sakowicz was disgusted at the sight of 'two amused Lithuanian "ladies" in the company of a certain "gentleman" who were on a day excursion to see the executions'. Because the weather was now cooler and the Jews were not told exactly where they were going, they wore as much as they could and included valuable apparel. During one day of shooting in early September, Sakowicz saw the Lithuanian commanding officer swaggering around in a woman's fur. The carnage supplied the basis for a grotesque economy. He noticed that 'when the trucks returned from the forests, the Lithuanian soldiers sitting inside were already dividing up the possessions'. Traffic went the other way, too: 'Lithuanian women came for the clothing.' On one occasion he heard a soldier say that he had taken an order for garments from a local and 'had gone to the "trouble" of choosing a woman from the fourth line whose height was about that of the villager'. The perception of Jews as a source of booty led Sakowicz to identify a fundamental difference between the Germans and the Lithuanians: 'For the Germans 300 Jews are 300 enemies of humanity; for the Lithuanians they are 300 pairs of shoes, trousers and the like.'[85]

Thanks to the increasing number of victims, the amount of alcohol, and the ill-discipline of both the guards and the shooters, several Jews were only wounded and crawled out of the mass graves once night fell. A few made it back to the ghetto, including Peyse Schloss, a sixteen-year-old girl who described her experiences to Herman Kruk. 'Few people knew we were in Ponary and few imagined what they were going to do with us. But we saw it with our own eyes, as the shootings were taking place no more than 200 yards from us. The men were numbed with blows to the head and only later were they shot. There were mountains of people lying. They all surrendered, obeying orders. All the work was done by the Lithuanians. They were only supervised by one German.' Peyse was in the last batch to be shot, at sunset, and was only hit in the arm. She clawed her way out and made it to safety with the help of kindly Lithuanians. Kruk added, 'Can the world not scream? Can history never take revenge?'[86]

By the end of the year the situation of the Vilnius ghetto stabilized. Thousands of Jews were now employed by the German army, producing fur and leather items, or working in the huge vehicle park. The ghetto developed the familiar panoply of institutions: there were five communal kitchens and a range of welfare and health services. Jacob Gens and the Order Service emerged as the dominant element. Noting that the Order Service men took bribes at the ghetto gates, Kruk complained that 'The homes of the Jewish police are full of everything: bread, butter, fat galore. Really, police work is the best livelihood.' The OS men established intimate relations with their German counterparts. On New Year's Eve Gens held a party attended by a gaggle of Jewish girls who were 'close to the Germans'. The Order Service organized merry events with 'girls, brandy and recently an orchestra' at which they were joined by Gestapo men. Gens used work for the Jews and bribes for the Germans to preserve the ghetto, but his tactics were not immediately obvious. Kruk lamented that the Lithuanians stole from the dead, while the Jewish council stole from the living.[87]

In Latvia the Germans established ghettos in Riga and Daugavpils. To create Riga's ghetto, situated in the run-down Moscow suburb, 27,000 Jews and 10,000 non-Jews had to be relocated during August, although the ghetto was not actually sealed until October. A Jewish council and an Order Service were set up, and a system for forced labour and provisioning put in place. Of the 30,000 ghetto inhabitants, over 15,000 were female and 5,000 were juveniles. Due to mobilization by the Red Army, evacuations and shootings, there were only about 8,000 men. Most of the adults were employed by the German army and navy, with thousands toiling at the docks unloading ships bringing supplies for Army Group North. Gertrude Schneider, who was a teenager when she entered the ghetto, later recalled that these outside workers were vital for bringing in food. In her memoir she recounted the emergence of something like normality: the hospital, the schools, and soup kitchens. The 'people began to get used to the grimness of their lives and it assumed a drab kind of stability. There was the belief that the central position of Riga, with its supply line to the Russian front, would ensure the need for Jewish workers and thus be of help to the survival of the ghetto inmates.' This was an illusion. There was constant bickering between Lohse and the Sipo-SD over who owned the Jews and their property. The civil administration provided the budget for the upkeep of the ghetto and intended to recoup the cost by exploiting Jewish labour; but the Sipo-SD insisted that the SS should be paid for Jewish workers. Nor did Lohse's officials fare much better with expropriated property and household goods. The cost of collecting rents from formerly Jewish-owned apartments outweighed the income derived from them, while much of the contents simply vanished into the hands of locals.[88]

The 15,000 Jews of Daugavpils were given orders to move into a ghetto in the Griva district. It consisted of little more than a collection of barracks and stables, once used by a Latvian cavalry regiment, surrounded by barbed wire. Hundreds more Jews were added from settlements in the surrounding countryside. The Germans called an Order Service and a Jewish council into being and the new leadership made efforts to construct a ghetto economy. In early August the ghetto rulers started demanding lists of unemployed Jews for resettlement. Initially the council complied, but they soon realized something was wrong. In fact the approximately 8,000 Jews removed from the ghetto on 8–9 and 18–19 August were murdered in forests or railway yards outside the town. Conditions for the remaining Jews improved once the population had been reduced but the Germans did not leave it at that. Another action in early November targeted non-working Jews, the ill and children: 3,000–5,000 were shot to death. A twelve-year-old Jewish boy, Syoma Shpungin, who lived through this period recalled after the war, 'It [the ghetto] was very crowded and dirty. And it was very cold . . . The belongings of the victims were kept by the executioners for themselves . . . The butchers were very often drunk.'[89]

Conditions at the killing site were described by a German, Heinrich Kittel, the commander of an infantry regiment who was secretly recorded in a British POW camp after he was captured in November 1944. 'I was lying in bed early one Sunday morning when I kept hearing two salvoes followed by small arms fire,' he told a fellow captive officer. He went to investigate and found himself amidst a crowd of spectators: 'Latvians and German soldiers were just standing there, looking in.' Kittel saw about sixteen Sipo-SD and sixty Latvians lined up at a trench where 'men, women and children . . . were counted off and stripped naked; the executioners first laid all the clothes in one pile. Then twenty women had to take up their position – naked – on the edge of the trench, they were shot down and fell into it.' His interlocutor then asked, 'How was it done?' Kittel elaborated: 'They faced the trench, then twenty Latvians came up behind and simply fired once through the back of their heads. There was a sort of step in the trench, so that they stood rather lower than the Latvians, who stood up on the edge and simply shot them through the head, and they fell down forwards into the trench. After that came twenty men and they were killed by a salvo in the same way.' Kittel was angered by what he saw and went to the senior Sipo officer to complain. '"Once and for all,"' Kittel told him, '"I forbid these executions outside, where people can look on. If you shoot people in the wood or somewhere no one can see, that's your own affair. But I absolutely forbid another day's shooting there. We draw our drinking water from deep springs; we're getting nothing but corpse water there."' Oblivious to his moral myopia, Kittel then got very excited and added, 'They seized three-year-old children by their hair, held them up, and shot them with a pistol and then threw them in.'[90]

After the first wave of mass shooting in the Bialystok district the situation stabilized. At the start of August, 43,000 Jews in the city were herded into two, widely separated ghettos. Efraim Barash, the head of the Jewish council, persuaded the Germans to include factories and workshops in the larger one and Jews were soon turning out footwear, clothing and furs for use by the German army. Buoyed-up by the success of his strategy of putting Jews to work, Barash enjoyed considerable authority. He presided over an elaborate ghetto organization and for a while the Jews enjoyed calm and reasonable conditions. The ghetto was not actually sealed until early November 1941 and evaded further purges because it had become so profitable to the Germans that Erich Koch, the Gauleiter, was able to repel efforts by the SS to remove the Jews. A similar dynamic occurred in Grodno, where about 25,000 Jews were sealed into a two-site ghetto.[91]

Further east, in Byelorussia, which under civilian administration became the Gebietskommissariat Weissruthenien, ghettos were formed at an uneven pace. Although the Minsk ghetto was established in July, Baranovichi and Novogrudok were unaffected until the end of the year. Nor was there much uniformity to orders for Jews to form councils, Order Service detachments, or even to wear the Star of David. Mass shootings occurred, but erratically and according to no obvious plan. In certain cases, they even triggered protests from civilian officials. On 27 October, the 11th Lithuanian Police Battalion under German command arrived in Slutsk, which had a Jewish community of about 7,000, with orders to liquidate the Jewish population. Heinrich Carl, the district commissioner, asked the commander to postpone the operation until he had sorted out essential workers and suggested forming two ghettos to facilitate the selection. The officer at first seemed to agree, but then unleashed his men, who began an indiscriminate massacre that brought factories and workshops to a standstill. Carl later addressed a letter to Wilhelm Kube, the Gebietskommissar, complaining about this action and describing how 'with indescribable brutality on the part of the German officers, and especially of the Lithuanian partisans, the Jews, including some Belorussians, were taken from their homes and concentrated together. The shots could be heard all over town and the corpses of Jews were piled in certain streets.' The operation was conducted so sloppily that 'some people who had been shot got out of the graves shortly after being covered'. He concluded, 'This day adds no glory to Germany and will not be forgotten . . . use all means to keep this police battalion well away from me.' Kube forwarded the letter to Lohse with a request that the officer should be disciplined and that skilled Jewish workers should be spared. It was not the principle of mass murder that bothered him, though. He urged the security forces to better coordinate executions with the civilian authorities and avoid alarming the locals. Lohse, in turn, sent the letter to Rosenberg, minister for the east, but he added nothing to the correspondence and the matter rested there. However, the incident was symptomatic of a wider conflict over policy between civilians and the SS that would flare up repeatedly until the end of the year.[92]

By contrast, the civil authorities in Slonim worked closely with the Lithuanian police unit sent in November to reduce the size of the Jewish population, which then stood at about 22,000. The Jews had been confined to a ghetto in a waterlogged quarter of the town called Zabinka. Thousands worked for the Germans in local quarries, in joinery workshops and at the railway station. Unusually, youngsters inside the ghetto began organizing an underground resistance almost immediately and acquired a small arsenal of rifles and pistols. In the autumn, when they got wind of the forthcoming action, they contacted local partisans. Other Jews prepared hideouts and dug bunkers. Unfortunately, they were not able to deflect the blow when it came. On 14 November, 9,000–10,000 Jews without work permits were removed and shot. The city commissioner, Gerhardt Erren, may not have known about the contacts between the ghetto Jews and the Soviet partisans, but he certainly knew about the adverse food situation. He subsequently informed Berlin that 'The Juden-Aktion of November 14, 1941 has greatly ameliorated the housing problem and also rid us of 10,000 unnecessary mouths to feed.'[93]

The strategically sensitive Pripet Marshes were an early target for the new German approach to the Jewish population. Between 27 July and 11 August, the 2nd SS Cavalry Regiment shot 6,526 'looters' in the Pripet area. The commander, Franz Magill, attempted to use the technique recommended by Himmler but informed his superiors that 'The driving of women and children into the marshes did not have the expected success, because the marshes were not so deep that one could sink.' Nevertheless, over a period of two weeks an estimated 25,000 Jews were butchered throughout the Pripet region.[94]

The wave of killing was particularly severe in the cities and towns located in the rear area of Army Group Centre, which remained under military administration. Here the combined effects of food shortages and security paranoia had a catastrophic impact. Ghettos were formed partly to restrict the ability of Jews to obtain food and so leave more for the local population, which was, in any case, under severe pressure due to army requisitioning. But they rarely lasted beyond the turn of the year. Instead, they came to function as holding pens from which Jews could be taken and massacred when sufficient manpower could be concentrated to do the job. The slaughter began in Borisov, where a ghetto had been constructed in August. In October, 7,000 Jews were taken from the ghetto to pits dug outside town and killed by men of Einsatzkommando 8. Over half the Jews of Vitebsk, a community with a glittering Jewish history, had either fled or been evacuated before the town was captured on 11 July. A ghetto was formed soon afterwards and was sealed in early September. There was hardly any time for ghetto organizations to develop before 8–10 October, when units of Einsatzkommando 9 massacred the population of 4,000. The 7,000 Jews in Bobriusk were ghettoized in October; three months later they were annihilated by the SS Cavalry Brigade, fresh from its triumphs in the Pripet Marshes. The tsunami of destruction rolled over Mogilev, where Einsatzkommando 8, reinforced by police units, slaughtered 6,500 Jews; Orsha, where 2,000 were shot; Gomel, where 7,000 were killed; and Polotsk, where another 7,000 were murdered.[95]

Two accounts may serve to give an impression of what these killing operations were like and also illustrate the attitude of the killers. The first is by Walter Mattner, a Viennese police officer, who described his experience at Mogilev in a letter to his wife dated 5 October 1941: 'I aimed calmly and shot with confidence at the women, children and numerous babies, aware that I have two babies of my own at home, and these hordes would treat them just the same, or even ten times worse, perhaps. The death we gave them was nice and quick, compared with the hellish suffering of the thousands and thousands in the GPU jails. The babies flew in great arcs and we shot them to pieces in the air before they fell into the ditch and the water. We need to finish off these brutes who have plunged Europe into war and who, even today, are prospecting in America.' The second is the deposition of a survivor of a massacre at Mstislavl, taken by a war crimes investigator in January 1944. Mstislavl was a small town in the Mogilev district, south-west of Smolensk. The Jews, who numbered about 1,300, worked as artisans and on a nearby collective farm. On 15 October 1941 a German police unit came to the town and ordered the Jews to assemble in the market square. Men and women were separated, and thirty elderly Jews were placed in a truck and driven away. 'From the assembled women the Germans selected the young ones, herded them into a shop, stripped them naked and subjected them to rape and torture. Anyone who resisted was shot on the public square.' Later in the day, the Jews were marched to a ditch. 'The fascist cannibals led the Jews in groups of ten up to the pits dug ahead of time, took their clothes and jewellery, then shot them. They killed the men in this way first, followed by the women with older children. The small children were thrown into the pit alive.' By the end of the year, the Germans had murdered 200,000 Jews in Soviet Byelorussia; barely 25,000 were left, mainly in isolated rural communities.[96]

Ghettos were enforced across Volhynia in the late summer of 1941, usually located in the worst parts of a particular city or town. But the Germans found it hard to contain such a numerous and widely dispersed population. Many remained open for months, so Jews wandered in and out searching for food and sanctuary elsewhere. Most communities were kitted out with a Jewish council, an Elder, and an Order Service, although none of them lasted long or became well established. Throughout the autumn, Einsatzkommandos and security units moved from town to town shooting Jews: for example, 17,000–18,000 in Rovno and 2,500 in Ostrog. The exceptionally large toll in Rovno was connected with the decision of the Reichkommissar, Erich Koch, to make the place his headquarters. However, there was not sufficient manpower to stage major actions in more than a few large centres. By the end of the year, three-quarters of Volhynian Jews were still living in their native towns and villages.[97]

The situation in east Galicia was especially confused. Hans Frank was hardly pleased that Lwow and the surrounding region, with its considerable Jewish population, had been added to the General Government. His first thought was simply to expel them all to the Pripet region and treat east Galicia as little more than a temporary dump. He devoted little time or effort to setting up a competent or conscientious administration. Instead, the enterprising and energetic SS police leader Odilo Globocnik stepped into the vacuum, grabbing the Jews for use on an ambitious project to construct a highway from Lwow to the Crimea, known as Durchgangstrasse IV. By the end of 1941, primitive work camps lined the route of the putative thoroughfare. Around 20,000 Jewish men were seized from cities and towns across east Galicia, though huge numbers perished due to the abysmal conditions in the camps and the harsh treatment meted out to them. Hundreds of Jews fled to Romania, Hungary and even the General Government to escape these round-ups. At the end of October when Frank realized that there was not going to be any mass deportation he seems to have despaired. He already presided over enormous, squalid and pestilential ghettos in the General Government and now there seemed no hope of removing the Jews to another territory. Bereft of any alternative, he acquiesced in the establishment of a ghetto in Lwow and other Jewish centres, in conjunction with a programme of mass shootings to eliminate non-working Jews or just to reduce the Jewish population.[98]

From September, Karl Lasch, the governor, and Fritz Katzmann, the HSSPF in the Galicia district, proceeded to create Jewish councils, register Jews for labour, and form ghettos. Katzmann's men, with Ukrainian collaborators, carried out a succession of huge massacres as the flip side of this process. On one day in Stanislawów, dubbed 'Bloody Sunday', 10,000–12,000 Jews were massacred in the old Jewish cemetery, including the entire Jewish council, which cast its lot with the victims. This left about 26,000 Jews to go into the ghetto although it was still disastrously overcrowded. The ghetto was not sealed until late December 1941. In Borislav, home to about 14,000 Jews, despite the outbreak of typhus no ghetto was created until the following May.[99]

The fate of the 135,000 Jews in Lwow was a grim catalogue of chaos and carnage. The local Ukrainians staged a second pogrom on 25–28 July to honour the memory of the nationalist leader Symon Petlyura who had been assassinated by a Jew in Paris in 1926. Mainly young Jewish men and women were taken to the prison where, according to Rabbi David Kahane, 'hair raising scenes unfolded'. Several thousand never returned. A Jewish council was then named which set about regulating housing, rations and forced labour. Edmund Kessler was relieved by the appointment of Jewish representatives, hoping that this would give 'a kind of legal status to the Jewish community'. When the Germans decreed the creation of a ghetto in early November, Moty Stromer saw this in a positive light. 'We were glad to have a place where we could live and keep some of our belongings,' he thought. Jews outside and Christians inside the designated area then started exchanging properties, often with people they knew. 'When it came to renting or exchanging apartments, the Christians only wanted to know if the Jewish apartments had gas, electricity, running water and bathrooms. They wanted comfort. None of the "new" Jewish quarters had these luxuries.' Rabbi Kahane gained a different impression of these transactions. He recalled that Christians were in no hurry to leave and 'For each square metre to be vacated by them, they demanded astronomical sums. Suits of clothing, English fabric, astrakhan furs, bedroom furniture, gold dollars just flew into the air. Even the smallest space was measured and sold. Each pitiful hole was bought with gold.' Few Jews were actually so well endowed; the vast majority were dirt-poor, and had little to exchange and, therefore, nowhere to go. Kessler noted that rich Jews aggravated the housing shortage by refusing to share their residences. In any case, a month later the Germans abandoned the plan when they realized it would cause too much disruption.[100]

The Jewish quarter offered only a pretence of security. On 12 November, German security police and Ukrainians surrounded the district and established a checkpoint under a bridge from which it was difficult to escape. Over a period of several days, around 10,000 Jewish residents who were not certified as working for German army installations or munitions firms were pulled out of the lines passing through this barrier and sent to killing sites outside the city. Kessler recalled that the guards 'set up an additional checkpoint to which mostly young women were brought. Under pretext of searching them for jewellery, hard currency and gold they were whipped, forced to totally disrobe, and sadistically violated, struck and kicked.' The women were then trucked to an area of sandy waste on the edge of an industrial suburb, machine-gunned to death and buried. German police and Ukrainian auxiliaries constantly invaded the Jewish residential streets, often targeting the homes of wealthy Jews. Stromer recollected that 'One night bandits who had been there before returned. They tied up the parents and raped the two daughters.' Meanwhile, the Order Service was instructed to seize men for forced labour. Jews sought desperately to evade these depredations. Stromer constructed a hiding place under an oven. To enter it he slid in feet first 'then with a big effort I would pull my arms into the oven and place them on my chest. After that, I would disguise my head with rags, and there I lay.'[101]

In the Soviet Ukraine in the weeks that the front was stationary, Einsatzgruppe C was able to carry out a number of large-scale massacres in conjunction with the formation of ghettos, although both policies were carried out inconsistently. In Zhitomir on 9 July the Einsatzgruppe shot about 5,000 Jews, half the pre-war Jewish population of the city. A ghetto was formed to hold the survivors, who were mainly workers, but it was liquidated about eight weeks later. The Einsatzgruppe proudly reported that 25–30 tons of linens, clothing, shoes, and household wares salvaged from the Jewish quarter were distributed to Volksdeutsche.[102]

In Berdichev, around 16,000–17,000 Jews had remained behind out of 25,000 (half of Berdichev's entire inhabitants). On 25 August they were forced into a ghetto in the Yatki district. A survivor described it to the famed Red Army war correspondent Vasily Grossman as 'the poorest area of town, an area of unpaved streets that never dried up. The neighbourhood consisted of ancient shacks, tiny single storied houses, and crumbling brick buildings. Weeds grew in the yards and everywhere were piles of junk, garbage, manure.' In two actions on 4 and 14–15 September, the Germans murdered first about 1,500, then about 12,000 Jews in a field near to the town's airport. According to Grossman's informant, 'Policemen, members of their families, and the mistresses of German soldiers rushed to loot the vacated apartments. Before the eyes of the living dead, the looters carried off scarves, pillows, feather mattresses. Some walked past the girls and took scarves and knitted woollen sweaters from women and girls who were awaiting their death.' Drunken SS men shot them in batches of forty, while the populace watched. Unfortunately, the pit dug by Soviet POWs was in dense, impervious clay. 'The pits were filled with blood since the clayey soil could no longer absorb any more, and the blood spilled over the edges, forming enormous puddles.' Those who were only wounded by the alcohol-befuddled shooters died 'by drowning in the blood that filled the pits'. Some, however, survived and were able to claw their way out in the darkness. The ghetto was liquidated on 3 November when almost all the remaining Jews were butchered. In Vinnitsa, two police battalions shot 10,000 out of the Jewish population of 17,000 and forced the rest into a ghetto. The decision to locate the Führer's advanced military headquarters in Vinnitsa doomed them. In Khmelnik, 7,000 Jews were massacred and the rest placed in a ghetto on the outskirts of town. The ghetto was eliminated in January 1942, after the residents had been robbed of all their warm clothing. They were gunned down, naked and shivering in an icy clearing in a pine forest. Some escaped the firing squads but 'wandered in the fields with no place to take refuge. Others froze to death and were found only in the spring when the snow melted.'[103]

The killing reached a crescendo at the end of September with the mass murder of 33,771 Jews on 29–30 September at the Babi Yar ravine on the edge of Kiev. German troops had marched into the city on 19 September, but dozens had been killed when powerful time-bombs went off in buildings being used by the military administration. With the arrival of Einsatzkommando 4a the military governor decided to punish the Jewish population as a reprisal. Posters instructed the Jewish residents to assemble on the morning of 29 September near the Jewish cemetery, on pain of death. Out of terror and in the hope of being reset-tled, thousands streamed to the rendezvous. A post-liberation account compiled by Lev Ozerov reported that 'Families baked bread for the journey, sewed knapsacks, rented wagons and two wheeled carts. Old women and men supported each other while mothers carried their babies in their arms or pushed baby carriages'. The columns were directed towards Babi Yar where 'an entire office operation with desks had been set up'. Thirty to forty at a time were processed, but their doc-uments were simply discarded. Instead they were beaten and pushed to an area that was overlooked by German and Ukrainian guards. There they were 'forced to strip naked: girls, women, children, old men. No exceptions were made. Rings were ripped from the fingers of the naked men and women, and those doomed people were forced to stand at the edge of a deep ravine, where the executioners shot them at point blank range. The bodies fell over the cliff, and small children were thrown in alive. Many went insane when they reached the place of execution'. Towards the end of the day, Yelena Yefimova Borodyansky-Knysh arrived at the lip of the ravine, clutching the hand of her little girl. She saw another woman try to protect her beautiful teenage daughter, only to be clubbed to death by the Germans. 'But they weren't in any hurry with the girl', Yelena remembered. 'Five or six Germans stripped her naked, but I didn't see what happened after that'. Soon it was Yelena's turn, but instead of waiting for the volley of rifle shots she hurled her child into the pit and threw herself on top of her. It was now almost dark and a German walked over the bodies, probing with a bayonet to check they were dead. Miraculously he missed Yelena and she was able to free herself from the jumble of cadavers, grab her child and make her way to a nearby village. Another Kiev survivor, Emilia Borisovna Kot-lova, responded to Ilya Ehrenburg's call for eye-witness accounts with a series of letters in January 1944 in which she recalled acts of defiance and resistance by Jews who realized the fate that awaited them. Old Jews said the traditional prayer 'Hear, O Israel' before dying. 'Young people fought with the executioners, shouting "The people will avenge you". Before killing them', she wrote, 'they still had time to rape the women.'[104]

After the fall of Kiev, the 1st Panzer Group and the 6th Army surged towards the Donets river and the Einsatzkommandos advanced again. However, they commonly discovered that most Jews had vanished from their path. Apart from exceptional circumstances, when cities were captured suddenly, the number of Jews falling into their hands diminished. This did not diminish the number of Jews killed, though, because now they were murdering every Jewish person they could. Much of the killing was done with the willing cooperation of their allies. Military operations in the south were a coalition effort, involving detachments of Romanians, Hungarians, Slovakians, as well as Volksdeutsche and local auxiliaries. So was genocide. While Germany's Axis allies could agree on little else, they shared a desire to be rid of the Jews.[105]

In the Ukrainian countryside, the Einsatzkommandos were surprised to come across Jewish rural settlements. They concluded that these places were populated by 'stupid' Jews who had failed to get off the land. Most communities were immediately wiped out anyway. During November and December, the spearheads of Army Group South captured cities that before the war had significant Jewish communities, including Nikolayev and Kherson on the Black Sea coast, Kursk and Kharkov, the industrial cities of Kremenchug, Dnepropetrovsk, Kirvoi Rog, Zaporozhe in the Don basin, and Mariupol on the Sea of Azov. In each place the Jews were annihilated either immediately or in stages, some as late as 1942.[106]

The experience of Jews in three places may speak for the fate of them all. The pre-war Jewish population of Dnepropetrovsk numbered 90,000 but the Germans found only 30,000 when the city was captured in mid-August. Of these they managed to slaughter about 25,000. Mikhail Petrovich Indik, a shop worker in a cooperative, was accidentally left behind when the Jews were evacuated so he was there to witness the murder and rape that followed. Indik escaped a mass shooting of 2,000 Jews on 13 October and survived in hiding thanks to his wife, who was Russian. At one point she was forced to put up with the attentions of a drunken policeman who lived next door to their home. From his hiding place, Indik could hear when the officer growled, 'Listen, you whore, when are you going to quit playing the role of an honest woman?' Like many other Russian, Ukrainian and Byelorussian women married to Jewish men, she endured a double jeopardy. Either they abandoned their menfolk or they went with them to the killing fields. If they hid their husbands they faced the routine perils of being a single women in unsettled times, aggravated by the risk that they could be sexually exploited by men hunting for Jews.[107]

Kharkov fell in late October. Immediately on taking the city German soldiers started looting Jewish homes. They were especially keen on clothing, probably because they were already feeling the cold and had no winter wear. Only half of the city's 20,000 Jews remained and were duly registered. When Soviet agents detonated bombs in several buildings, about 1,000 Jews were executed as a reprisal. During late December a ghetto was set up in a former factory but it was short-lived. Engineer Krivoruchko obeyed the order to go to the ghetto, trudging alongside the other Jews through the snow, robbed and beaten along the way. There was no food or even water in the buildings assigned to them so they had to drink melted ice. 'Robbery and murder were daily occurrences', he later testified. 'Usually, the Germans would burst into the room on the pretext of searching for weapons and steal anything that came to mind. In the event of resistance they dragged people out into the yard and shot them.' The starving Jews were easy prey when the Germans announced that they would be resettled. Hundreds left each day in trucks, but they got no further than pits beyond the city limits. Eventually Krivoruchko, too, was ordered out. At the end of the short journey he saw a ravine 'sealed off by a double row of sentries. On the edge of the ravine stood a truck with machine guns.' The people he was with panicked but the Germans clubbed them into the ravine and forced them to undress. Then they were machine-gunned. Krivoruchko saved himself by hopping back into a truck while the Germans were distracted and hiding under a tarpaulin. Back in the city he was concealed by his non-Jewish wife.[108]

Mariupol on the coast surrendered before its 10,500 Jews could get away. In early October, Sara Gleykh, a Jewish schoolgirl, began a diary of the subsequent events. The Germans plundered the city as soon as they were inside, seeking out food because they were at the end of their supplies. As usual, the Jews were registered and at the same time dispossessed of their valuables. On 20 October the Germans announced that all Jews would have to leave, but they got no further than ditches near an agricultural station a few miles away. When her turn came to undress and go into the pit, it was so full that Sara only had to step out onto the carcasses – one of whom she recognized as her mother. She screamed at the sight and lost consciousness. When she came to, it was dusk and she was covered with bodies, some still quivering with life. After the killers departed she dug herself out. She could hear Jews deeper beneath the mass of corpses still alive and unable to escape, but she could do nothing for them. 'When I had crawled out, I looked around: the wounded were writhing, groaning, attempting to get up and falling again.' A badly injured man told her and another girl to flee. 'The two of us, undressed except for our slips, and smeared with blood from head to toe, set off to seek refuge for the night.' They sought help at several dwellings but were repeatedly driven away. Eventually some kindly peasants gave them clothes and they started walking across the steppes. After days of wandering they reached a Red Army outpost.[109]

The bloodbath went on and on. Einsatzkommando 11a carried the tide of death down into the Crimea where, under the protective carapace of Manstein's 11th Army, they murdered 12,000 Jews in Simferopol, 2,000 in Yalta and 7,000 in Kerch. There was momentary confusion over whether the Krimchaks, converts to Judaism, and the Karaites, Jews who followed the Torah but rejected rabbinic Judaism, were really Jewish, but clarification soon arrived from Berlin. In a peculiar inversion of racial logic, the Krimchaks were slaughtered while the Karaites were spared. The 17,000 Jews living on collective farms that had been set up and funded by the American Jewish Agro-Joint project were all murdered, too.[110]

Transnistria and the Romanian killing operations

In south-west Ukraine, bordering Bukovina and Bessarabia, German policy ran up against the predilections of its allies. This area was the location of one of the first huge massacres and it became a zone of horrific violence. During August, Hungarian officials in the border region of Carpatho-Ruthenia, annexed to Hungary in 1938, decided to emulate the Romanians and expel the resident Jews, whom they considered aliens. This was a local initiative, implemented by Hungarian gendarmes under local commanders. Around 18,000 Jews were transported to the border and from there marched into former Soviet territory as far as Kamenets-Podolsk. This was what the Romanians had attempted a few weeks earlier, and the Germans were not pleased. However, instead of sending them back, this time Jeckeln took cognizance of the new instructions to dispose of Jews in the most radical fashion. He added the Jews from Hungary to some 8,000 Jewish men, women and children from Kamenets-Podolsk and had 23,600 shot over a three-day period.[111]

On 30 August, the Germans resolved their differences with the Romanians by handing them the area of land between the Dniester and the Bug, known as Transnistria, in return for the right to maintain bases there and control over the lines of communication to their armies in the southern USSR. The Tighina Convention, as it was called, cleared the way for the Romanians to use the region as a dumping ground for Jews expelled from their homes in Moldavia, Bukovina and Bessarabia. Consequently, Transnistria became one of the most ghastly killing grounds in eastern Europe. It was overwhelmingly rural, with an area of 40,000 square miles and an indigenous population of about 2.5 million, including roughly 300,000 Jews. Some two thirds of them were concentrated in Odessa, a city with an illustrious reputation in modern Jewish history as the birthplace of numerous writers, poets, political thinkers and musicians. That was until the territory was overrun by Romanian forces between 15 and 30 July. Odessa was surrounded but held out until 17 October, during which time up to half its Jews were evacuated or mobilized for military service and withdrawn by sea in a Dunkirk-style operation. Meanwhile, Sipo-SD units and Romanian killing squads murdered thousands of Jews in the cities of Transnistria, including Mogilev-Podolski, Tulchin and Balta.[112]

Once the territory was opened, the Romanian authorities began emptying the ghettos and camps in which Jews had been held for the previous weeks. It is estimated that about 66,000 Jews were force-marched eastwards and across the Dniester. Along the way they were systematically robbed by the police, gendarmes and army units assigned to escort them. Up to 25,000 died or were killed. Women were raped and murdered as a matter of course. One witness reported how a single Romanian contingent behaved: 'During the night, the members of the new detachment and their helpers would pick out girls from the throng and abuse them until dawn. During the day they managed to make a little money by "selling" a girl to a peasant.' Villagers congregated along the line of march would scrutinize the clothing Jews were wearing and identify attire they fancied; the guards would then shoot the wearer, strip the body, and sell the garb to their client. When the Jews reached the Dniester, officials of the Romanian National Bank relieved them of any currency and valuables they still possessed. The expulsions led to a local economic boom.[113]

The evacuation of the Chisenau ghetto between 8 and 13 October 1941 was accompanied by plunder, confiscations and body searches of women suspected of concealing valuables. The Jews were placed on trains that took them as far as Atachi on the Dniester; then they walked for days until they reached Tighana, Tiraspol, Orhei or Rezina where they were placed in makeshift camps, often converted pig farms, without any provisions or any way of making a living. By November only 130 Jews were left in Chisenau, allowed to stay thanks to enormous bribes and connections with corrupt local officials. In Cernauti things went quite differently, due to the exertions of the mayor, Traian Popovici. He vigorously contested the removal of professionals and skilled workers, fighting to get whole groups exempted from the deportations. Nevertheless, thousands left for northern Transnistria by train every day between 17 October and 15 November until only about 19,000 remained. In the absence of the city's Jewish citizens, production in its saw mills and chemical plants, metal works and textile mills ground to a halt. The Romanian authorities found themselves with a glut of vacant apartments and warehouses stuffed with plundered household goods. Antonescu's vision for the orderly redistribution of wealth from Jews to those he considered genuine Romanians turned sour and most of the bonanza went to opportunists, nicknamed 'Californians' by knowing locals. About 7,500 Jews were deported from Dorohoi county, too, even though it was in Romania. There local officials made fortunes selling exemptions to Jews who could afford them. In spite of the endemic corruption, so much property, precious metal, currency and assets flowed into the Romanian National Bank that gold backing for the lei rose from 2.1 billion in 1941 to 11.3 billion a year later.[114]

Transnistria now became the unwilling home to some 145,000 Jews. Less than half would survive more than twelve months. Having been stripped of valuables, cash, bedding, spare clothing, cooking utensils and food, they were directed to towns and villages where they found whatever shelter was available and scrounged for anything to eat. Many ended up in rough-hewn farm buildings. Rakhil Fradis-Milner and her family were amongst those who were further uprooted from the miserable camps to which they had been sent in July–August 1941. This time it was winter, and on the march her mother and nieces died of exhaustion and exposure. 'The last stops were the villages and collective farms around Bershad, in Balta County. The remains of the convoys were herded together there and housed in filthy pig and cow sheds with neither doors nor windows. Here typhus spread from filth, cold, and hunger, and hundreds of people were dying each day without help. After a few days, the dead were lying among the living.' Those deported from Cernauti to the Mogilev-Podolski area fared best. They arrived with their communal leaders and immediately began setting up self-help organizations. An engineer, Siegfried Jagendorf, persuaded local Romanian police officials to let him repair and start up an abandoned metal works, providing work for the deportees and products to exchange for food. He later expanded his activities to food-processing and textile plants. Jagendorf's enterprises offered a lifeline to the otherwise unemployed and destitute Jews. Their representatives also sent pleas for help to the Jewish leadership in Bucharest. Wilhelm Filderman, a wealthy businessman who led the Romanian Jews, responded by boldly addressing appeals to Antonescu. In a typical demonstration of the incoherent Romanian policy he won the regime's consent to send funds to the deportees. Those who ended up in camps in central and southern Transnistria suffered the worst. In these areas there were large communities of ethnic Germans who supported Selbstschutz (self-defence militia) units that were very willing to massacre the hapless communities of starving, disease-ridden Jews. But the most terrible fate was that of the Jews in Odessa.[115]

By the time the city capitulated, the Romanian besiegers had suffered heavy casualties and were in the mood for revenge. It is estimated that 8,000 Jews were slain over the two days following the Romanians' entry into the city. On 22 October, a time-bomb went off in the former Soviet secret police building that was being used as the HQ of a Romanian infantry division and the city commandant. Antonescu was furious at the further loss of life and determined on a terrible reprisal. Einsatzgruppe D reported that 'As a counter measure, the Romanians seem to be preparing to shoot the Jews in Odessa. To date, about 10,000 have been shot.' The retaliation was barbaric: dozens of Jewish men were strung up from the balconies of apartment buildings. A resident told Vera Inber, a post-liberation investigator, that 'There were thousands of them. At the feet of the hanged lay the bodies of those who had been tortured, mutilated and shot. Our town was a terrible sight, a town of the hanged.' Some 25,000 Jews were driven to nine warehouses in the Dalnic suburb. Once the Jews were packed inside, the Romanian army turned machine guns and artillery on them. When this method of destruction proved time-consuming, the buildings were doused in petrol and set on fire. Another 30,000 Jews of all ages, men and women, were force-marched out of the city towards the village of Bogdanovka, where they were butchered over a period of days. The rest of the Jewish population, about 40,000, were packed into a temporary ghetto in the Slobodka district. Jewish women were frequently separated out and raped en masse. A week later, Anna Morgulis, a middle-aged stenographer in an Odessa shipyard, was arrested on suspicion of sabotage and taken to a prison where she was beaten unconscious. 'That night, with impenetrable darkness all around us, thirty Romanian soldiers burst into our cell and, after throwing their coats onto the damp floor, threw themselves on us. We were all raped, even the old women. Some of the younger girls were driven insane. We, the older women – and there were women there even older than I was – sat there and wept.'[116]

Over the next weeks, and well into the winter, the Jews were removed by train and on foot from the miserable Slobodka quarter to ghetto-camps at Bogdanovka, Domanevka and Akhmetchetka in Golta county. They were joined by Jews driven out of the southern portion of Transnistria. Countless numbers died in the trains and on the roads. The odyssey of schoolboy Lev Rozhetsky took him first to Beryozovka Station, where he saw Jews being burned in pits. He was then marched through snow to Sirotskoe. There they were lodged in stables, but 'At night, drunken Romanian policemen and local bandits, armed with guns, knives, and clubs, burst into the stables, stabbing, killing, robbing, raping.' His column finally came to rest in a camp outside Domanevka, thirty miles from the rail-head. The conditions were nearly indescribable. Peasants sold the Jews scraps of food for exorbitant sums. Typhus carried off so many each day that the weakened survivors left the bodies to rot, having stripped them of clothing in the hope of exchanging it for something to eat. But most Jews did not have to endure these horrors for very long. The majority were massacred a few days or weeks after they arrived. In Bogdanovka, out of 48,000 in the camp at its peak, 30,000 were killed in mass shootings between 21 and 30 December and 3 and 9 January 1942. Karp Koneevich Sheremet, a Ukrainian and a native of Bogdanovka, later testified that 'Mass shootings . . . continued for days on end. They shot them beside the ravine outside the forestry collective, then burned them right away. There was a pause from 24 to 26 [December] because the execution detachment went to Golta to celebrate Christmas.' The 14,000 Jews held at Domanevka were almost all killed between 10 January and 18 March 1942. The Romanian guards and German Selbstschutz seemed to lose all inhibitions. One survivor recalled that 'the Romanians ripped the babies in half or grabbed them by the feet and smashed their heads on stones. The women had their breasts chopped off, and many whole families were either buried alive or burned alive in the bonfires.' The commandants of one village 'nightly sent their assistants to the camp to bring back pretty girls. They always derived a particular pleasure from watching the death agonies of these girls on the morning of the next day.' In Akhmetchetka 4,000 Jews were confined to a pig farm; most died of starvation and disease. Only about 3,000 Jews were left in the whole of Golta county by late 1943.[117]

The destruction of the Jews of Bukovina, Bessarabia and Trans-nistria was improvised and created all sorts of unforeseen problems. The Germans were bothered by the epidemic of typhus in settlements straddling their supply lines. Eventually this would lead to a decision that the Jews in Transnistria should be handed over to the Selbstschutz for disposal. During early 1942 these ethnic Germans shot about 33,000 Jews in Berezovka county alone. The Romanians had a different sort of headache. They quibbled with the Germans over who would get the homes and household property of the murdered Jews of Odessa. Their argument was somewhat weakened by the fact that there were not enough Romanians to fill the apartments vacated by Jews and nor was there sufficient transport to cart away the loot. The storage vaults of Odessa were filled to overflowing with looted pianos; there was no one left to play them.[118]

The crisis at the front and the crisis of anti-Jewish policy

At the end of 1941, Karl Jäger, commanding officer of Einsatzkom-mando 3, a sub-unit of Einsatzgruppe A, operating in Lithuania, provided his superiors with a detailed report of its homicidal activities over the previous six months. His men had killed 136,423 Jews: 46,403 men, 55,556 women and 34,464 children. The only Jews left were workers in three ghettos: 15,000 in Vilnius, 15,000 in Kaunus and 5,000 in Shauli. In fact, there were probably 10,000 more than his computa-tion since there were many unregistered or in hiding. Notwithstanding the incertitude concerning these gruesome statistics, the balance sheet for the massacres committed on the coat tails of Operation Barbarossa is staggering. There were only 6,500 Jews left in Latvia out of a pre-war Jewish population of about 95,000. The Jewish population of Byelorussia had been pared down from about 300,000 to 80,000–90,000. Some 200,000 Jews had been slaughtered in the Soviet Ukraine and around 90,000 in Transnistria.[119]

Yet however monstrous the achievement, it was only partial. Shortly after Jäger finished blowing his trumpet, Einsatzgruppe A informed Berlin that 139,000 Jews were still present in the Reichskommissariat Ostland. Between 270,000 and 290,000 Jews were also alive in Volhynia, Polesie and Podolia. No less than 522,000 were living in east Galicia and 90,000 were clinging to life in Transnistria. While the murder operations at the eastern reaches of the German advance had verged on the total, for logistical reasons and due to the concentration of the Jewish population, in the western regions nearly a million Jews remained.[120]

Though the Germans and their accomplices succeeded in inflicting unimaginable suffering and destruction of life on the Jews in the conquered parts of the USSR, the assault evolved haphazardly and turned into the customary incoherent jumble of mutually conflicting policies. There was little or no coordination with Germany's Axis partners, with the result that Hungary and Romania ended up taking action that ran counter to German interests. This was not sorted out until months into the campaign. Nor was there coordination between the SS and the civil authorities. When Hinrich Lohse, Reichskommissar for the Ostland, issued draft guidelines for the treatment of Jews, the security police were indignant. First they objected that he was treading on their turf and, second, that he had got it all wrong anyway. The Higher SS Police Leader Hans Prutzmann and Stahlecker, the Einsatzgruppe commander, protested to Berlin, where the ministry for the occupied eastern territories was quick to correct Lohse: the Sipo-SD had autonomy as far as Jews were concerned. Lohse's eventual directive of 16 August defined who was Jewish and mandated that Jews should be registered and marked. Their property and assets were to be confiscated and they were to be given a subsistence allowance. He ordered that Jews be cleared from rural areas and concentrated in urban ghettos, where they would receive rations according to what food could be spared. They would also perform forced labour. But the directive stressed that these were the minimum steps and were applicable where 'measures for the final solution' were not possible. In other words, if the Sipo-SD chose another fate for the Jews, Lohse was powerless to obstruct them.[121]

Friction arose repeatedly over the treatment of skilled workers. Heinrich Karl had objected to a Lithuanian police battalion wiping out the Jews who manned the workshops and factories in Slutsk, his city. Not long afterwards, Lohse raised the same issue with Stahlecker and HSSPF Krüger (who replaced Prutzmann). He formally inquired of the Ostministerium whether the elimination of Jews extended to those working for the Wehrmacht and the arms industries. Elements of the army, too, expressed reservations about the wanton destruction of skilled labour. The Armaments Inspectorate in the Ukraine accepted the need to remove 'superfluous eaters' from the cities and to eliminate hostile populations, but expressed concern over the risk of economic and reputational damage, not to mention the demoralizing effect on the troops who either saw or took part in brutish mass killings. Occasionally there was a principled protest. One Gebietskommissioner in the Ostland passed on the query 'if it was necessary to exterminate children . . . In no civilized country, not even in the middle ages, was it possible to execute pregnant women.'[122]

Ghettos, considered a ubiquitous feature of anti-Jewish policy, appeared late in the occupied areas of the USSR and were hardly standard practice. Furthermore, the rationale for them differed from place to place. To Army Group Centre they were a security measure; in the rear of Army Group North ghettos were a way to control food consumption. Some ghettos had a Jewish council and an Order Service, others did not. Whereas by late 1941 the ghettos in Poland had acquired an economic rationale, the temporary structures in the USSR were never more than detention camps.[123]

The absence of consistency with regards to ghettos can be traced back to a fundamental confusion over means and ends. Were Jews to be expelled, placed in ghettos, or put to death? Until October 1941, the hope was that Jews would be expelled into Siberia after the end of hostilities. In mid-September, EK 6 of Einsatzgruppen C commented that 'While a considerable number of Jews could be apprehended during the first weeks, it can be ascertained that in the central and eastern districts of the Ukraine, in many cases 70 per cent to 90 per cent and in some cases even 100 per cent of the Jewish population had bolted. The gratuitous evacuation of hundreds of thousands of Jews may be considered to be an indirect success of the work of the security police. As we hear mostly from the other side of the Urals, this is a considerable contribution to the solution of the Jewish question in Europe.' On 16 October 1941, Antonescu told his council of ministers that 'I have decided to evacuate all [Jews] from these regions. I still have about 10,000 Jews in Bessarabia who will be sent beyond the Dniester within several days and, if circumstances permit, beyond the Urals.' Yet by then, Himmler had already instructed his executioners to annihilate the Russian Jews to the last man, woman and child.[124]

In fact, when Himmler changed the nature of their mission, the evacuation of Soviet Jews was in full swing. In the first two weeks of the campaign the ability of Jews to flee was hindered by the speed of the German advance and the refusal of the Soviet security services to let refugees cross the old Russo-Polish border. As a result most of the Jews in eastern Poland were trapped. Thereafter the Jews were better able to escape and the Soviet regime put into place measures to evacuate the population from the path of the German armies. Jews were not evacuated as Jews, but because so many were skilled white-collar workers they benefited disproportionately from the policy to evacuate the staff and families of state agencies and industrial enterprises. The historian Yitzhak Arad estimates that about 5 per cent of Volhynian Jews managed to elude the Germans, while the proportion of Jews evading capture rose dramatically further into eastern Belarus, in the Russian Federation and in the eastern Ukraine. Although roughly one million Jews came under German occupation in the USSR, most of whom would perish, an equal number outran them or were pulled to safety by the Soviet state.[125]

The greatest failure of policy was military. On 2 October 1941, Army Group Centre launched Operation Typhoon, a last bid to capture Moscow and end the war before winter set in. At first all went well. The German armies made stunning gains, again thanks largely to the ineptitude of the Soviet commanders. Then the rain came and the front bogged down. When the frost arrived in mid-November and the attack resumed, it was little more than a desperate gamble. The troops were at the end of their tether, the army had used up all its replacements, and there were no more reserves. The transport system was barely able to supply the forward units with more than a portion of their requirements; fuel, fodder and ammunition took priority over winter clothing, condemning the miserable infantry to exposure and frostbite. On 6 December the Russians counter-attacked. Not only was the war going to last longer than the German leadership had anticipated, the eastern armies now found themselves fighting for survival against fresh Siberian divisions that Wehrmacht military intelligence did not even know existed.[126]

Defeat had multiple ramifications for anti-Jewish policy. The aim of solving the Jewish problem through expulsion to a territory beyond the living space of Germans had been premised on victory. That policy was now foiled, but the failure to end the war made it even more pressing to find a solution. The Third Reich faced a food crisis and a security crisis, both of which could be attributed to the Jews. Instead of postponing a reckoning with the Jewish question until the war was over, it had to be solved – and solved quickly – precisely because the war was not going to end soon. Finally, there was the international context. Germany had not knocked Russia out of the war, so Britain would stay in the fight and it was evident that the USA was edging towards the fray. Since in the minds of the Nazis the Jews were responsible for these developments, the Jews within their grasp would have to answer for them. The collision of military failure with failed Jewish policy would have devastating consequences for the Jews of the Third Reich.

The deportation of Jews from the Reich

Life for the remaining Jews in Nazi Germany was shabby, constricted and weighed down by apprehension. Confined to Jew-houses, limited to shopping at certain times, and banned from any cultural activities or outdoor recreation, they were almost completely cut off from the rest of society. In August 1940, the authorities confiscated the telephone in the Jew-house where Klemperer lived. A year later, he was prohibited from using the local lending library. The clothes Jews wore grew threadbare and their shoes deteriorated. Their diminishing rations and the poor quality of the food damaged their health. Those who fell ill found it arduous to get medical attention from the few remaining Jewish doctors and nurses. Although a high proportion were elderly and frail, 40,000 were forced to work for paltry remuneration. Indeed, by the end of 1940 they came to be seen as a valuable pool of skilled labour.[127]

During 1941, the remnant, including 'privileged Jews' and Jews in mixed marriages, came under increasing pressure. Local officials now demanded that Jews give up even the shared accommodation in Jew-houses. Some were motivated by the need to rehouse families whose homes were damaged or destroyed by RAF bombing, but the wave of evictions spread well beyond the cities struck by air raids. In Hanover, 100 Jews were forced to relocate to an old synagogue, 150 were jammed into a funeral parlour, and 200 into the communal offices. In Essen, the authorities provided a camp on the site of a disused coal mine. In Cologne they used barracks built for Russian prisoners of the Great War. Dresden Jews were housed in huts near a factory where most of them worked. In Breslau the 8,000–9,000 Jews were concentrated around the Storch Synagogue. They could only do business with one another, but somehow sustained a communal existence. The community ran a school for 500 children, a hospital, provided kosher food and organized cultural events. Eventually, the Breslau authorities evicted them from their homes, thirty apartments at a time, and shoved them into barracks that were little more than transit camps. This final dislocation left the many elderly Jews in utterly unfamiliar surroundings, battling with overcrowding and poor sanitation.[128]

As the world of the Jews shrank, the Germans benefited from the confiscation of their property. Gestapo men and Nazi Party officials were the first to grab the contents of vacated homes. What remained was auctioned off by the municipal pawnshops. In Hamburg the haul included 600 medical books and a top hat. Local people would approach the dealers with requests for specific items of household furniture. At a more rarefied level, the Museum of Art in Breslau applied for the best paintings from a private collection owned by Max Silberg. At no level of German society did there appear to be much concern about the fate of the Jews whose everyday articles and prized possessions found new owners.[129]

The Reichsvereinigung worked tirelessly to alleviate the conditions of the beleaguered communities. Much of its work was devoted to emigration. Even as Jews were dying in Polish ghettos and being slaughtered in Russia, the Central Office for Jewish Emigration was still pushing the orderly departure of Reich Jews. Hundreds who held visas for emigration to the USA were given exit papers and allowed to make their getaway, mainly via Spain and Portugal. Jews were now prepared to accept destinations that would once have been considered bizarre. In April 1940, thirty-five German and Austrian Jews arrived in Buena Tierra, a remote area of Bolivia, with the intention of constructing an agricultural settlement that would eventually absorb up to 1,200 refugees. The project was funded by the Sociedad Colonizadora de Bolivia, a joint venture between a local Jewish tycoon, Mauricio Hochschild, and the AJJDC. It proved too challenging, though, and the scheme faded. The 20,000 central European Jews who ended up in Bolivia preferred to cling to the more familiar urban jungle of La Paz. There they created Viennese-style coffee houses and cultural associations, while Lebensmittelgeschäft Brückner & Krill specialized in supplying them with continental delicacies. Across the Pacific, around 16,000 Jews from Mitteleuropa struggled to establish themselves in a corner of the international concession in Shanghai. In May 1940, Illo Koratkowski and her mother travelled by train 4,000 miles from Berlin via Moscow, Irkutsk and Harbin, to the Chinese port of Dairen where she boarded a ship to Shanghai. There her father awaited them. Victor Klemperer, however, was not among the lucky ones. 'New regulations about immigration into the USA,' he noted on 27 July 1941. 'Our affidavit . . . is thereby invalid. The new procedure means effectively that it will be impossible to get out in any foreseeable future. That suits us. All vacillation is now at an end. Fate will decide.'[130]

Klemperer was in no doubt that his fate would depend on the war, that there was a correlation between the regime's manipulation of anti-Semitism and developments on both the eastern front and the home front. Even though he was not allowed to own a radio he accurately monitored German military progress. In late July he noted, 'Advance into Russia appears to have come to a standstill; everyone knows or spreads rumours about heavy German losses.' The roller-coaster campaign was certainly taking a toll on domestic morale. Ulrich von Hassell calculated the popular mood using what he called his war 'barometer'. In early August after factoring in the evidence of heavy Russian resistance, mounting losses, and RAF air raids he came up with 'low barometer readings, a general feeling of endlessness and doom'. By the middle of the month he was alerted to the dissension between Hitler and his commanders and concluded that the war would persist into the winter. Klemperer, relying on fewer sources of information, reached the same prognosis. 'German position most precarious, total victory before onset of winter impossible, lasting through the winter next to impossible, given the shortage of raw materials.' He also learned that morale in the Rhineland, the target of regular RAF bombardment, and in Berlin 'which is frequently attacked, is said to be catastrophic'. Even the victory at Kiev and the pitiful sight of captured Russians did not deceive Reck-Malleczewan. He sardonically observed that the increasing use of synthetic products and food substitutes was responsible for the frequent bouts of biliousness in cafes.[131]

Foreign journalists, too, observed the deterioration. Howard Smith, one of the last American correspondents in Berlin, knew that even before the invasion of the USSR 'Germany was already actually scraping the bottom of Europe's economic bin.' Operation Barbarossa made things worse: 'the eastern front drained away already scarce fats so quickly that swift and huge reductions had to be made within a very short period'. Potatoes vanished from the shops and tomatoes disappeared into cans for the boys in Russia. In November beer consumption was reduced for the same reason. Smith noticed that bus and tram lines were quietly discontinued. 'The underground became shoddy, dirty, worn out.' Three-quarters of taxis were withdrawn from service and when lifts broke they went unrepaired. The rolling stock available to the Reichsbahn was reduced in order to replace 4,000 locomotives and freight wagons damaged in the east, half of the entire fleet servicing the eastern armies. 'Germany', he concluded 'has been winning itself to death.'[132]

Joseph Goebbels, an arch-realist in the privacy of his diary, could not deny the crisis. During July he acknowledged, 'Food situation in Berlin is very bad.' Even when harvest produce began to roll in, things were 'extraordinarily precarious'. On 24 August he admitted with a characteristic mixture of clarity and black humour, 'The mood of Germany has grown more serious. One is gradually becoming aware that the eastern campaign is no stroll to Moscow.' At the end of the month he acknowledged, 'we have underestimated Bolshevism'. Though there were up-ticks in morale, the trend was sober. Smith reckoned that by the third month of Operation Barbarossa 'a moral depression set in which joined the economic decline'. It was a watershed. Winter was approaching but victory was no closer. The euphoria that accompanied the offensive towards Moscow evaporated once the advance got bogged down, leaving people lower than ever and interested in only one thing: a final, decisive victory. Goebbels could not deliver that, but he could demonstrate that the Jewish enemy in Germany was beaten.[133]

Anti-Semitic propaganda had, of course, continued unabated since the war started. In October 1940 Goebbels scored one of his greatest successes as a film producer and propagandist with the release of *Jud Süß*, based on the story of a court Jew in the eighteenth century. It depicted 'the Jew' as avaricious, scheming, licentious and ruthless, but so skilfully that Germans attended in droves and applauded the movie. He followed it up with a documentary, *Der ewige Jude* (The Eternal Jew), intended to show the Ostjude as he really was. The film exploited the occupation of Poland to present scenes that would confirm the Nazi image of the eastern Jew. One segment cut from crowded streets in the Jewish district of Warsaw to hordes of rats swarming through a building. Some viewers were distressed by a deliberately gruesome sequence in an abattoir where cattle were slaughtered according to Jewish religious law. To Goebbels' disappointment, the documentary flopped. The head office of the SS reported that 'the disgusting character of what was presented as such, and most particularly the ritual slaughter scenes, were repeatedly cited as the main reason not to see the movie'. The SD office in Höxter commented rather more unflatteringly that people found it 'a bit boring'. Nevertheless the two films had a perceptible influence. Klemperer observed, 'Public Jew-baiting is rising again. Film propaganda Jew Süß and The Eternal Jew'. It was scant consolation that the latter disappeared from cinemas after a week.[134]

As his contribution to Operation Barbarossa, Goebbels ratcheted up the propaganda campaign. His articles, speeches, and directives to the press called particular attention to the 'alliance of plutocracy and Bolshevism', which was intended to explain the attack on the USSR and also to stigmatize American aid for both Britain and Russia. He was gifted an opportunity in July 1941 after an American Jew named Theodore Kaufman privately published a vitriolic book entitled *Germany Must Perish!*, which, amongst other things, demanded the sterilization of all Germans. Goebbels' press machine blew the influence of the book out of all proportion, claiming that its author, in truth a nonentity, had ties to the White House and was giving vent to American, or rather Jewish, plans for the Germans should the Third Reich be defeated. The SD welcomed publication of excerpts from the book which would 'show that this war is really one where the stakes are life or death'.[135]

Not coincidentally, the Gestapo and Nazi officials began to call for more draconian measures against the Jews in the Reich, specifically, marking them. The demand to render Jews visible was malicious but also practical. It related to the shortages of food and the belief that Jews were taking what should rightfully go to Germans. The SD in Bielefeld, for example, complained about the 'provocative' behaviour of Jews whose offence was to buy food in the market. The same office protested that a Jewish man married to an Aryan woman had bought 'pure coffee' in defiance of rationing restrictions. The NSDAP Gau office for racial policy in Munich raised the alternative possibility of an index of Mischlinge, since 'there is often an attempt to mask the degree of Jewish genetic background'.[136]

Against this febrile background, on 18 August Goebbels met with his officials at the Ministry of Propaganda to discuss Jewish policy. They assumed that it would only be a matter of time before the Jews were evacuated to the east, but agreed that until then they should be marked. When he had an audience with Hitler at the Führer headquarters later the same day Goebbels complained about the Jewish 'parasites' in Berlin and demanded that before they were removed they should be clearly indicated with a badge. Hitler agreed. He was, it seems, in a particularly vicious mood at this juncture and was in the habit of repeating his prophecy that the Jews would suffer for bringing about the war. He reiterated to Goebbels that 'In the east the Jews must pay the bill.' Closer to home, though, they would have to bear the marking that was already part of the Jewish way of life in Poland and the occupied USSR. On 1 September 1941, the Ministry of the Interior issued a decree that from the 19th of the month all Jews would have to wear a yellow Star of David with the word 'Jude' in gothic lettering at its centre. In the accompanying press comment, Nazi commentators explicitly linked the imposition to the war. The *Völkischer Beobachter* explained that 'The German soldier has met in the Eastern campaign the Jew in his most disgusting, most gruesome form. This experience forces the German soldier and the German people to deprive the Jews of every means of camouflage at home.'[137]

The application of the yellow star was greeted with enthusiasm by Nazis and those in tune with them, but more coolly by other Germans. The Gestapo men in Bielefeld rejoiced that now they could identify Jews on the street they could enforce all the many restrictions against them. The SD Head Office in Berlin claimed general public satisfaction, although it reported that some people were astonished to find so many Jews still around. The visibility of Jews actually ramped up demands for harsher action. The SD soon received complaints that Jews in mixed marriages were exempted and so remained indistinguishable as Jews. Shopkeepers whose premises were designated for Jewish use were alarmed that the discernible presence of Jews would deter their other customers. Leland Morris at the US Embassy informed Washington that many Germans were indeed 'unpleasantly surprised' to see that such numbers 'still live in good residential sections of the large cities occupying valuable apartments at a time of big shortage'. He added, however, that 'a very large proportion of Berliners have shown embarrassment and even sympathy rather than satisfaction at the display of Jewish badges'.[138]

Victor Klemperer certainly thought that the 'Jews' star did not meet with much public approval'. His perception was confirmed to some extent by the SD office tracking public opinion: it concluded that older and more religious people actually disapproved. Harry Flannery, who replaced William Shirer for CBS in Berlin, detected that 'most of the German people, even on this first day, paid no attention to the Jews'. Conversely, his colleague Howard Smith recalled that 'the day the Yellow Star was introduced, people all over Berlin were asking one another, why in God's name was a manoeuvre like this necessary? It was too obvious that the poor, wretched Jews living in Germany had nothing to do with the disappearance of foodstuffs and the failure of the High Command to conquer Russia in time'.[139]

The badge occasioned plenty of black humour. Since the order mandating the wearing of the star also forbade Jews from wearing medals, one wag suggested that the yellow star was the new 'Pour le Semité'. Flannery asserted that 'Jews wore it with visible pride' but gave no evidence of this. German Jews told another story. Klemperer keened to his diary, 'I feel myself shattered, cannot compose myself'. Ruth Andreas-Friedrich, a journalist in pre-Nazi Berlin and a member of the anti-Nazi underground, confided to her journal, 'It's here. As from today the Jews are outlawed, marked as outcasts by a Yellow Star of David that each one must wear on the left chest. We feel like crying abroad for help. But what good is our outcry. Those who would help us don't hear us – or perhaps don't want to. Thank God the greater part of the people are not pleased with the new decree. Almost everyone we meet is as much ashamed as we.'[140]

The marking of Jews in the Reich was but a prelude to their deportation, a tragedy that had been in the making for months. Back in July 1941, during the weeks when the Nazi elite was swollen with ambition, Heydrich had solicited from Göring the authority 'for making all necessary preparations with regard to organisational, practical and financial aspects for an overall solution of the Jewish question in the German sphere of influence'. Göring requested prompt delivery of the plan for 'the intended final solution', presumably since he and Heydrich anticipated that the war would be over in a matter of weeks or months, at which point it would be put into effect. But the war dragged on and Hitler repeatedly refused to countenance major deportations until it was over. During August, when Heydrich and Goebbels requested permission to set deportations in motion, they were told to wait. Hitler's resolve weakened once it became apparent that the war was going to continue into the next year. First of all, pressure was building up to deal with the housing shortage in Berlin. Since April 1941, Albert Speer's building inspectorate had been evicting Jews to provide homes for the victims of air raids. Nazi Party bosses in cities like Hamburg and Lübeck that had taken a pasting from the RAF were furious that Jews still occupied good apartments. In view of the 'catastrophic' housing situation why not deport them to the east? Overcrowding on trams and the railways occasioned similar grousing. Of course, the war was responsible for the declining standards of comfort, but Jews got the blame. Local authorities also reported anger amongst the parents of soldiers because they had to rub shoulders with Jews while their sons were engaged in the 'battle against Jews and Bolshevism'. Finally there was pressure on food supplies. Not only was the Wehrmacht consuming vast quantities of fats, meat and cereals, but the retention of millions of men at the front meant there were fewer hands to bring in the harvest. The regime could not afford to delay measures that would alleviate these pressures and distract attention from them at the same time. The final trigger may have been news that Stalin had ordered the forced resettlement of 400,000 ethnic Germans from the Volga region to Siberia. Ribbentrop met Hitler on 17 September and proposed that Germany retaliate by uprooting the Jews of central Europe to the eastern territories. Thus, between 15 and 17 September, Hitler finally ordered the deportation of Jews from the Reich and the Protectorate. The solution of the Jewish problem would go ahead regardless of what transpired on the eastern front. As he had predicted: the Jews would pay.[141]

Himmler, Heydrich and Eichmann now engaged in a round of meetings to implement the Führer's wish. It was no mean challenge. After all, there were almost 250,000 Jews in the Greater Reich and around 88,000 in the Protectorate. Notwithstanding success in the battle of Kiev the situation in the east was indeterminate. As in the case of all their previous schemes, the preparations were hasty and half-baked and they ran up against repeated obstacles that forced them to scale back their ambitions and improvise still further.

To begin they had to locate destinations for the Jews and, then, ensure that they would be received appropriately. On 18 September, Himmler informed Arthur Greiser by letter that, 'The Führer wishes the Altreich and the Protectorate to be cleared of and freed from Jews from West to East as soon as possible. Consequently, I shall endeavour, this year if possible, and initially as a first stage, to transport the Jews of the Altreich and the Protectorate to those Eastern territories which became part of the Reich two years ago, and then deport them even further eastwards next spring.' Then came the bad news: 'My intention is to take approximately 60,000 Jews of the Altreich and the Protectorate to spend the winter in Litzmannstadt ghetto which, I have heard, still has available capacity. I ask you not only to understand this step, which will certainly impose difficulties and burdens on your Gau, but to do everything in your power to support it in the interests of the Reich.' Greiser was dismayed, but after some hard negotiating agreed to take 20,000 Jews and 5,000 Roma into his domain. His consent was conditional on getting carte blanche to make room for the western Jews by removing 100,000 'sick' Polish Jews.[142]

In early October, Heydrich consulted with the ministry for the east concerning the dispatch of Reich Jews to locations under its nominal control. Minsk and Riga emerged as the two most likely destinations, since anywhere further east would strain transport resources and impinge on the rear of the German army groups. When the information reached Minsk that it would be necessary to accommodate 50,000 Jews from the Reich and the Protectorate the local Sipo-SD knew exactly what to do. There were no complications and no opposition. On 7 November, 12,000–17,000 non-working Jews were assembled in the ghetto and trucked to the Tuchinka ravine, where they were shot by detachments of German soldiers, Byelorussian police and Ukrainian auxiliaries. The first trainload of Reich Jews, comprising 990 cold, hungry, bedraggled and mostly elderly men and women, arrived the next day. They were taken to a special section of the ghetto that was segregated from the remaining Russian Jews. In a second massacre on 20 November, another 5,000–10,000 local Jews were murdered. These ghetto clearances were conducted with the customary mixture of avarice and barbarism. A survivor recalled that 'As soon as the small children got down from the trucks, the police took them from their parents and broke their spinal column against their knees. Small babies were thrown in the air and shot at or caught on bayonets and then flung into the trenches. Naked people were lined up next to the pit and shot with machine guns. Those who refused to undress were machine gunned in their clothing. If their clothing was of good quality, they were undressed after being killed.'[143]

Heydrich had meanwhile added the job of running the Protectorate to his already extensive list of offices. One of the first things he did was intensify the persecution of the Jews in Bohemia and Moravia. On 10 October, ten days after he was installed as Reich Protector in Prague, he told Karl-Hermann Frank, his secretary of state, Adolf Eichmann, and Hans Günther, who ran the Prague office for Jewish emigration, that he proposed to evacuate 5,000 Jews to the east in a few weeks and send the rest to a ghetto at a location still to be identified. At a press conference afterwards he announced his intentions to the world and added that the ghetto was nothing more than an 'interim' solution. In fact, he had absolutely no notion where the Jews would be housed, let alone what the permanent solution would be. Next day, Hans Günther called together the Jewish leadership in Prague and ordered them to come up with a list of suitable places. Even as they deliberated, five transports conveyed 5,000 Jews to Lodz, including the cream of the Prague Jewish intelligentsia, followed by 5,000 to Minsk and Riga. On 16 November, 1,000 Jews were sent from Brno (Brünn) to Minsk. A few days later, Karl Rahm, acting for Günther, selected the fortress town of Theresienstadt (Terezin in Czech) as the site for the ghetto. The first building team, comprising young Jewish men and skilled workers, was dispatched from Prague's Masaryk Station at 4.30 in the morning on 24 November 1941. By 10 a.m. they were at work, preparing the town for an influx of 60,000 Czech Jews.[144]

When Jeckeln, the new Higher SS Police Leader in the Ostland, informed Hinrich Lohse that he was expected to take 50,000 more Jews into the Riga ghetto, Lohse was taken aback. He protested to Rudolf Lange, commander of the Sipo-SD in Latvia and hence one of Heydrich's men, that it was an impossible undertaking. Where would they go? Jeckeln already had something in mind: they would make room for the Reich Jews in the ghetto by eliminating the Latvian Jews currently living there, much as he had wiped out communities in southern Russia, beginning with his exploits at Kamenets-Podolsk. Lohse seems to have been alarmed at this prospect and countered that there were useful workers in the ghetto. His dissension was ineffective. On 27 November, security police units, reinforced by order police, reorganized the ghetto into two parts and began selecting those who would be retained as a workforce. About 5,500 men and 300 women were segregated from the rest. Three days later, Latvian Sipo-SD and German police entered the ghetto and began rounding up people; they used such extreme violence that some 800 perished in the process. The 15,000 assembled Jews were then marched through snow and ice to the Rumbula forest where Jeckeln's experienced team (who had come with him from Ukraine) had excavated three massive pits, each with a ramp at one end so that the Jews could walk into their grave and lie down prior to being shot. The slaughter went on all day, but even though Jeckeln was able to draw on teams of Latvian policemen they could not quite finish the job. At nightfall the traumatized remnant were marched back to the ghetto.[145]

Numerous German soldiers and officers witnessed the carnage. One of them, a major general of pioneers called Walter Bruns, recalled the scene in a conversation that was secretly taped while he was a POW in Britain in 1945. He had an engineer's eye for detail: 'the pits were 24 metres in length and 3 metres in breadth – they had to lie down like sardines in a tin, with their heads in the centre. Above them were six men with submachine guns who gave them the coup de grâce. When I arrived those pits were so full that the living had to lie down on top of the dead; then they were shot and, in order to save room, they had to lie down neatly in layers. Before this, however, they were stripped of every-thing at one of the stations.' At these 'stations' they had to hand over jewellery, packs and suitcases. 'All good stuff was put into suitcases and the remainder thrown on a heap.' Further on they had to undress com-pletely: 'they were only permitted to keep on a chemise and knickers. They were all women and small two-year-old children.' He remembered the 'nasty remarks' made by the shooters such as '"Here comes a Jewish beauty!"' The image of one woman stuck in his mind. 'Talk about keep-ing the race pure,' he continued, 'at Riga they first slept with them and then shot them to prevent them from talking.' Bruns sent two other officers to observe the scenes so that they could support his formal complaint. Shortly afterwards steps were taken to conduct the mas-sacres with greater discretion.[146]

The Riga murders created a stink in Berlin, although not because of the dismay expressed by a few senior Wehrmacht officers. By chance, a transport of 950 Berlin Jews had arrived at the Skirotava Station on the same day and Jeckeln had them shot along with the locals. The murder of the Berlin deportees annoyed Lange because Reich Jews were under the control of the RSHA and Jeckeln, as HSSPF, had no jurisdiction over them. Lange made a formal protest to the RSHA, as a result of which Jeckeln was summoned to Berlin and given a mild reprimand by Himmler. After his return, the killing resumed. Now, though, the Jews knew the fate awaiting them and there was considerable resistance. During the action on 7–9 December they refused to assemble meekly and many sought to evade the German and Latvian police units. In the ensuing turmoil about 900 were gunned down in the ghetto, including members of the Jewish council and the Order Service. In spite of this disruption, roughly 10,000 Jews were driven to Rumbula and murdered there, mainly by Latvians under the command of Victor Arajs.[147]

The deportation of the Reich Jews had all the familiar hallmarks of improvisation, lack of resources, and partial success. Lange gave instructions to build a reception camp at Salaspils, a few miles south-east of Riga on the railway line between the capital and Daugavpils, but by the end of the year it was nowhere near complete. Instead, trainloads of incoming Jews were bundled into a special section of the ghetto or diverted to a concentration camp at Jungfernhof. Whereas Himmler had aimed to evacuate 70,000 Jews, he managed to uproot only 53,000. Because the Riga ghetto was 'full' and Salaspils was not operational, during November several trainloads of German Jews were diverted to Kaunus or Minsk. Since no one in authority had any interest in receiving them, the Jews reaching these destinations were shot on arrival. The massacre of 1,000 Jews from Breslau (from a transport that departed on 23 November) shocked the Kaunus ghetto. For days afterwards Jewish workers sorted the belongings taken from the doomed train: 'The finest possessions that the eye can see . . . the nicest foods, all prepared with a generous hand to last a long time, the best clothing, the rarest of medicines, and various professional instruments. An endless number of books – scientific, professional, Jewish books, prayer books, prayer shawls . . . they were so shockingly deceived. Their first step toward their new life was also their last – the pits of the 9th Fort.' Amongst the slain from Breslau were Willy Cohen, his wife and two daughters aged nine and three years old.[148]

Jews from the west began arriving in the Lodz ghetto in late October. Despite repeated protests to Berlin by Mayor Ventzki and the ghetto manager Friedrich Übelhör, by the end of the year the ghetto had absorbed nearly 20,000 from the Old Reich, Prague, Vienna and

Luxemburg. Yet no immediate steps were taken to thin out the existing population. Instead, Herbert Lange, the head of a Sonderkommando that had murdered the inmates of Polish asylums, was deployed to use the same techniques to get rid of unwanted Jews from the Wartheland. Lange had pioneered the use of gas vans. He arranged for the large storage compartment mounted on a furniture lorry to be made airtight. The victims were loaded into the back, the doors were sealed, and exhaust fumes from the engine were piped into it until they were asphyxiated. As a light touch, each lorry was painted to make it appear like one of an innocuous fleet of vehicles belonging to the Kaiser Kaffee Geschäft – a coffee company. Lange identified the small town of Chelmno as a suitable base for his operation and constructed a crude facility with barracks for his staff and the guard detail, cells for the Jewish labour force, sorting and storage units, and a burial site in a nearby forest. His first victims were several hundred Jews from the nearby towns of Kolo and Czachulec who were murdered on 8–10 December 1941, perhaps as a trial run. But Chelmno was just waiting for the Jews of Lodz. On 20 December the ghetto authorities informed Chaim Rumkowski that 20,000 Jews would have to be removed from the ghetto due to food shortages and the influx of German Jews. Rumkowski bargained the numbers down to half that, then set up a commission to determine who would go. 'The news of the coming resettlement', the authors of the ghetto chronicle noted, 'has created a mood of depression in the ghetto.'[149]

German Jews, preoccupied with their own fate, had no inkling that their imminent deportation was causing misery and horror 600 miles away. On 15 October, Jewish emigration from the Reich was prohibited. The title of Eichmann's office, IVB4 of the Gestapo, was adjusted to signify that it handled evacuation rather than emigration. Guidelines for the removal of the Jews began to flow from office IVB4 to Gestapo offices and police stations across the Reich. Jews who were scheduled for evacuation were given precise instructions and ordered to fill in numerous forms detailing their property and assets. At the appointed date and time they had to appear at the assembly place, a synagogue or communal building, with all the necessary documentation, a suitcase weighing no more than 50kg, a blanket, food for three days' travel, and 200 Reichsmarks. When leaving their apartments they had to make sure the gas was turned off, lock the front door and hand the key over to the police. Helpfully, the envelope that contained the instructions and forms issued to each deportee also included a key ring. At the point of departure, usually a suburban railway station or a freight yard, they had to hand over share certificates, foreign currency, bank savings books, and any precious objects, with the exception of wedding rings. Their identity cards were then stamped 'Evacuated'.[150]

To ensure that there was no legal impediment to the Reich taking all their property and assets the Interior Ministry promulgated the 11th supplement to the Reich Citizenship Law. This stated that any Jew who left Germany was automatically stripped of his or her nationality and forfeited his or her wealth to the state. Since Jews who were deported to Theresienstadt technically remained within the Greater Reich they were required to sign a document by which they exchanged their home and belongings for a new residence in the Reich ghetto.[151]

The Reichsvereinigung in Berlin and the IKG in Vienna tried to make the lot of the deportees as comfortable as possible. Food kitchens were stationed at the assembly areas and medical staff were in attendance. In Vienna, Jewish marshals actually escorted Jews to the trains, sometimes carrying their baggage for them. But the fact that Jewish officials were there to help Jews on their way gave the impression that the Jewish organizations were colluding in the deportation process. The exemption of these officials compounded the jaundiced opinion of those who passed through their hands. Large numbers of Jews preferred to take their own lives in surroundings that still offered a modicum of familiarity and consolation. Howard Smith noticed that the official Jewish newspaper in Berlin was filled with death notices on the eve of each transport. It is estimated that 4,000–5,000 Jews in the Reich capital died by their own hand rather than face the indignity and hardship of relocating to a strange, primitive land. Most of them were elderly and a high percentage were women. In a significant number of cases, women opted for suicide after their non-Jewish spouse, who shielded them from removal, had died or been killed (some were in the army). Some Nazi bureaucrats regarded it as a defeat when a Jew cheated deportation in this way. The district governor of Upper and Central Franconia, for example, reported that 'The Jew Dr Martin Israel Offenbacher avoided evacuation by committing suicide.' In 1943, Hannah Arendt wrote in an essay about refugees that 'Jewish suicides in the Third Reich, especially after the deportations began, were therefore acts of self-assertion rather than acts of resistance against the National Socialist murderers' policies.'[152]

In spite of all the efforts of the regime to prevent turf wars over the property of the deported and to regulate the disposal of their belongings, the enforced exodus generated the usual unseemly squabbles. Howard Smith recorded how 'their pitiful belongings were sold at public auctions, and good Aryans fought like jackals over a carcass to buy shabby objects the Reich war had made scarce'. The public sales were often conducted inside homes unsealed for the purpose; they were an 'ugly spectacle'. In Göttingen, the NSDAP office was 'swamped by requests for the assignment of apartments'. The Minden Gestapo office fought with the revenue office over the right to dispose of vacated properties. There were no public protests; the Churches remained silent. But there was private unease, especially once news of their fate leaked back to Germany. Klemperer got wind of the Riga massacre not long afterwards. A rumour, he wrote, 'but it is very credible and comes from various sources – evacuated Jews were *shot* in Riga, in groups, as they left the train'. Ulrich von Hassell recorded 'revulsion on the part of all decent people towards the scandalous measures taken against the Jews and prisoners in the east, and against harmless, and often distinguished Jews in Berlin and other large cities'.[153]

Those who boarded the transports endured a wretched three- or four-day journey only to arrive at what was, to them, the end of the world. Henry Rosenberg, deported from Hamburg to Minsk in early November, recalled: 'The carriages were not heated. With so many people and so much luggage it was not possible to settle down let alone sleep. People were so anxious that the slightest affront led to an altercation.' Since they arrived in darkness they were confined to the carriages until 5 a.m. when SS officers arrived and issued orders. 'We had to leave the train and assemble with our hand luggage in front of each carriage to be counted. Then we . . . were taken to the ghetto and told, "Anyone who runs away or refuses to obey orders will be shot. A hundred will be shot for every one who runs away."' He was sent with some other men to clear a school building which had been used to accommodate a group of local Jews prior to removal from the ghetto. 'The stoves were still burning, everything was strewn about, and the floor was covered with hundreds of corpses.' Russian Jews tried to get near, to look at the bodies. 'They cried and screamed and searched for their relatives among the dead. That is how we got to know that, in Minsk, on 9 November, 30,000 had been murdered.' Rosenberg was the only one from his transport to survive the war.[154]

From 10 December 1941, Jews from the Reich began to fill the spaces in Riga vacated by murdered Latvian Jews. The ghetto was divided into two parts, each surrounded by barbed-wire fencing. North of Ludzas Road, the 'small ghetto' was inhabited primarily by Latvian Jews. The German Jews occupied several blocks to the south, including an area for growing vegetables. Although transports delivered 20,000 German Jews to Riga, little over half that number were actually admitted to the ghetto. The old and the sick were taken from the railway station and shot. One of those who arrived was twenty-three-year-old Josef Katz, from Lübeck, who obtained permission from the Gestapo to accompany his mother when she received her deportation order. The Jews from his transport were sent to the Jungfernhof camp. In a postwar memoir Katz described his first impressions of the place: 'Several large barns, a few service buildings and off by itself the big house, that is all that awaits thousands of people at Camp Jungfernhof.' The next morning he saw a 'mountain of luggage, stoves and sleeping bags' covered by snow in the courtyard. 'The muddy roads are deeply rutted by the trucks and strewn with rubbish. Crowds are everywhere. The one pump in the camp is surrounded by people trying to wash up a little.' Within a few days, around 200 Jews had expired from cold, hunger, and the effects of hard labour. Katz, who was later transferred to the Salaspils camp, learned in January that his mother was dead. As he embarked on an odyssey that took him through one camp and one work detail after another, thoughts of revenge kept him going.[155]

The German, Austrian and Czech Jews deposited in Lodz were spared anything quite as horrific, although the sights that greeted them were shocking nonetheless. Oskar Rosenfeld was a fifty-eight-year-old writer who had been the Prague correspondent of the London *Jewish Chronicle* for many years. He started keeping a journal of his experiences soon after arriving. He saw 'Dreary mud huts . . . pools of sewage . . . stinking refuse . . . countless tired, crooked creatures . . . faces that had already overcome all misery, in which was written: We'll persevere, we'll survive you . . . shabby sundry stores, taverns, coffee houses, cigarette vendors, young girls and children who were selling something or other, the smell of things unknown in the West, young people in uniform with Zion stars on their arms, screams amidst the silence . . . This was the criminal quarter of Lodz, the ghetto of Litzmannstadt.'[156]

The newcomers were directed to hostels set up in school buildings and any other vacant premises. So many were elderly that the Jewish council created a special home for the aged filled only with German-speakers. Most of them could not work and, if they could, there were no jobs, so they sold off their possessions in order to supplement the paltry rations. At first this led to a boom and the cost of food on the black market shot up. According to the chronicle, 'Since the arrival of the transports from Germany, all the restaurants and pastry shops, half empty until then, have truly been besieged by newcomers . . . from the moment they arrived, the newcomers began selling their personal property and, with the cash they received, began to buy up literally everything available on the private food market.' The natives resented this inflation although the better-off were glad of the chance to obtain new clothing, footwear and cosmetics. Soon, however, the new arrivals began to run short of items. In a matter of weeks they could be seen wandering the ghetto, 'forever hungry and searching for food'. They surrounded the post office so that they could send beseeching postcards to relatives and friends in the Reich. Then they started to die off. Not a few succumbed to despair and committed suicide. The wife of a rabbi from Prague 'asked the sentry on duty at the border of the ghetto at the corner of Brzezinski Street to take her life'. She walked ten metres beyond the boundary and was killed with a head shot.[157]

Rumkowski struggled to keep a lid on inflation and stop the western Jews vacuuming up so much of the food that the rest of the ghetto went hungry. He warned German Jews to be careful about selling their possessions too quickly since there was no possibility of relief once they were destitute. And he warned the intellectuals to toe the line: 'watch your bones', he admonished the lawyers, professors and rabbis from Prague. The rest of the populace regarded the Reich Jews with suspicion because they had a cultural affinity with the ghetto overlords. The more street-wise despised them for their gullibility. Later, Polish Jews came to appreciate the cultural enrichment of the ghetto that flowed from the accession of so many artists, musicians, singers and actors. Few, however, had warm feelings for the converts who were added to the hundred-strong Christian community. At Christmas 1941, there was a minor sensation when forty Christian Jews attended a service conducted by a Carmelite nun from Vienna. Dawid Sierakowiak heard that some of these converts had 'sons at the front' and were suspected of being Nazi sympathizers.[158]

The war in the east and the Polish ghettos

Despite German hegemony across the continent, because of Operation Barbarossa the Jews in different parts of Europe experienced wildly diverging fates between June and December 1941. The invasion of the USSR brought a fathomless calamity on the Jews who lived in the path of the German armies and the Einsatzgruppen. For Jews in the General Government and the Wartheland, the invasion actually brought a measure of relief. The requirements of the German armed forces and war industries offered them an economic lifeline. In western Europe, Jewish life continued with a remarkable degree of normality. There was one exception to this trend: the assault on the Soviet state reversed the uneasy truce between communism and Nazism, sparking a wave of communist-led resistance from Paris to Belgrade. Given that the Nazis saw Jews behind any opposition to their cause, this eruption inevitably brought reprisals onto Jewish communities.[159]

Jews in the Polish ghettos were thrilled by news of the attack on the Soviet Union, an event many of them anticipated thanks to the numerous warning signs such as civil defence exercises. Dawid Sierakowiak in Lodz exclaimed, 'The entire ghetto is buzzing like one big beehive. Everybody feels that a chance for liberation is finally possible.' In Warsaw, Mary Berg was overjoyed: 'War between Germany and Russia! Who could have hoped it would come so soon!' Despite the run of German victories Emanuel Ringelblum astutely grasped the significance of *any* continuing Russian resistance and commented that 'The Soviet Army's stand is amazing the Jewish population.' Adam Czerniaków monitored the German advance closely, not least because his son was in Lwow. Like him, many Polish Jews anxiously followed the military bulletins with relatives in mind. By October, however, even Ringelblum was cast into gloom and Sierakowiak had become resigned: 'The war will take a long time, and our task now is to fight with all our strength to stay alive.' As the year drew to a close, German reverses and the entry of the United States into the war rekindled Jewish optimism. They gave Warsaw 'a new breath of hope'. Ghetto residents could scarcely conceal their glee when the Germans started confiscating furs from the Jewish population, a sure sign of how badly the Wehrmacht was equipped for winter warfare.[160]

In Lodz, the invasion led to an economic boom. In late August

1941, Sierakowiak boasted that 'The ghetto is developing more and more gloriously. A large number of new workshops and factories are being established . . . Hundreds of people are now finding employment, and everything appears to be going for the better.' The employment surge compensated for the loss of packages sent by relatives in the Soviet zone of Poland and the USSR, which amounted to about half the total volume received by the ghetto post office. Partly because of this the cost of food increased, but the rate of mortality fell. Towards the end of 1941, the ghetto was inundated with orders from the German army for winter equipment, including 56,000 white camouflage smocks. An essay in the ghetto chronicle dated January 1942 concluded that the food supply situation had been 'displaying a tendency towards complete stabilization. In the areas of basic items, the ghetto is quite regularly receiving food in quantities which correspond to the stated need.' Unfortunately, inequalities in the distribution meant that the 'upper 10,000' benefited at the expense of the masses. Those with means or in receipt of a bigger ration thanks to their work (or connections) were able to exchange vegetables for fats, sugar and meat. This pushed up prices on the open market beyond what most could afford and left them with inferior nourishment.[161]

Jews in other parts of the Wartheland and East Upper Silesia were barely affected by the cataclysm that unfolded to the east. On the contrary, Albrecht Schmelt found even more productive work for the Jewish labour force in the cities of East Upper Silesia, including Bedzin and Sosnowiec. By autumn 1941, he was employing approximately 17,000 Jews on road building, the railways, and producing items for the army. Operation Barbarossa saw a rapid expansion of Jewish employment in munitions factories as well as with private corporations that began to relocate to the region from areas coming under RAF bombardment. Consequently, aside from the restrictions and indignities already imposed on Jews, little changed. In Bielsko-Biala, Gerda Weissmann's family remained in the cellar of their former home. She started learning English and began a romance with a young boy. Letters arrived from her brother in Lwow. 'And so the winter passed,' she wrote, looking back on 1941. David Rubinowitz lived close enough to the Russo-German demarcation line to hear the opening salvoes of Operation Barbarossa, but other than that it hardly impinged on his life. A few miles away Jews were being massacred, but in the Kielce region conditions remained relatively stable. A ghetto was created in Kielce in March 1941 and sealed in October – with a population of about 30,000 Jews, including refugees and deportees into the city – but Jews in the small town where David lived were able to come and go much as they pleased. In September 1941 he was still collecting mushrooms and blackberries in the woods nearby.[162]

The transformation of the Warsaw ghetto economy began in May 1941 and was accelerated by the needs of the German army. On hearing of the invasion, Czerniaków noted tersely, 'It will be necessary now to work all day . . .' By early July, the Umschlagplatz, a rail freight yard on the northern border of the ghetto, was heaving with activity. During a visit Czerniaków saw: 'A vast area, huge warehouses, numerous personnel'. The depots were 'full of supplies for our productive enterprises'. The German army placed orders for mattresses, brushes, uniforms and footwear and employed Jews to repair and recondition equipment and clothing. Unfortunately, as Stanislaw Adler sagely observed, instead of operating a command economy and concentrating production into large units, Czerniaków perpetuated his laissez-faire approach. This resulted in a proliferation of small workshops that competed with one another, driving down profits and incomes. Yet this burgeoning created 'an illusion of abundance which infuriated the Nazi dignitaries' who inspected the ghetto economy. On the other hand, the cut-throat competition between producers made it even more attractive as a place for Germans to invest. As Adler noted, 'The ghetto constituted a real goldmine as far as the supply of cheap labour was concerned.' An increasing number of German private enterprises located into the ghetto between May 1941 and May 1942, providing employment, generating revenue, and allowing more food to be imported legally. For the first time, in October 1941 Czerniaków was able to contemplate a balanced budget.[163]

Nevertheless, starvation and disease continued to ravage the poorer sections of the population. One reason was the limitation that Auerswald imposed on the total amount of food that the ghetto could import. Czerniaków repeatedly called on him to increase the supply, but Auerswald was adamant. In August 1941 he told Czerniaków, 'the rations cannot be increased at this point because the newly captured territories absorb a lot of food'. Consequently, at the end of the year, Czerniaków calculated that the ghetto was importing 1.8 million zlotys' worth of food legally and 80 million zlotys' worth illegally. The Germans knew this too, and it confirmed their worst prejudices: first, that the Jewish residential district was sucking in food and, second, that the

Jews had the wherewithal to pay for it. Indeed, in early August 1941 smuggling was so effective that bread inside the ghetto was *cheaper* than outside. This profusion undermined Czerniaków's efforts to get access to the free market in Warsaw and reinforced the determination of the German ghetto administration not to increase the food allocation.[164]

Smuggling did little to alleviate the mass poverty and hunger because it was in the hands of private entrepreneurs who sold produce at the price the market could bear to those who could afford it. The dependants of men transferred to forced labour outside the ghetto, the unemployed, those unable to work because of age or infirmity, orphans and refugees, relied on public soup kitchens. The nutrition these institutions dispensed was inadequate. Czerniaków joked grimly, 'I write verse occasionally. A vivid imagination is needed for that, but never did I have the imagination to refer to the soup that we are doling out to the public as lunch.' Moreover, the crowded, unsanitary premises where they operated served to spread typhus and tuberculosis amongst the already weakened clientele. Mary Berg wrote that Grzybowska Street was 'always filled with hordes of beggars' because it was the site of a public kitchen and therefore a 'terrible breeding ground for typhus'.[165]

Michel Mazor recalled that 'the two sovereign powers ruling the ghetto were typhus and hunger'. Typhus raged through the ghetto in the spring and summer of 1941 and like hunger was aggravated by the social chasm dividing the Jewish population. Mary Berg recorded that 'setting people down in front of hospitals has become a daily occurrence. Mothers, unable to stand the sight of their child suffering without medical aid, hope that by this method they will succeed in getting the patients to a hospital.' By contrast, the well-off minority were able to buy serum to guard against typhus, some obtaining it by post from Switzerland. According to Mary, 'A lively trade in medicines is being carried out in the ghetto.' The publicly funded health service could not cope. When Czerniaków toured one of the hospitals he saw 'Corpses in the corridor and three patients in each bed'. It was not until the autumn that the health services were reorganized and Ludwig Hirszfeld was brought in to direct countermeasures against the epidemic.[166]

Of course, the callous attitude of the Germans was ultimately driving the tragedy. In October 1941, Auerswald amputated several blocks from the Jewish district, partly on the grounds that they straddled a German supply route. This resulted in the displacement of 6,000 people.

Yet inequality within Jewish society inflected the impact. Ringelblum noted that 'The Warsaw Jews viciously exploited the dilemma of those who were forced to move from Sienna Street,' charging 150–200 zlotys per month for a room. Exorbitant rents did not deter those like the Berg family with money and connections. Mary's father had been able to bribe his way into a job as a building janitor in July 1941 when Polish janitors were finally ordered out of the ghetto. These were coveted positions and most went to former Jewish professionals, especially lawyers. The job brought with it an armband that ensured exemption from forced labour, exemption from taxes, and extra food rations on top of a monthly salary of 200 zlotys. It also offered opportunities for backhanders from people sneaking in or out of a building after curfew. When the Bergs were forced to leave Sienna Street due to the contraction of the ghetto, they moved to 'a large comfortable apartment on Leszno, where there is even a piano'. Not only did they get a roomy place to live, her father again got work as a janitor. Few were as fortunate.[167]

Coincidentally, ten days after thousands were made homeless, the first snow came. Ringelblum knew what this would mean: 'the populace is trembling at the prospect of cold weather. The most fearful sight is that of freezing children. Little children with bare feet, bare knees, and torn clothing, standing dumbly in the street weeping ... Frozen children are becoming a general phenomenon.' Jews were not dying from the cold only because of a fuel shortage for which the Germans were responsible. Mary Berg reported that 'on the black market coal fetches fantastic prices and often cannot be obtained at all'. But when it was available, the rich could buy it. So the wealthy in the ghetto kept warm while freezing temperatures spelled catastrophe for the rest. According to Berg, in the tenements 'Most of the sewage pipes are frozen, and in many the toilets cannot be used. Human excrement is often thrown onto the street with the garbage.'[168]

The Jews in German-occupied western and southern Europe

During 1941, Helga Weiss, in Prague, continued to attend a makeshift Jewish school in an apartment. She accompanied her mother in the hours when it was permitted for Jews to go shopping. Meanwhile, her father idled away his time at home like all the other Jewish fathers who had been removed from their jobs or banned from business. In October she was forced to don the yellow star. In her diary she clinically analysed the reaction of Prague's denizens: 'One person will pass by me not noticing, at least apparently . . . another will smile sympathetically or encouragingly; with a third, a mocking and sneering jeer will cross his mouth.' She had to travel in the back of trams that were full of 'stars' but found the city centre 'swarming' with her own kind, visible for the first time. As autumn wore on, the rumours about transports turned into reality. By mid-October, Helga would start the school day by identifying who had gone and who was left. Adults packed rucksacks, purchased mess kits, and assembled hard-wearing, warm clothes. Children picked their favourite toys. Mothers made bread for the journey: in Prague, the deportations were associated with the aroma of home-cooking. Finally, the Weiss family received the summons to report at the assembly centre in the Messepalast, the Trade Fair Palace, for relocation to Theresienstadt. Over the next two days 'Aryan visitors' came by, some to console and others to snap up whatever the family could not take with them. At 5 a.m. on 7 December, Helga took a last look around the home in which she had grown up. The family had breakfast then caught the tram to the Trade Fair, hurried along the way by 'Ordners', the Jewish marshals.[169]

At the Messepalast they were issued with transportation numbers. Inside, the floor was marked with numbered squares, one square to each person. There was 'nothing but dirt, dust, an unbearably heavy atmosphere, suitcases and between them people stretched out'. A field kitchen stood in the courtyard, but it was so cold that water froze in the latrines. People slept fully clothed on the floor. The following day the men's hair was shaved and they were obliged to hand over their valuables, including the keys to their homes. At dawn the next morning they were told to assemble by number. A German officer informed them that they were going to a 'new land to avoid persecution'. They were then marched to a nearby station. 'Pedestrians stop on the pavements and stare curiously at us. Tears even appear in some of their eyes . . . the inhabitants of Prague don't get to see such a spectacle every day: people being led along main streets in broad daylight under military guard, carrying all their possessions on their backs. Children, pensioners, it doesn't matter, all with stars and transport numbers on their coats.' At eleven in the morning they were all seated in passenger carriages and at noon the transport left. Three hours later they arrived at Bohusovice Station, near Theresienstadt.[170]

On entering the ghetto the Jews were separated by gender. Helga and her mother were assigned to the Dresden barracks where they were allocated 1.2 square metres of space. 'We stick our feet in other people's faces,' she wrote, 'truly horrible. If you've not seen it with your own eyes you would never believe it . . .' Her father was sent to the Magdeburg barracks and employed for several days transporting suitcases. It was a mark of how assimilated these Czech Jews were that the year ended with a Christmas show.[171]

Throughout the second half of 1941, the Vichy regime continued to make the running with anti-Jewish policies in France. French-born Jews faced relentless exclusion from economic activity and the expropriation of their businesses. Thousands of foreign-born Jews languished in barren, ill-equipped internment camps. Nearly 15,000 German and Austrian Jews were confined to Gurs and Saint-Cyprien, while over 2,000 were held in the 'punishment camp' at Le Vernet. Some 3,000 who had emigration papers were cooped up in Les Milles, near Marseilles, awaiting the chance to leave France. Hundreds of Jewish men were transferred from the camps into Foreign Worker Units, forced to do hard labour on land reclamation schemes or canal digging. The pay was meagre, the rations were poor, and they laboured under a harsh disciplinary regime. Thousands more were under 'village arrest', scattered in towns and hamlets across the foothills of the Pyrenees, under the watchful eye of the local gendarme and the native inhabitants. Jewish relief agencies, funded largely by the AJJDC, conveyed food and money to the internees and others toiled to release as many as possible. They began with the children and by May 1942 had succeeded in rescuing almost all of them. Then they argued that adolescents and adults should be allowed out for the sake of family reunification. Thanks to these efforts, the Jewish camp population fell from around 40,000 at the start of 1941 to about 11,000 in November.[172]

During this period Raymond-Raoul Lambert was living comfortably with his family in the Free Zone, working with a committee bringing aid to refugees and internees. In early July he went to his local prefecture to complete the census on the Jews that was imposed on the south at the same time as the second Statut des Juifs was promulgated. There he encountered 'the classical disorder of official bureaucracy'. An office of 'Jewish Affairs' had appeared 'next to those for "Gun Permits" and "Permits to hold public dances"'. The clerk manning it was 'quite friendly, a bit embarrassed', although Lambert also noted that the officials handling Jewish affairs displayed an 'appalling sectarianism' and believed all the anti-Semitic propaganda that was spewed out by both the Germans and the French.[173]

A week later he travelled to Paris and met with Xavier Vallat, with whom he still enjoyed 'cordial' relations. The rapport between these two veterans, both of whom loathed the 'Boches', was a key factor in a dramatic new development. Theo Dannecker had been nagging Vallat to create a central Jewish representative body in France modelled on the Reichsvereinigung in Germany. Dannecker, who represented office IVB4 of the Gestapo, was in something of a competition with Carl-Theo Zeitschel, who headed the Jewish desk at the German Embassy, to devise a far-reaching anti-Jewish policy. In August, Zeitschel suggested to the ambassador, Otto Abetz, that it was now opportune to consider deporting the Jews from France. 'Progress in the conquest and occupation of vast territories in the East', he wrote, 'may bring about within a short time a definitive and satisfactory solution to the Jewish problem all over Europe.' Abetz discussed the proposal with Hitler, but the Führer was still opposed to any mass deportation until the war was over. In the meantime, Dannecker succeeded in winning over Vallat to his scheme for a centralized representation of the Jews, although only because the wily head of CGQJ insisted that it answer to Vichy. Vallat approached Lambert as the man to establish and lead just such a body.[174]

These machinations took place against the background of a deteriorating situation for the Jews in the occupied zone. Stalin's call for resistance against the Germans had galvanized the French Communist Party. Anti-German leaflets began to appear on the streets and demonstrations against the occupiers took place in July and August. The first German soldier to be killed by the underground was shot dead on 3 September 1941. This upsurge rattled the military administration and the security police, who called on the Vichy authorities to suppress communist agitation. The Vichy police responded by intensifying the repression of foreign Jews. Back in May, nearly 6,500 Polish, German, Austrian and Czech Jews had been ordered to report at police stations in Paris. Only 3,747 turned up, but they were immediately bundled off to internment camps at Pithiviers and Beaune-la-Roland. On 20 August the French police staged a 'rafle', or round-up, in the 11th arrondissement, a district popular with Jewish immigrants. This exercise netted over 4,232 foreign and French Jews, who were dispatched to a new camp in the Paris suburb of Drancy. Some 750 Jews, mainly French citizens, were subsequently released.[175]

Pressure on the Jews increased during the autumn. Two hundred thousand French people visited the exhibition on 'The Eternal Jew', an anti-Semitic extravaganza staged in Paris. The film *Jud Süß* played to enthusiastic audiences across the country. On 2–3 October, the chief of the security police in Paris, Helmut Knochen, tried to stampede the military administration into handing Jewish affairs over to the SS by secretly setting off bombs at a number of synagogues. The explosions were supposed to be evidence of popular anger against the Jews, justifying a crackdown, but the subterfuge was quickly exposed. Instead, the army emerged as the driving force of anti-Jewish measures. In response to a succession of attacks on German military personnel the military administration set in train a spate of arrests and executions that fell disproportionately on Jews. As a reprisal for the latest shooting incident, on 12 December 1941, the military administration ordered the arrest of 743 French Jews, mostly professionals and intellectuals. They were consigned to a detention camp at Compiègne-Royallieu.[176]

The round-ups and arrests nearly undermined Vallat's negotiations with Lambert. When the two met on 27 September, Vallat proposed the creation of a unified Jewish communal organization. It would operate separately in the two zones, but benefit from official protection in both. This would guarantee the continued distribution of aid and financial relief to refugees and displaced Jews as well as support for the panoply of education and welfare institutions in the north and the south. However, the Consistoire and the traditional leadership were appalled when they learned of Lambert's negotiations. They would not countenance a representative body resting on a racial definition of the Jews and refused to shelter under the same umbrella as those who were foreign-born. To men like Jacques Helbronner, Vallat's initiative spelled a form of ghetto and its implementation would be bound to deepen the isolation of Jews from French society. Lambert retorted that the Germans were determined to impose a unitary representation on them come what may, so it was better to reach an arrangement with the Vichy authorities, especially one that ensured the ability of the existing charities to continue their work. The leadership of the immigrant Jews was ambivalent: on the one hand they feared a trap, but on the other they were afraid that vital rescue and relief work would be choked off unless it received official sanction. While controversy raged in Paris, Lambert went ahead under his own steam. During November 1941 he concluded a deal with Vallat to set up the Union générale des israélites de France (UGIF), on the understanding that its work would be purely philanthropic and not political. It would not claim to represent the purely religious organizations, the Consistoire and the synagogues, and nor would it draw on funds that French Jews regarded as illegally confiscated.[177]

By an unfortunate coincidence, the law to underpin the existence of UGIF was published ten days before the arrests of 12 December. The conjunction of the two events caused consternation amongst French Jews; Lambert was immediately cast in the role of a collaborator. His haughty attitude and the fact that he was appointed to run UGIF did not help him to sell it. He confided to his journal, 'I am the only one capable of being secretary general – a heavy and very serious task ... the Jewish agencies, militants, the philanthropists, and those who I call the "Jewish princes" are agitated, jealous and already criticizing me.' He believed that in his new role he could fulfil his desire to 'remain both an excellent Jew and an excellent Frenchman', but others regarded him as a traitor.[178]

The formation of UGIF exposed the rift between native and foreign-born Jews in France: put simply, the Jewish population was splintering under the weight of persecution. Far from creating solidarity, the arrest of French and foreign Jews in December 1941 drove a sharper wedge between the two groups. Jean-Jacques Bernard, a half-Jewish playwright who was interned at Compiègne, evoked this gulf in a memoir penned soon after France was liberated. He recalled the feeling of the intellectuals, lawyers, and artists like himself who found themselves thrown together in jail by the Germans: 'in nearly all these Frenchmen no feeling of race existed. They considered themselves attacked as Frenchmen and only as Frenchmen.' At Compiègne they were joined by foreign-born Jews transferred from Drancy. These were 'nearly all Jews from central Europe, stateless people who had been driven from their own country and had come to find hospitality in France but had kept in their hearts the sense of being a Jewish community. This sentiment was generally unknown, and even resented by the majority of the Frenchmen arrested with me.' Conditions in the camp were grim: the barracks were unheated and the food was poor. In the space of a few weeks thirty men died, while Bernard's health steadily declined. Fearing the worst he declared in an oration to his fellow prisoners, 'if I have to die in this business, I shall have died for France; I don't want to be claimed by Judaism as a martyr'. Bernard was lucky: he never faced that choice. He was released and limped back to Paris where he could recuperate.[179]

In the Netherlands the same period saw the tightening of restrictions on Jewish life, but also German efforts to promote Jewish emigration. Jews were excluded from state education at all levels and driven out of the remaining sectors of the economy in which they were still active. Under a decree of 8 August 1941, their assets, including art works, were entrusted to the Lippmann–Rosenthal Bank, which acted as a front for state-sponsored larceny. Inevitably, the displacement of Jews from business and industry resulted in unemployment. In November the Germans required that idle Jews should be sent to work camps and gave the Jewish council the task of selecting and assembling them. Ominously, the Germans also instructed all German and stateless Jews to register, ostensibly for the purposes of emigration. Around 10 per cent refused and began the process of living underground.[180]

Until May 1941, German policy was still to expedite the emigration of as many Jews as possible. SS officials, frustrated that so few were departing, summoned Gertrude van Tijn to discuss ways to increase the numbers. Van Tijn suggested that the answer was to be found in Lisbon, which had turned into a bottle-neck for would-be emigrants. In early May the SS sent her to Portugal to meet with the Jewish relief agencies and Portuguese officials to try and unblock the flow. It was a successful mission: soon afterwards the AJJDC and HICEM chartered a ship to evacuate hundreds of refugees who had been unable to get passage to the USA. In return, the Portuguese lifted a temporary ban on accepting transmigrants. However, just when the SS had managed to accelerate Jewish emigration, the United States tightened immigration controls. In June 1941, President Roosevelt prohibited the transfer of funds to belligerent and neutral countries in Europe, crippling the work of the Jewish aid organizations. The following month, US consulates in Germany and German-occupied territory were shut down. Months before the Germans finally curtailed German Jewish emigration from areas under their control, the Americans had effectively ended the opportunity of escape.[181]

The turmoil Operation Barbarossa occasioned in France was nothing compared to the havoc it provoked in the German-occupied Balkans. On 6 April 1941, the Germans had invaded Yugoslavia in response to a coup d'état against the pro-Berlin government. Simultaneously they launched an attack on Greece in support of their hapless Italian allies. Although the Wehrmacht deployed a scratch force and fought the campaign on a shoestring, superior operational doctrine and tactics enabled them to destroy far more numerous armies. Yugoslavia surrendered on 17 April, Greece a week later. A British expeditionary force sent to Greece mainly to offer moral support withdrew to Crete and thence back to Egypt. As a result of these victories, about 80,000 Jews in Yugoslavia and approximately 77,000 in Greece fell under Axis control. Fully two thirds of the Greek Jews lived in Salonica, which had a Sephardi Jewish population of great antiquity and distinction. Yet, despite the fact that the Germans controlled the city, the Jews were left more or less undisturbed. The same was true for the Jews of central Greece, including 6,000 in Athens, living under Italian rule, and a similar number in eastern Thrace who were under Bulgarian administration.[182]

After Yugoslavia surrendered, the country was dismembered and its Jewish population spread between different overlords. Around 40,000 Jews ended up in the German client-state of Croatia; 15,000 in Serbia, which was little more than an autonomous region under direct German rule; about 16,000 in Backa, a block of land annexed to Hungary; 8,000 in western Macedonia, occupied by Bulgaria; and several thousand more in the coastal strip of Macedonia under Italian jurisdiction. Croatia was ruled by the Ustasha Party led by Ante Pavelić, whose creed was a mixture of Catholic conservatism and Croatian nationalism. Soon after the state gained its independence, the Ustasha government passed a slew of racial laws. In May 1941, Jews were compelled to wear the yellow badge. Following the invasion of the USSR, to which the Croats contributed a mobile brigade, the Jews were almost totally excluded from the economy and society. Some 20,000–25,000 were interned in a concentration camp constructed around a disused brick works at Jasenovac, about sixty miles south of Zagreb.[183]

Serbia was placed under a civilian administration and remained a backwater of German-controlled territory until Operation Barbarossa. The invasion of Russia triggered a popular uprising which soon had the Germans reeling. Harald Turner, the head of the administration, and the military commanders immediately assumed that the Jews were behind the insurgency. One month into the revolt, Felix Benzler, the Foreign Office representative in Belgrade, informed Berlin that the security forces planned 'extreme measures against the Communists who will be captured, and against the Jews, since it is obvious that they collaborate with the Communists'. Benzler requested permission to expel the Jews to Poland or Romania, but was told by Berlin to put them in concentration camps instead. Unfortunately, the camps were already full of dissident Serbs, so the head of the Jewish desk at the Foreign Ministry in Berlin consulted Eichmann about what to do with them. Eichmann responded curtly, 'shoot them'. But the advice was superfluous: the army had been shooting Jews as a reprisal measure for several weeks. In September, Hitler dispatched General Franz Böhme with two infantry divisions to suppress the insurrection before it spread further. He ordered that Jews should be held as hostages and executed. Even though most Jewish men were now interned, Turner continued to insist that they were a 'danger to public order and safety'. In the course of October and November about 6,000 Jewish men were shot as a reprisal and to break a rebellion that had absolutely nothing to do with them.[184]

Due to Operation Barbarossa, a certain uniformity began to appear in the German attitude towards the Jews across the continent. Towards the end of the year, developments in the war and Germany's international situation would begin a process of convergence that would tip the whole of European Jewry into a common, dreadful fate.

The widening war and Hitler's prophecy

In the autumn of 1941 the anti-Jewish policy of the Third Reich was in confusion. Hitler's September 1941 decision to permit the deportation of Jews from the Reich and the Protectorate to the east was made without much thought as to where they would go. Nor was there any firm policy about what would happen to them once they got there, wherever it was. Would they be warehoused in ghettos? Or shot? Would the deportation apply to Mischlinge and privileged Jews? If persons in these categories were sent east, would they be shot too? The deportations triggered a new wave of massacres and experiments with new techniques of mass killing, but these were hurriedly improvised local solutions to problems arising from decisions carelessly made in Berlin or Prague. By contrast, the Polish ghettos, with their massive Jewish populations, experienced months of relative stability and modest economic growth. Although conditions in the ghettos were appalling and the rate of mortality was unnaturally high, Jews and Germans had developed a mutually beneficial modus vivendi. Moreover, enclosed ghettos were not uniform: in swathes of East Upper Silesia, the Wartheland, the General Government, and even Galicia, Jews lived in demarcated residential districts or simply remained where they had clustered before the war. Having weathered the early depredations and anti-Jewish regulations, Jewish communities persisted in thousands of small towns and villages. The shtetl was still alive. Likewise in western Europe, Jews had adapted to life under occupation, cramped and impoverished by anti-Jewish restrictions though it was. The leading figures in the regime had no ideas for dealing with them beyond the vague notion that they would all be transported to the interior of the Soviet Union after the war was over. Not a single concrete step had been taken to organize such a massive deportation programme.[185]

However, the failure of Operation Barbarossa made the status quo untenable. First of all, the Third Reich was staring in the face of a European-wide food crisis. Famine had already taken hold in Greece, where the German army had devoured much of the available food. Germany was supplying three-quarters of the grain that Belgium required. The eastern armies had stripped Byelorussia bare of cereals, meat and fats. To compound the crisis, the invasion had so disrupted the harvest in the occupied Ukraine that only a fraction of what the Germans anticipated was actually brought in – and the army consumed 25 per cent of that. In order to supply viable rations to those elements of the population working for the Reich or serving the German army, Göring and Backe in effect revised the food plan. For workers to receive enough to function effectively, non-workers would get less or nothing at all. The Poles would have to shift for themselves; the elderly, children, POWs and Jews would starve. Even this was not enough to prevent belt-tightening in the Reich.[186]

The prolongation of the war also engendered a security crisis. While the Nazi leadership had anticipated that the invasion of the USSR would provoke an eruption of communist resistance they did not expect that it would be sustained, turning occupied Europe into a huge fifth column. Their reflex thinking was to see Jews behind the communists, who were, in turn, blamed for every manifestation of dissent, sabotage and violent resistance. Reprisals acted as a deterrent, but according to their perverse logic the massacres in the Soviet Union provided the Jews with even more reason to bring down the Reich. Hence Operation Barbarossa had transformed the entire Jewish population of Europe into a cunning, merciless adversary. Moreover, the perceived security threat represented an opportunity for Himmler and Heydrich to extend their powers. They had taken the lead in the war against partisans, Jewish-Bolsheviks, in the east: this very experience qualified them to take the leading role in the west. Anti-Jewish policy fused with security policy, with the SS in the driving seat.[187]

Finally, Germany's inability to knock out the Soviet Union had created a dangerous geo-strategic dilemma regarding the USA. In July 1941, Hitler had fantasized about launching an attack on America using enhanced naval forces and a Luftwaffe equipped with long-range bombers. Instead of gaining the capability to tackle the USA, Hitler was obliged to watch Roosevelt prepare his country for war and edge closer to combatant status. Despite the ideological gulf between them, the USA started sending military supplies and food aid to the Soviets. American troops occupied Iceland in July, taking over from the British, who had invaded the Danish-ruled island after the Nazi conquest of Denmark in May 1940. On 14 August 1941 Churchill and Roosevelt announced the Atlantic Charter, setting out their shared aspirations. Although it stopped short of military cooperation it was virtually a joint declaration of war on the Axis. During September and October there were several clashes between US Navy vessels and German U-boats. After the USS *Kearny* was attacked, Roosevelt solemnly told the American public, 'The shooting has started.' Within weeks he had achieved legislation for US merchant ships to be armed and permitted to venture into combat zones. The administration issued orders for the US Navy to 'shoot on sight' any German submarine that came within range.[188]

While Roosevelt believed that he had to move gradually, winning over the American public to the idea of entering the war, to Hitler it was obvious that the Jews were rushing the United States towards combat with the Reich. After the Japanese attack on Pearl Harbor on 7 December 1941, he resolved that he had nothing to lose by taking the initiative. Within hours of the news reaching him, he instructed the U-boat fleet to move to unrestricted warfare against American shipping and in a speech to the Reichstag on 11 December formally declared war on the United States. Even though he was relatively restrained in his comments about the Jewish enemy, he ensured that the German people understood who was to blame: 'That the Anglo-Saxon-Jewish-Capitalist World finds itself now in one and the same Front with Bolshevism does not surprise us National Socialists: we have always found them in company.'[189]

The extension of the war finally brought clarity and theoretical, if not practical, coherence to Nazi anti-Jewish policy. Germany was now involved in a global conflict engineered by the Jews, fighting a war, against Jewish-Bolshevism in Russia, against the Jewish-communist fifth column across Europe, and Jewish plutocracy in the USA and Britain. The Jewish population of the Reich and German-occupied Europe, who the Nazis had held hostage against such a prospect, no longer served that purpose. Instead they would pay the price, as Hitler had prophesied. In a series of meetings between 7 and 18 December, Hitler briefed the highest cadres of the Nazi Party and his most trusted aides about his new determination to punish the Jews during the war rather than wait to expel them from German living space in its aftermath. Having returned from a gathering on 12 December at which Hitler addressed the regional party bosses, Goebbels wrote, 'Concerning the Jewish question, the Führer is determined to make a clean sweep. He prophesied to the Jews that if once again they were to cause a world war, the result would be their own destruction. That was no figure of speech. The world war is here, the destruction of the Jews must be the inevitable consequence.'[190]

Four days later, Hans Frank, who attended this assembly, brought his administration in the General Government up to speed. Hitler had told them in Berlin, 'We must put an end to the Jews.' There was no room for compassion: 'they will disappear. They must go.' Frank informed his listeners that a major conference would be held the following month in Berlin to discuss the 'migration' of the Jews. 'But what is to happen to the Jews?' he asked rhetorically. 'Do you believe they will be lodged in settlements in the Ostland? In Berlin we were told: why all this trouble; we cannot use them in the Ostland or the Reichskommissariat [Ukraine] either; liquidate them yourselves.' To avoid any misconceptions about what this meant, Frank added, 'Gentlemen, I must ask you, arm yourselves against any thoughts of compassion. We must destroy the Jews wherever we encounter them and wherever it is possible, in order to preserve the entire structure of the Reich.' He even went as far as to speculate on how this goal was to be accomplished, revealing that the precise means were still unresolved. 'We have an estimated 2.5 million Jews in the General Government, perhaps with the half-Jews and all that that entails some 3.5 million. We cannot shoot these 3.5 million Jews, we cannot poison them, but nonetheless we will take some kind of action that will lead to a successful destruction.' That would be discussed in January.[191]

On 18 December, Otto Bräutigam at the ministry for the east wrote to Hinrich Lohse, ruler of the Ostland, that 'clarity on the Jewish question has been achieved through oral discussion: economic interests are to be disregarded on principle in the settlement of this question'. In other words, Lohse was to have no more qualms or objections about the mass killing of Jewish workers. Bräutigam's missive followed a meeting between his boss, Alfred Rosenberg, and Hitler, at which the former had raised the Jewish question. Rosenberg afterwards noted that Hitler told him 'they had burdened us with this war . . . It should come as no surprise when they above all suffered the consequences.' The same day as Bräutigam's communication, Himmler met Hitler. The topic in his appointment book stated simply, 'Jewish question/to be exterminated as partisans'. Since the Jews in the occupied areas of the USSR were already being 'exterminated as partisans' this suggests he was consulting with the Führer about plans to widen his murderous security operation to the Jewish communities across the rest of German-controlled Europe. The fate of the Jews had been decided.[192]

PART SIX

FINAL SOLUTION

1942

The war and the meeting at Wannsee

The end of 1941 saw Germany facing defeat on the Eastern Front. The Soviet offensive launched on 5–6 December fell on units that were under-strength, overstretched, ill-supplied, demoralized by sub-zero temperatures for which they were not equipped, and stranded in open country. While partisans harassed the Germans' extended lines of communication, security troops were being rushed to the front to stem Russian breakthroughs. Despairing of his generals, Hitler sacked the commander-in-chief, plus a clutch of senior generals, and took command into his own hands. He issued an order that each division, regiment and soldier had to stand and fight where they stood: there would be no repetition of 1815 or 1918. The 'Haltbefehl', or halt order, was actually successful: the Red Army exhausted itself in wave after wave of attacks on desperately defended German positions. The Wehrmacht was able to patch up the front line and the immediate crisis was averted. But Hitler and his courtiers knew that at best they had been given a brief second chance.[1]

By January 1942, the eastern armies of the Reich had lost 830,000 men or 25 per cent of their strength since the start of Operation Barbarossa. The loss of equipment was equally severe. Yet Hitler believed he had no alternative but to fight on and gamble everything, again, on a decisive victory. The easygoing confidence of summer 1941 gave way to a rather more businesslike approach to waging war. In mid-January, Göring demanded the reorganization of industry onto a war footing. Fritz Todt, the minister for armaments and munitions, set in train reforms to rationalize armaments production and convert civilian production lines to military ends. When Todt was killed in a plane crash, he was succeeded by Albert Speer, who was his equal in energy and clear-sightedness. On 21 March, Hitler appointed another hard-driving

Nazi, Fritz Sauckel, as plenipotentiary for labour mobilization. Sauckel found ways to squeeze more out of the German workforce, boosting the number of women in the factories, but devoted his efforts mainly to recruiting and then dragooning foreign labourers to work in the Reich. Bringing millions of foreigners into Germany raised the question of how they would be fed which, in turn, directed Backe's attention to the food supply and the revision of ration allowances. Each measure had an impact on Judenpolitik; cumulatively, the result was devastating.[2]

The economic ramifications of military failure were registered in Hitler's increasingly personal direction of the war. It was clear that in order to continue, the Reich needed to secure supplies of food, raw materials and, most critically, mineral oil. This now became Hitler's overriding goal. In late March, the high command presented him with operational plans for an offensive aimed at seizing the oil fields of the Caucasus. Success would throttle the Soviet economy and enable Germany to gird itself for the inevitable arrival of the Americans.[3]

Jewish policy at the turn of the year was framed against this tense and fluid background. On 29 November 1941, Heydrich had invited a number of senior civil servants, representatives of Nazi Party agencies, and leading lights of the RSHA to a meeting to discuss implementation of the mandate Göring gave him in July to deliver a 'comprehensive solution of the Jewish Question'. The participants were invited 'in the interest of achieving a common view among the central agencies involved in the relevant tasks'. The request to attend referred explicitly to the circumstances created by the transportation of Jews from the Reich and the Protectorate since mid-October.[4]

The convocation was intended to take place on 9 December, but the declaration of war on the USA compelled Heydrich to postpone it to 20 January. The venue was also shifted, to 56–58 Am Grossen Wansee, a handsome lakeside villa on the south-western outskirts of Berlin. As well as the change of date and location, the guest list changed slightly but significantly. Apart from the party men and the RSHA personnel, the original invitees included state secretaries or their equivalent from the ministry for the occupied eastern territories, the Interior Ministry, the Office of the Four Year Plan, the Ministry of Justice, the Foreign Office and the Reich Chancellery. The revised guest list included Hans Frank and HSSPF Friedrich-Wilhelm Krüger from the Government General (although in the event both sent their deputies). This was a noteworthy alteration. In December Heydrich seemed to be concerned

mainly with the deportation of Jews from the Reich and the Protectorate to the Reichskommissariat Ostland, which was to be represented at
the meeting by Herbert Lange. By 9 January, when the revised invitations were sent out, the inclusion of men responsible for the General
Government suggests either an oversight or a broadening of his purposes.[5]

There was, indeed, an ambiguity of purpose about the meeting at
Wannsee. Heydrich started by reiterating his appointment by Reich
Marshal Göring as plenipotentiary for 'the Preparation of the Final
Solution of the Jewish Question in Europe'. The meeting was convened,
he said, 'to obtain clarity on questions of principle' and to allow for
'prior joint consultation' with the aim of achieving harmony between
the relevant central agencies. Responsibility for handling the 'final solution' would lie essentially with Himmler and himself, 'without regard to
geographic boundaries'. This was an astonishing assertion of jurisdiction and gave the RSHA a bridgehead in every single country with a
Jewish population. However, Heydrich then reverted to more prosaic
matters. Drawing on a statistical summary drafted by Eichmann, he
gave a 'review of the struggle conducted up to now against this foe'. That
is to say, he gave an overview of the development of Judenpolitik in the
Third Reich from social and economic exclusion to forcing Jews out of
German living space. It was as if he went back to reading from a script
that had been composed only about Jews in the Reich. As he explained,
accelerated emigration had been the 'only possible provisional solution'
and it was taken in hand by the Sipo-SD through the central emigration
office for the Reich. Despite various difficulties, over 530,000 Jews had
departed legally from Germany, Austria and the Protectorate. But with
the coming of war forced emigration had run its course. It was to be
replaced by 'evacuation of the Jews to the East, as a further possible
solution, with the appropriate prior authorization by the Führer'.[6]

Heydrich described the forced emigration from the Reich as 'a provisional solution' that was 'supplying practical experience' in view of the
coming 'final solution'. This was at best an ex post facto rationalization
for the removal of the Reich Jews. The deportations had never before
been conceived in such terms and were, on the contrary, depicted at the
time (September–October 1941) as an end in themselves. Now they
were being retrospectively transformed into a rehearsal for something
far bigger.[7]

This 'final solution' would apply to eleven million Jews in countries that fell into two categories. First there were Germany, the Axis and client states, plus territories they occupied. Second there were England, the as yet unconquered portions of the USSR, and neutral or non-belligerent states, including Sweden, Switzerland, Turkey, Spain, Portugal and Ireland. Heydrich explained that the population figures for each country did not always accord with the preferred racial definition and pointed out that 'the handling of this problem in individual countries will encounter certain difficulties'. He named Hungary and Romania specifically as troublemakers. After a peculiar digression concerning the sociological make-up of Soviet Jewry he proceeded to enlarge on the 'final solution'. Jews would be 'utilized for work in the east', gathered into large labour columns segregated by gender, and deployed for road construction. They would move ever further east as the roads extended. In the process, all but the fittest would expire 'through natural reduction' and the remnant would be subject to 'special treatment'. In the concentration camps, Sonderbehandlung or 'special treatment' was already a euphemism for execution. He then spelled out why: history showed that the survivors of the road-building programme could become the germ cell of a 'new Jewish revival'. So, although the evacuation was not intended to deliver Jews to their deaths immediately it would ultimately eventuate in the destruction of the Jewish people.[8]

The plan was for Europe to be 'combed through from West to East', but starting with the Reich and the Protectorate, on account of 'the housing problem and other socio-political needs'. This awkward conjunction seems to indicate an earlier plan 'A' that had been just about the Reich merged into a later plan 'B' of far wider scope. Regardless, Heydrich hurried on to the detail: the Jews would be sent in groups first to 'transit ghettos' and then further eastwards. To ensure the smooth running of this procedure, previously bedevilled by pleas for exemptions, he proposed to strip out the elderly Jews (those over sixty-five) and those with severe war wounds and medals from the Great War. They would be 'admitted to the Jewish old-age ghetto' in Theresienstadt. Yet none of this could happen until the military situation was stabilized. Nor could it begin until appropriate arrangements were made in the countries occupied by or under the influence of Germany. Heydrich then jumped from essentially parochial issues to the European dimension, skipping any of the troublesome aspects that he anticipated in the Reich. This blasé approach would come back to haunt the plan.

Instead, he breezily declared that 'With regard to the handling of the final solution in European areas occupied by us and under our influence, it was proposed that the officials dealing with this subject in the Foreign Ministry should confer with the appropriate experts in the Security Police and the SD.' Heydrich did not foresee problems in Slovakia or Croatia, where the first steps had been taken. The Romanians had appointed a plenipotentiary for Jewish affairs, but it would be necessary to 'impose an adviser for Jewish questions on the Hungarians'. Nor could he see any difficulties rounding up Jews in either the occupied or the unoccupied zones of France. At this point Martin Luther interjected a warning that the evacuations might prove ticklish in the Scandinavian countries. By contrast, south-east and western Europe posed no challenge. Luther's reminder that the Foreign Office had a stake in the matter prompted a similar, lame intervention by Otto Hoffman of the Head Office for Race and Resettlement.

When Heydrich resumed, it was to deliver a long and complex categorization of Mischlinge and their fate, along with Jews in mixed marriages and Mischlinge in mixed marriages plus their children. This was, again, mainly pertinent to Germany rather than a European-wide 'final solution'. Half-Jews married to Germans who had German children or were particularly valuable to the Reich would be exempted from evacuation, but would have to submit to sterilization. If they refused, they would be evacuated. The reason for the inordinate attention he applied to this as against his airy treatment of almost everything else is that it was a highly sensitive and contentious issue in Germany. It touched on many thousands of families with impeccable racial credentials who had a relative married to a Jew or a Mischling. Wilhelm Stuckart of the Interior Ministry predicted that offering them a choice would lead to 'endless administrative work' and proposed instead compulsory sterilization of Mischlinge. The other potential flashpoint concerned the fate of Jews employed in the armaments industry. Erich Neumann, from the office of the Four Year Plan, objected that they should be retained until replacements could be found. His reservation reflected Göring's recent prioritization of war production and Heydrich agreed with alacrity.[9]

Towards the end of the discussion, Joseph Bühler, representing Hans Frank, piped up. He wanted it put on record that the Government General 'would welcome it' if the 'final solution' began there. They had no problem with transportation and the Jews played no significant role in the labour force; but they did present a menace to public health.

Furthermore, they destabilized the economy through their 'continuous black market dealings'. Notwithstanding his zeal, following a discussion of 'forms which the final solution might take' (that is to say methods of mass murder), Bühler and also Alfred Meyer, from the ministry for the occupied eastern territories, advocated 'certain preparatory work' so as to avoid causing alarm to the local populations.[10]

The meeting, which had convened around noon, broke up at about two o'clock in the afternoon. There had been a break in the middle, during which snacks and alcohol had been served. Afterwards, Eichmann retired to a quiet room with his line-manager Heinrich Müller, head of the Gestapo, and Heydrich. They had a smoke and a drink by the fireplace, which Eichmann later recalled was unusual for the normally abstemious Heydrich. It signified that the chief of the Sipo-SD was well pleased with the day's business. And yet, as with so many of Heydrich's pet projects, this one was deeply flawed and soon disintegrated. Indeed, Heydrich never lived to see the 'final solution' get into first gear. Over subsequent weeks Eichmann engaged in numerous meetings concerning the definition of Mischlinge and the question of their fate; neither was ever resolved. There was constant tension and argument over the retention of Jews for labour, with the Wirtschafts- und Verwaltungshauptamt (SS-WVHA, the SS Business and Administrative Head Office), tussling with the RSHA over the fate of Jews in the ghettos and the camps. Contrary to the scheme as laid out, the mass murder of Jews intensified first in the annexed territories, then the General Government, and after that in the occupied areas of the Soviet Union. The 'combing out' in the west did not get under way until the summer, and in France it did not get the sort of cooperation that Heydrich had lazily assumed. Above all, the scale of the task baulked even the fanatical agents of Eichmann's office IVB4, which was responsible for coordinating the deportations and driving them on. They would need more resources and more time, but the war did not permit either.[11]

There are numerous, puzzling features of the meeting in Wannsee. While mass killing using gas vans was already under way in Chelmno and an extermination camp, Vernichtungslager, with fixed-site gas chambers was under construction at Belzec in the General Government, Heydrich did not connect his plan with their operations – not even by means of cautious euphemisms. Then again, these murderous facilities could barely have handled deportees coming from all over Europe for 'special treatment'. In actuality, none of the killing sites that took shape over the following months was suited to the purposes laid out by the man directing the 'final solution'. Nor were many resources devoted to preparing for such a gargantuan enterprise. The mass murder facilities that were being developed were cheap, jerry-built affairs that soon proved hopelessly inadequate to the task expected of them. Once again, the centrality of the 'Jewish question' was not matched by resource allocation. Compared to the construction of coastal fortifications in north-west Europe, flak defences in the Reich, or practically any other aspect of the war effort, in material terms the war against the Jews was a sideshow. It was ill-planned, under-funded, and carried through haphazardly at breakneck speed. In one respect, though, it resembled the Reich war effort in 1942: the lack of manpower for the 'final solution' meant that the Germans would have to rely on their allies and local collaborators.[12]

Deportations from the Lodz ghetto to Chelmno death camp

On 1 January 1942, the Jewish population of the Lodz ghetto stood at 162,681, divided between approximately 67,000 men and 93,000 women. A few days into the new year, Rumkowski gave a sort of 'state of the union' speech in the House of Culture to an invited audience, including members of the Beirat, representatives of the workshops, and Jews from the recently arrived transports from central Europe. He acknowledged the shortage of food and fuel, blaming it in part on profiteers and the newcomers, but he took pride in having turned the ghetto into a productive centre, thereby keeping the 'policy makers' satisfied. They had compelled him to accept 20,000 more Jews into the ghetto, but he had consented to move out only 10,000 to make space for them. In deciding who would leave he intended to identify only those who were 'undesirable'. 'Friends,' he intoned, 'I predicted that hard times, perhaps very hard times would be coming, but I am certain that we will struggle though them if we eradicate the evil within ourselves.' He was sure that 'if the ghetto does its work well and in earnest the authorities will not apply any repressive measures'. So they had to drive up production and everyone had to work. 'They respect us,' he assured his audience, 'because we constitute a centre of productivity.'[13]

Meanwhile, the resettlement commission, comprising medical men and respected figures, drew up lists of who was to be removed. Activists in the various pre-war Jewish political parties put forward names. Rabbis were consulted and offered quickie divorces to men or women whose spouse was condemned to go. Rumkowski, however, turned the deportations into a punitive exercise and used them to reinforce his power. Those deemed criminals, shirkers, speculators, prostitutes and other 'undesirable' elements were arbitrarily included. The commission also picked on Jews only lately deported into the ghetto.[14]

The deportees were promised 10 Reichmarks and permitted to take clothing and food for the journey. These concessions made the process appear similar to the deportations into the Lodz ghetto or the removals for forced labour. Nobody had any suspicion that another fate awaited those sent out. Once the lists were issued, though, the Jews slated for departure did not meekly obey. Only about half reported at the assembly points where they were held overnight, and they were mostly the homeless with nowhere else to go or invalids with no chance of resisting. Consequently, the Order Service was dispatched to seize the rest. The ghetto chronicle stated baldly, 'From the start of the campaign the deportees have been brought in forcibly.' The recalcitrant were mainly taken in night raids, and as a punishment forfeited their luggage allowance. In this way, between 16 and 29 January 1942, the Jewish council and the OS assisted in the ejection of 10,103 Jews on fourteen transports, each comprising twenty freight cars carrying about fifty-five people per car.[15]

Shlomo Frank captured the first day of the deportations in his diary. The deportees were moved from the assembly points to Radogoszcz freight yard where they were loaded onto the waiting trains. 'Most of them – poor, broken, naked and starved. Their deportation was extraordinarily tragic. All of them cried mournfully. Mothers embraced little children . . . and screamed aloud. If we will die, you at least stay alive in order to be able to get revenge on those who are banishing us.'[16]

The transports travelled from Radogoszcz to the small town of Kolo, north-west of Lodz, where the Jews were disembarked. Those too old or frail to walk were taken by truck a short distance to a disused mill in the hamlet of Powiercie; the rest were escorted on foot. They were held there for twenty-four hours and then trucked to Chelmno the next morning. (In May 1942, following complaints from locals about the sight of these miserable processions, a narrow-gauge railway was laid down between Powiercie and Chelmno.) Once they were in Chelmno itself they were ushered into a partly ruined building, dubbed 'the mansion', and held in the basement. Here they were stripped of their belongings and told to undress so that they could be showered. They were then herded up a ramp, through an aperture in the wall of the building, and into the back of the gas vans.[17]

Initially, the vans used bottled carbon monoxide gas. In later models the exhaust fumes from the motor were piped into the rear compartment where the victims were packed together in the dark. They were asphyxiated on the journey to a nearby patch of woodland. Here, in a clearing known as the forest camp, Polish workers had excavated three mass graves. When a van arrived, the rear compartment was opened and a team of Jewish prisoners wearing shackles pulled the corpses out of the back and dragged them to the burial pits. At the end of each day these poor souls were forced to get into the pit themselves and were shot. The entire process was watched over by a few dozen SS men under the command of Hans Bothmann. The Polish gravediggers proved so helpful that eventually they became accomplices and provided additional manpower. An SS sergeant later testified that one perk of their job was raping Jewish women from the transports. 'It happened that sometimes a woman was selected from the Jews delivered for gassing for the work squad, which consisted of young men; probably the Poles themselves would choose her. I think that the Poles asked her if she would agree to have sexual intercourse with them. In the basement there was a room set aside for this purpose where the woman stayed one night or sometimes several days and was at the disposal of these Poles. Afterwards, she would be killed in the gas vans with the others.'[18]

There were few survivors of Chelmno: none of the deportees evaded their fate and only four Jews escaped from the work crew. Szlama Wiener (Shlomo Winer) was one of the first. He managed to get free around 19 January and reach the Jewish community in Grabow. From there he travelled to Piotrków and eventually made it into the Warsaw ghetto where he gave a deposition to Hersz Wasser, a member of the Oneg Shabat team. His account was later sent to London via the Polish underground.[19]

Wiener recalled that he was taken from his home town of Izbica Kujawska on 6 January and deposited in a cell in the basement of the mansion. At 7 a.m. the next morning he and some thirty other men were woken, given coffee and bread, and transported to the forest. They saw a van arrive and watched as the eight-man team was sent to unload it. These victims were actually Roma from the Lodz ghetto. Wiener described how 'The corpses were thrown out of the vans like garbage onto a heap. They were dragged by the feet and the hair. Two people stood at the edge of the ditch and threw the bodies into the grave. Two others were in the ditch and placed them in layers, face down, in such a way that the head of one was placed next to the feet of another . . . If there was an empty space, the corpse of a child was stuffed in there. The SS man stood up above with a pine branch in his hand and directed where to place the heads, legs, children and things.' At five in the afternoon the eight workers were ordered into the pit and shot. Wiener and the other workers, who had been performing various ancillary tasks, were then driven back to the makeshift barracks, where they wept copiously and recited prayers of mourning and penitence. The process was repeated the next day. This time, Wiener was assigned to clean excrement and other detritus from the interior of the van's cargo compartment. On the third day, he noticed that the clothing of the victims was adorned with the yellow star and realized that the Germans were murdering Jews. Over succeeding days the procedure changed somewhat, with the Germans paying more attention to plunder. 'After they were thrown out of the van, two German civilians approached and carried out a thorough search of the corpses, looking for valuables. They tore off necklaces, pulled rings off fingers, pulled out gold teeth. They even looked in the anuses and, with the women, genitalia.' The days of the work-Jews now began with the Shema, or prayers of repentance, and ended with Kaddish, the prayer recited by a mourner. Rather than continue the nauseating work, several committed suicide, sometimes helping to hang each other. On 13 January, the unloading crew discovered a live baby in one of the vans; it had been concealed in a pillow case. 'The SS men laughed. They shot the child with a machine gun and threw it into the grave.'[20]

That day, Michal Podchlebnik, one of Wiener's co-workers, spotted his wife, two children and parents amongst the cadavers. He did not give way to despair, though. Instead, Wiener and Podchlebnik discussed how they might escape and raise the alarm. On the 15th, Shlomo learned that his brother, mother and father were amongst the dead; he was now the sole survivor from a family of sixty. This convinced him that the Germans were killing the whole Jewish population. He escaped a few days later, squeezing through a loose window of the bus transporting the Jewish workforce between the forest and the base camp. Podchlebnik subsequently got away by a similar route.[21]

Notwithstanding these lapses in security, Chelmno was a highly efficient operation employing no more than eighty to a hundred SS guards and a handful of Polish labourers. It was also very profitable. The guards at the mansion carefully collected the clothing, jewellery, gold, silver and cash stripped from the Jews in the moments before they entered the gas van. The valuables and clothing were stored locally before being shipped in a fleet of trucks to warehouses in Lodz under the control of the German ghetto administration. There was so much clothing that in May the ghetto management claimed that they needed fuel for 900 trucks to transport it all. As the quantities piled up, Hans Biebow, the Kripo detachment in Litzmannstadt, and Göring's Haupttreuhandstelle Ost (responsible for Aryanization in the east) started to quarrel over who got the loot. Biebow sold off some of the best items to German officials and local Volksdeutsche. The criminal police helped themselves to a fair amount. The Nationalsozialistische Volkswohlfahrt, the Nazi welfare organization, ordered 3,000 men's suits and 1,000 items of women's clothing from the collection. Shortly after taking delivery they complained that some of the items were soiled and bloody, a few still bearing the yellow star.[22]

In February, after a three-week hiatus, the deportations resumed. Since there had been no information about the destination of the earlier transports or any word from the deportees, unease gripped the ghetto's inhabitants. According to the chronicle, 'This mystery is depriving the ghetto dwellers of sleep.' Undeterred by the 'mystery', the out-settlement commission extended the net to those on relief. But the Germans dispensed with enticements and the 7,000 Jews removed in this wave were handled much more roughly. Oskar Rosenfeld recorded that 'The police stormed the lodgings of the Jews marked for evacuation.' Often all they found were 'the corpses of children who had frozen to death'. The weather, hunger and disease were nearly as lethal as the Germans and those spared evacuation faced a daily battle to survive. In the short term, the removals made things harder. The Germans deliberately constricted the food supply to give Jews a motive for seeking their luck on the transports, while panicky food purchases by the evacuees drove up prices and aggravated the shortage of nutrition.[23]

After another three-week pause, the Germans decreed that 15,000 more had to go. This edict shocked the ghetto. According to Dawid Sierakowiak the news 'burst like thunder'. The chronicle remarked simply that 'March will long be remembered ... as the month of resettlement.' To fill the quota the commission listed people who were in receipt of welfare payments, anyone guilty of an infraction of ghetto regulations (no matter how minor), and anyone out of work – even if they had only recently become unemployed. Dawid struggled to understand why one thousand people were being driven out each day when 'the workshops are receiving huge orders and there is enough work for several months'. Although workers were exempted, only one other family member was protected, so many chose to go with their dependants. Rosenfeld raged that 'When they ran short of the required number of deportees, the Jewish police randomly hunted down people in the streets and herded them to the collection camp.' Hundreds concealed themselves in rudimentary hideouts or attempted desperate escapes from the columns on the way to Radogoszcz Station. In panic 120 Jews left for Warsaw, preferring their chances there. The chronicle referred to them as 'rats abandoning a sinking ship'. Dozens committed suicide. Throughout the turmoil Rumkowski remained uncharacteristically silent. The chronicle remarked sardonically that 'until now the chairman has never missed an occasion to deliver a speech'. Suddenly, on the second day of the Passover festival, the deportations were cancelled. Jews awaiting the trains were abruptly turned loose, their relief tempered by the realization that having sold all their worldly belongings they were destitute. Almost 25,000 Jews (9,267 men and 15,420 women) had been removed and over 2,200 were killed or died in the ghetto.[24]

Starvation now gripped the remaining inhabitants as never before. Jews from central Europe traded possessions they had brought with them; natives of the ghetto bartered their rations for food on the black market. Malnutrition destroyed morality. 'For the sake of bread, people turn into hypocrites, fanatics, boasters, miserable wretches,' Rosenfeld wrote from his vantage point in the statistical department of the Beirat. The Germans and Viennese died like flies. Czech Jews, who either spoke Yiddish or were able to grasp Polish, adapted better. But even Czechs who once prided themselves on their civility and culture degenerated physically and mentally. 'People had changed in three months of hunger,' Rosenfeld lamented. 'Almost everyone walked with a stooped back, had twitching legs. Illnesses of all sorts crept in. Even young people had pneumonia. Thousands tossed and turned in their cots in the prostrate position since their bones were hurting, and day dreamed of foodstuffs . . .' People died every day in the overcrowded apartments, houses and tenements but no one cared. 'Nobody gave a damn about the corpses. Complete indifference towards the fate of the dead or dying neighbour, whose presence did not inhibit any gaiety, laughter, trilling.' Hunger turned the Jews against one another, 'father against son, brother against brother, friend against friend'. Yet amidst these horrors the ghetto was still shocked by the exemplary execution of Max Hertz, who had tried to escape back to Germany. Eight hundred German and Austrian Jews were forced to assemble on the Sabbath to watch the Order Service carry out the hanging.[25]

A third wave of deportations commenced at the start of May. It followed a visit to Lodz by Himmler and marked a fundamental shift in Judenpolitik. For the first time Jews from the Reich were included; the taboo on killing them had been lifted (although, in line with the decisions taken at Wannsee, holders of the Iron Cross and the severely war-wounded were still exempted). Himmler also insisted that from this point the only grounds for sparing a Jew would be the capacity to work. Hence, a German medical commission arrived to examine the entire non-working population over the age of ten to determine who was capable of labour and, if not, liable to removal. Himmler also informed the ghetto administration that the non-productive Jews would be replaced by work Jews transferred in from communities around the Wartheland that were in the process of liquidation.[26]

The end of the ban on deporting German Jews meant that this time the Beirat was able to soften the blow on the ghetto by taking the majority of deportees from amongst the westerners. Many German Jews actually decided to go voluntarily. They were utterly demoralized, could not bear life in Lodz any longer, and harboured hopes that their unknown destination might offer some improvement.[27]

Nevertheless, the announcement of the medical commission had 'a staggeringly depressing effect' on the residents. The chronicle drew a picture of people 'walking around in a state of utter helplessness, seeking salvation, help and advice'. Dawid Sierakowiak described the news as a 'thunderbolt . . . The ghetto has gone mad. Thousands of endangered unemployed persons are struggling for work in every possible way, mostly using connections'. Of course, connections benefited the local Jews more than the newcomers, although Rumkowski sought to employ as many as possible through the Beirat. Thanks to the creation of new offices to handle the settlement of German Jews and the labour-intensive task of processing the clothing arriving from Chelmno, the Beirat's workforce was swollen to 12,880, or nearly 10 per cent of the working population. Those unfortunates who underwent examination were given an ink stamp on their chest. Hundreds, fearing this stigma, went into hiding only to be rooted out by the Order Service and man-handled before the SS doctors. Rosenfeld noted caustically that the Nazi medical men expressed surprise that so many of the Jews they examined were in poor health.[28]

Panic was heightened by information that the belongings of Jews from the communities in Kolo and Kutno were turning up in the ghetto warehouses, including backpacks that looked as if they had been prepared by deportees. Even so, the German Jews who were condemned to leave mostly accepted their fate. 'More than five months of hunger and cold, on bare floors, does not in the least dispose them to fight for life in the ghetto', concluded the chronicle. 'They say that wherever they may find themselves, things will not be any worse for them . . .' Local Polish Jews fell on the departing Reich Jews like 'hyenas'. A peculiar consequence of the forced exodus was the flood of clothing and goods onto the market; such was the profusion that prices fell and Polish Jews snapped up items they could only have dreamed of obtaining beforehand. The chroniclers did not hide their indignation that 'There have been many speculators who have made a good profit off the misfortunes of their brothers from the West. Ruthless and cruel, they have flocked around their victims like vultures on a battlefield.' The grotesque gender imbalance in the ghetto encouraged a different form of predation: single men with a work certificate had their pick of unemployed women willing to sign a marriage certificate. By contrast, Rosenfeld admired the stoicism of the Reich Jews. On the eve of their departure the men ate well, drank, and smoked their last cigarettes. Women went to the ghetto beauty parlour, 'getting their hair done before the deportation, eagerly embracing life'.[29]

They were not permitted to retain that dignity. The Order Service utilized the central prison as the collection point, so the deportees spent their penultimate night in the ghetto incarcerated like convicts. Then they were transferred to a transit camp in a school building in the Marysin district, close to the Radogoszcz Station. At four in the morning they were conveyed to the station on trams. At the side of the track the German criminal police tore away their baggage, backpacks and parcels. When word of this thievery reached others scheduled for expulsion they donned as much clothing as possible and filled their pockets with necessities. The chronicle described the strange spectacle: as 'their faces, cadaverously white or waxy yellow, swollen and despairing, sway disjointedly on top of disproportionately wide bodies that bend and droop under their own weight'. At 6.30 a.m., the Jews were embarked on the trains, seated in third-class passenger carriages. Since there was no platform, OS men had to help up the aged and infirm. Half an hour later they were gone.[30]

Many sought to preserve a last shred of dignity by taking their own lives. The chronicle charted a 'frenzy of suicides' throughout the deportations. The vast majority, unable or unwilling to end their own lives, impressed the chroniclers with their 'outward display of considerably greater self-control' than was common amongst their east European co-religionists.[31]

The May deportations carried off just under 11,000 Jews, most of them from central Europe. Over the same period Jews flooded in from surrounding towns, a brutal shuffling of populations that bemused Jewish onlookers. 'Must paint the zig-zag of in-and-outsettlings!' Oskar Rosenfeld jotted in his notebook; 'a. into the ghetto; b. Nuremberg, Cracow; c. Germans in; d. Poles out; e. Germans out; f. Neighbouring Poles in; g. some of the same out; h. Again Poles out. In the course of the confusion, thousands die.'[32]

The Jews who entered the ghetto brought with them chilling stories of selections, massacres and deportations. The chronicle recounted in great detail the fate of the Pabianice community, which was liquidated between 16 and 20 May. There had been about 9,000 Jews in the ghetto that was established in February 1940. The town had a thriving textile industry and around 1,400 Jews were employed in clothing manufacture. However, following an edict from Himmler that only working Jews would be allowed to live, a reinforced German police unit surrounded the ghetto and removed the inhabitants to an athletics field where they were divided into two categories, labelled 'A' and 'B' to denote whether they were considered capable of work or not. The non-working Jews were then removed; subsequently, they were dispatched to Chelmo and murdered. The remnant, numbering about 4,000, almost exclusively fit young men and women, were transferred to Lodz, which was now assuming the characteristics of a vast labour camp.[33]

These ghetto clearances were carried out with extreme violence. They were often preceded by executions to intimidate the population. While the cruelty was deliberate and instrumental, it stemmed just as much from the degeneration of men who were being employed day after day in such operations. Furthermore, the Sipo and order police were frequently assisted by non-uniformed militia composed of Volksdeutsche who lacked even a modicum of discipline. The civil administration was not only cognizant of the liquidations, its members participated in them. Hans Biebow often left his desk to take part in selections held during the deportations, hauling out those he considered prime labour for his ghetto enterprises. By mid-1942, about 97,000 Jews from Lodz, including Jews from central Europe and the inhabitants of ghettos across the Wartheland, had been murdered at Chelmno.[34]

Deportations from the Lublin ghetto to Belzec death camp

The onslaught against the Jewish population of the General Government commenced in March 1942, although plans to reduce the number of Jews had been mooted for much longer, and construction of a mass murder installation to dispose of 'useless' Jews had been under way at Belzec for months. By the end of the year the Jewish population in Hans Frank's domain was almost entirely annihilated and yet the decisions that led to this human cataclysm are obscure. Policy towards the Jews chopped and changed with bewildering frequency, while the ghastly, practical aspects of the mass killing display confusion and contradictions.[35]

In October 1941, Himmler had charged the SS police chief in Lublin, his protégé Odilo Globocnik, with responsibility for constructing a camp in the General Government with the sole purpose of murdering Jews en masse. It was to be a special, covert operation. Globocnik called in experts from the T-4 programme, notably Christian Wirth, to advise how this could best be done and to supervise construction of the necessary installations. Belzec, a former labour camp under Globocnik's control, was identified as a suitable site and Wirth got started. This was around early November. Considering that it was a small site with a few simple buildings, it took a surprisingly long time to complete. Compared with the speed at which the Wehrmacht and Luftwaffe were capable of erecting far larger base camps, supply dumps, airfields and fortifications, this suggests either a lack of urgency or lack of resources (which may amount to the same thing). Meanwhile, Globocnik assembled a staff of over 400 and recruited thousands of auxiliaries from

amongst Soviet POWs. Primarily Ukrainians, Byelorussians, Lithuanians and Latvians, they were trained at Trawniki, a labour camp on
the site of a disused sugar factory. By spring 1942 Globocnik had a
small army at his disposal consisting of 450 SS men, 2,000 security
police, 2,550 ex-Red Army 'volunteers' or Hilfswillige prepared at
Trawniki, 15,000 order police, and some 14,000 regular Polish and
Ukrainian police, not to mention thousands of ethnic Germans enrolled
in militia units. Most of these forces would have been available anyway,
yet only half of the men who were being specially trained at Trawniki (a
total of 5,500) were actually ready for deployment by mid-1942. More
puzzling, when Globocnik's men were let loose on the huge Jewish population in Lublin and its surrounding district, the gas chambers at
Belzec soon proved inadequate and the transport system clogged up.
Despite a period during which Wirth murdered local Jews to test the
gas chambers, no one seems to have calibrated the machinery of
destruction to the size of the population to be destroyed. This may be
understandable because the categories of those to be murdered were
altered several times, always enlarging the pool. This intensification
related to the shifting balance of power between the SS and the civil
administration and also the course of the war.[36]

The operation began with Lublin, the heart of Globocnik's empire
and the district that Himmler hoped would become an SS settlement
zone planned on racial-utopian lines. In early February, the German
authorities ordered the partition of the ghetto into two sections separated by a fence (that the Jewish council erected and paid for). Non-
working Jews were placed in ghetto A; those with documents certifying
that they were in the service of German-run enterprises went into
ghetto B. A month later the security police obliged all Jews in work to
get a new stamp on their identity papers signifying that they were
employed either on behalf of the Germans or by the Jewish council. A
week later, the Jewish council was told that non-working Jews had to be
resettled. The selection and assembly of deportees started on 16 March,
but the Jewish Order Service proved so ineffectual that the Germans
took over, sending in police units. The result was mayhem and bloodshed. Each day over 1,000 Jews were seized from ghetto A, marched,
dragged or carried to the Maharshal synagogue, which served as a collection point, then escorted in columns to the station in the Majdan
Tartarski district where they were embarked onto freight trains. Hermann Höfle, an SS major who was Globocnik's deputy and chief of staff,

personally supervised these savage evictions, stationing himself and his headquarters in a cafe located inside the ghetto. The cafe, run by a Jew called Shamai Grajer, had the convenience of a telephone and Grajer's waitresses plied the SS men with refreshments while they went about their business. When the deportations ceased on 29 March, 18,000 Jews had been forcibly removed and over a thousand shot or beaten to death on the streets of the ghetto.[37]

Desperate to halt the removals, the Jewish council offered a massive bribe to the SS. The Germans took the cash, jewellery, gold and 1,400kg of silver and then shot most of the councilmen. Instead of amelioration, the security police issued new identification documents to the denizens of ghetto B, sufficient for only about one in ten. The round-ups resumed on 1 April and were extended to the working Jews. This time, though, the Germans encountered more resistance and evasion. German police and auxiliaries had to search in basements and attics. Nevertheless, within a fortnight they had netted a further 12,000, who were passed on to Belzec. About 4,000 work Jews remained with Sipo permits, plus a roughly equal number of 'illegals', crammed into Majdan Tartarski. The security police conducted a census on 20 April and proceeded to hunt down those without proper documentation. Most were shot inside the diminished ghetto.[38]

The deportees made the relatively short rail journey from Lublin to Belzec, a distance of eighty miles, in a few hours. The camp that awaited them was compact, under 300 metres long on each of its four sides. It was enclosed by a barbed-wire fence, with guard towers at three corners and one overlooking the centre. The northern perimeter was contiguous with an anti-tank ditch, a relic of the camp's original function as one of a chain supplying labour to build fortifications on the old Russo-German demarcation line. A spur line extended from the Lublin–Lwow railway through a gateway into the camp. Trains were able to unload at a platform inside the reception area, but only twenty freight cars at a time. Since the average transport consisted of forty to sixty wagons this meant that the train had to be divided into sections, with the locomotive shunting back and forth two or three times. It also meant that Jews packed inside the dark, airless wagons could wait for up to six hours in baking heat or freezing cold. However, it was only a few metres from the platform to the wooden barracks, where men and woman were undressed and the women's hair shaved off so that it could be recycled for industrial purposes. An exit from these rooms opened onto a narrow barbed-wire corridor, known as 'the tube' by the camp staff, that led directly to the building housing the gas chambers. This structure was crudely assembled, with just a concrete floor and a double wooden wall filled with sand beneath a gabled roof. Initially, there were three gas chambers, each 4 by 8 metres and 2 metres high. The chambers had rubber-sealed airtight doors that were especially strong, to resist pressure from inside, and which could also be accessed from the outside to remove the dead. A dismounted Russian tank engine supplied the lethal fumes that were piped into the gas chambers. In another section of the camp, fenced off and concealed from the reception zone, there were four immense pits. After the dead were removed from the gas chambers, and after gold teeth had been removed from their mouths, the corpses were hauled to the pits by a Jewish work team. The Jews who laboured in and around the gas chambers had their living quarters in the sealed extermination area, known as camp II. Another Jewish labour force tidied up the wagons and the platform after each transport was unloaded, collected the belongings of the doomed, and shifted them in double-quick time to a large warehouse where they were roughly sorted. This group, numbering about 500, lived in a barracks in camp I.[39]

The camp personnel did not exceed 200. The first commandant was Christian Wirth, assisted by about a dozen SS men. A company of sixty to eighty Ukrainians, trained at Trawniki, provided the guards for the perimeter, the watchtower and the disembarkation area. When the Jews from Lublin were unloaded and assembled on the platform, Wirth or one of his subordinates gave a reassuring speech about how they were going to be resettled once they had cleaned up in the showers. They were told to hand over their valuables, but assured that they would get them back. Sometimes the Jews cheered when they heard this. Then the men were directed into the undressing room and through the haircutting room into the tube. They would all be dead within an hour. The women and children followed. Sometimes they had to stand naked and cold in the tube, waiting for the gas chambers to be made ready. Though the technology was elementary the engine was prone to break down.[40]

In mid-April the deportations from Lublin paused for several weeks because Jews were also pouring into Belzec from Lwow and other centres. Meanwhile the ghetto was replenished with Jews from central Europe. Before the process could restart, Wirth halted any further transports. Although the system had proved to work extremely well, the gassing facilities as originally conceived turned out to be far too small to cope with the influx. Moreover, the remit of the entire operation changed significantly, greatly increasing the expected volume of arrivals. So the first wooden gas chamber building was dismantled and replaced with a concrete and brick structure containing six cells, three on each side, opening off a central aisle.[41]

During March and June 1942, 85,000–90,000 German, Austrian, Czech and Slovak Jews were deported to Lublin and ghettos in the Lublin district. They were the first to be transported to the east under the rubric of the new 'final solution'. The Czech Jews had already been uprooted and came mainly from Theresienstadt; the trainloads of German Jews originated in cities across the Reich; the Slovak Jews were dispatched from places where they had been concentrated prior to removal under an agreement reached between the Slovak and the German authorities. The first wave of 25,000 arrived between 11 March and 20 April. They were stuffed into ghettos vacated by Polish Jews and the able-bodied were extracted to work in labour camps scattered across the district. They were not sent directly to Belzec or murdered on arrival. The second wave, from 22 April to 20 June, brought 61,000 Jews into the Lublin area and this time many transports went direct to the newly inaugurated death camp at Sobibor or the gas chambers at Majdanek, a mixed-function concentration and death camp on the outskirts of Lublin. The ghettos now served as selection sites where those deemed capable of work were cruelly parted from their loved ones. For the rest, the ghettos were little more than transit camps where they lingered miserably for days or weeks before being sent to a Vernichtungslager.[42]

When Belzec resumed its work, huge numbers of Jews were pumped into its maw from small towns across the Lublin district, from the ghettos where Jews from central Europe were held, and from cities in other districts of the General Government and Galicia. The intensification of the murder process was the outcome of an unusually large number of consultations between Himmler and Heydrich in late April and early May, framed by meetings between Himmler and Hitler on 23 April and 3 May. Parallel to these top-level exchanges, a fundamental shift in the balance of power occurred within the General Government between Frank's civil administration and the SS. In early May 1942, Krüger was appointed secretary of state for security in the General Government. On 3 June, a formal agreement gave the security police free rein over Jewish affairs and obviated the need for tiresome negotiations with the civil

21. The gate to the Riga ghetto, from outside the ghetto fence.

22. Jewish children in Lublin, photographed by a German soldier and labelled 'Jewish types', c.1941.

23 & 24. Scenes from a
market in the Warsaw ghetto,
taken by a member of the
Wehrmacht in the
early 1940s.

JUDENPOST 10
LITZMANNSTADT - GETTO

25. A Lodz ghetto stamp, bearing a portrait of Chaim Rumkowski.

26. A workshop in the Lodz ghetto, c. 1941–42.

27. A group of Jewish Latvian women forced to undress shortly before being shot by German troops in Liepaja, 15 December 1941.

28. A Jewish woman being abused during the pogrom in German-occupied Lvov, 30 June to 3 July 1941.

29. Jewish women from Kishinev, in Bessarabia, assembled under Romanian military guard prior to their execution by members of Einsatzkommando 11a at a site outside the city.

30. Jews in the Kaunus ghetto are boarded onto trucks during a deportation action. They were sent to the Koramei concentration camp in Estonia.

31. Anton Kaindl, the commandant of Sachsenhausen concentration camp, near Berlin, is greeted with the 'Heil Hitler' salute as prisoners stand to attention at roll call, February 1941.

32. Jewish prisoners at Drancy internment camp in Paris, 1942.

33. Members of the Ordedienst (Jewish Order Service) assist Jewish prisoners onto a deportation train in the Westerbork transit camp, c. 1942/43. They were possibly bound for Sobibor.

34. Hungarian Jews rescued from deportation by Raoul Wallenberg are escorted back to the Budapest ghetto, 28 November 1944.

35. A prison choir performing in a courtyard at Theresienstadt, c. 1943.

36. Jewish inmates of Theresienstadt, early 1945.

authorities. Over the next six months, some 57,000 Jews from the Lublin district would be sent to death camps, while 70,000 Jews would be shot in massacres conducted by German police units and auxiliaries throughout the region.[43]

The experience of the wretched deportees who arrived at Belzec during this period was captured in testimony by Rudolf Reder, who arrived from Lwow in mid-August. He escaped from the camp work-force in November 1942 and was hidden in the home of his former housekeeper in Lwow. Reder was in his early sixties and ran a soap-making business before the war. He was seized in a round-up and held overnight along with a mass of other Jews in an open field in the precincts of the Janowska labour camp. In the morning he was driven with hundreds of others onto a train. By this time, many Jews in the city had their suspicions about Belzec and throughout the journey individuals tried to escape from the box-cars. Many were shot by the security policemen accompanying the transport, one perched on each wagon and armed with a submachine gun. The train stopped repeatedly to let priority traffic use the line and arrived at noon, whereupon it was held in the siding for hours.

Eventually, Reder was disembarked onto the platform. He heard an SS man welcome the Jews and tell them they would have a shower and that everything would be all right. The men were then led away to a building marked 'Bade- und Inhalationsräume'. After a few minutes, prisoners appeared with stools and hair-cutting equipment: their job was to shave the women. It was 'at this moment that they were struck by the terrible truth. It was then that neither the women nor the men – already on their way to the gas – could have any illusions about their fate.' At that point, 'There were cries and shrieking. Some women went mad. Others, however, went to their death calmly, young girls in partic-ular.' Reder and a few other men were held to one side and then detailed to dig pits. But he could see as 'the women, naked and shaved, were rounded up with whips like cattle to the slaughter, without even being counted – "Faster, Faster" – the men were already dying. Two hours was the time it took to prepare for murder and for murder itself.' The SS men and Ukrainian guards 'counted 750 people for each gas chamber. Those women who tried to resist were bayoneted until the blood was running. Eventually all the women were forced into the chambers. I heard the doors being shut; I heard shrieks and cries; I heard desperate calls for help in Polish and Yiddish. I heard the blood-curdling wails of women and the squeals of children, which after a short time became one long, horrifying scream ... This went on for fifteen minutes. The engine worked for twenty minutes. Afterwards there was total silence.'

By this stage the old gas chamber building had been reconstructed with doors in the external wall through which to remove the dead. When the Ukrainians unbarred these openings this was the sight that greeted the eyes: 'the dead were in an upright position. Their faces were not blue. They looked almost unchanged, as if asleep. There was a bit of blood here and there from bayonet wounds. Their mouths were slightly open, hands rigid, often pressed against their chest. Those who were nearest to the now wide-open doors fell out by themselves. Like marionettes.' The Jewish work team was then commanded to do its job. 'We pulled out the corpses of the people so recently alive. We dragged them to pits with the help of leather straps while an orchestra played ... from morning until night.'[44]

Reder witnessed dozens of transports arrive while he was in Belzec and during his toil at the burial sites saw what became of them. 'We dug pits, enormous mass graves, and pulled bodies along ... There was a mountain of sand which we used to cover the pits when they were filled to overflowing. On average 450 people worked around the pits on a daily basis. What I found most horrible was that we were ordered to pile bodies to a height of about a metre above ground-level, and only then to cover them with sand. Thick, black blood ran from the mounds and covered the whole area like a sea ... Ankle deep we waded through the blood of our brothers. We walked over mounds of bodies.' After hours of this the men were in a daze. Some managed to pray, others moved around like zombies. The SS would sometimes entertain themselves by forcing the Jews to sing songs. After nearly four months Reder was assigned to accompany several SS men to Lwow to pick up some building material. While he was waiting in the truck he noticed that the escort had nodded off and seized his chance to escape. Only one other person is known to have survived Belzec.[45]

By then the Lwow ghetto had been repeatedly culled. For the first months of the year the Jewish population of roughly 110,000 enjoyed relative calm and benefited from a decent Jewish council with a succession of honest, hard-working chairmen. Until December 1941 it was possible to venture into the Aryan portion of the city to buy food to supplement the meagre official ration. For the poor, of course, there was no alternative to slow starvation, and typhus was endemic in their overcrowded lodgings. Notwithstanding the apparent tranquillity, rumours about massacres in other parts of Galicia triggered anxiety about local developments. In March 1942, the security police ordered the Jewish council to prepare a list of unemployed and 'asocial' Jews for resettlement. Rabbi David Kahane, now a member of the religious affairs department of the Jewish council, debated the meaning of this instruction with his colleagues. Fearing the worst they formed a delegation to the chairman of the council, a respected lawyer by the name of Henryk Landsberg. 'We got straight down to business,' Kahane recalled. 'We explained to him that in times of trial such as these we were duty bound to draw the attention of the leader of such a large Jewish community to the enormous responsibility associated with complying with the German orders. According to Jewish law and morality, he was to seek other ways. When our enemies come to us saying: "Bring one of you to us so that we may kill him. If not, we will kill you all" – it is better that all die and not one Jew be delivered to the enemy. This is what the Halakah [Jewish law] rules.' Landsberg retorted that the rabbis were no longer in the pre-war world and the Jewish council was 'an instrument to carry out the orders of the Gestapo'. On 19 March the council and the Order Service began to move against Jews on welfare and those without work certificates. However, the Order Service proved so ineffectual that the Germans took over, deploying their Ukrainian helpers. By the beginning of April 15,000 Jews had been seized and consigned to Belzec.[46]

After the action the Germans issued new work certificates to those employed in approved occupations plus an armband with an 'A' denoting a worker, Arbeiter. The wife of a worker got an armband with an 'H', signifying a homemaker, or Hausfrau. Because these identifiers were supposed to protect the bearer from arbitrary seizure there was a mad rush to get employment, with the Jewish council frantically trying to establish new enterprises to serve the Germans. Kahane and other rabbis were kept busy marrying women to men with the right armband, although some of them looked on this practice as the desecration of a holy institution and one that encouraged promiscuity. Many Jews struggled to preserve some shreds of normality and the dignity that came from observing time-honoured, spiritually consoling rituals. Moty Stromer recalled that 'It was our first Passover under the Germans. One morning before the holiday we baked matzoh in the kitchen . . . If I am not mistaken we had to hide on that day . . .' During the festive meal the assembled Jews 'shed more tears than the wine we drank'. Plenty of Jews trusted neither God nor the German work certificates. According to Rabbi Kahane, 'Engineers, architects, and artisans put their brains and hands to work to construct hideouts in cellars and attics. They built double walls that couldn't be found except by denunciation.' None of these devices was of much avail.[47]

In late June, the SS, who were now in total control of Jewish affairs in the General Government, staged a raid on the ghetto netting several thousand unemployed. They were taken to the Janowska labour camp on the edge of the city, where some were put to work in armaments factories; most were shot and buried in sandy gullies in one corner of the camp complex. This was a curtain-raiser to nearly two weeks of massive daily round-ups conducted with unimaginable ferocity by German and Ukrainian police. They paid scant attention to work permits and used dogs to sniff out those who were in hiding. Stromer, who clung to his job, looked on as thousands were sent to Janowska. 'People were shot to death in the streets. Wagons driving through the streets were commandeered to take the old and the sick to the assembly points.' There was no salvation from the citizens of Lwow. 'It was not enough that the Christians did not want to help the Jews, but there were special groups of Christians who pointed into the Jewish hideouts. Small Christian children would run through the streets yelling "Jew, Jew!" In this way they helped to destroy the Jews.'[48]

Rabbi Kahane made a desperate bid to secure help from the Metropolitan Sheptytsky, crossing Lwow to secure an interview with the aged cleric at the ecclesiastical palace. Sheptytsky said he would issue a pastoral letter calling on his flock not to abet the Germans in murder, although it was not published until November and did not specifically mention Jews. He adopted a similar tack in a private letter to the pope composed at the end of the month. However, the metropolitan's brother made arrangements for the abbess of the Studite convent to take in Kahane's daughter and promised to see if other Jewish children could be saved. Before he could get her to safety, Kahane and his family experienced days of sheer terror. When Ukrainian militia came to their building they joined other fugitives in the concealed bathroom of a Jew who had good papers. 'Can anyone grasp what goes on in the mind of a human being buried in a hideout like this, dreading the visit by the Gestapo?' he wrote later while in hiding at Sheptytsky's residence. 'Can anyone conceive of the terror seizing more than twenty people pressed together in a small bathroom when they hear the sounds of hard, heavy tread [sic] characteristic of the SS thugs, coming from the courtyard and up the staircase. Can anyone picture the frozen silence, the fainting glances, the heartbeat of twenty people imprisoned in a tiny room, at the time the German opens the door of the closet concealing the entrance to the bathroom?' Kahane and the others avoided discovery that time; but his mother and father were amongst the 40,000–50,000 deported to the death camps.[49]

The war machine and the killing machine

The expanding scope of anti-Jewish actions in the middle of 1942 and the lethal sorting of Jews into different categories was related to developments in the war. During May, June and July 1942 the Wehrmacht won a string of stunning victories. In early May the Germans crushed a Russian offensive to retake Kharkov. Shortly afterwards, the German 11th Army in the Crimea defeated a far superior Soviet force on the Kerch peninsula, clearing the way for an assault on Sebastopol. The great port-fortress fell on 4 July. In Libya, Rommel's combined German and Italian troops routed the British Eighth Army in the battle of Gazala and went on to capture Tobruk. The fuel and supply dumps that fell into Rommel's hands enabled the renamed Panzer Army Africa to make a dash for the Suez Canal. It looked as if nothing could stop them, until they ran into fresh British blocking positions at El Alamein. Rommel was just sixty miles short of Alexandria.[50]

However, the springtime triumphs of the German military were an illusion. They resulted from an ability to focus all the available offensive combat power in a specific theatre on a relatively limited battlefield. The Germans possessed operational and tactical superiority, but they were made to look even better by the ineptitude of Soviet and British generals. And, despite their success, they did not deliver a knock-out blow against the opposition. Indeed, the feats at Kharkov and in the Crimea were merely the preliminaries to 'Operation Blau'. This campaign required advances across a wide front, deep into enemy territory in search of the elusive strategic victory. It was 400 miles from Kharkov to Stalingrad and 700 miles from Rostov to Baku. In order to mount the attack into the Caucasus, with the goal of reaching the oil fields, Hitler was able to deploy forty fresh divisions, but half of them were Hungarian, Italian and Romanian. These units were poorly equipped, badly led, and had shaky morale. After a few weeks of good progress the German armies began to run out of fuel. Attrition took its toll of men and machines while Soviet resistance stiffened. By September the advance on both axes – towards Stalingrad and towards the oil fields – stalled short of their objectives.[51]

Between the victories of May and the stalemate of September 1942, Nazi anti-Jewish policy went through another metamorphosis, reflecting the oscillating fortunes of the Wehrmacht, the demands of the war economy, and morale on the home front. Since the start of the year, economic realities had played an important part in reshaping the Judenpolitik of the SS. Thanks to its control of the concentration camps the SS possessed a reservoir of cheap, expendable labour that could be put to work in its own enterprises or hired out to the military and civilian contractors. Himmler was intent on using this resource to transform the SS into an economic powerhouse, both to assist the war effort and to generate funds for its own growth. To this end he had instructed Richard Glücks, head of the inspectorate of concentration camps, to prepare for an influx of 150,000 Jews into labour camps in the Lublin district and into the camp at Auschwitz. He merged the head office of the SS that handled finance, business affairs, construction and administration with the main leadership office of the SS, placing the new headquarters unit, dubbed the Wirtschafts- und Verwaltungshauptamt (SS-WVHA, the SS Business and Administrative Head Office), under the capable management of Oswald Pohl. In March 1942, Himmler completed this horizontal integration by moving the inspectorate of concentration camps into the WVHA, too. When applied to Jews, the SS initiative to exploit the work potential of camp inmates translated into 'annihilation through labour' although this notion did not acquire doctrinal status until much later.[52]

At this point, Himmler was thinking in terms of eliminating 60 per cent of the Jews in the Lublin area, people who allegedly could not work, and retaining the balance for economic purposes. To be sure, Himmler and his colleagues did not envisage the long-term survival of this Jewish labour force. Jews with skills or capable of hard labour would be sweated until they either dropped dead or were no longer fit, in which case they would be murdered. Hence, the Jews deported to the General Government from western and central Europe in the spring were not immediately killed. Instead they were subjected to selections and a large part were sent to concentration and labour camps while the rest were dumped in ghettos. When Polish Jews in the ghettos were culled, those who were employed or possessed essential skills were spared while those unable to work went to the extermination camps.[53]

From late May into July, this policy of selective mass murder morphed into something even more threatening. The change was fed by security fears and anxiety about food supplies. On 18 May members of a communist resistance cell in Berlin consisting entirely of Jews set fire to an exhibition demonizing the USSR. The Jews, led by Herbert Baum, were mostly employed as forced labour in a Siemens electrical engineering plant. It did not take the Gestapo long to track them down (they were executed). The incident, though minor, fomented Himmler's security paranoia. Then, on 27 May, a group of Czech and Slovak soldiers from the Czechoslovak army-in-exile based in Britain mounted an assassination attempt on Heydrich in Prague. Heydrich was wounded and died in hospital a week later. Although the attack was masterminded by the Special Operations Executive in London, it reinforced Himmler's belief that he faced an upsurge of resistance activity across Europe that was rooted in the Jewish population. Over the days that Heydrich lay dying Himmler resolved that the Jews of Europe would be removed totally. He used the occasion of Heydrich's state funeral to tell senior officers of the SS and the police that 'Within a year we will definitely have completed the mass migration of the Jews; then no more will migrate.'[54]

However, due to the transport needs of the army in the first weeks of Operation Blau, there was a moratorium on all non-military rail traffic in the east. Instead, Himmler triggered deportations in central and western Europe and honed plans for the destruction of the Jews in the General Government. He obtained Hitler's backing for the allotment of trains once the ban was lifted and issued new guidelines to Krüger and Globocnik. On 19 July Himmler ordered Krüger, 'The resettlement of the entire Jewish population of the General Government should be implemented and completed by December 31, 1942.' After that date no people of Jewish origin were to remain except 'if they are in assembly camps in Warsaw, Krakow, Czestochowa, Radom, and Lublin. All projects that employ Jewish labour have to be completed by that date or transferred to the assembly camps.' The principle of selection on the basis of usefulness, capacity for labour, was scrapped and only those Jews already in work had any chance of survival. The ensuing

programme of mass extermination became known as Operation Reinhard.[55]

These revisions of Judenpolitik overlapped with another July crisis
in the management of the war. Operation Blau, as originally conceived,
was 'in ruins' and Hitler was obliged to improvise the rest of the campaign. This wobble was followed by jitters over rationing and morale on
the home front. On 5 August, Göring met with Nazi Party bosses in
Germany to review the food situation and on the following day transmitted instructions to the Reichskommissars in the occupied eastern
lands and army commanders to extract the maximum foodstuffs for the
Reich. When Karl Naumann, who ran the food department of Frank's
administration, pointed out that there was not enough even to feed just
the Poles, Herbert Backe retorted, 'The 3.5 million Jews [sic] remaining
in the General Government in Poland will have to be cleansed this year.'
On 24 August, Naumann passed on the message to his colleagues: 'The
maintenance of the estimated 1.5 million Jews in the population has
been abandoned, with the exception of 300,000 Jews who are useful
to the Reich because of artisan or other work skills ... The other 1.2
million Jews will no longer be given food.'[56]

The pressure to dispose of the Jews in Poland was now extreme:
policy had moved from presuming that Jews were useful unless proved
useless, to assuming they were useless unless proved useful. To make
matters worse, during July, the SS under Krüger established their un-
alloyed control over all the Jewish workers in the General Government.
This did not mean an end to friction over the utilization of Jewish
labour. Many Jewish workers were highly trained and possessed skills
that were not easily replaced; the managers of enterprises that relied on
them proved to be obstreperous. However, Sauckel's effort to pressgang
east Europeans to work in German industry was proving so successful
that there was no shortage of unskilled hands.[57]

The policy transition was to some extent reflected in the early
history of the second purpose-built extermination camp, Sobibor.
Construction work had started in March 1942 on the site of a hamlet
clustered beside the Chelm–Wlodowa railway line. A derelict chapel
and a post office that once served the community actually ended up
inside the camp precincts. But building proceeded so slowly that after
several weeks Globocnik appointed Franz Stangl, a veteran of T-4 who
was known for his efficiency and drive, to speed things up. Stangl visited Belzec to familiarize himself with the modus operandi of these new

killing centres and modelled Sobibor very closely on what he saw there. The western side of the perimeter, about 600 metres long, ran parallel to the rail line, with a siding outside and a spur line running inside the formidable three-layered barbed-wire fence. The SS buildings, Stangl's quarters, and barracks for the Ukrainian Trawniki men were situated in the Vorlager, or Fore-camp, in the southern sector opposite the platform. Here the transports were unloaded, twenty wagons at a time. The Jews were directed through a gateway into wooden buildings where valuables were confiscated and the victims undressed. They proceeded from there across a courtyard into a walkway lined on both sides by tall barbed-wire fencing. The processing area was designated camp II and included large sheds for storing the property of the doomed. It was 150 metres from camp II to the gas chamber building in camp III, and en route women were separated out so that their hair could be shaved. All the victims were then driven into the cells that were entered from a corridor runing along one side of the structure. Once the 400 Jews were packed inside the chambers, each 4 by 4 metres, carbon monoxide exhaust fumes were pumped in from a diesel engine housed in an adjacent shed. After about 30 minutes the bodies were removed through doors in the external wall and hauled a short distance to burial pits. A Jewish labour force, including women, was held in camp I, a camp within the camp, in the south-east corner. The entire facility was neat, tidy and well organized. Stangl had Jewish work Sonderkommandos to cover every phase of the operation. Security was tight. In addition to the five watchtowers, one centrally placed, the installation was surrounded by a minefield.[58]

In the first week of May 1942, Jews from the Zamość area and around Pulawy started arriving at Sobibor. They were completely unaware of what awaited them and were further disarmed by the deception the Germans practised. It was almost impossible to see from the wagons what was happening inside the camp and the first sight that greeted the deportees was a country railway station in a sylvan setting. Yaacov Freidberg, deported from the shtetl of Turobin in Krasnystaw county, described what happened next: 'the people were taken off rapidly and made to run to this place where they separated the men, women and children. That was a kind of half-way station. The people were put into a closed-in yard. The entire path lay between barbed wire fences, and, on the way, there were signs "To the Showers." Inside the yard, there were also large signs "To the Showers," and there were also signs "To the Cash Desk." The cash desk stood in a corner. There was a door there, and that was where the people assembled. Then Oberschar-fuehrer Michel would appear, whom we called "the preacher," and he addressed the people. His speeches were usually adapted to each trans-port. But, at that time, he would repeat the same story about what would happen there. They were going to the Ukraine where they would establish farms, they would have to work – work hard. And sometimes people used to ask questions: "What is going to happen to the women?" And he would reply: "If they want to live under better conditions, they, too, will have to work." After that, he would add: "You have to get undressed, but you must leave your belongings in order – we don't have much time – so that when you come out of the showers, it will not take long." The people believed him. They undressed, they arranged their possessions: money, gold and securities – these they handed over at the cash desk. In most cases, people handed over their money, but, at any rate, there were also some who buried the money and the gold in the sand – there was sand there – or in all sorts of corners, in the hope that on their return they would have some money. And then they walked through this narrow door, passing between two barbed wire fences, for a distance of three hundred meters.' Closer to the gas chamber the cor-ridor forked and the women went into the shaving shed. From this point the Ukrainians took over and all pretence ended, to be replaced by shouting, clubbing, and bayonets. Freidberg continued, 'They would stab them, cut off people's limbs, hit them continuously. They would urge them on with whips. All the time they kept them on the run. They did not allow people a moment to think of what was happening at all . . . We were on the outside of this yard and heard what was going on inside. The shrieking was terrible. And, afterwards, when we went in to remove the belongings, we saw enough horrors and a great deal of blood.'[59]

Women faced other horrors. From early June, the SS began to select young females to work in the camp laundry. Their numbers increased when an SS officer requisitioned fifteen more from a transport to knit warm winter woollens for the German guards. Ada Lichtman, deported from Mielec, was amongst the women spared immediate death. After she had been in the camp for a time, she was woken by cries. 'And what is the meaning of the screams? The Ukrainian guards are raping young girls before pushing them into the gas chambers.' One SS officer took a sixteen- or seventeen-year-old girl from a group of new arrivals and kept her as his 'mistress' for a while. Needless to say, the Jewish women could not afford to become or be seen to be pregnant. Lichtman recorded that one woman who gave birth in the camp was immediately stretchered to the death pits: the newborn baby was drowned in a latrine.[60]

About 57,000 Jews were murdered in Sobibor until late July when Stangl shut down the operation. The main reason for the pause was the need to strengthen the railway line running between Lublin and Chelm: it was unable to cope with the volume of traffic generated by the deportations. But it was also evident that the gassing facilities were too small. Hence, while the railway was being repaired, the gas chamber building was enlarged and three cells added. The doors to the chambers were now entered from a central corridor running the length of the building, though the bodies were extracted in the same way as before. Stangl also commissioned a narrow-gauge railway to run from the platform, past the gas chambers, to the mass graves. The corpses of those who died en route to Sobibor or Jews too feeble to walk were now transported by this means to the extermination area. The trucks doubled-up for removing corpses from the gas chambers to the pits. It also proved necessary to rethink the practice for disposing of the dead. The existing mass grave was filling up fast and the smell of putrefaction was unbearable. So the camp staff decided to begin burning the bodies immediately. At the base of a second, specially excavated pit, they constructed a sort of grille onto which the cadavers could be piled and incinerated. The treatment of the living changed as well as the handling of the dead. Previously, Jews had been sorted at Sobibor and several hundred sent to nearby forced labour camps. That practice now ceased and the only Jews saved from the gas chambers were those inducted into the camp's own Sonderkommandos. Sobibor had been adapted from a killing centre with facilities that were calibrated to a local or regional task to one that could service mass murder on a larger scale. Freidberg described the first version of the camp as 'primitive' compared to the revamped edition.[61]

When it resumed operating around 10 October, Sobibor swallowed up 2,400 Jews from Chelm county and 3,000 Jews from Lubartow the next day. Later that month it received 5,000 Jews from the ghetto-camp at Izbica, 3,300 from the Chelm ghetto, 5,000 from Wlodowa on one day alone, and 2,000 from Hrubieszow on another day. By the end of the year, Höfle reported to Berlin that 101,370 Jews had been murdered in what was to the killers an exemplary extermination camp.[62]

Deportations from the Warsaw ghetto

The first major Jewish community in Poland to feel the effect of the policy decisions made in Berlin and Lublin was the teeming Warsaw ghetto. In mid-1942 there were an estimated 400,000 Jews in the ghetto, including some 4,000 driven in from outlying districts in the spring plus 4,000 recently arrived German Jews. Starvation and disease were reducing this number at an appalling rate: 39,719 Jews died in the first six and half months of the year, which almost equalled the total for the whole of 1941.[63]

Adam Czerniaków charted the ominous signs in his journal, beginning with word from Hermann Probst, one of Auerswald's underlings, who warned him 'in connection with a certain official speech, that the future looks grim for the Jews'. Probst was referring to a menacing oration by Hitler at the Sportpalast on 30 January 1942 in which he stated 'the war will not end as the Jews imagine it will, namely with the uprooting of the Aryans, but the result of the war will be the complete annihilation of the Jews'. From February onwards Czerniaków heard disturbing rumours about expulsions and violent resettlements; he got word of the deportations from Lwow almost the day after they commenced. In mid-May, Ringelblum noted 'rumours about extermination squads that are wiping complete Jewish settlements off the face of the earth'. Mary Berg's uncle brought her family news from Lublin of massacres and deportations. Someone in the Order Service warned her that the same could happen in Warsaw, but she thought that 'To exterminate such a number of people seems impossible, inconceivable'. When Abraham Lewin heard about the fate of Jews in Lwow and learned that letters had stopped coming from Jews in Wloclawek, he concluded 'that all these places where there have been Jewish communities for 700 or 800 years are now judenrein'. Before the war, Lewin, scion of a Hassidic family, worked as a teacher in the Yehudia girls' school, where he met Emanuel Ringelblum. In 1940 he joined the directorate of Oneg Shabbat and started a detailed account of life in the ghetto. Falling back on his religious background, he wondered, 'what if Satan and his devils have triumphed? What if we have become the scapegoat and sacrifice for the whole sinful world?' Chaim Kaplan asked himself, what happened to the 40,000 Jews deported from Lublin? It was as though they had been 'swallowed up by stormy waters. But there is no doubt that they are no longer alive.' He was inclined to take Hitler at his word when, in a speech on 26 April 1942, he repeated his prophecy that the Jews would be exterminated because they started the war. 'There is an instinctive feeling', Kaplan reported, 'that some terrible catastrophe is drawing near for the Warsaw ghetto.'[64]

Jews monitored news of the war as anxiously as rumours about ghetto deportations, instinctively connecting the two and seeking portents of salvation. In early May they were cheered by the Russian offensive at Kharkov. Ringelblum explained that 'we try our utmost to see the war's end as imminent'. Within days such optimism became hard to sustain. Lewin was downcast when 'the megaphone announced the sad news of the fall of Kerch. The news hit me very hard. For the truth is, nowadays our hearts beat with the events taking place on Russian territory . . . Every shift in the balance in Hitler's favour fills us with boundless misery and despair.' The fall of Sebastopol sent a shudder through the population while Rommel's progrees in North Africa heaped anxiety upon anxiety. The veteran Zionist Chaim Kaplan worried that 'England has suffered a defeat and is fleeing to Egypt. And once the war is in Egypt who will wager that it will not spread from there into Palestine as well!'[65]

They took consolation where they could and the image of the meek, forgiving Jew is contradicted by the glee with which they received tidings of German setbacks. Lewin wrote that the bombing of German cities 'makes the pulse beat faster'. For Ringelblum the RAF's thousand-bomber raid on Cologne 'slaked our thirst for revenge somewhat. Cologne was an advance payment on the vengeance that must and shall be taken on Hitler's Germany for the millions of Jews they have killed . . . After Cologne I walked around in a good mood . . . my death is pre-paid.' Kaplan breathed a sigh of relief when Rommel was halted at El Alamein and looked forward to the British counter-attack. By mid-July he shrewdly perceived that the recent German successes meant little: 'Their victories on paper make no impression. A weakening is apparent in comparison with their power and might of last year.' Lewin considered it 'a certainty that the Anglo-American invasion of Europe, or the creation of a Second Front, must and will come to fruition in the near future'.[66]

The yearning for good news and dreams of liberation reflected the abysmal conditions inside the ghetto. Ringelblum raged against the inequality from which so many other evils flowed. 'During these days of hunger, the inhumanity of the Jewish upper class has clearly shown itself. The entire work of the Jewish Council is an evil perpetrated against the poor ... The finance politics of the Council are one great scandal ... In its name, indirect taxes are levied that fall heaviest on the poor.' Chaim Kaplan referred to the council as a 'leech'. Corruption was rampant at all levels of officialdom. 'The entire ghetto is a huge dung-hill', he complained, not least because janitors refused to clean their buildings unless bribed by the residents they were supposed to be serving. He alleged that during a round-up for forced labour in May 1942, the Order Service seized 800 men when the original German requisition was only for 400, and took bribes to free half of them. Venality was the least of their crimes in the eyes of Jews, who increasingly viewed them as collaborators. Lewin bemoaned the 'sad complicity of the Jewish police' in this raid.[67]

Czerniaków claimed to be doing his best to combat inequality and force the rich to share the burden of maintaining the ghetto. In early February 1942 he grumbled, 'A policy, which I am preparing, of exacting contributions from the rich to support the poor came under a barrage of criticism. To top it all, I was visited today by a delegation from the welfare shelters stating that over twenty per cent of their charges died of starvation.' The contradictions within ghetto society could not be more starkly highlighted than in Lewin's account of Szulc's restaurant. Here meals were served comparable to those before the war: 'Only smugglers, racketeers, important activists, members of the police, and other rich people to whom the times have been good can afford to eat there.' Smuggling remained a mainstay of the ghetto economy, for those who could afford to buy on the black market. He reported that 'Flour, potatoes, milk, butter, meat and other produce are brought into the ghetto. And out of the ghetto still pours a continual stream of possessions to the Aryan side. Jews are selling up everything they own.' Children formed the largest contingent involved in the illicit trade. 'Whole hosts of them can be seen climbing over the walls, crawling through the gaps ... and passing through the official entrances where gendarmes and Polish police stand guard.' He noticed that some Germans 'show a little mercy' and turn a blind eye while others 'hit the children with murderous blows'. Kaplan visited the cemetery, where he observed 'small, petty smuggling. The poor come here to smuggle – the impoverished and pauperized youth whose occupation is to bring in a few kilos of potatoes or onions. A whole family sustains itself from this.'

Those without agile children, sufficient food, or money, begged. In May, Ringelblum noticed that 'The beggars crowding the streets nowadays are different from last year's crop. Most of the beggars from the provinces have died out. The newcomers are a better class of people . . . speak a good, sometimes excellent Polish . . . well-dressed . . .'[68]

Moral standards wilted in the face of extreme inequality. Ringelblum maintained that 'Demoralization is spreading rapidly through the ghetto. While the poor become ever poorer and dress in rags, the girls are dressing up as though the war were nonexistent. There have been many cases of girls stealing from their parents, taking things from home to sell or barter for ornaments, or a hair wave . . .' Michel Mazor recalled that 'The main boulevard of the ghetto, Leszno Street, could boast at least twenty restaurants; there were as many, however, on Zelazna Street, Sienna Street, and elsewhere. Given the general poverty, young girls and women from all sorts of backgrounds offered their services as waitresses . . . no city in the world had as many beautiful and elegant women serving in cafes as did the short lived ghetto, with its Café des Arts, Splendide, Negresco etc. But right in front of these display windows, hordes of wretched beggars would pass, often collapsing from inanition.' The sight of such affluence and plenitude enraged Auerswald when he toured the ghetto and strengthened German prejudices against the 'useless eaters' who were allegedly stripping Poland of produce and forcing up prices for the rest of the population.[69]

The German Jews were amongst the most pathetic of the ghetto dwellers. When they made their first appearance they were an impressive sight. Mazor remembered going to visit them in the Little Ghetto. Their quarters were crowded but well kept. 'For me, having come straight out of the [main] ghetto, this was contact with the outside world. What struck me was the air of healthiness and optimism of the entire group, as well as the absence of any sign of fear for their fate.' Mary Berg observed that women and children who came off a transport from Danzig 'carried elegant luggage and were dressed far better than our own ghetto people'. Czerniaków, responsible for housing and feeding the deportees, paid less attention to their appearance. After nearly 2,000 had been deposited into his charge he wailed, 'We have no housing and no money'. To add insult to injury, the SS demanded gold from the Reich Jews, but 'there was not much of it'. In late April, 1,000 Czech Jews were crammed into the refugee shelters, too. Because they were not able to get work and their ration was inadequate to support life they slowly starved. The plight of the deportees from central Europe was only marginally less awful than that of deportees from the General Government. Mary Berg described them as 'ragged and barefoot, with the tragic eyes of those who are starving. Most of them are women and children. They become charges of the community, which sets them up in so-called hostels. There they die, sooner or later.'[70]

As in Lodz the gender imbalance in Warsaw was acute. Thousands of women parted from fathers, sons and brothers were left to fend for themselves. Mothers with young children and daughters of elderly parents were particularly hard hit since their role as carers made it difficult for them to work but they still had mouths to feed. At their most desperate such women were driven to cannibalism. Czerniaków recorded one case of a woman who ate flesh from the buttocks of her dead son. At another extreme 'a certain type of girl' could be observed – with make-up, dressed impeccably, hair coiffeured – who sought out protectors in return for sexual favours. Czerniaków noted archly that thanks to the inventiveness of the ghetto it was possible to obtain 'contraceptives made of baby pacifiers'.[71]

Italian troops passing through Warsaw central station en route to the Eastern Front in the spring of 1942 saw Jewish women employed as cleaners begging for scraps from the soldiers. One of them, Michaelangelo Pattoglio, recalled, 'A Jewish woman who is picking up trash from the train station speaks good Italian; she's a cultured person. She talks: we listen to her in astonishment . . . When they saw the Italian train, two or three hundred starving Polish Jews take off in a storm to talk to us, to ask for bread. They are starving.' Some Jewish women were so deep in despair that they offered themselves to the Italian men, a prospect that speaks volumes about the horrors they were escaping. Bartolomeo Fruterro, a regular soldier in an Alpini regiment, remembered, 'We put a woman doctor in our car, young, beautiful, and sharp. She speaks good Italian, says that the Germans are cremating all the Jews, that her life isn't worth anything, either. We are wily; we hide her well so the officers won't notice. The woman has a little white dress, all narrow pleats. We take it from her; she is left in her slip with a grey-green shirt over it. We give her food, take turns going to make love. A lot of other cars have their Jewish women, too; we travel that way for two days. But then the chaplain notices it, there's trouble, the major intervenes, and we have to leave the Jewish women at the first stations.'[72]

The inequalities in the ghetto provided the Germans with the material for a propaganda film that obscenely exaggerated them in order to confirm Nazi preconceptions about 'the Jew'. In early May 1942, a German army film unit arrived and started filming Jews in the workshops. The next day the filmmakers ordered Czerniaków to stage a meeting in his office and placed a large menorah on his desk to accentuate the Jewishness of the scenario. When they shot footage inside one of the few smart apartments on Leszno Street, he wrote, 'They are filming both extreme poverty and luxury . . . The positive achievements are of no interest to them.' A few days later the movie unit commandeered the *mikvah* (ritual bath), and rounded up twenty orthodox men and an equal number of elegantly dressed young women. Lewin retold what followed: 'They then forced the men and the women to strip completely naked. German officers divided them into pairs made of one from each sex from among the Jews. They matched young girls to old men, and conversely, young boys with old women. Then they forced the two sexes to commit a sexual act. These scenes, that is, the sexual scenes, were filmed.' Later, the Germans packed Jews into Szulcz's restaurant and filmed 'plutocrats' gorging. As a contrast, they staged a riot outside a bread shop.[73]

Jews did not remain passive in the face of such provocations. During late 1941 and early 1942, the political underground expanded its membership and the range of its activities. Neither the Jewish council nor the Germans showed much interest in internal Jewish politics and the activists were able to operate relatively freely. However, for the most part they remained focused on the welfare of their own members and did more or less what they had been doing before the war. The Bund ran a soup kitchen for workers affiliated to the union, tried to defend their interests in the workplace, and sponsored educational programmes for its youth wing. The Zionist youth movements maintained kitchens in their headquarters, which had the character of clubhouses, and conducted lively meetings to sustain morale. About 170 Zionist youth were able to work on a training farm in the Czerniaków suburb until November 1942. The farm served as a base for clandestine operations and was a hub for couriers, mainly young women, who circulated between ghettos delivering and picking up news. In mid-1942 there were no fewer than forty-seven underground newspapers circulating reports from across Poland and debating such issues as the appropriate ideological stance towards the USSR. The Oneg Shabbat organization was a hive for a particular sort of resistance activity, chronicling

German crimes in Warsaw and more widely. Ringelblum's team of reporters and interviewers provided essential evidence for dispatches to the west. These updates were carried by couriers of the Polish underground, men like Jan Karski. Through them the Bund remained in contact with its delegates in London as well as with the Polish government-in-exile. The Zionist movements had their own lines of communication to envoys based in Switzerland and Turkey, and each one thereby stayed in touch with party headquarters as well as the Jewish Agency in Palestine.[74]

During the first months of 1942 political activists in the ghetto started to receive information about the massacres of Jews in the German-occupied parts of the USSR and deportations from Jewish centres in Poland. The information was fragmentary and hard to assess, particularly since Warsaw Jews were enjoying a period of relative stability. The ghetto economy was functioning well and there were plenty of orders for the workshops. Nevertheless, it was impossible to ignore the testimony of Jews who had escaped the slaughters in Vilnius and the extermination centre at Chelmno. The call to arms addressed specifically to Jewish youth by the United Fighting Organization in Vilnius in January 1942 created a stir amongst the youth movements in Warsaw by claiming the Germans were intent on exterminating the Jews. Szlama Wiener, who escaped from Chelmno, was only the first of several fugitives to reach Warsaw with grim accounts of gas vans and ghetto clearances in the Wartheland. The problem facing activists in Warsaw was to work out whether these were local disasters or part of a general policy that would, sooner or later, extend to their ghetto. Those who credited the Germans with such outlandish ambitions 'were at a loss to cope with the news'. Apart from struggling with the implications of what such a phenomenon posed to the very idea of humanity, there were endless practical questions concerning how best to respond.[75]

In January, stirred by the Vilna declaration, Yitzhak Zuckerman, a leader of the Hechalutz-Dror left-wing Zionist youth group, approached the Bund with a proposition to cooperate in resistance work. The Bund was a larger organization and had more resources than the Zionist youth so their support was a necessary prerequisite. But Zuckerman was rebuffed. In March, the Poale Zion party made a similar overture but, again, the Bund rejected physical resistance. The party's negativity was partly based on a realistic appraisal of the situation the Jews confronted, although it was also ideologically unwilling to work with Jewish nationalists whom it traditionally despised. On 15 April, a meeting of its main youth cadres and veteran leadership declared that 'To call for active self-defence, as several, irresponsible organisations have done, is to call for mass suicide.' The left-wing Zionist youth groups and the left Poale Zion faction next went outside the ghetto to contact the Polish Workers' Party (Polska Partia Robotnicza, PPR), the reconstituted Polish Communist Party, to seek their cooperation. The PPR was more receptive, leading to the formation of the Anti-Fascist Bloc. It was the first broad-based resistance organization inside the ghetto, but the fact that it engaged with communists, hated enemies of the Bund, only further alienated Bundist sympathies. Months passed before Tsukunft, the Bund's youth wing, saw the value of this coalition and edged closer to joining a united resistance movement. In the interim the Anti-Fascist Bloc established a joint leadership, began training fighters, and started thinking how to defend the ghetto against a German assault. Its arsenal fell woefully short of its aspirations: in May 1942 it had one pistol. Moreover, its efforts to win support from the ghetto inhabitants and to raise money for arms purchases fell on stony ground.[76]

Just when the Jewish underground was beginning to coalesce, but before it had time to prepare itself for any engagement with the Germans or even to plan escape and evasion procedures, the Gestapo started taking an interest. This intelligence gathering was actually a prelude to the deportations but it led to discovery of the nascent resistance. On 17–18 April 1942, the Gestapo struck, killing fifty-two political activists. Raids in other ghettos led to the arrest or death of several leaders and couriers. The Bund and Tsukunft were shattered by this setback. The Zionist groups were no less disorientated. As the Germans intended, on the eve of the greatest action against the largest Jewish population in Poland, its political leadership was temporarily nonplussed and its ability to resist was severely degraded.[77]

Yet, by their own lights, the Jewish underground in the Warsaw ghetto did score a major victory against the Germans. On 21 May 1942, the Bund was able to smuggle out of Poland a letter informing its representatives in London that 700,000 Polish Jews had been murdered to date, specifying the use of poison gas, and asserting that this massacre was part of a programme for the total annihilation of the Jewish community. Details about the death camp at Chelmno and the new one at Treblinka were also supplied to the Polish government-in-exile. The raw material for these dispatches came from interviews conducted by Oneg

Shabbat with men who had escaped from the camps and from refugees who had evaded deportation from Lublin, Lwow and other places. The resulting intelligence formed the basis for a public relations offensive by the Bund in London and by the Polish exile leadership. It culminated in a broadcast on the BBC European service on 2 June 1942, breaking the silence about the systematic mass murder of Polish Jews. The Polish prime minister alluded to the catastrophe in a broadcast a week later. Afterwards, Ringelblum permitted himself a word of self-congratulation. It was 'a great day for O.S. This morning the English radio broadcast about the fate of Polish Jewry. They told everything we know so well: about Slonim and Vilna, Lemberg and Chelmno, and so forth.' After weeks when the ghetto felt utterly abandoned by an ignorant, uncaring world there was now a sign that they knew. Ringelblum rejoiced that 'it seems that all our interventions have finally achieved their purpose. There have been regular broadcasts over the English radio in the last few weeks, treating the cruelties perpetrated on the Polish Jews: Belzec and the like. Today there was a broadcast summarizing the situation: 700,000, the number killed in Poland . . . At the same time, the broadcast vowed revenge, a final accounting for all these deeds of violence. The Oneg Shabbat group has in this way fulfilled a great historical mission and has alerted the world to our fate and may save hundreds of thousands of Polish Jews from extermination.' Alas, the news reached the west too late and there was, in any case, little that could have been done to avert or mitigate the apocalypse that was about to engulf the Warsaw ghetto.[78]

In early June, Czerniaków detected stronger omens. He was immediately suspicious when the Germans required the extraction of Jews with foreign nationality to a secure place under their supervision, ostensibly until they could be exchanged for German nationals in Allied custody. Mary Berg was one of those affected by this measure; she and her family were amongst those taken to the Pawiak prison for safe-keeping. Survivors of the massive deportations from other ghettos flooded into Warsaw accompanied by rumours that the Germans would soon remove 70,000 local Jews. Czerniaków confided to his diary that he felt like a man on a sinking ship. As if to reassure himself, he took stock: 79,000 Jews were employed (50,000 in enterprises inside the ghetto). In June exports were valued at 12 million zlotys. Yet the rumours persisted and on 18 July, 'a day of foreboding', he challenged Auerswald to confirm or deny plans to resettle all but 120,000 Warsaw

Jews. Auerswald denied knowledge of any such proposals. Nonetheless, panic swept the streets and Czerniaków deliberately showed himself in public in order to calm people. On the same day, activists gathered to discuss how to respond should the rumours prove true. Hillel Seidman, a Jewish journalist who now worked for the Jewish council, recorded the discussions. Some participants maintained quite reasonably that it was impossible to deport half a million people. Optimists argued that the ghetto was serving the interest of the Germans anyway. Pessimists pointed to the destruction of other productive communities. In which case, what could they do? One rabbi recommended pleading with the Allies to make Jews citizens of Palestine and thereby Allied nationals. Another suggested warning the pope. 'Slowly but surely,' Seidman noted, 'realization dawns on the gathering that all our plans are un-realistic, impossible to carry out. The knowledge of our total help-lessness grows more tangible by the minute as we realize that we are condemned to our fate.'[79]

That fate was now hurtling towards them. On 21 July, the security police detained Czerniaków, his wife, and other members of the Jewish council. He was subsequently released but his colleagues were held as hostages. During a journey into the city on Jewish council business, Seidman spotted reinforced guard units at the gates and heard people talking about an imminent '*Aktion*'. By the time he returned the ghetto was in turmoil. Jews were struggling to obtain jobs and certificates proving they were employed. Women were marrying men, any men, who had labour permits.[80]

The following day, Czerniaków's darkest premonitions came true. At 10 a.m. Hermann Höfle appeared in his office, accompanied by two members of the team that had emptied the Lublin ghetto. They ordered him to arrange for 6,000 people to be ready for evacuation to the east by four in the afternoon and presented him with the categories of who would be included or excluded. The edict was later printed on a poster and plastered on walls across the ghetto. All Jews were to be deported to the east except: those employed by the Germans or working in German-owned firms; those fit to work (who would be collected and held in bar-racks); the Order Service and public health or medical workers; plus their close family members. Anyone ill or in hospital was also exempted. Deportees were permitted 15kg of baggage and told to bring with them to the assembly points their valuables as well as food for three days. Seidman, who was at the Jewish council, witnessed how 'with the speed of lightning, the news spreads: "Ausseidlung" [evacuation]. This terrible word sows the fear of death . . . I enter Czerniakow's boardroom. One look at him was enough – the chalk white face, the shaking hand, and staring eyes that see nothing.' Seidman left the building and found chaos outside, the streets filled with people dashing this way and that. He saw the Order Service already going to work to fill the quota. They started by seizing Jews in the refugee shelters and prisons, juveniles and beggars. By the end of the day, 6,250 Jews had been delivered to the Umschlagplatz, the goods yard and storage area (formerly the Transfer-stelle) that now functioned as a holding pen guarded by the Order Service and watched over by German security police.[81]

Early next morning, Hermann Worthoff, an SS lieutenant and a vet-eran of the Lublin clearances who served on Höfle's staff, came to Czerniaków's office with fresh instructions. Czerniaków haggled with him over categories to be exempted, focusing on the orphans in particu-lar. Worthoff told him to take up their case with Höfle; he required 7,000 to be deported. In reply to Czerniaków's question about how long this would go on, he answered, 'seven days a week'. Czerniaków later wrote, 'Throughout the town a great rush to start new workshops. A sewing machine can save a life.' But a sewing machine could not save the life of an orphan child or anyone else unable to operate one. Some time after that morning meeting Marceli Reich, the head of the council's translation department, found Czerniaków dead in his office. He had committed suicide. In a final note to his colleagues on the Jewish council he stated, 'I am powerless, my heart trembles in sorrow and compassion. I can no longer bear all this. My act will show everyone the right thing to do.' Unfortunately, few people gleaned the meaning of Czerniaków's final act. Ringelblum, never his greatest admirer, jotted scathingly, 'The suicide of Czerniaków – too late, a sign of weakness – should have called for resistance – a weak man.' To Kaplan, 'The first victim of the deportation decree was the president, Adam Czerniaków . . . He perpetuated his name by his death more than by his life.' Czer-niaków, 'who had a spark of purity in his heart, found the only way out worthy of himself'. Seidman, too, understood what had driven the chairman over the edge: 'he had suddenly realized the gaping chasm yawning in front of his kehillah. All his plans and hopes collapsed in front of cruel realities. Rather than become a mere tool of the enemy, he took his life and died with honour.' Czerniaków was buried hurriedly and secretly the next afternoon. That day, the fast of Tisha B'Av, when devout Jews commemorate the destruction of the temple in Jerusalem, 7,200 Jews were delivered to the Umschlagplatz.[82]

A pattern was established that was repeated, with variations, for the next six weeks. Höfle established his headquarters on Leszno Street in the centre of the ghetto. He delegated the day-to-day routine to the two Sipo-SD men assigned to the Jewish office of the Warsaw Gestapo, Karl Brandt and Gerhard Mende. Each morning they delivered written instructions to the Jewish council, now led by Mark Lichtenbaum, and the Order Service, commanded by Jozef Szerynski and Jacob Lejkin (who was in sole command for the first few days while his boss was held in prison). The guidelines stipulated the number of deportees, any new categories to be included, and the streets, buildings or workshops that were to be targeted. Seidman observed sardonically that the Germans would appear with maps that divided Warsaw block-by-block: 'the latest modern technology; after all, we are in the twentieth century'. The Order Service men would proceed to surround the designated location and herd the inhabitants into the courtyard or the street, where they checked their documents and picked out those exempt from deportation. SS men, German police or auxiliaries (Lithuanians, Latvians, Ukrainians) would then sweep the building or the whole block, shooting anyone they found still inside or in hiding. Finally, the deportees were escorted by the Order Service to the Umschlagplatz, where they were held until transport was available. Sometimes this could mean spending a day and a night in the open, in heat or rain, without food or sanitary facilities. The Umschlagplatz was strewn with debris and human excrement. However, this malodorous, crowded yard offered those slated for deportation the best chance of an escape. Here, Order Service men took hefty bribes to turn a blind eye while a deportee slipped away; workshop managers alerted to the fate of a valued employee would come looking for them to obtain their release; the family and protégés of Jewish councilmen were frequently rescued at this last moment, though usually at an extortionate cost.[83]

The round-ups did not go quite as smoothly or uniformly as the huge number seized each day would suggest. From 24 to 31 July, the volume of deportees ranged from just above 5,000 to just under 7,000 per day. On 5 and 6 August, the total exceeded 10,000. There was a pause in transports leaving the Umschlagplatz from 19 to 21 August, while outlying ghettos were emptied. A change of tactics over 6–11 September netted more than 54,000 Jews. Daily round-ups ceased on

12 September, although there were three subsequent lesser actions – including one in which the bulk of the Order Service was deported. As they progressed, the daily actions required more manpower, incentives or enhanced violence to succeed. On 25 July, the Order Service was forced to enrol hundreds of other Jewish council employees into its ranks because it lacked the personnel to cope with the task. Some deserted; a few preferred suicide to cooperation. In any case, it did not perform to the satisfaction of its real master. Five days later, after the number of deportees deposited at the Umschlagplatz had steadily fallen, the Germans lost patience with the OS and deployed German police and auxiliaries to carry out the *razzias* with them. At the same time, the Order Service put up notices that anyone going voluntarily to the Umschlagplatz would be given 3kg of bread and 1kg of jam. Since imports of food had practically ceased on 22 July and hunger was ubiquitous, this had a considerable effect. On 30 July, 1,500 Jews volunteered for deportation, 750 the next day, and 3,000 on 3 August. When the time came for the German and Czech Jews to go, they assembled under their own volition and marched to the trains, many of the men proudly wearing the medals earned fighting for or alongside the Germans during the Great War.[84]

The Order Service, which had once been lauded by the ghetto inhabitants, now turned into the most hated excrescence of German power. Chaim Kaplan railed that 'The deed is being carried out by the Jewish slaughterers . . . The criminal police force is the child of the criminal Judenrat.' Seidman was more careful in his remarks, stating that 'The Germans force the Judenrat and the Jewish police to assist in the mass deportations.' Lewin had no patience for such nuances: 'The police are carrying out the round-ups, and officials of the Jewish community wearing white armbands are assisting them.' He could find no justification for 'The savagery of the police during the round-ups, the murderous brutality. They drag girls from the rickshaws, empty out flats, and leave the property strewn everywhere.' Witnessing the extortion that customarily accompanied the blockades he condemned the 'terrible corruption of our police and their assistants. An outrage, an outrage!' After a month of constant round-ups he exploded: 'they beat viciously, they steal, and they loot and pillage like bandits in the forests. What degeneracy! Who has raised these bitter fruits among us?'[85]

Observers and diarists in the ghetto struggled to record the catastrophe. It defied comprehension and beggared the common vocabulary. Terror, hunger, exhaustion and frequent changes of residence made the task even harder. 'I haven't the strength to hold a pen in my hand,' Chaim Kaplan wrote after he heard news of the deportation decree. 'I'm broken, shattered. My thoughts are jumbled. I don't know where to start or stop.' Yet he continued to write. When friends asked why he bothered, he replied, 'I feel that continuing this diary to the very end of my physical and spiritual strength is a historical mission which must not be abandoned.' When Abraham Lewin's wife was seized he wrote, 'Eclipse of the sun, universal blackness. My Luba was taken away during a blockade . . . I have no words to describe my desolation.' The next day he went on with his diary. Over succeeding weeks, he interviewed escapees from Treblinka and continued to record the evidence of German crimes.[86]

'The ghetto has turned into an inferno,' Kaplan wrote on 27 July. 'Men have become beasts.' The Order Service ignored legitimate work papers and chased anyone to fill their quota. People caught in blockades tried to hide or fled over fences and roofs. Children and mothers fought against the OS men who beat them into submission with truncheons. 'The world', Lewin thought, 'has never seen such scenes. People are thrown into wagons like dogs, old people and the sick are taken to the Jewish cemetery and murdered there . . . The tragedies cannot be captured in words.' To Seidman, Warsaw became 'a factory of death'. When rabbis and academics were hauled out of the workshops, including his friends and colleagues of many years, he wailed, 'In our concern for our own survival, we were forced to be mere passive onlookers. How pitiful our lives now seem by comparison. Is this called living?' Observers tormented by extreme hunger were still shocked at the sight of Jews going voluntarily to the trains. Lewin was appalled to see twenty Ukrainians, fifty Jewish police and four Germans 'lead 3,000 Jews to the slaughter'. They went 'like lambs'. Seidman watched starving columns lured by the promise of a hunk of bread and some jam shuffling towards 'their final appointment with their slaughterers'.[87]

Yet there was opposition, evasion and resistance. The same day that Czerniaków took his life, sixteen leaders of the main political factions (except the Revisionist Zionists) conferred hastily about how they should react. The veteran trade unionist Bernard Goldstein summarized the Bund's line: 'We knew that armed resistance would doom the whole ghetto instead of only 60,000. And who, no matter how convinced that the whole ghetto was doomed in any case, could take upon himself the responsibility for precipitating such a catastrophe.' The historian, Zionist and former member of the Polish parliament Yitzhak Schipper also counselled against taking up arms. Zuckerman recalled him asking the young bloods at the gathering, 'Can one endanger the lives of other Jews?' The lesson of Jewish history was that they had 'no choice but to accept the sentence'. A representative of the Orthodox party Agudas-Israel assured the meeting that God would not permit the destruction of his people: 'the Lord gives and the Lord takes away'. The fact that the deportations seemed to affect only refugees and beggars encouraged the majority to defer any effort to obstruct the action. Zuckermen left the meeting depressed, but members of Hechalutz-Dror and the HaShomer HaTzair youth movement resolved to engage in passive resistance anyway. Next day they distributed leaflets warning Jews that the Umschlagplatz led only to death, and urged resistance. In a similar, though uncoordinated gesture, the Bund's illegal bulletin admonished Jews that they faced a 'campaign of extermination' and advised those who were condemned to deportation to resist 'tooth and nail'.[88]

Four days later, leading figures in Dror and HaShomer HaTzair met and established the Jewish Fighting Organization (Zydowska Organizacja Bejowa, ZOB). A delegation including Aryeh Wilner was sent to the Ayran side to establish contact with the Polish underground and secure weapons. Its mission accomplished, it returned, leaving Wilner to liaise with the Polish resistance. The Bund, meanwhile, sent people out of the ghetto to follow the deportation trains and ascertain the fate of the deportees. One of its agents, Zalman Friedrich, was able to meet men and women who had escaped from the Treblinka death camp. What he reported left the political leadership in no doubt of the stakes. Although the Bund did not join the ZOB for months, its younger activists were now on the path to militancy. However, the Jewish Fighting Organization was ineffectual and riven with arguments about tactics. Should it attempt to mount armed resistance in the ghetto or break out so its members could join partisan groups? Was its mission to frustrate the deportations or to strike back at the Germans for the sake of revenge? Indeed, who was the enemy? Should it fight the Jewish council and the Order Service? Partly because it lacked the wherewithal to do anything else, the ZOB started its campaign by attacking the most hated figures in the ghetto. On 20 August, a ZOB member, Israel Kanal, shot and wounded Szerynski; a leaflet announced that he was a victim of the Jewish Fighting Organization and denounced the entire Order

Service for collaborating with the Germans. By this stage the ZOB's arsenal had swollen to five pistols and eight grenades. Its fighters also began setting fire to German-owned or -run workshops. Tragically, on 3 September a German raid on the Landau workshop, where many of the underground were based, resulted in the discovery of the ZOB's weapons cache. Leading members of the organization, who were working at Landau's as a cover, were also arrested. The budding Jewish resistance was temporarily shattered. Amidst the daily pandemonium it was as much as the factions could do to preserve their own cadres. Organized opposition melted away.[89]

During August, the focus of the deportations shifted to welfare institutions, community organizations, and enterprises that were previously off-limits. On 5 August it was the turn of the defenceless children whom Czerniaków had earlier tried to save. Lewin noted tersely, 'They emptied Dr Korczak's orphanage with the Doctor at the head of 200 orphans.' His selflessness in accompanying the children to certain death immediately passed into legend, along with the display of courage by the infants who trooped in good order to the Umschlagplatz. Seidman grieved, 'Who knows how much potential, skill, talents and Jewish treasures are contained within these precious young souls, now condemned to death. Yet they march so quietly, so purposefully towards their untimely end.' Around the same time, Chaim Kaplan and his wife were taken. During his last days he was tormented equally by hunger, fear, and apprehension lest his testimony be swallowed up in the cataclysm: 'My utmost concern is for hiding my diary so that it will be preserved for future generations.' His final words in writing were a haunting question, 'If my life ends – what will become of my diary?'[90]

The Order Service, the Germans and their helpers, moved on to CENTOS, the other children's homes, Jewish Self-Help, and eventually the Jewish council itself. On 9 August it was ordered to relocate to smaller premises and commanded to give up 7,000 people from its employees and their families. The identity cards of essential community workers were invalidated and only those whose papers were stamped by the Sipo-SD were protected. Helen Szereszewska was rescued from the Umschlagplatz thanks to her husband, who was director of the finance department. After her narrow escape she moved into the council building and sat by her husband's desk from dawn to dusk. 'It was the same with all the Council staff', she recounted later, 'unless the wives and children worked they sat by their husband's desks ... Everyone provided cover for their families.' But the Germans were not done with the Jewish council. On 16 August the building was blockaded and a selection imposed, followed by another raid ten days later. 'The Council staff and their families were allocated three thousand numbers – to stay alive', Szereszewska recalled. She and her daughter, who was a clerk for the council, were amongst the super-privileged. 'But it doesn't mean that all the others had to perish,' she added rather casually. 'The others could hide in empty houses, could even hide in the cellars at the Council, or they could escape to the Aryan side. Many people leaped through the hole in the wall in the attic. You could jump out onto the heaps of rubble, into the empty spaces.' She did not say how many less fortunate than her survived through such expedients.[91]

Having cleared the southern segment of the ghetto, the Germans began striking at the workshops. In line with Himmler's order that the remaining Jewish employees in the General Government should be closely supervised, blocks of houses around each enterprise were cleared for use as barracks and then fenced off to create what were in effect labour camps. Jews had fought to get employment in these establishments and, thanks to sympathetic Jewish managers, several became a haven for members of the underground, Oneg Shabbat activists, rabbis and scholars. Now, the Germans purged the swollen workshops one by one, eliminating anyone who lacked a job. There were hideous scenes as women were parted from husbands, children from parents. In consternation Lewin exclaimed, 'the families are being deported (killed) and they want to leave behind only the working slaves for the time being. *What horror!* They are preparing to destroy us utterly.' Rabbi Huberband was one of 1,600 wrenched from the Brushmakers' on 18 August. Michael Zylberberg was luckier. Along with several rabbis he found shelter in the Landau workshop until he was picked out in a selection. He escaped from the Umschlagplatz with his wife, gained refuge in the Hoffman workshop, and survived a second selection there. His experience was not untypical.[92]

Wladyslaw Szpilman had stopped playing the piano in cafes once the deportations started and frantically tried to get work certificates for himself and his family. To add to his woes, they were evicted from their home in the small ghetto and scrambled to find new lodgings. For a while Szpilman, his sisters, brother-in-law and father were employed by a friend in one of the warehouses processing the belongings taken from deported Jews. It doubled up as barracks for the workforce, but offered limited protection. On 16 August there was a selection and Szpilman was ejected from the workforce along with his father and sister. In his post-war memoir he remembered how they finally succumbed to exhaustion and malnutrition: 'It was no use struggling any more.' The Order Service took them to the Umschlagplatz. 'When we arrived it was quite empty. People were walking up and down, searching for water. It was a hot, fine day in late summer.' He noticed that people avoided a certain section of the compound. 'Bodies lay there: the bodies of those killed yesterday for some crime or other, perhaps even for attempting to escape. Among the bodies of men were the corpses of a young woman and two girls with their skulls smashed to pieces. The wall under which the corpses lay showed clear traces of bloodstains and brain tissue.' The Szpilmans managed to settle down until more and more people began to pour in. All were oppressed by 'the atmosphere of leaden apathy reigning over the compound'. He spotted a young girl: 'Her dress was torn and her hair dishevelled, as if she had been fighting someone. She muttered to herself, "Why did I do it? Why did I do it?"' Whatever it was, it had failed to save her or her husband. The heat was now intense and the plaza was packed. There was no water. Some men talked of resistance, others argued it was folly. Szpilman's sister and brother-in-law turned up out of a sense of family solidarity. At around six o'clock, Germans arrived to select people fit for work. When the selection was completed, the train pulled in. Now the number of Order Service and SS men was reinforced, but Szpilman had lost the will to resist. 'We got ready to leave. Why wait. The sooner we were in the trucks the better.' Suddenly, an OS man who knew him pulled Szpilman back from the wagons and told him to scram. He was momentarily torn between flight and accompanying his mother, father, sisters and brother-in-law to what he instantly understood was death. 'Driven by compulsive animal fear, I ran for the streets, slipped into a column of [Jewish] Council workers just leaving the place, and got away through the gate that way.'[93]

In the final stages of the clearance, all forms of political, communal and family solidarity broke down. Lewin observed the survivors of selections 'thieving and looting insatiably'. He heard stories of mothers returning from the Umschlagplatz after making the most terrible choice of all: 'they were separated from their children aged 3 to 12 to 14, and if they had identity papers, they were freed'. Between 19 and 20 August the Order Service was redeployed to the ghetto of Otwock to assist the Germans deport the entire population of a town that was once a pretty resort favoured by the Jewish bourgeoisie. Towards the end, Lewin wrote, 'The human hand and pen are weary of describing all that has happened to the handful of Jews who are for the time being still alive, myself among them.'[94]

The action reached its horrendous climax on 6 September. The previous day the Germans ordered the entire Jewish population to assemble in the nine blocks above Gesia Street between Smocza and Zamenhofa Streets at the northern tip of the ghetto, on the pretext of being issued with new registration documents. It was a huge trap: the Germans distributed 32,000 fresh identity cards, sometimes in the form of a tin disc with a number stamped on it. Those employed by the Jewish council, Order Service men, labourers sorting the vast piles of belongings pouring in from Treblinka and the contents of empty apartments, plus workers in SS enterprises received numbers. Factory and workshop managers were obliged to list the workers they needed; they too received cards or discs. No dependants were allowed. Anyone without a number was hauled off to the adjacent Umschlagplatz. Huge sums changed hands as those without a number bargained for a place in a workshop while others who were lucky tried to buy sanctuary for a loved one. Armed with documents provided by the Jewish council, Seidman intervened to rescue Emanuel Ringelblum, Maurycy Orzech, a Bundist leader, and the poet Yitzhak Katzenelson. He saw money changing hands, people dodging past distracted guards, and SS officers 'in a jolly mood, laughing among themselves and cracking their whips against their shiny boots'. The process stretched over six agonizing days, in broiling heat. The Jews could eat and drink only what they had brought with them. Over 300 died in the 'cauldron', as it became known. Amidst the bedlam 2,648 were shot. When the blockade was lifted, 54,269 Jews had been removed. The great deportation was all but over. Roughly 10,300 Jews had been murdered in the ghetto, and another 11,580 had been sent to labour camps. According to the Germans' count, 253,742 Jews had departed via the Umschlagplatz.[95]

Since early August, the ghetto had a good idea of where they had gone. At first the information was sketchy and confused. On 6 August, Lewin jotted down 'Treblinka (the place of execution?)'. Three days later he wrote, 'It is now clear that 95 per cent of those [deported] are being taken to their deaths.' By 11 August the name Treblinka had more substance, although the details of what happened there were garbled. '15 kilometres before the station at Treblinka the Germans take over the train. When people get out of the train they are beaten viciously. Then they are driven into huge barracks. For five minutes heart rending screams are heard, then silence.' Finally, on 28 August, Lewin was one of those who heard an escapee, David Nowodworski, describe exactly what was going on at the death camp. 'From his words we put together a testimony of such stark anguish, so shattering, that it cannot be grasped and put into words. This is without doubt the greatest crime ever committed in the whole of history . . . God! Are we to be exterminated down to the last of us? Now it is certain that all those deported from Warsaw have been killed.' When Seidman heard similar testimony from Yaakov Rabinowitz, he could only write 'words fail; me . . . All I want to do is cry, cry, and cry.'[96]

Treblinka

Treblinka was the last extermination camp to be constructed and should have benefited from the experience gained at Belzec and Sobibor. In terms of location and layout it was similar to its precursors. The Germans picked a site near to an old labour camp on a spur line that branched off the local Malkinia–Seidlce railway that, in turn, connected with the main Warsaw–Bialystok railroad. The single-track spur ran along the western edge of the new camp, with a siding that extended through a gateway into the camp itself and alongside a platform that could accommodate twenty wagons at a time. Adjacent to the platform the Germans built a warehouse disguised as a train station. People disembarking from the wagons were assembled in a square, where an SS man informed them that they had to hand over their clothes and valuables before they were disinfected in shower rooms. Men and women were separated and then led into an enclosed area with two large barracks on either side. Men went into the one on the left and undressed; women and children went into the one on the right where they removed their clothing and where their hair was shaved off. These long wooden structures led out to a barbed wire corridor, 'the tube', that ended at the entrance to the gas chamber building. When it first opened, Treblinka had three chambers, each 4 by 4 metres and nearly 3 metres high. However, after several weeks these proved too small and two more were added. Even with this enlarged capacity Treblinka could not cope with the inflow of victims. Months after its inception a new gas chamber was opened with eight or ten cells of larger dimensions but lower in height. They had outward-opening trapdoors built into the exterior wall to enable removal of the dead. Jewish labourers dragged the corpses to mechanically excavated trenches and deep pits. The workforce servicing the gas chambers and the pits numbered about one hundred and lived in a self-contained barracks in the area known as the upper camp. Aside from the gas chamber building and the barracks for the workers, the space in the south-east corner was taken up by mass graves.[97]

The camp was shaped like a lopsided oblong, wider at the south and tapering towards the north. At the southern extremity, across the reception zone and the sorting yard, was the 'lazarette'. This mock first-aid hut was adorned with a red cross; in fact, it opened onto a pit which was used to dispose of the sick and the lame who could not make it to the gas chambers. A fire burned almost permanently in the depths of this cavity. Work Jews who could no longer function were also shot there and tossed into the flames. The Jewish workers who serviced the camp and served the SS lived in the lower camp in a horseshoe of huts known as 'the ghetto', an enclosed area that included a ground for morning and evening roll call. These prisoners cleaned the wagons after Jews had been disembarked, tidied up the platform and assembly square, removed the piles of belongings left behind by the victims, and sorted the huge quantities of clothing, personal effects and possessions of all kinds that spilled out of the bundles, backpacks and suitcases that were all that remained of the deportees. In the northern sector there were wooden buildings housing the quarters of the camp commandant, Dr Irmfried Eberl, and his office, several barracks for the Trawniki-trained Ukrainian guards, accommodation for the SS contingent, storage sheds, a garage and an armoury. At its greatest extent the entire complex was only 600 by 400 metres. The camp installations were surrounded by a barbed-wire fence, camouflaged with fresh foliage, and overlooked by five watchtowers on the perimeter plus one inside. An outer ring of barbed-wire entanglements and tank traps protected the whole area. Like Belzec, Treblinka had a small zoo for the amusement of the guards.[98]

When Treblinka opened for business on 23 July, Belzec and Sobibor had been operating for months and yet the builders and managers of Treblinka seemed to have ignored the lessons learned by the killers in those places. First of all, the gas chambers were too small and too few. This caused a backlog of victims who either stood around in the reception area or were held in the wagons. In either case, they had the chance to assess their situation and react defensively. It was no coincidence that there were more documented acts of resistance by arriving deportees here than at other camps. The unloading process was so chaotic and the security so lax that dozens of Jews managed to escape before they actually entered the camp, several by leaping into the wagons of trains returning to Warsaw. The complacent planning and incompetent management of the camp had ghoulish consequences that threatened to disrupt its smooth operation in other ways. So many Jews died in the box-cars en route or while they were held for hours in suffocating conditions that dozens of bodies had to be stacked on the platform. Many Jews broke out of the stationary wagons, were shot and lay where they fell. The corpses of those who expired on the tracks were chopped up by trains. Arms, legs and body parts were scattered beside the spur line. Due to lack of time or manpower or simply lack of concern, Eberl failed to clear away this mess, so each arriving trainload of Jews was alarmed at the sight that greeted them. Nor were the SS personnel able to arrange the disposal of corpses from the gas chambers fast enough. Rotting bodies began to accumulate in the upper camp. It turned out that little thought had been given to the implications of burying tens of thousands of dead in mass graves. So many were buried at the same time, hurriedly and under a thin layer of sand, that the gases forming in the decomposing cadavers caused eruptions. The smell and the sound of these gaseous blasts vied for repulsiveness. Far from being a sanitized death factory, Treblinka 'had the qualities of a crazed massacre'.[99]

The first transports made the sixty-mile journey from Warsaw on 23 July. Since they were travelling along a major supply route for the German armies in Russia, they were frequently obliged to make way for priority trains. The journey could therefore take hours and Jews in the freight cars that could not be accommodated immediately at the platform had to wait still longer in the hot, airless compartments. Whenever transports paused in populated areas, Poles would attempt to sell water to the Jews trapped inside. Yankiel Wiernik was seized in a round-up in Warsaw on 23 August. His transport was detained at Malkinia junction overnight and into the next day. Squinting out he saw 'peasants peddling bottles of water at 100 zlotys a piece'. Eddie Weinstein, deported from Losice in late August, recalled that Poles 'carried buckets of water over to the cars and filled the bottles that passengers pushed out at them. But they charged dearly for each bottle. Polish money was not good; they would only accept hard currency or valuables such as rings, earrings and brooches'. Sometimes the Poles split the proceeds with the guards.[100]

At four in the afternoon, Wiernik's train made the brief passage from Malkinia to the camp. 'Only on arriving there', he wrote in a war-time memoir composed while in hiding, 'did the horrible truth dawn on us. The camp yard was littered with corpses, some still in their clothes and some naked, their faces distorted with fright and awe, black and swollen, the eyes wide open, with protruding tongues, skulls crushed, bodies mangled. And, blood everywhere . . .' Once the train halted Weinstein was able to peek through a knot hole in the wall of his wagon. 'All along the platform, corpses were piled up'. When the surviving Jews clambered out 'we were struck by the sickening stench of burning'. His train had taken so long to reach Treblinka that many had died. 'We were ordered to remove from the train those who suffocated or lay motion-less. In every car there were corpses, lying in every conceivable posture.' The bodies, including those showing signs of life, were carried over to pits and tossed in. After a few hours he was assigned to Treblinka Station, a short way down the track, where he and other Jews were com-manded to clear up the detritus from previous trains. 'In addition to the bodies there were severed legs, arms, hands and other body parts lying between the railroad tracks.' Back at the camp a guard shot and wounded Weinstein. He survived the next week under piles of clothing in one of the sorting sheds. Fortunately the transports stopped over that period and there was relative calm. When the deportations resumed, he slipped into the work crew at the platform and toiled until he was able to sneak onto a wagon leaving the camp. Wiernik was not so nimble or lucky. He inserted himself into a group of workers shifting baggage from the reception area and survived his first night sleeping on open ground. At dawn he and the others with him were woken and forced to drag corpses to the pits. 'The corpses had already been lying around for quite some time and decomposition was already setting in, making the air foul with the stench of putrefaction. It often happened that an arm or a leg fell off when we put straps on them in order to drag them away. Thus we worked from dawn to dusk, without food or water, on what would some day be our own graves.'[101]

After four days of hauling cadavers, Wiernik was inducted into the regular workforce, the specialists who the Germans needed for skilled tasks: dentists and barbers to work at the gas chambers; builders, carpenters and sign-painters, to improve the camp structures; tailors, shoe-makers and metal workers to attend to the sartorial whims of the SS men and service the Ukrainians. The artisans who lived and worked in the 'ghetto' making boots, apparel, rings and other articles for the guards were dubbed 'Hofjuden' or court Jews. Wiernik, who was a trained joiner, was employed on the construction of the new gas chambers and the embellishment of the camp. In this role he was able to see most of what went on and witnessed the stream of transports when the camp resumed operations on 3 September. His testimony is one of the few that span the first frenzied phase of the camp's existence, the pause for reorganization, the second period of massive killing and the final months.[102]

Just under 200,000 Jews were deported from Warsaw to Treblinka and murdered there between 23 July and 28 August, roughly 5,400 per day. To this must be added some 51,000 Jews from the Radom district, 16,000 from the northern parts of the Lublin district, and an additional 45,000 Jews from towns around Warsaw like Otwock. This raises the average daily tally of murder to over 8,400 souls. The torrent of doomed humanity overwhelmed Eberl and his small complement of Germans and Ukrainians, although there is also evidence that the commandant was not up to the job. He failed to warn the Gestapo in Warsaw to slow down the deportations, call for reinforcements, or devise ways to handle the mass of arrivals more efficiently. Eberl's mismanagement came to light when Christian Wirth visited Treblinka in his capacity as the new inspector of the Operation Reinhard camps. He was accompanied by his boss, Odilo Globocnik. Even this pair, hardened to the business of mass atrocity as they were, could see there was a problem. Josef Oberhauser, Wirth's deputy, later recounted that 'In Treblinka everything was in a state of collapse. The camp was overstocked. Outside the camp, a train with deportees was unable to be unloaded as there was simply no more room. Many corpses of Jews were lying inside the camp. These corpses were already bloated.' Wirth relieved Eberl of his authority and arranged for Franz Stangl, commandant of Sobibor, to take over. Sobibor was temporarily dormant while the rail line serving the camp was strengthened to take the unusually frequent and heavy traffic generated by the mass killing programme, so Stangl had time on his hands. In the end, he stayed to run Treblinka, assisted by Kurt Franz, who had worked at Belzec. Together they cleaned up the place, although it was necessary to halt the transports for several days to get the job done. The new management also set about expanding the number and size of the gas chambers. In mid-October, the improved facility came on stream. It boasted a brick building with ten gas chambers, each 4 by 8 metres, leading off a central passageway. A Star of David was placed over the entrance and pot plants graced the steps up to the doorway. Skilled Jewish tradesmen did the actual work of building and decoration. One of them was Yankiel Wiernik. Later he wrote, 'The work on these gas-chambers lasted five weeks . . . We had to work from dawn to dusk under the ceaseless threat of beatings with whips and rifle-butts . . . [but] our spiritual sufferings were far worse. New transports of victims arrived each day. They were ordered to disrobe immediately and were led to the three gas chambers, going past us on the way. Many of us saw our children, wives and members of our families among the victims . . . We constructed death-chambers for ourselves and our brethren under such conditions.'[103]

On 3 September, the trains started rolling through Malkinia junction again, past the little Treblinka Station, and up the spur line to the camp. Amongst the first to arrive were the 52,000 Jews caught in the Warsaw ghetto 'cauldron', followed a few days later by 2,200 members of the Order Service and their families. However, after that there were no more transports from Warsaw until early 1943. Instead, deportees converged on Treblinka from ghettos across the General Government, including 40,000 from Czestochowa between 21 September and 5 October, 10,000 from Zelechow on 2 October, 11,000 from Ostrowiec on 11–12 October, and 22,000 from Piotrokow on 15–25 October. In total, approximately 380,000 Jews from the region, apart from Warsaw, ended up in the Treblinka death pits. They were followed by trainloads from the Bialystok district, with 38,900 from the county of Kelbasin alone. According to a report sent to Berlin by Hermann Höfle at the close of 1942, in 155 days the Treblinka extermination camp accounted for 713,555 lives – an average of 4,600 a day or nearly 200 per hour. It was the most lethal place on earth.[104]

Stangl made this astonishing throughput possible partly by reorganizing the camp so that experienced personnel attended to each stage of the murder process. Instead of relying on terrified groups of men plucked out of the crowd milling around the platform or the assembly square, he established permanent teams with specific tasks that they could master and perfect, carrying them out quickly and efficiently. There were Sonderkommandos to work on the platform, clean the wagons, remove the baggage and bundles, sort the stuff, process the valuables, and constantly ensure that the buildings looked bright and innocuous. In the extermination area, he mandated crews to clean the gas chambers, haul the dead, pull out the gold teeth, and man the pits. There were service and maintenance workers in both camps to ensure that the labourers were fed and that all the machinery ran smoothly. A sanitation team took care of the latrines. For the first time, women were brought into the camp to clean and cook for the Jews in the lower camp, the Hofjuden. Each team worked under a kapo who enforced discipline and acted as the eyes and ears of the SS.[105]

Yankiel Wiernik recorded how the improved system worked. Each time a new transport arrived the Jews were reassured on the platform that they were going to be resettled. All they had to do for the moment was surrender their valuables, get undressed and shower. At this stage, hope was their greatest enemy; only Jews who knew they had nothing to lose rebelled. Then 'the women and children were herded into the barracks at once, while the men were kept in the yard. The men were ordered to undress, while the women, naively anticipating a chance to take a shower, unpacked towels and soap. The brutal guards, however, shouted orders for quiet, and kicked and dealt out blows. The children cried, while the grownups moaned and screamed. This made things even worse; the whipping only became crueller. The women and girls were then taken to the "barber shop" to have their hair clipped. By now they felt sure that they would be taken to have a shower. Then they were escorted, through another exit, to Camp No. 2 where, in freezing weather, they had to stand in the nude, waiting their turn to enter the gas chamber, which had not yet been cleared of the last batch of victims. All through that winter, small children, stark naked and barefooted, had to stand out in the open for hours on end, awaiting their turn in the increasingly busy gas chambers. The soles of their feet froze and stuck to the icy ground. They stood and cried; some of them froze to death. In the meantime, Germans and Ukrainians walked up and down the ranks, beating and kicking the victims.' Once Jews were naked, confined to the barracks, the courtyard or the tube they were easy prey. Rifle butts, bayonets, whips and vicious dogs kept them in line and moving forward. The sadism shown by the guards was not simply for personal gratification: it was deliberately terrifying. But despite all Stangl's reforms, the process remained liable to disruption. In particular, the engine producing the fatal gas frequently malfunctioned, 'so the helpless victims had to suffer for hours on end before they died. Satan himself could not have devised a more fiendish torture. When the chambers were opened again, many of the victims were only half dead and had to be finished off with rifle butts, bullets or powerful kicks. Often people were kept in the gas chambers overnight with the motor not turned on at all. Overcrowding and lack of air killed many of them in a very painful way. However, many survived the ordeal of such nights; particularly the children showed a remarkable degree of resistance. They were still alive when they were dragged out of the chambers in the morning, but revolvers used by the Germans made short work of them . . .'[106]

The Ukrainian guards delighted in robbing the Jews and pilfering from their belongings when the eyes of the SS were turned the other way. In the surrounding villages they became well known for chucking around cash, jewellery and gold. Young women gravitated to the local taverns looking for a rich boyfriend or a guard willing to to pay for sex. Men selling trinkets hung around as near to the camp as they could get; it was a bonanza. In camp, the Ukrainians could freely indulge their appetites. Wiernik reported that 'When they had eaten and drunk their fill, the Ukrainians looked around for other amusements. They frequently selected the best looking Jewish girls from the transports of nude women passing their quarters, dragged them into their barracks, raped them and then delivered them to the gas chambers. After being outraged by their executioners, the girls died in the gas chambers with all the rest. It was a martyr's death.'[107]

The immediate impact on the Jewish prisoners of witnessing such horrors was unbearable. Many selected for the Sonderkommandos committed suicide shortly after learning what the camp was for and the fate that had befallen their loved ones. Chil Rajchman was deported to Treblinka from Lubartow in October 1942. He was put to work carrying bundles, sorting clothes and cutting hair, almost without respite. One day he was assigned to the corpse-carrying Sonderkommando and saw the technique for filling the pits: standing atop the bodies ready to receive a fresh cadaver tipped in by the corpse-carriers was 'a Jew, who lays the bodies out straight like herrings'. Some men were unable to stand this. 'Every morning,' Rajchman wrote in a memoir composed while hiding in Warsaw in 1944–5, 'we notice that there are people hanging in the barracks.' He recalled a father and his son who had 'been in this hell for two days. They decided to commit suicide. Having only one strap between them, they agreed that the father would hang himself first and after that the son would take him down and use the same strap to hang himself. That is in fact how it happened.' Sometimes one man would pull on the legs of another to speed his demise.[108]

However, the longer the work Jews hung on, the stronger became their will to fight back. They were inspired by increasingly regular instances of resistance from Jews arriving from ghettos that had been alerted to the fate awaiting deportees. The struggle began on the trains, with more and more attempting to hack their way through the floorboards. On 10 or 11 September, a deportee on a transport from Warsaw attacked an SS man, Max Bialas, with a concealed knife and fatally wounded him. Thereafter the Germans ordered the Jews to proceed to the undressing sheds with their hands in the air. But that did not stop melees breaking out on the platform. Before the year was out, Jews from Siedlce had to be subdued by gunfire. In October, ten Jews from Ostrowiec Swietokrzyski in Kielce district started resisting in the gas chamber building, forcing the guards to open fire. Rajchman was picked to help clean up the next day and saw 'The whole corridor of the structure with the three smaller gas chambers was filled with dead bodies. The floor was covered with ankle deep dried blood.' Two months later hundreds of young men from Grodno, transported from the Kelbasin labour camp, rioted on the threshold of the chambers. Again the guards and SS men resorted to their rifles and submachine guns, turning the building into a bullet-spattered bloodbath requiring extensive repairs and redecoration. The permanent labour force made such renovations possible in a very short time, but it also meant that the prisoners were able to observe more of what was going on and to form a cohesive community capable of resistance. When the transports slowed over the winter of 1942–3 hunger and disease took a toll on the workforce, but the remission gave them time to reflect and begin planning. Out of the deepest despair, the will to resist was crystallizing.[109]

The ghettos of the Ostland, Belarus and Ukraine

It was typical of the inconsistent and confused nature of Nazi anti-Jewish policy that while the Jews of the Wartheland and the General Government faced near-total extinction during 1942, the Jews penned inside the ghettos of the Baltic region and the district of Bialystok were left virtually undisturbed. There were equally sharp distinctions within the Ostland, between the northern part containing the ghettos of Vilnius and Kovno, and western Byelorussia, including the ghettos of Minsk, Novogrudok, Baranovichi, Slonim and Slutsk. In the southern portion of the Ostland, as across the Reichskommissariat Ukraine, the Germans engaged in a murderous 'second sweep' through Jewish population centres that had survived the first wave of mass shooting by the Einsatzgruppen, SS units, order police and auxiliaries between July and December 1942. In the far south, Einsatzgruppe D resumed its advance in the wake of Army Group South and began to perpetrate massacres on the model of the previous year. The second onslaught, like the first, was punctuated by arguments over the preservation of Jewish skilled labour. Hence the process appears erratic, with some towns being visited two or more times by killing units while, elsewhere, significant numbers were spared immediate execution. The 'second sweep' was generally associated with anti-partisan actions, and the resources devoted to wiping out Jewish communities cannot be disentangled easily from German efforts to suppress the escalating unrest in the occupied territories. Unlike 1941, this time the Germans and their collaborators encountered planned resistance, spontaneous opposition, carefully prepared evasion, and mass breakouts from ghettos. Sizeable groups of Jewish fugitives reached the forests and marshes in Volhynia, Polesie, Podolia and western Ukraine. Most roamed around individually or in small, disorganized clusters; few of them survived the subsequent Jew-hunts, the hostile attention of the local population, or the harsh environment. But some coalesced into partisan groups or found their way to existing guerrilla units. The Germans' tendency to conflate Jews with partisans began to acquire a tenuous hold in reality.[110]

The killing began in March, once the ground had thawed sufficiently for the Germans to prepare mass graves. This was also the moment at which the Russian winter offensive petered out and the Germans were able to redeploy security troops to the rear areas. The Minsk ghetto was amongst the first communities to be struck. There were 49,000 Jews there, including deportees from the Reich. The head of the Jewish council, Ilya Mushkin, was a communist and had long presided over secret contacts between the underground in the ghetto and Soviet resistance networks in the city. In Minsk the Germans' belief that Jews were associated with the partisans was certainly no fantasy. In February, the German civil authorities issued orders for the Jewish council to prepare the deportation of non-working inhabitants. The council refused to comply and was duly purged: Mushkin was arrested, tortured and executed. Due to this non-compliance, German security police with Latvian and Ukrainian auxiliaries had to comb through the ghetto, conducting round-ups that left hundreds dead. Einsatzgruppe A estimated that 3,412 Jews were shot in the operation on 2 March (timed to coincide with the Jewish festival of Purim), but the number was probably twice that. A tailor who worked in the October textile factory later told a war crimes investigator that Wilhelm Kube personally supervised the selection of skilled workers. The others were loaded onto trains that went in the direction of Molodechno, where they were shot. 'Along the route by which they were being transported,' he alleged, 'the German guards would come into the cars packed with people and select young, beautiful girls, take them away and rape them.' The Minsk Gestapo carried out a number of smaller massacres over the following months, often at night. These nocturnal raids were intended to strike at Jews identified as supporters of the partisans. 'Every night except Saturdays and Sundays,' recalled a survivor, 'the mobile gas vans rolled up to the gates of the ghetto.' However, the Sipo-SD men were unable to dislodge the underground. Instead, platoons of young men under the command of Hersh Smolar and Nahum Feldman were regularly smuggled out to join Soviet partisans in the nearby forests. The new chairman of the Jewish council, Moshe Yaffe, covertly supported their work until he was arrested and executed along with several colleagues. On 28–31 July, the Germans again separated those they declared useful from those deemed useless. Holders of work permits, now issued with a coloured patch for their garments, were held in a factory; the rest were corralled in Jubilee Square. About 25,000–30,000 Jews, including over 3,000 from Germany, were then removed from the ghetto, some in gas vans, others to killing sites such as the concentration camp at Maly Trostinets. By the end of the cull only 10,000–12,000 Jewish workers remained in Minsk.[111]

Massacres associated with the selection of work Jews occurred in dozens of other places. In Baranovichi, where 18,000 Jews lived in the ghetto, 6,000 work certificates were issued. Over 2,000 inhabitants were shot in early March, after which there was a long pause until the killers returned in the autumn and slaughtered a further 6,000 people. The Slutsk ghetto was divided into two sections, with 1,000 Jews in ghetto 'A' and 5,000 workers in ghetto 'B'. The non-employed Jews were shot. Slonim, where the population had long been divided between those with skills and those without, was the target of repeated round-ups between late April and late July. Here an anti-fascist committee had been in touch with local partisans for months and Jews started excavating bunkers as soon as the ghetto, containing 10,000–15,000 people (including Jews from surrounding villages), was sealed at the end of 1941. Gershon Kvint, second head of the Jewish council, provided cover for the resistance and encouraged Jews to defend themselves. Consequently, when the Germans attempted to eliminate those considered surplus to their needs they encountered fierce opposition. They had to burn the Jews out of their houses and faced gunfire from armed units of the underground. Eventually they threw in security police, Lithuanian auxiliaries, soldiers from the garrison and Organisation Todt construction workers; even Kube's chauffeur lent a hand. After days of mayhem, 800 artisans and professionals were confined to a small ghetto while hundreds more were moved to labour camps. Most of the former were shot in August and the ghetto was finally liquidated at the end of the year. Over the intervening months large groups made their way to the forests and joined partisan units or entered 'family camps' – camouflaged encampments maintained and defended by Jewish fighters.[112]

At the end of July, Wilhelm Kube wrote to Reichskommissar Lohse that Jews in Byelorussia were the 'main bearer of the partisan movement . . . Consequently, I and the SD would like it best if Jewry in the Generalbezirk Byelorussia was finally eliminated.' He intended to reduce them to a few thousand in work camps. 'Then there will be no further danger of partisans being able to rely to any great extent on Jewry . . . For the time being the essential requirements of the Wehrmacht, the main employer of the Jews, are being taken into consideration.' The Jewish inhabitants of Glubkoye, Doksytse and Luzhki were wiped out on this pretext, but in each case some Jews managed to evade the killers or escape to the forests. Four hundred and fifty men in the Order Service in Baranovichi went over to the partisans en masse. Dozens of Jews from Novogrudok, the survivors of earlier massacres plus deportees from other towns, defied the Germans and their own Jewish council to seek refuge with the forest fighters led by Tuvia Bielski and his brothers. In September 1942, an underground leadership crystallized and began planning a mass breakout in cooperation with the Bielskis, although this ambitious scheme did not come to fruition for many months. Five hundred Jews of Lida ignored the admonitions of their Jewish council and left for the woods. Throughout western Byelorussia small but significant numbers of Jews benefited from a conjunction of benign circumstances: thinly spread German garrisons, extensive swamps and dense woodland, and the presence of organized Soviet partisan units. Several of these were all-Jewish groups: Kube's apprehensions had been fulfilled, if not on anywhere near the scale that he imagined. Towards the end of the year, 8,350 Jews were killed in 'Operation Swamp Fever', an anti-partisan sweep. Most of them had fled from towns and villages, clinging on to life in marshes and timberland. When winter came only 15,000–16,000 working Jews were left alive in camps and ghettos in western Byelorussia; perhaps 6,000–7,000 were living precariously in the forests.[113]

The resumption of mass shootings in the Reichskommissariat Ukraine began a little later. The 8,000 Jews of Kobrin, in the north-west of the region, were visited first in July, when 3,000 were murdered, and finished off in October. The second assault met armed resistance and 500 Jews broke through the cordon around the town. Few, however, survived the ensuing manhunt. The ghetto in Brest-Litovsk (consisting of a small and a large section) had only been sealed in the previous December and until then young Jews had been able to establish ties with the communist resistance, accumulating a small arsenal. Conditions were miserable. An Italian soldier passing through Brest on a troop train recalled Jews begging for assistance at the station: 'all women, still elegant, high-class people. They came to ask us for a loaf of bread – say "bread, kaput" and let us know with gestures that the Germans are going to kill them all.' True to this prediction, most of the 18,000–20,000 Jews were murdered on 15–16 October 1942. Despite preparations to resist, a feint by the Germans lulled the Jewish underground into thinking they had deflected the blow. When the Germans returned they were caught off guard. Nevertheless, about 4,000 inhabitants were able to hide or resist and it was not until November that the ghetto was subdued. Pinsk, sitting astride a strategic artery of Army Group Centre repeatedly targeted by Soviet partisans, was identified by Himmler personally as a Jewish resistance nest. The ghetto, with 12,000–15,000 local Jews and deportees, was surrounded on 27 October and assaulted two days later. Hundreds of Jewish youngsters threw themselves at the lines of Germans and auxiliary police, but few got through. By early November the ghetto was emptied apart from 150 artisans and health workers. They too were shot before the end of the year. In Kamenets-Podolsk, in April 1942, the Germans entombed 2,500 Jews from the ghetto in a disused phosphate mine. The other half of the population were shot later in the autumn. And so it went on, in Staro Konstantinov, Sheptovska, Proskurov and dozens of other towns.[114]

At the start of 1942, there were approximately 270,000–290,000 Jews in Volhynia and Polesie, plus about 20,000 in Podolia. In late August, the Gebietskommissar met with Erich Koch and agreed that the area should be totally cleared of Jews. The subsequent operations followed a pattern with distinctive and revealing features. The mass shootings were carried out close to the doomed ghetto, in the open, and with no attempt at concealment. The Germans did not anticipate that the local Ukrainian population would protest or intervene. Although the Sipo-SD was in control of the process, the army and Organisation Todt assisted extensively when it came to excavating death pits and providing manpower for cordons or shooting parties. The bulk of the personnel came from order police and Ukrainian gendarmes or Schutzmannschaften, a high proportion of whom were ethnic Germans. Local collaboration was crucial for success. Once the forces for a clearance had been assembled they would proceed to the town and establish a cordon around the ghetto or Jewish residential district. The Jews would be ordered to assemble in a square or on a meadow or playing field where Sipo-SD men would inspect their papers, setting aside those with certificates indicating that they were employed by German-run enterprises. The unfortunates categorized as immediately expendable would be marched under a tight escort to pits dug on the outskirts, told to strip naked, and then shot by teams of riflemen. The property of the victims, in the ghetto and at the killing site, was then distributed or shipped to central storage facilities. Often local inhabitants descended on the deserted ghetto and stripped it bare even as the victims were being marched away.[115]

However, in distinction to the Einsatzgruppen operations in 1941, there was far more resistance and disruption. This was especially the case in ghettos assailed towards the end of the year. In Dubno, the ghetto was split in two and 5,000 Jews shot on 26–27 May. Deportees from the surrounding area took their place and were shot in October. In Kovel the ghetto was not established until May, but it was immediately used to separate working from non-working inhabitants. On 2 June, 6,000 were murdered in a nearby quarry. The rest were shot in mid-August, but about 1,000 fled before they could be executed. Most were caught over the following days and done to death. As the killing extended into the summer, more and more Jews were forewarned of what was coming. The Rovno ghetto, with 5,000 inhabitants, was cut down on 13 July, but many escaped to the forests. Hundreds amongst the 9,000 Jews in Kremenets evaded the two mass shootings on 15 July and 20 August. Around 2,000 Jews made their way out of Lutsk before the slaughterers arrived and dealt with the 15,000–16,000 who stayed. Tragically, most of the escapees found life in the wild impossible and drifted back to town, where they were rounded up and shot. When the Germans set about annihilating the Sarny ghetto in late August, 1,000 Jews, roughly one fifth of the population, rushed the fences and hundreds reached woodland. The 18,000 Jews in Ludmir were ghettoized in April and then divided the following month. In early September, 14,000 were shot, but large numbers managed to conceal themselves. The Germans paid a return visit two months later and massacred the 4,000–5,000 who thought they had survived the worst. Only a few hundred artisans were preserved. In just under seventy days, the Germans and their assistants had butchered 150,000 Jews.[116]

Jews who fled before an action or were able to escape during the chaos of a murder operation often fell victim to the Germans and their helpers in the days or weeks afterwards. In northern and eastern Volhynia their immediate survival was assisted by the swampy terrain and dense woods that lay within close reach of urban areas. The region was sparsely policed and the Germans tended to avoid the forests unless they were present in force on an anti-partisan mission. But it was a forbidding environment in the long-term. Without food, sturdy clothing, blankets or cooking utensils it was hard to endure for more than a short time – even in benign weather. Consequently it was common for starving Jews to drift back to their deserted ghetto thinking the coast was clear, only to face betrayal by the local collaborationist police. Sometimes the Germans would make a return sweep. Only the most wary and hardiest survived long enough to dig a bunker or form a group capable of extracting food from local peasants. In the western strip, bordering Galicia, there was less dense timberland and the population was far more hostile. To make matters worse the refugees were more likely to encounter Ukrainian guerrillas or Polish nationalist fighters who were murderously anti-Semitic, rather than the better-disciplined and marginally more welcoming Soviet partisans.[117]

In the western Ukraine, the slaughter was barely mitigated by the need for labour. The ghettos in Vinnitsa, Berdichev, Illintsy and Khmelnik were wiped out between March and June. A few hundred artisans clung to life here and there or eked out an existence in labour camps.

But by the end of 1942 there were no ghettos left in the Reichskommissariat Ukraine and almost no working Jews.[118]

The German army continued to preside over massacres in the areas
under its jurisdiction, such as Smolensk, where 2,000 Jews were executed in July, as well as the territories it overran during its heady
advance between June and September 1942. The fall of Sebastopol
enabled the Einsatzkommando in the Crimea to gun down 4,200 Jews
trapped in the port. Einsatzgruppe D was able to carry out a much more
formidable operation when the capture of Rostov delivered 16,000–
18,000 Jews into its hands. All were murdered between August 1942 and
February 1943. The Sipo-SD massacred unknown thousands of Jewish
refugees from the western USSR who had been evacuated to the Caucasus or sought refuge there under their own steam. Einsatzkommando
10 carried out several well-practised exercises when it entered conquered cities behind the spearheads of the 17th Army and 4th Panzer
Army. The victims included 13,000 in Krasnodar, 2,500 in Stavropol,
2,800 in Piatagorsk, and no less than 39,000–47,000 in the surrounding
districts. The murderers were temporarily befuddled when they encountered the mountain Jews of the Caucasus and paused for long scholarly
consultations with Berlin experts as to whether these Kalmyks and Nal-
chicks were Jews at all. The latter were declared non-racial Jews and left
alone, but only a handful of the former survived. About 7,000 of these
ancient Jewish tribesmen were exterminated. The Germans were
assisted in their work in the Crimea and the Caucasus by a battalion of
Muslims raised from captured Soviet prisoners of war.[119]

A thousand miles away, in the Galicia district, the army played a
contrary role by protesting against the wanton destruction of valuable
skilled workers. Between April and June 1942, while Belzec was undergoing reconstruction, the Sipo-SD and the SS police leaders resorted to
mass shootings to maintain the momentum of ghetto clearances. On 26
June, 6,000–8,000 Lwow Jews were shot in the precincts of the Janowska
camp as part of an effort by the security police to rationalize the number
of legitimate workers and, not coincidentally, to deny the civil authorities any role in the labour supply. From that point only Jews with
documents issued by the Sipo-SD would be spared execution. When the
'second sweep' erupted into Galicia, Jews with papers provided by the
army were snatched up, deported or shot. In mid-July, the 27,000 Jews
in the Przemysl ghetto were provided with 5,000 new work permits.
Then the ghetto was encircled and 13,000 permitless, workless Jews dis-

patched to Belzec. A month later, the Jewish population of Lwow was purged again. However, so many Jews were now attempting to escape from the trains to Belzec that they were stripped naked before they were put aboard in the hope that this would render them less inclined to break out. The number that smashed their way through the wagon floors of one transport was so numerous that the guards firing at them ran out of ammunition and were reduced to throwing stones at the fleeing cargo. In September the security police staged a final round-up, during which the Jewish council was hanged and 5,000–6,000 sent to Belzec. Afterwards the Germans ordered a census and issued 12,000 permits to the remnant working in SS-run enterprises or armaments factories. Similar, massive purges occurred in Stanislav, Tarnopol, Drohobych and Buczacz. The Jewish population in Stanislav was reduced from about 17,000 to 4,000 by a mixture of shootings and deportations to Belzec. The Tarnopol ghetto was brutally shrunk from around 12,000 down to 3,000 working Jews.[120]

With no end to these repeated decimations in sight, on 18 September, General Kurt von Gienanth, the senior army officer in the General Government, advised the army high command that 'The immediate removal of the Jews would cause a considerable reduction in Germany's war potential as well as supplies to the front . . .' He was not objecting to the murder of Jews as such; he merely wanted time for the army to find and train east European workers to replace them. Fritz Katzmann, the Higher SS Police Leader for Galicia, replied with a compromise. Working Jews could be held back from deportation as long as they were confined to camps under the control of the security police, in barracks adjacent to the industries they were serving. The employers of this labour force would have to provide quarters for the Jews and pay for them, too, guaranteeing the SS a profit. As a result of the army's self-interested intervention, 140,000–150,000 Jews remained alive. Towards the end of the year, Katzmann reported to the SS Head Office in Berlin that 254,989 Jews from the district had been 'evacuated or moved elsewhere'. But Himmler's aspiration to clear the General Government entirely of Jews had been thwarted.[121]

The war economy and the expansion of Auschwitz

The concentration camp outside the Polish town of Oswieçim in Upper Silesia, renamed Auschwitz following the German conquest of Poland, became a nodal point for the exploitation of labour by the SS and a focus of Himmler's ambitions to create an industrial empire. For all that, it did not impinge on the fate of the Jews until spring 1942. Then, for about six months, Jews from several countries were sent there for slave labour at the same time as it was used as a place to kill local Jews, mainly from East Upper Silesia, who were deemed surplus to the workforce. In July 1942 the much expanded camp was haphazardly integrated into the 'final solution'. Throughout the second half of the year, the extension camp at Birkenau was employed as a site for improvised mass murder while purpose-built killing facilities were being constructed. However, as with so many of his grandiose plans, Himmler's aspirations for Auschwitz took an inordinately long time to realize and when they reached maturity it looked as though the moment for them had passed.[122]

Auschwitz was conceived as a concentration camp in which to detain and terrorize Poles. It was the brainchild of Erich von dem Bach-Zelewski, when he was an SS police leader in occupied Poland in late 1939. One of his assistants located what seemed to be the ideal setting for a terror camp: a vacant Polish army barracks just outside the town, adjacent to a railway line and close to a junction with the main Katowice–Cracow railway. However, there were disadvantages: the buildings were in poor repair, the surrounding land was marshy, and both the sewage disposal system and fresh water supply were inadequate. In January 1940, Rudolf Höss, commandant of the Sachsenhausen concentration camp, led the last of several SS commissions to survey the site. He approved it. Three months later, Himmler appointed Höss to command the new establishment and it took all his drive plus ingenuity to obtain the necessary materials to complete the job. Höss did not lack for labour, though: he used 300 Jews from the town to do much of the heavy manual work. After that was completed, the Jews were banished; not a single Jew set foot inside Auschwitz concentration camp for almost two years. Instead, it was soon packed with Polish political prisoners who endured the customary SS camp regimen of pettifogging rules enforced by extreme violence. Höss brought with him from

Sachsenhausen thirty veteran prisoners, criminals, who served as the core of the internal prisoner administration, the kapos. They ensured that life in the camp was brutish and miserable.[123]

At this stage, Auschwitz consisted of twenty two-storey brick barracks to hold the prisoners, plus wooden stables and a former tobacco warehouse. The barracks complex was enclosed by barbed wire and entered through a gate that was topped off with a curvaceous wrought-iron sign announcing 'Arbeit Macht Frei', 'work is liberating'. As more prisoners arrived, the parade ground was partially built over and the enclosure became crowded with additional structures. An ammunition storage bunker located just outside was converted into a mortuary. From the start, mortality at Auschwitz was high and the Germans were keen to ensure that bodies were promptly disposed of. Corpses of deceased prisoners had to be transported to a municipal crematorium until the specialist firm Topf and Sons installed furnaces in the mortuary.[124]

In September 1940, Oswald Pohl, who ran SS business activities, saw Auschwitz and recognized its potential for economic development. The following month Himmler designated Auschwitz as the cornerstone of far-reaching plans to Germanize what used to be south-east Poland, employing tens of thousands of slave labourers to build the infrastructure. To begin with, about 80,000 Poles, including the entire Jewish population, were evicted from the town and its surroundings to be replaced by a few thousand ethnic Germans. To fund this gigantic project Himmler did a deal with the industrial conglomerate I. G. Farben. In March 1941, he toured the area in the company of senior executives from the corporation and offered them a site in the SS 'interest zone' complete with slave labour for the construction of a plant to manufacture synthetic oil, called Buna. In return for Monowitz, I. G. Farben agreed to provide capital and construction material to enlarge Auschwitz and build sub-camps. Subsequently, Himmler ordered the expansion of the main camp from 10,000 to 30,000 prisoners and the creation of an entirely new one to hold 100,000 anticipated prisoners of war from the Red Army. However, the invasion of Russia temporarily slowed development. In October, Karl Bischoff arrived from the SS main business office to take matters in hand. He reorganized the budget and increased the projected labour force from 97,000 to 125,000, without planning for any extra accommodation or amenities. In the event, the flood of prisoner labour from the Eastern Front never materialized.

The SS builders had to make do with a mere 10,000 Russians, who were assigned to the erection of a sprawling sub-camp on the site of a village called Brzezinka, about a mile away, renamed Birkenau by the Germans. The conditions for these men as they toiled through the winter were so abominable that only 2,000 were still alive the following February. The failure of Operation Barbarossa and the callous expenditure of human life in the course of building the second camp obliged Himmler to look elsewhere for slaves. Six days after the meeting at Wannsee to co-ordinate the 'final solution' across Europe, the Reichsführer of the SS gave instructions to Richard Glücks, director of the concentration camps, that 100,000 Jewish men and 50,000 Jewish women were to be sent to Auschwitz-Birkenau for use as labour. According to the historian of the concentration camps, Nikolaus Wachsmann, 'The decision to substitute Jews for Soviet POWs was taken impulsively at the top of the Nazi state.'[125]

Himmler's brusquely formulated instructions to Glücks created a paradox. On the one hand, preparations were under way for the mass extermination of Jews in Poland and Adolf Eichmann was beginning to plan the deportation of increased numbers of Jews from Germany, the Protectorate and western Europe to 'the east'. On the other hand, Himmler was diverting Jews capable of work into the concentration camp system, from which they had practically disappeared. In April, he specifically exempted Jews aged 16–35 from being sent to death camps. Instead, 17,000 Slovak Jews were sent to Auschwitz to enter the labour force there and another 40,000 went to camps in the Lublin district, although many would be murdered on arrival. Some 35,000 Polish Jews from Upper Silesian ghettos and labour camps were also shifted to Auschwitz and into work details. Jews arriving on transports from western Europe were inducted into the camp population for months before death became the routine fate of all but a few aboard the trains. This process turned Birkenau into a Jewish concentration camp and, eventually, reshaped the concentration camp population as a whole. To make matters even more puzzling, Birkenau was simultaneously being used as an improvised killing site where Jews who were capable of work were murdered.[126]

The apparent contradiction is partially explained by the febrile mood of the Nazi leadership between the winter crisis on the Russian front and the stumbling progress of Operation Blau. During the first three months of the year Nazi bosses accepted that it was not going to be a short war and grasped that it was necessary both to improve the performance of the war economy and deal with the shortage of labour. Himmler jumped on the crisis to strengthen the position of the SS, turning the population of the concentration camps into a labour resource for the war industries. The first SS strategy, exemplified by the I. G. Farben plant at Monowitz, was to use prisoners to construct plants on green-field sites near to existing camps. However, this approach largely foundered. Albert Speer, minister for armaments, did not want to lose control of weapons production to Himmler, and industry was reluctant to place itself in thrall to the SS. After much argument the SS conceeded that it made more sense to send prisoner labour to existing factories and house them in camps rather than start production units entirely from scratch. This marked a retreat from the triumphalist projects and overweening settlement schemes of the summer, when anything seemed possible, and reflected the awareness that a decisive victory had again eluded the Reich. On 25 September 1942, Hitler personally adjudicated a settlement under which the SS would in effect rent labour to industry. This agreement accelerated the development of SS-run labour camps servicing munitions factories in which the prisoners were predominantly Jewish. But the revaluation of Jewish workers did not mark a rupture with the previous months of unmitigated extermination.[127]

Under the September 1942 agreement, the SS were paid for Jewish labour at a rate of 3–4 Reichsmarks per person per day. Therefore, as soon as a Jew became unable to work he or she became a liability. Moreover, the apparently endless supply of Jews made it rational to examine and cull the workforce repeatedly to remove those no longer fit for the tasks they were expected to perform – the so-called 'selections' – and replace them. Jews unable to work were then sent to killing facilities to be murdered or just left to expire. Productivity standards also proved lethal. Because they were under-fed and usually ill, they tended to be less productive than non-Jewish workers. In the absence of better nutrition and medical care, the only way to improve their productivity was to extend the working day, which increased their inanition. Furthermore, since Jews were engaged predominantly in unskilled manual labour, notably construction, there was no need to train substitutes and no cost to letting them go. In other words, the drive to employ Jews was perfectly compatible with mass murder. Exploiting them for labour before murdering them actually compensated for the cost of deporting them in the first place. This procedure became known colloquially as 'annihilation through labour', although there was no comprehensive programme as such. In fact, the phrase was coined by the minister for justice, Otto Thierack, in September 1942, with reference to a specific mission to comb out prisons in the Reich and transfer certain categories of inmate to the concentration camps where they would be worked to death. The notion was applied retrospectively and inaccurately to the fate of the Jews. In actuality, work offered a lifeline to them and more would survive in labour camps than as fugitives from ghettos.[128]

The Jews enter Auschwitz

The first Jews to enter the Auschwitz concentration camp came from Slovakia. They were the victims of the Hlinka Slovak People's Party, which had ruled the country since it declared unilateral independence from Czecho-Slovakia in March 1939. The Hlinka Party was led by Jozef Tiso, a Roman Catholic priest, who became prime minister and then president of the new country. For Tiso, the 89,000 Jews of Slovakia were Christ-killers who could not be equal citizens in a Christian state. He stripped them of their rights and reduced them to second-class status. Other leading figures in the Hlinka movement – notably Vojtech Tuka, the minister of the interior and later prime minister, Alexander Mach, his successor, and Alexander Durcanscky, foreign minister – saw Jews as an alien, racial entity that had acquired political and economic power over the Slovaks. This faction aspired to expropriate the fabled wealth of the Jews and expel them completely. In fact, the Slovak Jewish population was quite humble: about 12,300 made their living from commerce and 22,000 were employees of one kind or another. Nevertheless, in November 1939, the hardliners succeeded in driving 7,500 Jews from border areas into Hungary and seizing their property. A little over a year later, the national assembly voted for a comprehensive solution to the Jewish question in Slovakia. A central office was set up to confiscate Jewish-owned assets, businesses and property. The Jews, meanwhile, were required to create a unitary representative body, the Ustredny Zidov, as the transmission mechanism for these measures. Within a year, 85 per cent of Jewish-run enterprises had been taken over and thousands of unemployed Jews were forced into labour camps. In September 1941 the racial anti-Semites in the government gained the upper hand in making anti-Jewish policy and promulgated a Jewish Codex that systematized all previous anti-Jewish legislation, placing it on a basis similar to the Nuremberg Laws. Jews were forced to wear a yellow star. Around 6,000 were expelled from the capital and dumped in internment camps. At this point, domestic Slovak anti-Semitism intersected with the anti-Jewish policies of the Third Reich and the needs of its war economy.[129]

For some time, the German government, desperate to get its hands on workers, had been requesting the Slovak authorities to send Slovak citizens to Germany as foreign labour. The Tiso government was not enthusiastic, but in early 1942 it came up with an alternative. Would the Reich be willing to accept Jews? There were now tens of thousands in labour camps at Novaky, Zilisna and Sered. By sending them to Germany the Slovaks could simultaneously appease the Nazi leaders and satisfy the desire to eject Jews from their country. The subsequent negotiations between the Slovak authorities and the Germans were conducted by Dieter Wisliceny. One of Eichmann's oldest colleagues, he had been sent to Bratislava in early September 1940 as an envoy of the Jewish office of the Gestapo to assist Hans Ludin, the German Ambassador, deal with Jewish questions. Although the Foreign Office was apprised of the conversations and had some input, the Slovak Jews thereby came under the jurisdiction of the RSHA: their fate served as a model for later deportations from western Europe directed by Eichmann's office within the remit of the 'final solution'. Yet the first trainloads to head towards Auschwitz had nothing to do with the 'final solution' itself. The Germans accepted the Slovak offer of Jews for forced labour and only men and women who were fit to work were summoned. They were entitled to take 50kg of baggage and each transport was accompanied by a doctor. Even so, the trains always left at night and at the border with the Reich the Hlinka guards made way for German police. The first trainload of Slovak Jews arrived in Auschwitz on 26 March 1942, consisting of 999 Jewish women dispatched from Poprad. Since the camp extension at Birkenau was nowhere near completion they were packed into the main camp in a section of barracks fenced off to serve as a temporary women's camp.[130]

The radical anti-Semites in the Slovak regime now saw an opening to rid themselves of the entire Jewish population and asked Wisliceny if the Reich would take non-working Jews, too. Following discussion of the terms on which this trade would rest, the Germans agreed. On 10

April 1942, Heydrich personally signed the contract with Prime Minister Tuka. The Reich would relieve the Slovaks of their unwanted Jewish
citizens, on condition that the Slovak government pay 500 Reichsmarks
per person to cover the cost of transport and accommodation. The
Slovaks kept the property the Jews left behind, but the Germans were
allowed to keep anything they took with them. The first transport carrying Jewish men, women and children from Slovakia departed the very
next day. By 20 October, 18,725 had been shipped to Auschwitz and
40,000 had ended up in the Lublin district. Most of the latter were murdered in Belzec and Sobibor. Around 8,000 evaded the transports by
fleeing to Hungary. An effective lobbying campaign playing on a growing unease in Catholic and government circles in Bratislava persuaded
the Slovaks to suspend the deportations 24,000 souls short of complete
destruction of the community.[131]

Four days after the first transport from Slovakia pulled up to the
Auschwitz station, a train chartered by the RSHA arrived from Compiègne in France carrying 1,112 Jewish prisoners. These were foreign
Jews who had been arrested in the round-ups of 14 May and 12 December 1941. They were shipped eastwards not as part of the 'final solution'
but at the initiative of the military administration in Paris as an alternative to the use of mass shootings in reprisal for resistance activity. The
mass execution of French citizens was Hitler's favoured response, but
the army believed that such a policy would only stimulate French
hostility. It was better, they argued, to make the punishment fall on Jews
and to use the already interned foreigners as a reservoir for punitive
deportations. The RSHA was willing to accede to this device since
the removals made room in the camps for more foreign Jews and more
hostages. Consequently, upon arrival, the first trainloads of Jewish
deportees from France were processed into the main camp and entered
the labour force. Further transports followed: on 5 June from Compiègne, on 22 June from Drancy, on 25 June from Pithiviers, on 28 June
from Beaune-la-Rolande, and on 17 July from Pithiviers. In each case
the prisoners went directly into the Auschwitz workforce. However,
within four to six weeks, 70–80 per cent of them were dead. It is estimated that from the 1,000 Jews on each of these transports, the number
of survivors ranged from 23 (on the first) to 59 (the convoy of 25
June).[132]

They perished due to the unremitting hard labour, brutal treatment
by kapos and SS guards, insufficient nourishment, and disease brought

on and aggravated by the abysmal sanitary conditions. On arrival, the men and women were shaved in the reception building, a number was tattooed on their right forearm, and they were kitted out with prisoner uniforms made of coarse cloth with faded blue-grey and white vertical stripes. All prisoners wore wooden-soled shoes that were ill-fitting and usually caused blisters that quickly turned septic. They were initially held in a quarantine unit before they were released into the main camp. From then on they were billeted in the overcrowded barracks, assigned a bunk that had barely more space than would be available inside a coffin. Lice spread easily in such circumstances and typhus raged through the main camp in the early summer of 1942. All prisoners (except those who were certified as sick) had to attend a roll call in the morning, at 4.30 a.m. in summer and 5.30 a.m. in winter, as well as in the evening after they had returned from work. This assembly, the 'Appell', could last for hours regardless of the weather.[133]

The work itself was arduous manual labour. Beginning in spring 1942, thousands of new arrivals were assigned to the Buna works, which involved a 4½-mile trek every morning and evening until late October when the Monowitz sub-camp (also known as Auschwitz-III) was opened. By the end of the year, I. G. Farben was employing 2,000 labourers, mostly Jewish, at the site alongside thousands of skilled foreign workers and German staff. Several thousand Jews were allotted to the Hermann Göring Works, which started production in 1942. Thousands more were distributed amongst sub-camps servicing the SS agricultural station at Rajsko, SS-run fishponds, poultry farms, and coalmines. A high proportion worked on the building site that was Birkenau. Prisoners manhandled wooden beams, steel joists, loads of bricks and mortar across boggy ground to the construction teams working on the prisoner accommodation and SS administration build-ings; they dug drainage canals in an attempt to lower the water table and control flooding; they laid out roads and paths, hauling massive concrete rollers to smooth the surfaces. For sustenance they received ersatz coffee in the morning and a slice of adulterated bread with mar-garine and a smear of jam; for lunch they were given some sort of soup, usually concocted from root vegetables; and in the evening they had a hot drink and another piece of bread. Sunday was a day of rest during which prisoners tried to obtain additional food. A few, privileged mem-bers of the internal camp hierarchy had access to a commissary that sold barely edible items such as salted snails to those who earned small cash payments. Those who received food parcels (permitted from mid-1942) bartered, sold or shared their precious supplements. Jews were not allowed to receive parcels and few had anything at all with which to trade.[134]

The poor diet caused diarrhoea and the bad water promoted dysentery. Due to the paucity of latrines, the long roll calls and the strict curfew at night, men and women regularly soiled themselves. The excrement contaminated sores on their lower body. Light injuries incurred in the course of labour or as a result of beatings usually went untreated and were easily infected by dirt or flies. Those who could no longer work were sent to the infirmary where the medical staff, drawn from the prison population but working under the supervision of SS doctors, struggled to provide treatment in the absence of basic medical supplies. Since July 1941, prisoners in Auschwitz too sick to work or suffering from contagious diseases had been murdered under the 14f13 programme at a facility in Lower Saxony. Individuals were also killed by SS doctors administering lethal injections. Following selections held in August, September and November 1942, hundreds of prisoners at a time, worn down by relentless toil and maltreatment in Monowitz and Birkenau, were killed in Auschwitz using Zyklon-B poison gas.[135]

The first occupants of Auschwitz-II, Birkenau, were the surviving Soviet prisoners of war who were moved there in March 1942 to continue their sacrificial labour. In August, the 17,000 mostly Jewish women who had by then arrived at Auschwitz were transferred from the grossly overcrowded quarters in the main camp to the rows of brick huts in section BIa. This became the Birkenau women's camp. A non-Jewish Polish prisoner, Seweryna Smaglewska, described the place in her post-war memoir: 'There were no roads, no paths between the blocks. In the depths of these dark dens, in bunks like multi-storied cages, the feeble light of a candle burning here or there flickered over naked, emaciated figures curled up, blue from the cold, bent over a pile of filthy rags, holding their shaved heads in their hands, picking out an insect with their scraggly fingers and smashing it on the edge of the bunk – that is what the barracks looked like in 1942.'[136]

In Block 30, two SS doctors, Carl Clauberg and Horst Schumann, began experiments in mass sterilization using X-rays and surgery. Clauberg was one of a number of Nazi medical experts invited by Himmler in mid-1942 to debate ways to sterilize large numbers of Jewish men and women quickly and cheaply. Himmler's objective was to resolve one of the issues raised at the Wannsee Conference and eliminate conflict over the fate of Mischlinge. Clauberg asked to try out his patent techniques on prisoners at Auschwitz and was allowed to rent space in one of the infirmary blocks in the women's camp. In late 1942 he was joined by Horst Schumann, who requested equipment and subjects with which to test his proposed methods. Having requisitioned male and female prisoners, Schumann subjected their genitals to X-rays of varying strength. Often this caused radiation burning and peritonitis which could, in turn, lead to fatal infections. The life expectancy of the human guinea pigs was further shortened when Schumann proceeded to extract the irradiated testicles and ovaries for examination.[137]

On the same day that the sixth convoy steamed into Auschwitz from France, the commandant's office was advised to expect another train from Drancy. When it was unloaded at Auschwitz on 19 July 1942, a selection took place on the platform and 375 Jews were immediately sent to the gas chambers. The Jews from four out of the next five transports were admitted to the camp without a selection and until early August a majority from the succeeding trains were sent for labour. But by then the scales had tipped in the direction of extermination. With a few exceptions, almost the entire trainload of Jews on each of convoys 15 to 43 from France was dead within a few hours of disembarking. They were the victims of a coordinated programme of deportations from western Europe intended to culminate in mass murder – the ultimate 'final solution'.[138]

Auschwitz and the 'final solution'

Auschwitz, unlike the extermination camps, was not designed for mass murder on an industrial scale so it was necessary for the camp administration to devise killing methods and ways of disposing of bodies while they were on the job. Far from being a smooth-running, clinical operation, this led to a great deal of trial and error. The first transports of Jews that came from East Upper Silesia in the spring of 1942 were unloaded at the ramp serving the main camp and walked or trucked to a one-storey building outside the main fence, on its eastern periphery. This construction contained the mortuary and crematorium for disposing of prisoners who expired or were executed. It had six ovens and the capacity to incinerate 340 bodies per day. The mortuary, which was 17

metres by 4.6 metres, with a low, flat concrete roof, was made airtight
and fitted with a strong, insulated door that could be screwed shut. The
room could hold up to 1,000 people if they were squeezed in, but the SS
discovered there was little point in killing that many at a time if there
was no quick way to get rid of the corpses. Once the victims were in the
room and the door was sealed, two or three SS men clambered up the
steep earthen embankment that surrounded it on three sides, donned
gas masks, removed the covering from vents that had been punched
through the roof, and emptied cans of Zyklon-B onto the throng below.
After they replaced the heavy lids the body heat of the people inside
caused the Zyklon-B crystals to vaporize; once the fumes were inhaled
people started to choke and death followed within minutes. The entire
process lasted about 20 minutes. When the SS were satisfied that the
victims were all dead the chore of removing the corpses and disposing
of them was handed to a team of Jewish prisoners. They too had to
improvise and find the best way to carry out their ghastly assignment.[139]

The learning curve of the SS and the prisoner detail that worked in
the crematoria, the Sonderkommando, was recorded by Filip Müller, a
twenty-year-old Slovak Jew from Sered. Müller was one of 4,500 Jews
deported to Auschwitz in April 1942. On arrival he entered the main
camp, but he was assigned to the crematoria as punishment for a trivial
offence. His first task was to go into the gas chamber, about which he
knew nothing, and undress the corpses. 'We were met by the appalling
sight of the dead – bodies of men and women lying higgledy-piggledy
among suit cases and rucksacks . . . I began to realize that there were
some people lying at my feet who had been killed only a short while
before.' With his keen eye he noticed the traces of a substance that must
have been toxic: 'where the crystals were scattered on the floor there
were no corpses, whereas in places further away, particularly around the
door, they were piled high.' Müller realized that as horrible as the work
was, it offered rich pickings for a starving man. SS supervision was
erratic and he was able to grab food from the baggage that lay everywhere. Unfortunately, when he was moved on to the cremation process
things went badly wrong. There were about twenty men in the Sonderkommando, not enough to perform all the jobs. In addition to stripping
the cadavers, they were commanded to cut off the women's hair and
package it, and extract gold teeth from the mouths of the dead. The
ovens were manned by others in the team, several of whom were
also greenhorns and completely ignorant about the technology. The

carcasses were dragged to the crematorium room and loaded onto retractable iron stretchers that slid in and out of the ovens, but if the tongs that the prisoners used to hold the corpses in place scraped the walls of the oven they could damage the fire-proof lining. Within minutes of Müller and his comrades attempting this manoeuvre they had accidentally dislodged a few firebricks in one of the ovens. The debris blocked a flue, resulting in the emission of dense, obnoxious smoke and an uncontrolled blaze. Eventually, firemen had to be called and the SS abandoned the effort. While three prisoners thought to be the culprits were shot (in fact, they had stopped work and were begging to die because they could not stand it), Müller and the Sonderkommando were ordered to load the hundreds of remaining cadavers onto trucks. They were then driven to a meadow where the exhausted Jews dumped them into a pit. Müller and the team returned to the camp to spend the night, and many more after it, in the punishment block.[140]

When the Sonderkommando was next summoned, Müller observed that the SS men had improved their technique. The transport consisted of 600 male and female Jews from Sosnowiec, mostly middle-aged, with some elderly and children. This time the SS required them to undress in the courtyard outside the crematoria building. Naturally, many were puzzled by this instruction and dawdled apprehensively while they tried to figure out what was going on. Their ruminations were cut short by shouts and beatings from the SS, who drove them inside. The Sonderkommando then swept up their clothing and belongings, making the place tidy for the next group. A different set of men handled the cremations so Müller's group only had to sort the clothing and valuables, which was now much easier. Three days later another transport was delivered and he noticed a further refinement. Two SS officers, Hans Aumeier and Maximilian Grabner, made speeches from the roof of the crematoria to the Jews in the courtyard, assuring them that they were about to be settled in a work camp. Grabner asked Jews to indicate if they had specific trades, reinforcing their sense of relief. Then they were told they had to be disinfected and showered. 'Cozened and deceived, hundreds of men, women and children . . . walked innocently and without a struggle into the large windowless chamber of the crematorium.' Once the Zyklon-B crystals were tipped through the vent, Grabner ordered the trucks that had delivered the Jews to run their engines. 'We could clearly hear the heart-rending weeping, cries for help, fervent prayers, violent banging and knocking and, drowning everything else, the noise of truck engines running at top speed.' Even so, the SS officers realized that this was hardly satisfactory. The gas chamber was too close to the main camp and too exposed; the disposal facilities were too constricted. Despite the construction of a new chimney the ovens could not cope with the volume of cremations. So the bulk of the killing was subsequently shifted to Birkenau.[141]

The new gas chambers at Birkenau were equally makeshift. To begin, the SS adapted a peasant farmhouse surviving from the demolished village of Breszinska. Prisoner craftsmen plastered the walls and blocked up the windows, leaving only a small aperture with a heavy wooden flap through which Zyklon-B could be poured in. The camp workshops also fashioned a strong, airtight door that was locked using a screw mechanism. The gas chamber was 15 by 6 metres and could accommodate 800 people. Crude wooden barracks were hastily erected in which the victims could undress before walking over to the so-called shower room. The converted farmhouse, known as Bunker 1, was adorned with signs announcing that it was a disinfection centre and the whitewashed gas chamber was kitted out with false showerheads. In nearby meadows prisoners dug burial pits and surrounded them with fences. Tracks were laid for trolleys to convey the bodies to the pits. In July, the transformation of a second farmhouse was completed in time for the mass deportations from France, Belgium and the Netherlands. Around then the Sonderkommando from Crematorium I, including Müller, was transferred to Birkenau, where conditions for them were much improved. However, the new layout was not quite so convenient for the SS. It was a 1½-mile walk from the ramp to the bunker and along the way the SS had to reassure the Jews that no harm would come to them. The column was trailed by an ambulance that was intended to convey a sense of concern for their well-being, although it was actually loaded with canisters of Zyklon-B.[142]

The SS soon discovered the same problem that was causing chaos at Treblinka at roughly the same time: as the hot summer wore on and the number of those murdered at Auschwitz and Birkenau climbed towards 200,000, fluids leaked from the decomposing corpses and the pits began to heave with noxious gases. 'A black, evil-smelling mass oozed out and polluted the ground-water in the vicinity,' Müller recalled. The Sonderkommando was called in to treat the bodies with lime and chlorine, but it was no use. During a visit to Birkenau in July 1942, during which he was treated to an exhibition of mass murder in the bunkers, Himmler ordained that the dead would have to be cremated from thereon. The remains of those already buried would have to be exhumed and inciner- ated, too.[143]

Reich Jews and the 'final solution'

The 'final solution' as a pan-European project had evolved slowly and erratically since the meeting at Wannsee, with repeated delays due both to the war and to second thoughts about the collaboration to be expected from Axis partners or subjugated countries. On 31 January 1942, Adolf Eichmann informed state police headquarters and the emi- gration offices that controlled Jewish affairs that 'The evacuation of Jews to the east which has recently been carried out in some regions rep- resents the beginning of the final solution of the Jewish question in the Old Reich, the Ostmark [Austria], and the Protectorate ... At present new possibilities for reception are being worked out, with the aim of deporting further contingents ...' However, difficulties with transport and the crisis on the eastern front prevented any new deportations for the moment. A few weeks later, on 6 March, he briefed the men respon- sible for Jewish affairs at Gestapo offices across the Reich to prepare for the evacuation of up to 55,000 Jews to the east. He envisaged 20,000 coming from Vienna, 18,000 from Prague and the rest from Germany. Jews with foreign nationality, Jews employed in war-related industries, the old and the young were to be excluded. To avoid wrangling over special cases, Theresienstadt was being cleared of Czech Jews and recast as the 'Reich ghetto' to accommodate prominent Jewish personalities, Jews with the Iron Cross or severe war wounds, and the elderly in gen- eral. That month another wave of deportations began that carried about 35,000 German Jews to Theresienstadt and 10,000 to ghettos in the east including Minsk, Warsaw and several other destinations in the General Government.[144]

The marking of German Jews and the first wave of deportations from the Reich had done little to appease the resentment that many Germans felt at the sight of Jews still in the country at a time when it was so hard pressed. It was not only true believers, who considered themselves members of the racial community, who vented their anger against this diminished, bedraggled remnant; those who were simply feeling the strain of wartime lashed out too. The SD in Höxter reported that citizens were furious when shopping hours for Jews were shifted to midday. This meant that good Germans either had to shop in the morning when it was cold or in the afternoon, after the Jews had allegedly snapped up the best produce. Citizens attending court were irritated to find officials still dealing with legal issues concerning Jewish people. Indeed, the greater visibility of Jews thanks to the yellow star, and the awareness that thousands had already been deported, acted as incitements. The RSHA Jewish department noted that a large part of the public saw the yellow badge as 'only a prelude to further, more drastic ordinances', with the goal of a final resolution of the Jewish Question'.[145]

The pressure on the remaining Jews was unrelenting. In June 1942, Victor Klemperer listed the indignities and impositions to which they were subjected. '1) To be home after 8 or 9 in the evening. Inspection! 2) Expelled from one's house. 3) Ban on wireless . . . telephone. 4) Ban on theatres, cinemas, concerts, museums. 6) Ban on using public transport: three phases a) omnibus banned, only front platform of tram permitted, b) all use banned, except to work, c) to work on foot, unless one lives 2½ miles away or is sick (but it is a hard fight to get a doctor's certificate). Also ban on taxi cabs, of course. 7) Ban on purchasing "food in short supply". 8) Ban on purchasing cigars or any kind of smoking materials. 9) Ban on purchasing flowers. 10) Withdrawal of milk ration card. 11) Ban on going to the barber. 12) Any kind of tradesman can only be called after application to the Community. 13) Complete surrender of typewriters, 14) of furs and woollen blankets, 15) of bicycles . . . 16) of deckchairs, 17) of dogs, cats, birds. 18) Ban on leaving city of Dresden, 19) on entering the railway station, 20) on setting foot on the Ministry embankment, in parks, 21) on using . . . roads bordering the Great Garden . . . on entering market halls. 22) Since 19 September the Jews' Star. 23) Ban on having reserves of foodstuffs at home . . . 24) Ban on lending libraries. 25) Because of the star, all restaurants are closed to us . . . 26) No clothing and 27) No fish card. 28) No special rations such as coffee, chocolate, condensed milk. 29) The special taxes. 30) The constantly contracting disposable allowance. Mine at first 600, then 320, now 185 RM. 31) Shopping restricted to *one* hour . . . But all together they are nothing as against the constant threat of house searches, of ill-treatment, of prison, concentration camp, and violent death.' Since any infraction of the regulations could lead to arrest and imprisonment his greatest fear was all too realistic. His diary becomes a litany of Jews shot in camps, deported or dead by their own hand.[146]

As fewer full Jews were left, more adverse attention fell on Misch-linge and those protected by mixed marriages. There were about 19,000 privileged Jews whose fate had been left unresolved at the Wannsee meeting, but the RSHA was accumulating evidence that backed its demand for their total eradication. Hence the Sicherheitsdienst in Minden informed the Berlin head office that people objected to the fact that privileged Jews could go about unmarked and unseen. It claimed that citizens with family members serving in Russia feared the danger posed by these invisible Jews. Such attitudes provided the rationale for pressurizing Aryan spouses to divorce their Jewish partners so that the latter could be dealt with summarily. Klemperer complained that his wife, Eva, was spat at and called a 'Jew's whore'. They were shoved from one Jew-house to another. Eva, however, remained true. By contrast, the marriage of Lilli and Ernst Jahn succumbed. The Nazi mayor of Immen-hausen, where Lilli still lived, repeatedly issued threats against her. She was forced to transfer all her financial assets and her share of their house to her husband. Even though his friends warned him of the likely consequences, Ernst eventually decided to divorce Lilli and marry his mistress, mother of his love-child. Lilli subsequently wrote to a friend, 'I feel infinitely lonely and forlorn'. She was now acutely vulnerable to deportation.[147]

With the cessation of emigration from the Reich and the increasing tempo of the evacuations, the Reichsvereinigung der Juden in Deutsch-land became enmeshed in the destruction of the community. It managed the lists of Jews to be deported, established transit centres through which they would pass on their way eastward, and supplied them with food and medical staff. Marshals of the Reichsvereinigung informed Jews of their fate, collected them, and escorted them to the assembly points prior to their departure. These marshals were usually accompanied by a member of the Gestapo, which fostered the appear-ance of collaboration. Even more disconcerting, representatives of the Reichsvereinigung collected the payment deportees made to cover the cost of their journey and passed the money on to the Gestapo. Its clerks and accountants documented the property they left behind. And yet its leadership continued to negotiate with the Nazi authorities, trying to wring concessions. It argued for the value of Jews working in the arma-ments industries and succeeded in getting them deferred. It added to the ranks of its own staff, finally reaching a total of 1,500 personnel temporarily exempted from deportation. It asked SS officials to withhold

Jews over sixty-five years old, aged invalids and decorated veterans of the Great War. Jews falling into these categories were indeed spared until June 1942, and then most were sent to Theresienstadt. Ultimately, the assassination of Heydrich and the resistance action by the Baum group undid the work of the Reichsvereinigung. By the summer, Klemperer observed, 'Murder is everywhere, reaching out for everyone, in ever more of a hurry.'[148]

Faced by the growing danger, more and more Jews remaining in Germany opted to go underground. Ruth Andreas-Friedrich became part of a network providing shelter for Jews on the run. Feeding them at a time of strict rationing was one of the challenges facing the helpers. In the midst of what she labelled the 'third migration', in June 1942, she noticed, 'A great many people with guilty looks are lugging shopping nets full of vegetables through the streets of Berlin.' Andreas-Friedrich also noted that Mischlinge were successfully petitioning the Reichssippenamt, the Race Kinship Office, to get their racial identity changed by proving that they had been born out of wedlock to two Aryan parents. 'Never before have there been so many marital infidelities, and so many daughters and sons ready under oath to assert their mother's vagaries.' Indeed the experts of the SD expressed 'astonishment' at the readiness of the Reichssippenamt to grant so many self-denying Jews a change of status that relieved them from the fear of deportation. It was hardly the case that all German Jews passively accepted their fate: evasion, concealment, flight and resistance now became an option for a significant number. It is estimated that from late 1942, 10,000–12,000 Jews removed their star (if they had ever worn one) and attempted to pass as Aryans or hid. In Berlin alone, 5,000 Jews chose to live illegally in the hope of avoiding deportation.[149]

Theresienstadt

Until the mass eviction of German Jews to Theresienstadt, the ghetto-camp had a predominantly Czech Jewish character. At the end of 1941 it accommodated 7,545 Jews from Prague and Brno. Over the next six months 26,524 Jews from all over Bohemia and Moravia were squeezed into the fortress. Between July and December 1942 the number of Czech Jewish arrivals doubled again, but during that time thousands were deported through what was in effect Theresienstadt's revolving door. They were replaced by approximately 53,000 German and 13,000 Austrian Jews, although many of them, too, were removed to the east after only a few weeks or months. From mid-1942 the internal administration as well as the external appearance and ambience of Theresienstadt changed to reflect the demographic transformation.[150]

Helga Weiss and her family were amongst the first Prague Jewish families to be forcibly replanted. Within weeks of their arrival they suffered two shocks. First, on 9 January 1942, nine young men were hanged for the apparently trivial crime of attempting to smuggle letters out of the ghetto. This atrocity was followed by news that 1,000 inhabitants were to be transported to Riga. Helga expressed the general disillusionment when she reflected, 'We thought at least now we're in Terezin we'd be spared any more of this.' Instead, from then on every day was lived under the threat of deportation. The terror of removal was juxtaposed with the pleasure of meeting friends and family as transports flooded in. There were so many reunions that Weiss remarked, 'Prague has come . . .'[151]

Until mid-1942, the deported Jews shared the fortress town with its indigenous inhabitants. But whereas the Czechs lived in family houses, the Jews were separated by gender and packed into the original barracks and living quarters adapted from other installations. In the Sudeten barracks fifty men lived in each room, stacked in bunks; the women in the Magdeburg barracks had slightly more space. Girls stayed with their mothers and boys with their fathers until they reached the age of twelve when youths moved into children's homes that offered more space, better facilities, and rooms for schooling. All adults except the old and the infirm were expected to join working parties, many of which operated outside the fortress walls. The ghetto was guarded by a detail of 120–150 Czech gendarmes. The Jews rarely saw a German.[152]

During the Czech period, Eichmann and his deputy Siegfried Seidl, who was responsible for running the ghetto on a day-to-day basis, appointed Jacob Edelstein as the Elder, with Otto Zucker as his deputy. Both men were Zionists with years of public service behind them. They presided over a council of thirteen elders who supervised several departments covering administration, building and maintenance, finance, labour and economic matters, and public heath. An 'Ordnungswache', or Order Watch, patrolled the streets and escorted Jews in and out of the ghetto confines. Crucially, the internal administration was responsible for maintaining a registry of all the residents and selected who would leave when the Germans ordained a deportation. The actual deportation lists were compiled by the Transport Committee. Since it was always the target of intense lobbying, during the days and hours before a deportation an Appeals Committee examined claims for exemption. On the surface, the categories were clearly set out by the Germans in guidelines issued to the council on 5 March 1942. Families with young children were not to be broken up. Men with decorations for military service or severe war wounds were exempted. Anyone who was sick, over the age of sixty-five years, or in a mixed marriage was not to be included. Anyone with foreign nationality (except Poles, Soviet citizens and people from Luxemburg) was held back. Finally, anyone on the first two transports from Prague was privileged; this included many who staffed the internal administration. Outside these formal categories there were many grounds for appealing and lobbying.[153]

Norbert Troller, a forty-six-year-old architect from Brno and veteran of the Great War, was deported to Theresienstadt in March 1942 after a spell of forced labour in a factory. On arrival he was allocated a bunk in the Sudeten barracks and commenced three weeks of manual work, as was customary for newcomers. Then he was assigned to the technical department, where he designed living quarters for the inmates and also the SS. Troller quickly learned that Theresienstadt was nothing like the end of the line and that survival depended on obtaining 'protection' from someone in the administration who could keep your name off the transportation lists. 'The concept of "protection"', he wrote in a memoir, 'was of such paramount importance for all of us that it overshadowed any other considerations.' Nevertheless, during the interval between the transports that departed each week Theresienstadt pulsated with life. 'There was work and leisure, concerns with sanitation, housing, health care, child care, record keeping, construction, theater, concerts, lectures, all functioning as well as possible under the circumstances.' But as soon as word came that another 1,000 to 2,000 people had to go within a few days the population could think of nothing except 'protection'.[154]

Troller coolly analysed the demoralizing effect of the struggle not to be transported. 'In fear of death one forgets, slowly at first, but then with considerable speed, the rules of ethics, of decency, of helpfulness . . . At any and all costs we try to prevent the execution of the death sentence on us and our loved ones . . . To escape that fate one had to do everything to be included in the privileged group of the "protected".' It was his good fortune to have skills that qualified him for the staff of the

Jewish administration. His boss in the architectural office shielded him from over twenty-five comb-outs. Troller was then able to do favours for even more influential ghetto figures and, ultimately, to get work from the SS. But he was still unable to protect his sister and her daughter, who were transported some six months after they had all arrived. Troller bewailed the system of drawing up lists and the 'psychological corruption' that affected individuals as they fought one another to avoid deportation. 'With devilish baseness and cunning they [the SS] . . . put the burden of selection on the Jews themselves; to select their own co-religionists, relatives, their friends. In the end this unbearable, desperate, cynical burden destroyed the community leaders who were forced to make the selections. The power of life and death forced on the Council of Elders was the main reason, the unavoidable force, behind the ever-increasing corruption in the ghetto . . .' But he knew he was not innocent. 'How can I forgive myself for having succumbed to egotistical, ruthless, incomprehensible actions towards my fellow sufferers whenever danger threatened . . .'[155]

In their determination to maintain a semblance of normal life, especially for the children, and preserve their humanity, the Jews of Theresienstadt supported an array of educational and cultural initiatives. Helga Weiss started attending classes and moved into a children's home where she studied Czech, geography, history and maths. The youths with whom she lived shared a plethora of books and went to shows performed in attics, the only free space available for such entertainments. 'Yesterday I went to see *The Kiss*. It's playing in Magdeburg, up in the loft. Even though it's sung only to the accompaniment of a piano, with no curtains or costumes, the impression it makes couldn't be greater even in the National Theatre.' Adults enjoyed these distractions and found more earthy satisfactions. Troller wryly observed men sneaking into the coal cellar of the women's barracks for prearranged liaisons with their wives, who emerged subsequently with 'coal-blackened backsides'. Marital infidelity became commonplace as traditional moral standards wilted under the threat of random extinction. Despite hunger and unmitigated body odours men and women formed relationships, some for love and others for more functional purposes. 'On the one hand, there was spontaneous, true, eternal love; on the other, we were faced with the continual threat of separation, sex, lust, a pressure cooker atmosphere, quick, quick, without fancy phrases, before the next transport to the east stops us . . .' For unmarried men like Troller, especially those who were privileged, there was no shortage of girlfriends. He and a friend constructed a *kumbal*, a cubby-hole, in which they could have privacy and entertain. There was a strict etiquette, though. A privileged worker who possessed a *kumbal* was expected to offer a gift to a visiting lady friend, such as food or cigarettes. But sometimes it was just a case of satisfying an urge. One afternoon Norbert's companion Lilly turned up at his place and announced, 'Nori – I need a fuck, come on.'[156]

The advent of thousands of elderly German Jews dampened the defiantly exuberant atmosphere in the ghetto cultivated by the younger Czechs, but enriched its cultural life. Amongst the newcomers in July 1942 were Philipp Manes and his wife. Manes was a sixty-seven-year-old veteran of the Great War and holder of the Iron Cross. He had run a fur agency in Berlin until he was put out of business by the Nazis and had spent the last few months working as a drill press operator in a factory. In his diary he detailed the last hours in the home where he had lived with his wife and where they had raised four children. 'It seemed inconceivable that we had to give up our entire estate, leave behind everything that we had acquired over the 37 years of our marriage ... All our possessions were to be appropriated by strangers. They would go through all the drawers and cupboards and throw out things that were worthless to them – our cherished possessions. Inconceivable.' But at 9.30 a.m. on the appointed morning, two Gestapo officers and two Jewish marshals came to escort them to a removal van that served as transport. Hours later they were disgorged at the Jewish Old People's Home on Grosse Hamburgerstrasse along with dozens of other deportees. The next day they were told their property had been expropriated because they were guilty of 'communist activity'. Manes, a staunch conservative, 'accepted this humiliation in silence'. Their passports were stamped 'evacuated from Berlin on 23 July' and 'with that our life as citizens of Germany ended'. At three o'clock the next morning they were transported to the Anhalter Station. 'We were cast out of the lives that we had made for ourselves, working for fifty years to see our business crowned with success ... and now here we are with the few effects that we can carry with us in bags and backpacks.'[157]

Along with their fellow, unwilling travellers they felt hopeful that Theresienstadt might live up to promise. What they actually found was shattering. First they were stripped of their valuables and their suitcases. For the rest of the summer Manes was condemned to wear the heavy winter clothes he had donned for the journey. They were led to a brick-walled stable and instructed to sleep on the ground. There was only a single water fountain and a disgusting communal latrine. Eventually they got their bedrolls and some personal items which they took with them to new quarters equipped with bunk beds. But this entailed the separation of men from women, and the planking for the bunks was riddled with bed bugs. Far from being a retirement home, Theresien-stadt was a daily battle for life. '"Ghetto" signifies a renunciation of or a moratorium on morals', Manes confided to his journal. 'When hunger triumphed over civilized behaviour and tore down all inhibitions, everyone gave themselves to one feeling and one goal: satiation at any price. Justice, security, property, and order simply yielded to this natural instinct. Those who have not witnessed how, at the end of the distribu-tion of food, old people plunged into empty vats, scraping them with their spoons, even scraping the tables where the food was served with knives, looking for leftovers, cannot understand how quickly human dignity can be lost.'[158]

After a few weeks Manes was asked by the administration to form an auxiliary to the Order Watch to assist disorientated or demented elderly Jews whose wanderings and distress caused discomfort to the rest of the populace. He used this position to start giving lectures, and before long was addressing audiences of a hundred. Eventually his talks evolved into a cultural programme employing sixty-five men and women. The lectures, play readings and poetry recitals in German brought much comfort to the Berliners and Viennese Jews who were otherwise utterly adrift in the Czech-speaking environment. Manes admired the Czech Jews for their patriotism and their Jewish pride, but he noted that they did not reciprocate this warmth. The two groups vied for power, contesting the distribution of privileges, work and rations. 'On the one side there was abundance and the good life, which was not shared; on the other, endless hunger.' Manes particularly resented the fact that Czech Jews were entitled to receive food parcels and seemed to get better rations from the kitchens. 'It has to be said', he admitted with a measure of self-reproach, 'the Jewish Czech does not love us. He sees us only as Germans.'[159]

Even after the non-Jewish population was evicted from the town, the arrival of the German and Austrian Jews caused acute overcrowd-ing. Combined with undernourishment due to the straitened food supply and bad sanitation, this sent the rate of mortality shooting upwards. In December 1941 just 48 Jews had died in the ghetto. The following March the number climbed to 259, but this was more or less in line with the increased population. In July 1942, there were on average 32 deaths per day, a total of 2,327 for August, and no fewer than 131 every day throughout September. According to Manes this was 'the time of the great dying of the old and the very old who, with their broken, weak bodies, their worn, uprooted souls; and their unrealizable longing for their far-off children, could not resist even a mild illness.'[160]

In September 1942 the Germans ordered the deportation of elderly Jews, to bring down the average age of the population and rebalance the number who were working. Helga Weiss was horrified at the sight of these transports. 'Altertransports. 10,000 sick, lame, dying, everyone over 65 ... Why send defenceless people away? ... can't they let them die here in peace? After all, that's what awaits them. The ghetto guards are shouting and running about beneath our windows; they're closing off the street. Another group is on its way ... Suitcases, stretchers, corpses. That's how it goes, all week long. Corpses on the two-wheeled carts and the living on the hearses ...' In two months, 17,780 aged prisoners exited the ghetto via the 'Schleuse' (sluice), the exit ramp that led down to Bohusovice Station. By the end of the year the proportion of ghetto residents aged over sixty-five years had fallen from 45 to 33 per cent .[161]

Seidl insisted that the council should be restructured to reflect the ratio of German, Austrian and Czech Jews. In October, Heinrich Stahl, one of the leaders of the Reichsvereinigung, was appointed deputy to Edelstein. At the start of 1943, by which time the population was equally divided between Czechs and Germans, Seidl ordered the formation of a triumvirate consisting of Edelstein, Paul Eppstein, a member of the Berlin Jewish leadership, and Josef Loewenherz, from Vienna. Not long afterwards Loewenherz dropped out of the picture and Seidl placed power in the hands of Eppstein, with the Viennese Benjamin Murmelstein as a deputy alongside Edelstein. For the next year and a half these men would determine who would live in Theresienstadt or depart on the transports.[162]

The 'final solution' in France

In France the 'final solution' evolved messily. Notwithstanding the aura of decisiveness at Wannsee and the apparently linear development of anti-Jewish policy in the subsequent months, what eventuated bears the hallmarks of opportunism and a last-minute concoction. A shift in the balance of power in France between factions in the French government and within the occupation administration certainly favoured a more radical approach to the Jews, but this was happenstance.

In February 1942, Xavier Vallat got into a row with Theodor Dannecker over the persecution of the Jews. He boasted that Vichy was doing more than the Germans and remonstrated against unilateral anti-Jewish actions by the military administration in the north. Vallat did not particularly care about the round-ups there; the Jews were merely pawns in his efforts to defend the sovereignty of the Vichy regime over the whole of France. However, his obstreperous attitude led Werner Best to dub him sarcastically the 'Commissioner for the Protection of Jews'. In April, Pierre Laval, who had been sacked as prime minister in December 1941, returned to office with a personal mission to wrest authority over French affairs from the Germans, even at the cost of intensified collaboration on certain matters. In May he removed the intransigent Germanophobe Vallat and appointed Louis Darquier de Pellepoix to run the Commissariat général aux questions juives. Darquier de Pellepoix was the founder of a veterans' organization and at one time or another a leading light in almost every far-right and anti-Semitic movement in France between the wars. He was an utterly disreputable man, who filled the CGQJ with cronies and skimmed money from Aryanized businesses. But his deputy, Joseph Antignac, was a cold and efficient administrator who worked well with the Germans. At around the same time, Laval promoted a gifted young prefect, René Bousquet, to head the French police service. Bousquet's representative in the occupied zone was Jean Leguay, an equally dynamic and effective civil servant.[163]

The new French team found themselves dealing with fresh faces on the German side. In February 1942, Otto von Stülpnagel resigned as the head of the military administration rather than approve ever more draconian repression and the mass shooting of hostages. He was replaced by his cousin, General Carl-Heinrich von Stülpnagel, who was more amenable to the high command's predilection for hostage taking and executions in reprisal for resistance activity. The following month, Himmler used the deteriorating security situation to warrant the appointment of Carl Oberg as the first Higher SS Police Leader for France. This step marked a decisive subtraction of power from the military administration. Oberg was placed in overall command of all

German security troops and aimed for the subordination of the French police too. The Sipo-SD was given executive power in the occupied zone and permitted to conduct arrests. This boded ill for the Jews since, as the SS Police Leader in the Radom district, Oberg had overseen the destruction of numerous Jewish communities. In May, Eichmann sent Herbert Hagen, one of his trusted lieutenants, to assist Helmut Knochen, chief of the security police. Hagen's role largely entailed pressing the French to adopt more rigorous anti-Jewish policies. Two months later Eichmann added Heinz Röthke, a former theology student, to the team responsible for enacting anti-Jewish policy. With this shift of power to the security apparatus, Werner Best dropped into the background and eventually left to take up the post of Reich Plenipotentiary in Denmark.[164]

Dannecker and Carl-Theo Zeitschel, who held the Jewish desk in the German Embassy, had long been pressing for the removal of Jews from France and had achieved a limited success with the transports from the internment camps. In early May, Heydrich visited Paris but at this time did not envisage mass deportations taking place for months. Shortly afterwards, though, Dannecker began negotiations with the railway authorities to obtain transports to take even larger numbers of Jews from France to the east. By chance, the senior German officer responsible for rail movements offered to make rolling stock available; suddenly the log jam was broken and developments accelerated. A week later, Abetz, the German Ambassador, informed Knochen that the embassy was awaiting a final decision from Berlin about the fate of Jews in France. On the same day, the military administration issued order No. 8, requiring that from 7 June all Jews in the occupied zone (except nationals of states allied to Germany) had to wear a yellow star with the word 'Juif' emblazoned on it. Objections by the Vichy government ensured that the star was not worn by Jews in the Free Zone. However, the Vichy authorities proved more tractable on other issues.[165]

On 11 June, the Judenreferenten (experts on Jewish affairs) posted to France, Belgium and the Netherlands by office IVB4 of the Gestapo were recalled to Berlin for an urgent consultation. According to Dannecker's notes, Eichmann told them that 'For military reasons the deportation of Jews from Germany to the Eastern areas of operations can no longer take place during the summer. The Reichsführer-SS has therefore ordered the transfer of large numbers of Jews from the South East (Romania) or from the Occupied Western areas to Auschwitz concentration camp for labour.' The deportees had to be aged between sixteen and forty and capable of hard labour, although 10 per cent of each transport could consist of Jews unfit for work. Jews in mixed marriages and citizens of neutral countries and states in the Axis were also excluded (as were Jews whom the Germans thought they could exchange for German citizens interned by the British and Americans). Eichmann set quotas of 15,000 Jews from the Netherlands, 15,000 from Belgium and 100,000 from France, encompassing both zones.[166]

Once Dannecker returned to Paris he issued guidelines for the forthcoming action and engaged in a round of conversations with Vichy officials. It is characteristic of German decision-making and policy implementation that the proposals in Berlin were honoured more in the breach. Although the deportations were supposedly intended to send a stream of labour to Auschwitz, unlike the transports that were sent in March and June only a diminishing fraction of the French deportees entered the labour force. Instead, most were murdered in gas chambers. Yet as we have seen these installations had not been prepared well in advance of the deportation schedule and were hurried, primitive contraptions. And, once again, the war disrupted German planning. With only three police battalions at their disposal, a maximum of 3,000 men, the Sipo-SD contingent in Paris did not have nearly enough personnel to conduct such a massive operation. Nor could any be spared from other theatres. Even after Eichmann abruptly scaled back the quota for France to 40,000, the Sipo-SD would still need the assistance of the Vichy regime. Thanks to the census of Jews in the occupied zone, the Jewish section of the Paris police held a card index with details of 149,793 Jews registered in the city. The gendarmes, the municipal police and the gardes mobiles took their orders not from the Germans but from the intendant of police in each prefecture and they, in turn, took their orders from the head of the police, René Bousquet. This gave the French considerable bargaining power and enabled them to set terms that contradicted German aspirations.[167]

While Laval and Pétain were happy to see the Germans remove foreign and stateless Jews from France and to empty the internment camps in both the north and the south – including children and families – they refused to let the Germans touch a Jew with French citizenship acquired by birth or by naturalization before 1927. Bousquet and Leguay would only agree to put the French police at the disposal of the Germans if they agreed to these conditions. When Dannecker demanded that they arrest 22,000 Jews in Paris and 10,000 in the un-occupied zone, including at least 40 per cent with French nationality, his French counterparts referred the matter to Laval. The result was a momentary crisis in German–French relations that threatened to derail Oberg's patient efforts to secure the collaboration of the French police force. On 30 June, Eichmann travelled to Paris and spent two days sorting things out. A subsequent memorandum noted that cooperation in the north was good, but in the south 'the French Government causes increasing difficulties'. A few days later, Oberg, Knochen and Hagen reached a compromise with Bousquet. The Germans would make do with foreign and stateless Jews, although they would come from both zones. French police would carry out the arrests in the north and the south, supplying the necessary manpower. As for taking children, Dannecker had to ask Berlin whether this was acceptable. The time it took to elicit a reply suggests that Eichmann had not reckoned on this part of the bargain.[168]

At the cost of surrendering unwanted Jews, Bousquet had managed to defend France's sovereignty over its citizens and extend the authority of the Vichy regime over a police operation in the occupied zone. The Germans had no choice but to agree to these terms, at least for the moment. Yet dependence on the Vichy regime actually left them dependent on French public opinion since their French partners could not ignore popular feeling. It was a risky deal.

The Jews were completely unaware of these machinations. In her diary entries for April and May 1942, Hélène Berr recorded her progress as a student at the Sorbonne, the merry round of parties and musical evenings, and weekends in the countryside with her boyfriend. Although Hélène worked as a volunteer for L'Entraide Temporaire, which provided assistance to Jewish children whose foreign-born parents were interned or deported, life continued normally for her family. The first measure to have an impact on them was the announce-ment that all Jews would be compelled to wear the yellow star. On 1 June she wrote, 'Maman came to tell me the news about the yellow star, and I pushed her away, saying "I'll talk about it later."' Hélène wrestled over whether or not to wear it and analysed what it meant for her iden-tity as a French woman and a Jew. While it was undoubtedly degrading, it was 'cowardly not to wear it vis-à-vis people who will'. She resolved that if she did, 'I want to stay very elegant and dignified at all times so that people can see what that means. I want to do whatever is most courageous.' For all her prognostications, when the day came to go out in public with the star on her coat it was an agonizing experience. She tried to keep her head high and maintain eye-contact with other pedestrians, but many looked away. She felt an odd sensation seeing other star-wearers, Jews who would formerly have been indistinguishable from anyone else. When some people smiled sympathetically, her eyes filled with tears. Taunted by children, however, she felt reduced to one identity: Jew. The next day on her way to the university she was forced to go to the last car of the tram. Once she reached the Sorbonne, 'I suddenly felt I was no longer myself, that everybody had changed, that I had become a foreigner, as if I were in the grip of a nightmare.'[169]

'There are no words for such infamy,' Raymond-Raoul Lambert growled in his journal, although as a resident of the Free Zone he was a spectator to events in the north. The star was the latest in a series of unpleasant twists since the return of Laval and the departure of Vallat. Until then, he believed he had made significant progress establishing UGIF and bringing succour to foreign and French Jews hit by the discriminatory policies of the Vichy regime or German repression. This was despite a wobbly beginning. At the end of 1941, Vallat had levied a punitive fine of 1 billion francs on the Jewish community and made UGIF responsible for collecting it. The fine dented the credibility of the new body and drew scathing criticism from the Consistoire. 'I accepted only collaboration at the technical level,' he averred defensively, depicting their opposition as purely selfish. 'The very wealthy Jews who are the majority of the Consistoire are afraid the Union [UGIF] will make them pay too much for the poor.' By March 1942, though, he sensed success and believed that UGIF was well established.[170]

Hélène Berr discovered the importance of the UGIF when her father was arrested for failing to wear the yellow star correctly. A German officer took him to a police station where he was charged and sent to Drancy internment camp. As soon as his family was notified, Hélène rushed to the Jewish desk at the police station carrying things he might need. Later she was able to send letters to her father via a UGIF office. Two weeks later, she registered with UGIF herself, although she could not suppress her feeling that it was dangerous to organize the Jews on a racial basis. 'I detest all those more or less Zionist movements that unwittingly play into the Germans' hands.' Nevertheless, before long she was working as a part-time volunteer in a UGIF office.[171]

Life went on. Hélène went into the country to pick raspberries, wandered in the Luxembourg Gardens, and visited favourite book-shops. Then, on 15 July, she noted, 'Something is brewing, something that will be a tragedy, maybe *the* tragedy.' She was warned that the Germans were planning a *rafle*, a round-up, of 20,000 Jews. 'A wave of terror has been gripping everybody else as well these past few days. It appears that the SS have taken command in France and that terror must follow.' Friends urged her to flee south.[172]

The rumours of an impending *rafle* were correct. Following Eichmann's two-day stay in the capital, the SS had settled the details of the first major action in France. Bousquet informed his lieutenants that the French police would have the lion's share of the operation. Nine thousand uniformed officers, supplemented by 400 members of a right-wing paramilitary association, would descend on six arrondissements at 4 a.m. on 16 July. Their target consisted of 28,000 non-French Jews, each named on lists supplied by the Jewish section of the Paris police. The officers were instructed to give the Jews enough time to take clothing and food for two days. If they vacated an apartment they had to ensure that the gas and electricity were turned off. The contents of the property had to be carefully noted before the residence was sealed. Fifty buses with blackened windows stood ready to convey the captives to assembly centres prior to sorting and deportation. The sorting was necessary because there were numerous excluded categories: pregnant women, women with children under two, wives of POWs, war widows, anyone married to a person who was exempt, and anyone registered as a UGIF employee.[173]

With military precision the arrest teams went to work, entering houses, apartment blocks, tenements, and hammering at doors with lists in hand. A contemporary publication by the resistance circulated a few months later gave an eyewitness account of what followed: 'They took away women and children over the age of two, women in the seventh and eighth, and even ninth month of pregnancy; sick people who were pulled out of their beds and carried on chairs or stretchers . . . it was especially the round-up of the children that must be emphasized. From the age of two they were considered candidates for the concentration camps! In a number of cases mothers were forcibly torn away from their little ones. Screaming and weeping filled the streets.' But the rumour mill had worked so effectively that thousands of men had taken care not to be at home. Foreign Jews who had grown used to police raids since the 1930s needed little warning and they knew what to do.

Many had prepared hiding places. A significant number of the police officers were unhappy at the job and leaked information to people they knew. Others knocked at a door once or twice and then gave up. Some turned a blind eye when they saw a Jew slipping out of a back entrance or down an alleyway. At the last moment the communist underground issued a warning in Yiddish, although it had limited distribution. By the end of the day the police had netted 11,363, far short of their goal. Further raids on 17 July brought the total up to 12,884. But this tally included 3,031 men, 5,802 women, and no fewer than 4,051 children.[174]

Nearly 5,000 were sent directly to Drancy, which now doubled as a transit camp. Over 8,000 Jews were bussed to the Vélodrome d'Hiver (popularly abbreviated to Vel' d'Hiv), a cycledrome in the 15th arrondissement, and held there for up to five days. Conditions in Vel' d'Hiv were terrible. It was very hot, but there was no water supply and only a few toilets. About a dozen nurses and doctors attempted to cope with a horde of distressed, dehydrated adults and children, many of whom were unwell when they were brought in. The scene was chaotic. A non-Jewish care worker who volunteered to help testified that 'Nothing had been done in advance for them. There wasn't even straw. The internees were "installed" on the bleachers or sitting on the ground. At night the children lay on the ground and the adults stayed seated . . . There was no food for the first two days. Those who had not brought provisions with them remained with empty stomachs. There was no water to drink or to wash with. The toilets, twelve in number, soon became blocked . . . The screams of the children were deafening. It drove you crazy.' The saving grace of this disorganization was that it allowed numerous Jews to slip out and escape.[175]

Between 19 and 22 July, the Jews in the Vel' d'Hiv were removed in batches on foot to the Gare d'Austerlitz from whence they went by train to the transit camps at Pithiviers and Beaune-la-Rolande. Here they made do in wooden barracks until the next stage of their grim odyssey. Prior to that, however, the Germans had to make a crucial decision: would the children be deported? The original plan excluded the very young and the very old. When French officials intimated that they were willing to include juveniles, Dannecker had asked Eichmann for instructions. It was not until 20 July that word came from Berlin: the children could be sent east too. As a result, between 31 July and 7 August, four trains carried adults with older children direct to Auschwitz. All of those on the first transport were registered in the camp;

the others were subject to selections. The transport of 5 August was the first from which the majority were murdered on arrival.[176]

The remaining children were sent to Drancy. At the trial of Adolf Eichmann in Jerusalem in 1961, Georges Wellers, a member of the Jewish camp staff, recalled the state they were in. 'These children arrived at Drancy after already having been completely neglected for two or three weeks at Beaune-la-Rolande and Pithiviers – they arrived with dirty, torn clothes in a very bad condition, often without buttons, often with one of their shoes completely missing, with sores on their bodies. They nearly all had diarrhoea; they were incapable of going down into the courtyard where there were lavatories. So sanitary slop pails were put on the landings, but the small infants were incapable of even using these slop pails which were too big for them . . .' The children were subsequently distributed amongst the transports that departed between 17 and 31 August. By then they had been sundered from their parents for weeks and were deeply distressed. Those with older siblings had someone to assist them; but many infants were entirely alone. Wellers described what it was like on the days children were deported. 'They were woken up early, at five o'clock in the morning; they were given coffee. They had woken up badly, in a bad mood. At five o'clock in the morning, even in the month of August in Paris, it is still very dark; it is still almost night, and when they wanted them to come down into the courtyard, it was usually very difficult. So the women volunteers tried through persuasion to get the older ones to come down first, but several times it happened that the children began to cry and struggle. It was impossible to bring them down into the courtyard of the camp, and so policemen had to go up into the rooms and take in their arms the children who were struggling and screaming. They took them down into the courtyard.'[177]

At Drancy the Germans confiscated whatever valuables the Jews had with them and filtered out anyone who had been detained inappropriately. Representatives of UGIF and Amelot, the immigrant welfare association, applied to the Germans to remove those who were French-born or protected under other headings. Nearly 1,000, including 192 French-born children, were plucked out. More controversially, UGIF supplied food and clothing to the detainees and equipped them for their journey to the east. Between 19 July and 31 August, sixteen transports departed from Le Bourget Station, near Drancy, with over 16,000 Jews on board.[178]

The *grand rafle* of 16–17 July rocked the Jews in France, but it did not immediately change them. Hélène Berr remarked in her diary on the following Saturday, 'On Thursday [16 July] I thought life might have ground to a halt. But it has gone on. It has resumed.' She returned to her studies in the library at the Sorbonne and maundered over a young man she fancied. Hélène did not panic, go underground or flee – although her family considered moving to the Free Zone. The assertion of normality was not for lack of information about the horrors that had spilled onto the streets of Montmartre and the Fauberg Saint-Denis. Rather, she felt defiant and she was boosted by the 'sympathy of the people in the street, on the metro. Men and women look at you with such goodness that it fills your heart with inexpressible feeling.' The assault on the Jews actually made her feel more in common with other French people. 'Superficial distinctions of race, religion and social class are no longer the issue ... there is unity against evil, and communion in suffering.' Hélène was also reassured to learn that army veterans and French citizens, like her father, who was still languishing in Drancy, were held back. A colleague at the UGIF office where she volunteered warned her that 'it would soon be the turn of women who were French citizens' but she seemed unable to grasp the implications for herself. Even as trains were rolling eastwards she lost herself in books and boys. 'We spent a marvellous afternoon in the library', she wrote on 26 July, 'listening to records, with the windows open to an infinitely tranquil yet buzzing sun-drenched garden.'[179]

It is estimated that 15,000 Jews, mainly men, successfully evaded the great round-up in Paris. The results were so poor that the Germans looked to the unoccupied zone to make up the numbers. Thousands of foreign-born Jews lived in the major cities there and thousands more, like Irène Némirovsky, had arrived from the north as refugees in 1940. The action on 16–17 July had triggered a further flight south, covertly assisted by UGIF and the Amelot committee. This influx had not gone unnoticed and there was considerable resentment against refugees. At a time of growing scarcity the newcomers were blamed for shortages and any with money were typically suspected of black market activity. Even so, identifying and locating Jews in the unoccupied zone was not straightforward. They were unmarked and, until December 1942, personal identification papers did not have to indicate if the bearer was Jewish. Unfortunately, though, Lambert had agreed to send the CGQJ the lists of Jews registered with UGIF in the south. The CGQJ immediately shared the information with the Sipo-SD. In any case, many of the foreign Jews were congregated in the internment camps and, hence, sitting ducks. Irène Némirovsky, who had found refuge at Issy-l'Évêque, was actually arrested on 13 July, before the main sweep, but was moved to Pithiviers and placed aboard a transport on 17 July packed with a thousand other foreign Jews. She died of 'flu' a month after her arrival in Auschwitz.[180]

René Bousquet had agreed with Dannecker to supply 10,000 Jews from the unoccupied zone. On 5 August he sent instructions to his prefects specifying who was to be included or excluded. Potential deportees had to be foreign Jews aged 18–60 years. The police were to leave pregnant women and nursing mothers, invalids, veterans of the Great War and their families, anyone married to a French citizen or with a French-born child, and essential workers. Any Jew married to someone in one of these categories was also exempted. The removals began with the camps, starting at Gurs, which was the miserable home of the Jews expelled from Baden Württemburg in 1940. In Noé, Récébédou, Rivesaltes, Le Vernet and Les Milles screening commissions briskly sifted out those who were exempt. The Jewish relief organizations used this sorting process as an opportunity to argue vigorously for every plausible case. OSE, the Jewish children's welfare organization, moved quickly to extract French-born youngsters. Agents of UGIF and rabbis who had served as military chaplains contested so many cases that even though 3,436 Jews were sent north to Drancy, the French authorities were still over 5,000 short of the target. Consequently, Bousquet relaxed the exemptions, ordered round-ups in the major cities, and sent police units to scour convents and remote villages. The results were still disappointing: in Marseilles, Nice and Lyons, Bousquet estimated that 40–75 per cent of the foreign Jews got away. Of 6,701 arrested Jews, 5,259 were eventually dispatched to Drancy. Further raids added another 1,113. By November, seventeen trains had carried 11,012 Jews from the Free Zone to Drancy and thence to Auschwitz.[181]

Raymond-Raoul Lambert anguished, 'the persecutions in the Occupied Zone are being redoubled. They are now arresting women and children, and deporting men *en masse* . . . Where is France now if it is letting innocent citizens be tortured without protest?' The deportations demanded a response, yet the leadership of the Jewish population found it hard to establish common ground. Lambert travelled to Vichy to meet Jacques Helbronner, president of the Consistoire, only to discover that

'The fate of the foreigners doesn't move him in the least.' When UGIF joined forces with the Consistoire to send a deputation to Laval, Helbronner refused to interrupt his summer holiday to join them. He insisted on keeping his privileged access to Laval to himself. The deputation that saw the Vichy premier on 6 August returned empty-handed. Laval insisted that it was 'legitimate for France to send foreigners to Germany; it can do anything it likes with them'. Lambert recorded that 'Mr Laval did not respond to the humanitarian and legal arguments put forward by the representatives of the charities . . .'[182]

Three days later, the head of UGIF was in the thick of efforts to save Jews in the Free Zone from deportation. It was symptomatic of the conflicted role played by UGIF that on the one hand he was supervising the provisioning of deportation trains, while on the other he was battling to get individuals deferred or released. On 10 August he went to the Marseilles prefecture with a list of French-born children in Les Milles and then to the camp itself, where he was forced to behold 'a heartrending spectacle. Buses are taking away seventy children from their parents who are to depart that evening. I have arranged for the children to leave first so they will not see their parents subjected to the roll call . . . We have to hold the fathers and mothers back as the buses leave the courtyard. What wailing and tears, what gestures as each poor father, faced with the moment of deportation, caresses the face of a son or daughter as if to imprint it on his fingertips! Mothers are screaming in despair and the rest of us cannot hold back our own tears . . '. The roll call was held under a blazing sun and many deportees collapsed. Some gendarmes showed their distaste for the mission, but the next day, 'brutal policemen who do not speak their language' loaded the Jews onto railroad cars. Forty were 'delivered up because they are Jews, by my country which had promised them asylum, and handed them over to those who will be their executioners. There are children, old people, war veterans, women, disabled people, old men . . . I cannot watch . . . I hide where I can weep.'[183]

Lambert returned to Vichy and demanded that police officials respect the privileges accorded to UGIF officials, war veterans and those holding emigration visas. On this trip he managed to see Darquier de Pellepoix, only to realize that the boss of the CGQJ was 'sidelined with regard to the deportation measures'. He cannily observed that 'This is a strange regime, whose victims are called upon to witness its administrative disorder.' Back at Les Milles in early September he again fought to get people deferred, but found himself rescuing deportees whom he had pulled off the trains days earlier. To his dismay, on one occasion he saw the police commander, desperate to fill two empty wagons, abandon any pretence of selection and arrange for the inmates to draw lots to determine who would board. When Lambert spotted that one of the victims was a distinguished Viennese publisher, he lost his composure. In his diary he reconstructed the scene: 'I can't stand it anymore! I rush across the courtyard like a madman. "You can't deport a Knight of the Legion d'Honneur," I tell the commandant. "Go and get him!" I push the guards apart, grab Fischer by the arm, and put him behind me . . .'[184]

By the beginning of September, the Germans had deported 32,130 Jews to Auschwitz on thirty-two transports. Yet they were still short of their target. The result was a further frenzy of round-ups in Paris aimed at Jews whose nationality had previously protected them. On 24 September, French police seized 1,594 Romanian Jews; five days later it was the turn of 1,700 Belgians; and on 5 November 1,060 Jews of Greek nationality. Eventually Knochen and Röthke were able to add 6,766 foreign Jews to the roster of the deported. However, they now faced a public opinion backlash and Vichy officials warned that massive actions were no longer desirable. The day after the Romanian Jews were grabbed, Knochen informed Himmler that 'It will no longer be possible to evacuate larger contingents of Jews.' The last transport departed from Drancy for Auschwitz on 11 November. By then, 42,500 Jews had been deported, most in just a five-week stretch from 26 July to 1 September. A handful stopped at Kosel, in Upper Silesia, where several hundred young men and women were taken off and assigned to slave labour, a faint trace of the original scheme to deport Jews to the east to replace the labour of Russian POWs.[185]

Until the large-scale round-ups in the summer of 1942, the French public had been largely indifferent to the fate of the Jews. The arrests and punitive deportations earlier in the year had met with silence from intellectuals, resistance circles and the Churches. However, the spectacle of women and children being herded through the streets and driven towards cattle trucks heading towards an 'unknown destination' provoked a wave of repulsion. Churchmen from all the main denominations gave voice to this disquiet. Just a few days after the *rafle* in Paris, Cardinal Suhard, Archbishop of Paris, addressed a letter of protest to Pétain and circulated the contents amongst his priests. The following month, Cardinal Gerlier, Archbishop of Lyons and Primate of Gaul, made a public declaration of dismay. He was echoed by Pastor Boegner, president of the Protestant Federation of France. On 23 August, Cardinal Saliège of Toulouse issued a powerfully worded pastoral letter: 'In our own diocese, the most disturbing scenes have taken place in the camps of Noé and Récébédou. Jews are human beings. Foreigners are human beings. All is not permitted against them, against these men, against these women, against these fathers and these mothers of families. They belong to humankind; they are our brothers as are so many others. A Christian may not forget this.' The cardinal's letter was subsequently used in a broadcast by the French service of the BBC. A month later, the National Council of the Reformed Church convened in emergency session to register the alarm of the Protestant population. Pastor Boegner reminded his community that Jesus was a Jew.[186]

The deportations occasioned a flurry of articles in the underground press. *Le Franc-Tireur* called on its readers to 'Expose the horrors of Paris; express your solidarity for all the victims – shelter them, hide them, refuse to allow France to be soiled.' *Libération* (in the southern zone) distributed 70,000 copies of an issue featuring accounts of the Vel' d'Hiv' atrocity. Father Chaillet, writing in *Cahiers du Témoignage Chrétien*, exclaimed, 'We must cry out to the unknowing and uncaring world our disgust and our indignation that such a manhunt could be conducted on our soil.' In October 1942, *Combat* declared that 'foreign Jews, the vanguard of French Jewry and all the French people, are suffering the Nazi persecution and enduring a painful martyrdom. Their martyrdom and persecution make them more precious. All those who suffer at the hands of the Germans, whether Jewish or not, whether Communists or not, are our brothers.' A communist leaflet urged those who read it to 'Shelter, protect, hide Jewish children and their families; save the honour of France.' In mid-September, Jean Moulin, head of the Gaullist resistance in occupied France, reported to the movement's London headquarters that 'The arrests of foreign Jews and their handing over to the Germans and even more so the disgraceful measure adopted with regard to Jewish children, of which the general public was initially unaware, have begun to stir the popular conscience.' It was the first time that Moulin had adverted explicitly to anti-Jewish measures. The Free French based in London amplified the clandestine press. There were seven references to the deportations in BBC French service transmissions between 1 August and 15 September 1942. André Labarthe, founder of the Gaullist journal in London *La France libre*, warned listeners, 'Frenchmen! You will not let this happen. You will unite against the rising plague in which you can all perish: Jews, Bretons, Lorrainers, Basques . . .' As Labarthe's words suggest, the Gaullists, no less than the Communists, were careful to frame the fate of the Jews in universalistic terms and to depict it as the prelude to an assault on all French people. Their admonitions were not fantasy; soon the resistance was inveighing against Sauckel's conscription of French workers for German industry, the Service du travail obligatoire (STO). Before the year was out, the focus of underground propaganda had shifted to the deportation of French workers. However, the enforcement of the STO gave a fillip to the resistance and stimulated support for men and women going into hiding to evade the taskmasters. Even if for the wrong reasons, it generated a sense of solidarity with Jews on the run, albeit in very different circumstances.[187]

From autumn 1942, the regime and the public had a sharper sense of what deportation entailed, even if the details were confused. As the public recoiled, the Vichy politicians reconsidered the strategy of co-operation. Their caution was deepened by a decisive turn in the war. After two weeks of heavy fighting against far stronger forces, on 4 November Rommel ordered what remained of the Italian–German force to retreat from the El Alamein line. Four days later, British and American troops invaded French-controlled Morocco and Algeria, pro-voking the Germans to occupy the Free Zone. Then news came from the eastern front that German forces were in deep trouble as the result of a major Soviet counter-offensive around Stalingrad. The Germans would never again enjoy such extensive collaboration with their anti-Jewish policy in France; on the contrary, they would encounter more and more obstruction.[188]

The 'final solution' in Belgium, the Netherlands and Norway

Although Eichmann issued uniform instructions to his Judenreferenten on 11 June, they had to operate under diverse conditions. In Belgium, Kurt Asche was hemmed in by the military administration and had few resources at his disposal. There was no Higher SS Police Leader in place and relatively few Sipo-SD personnel. However, he was able to obtain army support for certain measures. In November 1941 the army com-mand agreed to establish a unitary Jewish representative body, the

Association of Jews in Belgium (Association des Juifs en Belgique, AJB). The Germans appointed Chief Rabbi Solomon Ullmann as president, flanked by a number of equally respectable figures. Asche aspired to enrol all Jews in Belgium under the umbrella of the AJB, but they proved less than obliging. When the registration was carried out during March–April 1942, thousands ignored the threat of punishment for evasion. While the majority of Belgian Jews obeyed, the mass of foreign Jews steered clear. There was similar resistance to imposition of the yellow star. Even the AJB refused to assist the Germans distribute the hated badge. Anne Somerhausen, a left-wing parliamentarian who kept a diary during the occupation, marvelled that the stars appeared one day and then vanished the next.[189]

Moshe Flinker, a sixteen-year-old Dutch boy, was amongst the foreign Jews who opted to go unmarked. His family had moved from The Hague to Brussels in mid-1942 and started living there without the star. At great cost his father purchased residence permits that offered the family a degree of security. Torn from school, in an alien environment, Moshe had time on his hands to reflect on their situation. Orthodox in his beliefs and outlook, he interpreted the fate of the Jews through Jewish history and scripture. 'What other purpose could he [God] have in allowing such things to befall us?' he wondered. 'I feel certain that further troubles will not bring any Jews back to the paths of righteousness; on the contrary, I think that upon experiencing such great anguish they will think that there is no god at all in the universe . . .' The only way Moshe could make sense of the disaster was that it presaged redemption, that God would save his people and thereby prove his sovereignty over all mankind and all of creation. According to Moshe's philosophy, the Germans were tools of the Almighty.[190]

According to Eichmann's instructions the Sipo-SD was charged with deporting 10,000 Jews between 16 and 40 years of age, although 10 per cent of each projected transport could include non-working Jews. As in France, the Germans planned to begin with foreign and stateless Jews. Asche hoped to assemble them under the guise of a call-up for labour service, Arbeiteinsatz, issued by the AJB. In late July the notices went out over the name of Maurice Benedictus, a cigar manufacturer and member of the AJB council. However, the response was paltry. Asche was compelled to resort to *razzias* in the streets of districts in Antwerp, Brussels, Liège and Charleroi where the Jewish population was concentrated. For these to be effective he needed manpower, but the Belgian civil service and police authorities proved refractory. Apart from two large-scale operations in Antwerp in August, the local police played little part. Instead Asche relied on 1,800 Feldgendarmerie, military police, and paramilitary formations of the Belgian fascist parties, the Flemish Rexists and the Walloon Vlaams Nationaal Verbond, plus a unit of Flemish Waffen-SS volunteers. The Jews caught in the street raids followed those who had volunteered for labour service to Mechelen (Malines). Here the Sipo-SD had hurriedly established a transit camp in a former army barracks, the Dossin Casern, that was located conveniently close to major rail lines criss-crossing Belgium and also heading eastward.[191]

The Germans faced concerted resistance. Anne Somerhausen heard that mayors started quickly marrying Jewish women to Belgian men so that they would gain Belgian nationality. Soon after the labour call-up was announced, Jewish communists broke into the offices of the AJB and set fire to the files containing the names of registered Jews. On 29 August, a Jewish member of the communist Partisans Armés assassinated Robert Holzinger, the AJB official responsible for assembling Jews for deportation. Rabbi Ullmann, unwilling to give further legitimacy to the deportations, resigned from the AJB the following month. When the Sipo-SD reacted by arresting him and the rest of the Jewish leadership this only served further to undermine the appearance of an innocuous mobilization for labour service and thousands more Jews went underground. Meanwhile, Jewish communists and left-wing Zionists set up a Comité de Défense des Juifs, to help those going into hiding. The Comité was affiliated to the main Belgian underground, which was already well organized and strong.[192]

Despite the initially unpropitious circumstances and furious reaction, in just one hundred days the security police managed to net and deport 50 per cent more Jews than their quota required. Seventeen trains carried 16,882 Jews from Belgium to Auschwitz between 4 August and 31 October, sometimes departing at the rate of two per day.[193]

In the Netherlands, the Germans inaugurated the deportations by requiring Jewish refugees from the Reich to present themselves at the Central Office for Jewish Emigration, supposedly for labour service. When the responsibility for issuing the notices was handed down to the Jewish council there was unrest in its ranks and calls for non-cooperation. After an anguished session on 13 February 1942, the Joodse Raad, the Jewish council, agreed to comply. At this Heinz

Hesdörffer remarked bitterly, 'Dutch Jews rejoiced, glad to be rid of the German refugees and to be safe themselves. "We are Dutchmen, nothing can happen to us." But the joy was short-lived.' On 29 April, the Germans informed Abraham Asscher and David Cohen that from 2 May all Jews in the Netherlands would be obliged to wear the yellow star. Asscher and Cohen protested, but then referred the matter to an emergency meeting of the Jewish council. A majority agreed to accept the imposition and to distribute the badge. When Jews appeared on the streets bedecked with the star, they experienced a good deal of sympathy and there were countless gestures of solidarity. Locals joked that the Waterlooplein, heart of the Jewish quarter, should be renamed Place d'Étoile. But smiles did nothing to alleviate the relentless pressure from the German administration. Around the same time, Jews from the provinces were required to move into the Jewish district of Amsterdam, giving it more and more the character of a crowded ghetto. The council had to accommodate and support them.[194]

In April, Eichmann inspected Westerbork and told Willi Zöpf, his representative in the Netherlands, that transportations of Jews to the east would commence in the summer. At the meeting of Judenrefernten on 11 June he specified that 25,000 Jews would be deported from the Netherlands, with the customary exclusions. However, ten days later the number jumped to 40,000 to compensate for the decrease in the total anticipated coming from France. On 26 June, aus der Fünten summoned Abraham Asscher and Edwin Sluzker, an Austrian Jewish refugee who acted as the liaison with the Zentralstelle, and told them that the Jewish council had to arrange for Jewish men and women aged 16–40, including Dutch citizens, to report at the Zentralstelle for labour duty in Germany, at the rate of 800 per day. Again, Asscher and Cohen remonstrated and, again, the Joodse Raad held hours of agonizing deliberations. On 4 July, the Jewish leadership agreed to comply, on condition that the Germans agreed to a raft of exemptions. This suited German thinking perfectly: they had discovered from experience that as long as one group of Jews thought they were immune they would be willing to help remove another, saving the occupiers a great deal of manpower and effort as well as preserving the appearance of order.[195]

The very next day the call-up notices for the 'Arbeitseinsatz im Osten', labour service in the east, went out and 'all hell broke out at the headquarters of the Jewish council'. Jacob Presser, later to chronicle these events as a historian, recalled that 'People chased after papers, after exemptions, begged for a week's delay, produced doctor's certificates to the effect that they were dope addicts, mutilated or invalids . . . They lined up for specialists' certificates, legal advice, testimonials from their religious leaders or from the "friend" of an important German who might use his influence. If only one could find recognition as an "indispensable" Jew!' Corruption and favouritism proliferated. Heinz Hesdörffer, who had secured work with a refugee aid committee in Arnhem under the auspices of Gertrude van Tijn, witnessed the 'Dreadful scenes [that] took place in the hallways of the Nieuwe Keizersgracht [the Jewish council building] . . . Old men, pregnant women, children from the Amsterdam Jewish quarters in their shredded raggedy clothing, cheek by jowl with gentlemen and ladies of the Zuid, the most elegant neighbourhood, who had their summons in their pockets and also tried to save themselves until the last moment. Day and night the howling cries could be heard of those sentenced to death, but not everyone could be employed.'[196]

As in Belgium, thousands refused to obey the notices to report. Consequently, the Germans staged a massive raid on the Jewish quarter, grabbing 700 people whom they declared would be held hostage until 4,000 Jews heeded the summons. This tactic worked: for several weeks the Jewish council ensured that the quotas were filled. Jews poured into the courtyard of the Zentrallstelle building, where they were processed and shipped on to Westerbork via the Amsterdam central station. Nevertheless, by early August the numbers had fallen back again and the Germans staged further round-ups. They also adopted new tactics and began to raid the homes of Jews at night. A special battalion of the Amsterdam police carried out these nocturnal raids. The Schalkhaar unit, named after the police academy where it was trained, was formed in 1941 by the chief constable of the Amsterdam police, Sybren Tulp. It was recruited mainly from men with a military background and operated out of barracks, unlike the regular police. Tulp, a member of the Dutch Nazi Party, also set up a Jewish Bureau within the force. Led by a fanatical anti-Semite, Dahmen von Bucholz, the Bureau's mission was to pursue Jews suspected of infringing anti-Jewish regulations. Even with these extra resources it proved difficult to fill the trains departing from the central station for Westerbork. To make up the numbers, Hanns Rauter, the Higher SS Police Leader, emptied the labour camps where Dutch and foreign Jews had been working since 1941. Instead of using the Zentralstelle as the assembly point, the Germans pressed into use a theatre, the Hollandse Schouwburg, that was close to the Jewish district. From October, Jews seized in raids were sorted there before the unlucky were escorted to waiting deportation trains.[197]

On arrival at Westerbork, the Dutch Jews had an unwelcome surprise: the camp was run entirely by German Jews who had been incarcerated since late 1941, and who felt little sympathy for the newcomers. Spread over a 60-acre site surrounded by agricultural land, Westerbork had been established in 1939 to accommodate German Jewish refugees. It was equipped with a fine hospital, a quarantine unit and workshops. Inmates also laboured in farms and market gardens in the vicinity. During the first years of the occupation the camp was under the Dutch Ministry of Justice, but on 1 July 1942 the German security police took over and transformed it into a transit camp. The first commandant was Albert Gemmeker. He appointed Kurt Schlesinger, a German Jew, to head the internal camp administration. Schlesinger in turn appointed German Jews to most positions of power and took charge of the central registry which determined who would go east. Presser commented that 'these paladins, nearly all of them German Jews, had control over life and death and were accordingly flattered, influenced, bribed, envied and hated, and, indeed, loathed.' Schlesinger maintained order in the camp through the Ordedienst, Order Service, and the Fliegende Kolonne, flying column, many of whom were ex-soldiers. On Tuesdays, when the weekly transport was filled, these men ensured that the unfortunates selected for departure were boarded. Since the exterior of the camp was patrolled by Dutch police, the Germans were able to run it with the minimum of personnel.[198]

The Joodse Raad tried desperately to protect as many Jews as possible. Cohen asked for 35,000 exemptions and managed to get the Germans to grant 17,500. Those exempted received a number and a stamp in their identification papers. The fortunate included 1,500 baptized Jews, 1,800 whose racial status was under investigation, 800 who were protected by certain Germans, 3,800 working in the armaments, fur making and diamond cutting industries, plus 1,800 employees of the Jewish council. Unfortunately, a system that was supposed to create order and offer protection actually 'caused moral disruption on a vast scale'. In Presser's scathing analysis, 'by granting temporary privileges to a minority, they [the Germans] succeeded in liquidating the rest without too much fuss or bother'.[199]

For a considerable while, the Dutch Jewish leadership was not sure

about the meaning of 'Arbeitseinsatz im Osten'. They knew that deportation to Mauthausen was almost certainly a death sentence, but Dutch
and foreign Jews had been sent to forced labour on fortifications along
the North Sea coast for many months. The Germans added to their confusion by compelling nearly one hundred Dutch Jews who arrived in
Auschwitz-Birkenau to send home postcards indicating that they were
in good health. Rather than warn Jews or advise non-compliance, the
Jewish council sought to ease their passage eastwards. Gertrude van
Tijn's refugee committee turned its energies towards providing backpacks, mess tins, clothing and food for deportees. Nor did Dutch civil
servants raise their voice against the deportations; they kept up the
practice of avoiding conflict with the occupiers in order to preserve
authority over what they considered the core interests of the Dutch
people.[200]

Although broadcasts by the BBC Dutch service in the summer
of 1942 referred to the mass murder of Jews in Poland, only a minority
of Dutchmen connected this with the deportations. Most continued to
think that Jews were being sent to atrocious work camps. Nevertheless,
Jews did not meekly obey their leaders, be they foreign-born or Dutch
citizens. In December 1941, Lodewijk Visser, who had been removed
from the supreme court becasue he was a Jew, set up a committee to
defend Jewish rights and refused to accept an ID card stamped with a 'J'.
He died before his protest could have a wider impact, or before the Germans dealt with him. Walter Süsskind, a former businessman, organized
the rescue of hundreds of children from the Hollandse Schouwburg
until he was deported to Theresienstadt in 1943 (and from there to
Auschwitz-Birkenau, where he perished along with his family). Over
4,000 Jews used their Sephardi origins to get themselves classified as Portuguese nationals while several thousand more delayed deportation by
contesting whether they were Jewish at all. The Zionist youth movement
organized groups of a few dozen to head south, passing borders illegally
or with fake papers in the hope of reaching the Pyrenees and crossing
into Spain. By far the most common form of resistance lay in concealment. It is estimated that 25,000 Jews went underground, usually with
the assistance of friendly Dutch citizens. The best-known case is that of
the Frank family. But Anne Frank's father was untypical in terms of the
accommodation and resources at his disposal as well as the network of
loyal helpers he enjoyed. Few Jews could find a place to hide, let alone
people they could rely on to supply them with food and other necessar-

ies, even if they had the money for all that. In any case, most feared discovery and a sentence to Mauthausen, about which they knew something, more than deportation to a destination about which there was still ambiguity. Those who were still at large at the end of the year began to hope for a German military collapse and thought that if they could hold on for a bit longer they would be saved.[201]

Eichmann was greatly satisfied by the apparently smooth removal of Jews from the Netherlands. Between July and December 1942, forty-two transports carried 38,606 Jews eastwards, to Auschwitz-Birkenau. Eighteen trains stopped at Kosel in Upper Silesia, where 3,500 young men and women were disembarked to join the workforce in labour camps. The process was certainly less fraught with difficulty than France, where the Germans had to deal with an independent government that had its own mind and two distinct zones of operation, or Belgium, where their quarry proved both refractory and elusive. Yet the system of voluntary reporting failed in Holland, too, and the Germans were forced to resort to round-ups that required extensive manpower as well as causing sympathy for their quarry. The high number deported from the Netherlands was in part the result of the pre-existing reservoir of victims in Westerbork and workers in labour camps plus their families. This enabled the deportation of 12,000 Jews in October 1942 alone, which was over a third of the number deported that year and 10 per cent of the total extracted from the Netherlands.[202]

It was also an extremely profitable enterprise. By May 1943, the Germans had emptied 17,225 houses and apartments. Hundreds of barges and rail freight wagons took the loot back to Germany, where it was distributed to members of the racial community who had been bombed out of their homes. The Aryanization authorities took over 20,000 properties, 560 mortgages, and a vast haul of diamonds. The fictive Lippmann–Rosenthal Bank, Liro, absorbed stolen cash, bank accounts, life insurance policies and debts owed to Jewish financiers. Liro even had a 'branch' in Westerbork that served to pick the Jews clean before they were shunted to their deaths. The Germans prattled endlessly about the attachment of Jews to money and their legendary greed, but in the course of destroying the Dutch Jewish community they demonstrated venality and avarice on an epic scale.[203]

In November, the attention of the SS Head Office in Berlin suddenly turned to Norway, a country with a tiny Jewish population. The 2,173 Jews, including Jewish refugees like Ruth Maier, had been relatively

untroubled until early 1942, when Vidkun Quisling assumed the leadership of a collaborationist government and proceeded to demonstrate his
concordance with wider Nazi goals. But the operation against the Jews
there was probably the last-minute substitute for a bigger action against
the Jews of Denmark. Werner Best, who had arrived in Copenhagen
from France in September, rapidly assessed the situation and worked
out that a move against the Danish Jews would trigger unrest and jeopardize the smooth flow of vital foodstuffs to the Reich. Because
Terboven and Quisling controlled the police and security forces in
Norway, that country was a softer target. The order was transmitted to
the Norwegian police on 23 October and Jewish men were arrested
three days later. The operation 'had plainly been prepared in a rush',
though. The security police made the arrests in commandeered taxis. In
total, 770 Jews were caught and deported. Some 930 fled across the long
border into Sweden, where they were offered a safe haven.[204]

In March 1942, Ruth Maier was living with the Strøm family in
Lillestrøm when she was required to register with the police. Before
then, the main restrictions she faced were the result of her refugee
status. She was unable to get a work permit and had spent most of the
previous year working as a volunteer for the national labour service
scheme. She visited the American Embassy several times to inquire into
the opportunities for emigration, but she was told the quota was full
until early in the following year. In June 1941 she was forced to give up
work on a farm near Stavanger after she was joined by her close friend
Gunvor Hofmo. Gunvor had recently been jailed for political activities,
but anti-Semitism aggravated their situation. 'They made an issue of my
"racial affiliations" and Gunvor's political beliefs', Ruth explained in her
diary. In the autumn she returned to her adoptive family and took a
course in stenography in Oslo. While she was training she met a group
of Jewish men, the first Jews she had encountered for a while. The effect
was startling: 'they have this completely – how shall I put it? – erotic
effect on me. They awaken a feeling of love within me. I feel myself
drawn to them.' Despite this affinity, she never felt that she completely
belonged with the Jewish people. When she came across a detachment
of Austrian mountain troops on leave from the north, she 'wanted to
talk to them. My people, I wanted to be able to say. And yet they're not
my people at all.'[205]

Unhappy in her adoptive home, Ruth decided to move to Oslo and
found lodgings in a hostel. She worked for a small business that pro-

duced souvenirs, took a class in drawing, and enjoyed her independence. Her friendship with Gunvor had its ups and downs and she started flirting with a sculptor for whom she modelled. Then, on 27 September she wrote in her diary that Terboven, the Reichskommissar for Norway, 'has written to our hostel requesting to know who lives here. I'm now just waiting to be thrown out any day. I will try to remain calm, I will not be seen crying, nor begging to stay here. In such moments I feel solidarity with all those others around me who are suffering in their country. It's a shame it is the mere fact we are Jews that makes us martyrs.' Two days later she reported, 'They're arresting Jews. All male Jews between the ages of 16 and 72. Jewish shops are closed . . . I just feel sick. I'm no longer proud to be a Jew . . . I'm tired of hearing that Jews are being arrested again. I think: why do they *bother*? . . . Oh! Just leave us in *peace*!' Ruth refused to abandon her Jewish affiliations but insisted on locating her plight in the context of what other oppressed people were suffering. 'They torture us because we're Jews. I'd like to be able to destroy this boundary that makes Jews into Jews.' Her entry ends, 'Perhaps they'll fetch me, too. Qui sait?'[206]

They did. On 26 November the Germans followed up the seizure of Jewish men by apprehending women and children. In the early hours, a pair of Norwegian policemen led Ruth and two other Jewish women from the hostel to a car and drove them to the harbour where they were embarked on the liner *Donau* along with 530 others. It set sail in the afternoon, but she had enough time to smuggle out a farewell note to her friend Gunvor. 'I think it's just as well that it has happened this way. Why shouldn't we suffer when there's so much suffering? Don't worry about me. Perhaps I wouldn't even change places with you.' The *Donau* docked in Stettin and from there the prisoners were entrained for Auschwitz-Birkenau. On arrival, 186 were registered in the camp while the rest were murdered in the gas chambers. All trace of Ruth ends there; she was twenty-two years old.[207]

In Poland

Following the deportations of January to May 1942, stability returned to the Lodz ghetto. At the start of June the population stood at 104,469, including a fresh batch of Jews who had been relocated from liquidated ghettos elsewhere in the Wartheland. There was an abundance of work.

Thousands of people were employed just sorting the baggage and goods that flowed into Hans Biebow's storehouses from defunct Jewish communities – 20 tons of footwear alone. Enough sewing machines arrived to equip new workshops to take in more orders. And there was no shortage: in July a German purchasing commission toured the factories and left the inhabitants with enough work for months to come. The ghetto was now producing snow uniforms for the Wehrmacht, jump suits for parachutists, padded caps for panzer crews and straw boots for infantrymen in winter. The AEG corporation opened an electrical engineering plant in the ghetto. Dawid Sierakowiak exulted, 'The ghetto keeps developing . . . All kinds of workshops are being created.' He was made a clerk in one of the enterprises and celebrated the 'colossal orders' that were coming in. However, although 70,000–80,000 were employed, that was not enough to guarantee everyone's safety. Rumkowski began a drive to train children to operate sewing machines and work as tailors.[208]

Even as the workforce grew, the rations shrank. The death rate rose, and productivity declined. On 2 August, the chronicle blandly quoted a report by the head of the health department that 'The ghetto is plagued by starvation oedema.' An essayist for the chronicle put things more graphically: 'Pale shadows trudge through the ghetto, with oedemic swellings on their legs and faces, people deformed and disfigured, whose only dream is to endure, survive . . .' The chronicle charted 13,000 deaths in the first seven months of the year; it was becoming impossible to bury the dead fast enough. Daily existence turned into a grinding routine, as described by Dawid Sierakowiak: 'One buys rations, eats the little food there is in them, starves while eating it, and after that keeps waiting obstinately, cautiously, and unshakenly until the end of this cursed, devilish war; the workshops, home, meals, reading, night with bedbugs and cockroaches, and all over again without end, ultimately losing strength, with diminishing efficiency of body and mind.'[209]

What made their lot harder to bear was the awareness amongst the average ghetto dweller that not everyone was suffering equally. In May, Dawid attended a concert that should have been the occasion for celebrating what Oskar Rosenfeld saw as 'proof positive of the indestructability of the Jewish spirit'. Instead it gave him a chance to survey, 'The whole of select society gathered, bloated and dressed up. The gap between the various classes of people in the ghetto grows wider and wider. Some steal food themselves, others feed themselves officially, while the rest are swelling up and dying of hunger.' Dawid discovered that his own father was stealing food from him. Nor was Rosenfeld oblivious to the corruption and grotesque inequality in the ghetto. He remarked that 'while a hundred thousand people go hungry, a few gluttons have strawberry preserves, condensed milk, wine, liqueurs, fine cigarettes and so on.'[210]

Morale was further sapped by the stories that the survivors of ghetto clearances, such as in Pabiance and Brzeziny, brought in with them. On the one hand it appeared that the Germans were prepared to break up families and just retain those who were capable of work, while on the other, the ability to work was itself no guarantee of survival. Dawid noted ominously that 'there are no elderly, children, or sick among them. Those able to work and those unable to work were killed without distinction.' The ghetto was plunged into depression by news of the deportations from Warsaw and the death of Czerniaków. These savagely implemented population movements bemused chronicle writers. 'It is difficult to discern any guidelines in all of this,' they exclaimed. At the end of August the writers despaired that 'the decentralization of our ghetto by means of mass resettlement remains, to this day, unexplained, and the fact that Jews are being resettled here from small towns in the vicinity as well defies reason.'[211]

Then, on 1 September, the Germans struck Lodz again. In accordance with Himmler's July diktat that only working Jews should be allowed to live in occupied Poland, Rumkowski was told that 25,000 Jews, including all those aged under ten and over sixty-five, had to go. The ghetto was stunned. Rumkowski triggered a lock-down and reinforced the Order Service with the firemen while the resettlement committee pored over the census data, block by block, to determine who would be deported. The men of the Order Service were told that if the target was achieved, their families would be spared. Within hours of the announcement the OS and German police were emptying the hospital and the old people's homes. 'Scenes from Dante took place when the sick were being loaded,' Dawid reported. 'People knew they were going to their deaths! They even fought the Germans and had to be thrown onto the trucks by force.' The sick and lame hurled themselves out of windows and dragged themselves to safety, only to hear that the Order Service had taken their relatives instead of them. Rosenfeld, at the Jewish council building, was handed a scrap of paper from the old-age home on which was scrawled 'Please save me, the home is surrounded. Rosa Steiner, writer, Vienna.' All production ceased because 'everyone's running to secure work assignments for those in their family who are unemployed; parents of the unfortunate children are trying to save them by any means'. Rumkowski sealed the registry office to prevent the falsification of ages on birth certificates or the issuance of bogus death notices.[212]

Young women in the ghetto were in multiple jeopardy, victims of Jewish men as much as the Germans. When Lucille Eichengreen went to a factory manager to plead with him to employ her sister, aged twelve, he asked what she would give in return. After she explained that she had no money, the man grinned and told her 'that was not what he had in mind'. Lucille was stunned that such things could occur 'even among our own'. Avraham Cytryn made a similar proposal to his sister Lucie after their mother was seized. 'Everyone tells me I have a beautiful sister. What good does that do me? Why don't you become the mistress of one of the privileged ones in the ghetto?' He sent her to a certain man and she returned hours later, 'literally torn to bits'. Her unspeakable sacrifice was pointless: their mother had already been released.[213]

Four days after receiving the fatal order, Rumkowski addressed his people from a platform in Firefighters' Square. 'A grievous blow has befallen the ghetto,' he intoned in a shaky voice. 'They are asking from it the best that it possesses – the children and the old people.' He had not been blessed with children, he told them, but he had devoted his best years to their welfare. 'I never imagined that my own hands would have to deliver the sacrifice to the altar. In my old age, I must stretch out my hands and beg: Brothers and sisters give them over to me! Fathers and mothers: Give me your children!' He thought they would be left in peace after the hospitals and the homes for the elderly were emptied but 'it turned out that something different was predestined for us. The luck of the Jews is of course thus; always to suffer more and worse, particularly in wartime.' The day before, the Germans had said to him: send 20,000 or 'We will do it'. His only thought was: how many could he save? He consulted his closest colleagues and together concluded that, 'as difficult as this will be for us, we must take into our own hands the carrying out of the order. I have to carry out this difficult and bloody operation. I must cut off limbs in order to save the body! I must take children because, if not, others could also, God forbid, be taken.' At this point a great wailing rose from the crowd of thousands in the square. Rumkowski did not even attempt to offer consolation. Instead he confessed that 'I have come like a robber to take away from you the best from your own hearts!' He had asked to keep those aged over nine, but the Germans refused. So, he pleaded, let him have the children sick with tuberculosis, the ones doomed by ill-health. Then he began to fall apart, stuttering and repeating himself. 'A broken man is standing before you. Don't envy me. It is the most difficult decree I have ever had to carry out. I extend to you my broken, trembling arms and beg: Give the victims into my hands, in order through them to avoid additional victims, in order to protect a kehillah [community] of 100,000 Jews. They promised me so: if we ourselves will deliver the victims, here will be calm.' When adults shouted that they would go or urged Rumkowski to take children from large families he waved aside their protestations. 'I don't have any strength to conduct discussions with you,' he concluded and reminded the upturned faces of the fate that overcame the small communities around them. There was no alternative than to accede.[214]

In his diary of the great deportation, Josef Zelkowicz captured the last moments that mothers and fathers were able to spend with their ill-starred progeny. Fathers tried to remain calm; mothers fed and coddled their babies one last time. He reflected acridly that it was easy for the Beirat to call on the ordinary inhabitants to make the sacrifice when 'they managed to secure from the Germans exemptions from the deportation for children of the workshop directors, firemen, police, doctors, instructors, the Beirat, and the devil knows who else.' The Germans would get persons 'who, though able to work, will nevertheless be sacrificed to make up for the "connected" children and elderly.' At 7 a.m., he watched the Order Service 'load the old men and women onto the wagons like pieces of scrap metal'. In some places there was fighting as parents refused to hand over their young. Zelkowicz wondered, 'What happened to the Jewish police that prompted it to undertake this task? Were they driven out of their minds? Were their hearts excised and replaced with stones?' Or were they 'drugged' by the promise of protection for their relatives and extra rations? It went on for days. Elderly women dyed their hair and applied rouge to make themselves appear younger. 'People who are hiding their children in garrets, toilets, and other holes are losing their heads out of despair.' It was all to no avail. Notwithstanding the best efforts of the OS and the Elder's assurances, within days the Germans were in the ghetto. Hans Biebow himself took part in the round-ups, selecting those unfit for work from crowds of Jews herded into the courtyards of tenement blocks. In the course of the great action, 15,859 Jews were deported, 600 were shot in the ghetto and 20 were hanged for attempting to escape the maelstrom.[215]

Afterwards the ghetto looked and felt completely different. Rumkowski was a shrunken figure, his authority further diminished when the Germans redesignated his domain a labour camp and took a more direct role in its internal management. The medical services had completely collapsed and disease spread unchecked. Rosenfeld had the odd sensation that he was no longer among Jews since there was no one left wearing traditional Jewish garb, beards or side-curls. During the high holy days, everyone worked. But with the population now standing at 89,325 there was a bit more food to go round. On Simchat Torah, the festival to celebrate the start of a new cycle of readings from the five books of Moses, he attended a service at which a meal was served complete with schnapps, cognac, cholent (stew), peas, potatoes, meat and honeycakes. In November the Germans permitted the delivery of 5 million cigarettes – a year's supply. As the year drew to a close Dawid Sierakowiak was also cheered by the news of the Allied landings in North Africa, Rommel's retreat and tidings of a spectacular Russian offensive. The ghetto-cum-labour camp felt joy mixed with fear of German revenge.[216]

The Axis, the Allies and the 'final solution'

At the high point of the Wehrmacht's advance in the summer of 1942, when German spearheads were closing on Stalingrad and surging into the Caucasus, when it appeared that victory was just around the corner, the Jewish department of the Reichssicherheitshauptamt in Berlin in concert with the Foreign Office redoubled its efforts to persuade Axis partners and client states to settle the Jewish question in their respective countries by deporting their Jews to Germany. The results were mixed and the longer victory at the front was delayed, the harder the task became.

The Foreign Office began by politely asking the Bulgarians if it would be acceptable for the German authorities to deport Jews with Bulgarian citizenship who were resident in the Reich and other countries in western Europe. The Bulgarians agreed to this request, which removed at least one category of foreign Jews from the list of those excluded from round-ups. In August the Romanians gave their consent to a similar proposition. However, the Hungarian government flatly refused to allow the Germans to deport any of its nationals. Since March 1942, Miklós Kállay had been prime minister in Budapest and he was increasingly uneasy about every aspect of the alliance with Germany. In reply, the Wilhelmstrasse curtly advised the Hungarians to repatriate their Jewish nationals by the end of the year, after which they would be considered fair game. The Italians also rebuffed the German request, arguing that its Jewish citizens domiciled abroad fulfilled important functions for the domestic economy. Eichmann's men in office IVB4 of the RSHA had more success with Germany's lesser clients. In July, they triggered the deportation of Jews from Croatia. Most of the Jewish population there was already interned but at the end of the month those still at liberty were summoned for registration purposes. Two weeks later the first train steamed from Zagreb to Auschwitz bearing 1,200 Jews. Four transports followed, carrying 5,000 more to the gas chambers.[217]

To begin with it looked as if Romania would be equally complaisant. Deportations to Transnistria had largely ended, but in February 1942 the government imposed a central body – the Centralna Evreilor din Romania – on the Romanian Jews which portended nothing but ill. The following month all Jews aged 20 to 57 were obliged to register for forced labour and in early June Emil Dorian noted rumours sweeping the community to the effect that another wave of deportations was about to begin. Actually it was not until July that Gustav Richter, Eichmann's representative in Bucharest, met Deputy Prime Minister Mihai Antonescu to discuss the removal of Romanian Jews to camps in the Lublin area. Because he acted without consulting or going through the German Foreign Office there was a delay in the follow-up which was to prove critical. While on a visit to Hitler's Ukrainian headquarters in September Mihai Antonescu reiterated his commitment to the eradication of the Romanian Jews, but the government was actually having second thoughts. When the deportation experts in Berlin held a planning meeting on 26–27 September no one from Bucharest showed up. The following month Marshal Ion Antonescu halted the preparations to expel Romania's Jewish citizens and three days later suspended any further deportations to Transnistria. He informed Richter that 'with regard to the treatment of the Jews, I am not backing down, but I am not escalating either'. In fact, the regime had performed a complete U-turn. Not only had it safeguarded its Jewish population, it was now permitting Jews in Bucharest to send aid to the 90,000–95,000 surviving exiles in Transnistria.[218]

This change of direction was not prompted by any change of heart. Instead, Marshal Ion Antonescu had taken a long hard look at Romania's strategic situation. Having committed himself wholeheartedly to the operations in Russia, Romania was no closer to recovering the lost territory of Transylvania. Why should Romania divest itself of its Jewish citizens, who had some uses after all, when Hungary did not? Nor was the Romanian Jewish leadership passive. Wilhelm Filderman, the leader of the Romanian Jews, cleverly played on all these reservations in a series of memoranda that he submitted to Marshal Antonescu and sought to mobilize friendly intellectuals to petition the government. Such initiatives probably counted for much less than the failure of the German advance into the Caucasus. The German army ground to a halt far short of Baku, while the oil fields it had occupied were so comprehensively wrecked that it would take months for them to be reactivated. For the foreseeable future, the Third Reich would remain dependent on oil from the Ploesti fields. Marshal Antonescu held all the cards even before the Soviet onslaught rolled over his troops north and south of Stalingrad, entombing the German 6th Army. From that point he knew that Germany was a liability rather than a valuable ally.[219]

In July the Hungarians had proposed resettling Jews from the annexed area of Transylvania in Transnistria, but Himmler, at his most grandiose, had rejected this partial solution in favour of one that embraced the entire Hungarian Jewish population. Eichmann turned down a similar offer in late September, fearing that a round-up of foreign Jews in Hungary would alarm the country's Jewish citizens and make it harder to apprehend them later. Both Himmler and Eichmann were blind to the closing window of opportunity. By early October, when the Foreign Office consulted the Hungarian Ambassador in Berlin, Döme Sztójay, about the deportation of its nationals in western Europe, the Hungarian position had hardened. Sztójay informed the Wilhelmstrasse that Hungarian Jews in the Reich and other countries were deportable, but there would be no deportations from Hungary itself. A few days later the German Ambassador in Budapest belatedly addressed the Hungarian Foreign Office with a demand for the expulsion of all Jews from Hungarian territory. When the reply arrived over six weeks later, it was a flat no.[220]

A similar pattern emerged in Bulgaria, home to 48,400 Jews of whom 10 per cent lived in Sofia. The Bulgarian government had passed anti-Jewish laws in December 1940, symbolizing its pro-German stance more than as an expression of deep-rooted indigenous anti-Semitism. Jews were excluded from public service and the professions. They were obliged to live in certain areas, education was segregated, and Jews were subjected to punishing levels of taxation. The anti-Jewish laws used a racial definition of the Jews and forbade intermarriage with Bulgarians; however, protests by politicians, intellectuals and, especially, the Bulgarian Orthodox Church, led to the exception of baptized Jews. In 1941, Bulgaria was awarded chunks of Yugoslavia and Greece in return for letting the German army operate from its territory. These regions brought with them a further 15,000 Jews. During 1942 the government's anti-Jewish stance appeared to harden. A Commissariat for Jewish Affairs was established in August, headed by a notorious Jew-hater, Alexander Belev, and Jews aged 20 to 45 years were called up for labour service. The Bulgarians also cut adrift Jews with Bulgarian nationality in German-occupied countries. But they were less keen to see Jews deported from Bulgarian territory. In September and October the RSHA and then the Foreign Office engaged the Bulgarian authorities on the subject of deporting its Jewish citizens. However, the Bulgarians replied that they preferred to retain local Jews for compulsory labour.[221]

When the Germans sought to tackle the Jewish population in Greece they had to deal with the Italians, who occupied the bulk of the country. Although the largest community, numbering 55,000, lived in Salonica, which was under German control, 13,000 Jews were under Italian rule. The RSHA hoped to achieve a uniform action across the country, but this necessitated Italian accord. In July 1942 the Italians rejected the introduction of the yellow star. When the Germans imposed a harsh regime of forced labour on the Jews in Salonica, hundreds fled to the Italian zone where they were unmolested. Even when Mussolini agreed to the removal of Jews from the Italian-occupied areas of Croatia in August, the authorities in Rome exerted little pressure to make this happen. After the German Foreign Office prodded them in October, the Italians replied that they would prefer to intern the Jews in their zones rather than remove them. Internment in Croatia actually turned into a form of protection. Jews were shepherded into camps along the Dalmatian coast run by the Italian military, who had no intention of cooperating with the Germans. A month later the Russians began to pound Italian forces on the Don river. The collapse of the

Italian military position there and the reverses in North Africa would cast an even harsher light on subsequent German demands.[222]

The course of the war played as fundamental a role in shaping Allied responses to the fate of the Jews as it did in determining the posture that Germany's Axis partners adopted towards anti-Jewish measures. During the first half of 1942, information reached London and Washington about the fate of the Jews in German-occupied Europe but there was little that the Allies could do about it. Indeed, for Churchill, Britain and the Empire, the period from February to June 1942 was probably the nadir of military fortune and domestic morale during the war. On 11 February, two German battleships, the *Scharnhorst* and the *Gneisenau*, with the heavy cruiser *Prinz Eugen*, sailed undetected by the Royal Navy from Brest and passed through the supposedly impregnable English Channel to safe waters off the Netherlands. Four days later news arrived that Singapore had surrendered to the Japanese after a brief siege. Until August, a German innovation to the Enigma enciphering machine meant that the British code-breakers at Bletchley Park were unable to read transmissions to and from U-boats in the Atlantic. Shipping losses soared to levels that were all but unsustainable at just the time when the Americans were endeavouring to send men and supplies to Britain. On 20 June, while Churchill was at a summit meeting with President Roosevelt in Washington, he heard that Tobruk had fallen, leaving the road open for Rommel to dash for the Suez Canal. Until the end of July it looked as though the war was once again hanging in the balance.[223]

But what did the public know about the fate of the Jews? The London *Jewish Chronicle* was the only newspaper that regularly published reports of massacres of Jews in Poland and on the territory of the USSR, and even then its coverage was fragmentary. Few of these items received any kind of editorial comment. Some came from Soviet government spokesmen, but many were attributed to vague sources. It was not until June that the Polish government-in-exile and the Bund succeeded in drawing the media spotlight onto the mass murder of Jews in Poland using lethal gas at fixed-site extermination camps. On 25 June 1942, the eminently respectable *Daily Telegraph* published information that 700,000 Polish Jews had been murdered, naming Chelmno as one of the sites. The data came from Shmuel Zygielbojm, the Bund's representative on the Polish National Council in London. It had been collated by the Bund in Poland and transmitted to London via the Polish underground. The World Jewish Congress (WJC) followed up with a press conference chaired by Sidney Silverman, a Jewish Labour MP and WJC activist, and addressed by Ignacy Schwarzbart, the other Jewish member of the Polish exile council. The next morning, the *Daily Telegraph* reported that 1 million Jews had perished in Poland. These officially sanctioned bulletins and credible news reports opened the gateway to increased publicity. Every major UK national and local newspaper carried the latest story. But the *Jewish Chronicle* on 3 July devoted an editorial to the revelations that exemplified the problem journalists and the public had in grasping what they were being told: 'The hideous details now coming to hand of the wholesale butchery by the Germans of Jewish men, women, and children in Poland and Lithuania read like tales from the imagination of some drug-maddened creature seeking to portray a nightmare of hell. The average mind simply cannot believe the reality of such sickening revelations . . .' On 9 July both Schwarzbart and Zygielbojm appeared before the press accompanied by Brendan Bracken, the minister for information. From then on the fate of Polish Jews was a staple news item: newspaper readers learned about the deportations from Warsaw and the death of Czerniaków on almost the same day they occurred. On 11 December the *Jewish Chronicle* appeared with a black border of mourning around the front page, which announced that 2 million Jews had been done to death in German-occupied Europe.[224]

A similar dynamic occurred in the United States. Since America's entry into the war the persecution of the Jews had been awarded more coverage in the press, but it was never treated with the same urgency as reports of atrocities against Allied nationals. One reason was the informality of the sources and the absence of any official endorsement by government agencies. The president and the administration did not make any specific comment about the plight of Jews for fear of confirming German propaganda that Jewish interests were manipulating the White House. Hence the report from the Bund only made the front page in a few of the major US dailies; it was carried at the bottom of page 5 of the *New York Times* on 27 June. However, the *New York Times* on 22 July gave front-page treatment to a mass rally organized at Madison Square Gardens by the American Jewish Congress, B'nai Brith and the Jewish Labour Committee. The 20,000-strong audience heard messages from Roosevelt and Churchill pledging retribution against those guilty of war crimes.[225]

At the same time as the destruction of the Jews in Poland was becoming a news story, secret channels were conveying intelligence that the Germans had embarked upon a European-wide campaign of genocide. During July, a German industrialist named Eduard Schulte who had interests in the Auschwitz area learned of an order by Himmler to annihilate the Jews. At the end of the month, Schulte, who travelled regularly to Switzerland, conveyed this information to a Jewish business associate in Zurich, through whom it eventually reached Gerhard Riegner, a representative of the World Jewish Congress. Riegner distilled what he had learned into a brief summary and presented it to the British and American consulates in Geneva for transmission to, respectively, the Foreign Office and the State Department: 'Received alarming report stating that, in the Fuehrer's Headquarters, a plan has been discussed, and is under consideration, according to which all Jews in countries occupied or controlled by Germany numbering 3½ to 4 millions should, after deportation and concentration in the East, be at one blow exterminated, in order to resolve, once and for all the Jewish question in Europe. Action is reported to be planned for the autumn. Ways of execution are still being discussed including the use of prussic acid. We transmit this information with all the necessary reservation, as exactitude cannot be confirmed by us. Our informant is reported to have close connexions with the highest German authorities, and his reports are generally reliable. Please inform and consult New York.' Riegner relied on the diplomats to ensure that Sidney Silverman in London and Dr Stephen Wise in New York also got copies. Silverman was invited to the Foreign Office and handed the cable by sceptical officials just two days later. The even more suspicious State Department did not inform Wise until two weeks had elapsed. Even then US officials prevailed upon him not to go public until they had verified the information. Wise waited until 24 November before holding a press conference to disclose the staggering evidence that the Germans planned to kill four million Jews.[226]

Another source that convinced officials in Whitehall and Washington that Riegner's alarming cable was authentic came via the Polish government-in-exile. Since May 1942, the monthly bulletins of the Polish Home Army sent to London contained details about the mass murder of Jews in Belzec and Treblinka. In November, a courier for the underground, operating with the nom de guerre Jan Karski, reached London by a circuitous and dangerous route, bearing first-hand reports of conditions in the Warsaw ghetto in the wake of the deportations and in what he understood to be Belzec, but was probably a nearby labour camp. Karski, who was always escorted by a senior Polish diplomat who vouched for his bona fides, gave an account of what he had seen directly to the foreign secretary, Anthony Eden, in London, and later to President Roosevelt, telling them that nearly two million Jews had already been slaughtered. He also delivered a microfilm with crucial intelligence about the mass murders at Auschwitz, although the sensational nature of what he had to say about other crimes may inadvertently have obscured its significance.[227]

While officials were still weighing the validity of such reports about atrocities against the Jews, activists were organizing public protests and pressing for the government to react. In early September, the Labour Party in London convened a mass meeting addressed by the home secretary, Herbert Morrison. The American Jewish Congress summoned an emergency gathering of Jewish organizations to thrash out a programme for action that they could put to the administration, although there was little they could agree on that was in any way practical. On 3 December, representatives of the major organizations of the British Jewish community met with delegates of the governments-in-exile to formulate a response. Silverman declared that unless there was a major public protest soon the Jewish East End of London would explode with anger and frustration. As a result, a string of public events took place during December, commencing with a week of mourning and prayer, and culminating in a deputation to the foreign secretary two days before Christmas.[228]

On both sides of the Atlantic, civil servants and politicians pondered how best to meet the rising tide of indignation and demands for action. Neither country was prepared to admit Jewish refugees even if they were able to get out of Nazi-dominated Europe. During October, the US chargé d'affaires at Vichy, Somerville Pinkney Tuck, went out on a limb when he condemned the deportations during a face-to-face meeting with Laval. Not content with a verbal denunciation, Pinkney Tuck proposed to the State Department that the United States evacuate 4,000 of the most at-risk Jewish children in the internment camps. The secretary of state, Sumner Welles, was sympathetic to the idea, but Breckinridge Long, his assistant, vociferously objected to breaching the rules that restricted immigration. Despite a personal intervention by the president in favour of children's visas, the rescue plan was still mired in argument when the Germans occupied the Free Zone and it fell by the wayside.[229]

The safest gesture was to promise retribution once the war was over. On 7 October, the British and American governments announced the formation of a United Nations War Crimes Commission charged with collecting evidence for use in the trials of those responsible for atrocities. However, the release of information about the scale of Jewish suffering and losses in Poland created a surge of public feeling. Letters poured into the press from churchmen, labour activists and politicians, expressing sympathy, proposing more or less sensible counter-measures, and expecting a lead from the government. Feeling the heat, Roosevelt finally conceded to pleas from Wise and met a Jewish delegation at the White House on 8 December. But the Jews had few concrete proposals and Roosevelt had little to offer beyond a stentorian warning to the Nazis that perpetrators of war crimes would be punished. It was the first and last meeting the president had with representatives of American Jewry to discuss the plight of the Jews in Europe.[230]

Ten days later the US administration and the British government issued a joint statement on German war crimes. Eden read it out in the House of Commons in response to a staged question from Sidney Silverman. He told the hushed assembly that 'I regret to have to inform the House that reliable reports have recently reached His Majesty's Government regarding the barbarous and inhuman treatment to which Jews are being subjected in German-occupied Europe.' In particular he referred to the much publicized report from the Polish government-in-exile enumerating the Jewish dead at 1 million. He then recited from the joint statement being issued simultaneously in London, Washington and Moscow: '[T]he German authorities, not content with denying to persons of Jewish race in all the territories over which their barbarous rule has been extended the most elementary human rights, are now carrying into effect Hitler's oft repeated intention to exterminate the Jewish people in Europe. From all the occupied countries Jews are being transported, in conditions of appalling horror and brutality, to Eastern Europe. In Poland, which has been made the principal Nazi slaughter-house, the ghettoes established by the German invaders are being systematically emptied of all Jews except a few highly skilled workers required for war industries. None of those taken away are ever heard of again. The able-bodied are slowly worked to death in labour camps. The infirm are left to die of exposure and starvation or are deliberately massacred in mass executions. The number of victims of these bloody cruelties is reckoned in many hundreds of thousands of entirely innocent men, women and children.' The Allied governments 'condemn in the strongest possible terms this bestial policy of cold-blooded extermination'. After Eden had responded to questions, several of which pointedly asked what action the government proposed to take, a backbencher asked the Speaker of the House if it would be appropriate for the members to stand in silence for one minute 'in support of this protest against disgusting barbarism'. The Speaker said it was for the members to decide. As one they rose and stood, their heads bowed.[231]

PART SEVEN

TOTAL WAR

1943

The fortunes of war and the fluctuations of anti-Jewish policy

At the turn of the year 1942–3, Jews across Europe hoped the Allied landings in North Africa and the German defeat at Stalingrad would precipitate a German collapse. Emil Dorian in Bucharest wondered, 'Will this Christmas be the last Christmas of the war?' When Victor Klemperer heard of the Soviet breakthrough around Stalingrad he speculated, 'Perhaps it's coming to an end after all.' Four weeks later and he thought the Wehrmacht bulletins had '*never* sounded so pathetic . . . It can mean the beginning of the catastrophe.' Hillel Seidman, in Warsaw, remarked that religious Jews interpreted the battle of El Alamein as 'the beginning of the end' – not in the sense of Winston Churchill's rhetoric, but as heralding the final confrontation between Gog and Magog on the borders of the Holy Land. Herman Kruk, chronicler of the Vilna ghetto, noted that Jews started to wish each other 'May it increase', referring to the extent of the Red Army's advance. Now living under German occupation in the south of France, Raymond-Raoul Lambert wrote of the Anglo-American successes in North Africa that 'I really think the end will come in the autumn of '43.' After observing the ramshackle equipment of the occupiers and the age of the German soldiers, 'either very young or older,' he mused: 'Is this 1918 already . . . ?' But they all expressed a common dread: would the Germans turn on the Jews in rage at their defeats. Would they allow the Jews to survive? Lambert's question was universally shared: 'Can we hold on?'[1]

In fact, Allied military and diplomatic miscalculations, mirrored by German resilience and ruthlessness, ensured that Jewish suffering was both deepened and fatally prolonged. A secret Allied mission to incite an insurrection against Vichy rule in Algeria was bungled. In several places the invaders faced stiff opposition and the French only agreed to a ceasefire at the price of leaving the existing colonial regimes in place.

Even Vichy's anti-Jewish laws remained in force. British and American vanguards then raced for Tunis, which was hundreds of miles from the beachheads. When the leading echelon reached the Tunisian frontier it ran into strong German defensive positions. To their surprise, Hitler airlifted thousands of troops to shield the rear of the Afrika Korps. In the interim, Rommel's forces had retreated nearly 2,000 miles from the El Alamein position, evacuating Tripoli and abandoning Libya. At the start of February, what remained of the Afrika Korps crossed into Tunisia and occupied the Mareth Line, a chain of fortifications built by the French in the 1930s. But Rommel's armoured and mobile elements continued westwards and inflicted a sharp defeat on the Americans. Although the Italian–German bridgehead in Tunisia was unsustainable and amounted to a strategic folly, it held up Allied progress until early May 1943. In those crucial months the German high command could relax about an invasion of north-west Europe: it was clear that for the moment the Allies had committed themselves to a Mediterranean strategy.[2]

On the eastern front, Soviet commanders were surprised by the numbers of the German and Axis forces encircled in the Stalingrad pocket when the northern and southern pincers of their attack closed on 22 November 1942. The simultaneous crises in Tunisia and southern Russia exposed just how hopelessly overstretched the German armed forces had become. To add to their misery, on 19 December the Soviets unleashed a second wave of concentric attacks, smashing through the Italian 8th Army and threatening to sweep all the way to Rostov, cutting off the two German armies in the Caucasus. Hitler was forced to call off a relief effort to break through to the pocket, but insisted on supplying 6th Army by air rather than allowing it to surrender. The air-bridge was a costly failure. The 250,000 men in the Stalingrad pocket were condemned to two months of hunger and disease similar to the privations that the Jews of Warsaw and Lodz had suffered for over two years. Between 10 January and 2 February 1943, the Red Army finally crushed the pocket. However, Erich von Manstein, appointed by Hitler to overall command in the theatre, was able to extricate the bulk of Army Group A from the Caucasus and counter-attack the now over-extended Red Army. By March, he had managed to stabilize the front. When the thaw came and operations halted, the German armies were more or less back where they had started in May 1942. They had lost over half a million men, 220,000–250,000 in the Stalingrad battles alone, but they had not collapsed and there was potential for another, albeit limited, counter-stroke to capitalize on Manstein's earlier triumphs.[3]

While German reverses temporarily raised the spirits of beleaguered Jews, they had the opposite effect on the German public. The huge losses at Stalingrad and the end to any prospect that the war would soon be over caused morale to plunge. Hitler, shaken by the defeat, withdrew from the limelight, leaving Goebbels to fill the leadership vacuum with inspirational rhetoric and efforts to rationalize the war economy. Hatred and fear of the Jewish enemy were central to his approach. The start of the year saw not only a renewed propaganda drive against the Jews, but also a further wave of deportations from the Reich.[4]

The Jewish question always had a security dimension, but thanks to the Allied advances it acquired new geographical dimensions and a fresh urgency. Until the defeat of the Axis armies there, the 85,000 Jews of Tunisia were exposed to the attention of an Einsatzkommando that had originally been destined for Palestine. With Allied troops securely based in North Africa, the entire northern Mediterranean littoral beckoned as the location for the second front that Stalin demanded from the western allies. As a result, Jewish populations that had so far escaped the ministrations of the SS came into focus as a potential fifth column or a source of assistance for an Allied incursion. Hitler ordered the immediate occupation of southern France and strengthened German garrisons in the Balkans. Every Jewish community in these zones was now regarded as a potential resistance nest, a bridgehead for the Allies. Jews in port cities were particularly vulnerable to this fantastically exaggerated perception. Hence, Hitler decreed a major action against the alleged resistance in Marseilles in January 1943, while in February the RSHA turned its attention to Salonica, the great port city in north-east Greece. Paradoxically, further Allied successes in the Mediterranean – the invasion and surrender of Italy – would expose yet more Jews to persecution.[5]

The worsening military situation of the Reich also had an impact on anti-Jewish policy at the level of diplomatic relations. Having sought to enrol Europe in the anti-Bolshevik and anti-Jewish crusade in 1941–2, Hitler and the Nazi leadership now used the fear of Soviet conquest to strengthen the ties between Axis states. From Berlin's point of view the reaffirmation of shared objectives had to embrace merciless treatment of the Jews. According to the historian Peter Longerich, 'In the second half of the war . . . Judenpolitik was a main axis of Germany's occupation and alliance policies. In the view of the National Socialist leadership the more the war advanced the greater the significance of the systematic murder of the Jews for the solidarity of the German power bloc.' If so, this approach was a dismal failure. In every Axis capital the turn in the war enjoined a reconsideration of the alliance with Germany and a re-evaluation of anti-Jewish policy. Time and again, German diplomats met with a rebuff when they called for the deportation of Jewish populations. It was only when established governments foundered – usually due to military failure – and previously marginal, radical pro-Nazi groups seized power that the Reich again enjoyed full-hearted cooperation. As German manpower diminished precipitously, this cooperation acquired paramount importance. Indeed, it was the increasing precariousness of the Axis position that drove militants of various nationalities to serve the Germans. The first of these men were ideological warriors defending European civilization against the Asiatic hordes, but they were followed by desperados who had nothing to lose.[6]

Total war and the end of German Jewry

In a speech to a selected audience at the Sportpalast on 18 February 1943, two weeks after German radio announced the demise of 6th Army, Goebbels acknowledged the extent of the challenge facing Germany. There had been no choice but to take on the USSR, even though 'we did not properly evaluate the Soviet Union's war potential'. Now the people had to confront the danger of a Soviet victory. 'The goal of Bolshevism is Jewish world revolution. They want to bring chaos to the Reich and Europe, using the resulting hopelessness and desperation to establish their international, Bolshevist-concealed capitalist tyranny.' Goebbels then raised the spectre of atrocities that were the mirror image of those perpetrated by the Reich. 'A Bolshevization of the Reich would mean the liquidation of our entire intelligentsia and leadership, and the descent of our workers into Bolshevist-Jewish slavery . . . Behind the oncoming Soviet divisions we see the Jewish liquidation commandos, and behind them terror, the specter of mass starvation and complete anarchy.' Only National Socialist Germany was free of Jewish influence and, therefore, able to lead the fight against it. In an appeal to the millions listening on radio in Germany and beyond its borders he warned, 'The only choice now is between living under Axis protection or in a Bolshevist Europe.' He next linked the struggle against international Jewry with tough measures to improve Germany's war effort. 'Terrorist Jewry had 200 million people to serve it in Russia ... The masses of tanks we have faced on the Eastern Front are the result of 25 years of social misfortune and misery of the Bolshevist people. We have to respond with similar measures if we do not want to give up the game as lost.' Therefore he announced the closure of bars and nightclubs, the shutting down of luxury restaurants and shops, the cancellation of exemptions from military service, and initiatives to bring more women into the workforce. When Goebbels brought his peroration to its climax, asking the audience if they wanted total war, he was not just summoning them to the defence of Germany and Europe, or asking them to endorse cuts in living standards; he was exacting their sanction for total war against the Jews.[7]

In January 1943, there were approximately 50,000 Jews still living in the Reich. Most of the able-bodied men, like Victor Klemperer, were doing forced labour in war-related factories. But Hitler had long wanted to get rid of these last working Jews and Himmler now regarded them as a potential security threat. Moreover, with foreign labour pouring into the Reich there was no longer a reason to keep them. On 27 February, 7,000 Jews in Berlin who were employed in the armaments industry were arrested. Ruth Andreas-Friedrich described the events: 'Since six o'clock this morning trucks have been driving through Berlin, escorted by armed SS men. They stop at factory gates, in front of private houses; they load human cargo . . .' Amongst their number were thousands of men in mixed marriages who were supposed to be redeployed rather than removed entirely. Their Aryan wives did not know this, however, and started to congregate in the Rosenstrasse, where their men were being held, clamouring to give them food and clothing. Emboldened by their numbers and by the confusion of the police, who were taken aback by the demonstration and loath to disperse it by force, the women started calling for the release of their spouses. After a few days several thousand were reunited with their partners, but only after the sorting process was completed and 3,000 full Jews were deported. Andreas-Friedrich concluded, 'At least a few have come back – the so-called privileged ones: the Jewish partners in racially mixed marriages.' It was their previously established protected status, not their wives' spontaneous protests, that saved them.[8]

A similar combing out occurred in Dresden. On 28 February, Klemperer heard that the Hellerberg labour camp had been sealed off and about 3,000 Jews deported. Like the privileged ones in Berlin, Klemperer was spared. In April, though, he was summoned for forced labour and assigned to a paper-packaging works. He knew that the Gestapo's pursuit of Jews in mixed marriages was unrelenting, that his existence hung by a thread. In Höxter, at roughly the time of the factory action, the SD reported that a single Jew named Hartwig Stein was to be deported because his gentile spouse died. At the close of the year Klemperer learned of an eighty-eight-year-old man who was dispatched to Theresienstadt when his gentile spouse passed away. Between January and March 1943, the new anti-Jewish drive carried off 16,000 German Jews to Auschwitz-Birkenau.[9]

Now divorced from her husband Ernst, Lilli Jahn was easy meat for the Gestapo. In July 1943, the mayor of Immenhausen forced her to leave the town and move to nearby Kassel with her children. Her eldest son, Gerhard, was now a Flakhelfer, a member of an anti-aircraft gun crew, but this did not shield her from the Gestapo. At the end of August she was arrested for using the title 'Dr' and omitting Sarah from the nameplate of her apartment. She was sentenced to the Breitenau corrective labour camp. Nearly half of the other prisoners there were Jewish, working as slave labour in a chemical plant. The conditions were severe. Lilli was able to stay in touch with her children through a monthly letter written on the reverse side of a bottle label. She told a friend, 'Things are naturally far worse than I say in my letters to the children. Less than adequate food, insufficient clothing . . . You can't imagine what it's like.' Lilli begged her children to persuade Ernst, who had been drafted into a military hospital, to intercede for her. None of these appeals had any effect. On 17 March 1944, Lilli Jahn was transferred to Auschwitz and admitted into the camp. She was registered dead a month later.[10]

By mid-1943, the number of Jews left in the Reich had fallen to 32,000, of whom 18,500 were in Berlin. They were almost entirely in mixed marriages or protected for other reasons. But several thousand were in institutions maintained by the Reichsvereinigung or working for it. Alois Brunner, a member of Eichmann's team, began methodically emptying these facilities one after another. In May, he oversaw the dissolution of the former Jewish home for the aged on Grosse Hamburgerstrasse which had been converted into a Judenhaus. One of those deported was Lucie Adelsberger, a highly respected paediatrician and medical researcher, who had been incarcerated there for twelve months. In her post-war memoir she recalled that they were taken to an out-of-the-way freight station at Putlitzstrasse where the transport awaited. She was placed in the 'medical-wagon', which was slightly better than the others, but the thirty-six-hour journey was grim and debilitating. 'The air in the tightly sealed box-car, which hadn't been opened since the departure, is suffocating and pestilential . . . The pails of excrement are filled to overflowing and drip down their sides, and with every jolt of the train they spill over and splash on the people nearby who can't get out of the way because of the crush. The perimeter of the car is a barricade of baby carriages, for we have many infants in our group. They scream in their dirty diapers and refuse to be comforted because there's nothing to clean them up with and nothing to drink.' In the middle of the night on 19 May, the train pulled into the station at Auschwitz.[11]

On 10 June 1943 it was finally the turn of the Reichsvereinigung itself. Having maintained communal life for as long as possible and seen to the welfare of Jews up to the point of deportation, the leadership was sent to Theresienstadt. Several of its members were appointed to the Jewish council and continued in leading roles. The Gestapo appropriated the considerable assets of the Jewish community that they left behind. One Jewish organization remained in Berlin: the Jewish hospital on Iranischestrasse. It was occupied mainly by 800 privileged Jews and a few Jewish administrators. Several rooms housed Jews who worked directly for the Gestapo. These informers staved off deportation by cruising Berlin looking for so-called U-boats, Jews who had gone underground in response to the final deportation wave. Hundreds were in Berlin, living on false papers or hiding in places maintained by courageous people like Ruth Andreas-Friedrich. Both the hidden Jews and their helpers were perpetually at risk from Jews whose business was delivering them to the Gestapo.[12]

The military disasters and the slump in German morale were reflected in public attitudes towards anti-Jewish policy. The Allied declaration of 17 December 1942 on German war crimes was transmitted over the BBC German service, while a barrage of programmes during January and February alerted a significant portion of the German public to what was being done in their name or confirmed what they already suspected. 'Throughout the whole world there is increasing activity against us', Ulrich von Hassell responded in his diary. 'Atrocities in Poland are exploited very dramatically in the House of Commons. There is increasing nervousness here at home arising out of the anxiety over the outcome of the war and the fear of domestic disturbances.' He was strikingly well informed thanks to what he learned from an administrator in the General Government, a devoted member of the Nazi Party, who nevertheless deplored what was going on around him. 'It was so terrible that he could not endure it . . . Continual, indescribable mass murder of Jews.' The ex-diplomat was politically as well as temperamentally inclined to believe what he heard. Conversely, an SD informant in Schwabach, a town in northern Bavaria, reported that 'At the beginning of the month of December, there was generally a depressed mood in the local area among the population, especially due to the stories being told by soldiers at the front . . . One of the most powerful sources of alarm in circles connected with the church and in the rural population are at the moment the tales from Russia which speak about the shooting and extermination of the Jews. This news leaves a sense of great anxiety, emotional distress, and worry . . . As broad circles of the rural population see the situation, it is not yet certain that we will win the war, and if we do not, when the Jews return some day, they will take a horrible revenge.'[13]

The fear of Jewish revenge, coupled with the fear of defeat, was deliberately fostered by Goebbels. But linking Jewish vengeance to the menace of a Soviet victory was a double-edged sword. The more the regime's propaganda machine drew attention to actual Soviet atrocities or potential depredations, the more it caused Germans to reflect on the crimes committed by their own side. Many months after the surrender of the 6th Army, the district governor of Swabia reported that 'The shock of Stalingrad has still not completely dissipated. In many circles there are fears that the men taken prisoner there by the Russians could be killed as revenge for the supposed mass executions of Jews by Germans in the East.' This syndrome became particularly evident when Goebbels pounced on the discovery of mass graves containing the decomposed remains of some 4,500 Polish officers who had been massacred by the NKVD, the Soviet secret police, at Katyn in Byelorussia in mid-1940. Goebbels believed he could use the atrocity as a counterweight to Allied claims about German war crimes, as well as driving a wedge between the western allies and the USSR. It was also splendid proof of what he warned would befall countries in the path of the Red

Army, if the front buckled. However, the publicity blitz had unintended consequences.[14]

On the basis of what its agents were reporting, the Sicherheitsdienst head office at the RSHA confirmed that there was interest in the Katyn massacre and that it was generating 'hatred and fear of Bolshevism'. But there was also a conviction that the propaganda was hypocritical. 'We have no right to get upset about the measures of the Soviets because the Germans eliminated Poles and Jews in far greater numbers.' The SD office in Friedberg detected that 'Here and there, some say that our enemies would also find mass graves in the eastern territories we have conquered. These are not Poles, but Jews who have been systematically murdered by our troops. So one shouldn't make so much ado about such matters . . .' Hassell, briefed by his colleague in the General Government, was not fooled for a moment. He complained that while 'the gang tries in vain to befuddle world opinion about the Katyn massacres, the SS in Poland carries on most shamefully. Countless Jews have been gassed in specially built chambers, at least 100,000.' When the regime tried to pull off the same trick after uncovering more mass graves (in Vinnitsa, Ukraine), the SD in Berlin noted that the reports earned 'scant attention'. 'You can often hear the view expressed that we likewise were relentless in eradicating all elements of opposition in the East, especially the Jews. Stories from soldiers and other persons deployed in the East play a large role in this.' Later in the year, the Katyn revelation blended with rumours about efforts to destroy traces of the extermination of the Jews in the east. The SD in Bad Neustadt relayed a locally circulating story that an enemy government had sent an inquiry about the fate of German Jews to Hitler via the Red Cross. 'After that, the Führer had the Jews dug up and their remains burned, so that with a further retreat in the east, the Soviets do not get hold of any propaganda material like that discovered near Katyn.' German efforts to hide their crime backfired because of the success Goebbels had in exposing a Soviet one.[15]

Pervasive, if not always precise, knowledge of the dreadful fate that overcame the Jews, especially in the east, also informed German reactions to the strategic bombing campaign of the Royal Air Force. Since early 1942, RAF Bomber Command had switched from efforts to hit specific targets, such as factories, to area bombing that aimed to 'de-house' and demoralize civilians as well as damaging industrial production. The scale and destructiveness of these raids escalated steadily from the first 'thousand-bomber' raid on Cologne in May 1942 to the firestorm that gutted central Hamburg in July 1943. As the hail of incendiaries and explosives intensified, Germans cast around for explanations or scapegoats. In a demonstration of awareness, in which prudence jostled with guilt, they connected the 'terror bombing' (as Goebbels called it) to the 1938 November pogrom, Aryanization, and the deportations.[16]

The NSDAP branch in the Maxfeld district of Nuremberg caught indications that people now regretted the ejection of the city's Jews, although not out of any compassion for them: 'if the Jews had been retained as hostages, then we would have had an effective bargaining chip against the air raids'. People apparently believed that the RAF were deterred from bombing Augsburg because the shell of its synagogue was still standing. Similarly, the SD office in Würzburg passed on the view that the city 'will not be attacked by enemy planes since no synagogue was set on fire there. But others say that now the planes will be coming to Würzburg too, since the last Jew left the city a short time ago.' Victims of the raids on Barmen-Wuppertal, in the Ruhr, intimated 'that only the Jew, and no one else, is the cause behind such barbarism. They say that he is upset because his former property in Germany is now controlled by someone else.' After Cologne cathedral was badly damaged, the SD recorded local opinion that 'what is happening now is "punishment from God".' What Germans had done to synagogues was now being done to churches. Moving amongst the stunned populace of Schweinfurt after a major (and costly) daylight raid on the city's ball-bearing factory by the US Army Air Forces in August 1943, SD informants could often 'hear people say that this was retribution for what we did to the Jews in November 1938'.[17]

The linkage of bombing to Jewish revenge could be counterproductive in other ways. After Nazi propaganda tried to pin the destruction of the Eder and Möhne dams on the Jews, the SD in Halle commented on the press treatment: 'There was strong interest in publications stating that the attacks on the dams were caused by Jews. This plan triggered a heightened anti-Jewish mood ... On the other hand, some in the population held opposite views. Some persons speaking from Halle state that it was irresponsible for the NSDAP to engage in such measures towards the Jews. The Jews' revenge now on its way will, they say, be terrible when it comes and only the government is to blame. If the German side had not attacked the Jews, we would already have peace.' The Nazi Party Chancellery picked up a different strain of dissent. Seeing the dams as a valid military target that ought to have been better defended, other people concluded that 'the emphasis on the role of the Jews is quite incomprehensible'.[18]

North Africa and southern France

In addition to the troops that were rushed to Tunisia in November 1943, the RSHA sent Walter Rauff. He had formerly served as an adjutant to Heydrich and ran the technical department of the SS Head Office that coordinated development of the gas van in 1941–2. Rauff led a twenty-five-man Einsatzkommando that had originally been put together at the high tide of Rommel's advance into Egypt, with the intention of following the Afrika Korps into Palestine. Instead, it had languished in Athens and was redeployed on other duties until North Africa returned to the top of the exterminatory agenda.[19]

The Jews in Morocco, Algeria and Tunisia had been included in the list of targets drawn up for the Wannsee meeting, but so far they had been spared direct German persecution. Vichy anti-Jewish laws had been applied in Morocco and Algeria, though. Jewish businesses in Algeria were liquidated in late 1941 and in every city in Morocco where substantial numbers of Jews lived they were compelled to move back into the mellah, the old and usually dilapidated Jewish quarter. At least 2,000 European Jews were deported from Vichy France to Algeria to work in forced labour camps servicing construction of the Trans-Sahara railway. The regimen in these camps was as harsh as the terrain and it is estimated that hundreds perished. Jews were not freed from official discrimination until August 1943 when General de Gaulle's National Committee of French Liberation established its authority over the Maghreb.[20]

In Tunisia the Jews had fared better thanks to a benign colonial governor (the French resident-general Admiral Estéva), the peculiar nature of the European population, and Italian intervention. The European element in Tunisia was divided almost equally between French and Italian settlers. Although the French had gained control of Tunisia in 1881, the Italians used their nationals as a vehicle for influence and, ultimately, they hoped, to justify a transfer of sovereignty. Hence, Estéva was happy to persecute Jews with Italian citizenship but to soft-pedal the treatment of French Jews. Conversely, the Italians doggedly defended their citizens. This curious stand-off was suddenly overturned by the imposition of Axis power.[21]

Soon after his arrival, Rauff picked the Chief Rabbi of Tunis plus several community leaders to form a Jewish council and required them to supply 2,000 Jewish men aged 20–50 years for forced labour on defence works and airfield construction. When fewer than 150 reported for work, he seized hostages. Over the next few weeks, Rauff organized the registration of Jews, levied a compulsory fine of 20 million francs, and extorted 43kg of gold from the ancient Jewish community of Djerba. In April, he extended labour service to all Jewish adults. Many of them ended up in labour camps attached to airfields and dozens were killed when the landing strips were repeatedly bombed by Allied warplanes. Rauff had ambitions to evacuate all the Jews to Germany, but he only managed to extract twenty before the Italian–German bridgehead was crushed. He and his team were flown out on one of the last transport planes on 9 May 1943.[22]

The Allied success in Tunisia took so much longer than anticipated that it negated Anglo-American plans for a cross-Channel invasion in 1943. Instead, at the Casablanca conference in January 1943 the Americans reluctantly accepted British proposals for an assault on Sicily and then Italy. In anticipation of Allied designs on southern Europe, Hitler had sent the Wehrmacht into the Free Zone in southern France and ordered the arrest and deportation of Jews and communists whom he regarded as trail blazers for any Allied attack. Knochen required the Vichy police to evacuate Jews from all coastal areas and border strips as a further precautionary measure. The German security police considered the situation in the south to be particularly urgent because so many Jews had fled there in the wake of the great Paris round-ups. In Lyons the Jewish population had doubled while that of Marseilles had increased by 50 per cent. Fortunately for the overstretched Sipo, in mid-December 1942 the Vichy authorities required all Jews in the former Free Zone to have their ID cards stamped with the word 'Juif'. Joseph Antignac, head of the Section d'Enquête et de Contrôle, SEC (the anti-Jewish police), in the south, instigated thousands of investigations into the identity, credentials, property and activities of Jews.[23]

On 22 January 1943, the security police in collaboration with the French authorities launched Operation Tiger, to curb resistance activity in the port of Marseilles. Because the Germans regarded Jews as enemies per se, the security sweep turned into a major round-up of foreign and French Jews. Over seven days nearly 6,000 Jews were detained, of whom 3,000 were subsequently released. The rest were deported to Compiègne or Drancy, and from there to Majdanek or Sobibor. Lambert, who had been tipped off about the action, rushed to the city, which served as a hub for UGIF relief activity. Despite his remonstrations at the Prefecture and his protests to the chief of police, he was not even able to prevent the detention of certified UGIF employees. As a last resort, Lambert, along with the Chief Rabbi of Strasbourg, René Hirschler (the chief chaplain to Jewish members of the French armed forces), and Rabbi Israel Salzer, Chief Rabbi of Marseilles, addressed a telegram to Laval and Pétain: 'Confidential STOP As a result of extensive police operations carried out by the French authorities many French citizens all perfectly in compliance with the laws of our country notably veterans from Alsace and Lorraine returned prisoners young girls and minors have been arrested because they are Jews and some have been sent to an unknown destination STOP We protest with the last bit of our energy any such measures STOP We request with all our hearts not to be denied the chance in circumstances of this nature to procure the assistance authorized by Paris for our religion and our organizations.' They did not receive a reply. When it was all over, Lambert confessed to his diary, 'We have been through a time of fear such as I shall never forget.'[24]

The entire southern zone was now swept by raids. A young member of Eichmann's team who had recently been assigned to France, Klaus Barbie, was the driving force behind these manhunts. Under his direction the security police paid little attention to nationality or UGIF permits. Sipo-SD men rounded up Jews in Nîmes, Avignon, Carpentiers, Aix-en-Provence, and shipped them north at the rate of 40 per week. They hauled Jews off trains and dragged them out of UGIF offices. In response, an estimated 30,000 Jewish residents and refugees migrated to the Italian zone of occupation where German units were not permitted to operate and where Jews lived unmolested. Hundreds crossed the Pyrenees into Spain, many along perilous mountain tracks guided by *passeurs*. Some of these guides were members of resistance networks while others demanded fees as steep as the paths they traversed. Hundreds more made their way into Switzerland, legally or illegally. Most simply scattered. In the south, the Germans and the anti-Jewish police of the SEC lacked the file cards and census data that had previously enabled them to pinpoint Jews. They were reduced to labour-intensive screening operations and random document checks on the street, in cafes or public transport. Nor were the Jews at all passive or compliant. In the wake of the Marseilles debacle, Lambert and the UGIF leaders proceeded to decentralize relief and welfare work. They also established contact with the Jewish underground. Charities affiliated to UGIF now led a double existence, publicly dispensing aid and covertly helping Jews to disappear. OSE, the children's welfare agency, moved 6,000 children from homes and orphanages into hiding.[25]

However, neither the established communal notables nor the UGIF leadership alerted the Jewish population to the real meaning of deportation or confirmed the rumours about Treblinka and Auschwitz. The survivor-historian Jacques Adler subsequently charged both with dereliction of duty: 'At the Central Consistory, which had known since August 1942 that mass extermination was taking place in these camps, there was total silence. Not wanting to attract attention to itself, it neither denied nor confirmed the information. In Paris, the UGIF leadership remained silent, as if this issue was outside its concern.' To Adler, the Germans had succeeded in lulling the French Jewish population by targeting foreign and stateless Jews first, exploiting pre-existing divisions. 'The silence of French Judaism had helped deceive the Jewish population about the intended role of the imposed representation. French Judaism never really accepted the fact that French Jews were as exposed as the foreign Jews.' Until too late, 'there was no sense of solidarity'.[26]

To many Jews in the south such a warning would have been superfluous. On their own initiative thousands moved into the relative safety of the Italian zone. In November 1942, the Italian 4th Army had taken control of ten *départements* in the south-east, including the cities of Nice, Toulon and Grenoble. When Vichy police attempted to arrest and intern foreign Jews and 'undesirable aliens', Italian garrisons forcefully prevented them. The local military commander even tolerated a Jewish relief committee led by Angelo Donati, an Italian Jewish businessman, that provided Jewish refugees with identification papers which enabled them to reside legally in Nice and rendered them immune to police raids. This cavalier attitude to enemies of the Reich so appalled Knochen that he complained to Berlin. In January 1943, Himmler protested to Ribbentrop that the Italians were protecting Jews who were the 'origin of resistance activities and of communist propaganda in the region'. Ribbentrop took up the matter during an official visit to

Mussolini the following month. The Duce reacted by appointing a senior policeman, Guido Lospinoso, as chief of the Royal Inspectorate of Racial Police in the Italian zone of France. His task, supposedly, was to evacuate Jews to the interior where they could not aid an Allied invasion. However, Lospinoso moved with exquisite tardiness. When he got around to removing the Jews he did so in collaboration with Donati's aid committee. When SS officials, including Eichmann, demanded to see him to determine what on earth was happening he sidestepped meeting after meeting. Just when it appeared that he was about to authorize the handover of German and Austrian Jews, Mussolini was deposed and Italian assistance became academic in any case.[27]

For a period, the Germans seemed to be frustrated at every turn. Heinz Röthke complained, 'with or without promulgation of the denaturalization laws, we can no longer count on the collaboration of the French police in the arrest of Jews en masse. Unless the German military situation clearly improves within the coming days or weeks.' Yet the French refused to expatriate their own citizens and the majority of foreign Jews had either already been deported or gone to ground. This placed the Germans in a double-bind. To fill the deportation trains they needed both French cooperation and non-French victims; but unless they could render French Jews stateless, they could not get the assistance they needed to round them up. Helmut Knochen pressed Laval to denaturalize Jews who had become citizens since 1927, which would have greatly increased the pool, but Laval dragged his feet. The French premier was increasingly anxious about the likely outcome of the war and knew that anti-Jewish policy was one of the few bargaining chips he had left. Although he actually signed the necessary legislation on 20 June 1943, he withheld its publication. A week later, Knochen requested reinforcements from Berlin, only to receive a dusty reply on account of the 'extremely difficult situation as concerns manpower'. Nor could he expect reliable support from the anti-Jewish police of the CGQJ, the SEC. By late 1943, the CGQJ and the SEC, which were never competently staffed at the best of times, had degenerated into little more than self-serving bureaucracies and protection rackets. When officials received a denunciation against a Jew who was in hiding or making a living illicitly, they were as likely to seek a pay-off from the denounced person as to make an arrest. This did not mean that they were a negligible force. The relentless probing into documents and sporadic hunting expeditions always netted a few unfortunates. Each arrest and deportation generated a penumbra of terror.[28]

In June, Knochen did get some reinforcements in the form of Alois Brunner and half a dozen Sipo-SD men who had worked with him deporting Jews from Vienna and Salonica. Since March there had been no transports from Drancy, but now the hunt for Jews in France was stepped up. A series of raids by Sipo-SD teams caught the leadership of the semi-clandestine Amelot relief organization and disrupted a new communist-led welfare initiative dubbed Solidarité. Soon after his arrival in Paris, Brunner met leaders of UGIF-north and told them that henceforth they would be accountable to him rather than the CGQJ. To underline the new dispensation he dismissed the French police from Drancy and placed the camp under Sipo-SD management. He then reorganized the internal administration and compelled UGIF to provide supplies and maintenance. In anticipation of the denaturalization decree, he also instructed Sipo-SD staff to plan the mass arrest of 20,000 Jews in Paris, 6,000 across the northern zone and up to 30,000 in the south. When the denaturalization law failed to materialize, Brunner made do with what he had.[29]

He swept aside the remaining inhibitions about raiding UGIF-supported welfare facilities such as children's homes and hospitals or seizing UGIF personnel. In July he arrested André Baur, the vice president of the organization who was responsible for overseeing its activities in the north, on the pretext that he was to serve as a hostage against the return of a relative who had escaped from Drancy. The real reason was that Baur, who was French-born and possessed impeccable social credentials, had recently protested to Laval and the CGQJ about Brunner's tactics. As soon as he heard about Baur's detention, Lambert intervened with the Vichy authorities. After his efforts proved fruitless he fumed, 'The government, it seems to me, is nothing more than a fiction. Its executives shrink from taking responsibility.' Lambert now felt the burden of UGIF fall ever more heavily on his shoulders. He had just celebrated his forty-ninth birthday and was dreaming of retirement and, no less enticingly, revenge. When he heard of a heavy RAF raid on Bonn he asked himself, 'Shall I have the strength to preserve my humanity when the time comes to settle scores?' He was also thinking of posterity. In his diary on 20 August 1943 he sketched out a pamphlet defending his actions as the director of UGIF. True, he had cooperated with the Germans, but at least he had done some good, whereas the

Consistoire had achieved nothing by its policy of abstention. 'They pre-ferred their comfort to uncertainty and the heroism of struggle', he asserted. 'We chose the heroism of uncertainty and action, the reality of concrete effort.' The next day Raymond-Raoul Lambert was arrested along with his wife, three sons, and daughter who had been born in February 1942. She was named Marie-France, 'expressing affirmation and hope'. They were all held in Drancy until 7 December 1943 when they were transported to Auschwitz-Birkenau and murdered. André Baur, his wife and four children followed ten days later.[30]

Salonica and Sofia

Salonica, like Marseilles, was a strategically significant port on the north-ern shore of the Mediterranean. Knowing this, the Germans remained in occupation of the city and its environs after they completed the conquest of Greece in April 1940. The rest of the country was parcelled out between the Italians, who occupied the bulk, and the Bulgarians, who got Thrace and eastern Macedonia. A puppet government was installed in Athens led by Prime Minister Georgios Tsolakoglou, a general who used anti-Semitism to discredit his enemies and appease the Germans. Within a year of the occupation, German policies of extracting food, combined with the Allied blockade, produced famine conditions. Along with the rest of the population, the Jewish communities were badly hit by economic disruption and shortages.[31]

There were 70,000–80,000 Jews in Greece, divided into two commu-nities. The Romaniot Jews, whose presence dated from Roman times, were found in relatively small communities spread across the Pelopon-nese and the Greek islands. They were highly acculturated, Greek-speaking, and well-integrated into local society. Salonica, by contrast, was home to a Jewish community of some 53,000 Ladino-speaking Sephardi Jews, dating from the exodus of Spanish Jews from the Iberian peninsula after 1492. It comprised an elite of wealthy merchants and professionals, a large middling class of small traders and shopkeepers, and, uniquely, a working class of stevedores and manual labourers. Jews were so important to the workings of the port that it all but closed on major Jewish religious festivals. However, the salience of Jews in business and commerce stoked ethnic tension. During the inter-war years small but persistent anti-Jewish movements contributed to edgy relations between Christians and Jews in a city packed with Greek refugees from Anatolia who believed they had a right to homes and jobs.[32]

Nevertheless, under the German occupation the Jewish section was largely left alone – until the start of the war against the USSR. Then, in July 1941, the military government of Salonica, under Dr Max Merten, registered all Jewish males aged 18–45 for forced labour. On 11 July, 9,000 Jewish men were assembled in Plateia [Liberty] Square, where they were processed and made to perform humiliating exercises beneath a baking sun. Work columns were then assigned to airfield construction and road building. By December, most of the labourers had been released or ransomed back to the Jewish community.[33]

That month, Himmler pointed to the major security risk that the Jews allegedly posed to the port, but nothing much happened until the Allied landings in North Africa prompted the SS Head Office to take action. In January 1943, Eichmann sent his number two man, Rolf Günther, to reconnoitre the Jewish community. He was soon followed by Dieter Wisliceny and Alois Brunner. At the start of February they were assigned a company of order police with which to enforce anti-Jewish measures. They could also rely upon the support of the city's Greek governor, Vasilis Simonides, and the local police force. Just a few weeks earlier, the municipal authorities had sanctioned the destruction of the vast Jewish cemetery that lay close by the city centre and which many Salonicans had long considered an obstacle to urban development.[34]

Wisliceny and Brunner began by establishing a Jewish council, then registered the Jews and compelled them to wear the yellow star. Jews were limited to residence in three demarcated areas roughly equivalent to the existing Jewish districts. The poorest, known as the Baron Hirsch quarter, was conveniently close to a railway station and was chosen as a ghetto-cum-transit camp. During February, Jews were also forced to mark their businesses and homes, then expelled from the city's economic and social networks. The Chief Rabbi, Zvi Koretz, who led the Jewish council, proved to be a gullible and pliable instrument. The Germans could rely on an equally cooperative Jewish Order Service commanded by the German-speaking Jacques Albala and Vital Hasson, a former tailor. The Baron Hirsch quarter became Hasson's personal fiefdom, where he used his new-found power to extort money from fellow Jews. To members of the Jewish community like Dr Albert Menasche, all that was good and familiar now began to unravel with horrible speed. Menasche was a proud citizen: he had practised medicine in

Salonica for twenty years, had served in the Greek army, and was an accomplished amateur musician. Suddenly none of that mattered for him, his wife and daughter.[35]

On 1 March, panic swept through the community when the Jews were forced to declare all their assets. Koretz offered reassurance, but a few days later the Germans commenced a blockade of the Jewish districts and informed the Jewish council that the inhabitants were no longer permitted to move outside. All three areas were surrounded by barbed-wire fences and became, in effect, ghettos. When the Jews were forced to hand over the keys to their shops and businesses the local authorities were deluged with requests to buy or run these enterprises. Two weeks later, the Germans started to empty the Baron Hirsch quarter. The first train carried away 2,800 of the approximately 16,000 Jews confined there; it took five days for them to reach Auschwitz-Birkenau where most were murdered on arrival. Over the next fortnight four more transports departed for Auschwitz plus one that ended up in Treblinka. As the Baron Hirsch quarter was emptied, Jews were driven into it from the other ghettos. The moment they left their homes, locals descended on the vacated properties and stripped them so thoroughly that many were rendered uninhabitable. Between early April and early May, eleven more transports departed for Auschwitz. At the start of June only about 2,000 Jews were left, plus about a thousand rounded-up from communities in the surrounding countryside. Among them was Marco Nahon, a young doctor from Dimoteka, near the Turkish border. He was seized by a Sipo-SD unit along with other men from his small Jewish community in early May 1943 and held in the town's synagogue. The menfolk were forced to summon their wives and families until enough Jews had been assembled for a transport. The 740 unfortunates were then transferred to the Baron Hirsch ghetto. They were deported along with most of the Jewish council and administration on 1 June. Amongst them was Albert Menasche and his family. They had little idea where they were heading. 'In Salonika, we had vaguely heard people speak of this city,' he wrote in a post-war account, referring to their ignorance about Auschwitz.[36]

Koretz, Albala and other members of the administration were deported, though not to Poland. Their destination was a new concentration camp at Bergen-Belsen, near Celle, in northern Germany, recently established to hold Jews who the Germans considered plausible candidates to be exchanged for German nationals in Allied captivity. The transport to Bergen-Belsen also included several hundred Jews who had acquired (or claimed) Spanish nationality thanks to their Sephardi descent. When the final train departed on 10 August, carrying Jews who had previously been taken to do forced labour, 48,500 Jews had been savagely excised from the city. There was barely a murmur of protest from the Greek residents and a mere handful helped Jews to evade the Germans. Out of an ingrained sense of loyalty most young Jews chose to stay with their families. Only a few opted to defy the curfew and seek refuge with friends in the city or strike out for the mountains in search of partisans. Several hundred fugitives reached Athens with the assistance of the Italian consul, but this was to prove a temporary and precarious sanctuary.[37]

For months after the last Jews had vanished, Greek civilians and German soldiers looted the deserted districts. Wisliceny and Brunner had gone to some trouble to forestall such an eventuality by arranging for Governor Simonides to create a Service for the Disposal of Jewish Property, but the task was so enormous that the new body could not make progress quickly enough to satisfy local appetites. No fewer than twenty-seven warehouses bulged with household goods removed from Jewish homes. Only a fraction of the 2,000 businesses awaiting new management were properly evaluated and distributed. Instead, the disposal of Jewish property descended into chaos and corruption, doing little to relieve the city's housing shortage or revive its battered economy.[38]

Around the same time that Wisliceny and Brunner arrived in Salonica, Theo Dannecker was posted to Sofia in Bulgaria. He soon reached an agreement with Alexander Belev, head of the Commissariat for Jewish Affairs, for the deportation of 20,000 Jews from occupied Thrace and Macedonia. This was to be followed by the removal of 8,000 Jews from Bulgaria itself. Implementation of the plan commenced in early March, with Bulgarian troops and police rounding up 4,700 Jews in Thrace and over 7,000 in Macedonia, including 3,500 from the town of Skopje alone. The Thracian Jews were held in abysmal camps until 18–19 March when they were sent by train to Lom, on the Danube river, and loaded onto four barges that took them upstream to Vienna, where they were entrained for Treblinka. One barge sank en route, with the loss of most on board. The Macedonian Jews went overland to Treblinka in three transports.[39]

These measures had been taken with the knowledge and approval of the Bulgarian government, but when Belev set in motion the arrest of Jewish citizens in a number of provincial towns there was uproar. Several dozen professionals and intellectuals travelled to Sofia and met with Dimitar Peshev, the vice chairman of the National Assembly, to protest against the threat to Jewish friends and colleagues. Peshev was moved by what he heard about the fate of old men, women and children in Thrace and composed a petition against taking such steps against Bulgarian citizens. He managed to persuade forty-two members of the parliament to sign it. Simultaneously, Bishop Kiril of Plovdiv condemned the threatened deportations. These gestures caused the prime minister, Bogdan Filov, to order a postponement. Coincidentally, King Boris, the Bulgarian head of state, made an official visit to Hitler in Berchtesgaden at the end of March. Boris explained to his host that while he was happy to get rid of Jewish communists, he wanted to retain his Jewish subjects for labour. In May 1943, Belev tried again. This time the king intervened personally and threw his weight behind an alternative plan to disperse the 25,000 Jews of Sofia into the provinces. Despite protests and even street demonstrations by Jews in the capital, the evictions were carried out forcibly and not without harm to the victims. However, they were spared deportation, and the Allied invasion of Sicily in July 1943 finally dissuaded the Bulgarian government from further collusion with German anti-Jewish policy.[40]

The fate of the Jews remaining in Warsaw

In early January 1943, Himmler visited Warsaw. To his annoyance he discovered that despite his orders to clear the General Government of Jews and to incarcerate essential Jewish workers in SS-run camps, there were still at least 40,000 in the ghetto. He immediately issued orders that the working Jews were to be relocated to secure installations in the Lublin area. Himmler's grand plan was to combine security measures with SS business interests by transferring the workers and plant to enterprises operating under Globocnik's aegis. However, when Oswald Pohl, director of the WVHA, pointed out that this was impossible at such short notice, he accepted the principle of retaining a concentration camp in the city on condition that surplus Jews were removed. Amidst the welter of orders and counter-orders, the Jews of Warsaw took their fate into their own hands.[41]

The great deportation had left 36,000 Jews living in the ghetto legally with jobs and work certificates. The bulk of them inhabited a dozen blocks north of Gesia Street, between Bonifraska Street to the west and Smocza Street to the east. They included about 2,000 employed by the Jewish council, several hundred Order Service personnel and their families, outside workers, and no less than 4,000 employed in the Werterfassung (Centre for the Registration of Valuables), a compound consisting of storehouses where the property of the deported was stored and sorted. The Werterfassung was the biggest single employer in the ghetto. It was a vast recycling enterprise, with sections devoted to everything from mattresses, kitchenware and household furniture, to musical instruments. So many hands were needed that many illegals found work there. About 20,000 uncertified Jews lived wild in deserted apartments on streets long since cleared of their inhabitants. South of an officially uninhabited, sterilized strip, four large workshops and about half a dozen smaller German-run enterprises employed 20,000 Jews. The largest were the clothing factory on Lezno Street, originally established by Walther Többens in mid-1941, and Schultz's fur-making shop which also produced German army uniforms. The workforce lived in fenced-off barracks consisting of houses and tenements that had been knocked together. Near the southern limit of the old ghetto boundary, 4,000 Jews worked in the Brushmakers' Shop.[42]

The demography of the ghetto had changed as radically as its geography and economic structure. Three-quarters of the survivors were aged 20–50. The ratio of men to women had been reversed, so that there were now 100 males for every 78 females. There were almost no children: the only minors belonged to the families of privileged and protected Jews, the remnants of the Jewish council and the Order Service. The nutritional situation was much improved. Employees in the workshops were given sufficient rations to render smuggling unnecessary. However, the relative abundance of food did not mean that everyone ate as much as they wanted. Jews now started stockpiling supplies, provisioning hideouts that they suspected would one day be required. In the meantime, they toiled from sunup to sundown.[43]

'The days pass in gloom,' Abraham Lewin sighed in early October, 'bleak, full of grief and sorrow.' For Hillel Seidman everyday life had become an 'unending routine search for food, refuge, and ultimate safety'. Everything in the workshops was strictly regimented. Each worker had a number and identification papers attaching him to a

specific place. They lived in billets, without wives or children. Ringelblum remarked bitterly, 'slaves don't require families'. At dawn they
marched to work in columns, and sweated all day under the lash of
all-powerful masters. They had no personal possessions to speak of and
could not risk illness since there were no longer clinics or hospitals in
the ghetto. On second thoughts, Ringelblum concluded that they lived
'worse than slaves, because the latter knew they would remain alive . . .
The Jews are sentenced to death.' The religious and sociological character of the ghetto had been so cruelly engineered that it didn't need
schools or cheders. One of the surviving rabbis remarked to Seidman
that 'there are very few children left to religious families . . . Most of
these did not have any money or *protexia* [protection or patronage] and
were therefore unable to save their children. Those children who have
survived are mainly from the assimilationist ranks, who had both the
means and the influence.'[44]

Traumatized, hardly able to appreciate what was before their eyes,
those who had survived the bloody turmoil used the period of calm to
take stock as best they could. 'The present tragedy is so overwhelming
that none of us can accept or even evaluate its sheer enormity,' Seidman
wrote. 'Neither the public nor the individual are capable of understanding the catastrophe.' 'Have they really murdered a community of 300,000
Jews in Treblinka?' Lewin asked. 'It is so hard to believe in this appalling
and horrible truth; more than 300,000 Jews have been murdered in the
course of eight weeks.' Ringelblum questioned why there had been no
resistance. How could fifty SS men and 200 accomplices destroy such an
enormous, vibrant population? 'Why did we allow ourselves to be led
like sheep to the slaughter?' He found the explanation in German tactics
– the selections, the trick of making the workshops seem secure before
turning them into traps, the repeated blockades, the hunger and feeble-
ness of the victims. But he also excoriated the Jewish council and the
Order Service. 'They said not a single word of protest against this revolting assignment to lead their own brothers to the slaughter.' They had not
just been corrupted by the Germans: they exceeded them in malevolence. They had uncovered perfectly good hiding places and dragged
evaders to the Umschlagplatz. 'Where did Jews get such murderous violence? When in our history did we ever before raise so many hundreds
of killers?' To Seidman, the Order Service posed a 'difficult and painful
chapter'. He accounted for their behaviour in the light of his religious
beliefs. The Order Service men were happy to carry out German

commands because they were assimilated Jews who despised the Orthodox Jewish masses: converts, 'golden youth', an 'alien element, enemies to
their own people'. Ultimately, though, the Germans had contrived circumstances in which certain Jews 'could live only at the expense of our
fellow Jews'. 'Polish Jewry is finished', Lewin grieved, 'it exists no more.
Hitler has put an end to it.' Since Polish Jews were the demographic and
cultural reservoir of world Jewry, the global Jewish population had suffered a fatal blow.[45]

Yet, in a surprisingly short time, people recovered. On a sunny day
in early November, Lewin found himself watching Jews strolling on
Mila and Zamenhof streets. A new mood permeated the ghetto: a determination to resist and a desire for revenge. Meditating on the services
for Yom Kippur, the Day of Atonement, that marked the end of the
great action in 1942, Seidman shifted from speculation about the divine
response to the 'spirit of bitterness [that] holds sway everywhere . . .
Revenge is all that can bring some comfort now.' Stanislaw Adler sensed
'For almost everyone, there was a desire to endure and, as time passed
the desire for revenge grew stronger.' 'It seems to me', Ringelblum
declared, 'that people will no longer go to the slaughter like lambs.'
When Eliyahu Rozanski, a member of the Jewish Fighting Organization, assassinated Jacob Lejkin, the deputy commander of the Order
Service, there was widespread approval. The authority of the Jewish
council had evaporated and the Order Service were perceived as little
better than collaborators. Support was shifting to the youthful leaders
of the resistance. By tilting the generational and the gender balance of
the ghetto population as well as dissolving families, the Germans had
inadvertently created the optimum conditions for a rebellion.[46]

During the last two months of 1942, the Jewish underground parties finally achieved a unity of organization and purpose. Much of this
success was due to Mordechai Anielewicz, a charismatic young member
of the HaShomer HaTzair Zionist youth movement who had been
involved in underground activity in other parts of Poland over the previous two years. Anielewicz entered the ghetto around November 1942
and quickly assumed command of the Jewish Fighting Organization. In
order to convince the Polish underground that the Jews were viable
partners, the various factions agreed to create a Jewish National Committee alongside a unified command structure. Tsukunft, the youth
wing of the Bund, formally affiliated to the ZOB although its parent
organization baulked at the idea of joining a 'Jewish' national commit-

tee. Conversely, the Revisionist Zionist militia, the Zydowski Zwiazek Wojskowy (ZZW, Jewish Military Union), declined to do more than loosely coordinate with the ZOB because the latter included the Bund and the Communists. This was a serious breach since the ZZW boasted many former Polish Jewish army officers and had established a good rapport with the Home Army. As a result it was able to equip its 250 fighters with an impressive armoury. On a visit to their headquarters at 7 Muranowska Street, Ringelblum saw 'racks of different types of weapons, machine-guns, carbines, revolvers of different types, hand-grenades, bags of ammunition, and German uniforms . . .'[47]

The ZOB renewed its efforts to get arms and assistance from the Polish Home Army. Aryeh Wilner for the ZOB, Adolf Berman representing the Jewish National Committee, and the Bundist Leon Feiner, undertook the perilous work of liaison with the Polish underground outside the ghetto. These negotiations were neither easy nor straightforward. Hillel Seidman recalled a disappointing meeting with the Polish resistance during which his interlocutors declared 'we are not prepared to split the Polish underground arguing about the Jewish question'. When Seidman suggested they sabotage the railways carrying Jews to the death camps, he was met with silence. 'Not one strand of Polish society bothers to reply to our frantic calls for help,' he concluded angrily. In December, after repeated requests, the ZOB obtained a delivery of ten poor-quality pistols. It is estimated that by this time there were 600 activists ready to fight the Germans.[48]

To raise cash to buy more weapons the ZOB appealed to the wealthy and embarked on a campaign of forced taxation from those unwilling to contribute voluntarily. They made 'collections' from factory managers at the point of a gun. The Jewish council handed over 5 million zlotys. Meanwhile, a craze for bunker-building gripped the population. 'Everyone is making them', Ringelblum noted. 'Everywhere, in all the shops and elsewhere in the Ghetto, hiding places are being built. Their construction has actually become a flourishing specialized craft. Skilled workers, engineers etc., are making a living out of it.' Bunkers were designed to be habitable in cold weather and stocked with enough provisions to last for weeks. Some were 'equipped with gas, electricity, water, and toilets. Some of them cost thousands of zlotys.' Seidman visited one that was home to an entire yeshiva. Of course, only the well-off and well-connected could afford such havens. The poor relied on ingenuity. No one was sure if they would work anyway. Ringelblum concluded, 'the populace is afraid that at the crucial terrifying moment the Germans will discover some clever way of turning to naught all our efforts at self-rescue. Whether this is true or not, only the future will tell.'[49]

On 10 January 1943, rumours of a forthcoming deportation reached the ghetto. In fact, the Germans were not planning to murder the population; rather, the commander of the security police in the city, Ferdinand von Sammern-Frankenegg, aimed to remove illegal Jews and transfer the workshops to the Lublin area as per Himmler's orders. The ZOB did not know this. Anticipating a repeat of the 1942 deportations, its commanders gathered, but still could not agree whether it was time to show their hand. According to Seidman, the Polish underground signalled that it was not willing to offer assistance of any kind. He estimated the ZOB's arsenal as 143 revolvers and 4 carbines.[50]

The test came early in the morning of 18 January 1943 when German police, led by Order Service men, entered the ghetto and started hunting Jews without papers. As word of the incursion spread, streets and workshops emptied. In their frustration the Germans began to grab anyone they could find. The sortie took the Jewish fighting units by surprise and few were able to obtain weapons from the armouries or assemble in numbers. Instead, individual fighters acting largely on their own initiative engaged the Germans in gunfights on the streets. Up to a dozen Germans were killed in these chaotic encounters, but so were most of the Jewish combatants. Zuckerman and a comrade, Zacharia Artstein, found themselves at the top of a house on Zamenhof Street when four or five Germans barged in. 'I was sitting in a room with my gun cocked. We heard them, we heard the shouts: "Raus!" (Get out!) Then we heard them climbing the stairs . . . After they entered our room, he [Artstein] shot them in the back. Then we shot too and the Germans began running away. After the first shot they didn't even have time to take out their guns. They were so sure of themselves . . . I took the gun from the German who fell in the room. He was still alive, it was a pity to waste a bullet on him. But we did take their guns and grenades.' During the first day of the action, the Germans nabbed about 3,000 Jews. For the fighters though, 'a new period in our lives had begun'. Zuckerman later recalled, 'never in my life had I been so happy'.[51]

Anielewicz, who had been in the thick of the fray, met with ZOB commanders the following day to review their tactics. Instead of confronting the Germans head-on, they decided to fight from prepared positions and draw them into alleys, courtyards, and buildings where the enemy's superior firepower would be negated. There were a few more skirmishes over the next days, but the Germans avoided entering houses and the fighters stayed off the streets. Although they caught about 2,000 Jews alive, the raiders left about 1,000 ghetto dwellers dead. Their plans and their easy assumptions about Jewish behaviour had been disrupted for the first time. Zuckerman exalted, 'in all the months before, all the German had to do was yell "Raus!" and the Jews would come out. And this time, no Jew came out. This time, the Germans came up to us and we killed them.'[52]

The bunkers and malinas had worked, though survival in hiding for day after day was a chastening experience. The floor of Adler's bunker was covered by excrement and urine. It was very cold. Some of the Jews had typhus. There were women and a handful of terrified children. To stop them whimpering while Germans were in the vicinity, the infants were drugged. Adler recalled, 'a death-like silence pervades the shelter. Over three hundred people are listening, immobile and in suspense to the echo of resounding shots. The tension is extreme when the tramp of actual or imaginary SS men pass along the street close to the shelter, or when we hear sounds that indicate that the Germans are looking for something on the ground floor of the building just above. A concrete ceiling is all that separates us from them.'[53]

Dr Edward Reicher, a physician who had come to Warsaw from Lwow in 1941, described conditions in a typical small-scale malina. 'We slipped back beneath the floorboards into our rabbit hole,' he wrote in a wartime account reconstructed from memory after 1945. 'More and more people began to arrive. In the end, instead of thirty, there were seventy of us, counting friends and relatives of residents along with residents of adjoining buildings, including the elderly, the sick, and many children. How could we say no? It would have meant certain death. Seventy people in a space of 150 square feet, and only six and a half feet high. Standing one pressed against next, we could barely move. There wasn't enough air, and after a few hours we were running out of oxygen. There was no electricity. Our candles flickered and began to die. The sick and the elderly were suffering from the lack of air, but we were helpless to do anything for them. Upstairs the Germans were combing the building, floor by floor.' When a baby started to cry and its mother vainly attempted to soothe it, another woman attacked her and killed the infant. 'Where was God?' Reicher asked himself. 'Didn't he see what was happening here?'[54]

The happenings on 18–22 January, though small-scale in themselves, had an immense impact on the ghetto dwellers, the Poles, and the Germans. Zuckerman remembered that 'The January Uprising gave us wings, elevated us in the eyes of the Jews and enhanced our image as fighters, giving us a good name . . . The January events had extraordinary repercussions even in the Armia Krajowa [Home Army, AK], which had always eschewed us and now agreed to give us fifty pistols immediately. They also supplied us with grenades and the explosives we needed.' As the reputation of the ZOB soared, its commanders became the de facto leaders of the community. Edward Reicher recalled, 'Life in the ghetto changed. Now it was officially led by the young. The Jewish council was indeed the puppet of the German authorities. The lethargy of the older generation gave way to the energy of the young. They understood that the attitude of the previous generation had been a failure. If they didn't take things into their own hands, no one would do anything.' Bunker-building intensified still further, and architects designed underground shelters for civilians and as bases from which the combat units could operate. Support and money flowed to the ZOB and there was a tolerance for the 'collections' aimed at the ghetto elite. In the course of one such mission, Simha Rotem recalled, 'One of us knocked on the door and when it opened we burst in, identified the man of the house, stood facing him in a "persuasive" movement, and announced, "We've come to get your contribution for the ZOB." The Jew refused. I put the barrel of my revolver near him; he froze . . .' Rotem and his youthful comrades departed with the money. It helped towards the purchase of handguns, grenades and ammunition.[55]

Anielewicz and the military leadership learned hard lessons from the January engagement. They fashioned a more resilient command and control structure and resolved to keep fighting units permanently mobilized. Thanks to the cash and support in kind they were now getting, it was feasible for the activists to train all day or man look-out posts. They stationed 22 units, each consisting of 10–20 fighters from one political faction, at key points around the ghetto. In addition to around 200 handguns, they now had ten rifles, one submachine gun, hundreds of grenades, and explosives from which they manufactured bombs and mines. Zuckerman preferred handguns. Few Jews knew how to load or maintain rifles, and they were awkward to use in confined spaces; revolvers or pistols required less training and were easier to handle in small rooms, stairways and cellars. The fighters also manufactured

Molotov cocktails, although getting gasoline for them was far from easy. Rather than simply remain on standby, Anielewicz sent groups of fighters on regular missions. To prevent the dismantling of workshops and the subsequent transfer of employees to labour camps, combat groups set fire to them. They also fire-bombed the warehouses of the Werter-fassung, causing major damage. At least one of these raids resulted in a gunfight with workshop guards. Hit squads carried out several more assassinations, including Mieczyslaw Brzeznski, the commander of the Order Service at the Umschlagplatz, and Dr Alfred Nossig, an elderly German Jew suspected of working for the Gestapo.[56]

While some Jews trained to fight and others built bunkers, thousands opted to hide on the Aryan side. They joined a 'hidden city' that had its origins when the ghetto was first established. At that point Jews married to Poles, converts, and highly assimilated individuals who had business or social contacts willing to help them defy the German edict either resolved not to move in or made a quick exit. Over the next year or so, Jews inside the ghetto comforted themselves that however bad things were they stood a better chance of surviving inside than outside. Endless tales filtered back of Jews who were shot trying to leave or betrayed once they crossed the boundary. Since it was almost impossible to leave as a family unit it was only after families were shredded in the great deportation that large numbers of Jews felt liberated as well as desperate enough to take their chance. Yitzhak Zuckerman noticed that 'after September [1942], Jews started leaving in every possible way for the Aryan side of Warsaw; they looked for Polish friends and for apartments.' The exodus gained momentum after the January clashes. There was little doubt that, despite the bloody nose administered to the Germans, they would soon be back. Whereas the ghetto had once seemed the safer option than life in hiding, the pendulum swung the other way.[57]

Getting out was the easy part. Finding accommodation was much harder. To afford rent, often deliberately inflated if the landlord suspected the tenant was Jewish, it was necessary to have plenty of money. To buy food required a ration card and to move around meant getting identification papers. These were no less costly. But there was little point in getting documents if you looked and sounded like a Jew. Polonized Jews who spoke without a Yiddish accent, Jews who had fair hair, Jews with light-coloured eyes all stood a better chance of passing as Aryans. To survive in the Polish districts it was also essential to walk with a straight back and purposeful movements, to be cheerful and smile no matter what. Familiarity with Roman Catholicism and religious rituals was a big advantage since wrongly answering a question about either could give you away. Jews on the Aryan side were at permanent risk of exposure by anti-Semitic Poles or opportunists who saw Jews as the route to easy money. Zuckerman, who operated in Aryan Warsaw from April 1943 until the Home Army uprising of August 1944, recalled 'the danger from Polish blackmailers lurking on the other side who were as familiar as we were with the comings and goings. The blackmailers [shmaltsovniks – from the Polish for blackmail, 'szmalcownicy'] were one of the greatest dangers for a Jew seeking refuge on the Aryan side of Warsaw. Dozens of blackmailers were usually swarming around the exits and gates. They would rob the Jew by threatening to turn him over to the Germans; if they had a hope that this Jew had something left, they would follow him and extort something from him, down to his last cent. After they extorted everything from him, they would turn him over to the Polish police or the Germans.'[58]

However, in late 1942, the Polish underground government established the Council to Aid Jews, codenamed Zegota, to assist those who had gone into hiding or were masquerading as Aryans. At its height it is estimated that Zegota, in cooperation with the Jewish National Council and the Bund, was channelling money to 8,900 Jews. In March 1943, the civil leadership of the Polish underground issued a warning against betraying Jews in hiding. Shmaltsovniks who operated in public places increasingly had to reckon with reproaches from ordinary Poles who regarded any action on behalf of the Germans as treachery. While the underground authorities took little judicial action against those committing extortion or betraying Jews, interventions by members of the resistance induced the blackmailers to exercise greater caution and restrict their nefarious practices. The historian Gunnar S. Paulsson estimates that on the eve of the Warsaw Home Army uprising 28,000 Jews were concealed under one guise or another on the Aryan side. Wladyslaw Szpilman made his move in January, slipping away from an outside work party to an artist's studio secured for him by friends. So did Michael Zylberberg, joining his wife who had left the previous November. He dropped out of a labour column and made his way to the apartment where his wife was staying with a Polish woman. She was glad to keep his wife, he recalled, 'as she felt it was her patriotic duty to hide someone from the Germans'. He was less welcome and soon moved on. Stanislaw Adler left the ghetto in February, concealed in a cart carrying out dead bodies.[59]

On 13 April, shortly before the Passover festival, Yitzhak Zuckerman also left the ghetto. He was on a mission for the ZOB to make contact with the communist underground militia, the People's Army (Armia Ludowa, AL), to obtain weapons and support. On the sixth morning of the assignment he was woken by the sound of explosions coming from the ghetto: the German assault had begun. Initially it was directed by Ferdinand von Sammern-Frankenegg. He had at his disposal 9 officers and 821 other ranks drawn from a Waffen-SS panzergrenadier regiment, 6 officers and 228 men of an order police battalion, plus over 330 Ukrainian auxiliaries led by 2 German officers. For support he could call on army artillery, three armoured vehicles, and a dozen heavy machine guns. This time, however, the Jewish Fighting Organization had received advanced warning of German movements and its units were waiting. Simha Rotem, stationed at the Brushmakers', recalled that 'we saw German soldiers crossing the Nalewki intersection on their way to the Central Ghetto, walking in an endless procession. Behind them were tanks, armoured vehicles, light cannons, and hundreds of Waffen-SS units on motorcycles. "They look like they're going to war", he exclaimed to a comrade. Soon they could hear detonations and gunfire to the north. Marek Edelman commanded a Bundist unit in the path of the German advance. He watched the soldiers deploy as if on exercise. 'But no, they did not scare us and we were not taken by surprise. We were only awaiting an opportune moment. Such a moment presently arrived. The Germans chose the intersection at Mila and Zamenhof Streets for their bivouac area, and battle-groups barricaded at the four corners of the street opened concentric fire on them. Strange projectiles began exploding everywhere . . . German dead soon littered the street. The remainder tried to find cover in the neighbouring stores and house entrances, but their shelter proved insufficient.' The SS called up armoured vehicles, but the first one was hit by a Molotov cocktail and caught fire, causing the others to back away. After nearly an hour of combat the Germans pulled out. Another clash took place at the entrance to the ghetto at the junction of Nalewki and Gesia Streets, lasting for over six hours. Again, the Germans were repulsed. Meanwhile, the Revisionists beat off repeated assaults on their HQ at Muranowski Square. A Polish flag and a flag with a blue Star of David flew from the roof throughout the day, enraging the Germans and causing awe amongst Polish spectators who now crowded into vantage points to watch the astonishing spectacle of armed Jews throwing back attack after attack by Waffen-SS troops. The Germans managed to seize just 580 ghetto dwellers.[60]

The next day, the Germans turned their attention to the Brush-makers' quarter. Rotem's commander, Hanoch Gutman, waited till they advanced into the compound, then detonated the mine that had con-sumed so much time and energy. There was 'a tremendous explosion . . . crushed bodies of soldiers, limbs flying, cobblestones and fences crum-bling, complete chaos. I saw and I didn't believe: German soldiers screaming in panicky flight, leaving their wounded behind. I pulled out one grenade and then another and tossed them. My comrades were also shooting and firing at them. We weren't marksmen but we did hit some. The Germans took off.' They returned, with greater care, but were repulsed several times. Eventually, the Jewish combat units were forced to evacuate their stronghold because the building was on fire. The ZZW unit at Muranowska Square was finally dislodged too, and withdrew to the Aryan side. Beyond the ghetto, an Armia Ludowa contingent sup-ported the Jewish fighters by shooting up a German field gun crew. When the Germans called off the day's operation they were able to claim only 505 Jews for deportation.[61]

On 23 April 1943, Mordechai Anielewicz managed to scribble a letter to his comrade Yitzhak Zuckerman. 'I don't know what to write you,' he began hastily. 'Let's dispense with personal details this time. I have only one expression to describe: my feelings and the feelings of my comrades: things have surpassed our boldest dreams: the Germans ran away from the ghetto twice. One of our units held out for forty minutes, and the other one for more than six hours. The mine planted in the Brushmakers' area exploded. So far we have only had one casualty . . .' Anielewicz revelled in the information that SWIT radio, the Polish underground station, had transmitted an admiring account of the Jewish resistance. He was thrilled that the AL had conducted a support-ing attack. But he informed Zuckerman that 'we are switching to a system of guerrilla action'. They needed better, heavier weapons: rifles and submachine guns. Then he added details about the fate of the civil-ians: 'I can't describe to you the conditions in which the Jews are living. Only a few individuals will hold out. All the rest will be killed sooner or later. The die is cast. In all the bunkers where our comrades are hiding, you can't light a candle for the lack of oxygen . . .' The workshops had ceased to function and large expanses of the ghetto were on fire. 'Be well my friend. Perhaps we shall meet again. The main thing is the dream of my life has come true. I've lived to see a Jewish defence in the ghetto in all its greatness and glory.'[62]

The Germans had nothing to crow about. Goebbels fretted in his diary, 'From some of the occupied territories I am receiving signals about unpleasant matters. The fighting in the Warsaw ghetto is still continuing, using the military resources ... The Jews are putting up a desperate resistance ... The cause of this desperate resistance is, among other things, that the Jews are aware of what is in store for them when the resistance is broken. They cannot surrender.' Thanks to the failure of the first assaults, Sammern-Frankenegg was replaced by Jürgen Stroop, an SS-brigadier general who had gained plenty of experience on the eastern front. He cancelled further large-scale assaults and sent in small combat teams with engineers to destroy buildings and bunkers, setting alight entire blocks. Appeals by factory managers for Jews to leave the workshops and go peacefully were abandoned in favour of wholesale destruction of the ghetto.[63]

Over the following week, the fighting degenerated into isolated skirmishes with German patrols that ran into ZOB units. As they were driven from their fortified positions the fighters sought refuge in civilian bunkers. For the Jewish population, which had descended underground, conditions became hellish. 'The situation in the shelters is desperate and hopeless,' Simha Rotem wrote in an after-action report. 'Most palpable is the lack of air, water and food. Day after day passes. On the tenth day of the aktsia [action], the Ghetto is burned. Everywhere – sooty bodies. In the streets, in the courtyards, and in the cellars, people are burned alive. Because of (1) a lack of equipment, (2) a lack of food and water, (3) the impossibility of engaging the enemy in battle – since he is not within the Ghetto but is destroying the Ghetto from outside – we are forced to accept the idea of getting our people out to the forest to continue with our war.' On 29–30 April, Rotem went through the sewers to the Polish side in the hope of locating Home Army officers and arranging the evacuation of the Jewish fighters, most of whom were then still alive.[64]

At this point, the ZOB commanders confronted a gigantic flaw in their planning. As Zuckerman later admitted, 'We didn't have a rescue plan because we didn't figure that any of us would survive.' While fighting continued at points around the flaming ghetto, both Rotem and

Zuckerman cast around for means to extract the combat units and transport them either to safe houses or to the nearest forests where they could convert to partisan activity. But, as each day passed, the Germans uncovered more bunkers and forced more Jews to the Umschlagplatz. On 8 May a German force stumbled across the ZOB command bunker at 18 Mila Street. About 300 fighters were concentrated there. Some were killed in the exchange of gunfire and a few managed to tunnel through to adjacent basements and escape. Approximately 120, fearing that the Germans would pump in poison gas, took their own lives. Mordechai Anielewicz died, surrounded by the young men and women of the Jewish Fighting Organization.[65]

Twenty-four hours later, Rotem returned with sewer workers as guides. At moments he had to use his gun to force them deeper into the bowels of the smouldering ghetto. Once above ground he found little but ruination. Buildings were ablaze, bunkers were blown in, and only a few dazed Jews wandered through the rubble. He managed to collect forty survivors of the combat groups and took them back to the sewers. When they reached the exit there was no transport, so the exhausted, hungry fighters had to remain in the putrid tunnels for another twenty-four hours. On the morning of 10 May, Rotem heard the rescue lorry approach and threw a screen around the manhole cover. 'They begin coming out of the cistern. I don't recognise anyone, even though I knew them all, for these weren't people, but exhausted ghosts, barely tottering on their feet. A crowd of people gathers around, looked on, and said, "The cats are coming out."' The extraction team and the truck were provided by the Armia Ludowa. To Zuckerman's fury, the AK showed no interest in the ZOB remnant. To the contrary, 'they wanted to finish off not only the uprising but the rebels. As far as the AK was concerned, as fighters we weren't wanted anywhere on Polish soil.'[66]

During the confusion one group in the sewers was left behind. When they finally emerged they were wiped out. Only eighty fighters escaped the carnage in the ghetto to reach the Lomianki woods or safe houses in the city. Less than half of them survived subsequent encounters with German patrols, Polish nationalist partisans or shmaltsovniks. The Germans had suffered roughly sixteen dead and eighty-five wounded; the figures for the number of casualties amongst the Ukrainian auxiliaries is uncertain. By their reckoning, the Germans removed 53,667 Jews from the ghetto. At least 7,000 were killed in the fighting and 7,000 were sent directly to Treblinka. Over 8,000 endured on the Aryan side. The plan to transfer all the Jewish workers to camps in the Lublin area was never realized, but around 20,000 did end up as slave labour in Majdanek or other places where their lease on life was extended.[67]

Polish reactions to the uprising and the liquidation of the ghetto varied from admiration through compassion to glee. The AK and the AL mounted at least eleven supporting attacks on German targets outside and at least one AK unit may even have penetrated the ghetto to fight alongside the ZZW. In a press bulletin the Home Army high command praised the 'courageous, determined armed resistance ... the fighters of the Warsaw ghetto should be accorded full respect and support'. Broadcasting from London on 4 May, General Sikorski called on his countrymen 'to give all help and shelter to those being murdered'. He added that 'before all humanity, which has for too long been silent, I condemn these crimes'. But a Catholic underground paper saw the tragedy as an opportunity for the Jews to convert: 'Their souls will be cleansed and redeemed by the baptism of blood . . . they can be saved in the face of destruction by baptism and the true faith.'[68]

In fact, resistance on the site of the ghetto continued for several more weeks as groups of armed Jews who were based in undiscovered bunkers harassed German patrols. One was led by Zacharia Artstein who had fought side by side with Yitzhak Zuckerman in the house on Zamenhof Street. A handful of shelters remained undetected and were inhabited until the city was liberated. In a remarkable display of parsimony, the SS erected a concentration camp along what had been Gesia Street and brought in 4,000 foreign Jews to comb through the debris and recover anything of use. They succeeded in retrieving 30 million bricks and 6,000 tons of scrap metal. Conditions in the camp, KL Lublin-Arbeitslager Warschau, were horrible and prisoners were regularly shot. Their bodies were burned on pyres atop the rubble and ashes of the ghetto.[69]

The view from Washington, London and Bermuda

Jewish armed resistance in the Warsaw ghetto was reported in Britain and America within a short time and quite accurately. Information about the fighting in January 1943 was published in the London *Daily Telegraph* on 19 March headlined 'Warsaw Ghetto Plea to the Allies'. It was based on reports the paper had received via Shmuel Zygielbojm, the Bund representative on the exile Polish National Council. The Jewish Telegraphic Agency gave a solid account of the uprising in its bulletin dated 24 April, although the first substantial reports were not published in British newspapers until 7 May 1943. Then the *Manchester Guardian* gave the story a major spread, remarking that although the battle had begun on 19 April, the Germans had still not succeeded in suppressing Jewish opposition. It stated that 'This is the first instance of organised guerrilla resistance to the Germans by the Jews on any considerable scale.' The revolt was the lead story on the front page of the *Jewish Chronicle* the same day. A JTA bulletin on 12 May stated that resistance had been crushed, but two days later, the *Manchester Guardian* claimed that Jews were still holding out. As late as 25 May, *The Times* printed a short item headed 'Pogrom in Warsaw Ghetto. Jews' Desperate Fight'. This article was based on messages from the ghetto dated 28 April and 11 May which had been released by Zygielbojm's colleague Dr Ignacy Schwarzbart. Jewish resistance provided an inspiring story and the struggle was soon mythologized as 'Ghettograd', especially by left-wing journalists. However, this did little to affect the practical response of Allied government.[70]

In both Britain and America, the December 1942 declaration on Nazi war crimes had been followed by a great deal of agitation: letters were written to the press, public meetings were held, and committees were formed. Eleanor Rathbone was sceptical of its effect. She wrote to George Bell, Bishop of Chichester, 'I rather fear that the results may be that people will feel that they have discharged their consciences and that nothing more is needed.' She was especially dubious since the declaration made no reference to any concrete steps to help Jews. Determined to sustain the momentum generated by the government statement, in early January Rathbone and fellow independent MP Archibald Hill convened a meeting of Jewish and non-Jewish activists. Three weeks later they led an impressive deputation to see Anthony Eden. Rathbone followed this up with a pamphlet setting out a twelve-point plan to save the Jews in Europe entitled 'The Nazi Massacres of Poles and Jews: what rescue measures are practically possible'. On 9 March she founded the National Committee for Rescue from Nazi Terror. It included amongst its vice-presidents the archbishops of both Canterbury and York, and Sir William Beveridge, feted for his recent proposal for the creation of a welfare state. The campaigners were buoyed up by a Gallup poll, commissioned by the Committee, which revealed that 78 per cent of the public favoured admitting Jews facing death, 68 per cent on a temporary basis and 10 per cent indefinitely.[71]

Rathbone and her fellow campaigners did not know that a committee of the war cabinet, including the foreign secretary, the home secretary, and the secretary of state for the colonies (responsible for overseeing Palestine), had already deliberated on the matter. It had resolved to take no action for the present on the grounds that aid for refugees would divert resources from the war effort and barely dent the problem. The best solution for their plight was an Allied victory. Archibald Randall, the civil servant who handled refugee issues at the Foreign Office, wrote in a minute on 22 February 1943 responding to Rathbone's efforts that she was an 'impatient idealist' who 'knows very little'. He elaborated that 'The Jewish disaster is only part of the vast human problem of Europe under Nazi control; other parts are starving children, the deliberate extermination of Polish and Czech intelligentsia, forced labour and the spiritual perversion of youth.' Randall further objected that Hitler would never release large numbers of Jews and even if he did there was no shipping to transport them, nowhere for them to go, and nothing to feed them on. Yet, in the face of pleas for action from such luminaries as E. M. Forster, George Bernard Shaw and Rebecca West, who were joint signatories of a heartfelt letter that appeared in *The Times* on 16 February, the government realized it had to do something. Hence the Foreign Office began to explore joint action with the Americans and together they announced that a conference would shortly be held to discuss the 'refugee problem'.[72]

A similar movement of opinion built up in the United States. On 1 March 1943, the American Jewish Congress in collaboration with the AFL-CIO trades union federation and church organizations packed New York's Madison Square Gardens. Ten thousand people stood outside listening to the proceedings on the public address system. The speakers included Stephen Wise, Chaim Weizmann, Mayor Fiorello LaGuardia and Senator Robert Wagner. At its climax, the rally endorsed an eleven-point resolution that called on the administration to offer financial guarantees to states willing to accept Jewish refugees from German-controlled Europe and encourage neutrals to open their borders to those in flight. It also demanded the easing of immigration controls into the USA and Palestine. Finally, it asked the United Nations to set up an agency devoted to saving refugees. A Jewish Joint

Emergency Committee on European Jewish Affairs emerged in the aftermath of the rally to press for the realization of its demands.[73]

Eight days later, Madison Square Gardens played host to a very different kind of protest. A new body, styling itself the Emergency Committee to Save the Jewish People of Europe, mounted a spectacular and moving pageant entitled 'We Will Never Die'. It was the brainchild of two young Palestinian Jews who had arrived in the USA as envoys of the Revisionist Zionist underground army, the Irgun, in 1940. Hillel Kook (who used the nom de guerre Peter Bergson) and Samuel Merlin began their activity in the USA by covertly generating support for the Irgun and overtly campaigning for the creation of a Jewish army to contribute towards the liberation of the Jewish people under German rule. But when he read the *New York Times* report based on the Riegner telegram, Bergson abandoned this mission in favour of what he realized was the more urgent task of rescue. He collected a remarkable group of Jews and non-Jews from the worlds of politics, journalism and entertainment to publicize the Jewish catastrophe, raise money for rescue work, and prod the administration into taking definite steps to help. Unfortunately, the 'Bergson Boys' did not attempt to coordinate their activity with Stephen Wise or the established leadership of American Jewry. Instead, it appeared to Wise that they were dividing the Jewish community, diluting resources, and confusing the message it was trying to send to American politicians. Wise was particularly apprehensive that a noisy campaign would actually alienate the White House, so exerted himself to stifle Bergson's imaginative crusade. This certainly created the impression that American Jews were at each other's throats, but did little to stem the bandwagon that the Bergson Boys had set in motion. 'We Will Never Die' played to full houses in Washington, Philadelphia, Boston, Chicago and Los Angeles.[74]

On 11 March, James McDonald, the chair of the President's Advisory Committee on Political Refugees, added his weight to the campaign by issuing a statement echoing the programme of the Jewish Joint Emergency Committee. These Jewish and non-Jewish interventions had an effect on Congress, where the majority leader submitted a resolution to the Senate expressing support for rescue measures. Jewish lobbyists applied themselves to state legislatures across the country in pursuit of similar gestures. In April, Wise addressed a mass rally of 20,000 in the Chicago Stadium. Translating indignation into practical action, however, was proving immeasurably harder – not least because the British and American governments were determined to avoid being stampeded into inconvenient, costly or potentially embarrassing measures on behalf of the Jews. During a visit to Washington in March, Eden made it clear that the British government did not favour pressure on neutral countries to accept Jewish refugees or breaking the blockade to send food to starving ghettos. Breckinridge Long, the US assistant secretary of state who dealt with refugee matters, wrote candidly in his diary that 'One Jewish faction under the leadership of Rabbi Stephen Wise has been so assiduous in pushing their particular cause . . . that they are apt to produce a reaction against their interest . . . One danger in it all is that their activities may lend color to the charges of Hitler that we are fighting the war on account of and at the instigation and direction of our Jewish citizens.' He added that such activity 'might easily be a definite detriment to our war effort'.[75]

It was against this background that British and American officials came up with an international conference on the refugee question. The conference was held on Bermuda during 19–29 April 1943. The island location was deliberately selected because it was remote and immune to barracking by Jewish protesters. The only Jew who attended was Congressman Sol Bloom, a Roosevelt loyalist who chaired the House Foreign Affairs Committee. In any case, the delegates had precious little room for manoeuvre. The British only consented to attend if it was agreed in advance that the meeting would not recommend negotiations with the Germans, would not consider the exit of millions of people, and would rule out exchanging prisoners of war for civilians. Nor was there to be any question of violating the blockade. Every concrete proposal was shot down. For example, when the British suggested setting up camps in North Africa to accommodate Jewish refugees currently stuck in Spain, the Americans objected that importing Jews into the region would upset Arab feelings. The delegates were able to concur only on the desirability of encouraging neutral states to accept refugees and the usefulness of an Intergovernmental Committee on Refugees modelled on the defunct League of Nations High Commission. By contrast, there was no disagreement over the need for secrecy about the barren deliberations: the British delegation reported with satisfaction that they had been 'able to achieve very little'.[76]

The Bermuda conference served officials well on both sides of the Atlantic. Between January and April 1943 the promise of a high-level conclave deflected demands for further action and afterwards there was

the inevitable period of waiting for the report, during which campaigners lost heart. The cynicism of officials was exemplified in remarks
on the outcome of the talks made by Richard Law of the Foreign Office.
'We are subjected to extreme pressure from an alliance of Jewish organisations and archbishops', he began. 'There is no counter-pressure as yet
from the people who are afraid of an alien immigration into the country
because it will put their livelihood in jeopardy after the war. I have no
doubt in my mind that that feeling is widespread in England, but it is
not organised so we do not feel it.' The Americans were in a different,
tougher position because they were caught between a potent Jewish
lobby and widespread antipathy to refugees. They wanted to be seen to
act but actually do nothing. 'The Americans, therefore, while they must
do their utmost to placate Jewish opinion, dare not offend "American"
opinion.'[77]

Stephen Wise was not taken in so easily. Ten days after the State
Department delegation returned home, with no sign of an imminent
announcement of any results, he wrote to the president complaining
about the 'inexplicable absence of measures to save the Jews who can
still be saved – without of course, in the slightest, impairing the war
effort'. But Wise would not get to see the president until July 1943, when
Roosevelt simply repeated to him the promise of retribution against
German war criminals. Voices of concern were raised in the United
Kingdom too. Even before the conference was over, the *Jewish Chronicle*
wondered anxiously at the reason for the news blackout. The government promised a parliamentary debate on the outcome and then moved
to pack the benches with its supporters. Osbert Peake, the foreign office
minister, opened the debate on 19 May with an arid summary. Having
recited the meagre list of concrete proposals, he declared that in any
case 'these people are for the present mostly beyond the possibility of
rescue'. Furthermore, 'the rate of extermination is such that no measures
of rescue or relief, however large a scale, could be commensurate with
the problem'. In addition to the lack of shipping, the blockade and the
diversion of resources from winning a victory that alone could assure
them deliverance, he argued that an influx of refugees might provoke an
anti-Jewish reaction. This was rather more than Rathbone could
swallow. She retorted that 'It is an insult to the British people to suggest
that even those who "don't like Jews" would rather leave them to be
massacred than find asylum for a few thousand more of them.' Rathbone's close ally, the Conservative MP Victor Cazalet, railed that 'the

Jews are being exterminated today' and proclaimed it a Christian duty to save them. Their oratory bounced off the implacable government front bench. Rathbone was deflated. Cazalet died in an air crash a few weeks later. The momentum to rescue Jews that had been gained in the early spring was dissipated by summer 1943.[78]

By coincidence, the Bermuda conference opened on the same day that the Jewish fighters of Warsaw commenced their final stand. The unfolding tragedy was monitored daily by Zygielbojm and Schwarzbart but the Polish government-in-exile did not refer to it in any official statement until 4 May. Then General Sikorski devoted twenty-eight lines to the uprising out of a 271-line broadcast to his homeland. Sikorski called for aid and succour to the fighters and condemned the silence of the world, but his attention was elsewhere. The death throes of the Warsaw ghetto coincided with the revelations from Katyn, which placed the London Poles in an awful position. On the one hand, they wanted to denounce the Soviet atrocity and use it to show the western allies the malignancy of their partner in Moscow. On the other hand, to do so would be to reinforce German propaganda and put the Allied coalition at risk. Zygielbojm's frantic efforts to persuade the government-in-exile to do more came to nothing. On 11 May he told the Polish Jewish journalist Isaac Deutscher that he was contemplating a hunger strike to draw attention to the slaughter. The following day he committed suicide. In a last letter to the Polish president, Wladyslaw Raczkiewicz, Zygielbojm wrote, 'The responsibility for the crime of the murder of the whole Jewish nationality in Poland rests first of all on those who are carrying it out, but indirectly it also falls upon the whole of humanity, the people of the Allies, and their governments, who to this day, have not taken any real steps to halt this crime.' In a letter to the Bund representative in New York he explained that 'I hope that upon my death I will achieve what I failed to achieve in my life – real action to rescue at least a few . . . of the 300,000 Jews who have survived . . .' But in a personal note to his brother he suggested a different reason for taking his life: 'Why am I not with them in their last struggle? . . . What right have I to survive?'[79]

Ignacy Schwarzbart suggested to the foreign minister of the exile government, Count Raczyński, that they distribute Zygielbojm's final letter to the Polish president to British members of parliament prior to the debate on the Bermuda conference, in the hope of stinging them into a positive response. Polish officials refused because the suicide note contained criticism of their own failure to do more. Instead, the government-in-exile ignored the debate and the only newspaper that published the letter was the *Manchester Guardian*. Over the next year the government-in-exile usually showed an interest in publicizing the fate of Jews in Poland only when it wanted to prevent the Soviet-backed Jewish Anti-Fascist Committee from seizing the high ground. Aside from using the Jewish catastrophe to draw attention to the fate of Poland in general, it declined to get involved in rescue activities. Zygiel-bojm's gesture had been utterly futile.[80]

Confirmation that the Jews of Europe faced violent extinction reached the Yishuv, the Jewish community of Palestine, in the weeks after Rommel was driven back from El Alamein. This coincidence was important because until then the Jews in Palestine had been deeply afraid of a German breakthrough and found it hard to think of much beyond defensive measures. Their relief was now clouded by the appalling news from Poland, news that touched almost every member of the community. Yet the Jewish Agency executive seemed unable to devise an appropriate response. David Ben-Gurion and the leadership did not want to promote strikes and demonstrations that would disrupt the war effort. Nor did they want to foster a mood of hysteria. The National Council of the Yishuv, in consultation with the Jewish Agency, launched a month of mourning during December 1942 and January 1943, but it proved impossible to sustain. Cinemas, restaurants and businesses objected to the disruption caused by days of fasting and prayer. The secular labour movement, which set the tone for Jewish society, derided the very idea. Instead, the Jewish Agency focused on raising funds for relief and rescue efforts. Its delegates in Spain, Switzerland and Turkey were authorized to find ways around the Allied blockade so as to send money, food parcels and documents into German-dominated Europe. Papers conferring Palestinian citizenship made the holder eligible for exchange for German nationals interned in Palestine, and 800 Jews were saved in this way, while the mere possession of an immigration certificate could be the gift of life. However, because Ben-Gurion did not want to establish a powerful new body, the work was conduced by a committee of the Jewish Agency executive chaired by Yitzhak Gruenbaum. He was an underwhelming figure and failed to galvanize the public. Ultimately, the Joint Rescue Committee raised a fraction of the amount spent on land purchases for future settlements in Palestine and the envoys never had enough funds even for what they were able to achieve.

The Israeli historian Dina Porat found that by 1944 the 'debate over the proper response faded away'.[81]

The end of the ghettos in the General Government and Wartheland

The Warsaw ghetto uprising confirmed the worst fears and fantasies that animated the Nazi leadership. On 1 May 1943, Goebbels considered the most noteworthy news from the occupied territories to be 'the very stiff fighting between our police, including to some degree the army, and the insurgent Jews. The Jews have managed to fortify the ghetto for defence. The fighting there is very bitter ... it is a perfect example of what can be expected of these Jews when they have weapons in their hands.' In order to prevent further eruptions, on 19 June 1943, Hitler approved Himmler's proposal to liquidate the remaining Jewish population in the occupied eastern territories except for those in SS-controlled camps. When Himmler declared the entire General Government a 'Bandit Combat Zone' he signalled the seriousness of the security problem and, not coincidentally, acquired even more sweeping powers. Once again, real security issues connected with the course of the war, organizational self-interest, and fantastic anxieties about the menace posed by the Jewish enemy conjoined to have immediate, disastrous consequences.[82]

The decision to eradicate the Jews on the grounds of security, rather than ideology alone, put an end to months of prevarication, confusion, and bickering over the use of Jewish labour. At the start of the year there were still fifty-four ghettos and Jewish labour camps in the General Government servicing a range of enterprises. In pursuit of his earlier business plan Himmler had ordered Krüger, the Higher SS Police Leader for the General Government, to transfer Jews fit for work to premises controlled by the SS Business and Administration Head Office, the WVHA. The result was a wave of ghetto clearances and mass murder operations that dealt the final blow to the Radom ghetto, the Cracow ghetto and several others. Jewish workers were concentrated in a handful of camps, most notably Plaszow, outside Cracow. In March, Himmler's ambition to make the SS into a corporate giant took another stride with the establishment of Ostindustrie. This company, a partnership between the WVHA and Globocnik, was intended to manage camps supplying labour to munitions plants under SS stewardship. To obtain the necessary manpower and machinery, Himmler intended to appropriate the production units in Warsaw, Bialystok and Lodz and relocate them to the Lublin district. However, the behaviour of the Jews in Warsaw indicated that the proposed labour force was more combustible than the munitions it was intended to produce. Himmler's dream of becoming an industrial titan was superseded by the more familiar role of exterminator-in-chief. The Warsaw ghetto uprising thus accelerated the destruction of around 400,000 Jews still alive in German-occupied eastern Europe.[83]

In the Lublin district every remaining ghetto and labour camp was liquidated except for ten large installations, mostly part of Globocnik's business empire. He ran several that were devoted solely to sorting the property stolen from murdered Jews, with the largest at the old Lublin airfield. Nearly 5,500 worked in the Deutsche Ausrustungswerke (German Armaments Works, DAW), munitions plants adjacent to the Lipowa camp in Lublin. Despite the catastrophic failure to relocate their workshops from Warsaw, Többens set up anew in the Poniatowa camp and eventually employed 16,000 Jewish slave workers, while Schultz established production in the Trawniki camp using a workforce of about 6,300. Three thousand Jews were retained in Budzyn, serving a Heinkel plane factory. About 2,000 were utilized by the army in Deblin. Between March and November, 15,000 Jews were in eight factories run by Ostindustrie, manufacturing a range of products from glassware to pharmaceuticals. Ultimately, however, the utility and profitability of these enterprises would prove meaningless when weighed against the supposed threat the workers posed to German security.[84]

Around 20,000 Jews from Warsaw ended up in Majdanek, a hybrid concentration, labour and extermination camp. Majdanek started life in July 1941 when Himmler ordered the establishment of a camp to house Soviet prisoners of war on an extensive site in the Lublin suburb of Majdan Tartarski, adjacent to the Lublin–Zamość highway. Construction was delayed until the autumn and most of the POWs and Jews deployed for the job perished in the process. When it eventually began functioning it held under 10,000 inmates, three-quarters of whom were Jews. Most of these were from the Lublin district or the Warsaw ghetto. By mid-1943 the camp population had doubled but the proportion of Jews fell to just over half. Majdanek was now designated a concentration

camp under the SS Business and Administration Head Office. It supplied labour to warehouses where the booty from Operation Reinhard
was sorted and to workshops run by the DAW, producing clothing and
furniture for the German armed forces. Unusually, though, it was
equipped with gas chambers using Zyklon-B and also carbon dioxide.
Following the closure of Belzec, thousands of Jews from the Lublin
district and from central and western Europe were murdered there.
Between autumn 1942 and the end of 1943, about 8,500 Slovak Jews,
3,000 Czechs and 3,000 from other parts of Europe were directed to
Majdanek to be killed or selected for the labour force. Life in the camp
was dominated by the kapos, who were especially cruel. Thaddeus Stabholz, a physician who reached the camp from Warsaw after spending
nearly two weeks in a bunker, recalled that they once roasted a prisoner
over an open fire. His account of the time he spent there is a catalogue
of ceaseless brutality. Majdanek was so horrific that when he was transferred to Auschwitz-Birkenau to work as a camp doctor it marked a
significant improvement in his living conditions. Stabholz was especially lucky to have left the camp before November 1943, when the
entire Jewish population was wiped out in one day.[85]

In Galicia and western Ukraine between 140,000 and 150,000 Jews
were alive at the start of 1943. Belzec, which had been held in readiness
for the arrival of Romanian Jews, was shut down in December 1942 once
it was clear they would not be turning up. Since there was not enough
rail capacity to send Jews to either Treblinka or Sobibor, in January Fritz
Katzmann began the liquidation operations with a mass shooting of
10,000 Jews from the Lwow ghetto. The slaughter culminated in the execution of the Jewish council. The rump, containing about 25,000 Jews
(over half of them living 'wild'), was designated a 'Jews' camp' run by the
SS. In May, several thousand who had been employed in Wehrmacht
enterprises were moved to the Janowska camp, where prisoners had been
shot to make room for them. At the start of June, Katzmann proceeded
to liquidate what was left of the Lwow ghetto. In the opening stages his
policemen and auxiliaries encountered armed resistance and several
were killed. After a few days the Jews were overwhelmed. Some 3,000
perished in the ghetto, but 7,000 were inducted into Janowska where
hundreds were winnowed out in the course of selections. Katzmann's
killing units went on to murder the 6,000 Jews in Tarnopol, 4,000 in
Drohobych, 3,000 in Buczacz and thousands more in smaller ghettos. In
Tarnopol, the final action in July met an armed response and hundreds

of Jews fled the ghetto for the surrounding forests. Few, however, survived the Jew-hunts over the following months. In Drohobych, several
hundred essential workers in the petroleum industry were spared until
they, too, were sent to a camp. About 800 Jews from Buczacz found
refuge in the wooded hills around the town. Notwithstanding these
exceptions and 21,000 left in SS camps, at the end of June 1943 Katzmann
proclaimed Galicia Jew-free. His meticulous records indicate that
434,329 Jewish inhabitants had been killed.[86]

Katzmann's valedictory report to HSSPF Krüger, his superior, offers
an insight into the mentality of the SS and this cadre of the security
apparatus. It constructs anti-Jewish policy in a linear fashion, admitting
to conflicts with other agencies, but implying a steady purpose in SS
thinking throughout the period from June 1941 to June 1943. Katzmann
describes the first measures for marking Jews, curbing the black market
and forcing Jews to work. He brags about the creation of the camps to
supply labour for Durchgangstrasse IV, of which 160 kilometres had
been completed (in reality a derisory achievement). There is no mention of the wave of pogroms and mass killings in the summer of 1941,
although he acknowledges the difficulty posed by the importance of
Jews for all forms of manufacturing in the region. This required careful
management of the labour question, for which the civil administration
and Wehrmacht proved incompetent. Nor were the civilians able to
accomplish the creation of Jewish residential districts, exposing troops
passing through the region to the danger of typhus. Therefore the security police had to step in to take control of the housing situation and
revalidate work permits. In the course of ghettoization and reorganization of the labour force, many Jews were sent for 'special treatment'.
Katzmann does not elaborate on the reasons for this bifurcation. In
April 1942, the systematic evacuation of Jews from the district commenced. Thanks to the efforts of the security police, 255,000 Jews were
'resettled'. Again, Katzmann omits the messier aspects of this operation.
Instead, he explains how, in November 1942, he was forced to take all
Jews into SS-run camps in order to accelerate the process of rationalization. The last stage of clearing out the Jewish population was especially
hard: 'They not only tried to escape, and concealed themselves in the
most improbable places, drainage canals, chimneys, even in sewage pits,
etc. They barricaded themselves in catacombs of passages, in cellars
made into bunkers, in holes in the earth, in cunningly contrived hiding

places, in attics and sheds, inside furniture, etc. . . . As the number of Jews still remaining decreased their resistance became the greater. They used weapons of all types for their defense, and in particular those of Italian origin. The Jews bought these Italian weapons from Italian soldiers . . . Subterranean bunkers were discovered which had cleverly concealed entrances . . . so well hidden that they could not be found if one did not know where to look.' Katzmann concluded that 'Despite the extraordinary burden heaped upon every single SS-Police Officer during these actions, [the] mood and spirit of the men were extra-ordinarily good and praiseworthy from the first to the last day. Only thanks to the sense of duty of every single leader and man have we succeeded in getting rid of this PLAGUE in so short a time . . .'[87]

After this typically hyperbolic and self-pitying coda Katzmann offers a financial accounting that both undermines the notion of a fear-some enemy and reveals the Nazi money-grubbing obsession. 'Apart from furniture and large quantities of textiles, etc., the following were confiscated and delivered to Special Staff "Reinhard": . . . 97,581 kg. gold coins, 82,600 kg. silver chains, 6,640 kg. gold chains . . . 20,952 kg. gold wedding rings, 22,740 kg. pearls, 11,730 kg. gold teeth bridges, 28,200 kg. powder compacts silver or other metals . . . 343,100 kg. cigar-ette cases silver and other metal, 20,880 kg. gold rings with stones, 39,917 kg. brooches, earrings, etc., 6,166 kg. various pocket watches . . . 2,892 kg. pocket watches gold, 68 cameras, 98 binoculars, 7 stamp col-lections . . . 1 3.290 kg box corals . . . 1 suitcase of fountain pens and propelling pencils . . . 1 suitcase of cigarette lighters, 1 suitcase of pocket knives, 1 trunk of watch parts.' Katzmann's careful list was intended to allay any suspicion that the local SS had been lining their own pockets, yet by disavowing his venality he only highlighted the avarice of his employers. Katzmann evidently did not anticipate that his audience might raise an eyebrow at the juxtaposition of 'brutal methods' that were necessary to catch dangerous Jews with the fact that many of them were wearing brooches and pearl earrings or armed with nothing more lethal than fountain pens.[88]

As a counterpoint to Katzmann's point of view, the diary of Samuel Golfard captures the experience of Galician Jews in the first months of 1943. Golfard was living in Peremyshliany (Przemyslany), a small town with a Jewish population of about 3,000. Around 450 men of the com-munity were shot in November 1942, but over the following year the rest were largely left alone. This was partly because many of the working population were engaged in shale oil production. Nevertheless, they were forced into a tiny ghetto and at the end of the year, some 3,000 were deported to Belzec. Essential workers, including Golfard, were transferred to Jaktorow labour camp on the outskirts of town. Golfard started his diary by recapitulating the day on which his sister was taken. The 'Jewish militia' who assisted in the round-up were 'not better or worse than many Germans, who for a bottle of vodka or a can of sardines spared one's life. They were just somewhat cheaper.' Of the time he spent in Jaktorow, he wrote, 'I became convinced that there is no and has never been any racial solidarity among the Jews. Instead, here in camp, a solidarity of the rich and a solidarity of the poor existed, a solidarity of the sated and a solidarity of the hungry.' The only heroism he witnessed was 'the heroism of people walking to the gallows without a word of complaint'.[89]

From early April 1943, Golfard heard rumours of previously protected Wehrmacht workers being deported from Lwow. Anticipating an onslaught on their town, young men in the ghetto discussed armed resistance, but rejected Goldfard's militancy. 'Every one of them still has some expectations of hiding in a peasant's hovel or somewhere else, and they continue to reject any collective actions that might save their own lives.' The fate of those who did try their luck in the woods was hardly encouraging. He learned that six Jews who had escaped were caught and tortured before being executed. Some time later, Golfard left the ghetto. He was helped by a Pole, Tadeusz Jankiewicz and his family, but eventually the Germans caught him. Only his words, preserved by Jankiewicz, survived the cataclysm.[90]

The Jewish population in the district of Bialystok, which had remained relatively undisturbed during 1942, next faced destruction. The Bialystok ghetto, with a population of about 43,000, had been preserved thanks to the intervention of the German army and the East Prussian Nazi Party boss Erich Koch, who parried the murderous intentions of the RSHA by pointing to its value as a production centre. Grodno had not been so fortunate: about 6,000 Jews went from there to Auschwitz during November, leaving 17,000 work Jews and their families. Over 16,000 Jews from Volkovysk, which served as a place to concentrate Jews from around the region, were sent to Treblinka and 3,000 to Auschwitz by the end of the year. In January 1943, the SS Head Office renewed its calls to eliminate Jews from the Bialystok district. From 18–22 January, 11,500 were taken from Grodno to extermination camps. A few hundred workers were left until March, when the ghetto was finally dissolved. Some 10,000 Jews were also sent from the Pruzhany ghetto to Auschwitz. However, when the attention of the SS returned to Bialystok, Albert Speer, the minister for armaments, objected. Speer pointed out the difficulty of replacing skilled Jewish workers with Byelorussian peasants and argued for a stay of execution. Speer and Koch succeeded, partially. In early February, Eichmann's office started drawing up railway schedules for the deportation of just 10,000 Jews.[91]

Word of an Aktion triggered anguished debate within the official and underground leadership. Thanks to the long period of stability in Bialystok, and the sympathetic attitude of the Jewish council chairman, Efraim Barash, the ghetto had become a centre for Jewish resistance activity. Barash actually discussed tactics with Mordechai Tenenbaum, a member of the HaShomer HaTzair Zionist youth movement who had emerged as the leading personality of the fractious Jewish underground. Rather than leave the ghetto to fight as partisans, as many of his comrades argued, Tenenbaum believed they had a duty to stay in the ghetto and defend its people. When Barash intimated that the deportation would be partial, and that he had succeeded in making the ghetto workforce indispensable, Tenenbaum agreed it was the wrong time to resist. Nevertheless, while the youthful fighters held back there was spontaneous mass disobedience: Jews hid inside the ghetto and thousands sought refuge in the factories. One man threw acid in the face of a German officer, provoking a vicious reaction but doing little to slow the Aktion. Between 1 and 12 February, the Germans removed 10,000 Jews from the ghetto and shot 900 in its streets and buildings. Three transports took the victims to Treblinka, two to Auschwitz-Birkenau.[92]

With the collapse of his plans to ship men and machinery from Warsaw to Lublin in order to equip the Ostindustrie factories, in the summer Himmler again turned to Bialystok. His determination was fortified by increasing Soviet partisan activity in the area and uncertainty regarding the situation on the eastern front as a whole. But if the plant and equipment were removed, the ghetto would lose its raison d'être and the inhabitants knew what that entailed. So, to guard against any Warsaw-style debacle, Globocnik arranged for the factories to be protected before the population was tackled. On 15 August 1943, German forces surrounded the ghetto and Barash was given the bad news. Once more the underground leadership was caught on the hop and had little time to coordinate. Tenenbaum dispatched 200 fighters, with about 130 weapons and limited ammunition between them, to key defensive points but was unable to mobilize the entire ghetto population. At the eleventh hour the underground rushed out leaflets warning, 'all transports lead to death . . . You have nothing to lose! Work can no longer save you.' Instead, Jews were already assembling as instructed, with Barash taking the lead. At 9 a.m. the following day, when thousands of Jews were in the streets, packed and ready to depart, members of the resistance opened fire on German policemen. It was an uneven contest: by noon, most of the combat units were annihilated. Although isolated resistance continued, and increasing numbers of Jews preferred to hide than report for the transports, by 20 August the Germans had dispatched 12,000–13,000 Jewish workers to Lublin. As part of a proposed exchange scheme, nearly 2,000 children, mainly from orphanages, were removed from the assembly place and entrained for Theresienstadt. They were held there for six weeks until the scheme collapsed, at which point they were forwarded to Auschwitz-Birkenau and murdered. Fourteen transports carried the bulk of those deemed unfit for work to Treblinka; two took Jews to Auschwitz-Birkenau, where a fraction entered the labour force. Seventy fighters who had been awaiting an opportunity to break out were caught in a single bunker and shot in batches. Mordechai Tenenbaum committed suicide rather than let a German firing squad end his life.[93]

Himmler's aversion to ghettos and his greed for labour condemned the ghettos in East Upper Silesia that had provided work and stability for thousands of Jews. Between late June and mid-August 1943, 35,000 were deported from Sosnowicz and Bedzin to Auschwitz-Birkenau. About 6,000 Jews were redeployed as labour elsewhere. Gerda Weissmann, who was deported from her native Bielsko to Sosnowicz in mid-1942, was fortunate to have become part of the skilled labour force. From July 1942 until August 1943 she worked in a weaving mill in Bolkenhain. The female workers were accommodated in barracks attached to the factory, which had the reputation as 'one of the best labour camps for women in Germany'. After an unpleasant spell at a flax works in Märzdorf, she was transferred to a textile mill in Landshut, manufacturing parachutes. Again, the conditions in the camp were bearable. Gerda could not know that by this stage in the war employment in a German labour camp servicing a manufacturing enterprise offered the best terms of survival. The ghettos she left behind were all brutally dispersed.[94]

The tension in German policy-making between ideology and pragmatism, fanaticism and opportunism was exemplified by the fate of
Jews in the Wartheland and the Lodz ghetto during 1943. Himmler's
repugnance for any concentration of Jews outside SS supervision led to
the dissolution of roughly one hundred small camps in the Posen area,
dooming 11,000 Jewish workers. But when he turned to Lodz he faced a
similar coalition to the one that arrayed against him over the future of
Bialystok, except this time it met with greater success. Speer, Arthur
Greiser and the Wehrmacht's armaments department united in opposition to his demand to relocate the ghetto enterprises to Lublin.
Ironically, their case was helped by the visit of an SS investigatory commission that concluded the ghetto was uneconomical. This pessimistic
report quelled Himmler's appetite for a while.[95]

In fact, the period from January to June 1943 was the only time that
the Lodz ghetto showed a profit. It boasted 117 factories and workshops, sorting facilities and warehouses. As bombing disrupted production in the Reich, more factories located to Lodz out of range of the
RAF and US Army Air Forces. Nearly every one of the 85,804 Jews in
the ghetto was working. Nevertheless, their output was pitiful. Production was mostly un-mechanized and the manual workers were enfeebled
by lack of nutrition. From mid-1943 they were paid according to an
hourly rate that gave them no incentive to speed up. In any case, the pay
barely covered the cost of rations. The only way to boost productivity
was to extend the working day. By May, the labour force was working
twelve hours per shift, in two shifts. The combination of long hours and
poor food merely served to further erode its health and efficiency.[96]

Rumkowski, though, used economic success and the logic of total
war to validate his strategy and salvage his authority. On 13 March
1943, he told the ghetto: 'There is a war on and there is total mobilization in the Reich; new factories must be created, for which additional
workers must be found. From where are those workers to come? The
problem can only be solved by reorganisation, and it is better that we
face this inevitable fact soberly and undertake the necessary steps ourselves in order to prevent chaos.' Yet the counterproductive effects of
malnutrition, sickness, and inequality were transparent to the ghetto
chroniclers – who made less and less effort to conceal their disdain for
his regime. Not long after the chairman's pep talk, the chronicle quoted
a medical report that listed amongst the most common ghetto ailments,
'scurvy, pellagra, hunger oedema, and abscesses . . . bronchitis, pleurisy

... softening of the bones ...' A month later the writers stated that 'Except for a small elite that has everything and can obtain everything, ghetto dwellers are literally dragging their shoes behind them ...' Writing in the chronicle, Oskar Rosenfeld sardonically observed, 'The question: How much longer can this go on? is gradually becoming irrelevant. Death is flourishing. There are practically no births. The ghetto is liquidating itself.'[97]

Dawid Sierakowiak's diary testifies to the debilitating effect of endless labour and undernourishment. A few days before Rumkowski's oration he jotted, 'My unfortunate once-powerful father died today ...' Dawid himself was suffering from tooth decay, frostbitten feet, scabies and an intermittent fever. From his vantage point as a clerk in the ghetto administration, he was able to monitor the gap between the rich and the poor as well as the chairman's quirks. In March, Rumkowski visited his office with a commission to comb out those suitable for manual labour. The review included female employees, for whom the chairman had a certain weakness. 'He nearly jumped up when young girls paraded in front of him. Lunatics, perverts, and criminals like Rumkowski rule over us and determine our food allocation, work and health. No wonder the Germans don't want to interfere in ghetto matters; the Jews will kill one another perfectly well and, in the meantime, they will also squeeze maximum production out of one another.' Realizing that the Jews were in a race against time, Dawid despaired over the Allies' slow advances. He lost his race. On 15 April 1943 he wrote in his diary for the last time. Four months later he died from the combined effects of tuberculosis, malnutrition and exhaustion. He was nineteen years old.[98]

Moral standards withered in step with physical decay. In his private journal Rosenfeld documented the corruption at every level of ghetto society. Under the heading 'morality', he noted in February, 'Most personalities of "elevated social position" have official girlfriends, as they say here: love affairs. These girls and women have no shame and parade openly as the official mistresses of the respective candidates.' In a brief discussion of prostitution he remarked that 'one sees many pretty girls in the kitchens ... appetising, well groomed, round and meaty.' According to one of his informants, Rumkowski held orgies while he was in hospital for a spell. The Elder of the ghetto allegedly 'looked out the window, called girls inside. At one time, the wife of a doctor. She refused. Whereupon her name was found out and the Jewish police were sent to her apartment and demolished the furnishings ...' At the end of April, Rosenfeld briefly noted the case of a man who murdered a thirteen-year-old girl for food. He reported that people adopted children in order to claim an extra ration, but ate the food themselves while their diminutive charges starved.[99]

Even so, a religious and cultural life persisted amidst the degradation. Although Sabbath services and rest were impossible, pious Jews said the customary prayers when and where they could. Rosenfeld saw in the 'slender candles that street sellers offer to passers-by for Friday evenings ... a pitiful symbol of this life'. He celebrated Passover at the home of friends, 'with all the trimmings, even eggs'. In October, Yom Kippur was officially observed in the ghetto for the first time. There were over a hundred services and at each one the traditional prayers for the dead were recited. The chronicle commented that 'on Yom Kippur 1943, the ghetto has literally become a shtetl'. Ironically, the food supply improved in time for the fast. Rosenfeld sensed a 'Holiday atmosphere in the streets. Potato deliveries – pumpkins are rolling. Eyes are gleaming ...' Chanukkah at the end of the year was marked with menorahs, candles, gatherings and presents. Everyone was cheered by the conviction that it would be the last time the festival would be celebrated in the ghetto.[100]

It was indeed the last Chanukkah in the Lodz ghetto but it was not the last Chanukkah of the war and it was a near-miracle that the ghetto survived even this long. In September 1943, Himmler abandoned the notion of moving the machinery and key workers from Lodz to Lublin, but he reiterated his demand to Greiser that the ghetto should be reconfigured as a labour camp under SS control and merged into Ostindustrie. For several months, Greiser, backed by Albert Speer and the army, haggled with Himmler and Max Horn, the director of Ostindustrie. An SS commission of inquiry sent by Himmler to assess the ghetto concluded that it was woefully unproductive. But this may have been a part of the bargaining process, since Greiser's administration was demanding an astronomical amount in return for surrendering control to the SS. Finally, Greiser reached a deal with Himmler whereby he continued to run it, but with a population cut back to core workers.[101]

Liquidating the ghettos in the Ostland

The tussle over Jewish lives and labour coloured the fate of the last ghettos in the Reichskommisariat Ostland. At the start of 1943 an estimated

310,000–320,000 Jews were alive in Hinrich Lohse's domain, stretching from the Baltic into western Byelorussia. On 21 June, Himmler commanded his Higher SS Police Leader in the Ostland and the WVHA to collect them into concentration camps and end the practice of marching Jews from residential quarters to enterprises where they generated profits for private concerns. Instead, the machinery of production was to be moved into camps where it would operate under the direction of Oswald Pohl's technical experts. The SS would derive the financial benefits. Jews who were unable to work would be eliminated. Since Himmler saw no need for the camps to accommodate the unproductive families of workers, this policy spelled disaster.[102]

However, like Greiser and Biebow in Lodz, and Koch in Bialystok, Lohse was not going to part with such a lucrative asset without a struggle. Since 1942 he had been grappling with a severe manpower shortage. His labour managers were constantly shifting Jews from one urgent task to another, reconditioning Wehrmacht uniforms one moment and cutting peat the next. Joseph Katz, who had been deported from Lübeck in December 1941, initially worked for a market gardener supplying vegetables to the SS. He was switched to the Riga harbour workforce in July, followed by a spell toiling in the beet fields, and spent winter unloading coal or cement. This flexible workforce appreciated in value even as the SS tried to reduce it. With less and less financial support forthcoming from Berlin to sustain his administration, local sources of revenue bulked ever larger for Lohse. For nearly three months the two sides sparred, each making appeals to Berlin for backing. Eventually the security argument triumphed, Lohse backed down, and the fate of the Baltic Jews' ghettos was sealed.[103]

In June, Himmler assigned Erich von dem Bach-Zelewski to the Ostland to dissolve them and migrate the thinned-out Jewish workforce to concentration camps. The process took months. Eventually, nearly 8,000 inhabitants of the Riga ghetto were accommodated in a new concentration camp in the suburb known as Mezaparks. The camp, dubbed Kaiserwald, never contained all the Jews working in and around Riga, as Himmler intended. Instead, thousands employed by the army, Organisation Todt and on the docks were relocated to barracks erected close to where they toiled. Conditions in these barrack camps varied from one to another; few were as harsh as Kaiserwald, which was presided over by the SS and veteran prisoners transferred from Sachsenhausen. However, families that had survived intact in the ghetto were finally broken up by the process of 'barracking'. Around 2,000 Jews deemed unfit for work were sent to Auschwitz-Birkenau.[104]

The 20,000 Jews in the Vilnius ghetto had enjoyed relative tranquillity after the horrific massacres at Ponary in 1941. Although the United Partisan Organization (FPO, Fareynikte Partizaner Organizatsye) had raised the standard of revolt in January 1942, the ghetto actually settled into a comfortable routine. In early March 1942, Herman Kruk noted, 'In the Vilna ghetto, life begins to pulse again.' Under the guidance of the ghetto Elder, Jacob Gens, welfare, education and cultural institutions flourished. Despite the shocking news from Warsaw the ghetto behaved as if it were invulnerable. Gens even agreed to allocate men from the Order Service to participate with the Germans in Aktionen against nearby ghettos, notably Oszmiana. At the time of the Jewish New Year celebrations, in September 1942, the synagogues in the ghetto were full. There was a 'holiday mood'. It was only when news reached Vilnius about the liquidation of the Grodno ghetto that a chill ran through the inhabitants.[105]

In April 1943 the population reacted with panic when Jews began to arrive from Oszmiana and other destroyed ghettos bordering on the Bialystok district. The SS man who ran the ghetto, Franz Murer, offered reassurance, but the Jews began preparing for evasion and resistance. In early April 1943, Kruk went on a nocturnal tour of the ghetto and heard the tell-tale sound of work on malinas. 'In some houses, people don't get undressed. All night long, they work with spades, digging malinas and underground passages. The FPO is fully prepared.' Gens redoubled his efforts to increase the number of Jews in gainful employment, believing this would be the key to their survival. By June 1943 about 75 per cent of the entire population were working for German firms outside the ghetto and, increasingly, workshops within the perimeter.[106]

Despite bulging order books for the factories, in August the security police began to transfer Jews to concentration camps in Estonia. The first wave of 1,000 were abducted from their workplaces on 6 August; many resisted and several were gunned down. More widespread resistance was thwarted due to a tragedy that had occurred a few weeks earlier. Thanks to the chance detention of a local communist who cracked under torture, the German security police learned about the activity of Yitzhak Wittenberg, the leader of the FPO in the ghetto. They demanded that Gens hand him over or face the consequences. Gens arranged to meet Wittenberg but Lithuanian security police interrupted the discussions and took Wittenberg prisoner. When members of the FPO heard that Gens had detained their leader they launched a rescue mission and hustled him to safety. During 16 July, Gens and the Order Service launched a hunt for Wittenberg, hoping to persuade him to sur-render and thereby prevent a reprisal action. The ghetto dwellers, terrified of a German assault, clearly supported Gens. Wittenberg thus faced an appalling dilemma: he could launch an uprising at a time when the ghetto population was not ready, with incalculable consequences, or he could give himself up. Later that day he surrendered to Gens, who handed him over to the Germans; Wittenberg committed suicide in prison within hours of his detention. Disillusioned by the behaviour of the Jewish population, the FPO resolved not to resist in the ghetto and began a steady exodus to the forests.[107]

The willingness of the ghetto to trade the life of one man for its survival did nothing to avert the Germans' long-term plans. On 24 August and 1–4 September, a further 7,000 inhabitants were shipped out to newly constructed camps in Estonia, notably Vaivara and its sub-camp Klooga. At Vaivara the Jews were employed mainly in the extraction of oil from shale, at Klooga in peat cutting. By mid-September about 12,000 were left in Vilnius. Even though Gens had consistently cooperated with the Germans, he was executed. On 23 September, the Germans commenced the final liquidation. About 2,000 able-bodied Jews were sent to Estonia and a similar number to Kaiserwald. Some 4,000 deemed unfit for work were shipped to Sobibor. Several hundred were killed at the Ponary mass murder site where the destruction of Vilnius's Jewish community had begun in the wake of Operation Bar-barossa. Herman Kruk was amongst those relocated to Estonia. He was murdered in the Klooga camp a day before it was overrun by the Red Army in September 1944.[108]

For weeks after the last deportation, German police and Lithuanian collaborators combed the deserted district in search of Jews. Kazimierz Sakowicz clinically analysed the tactics they used: 'the Lithuanians have proven good psychologists of the Jews sentenced to die . . . They separ-ate 3–4 Jewish men and women and shoot the rest before their eyes. When it is the turn of the 3 or 4 they tell them "you will live", but they must reveal the hiding places. When one of them reveals one, he goes to the city to the ghetto, but immediately returns and dies. At the same time, a new "troika" of Judases is chosen . . .' In mid-October, the Germans were still shooting Jews in Ponary – 300 on one day. Only now they could not even be bothered to bury them.[109]

Like Vilnius, Kaunus had experienced a long stretch of quiet during 1942. The Jewish administration under Elchanan Elkes was able to create a network of institutions serving the population of 16,000. The food supply was adequate and there were no epidemics. A large proportion of the inhabitants worked, producing military clothing, gloves, brushes, saddles and bandages for the German army; over 3,000 were employed at a nearby airfield. In March 1943, as news trickled in of ghetto clearances elsewhere, the mood darkened. Despite promises from workshop managers that the labour force was too valuable to squander, the diarist Abraham Golub noted that people started to prepare underground shelters. Others girded themselves for armed resistance. The prospects were daunting. When the middle-aged Golub heard of Jews from the FPO in Vilnius making their way to the forest, he lamented, 'Not everyone can brave such conditions. Not everyone has a strong fist . . . Not everyone can be a hero.' The strained calm persisted. In April the ghetto celebrated Passover 'in full splendour'. News of German defeats in Russia and the invasion of Sicily in July cheered everyone, although Golub reckoned the Jews did not have time on their side.[110]

His pessimism was borne out when a German commission of inquiry visited the ghetto in late July. Although he did not know about the tug-of-war over Jewish labour that was going on between Lohse and Himmler, he was doubtful whether the busy workshops and ample orders would make any difference to their fate: 'The question of manpower does not play a major role in this decision, which is motivated primarily by what the Germans see as political and security problems.' In September a new SS captain arrived whose job was to break up the ghetto. During October, 2,700 Jews were removed and those designated fit for labour were sent to Estonia. Over the last months of the year, 5,000–6,000 Jews were redistributed amongst various barrack camps. About 8,000 remained in the ghetto, which was now arbitrarily redesignated a concentration camp in order to meet Himmler's criteria. In March 1944, Abraham Golub left the ghetto and went into hiding.[111]

There were some 21,000–23,000 Jews in the ghettos in Byelorussia at the start of 1943. The region was now infested with partisans and security weighed heavily on the mind of Wilhelm Kube, the

Generalkommissar. In April, he told a conference in Minsk that 'Last summer, when we undertook to solve the Jewish problem and began resettling them, the partisan movement was immediately weakened. Some of the Jews got away, escaped to the forests and reinforced the partisan movement.' There was a tiny element of truth in this diagnosis, but it was mainly a fantasy. The destruction of communities had begun long before the partisan menace was a reality. It resumed early in 1943 when the 4,000–5,000 Jews of Slutsk were murdered. The killing swept through Baranovichi, Novogrudok, Lida and Glubokoie, although hundreds of Jews were able to reach the forests. In September 1943, the Minsk ghetto, with about 9,000 inhabitants, was liquidated. Around 2,000 workers were passed over to Globocnik in Lublin. After sequestering 500 artisans deemed essential, 4,000 Jews were taken to the Maly Trostinets concentration camp and shot. Hundreds hid in the deserted ghetto and were the object of continuing sweeps for weeks afterwards. Kube was right about one thing. On 22 September 1943 he was killed by a bomb planted in his bedroom by a Soviet partisan.[112]

Revolts in Treblinka and Sobibor

The uprising in the Warsaw ghetto, followed by armed resistance in Vilnius and Bialystok, as well as the regularity with which Jews in ghettos slated for destruction now concealed themselves or fled, worried Himmler. Prone to anxiety at the best of times, the Reichsführer-SS fretted that even the SS-run camps in Poland were becoming a liability. His fears were confirmed by prisoner revolts in Treblinka and Sobibor. Although both sites were nearing the end of their genocidal mission, Himmler envisaged Sobibor continuing as a concentration camp. In any case, the notion that Jews could choose to disrupt their work was alarming. The SS was above all the guarantor of security for the Reich, but that role was impugned if it could not control small Jewish groups in its own, most high-security installations.[113]

The winter of 1942–3 had been especially cruel in Treblinka. Transports dried up and the work Jews faced starvation. Typhus broke out, which the Germans treated by shooting those too sick or weak to labour. The inmates were saved from inanition by the arrival of trains from the Balkans. While the Greek Jews went straight to the gas chambers, the Arbeitsjuden were able to plunder their belongings for food.

The pickings from this baggage were rich, unlike the pathetic bundles carried by the inhabitants of Bialystok and Warsaw who also ended in the death camp between February and May 1943. Up to late April, thirty-six transports delivered approximately 108,000 Jews to Treblinka. Then the pace slowed. Amongst the 24,000 who followed over the next three months were Warsaw Jews rooted out of bunkers, and the Jewish Order Service. Despite frantic attempts to conceal their past by getting rid of uniforms and insignia during the train journey, the work details in the camp took care to ensure that every one of the Order Service personnel went to the gas chambers. By contrast, they welcomed into their ranks a few survivors of the fighting. These militants helped to inspire the underground that had been developing in the camp for months.[114]

The impulse to revolt was quickened by signs that the Germans were winding up the camp's operations. In early spring, Himmler and Franz Stangl visited as part of a tour of Operation Reinhard camps and gave orders to exhume the bodies of Jews murdered during 1942 and burn them. The work began while the ground was still icy, as were the cadavers. It proved difficult to get the frozen corpses to ignite, until the arrival of a German nicknamed 'The Artist' who had made a special study of the problem. He ordered the work-Jews in the upper camp to dig pits, inside which they constructed raised grilles made of rail tracks. Dead bodies were heaped on top of the grille, and the pyre was then doused in petrol and set alight. Once there was sufficient heat the flesh began to thaw, then melt and produce fat that pooled at the bottom of the pit. 'It turned out that women burned easier than men,' Yankiel Wiernik remembered. 'Accordingly, corpses of women were used for kindling the fires.' When the fat ignited, the pyre generated enormous heat and consumed the carcasses that were tossed on top. Teams of inmates assisted by mechanical diggers worked in this hellish environment for week after week. The Germans also brought in mechanical diggers to scoop up the human remains. When fresh transports arrived, SS men threw children alive into the flames for sport, 'urging the mothers to jump heroically into the fire after their children, mocking them because of their cowardice'. The burning stretched into the summer when the heat from the pits and the hot weather made the work even more appalling. A sickening smell hung over the entire camp. However, as long as there were bodies to incinerate the Jewish slaves knew they would be kept alive. By July they could see that the job was nearing completion and began to fear for their lives.[115]

The preservation of the labour force, which had increased the efficiency of Treblinka, had also enabled an underground to develop amongst the Hofjuden. It crystallized around Julian Choronzycki, a physician who was part of the dental team, and a kapo named Marceli Galewski, who was known in the camp as Engineer Galewski. In the spring, Choronzycki was accidentally caught by SS guards with escape funds in his possession, but did not disclose anything about the underground before his execution. Engineer Galewski then took the lead, consulting with prisoners who had military training. They devised a plan to use youngsters who worked as servants in the SS barracks to get an impression of the key to the armoury, which was located in the section occupied by the garrison. On the appointed day these youths would sneak into the armoury and remove grenades and rifles. The weapons would be distributed to men who knew how to use them. Armed groups would then position themselves to take out the guards in the watchtowers, while others used petrol bombs to set fire to the gas chambers and key installations, particularly the fuel depot and the garage, where an armoured car was parked. In this way they hoped both to create a diversion and prevent the Germans from mounting a rapid pursuit. Yankiel Wiernik played a crucial part in the preparations because, thanks to his job, he was able to move through the camp and alert even the men in the gas chamber detail.[116]

The revolt was fixed for 2 August, a Sunday, when at least a few of the SS men and some of the Ukrainian guards would be off duty. During the afternoon members of the resistance took up their positions and waited for the arms to be distributed. The rebellion was timed to start at four in the afternoon, signalled by a single rifle shot. It did not go according to plan. The youngsters were able to bring only a few grenades and rifles from the armoury before one of the conspirators was seized by a suspicious guard. An hour earlier than intended, fearing that the ruckus would alert the whole garrison, one of the armed prisoners opened fire on the watchtower. This shot triggered the uprising, which quickly descended into chaos. Prisoners armed with Molotov cocktails managed to set the fuel dump alight although the armoured car was unscathed. Guards in the watchtowers opened fire on the Jews running this way and that across the camp grounds. If anything, the confusion helped, since the Germans could not identify where the breakout was taking place. Jews ran at the main gate, went over the wire of the inner fence or cut through it. They then had to cross a minefield and breach another barbed-wire entanglement. Dozens died in this zone, but they cleared the way for waves following them. The bodies of Jews shot down on the wire provided a bridge for others to scramble over. About 140 of the 500 prisoners managed to escape into nearby woods.[117]

The Treblinka uprising was not just the last throw of desperate men. In the tense hours before the revolt was due to begin, Wiernik reflected that 'We knew what this earth hid beneath its surface. We were the only witnesses of it. In silence we took leave of the ashes of our fellow Jews and vowed that, out of their blood, an avenger would arise.' If they succeeded in escaping they would be able to strike a double blow against the Germans, disabling the camp and carrying information about it to the outside world. For others, the mission was simpler. Willenberg later wrote, 'Down to the last man we thirsted for revenge, harbouring rage and murderous hate in our hearts.' Those who made it to the temporary safety of the woods had the satisfaction of being able to look back and see smoke rising from the camp, but they had not actually disabled the gas chambers. Two transports carrying nearly 8,000 Jews from Bialystok were murdered in Treblinka on 18 and 19 August. After that the Germans decided to shut it down and erase all trace of its existence.[118]

For the survivors, breaking out was only the beginning of a tortuous odyssey. Fewer than fifty would survive the subsequent manhunts or the perils of life in hiding. Chil Rajchman wandered in the woods for several weeks trying to find partisans. Some peasants gave him food and help; others chased him away. Eventually he reached the town of Piastow where a Gentile friend got him false papers. He lived as an Aryan for about a year until the Polish Home Army uprising forced him to take shelter in a bunker, where he endured for another three and a half months until the Red Army arrived. Richard Glazar and a pal tried to reach Hungary, walking the roads in the guise of impressed Czech labourers who had absconded and were making their way home. Eventually they were caught and imprisoned. Fortunately, the authorities sentenced them to forced labour and they were sent to a camp in Mannheim-Ludwigshafen in Germany. For the rest of the war Glazar worked in a metal foundry, dodging Allied bombs, until the Americans occupied the area. Samuel Willenberg made his way to Warsaw. He blended into the city's underworld and for a time was supported financially by the Bund and Zegota. Thanks to an amazing coincidence he bumped into Wiernik, who had also reached the Polish capital. Wiernik told him that he had written an account of Treblinka and given it to the underground for publication; it was circulated clandestinely the following year and made its way to Palestine and New York where it appeared in Yiddish and English. Willenberg later made contact with the Polish resistance and fought in the Warsaw uprising in August–September 1944.[119]

When Himmler visited Sobibor in early 1943 it was almost inactive. Much of the work that continued consisted of exhuming and cremating the dead murdered in 1942. Then, in March, the camp started to receive transports from the Netherlands. In all, nineteen trains brought 34,313 Dutch Jews to the gas chambers over the next five months. During this period, 3,500 French Jews were also murdered there. In addition, as its contribution to the liquidation of the ghettos, the death camp was used to kill almost 15,000 Jews from the General Government. Nearly 14,000 Jews were deported to Sobibor from doomed ghettos on the territory of the USSR, culminating in late September with a transport of Soviet Jewish POWs from Minsk. This shipment brought the total for those murdered at the camp during 1943 to 68,795. However, the Jewish soldiers from Minsk who were selected for the labour force were to prove the nemesis of Sobibor.[120]

As in Treblinka, the relative stability of the Jewish labour force allowed for the evolution of a resistance movement. It was initiated by Leon Feldhandler, the former chairman of the Jewish council in the small town of Zolkiewka in the Lublin district. Feldhandler had no military experience and had difficulty finding anyone he could trust who could advise how to stage an armed revolt. Instead, he contemplated bribing a few of the Ukrainian guards and concentrated on locating any whose loyalty to the Germans had been loosened by events in the war or whose greed overrode their sense of duty. It was not until the arrival of the Jewish soldiers that he had access to anyone with the requisite skills for a breakout. Even then, it took time for him to make contact with their leader, Alexander Pechersky – known as Sasha. Pechersky's men were horrified to learn where they were and after watching several hundred women being led to the gas chambers some resolved to escape at the earliest opportunity. However, Pechersky restrained them from attempting a small-scale breakout through a tunnel or the wire. While he was working out an alternative, he was introduced to Feldhandler. Despite language barriers they hit it off and agreed to arrange a mass escape embracing both the former POWs and the veterans of the labour force. Together they devised a plan of great subtlety and utter ruthlessness.[121]

The work-Jews provided numerous services for the SS men, making them coats, boots and jewellery. Feldhandler and Pechersky figured that if they chose a day when the commandant was on leave they could decapitate the garrison by luring his deputy and the SS non-commissioned officers to the workshops and murdering them one by one using axes and knives. That way they would also be able to get their side arms. At the same time, several prisoners who worked in the Ukrainian barracks would try to steal rifles. To hinder the inevitable pursuit, other teams would sabotage the vehicles in the garage and cut the phone wires from the commandant's office. All this had to be accomplished in sixty minutes. At the usual time for roll call they would assemble, but rather than wait to be counted they would march towards the main gate. As they passed the armoury a small unit would storm it in order to seize rifles that they could use in the forests. They hoped they would be able to exit along the access road which ran through the surrounding minefield and not have to fight their way out.[122]

On 14 October the underground moved into action. The first part of the plan went like clockwork and within an hour eight SS men and a Ukrainian were dead, although at least two of the SS staff were killed opportunistically by Jews stationed in the garage. The acting commandant did not make himself available to his assassins, so two prisoners went to his office and killed him there. A repairman, Shlomo Szmajzner, who went to fix the stove in the Ukrainians' quarters, returned with a couple of rifles jammed into a length of pipe. As planned, Feldhandler then attempted to assemble the entire 600-strong labour force. At this point the preparations began to fall apart. The supposed roll call resembled a mob and attracted the attention of an SS man, who was slain on the spot. Ukrainians in the watchtowers spotted the killing and opened fire, joined by a German NCO with a submachine gun who had escaped the assassinations. It proved impossible to rush the main gate. Instead, the prisoners stormed the fence in several places and rushed into the minefield. Out of about 550 prisoners, 320 made it past the perimeter. Although 170 were captured in the hours and days after the breakout, 150 managed to find refuge in the forests, many joining partisan groups. Others sought hiding places with local farmers. Their troubles were far from over.[123]

Toivi Blatt, a teenager from Izbica who had arrived in Sobibor in April 1943, initially stuck with Sasha Pechersky and his armed band of former POWs. But after a few days Pechersky sheared off with his men.

Blatt and the Polish Jews were left with one rifle, although Pechersky rationalized his action in an account he gave after the war. 'The Polish Jews turned westward towards Chelm. They could understand the language of the people there, and they knew all the roads. We, the people from Soviet Russia, turned eastward. Many were helpless: the Jews from Holland, the French and the Germans – none could speak to each other and there was gigantic space all around us.' Pechersky's group crossed the Bug river and eventually linked up with Soviet guerrillas. The rest of the Jews were mostly killed. Nearly a hundred were killed while in hiding and five fell in combat as partisans. Blatt reflected bitterly that 'daily life for a prisoner in Sobibor was actually in some ways more secure than that of Jews who were hiding on false papers, or in the forest, or in bunkers, freezing and searching for food, counting their every day as a miracle. In Sobibor we knew what to expect . . . Outside, there was a fierce struggle for existence.'[124]

Jew hunting in Poland

The chances of Jewish survival in Poland were indeed slim and the abysmal rate of success has obscured the efforts of those who attempted evasion or concealment. Yet recent studies reveal that, contrary to the myth of Jewish passivity, a significant proportion of town and village Jews in the General Government tried to elude the round-ups in mid- to late 1942 by fleeing to woodland or constructing hideouts. The Polish Canadian historian Jan Grabowski estimates that as many as 250,000 Jews sought to evade the deportations in this way. But barely 50,000 were alive by the end of the war. Few had prepared for flight and most found it nearly impossible to survive in the wild. Many returned to their homes after a few days or weeks, whereupon they were often caught in a second sweep by German security forces or handed over by the Polish police. In both cases, denunciation was frequently instrumental to their capture. Those who survived the first month or so gained valuable experience although typically they owed a lifeline to a peasant who supplied them with food in return for cash or items to sell. Whether they lived in bunkers in woodland or were concealed in an urban area, Jews needed helpers to exist. According to statistics from one county in central Poland, 70 per cent of Jews in hiding paid for support. This rendered them acutely vulnerable. The vast majority were betrayed or killed, usually when their resources expired. More than half of those who were succoured on an altruistic basis survived. Even then, making it through 1943 and into 1944 was a mountainous challenge.[125]

The Germans created a system that incentivized and terrorized Poles into doing their dirty work for them. In fact, without Poles who knew the local topography and knew how to identify a Jew the occupiers would have been helpless in the face of mass flight from the ghettos. Recognizing this, they offered bounty for handing over or killing Jews: cash rewards, a share of the valuables found on Jews, their clothing or just a bottle of vodka. And they compelled village elders to nominate hostages every week who would be shot if a Jew was found at large in the vicinity. Groups of Poles, usually led by a local authority figure such as an elder or a village policeman, would form a posse to follow up a lead in the hope of gain and in fear of a German reprisal if they did not. Sometimes, though, bands would set off on a Jew-hunt simply in the hope of uncovering a bunker and robbing the inhabitants. Jews who came to populated areas in search of food or work risked an encounter with the Polish police or watchmen who checked the identification papers of strangers as a matter of course. If they found Jews they either handed them over, usually having robbed them, or robbed and killed them without bothering the Germans. From late 1943, when Germans were thinly spread around the countryside and focused on anti-partisan duties, the Polish police had a free run. Women in hiding were especially at risk. When their money ran out they offered sex as payment for help, but many were sexually exploited in any case. Bands of Poles, including organized partisan units, would seek out Jewish family camps and raid them for their womenfolk.[126]

To the majority of Poles and Ukrainians, Jews were perceived not as humans in dire need of assistance, but as commodities to be traded or a source of enrichment. This perception was partly a result of ingrained prejudice, fortified by German propaganda, but it was also an opportunistic response to straitened and uncertain times. The Polish American scholar Jan Tomasz Gross has demonstrated that as a result of established stereotypes and the cruel environment created by the Germans, hunting and exploiting Jews was 'socially acceptable'. Extortion, torture, rape and murder were not activities on the fringe of society, conducted by marginal elements, but 'an accepted social practice'. Village elders, mayors, police officials, firemen, forest rangers and upstanding citizens all took part in Jew-hunts and sought to profit from the mythical wealth of the Jews. The same was true of Polish partisan units in the country-side, almost irrespective of their political stripe. Home Army units routinely refused to take in groups of fleeing Jews although they frequently accepted individual volunteers, especially if they did not look Jewish and kept quiet about their ethnicity. A significant proportion of Jews who survived in the forests recall encounters with AK units resulting in robbery, rape or murder. Almost as a matter of course, units of the National Armed Forces and Peasant Battalions slaughtered Jews with whom they collided in the forests. Some bands actively sought out Jews to rob and kill. Jewish fugitives recall that only the less numerous left-wing partisan organizations accepted them without question.[127]

Zygmunt Klukowski monitored the deportation of Jews from Zamość and his own town, Szczbrezesyn. After the first major action in Zamość he wrote with disgust in his diary, 'The way some Poles behave is completely out of line. During the massacre some even laughed. Some went sneaking into Jews' houses from the back, searching for what could be stolen.' By early August he recorded 'Some Poles are helping the Germans search for Jews.' During October, the Germans commenced the destruction of the Szczbrezesyn community. Now the local gendarmerie and Polish police were actively hunting for Jews and robbing them. They caught mainly old men, women and children. 'The younger men are in the forest', Klukowski noted. 'They are trying to organise and seek revenge.' So the hunt was extended to the countryside and the woods. Klukowski heard that Jewish fugitives were being robbed by partisans and bandits. In mid-November they started coming into town from the hills, surrendering to the gendarmerie because they were starving; some pleaded to be shot. 'It is hard to believe,' he wrote, but 'There are many people who see the Jews not as human beings but as animals that must be destroyed.' Six months later, in May 1943, Klukowski recorded bleakly that 'For some time now we have had no information at all concerning Jews in our region.'[128]

A similar story was repeated further east in Volhynia. Here Jews were caught in a brutal, many-sided struggle involving the Germans, the Polish Home Army, the UPA (the Ukrainian nationalist resistance movement) and Soviet partisans. Jews who escaped from ghettos frequently received aid from local Poles, who were likewise a threatened minority. They were admitted to Polish fighting units, not least because of their willingness to kill Ukrainians. Elements of the UPA routinely massacred Jewish individuals and bands they encountered, sparing only those who might provide them with useful services such as physicians or artisans. Soviet guerrillas were thin on the ground until 1943, but they offered the most hope to Jews and were ready to arm them. There were four all-Jewish partisan brigades in the Volhynia region, each 100–400 strong. Around 2,000 to 2,500 Jews lived in family camps, of whom about 1,500 survived to see the arrival of the Red Army. The historian Shmuel Spector estimated that 9 per cent of Jews who hid or fled were alive at the time of liberation, a stark indication of the horrendous conditions they faced in the natural environment and amongst the local populations.[129]

Due to the persistence of the German police in relentlessly hunting Jews and the attitude of the Polish or Ukrainian populations (depending on the region), until late 1943 it was statistically safer to be in a labour camp. Tragically, the death camp revolts jeopardized the relative safety of Jews who were in slave labour installations across the General Government and even further afield.

In the autumn, there were at least 50,000 Jews in labour camps run by the SS and the German armed forces. About 15,000 were in the Poniatowa camps, mostly producing clothing for the Többens firm. The output of items destined for the German armed forces was remarkable: each week Jewish workers produced 38,000 shirts, 18,000 pieces of underwear, 6,000 caps, over 7,000 pairs of socks, more than 4,000 packs and 2,400 belts for kit. Between 8,000 and 10,000 Jews, most relocated from the Warsaw ghetto, were employed in Schultz's factories. Some 18,000 Jewish prisoners in Majdanek, including the sub-camps in and around Lublin, toiled in DAW plants repairing uniforms, reconditioning vehicle engines, and making furniture for barracks. Since March 1943, thousands had been employed by Ostindustrie, repairing aircraft and manufacturing brushes. Yet this counted for little. On 19 October 1943, Hans Frank told a meeting in Cracow that 'The camps with Jews in the General Government constituted a great danger, and that the escape of the Jews from one of these camps [Sobibor] proved it.' Frank invited General Schindler of the armaments inspectorate and a representative of the SS to review all the camps with an eye to their future, but Himmler pre-empted the results. He ordered Friedrich Krüger, the HSSPF in the General Government, to terminate every single one.[130]

Krüger conferred with the SSPF in Lublin, Jacob Sporrenberg, about how to manage the operation, codenamed Unternehmen Erntefest, 'Harvest Festival'. The SS were afraid that if the liquidations proceeded in sequence, moving from one camp to another, there was a danger that Jews might be alerted to what was happening and prepare to resist. This was not something they could afford after so many embarrassing incidents during the year. So they resolved to assemble a force of 2,000–3,000 security police and strike simultaneously at each of the largest camps. Rather carelessly, though, they prefigured the action by ordering Jewish labourers in Majdanek, Poniatowa and Trawniki to dig zig-zag trenches. This afforded some Jewish prisoners an inkling of what was coming and there was, indeed, resistance. However, things went smoothly for the SS killers at Trawniki. They surrounded the camp in the early morning of 3 November and marched Jews in heavily guarded columns to the killing site. On arrival they were forced to strip, made to lie down in the ditch, and machine-gunned to death. The sound of shooting was partially obscured by loud music played over the camp's public address system. By mid-afternoon the Germans had shot 6,000. At Majdanek they used the same technique, but Jewish workers who were marched from the Lipowa Street camp to the ditches in Majdanek attempted to break through the SS cordon. Most were gunned down in the scrimmage. Elsewhere the combination of deception and over-whelming force was effective. At the end of the day the Germans had murdered 18,400 Jews, leaving 600 men and women to clean up. They were later shot too. The killing at Poniatowa did not begin until the fol-lowing morning. The Jews in one barrack refused to assemble for the short march to the killing field, whereupon the SS set fire to the build-ing. Everyone inside died. By half-past two in the afternoon 15,000 had been shot to death. The Germans spared 120 to tidy up, reducing this group by stages until there were 4 left. None survived. In all, the Ger-mans had massacred 43,000 people in under 48 hours. It was the largest single killing operation of the war.[131]

Nevertheless, in a manner characteristic of all such procedures, pockets of Jews clung to life. Several thousand continued to work for the Wehrmacht in Deblin and Biala Podlaska. Some 1,200 were kept by the Luftwaffe in Zamość. Those in Biala Podlaska and Zamość were eventually evacuated westward in April 1944. The Deblin labour force was not relocated until July 1944, when the men were sent to munitions plants in Germany. The women and children were shot. Approximately 3,000 were sheltered in the Budzyn and Krasnik labour camps not despite the fact that they were SS-controlled but *because* of this. Accord-ing to the Israeli historian David Silberklang, none other than Odilo

Globocnik 'set aside' Jewish skilled workers who were highly profitable or who he thought would be useful for future business ventures. In Krasnik they even kept their families with them. (Eventually they were evacuated westwards and many perished in sundry circumstances.) Handfuls of Jews persisted in farms and small food-processing enterprises across the region, partly because they were considered useful but also because they were simply overlooked.[132]

With the conclusion of Operation Harvest Festival, Globocnik was transferred to anti-partisan duties in northern Italy. On his departure he submitted a final accounting for Operation Reinhard. Meanwhile, teams of SS men and Ukrainians were attempting to remove any trace of the death camps in which roughly 1,700,000 Jews had been murdered. The erasure began at Belzec, where the dead had been exhumed and burned between March and April 1943. After the site was abandoned, Poles swarmed all over it, excavating the ash pits for valuables and dental gold. These digs were in danger of exposing what had gone on, so the SS returned and built a farmhouse that was manned by a small Ukrainian garrison. Their sole job was to stop Poles from grubbing around in the dirt. Treblinka was systematically dismantled from the end of August, using a Jewish labour force from Majdanek that was subsequently shot. A farm was erected in what had been the grounds of the camp and trees were planted around it, partly to make things more difficult for Polish treasure hunters. Plans to make Sobibor into a workshop for converting captured munitions were abandoned; the buildings were taken apart and the area transformed into a farm. Ukrainians were stationed there to deter scavengers. In fact, there was a huge amount of detritus at each location, especially bone fragments. Like so much else in the history of Operation Reinhard, Himmler's effort to conceal the crime was hastily conceived, inadequately prepared and poorly executed.[133]

Auschwitz-Birkenau redesigned for death

The closure of Treblinka and Sobibor left Auschwitz-Birkenau as the single mass extermination site in the genocidal armoury of the Third Reich. But the Birkenau of mid-1943 was a far cry from the Birkenau of mid-1942. As a result of decisions that remain obscure, between October 1941 and July 1942 the plans for a large mortuary and crematorium at Auschwitz that were designed to dispose of Soviet POWs who had expired in the camp metamorphosed into plans for an underground mortuary and surface-level crematorium at Birkenau that was, in turn, adapted to function as a gas chamber–crematorium complex. Crucially, the design of the subterranean mortuary was amended so that live humans could enter it down a staircase. By March 1943 the room previously designated as a Leichenkeller (corpse room) was redesignated an Auskleideraum (undressing room). Thus the naturally cool, sunken hall for the dead was transformed into an anteroom to an artificially ventilated room that was ostensibly for showering but actually served as the gas chamber.[134]

When it was completed, the undressing room was provided with benches and hooks for clothing. Banally familiar notices about the importance of cleanliness adorned the whitewashed walls. This facade was intended to deceive and reassure the victims until the last possible moment when they were ushered, or if necessary forced, into the killing room. The gas chamber, which was 30 by 7 metres, could take up to 2,000 people. It was fitted with a gas-tight and reinforced door that had a peephole so that SS personnel could monitor the progress of their murderous enterprise. The Zyklon-B pellets were inserted via covered openings set into the roof and fell through steel-mesh columns that marched along the centre of the underground chamber, mimicking the concrete pillars that supported the concrete ceiling. Electric fans were added to ventilate the chambers after each gassing. An electric-powered lift was installed to carry the corpses up to ground level, where there were five coke-fired ovens, each with three apertures, specially supplied by the leading German firm in the field, Topf and Sons. Other rooms on the ground floor provided space for melting down the dental gold extracted from the dead and washing and drying the hair shorn from the heads of murdered women. This building was given the designation Crematorium II.[135]

During August 1942, the construction department at Auschwitz prepared plans for three additional crematoria at Birkenau. Crematorium III was constructed opposite Crematorium II, on identical lines. Situated, respectively, just outside the boundary of the women's camp, BI, and the men's camp, BII, each semi-underground complex was enclosed by a barbed-wire fence and accessed via the road that led through the main gate between BI and BII. When all the ovens of Crematoria II and III were in continuous employment, they could reduce 1,440 humans to ash every day. However, the excavation of the underground chambers was arduous, time-consuming and costly. So the other two units, Crematoria IV and V, were built entirely above ground according to a different plan. They, too, were identically structured and faced each other like malign twins. Each contained three large rooms for gassing (approximately 11 by 8, 12 by 8, and 12 by 4 metres respectively). The third was subdivided for the convenience of killing smaller numbers of people. Zyklon-B was administered through flaps built into the exterior wall of each chamber. Since the buildings were more exposed to the elements than the underground death chambers in Crematoria II and III they were equipped with heating to ensure that the lethal crystals were immersed in warm air and thereby activated quickly. The corpses could be removed internally to the oven room where 768 bodies could be incinerated per day. But there were also outward-opening doors to allow the cadavers to be transported to pits where they could be burned in the open if necessary. This proved to be the case, since the ovens and chimneys of Crematoria IV and V were poorly designed to cope with the volume of business they came to handle, especially in mid-1944. Both buildings were fenced in and were surrounded by trees; later these orchards would provide shade for Jews waiting in all innocence for their turn to be ushered inside the phoney disinfection and shower rooms.[136]

At the same time as the camp's capacity for mass murder was increased, it acquired more importance as a source of plunder and a supply of labour. A separate compound was constructed containing thirty wooden storehouses that soon filled with the belongings removed from the ramp, where arriving Jews deposited their baggage, and the undressing rooms, where they left their footwear, clothing and remaining personal effects. Up to 1,600 Jews, mainly women, toiled in these large huts sorting the stuff and removing the yellow star from items of clothing. To the prisoners the compound was known as 'Canada', because it overflowed with plenty and offered endless opportunities for pilfering food and valuables. In February 1943 alone, 824 rail freight cars departed from Auschwitz for the Old Reich with textiles and leather goods. Most of the loot went to the Economics Ministry for recycling purposes, but over 200 loads of clothing, bedding, household linen and towels were sent to the Nazi Party office for the welfare of ethnic German settlers. Household items reached families in the Reich whose homes had been destroyed by bombing; stolen fountain pens were given to Luftwaffe pilots. There were so many prams that it took an hour for one shipment to reach the freight yard from 'Canada', pushed along five abreast. Without any sign of qualms as to their provenance, SS personnel and their wives would habitually pop into the Effektenlager to select such luxuries as a pair of shoes, a dress, some table napkins, a razor or a cigarette case. Every month or so, crates of valuables and fifteen to twenty suitcases laden with precious objects were driven in lorries under armed guard to the SS head office and the SS-WVHA in Berlin. Cash in numerous currencies, gold bars, silverware, diamonds, pearls and jewellery flowed from Auschwitz in an endless stream of loot, finally making their way into a special account at the Reichsbank in the fictitious name of Max Heiliger. It is estimated that between 1942 and 1944, six tons of dental gold were deposited in the vaults of the Reichsbank; there is little doubt that the bank officials knew where it had come from. Non-monetary gold, that is to say everything ranging from wedding rings to dental gold that had been melted down and re-smelted, was delivered by an SS officer named Melmer. The re-smelting was handled by Degussa (Deutsche Gold- und Silber-Scheindeanstalt), the same company that produced and supplied Zyklon-B to the SS.[137]

Kitty Hart, a sixteen-year-old Jewish girl from Bielsko in East Upper Silesia, was a member of the Kanadakommando. She and her mother had evaded ghettoization and deportation by working as foreign labourers in an I. G. Farben plant at Bitterfeld in Germany – until they were exposed as Jews. They were arrested and, after a spell in jail, in March 1943 were sent to Auschwitz. For a year she and her mother toiled in various work parties, getting weaker and weaker. Transfer to Birkenau saved her life, thanks to the incomparably better working conditions and the numerous perks. Fifteen years later, Kitty described how 'In one hut a group sorted nothing but shoes; in another only men's clothing was sorted; in another all women's; in still another only children's things. Then there was a hut named *Fressbaracke* where food just lay piled and rotting away, and in another hut valuables, jewelry, money and other precious things were sorted . . . At the very end of our hut was a big pile, from which we had to make up bundles of the invariable dozen of the same article. The clothes had to be folded neatly and then tied . . . Daily lorry loads were leaving with the stolen goods to be taken into Germany.' She added that 'All the clothing had to be fingered carefully along the seams for hidden jewelry and money.' This booty had to be dropped into baskets for collection, a practice that was keenly supervised by the guards. Kitty and other sorters tried to hide as much as they could for use by the camp underground and to prevent it enriching the Third Reich.[138]

Kitty was just one of tens of thousands of men and women from across Europe, non-Jews as well as Jews, who were directed to Auschwitz to provide labour for the industrial and agricultural concerns that sprouted around the camp. Unlike the phase from early 1941 to mid-1942, when deportees were assigned to Auschwitz specifically as forced labour and hence pre-selected, the transports that arrived thereafter were mostly unsorted. Consequently, the camp administration had to create a selection and admission system. Every trainload of new arrivals was assessed on the platform, where those deemed fit for labour or offering a skill that was useful to the camp were admitted. SS doctors made the selection based on the age of the deportee and an instantaneous evaluation of his or her physical strength. The elderly and the young, the sick and the lame were doomed. Visibly pregnant women and mothers with infants stood no chance. Those selected for the workforce were taken to one of two large buildings in camp BIa (women's camp) or BIb (men's camp), nicknamed the sauna, that functioned as a bath-house and disinfection facility. Here the prisoners (male and female) were divested of their clothing, all their body hair was shaven off, they were tattooed with a registration number, showered, and issued with prison garb. In the latter part of the war, inmates were often presented with garments recycled from dead prisoners or from the Canada compound. Kitty Hart remembered that 'We were stripped and under showers for some time, and still there were no clothes. Next came the disinfection – a dip in a foul-smelling, bluish green liquid. This over, the *Fryzerki*, the hairdressers, go to work. These were prisoners whose occupation was to shave our heads, under our armpits and between our legs. The command was, "Arms and legs out." It took only a few seconds. I touched my head. It felt queer and cold. I was thrown a heap of rags ... a vest, a pair of khaki breeches and a blouse which had been part of a Russian prisoner of war uniform.'[139]

In March 1943, the SS administration commenced construction of a central bathing, disinfection and delousing complex that became known as the Central Camp Sauna. It was located adjacent to the Canada compound and midway between the two pairs of gas chambers. Despite the importance that the SS administration attached to the 'sauna' for preventing the importation of disease, this relatively simple structure and its equipment did not actually begin to process new arrivals until January 1944.[140]

Whether they were processed in one of the older saunas or in the new building, for prisoners the experience marked a caesura in their lives, the transition into an environment where normal laws and values ceased to have any relevance. Marco Nahon arrived from Salonica with 740 Jews after a six-day journey, during which a woman gave birth in the box-car. Nahon, who had never heard of Auschwitz, was separated from his wife and daughter and taken to the quarantine barracks where every fresh intake was held for up to six weeks. There he was tattooed, disinfected, showered and handed the uniform of the Katzetnik, the inhabitant of a KZ, Konzentrationslager. In a memoir written in a displaced persons camp in the summer of 1945, he recollected how 'After arriving at the concentration camp in the morning with luggage, clothing, bedding, kitchen utensils, food etc., we find ourselves by evening robbed of everything, stripped to actual nakedness and completely destitute.'[141]

Another doctor, Lucie Adelsberger, arrived from Berlin a few days later. 'The first order of business', she recounted after the war, 'led us to the washhouse, the "sauna", where the actual processing began. We undressed, had our hair cut – no, actually our heads were shaved to stubble; then came the showers and finally the tattoos. This was where they confiscated the very last vestiges of our belongings; nothing remained, not our clothes or underwear, no soap, no towel, no needle, and no utensils, not even a spoon; no written document that could have identified us, no picture, no written message from a loved one. Our past was cut off, erased . . . We were put in prison garb, with no underwear, only a thin chemise . . . We were given wooden shoes with shreds of Jewish prayer shawls as foot-wrappings. Then we got our numbers burned into our left forearm and sewn onto our clothes with a triangular badge that identified each prisoner by color. We were cut off from the whole world out there, uprooted from our homeland, torn from our families, a mere number, of significance only for bookkeepers. Nothing remained but naked existence . . .' Adelsberger was drawn into the camp's prisoner staff because she was a physician; her first post was in the infirmary of the camp for Gypsies. Nahon was made a block-doctor. Their medical training levered them into privileged occupations that enhanced their survival chances and equipped them to observe what was happening around them. Hence physicians were amongst the earliest camp survivors to document conditions for the prisoners, not least the hierarchy that granted camp functionaries a slightly less tenuous hold on life.[142]

At the top of the pecking order were the kapos. These were men and women who the SS administration placed in charge of sections of the camp, blocks and kommandos (working parties). The first kapos in Auschwitz I, the main camp, were professional criminals transferred from German concentration camps. They were given rooms of their own, wore what they chose, could get their hair cut, and usually had a servant in the form of a young boy or a young woman who sometimes also provided sexual services. But they knew their cushioned existence depended on ensuring the submission of the other prisoners and extracting the maximum labour out of them. To these ends the guards permitted and encouraged them to employ massive violence, administering beatings with fists, boots and truncheons. Quite often the violence was whimsical or arbitrary, the point being to instil fear and subservience in the rest of the prisoners. Due to the expansion of Birkenau and the influx of Jewish prisoners, from 1942 onwards Jews also became kapos. Eliezer Gruenbaum, the son of Yitzhak Gruenbaum who chaired the Jewish Agency rescue committee, ended up as a deputy block chief in Auschwitz. Gruenbaum had rebelled against his father and become a communist. He was arrested in Paris by the Vichy authorities and deported to Auschwitz in June 1942. Thanks to the network of political prisoners that came to dominate the underground, he was given a sinecure as deputy Blockälteste. This involved having to control a thousand starving men stuffed into a freezing hut. In a post-war apologia, he explained that it was necessary to use force to distribute the rations with any equity. 'I tried various methods: distributing soup according to a list of young people, and also selecting those most in need . . . I was unsuccessful. You could deliver speeches, you could shout and plead . . . Second helpings had to be distributed with a cane.' After the war, survivors in Paris accused him of collaboration and gratuitous brutality, although a formal investigation was inconclusive.[143]

There were numerous occupations as a prisoner-functionary that carried advantages. The SS employed Jews as clerks and secretaries in their offices; the Aufnahmekommando were engaged in admitting prisoners, registering and tattooing them; Jewish doctors and medical orderlies staffed the infirmaries in the sub-camps and assisted the SS doctors in the main camp hospital, including the carrying out of medical experiments. Each hut had a record keeper, a Rapportschreiber. Large teams of prisoners collected the baggage and belongings of new arrivals off the ramp and tidied up the box-cars. Inmates were employed in the camp's printing office, post office and extensive maintenance services. Prisoners scrutinized every kommando and fought each other to get a plum job, using political or ethnic networks, bribery, betrayal and any means at their disposal. Nahon regarded the Elektrischer Kommando, which checked the high-voltage fences, as particularly benign. Those with technical skills worked in the SS motor pool as mechanics. Talented musicians were recruited to the camp orchestra, conducted by Alma Rose. Albert Menasche, the doctor deported from Salonica, found himself playing merry tunes on the flute a stone's throw from the gas chamber in which his beloved daughter had been murdered. Later he was transferred to work in the medical block at Birkenau. Jews like Kitty Hart who got work in the Kanadakommando were considered most fortunate: they worked indoors and had access to an almost unlimited supply of vittles and tradable items – if they were nimble and quick-witted enough to get away with 'organizing', the camp jargon for pilfering. Work parties outside the camp varied widely, depending on the nature of the employment, the character of the kapo and the degree of interaction with Germans. Some labour was back-breaking but factory work was bearable. Those condemned to open air toil fared worst; those who rubbed shoulders regularly with civilian staff or prisoners of war stood a chance of getting extra food or cigarettes that could be traded for rations. The worst occupation, usually regarded as the depth of depravity, offering no hope of survival or redemption, was the Sonderkommando that manned the gas chambers and the crematoria.[144]

The barracks housing prisoners and the infirmaries were mostly wooden structures, many originally designed as stables. Crudely manufactured wooden bunks stacked three high lined each side, with two or three prisoners crammed onto each level. A roughly constructed brick flue that ran the length of the hut conducting hot air from a stove at one end was the only source of warmth. The floor of the huts consisted of beaten earth and was liable to become a mess of excrement because many of the prisoners had diarrhoea or dysentery and there were no toilets. Instead, the latrines were located at the end of each row of huts, which was several minutes' walk away – more if the ground was muddy. The enfeebled prisoners were only allowed to use the latrines for short periods at certain times of the day, in any case. Getting to them was not only an energy-sapping race against nature, it was a provocation to SS guards who might at any time stop an inmate – with terrible results. Nahon's brother-in-law was beaten insensible for urinating in his hut.[145]

Each day was framed by the Appell, roll call. For Lucie Adelsberger 'Roll call in the concentration camp was the horror of the day.' The elder of each block and each sub-section had to account to his immediate superior and then the SS guard. This necessitated counting thousands and then tens of thousands, a task that took a long time even in ideal conditions. If the figures for a count did not reconcile with the SS record, the count had to be held again. This was often the case since prisoners died in their bunks and failed to appear, died unnoticed while on an outside work party, or dropped dead on the parade ground and were invisible from the end of the row where the enumerator passed. Roll calls could go on for hours in driving rain, freezing cold and scorching sun. 'Twice a day we stood at roll call,' Adelsberger recounted, 'in the dark hours before dawn prior to marching off to work (in the summer we got up at 3 a.m. and in the winter at 4) and again in the evening after work. Each time, the roll call lasted one to two hours, frequently much longer.' If the numbers did not tally, kapos and prisoner-functionaries were terrified in case this signified an escape. Prisoners might have to remain standing for up to forty-eight hours until the confusion was resolved. 'They stood in threadbare shreds of garments, in wooden clogs, or worn-out and split remnants of what had once been leather shoes, their hands wrapped in a few rags. And they stood still, for they were not allowed to move . . . forbidden to excuse themselves when bouts of diarrhoea caused the excrement to stream out like a waterfall.' Anyone who collapsed risked a beating. If a person collapsed a second time 'you never got up again'.[146]

Prisoners were tormented by hunger and thirst. Adelsberger diagnosed the effect as 'a nerve shattering pain, an attack on the whole personality'. She observed grimly that 'Hunger makes a person vicious and undermines her character.' The rations were not simply inadequate, the food was abysmal in quality. The monotonous diet of ersatz coffee and thin soup contained little nourishment while it was conducive to diarrhoea. Nahon regarded the feeding arrangements as a form of slow execution. Thanks to those who 'organized' food in the Canada compound or worked in the kitchens there was a black market in the camp and it was possible to obtain food in exchange for valuables or favours. But Nahon thought that the black market was confined more or less to the privileged elite. Since prisoners were sometimes forced to use their bowls as receptacles when they urinated or defecated in their bunks, the utensil intended to convey nutrition also risked infecting them with bacteria. Given the catastrophic sanitation, disease was endemic. Due to the impossibility of washing thoroughly and the lice-infested bunks and clothing, typhus flared up repeatedly. Prisoner doctors like Adelsberger and Nahon tried to stem the spread of disease and to cure those who succumbed but the task was all but hopeless, given the absence of basic medicines and the pervasive filth. The medical orderlies did not even have access to clean running water.[147]

Just as the Appell came to dominate each day, selections came to define longer periods in the camp's history. The first cull of prisoners was carried out by the SS in August 1942 to curb an outbreak of typhus. A year later, SS doctors organized the first examination of male prisoners and condemned 4,000 to the gas chambers because they were deemed unfit for work. On the eve of the Jewish holy day of Yom Kippur, 1943, the SS held a further selection, condemning 1,000 to death. Adelsberger recalled that 'The camp physician commandeered one or two more blocks and ordered the naked prisoners to pass by in single file. He then chose those who, because of weakness or under-nourishment, the edema of starvation, or because of scabies or sun-burn . . . were to go to the gas.' The numbers of the doomed were noted and they were immediately transferred to the 'selection block' to await their end. On the appointed day, this sub-section of the camp was locked down and the prisoners heard 'the screams of people being beaten, accompanied by the fury of SS commands and the barking of dogs; an hour or two later the chimneys were glowing'. Drawing on Greek mythology, Nahon compared selections to 'a kind of man-made Minotaur that gluts itself on human victims'.[148]

It is estimated that about half of all the Jews deported to Auschwitz were females and children who were murdered immediately. Yet about 30 per cent of the registered camp population consisted of Jewish women and, notwithstanding the imposed uniformity of camp life, gender significantly inflected their experiences. Jewish women from Slovakia were amongst the pioneers of Birkenau and consequently attained positions of authority within the women's camp. Krystyna Zywulska, sent to Auschwitz in June 1943, remarked bitterly in her post-war memoir that 'Slovene [sic] Jewesses' occupied the coveted posts of block seniors or 'blockovas'. Zywulska (whose real name was Sonia

Landau) also described the competition between national and ethnic groups for access to safe work parties. Slovak women had a head start in this respect, too. Helena Tischauer, who arrived from Slovakia in March 1942, acquired a job as a sign painter (which had been her pre-war vocation) and subsequently as a clerk. Thanks partly to these preferable occupations, she was one of the few women from those early Slovak transports to survive. Of the 28,000 women in the camp in early 1942, only about 5,400 were alive at the end of the year. The total rose to 56,000 in the course of 1943, but fully half of them died or were done to death. Due to the demand for labour and the influx of Hungarian Jewish women, the number reached about 47,000 in 1944.[149]

In addition to sickness and exhaustion, which men faced too, women were at risk due to pregnancy. Although mothers with infants were never admitted to the camp, young women who were in the early stages of pregnancy often passed through the selection. However, since it was not permitted to give birth in Auschwitz and mothers were doomed, such women eventually faced a horrible dilemma. Some opted to have an abortion in the form of an induced miscarriage. Others went to full term, with horrific consequences. Lucie Adelsberger explained, 'as soon as the newborn saw the light of day, the inconceivable happened: The Jewish child was forfeited to death and with him, his mother. Within a week both were sent to the gas chamber.' This practice posed a terrible quandary not just for the mother-to-be but also the medical staff in the women's camp. Adelsberger set out their thinking: 'Medical ethics prescribe that if, during labour, the mother and the child are in danger, priority must be given to saving the life of the mother. We prisoner physicians quietly acted in accordance with this regulation. The child had to die so that the mother might be saved.' Infanticide on these lines was so common that the doctors found it hard to obtain enough poison: 'We never had enough for them'. In parentheses, Adelsberger added that 'Many women never got over the shock of the death of their newborn infants and have forgiven neither themselves nor us.'[150]

Women were constantly at risk of sexualized violence. The shaving of body hair was the first assault; SS men routinely watched women in the shower room. Adelsberger recalled an SS officer who 'inspected us not only in a patronizing, offhanded, and condescending way, but as a man in an appraising, smirking, and lascivious manner. He interrogated the naked women one after the other . . . all the while gazing at the contours of their bodies, his eyes measuring our breasts and hips. And we were forced to respond to the quips and queries of this cooing man in his SS uniform with our unadorned words and our naked bodies, for this, too, was part of what it meant to be a prisoner in Birkenau.' On one occasion when the female inmates were disinfected, Zywulska remembered that 'Each one was rubbed under the arms and between the legs, a fact which caused the SS men standing at the sides, to burst into gales of laughter.' Women were also forced into the selections bereft of any clothing, exposed to the elements as well as the gaze of SS medical officials plus sundry guards.[151]

In extremis, women offered sex in exchange for food, clothing or protection from those such as barrack chiefs who had a modicum of power. Zywulska believed that female *blockovas* enjoyed the privilege of conducting liaisons with block leaders from the male sections while ordinary female prisoners had romantic and sexual relationships with other women. She was shocked to find that these affairs were often conducted amidst the squalor of the latrines, although her disgust was evoked as much by the display of lesbianism as by the excremental environment. One day while passing the toilet block, Zywulska espied 'Sitting on the boards in the space between, was a mannish looking German women, a black winkel [a criminal, signified by a black triangle]. On her knees sat a very feminine girl with long hair. She gazed at her partner in rapture, then she kissed her on the mouth. It was a long kiss. You couldn't imagine anything more revolting. This kind of "love" in these surroundings.'[152]

Judenpolitik in the context of military defeat

In mid-1943 the German military position in every theatre deteriorated. Paradoxically, however, Axis setbacks triggered a fresh offensive against the remaining Jews in German-dominated Europe and offered new opportunities for Himmler's men. The course of the war as much as Judenpolitik had an immediate and deleterious effect on the surviving Jewish populations.

On 9 July the British and Americans launched the invasion of Sicily, deploying a vast armada of ships and 180,000 troops. The success of the landings triggered open criticism of Mussolini in the Fascist Grand Council. Two weeks later King Vittorio Emanuele used his prerogative to replace him as prime minister with Marshal Pietro Badoglio. Immediately afterwards Mussolini was arrested. Nevertheless, it took over a month for the Allied forces, now approaching 480,000 men, to evict 60,000 Germans from the island.[153]

The fall of Mussolini and the conquest of Sicily prompted Allied hopes for the capitulation of Italy. It was even held possible that this would trigger a German collapse. Unfortunately, the political and military high commanders found themselves pursuing a muddled strategy and gifted Hitler an opportunity to recover his balance. At the Anglo-American conference in Casablanca in January 1943, the Americans had agreed to the invasion of Sicily but only on condition that the British concur with plans to invade north-west Europe in May 1944. The Americans grudgingly consented to a follow-on invasion of Italy if it looked as though the fascists were crumbling and if the invaders could expect help from the Italian army. With Sicily in the bag the debate reopened. The Allies concluded that they had to pursue the Germans and seek to knock out Italy completely. Yet the timetable for the projected landings in France required the transfer of the best American and British units to the United Kingdom. As a result, the forces available for a descent on the Italian mainland were much reduced. Meanwhile, Hitler had sent fourteen divisions to northern Italy and stationed powerful formations outside Rome to prevent his erstwhile ally from throwing in the towel. Consequently, the invasion of Italy, Operation Avalanche, was something of a gamble. It rested heavily on expectations of Italian cooperation and the assumption that the Germans would withdraw to the more defensible northern half of the peninsula.[154]

Instead, everything went awry. After much prevarication, Marshal Badoglio put out peace feelers to the Allies. The secret negotiations culminated in an armistice on 3 September 1943, the same day that the vanguard of the British Eighth Army crossed the straits of Messina to the mainland. But efforts to get the Italians to change sides came to naught. Badoglio did not help matters by fleeing with his government and the Italian high command, leaving Italian garrisons in Italy, France, Yugoslavia, Greece and the Greek islands without clear orders. When King Vittorio Emanuele broadcast the announcement of the Italian surrender he seemed to call on his people to avoid hostilities with either the Germans or the Allies. As a result, German troops were able to disarm most Italian units without meeting any resistance.[155]

When the Anglo-American invasion force came ashore in the Bay of Salerno on 9 September it was greeted with ferocious German counter-attacks. The Allies managed to cling on and finally broke out. Naples was occupied on 1 October, but bad weather and a tactically superior German defence slowed the northwards advance to a costly crawl. For the next seven months the under-powered and under-resourced Allied forces would prove unable to penetrate what Churchill had assured the Americans would be the 'soft underbelly' of Europe.[156]

To add to the imbroglio, Hitler ordered an SS commando mission to rescue Mussolini. The Duce was resurrected at the head of a puppet regime in northern Italy, the Italian Social Republic. Also known as the Republic of Salò, after the location of its headquarters on Lake Garda, it was to prove a final, vicious expression of fascist extremism and anti-Semitism.[157]

Although Hitler was momentarily shaken by Mussolini's fall, the Nazi regime did not come anywhere near to disintegration. The evaporation of fascism in Italy only redoubled Hitler's determination to clamp down on dissent within the Reich. On 10 August he appointed Himmler minister for the interior, signalling that domestic affairs were even more firmly in the hands of the security apparatus. However, military developments in the Mediterranean required the diversion of significant assets from the Russian front at a critical moment and contributed to the further decline of the Wehrmacht, even if the army was never in danger of falling apart.[158]

Indeed, in the wake of Stalingrad, Albert Speer had increased munitions production, making good the losses of 1942 and re-equipping the Wehrmacht for offensive operations. By spring 1943, Hitler reckoned that it was impossible to remain on the defensive. Rather, he hoped that by dealing a blow to the Soviets he could hang on to the raw materials and agricultural land of Ukraine and show his Axis partners that Germany was still in the fight. In March he issued orders for a concentric attack on the Red Army salient around Kursk, Operation Citadel. Although the Germans had assembled almost every effective offensive formation they possessed, the attack foundered – even before the invasion of Sicily gave Hitler a reason to call it off. At the beginning of August the Germans were back at their start line. For the rest of 1943 the Wehrmacht was forced back steadily on almost every sector from Leningrad to the Black Sea.[159]

As Germany's strategic position worsened, the Nazi leadership turned to anti-Semitism as if it were a secret weapon. Hitler referred to

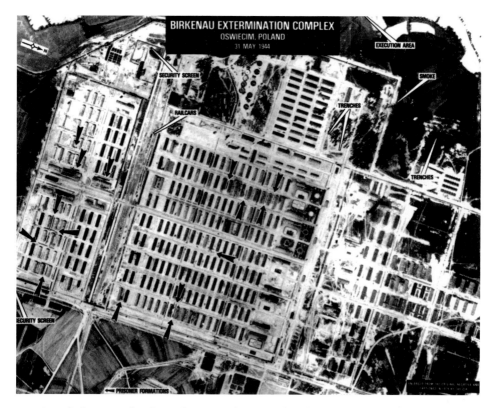

BIRKENAU EXTERMINATION COMPLEX
OSWIECIM, POLAND
31 MAY 1944

EXECUTION AREA

SECURITY SCREEN

SMOKE

RAILCARS

TRENCHES

TRENCHES

SECURITY SCREEN

PRISONER FORMATIONS

37. Aerial photograph of Auschwitz-Birkenau, taken by the 15th US Army Air Force in 1944. The photograph clearly demonstrates that the USAAF were flying over the camp and could therefore have bombed the approaches had they fully appreciated its function and had the will to intervene.

38. Hungarian
women and children
arriving at Auschwitz,
May/June 1944.

39. An elderly Jewish man
arriving at Auschwitz,
May/June 1944.

40. A transport of Hungarian women arriving at Auschwitz, with Sonderkommando in background, May/June 1944.

41. Victims being selected at Auschwitz, May/June 1944. Note the Sonderkommando members, left foreground.

42. One of the barracks at Bergen-Belsen shortly after the camp's liberation in April 1945.

Photo courtesy of the Wiener Library, London

Photo courtesy of the Wiener Library, London

43. Female SS guards supervised by British soldiers burying victims of Bergen-Belsen concentration camp in a mass grave, April 1945.

44. Aerial shot of the approaches to Treblinka, c. 1943.

45. Cover of the 1946 publication of Rudolf Reder's testimony from Belzec, in Polish. It shows the multi-lingual early efforts by survivors to give accounts of what befell the Jews.

46. DP Camp at Potsdamer Chaussee in Berlin-Zehlendorf, c. 1946.

47. Jewish detainees in a Cyprus internment camp hold a rally in support of immigration to Palestine, 1948.

48. The first train carrying Jews bound for Palestine pulls out of the station
at Bergen-Hohne, c. 1947.

Photo courtesy of the Wiener Library, London

the Jewish question with increasing frequency and urged Goebbels to use it relentlessly in propaganda. In early March, Goebbels confided to his diary, 'On the Jewish question especially, we are in it so deeply that there is no getting out any longer. And that is a good thing. Experience teaches that a movement and a people who have burned their bridges fight with much greater determination and fewer constraints than those that have a chance of retreat.' A few weeks later he added, 'The Führer issues instructions to set the Jewish question once more at the forefront of our propaganda in the strongest possible way.' Hitler instructed him to hammer home the message: 'the Jews are to blame; the Jews wanted the war; the Jews are making the war worse; and again and again the Jews are to blame'. True to his word, Hitler made a series of speeches in May 1943 in which he held the Jews responsible for the war and reiterated that they would pay the price.[160]

Himmler, too, used the fate of the Jews as a sort of blood bond to tie the civil and military leadership to the Nazi cause. To achieve this, however, he had to be more or less open about what had been done to the Jews. Thus at the same time as Jewish slaves were toiling in horrible conditions to obliterate the traces of German crimes, Himmler was in effect confessing to them and attempting to implicate the hierarchy of the Reich. During a long speech to senior SS personnel and leading members of the regime, including Albert Speer, in Posen on 4 October 1943, Himmler declared that 'Today I am going to refer quite frankly to a very grave chapter. We can mention it now among ourselves quite openly and yet we shall never talk about it in public. I'm referring to the evacuation of the Jews, the extermination of the Jewish people. Most of you will know what it is like to see 100 corpses lying side by side or 500 or 1,000 of them. To have coped with this and – except for cases of human weakness – to have remained decent, that has made us tough. This is an unwritten – never to be written – and yet glorious page in our history.' He then directly related the anti-Jewish measures to the war and evoked memories of Germany's defeat twenty-five years earlier. 'For we know how difficult we would have made it for ourselves if, on top of the bombing raids, the burdens and deprivations of the war, we still had Jews in every town as secret saboteurs, agitators, and trouble makers. We would probably have reached the 1916–17 stage ... We had the moral right ... the duty to our people to destroy this people which wanted to destroy us.' In early May 1944 he told senior army officers that 'The Jewish question has been solved in Germany and in the countries occupied by Germany. It was solved uncompromisingly, as was appropriate in view of the struggle in which we are engaged for the life of our nation, for the survival of our blood . . .' He explained that even women and children had to die because 'as Germans we must not permit hate-filled avengers to grow up with the result that our children and grand-children will then be obliged to confront them because we, the fathers and grandfathers, were too weak and cowardly . . .'[161]

The consequences of Italy's defeat

The adverse tide of the war did more than inspire furious rhetoric. Hitler attributed the surrender of Italy and rumbles of unease amongst his remaining Axis partners to Jewish influence. So he demanded the redoubling of efforts to scourge the Jews and used the continuing campaign of annihilation to implicate the elites in other countries so deeply that they could not afford a German defeat. The Italian collapse thus invigorated anti-Jewish policy just as it gave the Jew-hunters new fields in which to operate. Allied diplomatic bungling and uninspired operational decisions in the Mediterranean again thrust Jews into the firing line while offering them no escape or aid. The Jews of Italy and Jewish populations in the Italian-occupied areas of southern France, Serbia, and Greece were now at the mercy of the ever more vindictive Germans.[162]

In mid-1943 there were approximately 40,000 Jews on Italian territory, including refugees. The tightening of the anti-Jewish laws meant that by this time only half of Italian Jews had any livelihood; in May 1942, forced labour was introduced. A majority of the foreign Jews in the country had already been interned in camps or restricted to designated villages (so-called free internment) in remote areas since late 1940. Some 9,000, mainly foreign or stateless Jews, were in receipt of aid from the Delegation for the Assistance of Jewish Emigrants (Delegazione per l'Assistenza degli Emigranti Ebrei, DELASEM). Between 1939 and 1943, DELASEM helped roughly 5,000 Jewish emigrants leave Italy for various destinations. Only a small number were liberated in the opening months of the Allied invasion and they were mainly foreigners interned in the south, notably in the camp at Ferramonti in Calabria.[163]

The Allied landings seemed to promise speedy liberation for Luigi Fleischmann, a sixteen-year-old from Fiume whose family had been living under open internment in the village of Navelli in the Abruzzi, central Italy, since April 1942. Admitedly, life in Navelli was easygoing: the carabinieri exercised the loosest supervision over the Fleischmanns and three other Jewish families, one of which was British. At 11 a.m. each day they had to register with the police, a routine that was little more than a charade. 'The officials come out, glance at us and, from time to time, even count our number. Then they bark "OK, you can go now!"' The carabinieri told the Jews they were 'after all, human beings, not wild animals to be kept in a cage'. Luigi was free to roam the surrounding hills until the turn in the war threatened his idyll. First the police replaced their fascist insignia and then deserted altogether. Uncertain what might happen next, the Jews debated whether to stay put or go south. Since the Allies seemed relatively close they decided to remain. To their chagrin there was no rapid liberation; instead the Germans occupied the region and dug in. Observing the German reinforcements and defensive preparations Luigi wrote sadly in his diary, 'the Allies are taking their time'. When the front line bogged down for the winter they were about eighty miles away; they would not reach Navelli until June 1944.[164]

The sclerotic Allied advance allowed the Germans and their Italian collaborators to wreak havoc on the Jews. As usual, the intensity of the assault derived partly from the profusion of competing agencies. In October an Einsatzkommando of the Sipo-SD under Theo Dannecker was dispatched to Rome by Heinrich Müller. Himmler sent Karl Wolff as his Higher SS Police Leader to manage security matters – which included overseeing Jewish affairs. Ernst Kaltenbrunner, the head of the RSHA since January 1943, ordered the SD man on the spot, Herbert Kappler, to initiate an Aktion against Rome's Jewish community as soon as possible. In a wireless transmission on 11 October (intercepted and decoded by Bletchley Park), Kaltenbrunner instructed him that 'It is precisely the immediate and thorough eradication of the Jews in Italy which is in the special interest of the present internal political situation and the general security in Italy ... The longer the delay, the more the Jews who are doubtless reckoning on evacuation measures have an opportunity by moving to the houses of pro-Jewish Italians of disappearing completely.'[165]

The Jewish leadership, in particular the head of the Rome community Ugo Foa, responded sluggishly to the threat and allowed the Germans to get hold of files with the names and addresses of the membership. On 16 October, Kappler staged a razzia centred on the ancient Jewish quarter of Rome, once the site of the ghetto. In a few hours the German security police seized 1,257 Jews. Two days later a transport carried 1,007 Roman Jews to Auschwitz-Birkenau. It took five days to get there; most of the hungry, thirsty, exhausted deportees were murdered on arrival. Working through Ugo Foa and the president of the federation of Italian Jews, Dante Almansi, Kappler next extorted 50kg of gold from the terrified Jewish population. However, Kaltenbrunner's apprehensions were fulfilled. The bulk of the Jewish community took flight or found refuge with friends, in convents and in monasteries.[166]

Kappler and Dannecker had nowhere near enough men to repeat the mass round-up in Rome. Instead they resorted to sudden raids in Milan, Trieste, Turin, Florence, Genoa and Venice. Approximately 3,000 Jews were captured during October–November 1943, held in camps run by the German police, and shipped north to Auschwitz-Birkenau. Foreign Jews were most vulnerable: almost a quarter of the refugees and stateless Jews in the north perished due to these raids. By contrast only 12 per cent of Jews with Italian citizenship were deported. Thanks to local connections and local knowledge, they were more likely to find refuge with friends, sympathetic employees or kindly churchmen, most of the latter acting on their own initiative. Pope Pius XII maintained his public silence about the fate of the Jews, this time on the grounds that the wolf was at his door and it was prudent not to provoke a German incursion into the Vatican.[167]

From the beginning of 1944 the Germans were abetted by Mussolini's Salò Republic. Order Number 5, issued by the anti-Semitic interior minister, Guido Buffarini Guidi, enjoined the fascist police authorities in the north to locate and arrest all Jews except the elderly, Jews in mixed marriages, and baptized children. For the rest of the war, Italian fascist diehards in the National Republican Guard (Guardia Nazionale Repubblicana, GNR), the Brigate Nere (Blackshirts) and the Italian SS provided the manpower the Germans lacked. This collaboration was not completely harmonious; the Italians clashed with the Germans over the categories to be excluded, although these altercations were more about protecting Italian sovereignty than protecting certain classes of Jew. In February 1944, Friedrich Bosshammer took over from Dannecker and instituted a ruthless policy of emptying Jewish hospitals, old people's homes, and orphanages. The Sipo-SD took over a former POW camp at

Fossoli, in the province of Modena, and turned it into a collection point for Jews and resistance fighters destined for Auschwitz. Odilo Globocnik, who had been transferred from Lublin to Trieste to conduct anti-partisan operations, set up a concentration camp at San Sabba, a disused rice factory outside the city. His team, which included Christian Wirth, Franz Stangl, Kurt Franz and Josef Oberhauser, conducted a reign of terror along the northern Adriatic coastline. But they were only able to net about 1,000 Jews. Despite German ambitions to remove the entire Jewish population, only 6,806 Italian Jews (out of a possible 32,000) were deported, plus up to 1,000 foreign Jews (out of an estimated 8,000). Several hundred were also killed in Italy in the camps or in the course of Jew-hunts.[168]

Unwilling to sit waiting for the Allies to arrive, Luigi Fleischmann joined partisans operating in the Abruzzi. Radio Bari, in the liberated south, admonished Jews 'to escape from the Nazis and the fascists and [continued to] urge the Italians to help hide Jews'. Conversely, the official radio of the Salò Republic called on Italians to apprehend all Jews as enemies of the nation. Sadly, the protracted military campaign gave time for the Blackshirts and German police to swoop on neighbouring towns and villages. However, the Germans could expect limited cooperation. A police officer in Navelli tipped off the Fleischmann family that a raid was impending. The secretary of the commune gave Luigi's father a new identity card 'as well as an empty one that we could fill in with whatever details we wanted. He even put an official stamp on it and wished father all the best'.[169]

A similarly relaxed attitude had prevailed in the Italian zone of occupation in southern France between November 1942 and September 1943. Heinz Röthke grumbled to Helmut Knochen, 'The attitude of the Italians is, and was incomprehensible . . . In the last few months [he was writing in July 1943] there has been a mass-exodus of Jews from our occupation zone into the Italian Zone. The escape of the Jews is facilitated by the existence of thousands of flight-routes, the assistance given them by the French population, and the sympathy of the authorities, false identification cards, and also the size of the area which makes it impossible to seal off the zones of influence.' These frustrations were suddenly relieved by the Italian surrender and the immediate occupation of the region by German forces. On 10 September, Alois Brunner arrived in Nice with a fifteen-man Einsatzkommando and set up headquarters at the Hotel Excelsior near to the main railway station. On paper, Nice and its environs looked like a happy hunting ground. The Germans estimated that there were 25,000–30,000 Jews, including 15,000 who were foreign-born, just waiting to be rounded up. But Brunner suffered a crippling shortage of personnel. His job was made harder by the fact that Jews were not marked; even the identification cards of local Jews were clean, since the Vichy ordinance of late 1942 to stamp *Juif* in their papers had not been enforced by the Italians.[170]

Brunner could at least call on the Milice. This paramilitary outfit formed in January 1943 was led by a demobilized ex-serviceman, Joseph Darnand. It had started life as a veterans' movement in the Free Zone dedicated to supporting Marshal Pétain and fighting communism. With Vichy's blessing it developed into a quasi-police force, combating the resistance and, increasingly, hunting Jews. The Milice started to attract men who merely wanted to avoid obligatory labour service in Germany and opportunists who saw scope for blackmail and robbery. In mid-1943, Darnand secured the patronage of the SS. In return for offering loyalty to the Führer and enrolling in the Waffen-SS, he was able to obtain arms for his militia.[171]

Léon Poliakov, who had taken refuge under the Italian aegis, was working for an underground Jewish relief organization. Years later he recounted the desperate – though not ineffectual – methods to which the Sipo-SD and Miliciennes resorted. During the day, 'official black Citroëns cruised the streets of Nice, and passengers scrutinized passersby. At any moment, a pedestrian would be asked to get into a car. No useless questions or identification checks. The car went to the synagogue. There the victim was undressed and, if he was circumcised, he automatically took his place in the next convoy to Drancy . . .' Teams of security police raided hotels, *pensions* and rented accommodation. 'Members of the Milice, those jackals of the Gestapo, checked apartment buildings and made lists of names that sounded Jewish. Improvised physiognomists were posted in the stations.' But measuring the noses of rail passengers was hardly going to fill transports. So security police also raided the hotels in Nice and along the Riviera. There were no fewer than 170 such establishments and since the police could not visit more than ten per night Poliakov reckoned the odds were in his favour. 'Every night at the Hotel Lausanne, I told myself before going to bed that I had about a one in seventeen chance of being raided . . . Ah, those nights in Nice.'[172]

Thanks to trouser inspections in the synagogue and torture in the basement of the Excelsior, Brunner's Einsatzkommando was able to seize 1,100 Jews in Nice and a further 300 at locations along the coast. They also picked up around 400 Jews sheltering in villages inland. Yet, although they were able to send several transports northwards each month, between the start of September and the end of December they were able to catch less than 10 per cent of the Jews thought to be in the region. The failure of the operation was a testament to the increased awareness of the Jews, the strength of the underground networks they had created and their willingness to deliberately evade the occupier, the support of a significant segment of the population, and the weakness of the Germans.[173]

Such favourable conditions did not obtain in the other Italian zones of occupation that were taken over by the Germans. The Italian army of occupation along the Dalmatian coast had placed Jews under its protection in mid-1942 when the Germans started deporting Jews from Croatia. Around 3,000 were forcibly collected and transferred to the island of Arbe (Rab), where they were interned along with civilians of other nationalities in a concentration camp where mortality rates were high. After the Italian surrender the inmates moved to partisan-held territory on the mainland; some of them formed the 'Rab battalion' and joined the partisans. Some two hundred elderly and sick remained behind and were taken to Auschwitz to be murdered when the Germans occupied the island.[174]

Having disarmed the Italian garrisons in Greece and the Dodecanese, the Germans were able to extend the anti-Jewish regulations to these areas. In early September, Jürgen Stroop arrived in Athens as the HSSPF. He was aided by Walter Blume, the Sipo-SD commander. They were subsequently joined by Dieter Wisliceny and a handful of men from Eichmann's office. Eichmann had issued orders for the immediate detention of the Athens Jewish community, but the Chief Rabbi, Elias Barzilai, vanished before the Jew-hunting team could obtain names and addresses from him. Furthermore, his disappearance triggered a mass flight of Jews. Instead of being able to round them up at his convenience Stroop issued a decree requiring Jews to register with the authorities. Only a fraction obeyed. The Germans also faced obstruction from the Greek puppet government: Prime Minister Ioannis Rallis informed the German Foreign Office of his unwillingness to accept the removal of Greek Jewish citizens. Little was achieved until February 1944 when Wisliceny was recalled to Berlin and replaced by Toni Burger. On 23 March, Burger nabbed several dozen Jewish men who had appeared at the synagogue to register; they were forced to lead the Germans to other Jews, mainly women and children. A few days later, about 1,000 Jews were placed on a train heading to Auschwitz-Birkenau. At Larissa the train paused to take on board 1,700 Jews who had been rounded up in a simultaneous Aktion in Ioannina. This ancient Jewish community was wiped out in a day by SS troops with the assistance of the Wehrmacht Geheime Feldpolizei, the secret field police (GFP). The army also provided a fleet of eighty trucks to convey the Jews from the town to a camp at Larissa, where they were joined by Jews from other locations, notably Arta and Préveza. The transport, now numbering 2,700, rolled into Auschwitz on 11 April. At the selection on the ramp 320 men and 328 women were admitted into Birkenau; the rest were murdered.[175]

Burger was also responsible for arranging the removal of Jews from the Greek islands, although this was a complicated logistical operation and took much longer to organize. Burger visited Corfu in spring 1944 where he found approximately 2,000 Jews already registered with the German military administration. Overruling the protestations of the garrison commander, who feared that excising the Jews would cause local unrest, he set a date for the deportation. Lacking any manpower himself, Burger lined up the cooperation of the secret field police, the regular military police (the Feldgendarmerie), and the local Greek constabulary. On 9 June almost the entire Jewish population of the island was assembled at the Old Fort in Corfu city. Few tried to evade or escape the net, preferring to stay with their extended families. The Jews were loaded onto vessels provided by the German navy and shipped first to Lefkada and then to Patras on the mainland. From there they were entrained for the five-day journey to Auschwitz. At the same time as the Aktion on Corfu, nearly 500 Jews from Crete were drowned when the ship carrying them to Greece was torpedoed by a Royal Navy submarine. No such misfortunes befell the extraction of Jews from Rhodes and Cos in July. Again, Burger was able to call on regular army units and the navy to accomplish his mission. On 13 July the German authorities began to concentrate the 1,700 Jews on Rhodes in the city itself. In the interim they were sorted out and holders of Turkish passports were released. All were robbed. Ten days later the deportees were herded onto three small naval vessels which carried them to the mainland via Cos, where another 100 Jews were embarked. After awaiting transportation at the concentration camp of Chaidari they were included in a transport of 2,500 Jews that reached Auschwitz on

16 August. Six hundred were admitted into Birkenau; the remaining men, women and children were killed in the gas chambers.[176]

'Raining Death on Earth': deportations from western Europe

Eichmann's men managed to keep sending transports to Auschwitz-Birkenau throughout the latter half of 1943 and into 1944, but only with considerable difficulty. Had it not been for the reserve of doomed humanity in the concentration-transit camps at Drancy, Westerbork, Mechelen/Malines, Vught and Theresienstadt it would have been hard to fill the trains chartered by RSHA office IVB4.

In Paris there were still approximately 60,000 Jews, most of them French citizens and therefore immune to deportation unless they fell foul of the law. These Jews lived openly while wearing the yellow star; several thousand star-bearing children attended the public schools. There were over 800 UGIF personnel in the capital alone, helping ten times that number of Jews every day. More than 30,000 destitute Jews were being fed by UGIF soup kitchens. However, possession of a UGIF employee certificate was no longer a guarantee of immunity. In order to make up the numbers, the security police arrested UGIF staff and raided UGIF-maintained institutions including hospitals, orphanages and homes for the elderly. The range of previously exempted nationalities was also diminished: on 24–26 September the Sipo-SD snatched Jews with Hungarian, Spanish, Italian, Swiss, Portuguese, Swedish, Danish and Finnish passports. In February they took Turkish Jews. Some of these Jews were sent to the Bergen-Belsen exchange camp but most were consigned to the gas chambers at Birkenau. Between September and December 1943 they arrested an average of 380 Jews per month. In the provinces they managed to apprehend more: 315 in September, 597 in October, 877 in November and 421 in December. Amongst the victims were Jacques Helbronner, aged seventy, and his wife, who were caught in Lyons. Chief Rabbi Hirschler and his wife were taken in one of the last raids of the year, in Marseilles.[177]

Hélène Berr narrowly escaped a raid on her UGIF office in August 1943. Even though her boyfriend had fled to Spain and colleagues repeatedly urged her to leave Paris, she was determined to stay and bear witness. 'I have a duty to write because other people must know ... How will the world be cleansed unless it is made to understand the full extent of the evil it is doing?' As brave as she sounded in her diary, she was understandably rattled by the sights that greeted her day after day. Thanks to BBC radio transmissions she was no longer under any illusions as to what deportation portended: 'It is raining Death on Earth.'[178]

Even French Jews had to be wary of the CGQF. The special police devoted to Jewish affairs, under Joseph Antignac and Paty de Clam, sniffed around potential victims looking for any kind of legal irregularity that would justify an arrest warrant. The process of Aryanization ground on relentlessly. By May 1944, 42,227 Jewish-owned enterprises had been transferred to trustees. Over 9,600 properties had been sold, including 1,708 apartment buildings. Nearly 4,870 commercial enterprises had been disposed of and over 7,300 liquidated. This represented a massive transfer of wealth from the Jewish population to the state, much of which was siphoned off in corrupt deals.[179]

The intensification of the campaign against UGIF drove the agencies that sheltered beneath its umbrella to adopt covert tactics. The child welfare organization OSE, under the direction of Dr Joseph Weill, started moving children from its homes to church-run institutions. Weill, assisted by George Garel (a Russian-born Jew whose name was originally Garfinkel), made contact with Archbishop Saliège and through his support they were able to conceal 1,500 children, who it was thought would blend in with the students of Catholic boarding schools. By 1944, it is estimated that 6,000–7,000 children in the Paris region and 400 around Nice were in the care of Catholic and Protestant educational bodies. Hundreds of other children from centres including Strasbourg and Mulhouse were placed with individual families on farms and in villages. No fewer than 3,500 were accommodated in Le Chambon-sur-Lignon, a small town in the Cévennes. The population was entirely Protestant and its outlook was shaped by centuries of religious persecution. The town's pastor, André Trocmé, his wife Magda, and his deputy Edouard Thies, had begun aiding Jews after the fall of France. At first they provided homes for children who Quaker relief workers in Marseilles had extracted from the internment camps. After the deportations began and the south was occupied, Jews started making their way to the town in search of refuge. No one was turned away. Pastor Trocmé rallied the whole of his flock to support the rescue effort and eventually concluded elaborate arrangements with Jewish agencies that passed children and families into his care. Members of his community also led groups of fit young Jews across the mountains into Switzerland, following trails that Huguenots had travelled hundreds of years earlier. Le Chambon did not escape the attention of the Gestapo and the Milice. Trocmé and Thies were both arrested and detained for a time, and finally both had to go underground. But not a single Jew was abducted from the village. The historian Susan Zuccotti estimates that a further 800–1,000 Jews were hidden in homes, schools and on farms across the Protestant region.[180]

As well as evading the Germans, in the second half of 1943 more Jews joined the resistance and actively fought back. Communist Jews, immigrants and the young led the way. They constituted several all-Jewish units of the Francs-tireurs et partisans – main-d'œuvre immigrée (FTP–MOI). From June 1942 to July 1943, Jewish immigrants in the Paris region carried out nearly sixty operations against the German occupation forces. Many of the fighters were killed or captured, which amounted to certain death; by the end of 1943 the Jewish units had been destroyed or dissolved. Jewish boy scouts in the south went into the hills of the Massif Central and constituted the Armée Juive, an all-Jewish formation of the Maquis. Hundreds fought in the Maquis itself, including the young Claude Lanzmann – some openly as Jews, others concealing their identity.[181]

The deportation of Jews from Belgium, which resumed after a three-month hiatus in April 1943, also proved more arduous for the Germans than in the previous year. During March, the Belgian underground press carried articles indicating that trains from Mechelen/Malines carried Jews to their doom. BBC broadcasts about the mass murders in Poland also had an effect. Moshe Flinker heard that elderly people incapable of work were among Jews rounded up from the neighbourhood where he lived with his family. He had considered volunteering to go to the east; now he had second thoughts. Few Jews reported for 'labour service' any more and most immigrants had gone into hiding. Over sixty deportees escaped from the nineteenth transport from Mechelen, in early January 1943, before it even reached the frontier with Germany.[182]

Nevertheless, Kurt Asche, the Judenreferent in Brussels, continued to orchestrate raids on the Jewish immigrants' districts. The German police picked up Jews on the basis of document checks and denunciations. Jewish informers, notably Jacques Glogowski, also supplied a steady trickle of victims for the Dossin Barracks in Mechelen/Malines. By early April, Asche had enough Jews to fill a transport. It departed in the evening of 19 April carrying 1,631 Jews aged from 6 to 90 years. However, it had not progressed far when it was stopped by a man on the track waving a red lamp. He was Youra Livchitz, a Russian-born Jewish doctor who had been active in the resistance since 1942. After Jewish members of the resistance were arrested and sent to Mechelen/Malines, Livchitz hit on the idea of intercepting the deportation train and freeing as many of the deportees as possible. The underground was sceptical, but Livchitz recruited Jean Franklemon and Robert Maistriau to his project and in great haste they worked out a rudimentary plan. While the train was stationary, Franklemon and Maistriau attacked the bolts on the wagon doors with a pair of wire cutters. They were able to open one, allowing seventeen startled Jews to leap out before the police escort challenged Livchitz and started firing at them. Livchitz was the only one who was armed so they were forced to retreat. The train resumed its journey, but another 214 deportees managed to break free before it reached Germany. Many of them found refuge in Belgian homes.[183]

This daring rescue mission, which was unique in the annals of the deportations from western Europe, did nothing to stem the raids or interrupt the flow of trains. Prodded by Himmler, the Sipo-SD organized major *rafles* in Brussels and Antwerp on 3–4 September. Having steered clear of Jews with Belgian nationality to avoid upsetting the Belgian authorities, on 20 September the Germans began to deport them too. By the end of the year, a further 6,000 Jews had been sent from Belgium to Auschwitz via Mechelen/Malines. In 1944, Asche was able to dispatch four transports but they carried only 2,300 Jews. Among them were Moshe Flinker and his family, betrayed to the Germans on the eve of Passover. These last trainloads brought the total of deportees to 28,500, of whom just 1,000 were Belgian citizens.[184]

By comparison, deportations from the Netherlands to Auschwitz ran like clockwork. Following a pause for Christmas, transports from Westerbork recommenced on 11 January 1943 and departed weekly until 23 February. One trainload, carrying 1,000 patients and staff from a Jewish psychiatric institution, proceeded directly from Appeldoorn to Auschwitz. Due to the influx of Jews from Salonica, nineteen trains with 34,313 Jews were diverted to Sobibor between 2 March and 20 July 1943. This phase, which had no parallel in Belgium and France, was a cataclysm for the Dutch Jews. The duration and intensity of the deportations over this period helps to explain why the percentage of the

Jewish population of Holland that was murdered so greatly exceeded the proportion in either France or Belgium. Another reason lay in the establishment of a new camp at Vught, in January 1943. From 24 August to mid-November 1943, seven transports left Westerbork and one from Vught with a combined cargo of 8,127 Jews. Vught bulked larger in the following year. During 1944, eight trains departed from the two camps, taking 5,500 Jews directly into Birkenau, including several hundred women who provided human material for medical experiments. Nearly 4,000 were transferred to the exchange camp at Bergen-Belsen. This appalling catalogue of death still left 8,000–9,000 Jews who were in mixed marriages, part-Jewish or of disputed identity plus a few thousand foreign Jews shielded by their nationality.[185]

Hanns Rauter and Ferdinand aus der Fünten were able to fill these trains by maintaining a steady pressure on the Jewish community and striking easy targets such as the Appeldoorn sanatorium. After the grotesque spectacle of bewildered elderly, disabled and insane people being shoved into trucks taking them to the railway station, Sipo-SD men and Dutch collaborators repeated the procedure in other Jewish institutions across the Netherlands. On 21 May, aus der Fünten ordered the heads of the Joodse Raad to hand over 7,000 of its staff, arguing that with so few Jews left in Amsterdam it no longer required so many workers. Asscher and Cohen, the co-presidents, hastily convened an emergency meeting of the council to obtain its endorsement. Notwithstanding some dissent the members eventually ratified their decision. Gertrude van Tijn refused to engage in the selection and resigned from the administration, but it made no difference. For the next twenty-four hours, Jacob Presser recalled, 'there was once again utter chaos and panic' at the council building as individuals cajoled and bribed their way onto lists of essential personnel. During an all-night sitting, a special commission sorted the staff into three categories: 'A' equating to indispensable, 'B' signifying those doing important work, and 'C' for 'those who could be spared'. The next day the council presented the Germans with a list of 5,700 names, yet this was not enough. Not only had the council fallen short, many of those who were sent deportation notices refused to appear. Consequently, on 26 May, aus der Fünten sent the police to grab 3,000 from the Jewish quarter. Van Tijn was amongst them, but she was freed by the intervention of aus der Fünten. She and 1,500 other council members, employees and privileged Jews were exempted from deportation. The unprotected continued to fall victim to raids, house searches, document checks and denunciations. On 20 June, the last mass round-up by German police and Dutch collaborators caught 5,500 Jews, leaving the Jewish district all but deserted. A month later, the Jewish leadership was arrested at night, with the assistance of the Order Service men from Westerbork, and taken to the camp. Special workers and privileged Jews were scooped up in a final raid on the eve of the Jewish New Year in September 1943, after which there were no more Jews living openly in Amsterdam.[186]

However, this still left the Jews in mixed marriages untouched. Pursuing an idea that had been mooted at Wannsee and in subsequent discussions about Mischlinge, Willi Zöpf proposed that Jewish spouses be offered the choice of divorce or sterilization. Jacob Presser estimated that out of 8,610 Jews in mixed marriages 2,562 accepted sterilization, of whom 1,416 were female.[187]

The camp at Vught, officially known as Herzogenbusch concentration camp due to its proximity to the town of 's-Hertogenbosch, was instigated by Hanns Rauter in late 1942 to perform several functions. It was primarily intended to detain Dutch people who were implicated in resistance activity, but within its precincts Rauter created a section for Jews that masqueraded as a labour camp. In fact it was part of the deception strategy to lure Jews into voluntary deportation. The Jewish 'reception camp' was run by the WVHA and included facilities for diamond production, electrical engineering and clothing workshops. New arrivals were allowed to communicate with the outside world and receive food parcels. This was not entirely a ruse; Rauter hoped that by transferring production to the camp he could stymie complaints from manufacturers about the disruption of their workforce and curb annoying interventions by managers seeking to withdraw key employees from deportation lists. When it opened in January 1943 (typically, before the accommodation was actually ready), Vught held 450 Jews. Five months later it reached its peak capacity of 8,684. Transfers to Westerbork and shipments directly to Auschwitz, beginning in May 1943, reduced numbers so steadily that by the end of the year under 700 Jews remained in the barracks. The Jewish section, redesignated a transit camp, was wound up in February 1944 having served its purpose. Throughout its brief history (the main camp persisted until September 1944) the guards were mainly Dutch SS volunteers.[188]

For the inmates, Vught resembled Westerbork. In his camp diary David Koker, a brilliant student and Zionist activist aged twenty-two, noted divisions between Dutch and German Jews, stratification according to the peculiar values of the camp system, and the horrible tension of living under the threat of transportation. Koker's father was a diamond worker who had been exempted from deportation until February 1943, when his family was taken from their home at night and sent to the Hollandse Schouwberg. 'Picked up between 11 and 12 p.m.', David recorded in his first entry, dated 11 February. 'One police officer decent but anxious, and one unpleasant. I heard them coming.' They reached the new camp, which still smelled of fresh paint, after a two-hour walk from the station in a 'sad procession. Limping people, crying children'. Soon after settling in he noted the 'strong exclusiveness of the German-Jewish attitude'. At the inception of the Jewish camp the commandant had made a Berlin Jew, Richard Süsskind, the Elder and put him charge of the Ordedienst (OD, Order Service). As deportations loomed, David heard people complaining about 'the favouritism practiced by the administration. There's a lot of talk now about the German mentality.'[189] As the camp filled with Jews from the provinces the number of children grew to over 1,700. Then, in May, the German officials exposed the truth about Vught by ordaining the removal of those who could not work – including the children. David Koker witnessed the scenes as families, reluctant to part from their youngest members, assembled for departure. 'The parents have been a curse to their children. They've dragged them here. And now the children have become a curse to the parents: they're dragging them along to Poland. And this is all so wretched there's nothing more to be said.'[190]

Koker realized that a job was essential to avoid removal and succeeded in getting work as a registrar with the Philips electrical workshop. This kept him off the deportation trains and gave him the opportunity to find sheltered occupations for the rest of his family. By September he had worked his way into a position of authority in the Philips kommando and was able to manipulate the transportation lists. 'I slouch in my chair', he wrote on 1 September, 'look sadly at the assembly line, and try to keep the H[ess] girls, my last lovely refuge in this ugliness, from going on the transport.' As the Jewish population was decimated a mood of abandon permeated their ranks. In early November he noted, 'at the moment it's a total sex-crazed paradise in the women's camp', with men hopping in and out through hut windows and hurried liaisons in the latrines.[191]

David Koker took part in further selections after the camp

commandant determined that textile workers were no longer required. Women from the clothing shops, mothers and daughters facing separation from husbands and fathers, desperately sought work elsewhere. Those responsible for compiling the lists were beseeched by those who had no power and bullied by those who did. 'Our beautifully exact preferential lists are pointless. I tell everyone not to be under any illusions. And I have no intention of doing anything else.' He explained in his diary that 'To all these matters I bring an *angry* but nevertheless abstract sense of responsibility. I *have* to do this, this my job, it has to do with people, but it makes absolutely no difference who exactly is doing this.' All the same, once the transport had left bearing 1,152 Jews to Auschwitz, David wrote, 'When you've played at being providence for an evening, you go to bed with a moral hangover and great doubts.' He felt himself becoming 'some kind of Nietzschean' filled with a sense 'of freedom and power. And because of it, acting on behalf of people in whose doom you acquiesce becomes objective and functional.'[192]

During 1943 most of the transports carrying women and children from Vught went first to Westerbork. Heinz Hesdörffer, who had been arrested in Amsterdam on 4 March 1943 and consigned to the camp, observed their brief, unhappy sojourn. 'I will always remember these brave, caring mothers, with their wailing, tired little angels, whom they tried to calm down or gave them something to eat . . . these teary eyes, these young, pretty women's faces drawn in the deepest pain, scared about the fate of their family and themselves.' Fortunately, as a German Jewish refugee who had worked for various refugee committees, Hesdörffer knew a lot of German Jews in positions of authority and was quickly able to get a job that carried an exemption. Auschwitz conjured up nothing more than a vague sense of horror, but to avoid it, 'one did everything, gave every last penny'. He noted that 'there were young ladies who sold their honour in order to achieve a deferral'.[193]

Philip Mechanicus, a journalist in his early fifties, arrived in Westerbork in early November 1942 from the German police camp at Amersfort, where he had been imprisoned for failing to wear the yellow star. He was so brutalized by the German security police that he passed the first six months at Westerbork in the camp's well-appointed hospital. As soon as he was able, though, he started keeping a record of his experiences, characterizing himself as 'an official reporter giving an account of a shipwreck'.[194]

On Tuesday 1 June 1943, Mechanicus recorded a typical deportation day. 'The transports are as loathsome as ever. The wagons used were originally intended for carrying horses. The deportees no longer lie on straw, but on the bare floor in the midst of their food supplies and small baggage, and this applies even to invalids . . . There is a barrel, just one small barrel for all these people, in the corner of the wagon where they can relieve themselves publicly . . . With a bag of sand beside it, from which each person can pick up a handful to cover the excrement.' In another corner was a can of water with a tap. Once assembled outside their barracks, the 3,000 doomed Jews were marched to the transport by the OD along the main camp road known as the Boulevard des Misères. Each of the deportees had 'a bag of bread which is tied to their shoulder with a tape . . . and a blanket fastened to the other shoulder . . . Shabby emigrants who own nothing more than what they have on and what is hanging from them. Quiet men with tense faces and women breaking into frequent sobs. Elderly folk, hobbling along, stumbling over the poor road surface under their load and sometimes going through pools of muddy water. Invalids on stretchers . . .' OD men, supplemented by German regular police, Schutzpolizei (also called green police, because of their uniforms), manned a cordon around the train to prevent escapes. 'Any who dawdle or hesitate are assisted. They are driven into the train, or pushed, or struck, or pummelled, or persuaded with a boot, and kicked on board, both by the "Green Police" who are escorting the train and by OD men.' It seemed to Mechanicus that the Ordedienst had been 'recruited from the dregs of Jewish society, rough, coarse fellows, without refinement, human feelings or compassion; they just live for their cigarettes and an easy affair with women like themselves'. The Jews in the camp referred to them as the 'Jewish SS'. Once they were packed inside, representatives of Lippman–Rosenthal climbed up and forcibly divested the deportees of cash, fountain pens, watches and small valuables. After the wagons were all sealed, Albert Gemmeker, the commandant, waved his hand to signal the departure. Then 'Jewish Gestapo men who have been lined up to act as spies beside the train go along the track after the train has departed like hyenas in search of coins and banknotes.' Kurt Schlesinger, the senior Jewish official, and the SD men would ride it to the other side of the camp and jump off to save themselves the walk back to their office.[195]

Mechanicus also dissected the fraught relations between the Dutch and German Jews. 'The German Jews here play the leader, just as the

German Aryans are accustomed to play the leader ... many ask their Dutch fellow-Jews: what care and consideration have you ever given to us?' Having been in the camp for three years before the Dutch arrived, they occupied every position of influence – most importantly the registration department. 'They form, as it were, an almost exclusive association for the protection of the interests of German Jews. In this way they have, in point of fact, handed over the Dutch Jews to the Germans to suit their own convenience.' In early August 1943, Schlesinger invited Mechanicus, who was respected by both communities, to look at ways to lessen the mutual hostility. He suggested setting up an arbitration committee, composed equally of Dutch and German Jews, to resolve contested issues such as staffing the camp administration. Schlesinger (and Gemmeker) agreed.[196]

In September, the population of Westerbork fell to 6,000; much of the camp was empty. Mechanicus was preserved from deportation by Schlesinger who put him into a group of Jews with Palestine connections who the Germans considered might be suitable for exchange for German nationals held by the Allies. The fact that he had a non-Jewish wife and a child also qualified him for another protected list.[197] The most privileged Dutch Jews were held in a castle at Barnevald. From there 638 were transferred to Theresienstadt in mid-1944. They joined a few thousand who had been sent to the ghetto-camp in 1943 and early 1944 because it was considered more suitable to their high status and less likely to cause protests from influential non-Jews than sending them directly to Poland. Jacob Presser estimates that in total 4,897 Dutch Jews ended up in Theresienstadt, where their lives 'differed little from that of the rest'. No more than a quarter of them survived. For a while, though, their fate was intertwined with that of the Czech and German Jews who had been in the ghetto for up to two years.[198]

Theresienstadt, culture and catastrophe

At the start of February 1943 there were 44,672 Jews in Theresienstadt. During the course of the year 15,126 were added to their number, 12,696 died, and just over 17,000 were deported to Auschwitz. The new arrivals included 295 Dutch Jews in February and several hundred Danish Jews in October 1943. During this period, a spur line was constructed from the village of Bohusovice into the ghetto. More inmates got jobs in the expanding workshops and agricultural enterprises in the vicinity. Despite this, Ernst Kaltenbrunner, head of the RSHA, believed there were too many Jews. Accordingly, 7,000 were removed on five transports from 20 January to 1 February. Helga Weiss and her family only escaped one of the January expatriations thanks to her father's pull with the camp administration. However, Himmler then overruled Kaltenbrunner and there were actually no more transports until September. This period of stability seems to have been a consequence of the Allied declaration on Nazi war crimes. Himmler wanted to use Theresienstadt as proof that elderly German Jews evacuated from the Third Reich were, in fact, allowed to live in peace and safety. As part of this deception, in January the ghetto was given its own currency. The following month shops were set up at which inmates could purchase food and clothing. A library was opened. Theresienstadt's role as an advertisement for the Reich's humane treatment of the Jews acquired greater prominence from mid-1943 as a result of pressure from Allied and neutral countries for the Red Cross to be allowed to inspect it. In July, Anton Burger replaced Siegfried Seidl as commandant and accelerated the 'beautification' of the ghetto-camp.[199]

The stabilization of the population allowed cultural activities to flourish. A generation of brilliant young Czechs defied the effects of malnourishment, uncomfortable and cramped living quarters, and hard labour to write music and poetry, to paint and sketch. In an essay entitled 'Goethe and Ghetto', Victor Ullman, who was forty-five in 1943, argued that it was wholly right to devote energy to culture and creativity even in such an awful place. 'By no means did we sit weeping by the rivers of Babylon,' he wrote. 'Our endeavours in the arts were commensurate with our will to live.' This vitality gave birth to a stream of musical compositions, including settings of Yiddish folk songs and an opera, *The Emperor of Atlantis*, that is a subtle attack on fascism. The libretto was penned by Petr Kien, who showed huge promise as a poet and writer even though he was only twenty-two years old. Hans Krasa, a composer of note, rewrote his last pre-war work, an opera entitled *Brundibár* as an anti-fascist parable. Rafael Schächter, aged thirty-eight, had established himself as a performer before the Germans occupied Czechoslovakia. In Theresienstadt he set up a choir and conducted performances of works by Smetana, including *The Bartered Bride,* and a full rendering of Verdi's Requiem in the attic of one of the barracks. The only instrument at his disposal was a battered upright piano. Gideon

Klein and Pavel Haas, both students of Leoš Janáček and both in their mid-thirties, were avatars of modernism before their incarceration. Both composed works that were faithful to their training, yet managed to evoke Jewish suffering and traditional laments. Haas produced several excoriating satirical pieces for cabaret performances. By contrast, Zikmund Schul, only twenty-seven years old in 1943, wrote Jewish liturgical music. The art department of the ghetto administration was a refuge for several artists who were already acclaimed for their work. Fritz Taussig (a cartoonist and book illustrator whose real name was Bedrich Fritta), the departmental chief, created opportunities for Leo Haas, Petr Kien and Norbert Troller to create a visual record of the camp. Friedl Dicker-Brandeis, who had worked before the war as a textile designer, taught art to hundreds of children for whom painting and sketching was as much a therapeutic activity as a creative outlet. Their work, too, became a unique visual testimony to conditions in Theresienstadt.[200]

However, the survivor-historian Ruth Bondy offers a caveat to the list of cultural achievements and their impact on the ghetto-camp inhabitants. She recalls that during the eighteen months that she was imprisoned she saw only one opera performance and one play. '[M]any prisoners were not fortunate enough to see any, and not because they took no interest in culture. The hard labour, the hours standing in line for food, at a water faucet, for a toilet; the efforts undertaken to see one's parents or one's husband, wife, and children or a friend before the curfew . . . the widespread illness; the dread of the transports; mourning for a father or a mother who died in the ghetto – in short, the strength needed, first and foremost for day-to-day existence prevented much cultural activity.' She notes that it was also hard to get a ticket, while the 8 p.m. curfew effectively restricted audiences to the barrack where a performance took place. Needless to say, those with privileges and time did not face such obstacles.[201]

Suddenly, in early September 1943, the horror of the transports returned to Theresienstadt. Philipp Manes recalled how he and his circle lost their 'cozy sense of security . . . when, for the first time, the word "transport" sounded in our ears, like a dissonant trumpet blast. We could not grasp it. We did not believe it.' Burger announced that Jewish workers were needed for a new camp in the east. To signify that the deportees would be expected to function as a unit, Leo Janowitz, the secretary of the Council of Elders, was told he would accompany the transport along with Freddy Hirsch, a charismatic Zionist youth leader who helped to run the children's department. The two trains, carrying a total of 5,007 deportees, were actually destined for Auschwitz where they arrived on 6 September. But when the new arrivals were taken into Birkenau they were not subjected to either a selection or the usual initiation process. Instead, they were allowed to keep their hair, their clothing and their baggage. Families remained intact and they were conducted to sector BIIb, designated the Familienlager (family camp). Men and women were separated, but children were allowed to sleep with their mothers and older boys with their fathers. Eventually the adults were given work to perform and during the day Freddy Hirsch corralled the children into a separate building, Block 31, where they could be kept out of mischief and given schooling.[202]

Despite a clear view of the columns trudging to the gas chambers and the plumes of smoke that followed their disappearance, Hirsch and his co-workers constructed a near-normal routine for the 295 youngsters. He insisted they wash each morning (although the water was filthy) and ensured they had as decent a lunch as was possible. They were taught to respect each other's property so well that unlike the rest of the camp there was little theft or pilfering. Hirsch also arranged sporting and cultural activities, with special programmes for the Sabbath. The future historian Otto Dov Kulka, then aged nine, recalled that 'There I heard for the first time about the riveting developments in the Battle of Thermopylae and about the whole constellation of wars between the Persians and the Greeks. I also remember being so fascinated by this that I took in almost every word in the lessons . . '. Block 31 was 'the centre of the spiritual and cultural life of the place'.[203]

The family camp was part of the deception effort being orchestrated by Eichmann's office in Berlin. Since the Allied declaration on war crimes, Himmler had come under some pressure to explain what had happened to Jews who had been 'resettled' in the east. In March 1943, the Slovak government asked to make an inspection visit to the camps in Poland where Slovak Jews were supposedly relocated. For several months the press in the Allied and neutral countries, including Switzerland, had carried articles about the fate of the Jews. Historians who have examined the genesis of the Familienlager have concluded that it was probably intended to serve as a 'model camp' for inspection by the Red Cross, should the need arise. Hirsch was told to draw up a report specifically for the Swiss. Then again, given its proximity to the extermination facilities at Birkenau and the evidence of suffering that lay all around, this is not a wholly convincing explanation. It is just as likely to have been a ploy to deceive Jews in Theresienstadt. The inmates of the camp were encouraged to send back messages attesting to their health and the good local conditions. The family camp was also a useful way to relieve overcrowding in Theresienstadt on the eve of a visit by the Red Cross that actually did take place in June 1944. But the Jews who arrived in September, and those who followed them, were doomed to die in any case. When they were admitted into Auschwitz, the main registry created a card for each person indicating they would be subjected to Sonderbehandlung, special treatment, after six months. Special treatment was the Nazi euphemism for murder in the gas chambers.[204]

In December 1943, two more transports arrived from Theresienstadt carrying 5,007 Jews, including 353 children. Camp BIIb was now seriously overcrowded, plagued by malnutrition and disease. A quarter of the September transport had already perished when the period of grace it enjoyed elapsed on 7 March 1944. The 3,792 survivors were then moved to another compound where Hirsch, who suspected the worst, took his own life. During the night of 8 March, BIIb was locked down and the Jews there heard trucks and a commotion. The next morning no one was left of the September transports except some medical personnel and sick prisoners who had been in the infirmary, including Otto Dov Kulka and his mother.[205]

On 16, 17 and 18 May 1944 transports from Theresienstadt brought an infusion of 7,500 into the family camp, whose inhabitants no longer had any illusions about their future. The December deportees were supposed to be liquidated in June, but things changed between their admission to Birkenau and the date set for their termination. Crucially, the Red Cross was scheduled to make a visit to Theresienstadt on 23 June 1944, a week after the due date – so they were kept alive a little longer. Furthermore, the demand for labour meant that there would be a selection rather than a wholesale massacre. On 6 July 1944, approximately 3,500 were picked for work in Germany or in the environs of Auschwitz. Kulka was amongst the teenagers chosen to run errands or act as servants. The rest, 6,500, were murdered in the gas chambers on 14–16 July.[206]

Denmark, flight and rescue

The widespread perception that Germany was on the verge of collapse in the early months of 1943 encouraged the Danish population to rebel against German rule. Paradoxically, this upsurge nearly doomed the Jews of Denmark who had, until then, been spared any anti-Jewish measures. What transpired when the Germans finally moved against the Danish Jews in October 1943 almost instantly became the stuff of legend. After most of the Jews of Denmark escaped the German police raids and reached safety in Sweden it was claimed that the Danish king, Christian X, had appeared in public wearing the yellow star in solidarity with his Jewish subjects. His example and the courage of the Danish underground were held responsible for the miraculous rescue of 7,500 Jews. In fact, the king never wore a yellow star and nor were the Danish Jews ever required to do so. The successful flight of nearly all the Jewish community was less the result of heroic resistance to Nazi fanaticism than another example of hastily improvised and confused Judenpolitik coming to grief. Having said that, Jewish initiative and self-preservation were also vital in securing a relatively benign outcome to a potentially disastrous situation.[207]

Denmark had a Jewish population of about 8,000 at the start of the war. Jews had lived there since the seventeenth century and had become extremely well integrated after gaining full citizenship in the 1840s. The country had no anti-Semitic movement and its politicians believed that the best way to prevent one arising was by blocking large-scale Jewish immigration. Despite its proximity to the Third Reich, the country avoided an influx of Jewish refugees by maintaining extremely tight immigration controls. Only about 5,000 refugees of any type were allowed into Denmark between 1933 and 1939, and most were encouraged to leave quickly. Barely 1,500 German or stateless Jews managed to gain residence rights. Karl Steincke, the minister of justice, summed up the official attitude in April 1937 when he commented, 'One does not want to be inhumane, and one does not dare to be humane because of the consequences.'[208]

The German invasion on 9 April 1940 was accomplished swiftly and almost bloodlessly. In return for not resisting the German occupation the Danes were permitted to retain their armed forces and their entire system of government: the king, the prime minister, his cabinet, and parliament. Although the Communist Party was banned and its members of parliament arrested, Danish democracy was preserved. In March 1943 the country even went to the polls in a free general election: the local Nazi Party got 2 per cent of the vote. But the Germans were willing to swallow such embarrassments in view of the fact that Denmark supplied the Reich with a huge slice of its food consumption, meat and dairy products in particular. To ensure the flow of food imports and to obviate the need for a large garrison, Berlin was willing to grant the Danes extensive autonomy and treat them with kid gloves. The conviction that the Danes were fellow Aryans reinforced the determination to make the occupation a model of cooperation and amity.[209]

To preserve the policy of cooperation, the Germans did not press anti-Jewish legislation on the Danish authorities. Just months after the occupation, King Christian conferred with his prime minister on this issue and agreed that they would make the protection of the country's Jewish citizens a red line in their relations with the Third Reich. The government joined the Anti-Comintern Pact in November 1941 and allowed the Waffen-SS to enlist 6,000 men (out of twice as many volunteers) to fight on the Eastern Front. Yet when Göring urged the prime minister, Erik Scavenius, to deal with the 'Jewish question', Scavenius retorted that there was no 'Jewish question' in Denmark. At the Wannsee meeting in January 1942, German Foreign Office representatives warned that extracting the Jews from Denmark would be a sensitive matter. Unfortunately, the welling up of resistance to German occupation and exploitation in the autumn of 1942 provoked Hitler to demand a more punitive regime. In October 1942, Werner Best was transferred from Paris to Copenhagen as Reich plenipotentiary to implement the Führer's wishes.[210]

Best was confronted by escalating unrest and sabotage, culminating in a strike wave throughout August 1943. The commander of the garrison, General Hermann von Henneken, declared martial law and proceeded to disarm the Danish armed forces, including the navy. In response, the government resigned, leaving the country in the hands of senior civil servants. Fearing that the SS would move in and take control, Best sought police reinforcements and on 8 September suggested to Hitler that now would be a good time to deal with the Jews. This was somewhat odd, since Best had previously warned against any action against the local Jewish community, and, furthermore, his initiative led to the appointment of Rudolf Mildner as commander of the security police – giving the SS a foothold they had not enjoyed before. Ironically, Mildner immediately cautioned against a crack-down that would alienate the Danes. Henneken, too, pleaded for a postponement. But Best, who had a Machiavellian streak, was playing both ends against the middle. At the same time as inciting a nationwide round-up, he made sure the Jews were warned in good time. Best never intended to stage the sort of highly public, counterproductive mass arrests that had caused outrage in France in the summer of 1942; he could see a way to achieve much the same ends more cunningly and economically.[211]

During the last days of September, Rolf Günther carried out a scoping exercise for Eichmann's office, which would handle the round-ups and deportations. A ship was charted to carry Jews from Zealand to Germany and 1,800 order police were drafted in. While these preparation were being made, Best let the attaché for maritime affairs at the German Embassy, Georg Ferdinand Duckwitz, know that the security police were getting ready to snatch all the Danish Jews on 1 October. He was aware that Duckwitz – who was a less than enthusiastic supporter of the Nazi regime – had links with local politicians and, sure enough, the agitated attaché passed on the information to Hans Hedtoft, the leader of the Danish Social Democrats. Hedtoft, in turn, alerted Carl Henriques, the chairman of the Board of Representatives of the Copenhagen Jewish community. Since the next day, 29 September, was the eve of the Jewish New Year, when almost all Jews attended synagogue, it was easy to spread the word that the community was in peril. There was no formal announcement and no organized communal response. Instead, Jews individually and as families threw together a few belongings and headed for the countryside or the coast. Crucially, Henriques secured a meeting with the Swedish Ambassador, who had also heard from Duckwitz. The ambassador assured Henriques that should Jews attempt to enter his country 'Sweden is open'. No less important, American diplomats who were alerted to the impending crisis informed the Swedish government that the United States would cover the cost of accommodating Jewish refugees from Denmark.[212]

Sweden's open-door policy marked a fundamental shift that reflected internal political currents as well as a wider transformation of attitudes towards the Third Reich in the capitals of neutral and non-belligerent nations. From 1933–9, only about 2,000 German Jews were allowed to become permanent residents of the country and the border was officially sealed once war started. Until mid-1943, the Swedish

Foreign Ministry followed a policy of neutrality that in reality amounted to appeasing the Third Reich. Surrounded by German-occupied territory, militarily weak, and cut off from the democracies still at war with Hitler, the Swedes felt that their first priority was averting a German invasion. They permitted the Germans to transport troops across Swedish soil and pass naval vessels through Swedish waters. Almost all the country's massive iron ore production went to the German war effort, while key armaments industries exclusively supplied the Wehrmacht and Luftwaffe. The government quietly censored any criticism of Germany in the press, while private enterprises dealing with Germany discreetly removed Jewish employees. The Swedish Jewish community, numbering about 6,000, was otherwise unaffected.[213]

However, Swedes were shocked by the deportation of Jews from Norway and received the 1,100 Jews who fled to their territory with genuine warmth. Around the same time, Swedish diplomats were digesting information about the deportations and mass killings in Poland and Russia that reached them via secret channels in Germany, the press, and their own outposts abroad. This led the director of the Swedish Foreign Ministry, Gösta Engzell, to encourage the foreign service to extend aid and assistance to Jews who had connections to Sweden, a mandate open to generous interpretation. The Swedish Foreign Ministry badgered the Germans for information about the fate of Norwegian Jews with ties to Sweden and thereby put down a marker that Jews who possessed such affinities were in effect under Swedish diplomatic protection. By the time the Danish crisis erupted, the Swedish foreign service was primed to act supportively. Indeed, as soon as tidings of the planned deportation reached Stockholm the Foreign Ministry let it be known that Danish Jews with family or interests in Sweden were welcome.[214]

Knowledge that there was a haven within reach galvanized the Danish Jews. While civil servants vacillated over how best to meet the German threat and the Danish underground took cognizance of the developments, Jewish families made their getaway. On 30 September hundreds reached ports and fishing villages along the north-east coast of Zealand. Acting on their own initiative they sought out fishermen and skippers of boats willing to make the crossing to Sweden, offering handsome amounts to compensate for the risk. Within forty-eight hours, long before there was any organized response, about 500–600 had reached safety. They were mainly people with resources who could afford the 2,000 kroner that was the typical asking price of mariners on these first days. Those who did not have sufficient money took refuge in farms, boarding houses or churches, hoping to find someone willing to ferry them across the Öresund.[215]

On the evening of 1–2 October, 300 security police under Mildner's command, assisted by several hundred Danish SS volunteers, went to work, but it was not like any Aktion up to that time. Best issued instructions that they were not to damage property and were to knock on doors rather than batter them down. If there was no reply, they were to go. Nor did they pursue the action the next day; it fizzled out. The Germans succeeded in arresting only 580 Jews, mainly elderly and mainly in provinces where they had not been alerted to the danger. A single zealous Gestapo man, Hans Juhl, arrested 85 Jews in a church in Gilleleje. He was exceptional. Best did not deploy the full complement of order police put at his disposal and showed no interest in continuing the operation. Within hours he assured senior Danish civil servants that it was over. Remarkably, he sent a wireless message to the Foreign Ministry in Berlin announcing that 'Starting today, Denmark can be considered cleansed of Jews as no Jew can legally reside or work here anymore.'[216]

Believing the worst, however, the spectrum of Danish society rallied to the defence of their Jewish compatriots in a manner unprecedented throughout Europe during the war years. In the early evening on 1 October, the king addressed a personal letter to Best 'to emphasize that special actions taken against a group of people who for more than 100 years have enjoyed full civil rights in Denmark could have the most serious consequences'. Two days later, the bishops of the Lutheran Evangelical Church issued a pastoral letter to be read in every constituent church stating that 'Wherever Jews are persecuted for racial or religious reasons, it is the duty of the Christian Church to protest against such persecution.' The following day, politicians of every main party published a joint statement condemning the raids. The senior civil servant in charge of the Foreign Ministry, Nils Svennigsen, persuaded Best specifically to exclude people of mixed parentage and added that if anything bad happened to the arrested full Jews the policy of cooperation would be in tatters.[217]

Over the next few days, with Jews piled up in towns along the coast, the Danish resistance began to organize shiploads across the Öresund. On 6 October alone, one schooner carried 1,400 Jews to safety. By 9 October the total of Jewish escapees in Sweden reached about 4,500 and over the following week the remaining 2,000 Jews were successfully evacuated. The rescue operation encountered no opposition from the Danish coastguard or the German navy. Danish officers turned a blind eye to the traffic, while German naval assets, inadequate at the best of times, were focused on military objectives. Perhaps more pertinently, German coastal patrols were not given orders to intercept the vessels carrying Jews to Sweden. As soon as the Danish boats reached Swedish waters they were escorted and, if necessary, aided by Swedish naval patrols. The greatest danger they faced came from mechanical mishaps or bad weather: the Germans were not trying to intercept the maritime exodus.[218]

Nevertheless, the Danes had achieved what no other country in Europe had even attempted. A large part of the population, the nation's elite, and the entire underground had mobilized to save the Jewish community, acting boldly in the face of unknown odds. They did not know that the effort to seize the Jews was little more than an elaborate charade. In a report to Berlin on 5 October, Best explained that his task had been 'to cleanse the country of Jews and not to conduct a manhunt'. He had succeeded in pushing out the Jews while maintaining civil order and the essential supply of food to the Reich; pragmatism had trumped ideology. The historian Peter Longerich comments that the Danish operation was thus a turning point in anti-Jewish policy. Due to the reversal of German military fortunes her military allies and business partners were unwilling to toe the line any longer. Anti-Jewish measures, that had once been deployed to bind the Axis together, now threatened to divide it. 'The will to accomplish the policy of extermination reached its limit where Jewish policy threatened to lose its function within the system of occupation.' The action also exposed the confusion of purpose between Best and Eichmann's office. Ultimately, though, the Jews were able to escape because they acted quickly and boldly instead of relying on the civil authority to protect them. Unaware of the reasons for the lack of coordination or friction between the different elements of the Nazi machine they exploited the interstices and the availability of a nearby refuge and, with the help of many brave and decent people, slipped away.[219]

Allied knowledge and responses: the War Refugee Board

What did governments, politicians and the public know about Auschwitz by this stage in the war? Between April 1943 and March 1944 a stream of intelligence about the scale and activities of the camp, including reference to the use of poison gas, had reached the Polish government-in-exile. In early March 1943, Stefan Rowecki, the head of the Home Army, signed off a report to London stating that 520,000 Jews had been killed in the camp at Oswieçim. This message supplied the content for a front-page article in the *Polish Jewish Observer* on 3 September 1943, a subscription-only newspaper in London that served as a channel for the London Poles to disseminate information about the fate of Polish Jews. The article was summarized in the London *Jewish Chronicle* a week later, although inside the paper and without any editorial comment. The lack of urgency about publicizing such news or acting on it stemmed from the complex relationship between the exile governments and the major Allied powers as well as the priorities that determined how Jewish issues should be handled in Whitehall and Washington.[220]

During the critical months in spring 1943, the Polish government-in-exile was preoccupied by the fallout from the discovery of the mass graves of Polish officers murdered at Katyn. While the Poles hurled bitter criticism at Moscow, the British, on whom they depended, prioritized good relations with Stalin. As long as this row threatened the Allied coalition, Jewish matters were shoved to the background. Nor were the British keen to highlight the suffering of Jews in Europe in case this boosted demands to open Palestine to refugees. The whole point of the Bermuda conference had been to channel the desire to help the Jews into an innocuous dead end. Afterwards, the Foreign Office remained determined to avoid a clamour on the scale that pushed them to the declaration on German war crimes in December 1942. Consequently, during the latter part of 1943 when it was the sole death camp still in operation, information about Auschwitz and the scale of the mass killing going on there languished in the files of Polish officials and British civil servants.[221]

Even the British Jewish community was disinclined to raise the issue of atrocities too frequently. According to the Home Intelligence Reports collated for the Ministry of Information (MOI), the burst of publicity about German atrocities at the turn of the year had actually aggravated domestic anti-Semitism. The last summary of 1942 stated that there was 'no evidence that the popularity of the Jews in this country had increased'. There was 'greatest sympathy' for Jews abroad, but in England it was the 'general feeling that they badly want controlling'. In January 1943, the MOI concluded that publicity about German atrocities 'made people more aware of the Jews they do not like here'. Home Intelligence surveys in mid-1943 detected that people blamed Jews for rising house prices, the black market, and suspected them of evading both taxes and national service. When a pro-Jewish member of parliament suggested to Sir Richard Maconochie, the director of the BBC Home Service, that radio could do more to counteract anti-Semitism, Maconochie responded that tackling the subject on air 'would be only likely to make matters worse'. Consequently, for most of 1943 there was almost no pressure to keep the destruction of the European Jews at the forefront of public consciousness and little incentive for the British government to act. Instead, British Jews turned in on themselves and engaged in a period of infighting between the Zionist and non-Zionist factions of the community to determine who would lead and speak for Anglo-Jewry after the war.[222]

The situation in America was not much different until late 1943, when a fortuitous conjunction of personalities and politics broke the stasis that had afflicted approaches to the Jewish crisis in Europe. Following the dismal results of the Bermuda conference the Bergson group had continued to assail the administration over its policy, even mounting ad hominem attacks on the president in newspaper advertisements. In early October 1943, Bergson's emergency committee staged an eye-catching march on the White House by hundreds of Orthodox rabbis. Roosevelt spent the time while they were in town dedicating four bombers that had been delivered to the US Army Air Forces. In place of a meeting with the rabbinical representatives the White House issued a pallid statement about Jewish immigration to Palestine. A month later, Congressman Will Rogers Jnr, a member of the emergency committee, introduced a resolution into the House of Representatives calling for the establishment of a presidential commission to examine possible measures to rescue Jews in Hitler's Europe. A parallel resolution was brought to the Senate by Senator Guy Gillette. When the resolution came before the House Foreign Affairs Committee, its chairman, Sol Bloom, did not hide his animosity towards Bergson. Breckinridge Long was sent by the

State Department to give evidence and, they hoped, help to kill off the resolution. Instead, he gave a lamentable performance that strengthened those within the administration who were trying to do more for the Jewish cause.[223]

In particular, Henry Morgenthau, the secretary for the treasury, was incensed by the obstacles that the State Department erected to every undertaking, no matter how small, to bring relief to Jews in German-occupied Europe. He assembled an informal team of like-minded officials from his department, notably John Pehle and Josiah DuBois, and in December formally challenged Secretary of State Cordell Hull and Long to account for their stance. Convinced that it was time to alert the president to their obstructionism, Morgenthau commissioned DuBois to draw up an indictment, chronicling and analysing every block they had mounted. DuBois provocatively entitled his memorandum 'Report to the Secretary on the Acquiescence of this Government in the Murder of the Jews'. Although it was toned down, the version that Morgenthau submitted to Roosevelt did not pull any punches: it warned that a scandal could erupt over the perceived endeavours of an anti-Semitic cabal within the government. Just after noon on 16 January 1944, Morgenthau and members of his team went to the White House. After delivering an oral summary of the report, Morgenthau suggested that the president pre-empt a potentially ugly debate over the Rogers–Gillette resolution and approve the creation of an independent agency to devise and implement rescue work. Roosevelt agreed. On 22 January 1944 the War Refugee Board (WRB) came into existence by executive order.[224]

Roosevelt's thinking was influenced by the prospect of a re-election contest later that year, but the establishment of the WRB also reflected his maturation as a war leader and the increasing confidence of the United States as a military power. From the landings in North Africa until the invasion of Sicily, Roosevelt had been prepared to defer to Churchill on strategic issues and his general staff had followed suit. They all felt somewhat beholden to the British, who had been in the fight since it started, had made enormous sacrifices, and had a larger number of troops in the field. But by the start of 1944 Roosevelt had become disillusioned with the Mediterranean strategy sold to him by the British and plenty of young Americans had died in Sicily and Italy. The contribution of American industry to the Allied war machine now dwarfed British munitions production, while the build up of US forces for the invasion of north-west Europe meant that soon British troops would be a minority. Consequently, the president felt emboldened to set his own course, even at the cost of annoying the British. This independence of spirit applied to refugee matters as much as to the direction of the war. The WRB marked a fundamental breach in the Anglo-American consensus on the refugee question and the Jews. The British government certainly had no intention of emulating the White House. Addressing the cabinet, Foreign Secretary Eden dismissed the WRB as a device for '(1) placating the large Jewish vote and (2) spiking the guns of Congress'. Whitehall regarded the new agency with alarm and thereafter did its best to undermine the Board's activity.[225]

However laudable the intentions and ambitions behind its establishment, and however great the apprehension it inspired in the British Foreign Office, the WRB was hardly a formidable tool. Its remit was sweeping: 'to take action for the immediate rescue from the Nazis of as many as possible of the persecuted minorities of Europe, racial, religious or political and all civilian victims of enemy savagery . . . to take all measures within the Government's power to rescue the victims of enemy persecution who are in imminent danger of death and otherwise to assist such victims with all possible relief and assistance consistent with the successful prosecution of the war'. Yet it had a staff of only thirty to forty and relied heavily on the resources of the State Department. Fortunately, its director, John Pehle, was energetic, forceful and imaginative. In a short time the WRB inaugurated a mutually beneficial relationship with the much larger and well-endowed Office of Strategic Services (OSS), America's wartime intelligence and special operations agency. This cooperation would enhance the WRB's capabilities, but also enmesh it in the murky world of espionage.[226]

PART EIGHT

THE LAST PHASE

1944–1945

Hitler's hopes and Hungary's nemesis

Despite the setbacks and shocks of the previous year, at the start of 1944 Hitler reasoned that the war could still be brought to a successful conclusion. In his New Year message he both admonished the German people and sought to inspire them to one final effort: 'The year 1944 will make tough and severe demands on all Germans. The course of the war, in all its enormity, will reach its critical point . . .' He had some grounds for optimism. Although the combined RAF and USAAF bomber offensive had devastated one German city after another, civilian morale had not cracked. Industry had been disrupted, but Albert Speer had actually managed to increase armaments and munitions production. The Wehrmacht had been driven back relentlessly on the Russian front, but it was still possible to trade space for time in the east. By contrast, Hitler and his high command knew that time was running out for the Allied invasion of north-west Europe. It had to come in the late spring or summer of 1944, and they had prepared accordingly. Hitler ordered the diversion of new units and materiel to the west and invested massively in the Atlantic Wall, a chain of fortifications that stretched from Norway to the Pyrenees. He was convinced that he could smash the Allied bridgehead before it was securely established.[1]

Hitler could take comfort from recent events in Italy. At the start of the year an attempt by the British and Americans to outflank the stubbornly defended Gothic Line by landing several divisions at Anzio-Nettuno, within thirty miles of Rome, quickly developed into a bloody stalemate. The Germans came close to crushing the beachhead at Anzio and managed to keep the invaders bottled up for months. If the Germans could repeat this wherever the Allies came ashore in north-west Europe, Hitler thought that, at worst, he might be able to extract a separate peace from them. If the beachhead was wiped out, the Reich would be freed from the threat of invasion long enough for his western armies to be redeployed against the Soviets. Hitler knew the war could not be won, but he was not entirely deluded in thinking that he could achieve a stalemate, creating the conditions for a peace deal with either the western allies or Stalin.[2]

In Hitler's thinking, with the war hanging in the balance, it was more important than ever to root out and destroy the Jewish enemy. In his radio broadcast to the German people on 30 January 1944, he characterized the global conflict as a straightforward contest between Bolshevism, which he equated with world Jewry, and Germany for the survival of European civilization: 'there can be only one victor in this fight, and this will either be Germany or the Soviet Union! A victory by Germany means the preservation of Europe; a victory by the Soviet Union means its destruction . . . the fate of the German nation would be its complete extermination through Bolshevism. And this goal is also the openly admitted intention of international Jewry.' Only Germany could prevent 'a second triumphant Purim festival', meaning the slaughter of Gentiles, because it had cleansed itself of the Jews and created a united, racially pure Volksgemeinschaft. 'After all, only a state which is completely free of all antisocial focuses of infection at home can securely oppose Bolshevism abroad. Jewry itself has lost all power in our great Reich.' Towards the end of his speech Hitler harked back to his experience of defeat in 1918 and how he had transformed Germany since then. His message was that failure to prosecute the war against the Jews with undiminished ferocity could lead to a repeat of the scenario in 1917–18 when, as he saw it, the Jews undermined the morale of the German people and subverted the German army before they had been vanquished on the battlefield.[3]

The potential for Jewish subversion of the war effort played a fundamental role in Hitler's approach to his Axis partners. Any chance of victory depended on keeping the remaining elements of the Axis coalition together, but Hitler was especially nervous about Hungary. Since the Italian capitulation, German intelligence had monitored discussions within the Hungarian political leadership about the possibility of approaching the western allies to negotiate a way out of the war before the Red Army arrived on Hungary's borders. When the Hungarian prime minister, Miklós Kállay, appointed in March 1942, relaxed some of the anti-Jewish regulations and improved the treatment of the surviving Jewish labour servicemen, Hitler and Ribbentrop interpreted this as a sign of covert Jewish influence. Kállay's rejection of a request to com-mence the deportation of the Hungarian Jews in April 1943 was seen as proof that the Hungarian government had been suborned from within.[4]

Addressing senior army officers who were completing a course of ideological training in May 1944, Hitler drew together his anti-Jewish policy at home and its application abroad. Echoing his New Year speech he asserted that the elimination of the Jews from Germany was the con-dition for social unity and high morale. Only thus was the Volk able to withstand military reverses and relentless bombing. 'In removing the Jews I eliminated in Germany the possibility of creating some sort of revolutionary core or nucleus ... Look in contrast at other states. We have gained insight into a state which took the opposite route: Hungary. The entire state undermined and corroded, Jews everywhere, even in the highest places Jews and more Jews, and the entire state covered, I have to say, by a seamless web of agents and spies ... I have intervened here, too, and this problem will now also be solved.'[5]

After a request from Kállay to withdraw nine Hungarian divisions from the Eastern Front, Hitler's patience ran out. In early March 1944 he triggered Operation Margarethe, a plan for the occupation of Hungary that had been drawn up in the wake of Italy's default. Simultaneously he summoned the Hungarian head of state, Admiral Horthy, to a summit meeting at Schloss Klessheim near Salzburg, on 18 March. To Horthy's indignation, Hitler accused his Hungarian allies of treachery and attributed their waywardness to the persistence of Jewish influence. Since they had been too soft on the Jews, the Germans would have to take control. Horthy refused to sign a statement consenting to a German occupation, but it made no difference to the outcome. He was compelled to dismiss Kállay and appoint Döme Sztójay, the former Hungarian Ambassador in Berlin who was reliably pro-German, as the new prime minister. He also accepted a German demand to supply 100,000 Jews to the Reich as forced labour. Even as he was boarding his train home, two Wehrmacht divisions entered Hungary. Edmund Veesenmayer, the newly minted German plenipotentiary, and Ernst Kaltenbrunner, the head of the RSHA, joined Horthy en route. In Buda-pest they selected a new government to serve under Sztójay. Horthy remained in office, thereby conferring legitimacy on the imposed regime and by extension the anti-Jewish measures that it soon intro-duced.[6]

Many historians have viewed the invasion as a sign of Nazi insanity

– occupying the territory of an ally in order to seize its Jewish population and expending scarce resources on killing women and children when the war was as good as lost. However, although the eradication of Jewish influence in Hungary was fundamental to Hitler's decision to occupy the country, anti-Semitism alone did not drive the invasion and the Jewish tragedy that ensued from it. The occupation of Hungary and the destruction of the Hungarian Jews had a compelling, if perverted, logic. The primary aim was to keep Hungary in the Axis coalition and ensure that Hungarian armies remained in the field. The Germans also intended to squeeze everything they could out of the Hungarian economy at what they perceived to be a decisive moment in the war. The country had reserves of food, fuel and raw materials that the Germans considered were being poorly utilized. The Jews represented a part of this untapped potential. Despite the ravages inflicted by the local anti-Jewish laws, there was still considerable Jewish wealth in the country to plunder. Jews were heavily represented in the industrial and manufacturing sector of the Hungarian economy and ripe for expropriation. Finally, the Jewish population offered an immense pool of slave labour for the construction of underground factories intended to house the production lines for jet fighters and the V-1 flying bombs and V-2 rockets. Conversely, the occupation and the deportation of the Hungarian Jews had no adverse impact on the German war effort. It was a highly profitable enterprise that enriched the Hungarians and gave a boost to the German slave economy at a time when the Nazi leadership thought the war was still winnable.[7]

The fate of the Hungarian Jews

The Jewish population of Hungary, which had stood at around 445,000 in 1938, was greatly expanded by the award of territory from Czechoslovakia in November 1938 and March 1939, and from Romania in August 1940. These land transfers, implemented by the Axis as a reward for Hungarian fealty, added over 320,000 Jews. They were, however, poorly integrated into the native Magyarized Jewish community. To the Hungarian-speaking Neolog Jews in the capital, especially, the Jews in the 'liberated territories' seemed foreign and distant. Even the Hungarian Orthodox Jews, who had much in common with them, felt closer to their Hungarian compatriots.[8]

In one respect the Jews of Hungary were united. All sections of the Jewish population had been battered by waves of anti-Semitic legislation. In the last elections before the war, the far-right Arrow Cross movement, led by Ferenc Szálasi, won 30 per cent of the vote. Its parliamentary deputies clamoured for Nuremberg-style legislation to segregate the Jews. Intending to gratify the Nazis, rather than the Arrow Cross, in April 1940 the pro-German prime minister, Lászlo Bardossy, introduced a bill for the 'protection of the racial purity of the Magyar nation'. The legislation prohibited marriage between Christians and Jews, including the children of mixed marriages and certain converts. This stipulation aroused the wrath of the Churches, who insisted on their prerogative to bestow or withhold marriage rights. But the Church had nothing against the segregation and persecution of 'full Jews' and the bill was passed the following year. Miklós Kállay added to the roll of anti-Jewish statutes, if only as a device to appease Nazi Germany. In June 1942 he brought in a law to enable the expropriation of Jewish-controlled estates and thereby curtail Jewish influence in the countryside. A few weeks later, his government stripped the Jewish religion of the rights accorded to other denominations. This deprived key institutions of state funding and added to the financial burden on the community. By the time of the German occupation, laws passed by successive Hungarian governments and approved by Hungarian parliamentarians of their own volition, had impoverished large sections of the Jewish population, drained resources from communal organizations, and turned a religious community into a racial pariah.[9]

Greater damage resulted from the August 1940 call-up of Jewish men aged 25–60 to perform forced labour in auxiliary battalions attached to the army. The Hungarian military had already dismissed Jewish officers and NCOs and placed all Jewish servicemen in segregated units designated for manual labour. The first wave of new conscripts who joined them were issued with uniforms, too, and were commanded by Hungarian officers. Conditions were bearable, if harsh. However, when Hungary joined Operation Barbarossa the men in the labour battalions were subjected to great hardship, marching vast distances, carrying out arduous tasks under appalling conditions, ill-fed, poorly housed and badly treated. Although they were protected from the mass murder of Jews taking place all around them they were routinely used for mine-clearing operations and exposed to unnecessary danger. In the more permissive environment of the Eastern Front, anti-Semitic NCOs and officers robbed and tormented Jewish labour servicemen with virtual impunity. Several units were massacred. But the greatest loss of life resulted from the rout of the Hungarian army at Voronezh in January 1943, during which over 17,000 Jewish men in the labour battalions simply disappeared. It is estimated that at least 33,000 Hungarian Jewish males in the prime of life perished in Russia, leaving a population denuded of menfolk.[10]

Although Hungarian troops shielded the Jewish labour battalions from the Einsatzgruppen operations, they were not innocent of mass shootings and pogroms. In August 1941, Hungarian soldiers force-marched 18,000 'foreign Jews' from an internment camp at Korösmezo into German-occupied Ukraine and dumped them at Kamenets-Podolsk, where all but about 2,000 were subsequently massacred by an Einsatzkommando. A Hungarian army unit in Ujvidék (Novi Sad) in occupied Serbia shot about 700 Jews in a pogrom cum anti-partisan operation on 21–23 January 1942. News of these atrocities sparked a public uproar, leading to the fall of the Bardossy government and the appointment of Miklós Kállay.[11]

These blows had gravely strained communal resilience even before the Germans arrived. The man who orchestrated the final catastrophe was none other than Adolf Eichmann. During the first months of 1944 he and his men were at a loose end: the major centres of Jewish population in Europe outside Hungary had been annihilated and they were engaged in small-scale Jew-hunts in countries that no longer offered much support. Consequently, he was able to assemble an unusually large task force. On the eve of the invasion, 500–600 men of the Sipo-SD and SS gathered at Mauthausen concentration camp. The senior personnel included Hermann Krumey, Dieter Wisliceny, Franz Novak, Franz Abromeit, Otto Hunsche, Theo Dannecker, Siegfried Seidl and Richard Hartenberger, who had all at one time or another played a leading role in the destruction of Jewish communities. For the first time in his career, Eichmann took command in the field. The Einsatzkommando bearing his name set off for Hungary in the early hours of 19 March, pausing en route to celebrate its commander's birthday: he was thirty-seven years old.[12]

Eichmann reached Budapest on 21 March and set up headquarters at the Hotel Majestic in the Schwabenberg district. Later, he moved into a luxurious villa on Rose Hill that was stolen from its Jewish owner. However, he was not the only German official with an interest in Judenpolitik. As with every previous operation there was a bewildering tangle of agencies pursuing different goals and reporting up several chains of command. There was a contingent from the RSHA commanded by Hans Geschke, who was designated the BdS, commander of the Sipo-SD, in Hungary. Himmler sent Otto Winkelmann as the HSSPF with overall responsibility for all SS and Sipo-SD units, reporting directly to him. Winkelmann's second in command, Wilhelm Höttl, was in charge of SD counter-espionage operations. Himmler also dispatched Kurt Becher on a special mission to seize Jewish-owned industrial assets for the SS. Edmund Veesenmayer, of the German Foreign Office, had been invested by Hitler with 'plenipotentiary powers'. Finally, the Foreign Office sent Theodor Grell to man the Jewish desk at its Budapest embassy. This proliferation only increased the woes about to be inflicted on the Jews.[13]

Before Eichmann was installed on Rose Hill, Kaltenbrunner had met Döme Sztójay and Interior Ministry officials to agree the main lines of Jewish policy. They agreed on legislation to deprive Jews of their remaining rights and expropriate their wealth, and measures for their ghettoization, concentration, and deportation. These measures were to be enforced by Hungarian civil servants and the Hungarian gendarm- erie. Andor Jaross, the new interior minister, appointed László Endre and László Baky as secretaries of state with responsibility for political and administrative matters, including the 'Jewish Question'. Both were well known for their anti-Semitic views. Endre, a police administrator of long standing, had been a pro-Nazi activist since the early 1930s. Baky was a former army officer who had established a National Socialist Party in Hungary and served in parliament as a right-wing MP.[14]

Having learned painful lessons in France, and most recently in Den- mark, Eichmann was determined to achieve the cooperation of his Hungarian counterparts. They did not require much persuasion. He later recalled how 'At an informal meeting over a glass of Hungarian wine, I informed them that Himmler had issued an order to the German police and that he wanted the Hungarian Jews to be ghettoised, and then evac- uated to Auschwitz.' He added that the Germans did not want anyone over sixty or incapable of heavy manual labour. According to Eichmann the two spent most of the evening making merry because the Interior Ministry already had drafts of anti-Jewish legislation and little work was needed.[15]

Starting on 22 March, the regime promulgated the necessary laws for sequestering Jewish wealth and isolating Jews from the rest of society. The assets of Jewish citizens were frozen. They were obliged to register all their property and valuables, forbidden to own or drive vehicles or to use public transport. Their phones and radios were confiscated. Jews were totally removed from economic, professional or public life. The German occupation thereby facilitated a long-cherished ambition of Hungarian nationalists and anti-Semites. Men like Jaross and Endre believed that by confiscating and redistributing Jewish wealth they could create a utopian society for Hungarians. In reality, the elimination of Jews from the economy unleashed a bonanza as jobs, businesses and properties changed hands in a frenzy of greed.[16]

Eichmann was also determined to learn lessons from the events in Warsaw and to avoid Jewish resistance. Speed and deception were central to his strategy. As soon as they reached Budapest, Krumey and Wisliceny sent word for the Jewish leadership to assemble. The following morning, terrified communal representatives gathered at the Hotel Majestic, aware that overnight at least 200 Jews had already been arrested and incarcerated in the Kistarcsa internment camp. Within a few days 2,000 would be held there. Wisliceny and Krumey told them that Hungary's Jews were now under the control of the security police and ordered them to form a Jewish council. They were forbidden to communicate with Jews in the provinces and were threatened with dire punishment unless they maintained calm and order in the Jewish community. If they behaved well, no one would come to any harm. On 21 March a Jewish council was called into existence under the leadership of Samuel Stern, a highly respected figure with much communal experience.[17]

Ten days later Eichmann confronted the Jewish council in person. He told them that from 4 April the Jews would have to wear the yellow star. They were now going to work for the German war effort, but if they complied and worked hard they would be treated fairly. According to subsequent testimony by a member of the council, he said 'If the Jews went over to partisan operations he would kill them off without mercy. The Jews had to understand that nothing was being demanded of them except discipline and order. If there were discipline and order, then not only would Jewry have nothing to fear, but he would defend Jewry and it would live under the same good conditions as regards payment and treatment as all the other workers.' He assured them that he would 'prevent all plunder of Jewish possessions and that he would punish those seeking to enrich themselves from Jewish property'. The delegates should pass on this message to the Jewish community.[18]

Four days later, he attended a conference at the Ministry of the Interior to plan the deportations. The meeting was chaired by Baky and included senior members of the Eichmannkommando, Endre, and Lieutenant Colonel László Ferenczy, who commanded the 20,000 men of the Hungarian gendarmerie. They divided Hungary into six zones, roughly conforming to gendarmerie districts. In each one the Jews would first be registered, then removed from the countryside and concentrated in towns and cities. They would be stripped of their wealth and possessions and then transferred to ghettos from where they would be shipped to the Reich. The process would begin in the annexed eastern provinces, closest to the advancing Russians, so that it could be disguised as a security measure. This would also encourage Jews in the capital to comfort themselves that the measures were only targeting those who were 'foreign'. The conduct of the operation was entrusted to the chiefs of the gendarmerie and the police, aided by local officials ranging from mayors to schoolteachers.[19]

With a characteristic malice that showed a hatred of Judaism as well as Jews, the round-ups began at the start of the Passover festival, 16 April 1944. In twelve days, 194,000 Jews in Zone I, comprising Carpatho-Ruthenia and north-east Hungary, were driven into rapidly constructed temporary ghettos. Often these places were disused brickyards, derelict factories, farm buildings and pigsties without water or sanitation. The 98,000 Jews in Zone II, including Kolozsvar/Cluj and northern Transylvania, were evicted from their homes and herded into ghettos from 3 to 10 May. Zone III in northern Hungary, containing 53,000 Jews, was dealt with between 5 and 10 June. Zone IV in southern Hungary, which numbered 40,000 Jews, including the communities of Debrecen and Szeged, was targeted over 16–26 June. Finally, 29,000 Jews in Zone V in south-west Hungary were ghettoized from 30 June to 3 July. About 24,000 Jews in settlements around the capital were also incarcerated.[20]

Largely as a result of initiatives at the municipal level, steps were taken to separate the 200,000 Jews of the capital from the rest of the population and compress them into designated buildings known as 'yellow star houses'. Simultaneously Jews were restricted to certain bathhouses, restaurants, hotels and places of entertainment. Both the housing and the facilities apportioned to the Jews were inferior. Not

only were the city planners and officials engaging in anti-Jewish discrimination, they were engineering a redistribution of urban amenities.
Long-standing envy and avarice propelled the reshaping of the city as
much as ingrained prejudice. Ominously, in mid-May Endre intervened
with the lord mayor, Tibor Kaledy, to speed up the concentration of the
Jews. Apparently Kaledy's three-month schedule for completion of
the demographic reorganization was too protracted: the Jews were not
going to be around for that much longer.[21]

The so-called ghettos varied widely across Hungary, but all the Jews
who went into them experienced abuse and dispossession. In Sighet, a
city with a Jewish community of 10,000, where Hedi Fried lived, it 'consisted of several blocks surrounded by the fence. Those windows that
overlooked the main street outside were nailed fast and painted over.
The single street within the ghetto was crowded with people greeting
each other with wordless glances.' Hedi had recently qualified as a children's teacher; with her parents and sister she exchanged a bright, clean
and tidy apartment for a grubby, overcrowded room. They were obliged
to make an inventory of all their belongings and hand over all their
valuables on leaving. Bela Zsolt, a middle-aged writer in Nagyvarad
who had survived the labour battalions, found himself in the synagogue, which was the largest structure, amid a collection of buildings
that were surrounded by barbed wire. The city had one of the largest
Jewish populations outside Budapest, but the 21,000 Jews were jammed
into an assortment of dwellings. The overcrowding was intense and
soon people started dying. Zsolt fell sick and was thus placed in the synagogue, which functioned as a makeshift hospital. He lay surrounded by
dead bodies. 'Next to the terrible WC there is a laundry turned into a
morgue,' he explained in a post-war account, 'but by yesterday half a
dozen legs, naked and waxen, were hanging out of the half open door.'[22]

In addition to pitiable sanitation, overcrowding and hunger, the
Jews were victimized by the local population and the authorities. Peasants and tradesmen sold them food and drink through the fencing at
grossly inflated prices. Officials and gendarmes used more brutal and
systematic methods to extract wealth. Zsolt witnessed wealthy Jewish
citizens being dragged away to a nearby brewery that was used as a
torture and extortion centre. Later he watched the return 'one by one, of
the bloody parcels that had once been bankers, with aristocratic pretensions, feather wholesalers . . . patrician property owners, and the proud
proprietors of jewellery shops . . . Their heads were like watermelons

slashed in all directions . . .' Many had injuries to their genitals. To Zsolt, cupidity not anti-Semitism had turned the gendarmes into ravening beasts. 'They pretend to hate us as a pretext for taking our objects away . . . They are killing us for the sake of objects.'[23]

Women were routinely abused. Hedi recalled that on the eve of their deportation her family was taken from the ghetto to the synagogue, which served as an assembly centre, where 'the families were divided, the men crammed into the main hall, the women sitting on the floor of the gallery . . . The cock-feathers [gendarmes, who wore feathers in their uniform headgear] began to go through our belongings, looking for valuables. They called the women one by one, and female guards body-searched us in case we were hiding anything in our orifices.' These searches were also frequently carried out by male gendarmes.[24]

In a familiar scenario, even as the Jewish population was being uprooted and crammed into miserable holding pens, the Germans and their collaborators seemed at odds over what to do with them. Horthy and Sztójay had agreed to the shipment of 100,000 able-bodied Jews for labour in the Reich, but the more radical Baky, Endre and Ferenczy wanted to rid Hungary of every last Jew. Kaltenbrunner and the RSHA aspired to annihilate the entire Hungarian Jewish population, while Veesenmayer and the German Foreign Office adhered to the original understanding for labour deployment. On 14 April, Veesenmayer informed Berlin that the Hungarian prime minister had agreed to the deportation of 50,000 Jews to Germany for labour although he expected that Sztójay would approve the transfer of a further 50,000 in the following month. Three days later, at a conference at the Hungarian Interior Ministry, Ferenczy warned that conditions in the ghettos and transit camps in north-eastern Hungary were deteriorating fast; the Jews could not simply be left there. Eichmann then offered to take them all: those who could work and those who could not. Baky accepted. Thanks to a coalescence of Hungarian maximalists and German radicals, the fate of the Hungarian Jews was decided.[25]

Eichmann's logistical experts in Berlin and Budapest now started making the technical arrangements. Günther liaised with the WVHA to confirm that all the Jews would go to Auschwitz, in the first instance. Representatives of the Ministry for Labour, the Sipo and the Wehrmacht concurred that the Todt Organization would handle calls for Hungarian Jewish slave labour. Since about half of them would be female, Oswald Pohl, head of the WVHA, obtained agreement from

Himmler for women to be employed in heavy labour. At a meeting in Vienna on 4 May, Novak and Reichsbahn officials decided that four transports would depart daily from Hungary, carrying about 12,000 Jews, via Kosice and Tarnow to Auschwitz. Nothing was to interfere with military trains though. Finally, Veesenmayer and his foreign service team set up the necessary machinery to screen out foreign Jews.[26]

Ultimately, the whole operation depended on the Hungarians. Without their wholehearted collaboration it would have been impossible for Eichmann's kommando, even with the help of other Nazi agencies, to remove more than a fraction of such a huge Jewish population spread out over such a large area. And Eichmann had nothing but praise for the zeal and efficiency with which Hungarians at every level of society threw themselves into the task. Ferenczy led the way. At his headquarters in Munkacs he held regular briefing sessions for senior gendarmerie officers, police chiefs and local administrators. Every ghetto was assigned an embarkation point and a deportation date. Gendarmes were allotted to escort Jews to the railheads and accompany the trains until they reached the Hungarian border, where Germans would take over. Police chiefs, mayors, municipal clerks, tax officials, teachers and firemen would all play an active part in the eviction, pillage and deportation of their Jewish neighbours.[27]

The first trains actually left ahead of schedule, taking Jews from the internment camp in the Budapest suburb of Kistarcsa to Auschwitz-Birkenau. On 15 May deportations commenced from Zones I and II. Between 15 May and 7 June, ninety-two trains carried off 289,000 Jews from Carpatho-Ruthenia and northern Transylvania. From 11 to 16 June, twenty-three trains removed 59,000 Jews from Zone III. In just three days, beginning on 25 June, 41,500 Jews from Zone IV were deported on fourteen trains. In the final wave, on 4–8 July, eighteen transports loaded with over 55,000 Jews left for Auschwitz from Zone V and the area around Budapest. At this point Veesenmayer advised the Foreign Office in Berlin that 437,403 Jews had been deported to Auschwitz-Birkenau. Of these, 25–30 per cent were selected for labour; the rest were murdered on arrival. The speed, scale and totality of the destruction exceeded even the clearance of the Warsaw ghetto in July–September 1942.[28]

After one night in the assembly centre, Hedi Fried's family and 3,000 others were marched to Sighet station. 'Freight wagons stood before us, their windows nailed up. These were for us. A hundred of us were pushed into each wagon, which normally held eight horses. We were tired, hungry, thirsty and rather apathetic. We allowed ourselves to be shoved in . . .' At the beginning there was a semblance of order, but by the third day of the journey discipline broke down. 'The bucket in the corner began to overflow, and the smell of sweat, urine and excrement was nauseating. Our supply of water ran out, and thirst became unbearable. People began to beg and pray, wail and shriek.' Transports from the further reaches of Hungary could take up to a week to reach Auschwitz, if they were not delayed by disruption or forced to give way to priority military trains. In these cases the journey could be hellish.[29]

Few had any idea where they were going. After the war, survivors accused the Jewish leadership in Budapest of having failed to inform and warn Jews in the provinces about the true meaning of the deportations and what was happening at Auschwitz. Yet there was no lack of information about German atrocities and the fate of Jews in other countries. Hungarian Jews found it hard to believe that such things could happen to them, not least because their government had warded off similar horrors for so many years and because the war was apparently drawing to a close. Decades afterwards, Hedi Fried asked: 'Did we know of concentration camps? I don't remember. What I do remember is a Jewish refugee from Poland who came to our little town and was hidden by Aunt Lotti . . . My parents answered my questions [about him] evasively, whispering to each other of the horrors he had escaped, but I don't think anyone believed that such things might affect us. What had happened had happened in Germany, in Austria, in Czechoslovakia, in Poland, not in Hungary. We were Hungarian citizens; our fathers had fought in the Hungarian Army . . . Nothing could happen to us.' Bela Zsolt, who had witnessed the slaughter of Jews in the Soviet Union, knew better; he escaped from the Nagyvarad ghetto with his wife and made his way to Budapest where they found shelter with the assistance of friends.[30]

The War Refugee Board and rescue negotiations

For the first time during the war, in March 1944 in Hungary, the Allies were able to monitor a major German operation against the Jews as it unfolded. And, for the first time, in the War Refugee Board the Americans possessed an instrument specifically designed to respond to such a crisis. What is more, military developments gave them more leverage and options than they had ever possessed should they wish to aid the imperilled Jews. What ensued was one of the most dramatic, tragic and controversial episodes in the fate of the Jews and the Second World War.

On 5 April 1944, Himmler's personal representative in Budapest, Kurt Becher, successfully engineered the purchase of the Manfred-Weiss industrial combine for the SS. At a stroke Himmler acquired an industrial empire. In return for the sale, Becher enabled fifty members of the Weiss and Chorin families, Jews and converts who between them owned the bulk of shares in the concern, to leave Hungary for Switzerland and Portugal. This deal infuriated Eichmann on two counts: it brought great kudos to his rival Becher and trespassed on territory that he had controlled since 1938 – Jewish emigration. In order to counteract Becher's success Eichmann wanted a spectacular feat of his own.[31]

The opportunity came, thanks to the tangled skein that linked Jewish rescue activists in Slovakia and Hungary with the WRB, German military intelligence, and the OSS. In 1943, a group of Zionists in Budapest had formed a Relief and Rescue Committee to smuggle Jews from Slovakia and Poland via Hungary to safe havens. They were in touch with Rabbi Dov ber Weissmandel in Bratislava, Slovakia, who was the leading figure, with Gisi Fleischmann, in a clandestine underground organization known as the Working Group. In mid-1942 while the deportations from Slovakia were in full swing, the Working Group made contact with Dieter Wisliceny and offered him a huge bribe to halt the transports. Wisliceny took the money and when the deportations stopped in October 1942, as the Germans had always planned they would, he claimed the credit. His venality convinced Weissmandel and Fleischmann that they could arrest the machinery of destruction by judicious bribes. To this end, during 1943, they cooked up the Europa Scheme, a fantastically ambitious plan to obtain money from the Jewish Agency in Palestine to buy all the Jews in the German sphere of influence out of the threat of deportation. The viability of the scheme depended in part on being able to communicate with the Jewish Agency and to smuggle money and people across borders.[32]

Since early 1943, the Jewish Agency executive had stepped up its efforts to aid the Jews in German-dominated Europe and established outposts in Switzerland and Istanbul from which its envoys tried to maintain contact with Zionist groups in the Axis sphere. Palestinian

Jews crossed illicitly into areas under German control as couriers, while members of the Zionist underground groups in Slovakia, Poland, Hungary and Romania travelled in the other direction. By spring 1943, the Jewish Agency had a network of agents and couriers anchored in Istanbul operating across the Balkans. Teddy Kollek, one of Ben-Gurion's most trusted lieutenants, handled the Istanbul operation. Kollek started sharing his European agents and information with the British secret service. He also established a connection with the American intelligence agency, the Office of Strategic Services (OSS). The Americans were interested in Kollek's operation because he was running men into Hungary, and Washington was trying to induce the Hungarian leadership to defect from the Axis. These couriers, several of whom were part-Jewish, were recruited by the Relief and Rescue Committee. What Kollek did not know was that most of them were also on the payroll of the Abwehr, the German military intelligence, and were also known to Hungarian counter-espionage. In fact, the Hungarians had latched on to the Jewish couriers in the hope of using them to convey peace feelers to the Allies, and the Abwehr acquired their services for much the same reason.[33]

With German troops now in Hungary, the leading figures of the Budapest Relief and Rescue Committee, Otto Komoly, Reszo (Rudolf) Kasztner and Joel Brand, began to emulate the Slovakian Working Group and explore every route to Hungarian and German officials who they might be able to influence or bribe. On 24 March 1944, the committee's couriers arranged for Brand and Kasztner to meet Wisliceny, whereupon they offered the Nazi $2 million if he would mitigate the implementation of anti-Jewish policies. Wisliceny took a 'down-payment' of $200,000 and said he would see what he could do. These contacts continued for several weeks, during which even more money changed hands. Wisliceny meanwhile reported his conversations to Eichmann, who spotted an opening for a coup of his own. Around 25 April, Eichmann was introduced to Joel Brand. He told Brand that he would allow 1 million Jews to emigrate from Hungary if Brand could arrange the delivery of goods and materiel for the Reich. Specifically, he asked for 10,000 trucks for use on the Eastern Front plus various foodstuffs and 2 million bars of soap. He told the astonished Brand that he would make it possible for him to travel to Istanbul to meet Zionist representatives so as to convey this offer of 'goods for blood'. Eichmann had cleared his proposal with his superiors and was aspiring to land a very big fish indeed, one large enough to overshadow anything

delivered by Becher. But his pet project was complicated by the machinations of other SS officers in Budapest.[34]

Earlier in the year, the Abwehr, which was a nest of opposition to
the Nazis, had been purged and taken over by the foreign espionage service of the Sicherheitsdienst under Walter Schellenberg. The Abwehr's
part-Jewish agents, who doubled up as Zionist couriers, now found
themselves working for the SD. This development led to a further twist
in the unfolding plot. Gerhard Clages, the head of the SD intelligence
bureau in Budapest who now controlled the Zionist couriers, saw them
as a potential channel of communication with the western allies. This
was a gift, since his boss, Himmler, was eager to get a message to the
west that Germany would be interested in negotiating a separate peace
that would leave both sides free to concentrate on the Soviets. It is not
clear whether Himmler was serious about either releasing large numbers of Jews in return for a deal with the Allies or achieving a deal of
any kind, but Schellenberg spotted the opportunity for sowing suspicion
and dissension in the grand coalition simply by attempting such a
manoeuvre.[35]

When Brand next met Eichmann, on 14 May 1944, the day before
the first transports were due to leave for Auschwitz, he was confronted
by a panoply of SS officers, including Clages and Becher. To his surprise
he was ordered to travel to Istanbul with Bandi Grosz, a half-Jew with a
shady past who at various times had served the Zionists, the Germans,
the Hungarians and the OSS. Brand's mission was now more than just a
bid to save the Hungarian Jews; it was contaminated by a Machiavellian
ploy conjured up by the SS foreign intelligence bureau. Thanks to their
own spies the Allies knew this, but Brand had little idea that from the
outset his assignment was so compromised that it was doomed to fail.
As soon as he reached Istanbul he contacted Zionist officials and passed
on Eichmann's grotesque offer. A few days later he met a senior Jewish
Agency representative, who transmitted the gist to the agency executive
in Jerusalem. They prudently informed the British and asked for Brand
to be allowed to travel to Palestine to continue the negotiations. The
British agreed, but on 5 June arrested him while he was en route
through Syria. He was taken to Cairo, where he was detained for weeks
and closely interrogated. Brand was frantic, believing that his chance to
save a million lives was slipping away, and incredulous that the British
did not leap at the possibility. In fact, on 30 May the British war cabinet
had considered the bizarre proposition and vetoed any contacts with

the Germans. To ensure that the Soviets did not suspect any double-dealing, the Foreign Office also alerted Moscow to what was surely a scam. The Soviets concurred. Although the Jewish Agency sent Moshe Shertok, a senior official, to London to plead for the channels to be kept open, if only as a charade to delay the deportations, the Allies were unyielding. Chaim Weizmann and Shertok managed to see Anthony Eden on 6 July and reiterated the importance of dangling a bargain in front of the Germans, but they were rebuffed. On 19 July the British leaked the story to the press via the journalist and Labour Party intellectual Michael Foot. No one was more surprised than Ribbentrop, the German foreign minister, who apparently had no clue what was going on.[36]

Once the Brand mission had been exposed it lost any value for the Germans. However, Rudolf Kasztner and Hansi Brand (Joel's wife) had taken up where the hapless emissary had left off, trying to cajole or bribe Eichmann into holding Jews back from the transports. Cleverly they turned the silence from Istanbul to their advantage, arguing to Eichmann that unless the Germans made a gesture of goodwill why should anyone believe they were serious about letting Jews go? Impressed by this reasoning, in early June, Eichmann allowed Kasztner to bring 388 Jews from the eastern provinces to Budapest. After more hard bargaining, Kasztner was able to win Eichmann's consent for a train to carry Jews to Switzerland and safety. The train, which was soon fraught with controversy, was filled with representatives of the Zionist parties, leading rabbis, and those who could afford up to $1,000 for a place. Since members of Kasztner's own family and people from his home town of Cluj were on board, those less fortunate accused him of favouritism and corruption. On 30 June, the train with 1,684 Jewish passengers left Budapest; but it did not go to Switzerland. Instead Eichmann directed it to the 'exchange camp' at Bergen-Belsen. Most of the original complement eventually reached Switzerland on 6 December 1944.[37]

In addition, Eichmann told Kasztner that he would redirect 30,000 Jews to the Strasshof concentration camp in Austria, where they would be 'put on ice' pending the conclusion of the hoped-for deal with the Allies. Between 25 and 28 June, six or seven trains carrying about 18,000–20,000 Jews were sent to Strasshof via Vienna. Eichmann extracted a further payment of 5 million Swiss francs from his Jewish interlocutors for this favour. However, within a few days the ground shifted beneath his feet. As a result of international protests and the success of the Allied landings in Normandy, his Hungarian partners did a U-turn.[38]

At a press conference on 25 March, ostensibly to flag up the establishment of the WRB, President Roosevelt called on the German people to frustrate their government's intentions and reiterated the Allies' promise to collect evidence of war crimes and bring those guilty to justice. He invited neutral countries to open their borders to people fleeing Nazi persecution and announced that the US would set an example. The following month about 300 Jews liberated in southern Italy were evacuated to a refugee camp at Oswego in New York State. The United States also sent a stiff warning to the Hungarian regime that it would be held to account. Eight weeks later, Roosevelt addressed a personal message to Horthy, demanding that he halt the deportations and threatening him with retribution.[39]

The WRB spearheaded an international protest campaign. It requested the Vatican, the International Red Cross (ICRC), and a succession of neutral countries to register their concern with the Hungarian regime and do what they could to offer direct aid to Jews in peril. As a result, the Vatican finally broke its record of silence and inaction. Pope Pius XII appealed personally to Horthy, asking for the Hungarian government 'not to continue its war against the Jews'. Angelo Rotta, the papal nuncio in Budapest, conveyed the message himself, but confined the Vatican's mantle to baptized Jews. The ICRC sent a special envoy to Budapest, Friedrich Born, who started issuing Jews with protective papers carrying the Red Cross stamp. He later helped to set up safe houses for Jews under the Red Cross flag. Born appointed none other than Otto Komoly to run this scheme. Charles Lutz, an official at the Swiss Embassy, had the idea of taking over a building and conferring diplomatic status on it, then filling it with endangered Jews. The Glass House, as the first site was known, became a haven for youthful Zionists where they could forge documents and coordinate rescue work. King Gustav of Sweden added his voice to the international protests at the end of June. Swedish diplomats in the Budapest embassy, Carl Danielsson, Per Anger and Valdemar Langlet, each employed dozens of Jews, thereby giving them diplomatic protection. They also issued hundreds of documents placing the holders under Swedish protection. In July the Swedish trio were joined by Raoul Wallenberg, who was sent as a representative of the WRB.[40]

While this unprecedented whirl of rescue work offered thousands of Jews in Budapest a temporary lifeline, their longer-term fate was being determined on the landing grounds of Normandy. Operation Overlord commenced in the early hours of 6 June 1944 and by the end of the day it was clear that the Allies had secured a foothold in German-occupied France. Over the following month they expanded the bridgehead, slowly and at great cost against tenacious German resistance. By early July, though, it was obvious that the Germans were not going to crush the lodgement. Hitler's gamble in the west had failed. To compound Germany's dreadful strategic situation, on 22 June 1944 the Red Army opened a massive offensive that enveloped Army Group Centre, eliminated around 400,000 German troops, and carried the Soviet vanguard to the suburbs of Warsaw. The Germans were compelled to evacuate the Baltic territories and were swept out of Romania, which adroitly changed sides in August. To Admiral Horthy the writing was on the wall. Heavy bombing of the capital, which many Hungarians mistakenly saw as a direct response to the deportation of the Jews, encouraged his conviction that remaining in alliance with the Third Reich and doing Hitler's bidding would bring disaster.[41]

At the end of June Horthy reined in Endre and Baky, removing Jewish matters from their hands. Baky refused to accept his downgrading and conspired with the gendarmerie to stage a coup, install a Nazified regime, and continue the anti-Jewish policy. Horthy anticipated this move and rallied loyal army units to the capital. He had Baky and Endre arrested, ordered gendarmerie units to pull out of the city, told Veesenmayer that the deportations must stop, and demanded that the Gestapo leave. General Géza Lakatos, loyal to Horthy and antipathetic to the Germans, was appointed as the new prime minister. On 9 July, the deportation trains were halted on Horthy's orders. Undeterred, Eichmann sent a group of SD men to Kistarcsa camp where 1,500 Jews were being held. They forced the Jews onto a train to Auschwitz, but a Jewish official alerted members of the Jewish council, who raised the alarm with Horthy's entourage. The train was recalled. Infuriated by this, a few days later Eichmann summoned the Jewish council to the Hotel Majestic and detained them while his deputy, Kurt Novak, went to Kistarcsa with a detachment of security police and emptied the camp onto a waiting transport. The internment camp at Sarvar suffered the same fate. In these last manic operations, 3,000 Jews were conveyed to Auschwitz in defiance of the legitimate regime in Budapest.[42]

In fact, Horthy had not decided what should happen to the 150,000–200,000 Jews left in the capital and toyed with the idea of expelling them to camps in the countryside. In late July he announced that he was prepared to allow 40,000 Hungarian Jews to emigrate to Palestine, and informed the Germans that they could resume the deportations if they also permitted Jews to leave the country. Between them the Germans and the British killed the emigration plan. Eichmann warned Berlin that the Jews would send the healthiest and strongest emigrants to rebuild the Jewish people in their homeland, which was plainly undesirable. The British baulked at the prospect of thousands of Jews pouring into Palestine and vetoed any cooperation with the Hungarians. Nevertheless, the transports never resumed: on 25 July, Himmler confirmed the suspension of deportations. Eichmann went on holiday and his task force was wound up several weeks later.[43]

Death in Birkenau and forced labour in the concentration camps

Only a small minority of the approximately 440,000 Jews who were deported to Birkenau from Hungary spent more than a few hours in the camp. During the selections that took place on the ramp, between 25 and 30 per cent of the average transport carrying 3,000 people were selected to go into the labour pool. They were sent to the 'sauna' for processing and then into the 'quarantine camp' where they were held until they were assigned to a labour camp in Germany. The majority were escorted to the gas chambers and murdered within sixty minutes of arrival. If there was congestion, they might linger for a while longer. The speed and metronomic routine of the Aktion give the impression of a precisely choreographed and smoothly running operation, yet it was no more refined, scientific or clinical than the crudely constructed and brutally managed Action Reinhard camps.[44]

The occupation of Hungary was a surprise: no one in the concentration camp system or at Auschwitz was prepared for the implications. Late in the day, Rudolf Höss was recalled as commandant to handle the expected influx. Everything had to be arranged at speed and improvised, as usual. Filip Müller recalled that the crematoria ovens were overhauled and the chimneys cleaned out. In great haste, starting in late April, a spur line was laid to carry trains from the old ramp right into Birkenau. The surviving bunker was rehabilitated and incineration pits were dug in the meadows around it. In Müller's eyes the once pastoral scene to the rear of Crematorium V came to resemble 'a strange building site' as the pits, 40 by 50 metres and 2 metres deep, were excavated. Otto Moll, an SS officer with much experience of killing Jews and disposing of bodies, was added to the camp staff. To his despair, Müller saw the number of men in the Sonderkommando doubled to 900. A special 140-strong unit was assigned to the pits, where they were organized into teams to remove teeth and cut hair, carry the corpses to the pyre, stoke the flames and pour fat (collected in specially dug trenches) over the corpses to help them burn. Thirty-five men were detailed to collect the ash, sift out the bones and crush them with a specially manufactured device. The resulting human gravel was then poured into nearby rivers. Other groups were made ready to collect clothing and clear up the baggage. The Canada work detail was boosted to 2,000 sorters and bundlers.[45]

Hedi Fried's journey through Birkenau may stand for the tens of thousands of others who endured the experience. Immediately after the doors of her wagon were slid open, men in striped uniforms jumped up and started ejecting the exhausted, dehydrated passengers. Her father asked one of them where they were: 'Extermination camp', was all he replied, but it was enough. Harassed by shouts and blows the 3,000 people clustered on the ramp until a loudspeaker commanded men to form a column on the left, women on the right. Hedi kissed her father and then lost sight of him for ever. 'The long queue of women moved slowly towards a table where an SS man with his bloodhound was waving his stick like a conductor on a dais: "You right, you left, right, left, left."' She overheard members of a family ask to stay together, to be assured by the seated SS officer they would meet up later. 'Mothers reluctantly let go of their daughters; sisters parted from sisters.' When Hedi reached the desk she was sent to the left with her sister, while her mother went to the right. Her mother was told she would meet her daughters 'tomorrow'. After a momentary hug, they separated.[46]

Thanks to the extension of the rail track, veteran prisoners in sections BI and BII of Birkenau had a clear view of the selections and the long lines traipsing towards the crematoria. Evidently the newcomers had no notion of what was in store for them. There was almost never any resistance; the process seemed to work flawlessly. Adelsberger marvelled at their ignorance and anguished at their compliance. 'We watched as the people stood in the middle of the main street of Birkenau, their abandoned packs and sacks scattered about, thoroughly drenched by the rain or, more frequently, withering in the sun, with their children restlessly bopping here and there or clambering down the grass embankment. We used to count the baby carriages.' Some walked to Crematoria II and III where the Sonderkommando stood 'like hungry people in front of a grocery store'. Others made the trek around the central sauna to Crematoria IV and V where they disappeared into the birch groves. '[L]ess than an hour later the flames rose high behind these woods . . . The air was contaminated by the stench of burning bodies and singeing hair, and the smoke descended on the camp in swathes of ashes.' Albert Menasche was typical of the prisoners who by this time had become numb to the fate of others. 'Our only preoccupations were to avoid being hit by clubs, and above all, to get food . . . Those who went to their deaths no longer interested us.'[47]

The men of the Sonderkommando, like Filip Müller, witnessed what happened next. 'Long columns of those who during the selections had been chosen for the walk to the gas chambers struggled along the dusty roads, exhausted and in low spirits, mothers pushing prams, taking the older children by the hand. The young helped and supported the old and sick.' When they could not go directly into the undressing rooms of Crematoria IV and V they were guided to the beech grove where Moll offered words of encouragement, promising that they would soon get a shower and refreshment. An SS man who had been specially added to the guard detachment because he spoke Hungarian maintained the illusion of ordinariness until it was time for them to be ushered inside. At this point there was no longer any need for deception and any semblance of civility was abandoned. The SS men on duty at the gas chambers and crematoria were drunk for much of the time and seem to have lost whatever inhibitions they still possessed. Müller recalled that Moll would prowl through the undressing rooms before 'selecting a couple of naked young women and hustling them to one of the pits where corpses were being burnt'. Moll 'got a tremendous kick out of their terror. In the end he shot them from behind so that they fell forward into the burning pit.'[48]

Despite the frantic preparations, Birkenau proved unable to meet the challenge. The first Hungarian transport on 29 April was followed by up to 12,000 deportees per day, of whom 70–80 per cent were consigned to the gas chambers. Within days the ovens and chimneys in Crematoria IV and V overheated so that the pits had to be used constantly and not just when there was a heavy throughput, as had been anticipated. The sight and the smell when the pits were ignited at daybreak was repugnant. Müller recalled that 'Under the ever-increasing heat a few of the dead began to stir, writhing as though with some unbearable pain, arms and legs straining in slow-motion, and even their bodies straightening up a little ... Almost every corpse was covered with black scorch marks and glistened as if it had been greased. The searing heat had burst open their bellies: there was the violent hissing and spluttering of frying in great heat.' The ash-team had to spray water on the debris to cool it down so that they could collect the bones. The cold water falling on red-hot skulls caused them to explode. Hot ash blew into the eyes of the men working around the pits, blinding them.[49]

These macabre sights were hidden from the Jews selected to enter the camp labour force. While her mother went to the gas chamber, Hedi was marched to the 'bath-houses' with a column of women. Once inside they were told to undress and leave their valuables. 'We stripped ourselves naked and lined up before a man who cut off all our hair. We tried to hide our nakedness with our hands, but the SS guards went round and beat anyone who was not standing upright. My time came. I swallowed, tried to forget where I was and stood to attention before the "barber". He stood on a stool, swung his scissors and ripped off all my hair, everything. First with the scissors, then with a machine. First my head, then under my arms and lastly between my thighs.' After they were shorn they were given bits of soap, showered, and issued with prisoner garb. Luckily, these women were allowed to retain their shoes and Hedi located her own sturdy boots. Women and girls in fashionable pumps were soon in trouble. As dawn approached they were assembled for their first *Appell* and counted. Afterwards, the women were taken to a barracks where they digested what had befallen them as best they could and mourned for lost loved ones. Hedi was there for several days before she was returned to the 'sauna' and tattooed. Then she was embarked on a train that took her and several hundred others to Hamburg, where they were put to work clearing bomb damage.[50]

Approximately 25,000 of the 440,000 Hungarian Jews transported to Auschwitz-Birkenau were registered and admitted into the camp and about 80,000 were held for a few weeks until they were requisitioned for labour in the Reich. The torrent of Jews into concentration and labour camps in Germany dramatically reversed the state of affairs since 1942–43, when, on Himmler's orders, Jews had been eliminated from the camp system so completely that only 350 are known to have survived. Now, however, the clamour for labour was so urgent that Hitler revoked his decree that not a single Jew should be allowed onto German soil. The resulting flood of Hungarian Jews, plus 19,000 Polish Jews from Lodz, added a particular ethnic dimension to the final metamorphosis of the camp system.[51]

In September 1942 the six main concentration camps in Germany held 110,000 prisoners. By July 1943 that figure had doubled as the SS Business and Administration Head Office established new camps as part of its strategy to exploit labour and develop industrial interests. People arrested all over Europe were deported to the Reich to meet the demand for workers. The original concentration camps in Germany underwent phenomenal expansion: Buchenwald grew from just under 20,000 in mid-1943 to over 82,000 a year later. In August 1944 the overall camp population numbered 524,286 and reached its peak the following January, when a grand total of 714,211 inmates were registered. This exponential growth was a direct outcome of the drive to increase German arms output masterminded by Albert Speer and industry's demand for workers in response to successive waves of conscription that removed skilled German workers from the factory shop floor. Sub-camps sprang up all over the Reich to service industrial concerns and provide labour for farms, transport centres, and docks, and clearing bomb damage. Factory managers put in bids for slave workers and were none too fussy about how they were housed, fed, clothed or guarded. The camp system metastasized, with main camps such as Buchenwald and Mauthausen spawning numerous sub-camps that, in turn, developed satellite camps. During 1944 over 580 new camps came into being. And for the first time in the history of the Konzentrationslager, the Jews formed a substantial proportion of the prisoners.[52]

Jewish slave labour was predominant in two main areas. Himmler undertook to supply 100,000 labourers to the Jägerstab, the special staff created in March 1944 to accelerate the production of fighters and relocate assembly plants to underground sites. The SS also offered to provide the muscle power for the excavation of underground factories for the production of the V-1 flying bomb and the V-2 rocket that carried a 1-ton explosive payload. The facilities for producing the V (vengeance) weapons were located in the Harz Mountains, in Lower Saxony. The main camp there was at Nordhausen, a sub-camp of Buchenwald, also known by its code name as Dora-Mittelbau. Here about

60,000 prisoners toiled to enlarge existing tunnels driven into the hill-sides and carve out new ones. The first drafts of prisoners who arrived from mid-1943 until early 1944 actually lived in the tunnels, enduring abysmal conditions. Prisoners used oil drums as latrines, slept in damp bunks stacked against the side of rough-hewn cross-tunnels, and inhaled stale air filled with rock dust as well as noxious fumes from machine exhausts. The rate of mortality was so astronomical that an estimated 10,000 men died, far more than were ever killed by the rock-ets themselves. Prisoners were employed just to go through the tunnels each day picking up corpses and dragging them outside for disposal. Conditions improved somewhat when a barracks camp was opened in March 1944 to accommodate roughly 12,000 slave workers, the majority of whom were Hungarian and Polish Jews. Nevertheless, from the German point of view the project was a success: the facility produced 6,000 V-1 pilotless flying bombs and up to 700 missiles each month until the camp was shut down in March–April 1945.[53]

A second major concentration of Jewish slave labour was in the Eulen Mountains in Upper Silesia. The camps that spread across this region were offshoots of Gross-Rosen, which had been established in August 1940 to provide workers for an SS-run granite quarry. Gross-Rosen expanded from 7 barracks housing 1,500 prisoners to 22 blocks in early 1943, containing 16,000 men. There were no Jews until Himmler ordered the dissolution of Organisation Schmelt, whereupon valuable workers were spared deportation to the gas chambers at Auschwitz and transferred there instead. The infusion of Jews from Hungary and Lodz in mid-1944 raised the proportion of Jewish inmates to about one third of the total – which reached a peak of 98,000 in the main camp and dozens of satellite sites. Sub-camps provided labour for industrial plants run by I. G. Farben, Krupp, Telefunken and Flick, amongst many other concerns. Around 13,000 Jews were also employed excavating tunnels to house fighter-assembly plants and an under-ground headquarters for Hitler. The work regime was merciless and living conditions in the barracks were wretched. Sanitation and health declined precipitously when prisoners evacuated from Auschwitz began to arrive in early 1945. Gross-Rosen was actually intended to serve as a back-up for Auschwitz, but an orderly relocation proved impossible and the 'new Auschwitz' remained an SS fantasy.[54]

The final Jew-hunts and the last deportations

The destruction of the Hungarian Jews was paralleled by a final parox-
ysm of Jew-hunting wherever the Germans held sway. They were
abetted by fanatical anti-Semitic elements in society plus opportunists
and collaborators who were so implicated that they had nothing to lose
and much to gain by pillaging the Jewish remnant in their countries.
Instead of inspiring caution, the advance of the Allied armies accentuated the determination of Nazi true believers to wipe out the enemy
within. They obsessively pursued their Jewish quarry in order to exact
revenge for defeats on the battlefield and the relentless bombing campaign, as pre-emptive action to forestall Jewish-led retribution, and in
the conviction that Germany might just survive if purged of subversive
cells within the body politic.

In France the hard-pressed Jew-hunters gained a valuable ally in
Joseph Darnand, who replaced Bousquet as the head of the police at the
end of 1943. He brought to the job his allegiance to the SS, ideological
zeal, and the burgeoning ranks of the Milice. At roughly the same time,
the hopelessly corrupt Darquier de Pellepoix was ousted as director of
the CGQJ and effectively replaced by the lethally efficient Joseph Antignac. Knowing that an Allied landing was imminent and that the men of
Vichy would soon be fighting for their lives, Laval unleashed the security
apparatus on the resistance and the Jews. Between January and August
1944, France was more or less an anti-Semitic police state, although the
Vichy regime actually enjoyed a modest surge of popularity in reaction
to the death and devastation caused by Allied air raids.[55]

Helmut Knochen and Alois Brunner now abandoned any pretence
of deferring to Vichy sensibilities about the apprehension of Jews with
French citizenship. Between January and April, teams of Sipo-SD with
local collaborators mounted raid after raid in provincial cities, including
Laon, Saint-Quentin, Bordeaux, Reims, Poitiers, Troyes, Dijon, Nancy
and Limoges. They even swept through the Ardennes, netting 450
mainly foreign Jews who thought they had found safety on remote
farms and in secluded hamlets. Even though the Sipo snatch squads
routinely failed to reach more than 50–75 per cent of their target for
each raid, the numbers mounted up. In January they sent 1,520 Jews to
Drancy, just over 2,000 in February, a little more than 1,000 in March,
2,000 in April and 1,400 in May. Night raids in Paris succeeded in grab-

bing 730 non-French Jews in January, a hundred more than that in February, and between 200 and 425 each month until July. The security police and Milice also bulked up the numbers by swooping on UGIF offices and institutions, especially children's homes. In one of the most notorious of these child-snatching operations, Klaus Barbie seized forty-five children and eight members of staff at a home run by OSE in the village of Izieu near Lyons. In all, eight UGIF child-care centres were targeted by the Sipo-SD, consigning 258 children and 30 carers to Drancy and thence to Birkenau. Tragically, UGIF and OSE had delayed putting into operation a plan to disperse the children that might have saved them.[56]

Hélène Berr steadfastly refused to heed friends in Paris who urged her to go underground or flee the capital. To hide 'would mean hiding everyone' – her mother, father and sister, which was not straightforward. Nevertheless, the family took evasive measures, scattered and slept at different locations every night. Confronted by reports of raids and arrests she exclaimed, 'What a shame that one half of humanity is *manufacturing* evil and a tiny minority is trying to put it right.' In January she had a narrow escape when a concierge at the Sorbonne warned her of impending danger. On the night of 7 March, Hélène and her parents decided to stay in their apartment together. The next morning they were arrested. She was deported to Auschwitz-Birkenau on 27 March 1944, her twenty-third birthday. Her mother, Antoinette, died in the camp a month later. Her father, Raymond, perished in Auschwitz-Monowitz in September. Hélène was transferred to Belsen in November, where she became weaker and sicker. On 14 April 1945 she was so enfeebled by typhus that she was unable to get down from her bunk to attend a roll call. After a severe beating by a guard she died the same day.[57]

Brunner's men found more victims for the eastward-bound convoys in the spa town of Vittel, home to one of the strangest German internment camps. Located in the Vosges, Vittel boasted a number of comfortable hotels. After the fall of France the Germans appropriated several and wired them off from the others for use as detention centres for citizens of Allied countries. By early 1943 some 2,000 English were housed in the Hôtel des Sources, hundreds of Americans (including nuns) were lodged in the Hôtel Central, while elderly folk were accommodated in the Hôtel Continental. In early 1943 the Germans began to use the camp to warehouse Jews with foreign passports who they believed might be offered in exchange for German nationals interned in

Allied states. Mary Berg and her family benefited from this arrangement in January 1943. They were removed from the Pawiak prison in Warsaw and sent to Vittel by train via Poznan and Metz. When Mary arrived she described it as 'a paradise compared to our three years in the ghetto'. Her family had a decent room, there were shops and a cinema, and they were able to stroll through parkland inside the perimeter.[58]

However, this pretty spa acquired a more sinister function after the Warsaw ghetto uprising. The Germans knew that thousands of Jews had fled to the Ayran side and were living in hiding. To tempt them into the open the Gestapo employed Jews to circulate amongst the fugitives offering to sell them passports and travel papers issued by South American countries. The Jewish agents told a convincing story of how they obtained the documents and took a hefty payment. The Gestapo then let it be known that if the holders of such papers went to the Hôtel Polski they would be guaranteed protection. The scheme appeared so plausible that several veterans of the underground took it up. So did the poet and educator Yitzhak Katzenelson, who had escaped the ghetto with his eldest son Zvi in April 1943. (Katzenelson's wife and two younger sons had been sent to Treblinka the previous August.) Subsequently, Yitzhak and Zvi were amongst two trainloads who were sent to Vittel. On 22 May 1944, Katzenelson started a diary: 'My son and I are now in Vittel. We came with a group of Jews, all of whom were nationals of different . . . countries of South America. Zvi and I are nationals of Honduras.' After a year, an SD commission arrived to review the documents of potential exchange Jews. The passports held by Yitzhak and Zvi Katzenelson were among some 250 that were declared false. Father and son were transferred to Drancy on 18 April 1944 and ten days later shipped to Auschwitz where they were murdered. Hundreds of others who availed themselves of the Hôtel Polski were shot in the Pawiak prison or transported to Bergen-Belsen and thence to the gas chambers. Thanks to her mother's unimpeachable American credentials, Mary Berg and her family were allowed to depart for the USA via Lisbon on 1 March 1944. She began to work on the publication of her diary soon after she landed in New York.[59]

During the last, frenzied period of Jew-hunting in France, the Vichy authorities and the Germans employed bounty-hunters. In the south 200 informants were paid for denouncing fugitives. Seventeen agents worked with the Sipo-SD tracking down Jews in hiding. It was not uncommon for the French collaborators to blackmail Jews whom they discovered, keeping them alive until their funds were exhausted. The hunters then killed the Jews to conceal their own venality. It is estimated that at least 1,000 Jews were killed in southern France in the weeks prior to the liberation. An unknown number of German and foreign Jews who had been living under assumed identities or were concealed in remote locations simply disappeared. For weeks after the liberation bodies of unknown persons, thought to be Jews, turned up in woods, streams and roadside ditches. The Germans and their local auxiliaries also perpetrated several massacres. At Bourges, in central France, Sipo-SD men and Miliciennes murdered thirty-six Jews and tossed their bodies into a well. Seventy-three Jewish forced labourers who had been taken from Montluc prison in Lyons to repair an airfield at nearby Bron were gunned down on 17 August. When the retreating Germans finally emptied Montluc they shot dozens of Jews amongst several hundred resistance fighters.[60]

Between 20 January and 17 August 1944, seventeen transports from Drancy conveyed 14,833 Jews to Birkenau. This was just 2,200 fewer than the Germans had managed to deport during the whole of 1943, although nowhere near as intensive as the last six months of 1942. Regardless of Knochen's exhortations to round up all Jews regardless of their nationality, 30,000 French Jews wearing the yellow star continued to live openly in Paris. Many times that number, however, opted to evade the Germans with or without the aid of others. In the end, the Nazi diehards did not have the resources, manpower or time to come anywhere near to finishing their task in France. With Allied spearheads approaching Paris, Alois Brunner handed control of the camp to the Swedish consul general and boarded the last train out, taking with him fifty-one 'special' prisoners. He left behind 1,518 survivors.[61]

In the Netherlands, Rauter and aus der Fünten persisted with deportations even though they were scraping the barrel of eligible categories. From January until early September 1944, eight transports departed from Westerbork and Vught with 5,500 Jews. Smaller train-loads carried privileged individuals to Belsen, although this was often no more than a way-station to the gas chambers. The fact that Vught lasted this long was a mark of the continuing tug-of-war between the WVHA economists who wanted to utilize Jewish labour and the RSHA purists who wanted to kill every last Jew. In February 1944, Himmler visited Vught to see the facility for himself. David Koker caught sight of him during the inspection tour: 'A slight, insignificant-looking little man, with a rather good-humoured face . . .' The Reichsführer-SS seemed nervy, unfocused and erratic. Koker thought that all the Germans now looked worn down by ceaseless air-raids and talk of the impending invasion. Several weeks later a new commanding officer arrived: his mission was to shut the place down. Koker was amongst 285 Jews transferred to Westerbork. An intervention by the Philips company resulted in ninety of their workers, including David, his father and brother, returning to Vught. However, four days before the Allied landings in Normandy, Philips wound down its workshops at the camp. The three Kokers were put on a train to Birkenau, although they were tagged as valued workers by the WVHA. After seven weeks they were reassigned to a Telefunken factory at Langenbielau, near Reichenbach, producing radio transmitters. The camp serving the plant was a satellite of Gross-Rosen and conditions were harsh. David's father perished in early February 1945. Both brothers fell ill and narrowly avoided going to a 'croaking camp', one of the bleak sites used by the SS to dump sick and exhausted slave labourers. Instead, David was loaded onto a transport for Dachau that arrived on 28 February after a disastrously prolonged journey. When the wagons were opened, 80 per cent of the men on board were dead. David Koker was one of them.[62]

By the time that Koker rotated through Westerbork the camp was a shadow of its former self. So few Jews were arriving from Amsterdam that in late November 1943 the Germans actually cancelled a deportation train. By mid-February 1944 there were only 4,700 prisoners left, mostly on protected lists. Heinz Hesdörffer continued to lead a charmed life and was placed on a transport to Theresienstadt at the end of that month. Philip Mechanicus wandered past the deserted huts observing Allied planes flying overhead, musing when the war would end and whether it would end in time to save him. In early March 1944 along with other high-status prisoners he was transferred to Belsen, where he lingered for seven months. On 9 October 1944 he was moved to Birkenau with 120 'special' prisoners and shot three days later. Gertude van Tijn was luckier: her fate exemplifies the wild inconsistency of German anti-Jewish policy at an individual level. She was conveyed to Belsen on 15 March 1944 with 209 privileged Jews and spent six weeks in the quarantine section of the exchange camp. Towards the end of May the Germans began to process Jews for the exchange programme. In late June 1944 she finally departed along with 99 other Dutch Jews, 77 Jews of German origin, and 4 with Palestinian papers. During a stopover in

Vienna (where they were lodged at the same hostel in which the young Hitler had once lived), they were joined by 61 Jews from Vittel. Then they travelled by train via Budapest and Belgrade to Istanbul. There they boarded a ship for Haifa, where they arrived on 10 July 1944. The British authorities immediately placed them in a detention camp for illegal immigrants at Athlit. It had wooden barracks, barbed wire, watchtowers and armed guards, but that was where the similarity to Bergen-Belsen ended.[63]

Theresienstadt had experienced another period of relative quiet following the big deportations that led to the formation of the family camp in Birkenau. Then, in mid-May 1944, three large transports took another 7,500 people to refresh its population. Amongst them was Heinz Hesdörffer. When the family camp was finally liquidated he was one of those selected for labour and dispatched to the Schwarzheide concentration camp that supplied labour to a synthetic petrol plant. Three months elapsed before there were two more transports, each of 2,000 people. October 1944 was horrendous: over a period of nine days 14,400 Jews passed through the sluice and onto the trains. Helga Weiss and her mother volunteered to go. Otto Weiss had run out of options a few days earlier and departed along with Helga's boyfriend, Ota. 'We're following our men,' Helga told herself. After arriving in Birkenau they realized they had made a terrible mistake. Fortunately, they were selected for labour on the ramp and assigned to an aircraft factory in Freiberg after just one week. Helga left Birkenau sicker and weaker, scarred by the humiliating memory of being shaved and showered naked under the eyes of the SS, 'snotty-nosed boys, who must have been having great fun'. But they were alive: the majority of deportees from Theresienstadt went straight to the gas chambers. Indeed, it is difficult to detect any rationale for this last murderous spasm, since at the same time Jews in other places were being conserved for the labour force or traded with the Allies. The pattern of destruction may be explained by the fluctuating role that Theresienstadt played in German efforts to deceive the world about what was going on there and at Auschwitz. At this point the story of Theresienstadt intersects with the activity of the International Committee of the Red Cross on behalf of groups persecuted by the Germans.[64]

In October 1943, Werner Best had assured the Danish authorities that its Red Cross officials would be permitted to visit Theresienstadt to check on the conditions under which the 400 Jews deported there from

Denmark were being held. When the Danish Red Cross formally requested an inspection visit, the German Foreign Office and RSHA consented. This was the first time that any Red Cross officials were allowed into a ghetto or concentration camp. The German Red Cross, an autonomous national organization, showed little interest in such interventions. This was hardly surprising since its president was the senior medical officer of the SS. From 1940 onwards, the German government flatly rejected suggestions by the International Committee of the Red Cross in Geneva to send delegates into the concentration camps. Nor had it responded helpfully to requests for information about the destination and fate of Jewish deportees from various European countries. Then again, the ICRC had not exactly pressed the Germans. Its leadership was anxious not to jeopardize the organization's sacrosanct role of providing succour for prisoners of war by irritating Berlin. They were also ambivalent about intervening on behalf of people who were detained for political or 'racial' reasons. Even though ICRC officials received a great deal of information about the mass killing of Jews in Poland during 1942, they treated it with caution and scepticism. Unless they were absolutely certain of the facts they were unwilling to make a public statement on the matter that might provoke a German backlash; but they could not independently verify such reports as long as the Germans barred ICRC delegates from ghettos and camps. Hence, the world's pre-eminent humanitarian organization remained silent throughout the height of the slaughter. Even when the opportunity arose to visit Theresienstadt it was poorly handled.[65]

On 23 June 1944, Dr Maurice Rossel, a Swiss national who was part of the ICRC delegation in Berlin, and two members of the Danish Red Cross were escorted through Theresienstadt by Eberhard von Thadden, head of the Jewish desk at the German Foreign Office, and Karl Rahm, the commandant. They saw the results of the 'beautification' exercise that had been under way intermittently over the previous year: brightly painted buildings, well-stocked shops, a playing field where young boys kicked a football, a school choir, a bandstand in a town square, and benches where old people basked in the sun. Helga Weiss recalled that selected children were lined up to greet 'Uncle Rahm' and to complain that they had to eat 'sardines again'. Philipp Manes was rightly doubtful about the purpose of the Verschönerung and wondered, 'Is the town beautification being done for us . . . ?' But at least the food improved for a couple of days. The deputation had a brief interview with Paul

Eppstein, the Elder of the ghetto, but never asked him about the deportations or where previous inhabitants had gone. In fact, the previous month, 7,500 had been removed to mitigate the impression of overcrowding. Rossel's report gave the ghetto a clean bill of health and accepted the German lie that it was an 'Endlager', a final destination. Needless to say, the head office of the SS and Eichmann's bureau were highly satisfied with the outcome of the pantomime.[66]

As soon as the Red Cross visit was safely out of the way, Rahm began to reduce the ghetto. Eppstein was arrested and shot; he was replaced by Benjamin Murmelstein, who was reliably obsequious. Possibly suspecting plans for an uprising, Rahm ordered the transfer of 5,000 able-bodied men, ostensibly for work in the Reich. When Helga's father received his deportation slip and was unable any longer to evade transportation, she volunteered to accompany him. Manes thought, 'It was admirable, the way all the offices on these days worked on just a few hours of sleep. Everything was done to make the evacuation journey easy. Also, the German authorities were perfectly humane and acted only as facilitators.' This combination of ignorance and naiveté helps to explain why there was no resistance. Manes and his wife were put aboard the last transport that left for Birkenau on 28 October 1944. They were murdered seventy-two hours before the gas chambers ceased operating.[67]

Liquidating the last ghettos

While the Jews of Hungary were disappearing into the maw of Birkenau and Jews were being hunted all over western Europe, developments on the Eastern Front in the summer of 1944 heralded the death knell of the last surviving Jewish populations. The crushing success of the Soviet summer offensive against Army Group Centre left the southern flank of Army Group North dangling in thin air. Military logic suggested that the units shielding the Baltic should be withdrawn and concentrated to defend the borders of the Reich, but Hitler refused to contemplate any withdrawal. In August the vanguard of the Red Army reached the Baltic and briefly cut off the northern German armies. Now Hitler belatedly conceded the necessity of evacuating Estonia, although he stubbornly refused to pull German forces out of Latvia.

This Soviet advance precipitated the evacuation and liquidation of the remaining ghettos and camps in the Ostland.[68]

In July 1944 there were some 31,000–34,000 Jews in the Klooga and Lagedi (Estonia), Riga-Kaiserwald (Latvia), and Vilnius, Kaunus, Shauli (Lithuania) labour camps. These Jews were regarded as a valuable labour resource and arrangements were made for their transfer. Despite several horrible massacres, 20,000–23,000 were successfully relocated. The evacuation commenced in Estonia, when about half of the 8,000–9,000 slave labourers were shipped to Stutthof concentration camp, situated about twenty miles east of Danzig. This camp had been established in early September 1939 and had attracted a number of armaments works: it was to become the main reception centre for Jews from the Baltic region and initially functioned well in this respect. However, 2,500 Jews who were still in Klooga when the Red Army was a short distance away were shot to death, as were 500 in Lagedi on the Estonian coast. About 2,000 Jews were moved westward from the camp in Vilnius, where Jewish mechanics had been servicing and repairing German army vehicles. Three-quarters of the Jews in the Kaunus camp made the journey to the west by a variety of transport, some by ship and some by rail. Around 1,500 preferred to hide; they were all eventually discovered and executed. In early August, at the time of the first Soviet thrust, part of the Kaiserwald workforce was evacuated by ship to Stutthof, to be followed by the rest in late September when the Soviets resumed their push. These relatively well-managed departures, resulting in a relatively small proportion of deaths, stand in stark contrast to the chaotic and murderous evacuation that occurred just a few months later.[69]

Since the summer of 1944, Joseph Katz had been working for a German army motorized communications unit based in Riga. He observed the influx of Hungarian Jews but also noted the outflow of German settlers and installations being dismantled. Despite rumours that they were about to be cut off by the Red Army and repeated selections he somehow maintained his jocular, positive approach to daily existence. Indeed, things got better. He acquired a Hungarian girlfriend and they ate well since the Germans were now abandoning stockpiles of food. In September he was issued with fresh clothes and taken to Riga harbour for evacuation. He could hardly believe what was taking place: 'The sight is absolutely incredible. Jews whose lives weren't worth a damn are now being transported back to Germany.' Around the Jewish New Year they were disembarked at Danzig and taken on barges to

Stutthof. After being deported from Germany three years previously, he was back almost where he started.[70]

Amongst the Jews who did not leave were the chain gangs working under the SS officer Paul Blobel, who had been charged by Himmler with destroying the evidence of the mass shootings in 1941–2. From July 1943 onwards, Blobel's Einsatzkommando 1005 criss-crossed the killing sites of eastern Europe engaged in the appalling task of exhuming decomposed corpses and burning them. In September 1943 a unit of Einsatzkommando 1005 commenced this grisly work at the Ninth Fort outside Kaunus, where 45,000 Jews had been murdered. The closely guarded team of sixty-four Jewish labourers were stabled in the basement of the fort. As the weeks passed, they gelled as a group and began to consider escape. In October they were joined by a captured Soviet officer who was Jewish. He reorganized the resistance and initiated a bold plan to break out. On Christmas Day 1943, the Jews made their bid. The scheme worked perfectly and they all got clean away. Over the next few days, though, the security police tracked down many of the fugitives. Those who made their way into the Kaunus ghetto-labour camp fared best. Several of them later departed for the forests and fought as partisans. The unit of Einsatzkommando 1005 operating around Riga from January to September 1944 was not so fortunate. The men suffered terribly from malnutrition and disease, and the SS guards conducted repeated selections, killing those deemed unfit for the work. When the Red Army was about ten miles away the SS terminated the effort. For the sake of convenience, the 400–500 men were forced to climb onto the pyres and machine-gunned to death. The fires were then lit and the SS departed. Soon afterwards the Germans left the region for good.[71]

At the start of 1944, there were nearly 80,000 Jews in the Lodz ghetto. It had lasted so long thanks to the incoherence of Nazi anti-Jewish policy and the dysfunctional nature of the regime. The prolongation of the war, too, had played a part in its longevity. But its future was constantly under review and its immiserated inhabitants knew that their survival depended on the outcome of a struggle between German policy makers, on the one hand, and between the German and Allied armies, on the other. In February 1944, Arthur Greiser and Hans Biebow had concluded an agreement with Himmler and Pohl that the ghetto would be slowly wound down. It would remain the 'Gau-Ghetto' of the Wartheland, under Greiser's control, but Biebow would eliminate the non-working population. Ultimately, Greiser would get the real estate and the WVHA would receive the moveable property, which included the Jews.[72]

News that the Germans required the removal of 1,500 male workers, allegedly to alleviate the shortage of labour in Germany, caused panic. The chronicle recorded that 'Not even the dreadful famine in the ghetto mitigates the horror of resettlement for labour outside the ghetto. Although many people tell themselves that there is hope of better nourishment at a work site somewhere in the Reich, no one wishes to be separated from his family at this critical time in the war.' Only a fraction reported voluntarily; hundreds went into prepared hiding places. Rumkowski, who was told that if he did not supply the men the Germans would take them, duly sent in the Order Service and resorted to starvation tactics. Any man refusing to appear for transportation lost his ration card. In response, families reduced their already paltry food consumption in order to supply a pitiful amount to fathers, sons and brothers who were being concealed. For days the hunt went on. Without any pretence of neutrality the ghetto chroniclers commented that 'Even with the help of the other uniformed services, such as the Economic Police, and the Fire Department, it is hardly likely that the Order Service will succeed in searching the ghetto thoroughly and combing through all the hiding places in this squalid city in one day. Then, too, the police themselves are tired, and inhibited by their personal relationships with many of the hunted men, and finally, so corrupt that one can only be sceptical about the outcome.' All the same it was a one-sided contest: in March, 1,710 men left the ghetto. To the ghetto's delight word soon arrived that they really had been redeployed for labour and were well. Whether this was part of a deception plan is unclear, but it helped to reduce the resistance to the much larger out-settlements that followed in June and July 1944.[73]

Under the agreement with Himmler and Pohl to reduce the Jewish population to a minimum, Hans Bothmann and his Sonderkommando were recalled to resuscitate the killing centre at Chelmno. Speer made a last-ditch effort to preserve the workforce, but Greiser performed an abrupt U-turn and denounced his intervention to Himmler. In the middle of the month Otto Bradfisch, the chief of police for Lodz, served notice on Rumkowski that he had to deliver 500 men per week, soon to be increased to 3,000, to clear rubble in Germany. Rumkowski put out a call for volunteers and offered the incentive of immediate rations, but the chronicle reported widespread doubts about the sincerity of the summons. Confidence was further eroded when Biebow lost his temper with the Elder of the ghetto during a visit to his office and started punching him. Regardless, factory managers began drawing up lists of who could be released for deportation. Since the workshops operated on what the chronicle called a 'mishpoke' (Yiddish for family) basis, 'the managers will naturally sacrifice workers in whom they have no personal interest'. Consequently, the surviving German and Czech Jews were the first to go. The Reich Jews actually welcomed what they naively believed would be a ticket home: 'they still regard the ghetto milieu as a greater evil than collective-camp life on German soil'. Some hoped that with the end of the war approaching there would be more opportunities to escape and go underground if they were back in Germany. By contrast, Czech Jews besieged Oskar Singer, one of the few from Prague who was on the Beirat, seeking exemptions. Singer did his best to save as many of the Czech Jewish intellectuals as possible, including Josef Zelkowitz. Most western Jews lacked such connections and resorted to 'traditional tactics: by night they go into hiding at the apartments of others, hoping thereby to elude the Order Service . . .' The first transport left Radogoszcz on 23 June. When people noticed that the same wagons returned the next day, the truth became inescapable. The doomed resorted to ever more extreme measures. 'Shady deals that involve human lives are negotiated behind the scenes among the workshop managers . . . people are willing to sell themselves.' As the number of suicides rocketed, the Order Service staged night raids to make up numbers for the transports. Oskar Rosenfeld was revolted by the spectacle. 'A shameful, shocking street scene. Jews hunting other Jews like game. A real Jew-hunt, organised by Jews. But what is to be done; there is no choice.' Detachments of Order Service men would wait until workers assembled for their midday soup then throw a cordon around a street and grab whoever they could. 'We have learned something from our guards, after all. How to hunt human beings,' Rosenfeld quoted from 'a ghetto philosopher'. On 15 July, after twelve transports had removed 7,196 men to Chelmno, the deportation paused.[74]

The ghetto population had been reduced to 68,561 and for a few weeks it looked as if the familiar pattern would repeat itself. Orders flowed into the factories and work was resumed. According to the chronicle, 'The mood of the ghetto is rosy. Everyone is hopeful of a speedy end to the war.' Tragically, the very proximity of the Red Army, now just seventy miles away, triggered the final liquidation. And, paradoxically, the sights and sounds of impending German defeat acted like a narcotic on the ghetto. Each day planes adorned with the red star swarmed overhead. The Jews could see wounded German soldiers and Volksdeutch refugees streaming westward. They heard that the deportations from Hungary had been halted. Postcards arrived from former Lodz residents now working in munitions plants. Those who advocated caution and suggested it was time to prepare resistance were a tiny, ineffectual minority. The end of the war seemed so close, although few held their breath. In the last entry in his private journal, dated 28 July 1944, Oskar Rosenfeld wrote 'After so much suffering and terror, after so many disappointments, it is hardly surprising that they are not willing to give themselves over to anticipatory rejoicing. The heart is marred with scars, the brain encrusted with dashed hopes. And if, at long last, the day of "redemption" should be at the doorstep, it is better to let oneself be surprised than to experience yet another disappointment. That's human nature, this is the human mentality of Ghetto Litzmannstadt at the end of July 1944.'[75]

The final wave of deportations was ushered in by Rumkowski with an announcement on 2 August that 5,000 had to report daily for relocation. Biebow, Bradfisch and Rumkowski appealed to the workers, factory by factory, to comply voluntarily. When there was barely any response the German police started sealing off blocks of the ghetto, emptying them of Jews and readjusting the boundary. It took a month to decant the ghetto into the waiting box-cars, block by block. Biebow took an active part in these brutal clearances, killing and raping as he went. On 30 August 1944, Rumkowski and his family were placed aboard the last transport. Oskar Rosenfeld, Jozef Zelkowitz, and the others who chronicled his reign all perished in the gas chambers. Out of the 67,000 deported to Birkenau about 20,000 were allocated to labour camps in Germany. The rest were murdered. Two groups of 500 Jews were retained in Lodz to clear up; they included several factory managers who had been able to save themselves and their families. When they combed through deserted apartments, removing anything that could be recycled, the clean-up crews often came across the shrivelled bodies of men and women who had starved to death while in hiding.[76]

In a weird twist of fate, the Jewish workforce that had been assembled at Chelmno outlasted the ghetto whose destruction they were working on. One team of about forty men was employed sorting the belongings of the 7,000 people who were murdered there. Another group worked in the forest where the bodies were deposited, removing evidence of the killings. The forest workers were all shot in October, but the SS men became attached to the services provided by the sorting crew, which included tailors and shoe-makers. Nevertheless, it was clear to these men that their days were numbered and they planned a revolt. On 17 January 1945 the Germans got news that the Red Army had broken through to the east, and began to shoot the workforce in batches of five. Partway through the massacre one of the Jews succeeded in killing an SS man and grabbed his weapon. In the ensuing shootout, two managed to escape and survive the subsequent manhunt.[77]

False dawn: the war and the killing go on

The Germans were able to pursue a murderous Judenpolitik into the autumn of 1944 because the Allies failed to end either the war or the slaughter of the Jews. Crucially for the course of the war and, therefore, Jewish survival chances, Hitler grimly soldiered on while in neither the east nor the west were the Allies able to convert their enormous victories of the summer months into a knock-out blow. If German military failure had doomed the Jews in the first half of the war, they now suffered the consequences of Allied military failure.

The Nazi regime stayed in power despite successive hammer blows in the latter part of 1944 largely because Hitler's will and energy continued to pulse through the Nazi Party machine and into the battered, but still functioning arteries of government. Indeed, Hitler's popularity and that of the NSDAP enjoyed a resurgence, thanks to the failed coup mounted by disillusioned senior army officers on 20 July 1944. The conspiracy loosely conjoined a circle of civilian opponents long since committed to ending Hitler's rule, preferably by non-violent means, and high-ranking officers in German military intelligence, the reserve army, and certain field commands who for at least a year had been trying to kill him. While the civilian plotters, who included Ulrich von Hassell, inscribed the persecution of the Jews on their charge sheet against the regime, the soldiers were less concerned on that score. The officers were aware of the fate of Europe's Jews, not least because several of them had been in the thick of it on the Eastern Front. The criminality of the regime may have fed into their decision to assassinate the Führer, but it was not a significant factor. In their programme for a post-Nazi Germany, the conspirators did not include the full restoration of rights to German Jews. The sardonic diarist Reck-Malleczewen reflected on the aftermath of the bomb plot, 'Ah, now, gentlemen, this is a little late. You made this monster, and as long as things were going well you gave him whatever he wanted.'[78]

Instead of toppling Hitler, the bomb plot recharged Hitler's messianic belief that he alone could save the German people from defeat, Bolshevism, and the Jews. The conspiracy also confirmed his paranoid anti-Semitism that, in turn, fuelled the apparatus of persecution and murder. According to his secretary, Traudl Junge, after he recovered from the explosion at his headquarters Hitler proclaimed in a shaky voice, 'Those criminals who wanted to do away with me have no idea what would have happened to the German nation then. They don't know about the plans of our enemies who want to destroy Germany so that it can never rise again. If the Jews, with the hatred they feel, ever get power over us, then all will finally be over for Germany and European civilization.'[79]

The leader's warning that defeat would unleash an era of Jewish vengeance resonated with Germans on the home front and in uniform. In a letter to his mother in Magdeburg, Private K. Buthut, serving in the Baltic region, warned that the campaign was 'on a knife's edge'. 'You know of course that the Jew is going to take his blood revenge, mainly for the Party people. Unfortunately, I was also one who wore the Party uniform.' For safety's sake, Private Buthut asked his mother to burn the incriminating missive. The regime's apocalyptic jeremiads appeared to be vindicated when the Red Army briefly occupied the East Prussian village of Nemmersdorf in November 1944, raping, torturing and slaughtering those inhabitants who did not flee in time. Goebbels was able to use the horrific reports from Nemmersdorf to great effect in propaganda intended to fortify German resistance; but not everyone got the right message. The SD office in Stuttgart reported people saying that it was not a good idea to make a fuss about Soviet atrocities because 'any thinking individual who sees these murdered victims will immediately think of the atrocities that we committed in the enemy's territory, yes even in Germany. Didn't we slaughter the Jews by the thousand?' Nevertheless, the regime continued to pump out anti-Jewish propaganda as if this would make sense of the war and the quotidian misery of life. To Victor Klemperer this proved that 'the Jewish question represents the "essential core" and the quintessence of National Socialism'.[80]

Hitler's survival on 20 July would have meant nothing if the Allies had been able to pummel their way into the Reich before the end of the year. But that was not to be. From July to September 1944 the German armies reeled backwards on every front, yet the command-and-control system never broke down and ordinary soldiers demonstrated extraordinary resilience. As the Wehrmacht found itself backed up against the borders of the Reich, patriotism came into play, animating even those who had no special loyalty to Nazism. Moreover, Albert Speer was able to make up the massive losses of equipment thanks to the steps he had taken to boost production earlier in the year. The output of weapons and tanks peaked in the autumn before collapsing due to the shortage of fuel and raw materials and the disruption of transport by constant air bombardment.[81]

Conversely, the Allies let Germany off the hook. Once the British and Americans broke out of the Normandy bridgehead and began to speed across France they faced the question of where to direct their main axis of advance. In a bid to keep up the momentum, Montgomery persuaded Eisenhower to gamble on a lightning thrust from Belgium into the Netherlands using an 'airborne army' to seize bridges across the Meuse, Waal and Rhine rivers. Sadly, Operation Market Garden, launched on 17 September 1944, failed disastrously. The Wehrmacht won a last victory in the west and stalemate developed along the length of the 'West Wall', the defences running along Germany's border. Months would pass before the Allied advance was renewed, half a year before American and British troops crossed the Rhine.[82]

The Germans gained a breathing space in the east, too. By August 1944 the Red Army was nearing Warsaw and the line of the Vistula–Narva rivers, but it was outstripping its supply lines and running into stiffer opposition. The stabilization of the front had terrible consequences for Jews in hiding in Warsaw. On 2 August the Polish Home Army launched an uprising intended to gain control of the capital before the Red Army arrived. The revolt caught the Germans off guard but they recovered quickly and since Warsaw was a transport and supply hub, units were rushed in to choke off the rebellion. Although the Red Army was just a few miles away across the Vistula, it was too depleted to do more than mount a token relief effort. After eight weeks of appalling urban warfare the Home Army was forced to surrender. Hundreds of Jews, including Yitzhak Zuckerman and Samuel Willenberg, emerged from hiding to fight with the Poles. They included the inmates of a prison camp on Gesia Street who were freed by the insurgents in the first hours of the uprising and Jews who had successfully subsisted in bunkers and now surfaced only to find themselves under siege again. Several dozen were massacred by extremist elements of the Polish Home Army; many more perished in the chaos and mayhem of the fighting. The survivors were condemned to another three months of nerve-wracking evasion. In other parts of Poland the front line came to rest in areas where Jews were laid up in malinas or living on false papers. The sudden presence of German troops and frequent anti-partisan sweeps behind the lines meant that few surmounted this lethal coincidence.[83]

The chances of Jewish survival in Hungary were jeopardized by the protracted campaign to capture Budapest. Just when it seemed as if calm had been restored in the country, the SS intelligence service learned that Horthy was again in contact with the western allies, seeking a peace agreement. Although he was unable to obtain any assurance from the British or the Americans that they would support him if he broke with the Third Reich, on 15 October he announced on radio that Hungary was ending its alliance with Germany. Horthy anticipated that loyal units of the Hungarian army would hold the Germans at bay, but he miscalculated badly. While the army dithered the Germans took his son hostage and supported a counter-coup by Ferenc Szálasi, the leader of the rabidly anti-Semitic Arrow Cross movement. A few days later, Eichmann was back. He obtained agreement from Szálasi to secure 50,000 Jews for the construction of underground factories in the Reich. Since transport links were shattered, Eichmann planned to march the Jews by foot from Budapest to Vienna, a distance of more than 200 miles.[84]

Meanwhile, Szálasi's administration initiated the construction of a fenced-in ghetto around the great Dohnanyi Synagogue in district VII, the capital's Jewish quarter. With the arrival of Russian troops on the outskirts, between 20 and 26 October, Arrow Cross militia removed 35,000 Jewish men aged 16–60 and women aged 16–40 from the 'yellow-star houses', assembled them in labour battalions and sent them to the front, north and south of Budapest, to dig earthworks. In early November, the Szálasi regime ordered the mobilization of a further 25,000 Jews for labour in Germany. Police and militia scoured the Jewish residential blocks and sent anyone able-bodied to assembly centres in the Obuda brickyards in the suburbs. On 13 November, 27,000 Jews commenced the trek to the Reich on foot, guarded by Hungarian gendarmes. There was almost no provision to feed or house the marching columns, nor had accommodation been arranged. The many elderly people suffered terribly and soon started to fall by the wayside; impatient guards shot dozens every day. When the Jews reached their destinations they were in hardly any condition to work. These forced marches brought Eichmann into direct conflict with the international rescue effort, notably Raoul Wallenberg who repeatedly rescued Jews from the columns. Eichmann finally left Budapest hours before the Red Army completed its encirclement of the city on 26 December 1944. Even though he was gone, the misery of the Jews would drag on for another six ghastly weeks, during which thousands were slaughtered by Arrow Cross men.[85]

The Budapest ghetto measured 0.3 square kilometres. There was no space to bury the dead, so 3,000 corpses piled up alongside garbage and homeless refugees. A ghetto council created by the Arrow Cross regime struggled to maintain order and food supplies, but the Jews had to subsist on half of what was required to sustain life. With the Red Army encircling the capital, Arrow Cross militiamen directed their rage against the Jews, launching murderous excursions into the ghetto and Jew-houses. Groups of Jewish men were taken down to the Danube, where they were bound together and several shot so that they all toppled into the icy river. Those still alive were dragged under by the weight of the dead. It is estimated that 17,000 Jews perished in the besieged city, including several members of the Jewish council. One of the last casualties was Otto Komoly, who was dragged out of the Ritz Hotel to the Arrow Cross headquarters and murdered. On 17–18 January 1945 soldiers of the Red Army broke through the defences of Budapest and liberated Pest, the area where the ghetto was located and where most of the surviving Jews were domiciled. The Russians found about 70,000 in the ghetto and 50,000 either in hiding or living under foreign protection.[86]

For the last major deportation campaign of the war, the Germans returned to where they had begun three years earlier: Slovakia. After the cessation of the deportations in October 1942 around 20,000 Jews remained in the puppet state. The exact numbers are hard to determine since thousands fled to Hungary in 1942, but returned when that country fell victim to German rapaciousness. Most of those who survived the first onslaught in situ were protected by the authorities; they were deemed economically useful, were converts or were just well connected. During 1943 the German Foreign Office made repeated overtures to the Slovak government to permit deportations to resume, but Father Tiso's regime was more interested in finding out what had happened to those previously taken away. It had dark suspicions. For their part, the Jewish community obtained accurate information about Auschwitz-Birkenau when two escapees arrived in their midst in April 1944. The stability of the situation in Slovakia at this time enabled the Working Group to transmit the information to the west, making a vital if belated contribution to knowledge about the killing process. However, in August partisan forces triggered a long-planned national uprising that plunged eastern Slovakia into chaos and provoked a savage assault on the Jewish population which was blamed for the unrest. In fact, of course, Jews had nothing to do with the rebellion. It was hatched by dissidents within the Slovak regime who were in contact with the Czechoslovak exile government in London; the objective was to seize the passes over the Carpathian mountains in order to assist the advance of the Red Army. Unfortunately, the revolt went off at half cock and the Soviet spearheads failed to take the passes. Instead, the Germans were able to scrape together enough formations, mainly Waffen-SS units, to contain and crush the insurgents.[87]

Slovakia's Jews paid a heavy price for these operational blunders. Himmler put Gottlob Berger, chief of staff of the Waffen-SS and one of his closest aides, in charge of counter-measures. Berger assembled a force of 40,000 men to retake the liberated areas. He was succeeded by Hermann Höffle, a Waffen-SS general who brought with him an Einsatzgruppe devoted to hunting Jews. Once the rebellion was suppressed, Sipo-SD units assisted by the Hlinka Guard and Slovak militia initiated round-ups in every town and village with a Jewish population. Alois Brunner was posted to Bratislava, the Slovak capital, where he arrested the Judenzentrale (Jewish council) and seized files with lists of community members. The security police, assisted by Slovak SS and Hlinka guardsmen, then staged a succession of night raids on the homes of Jews. At the end of September, 1,800 were transported from the capital to the camp at Sered to join 5,000 already interned by the Slovak regime. Brunner routinely employed torture to force Jews into divulging the whereabouts of those in hiding. Amongst his victims was Gisi Fleischmann. She was eventually transferred to Birkenau, where she died on 17 October 1944. Eleven transports left Slovakia, mainly from Sered, between September 1944 and March 1945. About 8,000 Jews were deported to Auschwitz, 2,700 to Sachsenhausen and 1,600 to Theresianstadt. Thanks to the lateness of this Aktion, a large number of them survived the war. But thousands of Slovak Jews were killed in anti-partisan operations and Jew-hunts until the Red Army finally reached Bratislava in early April 1945.[88]

The Sonderkommando uprising in Birkenau

The continuing international silence about Auschwitz-Birkenau and the constant flow of transports from Hungary, then Lodz, Theresienstadt, and finally Slovakia spurred Jewish prisoners in the Sonderkommandos to consider an uprising to sabotage the killing facilities. Other Jewish inmates plotted to escape with the aim of getting information to the Allies and, hopefully, triggering some kind of action to disrupt the camp's homicidal routine.

The first successful escape with this end in mind was made by Alfred Wetzler and Rudolf Vrba, two Slovak Jews who had arrived in Birkenau in spring 1942. On 7 April 1944 they entered the partly built extension of Birkenau known as 'Mexico' and concealed themselves under a pile of timber. Their carefully thought-out plan was to remain in the hideout for three days until the Germans lifted the blockade around the camp that customarily trapped escapees. When the hue and cry died down, they made their move. Wetzler took with him the label from a can of Zyklon-B obtained at great risk by Filip Müller. Vrba, who had worked in the Canada compound for over a year and then in the registry office of the quarantine camp, carried in his head an astonishingly accurate summary of arrivals and the number of those murdered. After a walk lasting eleven days the pair reached Slovakia and made contact with the Jewish community, passing on all they knew and urging the Slovak Jewish leadership to inform the world.[89]

Since the Vrba–Wetzler report contained a warning about the impending fate of the Czech family camp, Rabbi Weissmandel and Gisi Fleischmann of the Working Group first sent summaries to the Czech legation in Switzerland. From there it was transmitted in mid-June to the British Foreign Office and the War Refugee Board. The Working Group also gave a copy to Rudolf Kasztner although, controversially, he did not publicize the contents to Hungarian Jews. The information came into his hands in the midst of the negotiations with Eichmann that he hoped would abort the deportations from Hungary, and he seems to have pre-ferred to sit on the explosive document. However, another member of the Relief and Rescue Committee, Miklos Krausz, sent a copy to a colleague in the Romanian Embassy who, in turn, forwarded it to George Mantello, a businessman who represented Romanian interests in Switzerland. Mantello instigated a press campaign that meant Birkenau was discussed in Swiss newspapers for several weeks. On 27 June, Churchill saw a copy that had been sent to Chaim Weizmann in London by Richard Lichtheim, the Jewish Agency delegate in Switzerland. He passed it on to Anthony Eden with a handwritten minute saying, 'What can be done? What can be said?' By this time the BBC home and foreign services were already giving more than usual coverage to the destruction of Jewish communities, with the focus on the deportations from Hun-gary. The Foreign Office was no longer able to manage the story.[90]

As a result of the information pouring in about the Hungarian deportations and the fine-grained report by Vrba and Wetzler (which was confirmed a few days later by another pair of escapees who reached Slovakia, Arnost Rosin and Czesław Mordowicz), Auschwitz jumped to the top of the agenda of organizations trying to save Jews from destruc-tion. In mid-May, the British military attaché in Bern, Switzerland, received a plea composed by Rabbi Weissmandel for the Allied air forces to bomb the railways leading to the camp. Quite independently his idea was echoed by Yitzhak Gruenbaum, the chairman of the rescue commit-tee of the Jewish Agency executive in Jerusalem. Jaromir Kopecky, at the Czech legation in Switzerland, also urged the Czechoslovak govern-ment-in-exile to put to the British government the case for bombing the camp. Richard Lichtheim transmitted a similar entreaty to London. Roswell McClelland, the WRB's man in Switzerland, cabled the same suggestion to John Pehle in Washington, who passed it on to John J. McCloy, assistant secretary of state at the War Department, at the end of June. Chaim Weizmann and Moshe Shertok first put the idea to the Foreign Office on 30 June and presented a memorandum to Eden a week later setting out proposals to mitigate the disaster in Hungary. The memorandum was drafted by Arthur Koestler and Michael Foot who, at Weizmann's invitation, had joined an informal group that met in response to the crisis. The proposed actions included issuing a warning of retribution to the Hungarians, interdicting the rail lines, and bombing the gas chambers. These Jewish appeals arrived at the height of the strug-gle in Normandy and it is noteworthy that they gained any traction at all with political leaders who were embroiled in the management of the entire war effort at a decisive, nerve-wracking moment. But neither the RAF nor the USAAF was willing to divert assets for such a mission and the politicians on both sides of the Atlantic were unwilling to press them overly much to do so.[91]

Churchill initially put his weight behind the request to the Air Ministry to investigate the possibility of bombing Auschwitz. After Eden suggested placing Weizmann's request before the cabinet, the prime minister retorted that there was no need for such extensive consultation. In his note to Eden he added, 'Get anything out of the Air Force you can and invoke me if necessary.' Eden did so, but two weeks later received a negative reply from Sir Archibald Sinclair, the secretary of state for air. Sinclair said he was 'informed' that interrupting the railways was 'out of our power'. Interdiction missions in Normandy had required 'an enormous concentration of bombers'. Hitting the gas chamber installations was 'out of the bounds of possibility for Bomber Command'. It was too far for a night attack and too hazardous and costly by daylight. Furthermore, such a raid might cause casualties to the inmates. Sinclair held out the possibility that the Americans might see things differently, but John J. McCloy had already negatived a request from the WRB on the grounds that it would involve 'the diversion of considerable air support' necessary to 'decisive operations'. Hence, both RAF and USAAF senior commanders accepted that bombing Auschwitz was technically feasible, but dissented on the grounds of its costliness, both in terms of possible casualties and the withdrawal of assets from a strictly combat role. They also doubted the effectiveness of such a mission. Had saving Jews been placed on a par with the war effort, there would not have been any basis for such objections. The US Fifteenth Air Force did bomb the I. G. Farben synthetic rubber plant at Auschwitz-Monowitz, just eleven miles away from Birkenau, in August 1944. The same month the RAF flew nineteen missions from bases in southern Italy to drop supplies to the Home Army in Warsaw. In the view of Richard Overy, historian of the air war, 'There is no doubt that had it been a priority target for the Allies, it certainly could have been bombed.' However, only military objectives were ever prioritized and there was a struggle between branches of the armed forces about what even these should be. The most senior ground commanders in France, such as Montgomery, had to argue tenaciously to persuade British Bomber Command to deploy its resources in support of the ground war.

Overy concludes that 'Appeals to help with civilian victims, whether refugees or those slated for genocide, were regarded as outside the remit of Allied military forces, whatever the moral force of the argument.'[92]

In the absence of any hint that outside intervention would be forth-coming, the men in the Sonderkommando went ahead with plans to sabotage the killing machine themselves. They believed their best chance of success lay in cooperation with the wider underground in the camp, making an attack on the gas chambers one facet of a general uprising. But the underground prevaricated. The non-Jewish prisoners knew that the Red Army was taking great strides westwards and wanted to delay such a risky undertaking until the Russians were closer. They believed that a revolt would have more chance of success if the Germans were tied down at the front and disorganized by Red Army attacks on their lines of communication. There would also be more chance that prisoners who broke out could survive until the Soviets arrived. As a result, the rebellion was postponed and postponed again. By July the transports had diminished in volume and instead the Sonderkomman-dos faced a different dilemma. While they had not been able to halt the mass murder of the Hungarian Jews, they now faced extinction them-selves.[93]

In September the SS started thinning out the crematorium crews, shooting 200 men who had been deceived into volunteering for other duties. On 7 October 1944, after the SS demanded that another 300 report for transfer to Lublin, the men in Crematorium IV refused to cooperate. A guard detachment arrived to forcibly remove them, but 'they showed an enormous courage refusing to budge'. According to Salman Lewental, a member of the Sonderkommando whose account of the events was buried in a jar prior to the evacuation of Auschwitz, 'They set up a loud shout, hurled themselves upon the guards with hammers and axes, wounded some of them, the rest they beat with what they could get at, they pelted them with stones . . .' Within minutes heavily armed SS reinforcements arrived and started pouring machine-gun fire into the mob. Before they were wiped out, though, the prisoners set fire to the building and succeeded in putting it out of commission. The crematorium workers at units II and III saw the flames and realiz-ing that their comrades had launched a rebellion spontaneously joined in. 'They pounced upon the obercapo, a Reichsdeutsche, and in a flash threw him alive into the burning furnace.' Filip Müller takes up the story in his memoir: 'The three hand-grenades and the arms *organized* over many months were hastily taken from their hiding places. With insulated pliers they cut the barbed wire in several places whereupon a large crowd intent on escaping pushed through . . . Suddenly someone threw a hand-grenade at the SS. As it went off there was great confusion among the SS men, for it had taken them completely unawares. The prisoners took advantage of this moment of surprise to escape through the holes in the barbed wire.' Some 200 men got a few miles before the SS surrounded them in a barn and massacred them. Müller survived by hiding in a flue during the fighting. He re-emerged a few days later and slipped into the workforce that was still operating Crematorium V and clearing up the mess.[94]

The Sonderkommando rebellion did not halt the mass murders. Transports continued to arrive at Birkenau from Theresienstadt and Slovakia, and the sole operating gas chamber continued in use until the beginning of November 1944. Then, as a matter of policy, Himmler ordered the SS to cease killing Jews. He was now more interested in preserving Jewish prisoners in the camps and using their redemption as a pretext for opening channels of communication to the Western allies in the pursuit of an armistice. Instead, prisoners were now employed to demolish the burned-out hulk of Crematorium IV, while the equipment was stripped out of the underground facilities at Crematoria II and III for shipment to the Reich, where it was anticipated it might be used elsewhere. Without transports coming into the camp the black market dried up and the food supply deteriorated. Müller noticed that it was curiously quiet. One of the SS men took to keeping rabbits in Crematorium V.[95]

The influx of the Hungarians and the bulging transports from Lodz, Theresienstadt and Slovakia propelled Birkenau far ahead of the other extermination camps in terms of the absolute number of Jewish victims. Between January and April 1944, transports had slowed down to about 6,000 victims per month. But from mid-May until mid-July, Birkenau accounted for the death of at least 300,000 Hungarian Jews. Over the next three months the deportations from Lodz, Theresienstadt and Sered brought the total murdered in 1944 to approximately 600,000. By the close of its career as an extermination centre, lasting two years and eight months, about 900,000 Jews had been killed at Birkenau, roughly 28,000 people per month.[96]

The evacuation of the camps, forced marches and massacres

Jews continued to die in stupendous numbers in the constricted territory of the Third Reich throughout the last weeks of its existence, even though the gas chambers at Birkenau had stopped operating. Indeed, in this last period Jewish policy went into reverse. Jews who had once been mercilessly expelled from the Reich were now gathered into it. Himmler, who had harangued his subordinates to exterminate them, issued orders to his SS to keep them alive. Anti-Jewish violence that had been banished from the Reich was now in evidence all over the place. Acts of spontaneous brutality and malice that had been held in check or carefully channelled, once again exploded into the open. Judenpolitik had turned full circle, exemplifying the incoherence that marked its birth. Almost the only consistent thread in this last manic period was Hitler's steady, unremitting, murderous Jew-hatred.

Each twist in Jewish policy in these last, confusing months can be traced back to the war. Hitler's refusal to contemplate surrender or armistice negotiations not only condemned the Jews to longer in captivity, it was due to the Jews that he held on. In his last New Year message to the Volk he mocked Allied assertions that defeat was imminent and forswore a repetition of November 1918. 'That is how the Jewish-international conspiracy has lived on hopes from the first day,' he raged. Again he raised the spectre of a terrible fate if Germany was defeated. 'We are aware of what the Anglo-American statesmen plan to do with the German Reich, what measures the Bolshevik rulers and the international Jews, who in the end are behind them, plan to take against the German Volk.' It would mean the deportation of 15–20 million Germans, enslavement, and starvation. After evaluating Hitler's New Year address, Victor Klemperer concluded that 'Each day teaches one anew that for the Third Reich this war really is the *Jewish war*, that no one can experience it as acutely and tragically as the star-wearing Jew who is held prisoner in Germany . . .'[97]

However, Hitler was losing control of Jewish policy just as he was losing control of his shrinking domain. On 12 January 1945 the Red Army launched its assault into the Reich and bounded from the Vistula to the Oder river, fifty miles from Berlin, within three weeks. In the west, the British and Americans breached the 'West Wall' and hammered their way through the Rhineland to reach the great river barrier, the last defensive line. The Americans crossed the Rhine on 7 March, the British a fortnight later. Unable to compel his armies to stop the onrushing enemy, Hitler placed his hopes in a miracle. When President Roosevelt died on 12 April he believed that this would rend the grand coalition, but nothing of the sort happened. Vice President Harry Truman assumed the reins of office in the White House and the Allied armies continued to grind forwards relentlessly. Five days later, 325,000 men trapped in a pocket defending the Ruhr industrial region surrendered; the Western Front disintegrated. At almost the same moment, the Soviets mounted a vast encircling attack on Berlin, cutting the capital off from the rest of the Reich on 24 April.[98]

Allied advances triggered a second and third wave of evacuations from the concentration camps. The basis for these actions was the general directive that Himmler issued to his Higher SS Police Leaders in June 1944 regarding the emergency evacuation of camps threatened by the enemy. The intention was to ensure that prisoners, a precious resource for the war effort, did not fall into enemy hands and to neutralize the threat of a slave revolt. But Himmler offered no specific guidelines about where evacuated prisoners should go, how they should be transported, who would supply them with food or where they would be quartered en route. This lack of clarity was to have disastrous effects. Himmler's police representatives simply ordered camp commandants to transfer the men and women in their charge, leaving all the details to them. In the conditions that prevailed in early 1945 this was asking for trouble. Transport and communication links were constantly interrupted by bombing or incursions by enemy ground forces. Rolling stock was in short supply and often inappropriate for transporting people. Food was scarce and no one was interested in feeding the despised concentration camp population. When prisoners removed from one camp arrived at another, the administration and the kapos insisted on feeding and housing 'their' people first. Absolutely no one cared about Jews.[99]

Most importantly for explaining the chaotic and murderous character of these later evacuations, the nature and behaviour of the guards changed fundamentally. By the start of 1945 able-bodied young men in the SS-Totenkopf units had been combed out for frontline duty and replaced by men who were sick, injured or elderly. Many replacements were ethnic Germans. They were supplemented by soldiers unfit for combat and aged members of the Volkssturm, the home guard raised by Goebbels for the last-ditch defence of the Reich. These men were badly trained, ill-disciplined, and liable to panic. Party officials, garrison units, police and Hitler Youth also contributed to guarding prisoners, especially when they came to rest at a town or village overnight. None had any investment in the preservation of the prisoner population and felt their first loyalty was to protecting their communities. Any sign of trouble could provoke gunfire. If news came that Red Army units were in the vicinity, jumpy guards were prone to kill single prisoners they thought were slowing the march or simply gun them down en masse so that they could get away faster.[100]

As the columns of men and women were transported or marched into the Reich they entered a society that had been systematically indoctrinated in racism for a decade, militarized and, more recently, brutalized by devastating bombing raids. The sight of filthy, malodorous, lice-ridden, bedraggled concentration camp inmates jabbering in a host of foreign tongues aroused fear: fear of contamination by disease and fear that they might break free and rampage through the German population. Although Jews made up a fraction of the columns, it was common for Germans to regard them all as the Jewish enemy. Yet the Israeli historian Daniel Blatman provides compelling evidence that the massacres were not driven by anti-Semitism. 'Killing was now a nihilistic act, committed locally and devoid of a guiding hand. It was backed by a certain consensus, but the identity and singularity of the victims was vague and undefined, apart from their broad and relatively illusory identity as an inferior group that did not deserve to live.' The decentralized, disorganized killing in the last weeks of the war resembled the violence of the November 1938 pogrom in that it was not centrally mandated or directed. It was a spontaneous eruption of hate from a society that had been trained to solve social problems, and the alleged threat that outsiders posed, by the application of lethal force.[101]

While they were never intended as such, the evacuations and forced marches between January and April 1945 caused such horrendous casualties that they were quickly labelled 'death marches', which is how they have entered the historical record. Ironically, although he issued ambiguous and sometimes contradictory orders, this was the opposite of what Himmler intended. Jews were caught up in the maelstrom incidentally and throughout the period the head of the SS was recasting himself as their protector.[102]

At the last count of the camp population in January 1945 there were 714,000 prisoners. Roughly 30–40 per cent of them were Jews, most of whom had entered the system through Auschwitz-Birkenau since May 1944. Although Jews had spread throughout the camps and were scattered in small pockets all over Germany, large numbers were clustered in the installations that had been created late in the war to provide labour for the underground factory programme – chiefly Dora-Mittelbau and the network of labour camps stemming from Gross-Rosen.[103]

The first major evacuation was from Auschwitz, commencing on 18 January 1945. Transfers during the second half of 1944 had already reduced the combined population of the main camp, Birkenau and Monowitz to just over 67,000. Plans had been laid to dissolve the camp entirely in the context of a wider evacuation of installations and population in Upper Silesia, but this larger scheme fell into disarray. Confusion amongst the SS staff meant that the evacuation was eventually undertaken late in the day with few preparations. There was no arrangement for provisioning or transport. Prisoners like Filip Müller 'organized' blankets and food supplies for themselves. Columns marched out of Birkenau on a snowy morning and made their way first to the main camp and Auschwitz railway station. Some entrained there but others had to walk as far as Gliewice before it was possible for the SS to load them onto transports. Lucie Adelsberger was thrown into a panic by the order to depart. She believed that the SS would kill the ailing prisoners in the infirmary where she was working and spent the last hours comforting them. Her column left at night and stumbled through snow to the main camp, the prisoners weighed down by blankets, clothing and food they had scrounged for what they thought would be a short march to the station. Instead they found themselves continuing along the highway. Their initial response was joy at leaving Birkenau and relief that they were not being killed, but by dawn as they became wearier and colder they realized their predicament. Anyone who could not keep up the pace or collapsed was shot. They could see 'nothing but snowscape, punctuated here and there by a dead body or two. They lay on the side of the road . . . and on top of snow drifts, all with bleeding head-wounds: women and men . . . Our ranks began to thin out as well, and now and again we heard the snap of the dreaded pistol.'[104]

Müller's group slogged on foot through the snow to Loslau where they embarked on a train to Mauthausen. From there they were moved to Melk, a sub-camp, where he joined about 8,000 others hacking tunnels into the rock. After a few weeks he was transferred to Gusen, another Mauthausen sub-camp, to work as an electrician in an aircraft factory. Müller had no qualifications as an electrical engineer but he realized he had to get away from the hard labour at Melk or he would die. Fortunately, the factory at Gusen was at a standstill and he idled away the time until yet another evacuation carried him to a barn near Gunskirchen that served as a temporary dumping ground for prisoners. Dozens lay on the floor of the barn and scattered around, dying of starvation and disease. He saved himself by climbing into the rafters and eking out a few pieces of bread until the arrival of American troops.[105]

Adelsberger's column wandered on and on, covering thirty miles by a roundabout route to Loslau where they were loaded onto open freight cars and transported to the Ravensbrück women's concentration camp. Of 18,672 women who left Birkenau, only about 10,000 arrived. Their hardships were not over. In addition to the brutality of the guards the Jewish women were treated badly by the veterans of the camp. Adelberger remembered that 'the absolutely worst part of this existence was the food and the way it was distributed. The "imperial Germans" were the first in line, and they ate their fill at our expense. Then we got our soup, in the same unwashed bowls the typhus patients and other dissipated, filthy or infected prisoners had used . . .'[106]

Marco Nahon was transferred from Auschwitz to Stutthof, from there to Ohrdruf, and then to the infirmary at Klavinkel, a small subcamp in a forest. He worked in the medical block where conditions were good until it, too, was evacuated and he joined a three-day march to Buchenwald. There Russian prisoners stole the last of his carefully husbanded rations. After three weeks he was moved on to Dachau, arriving in a state of near collapse.[107]

By the start of 1945, the shipyard where Josef Katz was supposed to be working was almost at a standstill, but he was not allowed a respite. Despite being ill he was forced to trudge away from the advancing British and even his indomitable spirit began to crack. It was 'the second time we were fleeing from our liberators'. He asked himself, 'What do they want from me? Why don't they let me die?' Josef was jolted out of his apathy by the sight of men being casually murdered along the line of march. Eventually they arrived at a half-deserted labour camp at Rieben in East Pomerania. The prisoners there refused to share any rations with the new arrivals and although they were barely able to stand upright forced them to work for German army officers who wanted manpower to construct defences. One by one the last survivors of the German transports to Riga as well as native Latvian Jews perished. Of the 500 who arrived with him, only 400 were alive two weeks later. Katz himself was in the camp infirmary when the Russians arrived on 7 March.[108]

Heinz Hesdörffer was evacuated by bus from the Schwarzheide labour camp to Sachsenhausen on 19 April. He arrived to find 40,000 people squeezed into an area designed to hold a quarter of that number. There were few Jews. After two days' respite he was on the move again, this time amidst a chaotic rabble barely controlled by the SS. Fortunately, Red Cross packages had reached the camp and he was able to get hold of food for the journey. Not even the guards seemed to know where they were heading – just as long as it was away from the Russians. Each morning prisoners afflicted by dysentery who were too sick to get up were shot where they lay. The Russians finally overtook the column at Grabow; he had survived.[109]

As well as the callous execution of individual prisoners unable to continue walking or to march at the start of a new day, the Germans committed numerous large-scale massacres. These atrocities occurred in the vicinity of towns and villages and often involved civilians. They were not specifically directed against Jews, but Jews formed a significant proportion of the victims. One of the most horrific occurred near Palmnicken on the coast of Pomerania. The catastrophe began when several thousand Jewish prisoners were evacuated from Stutthof and its sub-camps around Königsberg on 26 January 1945. About 1,500 were shot during a thirty-mile trek through freezing weather from the assembly point to a factory at Palmnicken. While the prisoners were quartered there for the night, news arrived that Soviet units were approaching and threatened to cut the line of retreat to Danzig. The roads were full of refugees and panic was in the air. For three days the guards and local officials argued about what to do with the roughly 3,000 prisoners at the factory. On the last day of January, SS men, Volkssturm, Hitler Youth, Organisation Todt workers and Ukrainian auxiliaries removed prisoners from the building to the bluffs and dunes overlooking the sea and cut them down with gunfire in batches of fifty. Piles of semi-clad, emaciated corpses piled up along the shoreline. Those who fled into the freezing waters died quickly from bullets or more slowly from exposure. Most of the 3,000 were massacred.[110]

The evacuation of Dora-Mittelbau and its sub-camps proceeded from early April. Many of the Jews forced to tramp through the snow had reached there only a few weeks previously from Auschwitz and were already enfeebled. On 9 April, about 2,000 reached the outskirts of a small town called Gardelegen, where they were accommodated in some cavalry barracks. Three days later, when US troops were known to be approaching, local Nazi Party officials assembled home guard units, Hitler Youth, police, and personnel from local army garrisons to deal with the menace it was believed the prisoners posed to the community. Approximately 1,000 were herded into a barn that was carpeted with straw. The Germans poured petrol on the straw and set it alight; those attempting to get out were shot. German prisoners who had served as kapos were allowed to join the killers and took part in the massacre. There were few survivors.[111]

The final wave of evacuations in April–May was the most chaotic and destructive. Of the 28,000 prisoners evacuated from Buchenwald to Flossenbürg on 6 April, only 20,000 arrived two weeks later. After orders were issued to empty the sub-camp at Ohrdruf the local SD set about murdering 1,500 political prisoners considered 'dangerous'. The camp had burgeoned from 1,000 prisoners to over 13,000 by March 1945, and most of the new prisoners had reached it in a wretched state. Three thousand were shot by the time the columns from Ohrdruf got to Buchenwald. The mass murder of prisoners was also carried out using Zyklon-B in improvised gas chambers in Ravensbrück, Dachau and Mauthausen. In some cases the victims were selected because they were sick, too weak to join a forced march, or were considered a security risk. Many, many more died as a result of deliberate neglect, starvation and epidemics. A temporary encampment in Buchenwald that was used to dump 17,000 prisoners between January and April claimed the lives of about 13,000 men. Historians estimate that 250,000 of the 718,000 inmates of the swollen prison camp system died between the beginning of January and the end of April 1945. Of these about half were Jews.[112]

Bergen-Belsen

The greatest death toll in a single place occurred at Bergen-Belsen. The calamity that unfolded there illustrates the inconsistency, improvisation, incompetence and sheer inhumanity of German policy towards the Jews.

Bergen-Belsen camp was originally established to hold prisoners of war in 1940. 'Stalag XIC 311' acquired a grim reputation the following year when up to 14,000 Soviet POWs died there. In April 1943 the SS constructed a new camp to hold Jews who were potential candidates for exchange for German nationals held by the Allies. This project was rooted in the notion that Jews had value as hostages in the eyes of the British and Americans, an idea that had animated the Nazis since 1933. Two exchanges did actually take place. In November 1942, Jews with Palestinian passports were swapped for members of the Templar community, German Christians, who had settled in the Holy Land. A second one, in July 1943, saw several dozen Jews held at Vittel go to Palestine. But Bergen-Belsen was symptomatic of a grander vision to use Jews to gain advantage for the Reich. In December 1942, Himmler won Hitler's agreement to ransom small numbers of Jews for foreign currency. Müller, head of the Gestapo, undertook to locate high-value prisoners and citizens of neutral countries for this purpose. During the spring of 1943, the German Foreign Office came up with a similar idea to use Jews for exchange schemes: their specialists envisaged a pool of 30,000 Jews. Bergen-Belsen was selected as a suitable location to hold them and was placed under the management of the WVHA. In April 1943 the 'exchange camp' received 2,400 Polish Jews with South American papers, including some from the Hotel Polski. They were followed by 350 Sephardi Jews with Turkish, Spanish and Portuguese nationality who were placed in a separate section for citizens of neutral states. Early in 1944, 3,670 Jews with connections to Palestine were transferred from the Netherlands to the 'star camp', so called because they wore the yellow star when they entered. By now Bergen-Belsen had a strangely cosmopolitan complexion: there were even Albanians and North Africans. Conditions were relatively benign. Under the first commandant, Adolf Haas, families stayed together, the inmates wore their own clothes and the work regimen was light.[113]

Abel Herzberg, a lawyer and editor of a Zionist newspaper in Amsterdam, was amongst the Dutch Jews interned in the 'star camp'. He had gone into hiding soon after the occupation, but was arrested in March 1943 along with his wife and imprisoned, first in the centre for VIPs at Barneveld and then in Westerbork. Thanks to their inclusion on a Palestine list they were transferred to Bergen-Belsen in January 1944. Herzberg described it in his camp diary as 'a sad, cheerless, grubby place on earth, somewhere on the heath, where everything that lives, or bears or brings life, has been hacked down, uprooted or burned. There is sand, grit and dust and nothing else. On it stand a number of rows of grey-green huts. Not a tree grows there, no flowers, not even grass.' The complex stretched along a main access road with the 'prisoner camp' to the north and the various enclosures for exchange prisoners to the south. It was surrounded by a double barbed-wire fence and watch-towers. In the summer 'it is scorching there. Nowhere in the camp is there paving or drainage. When it rains, the muster ground becomes either flooded, or a floating mass of mud and mire. With broken, half-rotten shoes on their feet, the people of Israel stand waiting for hours. In winter, shivering with cold, or soaked from the rain. Men, women, children.'[114]

In March 1944 the Germans started using part of Bergen-Belsen as a 'convalescent camp'. Prisoners from labour camps who could no longer work, including a high proportion of Jews, were sent there, but not to recover. There were no medical facilities, almost no food, and nowhere to house them except in already overcrowded huts or tents. They were sent there to die. Of 1,000 stricken prisoners transferred from Dora-Mittelbau because they could no longer lift a pick or carry a sack of cement, fewer than 60 lived. After the deportations from Hungary began, 1,684 Jews arrived as part of the deal between Kasztner and Eichmann. They were kept in a special compound pending the out-come of the negotiations. Hard on their heels came 4,000 Hungarian women who were placed in a 'women's camp' that comprised little more than tents. The infrastructure would have been unable to cope with these numbers at the best of times, but the erratic deliveries of food, the intermittent water supply and abysmal sanitation turned it into a charnel house. In the 'star camp' 4,000 people made do with one wash-house that had twelve taps – when the water supply was working. The camp for evacuated prisoners, which housed 8,000 souls, did not have *any* running water or latrines. Over the summer months typhus got a foothold and quickly reached epidemic proportions.[115]

Herzberg observed the consequences as the thousands of women poured in. 'It is swarming with fleas now. Lice, too, have arrived on the scene. But we? We think of the Polish women and feel profoundly contented. We are living in palaces.' Despite the mounting death toll, the inmates in the 'star camp' tried to preserve a degree of normality, schooling the hundreds of children and celebrating the Jewish festivals. But they were shaken by the sight of new batches coming from the east. Herzberg thought that Jews from Lodz were 'like animals. Com-pletely dishevelled and shattered. When food arrives, they behave like animals.' After 3,000 women, including some Dutch, were deposited in the women's camp he was shocked to hear about gas chambers – apparently for the first time. 'The most horrifying stories are being told. The children and all those not eligible for work are said to have been gassed. It is impossible to believe such an atrocity.' Anne Frank and her sister were amongst those Dutch women. After a storm devastated the encampment the women were squeezed into several barracks in the 'star camp'.[116]

Conditions deteriorated rapidly over the winter. Overcrowding was massively aggravated by the influx of 15,000 Jews evacuated from Auschwitz in December 1944. Indeed, Belsen came to supplant Gross-Rosen as the 'new' Auschwitz. Josef Kramer, who had previously been in charge of Birkenau, was appointed the new commandant. He brought with him kapos from Auschwitz and the full, draconian regimen of the concentration camps. Kramer cut the rations and did nothing to check the spread of typhus. The SS made no effort to pipe water into the prisoners' camp even though the numbers kept there soared. Herzberg reported that 'Every day now transports of thousands of people are arriving from concentration camps . . . there is a field full of corpses. And every day the carts trundle past filled with corpses and more corpses . . . the crematoria can no longer cope with the volume . . .' Typhus had had now entered the 'star camp' and started ravaging even those who were formerly privileged. By March, Bergen-Belsen's population reached 42,000; in April it touched 60,000 even though 7,000 were transferred to Theresienstadt. The mortality rate was astronomical: in March, 18,000 inmates died. During the first two weeks of April the death toll reached 9,000. It was impossible to dispose of the bodies fast enough, so corpses were stacked outside barracks. The living lay side by side with the dead in huts awash with excrement. Prisoners roamed the camp in search of food, dropped dead and lay where they fell. When Jews in the 'star camp' celebrated Passover, Herzberg remarked that 'There was no need for the bitter herbs', the customary mouthful to remind Jews of their suffering under the Pharaohs.[117]

Hedi Fried arrived a week later, on one of the last transports to reach Belsen. After a three-day journey sealed inside a box-car she was quartered in a hut much like the one she had left in Hamburg. However, no one issued any instructions and the only food to arrive was a thin vegetable 'soup'. There was a roll call in the evening and the morning, but apart from that the prisoners were left to their own devices. They got one ration of bread over the next few days and otherwise eked out the 'soup' and 'coffee'. Such was their thirst that 'Many of the girls went outside and drank from the filthy puddles in the yard.' Hedi took the opportunity to earn an extra ration by joining a team disposing of corpses. 'We were taken behind the barracks, where big heaps of bodies lay scattered, given spades and told to dig deep graves and bury the dead. I looked at the corpses and set to work without any feeling. They could just as well have been logs of wood.'[118]

On 15 April she was lying on her bunk, emaciated and apathetic, when she heard someone say that British soldiers were in the camp. They were the advance party of a force sent forward as the result of a local truce to prepare for the takeover of the camp. This unique arrangement came about because Kurt Becher, Himmler's special representative, had visited a few days earlier and ordered Kramer to surrender it intact rather than initiate an evacuation. This did not stop Kramer obeying instructions from the RSHA to relocate 7,000 'special' Jews, including most of those who had been held since 1943. They were supposed to go to Theresienstadt, but the rail system was so badly disrupted that the trains wandered southern Germany until they were intercepted by American or Russian troops. Those who remained, over 42,000, were the subject of discussions between senior Wehrmacht officers who crossed the British lines under a flag of truce on 12 April and staff officers at the headquarters of British VIII Corps. The Germans explained that there was a large concentration camp in the path of the British advance and it would be better to declare it a neutral zone rather than risk soldiers getting tangled up with typhus-ridden inmates or creating a situation in which the prisoners could break out and infect the population. Without having any clue about what they were letting themselves in for, the British agreed to an orderly handover. It took forty-eight hours for the fighting to die down sufficiently to allow the advance parties to move in. What they found stunned them and shocked the world.[119]

Lieutenant Colonel R. I. G. Taylor was the commanding officer of 63rd Anti-Tank Regiment of the Royal Artillery, which led the way. Cheering prisoners lined the road as they entered. 'A great number of them were little more than living skeletons with haggard yellowish faces. Most of the men wore a striped pyjamas type of clothing – others wore rags, while women wore striped flannel gowns or any other clothing they had managed to acquire. Many of them were without shoes and wore only socks and stockings. There were men and women lying in heaps on both sides of the track. Others were walking slowly and aimlessly about – a vacant expression on their starved faces.' Lieutenant Colonel M. W. Gonin, who commanded 11th Light Field Ambulance, which moved in on 17 April, testified soon afterwards that 'It was just a barren wilderness ... Corpses lay everywhere ... some in huge piles where they had been dumped by other inmates, sometimes they lay singly or in pairs where they had fallen as they shuffled along the dirt tracks. Those who died of disease usually died in the huts. When starvation was the chief cause of death they died in the open for it is an odd characteristic of starvation that its victims feel compelled to go on wandering until they fall down and die ... One saw women drowning in their own vomit because they were too weak to turn over, and men eating worms as they clutched half a loaf of bread purely because they had to eat worms to live and now could scarcely tell the difference between worms and bread.' Lieutenant Colonel J. A. D. Johnson, who led the 32d Casualty Clearing Station that got there a few days later, described the interior of the barracks. 'The prisoners were a dense mass of emaciated apathetic scarecrows huddled together in wooden huts, and in many cases without beds or blankets, and in some cases without any clothing whatsoever ... There were thousands of naked and emaciated corpses in various stages of decomposition lying unburied. Sanitation was to all intents and purposes non-existent.' It was not until two weeks after the handover that the British, using SS guards as forced labour, were able to bury the dead faster than people were dying.[120]

The endgame of Judenpolitik

The entry of British troops into Bergen-Belsen was a by-product of Himmler's desperate efforts to use Jews as pawns in his endgame with the western allies and the belated rescue efforts initiated by the WRB and the Swedes. Himmler had succeeded in establishing a line to the west thanks to the negotiations over the fate of Hungarian Jews in the summer and autumn of 1944. In November his representative, Kurt Becher, actually held talks with Roswell McClelland, the WRB agent in Switzerland and thus an employee of the US government. These talks did not have any immediate outcome, but helped to convince Himmler that it was time to halt the killing of Jews. The possibility of placing them under the protection of the Red Cross was then taken up by

Jean-Marie Musy, a Swiss politician and former president of the Swiss Confederation, who met Himmler several times in January 1945. Musy, who had been a forthright supporter of Nazi Germany earlier in the war, was trying to make up for his previous error of judgement, while Himmler was trying to use him as a conduit to the western leaders. As a result of these conversations, 1,210 Jews were transferred from Theresienstadt to Switzerland. Unfortunately, the publicity surrounding their arrival tipped off Hitler to what Himmler was doing and allowed the hardliners in the RSHA, Kaltenbrunner and Müller, to stymie further contacts.[121]

Himmler had other irons in the fire. He was using his Scandinavian-born masseur, Felix Kersten, as a channel to Jewish relief workers in Stockholm, the Swedish Red Cross and, ultimately, the Swedish government. Kersten was in contact with Hillel Storch, a Latvian Jew who had emigrated to Sweden, where he acted for the World Jewish Congress in addition to pursuing his own schemes to aid Jews in Poland. More importantly, since 1943 Kersten had functioned as a go-between conveying messages to the Swedish Foreign Ministry and the Red Cross on matters concerning the care of POWs. In February 1945, Himmler used him to set up a meeting with Count Folke Bernadotte, a former businessman and army officer who was the effective head of the Swedish Red Cross. Himmler proposed on humanitarian grounds that the Swedes should evacuate approximately 8,000 Scandinavians from the concentration camps. Subsequently he also addressed a letter to the Swedish Foreign Ministry claiming that he had released 2,700 Jews (to Switzerland), depicting this as part of a long-standing policy to assist Jewish emigration. Around the same time, via Kersten, Himmler alerted Storch to the catastrophic situation in Belsen. At this stage the British overruled any further contacts with Himmler, but Bernadotte set about organizing a rescue mission on behalf of Scandinavian nationals in the camp system. Under the auspices of the Swedish Red Cross he assembled a fleet of thirty-six white-painted buses, a dozen trucks, and a supply vehicle to cross to Denmark and thence drive to the Neuengamme concentration camp, outside Hamburg, where the Germans had promised to concentrate the Scandinavian prisoners. The mission was staffed by 308 personnel drawn mainly from the Swedish armed forces, including doctors and nurses. They had no explicit mandate to rescue Jews as Jews; Jewish people were only included if they happened to be Danish or Norwegian. In fact, of the 763 Norwegian Jews who had been deported only two or three remained alive, but nearly 500 Danish Jews were still in Theresienstadt. The buses set off on 8 March and travelled across northern Germany under constant threat of attack by trigger-happy Allied pilots. By early April they had removed 4,700 prisoners from Neuengamme, but not a single Jew had been saved.[122]

Himmler's real intentions now came to the fore. At a meeting with Bernadotte on 2 April he claimed that while Hitler was alive he could not contemplate peace negotiations but the following day he sent a message via Walter Schellenberg that he wanted Bernadotte to act as a mediator should the opportunity arise. Throughout this period Storch had been frantically lobbying the Swedish Foreign Ministry to include Jews in Bernadotte's mission. As a refugee, though, he lacked the right credentials to get much further and was replaced by Norbert Masur, a Swedish Jew who was also a member of the WJC. On 20–21 April, Masur met Himmler and Schellenberg. The Reichsführer-SS reiterated his claim that he had never sought the destruction of Jews who were not opposed to the Third Reich, and had arranged for Bergen-Belsen to be transferred to the Red Cross. He offered to release 1,000 Jewish women from Ravensbrück as a further show of good faith. Thanks to these conversations, Bernadotte's bus fleet included Ravensbrück in its itinerary. Between 12 and17 April the Swedes travelled deep into German-held territory to bring back 423 Danish Jews from Theresienstadt and several hundred more from the Ravensbrück women's camp. On that last mission one of the drivers and a dozen survivors were killed when Allied fighters strafed the column.[123]

On 29 April, Hitler learned of Himmler's efforts to initiate peace negotiations behind his back. The leader of the SS was stripped of his offices and ceased to be an interlocutor in efforts to rescue Jews. His final disgrace was to no purpose since the Allies were aware of these last-minute manoeuvres and had no intention of taking the bait. In any case, as Peter Longerich notes, Himmler did not keep his word: one of his last acts was to command the evacuation of the remaining camps under SS control, thereby setting in motion the last spasm of murders and massacres. It is not clear how many Jews were plucked from the camps during April, but at least 2,031 reached Sweden, including 1,615 who were stateless, 413 Danes and 3 Norwegians. At most this was 10 per cent of the total saved by the white buses at a time when Jews comprised 30–40 per cent of the camp population.[124]

German persecution of the Jews ended when Allied occupation

began. This phase is usually associated with the 'liberation' of the concentration camps, but more Jews were freed from fear of despoliation, deportation or death in the countries where they had always lived than in camps. 'Liberation' is also a misleading term because it suggests a joyful release that was hardly typical of what the survivors felt. In Romania, France and Belgium, Jews were freed from German rule seven to eight months *before* the war ended; large numbers of them enlisted in the Allied armies and joined the fight against Nazism, so for them the war only acquired a new dimension. Many families had relatives who were in areas still under German control and were hardly in a mood to rejoice until they got word of their loved ones. All faced the enormous task of recovering their rights, property, livelihoods and, in some cases, their children. For Jews in Poland the transition from German rule to Soviet occupation was even more fraught. Yitzhak Zuckerman recalled that 'for me, January 17, the day the Soviet forces entered Warsaw, was one of the saddest days of my life. I wanted to weep, and not tears of joy . . . When I saw the masses shouting for joy . . . suddenly the knowledge that there was no Jewish people sliced through me like a knife.' For Polish Jews, 'the orphaned, the last ones – what joy could we have?' Having bottled up his emotions for years he broke down. 'There had always been a sense of mission that gave us strength; but now it was over . . .'[125]

There was no single experience of 'liberation' at the end of the war and many Jews who passed under Allied control died soon afterwards. Approximately 90,000 Jews were inmates of concentration camps, although up to 30,000 did not survive much beyond the arrival of Allied troops. Thousands were in installations overrun by advancing units. Others were in camps handed over to Allied representatives, notably Bergen-Belsen. Theresienstadt was placed under Red Cross management a few days before the Red Army reached it. Hundreds were rescued from trains that had ground to a halt in the countryside, such as the evacuees from Belsen who clambered down from a stationary transport near the little town of Tröbitz, north of Dresden. Hundreds more just woke up on the morning of a forced march to find the SS guards had evaporated. In Berlin about 1,500 German Jews resurfaced, but ten times that number had persisted thanks to their 'privileged' status as partners in mixed marriages or as converts. Whereas the German Jews were mainly middle-aged, the camp and ghetto survivors were overwhelmingly young.[126]

A few examples will serve to illustrate the varied, bittersweet transition from slavery to freedom. Kitty Hart had been transferred from Auschwitz-Birkenau in November 1944 via Gross-Rosen to Langenbeilau (where David Koker briefly worked). After four months there she was marched over the Eulen Mountains to Tratenau and then moved on to an underground munitions factory. When the Allies approached she was evacuated again, pausing briefly in Bergen-Belsen, before ending up at a small camp serving a sugar refinery near Salzwedel. Americans swept past the camp on 13–14 April and the SS guards fled, but there was no handover of power. Instead, the prisoners broke out and sacked the nearby town. Kitty recalled this anarchic interlude as the 'happiest moment of my life'.[127]

Marco Nahon staggered into Dachau on 27 April after a ghastly ten-day trek from Ohrdruf during which the column had almost no food and suffered repeated air raids. Two days later he heard voices saying that the Americans were near. He dragged himself out of his hut and was borne to the fence by a cheering crowd. 'At the same time one of my most ardent wishes during captivity becomes reality. During my two years as a prisoner, I have fervently wanted to see those SS officers, so proud and so arrogant, being taken prisoners themselves. And now the moment has come. A group of SS officers, hands in the air, are being led away by the Americans, at the point of their bayonets.' He cried out, 'God granted that I should see those SS deprived of their liberty! Now I can die in peace!' Mercifully, he lived.[128]

In early April, Lucie Adelsberger was transferred from Ravensbrück to a small camp near Neustadt adjacent to an SS airfield. Here she and a group of other women endured the 'interminable waiting' for the war to end. When the Russians finally reached the camp on 2 May, 'We were incredulous and dumbstruck that first hour, when this inconceivable, unfathomable good fortune descended upon us. It was overwhelming, and it shattered us. Just as our starving bodies at first refused to digest the food we were now offered, so, too, were we unable to completely absorb our new freedom . . .'[129]

Helga Weiss and her mother were evacuated from the aircraft factory in Freiberg in January, marched to the local station and loaded onto a train destined for Flossenbürg. They travelled for five days in open coal wagons, stopping frequently in sidings due to priority traffic or disruption. Unable to proceed further they were held for a week at a small camp in Triebschitz in the Sudetenland. Helga now had frostbite.

Their journey resumed via Czechoslovakia, tantalizingly close to home. Finally, they were deposited in Mauthausen. Mother and daughter were now perilously weak, but the greatest threat came from other prisoners in the camp. 'The Gypsies are worse than the Germans,' Helga wrote. 'They beat us . . . and of the little food we get, they steal half, if not all of it.' At the start of May they observed guards changing into civilian clothes and disappearing. On 5 May Helga noticed a white flag over the main tower. Energy and joy surged through her body. 'I feel like dancing, whooping. We made it. We survived the war.' Two weeks later she and her mother were on a train back to Prague.[130]

Victor Klemperer and his wife took advantage of the chaos following the Allied bombing of Dresden on 13–15 February to shrug off their former identity. He removed the yellow star from his clothing and they masqueraded as refugees from the devastation. With assistance from Nazi Party welfare organizations Victor and his wife travelled to Bavaria, ending up in a small place near Aichach. In the first days of April the Nazi order toppled and the village officials fled. The Klemperers heard rumours that American troops had occupied nearby towns but none came to their village. There were no jeeps filled with GIs, cheers or flag waving: the Americans simply bypassed them. For Victor and Eva liberation meant 'No mayor, no Americans'. In June they made their way back to their old home in the suburbs of Dresden.[131]

EPILOGUE

With Berlin isolated, the command and control structures of the Third Reich finally disintegrated. No longer able to deny that his situation was beyond military salvation, that it was a matter of hours before Red Army soldiers swarmed over the Reich Chancellery, on 30 April Hitler committed suicide. Before then, however, he dictated his will and his 'political testament' to his secretary Traudl Junge. In it he blamed the Jews for the outbreak of war in 1939 and predicted that in centuries to come mankind would turn against 'international Jewry and its henchmen'. If in the meantime the inhabitants of Europe suffered massacre and slavery, the responsibility 'must be borne by the true culprits: the Jews'. Having called on his people and the armed services to opt for death rather than servitude, he nominated his successors – Admiral Dönitz as president and Goebbels as chancellor. He also settled some last scores by denouncing Göring and Himmler as traitors. Hitler's final words proved beyond doubt the centrality of the Jews in his world view and, hence, the singularity of the anti-Jewish policies that he propelled throughout his political career: 'Above all, I charge the leadership of the nation and their subjects with meticulous observance of the race-laws and merciless resistance to the universal poisoner of all peoples, international Jewry.'[1]

The Third Reich outlasted Hitler by a week. Military resistance in the west crumbled, but desperate fighting continued between German forces and the Red Army as long as Dönitz tried to obtain separate peace terms from the British and Americans. They refused to yield one iota on unconditional surrender across all fronts, so on 7 May the German high command signed the formal act of capitulation at the Supreme Allied Headquarters in Reims, France. A separate signing ceremony was held under Soviet auspices in Berlin, where fighting had actually terminated five days previously. The war was over. But the end of hostilities did not mark the end of Jewish suffering and for thousands of Jews the transition to peacetime marked little more than an abstract concept.[2]

Whatever situation they were in when the Allies reached them, the Jewish survivors were in dire need. Yet military personnel were hardly prepared or equipped for relief or rehabilitation work. This is not to say that the Allies failed to anticipate the problem of refugees: military units included civilian affairs officers and the military governments had branches for Displaced Persons (DPs). The main agency tasked with handling DPs in conjunction with the military was the United Nations Relief and Reconstruction Administration (UNRRA). But its first priority was to get people that had been uprooted by the war back home as fast as possible, and the magnitude of this mission was daunting. UNRRA was confronted with 20 million destitute people, including non-Jewish survivors of concentration camps, forced and slave labourers, prisoners of war, volunteer workers in Germany, and masses of refugees, amongst whom were people who had collaborated with the Germans plus millions of Volksdeutsche who had fled or were expelled from their homes. Sorting out who was who, and who deserved UNRRA assistance (which excluded anyone who had left home voluntarily or served the Germans), was itself a massive undertaking.[3]

There were also several Jewish relief organizations, chiefly the teams of social workers sent to Europe by the AJJDC and the Jewish Relief Unit (JRU), set up and sponsored by British Jews. However, the British and American military governments were initially wary of allowing them access to the survivors. Consequently, Jewish chaplains in the British and American forces were the first point of contact between those rescued from the Germans and Jews in the free world. Weeks passed before an organized Jewish relief effort touched those who needed it, and then it was often inadequate to the challenge.[4]

Allied policy towards the DPs, the Jewish DPs in particular, was deeply conflicted. At the Yalta conference in February 1945, Stalin, Roosevelt and Churchill had concurred in principle that citizens uprooted by the Germans or displaced by the war should be repatriated to their countries of origin. The military governments of the British, US and French zones of occupation in western Germany working with UNRRA succeeded in repatriating no less than 6 million with impressive speed. But they declined to forcibly return those who hailed from (or claimed to come from) territories annexed by the USSR, specifically the Baltic states and eastern Poland. As a result, by the end of 1945,

UNRRA was supporting three-quarters of a million 'non-repatriables' in DP camps. The Jews were initially a tiny sliver of this problem, but they were particularly troublesome. Few wanted to return to countries where their neighbours had turned on them and where they no longer had homes or means of living. Yet the Americans were not prepared to relax their immigration controls to enable them to leave Europe. The British government was equally determined to exclude Jewish refugees and until July 1947 actually considered repatriating German Jews who had arrived in the UK before the war. Nor were the British willing to expand Jewish immigration to Palestine. Rather, the Labour government that came to power in August 1945 committed itself to enforcing the restrictions on the Jewish population enshrined in the 1939 White Paper. Consequently, the Jewish survivors were condemned to a life in limbo.[5]

To their despair, 45,000 Jews found themselves confined to barbed-wire enclosures by order of the Allied military authorities in the British, American and French zones of occupation. Frequently these were the same concentration or labour camps where they had previously been held or not far away. The barracks were overcrowded and the amenities were basic. Moreover, the military administration and UNRRA refused to recognize Jews as a separate group with particular, urgent requirements. The Americans rejected criteria that had served as the basis of discrimination under Nazism, while the British feared that treating Jews like a national group would play into the hands of the Zionist movement, which was demanding the right for survivors to enter Palestine. As a result, Jews were corralled with Russians, Poles and Balts released from forced labour and were sometimes obliged to share quarters with evicted ethnic Germans who had been willing tools of the Nazis. This was a recipe for tension and there were frequent disturbances between Jews and non-Jews in the DP assembly centres. When information about the treatment of Jewish survivors was transmitted home by American Jewish army chaplains, it stirred indignation in the Jewish leadership. Responding to the numerous protests and the adverse publicity they generated, on 22 June 1945, President Truman asked Earl G. Harrison, the US representative on the Intergovernmental Committee for Refugees, to investigate and report back to him.[6]

Harrison duly travelled to Europe, accompanied by Joseph Schwartz of the AJJDC, and toured the DP camps accumulating impressions and evidence. The report he submitted to Truman ten weeks later transformed US policy and undermined Britain's stance towards the Jewish survivors. Harrison opened by stating that 'Up to this point they have been "liberated" more in a military sense than actually.' Three months after VE-Day, the estimated 100,000 Jewish DPs were still living behind barbed wire in crowded, insanitary quarters. In spite of pervasive physical and psychological afflictions, they were not getting any special medical supplies or treatment. Many still wore the clothes in which they had been released. They were offered little in the way of rehabilitation and were not even being helped to trace relatives. Although their plight could be alleviated by forcing the Germans to make amends, little was being done in that direction either. Indeed, Harrison argued, 'As matters now stand, we appear to be treating the Jews as the Nazis treated them except that we do not exterminate them. They are in concentration camps in large numbers under our military guard instead of S.S. troops. One is led to wonder whether the German people, seeing this, are not supposing that we are following or at least condoning Nazi policy.' As a prerequisite for any improvement he deemed it essential to acknowledge that the Jews had suffered more severely than any other group persecuted by the Germans and that, willy-nilly, they now identified themselves as a collective. He recommended that 'the Jews in Germany and Austria should have the first claim upon the conscience of the people in the United States and Great Britain'. In practice, following immediate aid, this entailed facilitating their emigration to Palestine. The vast majority no longer wished to stay in Europe and, knowing they could not enter the US under the current immigration controls, desired to start new lives in the only place likely to welcome them and provide the support they needed.[7]

Truman endorsed Harrison's report within days and instructed General Eisenhower, the supreme commander in Europe, to act on it at once. Jewish advisers were appointed to the US military government and survivors were relocated to Jewish-only sites. Relief began to pour in. During 1945, the AJJDC expended $317,000 on its European operation. Over the following year that sum increased more than tenfold and by 1947 the agency was spending $9 million on relief and rehabilitation – although by that time the numbers in need of aid had greatly increased.[8]

The DP camps in the US zones of occupation in Germany and Austria as well as those sprinkled the length of Italy became the arena for a wholly unexpected efflorescence of Jewish life. Within weeks of being freed, Jews started taking control of their fate and asserting their interests. Representative committees sprang up in each camp and, in July 1945, a gathering of delegates met at St Ottilien DP Camp to establish a unified voice for Jewish DPs in the US zone. These local representatives began to coordinate relief and rehabilitation activity with agents of the AJJDC and ORT, which provided education and vocational training. The camps became the arena for rituals through which Jews recovered a sense of agency. Where possible they engaged in the reburial of those who had been pitched into mass graves at the camps, at massacre sites, or dumped along the roads taken by forced marches. Internment according to Jewish rites not only gave some dignity back to the dead, it showed that, in the words of historian Margarete Myers Feinstein, the living had 'reclaimed control of their lives'. The performance of marriages was a more obviously positive gesture. Around 80 per cent of the survivors were aged 18–44 and most were either single or had lost a spouse. In normal conditions, Jewish law required that the surviving partner had to obtain proof of the other's death in order to remarry, but the religious authorities, only too aware of the likely circumstances, relaxed the standard of evidence in order to enable couples to start new married lives. The inevitable result was a baby boom, accompanied by rituals of circumcision and naming. This too was seen as 'a form of retaliation' against those who had sought to deny any future to the Jewish people.[9]

In a curious echo of the ghettos, the Americans permitted the Jewish DPs to establish a camp police. This was partly to maintain order without embroiling US military personnel (or, more pertinently, the German police) and to keep a lid on the burgeoning black market. It was also intended to contain vigilantism when survivors identified men or women who had served as kapos or abused positions of power in ghettos. Improvised honour courts presided over by survivors with legal backgrounds sought to adjudicate cases that came to light in this way. While they may have been ad hoc, the courts were able to draw upon shared experience to reach a balanced judgment about those accused of abuses and frequently expressed understanding for the behaviour of the arraigned. Only in the most egregious cases were the guilty excluded from the DP community and barred from access to welfare. Honour courts were also established by the renascent Jewish communities in Poland, France and Austria. They channelled anger and helped to prevent lynchings, but they were just as important as a symbolic exercise of autonomy, a demonstration that law once again ruled Jewish lives, and the reassertion of cherished values.[10]

The wider pursuit of justice inspired Jews in the camps and beyond to collect documents and testimony pertaining to the years of persecution. The work of documentation had begun as soon as Jews in eastern Poland were released from German rule. Survivors started chronicling the fate of Lublin Jews in July 1944 shortly after the city was liberated and soon came under the guidance of the professional historian Philip Friedman, who had survived the catastrophe in Lwow. By the following March a central historical commission based in Lodz was coordinating five branches. Their members contributed extensively to the official investigation and prosecution of war crimes in Poland. Friedman and Rachel Auerbach, a survivor of the Oneg Shabbat group, were members of the Main Commission for the Investigation of German Crimes that was constituted by the Polish provisional government in March 1945. He accompanied the investigation of Chelmno and she travelled to the site of Treblinka. Together they contributed to the reports on the death camps that the commission submitted to the Polish delegation to the International Military Tribunal at Nuremberg that commenced the trial of captured Nazi leaders in September 1945. Friedman also authored a forty-five-page overview of the destruction of Polish Jewry. Artur Eisenbach testified in the trial of Hans Biebow in Lodz and Nachman Blumenthal provided expert evidence against Rudolf Höss in Cracow. Blumenthal and Josef Kermisz also helped to document German crimes at Chelmno. In October 1947 these men and women established the Jewish Historical Institute in Warsaw. The central part of its already extensive collection comprised ten metal canisters containing part of the archive of Oneg Shabbat, recovered from the ruins of the ghetto.[11]

Historical commissions sprouted in almost every major DP camp in Germany too. Eventually their activity was coordinated by a central Jewish historical commission based in Munich. It amassed 5,000 statistical surveys and 1,000 eye-witness accounts. Dozens were published in its journal, *Fun Letsten Hurban* – contributing to an understanding of the catastrophe and inspiring further contributions. In France, Isaac Schneersohn resurrected the centre to chronicle German and French crimes that he had initiated in Grenoble under Vichy. Schneersohn was a Russian-born businessman and communal worker from a famous rabbinical family who had survived the occupation. He was a man of energy and vision, and his Centre de Documentation Juive Contemporaine (CDJC) attracted the talents of Léon Poliakov and Joseph Billig. They started to churn out collections of German documents evidencing the fate of the Jews in France while treading a delicate path between indicting Vichy and alienating French opinion. Schneersohn had wider ambitions and in 1947 convened a conference of Jewish historical commissions from across Europe, including representatives of the nascent Wiener Library in London (officially still called the Jewish Central Information Office), with the aim of coordinating the global research effort from Paris. The Yad Vashem Foundation in Palestine was unable to send anyone due to the crisis there, but made clear its belief that Jerusalem not Paris should become the main repository of documents and the base for studying the catastrophe.[12]

Many Jews felt the pull of Jerusalem. Thanks to their common fate and shared interests, notably the struggle to emigrate, the survivors in the camps in Germany and Austria developed a collective identity. They were dubbed 'She'erith Hapleitah' – the surviving remnant – by activists oriented towards Palestine and that is how they referred to themselves when interacting with the outside world. However, the seeming uniformity of life in the DP camps concealed internal divisions and conflicts.

Of the 20,000 Jewish survivors in the British zone about 12,000 were concentrated in the Hohne DP camp. It was located in a former army base, about two miles away from Bergen-Belsen, to which the living had been evacuated in May 1945. However, for the following year it was also used to accommodate DPs of various nationalities, a cause of much antagonism. The Jews were represented by a committee – grandly entitled the Central Committee of Liberated Jews – energetically chaired by Joseph Rosensaft, a survivor from Bedzin. Rosensaft's committee irritated the British authorities by campaigning noisily for the recognition of the Jews as a separate group and the right to emigrate to Palestine. There was unrest between different Jewish factions too. The survivors resented the late arrival of the Jewish Relief Unit and derided the help it brought. The JRU, in turn, brushed up against the better-resourced team from the AJJDC. Non-Zionist and Orthodox Jews felt marginalized by the predominantly secular, political leadership. Notwithstanding these internal divisions, the Belsen-Hohne DPs eventually supported a rich variety of initiatives. The camp boasted a kindergarten, a school and an ORT establishment for vocational training. There was a theatre, called 'Kazet', which presented dramatic reconstructions of life in the ghettos and camps as well as lighter entertainment. The residents had access to two Yiddish-language newspapers and there was even a publishing house. An honour court emerged, but its jurisdiction was contested by the internal police and it fell apart amidst acrimony.[13]

There was little cooperation between the DP camp Jews and the rump of German Jews living in the cities. Initially it was difficult for Jewish Germans to establish their credentials and avoid being treated as members of the vanquished nation, but they got scant sympathy from Jewish relief workers who could not understand why on earth they wanted to rebuild lives in Germany. About 90 per cent of the Jewish DPs were Polish and they felt little warmth for the German Jews who had survived in mixed marriages or as converts. Discord between the communities was aggravated by the fact that most of the relief was channelled into the Jewish DP camps. In reply, the German Jews left it to UNRRA to care for their east European brethren. The two groups had divergent practical concerns, too. Whereas German Jews were pre-occupied with the restitution of property, creating the basis for a renewed communal life, most east European Jews were focused on get-ting out. Even Polish Jews who went to live in urban areas kept to themselves: they were younger than the German Jewish survivors and had different priorities, such as starting families, looking for homes, and making a living (not always by legal means). In Frankfurt they established their own community and synagogue. In other centres German Jews tried to exclude them. The old antipathy between German Jews and Ostjuden was sharpened when the camp Jews were accused of black market activities and attracted anti-Semitic comments, even police raids.[14]

Efforts to create a unified representation of all the Jews in both zones foundered on the egos and ambitions of the men who dominated the representative committees in their respective domains. Since neither was prepared to accept subordinate status Rosensaft reigned supreme in Belsen-Hohne and the British zone while the Jews in the Bavarian camps formed their own central committee, led by Samuel Gringauz. Orthodox Jews felt better served by the Vaad Hatzalah, the council for rescue, supported by Orthodox Jews in the USA, which supplied their religious needs. Yet all had to contend with the persistence of anti-Semitic thinking among the German population.[15]

The state of affairs in the western zones of Germany was trans-formed by upheavals in Poland during 1946. Approximately 30,000–60,000 Jews emerged into freedom from hiding in the cities or the forests on Polish territory. About 20,000 were released from ghettos and camps, mainly in Czestochowa and East Upper Silesia. A few thousand more made their way back from camps in Germany and between 13,000 and 20,000 were demobilized from Russian or Polish military formations under Red Army command. However, the resurgence of the Jewish population was mainly due to the return of those deported to central Asia from Soviet-occupied Poland in 1939–41, including Jews who originally lived there and refugees from the German sector. Around 30,000 reached Poland in 1945 and a further 136,000 during 1946–7. The new Polish authorities directed the bulk of them to the areas annexed to Poland from western Germany – Lower and Upper Silesia and Szczecin (formerly Stettin). They poured into a country occupied by the Red Army and racked with civil strife. Polish nationalists and elements of the Home Army that had gone underground when the Red Army arrived routinely accused the Jews of collaboration with the Soviets. One underground leaflet in June 1945 stated, 'Power has been usurped by a gang of corrupt Jewish Communists who do the bidding of the Red Tsar Stalin . . .' Violence against the Jews was endemic, although only a proportion was politically motivated. It is estimated that about 200 Jews were killed on trains carrying them through Poland or ejected and shot by nationalist extremists. Hundreds more were murdered when they returned to their homes, victims of Poles who feared that they would otherwise have to give up property or wealth obtained from Jews while the Germans reigned. The danger was so great that Polish Jews often moved around in disguise or abandoned homes in remote areas for the relative safety of the cities. According to the best calculations a total of 600–750 Jews were done to death after the war, by Poles.[16]

For a brief, euphoric period the Central Committee of Polish Jews believed that notwithstanding the disorder there was a chance of reconstructing Jewish life in a new Poland under a progressive regime. Efforts and resources, mainly from the AJJDC, were devoted to schooling, health and welfare services, as well as cultural activities. But it was always an uphill struggle. The challenge was exemplified by the battle to retrieve Jewish children who had been placed with Christian families or in convents during the period of deportations. After the war the central committee set about recovering those whose identity and location were known, roughly 2,500. Where a parent or close relative was involved (about 10 per cent of cases) it was relatively easy to succeed, although 'financial compensation' was almost always demanded. When Jewish agencies made the approach it was often necessary to go to litigation. In either case, the cost of recovering children spiralled from 15,000 zlotys per child in 1945 to 50,000 zlotys a year later. By 1946, 239 orphans had been reclaimed for the Jewish community at a cost of 4.5 million zlotys. Rabbi Kahane, who had survived in Lwow, and the Chief Rabbi of Palestine, Isaac Herzog, who visited Poland, pleaded with Catholic Church leaders to instruct their flock to hand back Jewish children – but their appeals were ignored. The effort was further hindered by competition between secular Zionist organizations and religious rescuers, such as the British-based Rabbi Solomon Schonfeld. In any case, the arduous work of rebuilding Jewish life was suddenly rendered futile by the recurrence of pogroms on Polish soil.[17]

There had been an outbreak of collective anti-Jewish violence in Rzeszow in June 1945, after which 200 Jews abandoned the town. That attack had been triggered by an accusation of ritual murder. Two months later a mob in Cracow, inflamed by rumours that Jews had killed a Christian child, attacked the Kupa Synagogue. The attackers included Polish militiamen. One woman died in this incident and five other people were wounded. Nevertheless, these assaults lacked the resonance of the violence that claimed forty-two Jewish lives in Kielce on 4 July 1947. The target was a Jewish communal building where Jews were accused of concealing and slaughtering a Christian youth. In fact it housed over a hundred Jewish refugees, but despite the absurdity of the charge the local law officers did nothing to prevent repeated assaults, murder and looting. The assailants included police officials as well as armed workers. Conversely, the militia confiscated weapons from Jews in the hostel even though they had permits to carry them. When Yitzhak Zuckerman in Warsaw got news of the pogrom he armed himself and went to investigate. As he arrived 'bodies of Jews killed on the roads were brought in. I saw pregnant women whose stomachs were ripped open.' For him as for many other Jews who had vacillated in answer to the question whether to stay or to go, this was the answer. The phrase on everyone's lips was '*men geyt*', meaning 'we're off'. Zuckerman focused on evacuating the survivors of the atrocity and then dedicated himself to organizing emigration from Poland. The lacklustre response of the authorities and the attitude of the Church, which blamed Jewish communists, the so-called Zydo-Kommuna, for the tragedy, were as much an incentive to go as the horror itself. Over the next four months

100,000 Polish Jews streamed across the borders into Hungary and Czechoslovakia, making their way to Jewish DP camps in the American zone of Germany. Another 60,000 followed over the following three years. This exodus effectively extinguished the Jewish revival in Poland even before the Communist Party decided to clamp down on autonomous Jewish activity. Conversely, the influx into Germany transformed the camps and gave added salience to the plight of the Jewish DPs.[18]

In December 1945 there were only about 1,800 children in the Jewish DP camps of Germany and Austria. One month after the Kielce pogrom the number reached 16,000 and by the end of the year there were 26,500 Jewish children in the US zone alone. The Polish Jews who had been exiled to the USSR had departed and come back as family units. Although conditions in places such as Kazakhstan were harsh it was possible to preserve family life, marry, and have children. Now these Polish Jews brought their families to Germany, creating new demands on the relief agencies and also generating new possibilities. The overall Jewish population rose to 141,000 in the American zone and 50,000 in the British zone during 1946, peaking at about 190,000 in Germany plus some 60,000 in other refugee centres. Although the vast majority of the Jewish DPs were now Polish, only a small proportion had actually endured German camps and ghettos. All the same, they wanted to leave Europe and fixated on reaching either Palestine or America. Unable to work and unwilling to integrate into German society – even if they had been welcome, which they were not – they frittered away time in the camps, raising the spectre of 'demoralization'. Zuckerman observed caustically that 'Life in the camps was degenerate, a life of idleness supported by charity.' At the end of the year the lawyer and Zionist politician Zorach Warhaftig wrote that 'It can frankly be stated that eighteen months after the liberation the war is not yet over for European Jewry.'[19]

The dramatic expansion of the Jewish DP population fortified demands for the British to allow the refugees to settle in Palestine. After the Harrison report, the British government had approached the Americans to set up a joint committee to look into the Jewish DP problem and suggest solutions. They hoped that it would draw the Americans into the Palestine imbroglio and help relieve the pressure on them to solve it on their own accord. Between November 1945 and May 1946 the Anglo-American Committee of Inquiry visited DP camps and Jewish communities across Europe taking evidence, but the outcome was a bitter disappointment to Whitehall. A majority of members endorsed Harrison's findings and recommended the emigration of 100,000 Jews to Palestine. As more and more Polish Jews arrived in western Germany the pressure built up. Palestinian emissaries of Hamossad Le'aliyah Bet, the branch of the Haganah responsible for covert immigration, along with members of the Jewish Brigade, became increasingly active, channelling the new arrivals to ports in Italy and southern France where they embarked on rickety ships bound for the Jewish national home. In response, the Royal Navy strengthened its blockade of Palestine and the British government announced that illegal immigrants would be deported to camps on Cyprus. The tough new policy was a public relations disaster. World opinion was revolted by the fate of over 4,000 Jews on the ship *Exodus*, which had been purchased by the Haganah. It was intercepted by the navy on 18 July 1947. Newsreels showed Jews, only recently freed from Hitler's grip, being manhandled off *Exodus* and onto another vessel that took them back to Europe, eventually disembarking them in Hamburg – of all places.[20]

The camps on Cyprus presented a no less distressing image to the world. Nearly forty shiploads (carrying a total of 50,000 migrants) were consigned to two massive camps, one at Caraolos, close to Famagusta, and the other at Dekhelia, near Larnaca. At their peak capacity, 32,000 Jews were interned there. They lived in Nissan huts or in tents, baking during the summer and shivering in the winter. In an effort to alleviate conditions the AJJDC expended $30,000 per month on aid workers, food and supplies. In April 1947 some 10,000 internees took part in an open-air celebration of Passover. The British officers and guards were sympathetic on the whole, but they tried to prevent escapes and insisted on using armoured cars to escort groups of children going to nearby beaches for a swim. Despite the benign regimen 400 Jews were buried on the island, just 165 miles from 'the promised land'. Although 750 each month were permitted to make the short, final hop to Palestine, there was no disguising the fact that the British now held more Jews behind barbed wire than the Germans had done ten years previously.[21]

British endeavours to bar the Jews from Palestine not only backfired in the short term, they were futile. The Jewish inhabitants of the Yishuv were now in a state of open revolt and the security forces were unable to maintain order. After a last attempt to crush resistance using military force in early 1947, the British renounced the mandate and prepared to hand Palestine over to the United Nations. A special commission of the

UN set up to determine the future of Palestine recommended partition, a solution that won majority support at the UN general assembly the following November. British troops pulled out in May 1948 and the Jewish leadership under David Ben-Gurion proclaimed the state of Israel. With the way now open to unrestricted immigration the DP camps decanted their populations into the new state. Around 100,000 Jews arrived from Europe between June and December 1948. A quarter of a million immigrated the following year, including tens of thousands from Hungary, Yugoslavia, Bulgaria and Romania. Although some 30,000 Jews remained in DP centres in West Germany, too old or sick to move again or unwilling to start a new life in the Jewish state, the liminal world of the camps ended.[22]

Meanwhile, American opinion on immigration shifted fundamentally – although not out of sympathy for Europe's stranded Jews. Rather, change was driven by anti-communism and sympathy for DPs who claimed they could not return home for fear of persecution by the Soviets. In June 1948, Congress passed the first Displaced Persons Act, opening the way for 200,000 homeless Europeans to settle in the United States over two years. However, the Act stipulated that one third should be farmers and that nearly half had to originate from the Baltic states. Despite this blatant discrimination the Act marked a fundamental break with previous immigration policy. On 23 October 1948, the passenger ship SS *General Black* carried 813 Jews into New York, the first to arrive under the new dispensation. Eventually, nearly 140,000 would make their way to America.[23]

For the Jews who chose to remain in Europe, the post-war years were almost as beset and disillusioning as they were for those who fought to emigrate. They just had different battles to fight. Although their fate was no longer shaped by German militarism and interstate warfare, it was buffeted by civil strife and the fast-developing 'cold war' between the western allies and the USSR.

Years of persecution and official Jew-hatred had not softened attitudes towards the Jews in the victorious and liberated countries. On the contrary, the racist and anti-Semitic outlook fostered by Nazi propaganda persisted, while national feeling scaled new heights. The victors and the peoples of liberated Europe constructed mythic versions of the war that were a necessary foundation for peacetime reconstruction. In these accounts the victors had fought a 'good war': they had saved the Jews and therefore owed them nothing. In France, Belgium and the

Netherlands the post-war governments cultivated the impression that everything bad that had occurred between 1940 and 1945 had been caused by the Germans. With the exception of a few collaborators the people had been united in resisting the occupiers and had suffered terribly for this defiance: thousands had been executed, imprisoned and deported. In Paris, Brussels and Amsterdam the return of forced labourers sent to the Reich, POWs, and resistance fighters consigned to the concentration camps was stage-managed as a celebration of collective endurance and heroism. According to the historian Pieter Lagrou, the concentration camps became the 'cultural symbol of this narrative of national martyrdom'. The fate of the Jews did not fit well into this story; in fact, it was a dissonant element that raised awkward questions about how people had actually behaved under the occupation. Furthermore, in mid-1945 relatively little was known about the extermination centres in comparison to knowledge of the concentration camps to which dissident west Europeans had been sentenced. The Jewish survivors who trickled back to France, Belgium and the Netherlands could speak eloquently of the difference, but their number was minuscule set against the flood of POWs, conscripted workers and 'political deportees'. In any case, since Jews had been deported just for being Jewish and not because they had resisted the occupier their plight did not contribute to the myth of resistance and national suffering. Sensing this, many Jews chose to depict themselves as victims of fascism and to frame their post-war testimony or memoirs in such a way as to play down their Jewishness and the specific reasons for their persecution. As Lagrou writes, 'victims of racial persecution often preferred to see themselves as being victimised for their opinions rather than for what the persecutor had defined as their race ... persecution seemed more acceptable if it was somehow occasioned by a choice or an action or an opinion made by the victim'. Consequently, in the crucial months during which each nation's war story was crystallizing, the particular fate of its Jews was blurred, occluded or entirely suppressed. This distortion would seriously hamper contemporaneous efforts to obtain justice and redress for the Jewish victims of persecution and genocide.[24]

In France, the Jewish community re-emerged in the summer of 1944 following the liberation, but it immediately faced obstacles to re-integration and restitution. The provisional government abolished all the edicts passed by the Germans and the Vichy regime, but foreign and stateless Jews still laboured under discrimination. French men and women who had purchased property expropriated from the Jews rallied to defend what they considered had been obtained in good faith. The Association of Owners of Aryanized Property lobbied the authorities and organized demonstrations punctuated by anti-Semitic slogans. Jews attempting to recover businesses and homes were met with violence. In one incident in Paris in April 1945, six Jews were wounded and several arrested by police who took the side of the mob. Yet the Free French leadership, and later the provisional government under Charles de Gaulle, was reluctant to uphold the claims of dispossessed Jews for fear of alienating support at a febrile political moment. Instead they counselled the Jews to be patient and discreet.[25]

The victims did not entirely heed this admonition. In order to strengthen their voice, the Jews in France finally overcame their historic differences and formed a unified representative body, the Conseil Représentatif des Institutions juives de France (CRIF). The new body campaigned for compensation for those who had lost property and livelihoods, and demanded citizenship for foreign Jews as well as those who had fought for France. CRIF also took on the task of recovering Jewish children from convents and the homes of Christians. As in Poland this often necessitated legal action. None of this activity would have been possible without aid from the AJJDC: the Jewish population was largely impoverished and its institutions were in ruins, so AJJDC agents played a major role in the rebuilding.[26]

Notwithstanding the straitened circumstances, the CDJC continued to collect material pertaining to the Vichy regime and the occupation. As in Poland, the work of documentation was keyed into the search for justice. Billig and Poliakov moved temporarily to Nuremberg to assist the French delegation at the International Military Tribunal in the prosecution of Nazi crimes against humanity. In the process they accumulated a mass of records that provided the basis for a stream of publications from 1946 to 1949. The CDJC also published a monthly journal, *Le Monde Juif,* which carried the first fruits of historical research as well as reports by survivors. But only 2,500 out of the 76,000 Jews deported from France came home and their story was marginalized by the officially propagated myth of resistance. While militants sent to the camps received immediate financial compensation, Jews had to wait years for any assistance from the state.[27]

The first post-liberation government in Belgium seemed oblivious to what had befallen the Jews under German occupation and refused to

treat Jews differently from other citizens. Foreign-born Jews who surfaced from hiding, especially Germans, were subjected to internment as
enemy aliens. Illegal Jewish immigrants were actually expelled. Stateless
Jews as well as foreigners, who still comprised the majority of the Jewish
inhabitants, found themselves excluded from compensation for war
damage. However, all of the 5,900 Jewish deportees who returned did
initially receive state support thanks to the sympathetic outlook of the
communist minister of the interior. Grants were also extended to
2,791 orphaned Jewish children. Unfortunately, the Catholic Church
and many foster parents contested efforts by the Jewish community to
retrieve them. Belgian Jews resorted to the legal system to rectify this
grievance, only to find that the courts usually rejected claims based on
racial or religious grounds. Orthodox Jews showed less patience for
legal means; the Vaad Hatzalah used bribery and even abductions to get
orphans back. The report of the official Commission on War Crimes,
published in 1948, gave an accurate account of what had happened to
the Jews in Belgium, but it came too late to have much practical effect.
By spring 1946 anti-communism and the Cold War had produced a
rightward tilt in politics. Xenophobic and right-wing Catholic politicians accused the Jews of 'impertinence'. Sections of the press depicted
foreign Jews as an alien presence and blamed them for the black market.
The benefits that had been extended to foreign-born deportees and
orphans were rescinded. Jewish victims only gained recognition from
the state if they had engaged in resistance activity. The historian Frank
Caestecker concludes that 'The heritage of genocide was hardly felt in
public policy.'[28]

Just over 16,000 Jews survived the occupation in hiding in the
Netherlands. They were joined by 5,450 deportees – including nearly
1,000 who never went further than Westerbork. The Jewish population
had sustained catastrophic losses and the basis for communal existence
was virtually erased. Yet the government-in-exile saw no need to make
special provision for the Dutch Jews. Ironically, those who had risked
their lives to protect their Jewish neighbours were most insistent that
religious and racial categories should be banished from policy-making
in the post-war world. This reluctance had other, less elevated motives.
Many Dutch suspected that the ones who avoided deportation and
death had purchased their good fortune and possessed hidden riches.
Those who trickled back from eastern Europe were treated with disdain
due to their poor physical and mental condition. There was scant

understanding of what they had been through and little sympathy from Dutch people in the north of the country who had themselves endured a final winter of extreme privation. Camp survivors who reached the border were routinely detained along with Dutchmen who had gone to Germany voluntarily to work and sometimes found themselves being screened alongside members of the Dutch Nazi movement, the NSB. When the government set in train measures to compensate victims of German persecution, articles appeared in the press warning Jews not to strain the patience of those to whom they ought to feel gratitude. Anti-Jewish feeling in the immediate post-war period reached such a pitch that citizens who had hidden Jews preferred not to advertise their bravery.[29]

Dutch Jewish survivors faced particular difficulties in two areas. The despoliation of the community was almost total. Those who remained had to recover their own property and try to redeem heirless assets for use by the community – which was utterly bereft. Yet thousands of homes, businesses and parcels of land that had been expropriated, as well as millions of securities transferred to the Lippmann–Rosenthal pseudo-bank, were sold on to buyers who could argue genuinely or tactically that they had made the purchases in good faith. It would take years for Dutch Jews, working through government restitution agencies and the courts, to recover a fraction of the wealth systematically stolen from them. An even more sensitive and emotive issue was the fate of just over 2,000 Jewish war orphans in the custody of Christian foster families or institutions. The government established a commission to rule on these cases, but the Jewish members were in a minority and found themselves helpless when the chairman, Dr Gesina H. J. van der Molens, questioned the assumption that the deceased parents, who might not have been particularly religious, would have wanted their offspring removed from a Christian environment. 'According to some people', she declared, 'they must be given back to the Jewish community. In most cases the children were entrusted by their parents to resistance workers, and in other cases they, on their own, spirited them from the Germans. Does the Jewish community have the right to demand these children? Did these children really belong to the Jewish community alone?' The Jewish participants were so frustrated by the outcome of case after case that in mid-1946 they walked out of the commission. A plea by Chief Rabbi Herzog had no more effect and in June 1949 the community was driven to stage public protests. Long after the war was over the fate of Jewish war orphans continued to fester.[30]

Unusually for western Europe, the Jews in the Netherlands also set up an honour court to hear allegations of Jewish collaboration with the Germans. The defendants were David Cohen and Abraham Asscher, along with two dozen other members of the Jewish council. Asscher refused to recognize the proceedings, but Cohen (who was under pressure from the university where he had resumed his teaching position) fought to vindicate his conduct. In November 1947 the court ruled that the two men had behaved reprehensibly and punished them with exclusion from the community. They were then threatened with criminal charges by the body that the Dutch government had set up to deal with collaborators. The embarrassment caused by the ensuing public debate, and the relish with which some Dutch commentators appeared to off-load responsibility for the destruction of the community onto the Jews themselves, inspired the honour court to revise its verdict. This was by no means the end of the controversy. The moral dilemma faced by the council would echo on in the work of survivor historians, like Jacob Presser, for years to come.[31]

A fierce desire for justice and retribution animated Jews across the shattered continent. In the chaotic interlude between liberation and the re-establishment of order some survivors wreaked their own private revenge on local Germans. Jurek Kestenberg confessed to David Boder, a researcher from the United States who interviewed survivors in the DP camps in 1946, that he hunted down SS men and abused the German population in the vicinity of Buchenwald. Another interviewee, Benjamin Piskorz, recalled that 'I took a bit of revenge on the Germans.' He killed men and children. 'I also did some things with the Germans' children as the SS men did in Majdanek with the . . . Jewish children.' He explained he did it 'because the hate within me was so great'. Many years later, in his memoir, Yitzhak Zuckerman admitted that 'I was convinced that revenge operations should be carried out' but he preferred to execute individual war criminals rather than take indiscriminate action against any old German. By early 1945 he relented: 'I wouldn't issue any more death sentences.' Members of the Jewish Brigade in Austria and southern Germany also went after known SS personnel, although the extent of their extra-judicial activity remains vague. Aba Kovner, the leader of the Jewish partisan group that formed in Vilnius in early 1942, dedicated himself to mounting a major revenge operation. With other members of his unit he formed a group called 'Nakam', revenge in Hebrew, and set about obtaining enough toxin to kill thousands by contaminating the water system of a German metropolis. Their symbolic objective was Nuremberg. In the event the plan failed, although members of the groups succeeded in poisoning the bread delivered to a German POW camp, causing some fatalities. More typically, Jewish DPs treated the German population as legitimate targets for casual abuse (especially women), theft, and exploitation through the black market.[32]

The thirst for retribution was barely slaked by the outcome of war crimes trials held under Allied jurisdiction. The first of these was conducted under Royal Warrant by the British. During September–November 1945 a military court tried Josef Kramer, former commandant of Auschwitz, and over forty other members of the Camp SS, plus a few kapos taken into custody at Bergen-Belsen. In many ways this trial set the pattern for the others to follow. The charges ranged widely and certainly did not focus on the persecution and mass murder of Jews: the Allied prosecutors were chiefly interested in offences against Allied military personnel and citizens of Allied countries. What the Germans did to German Jews, for example, fell outside their jurisdiction. Jewish survivors gave evidence, but they were only a fraction of those who testified and the particularities of Judenpolitik got lost amidst the welter of exploitation and abuse that the Germans heaped on occupied populations. The same dilemma was writ large when it came to the International Military Tribunal at Nuremberg.[33]

The first assembly of delegates representing Jewish DPs, which met at St Ottilien in July 1945, passed a resolution calling on the Allies to ensure that Jews were included in the process under which justice would be exacted on the Germans by the victorious Allied powers. That never happened. The Allies had sufficient difficulty resolving their different approaches to a post-hostilities reckoning without complicating matters by involving Jewish jurists. Initially the British did not want to hold any trials at all and favoured the perfunctory investigation and summary execution of senior Nazis and members of the SS who fell into their hands. The Americans showed little interest in a judicial accounting until late 1944 when they were persuaded by the Russians that exemplary justice was called for. The four great powers were also edged in the direction of trials by the governments-in-exile which, since 1943, had been cataloguing German crimes. Their persistence led to the

creation of the UN War Crimes Commission that was intended to prepare cases against the perpetrators, although it was effectively sidelined
by the British and the Americans. During the summer of 1945 Allied
legal experts met in London to resolve these varied demands and came
up with the charter for a tribunal to be presided over by American,
British, Soviet and French judges, with legal teams from each country
taking responsibility for a portion of the charges. They agreed on four
chief counts: conspiracy against peace, the waging of aggressive war,
war crimes, and crimes against humanity. The men to be put on trial
comprised those at the apex of the civil and military echelon who had
been captured and remained alive. They included Göring, Wilhelm
Frick, Robert Ley, Hans Frank, Ribbentrop, Alfred Rosenberg, Fritz
Sauckel, Arthur Seyss-Inquart, Baldur von Schirach, Albert Speer,
Ernst Kaltenbrunner and Julius Streicher. Neurath, Hjalmar Schacht,
and Rudolf Hess, who had been out of the picture since the late 1930s,
were also selected for trial along with Keitel and Jodl of the army high
command and Admiral Dönitz. These men had presided over or fed
into most aspects of Judenpolitik at one time or another, and yet there
was no specific charge relating to crimes against the Jews.[34]

The World Jewish Congress tried to convince the chief American
prosecutor, Justice Robert Jackson, who oversaw the preparation of the
trial, that the annihilation of the Jewish people should be treated separately. They were assured that it would be subsumed under the newly
created and already somewhat controversial count of crimes against
humanity. One element of this count was genocide, newly defined by
the Polish Jewish jurist Raphael Lemkin, who had successfully lobbied
the Americans to adopt his jurisprudential innovation. But Jackson
refused to permit Chaim Weizmann to deliver an address to the tribunal coherently setting out the extent of German crimes against the
Jews. Consequently, the persecution of the Jews in the Third Reich
and the implementation of genocide emerged fitfully over the duration
of the proceedings between November 1945 and October 1946.[35]

This was not for lack of awareness or information. In his opening
peroration, Jackson referred to the 'common plan to exterminate the
Jews' and asserted that it 'was so methodically and thoroughly pursued
that [it] . . . largely succeeded'. Otto Ohlendorf was examined about the
Einsatzgruppen operations. Dieter Wisliceny disclosed information
about Eichmann and the workings of office IVB4 of the Gestapo, in
effect summarizing the 'final solution'. Bach-Zelewski was quizzed on

'anti-partisan' operations. The prosecution read into the court record Jürgen Stroop's report on the suppression of the Warsaw ghetto uprising, showing slides of the photographs that illustrated it. Rudolf Höss appeared as a defence witness for Kaltenbrunner, but described the mass-murder operations at Auschwitz-Birkenau. A French prisoner, Marie-Claude Vaillant-Couturier (who had testified at the Belsen trial), gave the inmates' perspective on the killing centre. A German engineer, Heinrich Graebe, gave a graphic account of a mass shooting in the Ukraine, all the more powerful for coming from a non-Jewish source. A handful of Jewish witnesses described Treblinka, Majdanek, and the fate of the Vilnius ghetto. Jacob Robinson, a lawyer attached to the World Jewish Congress, attended unofficially and supplied extensive statistical data amassed by the WJCs Institute of Jewish Affairs, which had been set up for the purpose of charting the depredations against the Jews. The official delegation from Poland passed on the results of the investigations into the extermination camps and the destruction of the Polish Jews. Léon Poliakov and Joseph Billig fed in German documents that gave evidence for the deportation of Jews from France. Rudolf Kasztner submitted the report of the Budapest Jewish rescue committee (originally prepared for the World Zionist Congress), giving fine detail on Eichmann's activity in Hungary and the disaster of the Hungarian Jews. Numerous Jewish lawyers, interrogators, psychologists, researchers, and translators laboured in support of the proceedings – including the Hollywood producer Budd Schulberg, who was in charge of preparing film evidence of Nazi crimes. And yet, the numbing detail presented day after day on a panoply of issues, and the relentless focus on the German conspiracy to wage war, obstructed a clear understanding of German policy towards the Jews and a nuanced appreciation of their fate.[36]

The Jewish population of Europe followed the trial avidly but greeted the outcome with mixed emotion. *Dos Naye Lebn*, a newspaper published in Lodz, proclaimed on 4 October 1946 that 'We have been overwhelmed with feelings of joy about the justice and joyous, holy revenge when we read about the death sentences for the twelve main murderers . . .' By contrast, *Le Monde Juif* for November 1946 wondered at the sparing treatment accorded to the fate of the Jews in the final judgement. Moyshe Feigenbaum, a leading light of the DP historical commissions, anticipated that it would be up to the Jews to supplement the trial record with their own experiences. The Nuremberg documents 'show only how the murderers behaved towards us, how they treated us and what they did with us. Do our lives in those nightmarish days consist only of such fragments? On what basis will the historian be able to create an image of what happened in the ghettos? ... Therefore each testimony of a saved Jew, every song from the Nazi era, every proverb, every anecdote and joke, every photograph is for us of tremendous value.'[37]

The partial comprehension of German anti-Jewish policy and its unprecedented character also account for the difficulty that Jews had in the parallel legal process of obtaining restitution and reparation. In 1945 there was simply no legal framework for dealing with state-sponsored larceny coupled with genocide on an international scale: it was necessary to invent a whole new language and to write new laws to deal with the claims of the living and the dead. Jewish organizations in the free world had begun mapping the extent of Jewish material losses during the war: the WJC established the Institute of Jewish Affairs and held a special conference in November 1944 to set out Jewish claims against the Germans and their partners in crime. A year later, Weizmann presented a memorandum to the Four-Power Conference in Paris that was considering the entire question of reparations to the countries exploited and plundered by the Germans. Nehemiah Robinson, Jacob's brother, set up an office of the WJC in Europe to press these demands. The Paris peace conference in November–December 1945 agreed to create a fund to compensate the victims of Nazi persecution and acknowledged that Jews would merit paramount consideration. A follow-up convention on reparations in June 1946 allotted over $50 million for the resettlement of non-repatriable displaced persons, including Jews. The funds were to come from 'non-monetary gold' discovered by the Allies at the end of the war in underground storage depots where the Germans had stashed plunder. The term 'non-monetary gold' was used to distinguish it from bullion that had been held by national banks, most of which was traced and returned; it was a euphemism for the residue of objects and personal belongings, such as wedding rings, smelted by the Germans. It included dental gold. Money would also be generated by the liquidation of heirless Jewish property and the disposal of sequestered German assets in neutral countries. Although 90 per cent of this sum was directed to the AJJDC and the Jewish Agency, it covered a fraction of the sums expended on the resettlement of Jews who left the Reich before 1939 and would not go far to cover the costs of maintaining the Jews in DP camps.[38]

The great powers refused to intervene at the level of restitution in particular countries or individual reparations. In the American and French zones the respective military governments passed laws to enable Jews to recovery property or receive compensation, leaving it to local agencies to work out, and then implement, the details. The British, afraid that the activities of the Zionist movement would benefit from recovered wealth, declined to act at all until 1949. As a result, the process was extremely uneven and riven with conflict. Survivors in West Germany submitted thousands of claims, although often the property in question had been reduced to rubble by bombing or fighting. In May 1947, Jewish organizations in the USA, Britain and France cooperated to set up the Jewish Restitution Successor Organization (JRSO) specifically to identify and evaluate heirless property; but the task was massive and there were huge problems of documentation. The JRSO abandoned any thought of obtaining recompense for household furnishings and personal items, lodging a universal claim based on a rough estimate of what had been plundered from the deportees from the Reich. While the Allies sent experts to recover treasures looted from national collections, it was left to an ad hoc body, Jewish Cultural Reconstruction, to track down artworks, devotional objects and rare books purloined from Jewish institutions. The team included the historian Salo Baron and Hannah Arendt. It achieved a great deal, but the thousands of paintings and antiques once owned by Jewish dealers and collectors or that once decorated Jewish homes across Europe lay beyond its purview. Unless there were survivors able to begin the arduous work of restitution this loot remained in the hands of the thieves and their beneficiaries.[39]

In Italy, which had changed sides during the war, Jewish efforts to achieve restitution were hampered by the myth that the country had never embraced the racial persecution of the Jews. Instead, every evil was blamed on the German occupation, 1943–5. No Italians faced trial for the despoliation, deportation or murder of Jews. Survivors had to go through a complicated legal process to prove that a property or business had been expropriated from them. The agency that handled such cases was the same one that had managed the dispossession of the Jews in the first place. Even if they were successful, Italian Jews had to pay back-taxes on a business or a residence and the costs of administering it while it was confiscated. When Jews who had been members of the

Fascist Party appealed to get their jobs back they were told that as fascists they were disqualified from any compensation.[40]

Even in the United Kingdom the war cast a perverted shadow over attempts by Jews to retrieve what was rightfully theirs. Hundreds of Jews from Axis countries found that their assets were frozen by the Custodian of Enemy Property. Afterwards those still alive usually succeeded in recovering their property; but many more who had entrusted a portion of their wealth to British financial institutions had perished. Instead of seeking heirs or handing the property to representative Jewish organizations, the British government appropriated the heirless assets and used them in a succession of bilateral compensation deals with other countries. Swiss banks would perpetrate a similar deception on a much, much larger scale.[41]

The lack of attention that the western allies paid to retribution, restitution and reparation was symptomatic of the swift redrawing of international relations in the post-war world. Already during the Potsdam peace conference in summer 1945 the strains were apparent between the western allies and the USSR. Anticipating the time when they would need Germany as part of the anti-Soviet alliance, by mid-1946 the British and the Americans were keener to promote reconstruction in their respective zones and to restore morale amongst the German population than to punish them and remind them of past misdeeds. For the same reasons, the Americans relented in their efforts to make neutral countries – chiefly Switzerland, Sweden and Spain – disgorge heirless Jewish assets or properties acquired at knock-down rates thanks to Aryanization. The Soviets were no less eager to win over the Germans. They knew that benign policies were more likely to legitimate and foster rule by the East German communists than continuing recrimination and ruination. The Jews were the great losers in this strategic repositioning. Even Jewish emigration from Europe to Palestine was adversely affected. As the western allies mustered their resources to counter what they perceived as the threat of Soviet expansion, the British became more attached to Palestine as a strategic base in the Middle East and less willing to alienate Arab feelings by permitting mass Jewish immigration.[42]

Jews in the fast-crystallizing Soviet bloc became increasingly isolated. In 1946 there were only about 6,000 Jews in the Soviet zone of Germany, including 2,500 of mixed parentage. They were embraced by the category of 'victims of fascism' but did not get any special assistance.

The official association of victims of Nazism offered some help reconsti-
tuting communities and for a few years aid trickled through from the
AJJDC, but they did not benefit from the restitution of private or
communal property. Unusually for German Jews, the community did
establish an honour court at the synagogue in Oranienburgerstrasse,
which had survived partially intact. It focused on the role of Jews who
bought their own lives by betraying Jews in hiding in Berlin. No fewer
than sixty-five were tried, of whom half were acquitted. Those found
guilty were excluded from the community and denied access to welfare.[43]

Stalin allowed democracy to survive in Czechoslovakia for three
years after the Red Army liberated Prague. During this period nearly
30,000 Jews returned to Slovakia from camps, forced labour and hiding.
A smaller number came back to Bohemia and Moravia. But the status of
survivors was confused. German Jews liberated in Theresienstadt were
slated for expulsion as enemy aliens. The government refused to reinstate
the pre-war treatment of Jews as a national minority, which meant that
they had to struggle against generic legislation for war compensation
that ignored the total devastation they had endured. Often the officials
who handled claims were the same men who staffed expropriation agencies under the Germans or for the Slovak regime. Efforts to retrieve
property frequently provoked a violent backlash. There were anti-Jewish
riots in Topalcany in September 1945 and in Bratislava in August 1946
following the promulgation of a restitution law. Paradoxically though,
the Prague government adopted a strongly pro-Zionist stance. This
accorded with the conviction in Moscow that a Jewish state in Palestine
would be dominated by socialists. Consequently, Czechoslovakia became
a corridor for Jews fleeing Poland and the authorities allowed the AJJDC
to provide aid en route. However, by 1948, Moscow was changing its
tune and the atmosphere chilled in this respect too. Eventually over
18,000 Czech Jews joined the exodus to Israel.[44]

In Hungary some 100,000 Jews survived the siege of Budapest and
the ghetto. They were completely stricken, though, and depended on
financial aid from the AJJDC. Eventually tens of thousands more made
their way back from the camps, bringing the total registered with the
community to 180,000. The World Jewish Congress led the fight to
restore their rights and recover their property, but it was a fruitless
endeavour. Once the communists monopolized power the work of
restitution ground to a halt and the community was subject to heavy

taxation. However, the left-wing government tackled the trial of collaborators with gusto. Baky, Endre and Jaross were tried and executed, while hundreds of lesser perpetrators were subjected to investigation and various degrees of punishment.[45]

A significant Jewish population remained in Romania, too. Around 50,000 deportees to Transnistria were left alive plus 65,000 Jews who had been uprooted from within the country. However, the post-Antonescu regime refused to allow back into the country Jews who could not prove that they were of Romanian birth. Tens of thousands remained trapped in the strip between the River Dneister and Soviet Ukraine, clamouring to emigrate. Eventually about 30,000 were permitted to leave for Israel. The remaining Romanian Jews received no compensation for their wartime ordeal and never recovered lost property. As in Hungary it suited the communists to stage trials of leading figures in the wartime government, notably Ion Antonescu, and a host of lesser officials. Crimes against the Jews featured in the accusations, but the scope and comprehensive nature of anti-Jewish measures were never spelled out clearly. The offence of anti-Semitism played second fiddle to the crime of being a fascist.[46]

The fons et origo of policy towards the Jewish remnant in countries under Soviet domination was, of course, Moscow. By 1945, Stalin had no more use for the Jewish Anti-Fascist Committee and the authorities once again refused to differentiate the fate of the Jews from the rest of the population. In reports of German atrocities and the liberation of the camps, the official media referred to fascist crimes against Soviet citizens, even if victims had been struck only because they were Jewish. Survivors in the liberated western territories of the USSR had to rebuild without any support from the state and were permitted to function collectively only as religious communities. For a period synagogues served as the address and channel for relief from the AJJDC and Jews in the west. One of the first activities by these reconstituted communities was to rebury the dead or to mark mass graves with memorials. There was no equivalent to the historical commissions in the USSR, but since 1944, Ilya Ehrenburg and Vasily Grossman had been recording testimony and collecting accounts by survivors in the wake of the advancing Red Army. They intended to publish these eye-witness statements and other evidence of the catastrophe in a 'Black Book'. However, during 1948 almost all forms of Jewish communal activity were choked off. The leading Yiddish writers associated with the Jewish Anti-Fascist

Committee were shot and the 'Black Book' was suppressed. It would not be until the end of the Cold War and the opening of archives in the former USSR that the full scale of Jewish suffering and loss in the USSR would be researched, transforming perspectives on the fate of the Jews across the whole of Europe during the Second World War.[47]

CONCLUSION

The fate of the Jews between 1933 and 1949 was rooted in anti-Semitism but it was shaped by war. Dislike and hatred of Jews was widespread in Europe before 1914, but the Great War created the conditions to super-heat these hostilities. The war made Hitler and it made large numbers of Germans receptive to his message – that the Jews were to blame for Germany's defeat, that they were a constant source of subversion, an enemy that had to be vanquished. The years of civil unrest after 1918, on top of the horror that trench warfare inflicted on servicemen and the effect of the blockade on the home front, coarsened German society and lowered inhibitions against illegality or violence. Cadres of young men emerged who conjured up military solutions to social issues and political questions, who believed in decisive action and the use of violence. The Nazi movement was infused with the spirit of the trenches and Hitler's leadership style reflected the German military practice of delegation, Auftragstaktik. Above all, Hitler and those around him were haunted by the defeat in November 1918 – which they attributed to the Jews. If, or when, Germany resumed a martial course, they were determined never to allow the Jews to commit such treachery again. They would strike first and destroy the Jewish enemy.

Hitler believed that Germany was at war with international Jewry, a contest on which hinged the fate of all mankind. Yet there was a puzzling gap between Nazi rhetoric and concrete policy. Judenpolitik in the first years of the Third Reich was erratic: it lacked consistency or central direction. Nevertheless, the Jews were the object of unremitting obloquy while at the same time the German population was schooled in hatred. The unofficial boycotts, sporadic violence, and a stream of legislation at local and national level sent out the message that Jews were fair game. Conversely, the practice of denying Jews the protection of the law or access to state benefits fortified the collective identity of the rest of the population as the Volksgemeinschaft – the racially defined people's community.

The regime assumed that world Jewry cared about the Jews in Germany and that their influence could sway governments in Whitehall and Washington. The early response of the Jewish diaspora and the international community tended to confirm that perception; it made German Jews hostage to the behaviour of both. Over time it became increasingly apparent that the Jews in Germany were hardly valuable hostages, but this reality did not impinge on Nazi thinking.

Preparations for war galvanized and focused Judenpolitik in 1936–7. The German economy was straining to meet the armament targets set by Hitler, so despoliation of the Jewish population offered an attractive income stream. This set a pattern for the future: when there were tough economic choices to make, the Jews would always be squeezed the hardest. Another pattern soon took shape. Every stage in the expansion of the Third Reich, starting with the occupation of Austria, was marked by ritualized violence against Jewish populations. The brutality and plunder in the newly acquired territories in turn radicalized attitudes and practices in the Reich itself.

While the personal predilections of Hitler and Goebbels played a major role in triggering the violence of 9–10 November 1938 that came to be known by the Germans as 'Kristallnacht', it was also a by-product of the bellicose mood generated by the Sudeten crisis. Hitler felt that his people had not shown enough enthusiasm for war, so exposure to massive violence would toughen them up. Many of the men and women who assaulted the Jews were letting off steam after a period of extreme tension. Yet none of this explains the elaborate and deliberate degradation of Judaism; the November pogrom was also the unrestrained expression of traditional Jew-hatred. Paradoxically, it provided the pretext for the adoption of more controlled, research-based methods of persecution advocated by the SD under Heydrich. Arguably, Goebbels' extra-marital affair with a Czech actress resulted in the SS gaining a dominant position in the formation and execution of Judenpolitik.

Once Germany was at war, the position of the Jews deteriorated sharply. The abuse and mass shooting of Jews in Poland marked a profound escalation of violence combined with a weakening of inhibitions. In this sense Operation Tannenberg was far more important in the course of anti-Jewish policy than the covert compulsory euthanasia project. The former was open and unashamed, the humiliation and killing of Jews openly celebrated; the latter was secret and stained with such ignominy that the perpetrators wished to conceal their deeds. But despite this extensive violence, the main thrust of German thinking was still directed towards a mixture of voluntary emigration and the forcible removal of Jews from areas of German habitation. The ghettos in Poland came into being when extrusion proved impractical and, like all previous Judenpolitik, ghettoization was muddled and inconsistently implemented. It generated further dilemmas for the Germans – from which they seemed miraculously freed by the defeat of France in the summer of 1940. Once again, though, the prospect of removing the Jews vanished like morning mist. As a result, conditions in the ghettos deteriorated and the death rate soared, although this was not a case of planned destruction. On the contrary, key figures in the German occupation authorities in Poland were converted to the idea of making the Polish Jews useful for the war effort. This policy created a nexus that proved hard to break once Berlin had resolved on the physical annihilation of all Jews.

The euphoria of the victory over France dissipated in the second half of 1940. Britain held out and Hitler found it impossible to cajole his allies and vassals into a strategy that might make her continued resistance impossible. Instead, Hitler opted to invade the USSR, dealing a blow against the Jewish-Bolshevik enemy, seizing the land and resources to maintain Germany's war economy, and providing a place to which Europe's Jews could be consigned finally. The invasion of the USSR was to be accompanied by a mass-murder campaign, Operation Tannenberg writ large. The military logisticians had also programmed mass death through starvation into their strategy: to compensate for the paucity of German resources Jews and Russians would starve. This was an unashamedly genocidal project, but it did not embrace or even impact on Jews in the rest of Europe. In fact, Operation Barbarossa generated a slight improvement in conditions in the Polish ghettos. Unfortunately, the attack on the USSR provoked resistance by communists across occupied Europe that was interpreted by Germans as evidence of Jewish subversion, the stirrings of the Jewish enemy. Reprisal actions against the Jews were taken by the army and civilian authorities in France and Serbia even before the SS considered such actions.

German military failure in the Russian campaign during 1941 triggered a further radicalization of anti-Jewish policy. Within weeks of the invasion, German armies inside Russia were being tormented by irregular forces operating in their rear areas, which they dogmatically attributed to Jewish incitement. The harassment of their supply lines by partisans only compounded the implications of failing to defeat Russia on schedule. Condemned to continue the war into 1942, the German leadership faced the prospect of a food and resource crisis. Morale on the home front was also flagging. Consequently, Hitler gave way to demands for the deportation of German Jews to the eastern occupied territories and towards the end of the year appears to have assented to a comprehensive solution of the 'Jewish question' across Europe. The trigger was most probably his decision to declare war on the United States, which in his mind formalized the state of hostilities between the two powers and brought into the open the global war that Germany was fighting. Driven by the determination to avoid another November 1918, and determined to punish the Jews in America by wreaking a terrible vengeance on their brethren in Europe, Hitler approved the physical annihilation of the Jews.

And yet, the European-wide genocide that unfolded from spring 1942 was no less haphazard than previous phases of anti-Jewish policy. It was low-cost and low-tech. The construction of extermination camps and the organization of deportations was never the highest priority; military exigencies always took precedence. Although the death camps were small-scale and crude constructions, it took months to build them and even then the killing apparatus was ill-designed, in need of modification. Even the manpower came mainly from non-German sources. Heydrich entrusted the planning to Adolf Eichmann, who had proved his mettle in promoting forced emigration and the logistics of mass deportations. But Eichmann had to reset the objectives to a more realistic level. The Germans managed to deport tens of thousands of Jews from western Europe in mid-1942, but they relied on extensive local assistance – which was not a given. Indeed, they would never achieve such numbers or such cooperation again over a comparable period. Apart from exceptional cases, such as Salonica in 1943 and Hungary in 1944, the Germans found themselves chasing ever more evasive Jews with ever more diminishing manpower at their disposal. Their greatest overall 'success' was in Poland, but here the Jews were already bottled up and the logistics were uncomplicated. Hence, over a quarter of a million Jews were conveyed from the prison-like ghetto of Warsaw to Treblinka in eight weeks on a few freight trains using one rail line.

When they resumed the deportations in early 1943, however, they faced extensive evasion and resistance.

Ultimately the genocidal assault was devastating, but this outcome was not due to the scientific killing machinery or the well-considered deception techniques that the Germans employed. Auschwitz-Birkenau has come to represent the apex of genocidal technology, although in fact the entire camp evolved in fits and starts with no clear design. Rather, the catastrophic rate of killing was due to German persistence, the active or passive cooperation of the populations amongst whom the Jews dwelt, and the duration of the murderous campaigns. This last factor was largely a consequence of Allied military failure.

Despite hopes of a German collapse in the winter of 1941–42, during the early spring or late summer of 1943, and autumn 1944, the Allies proved unable to administer a fatal blow against the German armed forces, while the Nazi state was sustained by a combination of resilience and repression. Most importantly, Hitler remained in place – willing on the war effort and the war against the Jews. In a startling reversal of Judenpolitik, however, he was persuaded to allow Jews to be exploited for labour in the concentration camps and in the Reich itself. Jewish policy thus came full circle, with some Jews protected to some slight degree thanks to their economic utility. Once again, though, anti-Jewish violence erupted on the streets of German towns, and ordinary Germans showed their racial superiority by casually murdering Jews in their vicinity. As in November 1938, the mayhem was decentralized, chaotic, and contrary to central orders.

During the last hours of his life and amidst the death agony of his empire, Hitler repeated his conviction that the Jews were the cause of Germany's misfortune and summoned his remaining followers not to repeat the humiliation of 1918. In this, at least, his Judenpolitik was consistent. Hitler's suicide and the destruction of Germany did not mark the end of Jewish suffering, though. The fate of the Jews continued to be determined by war – although now it was the Cold War and Britain's war against the Jews in Palestine. The immediate preoccupations of the western allies and the ideological fixation of the communists ensured that the Jewish survivors did not enjoy the retribution, restitution and reparation that they had longed for. There would be much unfinished business.

GLOSSARY

Abwehr German army counter-intelligence service

Abyssinia today, Ethiopia

AIZSARGI Aizsargi Organizacija, Latvian self-defence militia

AJA Anglo-Jewish Association. Self-appointed body of British Jews, est. 1871, to assist oppressed or impoverished Jewish communities abroad

AJB Association des Juifs en Belgique. Association of Jews in Belgium, German-imposed central organization of Jews in Belgium

AJC American Jewish Committee. Self-appointed representative body of American Jews, est. 1906, dominated by patrician, 'uptown' Jews

AJJDC (JDC) American Jewish Joint Distribution Committee. Also known as the Joint, est. 1914 to raise money for Jews abroad and to administer relief

AK Armia Krajowa. *Polish.* Home Army, the underground military organization in Poland under the orders of the Polish government-in-exile

Aktion lit. an action, term for German operation against Jews

AL Armia Ludowa. *Polish.* People's Army, underground military organization in Poland dominated by the Communist Party

Alpini elite Italian mountain troops

Älteste lit. eldest, term for German-appointed head of a Jewish council, titular leader of a ghetto

Altreich lit. Old Reich, term for territory of Germany within pre-March 1938 borders

Amelot committee semi-covert Jewish organization providing aid to Jews in Paris

American Jewish Committee *see* AJC

American Jewish Congress quasi-democratic representative body of American Jews, dominated by recent immigrants

American Jewish Joint Distribution Committee *see* AJJDC

Anglo-Jewish Association *see* AJA

Anschluss German term for the annexation of Austria

Appeasement policy of offering concessions to Hitler in order to preserve peace, associated with British prime minister Neville Chamberlain

Appell roll call of prisoners in a concentration camp

Arbeiter worker

Arbeitseinsatz im Osten term denoting labour service in the east

Arbeitsjuden work-Jews, usually referring to the semi-permanent labour force in a death camp

Armia Krajowa *see* AK

Armia Ludowa *see* AL

Arrow Cross extreme nationalist, right-wing Hungarian paramilitary organization

Aryan Nazi term for a member of the Aryan 'race'

Aryan paragraph form of attestation to being an Aryan, required of all public servants by the Nazi regime in Germany and applied in some occupied countries

Aryanization Nazi term for confiscating the businesses, property and assets of Jewish people

asocial catch-all Nazi term for those deemed criminals, beggars, vagrants, prostitutes, long-term unemployed, non-conformists

Association des Juifs en Belgique *see* AJB

Auftragstaktik German military doctrine for delegating to subordinate officers the responsibility for carrying out specific operations

Auskleideraum lit. undressing room

Ausseidlung lit. resettlement, Nazi euphemism for deportation to a death camp

autarky economic self-sufficiency

Bade- und Inhalationsräume lit. bath and inhalation rooms, term used to disguise gas chambers

BDM Bund der deutscher Mädel. Nazi organization for German girls aged fourteen to eighteen, equivalent of the Hitler Youth

Beirat term for Jewish council in Lodz ghetto

Berchtesgaden Hitler's rural retreat in Bavaria

Berghof complex of buildings at Berchtesgaden

Blitzkrieg lit. lightning war

Blockälteste lit. block elder, prisoner functionary in a concentration camp responsible for keeping order in a barracks

Blockova Polish slang term for female prisoner functionary in a concentration camp responsible for keeping order in a barrack block, derived from Russian

Blut und Boden blood and soil, term denoting racial ideology

B'nai Brith Jewish fraternal order, est. 1843 in USA

Board of Deputies of British Jews central representative body of British Jews, est. 1760

Bohemia and Moravia areas of Czechoslovakia occupied by Germany in March 1939 and denoted as the *'Protectorate'

Bolshevists general term for Russian communists, derived from Bolshevik Party, but in right-wing circles the term was often conflated with Jews

Bund Jewish Socialist Party and workers' movement in Poland

CBS Columbia Broadcasting Service. US broadcaster based in New York

CDJC Centre de Documentation Juive Contemporaine. Jewish documentation centre, est. 1943 in Grenoble and revived in 1945 in Paris to document the persecution of the Jews in France

CENTOS Central Organization for the Care of Orphans. Polish Jewish organization

Central British Fund for German Jewry fund-raising body based in London, devoted to aiding Jews in Nazi Germany and German Jewish refugees

Centralna Evreilor din Romania government-imposed central organization of Romanian Jews

Centralverein deutscher Staatsbürger jüdischen Glaubens *see* CV

Centre de Documentation Juive Contemporaine *see* CDJC

CGJ Council for German Jewry. Body created by British and American Jews in 1936 to coordinate aid for German Jews and German Jewish refugees

CGQJ Commissariat-général aux questions juives. Commissariat General for the Jewish Question, the main agency for enforcing anti-Jewish laws in Vichy France and expropriating the property and assets of Jewish people

Chanukkah Jewish religious festival celebrating the successful revolt of the Jews in ancient Judea against oppressive rule and the re-establishment of an independent Jewish polity

Comité de Défense des Juifs covert organization in Belgium to assist Jews

Commissariat-général aux questions juives *see* CGQJ

Confessing Church minority Protestant church movement in Germany established in opposition to the creation of the Nazi-aligned *German Christian Church

Conseil Représentatif des Institutions juives de France *see* CRIF

Consistoire central organization of French Jews created originally by Napoleon, mainly with religious functions

Council for German Jewry *see* CGJ

county commissioner cognate term for Landrat

CRIF Conseil Représentatif des Institutions juives de France. Post-1945 representative body of Jews in France

CV Centralverein deutscher Staatsbürger jüdischen Glaubens. Central Association of German citizens of the Jewish faith, est. 1893 to combat anti-Semitism

CV-Zeitung weekly newspaper of the *CV

DAF Deutsche Arbeitsfront. The German Labour Front, unitary successor organization to forcibly dissolved German trades unions

DAW Deutsche Ausrustungswerke. German Armaments Works, owned by the *SS

DDP Deutsche Demokratische Partei. German liberal party, est. 1919

deJewification term denoting the exclusion of Jews from society and the economy

DELASEM Delegazione per l'Assistenza degli Emigranti Ebrei. Delegation for the Assistance of Jewish Emigrants, Italian organization, est. 1939 initially to assist Jewish refugees in Italy to emigrate

Delegatura Polish term for the underground government in Poland responsible to the Polish government-in-exile in London

départements French administrative units, like counties

Der Angriff Nazi newspaper edited by Joseph Goebbels

Der Stürmer Nazi newspaper edited by Julius Streicher

Deutsch-Jüdischer Jugend German Jewish youth movement

Deutsche Arbeitsfront *see* DAF

Deutsche Ausrustungswerke *see* DAW

Deutsche Staatspartei successor to *DDP

Deutscher Vortrupp German Vanguard, a right-wing association of German Jews

DNVP Deutschnationale Volkspartei. German National People's Party, right-wing party in Weimar Germany

DP Displaced Person. Official UN term denoting people forced to leave their home due to persecution or warfare

Dror left-wing Zionist youth movement in Poland

Durchgangstrasse IV German term for road-building project in Ukraine

Economic Staff East German civilian-army unit established to exploit conquered territory in the USSR

EG Einsatzgruppe (Einsatzgruppen, pl.). Task force consisting of *Sipo, *SD and *Orpo personnel

Einsatzkommando *see* EK

Einzelaktion (Einzelaktionen, pl.) term denoting unauthorized anti-Jewish action

EK Einsatzkommando (Einsatzkommandos, pl.). Sub-unit of *EG

Fareynikte Partizaner Organizatsye (FPO) United Partisan Organization, Jewish fighting group established in Vilnius ghetto, January 1942

Feldgendarmerie German military police

Flakhelfer a member of a German anti-aircraft-gun crew

Fliegende Kolonne lit. flying column, term for special unit of the *Ordnungsdienst (Order Service) in Westerbork camp

14f13 code for programme to murder inmates of concentration camps too sick to work

FPO *see* Fareynikte Partizaner Organizatsye

francs-tireurs French term denoting guerrilla fighters or partisans

Francs-tireurs et partisans – main-d'œuvre immigrée (FTP-MOI) French partisans

Free Zone Zone Libre. Unoccupied zone of France, 1940–42

Freikorps right-wing militia formed of ex-servicemen in Germany, active 1918–22

FTP-MOI Francs-tireurs et partisans-main-d'œuvre immigrée. French partisans

Führer Chancellery Hitler's personal office

Funktionsbefehl a formal agreement between the *SD and the *Gestapo in 1937 demarcating spheres of action and responsibility

Gau one of the Nazi party administrative districts into which Germany was divided

Gauleiter leader of the Nazi Party organization in a particular *Gau

Gebietskommissar commissioner responsible for running a district in occupied USSR

Gebietskommissar administrative unit in occupied USSR

Gebietskommissar Weissrussin administrative unit covering most of Byelorussia (White Russia)

Geheime Feldpolizei the secret field police of the German armed forces

Geheime Staatspolizei the secret political police, usually known as Gestapo

Geltungsjuden lit. Jews by definition, people with two Jewish grandparents deemed Jewish under the Nuremberg Laws by virtue of certain criteria

Gemeinde community, legally defined organization of German Jews in a particular city or town

General Government German term for the area of occupied Poland not annexed to the Reich

Generalplan Ost plan for exploitation and settlement of conquered territory in the USSR

German Christian Church section of the Evangelical church that embraced Nazi racial doctrine and accepted Nazi-approved church leadership

German Zionist Federation *see* ZvfD

Germanization translation of the Nazi term for settling Germans and ethnic Germans in conquered territory as well as expelling native populations

Gestapa Prussian Gestapo

Gestapo *see* Geheime Staatspolizei

GFP *see* Geheime Feldpolizei

GPU Soviet secret police

Ha'avara agreement reached between Nazi Germany and the World Zionist Organization to enable German Jews to emigrate to Palestine with some of their assets by converting them into German goods

Hachshara agricultural training course for young Jews aiming to settle on collective farms, *kibbutzim, in Palestine

Hadassah American women's Zionist movement

Haganah semi-covert Jewish military organization in Palestine

HaShomer HaTzair left-wing Zionist youth movement

Hasidim generic Hebrew term for Orthodox Jewish sects in eastern Europe

Haupttreuhandstelle Ost Main Trustee Office for the East, created by Göring to oversee the pillage and economic exploitation of conquered territory in eastern Europe

Haushalt household

Hechalutz-Dror left-wing Zionist youth movement

HeHalutz Ha-Tsair left-wing Zionist youth movement

HICEM Paris-based aid organization uniting the US-based Hebrew Immigrant Aid Society of New York and the Jewish Colonisation Association

High Commission for Refugees League of Nations office for assisting refugees

Hilfskomitee German Jewish aid committee for emigrants and refugees

Hilfsverein der Deutschen Juden German Jewish welfare organization

Hilfswilliger volunteer, term denoting surrendered enemy personnel who opted to serve or fight with German military units

HJ Hitler Jugend. Hitler Youth

Hlinka Guard right-wing paramilitary organization in Slovakia

Hlinka Party right-wing Nationalist party in Slovakia

HSSPF Höhere SS- und Polizeiführer. Higher SS Police Leader: senior *SS and *Sipo-SD officer appointed by Himmler in occupied territories and responsible to him

Iberlebn *Yiddish.* lit. survival or overcoming
ICRC International Committee of the Red Cross
IKG Israelitische Kultusgemeinde. Central communal organization of Viennese Jews
Iron Guard right-wing paramilitary organization in Romania
Israelitische Kultusgemeinde *see* IKG
Israelitisches Familienblatt German Jewish weekly newspaper

JCA Jewish Colonization Association
JDC *see* AJJDC
Jewish Fighting Organization *see* ZOB
Jewish Refugees Committee later the German Jewish Aid Committee, body created by
    British Jews to aid German Jewish refugees in the UK
Jewish Relief Unit *see* JRU
JKB Jüdischer Kulturbund. German Jewish cultural organization established under
    Nazi supervision
Joodse Raad German-imposed Jewish council in Amsterdam
JRU Jewish Relief Unit. Mobile team sent by British Jews to provide medical and
    welfare aid to Jewish survivors in liberated north-west Europe
Judenaktion German operation against Jews
Judenhaus apartment building or house in Germany designated only for Jews
Judenpolitik anti-Jewish policy
Judenrat German-appointed Jewish council
Judenreferent official of the Jewish Department of the *Gestapo in the *RSHA, office
    IVB4, or agent of office IVB4 serving abroad
Jüdischer Frauenbund Association of Jewish Women
Jüdisches Nachrichtenblatt official gazette for Jewish people in Germany, published
    under Nazi supervision
Jüdische Rundschau weekly newspaper of the German Zionist movement
Jüdischer Abwehr Dienst Jewish defence service, established in Weimar Germany
Jüdischer Kulturbund *see* JKB
Jungvolk Nazi youth organization for ten- to fourteen-year-olds

Kaddish Jewish prayer recited by a mourner
kaftan traditional outer garment worn by Orthodox Jews in Eastern Europe
Kapo (Kapos, pl.) prisoner functionary in a concentration camp
Katzetnik inmate of a concentration camp
Kehilla Yiddish term for Jewish community, also denoting official communal body
kibbutz (kibbutzim, pl.) Jewish collective farm in Palestine
Kiddush cup cup used for drinking wine in celebration of the Sabbath
kike insulting term for Jew
Kindertransport train specially chartered by Jewish refugee agencies to evacuate
    Jewish children from Germany
KL Konzentrationslager concentration camp
KPD German Communist Party
Kraft Durch Freude Strength Through Joy, Nazi-run recreational organization

Krankenbehandler lit. carer for the sick

Kriegsmarine German navy

Kripo Kriminalpolizei. Criminal police

Kristallnacht lit. Night of Broken Glass, German term for anti-Jewish actions of
9–10 November 1938

Kulturbund Deutscher Juden German Jewish Cultural League, later the *JKB

kumbal Czech slang for a cubby-hole

Kurfürstendamm main shopping street in Berlin

Lebensraum lit. living space, Nazi term for land in eastern Europe deemed necessary
for the survival of the German people

lei unit of Romanian currency

Leichenkeller lit. corpse cellar, mortuary

Lippmann–Rosenthal Bank (Liro) Phony bank set up to hold expropriated property
and assets of Dutch Jews

Luftwaffe German air force

Machtergreifung lit. seizure of power, Nazi term for the takeover of Germany in 1933

Madagascar scheme Nazi plan to settle European Jews forcibly on the island of
Madagascar

Maghreb French-colonial territory of North Africa

malina *Polish.* hiding place

Maquis general term for French guerrilla fighters

matzoh unleavened bread, eaten by observant Jews during the festival of Passover

MBF Militärbefehlshaber in Frankreich. German military commander of occupied
France, based in Paris

mezuzah (mezuzot, pl.) small case affixed to the right-hand doorpost of Jewish homes
and businesses, containing words of scripture

Militärbefehlshaber in Frankreich *see* MBF

minyan (minyanim, pl.) *Hebrew.* quorum needed for a Jewish religious service

Mischling (Mischlinge, pl.) person defined as being of mixed race under the
Nuremberg Laws, including Mischling of the first degree and second degree

MOI Ministry of Information, Britain

Molotov cocktail home-made petrol bomb

NAACP National Association for the Advancement of Colored People

Nahplan lit. short-term plan

Nationalsozialistische Betriebszellenorganisation *see* NSBO

Nationalsozialistische Handwerks-, Handels-, und Gewerbe-Organisation *see*
NS-HAGO

Nationalsozialistische Volkswohlfahrt Nazi welfare organization

NCO non-commissioned officer

Nisko scheme Nazi plan to settle European Jews forcibly in the Lublin district of
Poland

non-Aryan Christian Jewish convert to Christianity

NSBO Nationalsozialistische Betriebszellenorganisation. National Socialist Company Cell Organization, party branch in a factory or office

NSDAP Nationalsozialistische Deutsche Arbeiterpartei. National Socialist German Workers' Party, Nazi Party, Nazis

NS-HAGO Nationalsozialistische Handwerks-, Handels-, und Gewerbe-Organisation. Nazi traders' association

Oberjude head Jew, Nazi term for head of a Jewish council

Operation Barbarossa German army plan for the invasion of the USSR

Operation Blau German army plan for thrust into the Caucasus in 1942

Operation Margarethe German plan for the occupation of Hungary

Operation Reinhard Nazi term for the annihilation of Polish Jews, 1942

Operation Sealion German army plan for the invasion of Britain, 1940

Operation Tannenberg *SS operation to eliminate opposition in Poland, 1939

Operation Tiger *SS operation to eliminate resistance in Marseille, 1943

Operation Typhoon German army plan to capture Moscow, October 1941

Ordedienst Order Service

Ordnungsdienst lit. Order Service, uniformed service instigated by Germans to keep order inside ghettos, usually referred to as Jewish police

Ordnungspolizei *see* Orpo

Ordnungswache lit. Order Watch, similar to *Ordnungsdienst (Order Service)

Organisation Todt German paramilitary construction organization, often utilizing slave labour

Organize concentration camp slang for obtaining food or valuables by barter or pilfering

Orpo Ordnungspolizei. The uniformed German police

ORT Jewish educational and vocational training organization

OSS Office of Special Services. US organization for covert military and intelligence operations

Ostindustrie *SS industrial enterprise in Poland

Ostjuden usually derogatory term for Yiddish-speaking east European Jews, usually derogatory

Ostland German administrative unit encompassing the Baltic states and part of Byelorussia

Ostmark Nazi term for Austria after the annexation

Ostministerium Ministry for the Occupied Eastern territories

OUN underground Ukrainian nationalist organization in Poland, working with the Germans 1939–41, later operating against Germans and Russians

Oyneg Shabas/Oneg Shabat semi-covert organization created by Emanuel Ringelblum to record the fate of Jews in the Warsaw ghetto and occupied Poland

Palestine between 1933 and 1948, under British rule, home to significant Jewish population aspiring towards nationhood but opposed by much larger Arab population

Palestine Office office to facilitate emigration to Palestine run by local Zionist
  organization
panzer tank
panzer group German armoured formation, roughly the size of a corps
Partisans Armés Belgian resistance group
passeurs guides who took refugees and escaping Allied military personnel from
  German-occupied France over the Pyrenees into Spain
Passover Jewish religious festival commemorating the Exodus from Egypt
Paulusbund organization devoted to aiding German Jewish converts to Christianity
Poale Zion Labour Zionist Party
pogrom anti-Jewish riot
Polonized assimilated to Polish culture, usually meaning Jews whose first language
  was Polish
Polska Partia Robotnicza *see* PPR
Popular Front socialist government in France, 1936–7
POW prisoner of war
PPR Polska Partia Robotnicza. Polish Workers' Party, reconstituted Polish Communist
  Party
protective custody Nazi term for detention in a concentration camp
Protectorate area of Czechoslovakia occupied by Germany in March 1939

rafle French term for round-up
Rapportschreiber prisoner functionary in a concentration camp responsible for
  recording and checking the number of inmates in a barrack block
Rassenschande a Nazi term meaning race shame or race mixing
razzia *Italian.* round-up
Rechtskonsulent (*Rechtkonsulenten*, pl.) Nazi term for Jewish legal consultant
Rechtsschutz lit. defence of rights, term for civil resistance
Rechtsstaat lit. state of law
Reich Chancellery office of the Chancellor of Germany
Reichsarbeitsdienst Reich Labour Service, compulsory year of labour
Reichsbahn German state railway
Reichsbank German state bank
Reichsbund jüdischer Frontsoldaten *see* RjF
Reichsführer-SS in full: Reichsführer-SS und Chef der Deutschen Polizei, Reich Chief
  of the SS and German Police – Himmler's title from June 1936
Reichskommissar governor of territory in occupied eastern Europe
Reichskommissar für die Festigung des deutschen Volkstums (RKFdV) Reich
  Commissariat for the Strengthening of Germandom, the organization responsible
  for settling ethnic Germans from Russia and the Baltic on annexed Polish land,
  headed by Himmler
Reichskommissariat Ukraine administrative unit of German-occupied Ukraine
Reichsmark unit of German currency
Reichssicherheitshauptamt *see* RSHA

Reichssippenamt the Race Kinship Office, *SS office to certify persons of Aryan status

Reichstag German federal parliament

Reichstatthalter governor

Reichsvereinigung der Juden in Deutschland Nazi imposed and appointed central organization of Jews in Germany, 1938–43

Reichsvertretung der deutschen Juden *see* RV

Resettlement Office office of the German city administration, Warsaw, responsible for relocating Jews to a ghetto in the city

Revisionist Zionists members of right-wing Zionist movement

Rexists extreme right-wing French-speaking movement in Belgium

RjF Reichsbund jüdischer Frontsoldaten. Association of Jewish combat veterans

RM *see* Reichsmark

Romanization Romanian version of Aryanization

RSHA Reichssicherheitshauptamt. The Reich Main Security Office, formed late 1939 to unite the *Gestapo, Criminal Police, *Sipo and *SD

RV Reichsvertretung der deutschen Juden. The Reich Representation of German Jews, the first centralized, representative body of German Jews, 1933–38 (from 1935 it was forced to change the nomenclature to Reichsvertretung der Juden in Deutschland, the representative body of Jews in Germany)

SA Sturmabteilung. Paramilitary Nazi Party organization, also known as Brownshirts

SCAP Service de Contrôle des Administrateurs Provisoires. Organization in Vichy France to appoint managers to run property and businesses expropriated from Jews

Schnellbrief lit. express letter, a summary for speedy transmission

Schupo Schutzpolizei. locally recruited collaborationist police force

Schutzmannschaften locally recruited collaborationist militia

Schutzpolizei *see* Schupo

Schutzstaffel *see* SS

SD Sicherheitsdienst. The security service of the *SS

SDHA Sicherheitsdiensthauptamt. SD Head Office, Berlin headquarters of the *SD

SEC Section d'Enquête et de Contrôle. The anti-Jewish police in Vichy France

Seder celebration on opening days of Passover festival

Selbstschutz self-defence militia formed by local ethnic Germans

Selection separation of Jews deemed capable of work from those deemed incapable, usually on arbitrary grounds, leading to the murder of those deemed incapable

Service de Controle des Administrateurs Provisoires (SCAP) organization in Vichy France that appointed managers to run property and businesses expropriated from Jews

Service du travail obligatoire *see* STO

Seuchensperrgebiet plagne-quarantine area

She'erith Hapleitah Hebrew term meaning the surviving remnant, referring to Jewish survivors in liberated Europe

shechita the slaughter of livestock according to Jewish religious law

Shema Jewish prayer

shtetl small town or rural settlement with large or majority Jewish population

Sicherheitsdienst *see* SD

Sicherheitsdiensthauptamt *see* SDHA

Sipo Sicherheitspolizei. Security police, comprising Gestapo and criminal police

Sipo-SD units of security police (*Sicherheitspolizei) and *SD, with personnel often belonging to both

SOE Special Operations Executive, British organization for covert military operations

Sonderbehandlung lit. special treatment, a euphemism for execution

Sonderkommando (Sonderkommandos, pl.) term for sub-unit of an *EK and also the Jewish workforce in the gas chambers and crematoria of the death camps

SPD German Social Democratic Party

Special Operations Executive British organization for covert military operations

Sperrgebiet quarantined area

SS Schutzstaffel. lit. protection detachment, set up in 1925 as Nazi Party bodyguard that evolved into a security and intelligence service with a military arm, headed by Himmler and intended to become a racial elite

SS-Totenkopf SS-Totenkopfverbände, lit. Death's Head Units, concentration camp guard force

SS-WVHA Wirtschafts- und Verwaltungshauptamt. The *SS Business and Administrative Head Office

Staatszionistische Partei right-wing German Zionist party

Stahlhelm Steel helmets, a paramilitary association of German war veterans

Stalag prisoner-of-war camp

Stapostelle (Stapostellen, pl.) Gestapo regional office

Star of David *see* Yellow Star

STO Service du travail obligatoire. Compulsory labour service in Germany forced on French civilians by the occupation regime

Sturmabteilung *see* SA

Sudetenland predominantly German-speaking strip of land along the western border of Czechoslovakia; its ethnic German inhabitants were known as Sudeten Germans

SWIT radio Polish underground radio station based in Britain

T-4 code name for the compulsory euthanasia project

tallit *Hebrew.* prayer shawl

tallit katan *Hebrew.* modified prayer shawl worn under the shirt

Tarbut Hebrew-language cultural organization

tefillin *Hebrew.* phylacteries, leather binding with box containing pieces of scripture, used by Orthodox Jewish men in morning prayer

The Thirteen slang term for the Office to Prevent Profiteering and Speculation, located at 13 Leszno Street in the Warsaw ghetto

Tisha B'Av Jewish day of mourning to commemorate destruction of the Temple in 70 CE

Torah scrolls parchment inscribed with the five books of Moses

TOZ Society for the Protection of Health, Jewish medical aid organization

Transferstelle lit. transfer office, the department of the German city administration in Warsaw responsible for supplying the ghetto with food and raw material

Tsukunft Yiddish for future, youth wing of the *Bund

UGIF Union générale des israélites de France. German-supervised central organization of French Jews, devoted to welfare, initially divided between the occupied and Free Zones

Umschlagplatz assembly and embarkation place for Jews sent to a death camp

Union générale des israélites de France *see* UGIF

UNRRA United Nations Relief and Reconstruction Administration. Organization created in 1943 to undertake relief work in liberated Europe

Unter der Linden main street in central Berlin

UPA Ukrainian nationalist resistance movement

Ustasha extreme right-wing nationalist movement in Croatia

Vaad Hatzalah council to aid religious Jews

Verband nationaldeutscher Juden the Association of German National Jews

Vernichtungslager extermination camp

Verschönerung lit. beautifying

Volk a people, a term with racial connotations

völkisch of the people, a term with racial overtones

Völkische Jungdeutsche Orden nationalist German youth movement

Völkischer Beobachter main Nazi Party newspaper

Volksdeutsch (Volksdeutsche, pl.) ethnic German

Volksgemeinschaft Nazi term for racial people's community

Volksgenossen lit. racial comrades

Vorkommando vanguard kommando

Waffen-SS military wing of the *SS, from 1939

Walloon Vlaams Nationaal Verbond right-wing separatist organization of French-speaking Belgians

Wartheland name given to the area of western Poland annexed to Germany, Gau Wartheland, also known as Warthegau

Wehrmacht German armed forces (Heer – army; Luftwaffe – air force; Kriegsmarine – navy)

Werterfassung storehouse of goods and valuables pillaged from Jews

Wilhelmstrasse term denoting the German Foreign Office and the government district in Berlin

Wirtschafts- und Verwaltungshauptamt *see* SS-WVHA

Workers' Circle left-wing Jewish organization

World Jewish Congress quasi democratic representative body of Jews around the world

World Zionist Organization central organization of Zionist movement

WRB War Refugee Board, USA

WVHA *see* SS-WVHA

yarmulke *Hebrew.* head covering, skull cap

Yellow Star (Star of David) imposed sign denoting the wearer to be a Jew by Nazi definition

Yishuv *Hebrew.* the Jewish population of Palestine

Yom Kippur Day of Atonement, the holiest day in the Jewish calendar

Youth Aliyah organization to assist Jewish youth to settle in Palestine

ZAHA Zentralausschuss für Hilfe und Aufbau. Central Committee for Assistance and Reconstruction, German Jewish welfare organization

Zegota Council to Aid Jews, created by the Polish underground government

Zentralausschuss für Hilfe und Aufbau *see* ZAHA

Zentralstelle für jüdische Auswanderung the Central Office for Jewish Emigration in Vienna, later replicated in Berlin, Prague and Amsterdam

Zionistische Vereinigung für Deutschland (ZvfD) German Zionist Federation

ZOB Zydowska Organizacja Bejowa. Jewish Fighting Organization, armed Jewish resistance movement in Warsaw ghetto

Zone Libre *see* Free Zone

ZTOS Jewish Self-Aid

ZvfD Zionistische Vereinigung für Deutschland. German Zionist Federation, the main German Zionist organization

Zydo-Kommuna derogatory Polish term identifying Jews with communists

Zydowska Organizacja Bejowa *see* ZOB

Zydowski Zwiazek Wojskowy *see* ZZW

Zyklon-B potassium cyanide

ZZW Zydowski Zwiazek Wojskowy. Jewish Military Union, armed organization of Revisionist Zionists in the Warsaw ghetto

BIBLIOGRAPHY

Reference works

Domarus, Max, *The Essential Hitler. Speeches and Commentary*, ed. Patrick Romane (Wauconda, IL: Bolchazy-Carducci, 2007)

Hayes, Peter and Roth, Kohn K. eds, *The Oxford Handbook of Holocaust Studies* (Oxford: Oxford University Press, 2010)

Laqueur, Walter, *The Holocaust Encyclopedia* (New Haven: Yale University Press, 2001)

Megargee, Geoffrey ed., *Encyclopedia of Camps and Ghettos, 1933–1945*, vol. 1, Parts A & B, *Early Camps, Youth Camps, and Concentration Camps and Subcamps under the SS-Business Administration Main Office (WVHA)* (Bloomington, IN: Indiana University Press, 2009)

———— ed., *Encyclopedia of Camps and Ghettos, 1933–1945*, vol. 2, *Ghettos in German-Occupied Eastern Europe* (Bloomington, IN: Indiana University Press, 2009)

Miron, Guy ed., *The Yad Vashem Encyclopedia of the Ghettos During the Holocaust* 2 vols (Jerusalem: Yad Vashem, 2009)

Niewyk, Donald and Nicosia, Francis eds, *The Columbia Guide to the Holocaust* (New York: Columbia University Press, 2000)

Patterson, David et al., *Encyclopedia of Holocaust Literature* (Westport, CT: Oryx Press, 2002)

Rozett, Robert and Spector, Shmuel eds, *Encyclopedia of the Holocaust* (New York: Facts on File, 2000)

Stone, Dan ed., *The Historiography of the Holocaust* (Houndmills: Palgrave Macmillan, 2004)

Synder, Louis L. ed., *Encyclopedia of the Third Reich* (New York: McGraw Hill, 1976)

United States Holocaust Memorial Museum, *Historical Atlas of the Holocaust* (New York: Macmillan, 1996)

Wistrich, Robert, *Who's Who in Nazi Germany* (New York: Macmillan, 1982)

Wyman, David ed., *The World Reacts to the Holocaust* (Baltimore: Johns Hopkins University Press, 1996)

Primary sources

Adelsberger, Lucie, *Auschwitz. A Doctor's Story*, trans. Susan Ray (Boston: Northeastern University Press, 1995)

Adelson, Alan ed., *The Diary of Dawid Sierakowiak*, trans. Kamil Turowski (London: Bloomsbury, 1996)

Adler, Stanislaw, *In the Warsaw Ghetto 1940–1943. An Account of a Witness*, trans. Sara Philip (Jerusalem: Yad Vashem, 1982)

Andreas-Friedrich, Ruth, *Berlin Underground*, trans. Barrows Mussey (London: Latimer House, 1948)

Arad, Y., Gutman, Y., Margaliot, A. eds, *Documents on the Holocaust* (Jerusalem: Yad Vashem, 1981)

Arad, Yitzhak, Krakowski, Shmuel, Spector, Shmuel eds, *The Einsatzgruppen Reports* (New York: Holocaust Library, 1982)

Avriel, Ehud, *Open the Gates! A Personal Story of 'Illegal' Immigration to Israel* (New York: Atheneum, 1975)

Bajohr, Frank and Strupp, Christoph eds, *Fremde Blicke auf das 'Dritte Reich'. Berichte ausländischer Diplomaten über Herrschaft und Gesellschaft in Deutschland 1933–1945* (Göttingen: Wallstein Verlag, 2011)

Barkai, Meyer ed., *The Fighting Ghettos*, (New York: Tower Book, 1962)

Ben-Sasson, Havi and Preiss, Lea, 'Twilight Days: Missing Pages from Avraham Lewin's Warsaw Ghetto Diary, May–July 1942', *Yad Vashem Studies*, 33 (2005), 7–60

Bernard, Jacques, *The Camp of Slow Death*, trans. Edward Owen Marsh (London: Gollancz, 1945 [first published 1944])

Berr, Hélène, *Journal*, trans. David Bellos (London: MacLehose Press, 2008)

Blatt, Thomas Toivi, *From the Ashes of Sobibor. A Story of Survival* (Evanston: Northwestern University Press, 1997)

Breitman, Richard et al. eds, *Advocate for the Doomed. The Diaries and Papers of James G. McDonald*, vol. 1, *1932–1935* (Bloomington: Indiana University Press, 2007)

————— et al. eds, *Refugees and Rescue. The Diaries and Papers of James G. McDonald*, vol. 2, *1935–45* (Bloomington: Indiana University Press, 2009)

CDJC, *Les Juifs en Europe (1939–1945). Rapports Présentés à la Première Conférence Européenne des Commissions Historiques et des Centres de Documentation Juifs* (Paris: Éditions du Centre, 1949)

Ciano, Count Galeazzo, *The Complete Unabridged Diaries of Count Galeazzo Ciano, Italian Minister of Foreign Affairs, 1936–1943*, ed. and trans. Robert L. Miller and Stanislaus Pugliese (London: Phoenix Press, 2002)

Cytryn, Avraham, *Youth Writing Behind the Walls. Notebooks from the Lodz Ghetto*, ed. Su Newman, trans. Chaya Naor (Jerusalem: Yad Vashem, 2005)

Czech, Danuta ed., *Amidst a Nightmare of Crime. Manuscripts of Prisoners in Cremation Squads Found at Auschwitz*, trans. Krystyna Michalik (New York: Howard Fertig, 1973)

————— ed., *Auschwitz Chronicle 1939–1945* (New York: Henry Holt, 1989)

————— et al. eds, *Auschwitz 1940–1945. Central Issues in the History of the Camp*, vol. V, Epilogue, trans. William Brand (Oswieçim: Auschwitz State Museum, 2000)

Diment, Michael, *The Lone Survivor. A Diary of the Lukacze Ghetto and Sryniukhy, Ukraine*, trans. Shmuel [Diment] Yahalom (New York: Holocaust Library, 1992)

Dobroszycki, Lucjan ed., *The Chronicle of the Lodz Ghetto 1941–1944*, trans. Richard Lourie, Joachim Neugroschel et al. (New Haven: Yale University Press, 1984)

Dodd, Martha, *My Years in Germany* (London: Gollancz, 1939)

Dodd, William E. and Dodd, Martha, *Ambassador Dodd's Diary* (London: Gollancz, 1939)

Dorian, Emil, *The Quality of Witness. A Romanian Diary 1837–1944*, ed. Marguerite Doria, trans. Mara Soceanu Vamos (Philadelphia: Jewish Publication Society of America, 1992)

Eberle, Henrik ed., *Letters to Hitler*, ed. Victoria Harris, trans. Steven Rendall, (London: Polity 2012)

Edelman, Marek, *The Ghetto Fights* (London: Bookmarks, 1990 [first published in English 1946])

Edelson, Alan ed., *The Diary of Dawid Sierakowiak*, trans. Kamil Turowski (London: Bloomsbury, 1996)

Ehrenburg, Ilya and Grossman, Vasily, *The Black Book*, trans. and ed. John Glad and James S. Levine (New York: Holocaust Library 1980)

Eichengreen, Lucille, *From Ashes to Life. My Memories of the Holocaust* (San Francisco: Mercury House, 1994)

Esh, Shaul ed., *Young Moshe's Diary*, trans. Hana'ar Moshe (Jerusalem: Yad Vashem, 1979)

Farbstein, Esther, 'A Close-up View of a Judenrat: the Memoirs of Pnina Weiss – Wife of a Member of the First Judenrat in Warsaw', *Yad Vashem Studies* 33 (2005), 61–99

Fest, Joachim, *Not Me. Memoirs of a German Childhood*, trans. Martin Chalmers (London: Atlantic Books, 2012)

Fleischmann, Luigi, *From Fiume to Navelli. A Sixteen-Year-Old's Narrative of the Fleischmann Family and Other Free Internees in Fascist Italy September 1943–June 1944* (Jerusalem: Yad Vashem, 2007)

François-Poncet, André, *The Fateful Years. Memoirs of the French Ambassador in Berlin 1931–38* (London: Hamish Hamilton, 1949)

Fried, Hedi, *The Road to Auschwitz. Fragments of a Life*, trans. Michael Meyer (Lincoln: University of Nebraska Press, 1990)

Fromm, Bella, *Blood and Banquets. A Berlin Social Diary* (London: Geoffrey Bles, 1942)

Garbarini, Alexandra et al. eds, *Jewish Responses to Persecution*, vol. 2, *1938–1940* (Lanham, MD: AltaMira Press, 2011)

Gedye, G. E. R., *Fallen Bastions* (London: Gollancz, 1939)

Gerhardt, Uta and Karlauf, Thomas eds, *The Night of Broken Glass. Eyewitness Accounts of Kristallnacht*, trans. Robert Simmons and Nick Somers (London: Polity, 2012)

Gibson, Hugh ed., *The von Hassell Diaries 1938–1944* (London: Hamish Hamilton, 1948)

Gissing, Vera, *Pearls of Childhood* (London: Robson Books, 1988)

Glaser-Heled, Galia and Bar-On, Dan, 'Displaced: the Memoir of Eliezer Gruenbaum at Birkenau – Translation and Commentary', *Shofar*, 27:2 (2009), 1–23

Glazar, Richard, *Trap with a Green Fence. Survival in Treblinka*, trans. Roslyn Theobald (Evanston: Northwestern University Press, 1995)

Goldstein, Bernard, *The Stars Bear Witness*, trans. and ed. Leonard Shatzkin (New York: Viking Press, 1949)

Grynberg, Henryk, *Children of Zion*, trans. Jacqueline Mitchell (Evanston: Northwestern University Press, 1994)

Halder, Franz, *The War Diary, 1939–1942*, ed. Charles Burdick and Hans-Adolf Jacobsen (Boulder: Westview Press,1988)

Harris, Mark Jonathan and Oppenheimer, Deborah eds, *Into the Arms of Strangers. Stories of the Kindertransport* (London: Bloomsbury, 2000)

Hart, Kitty, *I am alive* (London: Corgi Books, 1962)

Heberer, Patricia ed., *Children During the Holocaust* (Lanham, MD: AltaMira Press, 2011)

Heppner, Ernst G., *Shanghai Refuge. A Memoir of the World War II Jewish Ghetto* (Lincoln: University of Nebraska, 1993)

Herzberg, Abel J., *Between Two Streams. A Diary from Bergen-Belsen*, trans. Jack Santcross (London: Tauris Parke, 2008)

Hesdörffer, Heinz, *Twelve Years of Nazi Terror* (Pittsburgh: Rose Dog Books, 2008)

Hilberg, Raul et al. eds, *The Warsaw Diary of Adam Czerniakow* (Chicago: Ivan R. Dee, 1979)

Hitler, Adolf, *Mein Kampf*, trans. Ralph Manheim (London: Hutchinson, 1973 edn)

Hofmann, Michael ed. and trans., *Josef Roth. A Life in Letters* (London: Granta, 2012)

Huberband, Shimon, *Kiddush Hashem: Jewish Religious and Cultural Life in Poland During the Holocaust*, trans. David Fishman, ed. Jeffrey Gurock and Robert Hirt (New York: Ktav, 1987)

Isherwood, Christopher, *Goodbye to Berlin* (London: Vintage, 1998 edn)

Jarausch, Konrad H. ed., *Reluctant Accomplice. A Wehrmacht Soldier's Letters from the Eastern Front* (Princeton: Princeton University Press, 2011)

Johnson, Gaynor ed., *Our Man In Berlin. The Diary of Sir Eric Phipps, 1933–1937* (London: Palgrave, 2008)

The Judgment of Nuremberg 1946 (London: The Stationery Office, 1999, first published 1946)

Junge, Traudl, *Until the Final Hour. Hitler's Last Secretary*, ed. Melissa Müller, trans. Anthea Bell (London: Weidenfeld and Nicolson, 2003)

Kahane, David, *Lvov Ghetto Diary*, trans. Jerzy Michalowicz (Amhurst: University of Massachusetts Press, 1990)

Karski, Jan, *Story of a Secret State* (London: Penguin 2012 edn [first published 1944])

Katsh, Abraham ed., *Scroll of Agony. The Warsaw Diary of Chaim A. Kaplan* (New York: Macmillan, 1965)

Katz, Josef, *One Who Came Back. The Diary of a Jewish Survivor*, trans. Hilda Reach (Takoma Park, MD: Dryad Press, 2006)

Katzenelson, Yitzhak, *Vittel Diary [22.5.43–16.9.43]*, trans. Myer Cohen (Tel Aviv: Ghetto Fighters House, 1964)

Kaufman, Max, *Die Vernichtung Der Juden Lettlands* (Munich: Deutscher Verlag, 1947)

Kemp, Paul ed., *The Relief of Belsen, April 1945. Eyewitness Accounts* (London: Imperial War Museum, 1991)

Kerenji, Emil ed., *Jewish Responses to Persecution*, vol. 4, *1942–1943* (Lanham, MD: AltaMira Press, 2015)

Kessler, Renata ed., *The Wartime Diary of Edmund Kessler, Lwow, Poland, 1942–1944* (Boston: Academic Studies Press, 2010)

Klemperer, Victor, *I Shall Bear Witness. The Diaries of Victor Klemperer, 1933–41*, trans. and ed. Martin Chalmers (London: Weidenfeld and Nicolson, 1998)

———— *To the Bitter End. The Diaries of Victor Klemperer, 1941–45*, trans. and ed. Martin Chalmers (London: Weidenfeld and Nicolson, 1998)

Klukowski, Zygmunt, *Diary from the Years of Occupation 1939–1944*, trans. George Klukowski, ed. Andrew and Helen Klukowski (Chicago: University of Illinois Press, 1993)

Koestler, Arthur, *Scum of the Earth* (New York: Macmillan, 1941)

Koker, David, *At the Edge of the Abyss. A Concentration Camp Diary, 1943–1944*, trans. Michiel Horn and John Irons (Evanston: Northwestern University Press, 2012)

Krauss, Ota and Kulka, Erich, *The Death Factory*, trans. Stephen Joly (Oxford: Pergamon Press, 1966 [first published 1946])

Kruk, Herman, *The Last Days of the Jerusalem of Lithuania: Chronicles from the Vilna Ghetto and the Camps 1939–1944*, trans. Barbara Harshav, ed. Benjamin Harshav (New Haven: Yale University Press, 2002)

Kulka, Otto Dov, *Landscapes of the Metropolis of Death. Reflections on Memory and Imagination*, trans. Ralph Mandel (London: Allen Lane, 2013)

———— and Jäckel, Eberhard eds, *The Jews in the Secret Nazi Reports on Popular Opinion in Germany, 1933–1945*, trans. William Templer (New Haven: Yale University Press, 2011)

Kulkielko, Renya, *Escape from the Pit* (New York: Sharon Books, 1947)

Lafitte, François, *The Internment of Aliens* (London: Libris, 1988 [first published 1940])

Lambert, Raymond-Raoul, *Diary of a Witness 1940–1943*, trans. Isabel Best, ed. Richard I. Cohen (Chicago: Ivan R. Dee, 2007)

Lanzmann, Claude, *The Patagonian Hare. A Memoir*, trans. Frank Wynne (London: Atlantic Books, 2012)

Lederer, Zdenek, *Ghetto Theresienstadt*, trans. K. Weisskopf (London: Goldston, 1953)

Lengyel, Olga, *Five Chimneys* (New York: Ziff-Davis Publishing, 1947)

Levy, Isaac, *Witness to Evil. Bergen-Belsen 1945* (London: Peter Halban, 1995)

Lewin, Abraham, *A Cup of Tears. A Diary of the Warsaw Ghetto*, ed. Antony Polonsky, trans. Christopher Hutton (Oxford: Blackwell, 1988)

Limburg, Margarete and Ruebsaat, Hubert eds, *Germans No More. Accounts of Everyday Jewish Life, 1933–1938*, trans. Alan Nothangle (New York: Berghahn, 2006)

Lower, Wendy ed., *The Diary of Samuel Golfard and the Holocaust in Galicia* (Lanham, MD: AltaMira Press, 2011)

Lubrich, Oliver ed., *Travels in the Reich 1933–1945. Foreign Authors Report from Germany*, trans. K. Northcott, S. Wichmann, D. Krouk (Chicago: University of Chicago Press, 2010)

Manes, Philipp, *As if it were life. A WWII Diary from the Theresienstadt Ghetto*, trans. Janet Foster, Ben Barkow and Klaus Leist, eds. Ben Barkow and Klaus Leist (London: Palgrave, 2009)

Maschmann, Melita, *Account Rendered*, trans. Geoffrey Strachan (London: Abelard-Schuman, 1964)

Matthäus, Jürgen et al. eds, *Jewish Responses to Persecution*, vol. 3, *1941–1942* (Lanham, MD: AltaMira Press, 2013)

————— et al. eds, *War, Pacification, and Mass Murder, 1939. The Einsatzgruppen in Poland* (Lanham, MD: AltaMira Press, 2014)

————— and Roseman, Mark eds, *Jewish Responses to Persecution*, vol. 1, *1933–1938* (Lanham, MD: AltaMira Press, 2010)

Mazor, Michael, *The Vanished City*, trans. David Jacobson (New York: Maresilio, 1993 [first published 1955)]

Mechanicus, Philip, *Waiting for Death. A Diary*, trans. Irene R. Gibbons (London: Calder and Boyars, 1968)

Menasche, Doctor Albert (Number 124,454), *Birkenau (Auschwitz II). Memoirs of an Eye-Witness. How 72,000 Greek Jews Perished* (New York: Albert Martin, 1947)

Müller, Filip, *Eyewitness Auschwitz. Three Years in the Gas Chamber*, trans. and ed. Susanne Flatauer (Chicago: Ivan Dee, 1999 edn)

Nahon, Marco, *Birkenau. Camp of Death*, trans. J. H. Bowers, ed. Steven Bowman (Tuscaloosa: University of Alabama Press, 1989)

Neitzel, Sönke ed., *Tapping Hitler's Generals. Transcripts of Secret Conversations, 1941–45* (Barnsley: Front Line Books, 2007)

————— and Welzer, Harald, *Soldaten. On Fighting, Killing and Dying: The Secret Second World War Tapes of German POWs* (London and New York: Simon and Schuster, 2012)

Némirovsky, Irène, *Suite Française*, trans. Sandra Smith (London: Chatto and Windus, 2006)

Neurath, Paul Martin, *The Society of Terror. Inside the Dachau and Buchenwald Concentration Camps* (Boulder: Paradigm, 2005)

Noakes, J. and Pridham, G. eds, *Nazism 1919–1945. A Documentary Reader*, vol. 2, *State, Economy and Society 1933–1939* (Exeter: University of Exeter Press, 1997 edn)

———— *Nazism 1919–1945. A Documentary Reader*, vol. 3, *Foreign Policy, War and Racial Extermination* (Exeter: University of Exeter Press, 1997 edn)

Petzovsky, A. [Alexander Peshersky], 'The Outbreak in Sobivor', Meyer Barkai ed., *The Fighting Ghettos* (New York: Tower Books, 1962), 205–26

Poliakov, Léon, *L'Auberge des musiciens* (Paris: Mazarine, 1981)

Rajchman, Chil, *Treblinka. A Survivor's Memory 1942–1943*, trans. Solon Beinfeld (London: Quercus, 2011)

Reck-Malleczewen, Friedrich, *Diary of a Man in Despair*, trans. Paul Rubens (London: Duckbacks, 2000)

Reder, Rudolf, 'Belzec', trans. M. M. Rubel, *Polin*, 13 (2000), 268–89

Reicher, Edward, *Country of Ash. A Jewish Doctor in Poland, 1939–1945*, trans. Magda Bogin (New York: Bellevue, 2013)

Reich-Ranicki, Marcel, *The Author of Himself. The Life of Marcel Reich-Ranicki*, trans. Ewald Osers (London: Weidenfeld and Nicolson, 2001)

Revelli, Nuto ed., *Mussolini's Death March. Eyewitness Accounts of Italian Soldiers on the Eastern Front*, trans. John Penuel (Lawrence: University Press of Kansas, 2013)

Richardson, Horst Fuchs ed., *Your Loyal and Loving Son. The Letters of Tank Gunner Karl Fuchs, 1937–1941* (Washington DC: Brassey's, 2003)

Ringelblum, Emmanuel, *Polish–Jewish Relations During the Second World War*, trans. Dafna Allon et al., eds Joseph Kermish and Shmuel Krakowski (Evanston: Northwestern University Press, 1992

Rosenfeld, Oskar, *In the Beginning was the Ghetto. Notebooks from Lodz*, ed. Hanno Loewy, trans. Brigitte Goldstein (Evanston: Northwestern University Press, 2002)

Rotem (Kazik), Simha, *Memoirs of a Warsaw Ghetto Fighter. The past within me*, trans. and ed. Barbara Harshav (New Haven: Yale University Press, 1994)

Rubenstein, Joshua and Altman, Ilya eds, *The Unknown Black Book. The Holocaust in the German-Occupied Soviet Territories*, trans. Christopher Morris and Joshua Rubinstein (Bloomington: Indiana University Press, 2008)

Rubinowitz, David, *The Diary of David Rubinowitz*, trans. Derek Bowman (Edinburgh: Blackwood, 1981)

Sakowicz, Kazimierz, *Ponary Diary 1941–1943*, ed. Yitzhak Arad (New Haven: Yale University Press, 2005)

Schleunes, Karl ed., *Legislating The Holocaust. The Bernhard Loesener Memoirs and Supporting Documents* (Boulder: Westview Press, 2001)

Schroeder, Christa, *He Was My Chief. The Memoirs of Adolf Hitler's Secretary*, trans. Geoffrey Brooks (London: Frontline Books, 2009)

Schwarzschild, Leopold, *Chronicle of a Downfall. Germany, 1929–1939*, ed. Andreas Wesemann, trans. Michel Mitchell (London: I. B. Tauris, 2010)

Seidman, Hillel, *The Warsaw Ghetto Diaries*, trans. Yosef Israel (Jerusalem: Targum, 1997)

Shirer, William, *Berlin Diary. The Journal of a Foreign Correspondent, 1934–1941* (Baltimore: Johns Hopkins University Press, 2002 [orig. 1941])

Shneiderman, S. L. ed., *The Diary of Mary Berg* (Oxford: Oneworld, 2006)

Sloan, Jacob ed. and trans., *Notes from the Warsaw Ghetto. The Journal of Emmanuel Ringelblum* (New York: McGraw-Hill, 1958)

Smith, Howard K., *Last Train From Berlin* (London: Cresset Press, 1942)

Somerhausen, Anne, *Written in Darkness. A Belgian Woman's Record of the Occupation 1940–1945* (New York: Knopf, 1946)

Stabholz, Thaddeus, *Seven Hells*, trans. Jacques and Hilda Grunblatt (New York: Holocaust Library, 1990)

Strawczynski, Oskar, 'Ten Months in Treblinka (October 5, 1942 – August 2, 1943)', in Israel Cymlich, Oskar Strawczynski, *Escaping Hell in Treblinka* (Jerusalem: Yad Vashem, 2007), 127–86

Stromer, Moty, *Memoirs of an Unfortunate Person. The Diary of Moty Stromer*, trans. Elinor Robinson (Jerusalem: Yad Vashem, 2008)

Szereszewska, Helena, *Memoirs* (London: Vallentine Mitchell, 1997)

Szpilman, Wladyslaw, *The Pianist*, trans. Anthea Bell (London: Gollancz, 1999 [first published in Polish as *City of Death* in 1946])

Tischauer, Helen, interview by Dr David Boder, Feldafing, Germany, 23 September 1946 in Jürgen Matthäus ed., *Approaching an Auschwitz Survivor. Holocaust Testimony and its Transformations* (New York: Oxford University Press, 2009)

Tory [Golub], Avraham, *Surviving the Holocaust. The Kovno Ghetto Diary*, trans. Jerzy Michalowicz, ed. Martin Gilbert with Dina Porat (Cambridge, MA: Harvard University Press, 1990)

The Trial of Adolf Eichmann. Record of Proceedings in the District Court of Jerusalem, 9 vols. (Jerusalem: Israel Ministry of Justice, 1992–5)

Troller, Norbert, *Theresienstadt. Hitler's Gift To The Jews*, trans. Susan Cernyak-Spatz, ed. Joel Shatzky (Chapel Hill: University of North Carolina Press, 1991)

Trunk, Isaiah, *Lodz Ghetto. A History*, trans. and ed. Robert Shapiro (Bloomington: Indiana University Press, 2006)

Vági, Zoltan et al. eds, *The Holocaust in Hungary. Evolution of a Genocide* (Lanham, MD: AltaMira Press, 2013)

Vold, Jan Erik ed., *Ruth Maier's Diary. A Young Girl's Life under Nazism*, trans. Jamie Bullock (London: Harvill Secker, 2009)

Warhaftig, Zorach, *Uprooted: Jewish Refugees and Displaced Persons after Liberation* (New York: American Jewish Congress, 1946)

Wdowinski, David, *And We Are Not Saved* (London: W. H. Allen, 1964)

Weinstein, Eddie, *17 Days in Treblinka. Daring to Resist, and Refusing to Die* (Jerusalem: Yad Vashem, 2008)

Weiss, Helga, *Helga's Diary. A Young Girl's Account of Life in a Concentration Camp*, trans. Neil Bermel (London: Viking, 2013)

Weissmann Klein, Gerda, *All But My Life* (New York: Hill and Wang, 1995 edn)

Wetzler, Alfred, *Escape from Hell. The True Story of the Auschwitz Protocol*, trans. Ewald Osers, ed. Péter Várnan (New York: Berghahn, 2007)

Wiernik, Yankiel, *A Year in Treblinka* (New York: American Representation of the Jewish Workers Union of Poland, 1944)

Willenberg, Samuel, *Revolt in Treblinka* (Warsaw: Jewish Historical Institute, 2008 edn)

Zsolt, Bela, *Nine Suitcases*, trans. Ladislaus Löb (London: Jonathan Cape, 2004 [first published 1946–7])

Zuckerman, Yitzhak, *A Surplus of Memory. Chronicle of the Warsaw Ghetto Uprising*, trans. and ed. Barbara Harshav (Berkeley: University of California Press, 1993)

Zylberberg, Michael, *A Warsaw Diary* (London: Vallentine Mitchell, 1969)

Zywulska, Krystyna, *I came back*, trans. Krystyna Cenkalska (New York: Roy Publishers, 1951 [first published in Polish, 1946])

Domarus, Max, ed., *Hitler Speeches and Proclamations 1932–1945*, trans. Mary Fran Golbert (Wauconda, IL: Bolchazy-Carducci Publishers, 1990), digital version at http://www.pdfarchive.info/pdf/H/Hi/Hitler_Adolf_-_Hitler_Speeches_and_Proclamations.pdf

Goebbels, Joseph speech, 11 February 1943 http://www2.warwick.ac.uk/fac/arts/history/students/modules/hi369/reading/week8/goebbelstotal/

Hitler, Adolf speech, 30 January 1939 http://germanhistorydocs.ghi-dc.org/sub_document.cfm?document_id=2289

Hitler, Adolf speech, 9 December 1941 https://www.jewishvirtuallibrary.org/jsource/Holocaust/hitler_declares_war.html

Hitler, Adolf speech, 30 January 1942 www.worldfuturefund.org/.../Hitler%20Speeches/Hitler%20Speech%201942.

Hitler, Adolf speech, 30 January 1944.https://archive.org/stream/TheCompleteHitler-SpeechesAndProclamations-MaxDomarus/TheCompleteHitler-1932–1945-Vol1–4_djvu.txt

Report of the Conference on the Jewish Question at the Aviation Ministry on 12 November 1938 http://germanhistorydocs.ghi-dc.org/pdf/eng/English34.pdf

'Voices of the Holocaust' http://voices.iit.edu/

Secondary sources

Aalders, Gerard, *Nazi Looting. The Plunder of Dutch Jewry During the Second World War*, trans. Arnold and Erica Pomerans (Oxford: Berg, 2004)

Abitbol, Michel, *The Jews of North Africa in World War II* (Detroit: Wayne State University Press, 1989)

Adam, Uwe Dietrich, 'How Spontaneous was the Pogrom?', in Walter Pehle ed., *November 1938*, 73–94

Adamczyk-Garbowska, Monika, *Patterns of Return. Survivors' Postwar Journeys to Poland* (Washington DC: US Holocaust Memorial Museum, 2007)

Adler, Jacques, *The Jews of Paris and the Final Solution. Communal Response and Internal Conflicts, 1940–1944* (New York: Oxford University Press, 1987)

Aleksiun, Natalia, 'The Central Jewish Historical Commission in Poland, 1944–1947',
    in Finder et al. eds, *Polin*, vol. 20, *Making Holocaust Memory*, 74–97
————— 'The Polish Catholic Church and the Jewish Question in Poland, 1944–48',
    Yad Vashem Studies, 33 (2005), 143–70
Allen, Michael Thad, 'The Devil in the Details: The Gas Chambers of Birkenau,
    October 1941', *HGS*, 16:2 (2002), 189–216
————— *The Business of Genocide. The SS, Slave Labour, and the Concentration Camps*
    (Chapel Hill: University of North Carolina Press, 2002)
Allwork, Larissa, *Holocaust Remembrance Between the National and the Transnational.*
    The Stockholm International Forum and the First Decade of the International Task
    Force (London: Bloomsbury, 2015)
Alport, Nachum, *The Destruction of Slonim Jewry*, trans. Max Rosenfeld (New York:
    Holocaust Library, 1989)
Altman, Ilya, 'The History and Fate of *The Black Book* and *The Unknown Black Book*',
    in Rubenstein and Altman eds, *The Unknown Black Book*, xix–xxxix
Altshuler, Mordechai, 'Escape and Evacuation of Soviet Jews at the time of the Nazi
    Invasion: Policies and Realities', in Dobroscycki and Gurock eds, *The Holocaust in*
    the Soviet Union, 77–104.
Aly, Götz, 'Medicine against the Useless', in Götz Aly, Peter Chroust, Christian Pross
    eds, *Cleansing the Fatherland. Nazi Medicine and Racial Hygiene*, trans. Belinda
    Cooper (Baltimore: Johns Hopkins University Press, 1994)
————— *'Final Solution'. Nazi Population Policy and the Murder of the European Jews*
    (London: Arnold, 1999)
————— *Hitler's Beneficiaries. Plunder, Racial War and the Nazi Welfare State*, trans.
    Jefferson Chase (New York: Metropolitan Books, 2006)
————— and Heim, Susanne, *Architects of Annihilation. Auschwitz and the Logic of*
    Destruction, trans. A. G. Blunden (London: Weidenfeld and Nicolson, 2002)
Ancel, Jean, '"The New Invasion" – The Return of Survivors from Transnistria', in
    Bankier ed., *The Jews Are Coming Back*, 231–56
————— *The Economic Destruction of Romanian Jewry* (Jerusalem: Yad Vashem, 2007)
————— *The History of the Holocaust in Romania* (Lincoln: University of Nebraska
    Press, 2010)
Angress, Werner, *Between Fear and Hope. Jewish Youth in the Third Reich*, trans.
    Werner Angress and Christine Granger (New York: Columbia University Press,
    1988)
Angrick, Andrej, 'Annihilation and Labour: Jews and Thoroughfare IV in Central
    Ukraine', in Brandon and Lower eds, *The Shoah in Ukraine*, 190–223
————— and Klein, Peter, *The 'Final Solution' in Riga. Exploitation and Annihilation,*
    1941–1944, trans. Ray Brandon (New York: Berghahn, 2009)
Apostolou, Andrew, '"The Exception of Salonika". Bystanders and collaborators in
    Northern Greece', *Holocaust and Genocide Studies*, 14:2 (2000), 165–6
Arad, Gulie Ne'eman, *America, its Jews and the Rise of Nazism* (Bloomington: Indiana
    University Press, 2007)
Arad, Yitzhak, *Belzec, Sobibor, Treblinka. The Operation Reinhard Death Camps*
    (Bloomington: Indiana University Press, 1987)

———— *The Holocaust in the Soviet Union* (Lincoln: University of Nebraska Press, 2009)

Arens, Moshe, 'The Warsaw Ghetto Uprising: A Reappraisal', *Yad Vashem Studies*, 33 (2005), 101–42

Arnold, K. J. and Lübbers, G. C., 'The Meeting of the Staatssekretäre on 2 May 1941 and the Wehrmacht, A Document Up for Discussion', *Journal of Contemporary History*, 42:4 (2007), 613–26

Aronson, Shlomo, 'OSS X-2 and Rescue Efforts During the Holocaust', in Bankier ed., *Secret Intelligence and the Holocaust*, 65–104

———— *Hitler, the Allies and the Jews* (Cambridge: Cambridge University Press, 2004)

Ascher, Abraham, *A Community under Siege. The Jews of Breslau under Nazism* (Stanford: Stanford University Press, 2007)

Aschheim, Steven, *Brothers and Strangers. The East European Jew in German and German Jewish Consciousness, 1800–1923* (Madison: University of Wisconsin, 1999 edn)

Baden-Baden: http://www.yadvashem.org/yv/en/exhibitions/kristallnacht/baden.asp

Bajohr, Frank, *'Aryanization' in Hamburg. The Economic Exclusion of Jews and the Confiscation of their Property in Nazi Germany* (New York: Berghahn, 2002)

Ball, Simon, *The Bitter Sea* (London: Harper Press, 2009)

Bankier, David ed., *The Jews Are Coming Back. The return of the Jews to their countries of origin after WWII* (Jerusalem: Yad Vashem, 2005)

———— ed., *Probing the Depths of German Antisemitism. German Society and the Persecution of the Jews, 1933–1941* (Jerusalem: Yad Vashem, 2000)

———— ed., *Secret Intelligence and the Holocaust* (New York: Enigma Books, 2006)

———— and Gutman, Israel eds, *Nazi Europe and the Final Solution* (Jerusalem: Yad Vashem, 2009)

———— and Michman, Dan eds, *Holocaust and Justice. Representation and Historiography of the Holocaust in Post-War Trials* (Jerusalem: Yad Vashem, 2010)

Bánkowska, Aleksandra, 'Polish Partisan Formations during 1942–1944 in Jewish Testimonies', *Holocaust Studies and Materials* (2008), 103–22

Bardgett, Suzanne and Cesarani, David eds, *Belsen 1945. New Historical Perspectives* (London: Vallentine Mitchell, 2006)

Barkai, Avraham, 'The Final Chapter', in Meyer ed., *German-Jewish History in Modern Times*, vol. 4, 378–88

———— 'Self-Help in the Dilemma: "To Leave or to Stay?"', in Meyer ed., *Renewal and Destruction*, 313–32.

———— 'Shifting Organisational Relationships', in Meyer ed., *Renewal and Destruction*, 258–82

———— *From Boycott to Annihilation. The Economic Struggle of German Jews 1933–1945*, trans. William Templer (Hanover: University Press of New England, 1989)

Barkow, Ben, *Alfred Wiener and the Making of the Holocaust Library* (London: Vallentine Mitchell, 1997)

Bartov, Omer, *Hitler's Army. Soldiers, Nazis, and War in the Third Reich* (New York: Oxford University Press, 1992)

———— *Murder in Our Midst. The Holocaust, Industrial Killing and Representation* (New York: Oxford University Press, 1996)

Bauer, Yehuda, *The Death of the Shtetl* (New Haven: Yale University Press, 2009)

———— *Jews for Sale? Nazi-Jewish Negotiations, 1933–1945* (New Haven: Yale University Press, 1994)

———— *Rethinking the Holocaust* (New Haven: Yale University Press, 2001)

Beevor, Anthony, *The Second World War* (London: Weidenfeld and Nicolson, 2012)

Beker, Avi ed., *The Plunder of Jewish Property during the Holocaust* (New York: New York University Press, 2001)

Bellamy, Chris, *Absolute War. Soviet Russia in the Second World War* (London: Pan, 2007)

Bender, Sarah, *The Jews of Bialystok during World War II and the Holocaust* (Waltham, MA: Brandeis University Press, 2008)

Ben-Sefer, Ellen, 'Forced Sterilization and Abortion as Sexual Abuse', in Hedgepeth and Saidel eds, *Sexual Violence Against Jewish Women During the Holocaust*, 150–73

Bentwich, Norman, *They Found Refuge* (London: Cresset Press, 1956)

Benz, Wolfgang, *The Holocaust*, trans. Jane Sydenham-Kwiet (New York: Columbia University Press, 1995)

Beorn, Waitman Wade, *Marching Into Darkness. The Wehrmacht and the Holocaust in Belarus* (Cambridge, MA: Harvard University Press, 2014)

Berenbaum, Michael and Peck, Abraham eds, *The Holocaust in History. The Known, the Unknown, the Disputed, and the Reexamined* (Indiana: Indiana University Press, 1998)

Bergen, Doris, *Twisted Cross: The German Christian Movement in the Third Reich* (Chapel Hill: University of North Carolina Press, 1996)

———— *War & Genocide. A Concise History of the Holocaust*, 2nd edition (Lanham MD: Rowan and Littlefield, 2009)

Bergerson, Andrew Stuart, *Ordinary Germans In Extraordinary Times. The Nazi Revolution in Hildesheim* (Bloomington: Indiana University Press, 2004)

Bernstein, Michael André, *Foregone Conclusions: Against Apocalyptic History* (Berkeley: University of California Press, 1994)

Bessel, Richard, *Germany 1945. From War to Peace* (London: Simon and Schuster, 2009)

Black, Jeremy, *The Holocaust* (London: The Social Affairs Unit, 2008)

Black, Peter R., 'Auxiliaries for Operation Reinhard: Shedding Light on the Trawniki Training Camp Through Documents from Behind the Iron Curtain', in Bankier ed., *Secret Intelligence and the Holocaust*, 327–66

Blatman, Daniel, 'The Death Marches, January–May 1945: Who Was Responsible for What?', *Yad Vashem Studies* 28 (2000), 155–202

———— *The Death Marches. The Final Phase of Nazi Genocide*, trans. Chaya Galai (Cambridge, MA: Harvard University Press, 2011)

————— *For Our Freedom and Yours. The Jewish Labour Bund in Poland 1939–1949* (London: Vallentine Mitchell, 2003)

Blood, Philip, *Hitler's Bandit Hunters. The SS and the Nazi Occupation of Europe* (Washington DC: Potomac Books, 2008)

Bloxham, Donald, *The Final Solution. A Genocide* (Oxford: Oxford University Press, 2009)

————— *Genocide on Trial. War Crimes Trials and the Formation of Holocaust History and Memory* (Oxford: Oxford University Press, 2001)

Blumenson, Martin, *The Duel for France, 1944* (New York: DaCapo Press, 1963)

Bogner, Nahum, *At the Mercy of Strangers. The Rescue of Jewish Children with Assumed Identities in Poland* (Jerusalem: Yad Vashem, 2009)

Bolchover, Richard, *British Jewry and the Holocaust* (Cambridge: Cambridge University Press, 1993)

Bondy, Ruth, *Trapped. Essays on the History of the Czech Jews, 1939–1943* (Jerusalem: Yad Vashem, 2008)

Boog, Horst, 'The Luftwaffe Assault', in Paul Addison and Jeremy A. Crang eds, *The Burning Blue. A New History of the Battle of Britain* (London: Pimlico, 2000), 39–54

Boom, Bart van der, 'Ordinary Dutchmen and the Holocaust: a summary of findings', in Romijn et al. eds, *The Persecution of the Jews in the Netherlands*, 29–52

Borut, Jacob, 'Antisemitism in Tourist Facilities in Weimar Germany', *Yad Vashem Studies*, 28 (2000), 7–50

Bowman, Steven M., *The Agony of Greek Jews 1940–1945* (Stanford: Stanford University Press, 2009)

Braham, Randolph, 'Hungarian Jews', in Gutman and Berenbaum eds, *Anatomy of the Auschwitz Death Camp*, 456–68

————— ed., *Jewish Leadership during the Nazi Era: Patterns of Behaviour in the Free World* (New York: Columbia University Press, 1985)

————— *The Politics of Genocide. The Holocaust in Hungary* (Detroit: Wayne State University Press, 2000)

————— *The Politics of Genocide. The Holocaust in Hungary*, 2 vols (New York: Columbia University Press, 1994 edn)

————— and Miller, Scott eds, *The Nazis' Last Victims. The Holocaust in Hungary* (Detroit: Wayne State University Press, 1998)

Branche, Raphaelle and Virgili, Fabrice eds, *Rape in Wartime* (London: Palgrave, 2012)

Brandon, Ray and Lower, Wendy eds, *The Shoah in Ukraine. History, Testimony, Memorialization* (Bloomington: Indiana University Press, 2010)

Breitman, Richard, 'Himmler and Bergen-Belsen', in Reilly et al. eds, *Belsen in History and Memory*, 72–84

————— 'Nazi Espionage: The Abwehr and SD Foreign Intelligence', in Breitman et al. eds, *US Intelligence and the Nazis*, 93–120

————— 'New Sources on the Holocaust in Italy', *Holocaust and Genocide Studies*, 16:3 (2002), 402–14

————— 'Other Responses to the Holocaust', in Breitman et al. eds, *US Intelligence and the Nazis*, 45–64

————— et al. eds, *US Intelligence and the Nazis* (New York: Cambridge University Press, 2005)

————— and Lichtman, Alan J., *FDR and the Jews* (Cambridge, MA: Harvard University Press, 2013)

Brenner, Michael, *After the Holocaust: Rebuilding Jewish Lives in Postwar Germany*, trans. Barbara Harshav (Princeton: Princeton University Press, 1999)

————— *The Renaissance of Jewish Culture in Weimar Germany* (New Haven: Yale University Press, 1996)

Breughel, J. W., 'The Bernheim petition: A challenge to Nazi Germany in 1933', *Patterns of Prejudice*, 17:3 (1983), 17–25

Bridgman, John, *The End of the Holocaust and the Liberation of the Camps* (London: Batsford, 1990)

Browder, George C., *Hitler's Enforcers. The Gestapo and the SS Security Service in the Nazi Revolution* (New York: Oxford University Press, 1996)

Browning, Christopher, *Ordinary Men. Reserve Police Battalion 101 and the Final Solution in Poland* (New York: Harper Collins, 1992)

————— with Matthäus, Jürgen, *The Origins of the Final Solution: The Evolution of Nazi Jewish Policy, September 1939–March 1942* (London: William Heinemann, 2004)

Bruttmann, Tal, *La logique des bourreaux 1943–1944* (Paris: Hachette, 2006)

Bryant, Chad, *Prague in Black. Nazi Rule and Czech Nationalism* (Cambridge, MA.: Harvard University Press, 2007)

Büchler, Yehoshua, 'Reconstruction Efforts in Hostile Surroundings – Slovaks and Jews after World War II', in Bankier ed., *The Jews Are Coming Back*, 257–76

————— and Bauer, Yehuda, 'Document: A Preparatory Document for the Wannsee "Conference"', *Holocaust and Genocide Studies*, 9:1 (1995), 121–9

Buggeln, Marc, *Slave Labour in Nazi Concentration Camps*, trans. Paul Cohen (New York: Oxford University Press, 2014)

Burleigh, Michael, *Death and Deliverance. 'Euthanasia' in Germany 1900–1945* (Cambridge: Cambridge University Press, 1994)

————— *The Third Reich. A History* (London: Macmillan, 2000)

————— and Wipperman, Wolfgang, *The Racial State. Germany 1933–1945* (Cambridge: Cambridge University Press, 1991)

Burletson, Louise, 'The State, Internment and Public Criticism in the Second World War', in Cesarani and Kushner eds, *The Internment of Aliens*, 101–24

Burrin, Philippe, *Hitler and the Jews* (London: Edward Arnold, 1994)

Büttner, Ursula, 'The "Jewish Problem Becomes a Christian Problem". German Protestants and the Persecution of the Jews in the Third Reich', in Bankier ed., *Probing the Depths of German Antisemitism*, 431–59.

Caestecker, Frank, 'The Reintegration of Jewish Survivors into Belgian Society, 1943–1947', in Bankier ed., *The Jews Are Coming Back*, 72–107

Callil, Carmen, *Bad Faith. A Forgotten History of Family and Fatherland* (London: Cape, 2006)

Caplan, Jane and Wachsmann, Nikolaus eds, *Concentration Camps in Nazi Germany.*
The New Histories (London: Routledge, 2010)

Caron, Vicki, *Uneasy Asylum. France and the Jewish Refugee Crisis 1933–1942*
(Stanford: Stanford University Press, 1999)

Carpi, Daniel, *Between Mussolini and Hitler. The Jews and the Italian Authorities in*
France and Tunisia (Hanover, NH: Brandeis University Press, 1994)

Caune, Andris et al. eds, *Latvia in World War II* (Riga: University of Latvia, 2000)

Cesarani, David, 'Jewish Victims of the Holocaust and Swiss Banks', *Dimensions*, 191
(1997), 3–6

———— 'A Brief History of Bergen-Belsen', in Bardgett and Cesarani eds, *Belsen 1945*,
13–21

———— 'British reactions to the Warsaw Ghetto Uprising', in Grinberg ed., *Fifty Years*
After, 133–44

———— 'The International Military Tribunal at Nuremberg: British Perspectives', in
Reginbogin and Safferling eds, *Die Nürnburger Prozesse*, 31–8

———— 'Introduction' in Harris and Oppenheimer eds, *Into the Arms of Strangers*,
1–16

———— 'The London Jewish Chronicle and the Holocaust', in Shapiro ed., *Why Didn't*
the Press, 175–95

———— 'The Transformation of Communal Authority in Anglo-Jewry, 1914–1940', in
Cesarani ed., *The Making of Modern Anglo-Jewry*, 115–40

———— *Arthur Koestler. The Homeless Mind* (London: Heinemann, 1998)

———— *Eichmann. His Life and Crimes* (London: Heinemann, 2004)

———— ed., *The Final Solution. Origins and Implementation* (London: Routledge,
1994)

———— ed., *Genocide and Rescue. The Holocaust in Hungary 1944* (Oxford: Berg, 1997)

———— ed., *Holocaust. Critical Concepts in Historical Studies*, 6 vols (London:
Routledge, 2004)

———— *The Holocaust. A Teacher's Guide* (London: Holocaust Educational Trust,
1998)

———— *The Jewish Chronicle and Anglo-Jewry, 1841–1991* (Cambridge: Cambridge
University Press, 1994)

———— *Major Farran's Hat. Murder, Scandal and Britain's War against Jewish*
Terrorism, 1945–1948 (London: Heinemann, 2009)

———— ed., *The Making of Modern Anglo-Jewry* (Oxford: Blackwell, 1990)

———— 'Striped Pyjamas', *Literary Review, May*, 2011, at http://www.literaryreview.
co.uk/cesarani_10_08.html

———— and Kushner, Tony eds, *The Internment of Aliens in Twentieth Century*
Britain (London: Frank Cass, 1993)

———— and Levine, Paul, *'Bystanders' to the Holocaust: A Re-evaluation* (London:
Frank Cass, 2002)

Chadwick, W. R., *The Rescue of the Prague Refugees 1938/39* (Padstow: Troubador
Publishing, 2010)

Charney, Frederick B., *The Bulgarian Jews and the Final Solution 1940–44* (Pittsburgh:
University of Pittsburgh Press, 1972)

Chrostowski, Witold, *The Extermination Camp Treblinka* (London: Valentine Mitchell, 2003)

Citino, Robert M., *Death of the Wehrmacht. The German Campaigns of 1942* (Lawrence: University of Kansas Press, 2007)

———— *The German Way of War. From the Thirty Years War to the Third Reich* (Lawrence: University of Kansas Press, 2008)

———— *The Wehrmacht Retreats. Fighting a Lost War, 1943* (Lawrence: University of Kansas Press, 2012)

Clark, Lloyd, *Crossing the Rhine. Breaking into Nazi Germany 1944 and 1945 – The Greatest Airborne Battles in History* (New York: Grove Press, 2008)

Clifford, Rebecca, *Commemorating the Holocaust. The Dilemmas of Remembrance in France and Italy* (Oxford: Oxford University Press, 2013)

Cohen, Asher, Cochavi, Yehoyakim and Gelber, Yoav eds, *The Shoah and the War* (New York: Peter Lang, 1992)

Cohen, Boaz, 'Dr Jacob Robinson, the Insitute of Jewish Affairs and the Elusive Jewish Voice in Nuremberg', in Bankier and Michman eds, *Holocaust and Justice*, 81–100

Cohen, Richard I., *The Burden of Conscience. French Jewry's Response to the Holocaust* (Bloomington: Indiana University Press, 1987)

Cohen, Susan, *Rescue the Perishing. Eleanor Rathbone and the Refugees* (London: Vallentine Mitchell, 2010)

Cole, Tim, *Holocaust City. The Making of a Jewish Ghetto* (London: Routledge, 2002)

Collingham, Lizzie, *The Taste of War. World War Two and the Battle for Food* (London: Allen Lane, 2011)

Confino, Alon, *A World Without Jews. The Nazi Imagination. From Persecution to Genocide* (New Haven: Yale University Press, 2014)

Conradi, Peter, *Hitler's Piano Player. The Rise and Fall of Ernst Hanfstaengl, Confidant of Hitler, Ally of FDR* (London: Duckworth, 2005)

Csosz, László, 'Agrarian reform and race protection: the implementation of the Fourth Jewish Law', in Molnár ed., *The Holocaust in Hungary*, 180–97

Czech, Danuta, 'The Auschwitz Prisoner Administration', in Gutman and Berenbaum eds, *Anatomy of the Auschwitz Death Camp*, 362–78

Dallas, Gregor, *Poisoned Peace. 1945 – The War That Never Ended* (London: John Murray, 2005

Dawidowicz, Lucy, *The War Against the Jews* (London: Penguin, 1975)

Davies, Norman, *Rising '44. 'The Battle for Warsaw'* (London: Pan, 2004)

Dean, Martin, 'The Development and Implementation of Nazi Denaturalization and Confiscation Policy up to the Eleventh decree to the Reich Citizenship Law', *Holocaust and Genocide Studies*, 16:2 (2002), 217–42

———— 'Seizure, Registration and Sale: The Strange case of the German Administration of Jewish Moveable Property in Latvia (1941–1944)', in Caune et al. eds, *Latvia in World War II*, 372–8

———— 'Soviet Ethnic Germans and the Holocaust in the Reich Commissariat Ukraine, 1941–1944', in Brandon and Lower eds, *The Shoah in Ukraine*, 248–71

BIBLIOGRAPHY

————— *Collaboration in the Holocaust* (Houndmills: Macmillan, 2000)

————— *Robbing the Jews. The Confiscation of Jewish Property in the Holocaust, 1933–1945* (New York: Cambridge University Press, 2008)

————— et al., Goschler, Constantin, and Ther, Philipp, *Robbery and Restitution. The Conflict over Jewish Property in Europe* (New York: Berghahn, 2007)

Delage, Christian, 'The Judicial Construction of the Genocide of the Jews at Nuremberg: Witnesses on the Stand and the Screen', in Bankier and Michman eds, *Holocaust and Justice*, 101–13

Deletant, Dennis, 'Transnistria and the Romanian Solution of the "Jewish Problem"', in Brandon and Lower eds, *The Shoah in Ukraine*, 156–89

————— *Hitler's Forgotten Ally. Ion Antonescu and His Regime, Romania 1940–1944* (Houndmills: Palgrave Macmillan, 2006)

Dembowski, Peter, *Christians in the Warsaw Ghetto. An Epitaph for the Unremembered* (Chicago: University of Notre Dame Press, 2005)

d'Este, Carlo, *Warlord. A Life of Churchill at War, 1874–1945* (London: Allen Lane, 2009)

Dieckmann, Christoph, 'The Role of the Lithuanians in the Holocaust', in Beate Kosmola and Feliks Tych eds, *Facing the Nazi Genocide: Non-Jews and Jews in Europe* (Berlin: Metropol, 2004), 149–68

Dinnerstein, Leonard, *America and the Survivors of the Holocaust* (New York: Columbia University Press, 1982)

Dipper, Christof, '20 July and the "Jewish Question"' in Bankier ed., *Probing the Depths of German Antisemitism*, 463–78

Dirks, Christian, 'Snatchers: The Berlin Gestapo's Jewish Informants' in Meyer, Simon and Schütz eds, *Jews in Nazi Berlin*, 249–73

Dobroscycki, Lucjan and Gurock, Jeffrey S. eds, *The Holocaust in the Soviet Union* (Armonk, NY: M. E. Sharpe, 1993)

Doerry, Martin, *My Wounded Heart. The Life of Lilli Jahn*, trans. John Brownjohn (London: Bloomsbury, 2004)

Don, Yehuda, 'Economic Implications of the Anti-Jewish Laws in Hungary', in Cesarani ed., *Genocide and Rescue. The Holocaust in Hungary 1944*, 47–76

Doorslaer, Rudi van, 'The Expropriation of Jewish Property and Restitution in Belgium', in Dean, Goschler and Ther eds, *Robbery and Restitution*, 155–70

Dreisziger, Nándor ed., *Hungary in an Age of Total War (1938–1948)* (New York: Columbia University Press, 1998)

Dwork, Debórah and Pelt, Robert Jan van, *Holocaust. A History* (London: John Murray, 2002)

Edgerton, David, *Britain's War Machine* (London: Penguin, 2011)

Embacher, Helga, 'Viennese Jewish Functionaries on Trial. Accusations, Defense Strategies and Hidden Agendas', in Finder and Jockusch eds, *Jewish Honor Courts*, 165–96

Engel, David, 'Why Punish Collaborators?' in Finder and Jockusch eds, *Jewish Honor Courts*, 29–48

————— *Facing a Holocaust: The Polish Government-In-Exile and the Jews, 1943–1945* (Chapel Hill: University of North California Press, 1993)

————— *The Holocaust. The Third Reich and the Jews* (London: Longman, 1999)

————— *In the Shadow of Auschwitz. The Polish Government-in-Exile and the Jews, 1939–1942* (Chapel Hill: University of North Carolina Press, 1987)

Engelking, Barbara and Leociak, Jacek, *The Warsaw Ghetto. A Guide to the Perished City*, trans. Emma Harris (New Haven: Yale University Press, 2009)

Epstein, Barbara, *The Minsk Ghetto 1941–1943. Jewish Resistance and Soviet Internationalism* (Berkeley: University of California Press, 2008)

Epstein, Catherine, *Model Nazi. Arthur Greiser and the Occupation of Western Poland* (Oxford: Oxford University Press, 2010)

Evans, Richard J., *The Coming of the Third Reich* (London: Allen Lane, 2003)

————— *The Third Reich in Power 1933–1939* (London: Penguin, 2005)

————— *The Third Reich at War 1939–1945* (London: Allen Lane, 2008)

Ezergailis, Andrew, *The Holocaust in Latvia 1941–1944* (Riga: The Holocaust Institute of Latvia, 1996)

Farbstein, Esther, *Hidden Thunder. Perspectives on Faith, Halacha, and Leadership during the Holocaust* (Jerusalem: Mossad Harav Kook, 2007)

Favez, Jean-Claude, *The Red Cross and the Holocaust*, trans. John and Beryl Fletcher (Cambridge: Cambridge University Press, 1999)

Feldman, Gerald D., *Allianz and the German Insurance Business, 1933–1945* (Cambridge: Cambridge University Press, 2001)

Feldman, Jackie, *Above the death pits, beneath the flag. Youth voyages to Poland and the performance of Israeli national identity* (New York: Berghahn, 2008)

Felstiner, Mary, 'Alois Brunner: "Eichmann's Best Tool"', *Simon Wiesenthal Centre Annual*, 3 (1986), 1–46

Ferguson, Niall, *High Financier. The Lives and Time of Siegmund Warburg* (London: Allen Lane, 2011)

Fest, Joachim, *Plotting Hitler's Death. The German Resistance to Hitler 1939–1945*, trans. Bruce Little (London: Weidenfeld and Nicolson, 1996)

Finder, Gabriel, 'Judenrat on Trial. Postwar Polish Jewry Sits in Judgment on Its Wartime Leadership', in Finder and Jockusch eds, *Jewish Honor Courts*, 83–106

————— et al. eds, *Polin*, vol. 20, *Making Holocaust Memory* (Portland, OR: Littman Library, 2008)

————— and Cohen, Judith, '*Memento Mori: Photographs from the Grave*', in Finder et al. eds, Polin, vol. 20, *Making Holocaust Memory*, 3–54

————— and Jockusch, Laura eds, *Jewish Honor Courts: Revenge, Retribution, and Reconciliation in Europe and Israel After the Holocaust* (Detroit: Wayne State University Press, 2014)

Fink, Carole, *Defending the Rights of Others. The Great Powers, the Jews and International Minority Protection* (Cambridge: Cambridge University Press, 2004)

Fischer, Albert, 'The Ministry of Economics and the Expulsion of the Jews from the

German Economy', in Bankier ed., *Probing the Depths of German Antisemitism*, 213–25

Fishman, J. S., 'The Reconstruction of the Dutch Jewish Community and its Implications for the Writing of Contemporary Jewish History', *Proceedings of the American Academy for Jewish Research*, 45 (1978), 67–101

Fleming, Michael, *Auschwitz, the Allies and Censorship of the Holocaust* (Cambridge: Cambridge University Press, 2014)

Fox, J. P., 'Great Britain and the German Jews, 1933', *Wiener Library Bulletin*, 36:26/7 (1972), 40–6

Foxman, Abraham H., 'The Resistance Movement in the Vilna Ghetto', in Suhl ed., *They Fought Back*, 148–59

Fraenkel, Daniel, 'Jewish Self-Defence under the Constraints of National Socialism: the Final Years of the Centralverein', in Bankier ed., *Probing the Depths of German Antisemitism*, 339–59

Friedlander, Henry, *The Origins of Nazi Genocide. From Euthanasia to the Final Solution* (Chapel Hill: University of North Carolina, 1995)

Friedländer, Saul, *Nazi Germany and the Jews*, vol. 1, *The Years of Persecution, 1933–1939* (London: Weidenfeld and Nicolson, 1997)

——— *Nazi Germany and the Jews*, vol. 2, *The Years of Extermination 1939–1945* (London: Weidenfeld and Nicolson, 2007)

Friedman, Philip, *Roads to Extinction: Essays on the Holocaust*, ed. Ada June Friedman (Philadelphia: Jewish Publication Society of America, 1980)

Friedrich, Thomas, *Hitler's Berlin. Abused City* (London: Yale, 2012)

Frieser, Karl-Heinz, *The Blitzkrieg Legend. The 1940 Campaign in the West* (Annapolis: Naval Institute Press, 2012)

Friling, Tuvia, 'Istanbul 1942–1945: The Kollek-Avriel and Berman-Ofner networks', in Bankier ed., *Secret Intelligence and the Holocaust*, 105–56

———, Ioanid, Radu and Ionescu, Mihail E. eds, *Final Report of the International Commission on the Holocaust In Romania* (Iasi: Polirom, 2005)

Fritz, Stephen, *Frontsoldaten. The German Soldier in World War II* (Lexington: University Press of Kentucky, 1995)

——— *Ostkrieg. Hitler's War of Extermination in the East* (Lexington: University of Kentucky Press, 2011)

Fritzsche, Peter, *Germans into Nazis* (Cambridge MA: Harvard University Press, 1998)

——— *Life and Death in the Third Reich* (Cambridge, MA: Harvard University Press, 2008)

Fromjimovics, Kinga, 'Different Interpretations of Reconstruction: The AJDC and the WJC in Hungary after the Holocaust', in Bankier ed., *The Jews Are Coming Back*, 277–92

Gafny, Emunah Nachmany, *Dividing Hearts. The Removal of Jewish Children from Gentile Families in Poland in the Immediate Post-Holocaust Years* (Jerusalem: Yad Vashem, 2009)

Garrard, John and Garrard, Carol, *The Bones of Berdichev. The Life and Fate of Vasily Grossman* (New York: Free Press, 1996)

Geissbühler, Simon, 'The Rape of Jewish Women and Girls During the First Phase of the Romanian Offensive in the East, July 1941. A Research Agenda and Preliminary Findings', *Holocaust Studies* 19:1 (2013), 59–80

Gellately, Robert, *Backing Hitler: Consent and Coercion in Nazi Germany* (Oxford: Oxford University Press 2001)

———— *The Gestapo and German Society. Enforcing Racial Policy 1933–1945* (Oxford: Clarendon Press, 1990)

———— and Stolzfus, Nathan eds, *Social Outsiders in Nazi Germany* (Princeton: Princeton University Press, 2001)

Geller, Jay, *Jews in Post-Holocaust Germany, 1945–1953* (New York: Cambridge University Press, 2005)

Gerlach, Christian, 'The decision making process for the deportation of Hungarian Jews', in Molnár ed., *The Holocaust in Hungary*, 473–81

———— 'German Economic Interests, Occupation Policy, and the Murder of the Jews in Belorussia, 1941/43', in Herbert ed., *National Socialist Extermination Policies*, 210–39

———— 'The Wannsee Conference, the Fate of German Jews, and Hitler's Decision in Principle to Exterminate All European Jews', *Journal of Modern History*, 70 (1998), 759–812

———— *Krieg, Ernährung, Völkermord. Deutsche Vernichtungspolitik im Zweiten Weltkrieg* (Zurich: Pendo, 2001)

———— and Aly, Götz, *Das letze Kapitel: Realpolitik, Ideologie und der Mord an den ungarischen Juden 1944/45* (Stuttgart: dva, 2002)

Gerwarth, Robert, *Hitler's Hangman. The Life of Reinhard Heydrich* (London: Yale University Press, 2011)

Gewirtz, Sharon, 'Anglo-Jewish responses to Nazi Germany, 1933–1939. The Anti-Nazi Boycott and the Board of Deputies of British Jews', *Journal of Contemporary History*, 26 (1991), 255–76

Gigliotti, Simone, *The Train Journey. Transit, Captivity and Witnessing the Holocaust* (London: Berghahn, 2009)

Gilbert, Shirli, '"We Long for a Home". Songs and Survival among Jewish Displaced Persons', in Patt and Berkowitz eds, *'We Are Here'*, 289–307

Gilbert, Martin, *Auschwitz and the Allies* (London: Michael Joseph, 1981)

———— *The Holocaust. The Jewish Tragedy* (London: Collins, 1986)

———— *Sir Horace Rumbold. Portrait of a Diplomat 1869–1941* (London: Heinemann, 1973)

Gildea, Robert, *Marianne in Chains. In Search of the German Occupation, 1940–1945* (London: Macmillan, 2002)

Giles, Geoffrey, 'The Institutionalisation of Homosexual Panic in the Third Reich', in Gellately and Nathan eds, *Social Outsiders in Nazi Germany*, 233–47

Gillman, Leni and Gillman, Peter, *'Collar the Lot!' How Britain Interned and Expelled its Wartime Refugees* (London: Quartet, 1980)

Gittelman, Zvi, 'Soviet Reactions to the Holocaust, 1945–1991', in Dobroscycki and Gurock eds, *The Holocaust in the Soviet Union*, 3–27

———— ed., *Bitter Legacy. Confronting the Holocaust in the USSR* (Bloomington: Indiana University Press, 1997)

Goeschel, Christian, 'Suicides of German Jews in the Third Reich', *German History*, 25:1 (2007), 24–45

Golczewski, Frank, 'Shades of Grey: Reflections on Jewish-Ukrainian and German-Ukrainian Relations in Galicia', in Brandon and Lower eds, *The Shoah in Ukraine. History, Testimony, Memorialization*, 114–55

Goldhagen, Daniel Jonah, *Hitler's Willing Executioners. Ordinary Germans and the Holocaust* (London: Little Brown, 1996)

Golz, Anna von der, *Hindenburg. Power, Myth and the Rise of the Nazis* (Oxford: Oxford University Press, 2009)

Goschler, Constantin, 'The Attitude Towards Jews in Bavaria after the Second World War', in Moeller ed., *West Germany Under Construction*, 231–50

Grabowski, Jan, 'Rural Society and the Jews in Hiding: Elders, Night Watchers, Firefighters, Hostages and Manhunts', *Yad Vashem Studies*, 40 (2012), 49–74

———— *Hunt for the Jews. Betrayal and Murder in German-Occupied Poland* (Bloomington: Indiana University Press, 2014)

Graml, Hermann, *Anti-Semitism in the Third Reich* (Oxford: Berghahn, 1988)

Gregor, Neil, *How to Read Hitler* (London: Granta, 2005)

Greif, Gideon, *We Wept Without Tears. Testimonies of the Jewish Sonderkommando from Auschwitz* (New Haven: Yale University Press, 2005)

Grenville, J. A. S., *The Jews and Germans of Hamburg. The Destruction of a Civilization 1790–1945* (London: Routledge, 2012)

Griffioen, Pim and Zeller, Ron, 'Comparing the Persecution of the Jews in the Netherlands, France and Belgium', in Romijn et al. eds, *The Persecution of the Jews in the Netherlands*, 55–91

Grinberg, Daniel ed., *Fifty Years After. Papers from the Conference organized by the Jewish Historical Institute of Warsaw, 29–31 March 1993* (Warsaw: Jewish Historical Institute, 1994)

Grobman, Alex, *Battling for Souls. The Vaad Hatzala Rescue Committee in Post-war Europe* (Jersey City, NJ: Ktav, 2004)

———— *Rekindling the Flame. American Chaplains and the Survivors of European Jewry, 1944–1945* (Detroit: Wayne State University Press, 1993)

Gross, Jan Tomasz, 'The Jewish Community in the Soviet-Annexed Territories on the Eve of the Holocaust', in Dobroscycki and Gurock eds, *The Holocaust in the Soviet Union*, 155–79

———— *Fear: Anti-Semitism in Poland after Auschwitz: An Essay in Historical Interpretation* (Princeton: Princeton University Press, 2006)

———— *Neighbors. The Destruction of the Jewish Community in Jedwabne, Poland* (Princeton: Princeton University Press, 2001)

———— with Gross, Irena Grudzinska, *Golden Harvest. Events at the Periphery of the Holocaust* (New York: Oxford University Press, 2012)

Gruber, Ruth, *Haven. The Dramatic Story of 1,000 World War II Refugees and How They Came to America* (New York: Three Rivers Press, 2000 edn)

Gruner, Wolf, 'Public Welfare and the German Jews', in Bankier ed., *Probing the Depths of German Antisemitism*, 78–105

—————— *Jewish Forced Labour Under the Nazis. Economic Needs and Racial Aims, 1938–1944*, trans. Kathleen M. Dell'Orto (New York: Cambridge University Press, 2006)

Guenther, Irene, *Nazi Chic? Fashioning Women in the Third Reich* (Oxford: Berg, 2004)

Gutman, Israel, 'Introduction: The Distinctiveness of the Lodz Ghetto', in Trunk ed., *Lodz Ghetto*, xxix–lvii

Gutman, Yisrael, *The Jews of Warsaw 1939–1943. Ghetto, Underground, Revolt*, trans. Ina Friedman (Bloomington: Indiana University Press, 1982)

—————— and Berenbaum, Michael eds, *Anatomy of the Auschwitz Death Camp* (Bloomington: Indiana University Press, 1994)

—————— and Haft, Cynthia eds, *Patterns of Jewish Leadership in Nazi Europe 1933–1945* (Jerusalem: Yad Vashem, 1979)

Gutterman, Bella, *A Narrow Bridge to Life. Jewish Forced Labour and Survival in the Gross-Rosen Camp System, 1940–1945*, trans. IBRT (New York: Berghahn, 2008)

Haan, Ido de 'An Unresolved Controversy: The Jewish Honour Court in the Netherlands, 1946–50', unpublished paper, 1 November 2014, Lessons and Legacies, XIII

Hadley, Karen, 'Lessons from Auschwitz', *History Today*, September 2010, 4–5

Halbmayr, Brigitte, 'Sexualized Violence against Women during Nazi "Racial" Persecution', in Hedgepeth and Saidel eds, *Sexual Violence Against Jewish Women During the Holocaust*, 29–44

Hallie, Philip, *Lest Innocent Blood be Shed* (New York: Harper, 1994)

Hamann, Brigitte, 'Hitler and Vienna', in Mommsen ed., *The Third Reich Between Vision and Reality*, 23–37

—————— *Hitler's Vienna. A Dictator's Apprenticeship* (Oxford: Oxford University Press, 1999)

Harris, Jeremy D., 'Broadcasting the Massacres. An analysis of the BBC's contemporary coverage of the Holocaust', *Yad Vashem Studies*, 25 (1996), 65–98

Hastings, Max, *Finest Years. Churchill as Warlord 1940–45* (London: Harper Press, 2009)

Hayes, Peter, *From Cooperation to Complicity. Degussa in the Thrid Reich* (New York: Cambridge University Press, 2004)

Headland, Ronald, *Messages of Murder. A Study of the Reports of the Security Police and the Security Service, 1941–1945* (Toronto: Associated University Press, 1992)

Heberer, Patricia and Matthäus, Jürgen eds, *Atrocities on Trial. Historical Perspectives on the Politics of Prosecuting War Crimes* (Lincoln: University of Nebraska Press, 2008).

Hedgepeth, Sonja M. and Saidel, Rochelle G. eds, *Sexual Violence Against Jewish Women During the Holocaust* (Waltham, MA: Brandeis University Press, 2010)

Heer, Hannes, 'The Logic of Extermination: The Wehrmacht and the Anti-Partisan War', in Heer and Naumann eds, *War of Extermination*, 92–126

———— and Naumann, Klaus eds, *War of Extermination. The German Military in World War II 1941–1944* (New York: Berghahn, 2000)

Heller, Celia, *On the Edge of Destruction: The Jews of Poland Between the Two World Wars* (Detroit: Wayne State University Press, 1994)

Herbert, Ulrich, 'The German Military Command in Paris and the Deportation of the French Jews', in Herbert ed., *National Socialist Extermination Policies*, 128–62

———— ed., *National Socialist Extermination Policies. Contemporary Perspectives and Controversies* (New York: Berghahn, 2000)

Herczl, Moshe, *Christianity and the Holocaust of Hungarian Jewry*, trans. Joel Lerner (New York: New York University Press, 1991)

Herf, Jeffrey, *Divided Memory. The Nazi Past in the Two Germanys* (Cambridge, MA: Harvard University Press, 1997)

———— *The Jewish Enemy. Nazi Propaganda During World War II and the Holocaust* (Cambridge MA: Harvard University Press, 2009)

Herzog, Dagmar ed., *Lessons and Legacies*, vol. VII, *The Holocaust in International Perspective* (Evanston, IL: Northwestern University Press, 2006)

Heschel, Susannah, *The Aryan Jesus. Christian Theology and the Bible in Nazi Germany* (Princeton: Princeton University Press, 2008)

Hett, Benjamin Carter, *Crossing Hitler. The Man Who Put the Nazis on the Witness Stand* (New York and Oxford: Oxford University Press, 2008)

Hilberg, Raul, *The Destruction of the European Jews*, vol. 2 (New York: Holmes & Meier, 1985 edn), 718–30

———— and Staron, Stanislaw, 'Introduction', in Hilberg et al. eds, *The Warsaw Diary of Adam Czerniakow*, 25–72

Himka, John-Paul, 'Metropolitan Andrey Sheptytsky and the Holocaust', *Polin*, 26 (2014), 337–60.

Hinrichsen, Klaus, 'Visual Art Behind the Wire', in Cesarani and Kushner eds, *The Internment of Aliens in Twentieth Century Britain*, 188–241

HMDT Statement of Commitment, http://hmd.org.uk/genocides/holocaust

Holocaust Education and Development Programme, *Teaching About the Holocaust in English Secondary Schools* (London: Institute of Education, 2009)

Hondius, Dienke, 'Bitter Homecoming. The Return and Reception of Dutch and Stateless Jews in the Netherlands', in Bankier ed., *The Jews Are Coming Back*, 108–36

———— *Return. Holocaust Survivors and Dutch Anti-Semitism*, trans. David Colmer (Westport, CT: Praeger, 2003)

Horowitz, Gordon J., *Ghettostadt. Lodz and the Making of a Nazi City* (Cambridge, MA: Belknap Press, 2008)

Hull, Isabel V., *Absolute Destruction. Military Culture and the Practices of War in Imperial Germany* (Ithaca, NY: Cornell University Press, 2005)

Imlay, Talbot and Horn, Martin, *The Politics of Industrial Collaboration during World War II. Ford France, Vichy and Nazi Germany* (Cambridge: Cambridge University Press, 2014)

Ingrao, Christian, *Believe and Destroy. Intellectuals in the SS War Machine*, trans. Andrew Brown (London: Polity, 2013)

Ioanid, Radu, 'The Holocaust in Romania: the Iasi Pogrom of June 1941', *Central European History* 2:2 (1993), 119–48

———— *The Holocaust in Romania. The Destruction of Jews and Gypsies under the Antonescu Regime, 1940–1944* (Chicago: Ivan R. Dee, 2000)

Iwaszko, Tadeusz, 'The Housing, Clothing and Feeding of the Prisoners', in Iwaszko et al. eds, *Auschwitz 1940–1945*, vol. II, 89–98

———— et al. eds, *Auschwitz 1940–1945. Central Issues in the History of the Camp*, vol. II, *The Prisoners – Their Life and Work* (Oswiecim: Auschwitz-Birkenau State Museum, 2000)

Jäckel, Eberhard, *Hitler's World View. A Blueprint for Power* (Cambridge, MA: Harvard University Press, 1981)

Jackson, Julian, *France 1940–1944. The Dark Years* (Oxford: Oxford University Press, 2001)

Jensen, M. B. and Jensen, S. L. B. eds, *Denmark and the Holocaust* (Copenhagen: Institute for International Studies, 2003)

Jockusch, Laura, 'Rehabilitating the Past. Jewish Honor Courts in Allied-Occupied Germany', in Finder and Jockusch eds, *Jewish Honor Courts*, 49–82

———— *Collect and Record! Jewish Holocaust Documentation in Early Postwar Europe* (New York: Oxford University Press, 2012)

Johnson, Eric A., *Nazi Terror. The Gestapo, Jews and Ordinary Germans* (London: John Murray, 1999)

Jones, Michael, *The Retreat. Hitler's First Defeat* (London: John Murray, 2009)

Judt, Tony, *Postwar. A History of Europe Since 1945* (London: Heinemann, 2005)

Kallis, Aristotle, *Genocide and Fascism. The Eliminationist Drive in Fascist Europe* (London: Routledge, 2009)

Kaplan, Marion, 'Changing Roles in Jewish Families' in Nicosia and Scrase eds, *Jewish Life in Nazi Germany*, 15–25

———— *Between Dignity and Despair. Jewish Life in Nazi Germany* (New York: Oxford University Press, 1998)

Karas, Joza, *Music in Terezin 1941–1945* (New York: Beaufort Books, 1988)

Karlsson, Klas-Göran and Zander, Ulf eds, *The Holocaust – Post-War Battlefields. Genocide as Historical Culture* (Malmo: Sekel Bokförlag, 2006)

Karny, Miroslav, 'The Vrba and Wetzler Report', in Gutman and Berenbaum eds, *Anatomy of the Auschwitz Death Camp*, 553–68

Karsai, László, 'Anti-Jewish laws and decrees in Hungary, 1920–1944', in Molnár ed., *The Holocaust in Hungary*, 143–66

———— 'The Last Phase of the Hungarian Holocaust: The Szálasi regime and the Jews', in Braham and Miller eds, *The Nazis' Last Victims*, 103–16

———— and Molnár, Judit eds, *The Kastzn Report. The Report of the Budapest Jewish Rescue Committee, 1943–1945* (Jerusalem: Yad Vashem, 2013)

Kassow, Samuel D., *Who Will Write Our History? Emanuel Ringelblum, the Warsaw Ghetto, and the Oyneg Shabas Archive* (Bloomington: Indiana University Press, 2007)

Katzburg, Nathaniel, *Hungary and the Jews 1920–1943* (Ramat Gan: Bar Ilan University Press, 1981)

Kay, Alex J., *Exploitation, Resettlement, Mass Murder. Political and Economic Planning for German Occupation in the Soviet Union, 1940–41* (New York: Berghahn, 2006)

———— Rutherford, Jeff and Stahel, David eds, *Nazi Policy on the Eastern Front, 1941. Total War, Genocide and Radicalisation* (Rochester NY: University of Rochester Press, 2012)

Keren, Nili, 'The Family Camp', in Gutman and Berenbaum eds, *Anatomy of the Auschwitz Death Camp*, 428–40

Kershaw, Ian, 'Improvised Genocide? The Emergence of "the Final Solution" in the Warthegau', *Transactions of the Royal Historical Society*, 6th series, vol. 2 (1992), 51–78

———— '"Working Towards the Führer." Reflections on the Nature of the Hitler Dictatorship', *Contemporary European History*, 2:2 (1993), 103–18

———— *Fateful Choices. Ten Decisions that Changed the World 1940–1941* (London: Allen Lane, 2007)

———— *Hitler 1889–1936. Hubris* (London: Allen Lane, 1998)

———— *Hitler 1936–1945. Nemesis* (London: Allen Lane, 2000)

———— *The Nazi Dictatorship. Problems and Perspectives of Interpretation* (London: Arnold, 2000 edn)

Kertzer, David, *The Popes Against the Jews. The Vatican's Role in the Rise of Modern Anti-Semitism* (New York: Knopf, 2001)

Klarsfeld, Serge, 'The Influence of the War on the Final Solution in France', in Cohen, Cochavi, Gelber eds, *The Shoah and the War*, 271–91

Knoch, Habbo and Buchholz, Marlis et al. eds, *Bergen-Belsen* (Göttingen: Wallstein Verlag, 2010)

Kochan, Lionel, *Pogrom. November 10, 1938* (London: André Deutsch, 1957)

Kochan, Miriam, 'Women's Experience of Internment', in Cesarani and Kushner eds, *The Internment of Aliens in Twentieth Century Britain*, 147–66

———— *Britain's Internees in the Second World War* (London: Macmillan, 1983)

Kochavi, Arieh, 'The Role of Genocide in the Preparations for the Nuremberg Trials', in Bankier and Michman eds, *Holocaust and Justice*, 59–80

———— *Post-Holocaust Politics: Britain, the United States, and Jewish Refugees, 1945–1948* (Chapel Hill and London: University of North Carolina, 2002)

———— *Prelude to Nuremberg. Allied War Crimes Policy and the Question of Punishment* (Chapel Hill: University of North Carolina Press, 1998)

Kolb, Eberhard, *The Weimar Republic*, trans. P. S. Falla (London: Routledge, 1988)

Kolinsky, Eva, *After the Holocaust: Jewish Survivors in Germany after 1945* (London: Pimlico, 2004)

Königsweder, Angelika and Wetzel, Juliane, *Waiting for Hope. Jewish Displaced Persons in Post-World War II Germany*, trans. John Broadwin (Evanston: Northwestern University Press, 2001)

Koonz, Claudia, 'On Reading a Document: SS-Man Katzmann's "Solution of the Jewish Question in the District of Galicia"', The Raul Hilberg Lecture, University of Vermont, 2 November 2005 at https://www.uvm.edu/~uvmchs/documents/ KoonzHilbergLecture_002.pdf

————— The Nazi Conscience (Cambridge, MA: Harvard University Press, 2003)

Kosmola, Beate and Tych, Feliks eds, Facing the Nazi Genocide: Non-Jews and Jews in Europe (Berlin: Metropol, 2004)

Krakowski, Shmuel, Chelmno. A Small Village in Europe. The First Nazi Mass Execution Camp (Jerusalem: Yad Vashem, 2009)

————— 'The Number of Victims', in Gutman and Berenbaum eds, Anatomy of the Auschwitz Death Camp, 61–76

————— The War of the Doomed. Jewish Armed Resistance in Poland, 1942–1944, trans. Ora Blaustein (New York: Holmes and Meier, 1984)

Kranzler, David, Holocaust Hero. Solomon Schonfeld (Jersey City: Ktav, 2004)

Kühne, Thomas, Belonging and Genocide. Hitler's Community, 1918–1945 (New Haven: Yale University Press, 2010)

————— and Lawson, Tom eds, The Holocaust and Local History (London: Vallentine Mitchell, 2011)

Kurlander, Eric, Living With Hitler. Liberal Democrats in the Third Reich (London: Yale University Press, 2009)

Kushner, Tony, 'Clubland, Cricket Tests and Alien Internment, 1939–40', in Cesarani and Kushner eds, The Internment of Aliens in Twentieth Century Britain, 79–101

————— The Holocaust and the Liberal Imagination (Oxford: Blackwell, 1994)

————— The Persistence of Prejudice. Antisemitism in British Society during the Second World War (Manchester: Manchester University Press, 1989)

Kwiet, Konrad, 'Rehearsing for Murder: The Beginning of the Final Solution in Lithuania in June 1941', Holocaust and Genocide Studies, 12:1 (1998), 3–26

————— 'Without Neighbours: Daily Living in Judenhauser', in Nicosia and Scrase eds, Jewish Life in Nazi Germany, 117–48

Lagrou, Pieter, 'Return to a Vanished World. European Societies and the Remnants of their Jewish Communities, 1945–1947', in Bankier ed., The Jews Are Coming Back, 1–24

————— The Legacy of Nazi Occupation: Patriotic Memory and National Recovery in Western Europe, 1945–1965 (Cambridge: Cambridge University Press, 1999)

Lamberti, Marjorie, Jewish Activism in Imperial Germany. The Struggle for Civic Equality (New Haven: Yale University Press, 1978)

Langbein, Hermann, Against All Hope. Resistance in the Nazi Concentration Camps 1938–1945 (New York: Continuum, 1994)

Lange, Anders, A survey of teachers' experiences and perceptions in relation to teaching about the Holocaust (Stockholm: The Living History Forum, 2008)

Langer, Lawrence, Holocaust Testimonies. The ruins of memory (New Haven: Yale University Press, 1991)

Langerbein, Helmut, Hitler's Death Squads. The Logic of Mass Murder (College Station, TX: Texas A&M University, 2004)

Laqueur, Walter, *The Terrible Secret. Suppression of the Truth about Hitler's Final Solution* (London: Penguin, 1980)

———— and Breitman, Richard, *Breaking the Silence. The Secret Mission of Eduard Schulte, who brought the world news of the Final Solution* (London: Bodley Head, 1986)

Lasik, Aleksander et al. eds, *Auschwitz 1940–1945. Central Issues in the History of the Camp*, vol. I, *The Establishment and Organisation of the Camp* (Oswiecim: Auschwitz-Birkenau State Museum, 2000)

Lattek, Christine, 'Bergen-Belsen: From "Privileged" Camp to Death Camp', in Reilly et al. eds, *Belsen in History and Memory*, 37–51

Laub, Morris, *Last Barrier to Freedom: Internment of Jewish Holocaust Survivors on Cyprus, 1946–1949* (Berkeley, CA: Judah Magnes Museum, 1985)

Laub, Thomas, 'The development of German Policy in Occupied France, 1941, Against the background of the war in the East', in Kay, Rutherford and Stahel eds, *Nazi Policy on the Eastern Front, 1941*, 281–313

———— *After the Fall. German Policy in Occupied France 1940–1944* (Oxford: Oxford University Press, 2010)

Lavsky, Hagit, *New Beginnings. Holocaust Survivors in Bergen-Belsen and the British Zone in Germany, 1945–1950* (Detroit: Wayne State University Press, 2002)

Lee, Carol Ann, *Roses from the Earth. The Biography of Anne Frank* (London: Viking, 1999)

Leff, Lurel, *Buried by the Times. The Holocaust and America's Most Important Newspaper* (New York: Cambridge University Press, 2005)

Leitz, Christian, *Nazi Germany and Neutral Europe during the Second World War* (Manchester: Manchester University Press, 2000)

Levine, Paul, 'Swedish neutrality during the Second World War: tactical success or moral compromise', in Wylie ed. *European Neutrals and Non-Belligerents During the Second World War*, 304–30

———— *From Indifference to Activism, Swedish Diplomacy and the Holocaust 1938–44* (Uppsala: Studia Historica Upsaliensia, 1998)

———— *Raoul Wallenberg in Budapest. Myth, History and Holocaust* (London: Vallentine Mitchell, 2010)

Levy, Daniel and Sznaider, Natan, *The Holocaust and Memory in a Global Age*, trans. Assenka Oksiloff (Philadelphia: Temple University, 2006)

Levy, Richard S., *The Downfall of the Anti-Semitic Political Parties in Imperial Germany* (New Haven: Yale University Press, 1975)

Lewy, Guenter, *The Catholic Church and Nazi Germany* (New York: DaCapo, 2000 edn)

———— *The Nazi Persecution of the Gypsies* (Oxford: Oxford University Press, 2000)

Lidegaard, Bo, *Countrymen. The Untold Story of How Denmark's Jews Escaped the Nazis* (London: Atlantic Books, 2013)

Lifton, Robert Jay, *The Nazi Doctors. Medical Killing and the Psychology of Genocide* (New York: Basic Books, 2000 edn)

———— and Hackett, Amy, 'Nazi Doctors', in Gutman and Berenbaum eds, *Anatomy of the Auschwitz Death Camp*, 301–16

Lipman, V. D., 'Anglo-Jewish Attitudes to the Refugees from Central Europe 1933–1939', in Mosse ed., *Second Chance*, 519–32

Lipstadt, Deborah, *Beyond Belief. The American Press and the Coming of the Holocaust 1933–1945* (New York: Free Press, 1986)

Litvak, Josef, 'Jewish Refugees from Poland in the USSR, 1939–1946', in Zimmerman ed., *Contested Memories*, 123–50

Löb, Ladislaus, *Dealing with Satan. Kasztner's Daring Rescue Mission* (London: Jonathan Cape, 2008)

Lohalm, Uwe, 'Local Administration and Nazi Anti-Jewish Policy', in Bankier ed., *Probing the Depths of German Antisemitism*, 109–46

London, Louise, 'British Government Policy and Jewish Refugees 1933–45', *Patterns of Prejudice*, 23:4 (1989), 35–43

———— *Whitehall and the Jews* (Cambridge: Cambridge University Press, 2000)

Longerich, Peter, *Goebbels. A Biography*, trans. Alan Bance, Jeremy Noakes and Lesley Sharpe (London: Bodley Head, 2015)

———— *Heinrich Himmler. A Life*, trans. Jeremy Noakes and Lesley Sharpe (Oxford: Oxford University Press, 2012)

———— *Holocaust. The Nazi Persecution and Murder of the Jews* (Oxford: Oxford University Press, 2010)

Lower, Wendy, 'Axis Collaboration, Operation Barbarossa and the Holocaust in the Ukraine', in Kay, Rutherford and Stahel eds, *Nazi Policy on the Eastern Front, 1941*, 186–219

———— *Nazi Empire Building and the Holocaust in the Ukraine* (Chapel Hill: University of North Carolina Press, 2005)

Lozowick, Yaacov, *Hitler's Bureaucrats. The Nazi Security Police and the Banality of Evil*, trans. Haim Watzman (New York: Continuum, 2002)

Ludi, Regula, '"Why Switzerland?" Remarks on a Neutral's Role in the Nazi Program of Robbery and Allied Postwar Restitution Policy', in Dean, Goschler and Ther eds, *Robbery and Restitution*, 182–210

———— *Reparations for Nazi Victims in Postwar Europe* (New York: Cambridge University Press, 2010)

Lukacs, John, *The Hitler of History. Hitler's Biographers on Trial* (London: Weidenfeld and Nicolson, 2000)

Lusane, Clarence, *Hitler's Black Victims. The Historical Experience of Afro-Germans, European Blacks, Africans, and African Americans in the Nazi Era* (London: Routledge, 2003)

Mallman, Klaus-Michael and Cupers, Martin, *Nazi Palestine. The Plans for the Extermination of the Jews in Palestine*, trans. Krista Smith (London: Enigma Books, 2010)

Mankowitz, Zvi, *Life Between Memory and Hope: The Survivors of the Holocaust in Occupied Germany* (Cambridge: Cambridge University Press, 2002)

Manoschek, Walter, '"Coming Along to Shoot Some Jews?" The Destruction of the Jews in Serbia', in Heer and Naumann eds, *War of Extermination*, 39–52

Marrus, Michael, 'The Holocaust at Nuremberg', *Yad Vashem Studies*, 26 (1998), 5–42

———— *'The Shoah and the Second World War: Some Comments on Recent Historiography'*, in Cohen, Cochavi, Gelber eds, The Shoah and the War, 1–24

———— *The Nuremberg War Crimes Trial 1945-1946. A Documentary History* (New York: Bedford/St Martin's, 1997)

———— *The Unwanted. Refugees in the Twentieth Century* (New York: Oxford University Press, 1985)

———— and Paxton, Robert O., *Vichy France and the Jews* (New York: Schocken, 1983)

Matthäus, Jürgen, 'Controlled Escalation: Himmler's Men in the Summer of 1941 and the Holocaust in the Occupied Soviet Territories', *Holocaust and Genocide Studies*, 21:2 (2007), 218–42

———— 'Evading Persecution. German Jewish Behaviour Patterns after 1933', in Nicosia and Scrase eds, *Jewish Life in Nazi Germany*, 47–70

———— 'Operation Barbarossa and the Onset of the Holocaust, June–December 1941', in Browning, *The Origins of the Final Solution*, 244–308

Mawdsley, Evan, *Thunder in the East. The Nazi–Soviet War 1941-1945* (London: Arnold, 2007)

Mazower, Mark, *Hitler's Empire. Nazi Rule in Occupied Europe* (London: Allen Lane, 2008)

———— *Inside Hitler's Greece. The Experience of Occupation, 1941–1944* (London: Yale University Press, 1993)

———— *Salonica. City of Ghosts. Christians, Muslims and Jews 1430-1950* (London: Harper Collins, 2004)

Mazurek, Jerzy, '"Jozek, what are you doing?" The Massacre of Jews Committed by the AK in the Village of Kosowice', *Holocaust Studies and Materials* (2013), 405–32

McQueen, Michael, 'Nazi Policy Towards the Jews in the Reichskommissariat Ostland, June–December 1941', in Gitelman ed., *Bitter Legacy. Confronting the Holocaust in the USSR*, 91–103

Meershoek, Guus, 'The Amsterdam Police and the Persecution of the Jews', in Berenbaum and Peck eds, *The Holocaust in History*, 284–300

Meeuwnwoord, Marieke, 'The Holocaust in the Netherlands: new research of camp Vught', in Romijn et al. eds, *The Persecution of the Jews in the Netherlands*, 93–103

Megargee, Geoffrey, *Inside Hitler's High Command* (Lawrence: University of Kansas Press, 2000)

———— *War of Annihilation. Combat and Genocide on the Eastern Front, 1941* (Lanham, MD: Rowman and Littlefield, 2006)

Melvin, Hugo, *Manstein. Hitler's Greatest General* (London: Phoenix, 2010)

Mendes-Flohr, Paul, 'Jewish Cultural Life under National Socialism', in Meyer ed., *German-Jewish History in Modern Times*, vol. 4, *Renewal and Destruction: 1918–1945*, 283–312

Merridale, Catherine, *Ivan's War: Life and Death in the Red Army, 1939–1945* (New York: Henry Holt, 2006)

Meyer, Beate, 'Between Self-Assurance and Forced Collaboration. The Reich

Association of Jews in Germany, 1939–1945', in Nicosia and Scrase eds, *Jewish Life in Nazi Germany*, 149–69

———— 'The Mixed Marriage: A Guarantee of Survival or a Reflection of German Society during the Nazi Regime?', in Bankier ed., *Probing the Depths of German Antisemitism*, 54–76

———— Simon, Hermann and Schütz, Chana eds, *Jews in Nazi Berlin: From Kristallnacht to Liberation* (Chicago: University of Chicago Press, 2009)

Meyer, Michael ed., *German-Jewish History in Modern Times*, vol. 3, *Integration in Dispute 1871–1918* (New York: Columbia University Press, 1997)

———— ed., *German-Jewish History in Modern Times*, vol. 4, *Renewal and Destruction: 1918–1945* (New York: Columbia University Press, 1998)

Michaelis, Meir, 'Italian Policy up to the Armistice', in Cohen, Cochavi, Gelber eds, *The Shoah and the War*, 283–300

———— *Mussolini and the Jews. German-Italian relations and the Jewish Question in Italy 1922–1945* (Oxford: Oxford University Press, 1971)

Michman, Dan, 'Problematic National Identity, Outsiders and Persecution: Impact of the Gentile Population's Attitude in Belgium on the Fate of the Jews in 1940–1944', in Bankier and Gutman eds, *Nazi Europe and the Final Solution*, 455–68

———— ed., *Belgium and the Holocaust* (Jerusalem: Yad Vashem, 1998)

———— *The Emergence of the Jewish Ghettos During the Holocaust*, trans. L. J. Schramm (New York: Cambridge University Press, 2011)

Moeller, Robert G. ed., *West Germany Under Construction. Politics, Society, and Culture in the Adenauer Era* (Ann Arbor: University of Michigan Press, 1997)

Mogenson, Michael, 'October 1943 – the Rescue of the Danish Jews', in Jensen and Jensen eds, *Denmark and the Holocaust*, 33–61

Molnár, Judit, 'Gendarmes Before the People's Court', in Molnár ed., *The Holocaust in Hungary*, 677–84

———— ed., *The Holocaust in Hungary in A European Perspective* (Budapest: Balassi Kiadó, 2005)

Mommsen, Hans, 'Hitler's Reichstag Speech, 30 January 1939', *History and Memory* 9:1/2 (1997), 142–61

———— ed., *The Third Reich Between Vision and Reality. New perspectives on German history, 1918–1945* (Oxford: Berg, 2001)

Montague, Patrick, *Chelmno and the Holocaust. The Story of Hitler's First Death Camp* (London: I. B. Tauris, 2012)

Moore, Bob, *Survivors. Jewish Self-Help and Rescue in Nazi-Occupied Western Europe* (Oxford: Oxford University Press, 2010)

———— *Victims and Survivors. The Nazi Persecution of the Jews in the Netherlands 1940–1945* (London: Arnold, 1997)

Moorhead, Caroline, *Village of Secrets: Defying the Nazis in Vichy France* (London: Chatto and Windus, 2014)

Móscy, István, 'Hungary's Failed Strategic Surrender: Secret Wartime Negotiations with Britain', in Dreisziger ed., *Hungary in an Age of Total War*, 86–106

Moser, Jonny, 'Depriving Jews of their Legal Rights in the Third Reich', in Pehle ed., *November 1938*, 123–38

——— 'Nisko: The First Experiment in Deportation', *Simon Wiesenthal Centre Annual*, 2 (1985), 1–30

Mosse, Werner E. ed., *Second Chance. Two centuries of German-speaking Jews in the United Kingdom* (Tübingen: J. C. B. Mohr, 1992)

Motadel, David, *Islam and Nazi Germany's War* (Cambridge, MA: Harvard University Press, 2014)

Musial, Bogdan, 'The Origins of Operation Reinhard', *Yad Vashem Studies*, 28 (1999), 112–53

Myers Feinstein, Margarete, 'Jewish Observance in Amalek's Shadow: Mourning, Marriage, and Birth Rituals among Displaced Persons in Germany', in Patt and Berkowitz eds, *'We Are Here'*, 257–88

——— *Holocaust Survivors in Postwar Germany* (New York: Cambridge University Press, 2010)

Neillands, Robin, *The Battle for the Rhine 1944* (London: Cassell, 2005)

Neitzel, Sönke and Welzer, Harald, *Soldaten. On Fighting, Killing and Dying. The Secret Second World War Tapes of German POWs*, trans. Jefferson Chase (London: Simon and Schuster, 2012)

Neufeld, Michael J. and Berenbaum, Michael eds, *The Bombing of Auschwitz* (New York: St Martin's Press, 2000)

Nicholas, Lynn H., *The Rape of Europa, The Fate of Europe's Treasures in the Third Reich and the Second World War* (London: Papermac, 1994)

Nicosia, Francis, 'German Zionism and Jewish Life in Nazi Berlin', in Nicosia and Scrase eds, *Jewish Life in Nazi Germany*, 89–116

——— *Zionism and Anti-Semitism in Nazi Germany* (New York: Cambridge University Press, 2008)

——— and Scrase, David eds, *Jewish Life in Nazi Germany. Dilemmas and Responses* (New York: Berghahn, 2012)

Nidam-Orvieto, Iael, 'The Impact of the Anti-Jewish Legislation on Everyday Life and the Response of Italian Jews, 1938–1943', in Zimmerman ed., *Jews in Italy under Fascist and Nazi Rule*, 158–81

Niewyk, Donald, 'Solving the "Jewish Problem": continuity and change in German antisemitism, 1871–1945', in Cesarani ed., *Holocaust. Critical Concepts in Historical Studies*, vol. 1 (London: Routledge, 2004), 50–90

——— *The Jews in Weimar Germany* (New Brunswick: Transaction Books, 2001 edn)

Niznansky, Eduard, 'Expropriation and Deportation of Jews in Slovakia', in Kosmola and Tych eds, *Facing the Nazi Genocide*, 205–30

Nordlund, Sven, '"The War is Over – Now You Can Go Home!" Jewish Refugees and the Swedish Labour Market in the Shadow of the Holocaust', in Cesarani and Levine, *'Bystanders' to the Holocaust*, 171–98

O'Neill, Robin, 'Belzec – The Forgotten Death Camp', *East European Jewish Affairs*, 28:2 (1998–9), 49–62

Obenhaus, Herbert, 'The Germans: An Antisemitic People. The press campaign after 9 November 1938', in Bankier ed., *Probing the Depths of German Antisemitism*, 147–80

Ofer, Dalia, *Escaping the Holocaust. Illegal Immigration to the Land of Israel, 1939–1944* (New York: Oxford University Press, 1990)

Overy, Richard, *The Bombing War. Europe 1939–1945* (London: Penguin, 2013)

Passelecq, Georges and Suchecky, Bernard, *The Hidden Encyclical of Pius XI*, trans. Steven Rendall (New York: Harcourt Brace, 1997)

Patt, Avinoam J. and Berkowitz, Michael, eds, *'We Are Here'. New Approaches to Jewish Displaced Persons in Postwar Germany* (Detroit: Wayne State University Press, 2010)

Paucker, Arnold and Kwiet, Konrad, 'Jewish Leadership and Jewish Resistance', in Bankier ed., *Probing the Depths of German Antisemitism*, 371–94

Paulsson, Gunnar S., *Secret City. The Hidden Jews of Warsaw 1940–1945* (New Haven: Yale University Press, 2002)

Pavan, Ilaria, 'Indifference and Forgetting: Italy and its Jewish Community, 1938–1970', in Dean et al., *Robbery and Restitution*, 155–70

Pearce, Andy, *Holocaust Consciousness in Contemporary Britain* (London: Routledge, 2014)

Peck, Jeffrey M., 'Germany', in Wyman ed., *The World Reacts to the Holocaust*, 447–72

Pehle, Walter ed., *November 1938*, trans. William Templer (Oxford: Berg, 1991)

Pelt, Robert Jan van, 'Introduction: David Koker and his diary', in Koker, *At the Edge of the Abyss*, 3–71

———— 'A Site in Search of a Mission', in Gutman and Berenbaum eds, *Anatomy of the Auschwitz Death Camp*, 93–157

———— and Dwork, Debórah, *Auschwitz 1270 to the Present* (New Haven: Yale University Press, 1996)

Penkower, Monty Noam, *The Swastika's Darkening Shadow. Voices Before the Holocaust* (New York: Palgrave Macmillan, 2013)

Perego, Simon, 'Jurys d'honneur. The Stakes and Limits of Purges Among Jews in France After the Liberation', in Finder and Jockusch eds, *Jewish Honor Courts*, 137–64

Peresztegi, Agnes, 'Reparation and Compensation in Hungary, 1945–2003', in Molnár ed., *The Holocaust in Hungary*, 648–64

Person, Katarzyna, 'Jews Accusing Jews. Denunciations of Alleged Collaborators in Jewish Honor Courts', in Finder and Jockusch eds, *Jewish Honor Courts*, 225–46

———— *Assimilated Jews in the Warsaw Ghetto, 1940–1943* (Syracuse: Syracuse University Press, 2014)

Persson, Sune, *Escape from the Third Reich*, trans. Graham Long (Barnsley: Skyhorse, 2009)

Petropoulos, Jonathan and Roth, John K. eds, *Gray Zones. Ambiguity and Compromise in the Holocaust and its Aftermath* (New York: Berghahn, 2005)

Philipponnat, Olivier and Lienhardt, Patrick, *The Life of Irène Némirovsky 1903–1942*, trans. Euan Cameron (London: Vintage, 2011)

Picciotto, Liliana, 'The Shoah in Italy: Its History and Characteristics', in Zimmerman ed., *Jews in Italy under Fascist and Nazi Rule, 1922–1945*, 210–14

———— 'Statistical Tables on the Holocaust in Italy with an Insight into the Mechanics of the Deportations', *Yad Vashem Studies*, 33 (2005), 307–46

Pinchuk, Ben Cion, 'Facing Hitler and Stalin. On the Subject of Jewish "Collaboration" in Soviet Occupied Eastern Poland, 1939–1941', in Zimmerman ed., *Contested Memories*, 61–8

Pine, Lisa, *Nazi Family Policy, 1933–1945* (Oxford: Berg, 1997)

Piper, Franciszek, 'The Exploitation of Prisoner Labor', in Tadeusz Iwaszko et al. eds, *Auschwitz 1940–1945*, vol. II, 71–136

———— 'Gas Chambers and Crematoria', in Gutman and Berenbaum eds, *Anatomy of the Auschwitz Death Camp*, 157–82

———— *Auschwitz 1940–1945. Central Issues in the History of the Camp*, vol. III, *Mass Murder* (Oswiecim: Auschwitz-Birkenau State Museum, 2000)

Podolsky, Anatoly, 'The Tragic Fate of Ukrainian Jewish Women Under Nazi Occupation, 1941–1944', in Hedgepath and Saidel eds, *Sexual Violence*, 93–107

Pohl, Dieter, 'Hans Krüger and the Murder of the Jews in the Stanislawow Region', *Yad Vashem Studies*, 26 (1998), 239–64

———— 'The Holocaust and the concentration camps', in Caplan and Wachsmann eds, *Concentration Camps in Nazi Germany*, 149–66

———— 'The Murder of the Jews in the General Government', in Herbert ed., *National Socialist Extermination Policies*, 86–7

———— 'The Murder of Ukraine's Jews under German Military Administration and in the Reich Commissariat Ukraine', in Brandon and Lower eds, *The Shoah in Ukraine*, 23–76

———— *Von der 'Judenpolitik' zum Judenmord. Der Distrikts Lublin des Generalgouvernement 1939–1944* (Frankfurt am Main: Peter Lang, 1993)

Polonsky, Antony, *The Jews in Poland and Russia*, vol. II, *1881–1914* (Oxford: Littman Library, 2010)

———— *The Jews in Poland and Russia*, vol. III, *1914–2008* (Oxford: Littman Library, 2012)

———— and Michlic, Joanna B. eds, *The Neighbours Respond. The Controversy Over the Jedwabne Massacre in Poland* (Princeton: Princeton University Press, 2004)

Porat, Dina, 'The Holocaust in Lithuania. Some Unique Aspects', in Cesarani ed., *The Final Solution. Origins and Implementation*, 159–74

———— *The Blue and the Yellow Stars of David. The Zionist Leadership in Palestine and the Holocaust, 1939–1945*, trans. David Ben-Nahum (Cambridge, MA: Harvard University Press, 1990)

Porch, Douglas, *Hitler's Mediterranean Gamble. The North African Campaign and the Mediterranean in Campaigns in World War II* (London: Cassell, 2004)

Poznanski, Renée, 'French Apprehensions, Jewish Expectations: From a Social Imaginary to a Political Practice', in Bankier ed., *The Jews are Coming Back*, 25–57

————— 'French Public Opinion and the Jews during World War II: Assumptions of the Clandestine Press', in Kosmola and Tych eds, *Facing the Nazi Genocide*, 117–35

————— 'The French Resistance: An Alternative Society for the Jews?' in Bankier and Gutman eds, *Nazi Europe and the Final Solution*, 411–34

————— *Jews in France during World War II*, trans. Nathan Bracher (Hanover: Brandeis University Press, 2001)

Press, Bernhard, *The Murder of the Jews in Latvia 1941–1945* (Evanston: Northwestern University Press, 2000)

Pressac, Jean-Claude with Pelt, Robert Jan van, 'The Machinery of Mass Murder at Auschwitz', in Gutman and Berenbaum eds, *Anatomy of the Auschwitz Death Camp*, 183–245.

Presser, Jacob, 'Introduction', in Mechanicus, *Waiting for Death*, 5–10

————— *Ashes in the Wind. The Destruction of Dutch Jewry*, trans. Arnold Pomerans (London: Souvenir Press, 2010 edn)

Pulzer, Peter, 'The First World War', in Meyer ed., *German-Jewish History in Modern Times*, vol. 3, *Integration in Dispute 1871–1918*, 360–84

————— *The Rise of Political Anti-semitism in Germany and Austria* (London: Peter Halban, 1988 edn).

Rabinovici, Doron, *Eichmann's Jews. The Jewish Administration of Holocaust Vienna, 1938–1945*, trans. Nick Somers (London: Polity, 2011)

Rayski, Adam, *The Choice of the Jews Under Vichy. Between Submission and Resistance*, trans. Will Sayers (Notre Dame: University of Notre Dame Press, 2005)

Redlich, Simon, 'Metropolitan Andreii Sheptyts'kyi and the Complexities of Ukrainian Jewish Relations', in Gitelman ed., *Bitter Legacy Confronting the Holocaust in the USSR*, 61–90

Rees, Lawrence, *Auschwitz. The Nazis and the 'Final Solution'* (London: BBC Books, 2005)

————— *The Nazis. A Warning from History* (London: BBC Books, 1997)

Reginbogin, H. R. and Safferling, C. J. M. eds, *Die Nürnburger Prozesse. Völkerstrafrecht seit 1945* (Munich: K. G. Saur, 2006)

Reilly, Jo et al. eds, *Belsen in History and Memory* (London: Frank Cass, 1997)

Reinharz, Judah, *Fatherland or Promised Land. The Dilemma of the German Jew, 1893–1914* (Ann Arbor: University of Michigan Press, 1975)

Rigg, Bryan Mark, *Lives of Hitler's Jewish Soldiers* (Lawrence: University of Kansas Press, 2009)

Roberts, Mary Louise, *What Soldiers Do. Sex and the American GI in World War II France* (Chicago: Chicago University Press, 2013)

Ro'i, Yaacov, 'The Reconstruction of Jewish Communities in the USSR, 1944–1947', in Bankier ed., *The Jews Are Coming Back*, 186–205

Römer, Felix, 'The Wehrmacht in the War of Ideologies. The Army and Hitler's Criminal Orders on the Eastern Front', in Kay, Rutherford and Stahel eds, *Nazi Policy on the Eastern Front, 1941*, 73–100

Romijn, Peter, 'The "Lesser Evil" – the case of the Dutch local authorities and the

Holocaust', in Romijn et al. eds, *The Persecution of the Jews in the Netherlands*, 13–28

———— et al. eds, *The Persecution of the Jews in the Netherlands, 1940–1945* (Amsterdam: Vossiuspers, 2012)

Roseman, Mark, *The Villa, The Lake, The Meeting. Wannsee and the 'Final Solution'* (London: Allen Lane, 2002)

Rosen, Alan, *The Wonder of Their Voices. The 1946 Holocaust Interviews of David Boder* (New York: Oxford University Press, 2010)

Rosenbaum, Ron, *Explaining Hitler, The Search for the Origins of his Evil* (New York: Macmillan, 1998)

Rossino, Alexander, *Hitler Strikes Poland. Blitzkrieg, Ideology, and Atrocity* (Lawrence: University of Kansas Press, 2003)

Rothkirchen, Livia, 'Czechoslovakia', in Wyman ed., *The World Reacts to the Holocaust*, 156–200

———— 'Gateway to Death: The Unique Character of Terezin (Theresienstadt)', in Rothkirchen, *The Jews of Bohemia & Moravia*, 233–47

———— *The Jews of Bohemia & Moravia. Facing the Holocaust* (Lincoln: University of Nebraska Press, 2005)

Rozett, Robert, 'International Interventions: The Role of Diplomats in Attempts to Rescue Jews in Hungary', in Braham and Miller eds, *The Nazis' Last Victims*, 137–52

———— *Conscripted Slaves. Hungarian Jewish Forced Labourers on the Eastern Front during the Second World War* (Jerusalem: Yad Vashem, 2014)

Rünits, Lone, 'The Politics of Asylum in Denmark in the Wake of Kristallnacht – A Case Study', in Jensen and Jensen eds, *Denmark and the Holocaust*, 14–32

Rutherford, Jeff, *Combat and Genocide on the Eastern Front. The German Infantry's War, 1941–1944* (Cambridge: Cambridge University Press, 2014)

Rutherford, Philip T., *Prelude to the Final Solution. The Nazi Programme for Deporting Ethnic Poles, 1939–1941* (Lawrence: University of Kansas Press, 2007)

Ryan, Donna F., *The Holocaust and the Jews of Marseille. The Enforcement of Anti-Semitic Policies in Vichy France* (Urbana: University of Illinois Press, 1996)

———— and Schuman, John S. eds, *Deaf People in Hitler's Europe* (Washington DC: Gallaudet University Press, 2002)

Saerens, Lieven, 'Antwerp's Attitude Towards the Jews from 1918 to 1940 and Its Implications for the Period of Occupation', in Michman ed., *Belgium and the Holocaust*, 159–67

Safrian, Hans, 'Expediting Expropriation and Expulsion. The Impact of the "Vienna Model" on anti-Jewish policies in Nazi Germany, 1938', *Holocaust and Genocide Studies*, 14:3 (2000), 390–414

———— *Eichmann's Men*, trans. Ute Stargardt (New York: Cambridge University Press, 2010)

Sagi, Nana, *German Reparations: A History of the Negotiations* (London: Macmillan, 1986)

Saidel, Rochelle G., *Mielec, Poland. The Shtetl that Became a Nazi Concentration Camp* (Jerusalem: Geffen, 2012)

Sammartino, Annemarie, *The Impossible Border. Germany and the East, 1914–1922* (Ithaca, NY: Cornell University Press, 2010)

Sandkühler, Thomas, 'Anti-Jewish Policy and the Murder of the Jews in the District of Galicia, 1941/42', in Herbert ed., *National Socialist Extermination Policies*, 104–27

Sarfatti, Michele, 'Characteristics and Objectives of the Anti-Jewish Racial Laws in Fascist Italy, 1938–1943', in Zimmerman ed., *Jews in Italy under Fascist and Nazi Rule*, 71–80

———— *The Jews in Mussolini's Italy. From Equality to Persecution*, trans. John and Anne C. Tedeschi (Madison: University of Wisconsin Press, 2006)

Satloff, Robert, *Among the Righteous. Lost Stories from the Holocaust's Long Reach Into Arab Lands* (New York: Public Affairs, 2006)

Schaft, Gretchen and Zeidler, Gerhard, *Commemorating Hell. The Public Memory of Mittlebau-Dora* (Urbana: University of Illinois Press, 2011)

Scheck, Rafael, *Hitler's African Victims. The German Army Massacres of Black French Soldiers in 1940* (New York: Cambridge University Press, 2006)

Schelvis, Jules, *Sobibor. A History of a Nazi Death Camp*, trans. Karin Dixon, ed. Bob Moore (Oxford: Berg, 2007)

Scheren, Jos, 'Aryanization, Market Vendors, and Peddlers in Amsterdam', *Holocaust and Genocide Studies*, 14:3 (2000), 415–29

Schleunes, Karl A., *The Twisted Road to Auschwitz. Nazi Policy Towards German Jews 1933–1939* (Urbana: University of Illinois Press, 1990 edn)

Schmidt, Ulf, *Karl Brandt. The Nazi Doctor. Medicine and Power in the Third Reich* (London: Hambledon Continuum, 2007)

Schneider, Gertrude, 'The Two Ghettos in Riga, Latvia, 1941–43', in Dobroscycki and Gurock eds, *The Holocaust in the Soviet Union*, 181–94

Schorsch, Ismar, *Jewish Reactions to German Anti-Semitism, 1870–1914* (New York: Columbia University Press, 1972)

Schreiber, Jean-Philippe, 'Belgium and the Jews under Nazi Rule: Behind the Myths', in Bankier and Gutman eds, *Nazi Europe and the Final Solution*, 469–88

Schreiber, Marion, *The Twentieth Train*, trans. Shaun Whiteside (London: Atlantic Books, 2004)

Sebag-Montefiore, Hugh, *Dunkirk. Fight to the Last Man* (London: Penguin, 2007)

Segev, Tom, *1949. The First Israelis* (New York: Henry Holt, 1998)

———— *Simon Wiesenthal. His Life and Legends* (London: Cape, 2010)

Seul, Stephanie, 'The Representation of the Holocaust in the British Propaganda Campaign directed at the German Public, 1938–1945', *Leo Baeck Year Book*, 52 (2007), 267–306

Shapiro, Robert Moses ed., *Why Didn't The Press Shout? American and International Journalism During the Holocaust* (New York: Yeshiva University Press, 2003)

Sharples, Caroline and Jensen, Olaf eds, *Britain and the Holocaust. Remembering and Representing War and Genocide* (London: Palgrave Macmillan, 2013)

Shatzkes, Pamela, *Holocaust and Rescue. Impotent or Indifferent? Anglo-Jewry 1938–1945* (Basingstoke: Palgrave, 2002)

Shelach, Menachem, 'The Murder of the Jews in Serbia and the Serbian Uprising in July 1941', in Cohen, Cochavi, Gelber eds, *The Shoah and the War*, 161–75

Shephard, Ben, *After Daybreak. The Liberation of Belsen, 1945* (London: Jonathan Cape, 2005)

Shepherd, Naomi, *Wilfred Israel. German Jewry's Secret Ambassador* (London: Weidenfeld and Nicolson, 1984)

Sherman, A. J., *Island Refuge. Britain and Refugees from the Third Reich 1933–1939,* (Ilford: Frank Cass, 1994)

Silberklang, David, *Gates of Tears. The Holocaust in the Lublin District* (Jerusalem: Yad Vashem, 2013)

Skibinska, Alina, 'The Return of Jewish Holocaust Survivors and the Reaction of the Polish Population', in Tych and Adamczyk-Garbowska, *Jewish Presence and Absence,* 25–66

———— with Mazurek, Jerzy, '"Barwy Biale" on their way to Aid Fighting Warsaw: The Crimes of the Home Army against the Jews', *Holocaust Studies and Materials (2013),* 433–80

———— and Tokarska-Bakir, Joanna, '"Barabasz" and the Jews: From the History of the "Wybraniecki" Home Army Partisan Detachment', *Holocaust Studies and Materials* (2013), 13–78

Slany, Willliam Z., *US and Allied Efforts to Recover and Restore Gold and Other Assets Stolen or Hidden by Germany During World War II. A Preliminary Study* (Washington: US State Department, 1997)

Smolar, Hersh, 'The History of the Minsk Ghetto', in Ehrenburg and Grossman, *The Black Book,* 139–40

Snyder, Timothy, 'The Holocaust: the ignored reality', *New York Review of Books,* 16 July 2009, http://www.nybooks.com/articles/archives/2009/jul/16/holocaust-the-ignored-reality/

———— *Bloodlands. Europe Between Hitler and Stalin* (London: Bodley Head, 2010)

Sompolinsky, Meier, *Britain and the Holocaust. The Failure of Anglo-Jewish Leadership* (Brighton: Sussex Academic Press, 1999)

Spector, Shmuel, 'The Holocaust of the Ukrainian Jews', in Gitelman ed., *Bitter Legacy,* 43–60

———— *The Holocaust of Volhynian Jews 1941–1944,* trans. Jerzy Michalowicz (Jerusalem: Yad Vashem, 1990)

Spitzer, Leo, *Hotel Bolivia. The Culture of Memory in a Refuge from Nazism* (New York: Hill and Wang, 1998)

Stafford, David, *Endgame 1945. Victory, Retribution, Liberation* (London: Little Brown, 2007)

Stahel, David, 'Radicalizing Warfare. Command and the Failure of Operation Barbarossa', in Kay, Rutherford and Stahel eds, *Nazi Policy on the Eastern Front, 1941,* 19–44

———— *Kiev 1941. Hitler's Battle for Supremacy in the East* (Cambridge: Cambridge University Press, 2012)

———— *Operation Barbarossa and Germany's Defeat in the East* (Cambridge: Cambridge University Press, 2009)

Stargardt, Nick, 'Speaking in public about the murder of the Jews: What did the

Holocaust mean to the Germans?', in Wiese and Betts eds, *Years of Persecution, Years of Extermination*, 133–55

Stave, Bruce M. and Palmer, Michele with Present, Leslie Frank, *Witnesses to Nuremberg. An Oral History of American Participants at the War Crimes Trials* (New York: Twayne, 1998)

Steinbacher, Sybille, 'In the Shadow of Auschwitz. The Murder of the Jews of East Upper Silesia', in Herbert ed., *National Socialist Extermination Policies*, 276–305

———— *Auschwitz. A History* (London: Penguin, 2005)

Steinberg, Jonathan, *All or Nothing. The Axis and the Holocaust 1941–43* (London: Routledge, 1990)

Steinberg, Maxime, 'The Jews in the Years 1940–1944: Three Strategies for Coping with a Tragedy', in Michman ed., *Belgium and the Holocaust*, 347–72

———— 'The Judenpolitik in Belgium within the West European Context: Comparative Observations', in Michman ed., *Belgium and the Holocaust*, 190–221

———— 'The Trap of Legality: the Association of the Jews in Belgium', in Gutman and Haft eds, *Patterns of Jewish Leadership in Nazi Europe 1933–1945*, 353–76

Steinhart, Eric, *The Holocaust and the Germanization of Ukraine* (New York: Cambridge University Press, 2015)

Steinweis, Alan, *Art, Ideology and Economics in Nazi Germany. The Reich Chambers of Music, Theater and the Visual Arts* (Chapel Hill, NC: University of North Carolina Press, 1993)

———— *Kristallnacht 1938* (Cambridge MA: Harvard University Press, 2009)

Stern, Frank, 'The Historic Triangle: Occupiers, Germans and Jews in Postwar Germany', in Moeller ed., *West Germany Under Construction*, 199–230

Stockings, Craig and Hancock, Eleanor, *Swastika over the Acropolis. Reinterpreting the Nazi Invasion of Greece in World War II* (Leiden: Brill, 2013)

Stoltzfus, Nathan, *Resistance of the Heart. Intermarriage and the Rosenstrasse Protest in Nazi Germany* (New York: Norton, 1996)

Stone, Dan, *The Liberation of the Camps: The End of the Holocaust and Its Aftermath* (London: Yale University Press, 2015)

Strauss, Herbert, 'Jewish Emigration from Germany. Nazi Policies and Jewish Responses (1)', *Leo Baeck Institute Year Book*, 25 (1980), 312–59

———— 'Jewish Emigration from Germany. Nazi Policies and Jewish Responses (II)', *Leo Baeck Institute Year Book*, 26 (1981), 343–8

Strzelcki, Andrzej, 'The History, role and operation of the "Central Camp Sauna" in Auschwitz II-Birkenau', in Swiebocka ed., *The Architecture of Crime. The 'Central Sauna' in Auschwitz II-Birkenau*, 11–16

———— 'The Liquidation of the Camp', in Czech et al. eds, *Auschwitz 1940–1945*, vol. V, 16–20

Strzelecka, Irena, 'Hospitals', in Gutman and Berenbaum eds, *Anatomy of the Auschwitz Death Camp*, 379–92

———— 'The Hospitals at Auschwitz Concentration Camp', in Iwaszko et al. eds, *Auschwitz 1940–1945*, vol. II, 291–346

———— 'Quarantine on Arrival', in Iwaszko et al. eds, *Auschwitz 1940–1945*, vol. II, 45–50

———— 'Women', in Gutman and Berenbaum eds, *Anatomy of the Auschwitz Death Camp*, 393–411

———— 'Women in the Auschwitz Concentration Camp', in Iwaszko et al. eds, *Auschwitz 1940–1945*, vol. II, 177–200

———— and Setkiewicz, Piotr, 'The Construction, Expansion and Development of the Camp and its Branches', in Lasik et al. eds, *Auschwitz 1940–1945*, vol. I, 63–80

Strzelecki, Andrzej, 'Plundering the Victims' Property', in Iwaszko et al. eds, *Auschwitz 1940–1945*, vol. II, 137–70

Sturdy-Colls, Caroline, 'Gone but not Forgotten: Archaeological Approaches to the Site of the former Treblinka Extermination Camp in Poland', *Holocaust Studies and Materials* (2013), 253–89

Suhl, Yuri ed., *They Fought Back. The Story of the Jewish Resistance in Nazi Europe* (New York: Schocken, 1967)

Swiebocka, Teresa ed., *The Architecture of Crime. The 'Central Sauna' in Auschwitz II-Birkenau*, trans. William Brand (Oswiecim: Auschwitz-Birkenau State Museum, 2001)

Swiebocki, Henryk, *Auschwitz 1940–1945. Central Issues in the History of the Camp*, vol. IV, *The Resistance Movement* (Oswięcim: Auschwitz-Birkenau State Museum, 2000)

Tal, Uriel, *Christians and Germans in Germany. Religion, Politics and Ideology in the Second Reich, 1870–1914* (London: Cornell University Press, 1975)

Tec, Nechama, *Defiance. The Bielski Partisans* (New York: Oxford University Press, 1993)

Teveth, Shabetai, *Ben-Gurion and the Holocaust* (New York: Harcourt Brace, 1995)

Thacker, Toby, *Joseph Goebbels. Life and Death* (London: Palgrave Macmillan, 2009)

Todorov, Tzvetan, *The Fragility of Goodness. Why Bulgaria's Jews Survived the Holocaust*, trans. Arthur Denner (London: Weidenfeld and Nicolson, 1999)

Tooze, Adam, *The Wages of Destruction: The Making and Breaking of the Economy* (London: Allen Lane, 2006)

Trunk, Isaiah, *Judenrat. The Jewish Councils in Eastern Europe under Nazi Occupation* (Lincoln: University of Nebraska, 1996)

———— ed., *Lodz Ghetto. A History*, trans. and ed. Robert Moses Shapiro (Bloomington: Indiana University Press, 2006)

Turner Jr, Henry Ashby, 'Two Dubious Third Reich Diaries', *Central European History* 33:3 (2000), 415–22

———— *Hitler's Thirty Days to Power: January 1933* (London: Bloomsbury, 1996)

Tych, Feliks and Adamczyk-Garbowska, Monika, *Jewish Presence in Absence. The Aftermath of the Holocaust in Poland, 1944–2010*, trans. Grzegorz and Jessica Taylor Kucia (Jerusalem: Yad Vashem, 2014)

Unger, Michael, 'The Lodz Ghetto', in Josef Zelkowitz, *In Those Terrible Days. Writings from the Lodz Ghetto*, ed. Michael Unger, trans. Naftali Greenwood (Jerusalem: Yad Vashem, 2002)

Ungváry, Krisztián, *The Battle for Budapest. 100 Days in World War II* (London: I. B. Tauris, 2003)

Vat, Dan van der, *The Good Nazi. The Life and Lies of Albert Speer* (London: Weidenfeld and Nicolson, 1997)

Vernant, Jacques, *The Refugee in the Post-War World* (London: Allen and Unwin, 1953)

Vilhjálmsson, Vilhjálmur Örn, 'The King and the Star. Myths created during the Occupation of Denmark', in Jensen and Jensen eds, *Denmark and the Holocaust*, 102–117

Volkov, Shulamit, *Germans, Jews, and Antisemites. Trials in Emancipation* (Cambridge: Cambridge University Press, 2006)

Wachsmann, Nikolaus, 'The dynamics of destruction: the development of the concentration camps, 1933–1945', in Caplan and Wachsmann eds, *Concentration Camps in Nazi Germany*, 17-43
———— *Hitler's Prisons. Legal Terror in Nazi Germany* (London: Yale University Press, 2004)
———— *KL. A History of the Nazi Concentration Camps* (London: Little Brown, 2015)

Wagner, Jens-Christian, 'Work and extermination in the concentration camps', in Caplan and Wachsmann eds, *Concentration Camps in Nazi Germany*, 127-48

Waite, Robert G., '"Reliable Local Residents": Collaboration in Latvia, 1941–1945', in Caune et al. eds, *Latvia in World War II*, 114–42

Wallis, Russell, *Britain, Germany and the Road to the Holocaust. British Attitudes towards Nazi Atrocities* (London: I. B. Tauris, 2014)

Wasserstein, Bernard, 'Patterns of Jewish Leadership in Great Britain during the Nazi Era', in Braham ed., *Jewish Leadership during the Nazi Era*, 29–43
———— *The Ambiguity of Virtue. Gertrude van Tijn and the Fate of the Dutch Jews* (London: Harvard University Press, 2014)
———— *Britain and the Jews of Europe, 1939–1945* (London: Leicester University Press, 1999 edn)

Watt, Richard M., *The Kings Depart. The German Revolution and the Treaty of Versailles 1918–1919* (London: Penguin, 1972)

Weber, Thomas, *Hitler's First War. Adolf Hitler, the Men of the List Regiment, and the First World War* (Oxford: Oxford University Press, 2010)

Weil, Patrick, 'The Return of the Jews in the nationality or in the territory of France (1943–1973)', in Bankier ed., *The Jews are Coming Back*, 57–71

Weinberg, Gerhard, 'German plans for victory, 1944–1945', in Weinberg, *Germany, Hitler and World War II*, 274–86
———— *Germany, Hitler & World War II* (Cambridge: Cambridge University Press, 1994)
———— *A World at Arms. A Global History of World War II* (Cambridge: Cambridge University Press, 1994)

Weindling, Paul, *Health, Race and German Politics between National Unification and Nazism 1870–1945* (Cambridge: Cambridge University Press, 1989)

Weiss, Yfat, 'The "Emigration Effort" or "Repatriation", in Bankier ed., *Probing the Depths of German Antisemitism*, 360–70

Welch, David, 'Manufacturing a Consensus: Nazi Propaganda and the Building of a "National Community" (Volksgemeinschaft)', *Central European History* 2:1 (1993), 1–15

—— *The Third Reich. Politics and Propaganda* (London: Routledge, 1994)

Westerman, Edward B., *Hitler's Police Battalions. Enforcing Racial War in the East* (Lawrence: University of Kansas Press, 2005)

Wette, Wolfram, *The Wehrmacht. History, Myth, Reality*, trans. Deborah Lucas Schneider (Cambridge, MA: Harvard University Press, 2006)

Wiese, Christian and Betts, Paul eds, *Years of Persecution, Years of Extermination. Saul Friedländer and the Future of Holocaust Studies* (London: Continuum, 2010)

Wiesen, S. Jonathan, *Creating the Nazi Marketplace. Commerce and Consumption in the Third Reich* (New York: Cambridge University Press, 2011)

Wildt, Michael, 'Before the "Final Solution": The *Judenpolitik* of the SD, 1935–1938', *Leo Baeck Institute Year Book*, 43 (1998), 241–69

—— *Hitler's Volksgemeinschaft and the Dynamics of Racial Exclusion. Violence against the Jews in Provincial Germany, 1919–1939*, trans. Bernard Heise (New York: Berghahn, 2012)

—— *An Uncompromising Generation. The Nazi Leadership of the Reich Main Security Office*, trans. Tom Lampert (Madison: University of Wisconsin Press, 2009)

Witte, Peter, 'Two Decisions Concerning the "Final Solution of the Jewish Question": Deportations to Lodz and Mass Murder in Chelmno', *Holocaust and Genocide Studies*, 9:3 (1995), 318–46

—— and Tyas, Stephen, 'A New Document on the Deportation and Murder of Jews During "Einsatz Reinhardt" 1942', *Holocaust and Genocide Studies*, 15:3 (2001), 468–86

Wolf, Diane L., *Beyond Anne Frank. Hidden Children and Postwar Families in Holland* (Berkeley: University of California Press, 2007)

Wood, E. Thomas and Jankowski, Stanislaw, *Karski. How One Man Tried to Stop the Holocaust* (New York, John Wiley, 1994)

Wood, Stephen and Locke, Ian, '"Ex-Enemy Jews": the Fate of the Assets of Holocaust Victims and Survivors in Britain', in Beker ed., *The Plunder of Jewish Property during the Holocaust*, 209–26

Wünschmann, Kim, *Before Auschwitz. Jewish Prisoners in the Prewar Nazi Concentration Camps* (Cambridge, MA: Harvard University Press, 2015)

Wyden, Peter, *Stella: One Woman's True Tale of Evil, Betryal, and Survival in Hitler's Germany* (New York: Doubleday, 1992)

Wylie, Neville ed., *European Neutrals and Non-Belligerents During the Second World War* (Cambridge: Cambridge University Press, 2002)

Wyman, David S., *The Abandonment of the Jews. America and the Holocaust 1941–1945* (New York: Pantheon, 1985 edn)

—— *Paper Walls. America and the Refugee Crisis 1938–1941* (New York: Pantheon, 1995)

————— and Medoff, Rafael, *A Race Against Death. Peter Bergson, America, and the Holocaust* (New York: The New Press, 2002)

Wyman, Mark, *Europe's Displaced Persons, 1945–1951* (Toronto: Associated University Presses, 1986)

Yahil, Leni, *The Holocaust. The Fate of European Jewry* (New York: Oxford University Press, 1990)

Zariz, Ruth, 'Exchange of Populations as a Means of Jewish Salvation', in Cohen, Cochavi, Gelber eds, *The Shoah and the War*, 405–16

Zbikowski, Andrzej, 'The Post-War Wave of Pogroms and Killings', in Tych and Adamczyk-Garbowska, *Jewish Presence and Absence*, 67–94

Zimmerman, Joshua D. ed., *Contested Memories. Poles and Jews During the Holocaust and Its Aftermath* (New Brunswick: Rutgers University Press, 2003)

————— ed., *Jews in Italy under Fascist and Nazi Rule, 1922–1945* (New York: Cambridge University Press, 2005)

Zuccotti, Susan, *The Holocaust, the French, and the Jews* (New York: Basic Books, 1993)

————— *The Italians and the Holocaust. Persecution, Rescue and Survival* (London: Peter Halban, 1987)

————— *Under His Very Windows, The Vatican and the Holocaust in Italy* (New Haven: Yale University Press, 2000)

Zucker, Bat-Ami, *In Search of Refuge. Jews and US Consuls in Nazi Germany 1933–1941* (London: Vallentine Mitchell, 2001)

Zweig, Ronald, 'The War Refugee Board and American Intelligence', in Cohen, Cochavi, Gelber eds, *The Shoah and the War*, 293–416

————— *Britain and Palestine During the Second World War* (London: Boydell Press, 1986)

————— *German Reparations and the Jewish World: A History of the Claims Conference* (Boulder: Westview Press, 1987)

————— *The Gold Train. The Destruction of the Jews and the Second World War's Most Terrible Robbery* (London: Penguin, 2000)

NOTES

The following short forms have been used:

Ambassador Dodd's Diary –William E. Dodd and Martha Dodd, *Ambassador Dodd's Diary* (London: Gollancz, 1939)

Berg Diary – S. L. Schneiderman ed., *The Diary of Mary Berg* (Oxford: Oneworld, 2006)

Berr Journal – Hélène Berr, *Journal*, trans. David Bellos (London: MacLehose Press, 2008)

The Black Book – Ilya Ehrenburg and Vasily Grossman eds, *The Black Book*, trans. John Glad and James S. Levine (New York: Holocaust Library, 1981)

Czerniakow Diary – Raul Hilberg et al. eds, *The Warsaw Diary of Adam Czerniakow* (Chicago: Ivan R. Dee, 1979)

Documents on the Holocaust – Y. Arad, Y. Gutman, A. Margaliot eds, *Documents on the Holocaust* (Jerusalem: Yad Vashem, 1981)

Dorian Diary – Emil Dorian, *The Quality of Witness. A Romanian Diary 1837–1944*, ed. Marguerite Doria, trans. Mara Soceanu Vamos (Philadelphia: Jewish Publication Society of America, 1992)

Einsatzgruppen Reports – Yitzhak Arad, Shmuel Krakowski, Shmuel Spector eds, *The Einsatzgruppen Reports* (New York: Holocaust Library, 1982)

Fremde Blicke – Frank Bajohr and Christop Strupp eds, *Fremde Blicke auf das 'Dritte Reich'. Berichte ausländischer Diplomaten über Herrschaft und Gesellschaft in Deutschland 1933–1945* (Göttingen: Wallstein Verlag, 2011)

Fromm Diary – Bella Fromm, *Blood and Banquets. A Berlin Social Diary* (London: Geoffrey Bles, 1942)

Germans No More – Margarete Limburg and Hubert Ruebsaat ed., *Germans No More. Accounts of Everyday Jewish Life, 1933–1938*, trans. Alan Nothangle (New York: Berghahn, 2006)

HGS – *Holocaust and Genocide Studies*

Jewish Responses, vol. I – Jürgen Matthäus and Mark Roseman eds, *Jewish Responses to Persecution*, vol. I, *1933-1938* (Lanham, MD: AltaMira Press, 2010)

Jewish Responses, vol. II – Alexandra Garbarini et al. eds, *Jewish Responses to Persecution*, vol. II, *1938–1940* (Lanham, MD: AltaMira Press, 2011)

Kaplan Diary – Abraham Katsh ed., *Scroll of Agony. The Warsaw Diary of Chaim A. Kaplan* (New York: Macmillan, 1965)

Klemperer Diaries – Victor Klemperer, *I Shall Bear Witness. The Diaries of Victor*

Klemperer, 1933–41, trans. and ed. Martin Chalmers (London: Weidenfeld and Nicolson, 1998)

Lambert Diary – Raymond-Raoul Lambert, *Diary of a Witness 1940–1943*, trans. Isabel Best, ed. Richard I. Cohen (Chicago: Ivan R. Dee, 2007)

Letters of Karl Fuchs – Horst Fuchs Richardson ed., *Your Loyal and Loving Son. The Letters of Tank Gunner Karl Fuchs, 1937–1941* (Washington DC: Brassey's, 2003)

Lodz Ghetto Chronicle – Lucjan Dobroszycki ed., *The Chronicle of the Lodz Ghetto 1941–1944*, trans. Richard Lourie, Joachim Neugroschel et al. (New Haven: Yale University Press, 1984)

Lewin Diary – Abraham Lewin, *A Cup of Tears. A Diary of the Warsaw Ghetto*, ed. Antony Polonsky, trans. Christopher Hutton (Oxford: Blackwell, 1988)

McDonald Diaries, I – Richard Breitman et al. eds, *Advocate for the Doomed. The Diaries and Papers of James G. McDonald*, vol. 1, *1932–1935* (Bloomington: Indiana University Press, 2007)

McDonald Diaries, II – Richard Breitman et al. eds, *Refugees and Rescue. The Diaries and Papers of James G McDonald*, vol. 2, *1935–45* (Bloomington: Indiana University Press, 2009)

The Night of Broken Glass – Uta Gerhardt and Thomas Karlauf eds, *The Night of Broken Glass. Eyewitness Accounts of Kristallnacht*, trans. Robert Simmons and Nick Somers (London: Polity, 2012)

Phipps Diary – Gaynor Johnson ed., *Our Man In Berlin. The Phipps Diary 1933–1937* (London: Palgrave, 2008)

Ringelblum Notes – Jacob Sloan ed. and trans., *Notes from the Warsaw Ghetto. The Journal of Emmanuel Ringelblum* (New York: McGraw-Hill, 1958)

Ruth Maier's Diary – Jan Erik Vold ed., *Ruth Maier's Diary. A Young Girl's Life under Nazism*, trans. Jamie Bullock (London: Harvill Secker, 2009)

Sakowicz Diary – Kazimierz Sakowicz, *Ponary Diary 1941–1943*, ed. Yitzhak Arad (New Haven: Yale University Press, 2005)

Secret Nazi Reports – Otto Dov Kulka and Eberhard Jäckel eds, *The Jews in the Secret Nazi Reports on Popular Opinion in Germany, 1933–1945*, trans. William Templer (New Haven: Yale University Press, 2011)

Seidman Diaries – Hillel Seidman, *The Warsaw Ghetto Diaries*, trans. Yosef Israel (Jerusalem: Targum, 1997)

Shirer Diary – William L. Shirer, *Berlin Diary. The Journal of a Foreign Correspondent, 1934–1941* (Baltimore: Johns Hopkins University Press, 2002 [orig. 1941])

Sierakowiak Diary – Alan Edelson ed., *The Diary of Dawid Sierakowiak*, trans. Kamil Turowski (London: Bloomsbury, 1996)

Tory Diary – Avraham Tory [Golub], *Surviving the Holocaust. The Kovno Ghetto Diary*, trans. Jerzy Michalowicz, ed. Martin Gilbert with Dina Porat (Cambridge MA: Harvard University Press, 1990)

The Unknown Black Book – Joshua Rubinstein and Ilya Altman eds, *The Unknown Black Book. The Holocaust in the German-Occupied Soviet Territories*, trans. Christopher Morris and Joshua Rubinstein (Bloomington: Indiana University Press, 2008)

Vilna Ghetto Chronicles – Herman Kruk, *The Last Days of the Jerusalem of Lithuania:*

Chronicles from the Vilna Ghetto and the Camps 1939–1944, trans. Barbara
Harshav, ed. Benjamin Harshav (New Haven: Yale University Press, 2002)
Von Hassell Diaries – Hugh Gibson ed., *The von Hassell Diaries 1938–1944* (London:
Hamish Hamilton, 1948)
Weiss Diary – Helga Weiss, *Helga's Diary. A Young Girl's Account of Life in a
Concentration Camp*, trans. Neil Bermel (London: Viking, 2013)

Introduction

1 Daniel Levy and Natan Sznaider, *The Holocaust and Memory in a Global Age*,
   trans. Assenka Oksiloff (Philadelphia: Temple University, 2006); Klas-Göran
   Karlsson and Ulf Zander eds, *The Holocaust – Post-War Battlefields. Genocide as
   Historical Culture* (Malmo: Sekel Bokförlag, 2006); Rebecca Clifford,
   Commemorating the Holocaust. The Dilemmas of Remembrance in France and Italy
   (Oxford: Oxford University Press, 2013); Caroline Sharples and Olaf Jensen eds,
   Britain and the Holocaust. Remembering and Representing War and Genocide
   (London: Palgrave Macmillan, 2013); Andy Pearce, *Holocaust Consciousness in
   Contemporary Britain* (London: Routledge, 2014); Larissa Allwork, *Holocaust
   Remembrance Between the National and the Transnational. The Stockholm
   International Forum and the First Decade of the International Task Force* (London:
   Bloomsbury, 2015).
2 For important, but all too rare, evidence-based assessments of what teachers
   know and what school students learn in two countries that pioneered 'Holocaust
   education' see Holocaust Education and Development Programme, *Teaching
   About the Holocaust in English Secondary Schools* (London: Institute of Education,
   2009); Anders Lange, *A survey of teachers' experiences and perceptions in relation
   to teaching about the Holocaust* (Stockholm: The Living History Forum, 2008).
   More recent, as yet unpublished, research by the Holocaust Education and
   Development Programme (now the Centre for Holocaust Education) reveals that
   knowledge levels amongst school students exposed to teaching on the subject
   remains patchy. On the perils of fiction for young adults, see David Cesarani,
   'Striped Pyjamas', *Literary Review*, May 2011, accessible at http://www.
   literaryreview.co.uk/cesarani_10_08.html. Jackie Feldman, *Above the death pits,
   beneath the flag. Youth voyages to Poland and the performance of Israeli national
   identity* (New York: Berghahn, 2008); Karen Hadley, 'Lessons from Auschwitz',
   History Today, September 2010, 4–5, on the work of the UK-based Holocaust
   Educational Trust.
3 Timothy Snyder, 'The Holocaust: the ignored reality', *New York Review of Books*,
   16 July 2009, accessible at http://www.nybooks.com/articles/archives/2009/jul/16/
   holocaust-the-ignored-reality/ wrote compellingly about this disparity, although
   his extended analysis and explanation for why so many Jews died in the area he
   dubbed the 'Bloodlands' was more contentious; see his *Bloodlands. Europe
   Between Hitler and Stalin* (London: Bodley Head, 2010).
4 For an interpretation of testimony offering little in the way of redemption, see

Lawrence Langer, *Holocaust Testimonies. The ruins of memory* (New Haven: Yale University Press, 1991). It is significant that he drew on the Yale Fortunoff Video Archive for Holocaust Testimonies that recorded survivors' testimony on video in the late 1970s and 1980s. Thanks to the timing it was able to capture the fate of witnesses such as 'Magda F., whose husband, parents, brothers, three sisters, and all their children were engulfed in the tide of Nazi mass murder'.

5 For research on some of these fraught issues, see Jonathan Petropoulos and John K. Roth eds, *Gray Zones. Ambiguity and Compromise in the Holocaust and its Aftermath* (New York: Berghahn, 2005) and Sonia M. Hedgepeth and Rochelle G. Saidel eds, *Sexual Violence Against Jewish Women During the Holocaust* (Waltham, MA: Brandeis University Press, 2010).

6 See, for example, Thomas Kühne and Tom Lawson eds, *The Holocaust and Local History* (London: Vallentine Mitchell, 2011); Donald Bloxham, *The Final Solution. A Genocide* (Oxford: Oxford University Press, 2009), 1–10.

7 Michael Burleigh, *The Third Reich. A History* (London: Macmillan, 2000); Peter Longerich, *Holocaust. The Nazi Persecution and Murder of the Jews* (Oxford: Oxford University Press, 2010); Ian Kershaw, *Hitler 1889–1936. Hubris* (London: Allen Lane, 1998) and *Hitler 1936–1945. Nemesis* (London: Allen Lane, 2000); Richard J. Evans, *The Coming of the Third Reich* (London: Allen Lane, 2003); *The Third Reich in Power 1933–1939* (London: Allen Lane, 2005); *The Third Reich at War 1939–1945* (London: Allen Lane, 2008); Saul Friedländer, *Nazi Germany and the Jews*, vol. 1, *The Years of Persecution 1933–1939* (London: Weidenfeld and Nicolson, 1997) and *Nazi Germany and the Jews*, vol. 2, *The Years of Extermination 1939–1945* (London: Weidenfeld and Nicolson, 2007); Christopher Browning with Jürgen Matthäus, *The Origins of the Final Solution* (London: Heinemann, 2004).

8 For books based on two award-winning BBC documentary series, see Lawrence Rees, *The Nazis. A Warning from History* (London: BBC Books, 1997); Lawrence Rees, *Auschwitz. The Nazis and the 'Final Solution'* (London: BBC Books, 2005). Wolfgang Benz, *The Holocaust*, trans. Jane Sydenham-Kwiet (New York: Columbia University Press, 1995); David Engel, *The Holocaust. The Third Reich and the Jews* (London: Longman, 1999); Jeremy Black, *The Holocaust* (London: The Social Affairs Unit, 2008); Doris Bergen, *War & Genocide. A Concise History of the Holocaust*, 2nd edition (Lanham MD: Rowan and Littlefield, 2009); Bloxham, *The Final Solution*. The exceptional one-volume history is Debórah Dwork and Robert Jan van Pelt, *Holocaust: A History* (London: John Murray, 2002).

9 For analysis and assessments, see Christian Wiese and Paul Betts eds, *Years of Persecution, Years of Extermination. Saul Friedländer and the Future of Holocaust Studies* (London: Continuum, 2010).

10 For a discussion of these issues, see 'What was the Holocaust' and 'Comparisons with other genocides' in Yehuda Bauer, *Rethinking the Holocaust* (New Haven: Yale University Press, 2001), 1–13, 39–67 and Donald Niewyk and Francis Nicosia, *The Columbia Guide to the Holocaust* (New York: Columbia University Press, 2000), 45–52; Omer Bartov, 'Antisemitism, the Holocaust, and Reinterpretations of National Socialism' in his *Murder in Our Midst. The*

Holocaust, Industrial Killing and Representation (New York: Oxford University Press, 1996), 53–70. The linguistic determinism is not quite the same for languages other than English. However it is common for Holocaust and *Shoah* to be incorporated into German, French and Italian, too.

11 David Cesarani, *The Holocaust. A Teacher's Guide* (London: Holocaust Educational Trust, 1998); the HMDT statement is accessible at http://hmd.org.uk/genocides/holocaust; Michael André Bernstein, *Foregone Conclusions: Against Apocalyptic History* (Berkeley: University of California Press, 1994).

12 Eberhard Jäckel, *Hitler's World View. A Blueprint for Power* (Cambridge MA: Harvard University Press, 1981), 52–61; Philippe Burrin, *Hitler and the Jews* (London: Edward Arnold, 1994), 17–39; Jeffrey Herf, *The Jewish Enemy. Nazi Propaganda During World War II and the Holocaust* (Cambridge MA: Harvard University Press, 2009), 3–13.

13 David Cesarani ed., *The Final Solution: Origins and Implementation* (London: Routledge, 1994), 4–14; Ian Kershaw, *The Nazi Dictatorship. Problems and Perspectives of Interpretation* (London: Arnold, 2000 edn), 69–133; Longerich, *Holocaust*, 1–8, 40–61, 70–2, 423–7. The classic statement of haphazardly developing anti-Jewish policy, first published in 1970, remains Karl A. Schleunes, *The Twisted Road to Auschwitz. Nazi Policy Towards German Jews 1933–1939* (Urbana: University of Illinois Press, 1990 edn).

14 Karl-Heinz Frieser, *The Blitzkrieg Legend. The 1940 Campaign in the West* (Annapolis, MD: Naval Institute Press, 2012); Robert M. Citino, *Death of the Wehrmacht. The German Campaigns of 1942* (Lawrence: University of Kansas Press, 2007), 3–34; Geoffrey P. Megargee, *Inside Hitler's High Command* (Lawrence: University of Kansas Press, 2000), 323–4.

15 Martin Gilbert, *The Holocaust. The Jewish Tragedy* (London: Collins, 1986), 154; Michael Marrus, 'The *Shoah* and the Second World War: Some Comments on Recent Historiography', in Asher Cohen, Yehoyakim Cochavi and Yoav Gelber eds, *The Shoah and the War* (New York: Peter Lang, 1992), 1–24. Gerhard Weinberg, *A World at Arms. A Global History of World War II* (Cambridge: Cambridge University Press, 1994) was the first military history of the conflict to integrate the fate of the Jews. See also his essay 'The "Final Solution" and the war in 1943' in his *Germany, Hitler & World War II* (Cambridge: Cambridge University Press, 1994), 217–44. In exemplary fashion, Stephen G. Fritz, *Ostkrieg. Hitler's War of Extermination in the East* (Lexington, KY: University of Kentucky Press, 2011), skilfully weaves the fate of the Jews into all aspects of the Russo-German war.

16 See Parts 5–6.

17 Thomas Weber, *Hitler's First War. Adolf Hitler, the Men of the List Regiment, and the First World War* (Oxford: Oxford University Press, 2010), *passim* but particularly 229–30, 338; Megargee, *Inside Hitler's High Command*, 65–6.

18 See Herf, *The Jewish Enemy*.

19 Robert M. Citino, *The German Way of War: From the Thirty Years War to the Third Reich* (Lawrence: University of Kansas Press, 2008); Isabel V. Hull, *Absolute*

Destruction. Military Culture and the Practices of War in Imperial Germany (Ithaca, NY: Cornell University Press, 2005).

20 David Stahel, *Operation Barbarossa and Germany's Defeat in the East* (Cambridge: Cambridge University Press, 2009), 33–138; Megargee, *Inside Hitler's High Command*, 87–141.

21 Adam Tooze, *The Wages of Destruction: The Making and Breaking of the Nazi Economy* (London: Allen Lane, 2006), 513–51; Lizzie Collingham, *The Taste of War. World War Two and the Battle for Food* (London: Allen Lane, 2011), 30–7, 157–64.

22 Ian Kershaw, *Fateful Choices. Ten Decisions that Changed the World 1940–1941* (London: Allen Lane, 2007), 382–470.

23 Ian Kershaw, "'Working Towards the Führer.' Reflections on the Nature of the Hitler Dictatorship', *Contemporary European History*, 2:2 (1993), 103–18.

24 Citino, *The German Way of War*, 16–17; Michael Wildt, *An Uncompromising Generation. The Nazi Leadership of the Reich Main Security Office*, trans. Tom Lampert (Madison, WI: University of Wisconsin Press, 2009), 21–36, 72–80.

25 Götz Aly, *Hitler's Beneficiaries. Plunder, Racial War and the Nazi Welfare State*, trans. Jefferson Chase (New York: Metropolitan Books, 2006).

26 Jan Tomasz Gross with Irena Grudzinska Gross, *Golden Harvest. Events at the Periphery of the Holocaust* (New York: Oxford University Press, 2012).

27 Hedgepeth and Saidel eds, *Sexual Violence Against Jewish Women*, 1–5; Catherine Merridale, *Ivan's War: Life and Death in the Red Army, 1939–1945* (New York: Henry Holt, 2006), 266–77; Dagmar Herzog ed., *Lessons and Legacies*, vol. VII, *The Holocaust in International Perspective*, Part III 'Gender and Sexual Violence' (Evanston, IL: Northwestern University Press, 2006), 159–215; Mary Louise Roberts, *What Soldiers Do. Sex and the American GI in World War II France* (Chicago: Chicago University Press, 2013), 195–236; Raphaelle Branche and Fabrice Virgili eds, *Rape in Wartime* (London: Palgrave, 2012).

28 For the fate of 'other victims', see Michael Burleigh, *Death and Deliverance. 'Euthanasia' in Germany 1900–1945* (Cambridge: Cambridge University Press, 1994); Guenter Lewy, *The Nazi Persecution of the Gypsies* (Oxford: Oxford University Press, 2000); Robert Gellately and Nathan Stolzfus eds, *Social Outsiders in Nazi Germany* (Princeton: Princeton University Press, 2001); Donna F. Ryan and John Schuman eds, *Deaf People in Hitler's Europe* (Washington DC: Gallaudet University Press, 2002); Clarence Lusane, *Hitler's Black Victims. The Historical Experience of Afro-Germans, European Blacks, Africans, and African Americans in the Nazi Era* (London: Routledge, 2003).

29 Avinoam J. Patt and Michael Berkowitz eds, *'We Are Here'. New Approaches to Jewish Displaced Persons in Postwar Germany* (Detroit: Wayne State University Press, 2010); Emunah Nachmany Gafny, *Dividing Hearts. The Removal of Jewish Children from Gentile Families in Poland in the Immediate Post-Holocaust Years* (Jerusalem: Yad Vashem, 2009); Nahum Bogner, *At the Mercy of Strangers. The Rescue of Jewish Children with Assumed Identities in Poland* (Jerusalem: Yad Vashem, 2009), 183–295; Regula Ludi, *Reparations for Nazi Victims in Postwar Europe* (New York: Cambridge University Press, 2010); Patricia Heberer and

Jürgen Matthäus eds, *Atrocities on Trial. Historical Perspectives on the Politics of Prosecuting War Crimes* (Lincoln: University of Nebraska Press, 2008).

Prologue

1 This account relies on the excellent analysis and narrative of Henry Ashby Turner Jr, *Hitler's Thirty Days to Power: January 1933* (London: Bloomsbury, 1996).

2 André François-Poncet, *The Fateful Years. Memoirs of the French Ambassador in Berlin 1931–38* (London: Hamish Hamilton, 1949), 47–8.

3 Turner Jr, *Hitler's Thirty Days to Power*, 155–6.

4 François-Poncet, *Fateful Years*, 48.

5 Evans, *Coming of the Third Reich*, 305–8.

6 Leopold Schwarzschild, *Chronicle of a Downfall. Germany, 1929–1939*, ed. Andreas Wesemann, trans. Michel Mitchell (London: I. B. Tauris, 2010), vi–xii, 97–9.

7 'Chancellor Hitler', 4 February 1933, in Schwarzschild, *Chronicle of a Downfall*, 97–9.

8 Sir Horace Rumbold to the Foreign Office, 18 August 1931, 21 August 1932, 27 January 1933, 3 October 1938 (on Jews), cited in Martin Gilbert, *Sir Horace Rumbold. Portrait of a Diplomat 1869–1941* (London: Heinemann, 1973), 319, 360–1, 366, 368.

9 Georges Simenon, 'Hitler in the Elevator', in Oliver Lubrich ed., *Travels in the Reich 1933–1945. Foreign Authors Report from Germany*, trans. K. Northcott, S. Wichmann, D. Krouk (Chicago: University of Chicago Press, 2010), 34–5.

10 Jürgen Matthäus and Mark Roseman, *Jewish Responses to Persecution*, vol. I, *1933–1938* (Lanham MD: AltaMira Press, 2011), 1–2.

11 *Jewish Responses*, vol. I, 8–9.

12 Ibid, 10–11.

13 Joseph Roth to Stefan Zweig, February 1933 in *Josef Roth. A Life in Letters*, ed. and trans. Michael Hofmann (London: Granta, 2012), 237.

14 Abraham Ascher, *A Community under Siege. The Jews of Breslau under Nazism* (Stanford: Stanford University Press, 2007), 65–6; J. A. S. Grenville, *The Jews and Germans of Hamburg* (London: Routledge, 2012), 52–3, 58–9.

15 Friedländer, *Nazi Germany and the Jews*, vol. 1, 14–15; Matthäus and Roseman, Introduction, *Jewish Responses*, vol. I, xiv–xvi, xxx–xxxvi.

16 Marion Kaplan, *Between Dignity and Despair. Jewish Life in Nazi Germany* (New York: Oxford University Press, 1998), 10–11.

17 Kaplan, *Between Dignity and Despair*, 10–11. Donald Niewyk, *The Jews in Weimar Germany* (New Brunswick: Transaction Books, 2001), 16–20.

18 Niewyk, *The Jews in Weimar*, 13–16.

19 Donald Niewyk, *The Jews in Weimar*, 18–21; Steven Aschheim, *Brothers and Strangers. The East European Jew in German and German Jewish Consciousness, 1800–1923* (Madison: University of Wisconsin, 1999 edn), 215–45; Annemarie Sammartino, *The Impossible Border. Germany and the East, 1914–1922* (Ithaca,

NY: Cornell University Press, 2010); Michael Brenner, *The Renaissance of Jewish Culture in Weimar Germany* (New Haven: Yale University Press, 1996), 33, 51–65.

20 Peter Pulzer, *The Rise of Political Anti-semitism in Germany and Austria* (London: Peter Halban, 1988 edn).

21 Richard S. Levy, *The Downfall of the Anti-Semitic Political Parties in Imperial Germany* (New Haven: Yale University Press, 1975).

22 Shulamit Volkov, *Germans, Jews, and Antisemites. Trials in Emancipation* (Cambridge: Cambridge University Press, 2006), 100–28; Uriel Tal, *Christians and Germans in Germany. Religion, Politics and Ideology in the Second Reich, 1870–1914* (London: Cornell University Press, 1975); Donald Niewyck, 'Solving the "Jewish Problem": continuity and change in German antisemitism, 1871–1945', in David Cesarani ed., *Holocaust. Critical Concepts in Historical Studies*, vol. 1 (London: Routledge, 2004), 50–90.

23 Ismar Schorsch, *Jewish Reactions to German Anti-Semitism, 1870–1914* (New York: Columbia University Press, 1972); Judah Reinharz, *Fatherland or Promised Land. The Dilemma of the German Jew, 1893–1914* (Ann Arbor: University of Michigan Press, 1975); Marjorie Lamberti, *Jewish Activism in Imperial Germany. The Struggle for Civic Equality* (New Haven: Yale University Press, 1978).

24 Peter Pulzer, 'The First World War', in Michael Meyer ed., *German-Jewish History in Modern Times*, vol. 3, *Integration in Dispute 1871–1918* (New York: Columbia University Press, 1997), 360–84.

25 Eberhard Kolb, *The Weimar Republic*, trans. P. S. Falla (London: Routledge, 1988), 3–21.

26 Kolb, *The Weimar Republic*, 35–8; Sammartino, *The Impossible Border*, 46–65.

27 Kolb, *The Weimar Republic*, 23–33.

28 Peter Fritzsche, *Germans into Nazis* (Cambridge MA: Harvard University Press, 1998), 93–136; Evans, *Coming of the Third Reich*, 103–12.

29 Michael Wildt, *Hitler's Volksgemeinschaft and the Dynamics of Racial Exclusion. Violence against the Jews in provincial Germany, 1919–1939*, trans. Bernard Heise (New York: Berghahn, 2012), 20–70. Niewyk, *The Jews in Weimar*, 49–53, minimizes the extent and impact of anti-Semitic politics.

30 Richard M. Watt, *The Kings Depart. The German Revolution and the Treaty of Versailles 1918–1919* (London: Penguin, 1972), 235–6; Evans, *Coming of the Third Reich*, 156–161; Wildt, *Hitler's Volksgemeinschaft*, 53–4; Aschheim, *Brothers and Strangers*, 243–5.

31 Kolb, *The Weimar Republic*, 57–61, 70–2.

32 Niewyk, *The Jews in Weimar*, 84–95; Aschheim, *Brothers and Strangers*, 220–3.

33 Ben Barkow, *Alfred Wiener and the Making of the Holocaust Library* (London: Vallentine Mitchell, 1997); for an example of Jewish defence work, see Jacob Borut, 'Antisemitism in Tourist Facilities in Weimar Germany', *Yad Vashem Studies*, 28 (2000), 7–50; Kershaw, *Hitler 1889–1936*, 330–2.

34 Adolf Hitler, *Mein Kampf*, trans. Ralph Manheim (London: Hutchinson, 1973 edn); Neil Gregor, *How to Read Hitler* (London: Granta, 2005).

35 Evans, *Coming of the Third Reich*, 196–8; Gilbet, *Sir Horace Rumbold*, 339; *Phipps Diary*, 31. For varied historical interpretations, see Ron Rosenbaum, *Explaining*

Hitler, The Search for the Origins of His Evil (New York: Macmillan, 1998) and John Lukacs, *The Hitler of History. Hitler's Biographers on Trial* (London: Weidenfeld and Nicolson, 2000).

36 Kershaw, *Hitler 1889–1936*, 10–26, 29–60. Brigitte Hamann, 'Hitler and Vienna', in Hans Mommsen ed., *The Third Reich Between Vision and Reality. New perspectives on German history, 1918–1945* (2001), 23–37 and more fully in Brigitte Harmann, *Hitler's Vienna. A Dictator's Apprenticeship* (Oxford: Oxford University Press, 1999).

37 Kershaw, *Hitler 1889–1936*, 81–105; Weber, *Hitler's First War*, part 1.

38 Kershaw, *Hitler 1889–1936*, 116–25, 137–65.

39 Ibid, 170–9.

40 Ibid, 192–3, 200–19.

41 Ibid, 224–34.

42 Ibid, 262–79; Fritzsche, *Germans into Nazis*, 173–81, 186–204; Evans, *Coming of the Third Reich*, 207–26.

43 Wildt, *Hitler's Volksgemeinschaft*, 59–64.

44 Kershaw, *Hitler 1889–1936*, 302–4, 309–11; Fritzsche, *Germans into Nazis*, 161–72. 'The Weimar Constitution Ten Years On', 10 August 1929, in Schwarzschild, *Chronicle of a Downfall*, 2–5.

45 Evans, *Coming of the Third Reich*, 232–42.

46 Kershaw, *Hitler 1889–1936*, 333–5.

47 14 October, 25 December 1930, *Fromm Diary* 31, 32–3. For a caveat to Fromm's contemporary record of events, see Henry Ashby Turner Jr, 'Two Dubious Third Reich Diaries', *Central European History* 33:3 (2000), 415–22.

48 Fritzsche, *Germans into Nazis*, 208–9.

49 Thomas Friedrich, *Hitler's Berlin. Abused City* (London: Yale, 2012), 186–9, 200–1, 236–41; Wildt, *Hitler's Volksgemeinschaft*, 64–6.

50 Friedrich, *Hitler's Berlin*, 242.

51 29 January 1932, *Fromm Diary*, 43; Kershaw, *Hitler 1889–1936*, 340–56.

52 Kershaw, *Hitler 1889–1936*, 360–5.

53 Toby Thacker, *Joseph Goebbels. Life and Death* (London: Palgrave Macmillan, 2009), 13–28, 36–54, 56–74, 78–98; Peter Longerich, *Goebbels. A Biography*, trans. Alan Bance, Jeremy Noakes and Lesley Sharpe (London: Bodley Head, 2015), 36–94, 168–74.

54 Anna von der Golz, *Hindenburg. Power, Myth and the Rise of the Nazis* (Oxford: Oxford University Press, 2009), 153–7; Friedrich, *Hitler's Berlin*, 267–72.

55 'An Imaginary Speech by Brüning', 20 September 1930, 'Let him have a go', 30 April 1932, in Schwarzschild, *Chronicle of a Downfall*, 44–51, 69–73.

56 Friedrich, *Hitler's Berlin*, 274–5; Evans, *Coming of the Third Reich*, 272–82.

57 Kershaw, *Hitler 1889–1936*, 366–8.

58 Ibid, 367–70.

59 Ibid, 370–5, 380–91; Turner Jr, *Hitler's Thirty Days to Power*, 11–13.

60 Turner Jr, *Hitler's Thirty Days to Power*, 17–29.

61 'Twilight', 30 December 1932, in Schwarzschild, *Chronicle of a Downfall*, 89–91

62 Turner Jr, *Hitler's Thirty Days to Power*, 41–52, 58–68, 74–7.

63 Ibid, 70–1, 109–33.

64 Ibid, 133–48.

65 *Jüdische Rundschau* quoted in Jewish Telegraphic Agency, 9 January 1933, in Monty Noam Penkower, *The Swastika's Darkening Shadow. Voices Before the Holocaust* (New York: Palgrave Macmillan, 2013), 119–20.

66 Siegmund Warburg to Mauritz Philipson, 15, 17 September 1930 cited in Niall Ferguson, *High Financier. The Lives and Times of Siegmund Warburg* (London: Allen Lane, 2010), 77–8; Turner Jr, *Hitler's Thirty Days to Power*, 22, 196.

67 Cited in Friedrich, *Hitler's Berlin*, 183.

68 Joachim Fest, *Not Me. Memoirs of a German Childhood*, trans. Martin Chalmers (London: Atlantic Books, 2012), 39; cited in Turner Jr, *Hitler's Thirty Days to Power*, 158.

69 Sir Horace Rumbold to Sir John Simon, 27 January, 4 and 10 February 1933, in Gilbert, *Sir Horace Rumbold*, 366, 368.

70 1 September 1932, in Richard Breitman et al. eds, *Advocate for the Doomed. The Diaries and Papers of James G. McDonald 1932-1935* (Bloomington: Indiana University Press, 2007), 13–14, 15. On Hanfstaengl see Peter Conradi, *Hitler's Piano Player. The Rise and Fall of Ernst Hanfstaengl, Confidant of Hitler, Ally of FDR* (London: Duckworth, 2005).

71 Grenville, *The Jews and Germans of Hamburg*, 57.

72 Melita Maschmann, *Account Rendered*, trans. Geoffrey Strachan (London: Abelard-Schuman, 1964), 11.

One – The First Year: 1933

1 Tooze, *The Wages of Destruction*, 37.

2 Evans, *Coming of the Third Reich*, 314–27; François-Poncet, *Fateful Years*, 49–54.

3 Evans, *Coming of the Third Reich*, 328–37.

4 Nikolaus Wachsmann, 'The Dynamics of destruction: the development of the concentration camps, 1933–1945', in Jane Caplan and Nikolaus Wachsmann eds, *Concentration Camps in Nazi Germany. The New Histories* (London: Routledge, 2010), 18–20.

5 Christopher Isherwood, 'Berlin Diary (Winter 1932-3)', *Goodbye to Berlin* (London: Vintage, 1998 edn), 251. The diary was first published in 1935.

6 Evans, *Coming of the Third Reich*, 339–40.

7 'Fait Accompli', 11 March 1933 in Schwarzschild, *Chronicle of a Downfall*, 100–2.

8 Avraham Barkai, *From Boycott to Annihilation. The Economic Struggle of German Jews 1933-1945*, trans. William Templer (Hanover, NH: University Press of New England, 1989), 13–17; Wildt, *Hitler's Volksgemeinschaft*, 77–109; *Jewish Responses*, vol. I, 11–12.

9 Wildt, *Hitler's Volksgemeinschaft*, 80–1; Report by the Mayor of Gollnow, 14 March 1933, in Otto Dov Kulka and Eberhard Jäckel eds, *The Jews in the Secret Nazi Reports on Popular Opinion in Germany, 1933-1945*, trans. William Templer (New Haven: Yale University Press, 2011), 4–6.

10 Prussian Political Police, Berlin, reporting communication from Breslau Police Superintendent, 11 March 1933, in *Secret Nazi Reports*, 3–4.

11 Police HQs Bochum, Dortmund, Oberhausen reports to Highert Police Leader, West, for 27–28 March 1933, *Secret Nazi Reports*, 6–7.

12 *Jewish Responses*, vol. I, 27–9; Benjamin Carter Hett, *Crossing Hitler. The Man Who Put the Nazis on the Witness Stand* (New York and Oxford: Oxford University Press, 2008), 159–63; Kim Wünschmann, *Before Auschwitz. Jewish Prisoners in the Prewar Nazi Concentration Camps* (Cambridge, MA: Harvard University Press, 2015), 19–57. For the assault on Judaism, see Alon Confino, *A World Without Jews. The Nazi Imagination. From Persecution to Genocide* (New Haven: Yale University Press, 2014), 27–39.

13 Gilbert, *Sir Horace Rumbold*, 370–3; Richard Breitman and Alan J. Lichtman, *FDR and the Jews* (Cambridge, MA: Harvard University Press, 2013), 55–6.

14 20, 21 March 1933, *McDonald Diaries*, I, 24–5. For similar protests in France, see Vicki Caron, *Uneasy Asylum. France and the Jewish Refugee Crisis 1933–1942* (Stanford: Stanford University Press, 1999), 96–7.

15 Breitman and Lichtman, *FDR and the Jews*, 52–3.

16 Ibid, 54.

17 Ibid, 56–9.

18 David Cesarani, *The Jewish Chronicle and Anglo-Jewry, 1841–1991* (Cambridge: Cambridge University Press, 1994), 145–6.

19 J. P. Fox, 'Great Britain and the German Jews, 1933', *Wiener Library Bulletin*, 36:26/7 (1972), 40–6; Sharon Gewirtz, 'Anglo-Jewish responses to Nazi Germany, 1933–1939. The Anti-Nazi Boycott and the Board of Deputies of British Jews', *Journal of Contemporary History* 26 (1991), 255–76.

20 *Jewish Chronicle*, 2 April 1933, 21 and 28 July 1933. David Cesarani, 'The Transformation of Jewish Communal Authority in Anglo-Jewry, 1914–1940', in David Cesarani ed., *The Making of Modern Anglo-Jewry* (Oxford: Blackwell, 1990), 126–7.

21 Moffat journal entry for 22 February 1933 cited in *McDonald Diaries*, I, 25.

22 Gilbert, *Sir Horace Rumbold*, 373–5.

23 François-Poncet, *Fateful Years*, 71.

24 Gulie Ne'eman Arad, *America, Its Jews and the Rise of Nazism* (Bloomington: Indiana University, 2007), 145.

25 27 March 1933, *Fromm Diary*, 88. Arad, *America, its Jews and the Rise of Nazism*, 144–5; Saul Friedländer, *Nazi Germany and the Jews*, vol. 1, 19–21; Longerich, *Goebbels*, 218–19.

26 23 March 1933, *Fromm Diary*, 86–7. Breitman and Lichtman, *FDR and the Jews*, 56; Fox, 'Great Britain and the German Jews'.

27 Messersmith journal entry for 31 March 1933 cited in *McDonald Diaries*, I, 32; Frank Bajohr and Christoph Strupp eds, *Fremde Blicke auf das 'Dritte Reich'. Berichte ausländischer Diplomaten über Herrschaft und Gesellschaft in Deutschland 1933–1945* (Göttingen: Wallstein Verlag, 2011), 362. I would like to thank Dr Rudolf Mühs for bringing this volume to my attention.

28 Lucy Dawidowicz, *The War Against the Jews* (London: Penguin, 1975), 83–5;

Martin Gilbert, *Holocaust*, 86, actually inverts the order of events; Hermann Graml, *Anti-Semitism in the Third Reich* (Oxford: Berghahn, 1988), 91, 93–6, sees the boycott as a device to overcome opposition to anti-Semitism; Leni Yahil, *The Holocaust: The Fate of European Jewry* (Oxford: Oxford University Press, 1990), 60–3, explains it as a tool to extend Nazi influence and discomfort opponents; Wolfgang Benz, *The Holocaust*, trans. Jane Sydenham-Kwiet (New York: Columbia University Press, 1999), 15–17, treats the stated reason for the boycott as an 'excuse' for a move that would let the population know where policy was trending; Debórah Dwork and Robert Jan van Pelt, *Holocaust: A History* (London: John Murray, 2002), 69–70, regard it as a 'pre-emptive strike'.

29 Victor Klemperer, *I Shall Bear Witness. The Diaries of Victor Klemperer, 1933–41*, trans. and ed. Martin Chalmers (London: Weidenfeld and Nicolson, 1998), 27, 30 March 1933, 9.

30 McDonald to FPA, 3 April 1933 and diary 1 April 1933, *McDonald Diaries*, I, 28, 33.

31 29 March 1933, *Fromm Diary*, 88–9; District Governor Lower Bavaria and Upper Palatinate, 'Report for the Second Half of March', 30 March 1933; Bad Kissingen Municipal Council, 'Report for the Second Half of March', 31 March 193; reports to Higher Police Leader in the West, 30 March–1 April, *Secret Nazi Reports*, 7, 7–8, 8.

32 Messersmith to Secretary of State Hull, 'With further reference to the manifold aspects of the anti-Jewish movement in Germany', 31 March 1933, cited in Bat-Ami Zucker, *In Search of Refuge. Jews and US Consuls in Nazi Germany 1933–1941* (London: Vallentine Mitchell, 2001), 67.

33 *Jewish Responses*, vol. I, 15; 3 April 1933, *McDonald Diaries*, I, 27; 31 March 1933, *Klemperer Diaries*, I, 9–10.

34 3 April 1933, *Klemperer Diaries*, I, 9; *Jewish Responses*, vol. I, 19–20; Abraham Ascher, *A Community under Siege*, 82. Avraham Barkai, *From Boycott to Annihilation*, 17–25.

35 Ralph C. Busser, 'Present Operation and Effect of the Anti-Jewish Movement in Central Germany', 5 April 1933, *Fremde Blicke*, 364–5.

36 Edwin Landau in Margarete Limburg and Hubert Ruebsaat ed, *Germans No More. Accounts of Everyday Jewish Life, 1933–1938*, trans. Alan Nothangle (New York, Berghahn, 2006), 10–11.

37 Henriette Necheles-Magnus in *Germans No More*, 19–21; Grenville, *The Jews and Germans of Hamburg*, 82–5.

38 1 April 1933, *McDonald Diaries*, I, 33; Gilbert, *Sir Horace Rumbold*, 375.

39 George Messersmith, 'With Reference to the Boycott Against Jewish Business Establishments and with further reference to the Manifold Appeals of the Anti-Jewish Movement in Germany', 3 April 1933, *Fremde Blicke*, 363–4.

40 Wildt, *Hitler's Volksgemeinschaft*, 77–109; Evans, *Coming of the Third Reich*, 431–8.

41 George Messersmith, 'Uncertainty as to the Developments in the Economic and Financial Situation in Germany', 9 May 1933; Charles M. Hathaway, Munich, report, 13 May 1933, *Fremde Blicke*, 372–3.

42 Evans, *Coming of the Third Reich*, 374–89; Friedländer, *Nazi Germany and the Jews*, vol. 1, 28–31.

43 Evans, *Coming of the Third Reich*, 342–8.

44 Richard J. Evans, *The Third Reich in Power, 1933–1939* (London: Penguin, 2005), 20–1, 81–5; Zucker, *In Search of Refuge*, 73–4; Nikolaus Wachsmann, *Hitler's Prisons. Legal Terror in Nazi Germany* (London: Yale University Press, 2004), 113–18; Nikolaus Wachsmann, *KL. A History of the Nazi Concentration Camps* (London: Little Brown, 2015), 38–60.

45 Evans, *The Third Reich in Power*, 52–5, 77, 96–104. Robert Gellately, *Backing Hitler: Consent and Coercion in Nazi Germany* (Oxford: Oxford University Press, 2001).

46 Evans, *The Third Reich in Power*, 120–40, 261–5; Longerich, *Goebbels*, 212–13, 222–7, 240–2; Alan Steinweis, *Art, Ideology and Economics in Nazi Germany. The Reich Chambers of Music, Theater and the Visual Arts* (Chapel Hill: University of North Carolina Press, 1993), 32–48; David Welch, *The Third Reich. Politics and Propaganda* (London: Routledge, 1993), 17–47.

47 Confino, *World Without Jews*, 39–45; Joseph Roth to Stefan Zweig, 6 April 1933, *Josef Roth. A Life in Letters*, 251; *Jüdische Rundschau*, 12 May 1933, *Jewish Responses*, vol. I, 41–2.

48 Evans, *The Third Reich in Power*, 419–41, 465–75, 484–8.

49 Evans, *The Third Reich in Power*, 507–10, 516–19, 529–35. Michael Burleigh and Wolfgang Wipperman, *The Racial State. Germany 1933–1945* (Cambridge: Cambridge University Press, 1991); Lisa Pine, *Nazi Family Policy, 1933–1945* (Oxford: Berg, 1997), 8–46; Donna F. Ryan and John S. Schuman eds, *Deaf People in Hitler's Europe* (Washington DC: Gallaudet University Press, 2002), 11–97, 121–63; Geoffrey Giles, 'The Institutionalisation of Homosexual Panic in the Third Reich', in Robert Gellately and Nathan Stolzfus eds, *Social Outsiders in Nazi Germany* (Princeton: Princeton University Press), 233–47.

50 Andrew Stuart Bergerson, *Ordinary Germans In Extraordinary Times. The Nazi Revolution in Hildesheim* (Bloomington: Indiana University Press, 2004), 131–64.

51 Fritzsche, *Germans into Nazis*, 211–30; Peter Fritzsche, *Life and Death in the Third Reich* (Cambridge, MA: Harvard University Press, 2008), 20–4, 35–52, 56–65, 76–91; S. Jonathan Wiesen, *Creating the Nazi Marketplace. Commerce and Consumption in the Third Reich* (New York: Cambridge University Press, 2011), 39–49, 53–60. Irene Guenther, *Nazi Chic? Fashioning Women in the Third Reich* (Oxford: Berg, 2004).

52 Fritzsche, *Life and Death in the Third Reich*, 96–108; Thomas Kühne, *Belonging and Genocide. Hitler's Community, 1918–1945* (New Haven: Yale University Press, 2010), 42–6; Claudia Koonz, *The Nazi Conscience* (Cambridge, MA: Harvard University Press, 2003), 144–5.

53 Maschmann, *Account Rendered*, 10–12, 17–22, 24–6.

54 'Caught up in the nationalist revolution', 1 July 1933 in Schwarzschild, *Chronicle of a Downfall*, 111. Fritzsche, *Life and Death in the Third Reich*, 5–8, 50–4; Koonz, *The Nazi Conscience*, 131–9, 201–14; Welch, *The Third Reich. Politics and Propaganda*, 50–89, and his 'Manufacturing a Consensus: Nazi Propaganda and

the Building of a "National Community" (Volksgemeinschaft)', *Central European History* 2:1 (1993), 1–15.

55 Fritzsche, *Life and Death in the Third Reich*, 96–108, 123–4; Koonz, *The Nazi Conscience*.

56 Longerich, *Holocaust*, 31–2.

57 Grenville, *The Jews and Germans of Hamburg*, 111–13.

58 Francis Nicosia and David Scrase eds, *Jewish Life in Nazi Germany. Dilemmas and Responses* (New York: Berghahn, 2012), 4–5; Longerich, *Holocaust*, 40–1; Friedländer, *Nazi Germany and the Jews*, vol. 1, 12–13.

59 Annemarie Schwarzenbach to Klaus Mann, 8 April 1933 in Lubrich ed., *Travels in the Reich*, 37–9; *Secret Nazi Reports*, 633; Wildt, *Hitler's Volksgemeinschaft*, 201–2.

60 NSDAP District Office report, 15 July 1933; District Governor, Lower Franconia, reports, 8 August and 6, 20 September 1933, *Secret Nazi Reports*, 12, 14, 17.

61 Martha Dodd, *My Years in Germany* (London: Gollancz, 1939), 28–30.

62 Stapostelle Government District Kassel, August report, 29 August 1933, *Secret Nazi Reports*, 16; *Jewish Responses*, vol. I, 37.

63 Martin Doerry, *My Wounded Heart. The Life of Lilli Jahn*, trans. John Brownjohn (London: Bloomsbury, 2004), 1–50 and 51–2, 55–6, 60–2 for letters to Leo and Hanne Barth, 5 February and 2 April 1933.

64 Raymond Geist to State Department, 15 December 1933, *Fremde Blicke*, 395; Reich Economic Ministry circular, 16 December 1933, *Secret Nazi Reports*, 666.

65 *Jewish Responses*, vol. I, 33–4.

66 Siegmund Warburg diary, 6 March 1933, in Ferguson, *High Financier*, 78–80.

67 Warburg diary, 6, 9, 11 March 1933, in Ferguson, *High Financier*, 79–80.

68 Warburg diary, 21 March 1933, in Ferguson, *High Financier*, 79–80.

69 *Jewish Responses*, vol. I, 21–2, 48–52, 56–7.

70 *Jewish Responses*, vol. I, 5–6; 3 April 1933, *Klemperer Diaries*, I, 9; Edwin Landau in *Germans No More*, 10–11.

71 Y. Arad, Y. Gutman, A. Margaliot eds, *Documents on the Holocaust* (Jerusalem: Yad Vashem, 1981), 37–9.

72 25 April 1933, *Klemperer Diaries*, I, 15.

73 8 April 1933, 6 May 1933, *McDonald Diaries*, I, 43, 47–8, 59; Gilbert, *Sir Horace Rumbold*, 379–80.

74 Breitman and Lichtman, *FDR and the Jews*, 61; Gewirtz, 'Anglo-Jewish responses to Nazi Germany', 259, 265–6; Cesarani, 'The Transformation of Jewish Communal Authority', 127–8.

75 16 June, 3 July, 4 July, 13 July 1933, William E. Dodd and Martha Dodd, *Ambassador Dodd's Diary* (London: Gollancz, 1939), 18–20, 22–3, 24, 25, 40–1.

76 23 August, 14 September, 17 October 1933, *Ambassador Dodd's Diary*, 50, 61–3. For a critical assessment of the diary, see Richard Breitman, 'Conclusion' in *McDonald Diaries*, I, 793–5.

77 21 November 1933, *Phipps Diary*, 31.

78 13 May, 18 August 1933, *McDonald Diaries*, I, 68–9, 82–3, 229.

79 Kurt Sabatzky in *Germans No More*, 45. In his case the Gestapo successfully appealed.

80 *Jewish Responses*, vol. I, 3.

81 Avraham Barkai, 'Shifting Organisational Relationships', in Michael Meyer ed., *German-Jewish History in Modern Times*, vol. 4, *Renewal and Destruction 1918–1945* (New York: Columbia University Press, 1998), 260–1; *Jewish Responses*, vol. I, 45–7; Grenville, *The Jews and Germans of Hamburg*, 111–13.

82 Avraham Barkai, 'Self-Help in the Dilemma: "To Leave or to Stay?"', in Meyer ed., *Renewal and Destruction*, 314–15; Alexander Szanto in *Germans No More*, 131–42; Ascher, *A Community under Siege*, 89–110.

83 Paul Mendes-Flohr, 'Jewish Cultural Life under National Socialism', in Meyer ed., *Renewal and Destruction*, 301–3.

84 Francis Nicosia, *Zionism and Anti-Semitism in Nazi Germany* (New York: Cambridge University Press, 2008), 78–90, 145–50, 211–20, and his 'German Zionism and Jewish Life in Nazi Berlin', in Nicosia and Scrase eds, *Jewish Life in Nazi Germany*, 96–102.

85 Nicosia, *Zionism and Anti-Semitism in Nazi Germany*, 91–3.

86 Kurt Bauman in *Germans No More*, 118–27; Mendes-Flohr, 'Jewish Cultural Life under National Socialism', in Meyer ed., *Renewal and Destruction*, 284–92; Steinweis, *Art, Ideology and Economics in Nazi Germany*, 121–3.

87 Roth to Zweig, 29 November 1933, *Josef Roth. A Life in Letters*, 287–8; 9 October 1933, *Klemperer Diaries*, I, 33.

88 *Jewish Responses*, vol. I, 79–80, 83–4; 14 November 1933, *Klemperer Diaries*, I, 39–40.

89 Stapostelle Government District Kassel, 'Report on the Activity of Jewish Associations', 9 November 1933; Police HQ Nuremberg-Fürth, 'Political News', 4 December 1933, *Secret Nazi Reports*, 19–20, 21.

90 Michael Marrus, *The Unwanted. Refugees in the Twentieth Century* (New York: Oxford University Press, 1985), 128–30; Herbert Strauss, 'Jewish Emigration from Germany. Nazi Policies and Jewish Responses (1)', *Leo Baeck Institute Year Book*, 25 (1980), 312–59.

91 Louise London, *Whitehall and the Jews* (Cambridge: Cambridge University Press, 2000), 25–33; Caron, *Uneasy Asylum*, 14–17.

92 Caron, *Uneasy Asylum*, 43–59. Even though France felt obligated towards the population of the Saar which had lived under French rule from 1919 to 1934, it accepted German and German Jewish refugees from the Saar in the wake of the January 1934 plebiscite grudgingly and did not amend the restrictions on their ability to work.

93 *Jewish Responses*, vol. I, 72–4.

94 Caron, *Uneasy Asylum*, 99–115; 12 December 1933, *McDonald Diaries*, I, 218.

95 Caron, *Uneasy Asylum*, 97–8; 13 December 1933, *McDonald Diaries*, I, 218.

96 Roth to Zweig, 7 November 1935, *A Life in Letters*, 426–8.

97 London, *Whitehall and the Jews*, 25–33; V. D. Lipman, 'Anglo-Jewish Attitudes to the Refugees from Central Europe 1933–1939', in W. E. Mosse ed., *Second Chance. Two centuries of German-speaking Jews in the United Kingdom* (Tübingen: J. C. B. Mohr, 1992), 519–31.

98 Breitman and Lichtman, *FDR and the Jews*, 59–60; Zucker, *In Search of Refuge*, 50.

99 6, 12 September and 15, 17 November 1933, *McDonald Diaries*, I, 99–100, 152, 161, 172.

100 10, 26 October, 11, 18, 21, 22–3 November, 6, 15 December 1933, *McDonald Diaries*, I, 108–10, 133–47, 176, 180–2, 187, 205–6, 223–4. On Palestine, see also 9 April, 18 October 1934, *McDonald Diaries*, I, 345–6, 515–17.

101 Moffat journal, 5 January, 3 March 1934, cited in *McDonald Diaries*, I, 258, 311. For meetings with FDR, see 16 January, 5 May, 17 December 1934, *McDonald Diaries*, I, 261–4, 383–4, 575. On business of the High Commission, 30 January, 13 November, 17, 21 December 1934, *McDonald Diaries*, I, 276–7, 553–4, 575, 585.

Two – Judenpolitik: 1934–1938

1 2 February 1934, *Klemperer Diaries*, I, 51; Roth to Zweig, 18 February 1934, *A Life in Letters*, 310; 'Severing rules in Europe', 3 February 1934, in Schwarzschild, *Chronicle of a Downfall*, 115–18.

2 22 January 1934, *Phipps Diary* 38–9. Tooze, *The Wages of Destruction*, 59–66, 71–98.

3 Dodd, 'Internal Political Situation', 20 April 1934, *Fremde Blicke*, 405–6; *Fromm Diary*, 142–3; 13 May, 13 June 1934, *Klemperer Diaries*, I, 62, 67.

4 21 June 1934, *Ambassador Dodd's Diary*, 125–8. Evans, *The Third Reich in Power*, 27–31.

5 Evans, *The Third Reich in Power*, 31–41.

6 4, 11 July 1934, *Phipps Diary* 63, 65–6; 1, 8, 13 July 1934, *Ambassador Dodd's Diary*, 129–34; Roth to Zweig, 24 July 1935, *A Life in Letters*, 411–13.

7 Peter Longerich, *Heinrich Himmler. A Life*, trans. Jeremy Noakes and Lesley Sharpe (New York: Oxford University Press, 2012), 13–73, 88– 100, 110–127, 160–76; Robert Gerwarth, *Hitler's Hangman. The Life of Reinhard Heydrich* (London: Yale University Press, 2011), 78–80.

8 12 September 1934, *Phipps Diary* 70–1; Ambassador Dodd, 'Discontent Among Germans with the Nazi Regime', 14 November 1934, *Fremde Blicke*, 422; 4, 21 August 1934, *Klemperer Diaries*, I, 77, 79.

9 *Jewish Responses*, vol. I, 97–8, 127–8; Wildt, *Hitler's Volksgemeinschaft*, 114–27.

10 Dawidowicz, *The War Against the Jews*, 92–3; Gilbert, *Holocaust*, 42–3; Graml, *Anti-Semitism in the Third Reich*, 106–11; Yahil, *The Holocaust*, 67–8. Compare: Longerich, *Holocaust*, 41–3; *Jewish Responses*, vol. I, 95–8.

11 *Secret Nazi Reports*, 671.

12 Eric Kurlander, *Living With Hitler. Liberal Democrats in the Third Reich* (London: Yale University Press, 2009), 8–9, 14–15, 60–5, 155; Barkai, *From Boycott to Annihilation*, 59–63; compare with Albert Fischer, 'The Ministry of Economics and the Expulsion of the Jews from the German Economy', in David Bankier ed., *Probing the Depths of German Antisemitism. German Society and the Persecution of the Jews, 1933–1941* (Jerusalem: Yad Vashem, 2000), 213–25.

13 31 January, 7 February, 20 and 21 April 1934, *McDonald Diaries*, I, 279, 290–3, 366–7.

14 10 February, 5, 7 March, 4, 12 July 1934, *Ambassador Dodd's Diary*, 92, 98–9, 100–1, 130, 136. Breitman and Lichtman, *FDR and the Jews*, 107.

15 9, 18, 24, 28 May, 1, 13 June 1934, *Ambassador Dodd's Diary*, 111–13, 116–17, 121, 134.

16 31 August 1934, *Ambassador Dodd's Diary*, 167; 30 May 1934, *Phipps Diary*, 58–60; Raymond Geist, 'Situation of the Jews in Germany', 28 July 1934, *Fremde Blicke*, 416–17.

17 *Jewish Responses*, vol. I, 107–8; Fraenkel, 'Jewish Self-Defence under the Constraints of National Socialism: the Final Years of the Centralverein', in Bankier ed., *Probing the Depths of German Antisemitism*, 348–51.

18 *Jewish Responses*, vol. I, 108.

19 Hertz to Hitler, 27 April 1934, Henrik Eberle ed., *Letters to Hitler*, ed. Victoria Harris, trans. Steven Rendall, (London: Polity 2012), 130; Grenville, *Jews and Germans*, 110–11.

20 *Jewish Responses*, vol. I, 95–8, 104–5, 112, 117–20; Fraenkel, 'Jewish Self-Defence under the Constraints of National Socialism: the Final Years of the Centralverein' in Bankier ed., *Probing the Depths of German Antisemitism*, 339–59.

21 Barkai, 'Jewish Life Under Persecution', and 'Self-Help in the Dilemma: "To Leave or to Stay?"', in Meyer ed., *Renewal and Destruction*, 242–4, 314–16; Barkai, *From Boycott to Annihilation*, 80–8.

22 25 June 1934, *Phipps Diary* 60–1; Ascher, *A Community under Siege*, 122–3; Barkai, *From Boycott to Annihilation*, 241.

23 Norman Bentwich, *They Found Refuge* (London: Cresset Press, 1956), 26–7; Moffat journal, 29 May 1934, cited in *McDonald Diaries*, I, 398. 13, 23 June, 23 July 1934, *McDonald Diaries*, I, 398, 439, 458.

24 Diary entry, 26 January 1934, and McDonald to Rosenberg, 27 July 1934, *McDonald Diaries*, I, 269, 447.

25 26 April 1934, *McDonald Diaries*, I, 376; Smallbones to Phipps, 24 February 1934, 400–1; Raymond Geist, 'Situation of the Jews in Germany', 28 July 1934, *Fremde Blicke*, 416–17; 29 October 1934, *Ambassador Dodd's Diary*, 192; Naomi Shepherd, *Wilfred Israel. German Jewry's Secret Ambassador* (London: Weidenfeld and Nicolson, 1984), 81–91.

26 Gestapa Berlin, report for 1 November 1933–10 January 1934, 10 January 1934; Central Office for the Commander of the Political Police, report for February–March, 14 April 1934; District Government Swabia and Neuberg, August Report, 6 September 1934 and Gendarmerie Bad Neustadt, October Report, 24 October 1934; Stapostelle Berlin Region, September report, 4 October 1934; Chief of Police, Dresden, report for 6–12 December 1934, 13 December 1934; Chief of Police, Berlin, report for November–December 1934, 18 January 1935, *Secret Nazi Reports*, 26–7, 29–30, 60, 61, 67, 73–4, 74–5.

27 Fichte to Hitler, 2 February 1934, Falkstein to Hitler, 5 February 1934, Barth to Hitler, 4 March 1934, in Eberle ed., *Letters to Hitler*, 115–18, 118–19, 119–20.

28 Gestapa Berlin, II 1 B 2, report, November 1934, *Secret Nazi Reports*, 67–9.

29 Stapostelle Government District Kassel, October report, 5 November 1934, *Secret Nazi Reports*, 65–6.

30 Stapostelle Government District Kassel, November report, 5 December 1934; Interior Ministry of Braunschweig report, 14 December 1934; District Office, Alzenau, Lower Franconia, November report, 27 November 1934; Military Police Squad 1/V Frankfurt-am-Main, report for 23 December 1934, 25 December 1934, *Secret Nazi Reports*, 69, 71, 72–3, 91–2.

31 Stapostelle Cologne Government District, September report, 1 October 1934; Stapostelle Government District Koblenz, October 1934 report; 62, 66–7; 13 June 1934, *Klemperer Diaries*, I, 64–5; Raymond Geist, 'Situation of the Jews in Germany', 28 July 1934, *Fremde Blicke*, 416–17.

32 *Jewish Responses*, vol. I, 130–2; *Secret State Reports*, 83 (State Minister for Hesse, Report, 11 January 1935), and 96 (County Commissioner, Woldhagen, Report, 27 December 1934).

33 *CV-Zeitung*, 20 December 1934 in *Jewish Responses*, vol. I, 146; 16 December 1934, 15 January 1935, *Klemperer Diaries*, I, 97, 104–5.

34 20 June 1935, *Klemperer Diaries*, I, 121.

35 *Jewish Responses*, vol. I, 152; Grenville, *Jews and Germans*, 126.

36 Longerich, *Himmler*, 187–9, 209–13, 214–18; Gerwarth, *Hitler's Hangman*, 84–98.

37 *Jewish Responses*, vol. I, 108–11; Gestapo Head Office (Gestapa) Berlin, 'The Jews in Germany', April 1934, *Secret Nazi Reports*, 31–7.

38 Gestapa Berlin Department II/1 B 2 report, November 1934, 24 October 1934, *Secret Nazi Reports*, 68–9. Gerwarth, *Hitler's Hangman*, 87–90.

39 SD Main Office, 'Situation Report', May–June 1934; SD Main Office J I/6, 'Situation Report', n.d. January 1936, *Secret Nazi Reports*, 43–4, 186–8. George C. Browder, *Hitler's Enforcers. The Gestapo and the SS Security Service in the Nazi Revolution* (New York: Oxford University Press, 1996), 78–82; cf. Michael Wildt, 'Before the "Final Solution": The *Judenpolitik* of the SD, 1935–1938', *Leo Baeck Institute Year Book*, 43 (1998), 241–69 and Nicosia, *Zionism and Anti-Semitism in Nazi Germany*, 111–21, 228–48.

40 *Jewish Responses*, vol. I, 108, 153; Wildt, 'Before the "Final Solution"', 241–8; David Cesarani, *Eichmann. His Life and Crimes* (London: Heinemann, 2004), 40–7.

41 Cesarani, *Eichmann*, 18–48.

42 Nicosia, *Zionism and Anti-Semitism in Nazi Germany*, 118–21; Wildt, 'Before the "Final Solution"', 248–50.

43 District Governor Koblenz, report for December 1934–January 1935, 3 February 1935; Stapostelle Police District Berlin, February 1935 report; District Government Lower Franconia and Aschaffenburg, 'Political and Economic Situation', 8 February 1935; County Commissioner Fritzlar-Homberg, January–February 1935 report, *Secret Nazi Reports*, 101–2, 102–3, 104–5, 108.

44 *Secret Nazi Reports*, 134; William L. Shirer, *Berlin Diary. The Journal of a Foreign Correspondent, 1934–1941* (Baltimore: Johns Hopkins University Press, 2002 [orig. 1941]), 36; Virginia Woolf diary, 9 May 1935, in Lubrich ed., *Travels in the Reich*, 73–5; 22 May 1935, *Ambassador Dodd's Diary*, 255–6.

45 Stapostelle Government District Lüneburg, daily report, 20 December 1934; Gendarmerie, Bad Neustadt, report for 18/19 December, 21 December 1934; Governor of Silesia, April–May 1935 report; Stapostelle Police District Berlin, report June 1935; Stapostelle Government District Breslau, 5 July 1935; Stapostelle Government District Königsberg, report June 1935; Stapostelle Police District Berlin, July 1935 report, *Secret Nazi Reports*, 80, 90, 127, 130, 132, 134, 137–9.

46 Stapostelle Breslau, 3 August 1935; Stapostelle Government District Minden, report for August 1935, 4 September 1935, *Secret Nazi Reports*, 140, 146–7.

47 District Governor Wiesbaden, 'Political Situation Report', 30 April 1935; Stapostelle Police District Berlin, 'General Overview', 13 June 1935 and June 1935 report; Stapostelle Government District Münster, May 1935 report, 6 June 1935; *Secret Nazi Reports*, 121–2, 123, 126–7, 130–1.

48 Samuel W. Honaker, US consul-general, Stuttgart, 'Recent Developments in the Anti-Semitic Agitation in Stuttgart', 23 August 1935, *Fremde Blicke*, 429–30.

49 District Governor Wiesbaden, May–June report, 1 July 1935; Stapostelle Government District Cologne, report for June, 7 July 1935; County Commissioner in Hünfeld, May–June 1935 report, 1 July 1935, *Secret Nazi Reports*, 133–4, 135–6, 137.

50 Stapostelle Police District Berlin, report for July 1935, *Secret Nazi Reports*, 137–9; Martin Gumpert in *Germans No More*, 71–3.

51 17 April, 30 June, 21 July, 11 August 1935, *Klemperer Diaries*, I, 113, 114, 124; 21 August 1935, Richard Breitman et al. eds, *Refugees and Rescue. The Diaries and Papers of James G. McDonald 1935–1945* (Bloomington: Indiana University Press, 2009), 8–9; *Jewish Responses*, vol. I, 162–3.

52 District Governor Upper and Central Franconia, report for second half of September, 6 October 1933; NSDAP District Office for Municipal Policy, Kempten, 'Report on the Prevailing Mood', 3 January 1935, *Secret Nazi Reports*, 18, 94. Longerich, *Holocaust*, 57–8.

53 *Jüdische Rundschau*, 10 May 1935; CV circulars, 15 April and 31 May 1935, RV report, 19 August 1935, *Jewish Responses*, vol. I, 157, 158–9, 159–60, 173.

54 *Secret Nazi Reports*, liii–liv; Wildt, *Hitler's Volksgemeinschaft*, 133–54, 188–9; Grenville, *Jews and Germans*, 126; Confino, *World Without Jews*, 56–61. Stapostelle Government District Frankfurt/Oder, daily report, 5 August 1935, *Secret Nazi Reports*, 141.

55 J. Noakes and G. Pridham eds, *Nazism 1919–1945. A Documentary Reader*, vol. 2, *State, Economy and Society 1933–1939* (Exeter: University of Exeter Press, 1997 edn), 531–3; *Documents on the Holocaust*, 73–5; Grenville, *Jews and Germans*, 130–1.

56 Wildt, *Hitler's Volksgemeinschaft*, 188–9; B. C. Newton to Samuel Hoare, on 'Situation of the Jews in Germany based on assessments from consulates in Frankfurt a. M., Munich and Breslau', 9 September 1935, *Fremde Blicke*, 431; 22 August 1935, *McDonald Diaries*, II, 10, 20; Longerich, *Holocaust*, 57–9.

57 2 August 1935, *Ambassador Dodd's Diary*, 273–4; Kershaw, *Hitler, 1889–1936*, 559–68.

58 For an early proposal for segregation and turning the Jews into a 'national

minority' as an alternative to 'physical extermination', see Interior Ministry of Württemberg situation report on the Jewish Question, 30 November 1933, *Secret Nazi Reports*, 22–5. Kershaw, *Hitler, 1889–1936*, 568–71; Karl A. Schleunes ed., *Legislating The Holocaust. The Bernhard Loesener Memoirs and Supporting Documents* (Boulder, CO: Westview Press, 2001).

59 *Documents on the Holocaust*, 77–82, 82–3; Evans, *The Third Reich in Power, 1933–1939*, 539–43.

60 J. Noakes and G. Pridham eds, *Nazism 1919–1945*, 1997 edn., vol. 2, 533–41.

61 Grenville, *Jews and Germans*, 131–3; Friedländer, *Nazi Germany and the Jews*, vol. 1, 135–55. Compare with Longerich, *Holocaust*, 52–61.

62 11 November 1935, *Phipps Diary*, 122.

63 W. E. B. DuBois articles from the *Pittsburgh Courier* in Lubrich ed., *Travels in the Reich*, 135–49.

64 *Jewish Responses*, vol. I, 179–81; Friedländer, *Nazi Germany and the Jews*, vol. 1, 162–3; Grenville, *Jews and Germans*, 139–40.

65 Statement of the Reichsvertretung, 22 September 1935, *Documents on the Holocaust*, 84–6; *Jewish Responses*, vol. I, 190–1.

66 Willy Cohn diary, 15, 19 September 1935, *Jewish Responses*, vol. I, 187–9.

67 Luise Solmitz diary, 15 September, 15 November 1935, *Jewish Responses*, vol. I, 185–6, 196–7.

68 Jürgen Matthäus, 'Evading Persecution. German Jewish Behaviour Patterns after 1933', in Nicosia and Scrase eds, *Jewish Life in Nazi Germany*, 47–70.

69 Doerry, *My Wounded Heart*, 68–72.

70 6 October 1935, *Klemperer Diaries*, I, 128; Leo Baeck, Prayer for the Eve of the Day of Atonement, 10 October 1935, *Documents on the Holocaust*, 87–8.

71 31 October 1935, *Klemperer Diaries*, I, 132; Bernard Kahn to AJJDC European Executive Council, 29 November 1935; Dr Karl Rosenthal to CV HQ, 26 September 1935; Yom Kippur precautions, 7 October 1935, *Jewish Responses*, vol. I, 199–200, 201, 217–18.

72 Werner Angress, *Between Fear and Hope. Jewish Youth in the Third Reich*, trans. Werner Angress and Christine Granger (New York: Columbia University Press, 1988), 43–59.

73 McDonald to James Rosenberg, 18 September 1935 and to Felix Warburg, 10 October 1935, *McDonald Diaries*, II, 29, 45; Bernard Kahn to AJJDC European Executive Council, 29 November 1935, *Jewish Responses*, vol. I, 217–18; Raymond Geist, 'The German Economic Situation with Particular Reference to the Political Outlook', 12 November 1935, *Fremde Blicke*, 442.

74 5, 12 February, 11 April 1935, *McDonald Diaries*, I, 617–18, 622.

75 30 December 1935, *McDonald Diaries*, I, 102–3.

76 31 July 1935, *McDonald Diaries*, I, 788–89; Bentwich, *They Found Refuge*, 28–9.

77 Bentwich, *They Found Refuge*, 30–3; *McDonald Diaries*, II, 110.

78 CV report on Situation in Pomerania, 6 November 1935, *Jewish Responses*, vol. I, 201–2; Stapostelle Government District Arnsberg, report for September 1935; Stapostelle Government District Cologne, September 1935 report, 18 October 1935; County Commissioner, Melsungen, September–October 1935 report, 24

October 1935; Stapostelle Government District Breslau, overview, 2 January 1936, *Secret Nazi Reports*, 153–4, 154–5, 171–2, 178.

79 Trier District Governor, report for April–May 1935, 6 June 1935; Stapostelle Police District Berlin, September report 1935; Stapostelle Government District Magdeburg, September 1935 report, 5 October 1935; Stapostelle Government District Minden, September report, 3 October 1935 and report for 8 November to 7 December 1935; Government District Minden, State Lippe and Hameln-Pyrmont, report for September 1935, *Secret Nazi Reports*, 128, 151–2, 155, 156–7, 159–60, 177–8.

80 Evans, *The Third Reich in Power*, 222–33, 234–53; Guenter Lewy, *The Catholic Church and Nazi Germany* (New York: DaCapo, 2000 edn), 151–6, 168–71; Ursula Büttner, 'The "Jewish Problem Becomes a Christian Problem". German Protestants and the Persecution of the Jews in the Third Reich', in Bankier ed., *Probing the Depths of German Antisemitism*, 431–59.

81 NSDAP District Directorate Eichstätt, May 1935; Stapostelle Government District Aachen, August report, 5 September 1935; Stapostelle Königsberg, October 1935, *Secret Nazi Reports*, 129, 144, 169.

82 District Governor Upper and Central Franconia, August 1935 report, 9 September 1935; County Commissioner Gelnhausen, July–August 1935 report, 31 July 1935, *Secret Nazi Reports*, 149, 151; Smallbones to B. C. Newton, 4 September 1935, *Fremde Blicke*, 431–2. Evans, *The Third Reich in Power*, 225–30; Susannah Heschel, *The Aryan Jesus. Christian Theology and the Bible in Nazi Germany* (Princeton: Princeton University Press, 2008), 26–66; Doris Bergen, *Twisted Cross: The German Christian Movement in the Third Reich* (Chapel Hill, NC: University of North Carolina Press, 1996).

83 Stapostelle Government District Trier, September report, 5 October 1935; NSDAP Main Office for Municipal Policy, 25 October 1935; Stapostelle Government District Magdeburg, report for November, 5 December 1935; Stapostelle Government District Breslau, overview, 2 January 1936; Stapostelle Police District Berlin, January 1936; Stapostelle Government District Arnberg, February 1936; Gestapa Baden, report February 1936, *Secret Nazi Reports*, 157, 158, 175, 178, 190–1, 195, 196.

84 County Commissioner Bad Kissingen, September report, 27 September 1935; SDHA Office Dept. II/112, 'The Situation of the Jews in Germany at the Moment', 13 September 1936, *Secret Nazi Reports*, 158–9, 213–14. Frank Bajohr, '*Aryanization' in Hamburg. The Economic Exclusion of Jews and the Confiscation of their Property in Nazi Germany* (New York: Berghahn, 2002), 43–88, 115–25, illustrates its patchiness and complexity.

85 Uwe Dietrich Adam quoted in *Jewish Responses*, vol. I, 179; Yahil, *The Holocaust*, 70; Karl A. Schleunes, *The Twisted Road to Auschwitz. Nazi Policy Towards German Jews 1933–1939* (Urbana: University of Illinois Press, 1990 edn), 126; Evans, *The Third Reich in Power*, 571–3.

86 *Jewish Responses* vol. I, 177–9; Wildt, *Volksgemeinschaft*, 215–18; Longerich, *Holocaust*, 61–7.

87 23 January 1936, *Shirer Diary*, 45; *Fromm Diary*, 194.

88 Grenville, *Jews and Germans*, 140; Stapostelle Government District Aachen, February report, 5 March 1936 and Stapostelle Police District Berlin, February report, 6 March 1936, *Secret Nazi Reports*, 193–5; 11 February 1936, *Klemperer Diaries*, I, 146.

89 28 October 1935, *McDonald Diaries*, I, 62–4; Smallbones to Newton, 4 September 1935, *Fremde Blicke*, 431–2; WJC report on 'The Situation of the Jews in Germany', January 1936, *Jewish Responses*, vol. I, 197–9.

90 *Jewish Responses*, vol. I, 216; Government District Koblenz, November report, 5 December 1935; Stapostelle Government District Hanover, December report, 6 January 1936; Stapostelle Government District Wiesbaden, 4 January 1936; Gendarmerie, Butzbach report, 27 February 1936, *Secret Nazi Reports*, 175–6, 180, 184, 200.

91 District Governor, Kassel, January–February report, 4 March 1936; County Commissioner in Mayen, March report, 28 March 1936; District Governor of Lower Bavaria and Upper Palatinate, June report, 7 July 1936; Gendarmerie, Gunzenhausen, March report, 31 March 1936; District Governor of the Palatinate, June report, 8 July 1936; Mayor of Haigerloch, 29 October 1937, *Secret Nazi Reports*, 200–1, 205–6, 208–9, 266.

92 CV Head Office to Reich Economic Ministry, 30 October 1935, *Jewish Responses*, vol. I, 203–5; 14 October 1935, *McDonald Diaries*, II, 48; Shepherd, *Wilfred Israel*, 106, 131–3.

93 Stapostelle Government District Cologne, August report, 3 September 1935, *Secret Nazi Reports*, 145. Barkai, *From Boycott to Annihilation*, 59–63.

94 François-Poncet, *Fateful Years*, 221. Eric Kurlander, *Living With Hitler. Liberal Democrats in the Third Reich* (London: Yale University Press, 2009), 8–9, 14–15, 60–5, 155; cf. Albert Fischer, 'The Ministry of Economics and the Expulsion of the Jews from the German Economy', in Bankier ed., *Probing the Depths of German Antisemitism*, 213–25.

95 5, 9 September 1935, *McDonald Diaries*, II, 20–1, 24–5; 27 November 1935, *Ambassador Dodd's Diary*, 287.

96 3 December 1935, *Phipps Diary*, 131–3. Bella Fromm shared this view of Schacht, *Fromm Diary*, 168–9.

97 Evans, *The Third Reich in Power*, 631–7. 8, 31 March 1936, *Klemperer Diaries*, I, 149, 151–2.

98 It is not mentioned in Gilbert, *Holocaust*, or Dwork and van Pelt, *Holocaust*; Yahil, *The Holocaust*, 90, notes its significance for 'economic policy toward the Jews'; Dawidowicz, *The War Against the Jews*, 127–8, treats it as a precursor to the expropriation of the Jews.

99 Evans, *The Third Reich in Power*, 351–7; Tooze, *The Wages of Destruction*, 71–86, 207–13, 214–29; Wiesen, *Creating the Nazi Marketplace*, 12–16.

100 Noakes and Pridham eds, *Nazism 1919–1945*, vol. 2, 281–7.

101 Longerich, *Holocaust*, 61–7; Friedländer, *Nazi Germany and the Jews*, vol. 1, 179–89.

102 Grenville, *Jews and Germans*, 141–7; 12 September 1936, *Ambassador Dodd's Diary*, 356–7; 22, 30 October 1935, *Phipps Diary*, 184–7.

103 Longerich, *Holocaust*, 90–4; Friedländer, *Nazi Germany and the Jews*, vol. 1, 194–203, 204–10; Evans, *The Third Reich in Power*, 524–35; Lewy, *The Nazi Persecution of the Gypsies*, 17–20, 24–35.

104 Longerich, *Himmler*, 204.

105 SDHA, II/112, Proposal for consultation between Heydrich and Reich Interior Ministry, 20 November 1936, *Secret Nazi Reports*, 219–20. Longerich, *Holocaust*, 90–4; Friedländer, *Nazi Germany and the Jews*, vol. 1, 194–203, 204–10.

106 Longerich, *Holocaust*, 64.

107 26 April 1936, Kurt Rosenberg diary, *Jewish Responses* vol. I, 261; 13, 16 August 1936, *Klemperer Diaries*, I, 174–5, 176.

108 14 September 1936, Mally Dienemann diary, *Jewish Responses*, vol. I, 263–4; 14 September, 8 December 1936, *Klemperer Diaries*, I, 182, 193.

109 Grenville, *Jews and Germans*, 148–9; *Jewish Responses*, vol. I, 259–60.

110 Report of Reichsvertretung meeting on 15 June 1937 and David Glick report to AJJDC, mid 1937, *Jewish Responses*, vol. I, 264–8; Nicosia, *Zionism and Anti-Semitism in Germany*, 181–206.

111 SDHA Dept. II/112, 'On the Jewish Problem', January 1937, *Secret Nazi Reports*, 227–33. Emphasis in original. Wildt, 'Before the "Final Solution"', 258–9, and *Judenpolitik*, 32–3.

112 Guidelines for SD Officers, 21 April 1937, Wildt, *Judenpolitik*, 110–15.

113 SDHA Dept. II/112 (1 January–31 March 1937), 8 April 1937, *Secret Nazi Reports*, 243–5.

114 SDHA Dept. II/112 (1–15 April 1937), 19 April 1937 and (15–30 April), 4 May 1937, *Secret Nazi Reports*, 243–5, 248–9; 17 March, 29 November 1937, *Ambassador Dodd's Diary*, 394–5, 439.

115 SDHA Dept . II/112, report for 1–15 July 1937 and 1–15 September 1937, 17 September 1937, *Secret Nazi Reports*, 256–9, 262. Wildt, 'Before the "Final Solution"', 255, and *Judenpolitik*, 34–5. Carole Fink, *Defending the Rights of Others. The Great Powers, the Jews and International Minority Protection* (Cambridge: Cambridge University Press, 2004), 278–9, 331, 334. J. W. Breughel, 'The Bernheim petition: A challenge to Nazi Germany in 1933', *Patterns of Prejudice*, 17:3 (1983), 17–25.

116 SDHA Dept. II/112, reports for 1–15 July, 1–15 August, 16–30 November 1937, *Secret Nazi Reports*, 256–61, 270–1.

117 Herbert Strauss, 'Jewish Emigration from Germany. Nazi Policies and Jewish Responses (II)', *Leo Baeck Institute Year Book*, 26 (1981), 343–8.

118 Nicosia, *Zionism and Anti-Semitism in Nazi Germany*, 123–6.

119 SDHA Dept. II/112, reports for 1–15 July, 1–15 August, 16–30 November 1937, *Secret Nazi Reports*, 256–61, 270–1. Cesarani, *Eichmann*, 53–6.

120 Willy Cohn diary, 27 June 1933, *Jewish Responses*, vol. I, 66–7.

121 Bavarian Political Police, October report, 1 November 1935; Stapostelle Government District Düsseldorf, October report, 6 November 1935; SD Main Office Dept. II/112 April–May report, 25 June 1936, *Secret Nazi Reports*, 161, 166–7, 206–7; Erich Sonnemann to Heinz Kellermann, n.d., *Jewish Responses*, vol. I, 228.

122 Willy Cohn diary, 26 March–3 May 1937, *Jewish Responses*, vol. I, 222, 230–2; 26
     January 1934, *McDonald Diaries*, I, 270. Nicosia, *Zionism and Anti-Semitism in
     Nazi Germany*, 208; Barkai, 'Self-Help in the Dilemma', 320–3.
123 *Jewish Responses*, vol. I, 222–4; Grenville, *Jews and Germans*, 115; Kaplan,
     Between Dignity and Despair, 62–73, on the family as well as the financial
     dilemmas of emigration.
124 Caron, *Uneasy Asylum*, 142–57.
125 Breitman and Lichtman, *FDR and the Jews*, 94–5; Zucker, *In Search of Refuge*,
     87–90.
126 SDHA II/112, report for 1–15 November, 18 November 1937, *Secret Nazi Reports*,
     268–9; *Jewish Responses*, vol. I, 234–5, 307–10.
127 District Governor Upper and Central Franconia, April report, 5 May 1937; SDHA
     II/112, report for 1–15 September, 17 September 1937, *Secret Nazi Reports*, 252,
     262. Barkai, *From Boycott to Annihilation*, 69–77.
128 Mayor, Bad Nauheim, August report, 27 August 1937; County Commissioner,
     Gelnhausen, situation report on the Jews, 30 November 1937; Gendarmerie,
     Cham, November report, 28 November 1937; Stapostelle, Munich, Dept. II 2 A,
     October report, 1 November 1937, *Secret Nazi Reports*, 261–2, 264, 271–2. SD
     Upper Division East, Dept II/112 Annual Report for 1937, 8 January 1938; SD
     Upper Division Southeast Dept II/112, Annual Report for 1937, 14 January 1938;
     SD Upper Division Northwest, Dept II/112, Annual Situation Report for 1937, 14
     January 1938; SD Upper Division South, Annual Report for 1937, *Secret Nazi
     Reports*, 273–8.
129 SDHA Central Dept. II/1, Situation report, 1–31 January 1938, *Secret Nazi
     Reports*, 282–5; François-Poncet, *Fateful Years*, 221. Evans, *The Third Reich in
     Power*, 358–61; Bajohr, 'Aryanization' in Hamburg*, 174–7.
130 SDHA Dept. II/112, 'Short report for "C" on Jewry', 12 November 1937, *Secret
     Nazi Reports*, 267–8.
131 SDHA Central Dept. II/1, Situation Report, 1–31 January 1938; SD Upper
     Division Northwest, Dept II/112, Annual Situation Report for 1937, 14 January
     1938; SD Main Office, II/112, report for February 1938, 4 March 1938, *Secret Nazi
     Reports*, 273–4, 282–5, 286–8.
132 J. Webb Benton, US consul, 'The Church Question in Bremen and Oldenburg', 14
     April 1937, *Fremde Blicke*, 469–70. Lewy, *The Catholic Church and Nazi Germany*,
     156–9; Georges Passelecq and Bernard Suchecky, *The Hidden Encyclical of Pius
     XI*, trans. Steven Rendall (New York: Harcourt Brace, 1997), 100–10.
133 10, 17 April, 23 June, 29 December 1937, *Ambassador Dodd's Diary*, 402, 405,
     425, 449–50.
134 SDHA Dept. II/112, 'Jews in Danzig', 16 June 1937, *Secret Nazi Reports*, 254–5.
135 18 October 1936, 13 July 1937, *Klemperer Diaries*, I, 190, 220.
136 17 August, 27 October 1937, 23 February 1938, *Klemperer Diaries*, I, 224, 229–30,
     240–1.
137 Heinemann Stern in *Germans No More*, 77–9.
138 Ibid, 99–102.
139 Mayor's report, Amt Altenrüthen, 22 May 1937, *Secret Nazi Reports*, 253.

140 Marion Kaplan, 'Changing Roles in Jewish Families', in Nicosia and Scrase eds, *Jewish Life in Nazi Germany*, 15–25.

141 Gerta Pfeffer in *Germans No More*, 65–7; Kaplan, 'Changing Roles in Jewish Families', 20.

142 Robert Gellately, *The Gestapo and German Society. Enforcing Racial Policy 1933–1945* (Oxford: Clarendon Press, 1990), 160–4. Hans Kosterlitz in *Germans No More*, 74–6.

143 Stapostelle Government District Breslau, overview, 2 January 1936; District Office Bad Brückenau, 'Surveillance of Jews in Bad Brückenau', 9 October 1936; Chief Public Prosecutor Mannheim, Report for November and December 1936, 21 January 1957; State Public Prosecutor Karlsruhe, bi-monthly situation report, 30 October 1939, *Secret Nazi Reports*, 178, 217, 225, 331.

Three – Pogrom: 1938–1939

1 31 January, 23 February 1938, *Klemperer Diaries*, I, 239, 241.

2 Evans, *The Third Reich in Power*, 359–60.

3 The full protocol is in J. Noakes and G. Pridham eds, *Nazism 1919–1945. A Documentary Reader*, vol. 3, *Foreign Policy, War and Racial Extermination* (Exeter: University of Exeter Press, 1997 edn), 680–7.

4 François-Poncet, *Fateful Years*, 226–7; Evans, *The Third Reich in Power*, 642–5.

5 G. E. R. Gedye, *Fallen Bastions* (London: Gollancz, 1939), 224–77, 281–99; Evans, *The Third Reich in Power*, 646–52.

6 Carl Zuckmayer's 1966 memoir, *Als wär's ein Stück von mir*, cited in Hans Safrian, *Eichmann's Men*, trans. Ute Stargardt (New York: Cambridge University Press, 2010), 20.

7 Doron Rabinovici, *Eichmann's Jews. The Jewish Administration of Holocaust Vienna, 1938–1945*, trans. Nick Somers (London: Polity, 2011), 17–25.

8 Gedye, *Fallen Bastions*, 296–304; 19 March 1938, *Shirer Diary*, 100.

9 27 September 1938, *Ruth Maier's Diary. A Young Girl's Life under Nazism*, ed. Jan Erik Vold, trans. Jamie Bullock (London: Harvill Secker, 2009), 89–90; Gedye, *Fallen Bastions*, 308.

10 Gedye, *Fallen Bastions*, 309–10, 354–6. Friedländer, *Nazi Germany and the Jews*, vol. 1, 240–7.

11 Graml, *Anti-Semitism in the Third Reich*, 134–6, depicts the violence that accompanied the Anschluss and the increasing persecution of Jews in the Old Reich in early 1938 as 'parallel'; compare to Hans Safrian, 'Expediting Expropriation and Expulsion. The Impact of the "Vienna Model" on anti-Jewish policies in Nazi Germany, 1938', *HGS*, 14:3 (2000), 390–414.

12 Mark Mazower, *Hitler's Empire. Nazi Rule in Occupied Europe* (London: Allen Lane, 2008), 47–9; Evans, *The Third Reich in Power*, 646–57.

13 Longerich, *Himmler*, 403–4; Safrian, *Eichmann's Men*, 19–24.

14 22, 25 March 1938, *Shirer Diary*, 110–11; Gedye, *Fallen Bastions*, 307, 309–10.

15 SDHA Dept. II/112, report for January–March 1938, *Secret Nazi Reports*, 292–3;

Wildt, 'Before the "Final Solution"', 263–4 and *Judenpolitik*, 52–5; Leo Lauterbach to Executive of the WZO, 29 April 1938, *Documents on the Holocaust*, 92. Rabinovici, *Eichmann's Jews*, 34–6.

16 Rabinovici, *Eichmann's Jews*, 34–6, 40–6; Cesarani, *Eichmann*, 61–5.

17 Evans, *The Third Reich in Power*, 647; Safrian, 'Expediting Expropriation and Expulsion', 390–4.

18 Safrian, 'Expediting Expropriation and Expulsion', 392–4.

19 Martin Dean, *Robbing the Jews. The Confiscation of Jewish Property in the Holocaust, 1933–1945* (New York: Cambridge University Press, 2008), 108–11.

20 Safrian, 'Expediting Expropriation and Expulsion', 392–4; compare, Götz Aly and Susanne Heim, *Architects of Annihilation. Auschwitz and the Logic of Destruction*, trans. A. G. Blunden (London: Weidenfeld and Nicolson, 2002), 16–23.

21 Rabinovici, *Eichmann's Jews*, 28–30, 46–7.

22 Ibid, 48–50.

23 Ibid, 50–2; cf. Safrian, *Eichmann's Men*, 31.

24 Safrian, *Eichmann's Men*, 31–4.

25 Margarete Neff-Jerome and Philip Flesch memoirs in *Jewish Responses*, vol. I, 279–81, 285–6; Zuckerman to Goldmann, 5 April 1938 and anonymous report (document 10-7), June 1938, in *Jewish Responses*, vol. I, 278, 282–5.

26 Gedye, *Fallen Bastions*, 305; JTA report, June 1938, *Jewish Responses*, vol. I, 285 for the estimated number of suicides.

27 12 March 1938, *Shirer Diary*, 104.

28 London, *Whitehall and the Jews*, 58–68, 72–8.

29 Caron, *Uneasy Asylum*, 117–41, 142–7, 171–80.

30 Breitman and Lichtman, *FDR and the Jews*, 101–2; Zucker, *In Search of Refuge*, 173–5.

31 *McDonald Diaries*, II, 122–3, 124; Arad, *America, its Jews and the rise of Nazism*, 195–7.

32 *McDonald Diaries*, II, 121. David Wyman, *Paper Walls. America and the Refugee Crisis 1938–1941* (New York: Pantheon, 1995), 47–9.

33 Fest, *Not Me*, 76.

34 14 March 1938, Willy Cohn diary, *Jewish Responses*, vol. I, 277–8; 20, 30 March, 5 April 1938, *Klemperer Diaries*, I, 241–2.

35 Schleunes, *Twisted Road*, 218.

36 27 April 1938, Luise Solmitz diary, *Jewish Responses*, vol. I, 291; 29 June 1938, *Klemperer Diaries*, I, 249; Ascher, *A Community under Siege*, 128–34.

37 SDHA, Dept. II/112, July 1938 report, *Secret Nazi Reports*, 319–21; Bajohr, 'Aryanization' in Hamburg, 185–221 on the stampede in Hamburg and the fate of M. M. Warburg.

38 Barkai, *From Boycott to Annihilation*, 121–4, 125–6, 128. For the fashion industry, see Guenther, *Nazi Chic? Fashioning Women in the Third Reich*, 158–65.

39 SDHA, Dept. II/112, March 1938 report, *Secret Nazi Reports*, 291–3; Barkai, *From Boycott to Annihilation*, 121–3; Friedländer, *Nazi Germany and the Jews*, vol. 1, 260–5.

40 Barkai, *From Boycott to Annihilation*, 117; *Jewish Responses*, vol. I, 292.

41 District Governor of Upper and Central Franconia, February 1938 report, 9 March 1938; NSDAP District Leadership Königshofen-Hofheim, 'Report on the Prevailing Mood', 2 May and 30 May 1938; *Secret Nazi Reports*, 288, 299, 306.

42 CV Regional Office, Württemberg to CV HQ, 1 June 1938, *Jewish Responses*, vol. I, 295–6; District Governor of Lower Franconia and Aschaffenburg, March 1938 report, 9 April 1938; District Governor Palatinate, April 1938 report, 10 May 1938; Gendarmerie Hösbach, 'Events in Goldbach, Special Operations Against Jews', 19 April 1938; District Governor of Lower Bavaria and Upper Palatinate, July 1938 report, 8 August 1938, *Secret Nazi Reports*, 294–5, 296–7, 298–9, 324.

43 SDHA, Dept. II/112, April–May report, May 1938, *Secret Nazi Reports*, 300–2.

44 Evans, *The Third Reich in Power*, 576–7; Wachsmann, *KL*, 139–51.

45 Wünschmann, *Before Auschwitz*, 184–96.

46 Ibid, 168–84.

47 Hugh R. Wilson, 'Demonstrations Against Jewish Shops', 22 June 1938, *Fremde Blicke*, 484; SDHA, Dept. II/112, report, 1 July 1938, *Secret Nazi Reports*, 306–7.

48 28 June 1938, *Fromm Diary*, 235–7.

49 Longerich, *Holocaust*, 102–5.

50 Breitman and Lichtman, *FDR and the Jews*, 102–9; Caron, *Uneasy Asylum*, 182–6.

51 London, *Whitehall and the Jews*, 82–92; *McDonald Diaries*, II, 136, 139–40; 7 July 1938, *Shirer Diary*, 120.

52 Marrus, *The Unwanted*, 170–4.

53 SDHA, Dept. II/112, report, 1–31 August, 8 September 1938, *Secret Nazi Reports*, 325–7; Friedländer, *Nazi Germany and the Jews*, vol. 1, 262–3.

54 Aristotle Kallis, *Genocide and Fascism. The Eliminationist Drive in Fascist Europe* (London: Routledge, 2009), 87–138.

55 Radu Ioanid, *The Holocaust in Romania. The Destruction of Jews and Gypsies under the Antonescu Regime, 1940–1944* (Chicago: Ivan R. Dee, 2000), xix–xx, 5–19; Jean Ancel, *The Economic Destruction of Romanian Jewry* (Jerusalem: Yad Vashem, 2007), 9–12.

56 Ancel, *The Economic Destruction of Romanian Jewry*, 33–50.

57 14, 17, 25 January 1938, Emil Dorian, *The Quality of Witness. A Romanian Diary 1837–1944*, ed. Marguerite Doria, trans. Mara Soceanu Vamos (Philadelphia: Jewish Publication Society of America, 1992), 13–19.

58 Nathaniel Katzburg, *Hungary and the Jews 1920–1943* (Ramat Gan: Bar Ilan University Press, 1981), 25–31.

59 Katzburg, *Hungary and the Jews*, 32–43. Zoltan Vagi, Laszlo Csosz and Gabor Kadar eds, *The Holocaust in Hungary. Evolution of a Genocide* (Lanham MD: AltaMira Press, 2013), xxx–xxxviii, 1–2.

60 Katzburg, *Hungary and the Jews*, 80–93.

61 Vagi, Csosz and Kadar eds, *The Holocaust in Hungary*, 3–6.

62 Ibid, 6–9; Katzburg, *Hungary and the Jews*, 114–38; Moshe Herczl, *Christianity and the Holocaust of Hungarian Jewry*, trans. Joel Lerner (New York: New York Universaity Press, 1991), 11–127; Yehuda Don, 'Economic Implications of the Anti-Jewish Legislation', in David Cesarani ed., *Genocide and Rescue. The Holocaust in Hungary 1944* (Oxford: Berg, 1997), 47–76.

63 Michele Sarfatti, *The Jews in Mussolini's Italy. From Equality to Persecution*, trans. John and Anne C. Tedeschi (Madison: University of Wisconsin Press, 2006), 3–41, 66–7, 116–17.

64 David Kertzer, *The Popes Against the Jews. The Vatican's Role in the Rise of Modern Anti-Semitism* (New York: Knopf, 2001), 133–65, 213–36; Sarfatti, *The Jews in Mussolini's Italy*, 42–53; Meir Michaelis, *Mussolini and the Jews. German-Italian Relations and the Jewish Question in Italy 1922–1945* (Oxford: Oxford University Press, 1971), 10–52; 15 May 1934, *McDonald Diaries*, I, 393–4.

65 Sarfatti, *The Jews in Mussolini's Italy*, 96–121; Michaelis, *Mussolini and the Jews*, 80–103, 107–52, attributes the official adoption of anti-Semitism to coordination with Nazi Germany.

66 6 September, 3 December 1937 and 20 April 1938, Count Galeazzo Ciano, *Diary 1937–1943. The complete unabridged diaries of Count Galeazzo Ciano, Italian Minister of Foreign Affairs, 1936–1943*, ed. and trans. Robert L. Miller and Stanislaus Pugliese (London: Phoenix Press, 2002), 6, 32, 83.

67 15, 17 July 1938, *Ciano Diary*, 109–110; Sarfatti, *The Jews in Mussolini's Italy*, 121–9.

68 20 April, 4 June 1938, *Ciano Diary*, 83, 99; Michele Sarfatti, 'Characteristics and Objectives of the Anti-Jewish Racial Laws in Fascist Italy, 1938–1943', in Joshua D. Zimmerman ed., *Jews in Italy under Fascist and Nazi Rule, 1922–1945* (New York: Cambridge University Press, 2005), 71–80.

69 6 October, 6, 28 November 1938, *Ciano Diary*, 139, 153, 161; Sarfatti, *The Jews in Mussolini's Italy*, 129–57.

70 Breitman and Lichtman, *FDR and the Jews*, 143–4; Iael Nidam-Orvieto, 'The Impact of the Anti-Jewish Legislation on Everyday Life and the Response of Italian Jews, 1938–1943', in Zimmerman ed., *Jews in Italy under Fascist and Nazi Rule, 1922–1945*, 158–81.

71 Evans, *The Third Reich in Power*, 665–73.

72 28 June 1938, *Fromm Diary*, 237; 5 October 1938, *Ruth Maier's Diary*, 96.

73 *Jewish Responses*, vol. I, 328; 18, 20 June 1938, *Fromm Diary*, 239–40.

74 24 August 1938, *Klemperer Diaries*, I, 255; 24, 25 August 1938, Luise Solmitz diary, *Jewish Responses*, vol. I, 329–30; François-Poncet, 'Report on The Persecution of the Jews', 9 August 1938, *Fremde Blicke*, 486–7.

75 SD Lower Division, Wiesbaden, 30 September 1938; SDHA, Dept. II/112, September report, 8 October 1938, *Secret Nazi Reports*, 330.

76 SD District Office, Hanau, Dept. II/112, 23, 27 May 1938; SDHA, Dept. II 1, extract from daily information, 5 August 1938; District Governor of Upper and Central Franconia, August report, 7 September 1938; District Governor Palatinate, August 1938 report, 12 September 1938; District Governor Main Franconia, September 1938 report, 10 October 1938; District Governor Palatinate, October 1938 report, 9 November 1938, *Secret Nazi Reports*, 303–4, 322, 323–4, 331–2, 338–9.

77 Evans, *The Third Reich in Power*, 673–7.

78 'Taking Stock after Munich', 8 October 1938 and 'On the Record', 29 October

1938, in Schwarzschild, *Chronicle of a Downfall*, 177–8. Kershaw, *Hitler 1936–1945. Nemesis* (London: Allen Lane, 2000), 123–5.

79 2 October 1938, *Klemperer Diaries*, I, 257–8.

80 Geist to Messersmith, 28 October 1938, *McDonald Diaries*, II, 143–4.

81 12 July 1938, *Klemperer Diaries*, I, 250.

82 5 October 1938, *Ruth Maier's Diary*, 95–8.

83 16 October 1938, *Ruth Maier's Diary*, 98–9. Longerich, *Holocaust*, 108.

84 Noakes and Pridham eds, *Nazism 1919–1945*, 1997 edn., vol. 3, 113–14.

85 Fritzsche, *Life and Death in the Third Reich*; Kühne, *Belonging and Genocide*.

86 SDHA, Dept. II/112, October report, 1 November 1938, *Secret Nazi Reports*, 334–5, 335–6. Longerich, *Holocaust*, 109–10; Alan Steinweis, *Kristallnacht 1938* (Cambridge MA: Harvard University Press, 2009), 16–17.

87 *Jewish Responses*, vol. I, 345–7. Broniatowski eventually managed to emigrate to the USA where he joined his sons.

88 Mally Dienemann diary, 1 November 1938, *Jewish Responses*, vol. I, 343–4; Yfat Weiss, 'The "Emigration Effort" or "Repatriation"', in Bankier ed., *Probing the Depths of German Antisemitism*, 360–70.

89 Polish consuls in Germany immediately alerted their Foreign Office to the deportations. Feliks Chiczewiski warned that the Germans were seeking the 'total destruction' of the Jews in Germany: Chiczewiski to Polish Foreign Ministry, 26 October 1938, *Fremde Blick*, 495; AJJDC report, 18 November 1938, *Jewish Responses*, vol. I, 348–9.

90 Steinweis, *Kristallnacht*, 17–18. It is possible that Grynszpan was actually seeking out Rath, with whom he may have had a homosexual relationship.

91 Steinweis, *Kristallnacht*, 21–2, 27–8, 38–9; Longerich, *Goebbels*, 391–400.

92 Friedländer, *Nazi Germany and the Jews*, vol. 1, 269–71.

93 Steinweis, *Kristallnacht*, 39–43.

94 Friedländer, *Nazi Germany and the Jews*, vol. 1, 27–8; Steinweis, *Kristallnacht*, 59–71; Uwe Dietrich Adam, 'How Spontaneous was the Pogrom?', in Walter Pehle ed., *November 1938*, trans. William Templer (Oxford: Berg, 1991), 73–94. Compare Kulka and Jaeckel, 'Introduction', *Secret Nazi Reports*, liii–lvii and Longerich, *Holocaust*, 109–13, which depict the events as more purposeful, a continuity of previous Judenpolitik. Graml, *Anti-Semitism in the Third Reich*, 5–29.

95 Uwe Dietrich Adam, 'How Spontaneous was the Pogrom?', in Pehle ed., *November 1938*, 73–80; Steinweis, *Kristallnacht*, 48–53; Grenville, *The Jews and Germans*, 172–4.

96 Dawidowicz, *The War Against the Jews*, 136–7; Gilbert, *Holocaust*, 69–73, gives no explanation of how, as against why, the pogrom occurred. Compare the still serviceable account by Lionel Kochan, *Pogrom. November 10, 1938* (London: André Deutsch, 1957) and Graml, *Anti-Semitism in the Third Reich*, 6–29.

97 Steinweis, *Kristallnacht*, 77–8, drawing on testimonies given to the Central Information Office (Wiener Library); Merecki testimony in Uta Gerhardt and Thomas Karlauf eds, *The Night of Broken Glass. Eyewitness Accounts of Kristallnacht*, trans. Robert Simmons and Nick Somers (London: Polity, 2012),

36–52. See Confino, *World Without Jews*, 114–27, for the attack on Judaism.

98 Steinweis, *Kristallnacht*, 74–6, 78; District Governor of Lower Bavaria and Upper Palatinate, November 1938 report, 8 December 1938, *Secret Nazi Reports*, 366–7.

99 Steinweis, *Kristallnacht*, 78–82; Gestapo Office Dept. II/B2, Bielefeld, 'Protest Operation Against Jews on 10 November 1938', 26 November 1938; District Officer, Garmisch-Partenkirchen, 'Actions Against the Jews', 10 November 1938, *Secret Nazi Reports*, 358–60, 377.

100 Gestapo Office Dept. II/B2, Bielefeld, report, 26 November 1938; Chief Public Prosecutor, Mossbach, report, 24 November 1938, *Secret Nazi Reports*, 358, 384. Kaplan, *Between Dignity and Despair*, 122–5. This is one reason for dispensing with the term Kristallnacht or Night of Broken Glass usually employed to name the events of 9–10 November.

101 Steinweis, *Kristallnacht*, 117–18; Rabinovici, *Eichmann's Jews*, 58.

102 Friedländer, *Nazi Germany and the Jews*, vol. 1, 278–9; Steinweis, *Kristallnacht*, 114–18.

103 Steinweis, *Kristallnacht*, 64–7.

104 Ibid, 63–71.

105 Thomas Karlauf, 'Introduction' in *The Night of Broken Glass*, 11–13, and testimony of Hugo Moses, 19; *Jewish Responses*, vol. I, 331–6.

106 Rudolf Bing testimony in *The Night of Broken Glass*, 58–62.

107 Ibid, Hugo Moses testimony in ibid, 19–34.

108 10–12 November 1938, Luise Solmitz diary, *Jewish Responses*, vol. I, 352–3.

109 Toni Lessler memoir, *Jewish Responses*, vol. I, 354–5.

110 Rabinovici, *Eichmann's Jews*, 57–9; Siegfried Merecki testimony in *The Night of Broken Glass*, 36–52.

111 11, 13 November 1938, *Ruth Maier's Diary*, 99, 102–4.

112 Cesarani, *Eichmann*, 71; SDHA, II/1 report for 1938, *Secret Nazi Reports*, 425–6.

113 Steinweis, *Kristallnacht*, 99–101.

114 Ibid, 103, 127–30; Herbert Obenhaus, 'The Germans: An Antisemitic People. The press campaign after 9 November 1938', in Bankier ed., *Probing the Depths of German Antisemitism*, 147–80.

115 Circular received by the Bielefeld Gestapo Office Dept. II/B2, 14 November 1938, *Secret Nazi Reports*, 343–8.

116 Minden city, report for 10 November 1938, 18 November and Minden District Governor, 5 December 1938; Lemgo, Mayor's report on 'The Operation Against the Jews', 17 November 1938; Amt Borgentreich, Mayor's report on 'Operation Against the Jews on 10 November 1938', 17 November 1938; Atteln, Mayor's report, 17 November 1938; *Secret Nazi Reports*, 353 and 365, 356, 357–8, 368.

117 County Commissioner, Halle in Westphalia, report on 'Operation Against Jews', 18 November 1938; Bielefeld, Lord Mayor's report on 'Action Against the Jews on 9/10 November 1938', 22 November 1938, *Secret Nazi Reports*, 348–50, 350–2.

118 Bielefeld County Commissioner report on 'Operation Against the Jews on 10 November 1938', 18 November 1938; Bielefeld Stapostelle Dept. II/B2, 'Protest Operation Against Jews on 10 November 1938', 26 November 1938, *Secret Nazi Reports*, 356, 358–60.

119 SD District Officer Kochem, November report, 25 November 1938; Muggendorf
    Gendarmerie, situation report, 26 November 1938, *Secret Nazi Reports*, 361–2,
    385.

120 Edwin C. Kemp, US consul, 'Anti-Jewish Demonstration in Bremen', 10 November
    1938; Samuel W. Honaker, US consul general, Stuttgart, 'Anti-Semitic Persecution
    in the Stuttgart Consular District, 12 November 1938; Hugh R. Wilson, 'Pogrom
    in Berlin and Reich and Popular Reaction', 16 November 1938, *Fremde Blicke*,
    498, 504–5, 515.

121 British consul, Frankfurt-am-Main, 16 November 1938; Smallbones to Ogilvie-
    Forbes, 'Report on the Mistreatment of imprisoned Jews in the
    Konzentrationslager during the Nazi pogrom', 24 December 1938, *Fremde Blicke*,
    515–16, 523–4.

122 County Commissioner, Bielefeld, report on 'Operation Against the Jews on 10
    November 1938', 18 November 1938; Mayor of Amt Neuhaus, report on
    'Operation Against Jews on 10 November 1938', 17 November 1938; County
    Commissioner Höxter, 'Operation Against the Jews', 18 November 1938;
    Lippspringe, mayor's report on 'Operation Against Jews', 17 November 1938;
    County Commissioner, Paderborn, report on 'Operation Against the Jews on 10
    November 1938', 23 November 1938, *Secret Nazi Reports*, 352, 354, 355, 356, 363,
    371. See also, Kochem SD District Officer, November report, 25 November 1938;
    SD Upper Division West, Dept. II/112 Annual report for 1938; on arrest of clergy
    see District Governor, Upper and Central Franconia, report for November 1938,
    8 December 1938 and Muggendorf Gendarmerie monthly report, 26 December
    1938, 361–2, 366–7, 396–7, 408–10.

123 SD District Office, Gotha, report for October–December 1938; District Office
    Ebermannstadt, report for November 1938, 2 December 1938; District Court
    President, Trier, report for October–December 1938, *Secret Nazi Reports*, 373–6,
    386–7, 387–8.

124 County Commissioner, Halle in Westphalia, report on 'Operation Against Jews',
    18 November 1938, *Secret Nazi Reports*, 350–2. Steinweis, *Kristallnacht*, 82–5.
    Information on Baden-Baden from http://www.yadvashem.org/yv/en/exhibitions/
    kristallnacht/baden.asp

125 SDHA, Dept. II/112, November report, 7 December 1938; also NSDAP Main
    Office for Training, 18 January 1939 and SD Upper Division, North, Dept. II/112,
    report for 1938, 20 January 1939, *Secret Nazi Reports*, 340–3, 368–9, 417–19.

126 25 November, 20 December 1938, Ulrich von Hassell, *The Von Hassell Diaries
    1938–1944*, ed. Hugh Gibson (London: Hamish Hamilton, 1948), 20–1, 25.

127 Karl Fuchs to his parents, 23 November 1938 in Horst Fuchs Richardson ed. and
    trans., *Your Loyal and Loving Son. The Letters of Tank Gunner Karl Fuchs, 1937–
    1941* (Washington DC: Brassey's, 2003), 36.

128 Maschmann, *Account Rendered*, 51–2.

129 Steinweis, *Kristallnacht*, 107–8; Grenville, *The Jews and Germans*, 378–9. Philipp
    Flesch memoir, *Jewish Responses*, vol. I, 355–6.

130 Paul Martin Neurath, *The Society of Terror. Inside the Dachau and Buchenwald
    Concentration Camps* (Boulder, CO: Paradigm, 2005), 123–5, 249–55.

131 Wünschmann, *Before Auschwitz*, 196–208.

132 Steinweis, *Kristallnacht*, 112–14.

133 Karl Schwabe testimony in *The Night of Broken Glass*, 95–109.

134 Hans Reichmann memoir, *Jewish Responses*, vol. I, 359–63.

135 Hertha Nathorff testimony in *The Night of Broken Glass*, 148–64.

136 Mally Dienemann memoir in *Jewish Responses*, vol. I, 363–6. Kaplan, *Between Dignity and Despair*, 129–31, 133–8.

137 SDHA II/1, report for 1938, *Secret Nazi Reports*, 419–31.

138 Steinweis, *Kristallnacht*, 103–7.

139 The only easily available printed sources for the conference are severely truncated and quite unrepresentative of the content or tone of the gathering: Noakes and Pridham eds, *Nazism 1919–1945*, vol. 2, 558–60, 566 and *Documents on the Holocaust*, 108–15. For the full protocol (only part of which survived) see 'Stenographic Report of the Conference on the Jewish Question at the Aviation Ministry on 12 November 1938; suppression of Jews from the German economy; seizure of insurance payments for the losses sustained by Jews on 10 November and other anti-Jewish measures', http://germanhistorydocs.ghi-dc.org/pdf/eng/English34.pdf

140 For this and subsequent paragraphs, see 'Stenographic Report of the Conference on the Jewish Question at the Aviation Ministry on 12 November 1938'.

141 The important, and usually overlooked, ramifications of the insurance question are lucidly set out in Gerald D. Feldman, *Allianz and the German Insurance Business, 1933–1945* (Cambridge: Cambridge University Press, 2001), 190–205.

142 Feldman, *Allianz*, 205–28.

143 For this and subsequent paragraphs, see 'Stenographic Report of the Conference on the Jewish Question at the Aviation Ministry on 12 November 1938'.

144 On Madagascar, see Caron, *Uneasy Asylum*, 146–57, 220–2.

145 Jonny Moser, 'Depriving Jews of their Legal Rights in the Third Reich', in Pehle ed., *November 1938*, 123–38; Wolf Gruner, 'Public Welfare and the German Jews' and Uwe Lohalm, 'Local Administration and Nazi Anti-Jewish Policy', in Bankier ed., *Probing the Depths of Antisemitism*, 78–105, 109–46.

146 Dean, *Robbing the Jews*, 116, 119–20; Safrian, 'Expediting Expropriation and Expulsion', 390–414.

147 Special Report by the Mayor of Berlin, 5 January 1939, *Secret Nazi Reports*, 403–5; Evans, *The Third Reich In Power*, 595–7.

148 Dean, *Robbing the Jews*, 126–7, 135–6; Ascher, *A Community under Siege*, 178–9.

149 Wolf Gruner, *Jewish Forced Labour Under the Nazis. Economic Needs and Racial Aims, 1938–1944*, trans. Kathleen Dell'Orto (New York: Cambridge University Press, 2006), 5–8.

150 NSDAP Reich Directorate Main Office for Municipal Policy, 15 January 1939, *Secret Nazi Reports*, 367; Moser, 'Depriving Jews of their Legal Rights', 131.

151 Dean, *Robbing the Jews*, 135–6.

152 Friedländer, *Nazi Germany and the Jews*, vol. 1, 286–90; Grenville, *The Jews and Germans*, 182–3.

153 Safrian, *Eichmann's Men*, 36–8; Beate Meyer, 'Between Self-Assurance and Forced

Collaboration. The Reich Association of Jews in Germany, 1939–1945', in Nicosia and Scrase eds, *Jewish Life in Nazi Germany*, 149–69.

154 Kushner, *The Holocaust and the Liberal Imagination* (Oxford: Blackwell, 1994), 48–56; London, *Whitehall and the Jews*, 105–6.

155 Susan Cohen, *Rescue the Perishing. Eleanor Rathbone and the Refugees* (London: Vallentine Mitchell, 2010), 101–119; A. J. Sherman, *Island Refuge. Britain and Refugees from the Third Reich, 1933–1939* (Ilford: Cass, 1994), 170–83.

156 London, *Whitehall and the Jews*, 99–101.

157 Sherman, *Island Refuge*, 183–5; London, *Whitehall and the Jews*, 108–11, 114–16; Shepherd, *Wilfred Israel*, 125–31, 145, 146–9.

158 Deborah E. Lipstadt, *Beyond Belief. The American Press and the Coming of the Holocaust, 1933–1945* (New York: Free Press, 1986), 98–109; Breitman and Lichtman, *FDR and the Jews*, 113–15.

159 Zucker, *In Search of Refuge*, 71, 125–8; Moffat diary, 29, 30 October, cited in *McDonald Diaries*, II, 145 and 146–7.

160 Wyman, *Paper Walls*, 75–98.

161 Caron, *Uneasy Asylum*, 195–200, 202–3.

162 'A Model', 12, 19, November 1938, in Schwarzschild, *Chronicle of a Downfall*, 186–94.

163 25, 27 November, 15 December 1939, *Klemperer Diaries*, I, 261–3, 268–71.

164 Heinz Hesdörffer, *Twelve Years of Nazi Terror* (Pittsburgh: Rose Dog Books, 2008), 1–5, 11–15.

165 Caron, *Uneasy Asylum*, 164–5, 174–7.

166 Ernest G. Heppner, *Shanghai Refuge. A Memoir of the World War II Jewish Ghetto* (Lincoln: University of Nebraska Press, 1993), 3–18, 28–32.

167 Rabinovici, *Eichmann's Jews*, 63–5, 82–5; Ehud Avriel, *Open the Gates! A Personal Story of 'Illegal' Immigration to Israel* (New York: Atheneum, 1975), 39–100.

168 3, 27 November, 9, 11 December 1938, 30 January, 1 February 1939, *Ruth Maier's Diary*, 100–1, 106–7, 110–14, 123, 126–7.

169 Bentwich, *They Found Refuge*, 65–72.

170 London, *Whitehall and the Jews*, 111–28.

171 David Cesarani, 'Introduction' in Mark Jonathan Harris and Deborah Oppenheimer eds, *Into the Arms of Strangers. Stories of the Kindertransport* (London: Bloomsbury, 2000), 1–16.

172 Shepherd, *Wilfred Israel*, 146–9; Harris and Oppenheimer eds, *Into the Arms of Strangers*, 77–8, 99, 112–13, 119–22; Vera Gissing, *Pearls of Childhood* (London: Robson Books, 1988), 100–1; W. R. Chadwick, *The Rescue of the Prague Refugees 1938/39* (Padstow: Troubador Publishing, 2010), 44–5; David Kranzler, *Holocaust Hero. Solomon Schonfeld* (Jersey City, NJ: Ktav, 2004), 50–7, 58–61.

173 Excerpts from Hitler's Speech to the First Greater German Reichstag, 30 January 1939, http://germanhistorydocs.ghi-dc.org/sub_document.cfm?document_id=2289

174 5, 24 February 1939, *Klemperer Diaries*, I, 281–2. Hans Mommsen, 'Hitler's Reichstag Speech, 30 January 1939', *History and Memory* 9:1/2 (1997), 142–61;

compare to Friedländer, *Nazi Germany and the Jews*, vol. 1, 307–14, who reads the speech as a prophecy of extermination.

175 Evans, *The Third Reich in Power*, 599, estimates 269,000 in December 1938 falling to 188,000 in May and 164,000 in September 1939. Discrepancies arise because the German authorities included part-Jews, roughly 25,000 foreign Jews and 20,000 Jewish converts to Christianity; compare to Avraham Barkai, 'Exclusion and Persecution: 1933–1938' in Meyer ed., *Renewal and Destruction*, 231–4. SD Upper Division Elbe II/112 report for 1938, 18 January 1939; for churchmen who persisted in associating with or defending Jews, SD District Office, Knochen, report for January 1939, 24 January 1939, and District Governor Upper and Central Franconia, February report, 7 March 1939, *Secret Nazi Reports*, 410–16, 441–2, 445–6. Friedländer, *Nazi Germany and the Jews*, vol. 1, 316–17.

176 NSDAP Cell, Herne, 'Report on the Prevailing Mood', 13 March 1939, *Secret Nazi Reports*, 448–9. Also, SDHA, Dept. II/112, report for June 1939, 8 July 1939 and District Governor Palatinate, report for July, 10 August 1939, *Secret Nazi Reports*, 458, 464.

177 SDHA, Dept. II/112, report, 15 June 1939 and report for June 1939, 8 July 1939, *Secret Nazi Reports*, 454–5, 457–8.

178 Evans, *The Third Reich in Power*, 565–70; Beate Meyer, 'The Mixed Marriage: A Guarantee of Survival or a Reflection of German Society during the Nazi Regime?', in Bankier ed., *Probing the Depths of German Antisemitism*, 54–77.

179 Doerry, *My Wounded Heart*, 86.

180 7 April 1939, *Klemperer Diaries*, I, 284–5; Ascher, *A Community under Siege*, 208; NSDAP branch Castrop-Rauxel, 'Report on the Prevailing Mood', 20 December 1938; SD Upper Division East, II/112, annual report for 1938, 13 January 1939, *Secret Nazi Reports*, 395–6, 397–403.

181 Hedwig Jastrow, suicide note, 29 November 1939, *Jewish Responses*, vol. I, 369.

182 Gendarmerie, Bad Reichenhall, report, 15 December 1938; SD Lower Division Württemberg-Hohenzollern, report for January–March 1939, 1 April 1939, *Secret Nazi Reports*, 393–4, 339–41.

183 Kershaw, *Hitler 1936–1945*, 163–9.

184 *Weiss Diary*, 10.

185 Evans, *The Third Reich in Power*, 681–6; Mazower, *Hitler's Empire*, 58–62; Chad Bryant, *Prague in Black. Nazi Rule and Czech Nationalism* (Cambridge, MA.: Harvard University Press, 2007), 28–36, 76–80.

186 'The Ides of March', 25 March 1939, in Schwarzschild, *Chronicle of a Downfall*, 197–9; Breitman and Lichtman, *FDR and the Jews*, 142–3; 7, 20 April 1939, *Klemperer Diaries*, I, 284–5, 286–7.

187 SDHA, II 1, report January–March 1939, *Secret Nazi Reports*, 434–9; Bryant, *Prague in Black*, 50–2, 58, 82–4; *Weiss Diary*, 10–12.

188 SDHA, II 1, report January–March 1939, *Secret Nazi Reports*, 436; Cesarani, *Eichmann*, 74.

189 London, *Whitehall and the Jews*, 142–53, 153–66; Pamela Shatzkes, *Holocaust and Rescue. Impotent or Indifferent? Anglo-Jewry 1938–1945* (Basingstoke: Palgrave, 2002), 57–63.

190 Breitman and Lichtman, *FDR and the Jews*, 151–6; Wyman, *Paper Walls*, 52–6.

191 *McDonald Diaries*, II, 164–77.

192 Breitman and Lichtman, *FDR and the Jews*, 136–8. One died of natural causes en route. Many were eventually murdered by the Nazis.

193 SDHA, II/112, report, 15 June, 8 July 1939, *Secret Nazi Reports*, 454–5.

194 11, 17, 24 February, 4, 22, 29 March, 12 April, 1, 7, 30 June 1939, *Ruth Maier's Diary*, 128–30, 130–1, 131–2, 133–6, 138–9, 144, 150–1, 151–4, 165.

195 Evans, *The Third Reich in Power*, 689–705; Kershaw, *Hitler 1936–1945*, 166–8, 177–80, 186–96.

196 28 August 1939, *Klemperer Diaries*, I, 292–3; 26 August 1939, *Ruth Maier's Diary*, 182–3.

197 Evans, *The Third Reich in Power*, 703.

198 Kershaw, *Hitler 1936–1945*, 211–23.

199 1 September 1939, *Weiss Diary*, 12; 3 September 1939, *Klemperer Diaries*, I, 293–5. Kershaw, *Hitler 1936–1945*, 224–5; Evans, *The Third Reich in Power*, 703–4.

Four – War: 1939–1941

1 Kershaw, *Hitler 1936–1945*, 190–7, 200–23; Anthony Beevor, *The Second World War* (London: Weidenfeld and Nicolson, 2012), 24–38.

2 Herf, *The Jewish Enemy*, 5–9, 13, 61–2, 72–3; 4 October, 2 November, 31 December 1939, 9 January 1940, *Shirer Diary*, 230, 242, 271, 275.

3 Longerich, *Holocaust*, 132–5.

4 Alexandra Garbarini ed., *Jewish Responses to Persecution*, vol. II, *1938–1940* (Lanham MD: AltaMira Press, 2012), xxix–xxx.

5 Tooze, *The Wages of Destruction*, 292–316. The comparative weakness of Germany is set out in David Edgerton, *Britain's War Machine* (London: Penguin, 2011), 11–85.

6 Collingham, *The Taste of War*, 20–6, 26–30, 155–64; Götz Aly, *Hitler's Beneficiaries. Plunder, Racial War, and the Nazi Welfare State*, trans. Jefferson Chase (New York: Metropolitan Books, 2006) is the most extreme statement of this thesis.

7 Omer Bartov, *Hitler's Army. Soldiers, Nazis, and War in the Third Reich* (New York: Oxford University Press, 1992), 109–18; Wolfram Wette, *The Wehrmacht. History, Myth, Reality*, trans. Deborah Lucas Schneider (Cambridge, MA: Harvard University Press, 2006), 69–73, 76–9, 85–9.

8 Alexander Rossino, *Hitler Strikes Poland. Blitzkrieg, Ideology, and Atrocity* (Lawrence: University of Kansas Press, 2003), 221–2; Sönke Neitzel and Harald Welzer, *Soldaten. On Fighting, Killing and Dying. The Secret Second World War Tapes of German POWs*, trans. Jefferson Chase (London: Simon and Schuster, 2012), 34–8, 55.

9 2 August 1939, Franz Halder, *The War Diary, 1939–1942*, ed. Charles Burdick and Hans-Adolf Jacobsen (Boulder: Westview Press, 1988), 31–2; Rossino, *Hitler Strikes Poland*, 2–11; Richard J. Evans, *The Third Reich at War* (London, 2008), 4.

10 Rossino, *Hitler Strikes Poland*, 11–18, 36–57; Gerwarth, *Hitler's Hangman*, 136–8.

11 Dawidowicz, *The War Against the Jews*, 148–54, depicts the opening weeks of war and the first anti-Jewish measures as 'a guidepost in the chronology of the Final Solution. [It] testifies that a master plan for annihilating the Jews had already been conceived'; Gilbert, *Holocaust*, 88–9.

12 Rossino, *Hitler Strikes Poland*, xiv.

13 Beevor, *The Second World War*, 24–38.

14 Rossino, *Hitler Strikes Poland*, 60–87; Wildt, *An Uncompromising Generation*, 217–41.

15 Rossino, *Hitler Strikes Poland*, 121–2, 158–61, 171–2, 191–208, 217–19; Neitzel and Welzer, *Soldaten*, 44–73.

16 Rossino, *Hitler Strikes Poland*, 90–115.

17 Ibid, 99–101, 103–7, 109–110.

18 10, 11 and 20 September 1939, Halder, *War Diary*, 52, 54–5, 59.

19 19 September 1939, Halder, *War Diary*, 57; Rossino, *Hitler Strikes Poland*, 116–17.

20 Rossino, *Hitler Strikes Poland*, 116–18; Gerwarth, *Hitler's Hangman*, 142–7.

21 Christopher R. Browning, *The Origins of the Final Solution: The Evolution of Nazi Jewish Policy, September 1939–March 1942* (London: William Heinemann, 2004), 19–20, 72–80; Rossino, *Hitler Strikes Poland*, 153–85.

22 Antony Polonsky, *The Jews in Poland and Russia*, vol. III, *1914–2008* (Oxford: Littman Library, 2012), 59–66, 69–97, 98–149, 184–92.

23 Polonsky, *The Jews in Poland and Russia*, vol. III, 43–54, 66–97, 167–83. See also Celia Heller, *On the Edge of Destruction: The Jews of Poland Between the Two World Wars* (Detroit: Wayne State University Press, 1994).

24 Rossino, *Hitler Strikes Poland*, 210.

25 Konrad H. Jarausch ed., *Reluctant Accomplice. A Wehrmacht Soldier's Letters from the Eastern Front* (Princeton: Princeton University Press, 2011), 67–8, 89–90.

26 Abraham Katsh ed., *Scroll of Agony. The Warsaw Diary of Chaim A. Kaplan* (New York: Macmillan, 1965), 1 September 1939, 19–22; Wladyslaw Szpilman, *The Pianist*, trans. Anthea Bell (London: Gollancz, 1999 [first published in Polish as *City of Death* in 1946]), 35; Alan Edelson ed., *The Diary of Dawid Sierakowiak*, trans. Kamil Turowski (London: Bloomsbury, 1996), 26 August 1939, 29.

27 Shimon Huberband, *Kiddush Hashem: Jewish Religious and Cultural Life in Poland During the Holocaust*, trans. David Fishman, ed. Jeffrey Gurock and Robert Hirt (New York: Ktav, 1987), 2–10 September 1939, 7–32, 33–5, 37.

28 9, 10, 13 September 1939, *Sierakowiak Diary*, 36–7, 38.

29 14–15 and 14–23 September 1939, Huberband, *Kiddush Hashem*, 39–54, and on beard cutting, 188–92.

30 1, 2, 4, 5, 7, 10 October 1939, *Kaplan Diary*, 41–3, 45–6.

31 Helena Szereszewska, *Memoirs* (London: Vallentine Mitchell, 1997), 1–5.

32 4, 22, 25, 28 October 1939, *Sierakowiak Diary*, 47, 54, 55, 55–6.

33 Zygmunt Klukowski, *Diary from the Years of Occupation 1939–1944*, trans. George Klukowski, ed. Andrew and Helen Klukowski (Chicago: University of Illinois Press, 1993), 20 September, 14, 15 October 1939, 28–9, 40–1.

34 13 October 1939, *Kaplan Diary*, 49–50; 29 September 1939, *Klukowski Diary*, 33.

35 Kershaw, *Hitler 1936–1945*, 237–40; Mazower, *Hitler's Empire*, 79–81; Philip T. Rutherford, *Prelude to the Final Solution. The Nazi Programme for Deporting Ethnic Poles, 1939–1941* (Lawrence: University of Kansas Press, 2007), 40–51.

36 Longerich, *Himmler*, 434–6; Gerwarth, *Hitler's Hangman*, 149–51; Rutherford, *Prelude to the Final Solution*, 53, 60–2.

37 Rutherford, *Prelude to the Final Solution*, 54–5.

38 Rutherford, *Prelude to the Final Solution*, 52–7; Evans, *The Third Reich at War*, 28–35.

39 Catherine Epstein, *Model Nazi. Arthur Greiser and the Occupation of Western Poland* (Oxford: Oxford University Press, 2010), 125–35; Rutherford, *Prelude to the Final Solution*, 58–61. In 1940, Silesia would be split into two: Lower Silesia, under Karl Hanke, and Upper Silesia, under Karl Bracht.

40 Longerich, *Himmler*, 437–8, 469–72; Wildt, *An Uncompromising Generation*, 160–72; Evans, *The Third Reich at War*, 13–14, 15–16, 23; Dieter Pohl, *Von der 'Judenpolitik' zum Judenmord. Der Distrikts Lublin des Generalgouvernement 1939–1944* (Frankfurt am Main: Peter Lang, 1993), 37–9.

41 Rossino, *Hitler Strikes Poland*, 92–4; Longerich, *Himmler*, 439–40.

42 20 September 1939, Halder, *War Diary*, 59; Rutherford, *Prelude to the Final Solution*, 43–6.

43 For this and the following paragraphs, see *Documents on the Holocaust*, 173–8. The text and the translation differ from Noakes and Pridham eds, *Nazism 1919–1945*, (1997 edn.), vol. 3, 1051–2.

44 Rossino, *Hitler Strikes Poland*, 95–6; Gerwarth, *Hitler's Hangman*, 154–7.

45 Gerwarth, *Hitler's Hangman*, 154–5; Rutherford, *Prelude to the Final Solution*, 48; Browning, *The Origins of the Final Solution*, 25–8; Dan Michman, *The Emergence of the Jewish Ghettos During the Holocaust*, trans. L. J. Schramm (New York: Cambridge University Press, 2011), 65–89.

46 Jonny Moser, 'Nisko: The First Experiment in Deportation', *Simon Wiesenthal Centre Annual*, 2 (1985), 1–30. For updated versions of these events, see also Safrian, *Eichmann's Men*, 51–2; Rabinovici, *Eichmann's Jews*, 89–93.

47 Moser, 'Nisko', 10–30; Safrian, *Eichmann's Men*, 52–6.

48 Cesarani, *Eichmann*, 80; *Jewish Responses*, vol. II, 316–18.

49 'The initial period of the deportations served as a preparatory or experimental phase for the mass deportations of Jews from Poland and from all of Europe to the extermination camps.' Yahil, *The Holocaust*, 150–2; Gilbert, *Holocaust*, 93–4, describes the deportation as 'a new policy'. Cf. Browning, *The Origins of the Final Solution*, 36–43; Longerich, *Himmler*, 151–4.

50 Epstein, *Model Nazi*, 135–55.

51 Rutherford, *Prelude to the Final Solution*, 63–85.

52 Ibid, 86–104.

53 Epstein, *Model Nazi*, 166–9; Browning, *The Origins of the Final Solution*, 43–53.

54 Browning, *The Origins of the Final Solution*, 52–3; Safrian, *Eichmann's Men*, 63–4. For the evolution of the SD Jewish office, its structure, staffing and policies, see Yaacov Lozowick, *Hitler's Bureaucrats. The Nazi Security Police and the Banality of Evil*, trans. Haim Watzman (New York: Continuum, 2002), esp. 10–73.

55 Rutherford, *Prelude to the Final Solution*, 110–11, 113–19, 120–5; Browning, *The Origins of the Final Solution*, 53–61.

56 Rutherford, *Prelude to the Final Solution*, 130–2; Browning, *The Origins of the Final Solution*, 61–5.

57 Rutherford, *Prelude to the Final Solution*, 170–2; Longerich, *Himmler*, 455–7; Gerwarth, *Hitler's Hangman*, 154–7.

58 Longerich, *Holocaust*, 148–52, 160–1; Yisrael Gutman, *The Jews of Warsaw 1939–1943. Ghetto, Underground, Revolt*, trans. Ina Friedman (Bloomington: Indiana University Press, 1982), 1–15; 1 December 1939, *Kaplan Diary*, 80.

59 *Jewish Responses*, vol. II, 146; Michman, *The Emergence of the Jewish Ghettos*, 75–9.

60 Michman, *The Emergence of the Jewish Ghettos*, 79–82.

61 18 November 1939, *Czerniaków*, 89; Gutman, *The Jews of Warsaw*, 48–50; Michman, *The Emergence of the Jewish Ghettos*, 83; *Jewish Responses*, vol. II, 388–9. See also Esther Farbstein, 'A Close-up View of a Judenrat: the Memoirs of Pnina Weiss – Wife of a Member of the First Judenrat in Warsaw', *Yad Vashem Studies* 33 (2005), 61–99.

62 21, 27 October 1939, *Kaplan Diary*, 55–6, 59, 80; Michael Zylberberg, *A Warsaw Diary* (London: Vallentine Mitchell, 1969), 20–2; S. L. Schneiderman ed., *The Diary of Mary Berg* (Oxford: Oneworld, 2006), 15 October, 3 November 1939, 9–11; 15, 16 November 1939, *Sierakowiak Diary*, 62–3.

63 Epstein, *Model Nazi*, 231–3; Aly, *Hitler's Beneficiaries*, 184–5.

64 21 November 1939, *Kaplan Diary*, 55–6; Barbara Engelking and Jacek Leociak, *The Warsaw Ghetto. A Guide to the Perished City*, trans. Emma Harris (New Haven: Yale University Press, 2009), 381–3.

65 21 November 1939, *Sierakowiak Diary*, 64; Engelking and Leociak, *The Warsaw Ghetto*, 143–4.

66 21 November, 16 December 1939, *Kaplan Diary*, 55–6, 87; 18 December 1939, *Berg Diary*, 13–14.

67 Isaiah Trunk, *Judenrat. The Jewish Councils in Eastern Europe under Nazi Occupation* (Lincoln: University of Nebraska, 1996), 1–13, 21–5.

68 Trunk, *Judenrat*, 14–17, 29–35.

69 4 October 1939, *Czerniaków Diary*, 78; Bernard Goldstein, *The Stars Bear Witness*, trans. and ed. by Leonard Shatzkin (New York: Viking Press, 1949), 34–8. Goldstein's memoir was first published in 1947 in Yiddish in New York with the title *Finf Yor in Warshaver Getto* (Five Years in the Warsaw Ghetto*)*. Gutman, *The Jews of Warsaw*, 36–8.

70 16, 31 October 1939, 13 January, 10 February 1940, *Czerniaków Diary*, 84, 86, 107, 116; on financial matters, see 21 December 1939, 9, 16 January, 26 February, 16 March 1940, *Czerniaków Diary*, 101, 106, 108, 121. Gutman, *The Jews of Warsaw*, 21–7, 36–42; *Jewish Responses*, vol. II, 375–82.

71 Trunk, *Judenrat*, 43–8.

72 *Jewish Responses*, vol. II, 189–213; Engelking and Leociak, *The Warsaw Ghetto*, 292–301.

73 16 November 1939, *Sierakowiak Diary*, 63.

74 30 November, 11, 20 December 1939, 5 January 1940, *Czerniaków Diary*, 94, 98, 101, 105; Szpilman, *The Pianist*, 54; 30 November 1939, *Kaplan Diary*, 78; also 20 December 1939, *Klukowski Diary*, 62.

75 *Jewish Responses*, vol. II, 154–5; 27 November 1939, *Kaplan Diary*, 77; 1 November 1939, *Klukowski Diary*, 47; 28 November 1939, *Sierakowiak Diary*, 65–6; Szereszewska, *Memoirs*, 6, 10, 11; Yitzhak Zuckerman, *A Surplus of Memory. Chronicle of the Warsaw Ghetto Uprising*, trans. and ed. Barbara Harshav (Berkeley: University of California Press, 1993), 19–29.

76 Isaiah Trunk, *Lodz Ghetto. A History*, trans. and ed. by Robert Shapiro (Bloomington: Indiana University Press, 2006), 9–10; Gordon J. Horowitz, *Ghettostadt. Lodz and the Making of a Nazi City* (Cambridge, MA: Belknap Press, 2008), 26–9; Epstein, *Model Nazi*, 169–70.

77 Trunk, *Lodz Ghetto*, 12–15; Horowitz, *Ghettostadt*, 42–52.

78 Trunk, *Lodz Ghetto*, 15–16; Horowitz, *Ghettostadt*, 34–42.

79 Horowitz, *Ghettostadt*, 16–20; Michael Unger 'Introduction' to Josef Zelkowitz, *In Those Terrible Days. Writings from the Lodz Ghetto*, trans. Naftali Greenwood, ed. Michael Unger (Jerusalem: Yad Vashem, 2002), 20–1.

80 Trunk, *Lodz Ghetto*, 34–53; Horowitz, *Ghettostadt*, 56–9.

81 Trunk, *Lodz Ghetto*, 83–4; Horowitz, *Ghettostadt*, 64–7; Yisrael Gutman, 'Introduction: The Distinctiveness of the Lodz Ghetto', in Trunk, *Lodz Ghetto*, xli–xlii.

82 Michman, *The Emergence of the Jewish Ghettos*, 84–9; Longerich, *Holocaust*, 166–7; Rutherford, *Prelude to the Final Solution*, 171–2.

83 4, 20 April, 28 May 1939, David Rubinowitz, *The Diary of David Rubinowitz*, trans. Derek Bowman (Edinburgh: Blackwood, 1981), 3–4; see also the memoir Renya Kulkielko, *Escape from the Pit* (New York: Sharon Books, 1947), 7–24.

84 Gerda Weissmann Klein, *All But My Life* (New York: Hill and Wang, 1995 [first published 1957]), 3–21; Sybille Steinbacher, 'In the Shadow of Auschwitz. The Murder of the Jews of East Upper Silesia', in Ulrich Herbert ed., *National Socialist Extermination Policies. Contemporary German Perspectives and Controversies* (New York: Berghahn, 2000), 291–2; Gruner, *Jewish Forced Labour Under the Nazis*, 214–22.

85 Entry for January 1940 in Jacob Sloan ed. and trans., *Notes from the Warsaw Ghetto. The Journal of Emmanuel Ringelblum* (New York: McGraw-Hill, 1958), 7–13; 15, 25 March, 13, 16, 22 April 1940, *Czerniaków Diary*, 131–2, 140–1; Engelking and Leociak, *The Warsaw Ghetto*, 145–7, 311–16.

86 Engelking and Leociak, *The Warsaw Ghetto*, 412–13, 416–18.

87 Ibid, 459–77.

88 Goldstein, *The Stars Bear Witness*, 41–4; 4, 14, 19, 30 December 1939, 5, 8 January, 21, 23 February, 9 March 1940, *Kaplan Diary*, 82, 86–7, 88, 93–4, 96–7, 100, 122–4.

89 27 December 1939, 28 April 1940, *Berg Diary*, 14, 19–20.

90 Zuckerman, *A Surplus of Memory*, 40–57, 62–6, 74–5; Engelking and Leociak, *The Warsaw Ghetto*, 343–51; 10 March 1940, *Czerniaków Diary*, 130; 24 March, 23–30

April 1940, Huberband, *Kiddush Hashem*, 55–9; 24 April 1940, *Kaplan Diary*, 140–1.

91 Gutman, *The Jews of Warsaw*, 23–4; 14 January 1940, *Kaplan Diary*, 101–2.

92 5 April 1940, 10 January 1941, *Berg Diary*, 17–18, 37; February, March, April 1940, *Ringelblum Notes*, 17, 20–1, 24, 34.

93 24, 26–8 March 1940, *Czerniakow Diary*, 131, 132–3; 10 January 1940, *Berg Diary*, 17; 28 March 1940, *Kaplan Diary*, 134–5; Goldstein, *The Stars Bear Witness*, 51–3; Emmanuel Ringelblum, *Polish–Jewish Relations during the Second World War*, trans. Dafna Allon et al., eds Joseph Kermish and Shmuel Krakowski (Evanston, IL: Northwestern University Press, 1992), 49–53.

94 14 February, 18, 29, 30 March, 1, 2, 4, 9, 13 April, 10 May 1940, *Czerniaków Diary*, 117, 130, 134–6, 138, 140, 147–8; Engelking and Leociak, *The Warsaw Ghetto*, 56–60; Gutman, *The Jews of Warsaw*, 50–2; Michman, *The Emergence of the Jewish Ghettos*, 83–4.

95 Grenville, *The Jews and Germans*, 202, 207–12; Luise Solmitz diary, 8 August 1939, *Jewish Responses*, vol. II, 100; Friedländer, *Nazi Germany and the Jews*, vol. 2, 51–2. See Bryan Mark Rigg, *Hitler's Jewish Soldiers* (Lawrence: University of Kansas Press, 2009).

96 Howard K. Smith, *Last Train From Berlin* (London: Cresset Press, 1942), 37–48; Ralph Getsinger, US vice-consul, 'Hamburg After Two Months of War', 10 November 1939, *Fremde Blicke*, 543–4; SD District Office, Worms, 'Political Report on the Prevailing Mood', 14 September 1939, *Secret Nazi Reports*, 471–2; 10 September 1939, *Klemperer Diary*, I, 296–7.

97 Stapostelle, Cologne, 'Allocation of Special Food Shops for Jews', 29 September 1939; District Governor of Upper and Central Franconia, report for September 1939, 6 October 1939; District Governor of Lower Bavaria and Upper Palatinate, report for September 1939, 9 October 1939, *Secret Nazi Reports*, 472–3, 474–5; Konrad Kwiet, 'Without Neighbours. Daily Living in *Judenhäuser*', in Nicosia and Scrase eds, *Jewish Life in Nazi Germany*, 117–48; Ascher, *A Community under Siege*, 209; 9 December 1939, *Klemperer Diary*, I, 307.

98 NSDAP District Leadership Kitzingen-Gerolzhofen, 'Report on the Prevailing Mood', 11 September 1939 and Sandberg Gendarmerie, report for September 1939, 28 September 1939; SD District Office, Bad Kissingen, report, 27 November 1939; District Governor Upper and Central Franconia, report for November 1939, 7 December 1939; RSHA, Office III (SD), 'Reports from the Reich', 10 April 1940, *Secret Nazi Reports*, 476–7, 483, 484, 495; 31 March 1940, *Klemperer Diary*, I, 316; Grenville, *Jews and Germans*, 212.

99 19, 29 April, 22, 26 May, 6 June 1940, *Klemperer Diary*, I, 317–18, 318–20, 324–6, 328.

100 NSDAP Munich District, Office for Racial Policy, 'Activity Report', 23 April 1940; Mayor, Bad Nauheim, 'The Political Situation', 22 May 1940, Mayor of Schwandorf, 'Report for May', 31 May 1940, *Secret Nazi Reports*, 497–8, 498–9; Grenville, *Jews and Germans*, 202; Rigg, *Hitler's Jewish Soldiers*.

101 SD Regional Division Leipzig, 'Report on the Domestic Situation', 13 October 1939; Emigration Consulting Office, Cologne, report for October–December

1939; District Governor of Upper and Central Franconia, 'Report for March 1940', 7 April 1940, *Secret Nazi Reports*, 479, 488–9, 493–4; 27 February 1940, *Shirer Diary*, 291–3; Grenville, *Jews and Germans*, 198–9; Rabinovici, *Eichmann's Jews*, 82–5; Friedländer, *Nazi Germany and the Jews*, vol. 2, 83–9.

102 For the deep background, see Paul Weindling, *Health, Race and German Politics between National Unification and Nazism 1870–1945* (Cambridge: Cambridge University Press, 1989); Götz Aly, 'Medicine against the Useless', in Götz Aly, Peter Chroust, Christian Pross eds, *Cleansing the Fatherland. Nazi Medicine and Racial Hygiene*, trans. Belinda Cooper (Baltimore: Johns Hopkins University Press, 1994), 22–98, for an overview.

103 Evans, *The Third Reich at War*, 75–93; Longerich, *Holocaust*, 135–41; Kershaw, *Hitler 1936–1945*, 252–61; Michael Burleigh, *Death and Deliverance. 'Euthanasia' in Germany 1900–1945* (Cambridge: Cambridge University Press, 1994), 3–4, 93–111, 113–29, 130–45; Ulf Schmidt, *Karl Brandt. The Nazi Doctor. Medicine and Power in the Third Reich* (London: Hambledon Continuum, 2007), 117–33, 133–46.

104 Burleigh, *Death and Deliverance*, 145–61. In general, see Henry Friedlander, *The Origins of Nazi Genocide. From Euthanasia to the Final Solution* (Chapel Hill: University of North Carolina Press, 1995).

105 Schmidt, *Karl Brandt*, 146–53; Burleigh, *Death and Deliverance*, 162–80; Evans, *The Third Reich at War*, 93–101.

106 21 September, 25 November 1940, *Shirer Diary*, 512, 569–75; Paul M. Dutko, 'Mysterious Deaths of Mental Patients from Leipzig Consular District and the Connections Therewith of the Black Guard (SS)', 16 October 1940, *Fremde Blicke*, 552–3.

107 Grenville, *The Jews and Germans*, 214–15; Garbarini ed., *Jewish Responses*, vol. II, 11; 21 May, 2 November 1941, *Klemperer Diary*, I, 368–9, 423.

108 Beevor, *The Second World War*, calls the T-4 programme the 'blueprint' for genocide; Friedlander, *The Origins of Nazi Genocide*, 284, calls it 'the model for the Final Solution'; Schmidt, *Karl Brandt*, 207–23, 233–49. Cf. Wachsmann, *KL*, 240–58 on 14f13.

109 Robert Jay Lifton, *The Nazi Doctors. Medical Killing and the Psychology of Genocide* (New York: Basic Books, 2000 edn), 45–76, 134–9, 142–4; Friedlander, *The Origins of Nazi Genocide*, 21–2. Wachsmann, *KL*, 240–88, argues that the 14f13 programme and the mass execution of Soviet POWS in the concentration camps in 1941 was, however, a crucial stage in developing the techniques and the experienced personnel for carrying out genocide.

110 Letters dated 12, 15 November, 22 December 1939, Jarausch ed., *Reluctant Accomplice*, 103–5, 105–7, 109, 118–20.

111 Letters dated 31 March, 7 April 1940, Jarausch ed., *Reluctant Accomplice*, 176–9, 180.

112 Maschmann, *Account Rendered*, 50, 60, 62–6, 80–5.

113 19 October, 25 December 1939, 11 March 1940, *Von Hassell Diaries*, 75–7, 95, 114–15.

114 19 November 1939, 27 January 1940, *Shirer Diary*, 250, 285–6.

115 Russell Wallis, *Britain, Germany and the Road to the Holocaust. British Attitudes towards Nazi Atrocities* (London: I. B. Tauris, 2014), 204–6; David Cesarani, 'The London Jewish Chronicle and the Holocaust', in Robert Moses Shapiro ed., *Why Didn't The Press Shout. American and International Journalism During the Holocaust* (New York: Yeshiva University Press, 2003), 180–1.

116 David Engel, *In the Shadow of Auschwitz. The Polish Government-in-Exile and the Jews, 1939–1942* (Chapel Hill: University of North Carolina Press, 1987), 8, 52–3, 60–78; cf. E. Thomas Wood and Stanislaw Jankowski, *Karski. How One Man Tried to Stop the Holocaust* (New York, John Wiley, 1994), 44–55. Jan Karski, *Story of a Secret State* (London: Penguin 2012 edn), 101–35, recalls the mission but the account, originally written and published in 1944, was coy about details.

117 Ronald Zweig, *Britain and Palestine During the Second World War* (London: Boydell Press, 1986), 1–5.

118 Bernard Wasserstein, *Britain and the Jews of Europe, 1939–1945* (London: Leicester University Press, 1999 edn), 43–54; Dalia Ofer, *Escaping the Holocaust. Illegal Immigration to the Land of Israel, 1939–1944* (New York: Oxford University Press, 1990), 4–7, 128–44.

119 London, *Whitehall and the Jews*, 169–86; Leni and Peter Gillman, *'Collar the Lot!' How Britain Interned and Expelled its Wartime Refugees* (London: Quartet, 1980), 23–68.

120 Michael Fleming, *Auschwitz, the Allies and Censorship of the Holocaust* (Cambridge: Cambridge University Press, 2014), 47–8 and generally, 50–1; Wallis, *Britain, Germany and the Road to the Holocaust*, 203–4; Kushner, *The Holocaust and the Liberal Imagination*, 123–6, 128–34. The level of censorship was even more extreme in the case of BBC German Service broadcasts to Germany, which at this time were virtually required by the Foreign Office to exclude any mention of Jews: see Stephanie Seul, 'The Representation of the Holocaust in the British Propaganda Campaign directed at the German Public, 1938–1945', *Leo Baeck Year Book*, 52 (2007), 267–306.

121 Breitman and Lichtman, *FDR and the Jews*, 162–75; Zucker, *In Search of Refuge*, 99–102, 130–1, 151–5, 165–6.

122 Lurel Leff, *Buried by the Times. The Holocaust and America's Most Important Newspaper* (New York: Cambridge University Press, 2005), 59–74; Lipstadt, *Beyond Belief*, 136–49.

123 Bernard Wasserstein, 'Patterns of Jewish Leadership in Great Britain', in Randolf Braham ed., *Jewish Leadership During the Nazi Era: Patterns of Behavior in the Free World* (New York: Columbia University Press, 1985), 29–34.

124 *Jewish Responses*, vol. II, 190–2, 200.

125 Dina Porat, *The Blue and the Yellow Stars of David. The Zionist Leadership in Palestine and the Holocaust, 1939–1945* (Cambridge MA: Harvard University Press, 1990), 5–16, 17–22.

126 Tooze, *The Wages of Destruction*, 334–66; 30 October, 12 November, 31 December 1939, 22 January, 27 February, 4 March, 1, 4 April 1940, *Shirer Diary*, 241, 248, 271, 280–1, 291–2, 294–5, 323; Friedrich Reck-Malleczewen, *Diary of a Man in Despair*, trans. Paul Rubens (London: Duckbacks, 2000), 131.

127 10 May 1939, *Shirer Diary*, 331–5; Kershaw, *Hitler 1936–1945*, 283–300.

128 Hugo Melvin, *Manstein. Hitler's Greatest General* (London: Phoenix, 2010), 132–55; Karl-Heinz Frieser, *The Blitzkrieg Legend* (Annapolis, MD: Naval Institute Press, 2012), 60–99.

129 Frieser, *The Blitzkrieg Legend*, 102–314.

130 Longerich, *Himmler*, 458–61, 490–8; Gerwarth, *Hitler's Hangman*, 174. Hugh Sebag-Montefiore, *Dunkirk. Fight to the Last Man* (London: Penguin, 2007), 293–315, 345–61.

131 Rafael Scheck, *Hitler's African Victims. The German Army Massacres of Black French Soldiers in 1940* (New York: Cambridge University Press, 2006); cf. Clarence Lusane, *Hitler's Black Victims. The Historical Experience of Afro-Germans, European Blacks, Africans and African Americans in the Nazi Era* (New York: Routledge, 2003). For a brief, balanced overview, see Michael Burleigh and Wolfgang Wipperman, *The Racial State. Germany 1933–1945* (Cambridge: Cambridge University Press, 1991), 128–30.

132 Frieser, *The Blitzkrieg Legend*, 12–59, 255–60.

133 Mazower, *Hitler's Empire*, 100–110; Evans, *The Third Reich at War*, 373–97.

134 Julian Jackson, *France 1940–1944. The Dark Years* (Oxford: Oxford University Press, 2001), 126–36; Robert Gildea, *Marianne in Chains. In Search of the German Occupation, 1940–1945* (London: Macmillan, 2002), 43–64.

135 Jackson, *France 1940–1944*, 142–54; Friedländer, *Nazi Germany and the Jews*, vol. 2, 67–9; *Jewish Responses*, vol. II, xxxi–xxxiii.

136 Noakes and Pridham eds, *Nazism 1919–1945* (1997 edn.), vol. 3, 932–4; Rutherford, *Prelude to the Final Solution*, 139–40; Longerich, *Himmler*, 508.

137 *Documents on the Holocaust*, 216–18; Longerich, *Holocaust*, 161–4; Browning, *The Origins of the Final Solution*, 81–2.

138 Cesarani, *Eichmann*, 84–7; Gerwarth, *Hitler's Hangman*, 178–81.

139 Browning, *The Origins of the Final Solution*, 86–9; Grenville, *The Jews and Germans*, 213; Friedländer, *Nazi Germany and the Jews*, vol. 2, 81–2, 103; Meyer, 'Between Self-Assurance and Forced Collaboration', 154–5; 7 July 1940, *Klemperer Diary*, I, 331–2; 17 July 1940, *Shirer Diary*, 451.

140 Götz Aly, *'Final Solution'. Nazi Population Policy and the Murder of the European Jews* (London: Arnold, 1999), 92; 1 July 1940, *Czerniaków Diary*, 169.

141 Longerich, *Holocaust*, 171–3; Gerwarth, *Hitler's Hangman*, 182–3; Grenville, *The Jews and Germans*, 213–14; Meyer, 'Between Self-Assurance and Forced Collaboration', 154–5; *Jewish Responses*, vol. II, 333–43.

142 Kershaw, *Fateful Choices*, 11–53.

143 Horst Boog, 'The Luftwaffe Assault', in Paul Addison and Jeremy A. Crang eds, *The Burning Blue. A New History of the Battle of Britain* (London: Pimlico, 2000), 39–54; Megargee, *Inside Hitler's High Command*, 87–92.

144 Gillman, *'Collar the Lot!'*, 69–89.

145 Gillman, *'Collar the Lot!'*, 91–114, 131–45, 147–59, 161–7; Wasserstein, *Britain and the Jews of Europe*, 77–83; Tony Kushner, 'Clubland, Cricket Tests and Alien Internment, 1939–40', in David Cesarani and Tony Kushner eds, *The Internment of Aliens in Twentieth Century Britain* (London: Cass, 1993), 79–101.

146 Louise Burletson, 'The State, Internment and Public Criticism in the Second World War', in Cesarani and Kushner eds, *The Internment of Aliens*, 101–24. For contemporary criticism, see François Lafitte, *The Internment of Aliens* (London: Libris, 1988) first published in September 1940.

147 For the experience of internees see Miriam Kochan, *Britain's Internees in the Second World War* (London: Macmillan, 1983) and Cesarani and Kushner eds, *The Internment of Aliens*, 147–66, 188–241.

148 David Cesarani, *Arthur Koestler. The Homeless Mind* (London: Heinemann, 1998), 156–60; Arthur Koestler, *Scum of the Earth* (New York: Macmillan, 1941), 96, 107–8.

149 Caron, *Uneasy Asylum*, 240–59, 316.

150 Ibid, 259–63; Cesarani, *Arthur Koestler*, 159–63; Renée Poznanski, *Jews in France during World War II*, trans. Nathan Bracher (Hanover, NH: Brandeis University Press, 2001), 56–9; Michael R. Marrus and Robert O. Paxton, *Vichy France and the Jews* (New York: Schocken, 1983), 112–14, 161–4.

151 Léon Poliakov, *L'Auberge des musiciens* (Paris: Mazarine, 1981), 79; Poznanski, *Jews in France during World War II*, 26.

152 2, 15 July 1940, *Lambert Diary*, 3–6, 6–10, which also contains a vivid description of the flight south from Paris.

153 Marrus and Paxton, *Vichy France and the Jews*, 3–4; Caron, *Uneasy Asylum*, 323–38.

154 Marrus and Paxton, *Vichy France and the Jews*, 3–21, 34–54; Jacques Adler, *The Jews of Paris and the Final Solution. Communal Response and Internal Conflicts, 1940-1944* (New York: Oxford University Press, 1987), 16.

155 2, 19 October 1940, *Lambert Diary*, 21, 22–3.

156 Adler, *The Jews of Paris and the Final Solution*, 35–7; Poznanski, *Jews in France during World War II*, 42–6.

157 Susan Zuccotti, *The Holocaust, the French, and the Jews* (New York: Basic Books, 1993), 38–50; Poznanski, *Jews in France during World War II*, 66–8. Irène Némirovsky, *Suite Française*, trans. Sandra Smith (London: Chatto and Windus, 2006), 6–156 dramatizes the exodus which she witnessed.

158 Zuccotti, *The Holocaust, the French, and the Jews*, 65–75; Poznanski, *Jews in France during World War II*, 50–2, 66–8; Caron, *Uneasy Asylum*, 331–9, 342–5; Marrus and Paxton, *Vichy France and the Jews*, 165–73.

159 Marrus and Paxton, *Vichy France and the Jews*, 78–83; Jackson, *France 1940-1944*, 170–1; Talbot Imlay and Martin Horn, *The Politics of Industrial Collaboration during World War II. Ford France, Vichy and Nazi Germany* (Cambridge: Cambridge University Press, 2014), 53–8; Lynn H. Nicholas, *The Rape of Europa, The Fate of Europe's Treasures in the Third Reich and the Second World War* (London: Papermac, 1994), 119–40.

160 Caron, *Uneasy Asylum*, 331–9.

161 Zuccotti, *The Holocaust, the French, and the Jews*, 51–7, 60–1; Poznanski, *Jews in France during World War II*, 31–42; Marrus and Paxton, *Vichy France and the Jews*, 101–2.

162 Serge Klarsfeld, 'The Influence of the War on the Final Solution in France', in Cohen, Cochavi, Gelber eds, *The Shoah and the War*, 271–91.

163 Marrus and Paxton, *Vichy France and the Jews*, 96–100; Poznanski, *Jews in France during World War II*, 68–74.

164 Adler, *The Jews of Paris and the Final Solution*, 17–26; Poznanski, *Jews in France during World War II*, 105–18; 24 February 1941, *Lambert Diary*, 28–9.

165 Lieven Saerens, 'Antwerp's Attitude Towards the Jews from 1918 to 1940 and Its Implications for the Period of Occupation', and Maxime Steinberg, 'The Judenpolitik in Belgium Within the West European Context: Comparative Observations', in Dan Michman ed., *Belgium and the Holocaust* (Jerusalem: Yad Vashem, 1998), 159–67, 200–8.

166 Steinberg, 'The Judenpolitik in Belgium', 200–1.

167 Bob Moore, *Victims and Survivors. The Nazi Persecution of the Jews in the Netherlands 1940–1945* (London: Arnold, 1997), 20–8.

168 Jacob Presser, *Ashes in the Wind. The Destruction of Dutch Jewry*, trans. Arnold Pomerans (London: Souvenir Press, 2010 edn), 4–6.

169 Peter Romijn, 'The "Lesser Evil" – the case of the Dutch local authorities and the Holocaust', in Peter Romijn et al. eds, *The Persecution of the Jews in the Netherlands, 1940–1945* (Amsterdam: Vossiuspers, 2012), 13–26.

170 Presser, *Ashes in the Wind*, 7–32.

171 Ibid, 33–45.

172 Jos Scheren, 'Aryanization, Market Vendors, and Peddlers in Amsterdam', *HGS*, 14:3 (2000), 415–29; Michman, *The Emergence of the Jewish Ghettos*, 95–101; Presser, *Ashes in the Wind*, 47–50.

173 Presser, *Ashes in the Wind*, 50–7; Moore, *Victims and Survivors*, 63–73.

174 Bart van der Boom, 'Ordinary Dutchmen and the Holocaust: a summary of findings', in Romijn et al. eds, *The Persecution of the Jews in the Netherlands*, 29–52, esp. 36–9.

175 9 April, 10, 15, 27 May, 17, 22 June 1940, *Czerniaków Diary*, 138, 148, 150, 154, 161, 164; 4, 16 May 1940, *Ringelblum Notes*, 37, 40; 9, 11 April, 10 May, 14 June, 6 July 1940, *Kaplan Diary*, 138–9, 150–1, 162–3, 170; 20 May, 16 June 1940, *Berg Diary*, 20.

176 Megargee, *Inside Hitler's High Command*, 87.

177 Kershaw, *Fateful Choices*, 65–80; Megargee, *Inside Hitler's High Command*, 87–92; Weinberg, *A World at Arms*, 179–86.

178 Kershaw, *Fateful Choices*, 65–90, 259–63; Alex J. Kay, *Exploitation, Resettlement, Mass Murder. Political and Economic Planning for German Occupation in the Soviet Union, 1940–41* (New York, Berghahn, 2006), 26–38.

179 Fritz, *Ostkrieg. Hitler's War of Extermination in the East*, 35–52.

180 Longerich, *Holocaust*, 173–6; Browning, *The Origins of the Final Solution*, 99–101; Cesarani, *Eichmann*, 89. The newly discovered diary of Alfred Rosenberg supports the contention that the Madagascar solution was superseded by the prospect of conquests in the east. See entry for 28 March 1941, http://collections. ushmm.org/view/2001.62.14?page=505 I am grateful to Jürgen Matthäus for bringing this to my notice and allowing me to see the MS of the forthcoming

publication, Jürgen Matthäus and Frank Bajohr eds, *The Political Diary of Alfred Rosenberg and the Onset of the Holocaust* (Lanham, MD: Rowman and Littlefield, 2015).

181 Browning, *The Origins of the Final Solution*, 112–14; Wildt, *An Uncompromising Generation*, 264–7.

182 Trunk, *Lodz Ghetto*, 49, 148–59, 168–9; Browning, *The Origins of the Final Solution*, 116–20; Horowitz, *Ghettostadt*, 92–102; Unger, 'Introduction' to Josef Zelkowitz, *In Those Terrible Days*, 23–4, 33; Epstein, *Model Nazi*, 178–80.

183 Trunk, *Lodz Ghetto*, 70–1, 323-4; Horowitz, *Ghettostadt*, 70–4.

184 Trunk, *Lodz Ghetto*, 40–2, 70–2.

185 Ibid, 65–7, 172–4.

186 Ibid, 104–7.

187 Ibid, 107–17.

188 Ibid, 198–223.

189 Ibid, 58–60.

190 Ibid, 298–303.

191 Unger, 'Introduction' to Josef Zelkowitz, *In Those Terrible Days*, 24–5; Gutman, 'Introduction: The Distinctiveness of the Lodz Ghetto', in Trunk, *Lodz Ghetto*, xliv–li; Trunk, *Lodz Ghetto*, 304–8, 325–33.

192 Trunk, *Lodz Ghetto*, 54–8, 84–7; 27 April 1941, *Sierakowiak Diary*, 83–4.

193 Trunk, *Lodz Ghetto*, 334–42.

194 Ibid, 342–9.

195 Trunk, *Lodz Ghetto*, 348–9; Zelkowicz, *In Those Terrible Days*, 76–84, quote on 80.

196 Trunk, *Lodz Ghetto*, 303–5, 349–55; Zelkowicz, *In Those Terrible Days*, 129–39, quote on 131.

197 Trunk, *Lodz Ghetto*, 303–5, 355–7; Zelkowicz, *In Those Terrible Days*, 135.

198 12, 14, 15, 19 January 1941, Lucjan Dobroszycki ed., *The Chronicle of the Lodz Ghetto 1941-1944*, trans. Richard Lourie, Joachim Neugroschel et al. (New Haven: Yale University Press, 1984), ix–xvii, 4–5, 8–9, 10, 12.

199 23, 24, 30 January, 6, 8 March 1941, *Lodz Ghetto Chronicle*, 14–16, 20, 31, 33; Zelkowicz, *In Those Terrible Days*, 205–32.

200 10 April, 7 June 1941, *Lodz Ghetto Chronicle*, 44–5, 59–60; 16 April, 3 May 1941, *Sierakowiak Diary*, 80, 86; Gutman, 'Introduction: The Distinctiveness of the Lodz Ghetto', in Trunk, *Lodz Ghetto*, xliv–xlv; Horowitz, *Ghettostadt*, 129–31.

201 1, 26 March, 22 July 1941, *Lodz Ghetto Chronicle*, 22–4, 37, 65–6; 6, 7, 11 April, 16, 31 May, 23 August 1941, *Sierakowiak Diary*, 77, 79, 91–2, 96–7, 121; Zelkowicz, *In Those Terrible Days*, 140, 191–3.

202 4 March, 4 August 1941, *Lodz Ghetto Chronicle*, 28–9, 72; 27, 30 April, 10 May, *Sierakowiak Diary*, 83–4, 85, 88–9.

203 6 June 1941, *Sierakowiak Diary*, 98; 5, 10–24 March 1941, *Lodz Ghetto Chronicle*, 30, 35; Horowitz, *Ghettostadt*, 131–2.

204 1, 16 July, 9, 19 August, 3, 14, 30 September 1940, *Czerniaków Diary*, 169, 174, 181–3, 193, 197, 203; Gutman, *The Jews of Warsaw*, 48–55, 57–61.

205 The ghetto decree was actually published on Yom Kippur, the holiest day of the

Jewish ritual calendar, 12 October 1940, *Czerniaków Diary*, 206; Engelking and Leociak, *The Warsaw Ghetto*, 39–40, 62–75.

206 12, 13, 14, 18–20 October 1940, *Czerniaków Diary*, 206–7, 208–9; Szereszewska, *Memoirs*, 14, 18–19, 27, 32; 12 July 1940, *Berg Diary*, 31–3.

207 Goldstein, *The Stars Bear Witness*, 64; 20 November 1940, *Berg Diary*, 28–9.

208 Stanislaw Adler, *In the Warsaw Ghetto 1940–1943. An Account of a Witness*, trans. Sara Philip (Jerusalem: Yad Vashem, 1982), 31–6; 2 November 1940, *Berg Diary*, 27; 15 September, 10, 14, 17, 22 October, 17, 19 November 1940, *Kaplan Diary*, 195–6, 209–13, 225–6. See also 19 November 1940, *Ringelblum Notes*, 86–7, on the shock of being closed in.

209 Gutman, *The Jews of Warsaw*, 66–72, 113; Engelking and Leociak, *The Warsaw Ghetto*, 33–6.

210 Engelking and Leociak, *The Warsaw Ghetto*, 380–406

211 20, 25 November 1940, *Czerniaków Diary*, 218–19, 220; Engelking and Leociak, *The Warsaw Ghetto*, 33–6, 149–59, 367–9.

212 Gutman, *The Jews of Warsaw*, 80–3; Engelking and Leociak, *The Warsaw Ghetto*, 159–61. 27 October 1940, *Kaplan Diary*, 215–16; Adler, *In the Warsaw Ghetto*, 14, 69–70; 26 April 1941, *Ringelblum Notes*, 164–5; 12, 20 February, 4 November 1940, *Czerniakow Diary*, 117, 119–20, 212–13.

213 3, 4 September 1940, *Czerniaków Diary*, 193, 205; 29 August, 14 September 1940, *Kaplan Diary*, 19–91, 194–5. Engelking and Leociak, *The Warsaw Ghetto*, 143–7, 149–59.

214 Gutman, *The Jews of Warsaw*, 86–94; Engelking and Leociak, *The Warsaw Ghetto*, 190–213, 445.

215 22 December 1940, *Berg Diary*, 32–4; 21 December 1940, *Kaplan Diary*, 234; Adler, *In the Warsaw Ghetto*, 7–8, 23–5, 26–8, 44–8, 50–3.

216 Engelking and Leociak, *The Warsaw Ghetto*, 218–28; Huberband, *Kiddush Hashem*, 136–40.

217 Engelking and Leociak, *The Warsaw Ghetto*, 407–11, 412–19, 419–31.

218 Ibid, 446–59.

219 2 November, 16 December 1940, *Kaplan Diary*, 229–30, 232–3; Adler, *In the Warsaw Ghetto*, 94; see also, 15 December 1940, 12 June 1941, *Berg Diary*, 30–2, 64–5.

220 Gutman, *The Jews of Warsaw*, 62–5, 109–10; Engelking and Leociak, *The Warsaw Ghetto*, 233–42, 280–92.

221 16 August, 11 September 1940, *Berg Diary*, 23–7; Goldstein, *The Stars Bear Witness*, 71–2, 85–6; Michel Mazor, *The Vanished City*, trans. David Jacobson (New York: Maresilio, 1993), 157–65; Gutman, *The Jews of Warsaw*, 102–6; Samuel D. Kassow, *Who Will Write Our History? Emanuel Ringelblum, the Warsaw Ghetto, and the Oyneg Shabas Archive* (Bloomington, Indiana University Press, 2007), 90–106, 112–28; Engelking and Leociak, *The Warsaw Ghetto*, 258–76, 292–300.

222 Zylberberg, *A Warsaw Diary*, 23–5; 17 February, 4 April 1941, *Berg Diary*, 40–1, 45–6; 15, 23, 25 September, 5 October 1940, 15 February 1941, *Kaplan Diary*,

195–6, 198–200, 204–5, 242; Engelking and Leociak, *The Warsaw Ghetto*, 243–50, 317–29, 343–59, 440–1.

223 Goldstein, *The Stars Bear Witness*, 83–5; 20 February 1941, *Kaplan Diary*, 244–5; 2 January, 9, 20 April 1941, *Berg Diary*, 35–6, 46–7, 48–53; Adler, *In the Warsaw Ghetto*, 263–6; 27 February 1941, *Ringelblum Notes*, 132; Engelking and Leociak, *The Warsaw Ghetto*, 530–9; Katarzyna Person, *Assimilated Jews in the Warsaw Ghetto, 1940–1943* (Syracuse: Syracuse University Press, 2014), 100–33.

224 2, 25 October, 26 December 1940, 19 February 1941, *Kaplan Diary*, 202–3, 214–15, 234–6, 244; 17 April 1941, *Ringelblum Notes*, 154–5; Engelking and Leociak, *The Warsaw Ghetto*, 641–6.

225 Huberband, *Kiddush Hashem*, 193–8, 207–10; Kassow, *Who Will Write Our History?*, 165–9.

226 24 December 1940, 11 December 1941, *Berg Diary*, 34, 111–13; 9 January 1941, *Kaplan Diary*, 237; 27 July 1941, *Czerniaków Diary*, 262–3; mid-September 1941, *Ringelblum Notes*, 215–16; Zylberberg, *A Warsaw Diary*, 48–9. Person, *Assimilated Jews in the Warsaw Ghetto*, 38–48; Peter Dembowski, *Christians in the Warsaw Ghetto. An Epitaph for the Unremembered* (Chicago: University of Notre Dame Press, 2005).

227 September 1941, *Ringelblum Notes*, 215–16; Edward Reicher, *Country of Ash. A Jewish Doctor in Poland, 1939–1945*, trans. Magda Bogin (New York: Bellevue, 2013), 63–4; 5 November 1940, *Kaplan Diary*, 220–1; Goldstein, *The Stars Bear Witness*, 53–4.

228 1, 28 July 1940, *Czerniaków Diary*, 168–9, 178; 10 March, 6, 17 April 1941, *Ringelblum Notes*, 135–6, 146, 156; Gutman, *The Jews of Warsaw*, 107–10, 114.

229 20 May 1941, *Berg Diary*, 51–2; Szpilman, *The Pianist*, 13–14, 16–17.

230 31 July 1941, *Berg Diary*, 81–2; Adler, *In the Warsaw Ghetto*, 68, 256–7; 5 January 1941, *Ringelblum Notes*, 12–21; Reicher, *Country of Ash*, 69–78; Kassow, *Who Will Write Our History?*, 239–59.

232 Adler, *In the Warsaw Ghetto*, 253, 257–8; 18 March, 26 April 1941, *Ringelblum Notes*, 141, 159–61.

232 12 June 1941, *Berg Diary*, 59–60; Mazor, *The Vanished City*, 15; Engelking and Leociak, *The Warsaw Ghetto*, 311–16.

233 28 February, 11 May, 26, 30 August 1941, *Ringelblum Notes*, 129, 174, 197, 205–6; Goldstein, *The Stars Bear Witness*, 80.

Five – Barbarossa: 1941

1 Gilbert, *Holocaust*, 154; see also Dawidowicz, *The War Against the Jews*, 157–63, who asserts that 'The plans to wage war against Russia were always in Hitler's thoughts.' Dawidowicz inverts the strategic dénouement by claiming that Hitler attacked Britain and France in order to clear the way for an attack on the USSR.

2 25, 26 July, 8 August 1940, *Shirer Diary*, 459–61, 467; Sydney B. Redecker, US Consul, 'Political Report No. 2, Frankfurt-am-Main', 16 January 1941 in *Fremde*

Blicke, 554–6. Tooze, *The Wages of Destruction*, 386–90; Collingham, *The Taste of War*, 35.

3 13 July, 22, 31 July 1940, *Halder Diary*, 227, 230, 241–6; Kay, *Exploitation, Resettlement, Mass Murder*, 26–42; Tooze, *The Wages of Destruction*, 420–5; Kershaw, *Hitler 1936–1945*, 323–4; Mazower, *Hitler's Empire*, 129–36.

4 Kay, *Exploitation, Resettlement, Mass Murder*, 47–50; Mazower, *Hitler's Empire*, 147–8; Collingham, *The Taste of War*, 36–7.

5 23 December 1940, *Halder Diary*, 309–10; Fritz, *Ostkrieg*, 57–9; Kay, *Exploitation, Resettlement, Mass Murder*, 56–63, 123–39. Cf. K. J. Arnold and G. C. Lübbers, 'The Meeting of the Staatssekretäre on 2 May 1941 and the Wehrmacht, A Document Up for Discussion', *Journal of Contemporary History*, 42:4 (2007), 613–26.

6 14, 17, 30 March 1941, *Halder Diary*, 332–9, 345–6. David Stahel, *Operation Barbarossa and Germany's Defeat in the East* (Cambridge: Cambridge University Press, 2009), 33–95.

7 'Orders for Special Areas in Connection with Directive 21', 19 May 1941, *Documents on the Holocaust*, 375. Fritz, *Ostkrieg*, 65–70; Geoffrey P. Megargee, *War of Annihilation. Combat and Genocide on the Eastern Front, 1941* (Lanham MD: Rowman and Littlefield, 2006), 33–41. The best overview and analysis of the Russo-German war is Evan Mawdsley, *Thunder in the East. The Nazi–Soviet War 1941–1945* (London: Arnold, 2007).

8 'Guidelines for the Treatment of Political Commissars', 6 June 1941, *Documents on the Holocaust*, 376–7. Felix Römer, 'The Wehrmacht in the War of Ideologies. The Army and Hitler's Criminal Orders on the Eastern Front', in Alex J. Kay, Jeff Rutherford and David Stahel eds, *Nazi Policy on the Eastern Front, 1941. Total War, Genocide and Radicalisation* (Rochester NY: University of Rochester Press, 2012), 73–100; Wolfram Wette, *The Wehrmacht. History, Myth, Reality*, trans. Deborah Lucas Schneider (Cambridge, MA: Harvard University Press, 2006), 90–5.

9 Shlomo Aronson, *Hitler, the Allies and the Jews* (Cambridge: Cambridge University Press, 2004), 58–61; Beevor, *The Second World War*, 159; Friedländer, *Nazi Germany and the Jews*, vol. 2, 131–4, 187–9.

10 Kay, *Exploitation, Resettlement, Mass Murder*, 96–114; Browning, *The Origins of the Final Solution*, 213–14; Longerich, *Holocaust*, 179–81; Longerich, *Himmler*, 516–28; Gerwarth, *Hitler's Hangman*, 182–5.

11 Christian Ingrao, *Believe and Destroy. Intellectuals in the SS War Machine*, trans. Andrew Brown (London: Polity, 2013), 138–48; Helmut Langerbein, *Hitler's Death Squads. The Logic of Mass Murder* (College Station, TX: Texas A&M University, 2004), 27–30.

12 Cf. Browning, *The Origins of the Final Solution*, 224–34 and Longerich, *Holocaust*, 181–91.

13 Wildt, *An Uncompromising Generation*, 268–79; Yitzhak Arad, Shmuel Krakowski, Shmuel Spector eds, *The Einsatzgruppen Reports* (New York: Holocaust Library, 1982), x–xiii.

14 Ronald Headland, *Messages of Murder. A Study of the Reports of the Security Police*

and the Security Service, 1941–1945 (Toronto: Associated University Press, 1992), 27–36, 37–47; Longerich, *Himmler*, 520; Jürgen Matthäus, 'Controlled Escalation: Himmler's men in the Summer of 1941 and the Holocaust in the Occupied Soviet Territories', *HGS*, 21:2 (2007), 218–42.

15 2 July 1941, Chief of the Sipo-SD to HSSPF, *Documents on the Holocaust*, 377–8 and a fuller version Noakes and Pridham eds, *Nazism 1919–1945* (1997 edn.), vol. 3, 1091–2; Browning, *The Origins of the Final Solution*, 227–8; Longerich, *Himmler*, 517–26; Gerwarth, *Hitler's Hangman*, 185–9. The idea for local pogroms may have come from Alfred Rosenberg.

16 Antony Polonsky, *The Jews in Poland and Russia*, vol. II, *1881–1914* (Oxford: Littman Library, 2010), 3–86.

17 Polonsky, *The Jews in Poland and Russia*, vol. III, 240–96.

18 Shmuel Spector, *The Holocaust of Volhynian Jews 1941–1944*, trans. Jerzy Michalowicz, (Jerusalem: Yad Vashem, 1990), 7–22; Polonsky, *The Jews in Poland and Russia*, vol. III, 376–94. On Bialystok, Sarah Bender, *The Jews of Bialystok during World War II and the Holocaust* (Waltham, MA: Brandeis University Press, 2008), 18–88.

19 Polonsky, *The Jews in Poland and Russia*, vol. III, 205–38.

20 Andrew Ezergailis, *The Holocaust in Latvia 1941–1944* (Riga: The Holocaust Institute of Latvia, 1996), 58–69; Bernhard Press, *The Murder of the Jews in Latvia 1941–1945* (Evanston: Northwestern University Press, 2000), 3–23, 25–32.

21 Spector, *The Holocaust of Volhynian Jews*, 22–34; Nachum Alport, *The Destruction of Slonim Jewry*, trans. Max Rosenfeld (New York: Holocaust Library, 1989), 9–10; Moty Stromer, *Memoirs of an Unfortunate Person. The Diary of Moty Stromer*, trans. Elinor Robinson (Jerusalem: Yad Vashem, 2008), 30; Tom Segev, *Simon Wiesenthal. His Life and Legends* (London: Cape, 2010), 41–2. Henryk Grynberg, *Children of Zion*, trans. Jacqueline Mitchell (Evanston: Northwestern University Press, 1994), 55–117 offers a panorama of experiences under Soviet rule, the deportations and life in Siberian and central Asian camps.

22 Polonsky, *The Jews in Poland and Russia*, vol. III, 384–94, 399–411; Ben Cion Pinchuk, 'Facing Hitler and Stalin. On the Subject of Jewish "Collaboration" in Soviet Occupied Eastern Poland, 1939–1941', and Josef Litvak, 'Jewish Refugees from Poland in the USSR, 1939–1946', in Joshua D. Zimmerman ed., *Contested Memories. Poles and Jews During the Holocaust and Its Aftermath* (New Brunswick: Rutgers University Press, 2003), 61–8 and 123–50; Jan T. Gross, 'The Jewish Community in the Soviet-Annexed Territories on the Eve of the Holocaust', in Lucjan Dobroscycki and Jeffrey S. Gurock eds, *The Holocaust in the Soviet Union* (Armonk, NY: M. E. Sharpe, 1993), 155–79.

23 Fritz, *Ostkrieg*, 77–91; Stahel, *Operation Barbarossa*, 153–86; for a summary of Einsatzgruppen operations, see Longerich, *Holocaust*, 195–206.

24 Chris Bellamy, *Absolute War. Soviet Russia in the Second World War* (London: Pan, 2007), 179–98.

25 30 June, 6, 18 July 1941, *Einsatzgruppen Reports*, 10, 36. Konrad Kwiet, 'Rehearsing for Murder: The Beginning of the Final Solution in Lithuania in June 1941', *HGS*, 12:1 (1998), 3–26. The 'Operational Situational Reports' of the

Einsatzgruppen were dated and numbered sequentially, but each 'sitrep' summarized despatches from more than one EG or EK, often combined information from a few, and frequently covered several days if not longer. To avoid confusion and clutter only the date of a report will be given and it will usually only be tied to a specific unit if just one is mentioned.

26 30 June 1941, *Einsatzgruppen Reports*, 1; 22 June, 7 July, 4 August 1941, Avraham Tory [Golub], *Surviving the Holocaust. The Kovno Ghetto Diary*, trans. Jerzy Michalowicz, ed. Martin Gilbert with Dina Porat (Cambridge MA: Harvard University Press, 1990), vii–xxiv, 3–5, 7–8, 23–8; 'An appeal to the nations of the world. From the diary of Dr Victor Kutorga' [1941], in Joshua Rubinstein and Ilya Altman eds, *The Unknown Black Book. The Holocaust in the German-Occupied Soviet Territories*, trans. Christopher Morris and Joshua Rubinstein (Bloomington: Indiana University Press, 2008), 278–82.

27 Michael McQueen, 'Nazi Policy Towards the Jews in the Reichskommissariat Ostland, June–December 1941', in Zvi Gitelman ed., *Bitter Legacy. Confronting the Holocaust in the USSR* (Bloomington: Indiana University Press, 1997), 91–103; Christoph Dieckmann, 'The Role of the Lithuanians in the Holocaust', in Beate Kosmola and Feliks Tych eds, *Facing the Nazi Genocide: Non-Jews and Jews in Europe* (Berlin: Metropol, 2004), 149–68.

28 8, 10 July 1941, *Tory Diary*, 15–18.

29 Yitzhak Arad, *The Holocaust in the Soviet Union* (Lincoln: University of Nebraska Press, 2009), 141–7.

30 13 July 1941, *Einsatzgruppen Reports*, 22–3; 4–7, 9–10, 12, 20 July, Herman Kruk, *The Last Days of the Jerusalem of Lithuania: Chronicles from the Vilna Ghetto and the Camps 1939–1944*, trans. Barbara Harshav, ed. Benjamin Harshav (New Haven: Yale University Press, 2002), 46–7, 50–1, 56–7, 60–1, 66, 70–2; 11 July 1941, Kazimierz Sakowicz, *Ponary Diary 1941–1943*, ed. Yitzhak Arad (New Haven: Yale University Press, 2005), 11–13, 13–14.

31 11, 13–19, 23 July, *Sakowicz Diary*, 11–13, 13–14.

32 'Accounts of local inhabitants Nesta Miselevich, Veksler, and Yazhgur', *The Unknown Black Book*, 301–3.

33 16 July 1941, *Einsatzgruppen Reports*, 26–8; Ezergailis, *The Holocaust in Latvia*, 145–62, 173–86, 208–11.

34 16 July 1941, *Einsatzgruppen Reports*, 26–8; Andrej Angrick and Peter Klein, *The 'Final Solution' in Riga. Exploitation and Annihilation, 1941–1944*, trans. Ray Brandon (New York: Berghahn, 2009), 65–7, 70; Ezergailis, *The Holocaust in Latvia*, 217–18. Max Kaufman survived and while in a camp for displaced persons in Germany wrote one of the first accounts of the destruction of the Latvian Jews, *Die Vernichtung Der Juden Lettlands* (Munich: Deutscher Verlag, 1947).

35 For the routes of the units, see Arad, *The Holocaust in the Soviet Union*, 126–9.

36 Arad, *The Holocaust in the Soviet Union*, 150–2, 163–7; Bender, *The Jews of Bialystok*, 90–8; Edward B. Westerman, *Hitler's Police Battalions. Enforcing Racial War in the East* (Lawrence: University of Kansas Press, 2005), 171–7.

37 Polonsky, *The Jews in Poland and Russia*, vol. III, 421–4.

38 Jan T. Gross, *Neighbors. The Destruction of the Jewish Community in Jedwabne*,

Poland (Princeton: Princeton University Press, 2001), 22–101; Spector, *The Holocaust of Volhynian Jews*, 64–7; cf. Longerich, *Holocaust*, 192–205. For debate about the methodology for investigating these events and interpreting them, see Antony Polonsky and Joanna B. Michlic eds, *The Neighbors Respond. The Controversy Over the Jedwabne Massacre in Poland* (Princeton: Princeton University Press, 2004), esp. 209–385.

39 5 August 1941, *Einsatzgruppen Reports*, 67–8; Arad, *The Holocaust in the Soviet Union*, 151–2; Hersh Smolar, 'The History of the Minsk Ghetto', in Ilya Ehrenburg and Vasily Grossman eds, *The Black Book*, trans. John Glad and James S. Levine (New York: Holocaust Library, 1981), 139–40; Barbara Epstein, *The Minsk Ghetto 1941–1943. Jewish Resistance and Soviet Internationalism* (Berkeley: University of California Press, 2008), 77–87.

40 Einsatzgruppe B reports, 23, 24 July 1941, *Einsatzgruppen Reports*, 42–4, 45–6. A long report on the 'Jewish Question in the Byelorussian Territories', transmitted to Berlin on 27 July 1941, reads as if it was the first time the Sipo-SD had paid serious attention to this issue, *Einsatzgruppen Reports*, 47–50.

41 3, 5, 6, 16 July 1941, *Einsatzgruppen Reports*, 4, 8–9, 12, 31–3; Frank Golczewski, 'Shades of Grey: Reflections on Jewish-Ukrainian and German-Ukrainian Relations in Galicia', in Ray Brandon and Wendy Lower eds, *The Shoah in Ukraine. History, Testimony, Memorialization* (Bloomington: Indiana University Press, 2010), 114–55; Simon Redlich, 'Metropolitan Andreii Sheptyts'kyi and the Complexities of Ukrainian Jewish Relations' in Gitelman ed., *Bitter Legacy*, 61–90.

42 L. Herts and Naftali Nacht, 'The Murder of the Jews in Lvov', *The Black Book*, 109; Arad, *The Holocaust in the Soviet Union*, 89–91; Renata Kessler ed., *The Wartime Diary of Edmund Kessler, Lwow, Poland, 1942–1944* (Boston: Academic Studies Press, 2010), 33–7; David Kahane, *Lvov Ghetto Diary*, trans. Jerzy Michalowicz (Amhurst MA: University of Massachusetts Press, 1990), 6–7.

43 6, 11 July 1941, *Einsatzgruppen Reports*, 12, 19.

44 Spector, *The Holocaust of Volhynian Jews*, 64–71, 72–100.

45 EG C report, 29 July 1941, *Einsatzgruppen Reports*, 55–7.

46 For the routes of the Einsatzgruppen units, see Arad, *The Holocaust in the Soviet Union*, 126–9; Dennis Deletant, *Hitler's Forgotten Ally. Ion Antonescu and His Regime, Romania 1940–1944* (Houndmills: Palgrave Macmillan, 2006), 83–7.

47 Deletant, *Hitler's Forgotten Ally*, 12–25; Jean Ancel, *The History of the Holocaust in Romania* (Lincoln: University of Nebraska Press, 2010), 71–82 and *The Economic Destruction of Romanian Jewry*, 48–63.

48 Ioanid, *The Holocaust in Romania*, 38–43; Ancel, *The History of the Holocaust in Romania*, 71–82; 9 August 1940, *Dorian Diary*, 112–13.

49 Ioanid, *The Holocaust in Romania*, 45–51; Ancel, *The Economic Destruction of Romanian Jewry*, 69–86, 86–124; 25 June 1940, 10 January 1941, *Dorian Diary*, 99–100, 135–6.

50 Deletant, *Hitler's Forgotten Ally*, 52–67; Ancel, *The Economic Destruction of Romanian Jewry*, 127–32; 24 January, 2, 5 February, March 1941, *Dorian Diary*, 137–9, 140–4, 148–9.

51 Ancel, *The Economic Destruction of Romanian Jewry*, 148–70; Ioanid, *The Holocaust in Romania*, 111.

52 Ancel, *The Economic Destruction of Romanian Jewry*, 307–22; Ancel, *The History of the Holocaust in Romania*, 445–56; Ioanid, *The Holocaust in Romania*, 63–90 and 'The Holocaust in Romania: the Iasi Pogrom of June 1941', *Central European History* 2:2 (1993), 119–48; 11, 13 August 1941, *Dorian Diary*, 166, 167.

53 11, 17, July 1941, *Einsatzgruppen Reports*, 16–19, 34–5; Einsatzgruppe D report, 21 July 1941, cited in Ioanid, *The Holocaust in Romania*, 108; Ioanid, *The Holocaust in Romania*, 90–108; Ancel, *The History of the Holocaust in Romania*, 171–5; Friedländer, *Nazi Germany and the Jews*, vol. 2, 225–7, comments that the Romanians were 'outperforming Otto Ohlendorf's Einsatzgruppe D'.

54 Ancel, *The History of the Holocaust in Romania*, 176–91; Dennis Deletant, 'Transnistria and the Romanian Solution of the "Jewish Problem"', in Brandon and Lower eds, *The Shoah in Ukraine*, 156–67.

55 Rakhil Fradis-Milner to Rakhil Kovnator, 25 September 1944, *The Unknown Black Book*, 157–61; EG D report, 23 August 1941, *Einsatzgruppen Reports*, 105–6.

56 E. Grosberg statement, *The Black Book*, 92–3; Ioanid, *The Holocaust in Romania*, 111–42; Simon Geissbühler, 'The Rape of Jewish Women and Girls During the First Phase of the Romanian Offensive in the East, July 1941. A Research Agenda and Preliminary Findings', *Holocaust Studies* 19:1 (2013), 59–80.

57 Christa Schroeder, *He was My Chief. The Memoirs of Adolf Hitler's Secretary*, trans. Geoffrey Brooks (London: Frontline Books, 2009), 89–90; 24, 30 June, 3, 8, July 1941, *Halder Diary*, 416–21, 437–8, 444–6, 501–4; Fritz, *Ostkrieg*, 82–111.

58 Jürgen Matthäus, 'Operation Barbarossa and the Onset of the Holocaust, June–December 1941', in Browning, *The Origins of the Final Solution*, 265–7; Kay, *Exploitation, Resettlement, Mass Murder*, 180–5.

59 Kay, *Exploitation, Resettlement, Mass Murder*, 99–101; Matthäus, 'Operation Barbarossa', 277–84; Arad, *The Holocaust in the Soviet Union*, 96–101; Longerich, *Holocaust*, 239–40.

60 28 June 1941, *Halder Diary*, 429–31; Stahel, *Operation Barbarossa*, 160, 199, 254–7; Omer Bartov, *Hitler's Army. Soldiers, Nazis, and War in the Third Reich* (New York: Oxford University Press, 1992), 127–30.

61 10, 25 July 1941, *Halder Diary*, 463–5, 485; Megargee, *Inside Hitler's High Command*, 134–5; Stahel, *Operation Barbarossa*, 228–45.

62 Megargee, *Inside Hitler's High Command*, 112–24; Fritz, *Ostkrieg*, 81–91, 116–34, 148–62, 182–93; Stahel, *Operation Barbarossa*, 209–300.

63 24 July, 22 August 1941, *Halder Diary*, 485, 514–15; Megargee, *Inside Hitler's High Command*, 131–7; Stahel, *Operation Barbarossa*, 423–38.

64 David Stahel, *Kiev 1941. Hitler's Battle for Supremacy in the East* (Cambridge: Cambridge University Press, 2012); cf. Mawdsley, *Thunder in the East*, 69–74.

65 10 August, 13 September 1941, *Halder Diary*, 504–6, 529–35. David Stahel, 'Radicalizing Warfare. Command and the Failure of Operation Barbarossa', in Kay, Rutherford and Stahel eds, *Nazi Policy on the Eastern Front, 1941*, 19–44; Kershaw, *Hitler 1936–1945*, 405–20; Megargee, *War of Annihilation*, 57–71, 89–96, 108–15. Cf. Arad, *The Holocaust in the Soviet Union*, 129–33, rejecting arguments

that the food crisis or security were reasons for the escalation of killing and arguing that they merely served as pretexts.

66 3 October 1941, *Halder War Diary*, 545; Philip Blood, *Hitler's Bandit Hunters. The SS and the Nazi Occupation of Europe* (Washington DC: Potomac Books, 2008), 63.

67 Proclamation of OKW, 12 September 1941, *Documents on the Holocaust*, 387; Stephen G. Fritz, *Frontsoldaten, The German Soldier in World War II* (Lexington KY: University Press of Kentucky, 1995), 199.

68 Longerich, *Holocaust*, 204–11, 214–18; Longerich, *Himmler*, 529–37; Gerwarth, *Hitler's Hangman*, 195–6, 197–201. Longerich, *Holocaust*, 181–2, argues that Himmler envisaged a three-phase, expanding deployment of killing units in line with operational possibilities, first, in the army rear areas, then in the Army Group rear areas, and finally the zones of civil administration. Christian Gerlach, *Krieg, Ernärung, Völkermord. Deutsche Vernichtungspolitik im Zweiten Weltkrieg* (Zurich: Pendo, 2001), 11–78, sets out the case for planned measures to eliminate 'useless eaters'.

69 Longerich, *Holocaust*, 218–31; Matthäus, 'Operation Barbarossa', 253–77. Matthäus, 'Operation Barbarossa', 261–2, suggests that the mass killing moved from a 'utopian' to a practical phase, but his own evidence of the severely technical approach to annihilating populations implies that both thinking and practice moved in the reverse direction.

70 Longerich, *Holocaust*, 239–40; Dieckmann, 'The Role of the Lithuanians', 157–61; Robert G. Waite, '"Reliable Local Residents": Collaboration in Latvia, 1941–1945', in Andris Caune et al. eds, *Latvia in World War II* (Riga: University of Latvia, 2000), 114–42.

71 Westerman, *Hitler's Police Battalions*, 15–16, 68–87, 100–14, 185–91.

72 For contrasting explanations of how Germans could kill such vast numbers of Jews in cold blood, see Daniel Jonah Goldhagen, *Hitler's Willing Executioners. Ordinary Germans and the Holocaust* (London: Little Brown, 1996), 181–280; Christopher R. Browning, *Ordinary Men. Reserve Police Battalion 101 and the Final Solution in Poland* (New York: Harper Collins, 1992); Westerman, *Hitler's Police Battalions*. On the role of the German army, see Hannes Heer and Klaus Naumann eds, *War of Extermination. The German Military in World War II 1941–1944* (New York: Berghahn, 2000).

73 10, 12, 15, 22, 29 August, 23 September, 9 October, 14 November 1941, *Einsatzgruppen Reports*, 82, 84, 88–9, 104–5, 114–16, 148–55, 177–9, 231–5; 3 October 1941, *Halder War Diary*, 545. See also Jeff Rutherford, *Combat and Genocide on the Eastern Front. The German Infantry's War, 1941–1944* (Cambridge: Cambridge University Press, 2014), 128–45.

74 Longerich, *Holocaust*, 242–7; cf. Waitman Wade Beorn, *Marching Into Darkness. The Wehrmacht and the Holocaust in Belarus* (Cambridge, MA: Harvard University Press, 2014), 92–118.

75 Fritz, *Frontsoldaten*, 55–6, 58–9, 195–7; Bartov, *Hitler's Army*, 160–1. The samples quoted by Bartov are taken mainly from a collection published by the Germans in 1941, *Deutsche Soldaten sehen die Sowjetunion*, but his conclusions are confirmed

by Fritz, who trawled through numerous field post collections and private archives. See also, Neitzel and Welzer, *Soldaten. On Fighting, Killing and Dying. The Secret Second World War Tapes of German POWs*, 34–6, 44–76, 142–9.

76 Fuchs to Madi, 3, 25 June, 5 July, 5 August 1941; Fuchs to his father, 4 August 1941, *Letters of Karl Fuchs*, 105, 110, 112, 118, 120. Fuchs was killed in the final lunge towards Moscow.

77 Bartov, *Hitler's Army*, 130–1. Hannes Heer, 'The Logic of Extermination: The Wehrmacht and the Anti-Partisan War', in Heer and Naumann eds, *War of Extermination*, 92–126.

78 Matthäus, 'Operation Barbarossa', 290–3; Ingrao, *Believe and Destroy*, 161–200; Longerich, *Himmler*, 534–5. Eichmann's comments were made to an ex-Nazi journalist in Buenos Aires in 1955 or 1956 and repeated to his interrogator after he was captured and taken to Israel to stand trial for his crimes in 1960: *The Trial of Adolf Eichmann. Record of Proceedings in the District Court of Jerusalem*, 9 vols (Jerusalem: Israel Ministry of Justice, 1992–5), vol. 7, 212–13.

79 EG A reports, 10 August, 19 September 1941, *Einsatzgruppen Reports*, 82, 138; 'An Appeal to the Nations of the World', from the diary of Dr Viktor Kuturga, *The Unknown Black Book*, 286.

80 4 August–1 October 1941, *Tory Diary*, 26–39.

81 EG A, 16 August 1941, *Einsatzgruppen Reports*, 91; 8, 10 July, 4 August, *Tory Diary*, 15–18, 23–8; Dieckmann, 'The Role of the Lithuanians', 162–5; Dina Porat, 'The Holocaust in Lithuania. Some Unique Aspects', in David Cesarani ed., *The Final Solution. Origins and Implementation* (London: Routledge, 1994), 159–74.

82 28 October 1941, *Tory Diary*, 43–59.

83 5, 6, September, 1 October 1941, *Vilna Ghetto Chronicles*, 94–6, 122–3; Yitzhak Arad commentary in *Sakowicz Diary*, 22–7, 30–4, 43–5.

84 23–27 August, 2 September 1941, *Sakowicz Diary*, 13–14, 20–1, 27–9.

85 2 September, 25 October, 21 November 1941, *Sakowicz Diary*, 27–9, 34–6, 40.

86 4 September 1941, *Vilna Ghetto Chronicles*, 91–2.

87 5, 6, 16–17 September, 1 October, 22, 25, 31 December, *Vilna Ghetto Chronicles*, 94–6, 113–15, 122, 133–6, 149, 160.

88 Angrick and Klein, *The 'Final Solution' in Riga*, 101–18; Gertrude Schneider, 'The Two Ghettos in Riga, Latvia, 1941–43', in Dobroscycki and Gurock eds, *The Holocaust in the Soviet Union*, 183–5; Martin Dean, 'Seizure, Registration and Sale: the strange case of the German Administration of Jewish Moveable Property in Latvia (1941–1944)', in Caune et al. eds., *Latvia in World War II*, 372–8.

89 Arad, *The Holocaust in the Soviet Union*, 148–9; 'The story of Syoma Shpungin', *The Black Book*, 347–8.

90 Sönke Neitzel ed., *Tapping Hitler's Generals. Transcripts of Secret Conversations, 1941–45* (Barnsley: Front Line Books, 2007), 204–5.

91 Bender, *The Jews of Bialystok*, 98–108.

92 Arad, *The Holocaust in the Soviet Union*, 155–6.

93 Alport, *The Destruction of Slonim Jewry*, 50–102.

94 'Report on the Course of the Action in the Pripet 27 July–11 August', *Documents on the Holocaust*, 414–15.

95 Christian Gerlach, 'German Economic Interests, Occupation Policy, and the Murder of the Jews in Belorussia, 1941/43', in Ulrich Herbert ed., *National Socialist Extermination Policies. Contemporary Perspectives and Controversies* (New York: Berghahn, 2000), 210–39.

96 Ingrao, *Believe and Destroy*, 159; 'Liquidation of the Jews in Mstislavl', *The Unknown Black Book*, 274–5.

97 Spector, *The Holocaust of Volhynian Jews*, 101–6.

98 Thomas Sandkühler, 'Anti-Jewish Policy and the Murder of the Jews in the District of Galicia, 1941/42', in Herbert ed., *National Socialist Extermination Policies*, 104–27; Andrej Angrick, 'Annihilation and Labour: Jews and Thoroughfare IV in Central Ukraine', in Brandon and Lower eds., *The Shoah in Ukraine*, 190–223.

99 Arad, *The Holocaust in the Soviet Union*, 223–8.

100 Ibid, 225–6; Kahane, *Lvov Ghetto Diary*, 34; Stromer, *Memoirs*, 67; *Kessler Diary*, 45, 50–52.

101 Stromer, *Memoirs*, 79, 83–4; Kahane, *Lvov Ghetto Diary*, 36–7.

102 19, 28 September 1941, *Einsatzgruppen Reports*, 140, 174.

103 Vasily Grossman, 'The Murder of the Jews in Berdichev' and 'In the Vinnitsa Region' by R. Kovnator, *The Black Book*, 13–24, 28–32.

104 EG C reports, 28 September, 2, 27 October 1941, *Einsatzgruppen Reports*, 164–5, 168, 210–13; Lev Ozerov, *The Black Book*, 3–12; Anatoly Podolsky, 'The Tragic Fate of Ukrainian Jewish Women Under Nazi Occupation, 1941–1944', in Hedgepath and Saidel eds, *Sexual Violence*, 93-107, esp. 98-100.

105 9 August 1941, *Einsatzgruppen Reports*, 77–8; Wendy Lower, 'Axis Collaboration, Operation Barbarossa and the Holocaust in the Ukraine', in Kay, Rutherford and Stahel eds., *Nazi Policy on the Eastern Front, 1941*, 186–219; Wendy Lower, *Nazi Empire Building and the Holocaust in the Ukraine* (Chapel Hill: University of North Carolina Press, 2005), 69–86; Shmuel Spector, 'The Holocaust of the Ukrainian Jews', in Gitelman ed., *Bitter Legacy*, 43–60.

106 Arad, *The Holocaust in the Soviet Union*, 181–4.

107 The experience was recorded by G. Munblit, *The Black Book*, 59–60.

108 16 January, 4 February 1942, *Einsatzgruppen Reports*, 289; 'The Recollections of Engineer S S Krivoruchko', *The Unknown Black Book*, 99–103.

109 'The Diary of Sara Gleykh', edited by Ilya Ehrenburg, *The Black Book*, 70–6.

110 Arad, *The Holocaust in the Soviet Union*, 201–11.

111 7, 28, August, 11 September 1941, *Einsatzgruppen Reports*, 76, 112–13, 128–9; Randolph Braham, *The Politics of Genocide. The Holocaust in Hungary*, 2 vols (New York: Columbia University Press, 1994 edn), vol. 1, 207–14.

112 Ancel, *The Economic Destruction of Romanian Jewry*, 252–56; Dennis Deletant, 'Transnistria and the Romanian Solution of the "Jewish Problem"', in Brandon and Lower eds, *The Shoah in Ukraine*, 167–72.

113 Ancel, *The Economic Destruction of Romanian Jewry*, 186–91; Ioanid, *The Holocaust in Romania*, 142–75; Podolsky, 'The Tragic Fate of Ukrainian Jewish Women', 102–3.

114 Ancel, *The Economic Destruction of Romanian Jewry*, 201–16, 216–24.

115 Fradis-Milner, 25 September 1944, *The Unknown Black Book*, 158–9; Ioanid, *The Holocaust in Romania*, 195–212; Ancel, *The Economic Destruction of Romanian Jewry*, 256–71.

116 26 October 1941, *Einsatzgruppen Reports*, 209; 'Odessa', based on eye-witness reports collated by Vera Inber, *The Black Book*, 77–91; 'The story of Anna Morguilis from Odessa', *The Unknown Black Book*, 115–18; Ancel, *The Economic Destruction of Romanian Jewry*, 280–2; Ioanid, *The Holocaust in Romania*, 177–82.

117 'Odessa', based on eye-witness reports collated by Vera Inber, *The Black Book*, 85–6; 'Recollections and verses of the schoolboy Lev Rozhetksy, April 4–August 16, 1944', *The Unknown Black Book*, 121–32, also testimony from survivors Bogdanovska camp, collected in May 1944, *The Unknown Black Book*, 138–41; Ancel, *The Economic Destruction of Romanian Jewry*, 282–88; Ioanid, *The Holocaust in Romania*, 182–93, 195–210.

118 Ancel, *The Economic Destruction of Romanian Jewry*, 290–306; Ioanid, *The Holocaust in Romania*, 187–92. On the role of the Selbstschutz see Eric Steinhart, *The Holocaust and the Germanization of Ukraine* (New York: Cambridge University Press, 2015), 113–56.

119 Jäger Report, *Documents on the Holocaust*, 398–400; Arad, *The Holocaust in the Soviet Union*, 261, 274.

120 11 January 1942, *Einsatzgruppen Reports*, 268–9; Gerlach, 'German Economic Interests', 224; Dieter Pohl, 'The Murder of Ukraine's Jews under German Military Administration and in the Reich Commissariat Ukraine', in Brandon and Lower eds, *The Shoah in Ukraine*, 43.

121 'Provisional Directive Concerning the Treatment of Jews', 13 August 1941, *Documents on the Holocaust*, 394–5; Matthäus, 'Operation Barbarossa', 283–7; Angrick and Klein, *The 'Final Solution' in Riga*, 98–9; Arad, *The Holocaust in the Soviet Union*, 110–11.

122 Hinrich Lohse to Reich Minister for the Occupied Eastern Territories, 15 November 1941 and Otto Brautigan to Lohse, 18 December 1941, *Documents on the Holocaust*, 394–5; Armaments Inspectorate Ukraine to Office of the Industrial Armaments Division, General Thomas, 2 December 1941, *Documents on the Holocaust*, 417–19; Arad, *The Holocaust in the Soviet Union*, 155–6, 158–62. Cf. Longerich, *Holocaust*, 231–2.

123 Michman, *The Emergence of the Jewish Ghettos*, 105–20.

124 EG C report, 12 September 1941, *Einsatzgruppen Reports*, 130–1; Ioanid, *The Holocaust in Romania*, 142.

125 Arad, *The Holocaust in the Soviet Union*, 75–7; Mordechai Altshuler, 'Escape and Evacuation of Soviet Jews at the time of the Nazi Invasion: Policies and Realities', in Dobroscycki and Gurock eds, *The Holocaust in the Soviet Union*, 77–104.

126 2–6 October, 11, 21, 23, 30 November, 4 December 1941, *Halder Diary*, 543–5, 562–3, 570–3, 577–9; Fritz, *Ostkrieg*, 135–65, 182–93.

127 11 August, 21 October 1940, *Klemperer Diary*, I, 336–7, 344; Browning, *The Origins of the Final Solution*, 169, 172–8; Grenville, *The Jews and Germans*, 216–17.

128 Kwiet, 'Without Neighbours', 117–48; Ascher, *A Community under Siege*, 209–10, 219–26, 228–9, 230–8.

129 Grenville, *The Jews and Germans*, 250–1; Ascher, *A Community under Siege*, 216–19.

130 Browning, *The Origins of the Final Solution*, 193–7; Meyer, 'Between Self-Assurance and Forced Collaboration', in Nicosia and Scrase eds, *Jewish Life in Nazi Germany*, 150–4; 8 July, 7 August, 6 October 1940, District Governor, Upper and Central Franconia; Cologne Emigration Office, reports for July–September 1940 and January–March 1942, *Secret Nazi Reports*, 500, 502, 506, 578; 27 July 1941, *Klemperer Diary*, I, 405; Leo Spitzer, *Hotel Bolivia. The Culture of Memory in a Refuge from Nazism* (New York: Hill and Wang, 1998), 112–22, 146–7; Heppner, *Shanghai Refuge. A Memoir of the World War II Jewish Ghetto*, 60–70.

131 2, 18 August, 20 November 1941, *Von Hassell Diaries*, 185–8, 191, 193, 200–1; 27 July, 2 September 1941, *Klemperer Diary*, I, 405, 409; Reck-Malleczewen, *Diary of a Man in Despair*, 141–2, 154–7.

132 Smith, *Last Train From Berlin*, 56, 85–6, 90–1, 99–100, 103–4.

133 Goebbels diary cited in Fritz, *Ostkrieg*, 121, 135–6; Smith, *Last Train From Berlin*, 56–7, 58–65, 74–5.

134 On *Jud Süß*: SD District Office, Bielefeld, 8, 15 October 1940 and RSHA Dept III (SD), 'Reports from the Reich', 28 November 1940; on *Der ewige Jude*, RSHA Dept III (SD), 'Reports from the Reich', 20 January 1941 and SD District Office, Höxter, 'Film Programme', 7 February 1941, *Secret Nazi Reports*, 507, 511–12, 515–17; 10 December 1940, *Klemperer Diary*, I, 347–8; Thacker, *Joseph Goebbels*, 221–3, 225–6.

135 RSHA Dept III (SD), 'Reports from the Reich', 31 July 1941, *Secret Nazi Reports*, 529–30; Smith, *Last Train From Berlin*, 138–9; Herf, *The Jewish Enemy*, 103–16; Breitman and Lichtman, *FDR and the Jews*, 184–5.

136 NSDAP Gau Munich-Upper Bavaria Office for Racial Policy, report, 14 October 1940; SD Main District Office, Bielefeld, 30 November 1940 and 5 August 1941 report on 'Mood Against the Jews', *Secret Nazi Reports*, 509, 510, 532–3.

137 Thacker, *Joseph Goebbels*, 233–6; Longerich, *Goebbels*, 486–92; Kershaw, *Hitler 1936–1945*, 472–4; Friedländer, *Nazi Germany and the Jews*, vol. 2, 238–9, 251–6.

138 SD District Office, Bielefeld, report, 13 September; SD Office Minden, 'Marking of the Jews', 26 September; District Governor, Augsburg, report for September, 8 October; Gendarmerie, Urspringen, 'Behaviour of the Jews in Urspringen', 19 September; RSHA Dept III (SD), 'Reports from the Reich', 9 October 1941, *Secret Nazi Reports*, 537, 539–40, 542–3, 547, 548–9; Leland B. Morris, US Embassy, to State Department, 30 September 1941, *Fremde Blicke*, 561–2.

139 17 January 1942, *Klemperer Diary*, II, 6; RSHA Dept III (SD), 9 October; SD District Office Paderborn, report, 11 October 1941, *Secret Nazi Reports*, 548–9, 549; Smith, *Last Train From Berlin*, 143; Harry Flannery, *Assignment to Berlin* (New York: Knopf, 1942), 295–7; Friedländer, *Nazi Germany and the Jews*, vol. 2, 251–6.

140 Flannery, *Assignment to Berlin*, 143; 15 September 1941, *Klemperer Diary*, I, 410–11; Ruth Andreas-Friedrich, *Berlin Underground*, trans. Barrows Mussey (London: Latimer House, 1948), 65.

141 Kershaw, *Hitler 1936–1945*, 476–81; Peter Witte, 'Two Decisions Concerning the "Final Solution of the Jewish Question": Deportations to Lodz and Mass Murder in Chelmno', *HGS*, 9:3 (1995), 318–46; Matthäus, 'Operation Barbarossa', 285–94; Dan van der Vat, *The Good Nazi. The Life and Lies of Albert Speer* (London: Weidenfeld and Nicolson, 1997), 95–6; Smith, *Last Train From Berlin*, 97–8; Mayor of Siegburg, 'Consolidating the Jews in the City of Siegburg Together Under One Roof', 4 June 1941; Mayor, Forschheim, report, 30 September, demanding relocation of Jews to outskirts; SD Bielefeld, 4 November; NSDAP Lübeck district leadership, 'Report on the Prevailing Mood', 10 November 1941, *Secret Nazi Reports*, 526, 545–6, 551–2. Aly, *Hitler's Beneficiaries*, 117–18; Collingham, *The Taste of War*, 157–64.

142 Witte, 'Two Decisions Concerning the "Final Solution of the Jewish Question"'; Matthäus, 'Operation Barbarossa', 300–6; Cesarani, *Eichmann*, 95–7; Epstein, *Model Nazi*, 184–6; Gerwarth, *Hitler's Hangman*, 206.

143 Epstein, *The Minsk Ghetto*, 77–9; Arad, *The Holocaust in the Soviet Union*, 152–5; Smolar, 'The History of the Minsk Ghetto', *The Black Book*, 152–3.

144 Livia Rothkirchen, *The Jews of Bohemia & Moravia. Facing the Holocaust* (Lincoln: University of Nebraska Press, 2005), 123–8; Zdenek Lederer, *Ghetto Theresienstadt* (London: Edward Goldston, 1953), 13–14. See Gerwarth, *Hitler's Hangman*, 201–5 for a more up-to-date interpretation of Heydrich's decision to clear the Protectorate of Jews.

145 Angrick and Klein, *The 'Final Solution' in Riga*, 131–48.

146 Major General Bruns, recorded 25 April 1945, Neitzel ed., *Tapping Hitler's Generals*, 227–8.

147 Angrick and Klein, *The 'Final Solution' in Riga*, 154–8.

148 Browning, *The Origins of the Final Solution*, 492–4; Angrick and Klein, *The 'Final Solution' in Riga*, 235–9; Jürgen Matthäus et al. eds, *Jewish Responses to Persecution*, vol. III, *1941–1942* (Lanham MD: AltaMira Press, 2013), 156–9; Ascher, *A Community under Siege*, 246–53.

149 Browning, *The Origins of the Final Solution*, 392–8; Epstein, *Model Nazi*, 186–7; Trunk, *Lodz Ghetto*, 228; Gutman, 'The Distinctiveness of the Lodz Ghetto', xlviii; Ian Kershaw, 'Improvised Genocide? The Emergence of "the Final Solution" in the Warthegau', *Transactions of the Royal Historical Society*, 6th series, vol. 2 (1992), 51–78; Patrick Montague, *Chelmno and the Holocaust. The Story of Hitler's First Death Camp* (London: I. B. Tauris, 2012), 14–27, 50–65; 20 December 1941, *Lodz Ghetto Chronicle*, 96–7.

150 Browning, *The Origins of the Final Solution*, 374–88; Grenville, *The Jews and Germans*, 217–18; Cesarani, *Eichmann*, 121–2.

151 Grenville, *Jews and Germans*, 241; Martin Dean, 'The Development and Implementation of Nazi Denaturalization and Confiscation Policy up to the Eleventh decree to the Reich Citizenship Law', *HGS*, 16:2 (2002), 217–42 and *Robbing the Jews*, 161–71, 222–43.

152 Kaplan, *Between Dignity and Despair*, 179–89; Rabinovici, *Eichmann's Jews*, 116–22; Smith, *Last Train From Berlin*, 138–40; 7 April 1942 District Governor, Upper

and Central Franconia, *Secret Nazi Reports*, 580–1; Christian Goeschel, 'Suicides of German Jews in the Third Reich', *German History*, 25:1 (2007), 24–45.

153 Smith, *Last Train From Berlin*, 140; SD District Office Minden, report, 19 December 1941 and Party District Chief Göttingen, 'Report to Göttingen Gestapo', 19 December 1941, *Secret Nazi Reports*, 567, 570; 13 January 1942, *Klemperer Diary*, II, 5; 1 November 1941, *Von Hassell Diaries*, 201.

154 Grenville, *Jews and Germans*, 222–4.

155 Angerick and Klein, *The 'Final Solution' in Riga*, 101–11; Josef Katz, *One Who Came Back. The Diary of a Jewish Survivor*, trans. Hilda Reach (Takoma Park, MD: Dryad Press, 2006), 13–25.

156 Oskar Rosenfeld, *In the Beginning was the Ghetto. Notebooks from Lodz*, ed. Hanno Loewy, trans. Brigitte Goldstein (Evanston: Northwestern University Press, 2002), 4–11, 12–13.

157 Horowitz, *Ghettostadt*, 132–42; entry on November, 1, 4, 13 December 1941, 1–5 January 1942, *Lodz Ghetto Chronicle*, 80–1, 85–6, 91–2, 93–4, 109–10.

158 Entry on November and 1, 2, 4, 13, 23–25 December 1941, 1–5 January 1942, *Lodz Ghetto Chronicle*, 83, 85–7, 87–9, 91–2, 93–4, 99–100, 111–15; 16, 17, 19, 20 October 1941, *Sierakowiak Diary*, 141–2; Trunk, *Lodz Ghetto*, 308–11.

159 Christian Gerlach, 'The Wannsee Conference, the Fate of German Jews, and Hitler's Decision in Principle to Exterminate All European Jews', *Journal of Modern History*, 70 (1998), 759–812.

160 23 June 1941, *Sierakowiak Diary*, 105; 26 June, 9 December 1941, *Berg Diary*, 87, 111; 20 August, n.d. October 1941, January 1942, *Ringelblum Notes*, 197–202, 251–2, 254; 26–28 December 1941, *Lodz Ghetto Chronicle*, 116.

161 24 August 1941, *Sierakowiak Diary*, 121–3; 23–25 June, 26–28 December 1941, 6–9 January 1942, *Lodz Ghetto Chronicle*, 62, 101, 116–19; 'At the Paper Ressort', *Lodz Ghetto Chronicle*, 235–48. *Ressort* was a corruption of *Arbeitsressort* – factory or workshop.

162 Gruner, *Jewish Forced Labour Under the Nazis*, 220–2; Weissmann Klein, *All But My Life*, 36–54; 4, 10 July, 4 August, 16 September, 1 November, 12 December 1941, *Diary of David Rubinowitz*, 16–18, 20, 22, 24, 26.

163 Adler, *In the Warsaw Ghetto*, 82–5, 221–3, 225–8, 238–9; 1, 12, 23 May, 22 June, 4 July, 18 October 1941, *Czerniaków Diary*, 228, 234, 240–1, 251, 254, 289–90.

164 21, 28 May, 3 June, 19 August, 21 November 1941, *Czerniaków Diary*, 239–40, 243, 245–6, 247, 268–9, 300–1; September 1941, *Ringelblum Notes*, 216–17. Cf. Raul Hilberg and Stanislaw Staron, 'Introduction', in *Czerniaków Diary*, 55–6.

165 23 August 1941, *Czerniaków Diary*, 271; 31 July 1941, *Berg Diary*, 80–3.

166 Mazor, *The Vanished City*, 120–1; 29 July 1941, *Berg Diary*, 75–6; 14 October 1941, *Czerniaków Diary*, 288.

167 October 1941, *Ringelblum Notes*, 222–3; 1, 27 July, 1 October 1941, *Berg Diary*, 69, 74, 96–8.

168 November 1941, *Ringelblum Notes*, 233–4; 22 November, 1 December 1941, *Berg Diary*, 107–10, 110–11.

169 5, 12, 15, 28 October, 4, 7 December 1941, *Weiss Diary*, 12–18, 18–22, 22–3, 30–1, 33–5.

170 7 December 1941 [entry undated, 9 December 1941], *Weiss Diary*, 35–9, 40–5.

171 [9–10 December, undated entries], 13, 14 [entry undated, 24] December 1942, *Weiss Diary*, 46–50, 50–6.

172 Poznanski, *Jews in France during World War II*, 172–99.

173 15, 22 June, 8 July, 2 August 1941, *Lambert Diary*, 43–3, 43–50, 54–5, 61–5.

174 8 July 1941, *Lambert Diary*, 54–5; Klarsfeld, 'The Influence of the War on the Final Solution in France', 271–81.

175 Thomas Laub, 'The development of German Policy in Occupied France, 1941, Against the background of the war in the East', in Kay, Rutherford and Stahel eds, *Nazi Policy on the Eastern Front, 1941*, 281–313; Adler, *The Jews of Paris and the Final Solution*, 37–41; Poznanski, *Jews in France during World War II*, 56–7, 207–9.

176 Ulrich Herbert, 'The German Military Command in Paris and the Deportation of the French Jews', in Herbert ed., *National Socialist Extermination Policies*, 128–62; Poznanski, *Jews in France during World War II*, 209–10.

177 Poznanski, *Jews in France during World War II*, 131–5; Adler, *The Jews of Paris and the Final Solution*, 81–102.

178 3 October, 30 November, 2, 11 December 1941, *Lambert Diary*, 71–2, 76–7, 77–9, 79–83.

179 Jean-Jacques Bernard, *The Camp of Slow Death*, trans. Edward Owen Marsh (London: Gollancz, 1945; originally published as *Camp de la mort lente* [Paris: Albin Michel, 1944]), 23, 41–2.

180 Moore, *Victims and Survivors*, 81–8; Presser, *Ashes in the Wind*, 76–97; Dean, *Robbing the Jews*, 264–76.

181 Bernard Wasserstein, *The Ambiguity of Virtue. Gertrude van Tijn and the Fate of the Dutch Jews* (London: Harvard University Press, 2014), 102–10.

182 Mark Mazower, *Inside Hitler's Greece. The Experience of Occupation, 1941–1944* (London: Yale University Press, 1993), 235–8. On the military campaign, see Craig Stockings and Eleanor Hancock, *Swastika over the Acropolis. Reinterpreting the Nazi Invasion of Greece in World War II* (Leiden: Brill, 2013).

183 Leni Yahil, *The Holocaust. The Fate of European Jewry* (New York: Oxford University Press, 1990), 349–52.

184 Menachem Shelach, 'The Murder of the Jews in Serbia and the Serbian Uprising in July 1941', in Cohen, Cochavi, Gelber eds, *The Shoah and the War*, 161–75; Walter Manoschek, '"Coming Along to Shoot Some Jews?" The Destruction of the Jews in Serbia', in Heer and Naumann eds, *War of Extermination*, 39–52.

185 Matthäus, 'Operation Barbarossa', 294–307.

186 Collingham, *The Taste of War*, 164–70, 180–99, 199–205, 353–79; cf. Tooze, *The Wages of Destruction*, 538–45.

187 Longerich, *Himmler*, 542–6; Longerich, *Holocaust*, 260–71; Gerwarth, *Hitler's Hangman*, 222–7; Evans, *The Third Reich at War*, 233.

188 Breitman and Lichtman, *FDR and the Jews*, 185–90.

189 Kershaw, *Fateful Decisions*, 184–242, 298–330; For Hitler's speech, see https://www.jewishvirtuallibrary.org/jsource/Holocaust/hitler_declares_war.html

190 Thacker, *Joseph Goebbels*, 236–43; Longerich, *Goebbels*, 506–7 translates the entry slightly differently; Browning, *The Origins of the Final Solution*, 407–8.

191 Browning, *The Origins of the Final Solution*, 408–9; Kershaw, *Hitler 1936–1945*, 461–75, 484–7.

192 Longerich, *Holocaust*, 297–8; Longerich, *Himmler*, 551–3.

Six – Final Solution: 1942

1 Fritz, *Ostkrieg*, 199–215; Michael Jones, *The Retreat. Hitler's First Defeat* (London: John Murray, 2009).

2 Fritz, *Ostkrieg*, 224–6, 226–30; Collingham, *The Taste of War*, 199–205.

3 Weinberg, *A World At Arms*, 408–11; Fritz, *Ostkrieg*, 230–6.

4 Mark Roseman, *The Villa, The Lake, The Meeting. Wannsee and the 'Final Solution'* (London: Allen Lane, 2002), 55–9.

5 Roseman, *The Villa, The Lake, The Meeting*, 60–4, 65–7. Yehoshua Büchler and Yehuda Bauer, 'Document: A Preparatory Document for the Wannsee "Conference"', *HGS*, 9:1 (1995), 121–9, reveal that the General Government was included in an attempt to bring the civil administration to heel. Cf. Christian Gerlach, 'The Wannsee Conference, the Fate of German Jews, and Hitler's Decision in Principle to Exterminate All European Jews', *Journal of Modern History*, 70 (1998), 759–812, arguing that the conference was originally called only to discuss the fate of Jews from the Greater Reich and Protectorate, but between 29 November and 8 January 1942 (when the revised invitations were sent out) mutated into a meeting to plan the fate of Jews across Europe.

6 *Documents on the Holocaust*, 249–53; for an alternative translation, see Roseman, *The Villa, The Lake, The Meeting*, 108–11; cf. Cesarani, *Eichmann*, 112–14.

7 Cf. Gerlach, 'The Wannsee Conference' and Longerich, *Holocaust*, 305–10.

8 *Documents on the Holocaust*, 253–6; Roseman, *The Villa, The Lake, The Meeting*, 111–13.

9 *Documents on the Holocaust*, 257–60; Roseman, *The Villa, The Lake, The Meeting*, 114–17.

10 *Documents on the Holocaust*, 260–1; Roseman, *The Villa, The Lake, The Meeting*, 117–18.

11 Cesarani, *Eichmann*, 114, 119–24; Gerlach, 'The Wannsee Conference'.

12 Friedländer, *Nazi Germany and the Jews*, vol. 2, 339–45; Wachsmann, *KL*, 292–4.

13 4 January 1942, *Lodz Ghetto Chronicle*, 111–16.

14 Gutman, 'The Distinctiveness of the Lodz Ghetto', xlviii–liii; Horowitz, *Ghettostadt*, 145–55; Trunk, *Lodz Ghetto*, 228–9.

15 Essay covering January–March 1942, *Lodz Ghetto Chronicle*, 120–1, 124–5; Shmuel Krakowski, *Chelmno. A Small Village in Europe. The First Nazi Mass Execution Camp* (Jerusalem: Yad Vashem, 2009), 57–66.

16 17 January 1942, diary of Shlomo Frank, cited in Trunk, *Lodz Ghetto*, 230–1.

17 Montague, *Chelmno and the Holocaust*, 66–72.

18 Ibid, 51–9, 76–85, 91–6.

19 Krakowski, *Chelmno*, 68–80.

20 Montague, *Chelmno and the Holocaust*, 96–113.

21 Ibid, 128–36.

22 Ibid, 76–82, 85–90; Krakowski, *Chelmno*, 183–91.

23 22–28 February 1942 and essay on the resettlement action, *Lodz Ghetto Chronicle*, 127–9.

24 21, 24, 26, 27, 29, 30 March 1942, *Sierakowiak Diary*, 149–50; Rosenfeld, *In the Beginning was the Ghetto*, 31–2; entry for March and 1 April 1942, *Lodz Ghetto Chronicle*, 133–40, 140–4.

25 17 February 1942 and undated notes, Rosenfeld, *In the Beginning was the Ghetto*, 14–16, 20–3, 24, 28–9; February 1942, *Lodz Ghetto Chronicle*, 129–31, 133–5.

26 Horowitz, *Ghettostadt*, 161–6; Longerich, *Himmler*, 563–7; Longerich, *Holocaust*, 323.

27 Horowitz, *Ghettostadt*, 166–7; Trunk, *Lodz Ghetto*, 222–38.

28 16, 18, 21–24 April 1942, *Lodz Ghetto Chronicle*, 147–50, 150–2; 19, 20, 23, 24 April 1942, *Sierakowiak Diary*, 155–7, 158; 19 April 1942, Rosenfeld, *In the Beginning was the Ghetto*, 34–5; Trunk, *Lodz Ghetto*, 38–9.

29 29–30 April, 1 May 1942, *Lodz Ghetto Chronicle*, 153–8, 159; 1, 5 May 1942, *Sierakowiak Diary*, 161, 163; 4 May 1942, Rosenfeld, *In the Beginning was the Ghetto*, 39–41.

30 4, 6–7 May 1942, *Lodz Ghetto Chronicle*, 160, 161–5; undated notes, 1942, Rosenfeld, *In the Beginning was the Ghetto*, 103–5.

31 7, 8, 12, 17 May 1942, *Lodz Ghetto Chronicle*, 165–7, 170–2, 174–7.

32 On contradictory German policies, see Gruner, *Jewish Forced Labour Under the Nazis*, 189–91; 12, 19, 23, 26 May 1942, Rosenfeld, *In the Beginning was the Ghetto*, 58–62.

33 18 May 1942, *Lodz Ghetto Chronicle*, 177–81.

34 Montague, *Chelmno and the Holocaust*, 183–8.

35 Dieter Pohl, 'The Murder of the Jews in the General Government', in Herbert ed., *National Socialist Extermination Policies*, 86–7 and David Silberklang, *Gates of Tears. The Holocaust in the Lublin District* (Jerusalem: Yad Vashem, 2013), 221–8, argue that a decision to murder masses of Jews was taken by Himmler and Odilo Globocnik in October 1941.

36 Silberklang, *Gates of Tears*, 228–51; Thomas Sandkühler, 'Anti-Jewish Policy and the Murder of the Jews in the District of Galicia, 1941/42', in Herbert ed., *National Socialist Extermination Policies*, 104–27; cf. Bogdan Musial, 'The Origins of Operation Reinhard', *Yad Vashem Studies*, 28 (1999), 112–53 and Dieter Pohl, 'Hans Krüger and the Murder of the Jews in the Stanislawow Region', *Yad Vashem Studies*, 26 (1998), 239–64; Peter R. Black, 'Auxiliaries for Operation Reinhard: Shedding Light on the Trawniki Training Camp Through Documents from Behind the Iron Curtain', in David Bankier ed., *Secret Intelligence and the Holocaust* (New York: Enigma Books, 2006), 327–36, on the limited number of trained men actually available for 'Operation Reinhard' at the outset.

37 Silberklang, *Gates of Tears*, 230–1, 260–79, 281–9.

38 Ibid, 286–7, 289–90.

39 Yitzhak Arad, *Belzec, Sobibor, Treblinka. The Operation Reinhard Death Camps* (Bloomington: Indiana University Press, 1987), 23–9.

40 Ibid, 68–74.

41 Ibid, 73; Robin O'Neill, 'Belzec – The Forgotten Death Camp', *East European Jewish Affairs*, 28:2 (1998–9), 49–62.

42 Silberklang, *Gates of Tears*, 290–306; Arad, *Belzec, Sobibor, Treblinka*, 383–9.

43 Silberklang, *Gates of Tears*, 307–35; Longerich, *Himmler*, 563–7; Pohl, 'The Murder of the Jews in the General Government', 88–9.

44 Rudolf Reder, 'Belzec', trans. M M Rubel, *Polin*, 13 (2000), 268–89, here 271–5. Reder's memoir was written in Polish with the assistance of Nella Rost, a researcher for the Jewish historical commissions that after the liberation of Poland collected evidence of crimes against the Jews. It was published in 1946 by the Jewish Historical Commission in Lwow.

45 Reder, 'Belzec', 280–8.

46 Kahane, *Lvov Ghetto Diary*, 43–4, 44–9; Esther Farbstein, *Hidden Thunder. Perspectives on Faith, Halacha, and Leadership during the Holocaust*, (Jerusalem: Mossad Harav Kook, 2007), 187–200, on the typical refusal of rabbis to condone handing over Jews to the Germans even to save the lives of other Jews.

47 Stromer, *Memoirs*, 85; Kahane, *Lvov Ghetto Diary*, 50–6; Farbstein, *Hidden Thunder*. 327–41.

48 Stromer, *Memoirs*, 113.

49 Kahane, *Lvov Ghetto Diary*, 57–72; John-Paul Himka, 'Metropolitan Andrey Sheptytsky and the Holocaust', *Polin*, 26 (2014), 337–60.

50 Robert Citino, *Death of the Wehrmacht. The German Campaigns of 1942* (Lawrence: University Press of Kansas, 2007), 50–84, 85–114, 116–48; Hayward, *Stopped at Stalingrad*, 65–119; Fritz, *Ostkrieg*, 236–66.

51 Citino, *Death of the Wehrmacht*, 152–82, 223–58; Fritz, *Ostkrieg*, 266–97.

52 Longerich, *Himmler*, 557–61; Michael Thad Allen, *The Business of Genocide. The SS, Slave Labour, and the Concentration Camps* (Chapel Hill: University of North Carolina Press, 2002), 154–64; Jens-Christian Wagner, 'Work and extermination in the concentration camps', in Jane Caplan and Nikolaus Wachsmann eds, *Concentration Camps in Nazi Germany. The New Histories* (London: Routledge, 2010), 132–6, 139–41; Wachsmann, *KL*, 289–97, 393–403.

53 Longerich, *Holocaust*, 314–20; Gruner, *Jewish Forced Labour Under the Nazis*, 257–9; Wachsmann, *KL*, 297–9, 306–25.

54 Friedländer, *Nazi Germany and the Jews*, vol. 2, 345–51; Longerich, *Holocaust*, 332–4; Longerich, *Himmler*, 568–71.

55 Longerich, *Himmler*, 572–3; Silberklang, *Gates of Tears*, 312–13; Gruner, *Jewish Forced Labour Under the Nazis*, 259–61. Confusingly, the name of the operation was probably coined before the assassination of Heydrich and not even the Nazis used a uniform spelling: Witte and Tyas, 'A New Document on the Deportation and Murder of Jews During "Einsatz Reinhardt" 1942', 474–5.

56 Citino, *Death of the Wehrmacht*, 168–76, 221–5; Longerich, *Holocaust*, 341–4; Aly, *Hitler's Beneficiaries*, 173–4; Fritz, *Ostkrieg*, 220–4.

57 Longerich, *Himmler*, 573–4; Gruner, *Jewish Forced Labour Under the Nazis*, 261–8.

58 Arad, *Belzec, Sobibor, Treblinka*, 30–6; Jules Schelvis, *Sobibor. A History of a Nazi Death Camp*, trans. Karin Dixon, ed. Bob Moore (Oxford: Berg, 2007), 23–39.

59 Testimony of Yacov Freidberg, session 64, 4 June 1961, *The Trial of Adolf Eichmann*, vol. III (Jerusalem: State of Israel Ministry of Justice, 1993), 1167–71; Arad, *Belzec, Sobibor, Treblinka*, 75–80.

60 Arad, *Belzec, Sobibor, Treblinka*, 114–15; Rochelle G. Saidel, *Mielec, Poland. The Shtetl that Became a Nazi Concentration Camp* (Jerusalem: Geffen, 2012), 88–9.

61 Arad, *Belzec, Sobibor, Treblinka*, 123–4; Schelvis, *Sobibor*, 103–13; Freidberg, *The Trial of Adolf Eichmann*, vol. III, 1167.

62 Arad, *Belzec, Sobibor, Treblinka*, 123–4 and Appendix A, 390–1.

63 Engelking and Leociak, *The Warsaw Ghetto*, 47–51.

64 31 January, 16 February, 13, 18 March, 1 April 1942, *Czerniaków Diary*, 320, 326, 335, 339; 10 April, 8 May 1942, *Ringelblum Notes*, 256–7, 261–4; 15 April, 8 May 1942, *Berg Diary*, 134–5, 145; 25, 30 May, 4 June 1942, Abraham Lewin, *A Cup of Tears. A Diary of the Warsaw Ghetto*, ed. Antony Polonsky, trans. Christopher Hutton (Oxford: Blackwell, 1988), 96–7, 106–8, 118; Havi Ben-Sasson and Lea Preiss, 'Twilight days: Missing Pages from Avraham Lewin's Warsaw Ghetto Diary, May–July 1942', *Yad Vashem Studies*, 33 (2005), 7–60, here entry 14 June 1942, 26; 3, 21 June 1942, *Kaplan Diary*, 286–7, 297–8. For Hitler's 30 January 1942 speech see Max Domarus ed., *Hitler Speeches and Proclamations 1932–1945*, trans. Mary Fran Golbert (Wauconda, IL: Bolchazy-Carducci Publishers, 1990), digital version at http://www.pdfarchive.info/pdf/H/Hi/Hitler_Adolf_-_Hitler_Speeches_and_Proclamations.pdf, 2570–9.

65 8 May 1942, *Ringelblum Notes*, 260–1; 16 May 1942, *Lewin Diary*, 73–7; 21 June 1942, *Czerniaków Diary*, 368; 27 June, 2 July 1942, *Kaplan Diary*, 302–3, 305–6.

66 26 June 1942, *Ringelblum Notes*, 301; 26 May, 2 June 1942, *Lewin Diary*, 95–6, 114; 6, 13 July 1942, *Kaplan Diary*, 307–8, 312–14.

67 January 1942, *Ringelblum Notes*, 245–6; 23 May 1942, *Kaplan Diary*, 277–8; see also 30 May 1942, *Lewin Diary*, 106–8.

68 2 February 1942, *Czerniaków Diary*, 321; 18, 22 May, 9 June 1942, *Lewin Diary*, 77–8, 89, 125–8; 7 May 1942, *Kaplan Diary*, 267–8; 28 May 1942, *Ringelblum Notes*, 282.

69 30 May 1942, *Ringelblum Notes*, 288–9; Mazor, *Vanished City*, 41–3.

70 30 May 1942, *Ringelblum Notes*, 288; Mazor, *Vanished City*, 114–15; 4, 8, 14, 27 April 1942, *Czerniaków Diary*, 340–1; 27 February, 12 June 1942, *Berg Diary*, 128–30, 159.

71 20, 25 February 1942, *Czerniaków Diary*, 328, 330; 21 May 1942, *Lewin Diary*, 84.

72 Oral history interviews with Bartolomeo Fruterro, Michaelangelo Pattoglio, in Nuto Revelli ed., *Mussolini's Death March. Eyewitness Accounts of Italian Soldiers on the Eastern Front*, trans. John Penuel (Lawrence: University Press of Kansas, 2013), 219–25, 239–61, here, 220 and 242–3.

73 2, 12, 13, 15 May, *Czerniaków Diary*, 349, 352–4; 8 May 1942, *Berg Diary*, 143–5; 13, 16, 19, 23 May 1942, *Lewin Diary*, 71–2, 80, 90; see also 14, 19 May 1942, *Kaplan Diary*, 271–2, 274–6.

74 Gutman, *The Jews of Warsaw*, 122–32, 132–44, 144–5, 146–54; Daniel Blatman, *For Our Freedom and Yours: The Jewish Labour Bund in Poland 1939–1949* (London: Vallentine Mitchell, 2003), 44–55; Engelking and Leociak, *The Warsaw Ghetto*, 659–72, 673–85.

75 Engelking and Leociak, *The Warsaw Ghetto*, 680–1; Gutman, *The Jews of Warsaw*, 162–7.

76 Engelking and Leociak, *The Warsaw Ghetto*, 681–3; Blatman, *For Our Freedom and Yours*, 90–6; Gutman, *The Jews of Warsaw*, 170–6; Zuckerman, *A Surplus of Memory*, 170–5, 181–4.

77 17 April 1942, *Czerniaków Diary*, 342–5; Engelking and Leociak, *The Warsaw Ghetto*, 683–5; Blatman, *For Our Freedom and Yours*, 97–101; Gutman, *The Jews of Warsaw*, 176–80.

78 26 June 1942, *Ringelblum Notes*, 295–6; Engelking and Leociak, *The Warsaw Ghetto*, 657–72.

79 3, 13, 17 June, 11, 18, 19 July 1942, *Czerniaków Diary*, 362, 366–7, 378, 381–2; 15, 30 June 1942, *Berg Diary*, 149–50; 17, 18 July 1942, Hillel Seidman, *The Warsaw Ghetto Diaries*, trans. Yosef Israel (Jerusalem: Targum, 1997), 33–40, 44–8.

80 21 July 1942, *Czerniaków Diary*, 383–4; 21 July 1942, *Seidman Diaries*, 48–51.

81 22 July 1942, *Czerniaków Diary*, 384–5; 21 July 1942, *Seidman Diaries*, 52–3; Engelking and Leociak, *The Warsaw Ghetto*, 212–13, 704–5.

82 July–December, *Ringelblum Notes*, 316; 26 July 1942, *Kaplan Diary*, 323–5; 23, 24 July 1942, *Seidman Diaries*, 57–9, 60. See also Marcel Reich-Ranicki, *The Author of Himself. The Life of Marcel Reich-Ranicki*, trans. Ewald Osers (London: Weidenfeld and Nicolson, 2001), 163–75.

83 Engelking and Leociak, *The Warsaw Ghetto*, 698–700; 24 July 1942, *Seidman Diaries*, 60–2.

84 Engelking and Leociak, *The Warsaw Ghetto*, 703–15; Adler, *In the Warsaw Ghetto*, 268–75. Adler, an administrative officer with the Order Service, is suspiciously vague about his activities during the period.

85 27, 29 July 1942, *Kaplan Diary*, 325–7, 329–31; 24, 26 July, 23 August, 1942, *Lewin Diary*, 136–7, 138–9, 163–4; 23 July 1942, *Seidman Diaries*, 57–8.

86 22, 26 July 1942, *Kaplan Diary*, 319–21, 323–5; 12, 24, 28 August 1942, *Lewin Diary*, 153–4, 163–4, 170.

87 27 July 1942, *Kaplan Diary*, 325–6; 28 July, 1, 9 August 1942, *Lewin Diary*, 140, 144–5, 150–1; 29 July, 27 August 1942, *Seidman Diaries*, 66–8, 84–6.

88 Gutman, *The Jews of Warsaw*, 228–36; Zuckerman, *A Surplus of Memory*, 193–4; Goldstein, *The Stars Bear Witness*, 108–12; Marek Edelman, *The Ghetto Fights* (London: Bookmarks, 1990; first published in Polish in 1945, in English 1946), 55–6.

89 Gutman, *The Jews of Warsaw*, 236–49; Zuckerman, *A Surplus of Memory*, 202–4, 218–22; Goldstein, *The Stars Bear Witness*, 118–19; 21 August 1942, *Lewin Diary*, 161–2.

90 7 August 1942, *Lewin Diary*, 76–9; 12 August 1942, *Seidman Diaries*, 75–8; 4 August 1942, *Kaplan Diary*, 337–8.

91 Engelking and Leociak, *The Warsaw Ghetto*, 718–19; 10 August 1942, *Seidman Diaries*, 72–3; Szereszewska, *Memoirs*, 60–1, 96–7, 105.

92 18 August 1942, *Lewin Diary*, 159–60; Zylberberg, *A Warsaw Diary*, 67–70, 71–5.

93 Szpilman, *The Pianist*, 94–7, 98–107.

94 16, 19, 20 August, 11 September 1942, *Lewin Diary*, 157–8, 160–1, 176–9.

95 8 September 1942, *Seidman Diaries*, 113–17; Engelking and Leociak, *The Warsaw Ghetto*, 727–30; Gutman, *The Jews of Warsaw*, 221.

96 6, 9, 11, 28 August 1942, *Lewin Diary*, 148, 150–1, 152–3, 170–1; 2 September 1942, *Seidman Diaries*, 100–7.

97 For this and the following paragraph, see Arad, *Belzec, Sobibor, Treblinka*, 37–43.

98 See also Witold Chrostowski, *The Extermination Camp Treblinka* (London: Valentine Mitchell, 2003), 24–54.

99 Arad, *Belzec, Sobibor, Treblinka*, 89–99; Longerich, *Holocaust*, 33.

100 Yankiel Wiernik, *A Year in Treblinka* (New York: American Representation of the Jewish Workers Union of Poland, 1944), 6–8; Eddie Weinstein, *17 Days in Treblinka. Daring to Resist, and Refusing to Die* (Jerusalem: Yad Vashem, 2008), 36–7.

101 Wiernik, *A Year in Treblinka*, 9–10; Weinstein, *17 Days in Treblinka*, 39–62.

102 Wiernik, *A Year in Treblinka*, 11–55.

103 Arad, *Belzec, Sobibor, Treblinka*, 89–92, 119–20; Wiernik, *A Year in Treblinka*, 18.

104 Arad, *Belzec, Sobibor, Treblinka*, 127–8 and Appendix A, 392–7; the Höfle telegram was intercepted by British signals intelligence at Bletchley Park and decoded: Peter Witte and Stephen Tyas, 'A New Document on the Deportation and Murder of Jews During "Einsatz Reinhardt" 1942', *HGS*, 15:3 (2001), 468–86, here 469–70.

105 Arad, *Belzec, Sobibor, Treblinka*, 109–13; Chrostowski, *The Extermination Camp Treblinka*, 45–52.

106 Wiernik, *A Year in Treblinka*, 18–22; see also Oskar Strawczynski, 'Ten Months in Treblinka (October 5, 1942 – August 2, 1943)', in Israel Cymlich, Oskar Strawczynski, *Escaping Hell in Treblinka* (Jerusalem: Yad Vashem, 2007), 127–86.

107 Arad, *Belzec, Sobibor, Treblinka*, 162–4; Wiernik, *A Year in Treblinka*, 22.

108 Chil Rajchman, *Treblinka. A Survivor's Memory 1942–1943*, trans. Solon Beinfeld (London: Quercus, 2011), 43–6, 91.

109 Arad, *Belzec, Sobibor, Treblinka*, 254–6; Rajchman, *Treblinka*, 63–4; Wiernik, *A Year in Treblinka*, 22. In a memoir written in Czech soon after the war, Richard Glazar, *Trap with a Green Fence. Survival in Treblinka*, trans. Roslyn Theobald (Evanston: Northwestern University Press, 1995), 45–58, recalled how 'stabilization' allowed the prisoners to act collectively. Glazer was deported to Treblinka from Czechoslovakia in mid-October 1942.

110 Arad, *The Holocaust in the Soviet Union*, 251–73, 287–97.

111 Ibid, 251–2, 255–6; Epstein, *The Minsk Ghetto*, 104–6, 133–47; EG A report, 9 March 1942, *Einsatzgruppen Reports*, 307–8; 'From the notes of the Partisan A Mikhail Grichanik' and 'Accounts of Perla Aginskaya and others', *The Unknown Black Book*, 240, 245–6.

112 Arad, *The Holocaust in the Soviet Union*, 256–8; Alport, *The Destruction of Slonim Jewry*, 125–42, 156–70, 195–221, 244–54.

113 Arad, *The Holocaust in the Soviet Union*, 491–3, 505–10; Nechama Tec, *Defiance. The Bielski Partisans* (New York: Oxford University Press, 1993), 40–93.

114 Arad, *The Holocaust in the Soviet Union*, 266–71; interview with Francesco Rossi in Revelli ed., *Mussolini's Death March*, 315–16.

115 Spector, *The Holocaust of Volhynian Jews*, 172–87; Martin Dean, *Collaboration in the Holocaust* (Houndmills: Macmillan, 2000), 78–104; Martin Dean, 'Soviet Ethnic Germans and the Holocaust in the Reich Commissariat Ukraine, 1941–1944', in Brandon and Lower eds, *The Shoah in Ukraine*, 248–71.

116 Spector, *The Holocaust of Volhynian Jews*, 189–206; Arad, *The Holocaust in the Soviet Union*, 263–73.

117 Spector, *The Holocaust of Volhynian Jews*, 227–31; Arad, *The Holocaust in the Soviet Union*, 493–5; Yehuda Bauer, *The Death of the Shtetl* (New Haven: Yale University Press, 2009), 66–7, 94–118, 122–51.

118 Arad, *The Holocaust in the Soviet Union*, 271–2.

119 Ibid, 283–91, 292–7; Klaus-Michael Mallman and Martin Cüppers, *Nazi Palestine. The Plans for the Extermination of the Jews in Palestine*, trans. Krista Smith (London: Enigma Books, 2010), 185–8. On the collaboration of Muslims in the USSR and more widely, see David Motadel, *Islam and Nazi Germany's War* (Cambridge, MA: Harvard University Press, 2014), esp. 133-77.

120 Arad, *The Holocaust in the Soviet Union*, 274–83; Arad, *Belzec, Sobibor, Treblinka*, 249–52.

121 Arad, *The Holocaust in the Soviet Union*, 283–5.

122 Robert Jan van Pelt, 'A Site in Search of a Mission', in Yisrael Gutman and Michael Berenbaum eds, *Anatomy of the Auschwitz Death Camp* (Bloomington: Indiana University Press, 1994), 93–157; Wachsmann, *KL*, 289–314.

123 Sybille Steinbacher, *Auschwitz. A History* (London: Penguin, 2005), 22–44; Irena Strzelecka and Piotr Setkiewicz, 'The Construction, Expansion and Development of the Camp and its Branches', in Aleksander Lasik et al. eds, *Auschwitz 1940-1945. Central Issues in the History of the Camp*, vol. 1, *The Establishment and Organisation of the Camp*, trans. William Brand (Oswięçim: Auschwitz-Birkenau State Museum, 2000), 63–80; Robert Jan van Pelt and Debórah Dwork, *Auschwitz 1270 to the Present* (New Haven: Yale University Press, 1996), 163–96; Henryk Swiebocki, *Auschwitz 1940-1945. Central Issues in the History of the Camp*, vol. IV, *The Resistance Movement*, trans. William Brand (Oswięçim: Auschwitz-Birkenau State Museum, 2000), 65–79.

124 Van Pelt and Dwork, *Auschwitz*, 168–71.

125 Steinbacher, *Auschwitz*, 45–51, 89–95; van Pelt and Dwork, *Auschwitz*, 197–211, 262–75; Wachsmann, *KL*, 295.

126 Dieter Pohl, 'The Holocaust and the concentration camps', in Caplan and Wachsmann eds, *Concentration Camps in Nazi Germany*, 149–66, esp. 151–2, 154; Wachsmann, *KL*, 299–302.

127 Nikolaus Wachsmann, 'The dynamics of destruction. The development of the concentration camps, 1933–1945', and Jens-Christian Wagner, 'Work and

extermination in the concentration camps', 17–43, esp. 29–31, and 127–48, esp. 132–5; Wachsmann, *KL*, 361–8, 393–410.

128 Pohl, 'The Holocaust and the concentration camps', 151–2; Wagner, 'Work and extermination in the concentration camps', 136–7, 139–41; Wachsmann, *KL*, 344–8, 474–9.

129 Eduard Niznansky, 'Expropriation and Deportation of Jews in Slovakia', in Kosmola and Tych eds, *Facing the Nazi Genocide*, 205–30.

130 Van Pelt and Dwork, *Auschwitz*, 300–1; Raul Hilberg, *The Destruction of the European Jews*, vol. 2 (New York: Holmes & Meier, 1985 edn), 718–30; Wachsmann, *KL*, 295–7; 26 March 1942, Danuta Czech, *Auschwitz Chronicle 1939–1945* (New York: Henry Holt, 1990), 148.

131 Franciszek Piper, *Auschwitz 1940–1945. Central Issues in the History of the Camp*, vol. III, *Mass Murder*, trans. William Brand (Oswięcim: Auschwitz-Birkenau State Museum, 2000), 32–5; Longerich, *Holocaust*, 324–6.

132 30 March, 7, 24, 27 June, 19, 21 July 1942, *Auschwitz Chronicle*, 151, 176, 180, 187, 189, 200, 201; Herbert, 'The German Military Command in Paris and the Deportation of the French Jews', 143–4; Zuccotti, *The Holocaust, the French, and the Jews*, 88–90.

133 Irena Strzelecka, 'Quarantine on Arrival', Tadeusz Iwaszko, 'The Housing, Clothing and Feeding of the Prisoners' and Irena Strzelecka, 'The Working Day for the Auschwitz Prisoners', in Tadeusz Iwaszko et al. eds, *Auschwitz 1940–1945. Central Issues in the History of the Camp*, vol. II, *The Prisoners – Their Life and Work*, trans. William Brand (Oswięcim: Auschwitz-Birkenau State Museum, 2000), 45–50, 51–64, 65–70; Steinbacher, *Auschwitz*, 29–40, 51–60.

134 Franciszek Piper, 'The Exploitation of Prisoner Labor', in Iwaszko et al. eds, *Auschwitz 1940–1945*, vol. II, 71–136; Steinbacher, *Auschwitz*, 29–40, 51–60; Wachsmann, *KL*, 344–50.

135 Irena Strzelecka, 'The Hospitals at Auschwitz Concentration Camp', in Iwaszko et al. eds, *Auschwitz 1940–1945*, vol. II, 291–346.

136 Irena Strzelecka, 'Women in the Auschwitz Concentration Camp' in Iwaszko et al. eds, *Auschwitz 1940–1945*, vol. II, 177–200, here 185.

137 Strzelecka, 'The Hospitals at Auschwitz Concentration Camp', 347–56; Robert Jay Lifton and Amy Hackett, 'Nazi Doctors' and Irena Strzelecka, 'Women', in Gutman and Berenbaum eds, *Anatomy of the Auschwitz Death Camp*, 393–411, 301–16; Wachsmann, *KL*, 427–43.

138 Piper, *Auschwitz 1940–1945*, vol. III, 28–9; Longerich, *Holocaust*, 327–9.

139 Piper, *Auschwitz 1940–1945*, vol. III, 121–33; Wachsmann, *KL*, 299–314, 350–3.

140 Filip Müller, *Eyewitness Auschwitz. Three Years in the Gas Chamber*, trans. and ed. Susanne Flatauer (Chicago: Ivan Dee, 1999 edn), 11–22. Müller first wrote up his experiences in 1946 and they were published in summary form in Ota Krauss and Erich Kulka, *Továrna na smrt* (Prague: Orbis, 1946), which appeared in English as *The Death Factory*, trans. Stephen Joly (Oxford: Pergamon Press, 1966), 156–60. He expanded his testimony in the 1960s with the 'literary collaboration' of Helmut Freitag.

141 Müller, *Eyewitness Auschwitz*, 31–9.

142 Piper, *Auschwitz 1940–1945*, vol. III, 134–8.

143 Ibid, 138–40; Müller, *Eyewitness Auschwitz*, 50–3.

144 Longerich, *Holocaust*, 320–2.

145 RSHA, Dept. III (SD), 'Reports from the Reich', 29 January 1942; SD District Office Höxter, 'Store Hours for Selling to Jews', 19 January 1942; RSHA, Dept. III (SD), 'Reports from the Reich', 2 February 1942, *Secret Nazi Reports*, 571–2, 572–3, 574–5.

146 2, 6 June, 19 August 1942, *Klemperer Diary*, II, 61–3, 84–5, 120–1.

147 Grenville, *The Jews and Germans*, 225, 254–5; Meyer, 'Between Self-Assurance and Forced Collaboration', 168–9; SD District Office Minden, report, 21 February 1942, *Secret Nazi Reports*, 576; 23 May, 13, 21 November 1942, *Klemperer Diary*, II, 54, 157, 160–1; Doerry, *My Wounded Heart*, 95–8. See also, Beate Meyer, 'The Mixed Marriage: A Guarantee of Survival or a Reflection of German Society during the Nazi Regime?', in Bankier ed., *Probing the Depths of German Antisemitism*, 54–76.

148 Meyer, 'Between Self-Assurance and Forced Collaboration', 155–62; Grenville, *The Jews and Germans*, 239–40, 244; 25, 27 July 1942, *Klemperer Diary*, II, 102–3, 105.

149 Arnold Paucker and Konrad Kwiet, 'Jewish Leadership and Jewish Resistance', in Bankier ed., *Probing the Depths of German Antisemitism*, 381–2; 23 February, 9, 19 June 1942, Andreas-Friedrich, *Berlin Underground*, 68–9, 70, 71; 10 August 1942, *Secret Nazi Reports*, 601–2.

150 Zdenek Lederer, *Ghetto Theresienstadt*, trans. K. Weisskopf (London: Goldston, 1953), 35–44, 247–50 for statistical summary; Livia Rothkirchen, 'Gateway to Death: The Unique Character of Terezin (Theresienstadt)', in Rothkirchen, *The Jews of Bohemia & Moravia*, 233–47.

151 Lederer, *Ghetto Theresienstadt*, 20–3; n.d., *Weiss Diary*, 56–7, 61–6.

152 Lederer, *Ghetto Theresienstadt*, 17–24, 59–73.

153 Ibid, 24–8.

154 Norbert Troller, *Theresienstadt. Hitler's Gift To The Jews*, trans. Susan Cernyak-Spatz, ed. Joel Shatzky (Chapel Hill: University of North Carolina Press, 1991), 8–17, 30–1, 34–5.

155 Troller, *Theresienstadt*, 34, 39–40, 44.

156 *Weiss Diary*, 63–4, 67–70; Troller, *Theresienstadt*, 77–8, 89–98, 118–24.

157 March–July 1942, 19, 23 July 1942, Philipp Manes, *As if it were life. A WWII Diary from the Theresienstadt Ghetto*, trans. Janet Foster, Ben Barkow and Klaus Leist, eds Ben Barkow and Klaus Leist (London: Palgrave, 2009), 1–5, 13–15, 19.

158 *Manes Diary*, 23–30, 40, 42–3.

159 Ibid, 44–52, 70–2.

160 Lederer, *Ghetto Theresienstadt*, 48–50; *Manes Diary*, 64–8.

161 Lederer, *Ghetto Theresienstadt*, 50–1; *Weiss Diary*, 72–3.

162 Lederer, *Ghetto Theresienstadt*, 39–51.

163 Marrus and Paxton, *Vichy France and the Jews*, 116–18, 222–6; Poznanski, *Jews in France during World War II*, 251–3. On Darquier de Pellepoix, see Carmen Callil, *Bad Faith. A Forgotten History of Family and Fatherland* (London: Cape, 2006).

164 Thomas J. Laub, *After the Fall. German Policy in Occupied France 1940–1944*

(Oxford: Oxford University Press, 2010), 181–8; Marrus and Paxton, *Vichy France and the Jews*, 222–7.

165 Laub, *After the Fall*, 228–9.

166 Marrus and Paxton, *Vichy France and the Jews*, 228–9.

167 Ibid, 241–2.

168 Serge Klarsfeld, 'The Influence of the War on the Final Solution in France', in Cohen, Cochavi, Gelber eds, *The Shoah and the War*, 271–81; Zuccotti, *The Holocaust, the French, and the Jews*, 97–102.

169 7, 8, 15 April, 1, 8, 9 June 1942, Hélène Berr, *Journal*, trans. David Bellos (London: MacLehose Press, 2008), 15–29, 48, 50–1, 53–5.

170 8 January, 11 February, 29 March 1942, *Lambert Diary*, 89–95, 100–5, 111–13; cf. Adler, *The Jews of Paris and the Final Solution*, 81–102.

171 24 June, 2, 6 July 1942, *Berr Journal*, 67–76, 84–5, 93.

172 15 July 1942, *Berr Journal*, 97.

173 Marrus and Paxton, *Vichy France and the Jews*, 248–9.

174 Adam Rayski, *The Choice of the Jews Under Vichy. Between Submission and Resistance*, trans. Will Sayers (Notre Dame: University of Notre Dame Press, 2005), 88–95; Zuccotti, *The Holocaust, the French, and the Jews*, 104–8.

175 Rayski, *The Choice of the Jews Under Vichy*, 90; Zuccotti, *The Holocaust, the French, and the Jews*, 111–16.

176 Zuccotti, *The Holocaust, the French, and the Jews*, 112–13;

177 Testimony of Georges Wellers, session 32, 9 May 1961, *The Trial of Adolf Eichmann*, vol. II, 583–5.

178 Poznanski, *Jews in France during World War II*, 260–2; cf. Adler, *The Jews of Paris and the Final Solution*, 109–29.

179 18, 19, 21, 22, 23, 24, 26 July 1942, *Berr Journal*, 98–110.

180 Marrus and Paxton, *Vichy France and the Jews*, 181–6, 246–9; Poznanski, *Jews in France during World War II*, 270–2; Adler, *The Jews of Paris and the Final Solution*, 43–6; Donna F. Ryan, *The Holocaust and the Jews of Marseille. The Enforcement of Anti-Semitic Policies in Vichy France* (Urbana: University of Illinois Press, 1996), 79–107, 163–6. Olivier Philipponnat and Patrick Lienhardt, *The Life of Irène Némirovsky 1903–1942*, trans. Euan Cameron (London: Vintage, 2011), 1–5, 369–84

181 Zuccotti, *The Holocaust, the French, and the Jews*, 118–34.

182 21 July, 6 September, 4 October 1942, *Lambert Diary*, 127–8, 132–3, 134–7; Poznanski, *Jews in France during World War II*, 288–91.

183 11 October 1942, *Lambert Diary*, 137–40; Adler, *The Jews of Paris and the Final Solution*, 109–29.

184 11 October 1942, *Lambert Diary*, 142–4.

185 Laub, *After the Fall*, 234–6; Klarsfeld, 'The Influence of the War on the Final Solution in France', 277–8; Zuccotti, *The Holocaust, the French, and the Jews*, 157–62; Marrus and Paxton, *Vichy France and the Jews*, 260–2.

186 Marrus and Paxton, *Vichy France and the Jews*, 270–82; Poznanski, *Jews in France during World War II*, 292–302; Ryan, *The Holocaust and the Jews of Marseille*, 169–71.

187 Renée Poznanski, 'French Public Opinion and the Jews during World War II: Assumptions of the Clandestine Press', in Kosmola and Tych eds, *Facing the Nazi Genocide*, 117–35, esp. 123–33 and her 'The French Resistance: An Alternative Society for the Jews?' in David Bankier and Yisrael Gutman eds, *Nazi Europe and the Final Solution* (Jerusalem: Yad Vashem, 2009), 411–34.

188 Klarsfeld, 'The Influence of the War on the Final Solution in France', in Cohen, Cochavi, Gelber eds, *The Shoah and the War*, 277–8.

189 Maxime Steinberg, 'The Jews in the Years 1940–1944: Three Strategies for Coping with a Tragedy' and 'The Judenpolitik in Belgium within the West European Context: Comparative Observations', in Michman ed., *Belgium and the Holocaust*, 205–13, 353–62; Anne Somerhausen, *Written in Darkness. A Belgian Woman's Record of the Occupation 1940–1945* (New York: Knopf, 1946), 144–8.

190 24 November, 2 December 1942, Shaul Esh ed., *Young Moshe's Diary*, trans. Hana'ar Moshe (Jerusalem: Yad Vashem, 1979), 19–26, 30–1.

191 Pim Griffioen and Ron Zeller, 'Comparing the Persecution of the Jews in the Netherlands, France and Belgium', in Romijn et al. eds, *The Persecution of the Jews in the Netherlands,* 55–91.

192 Maxime Steinberg, 'The Trap of Legality: the Association of the Jews in Belgium', in Yisrael Gutman and Cynthia Haft eds, *Patterns of Jewish Leadership in Nazi Europe 1933–1945* (Jerusalem: Yad Vashem, 1979), 353–76, esp. 353–68; Bob Moore, *Survivors. Jewish Self-Help and Rescue in Nazi-Occupied Western Europe* (Oxford: Oxford University Press, 2010), 171–7; Somerhausen, *Written in Darkness*, 144–8. See also, Dan Michman, 'Problematic National Identity, Outsiders and Persecution: Impact of the Gentile Population's Attitude in Belgium on the Fate of the Jews in 1940–1944' and Jean-Philippe Schreiber, 'Belgium and the Jews under Nazi Rule: Behind the Myths', in Bankier and Gutman eds, *Nazi Europe and the Final Solution*, 455–68 and 469–88.

193 Steinberg, 'The Jews in the Years 1940–1944: Three Strategies for Coping with a Tragedy', 347–50; Yahil, *The Holocaust*, 393–4; Longerich, *Holocaust*, 362–3.

194 Wasserstein, *The Ambiguity of Virtue,* 128–33; Hesdörffer, *Twelve Years of Nazi Terror,* 18; Presser, *Ashes in the Wind,* 118–37.

195 Presser, *Ashes in the Wind,* 135–43; Wasserstein, *The Ambiguity of Virtue,* 138–40.

196 Presser, *Ashes in the Wind,* 141; Hesdörffer, *Twelve Years of Nazi Terror,* 22–3.

197 Presser, *Ashes in the Wind,* 143–53, 158–64, 170–3; Guus Meershoek, 'The Amsterdam Police and the persecution of the Jews', Michael Berenbaum and Abraham Peck eds, *The Holocaust in History, the Known, the Unknown, the Disputed, and the Reexamined* (Indiana: Indiana University Press, 1998), 284–300.

198 Presser, *Ashes in the Wind,* 407–9, 415–28; Jacob Presser, 'Introduction', in Philip Mechanicus, *Waiting for Death. A Diary*, trans. Irene R. Gibbons (London: Calder and Boyars, 1968), 5–10.

199 Presser, *Ashes in the Wind,* 164–9.

200 Ibid, 246–54, 264–77, 348–56; Wasserstein, *The Ambiguity of Virtue,* 141–2, 146–8.

201 Presser, *Ashes in the Wind,* 378–84, 383–400; Van der Boom, 'Ordinary Dutchmen and the Holocaust: A Summary of Findings', 38–48.

202 Griffioen and Zeller, 'Comparing the Persecution of the Jews in the Netherlands, France and Belgium', in Romijn et al. eds, *The Persecution of the Jews in the Netherlands*, 55–92; Presser, *Ashes in the Wind*, 68–73, 357–71, 371–74.

203 Gerard Aalders, *Nazi Looting. The Plunder of Dutch Jewry During the Second World War*, trans. Arnold and Erica Pomerans (Oxford: Berg, 2004), 11–83, 104–63, 175–83, 185–201, 203–9.

204 Longerich, *Holocaust*, 370–2.

205 22 April, 8 June, 22 November 1941, 20 June 1942, *Ruth Maier's Diary*, 324–5, 341, 373–4, 393–4.

206 27, 29 September 1942, *Ruth Maier's Diary*, 405, 406–7.

207 Ibid, 411–12.

208 1, 4, 8–10 June; 2, 21, 23, July; 4 August 1942, *Lodz Ghetto Chronicle*, 194, 199–200, 203, 217–18, 226, 236; 26 June, 22 July, 26 August 1942 *Sierakowiak Diary*, 189, 198, 210–11; Horowitz, *Ghettostadt*, 196, 199–201.

209 25, 28 June, 2, 30, 31 July, 28 August 1942, *Lodz Ghetto Chronicle*, 212, 214–15, 217–18, 232–4, 244–5; 11 August 1942 *Sierakowiak Diary*, 205.

210 27, 29, 30 May 1942 *Sierakowiak Diary*, 174, 176–7; 9 June, 6–8 August 1942, Rosenfeld, *In the Beginning was the Ghetto*, 69–70, 115.

211 20–21 May, 27 July, 28, 30 August 1942, *Lodz Ghetto Chronicle*, 181–2, 231, 244–6; 27 July, 12, 27 August 1942, *Sierakowiak Diary*, 200, 205, 211.

212 4, 14 September 1942, *Lodz Ghetto Chronicle*, 248–50, 250–8; 1–4 September 1942 *Sierakowiak Diary*, 212–18; 1–3 September 1942, Rosenfeld, *In the Beginning was the Ghetto*, 119–22; Horowitz, *Ghettostadt*, 203–13.

213 Lucille Eichengreen, *From Ashes to Life: My Memories of the Holocaust* (San Francisco: Mercury House, 1994), 48–9; Avraham Cytryn, *Youth Writing Behind the Walls. Notebooks from the Lodz Ghetto*, ed. Su Newman, trans. Chaya Naor, (Jerusalem: Yad Vashem, 2005), 247–50.

214 Trunk, *Lodz Ghetto*, 272–5.

215 1–12 September 1942, Zelkowicz, *In Those Terrible Days*, 251–349.

216 25 September, 5 November, 3 December 1942, *Lodz Ghetto Chronicle*, 261–2, 285, 296; September 1942, Rosenfeld, *In the Beginning was the Ghetto*, 136–7; 21 November 1942, *Sierakowiak Diary*, 234.

217 Longerich, *Holocaust*, 363–5.

218 11 February, 10 March, 7 June 1942, *Dorian Diary*, 195, 199–200, 211–12; Ioanid, *The Holocaust in Romania*, 238–48; cf. Ancel, *The History of the Holocaust in Romania*, 470–84.

219 Ancel, *The History of the Holocaust in Romania*, 486–99; Longerich, *Holocaust*, 365–6, 369–70.

220 Vagi, Csoz and Kadar eds, *The Holocaust in Hungary*, 61–5; Longerich, *Holocaust*, 367, 371–2.

221 Longerich, *Holocaust*, 367–8, 370–1; Frederick Charny, *The Bulgarian Jews and the Final Solution 1940–44* (Pittsburgh: University of Pittsburgh Press, 1972), 35–84.

222 Longerich, *Holocaust*, 368, 372; Susan Zuccotti, *The Italians and the Holocaust. Persecution, Rescue and Survival* (London: Peter Halban, 1987), 75–8

223 Max Hastings, *Finest Years. Churchill as Warlord 1940–45* (London: Harper Press, 2009), 234–53, 295–8.

224 Cesarani, *The Jewish Chronicle and Anglo-Jewry 1841–1991*, 176–9; Richard Bolchover, *British Jewry and the Holocaust* (Cambridge: Cambridge University Press, 1993), 8–10; Walter Laqueur, *The Terrible Secret. Suppression of the Truth about Hitler's Final Solution* (London: Penguin, 1980), 67–76.

225 Breitman and Lichtman, *FDR and the Jews*, 194–8; Leff, *Buried by the Times*, 140–58; Lipstadt, *Beyond Belief*, 159–73, 180–7.

226 Walter Laqueur and Richard Breitman, *Breaking the Silence. The Secret Mission of Eduard Schulte, who brought the world news of the Final Solution* (London: Bodley Head, 1986), 96–117, 123–34, 136–7.

227 Arad, *Belzec, Sobibor, Treblinka*, 349–59; Fleming, *Auschwitz, the Allies and Censorship of the Holocaust*, 148–57.

228 Bernard Wasserstein, 'Patterns of Jewish Leadership in Great Britain during the Nazi Era', in Braham ed., *Jewish Leadership during the Nazi Era*, 29–43; Breitman and Lichtman, *FDR and the Jews*, 199–201. For contrasting interpretations of the British-Jewish response, Meier Sompolinsky, *Britain and the Holocaust. The Failure of Anglo-Jewish Leadership* (Brighton: Sussex Academic Press, 1999), 55–75, Pamela Shatzkes, *Holocaust and Rescue. Impotent or Indifferent? Anglo-Jewry 1938–1945* (London: Palgrave, 2002), 110–16 and Bolchover, *British Jewry and the Holocaust*, 54–73. On the USA, see Ne'eman Arad, *America, its Jews and the rise of Nazism*, 213–20.

229 Breitman and Lichtman, *FDR and the Jews*, 202–4. For a critical appraisal of American Jewish responses and the administration, see David Wyman, *The Abandonment of the Jews. America and the Holocaust 1941–1945* (New York: Pantheon, 1985 edn), 19–58.

230 Breitman and Lichtman, *FDR and the Jews*, 204–6; cf. Wyman, *The Abandonment of the Jews*, 61–78.

231 17 December 1942, *Hansard*, Series 5, vol. 385, cols 2082–7; Wasserstein, *Britain and the Jews of Europe*, 151–63.

Seven – Total War: 1943

1 15, 26 November, 11, 22 December 1942, 24 January 1943, *Klemperer Diary*, II, 157, 162, 166, 169, 184; 17 January 1943, *Seidman Diaries*, 409; 12 November 1942, 6 January 1943, *Vilna Ghetto Chronicles*, 409, 445; 29 November, 2, 18 December 1942, *Lambert Diary*, 152, 155, 158.

2 Citino, *Death of the Wehrmacht*, 267–88 and his *The Wehrmacht Retreats. Fighting a Lost War, 1943* (Lawrence: University of Kansas Press, 2012), 4–40; Simon Ball, *The Bitter Sea* (London: Harper Press, 2009), 158–211; Douglas Porch, *Hitler's Mediterranean Gamble. The North African Campaign and the Mediterranean in Campaigns in World War II* (London: Cassell, 2004), 348–414.

3 Fritz, *Ostkrieg*, 303–26; Citino, *Death of the Wehrmacht*, 289–302 and *The Wehrmacht Retreats*, 31–74; Hayward, *Stopped at Stalingrad*, 227–310.

4 Kershaw, *Hitler 1889–1936*, 550–5, 561–77; Evans, *The Third Reich at War*, 420–32; Fritz, *Ostkrieg*, 326–36.

5 Mallman and Cüppers, *Nazi Palestine*, 116–24, 167–84; Longerich, *Holocaust*, 390–6; Longerich, *Himmler*, 647–9, 662–3.

6 Longerich, *Holocaust*, 374.

7 Herf, *The Jewish Enemy*, 190–6; For the text of Goebbels' speech, http://www2.warwick.ac.uk/fac/arts/history/students/modules/hi369/reading/week8/goebbelstotal/

8 28 February, 7 March 1943, Andreas-Friedrich, *Berlin Underground*, 81–3; Longerich, *Holocaust*, 386. Nathan Stoltzfus, *Intermarriage and the Rosenstrasse Protest in Nazi Germany* (New York: Norton, 1996), casts the protest in a more idealistic light.

9 17 January, 28 February, 25 April 1943, 5 December 1944, *Klemperer Diary*, II, 182, 196, 206–9, 364; SD District Office Höxter, 'Jew Hartwig Stein', 27 February 1943, *Secret Nazi Reports*, 611; Grenville, *The Jews and Germans*, 251–2.

10 Doerry, *My Wounded Heart*, 97–112, 114–16, 121–3, 149–233, 241–9.

11 Lucie Adelsberger, *Auschwitz. A Doctor's Story*, trans. Susan Ray (Boston: Northeastern University Press, 1995), 13–17, 21–2.

12 Meyer, 'Between Self-Assurance and Forced Collaboration', 159–61; Avraham Barkai, 'The Final Chapter', in Michael Meyer ed., *German History in Modern Times*, vol. 4, 378–88; 1 December 1942, Andreas-Friedrich, *Berlin Underground*, 76. See also Christian Dirks, 'Snatchers: The Berlin Gestapo's Jewish Informants', in Beate Meyer, Hermann Simon and Chana Schütz eds, *Jews in Nazi Berlin: From Kristallnacht to Liberation* (Chicago: University of Chicago Press, 2009), 249–73 and Peter Wyden, *Stella: One Woman's True Tale of Evil, Betryal, and Survival in Hitler's Germany* (New York: Doubleday, 1992).

13 20 December 1942, *Von Hassell Diaries*, 249–50; SD District Office Schwabach, report for December 1942, 23 December 1942, *Secret Nazi Reports*, 607–8; Jeremy D. Harris, 'Broadcasting the Massacres. An analysis of the BBC's contemporary coverage of the Holocaust', *Yad Vashem Studies*, 25 (1996), 65–98; Eric A. Johnson, *Nazi Terror. The Gestapo, Jews and Ordinary Germans* (London: John Murray, 1999), 444–57.

14 District Governor Swabia , report for May 1943, 10 June 1943, *Secret Nazi Reports*, 623; Herf, *The Jewish Enemy*, 201–9. Other mass graves were later discovered, bringing the total to 22,000.

15 RSHA, Dept. III (SD), 'Reports from the Reich', 19 April 1943; SD District Office Friedberg, III A4, 'Mood and Situation', 23 April; RSHA, Dept. III (SD), 'Reports on Domestic Questions', 26 July 1943; SD District Office Bad Neustadt, 'General Mood and Situation', 15 October 1943, *Secret Nazi Reports*, 615–17, 618–19, 629–30, 635; 15 May 1943, *Von Hassell Diaries*, 272.

16 Nick Stargardt, 'Speaking in public about the murder of the Jews: What did the Holocaust mean to the Germans?', in Christian Wiese and Paul Betts eds, *Years of Persecution, Years of Extermination. Saul Friedländer and the Future of Holocaust Studies* (London: Continuum, 2010), 133–55, esp. 140–9; cf. Richard Overy, *The*

Bombing War. Europe 1939-1945 (London: Penguin, 2013), 289–301, 323–38, 447–8.

17 NSDAP Local Branch, Nuremberg-Maxfeld, 'Ideological Situation Report', 9 April 1943; SD District Office Friedberg, report, 14 May; Gendarmerie, Sandberg, general report, 28 June 1943; RSHA, Dept. III (SD), 'Reports on Domestic Questions', 8 July 1943; SD District Office Würzburg, 'General Mood and Situation', 3 August 1943; SD District Office Schweinfurt, 'General Mood and Situation', 6 September 1943, *Secret Nazi Reports*, 614–15, 628, 629, 631, 634.

18 SD Regional Division Halle/S. III C 4, 'General Guidance of the Press', 22 May 1943; NSDAP Party Chancellery II B4, 'Extracts from Reports of Gau Head Offices and Other Offices', 29 May 1943, *Secret Nazi Reports*, 622, 624–5.

19 Mallman and Cüppers, *Nazi Palestine*, 116–24, 154–66, 167–84.

20 Robert Satloff, *Among the Righteous. Lost Stories from the Holocaust's Long Reach Into Arab Lands* (New York: Public Affairs, 2006), 30–7, 57–61 and in general, see Michel Abitbol, *The Jews of North Africa in World War II* (Detroit: Wayne State University Press, 1989).

21 Daniel Carpi, *Between Mussolini and Hitler. The Jews and the Italian Authorities in France and Tunisia* (Hanover, NH: Brandeis University Press, 1994), 195–9, 200–27.

22 Mallman and Cüppers, *Nazi Palestine*, 170–6, 184; Carpi, *Between Mussolini and Hitler*, 228–40.

23 Weinberg, *A World at Arms*, 431–8; Citino, *The Wehrmacht Retreats*, 165–70; Marrus and Paxton, *Vichy France and the Jews*, 302–6; Poznanski, *Jews in France during World War II*, 356–65.

24 1 February 1943, *Lambert Diary*, 163–9; Ryan, *The Holocaust and the Jews of Marseille*, 1–9, 180–93; Zuccotti, *The Holocaust, the French, and the Jews*, 173.

25 18 May 1943, *Lambert Diary*, 180–8; Poznanski, *Jews in France during World War II*, 394–421.

26 Adler, *The Jews of Paris and the Final Solution*, ix-xiii, 202. See also, Richard I. Cohen, *The Burden of Conscience. French Jewry's Response to the Holocaust* (Bloomington: Indiana University Press, 1987), 94–8, 173–8 and Rayski, *The Choice of the Jews Under Vichy*, 151–3, 230–1.

27 Cesarani, *Eichmann*, 144; Carpi, *Between Mussolini and Hitler*, 102–32, 136–63, 183–4; cf. Sarfatti, *The Jews in Mussolini's Italy*, 161.

28 Klarsfeld, 'The Influence of the War on the Final Solution in France', 278–80; Zuccotti, *The Holocaust, the French, and the Jews*, 178.

29 Safrian, *Eichmann's Men*, 174–5; Mary Felstiner, 'Alois Brunner: "Eichmann's Best Tool"', *Simon Wiesenthal Centre Annual*, 3 (1986), 1–46.

30 11 February 1942, 18, 20 August 1943, *Lambert Diary*, 95, 197–9; for Lambert's fate, see Richard I. Cohen, 'Introduction' in *Lambert Diary*, lxi–lxiv; Adler, *The Jews of Paris and the Final Solution*, 149–57; Cohen, *The Burden of Conscience*, 89–92, 128–30.

31 Mazower, *Inside Hitler's Greece*, 15–22.

32 Steven M. Bowman, *The Agony of Greek Jews 1940–1945* (Stanford: Stanford University Press, 2009), 2, 28–9, 50–3; Andrew Apostolou, '"The Exception of

Salonika". Bystanders and collaborators in Northern Greece', *HGS*, 14:2 (2000), 165–6; Mark Mazower, *Salonica. City of Ghosts. Christians, Muslims and Jews 1430–1950* (London: Harper Collins, 2004), 421–4.

33 Safrian, *Eichmann's Men*, 150–4.

34 Mazower, *Salonica*, 421–4; Bowman, *The Agony of Greek Jews*, 59–62; Safrian, *Eichmann's Men*, 154–7.

35 Mazower, *Salonica*, 424–33; Bowman, *The Agony of Greek Jews*, 62–6; Safrian, *Eichmann's Men*, 157–62; Doctor Albert Menasche (Number 124,454), *Birkenau (Auschwitz II). Memoirs of an Eye-Witness. How 72,000 Greek Jews Perished* (New York: Albert Martin, 1947), 9–17.

36 Mazower, *Salonica*, 431–4; Bowman, *The Agony of Greek Jews*, 80–93; Hilberg, *The Destruction of the European Jews*, vol. 2, 692–701; Menasche, *Birkenau*, 17; Marco Nahon, *Birkenau. Camp of Death*, trans. J. H. Bowers, ed. Steven Bowman (Tuscaloosa: University of Alabama Press, 1989), 21–9.

37 Mazower, *Salonica*, 434–42; Bowman, *The Agony of Greek Jews*, 138–54, 162–72.

38 Mazower, *Salonica*, 443–9; Safrian, *Eichmann's Men*, 162–7.

39 Frederick B. Charney, *The Bulgarian Jews and the Final Solution 1940–44* (Pittsburgh: University of Pittsburgh Press, 1972), 69–100, 101–14, 122–8; cf. Tzvetan Todorov, *The Fragility of Goodness. Why Bulgaria's Jews Survived the Holocaust*, trans. Arthur Denner (London: Weidenfeld and Nicolson, 1999), 7–9.

40 Charney, *The Bulgarian Jews and the Final Solution*, 90–100, 142–57; Todorov, *The Fragility of Goodness*, 19–26, 27–40, and extract from the unpublished memoir by Dimitar Peshev, 137–83.

41 Engelking and Leociak, *The Warsaw Ghetto*, 763; Longerich, *Himmler*, 664; Gutman, *The Jews of Warsaw*, 277–9.

42 Engelking and Leociak, *The Warsaw Ghetto*, 93–8, 396–9, 477–81, 749–53.

43 Gutman, *The Jews of Warsaw*, 268–70, 273–4; Adler, *In the Warsaw Ghetto*, 275, 281–2.

44 5 October 1942, *Lewin Diary*, 187–8; 27 November 1942, 11 January 1943, *Seidman Diaries* 164–7, 209–10; 15 October 1942, *Ringelblum Notes*, 320–1.

45 16 October, 1 November, 29 December 1942, *Lewin Diary*, 189–90, 195–7, 232; 15 October 1942, *Ringelblum Notes*, 310–14, 329–32; 12 October 1942, *Seidman Diaries*, 152–7.

46 21 September 1942, *Seidman Diaries*, 128–30; Adler, *In the Warsaw Ghetto*, 282; 15 October 1942, *Ringelblum Notes*, 325; Gutman, *The Jews of Warsaw*, 283–5, 301–2.

47 Gutman, *The Jews of Warsaw*, 285–91; Blatman, *For Our Freedom and Yours*, 104–5; Engelking and Leociak, *The Warsaw Ghetto*, 757–62; Zuckerman, *A Surplus of Memory*, 244–55; 30 November, 9 December 1942, *Seidman Diaries*, 165–8, 175–9. On the Revisionist Zionist element, David Wdowinski, *And We Are Not Saved* (London: W. H. Allen, 1964), 81–2; Gutman, *The Jews of Warsaw*, 293–7; Engelking and Leociak, *The Warsaw Ghetto*, 762–3.

48 Gutman, *The Jews of Warsaw*, 297–301; Zuckerman, *A Surplus of Memory*, 248–55; 30 November, 9 December 1942, *Seidman Diaries*, 165–8, 175–9.

49 10, 11, 13 January 1943, *Seidman Diaries*, 197–204, 210–14, 230–4; 14 December 1942, *Ringelblum Notes*, 338–44.

50 11 January 1943, *Seidman Diaries*, 210–14; Gutman, *The Jews of Warsaw*, 278–80.

51 Gutman, *The Jews of Warsaw*, 307–12; Zuckerman, *A Surplus of Memory*, 283–4, 285, 288.

52 Engelking and Leociak, *The Warsaw Ghetto*, 763–6; Zuckerman, *A Surplus of Memory*, 285.

53 Adler, *In the Warsaw Ghetto*, 297–301, 305–17.

54 Reicher, *Country of Ash*, 117–22.

55 Engelking and Leociak, *The Warsaw Ghetto*, 766–75; Gutman, *The Jews of Warsaw*, 317–20, 320–3, 350–4; Reicher, *Country of Ash*, 114–15; Zuckerman, *A Surplus of Memory*, 317; Simha Rotem (Kazik), *Memoirs of a Warsaw Ghetto Fighter. The past within me*, trans. and ed. Barbara Harshav (New Haven: Yale University Press, 1994), 28–9.

56 Gutman, *The Jews of Warsaw*, 336–46; Engelking and Leociak, *The Warsaw Ghetto*, 773; Zuckerman, *A Surplus of Memory*, 288, 292–5, 307–8.

57 Gunnar S. Paulsson, *Secret City. The Hidden Jews of Warsaw 1940–1945* (New Haven: Yale University Press, 2002), 28–35, 78–90, 98–137; Zuckerman, *A Surplus of Memory*, 276–7.

58 Paulsson, *Secret City*, 147–59; Zuckerman, *A Surplus of Memory*, 276–7.

59 Engelking and Leociak, *The Warsaw Ghetto*, 740–5; Paulsson, *Secret City*, 20–1, 147–59; Blatman, *For Our Freedom and Yours*, 155–9; Szpilman, *The Pianist*, 126–35; Zylberberg, *A Warsaw Diary*, 82–4; Adler, *In the Warsaw Ghetto*, 315–30. Hillel Seidman also left at around this time.

60 Engelking and Leociak, *The Warsaw Ghetto*, 775–82; Zuckerman, *A Surplus of Memory*, 344, 350–1; Rotem, *Memoirs of a Warsaw Ghetto Fighter*, 33–4; Marek Edelman, *The Ghetto Fights* (London: Bookmarks, 1990; first published in English, 1946), 75–6.

61 Engelking and Leociak, *The Warsaw Ghetto*, 775–82; Rotem, *Memoirs of a Warsaw Ghetto Fighter*, 34; Moshe Arens, 'The Warsaw Ghetto Uprising: A Reappraisal', *Yad Vashem Studies*, 33 (2005), 101–42.

62 Zuckerman, *A Surplus of Memory*, 357.

63 Engelking and Leociak, *The Warsaw Ghetto*, 779.

64 Rotem, *Memoirs of a Warsaw Ghetto Fighter*, 39–42, 162.

65 Engelking and Leociak, *The Warsaw Ghetto*, 779–89.

66 Zuckerman, *A Surplus of Memory*, 263–5, 382–4; Rotem, *Memoirs of a Warsaw Ghetto Fighter*, 168–9; Edelman, *The Ghetto Fights*, 84–5; Gutman, *The Jews of Warsaw*, 420–5.

67 Shmuel Krakowski, *The War of the Doomed. Jewish Armed Resistance in Poland, 1942–1944*, trans. Ora Blaustein (New York: Holmes and Meier, 1984), 161–216 and Gutman, *The Jews of Warsaw*, 365–92, for an overview of the uprising and estimation of casualties; Zuckerman, *A Surplus of Memory*, 382–403, 789–96.

68 Gutman, *The Jews of Warsaw*, 401–15.

69 Engelking and Leociak, *The Warsaw Ghetto*, 801–6.

70 David Cesarani, 'British reactions to the Warsaw Ghetto Uprising', in Daniel

Grinberg ed., *Fifty Years After. Papers from the Conference organized by the Jewish Historical Institute of Warsaw, 29–31 March 1993* (Warsaw: Jewish Historical Institute, 1994), 133–44; for the US response, see Lipstadt, *Beyond Belief,* 216–17.

71 Cohen, *Rescue the Perishing,* 173–4, 181–94; Louise London, 'British Government Policy and Jewish Refugees 1933–45', *Patterns of Prejudice,* 23:4 (1989), 35–43.

72 Cohen, *Rescue the Perishing,* 188–9; Wasserstein, *Britain and the Jews of Europe,* 164–9.

73 Breitman and Lichtman, *FDR and the Jews,* 217–18; cf. Wyman, *The Abandonment of the Jews,* 79–92.

74 Breitman and Lichtman, *FDR and the Jews,* 218–25; cf. David S. Wyman and Rafael Medoff, *A Race Against Death. Peter Bergson, America, and the Holocaust* (New York: The New Press, 2002), 13–46.

75 Breitman and Lichtman, *FDR and the Jews,* 220; *McDonald Diaries,* II, 310.

76 Wasserstein, *Britain and the Jews of Europe,* 169–80; Wyman, *The Abandonment of the Jews,* 104–23; Kushner, *The Holocaust and the Liberal Imagination,* 182–90; Breitman and Lichtman, *FDR and the Jews,* 224–5; *McDonald Diaries,* II, 305, 308–9.

77 Wasserstein, *Britain and the Jews of Europe,* 180–1.

78 Breitman and Lichtman, *FDR and the Jews,* 226–7; Wasserstein, *Britain and the Jews of Europe,* 181–3; Cohen, *Rescue the Perishing,* 194–8.

79 Blatman, *For Our Freedom and Yours,* 145–50; David Engel, *Facing a Holocaust: The Polish Government-In-Exile and the Jews, 1943–1945* (Chapel Hill: University of North California Press, 1993), 70–6.

80 Engel, *Facing a Holocaust,* 76–7, 81–9, 89–94. Cf. Fleming, *Auschwitz, the Allies and Censorship of the Holocaust,* arguing that the Polish government-in-exile was hamstrung by British resistance to publicizing the plight of Polish Jews and used its own channels to make the information available to those who wanted to use it.

81 Porat, *The Blue and the Yellow Stars of David,* 49–62, 64–9, 80–9, 110–36, 144–9. On the controversial question of Ben-Gurion's attitude to rescue, see also Shabetai Teveth, *Ben-Gurion and the Holocaust* (New York: Harcourt Brace, 1995). Avriel, *Open the Gates!,* 123–73, recalls the tribulations and accomplishments of a key Zionist envoy.

82 Gutman, *The Jews of Warsaw,* 427–8; Longerich, *Holocaust,* 376–9.

83 Longerich, *Holocaust,* 379; Bender, *The Jews of Bialystok,* 221–4; Gruner, *Jewish Forced Labour,* 266–72; Silberklang, *Gates of Tears,* 390–3.

84 Silberklang, *Gates of Tears,* 309–402.

85 Silberklang, *Gates of Tears,* 250–1; Thaddeus Stabholz, *Seven Hells,* trans. Jacques and Hilda Grunblatt (New York: Holocaust Library, 1990), 29–89.

86 Arad, *The Holocaust in the Soviet Union,* 334–40; Longerich, *Holocaust,* 379.

87 *Documents on the Holocaust,* 335–41; for a more extensive version but a different translation see *The Diary of Samuel Golfard and the Holocaust in Galicia,* ed. Wendy Lower (Lanham MD: AltaMira Press, 2011), 101–6.

88 *Documents on the Holocaust,* 335–41; Claudia Koonz 'On Reading a Document: SS-Man Katzmann's "Solution of the Jewish Question in the District of Galicia"',

The Raul Hilberg Lecture, University of Vermont, 2 November 2005 at https://www.uvm.edu/~uvmchs/documents/KoonzHilbergLecture_002.pdf

89 26, 30 January 1943, *The Diary of Samuel Golfard*, 55, 72.

90 5, 14 April 1943, *The Diary of Samuel Golfard*, 89, 93 and Wendy Lower, 'Introduction', 28–47 and 'Related Documents', 123–35 in the same volume.

91 Arad, *The Holocaust in the Soviet Union*, 258–60; Bender, *The Jews of Bialystok*, 169–72, 185–92, 194.

92 Bender, *The Jews of Bialystok*, 155–69, 177–84, 193–203, 204–11.

93 Ibid, 252–69, 269–73.

94 Klein, *All But My Life*, 114–42, 145–52, 153–66; Silberklang, *Gates of Tears*, 431–4; Bella Gutterman, *A Narrow Bridge to Life. Jewish Forced Labour and Survival in the Gross-Rosen Camp System, 1940–1945*, trans. IBRT (New York: Berghahn, 2008), 51–2; Marc Buggeln, *Slave Labour in Nazi Concentration Camps*, trans. Paul Cohen (New York: Oxford University Press, 2014), esp. 83–139.

95 3 March, 8 April 1943, *Lodz Ghetto Chronicle*, 322, 333; Gutman, 'The Distinctiveness of the Lodz Ghetto', xlv; Trunk, *Lodz Ghetto*, 172–4; Epstein, *Model Nazi*, 257–67; Horowitz, *Ghettostadt*, 234–37, 267–71.

96 Epstein, *Model Nazi*, 257–67; Gutman, 'The Distinctiveness of the Lodz Ghetto', xl–xlii; Trunk, *Lodz Ghetto*, 159–64; Horowitz, *Ghettostadt*, 237–41.

97 13, 19 March, 21 April, 1, 7 August 1943, *Lodz Ghetto Chronicle*, 323–4, 325, 337, 355–7, 367.

98 20 February, 6, 8, 11 March 1943, *Sierakowiak Diary*, 250, 252, 253, 256–7, 263.

99 23 February, 30 April, 6, 26 May, 8–9 July 1943, Rosenfeld, *In the Beginning was the Ghetto*, 159, 167 (undated essay), 187, 189, 191, 195.

100 10 April, 11 October, 25 October 1943, *Lodz Ghetto Chronicle*, 333–4, 395–7, 421–3; 20 April, 8 October, 28 December 1943, Rosenfeld, *In the Beginning was the Ghetto*, 185, 204, 241–3

101 Gutman, 'The Distinctiveness of the Lodz Ghetto', xlv–xlvi; Trunk, *Lodz Ghetto*, 248–54.

102 Arad, *The Holocaust in the Soviet Union*, 312–14; Angrick and Klein, *The 'Final Solution' in Riga*, 278–80, 366–72.

103 Katz, *One Who Came Back*, 43–9, 65–79, 88–102; Arad, *The Holocaust in the Soviet Union*, 314–15; Angrick and Klein, *The 'Final Solution' in Riga*, 336–46, 372–5.

104 Arad, *The Holocaust in the Soviet Union*, 321–2; Longerich, *Holocaust*, 383–4; Angrick and Klein, *The 'Final Solution' in Riga*, 379–90.

105 8 March, 12, 15, 17 September, 28 October, 28 December 1942; 25 February 1943, *Vilna Ghetto Chronicles*, 226–8, 356, 357, 360, 387–9, 439, 464.

106 5, 9 April 1943, *Vilna Ghetto Chronicles*, 500–2, 507–8; 4, 5 April 1943, *Sakowicz Diary*, 69–83; Arad, *The Holocaust in the Soviet Union*, 315–17.

107 Philip Friedman, *Roads to Extinction*, 372–7; Abraham H. Foxman, 'The Resistance Movement in the Vilna Ghetto', in Yuri Suhl ed., *They Fought Back. The Story of the Jewish Resistance in Nazi Europe* (New York: Schocken, 1967), 148–58.

108 1 July 1943, *Vilna Ghetto Chronicles*, 580; 24 September 1943, *Sakowicz Diary*, 118–19; Arad, *The Holocaust in the Soviet Union*, 318–19.

109 6, 11 October 1943, *Sakowicz Diary*, 127–9, 130–2.

110 January–December 1942, 4, 10 March, 19, 21 April, 8, 28 May 1943, *Tory Diary*, 65–89, 248–51, 299–302, 303–4, 324–6, 355–6; Arad, *The Holocaust in the Soviet Union*, 319.

111 Entry for 28 September 1943 and letter by Elchanan Elkes, 11 November 1943, *Tory Diary*, 481–6, 507.

112 Longerich, *Holocaust*, 382–5; Arad, *The Holocaust in the Soviet Union*, 326–9.

113 Arad, *Belzec, Sobibor, Treblinka*, 165–9.

114 Chrostowski, *The Extermination Camp Treblinka*, 100; Arad, *Belzec, Sobibor, Treblinka*, 219–22; Wiernik, *A Year In Treblinka*, 30–2; Willenberg, *Revolt in Treblinka*, 105–12, 127–9, 158–60; Glazar, *Trap with a Green Fence*, 69–76, 89–96.

115 Arad, *Belzec, Sobibor, Treblinka*, 171–2, 173–7; Wiernik, *A Year In Treblinka*, 26–8, 40–1; Rajchman, *Treblinka*, 69–78.

116 Wiernik, *A Year In Treblinka*, 35–8; Rajchman, *Treblinka*, 101–2; Willenberg, *Revolt in Treblinka*, 175–8; Glazar, *Trap with a Green Fence*, 111–12.

117 Wiernik, *A Year In Treblinka*, 44–6; Rajchman, *Treblinka*, 102–3; Willenberg, *Revolt in Treblinka*, 178–82; Glazar, *Trap with a Green Fence*, 137–45.

118 Wiernik, *A Year In Treblinka*, 44; Willenberg, *Revolt in Treblinka*, 179.

119 Rajchman, *Treblinka*, 106–11; Glazar, *Trap with a Green Fence*, 146–88; Willenberg, *Revolt in Treblinka*, 150–72, 224–63.

120 Arad, *Belzec, Sobibor, Treblinka*, 147–9; Jules Schevlis, *Sobibor. A History of a Nazi Death Camp*, trans. Karin Dixon (New York: Berg, 2007), 198–208, 216–20.

121 Arad, *Belzec, Sobibor, Treblinka*, 299–314.

122 Ibid, 315–21; Thomas Toivi Blatt, *From the Ashes of Sobibor. A Story of Survival* (Evanston: Northwestern University Press, 1997), 139–44.

123 Arad, *Belzec, Sobibor, Treblinka*, 322–42; Blatt, *From the Ashes of Sobibor*, 145–53, 232–3.

124 Blatt, *From the Ashes of Sobibor*, 155–71, 173; A. Petzovsky [Alexander Peshersky], 'The Outbreak in Sobivor', in Meyer Barkai ed., *The Fighting Ghettos* (New York: Tower Books, 1962), 205–26. This anthology is an abbreviated translation of *The Book of the Fighting Ghettos*, edited by Yitzhak Zuckerman. On the survival of death camp escapees in general, see Arad, *Belzec, Sobibor, Treblinka*, 342–8.

125 Jan Grabowski, *Hunt for the Jews. Betrayal and Murder in German-Occupied Poland* (Bloomington: Indiana University Press, 2014), 1–4, 59–65, 134–48, and 'Rural Society and the Jews in Hiding: Elders, Night Watchers, Firefighters, Hostages and Manhunts', *Yad Vashem Studies*, 40 (2012), 49–74.

126 Grabowski, *Hunt for the Jews*, 63–86, 101–20, 137–48.

127 Gross with Gross, *Golden Harvest*, 50–4, 91–114; Grabowski, *Hunt for the Jews*, 101–20; Aleksandra Bánkowska, 'Polish Partisan Formations during 1942–1944 in Jewish Testimonies', *Holocaust Studies and Materials* (2008), 103–22; Alina Skibinska and Joanna Tokarska-Bakir, '"Barabasz" and the Jews: From the History of the "Wybraniecki" Home Army Partisan Detachment', *Holocaust Studies and*

Materials (2013), 13–78; Jerzy Mazurek, "'Jozek, what are you doing?" The Massacre of Jews Committed by the AK in the Village of Kosowice', *Holocaust Studies and Materials* (2013), 405–32; Alina Skibinska with Jerzy Mazurek, "'Barwy Biale" on their way to Aid Fighting Warsaw: The Crimes of the Home Army against the Jews', *Holocaust Studies and Materials* (2013), 433–80.

128 8 May, 8 August, 24 October, 17, 26 November 1942, 28 May 1943, Klukowski, *Diary*, 195–6, 209, 221, 225, 226–7, 256.

129 Spector, *The Holocaust of Volhynian Jews*, 257–326, 327–32, 356–61.

130 Longerich, *Himmler*, 666–7; Longerich, *Holocaust*, 382; Arad, *Belzec, Sobibor, Treblinka*, 365–9; Pohl, *Von der 'Judenpolitik' zum Judenmord*, 166–71.

131 Silberklang, *Gates of Tears*, 403–9.

132 Ibid, 409–30, 432–3.

133 Arad, *Belzec, Sobibor, Treblinka*, 370–6; Caroline Sturdy-Colls, 'Gone but not Forgotten: Archaeological Approaches to the Site of the former Treblinka Extermination Camp in Poland', *Holocaust Studies and Materials* (2013), 253–89.

134 Van Pelt and Dwork, *Auschwitz*, 320–4 and central plates 'Blueprints of Genocide' and Jean-Claude Pressac with Robert Jan van Pelt, 'The Machinery of Mass Murder at Auschwitz', in Gutman and Berenbaum eds, *Anatomy of the Auschwitz Death Camp*, 183–245. Cf. Michael Thad Allen, 'The Devil in the Details: The Gas Chambers of Birkenau, October 1941', *HGS*, 16:2 (2002), 189–216, arguing that several documents suggest the SS designers may have considered using the underground rooms for poison gas much earlier.

135 Piper, *Auschwitz 1940–1945*, vol. III, 144–68 and his 'Gas Chambers and Crematoria', in Gutman and Berenbaum eds, *Anatomy of the Auschwitz Death Camp*, 157–82.

136 Piper, *Auschwitz 1940–1945*, vol. III, 167–73.

137 Andrzej Strzelcki, 'Plundering the Victims' Property', in Iwaszko et al. eds, *Auschwitz 1940–1945*, vol. II, 137–65; Willliam Z. Slany, *US and Allied Efforts to Recover and Restore Gold and Other Assets Stolen or Hidden by Germany During World War II. A Preliminary* Study (Washington: US State Department, 1997), 162–5; Peter Hayes, *From Cooperation to Complicity. Degussa in the Third Reich* (New York: Cambridge University Press, 2004), 181–4, 283–96; Wachsmann, *KL*, 376–81.

138 Kitty Hart, *I am alive* (London: Corgi Books, 1962), 69–70.

139 Andrzej Strzelcki, 'The History, role and operation of the "Central Camp Sauna" in Auschwitz II-'Birkenau', in Teresa Swiebocka ed., *The Architecture of Crime. The 'Central Sauna' in Auschwitz II-Birkenau*, trans. William Brand (Oswięcim: Auschwitz-Birkenau State Museum, 2001), 11–16; Hart, *I am alive*, 40–1.

140 Strzelcki, 'The History, role and operation of the "Central Camp Sauna"', 24–9.

141 Nahon, *Birkenau*, 21–9, 30–2, 33–41.

142 Adelsberger, *Auschwitz. A Doctor's Story*, 29–31; Nahon, *Birkenau*, 45–6.

143 Piper, 'The Exploitation of Prisoner Labour', in Tadeusz Iwaszko et al. eds, *Auschwitz 1940–1945*, vol. II, 89–98; Galia Glaser-Heled and Dan Bar-On, 'Displaced: the memoir of Eliezer Gruenbaum at Birkenau – Translation and Commentary', *Shofar*, 27:2 (2009), 1–23, here 6.

144 Danuta Czech, 'The Auschwitz Prisoner Administration', in Gutman and Berenbaum eds, *Anatomy of the Auschwitz Death Camp*, 362–78; Menasche, *Birkenau*, 17–58; Adelsberger, *Auschwitz. A Doctor's Story*, 73–80; Nahon, *Birkenau*, 68–72; Wachsmann, *KL*, 499–521.

145 Adelsberger, *Auschwitz. A Doctor's Story*, 37–8; Nahon, *Birkenau*, 46–7; van Pelt and Dwork, *Auschwitz*, 262–8.

146 Adelsberger, *Auschwitz. A Doctor's Story*, 47–8.

147 Nahon, *Birkenau*, 42–3, 61–6; Adelsberger, *Auschwitz. A Doctor's Story*, 43–6, 50–4; Irena Strzelecka, 'Hospitals', in Gutman and Berenbaum eds, *Anatomy of the Auschwitz Death Camp*, 379–92.

148 Strzelecka, 'Hospitals', Gutman and Berenbaum eds, *Anatomy of the Auschwitz Death Camp*, 398–91; Adelsberger, *Auschwitz. A Doctor's Story*, 65–6; Nahon, *Birkenau*, 95.

149 Irena Strzelecka, 'Women', in Gutman and Berenbaum eds, *Anatomy of the Auschwitz Death Camp*, 412–17; Krystyna Zywulska, *I came back*, trans. Krystyna Cenkalska (New York: Roy Publishers, 1951 [first published in Polish, 1946]), 22, 50, 68; Helen Tischauer interview by Dr David Boder, Feldafing, Germany, 23 September 1946 in Jürgen Matthäus ed., *Approaching an Auschwitz Survivor. Holocaust Testimony and its Transformations* (New York: Oxford University Press, 2009), 124–8, 138, 145–6, 149–50.

150 Adelsberger, *Auschwitz. A Doctor's Story*, 100–1; Zywulska, *I came back*, 96–7; Ellen Ben-Sefer, 'Forced Sterilization and Abortion as Sexual Abuse', in Hedgepeth and Saidel eds, *Sexual Violence Against Jewish Women*, 150–73, esp. 160–4.

151 Adelsberger, *Auschwitz. A Doctor's Story*, 85–6; Zywulska, *I came back*, 61–2; Brigitte Halbmayr, 'Sexualized Violence against Women during Nazi "Racial" Persecution in Hedgepeth and Saidel eds, *Sexual Violence Against Jewish Women*, 29–44, esp. 33–8.

152 Zywulska, *I came back*, 61, 107; Halbmayr, 'Sexualized Violence', 35.

153 Porch, *Hitler's Mediterranean Gamble*, 415–51; Citino, *The Wehrmacht Retreats*, 165–97.

154 Porch, *Hitler's Mediterranean Gamble*, 452–62.

155 Ibid, 462–74; Citino, *The Wehrmacht Retreats*, 241–54.

156 Porch, *Hitler's Mediterranean Gamble*, 485–503, 507–12; Citino, *The Wehrmacht Retreats*, 255–65.

157 Sarfatti, *The Jews in Mussolini's Italy*, 178–83.

158 Longerich, *Himmler*, 681–4; Kershaw, *Hitler 1936–1945*, 599.

159 Tooze, *The Wages of Destruction*, 550–84; Fritz, *Ostkrieg*, 329–30, 336–53, 364–84; Citino, *The Wehrmacht Retreats*, 116–44, 212–37.

160 Friedländer, *Nazi Germany and the Jews*, vol. 2, 472–6, 538; Kershaw, *Hitler 1936–1945*, 581–4, 588–9; Herf, *The Jewish Enemy*, 211–13; Fritz, *Ostkrieg*, 360–1.

161 Longerich, *Himmler*, 689–90, 694–5; Kershaw, *Hitler 1936–1945*, 603–6, 636–7; Friedländer, *Nazi Germany and the Jews*, vol. 2, 540–5; van der Vat, *The Good Nazi*, 164–9.

162 Longerich, *Holocaust*, 401–3.

163 Meir Michaelis, 'Italian Policy up to the Armistice', in Cohen, Cochavi, Gelber eds, *The Shoah and the War*, 283–300; Liliana Picciotto, 'Statistical Tables on the Holocaust in Italy with an Insight into the Mechanics of the Deportations', *Yad Vashem Studies*, 33 (2005), 307–46; Sarfatti, *The Jews in Mussolini's Italy*, 161–74.

164 Luigi Fleischmann, *From Fiume to Navelli. A Sixteen-Year-Old's Narrative of the Fleischmann Family and Other Free Internees in Fascist Italy September 1943–June 1944* (Jerusalem: Yad Vashem, 2007), 14–16, 19–20.

165 Liliana Picciotto, 'The Shoah in Italy: Its History and Characteristics', in Zimmerman ed., *Jews in Italy under Fascist and Nazi Rule, 1922-1945*, 210–14; Richard Breitman, 'New Sources on the Holocaust in Italy', *HGS*, 16:3 (2002), 402–14.

166 Zuccotti, *The Italians and the Holocaust*, 101–37.

167 Ibid, 144–6, 154–65, 210–17 and Zuccotti, *Under His Very Windows, The Vatican and the Holocaust in Italy* (New Haven: Yale University Press, 2000), 150–70, 202–99; Friedländer, *Nazi Germany and the Jews*, vol. 2, 559–69.

168 Picciotto, 'The Shoah in Italy', 214–21; Sarfatti, *The Jews in Mussolini's Italy*, 187–96; Zuccotti, *The Italians and the Holocaust*, 166–99.

169 8, 24 December 1943, 6 March 1944, Fleischmann, *From Fiume to Navelli*, 58–9, 78–80, 115–16; Sarfatti, *The Jews in Mussolini's Italy*, 202–10

170 Zuccotti, *The Holocaust, the French, and the Jews*, 82–9, 167, 181–2.

171 Jackson, *France 1940-1944*, 230–1.

172 Poliakov's reminiscences from his memoir, *L'auberge des musiciens*, quoted in Zuccotti, *The Holocaust, the French, and the Jews*, 181–2.

173 Zuccotti, *The Holocaust, the French, and the Jews*, 164–6.

174 Zuccotti, *The Italians and the Holocaust*, 76–8; Jonathan Steinberg, *All or Nothing. The Axis and the Holocaust 1941-43* (London: Routledge, 1990), 131–4.

175 Mazower, *Inside Hitler's Greece*, 250–3; Safrian, *Eichmann's Men*, 181–5; 11 April 1944, Czech, *Auschwitz Chronicle*, 609.

176 Longerich, *Himmler*, 691–2; Zuccotti, *The Italians and the Holocaust*, 80–2; Mazower, *Inside Hitler's Greece*, 252–6; Safrian, *Eichmann's Men*, 185–8.

177 Poznanski, *Jews in France during World War II*, 321–32, 336–51; Friedländer, *Nazi Germany and the Jews*, vol. 2, 550–5; Zuccotti, *The Holocaust, the French, and the Jews*, 157–65, 187–9; Safrian, *Eichmann's Men*, 175–7.

178 25 August, 10, 28, October, 1 November 1943, *Berr Journal*, 155, 155–9, 186, 193–6.

179 Poznanski, *Jews in France during World War II*, 238–46; Marrus and Paxton, *Vichy France and the Jews*, 152–6.

180 Zuccotti, *The Holocaust, the French, and the Jews*, 227–31; Philip Hallie, *Lest Innocent Blood be Shed* (New York: Harper, 1994), 129–38; Caroline Moorhead, *Village of Secrets: Defying the Nazis in Vichy France* (London: Chatto and Windus, 2014), 141–50, 190–205, 218–21, 224–34.

181 Poznanski, *Jews in France during World War II*, 351–5; Zuccotti, *The Holocaust, the French, and the Jews*, 260–78; Claude Lanzmann, *The Patagonian Hare. A Memoir*, trans. Frank Wynne (London: Atlantic Books, 2012), 91–111.

182 Longerich, *Holocaust*, 387–8; 13, 15 January 1943, *Young Moshe's Diary*, 60–2;

Marion Schreiber, *The Twentieth Train*, trans. Shaun Whiteside (London: Atlantic Books, 2004), 162–3, 170–1.

183 Schreiber, *The Twentieth Train*, 210–30; 7 March 1944, Anne Somerhausen, *Written in Darkness. A Belgium Woman's Record of the Occupation 1940–1945* (New York: Knopf, 1946), 261–2 (Somerhausen repeatedly muddles dates, which makes her 'diary' a less than reliable source).

184 Longerich, *Holocaust*, 387–8; Shaul Esh, 'Introduction', *Young Moshe's Diary*, 6–8. Moshe's sisters and a younger brother survived.

185 Presser, *Ashes in the Wind*, 482–4; Moore, *Victims and Survivors*, 103–5; Griffioen and Zeller, 'Comparing the Persecution of the Jews in the Netherlands, France and Belgium', in Romijn et al. eds, *The Persecution of the Jews in the Netherlands*, 72–4, 77–8.

186 Romijn, 'The "Lesser Evil"', in Romijn et al. eds, *The Persecution of the Jews in the Netherlands*, 23–5; Presser, *Ashes in the Wind*, 178–94, 202–13; Moore, *Victims and Survivors*, 104–5; Wasserstein, *The Ambiguity of Virtue*, 171–80.

187 Presser, *Ashes in the Wind*, 195–202.

188 Ibid, 464–78; Marieke Meeuwnwoord, 'The Holocaust in the Netherlands: new research of camp Vught', in Romijn et al. eds, *The Persecution of the Jews in the Netherlands*, 93–103; Robert Jan van Pelt, 'Introduction' to David Koker, *At the Edge of the Abyss. A Concentration Camp Diary, 1943–1944*, trans. Michiel Horn and John Irons (Evanston: Northwestern University Press, 2012), 58–9; Moore, *Victims and Survivors*, 101.

189 Van Pelt, 'Introduction' and 11, 22, 23, February, 23 March 1943, Koker, *Diary*, 23–42, 77–8, 105, 109, 152.

190 8, 9, 10 May 1943, Koker, *Diary*, 190–2.

191 23 May, 7 July, 16 August, 1, 30 September, 7 November 1943, Koker, *Diary*, 198–200, 221–2, 243, 251–3, 264, 281–2.

192 11, 15, 27 November 1943, Koker, *Diary*, 285–6, 289, 294–5.

193 Hesdörffer, *Twelve Years of Nazi Terror*, 53–4, 57, 60–2, 65 (on the Vught transports).

194 29 May 1943, Mechanicus, *Diary*, 16–17.

195 1 June 1943, Mechanicus, *Diary*, 25–7.

196 3 June, 3 July, 4, 27 August 1943, Mechanicus, *Diary*, 29–33, 73–4, 112, 140.

197 14 September 1943, Mechanicus, *Diary*, 155–8.

198 Presser, *Ashes in the Wind*, 235–8, 529–35.

199 Lederer, *Ghetto Theresienstadt*, 52–3, 88–95; Rothkirchen, *The Jews of Bohemia and Moravia*, 242–3; 14 January 1943, *Weiss Diary*, 77.

200 Lederer, *Ghetto Theresienstadt*, 122–31; Rothkirchen, *The Jews of Bohemia and Moravia*, 265–83; Joza Karas, *Music in Terezin 1941–1945* (New York: Beaufort Books, 1988), 9–84, 93–161.

201 Ruth Bondy, *Trapped. Essays on the History of the Czech Jews, 1939–1943* (Jerusalem: Yad Vashem, 2008), 11–12.

202 Bondy, *Trapped*, 152–3, 156–9; *Manes Diary*, 112–15.

203 Bondy, *Trapped*, 159–69; Nili Keren, 'The Family Camp', in Gutman and Berenbaum eds, *Anatomy of the Auschwitz Death Camp*, 428–40; Otto Dov Kulka,

Landscapes of the Metropolis of Death. Reflections on Memory and Imagination, trans. Ralph Mandel (London: Allen Lane, 2013), 18–19.

204 Kulka, *Landscapes of the Metropolis of Death*, 105–14; Bondy, *Trapped*, 152–5; Rothkirchen, *The Jews of Bohemia and Moravia*, 247–64; Cesarani, *Eichmann*, 136–7, 149–50.

205 Kulka, *Landscapes of the Metropolis of Death*, 30.

206 Bondy, *Trapped*, 175–6; Kulka, *Landscapes of the Metropolis of Death*, 30, 34.

207 Longerich, *Himmler*, 397–401; Vilhjálmur Örn Vilhjálmsson, 'The King and the Star. Myths created during the Occupation of Denmark', in M. B. Jensen and S. L. B. Jensen eds, *Denmark and the Holocaust* (Copenhagen: Institute for International Studies, 2003), 102–17.

208 Lone Rünits, 'The Politics of Asylum in Denmark in the Wake of Kristallnacht – A Case Study', in Jensen and Jensen eds, *Denmark and the Holocaust*, 14–32; Bo Lidegaard, *Countrymen. The Untold Story of How Denmark's Jews Escaped the Nazis* (London: Atlantic Books, 2013), 12–13.

209 Lidegaard, *Countrymen*, 20–1; Collingham, *The Taste of War*, 175.

210 Lidegaard, *Countrymen*, 26–31.

211 Longerich, *Holocaust*, 397–401; Lidegaard, *Countrymen*, 31–45; Michael Mogenson, 'October 1943 – the Rescue of the Danish Jews', in Jensen and Jensen eds, *Denmark and the Holocaust*, 33–61, esp. 35–8.

212 Lidegaard, *Countrymen*, 80–93, 96–8.

213 Christian Leitz, *Nazi Germany and Neutral Europe during the Second World War* (Manchester: Manchester University Press, 2000), 49–84; Paul Levine, 'Swedish neutrality during the Second World War: tactical success or moral compromise', in Neville Wylie ed., *European Neutrals and Non-Belligerents During the Second World War* (Cambridge: Cambridge University Press, 2002), 304–30; Sven Nordlund, '"The War is Over – Now You Can Go Home!" Jewish Refugees and the Swedish Labour Market in the Shadow of the Holocaust', in David Cesarani and Paul Levine eds, *'Bystanders' to the Holocaust: A Re-evaluation* (London: Frank Cass, 2002), 171–98.

214 *From Indifference to Activism, Swedish Diplomacy and the Holocaust 1938–44* (Uppsala: Studia Historica Upsaliensia, 1998), 66–9, 92–5, 114–30, 134–43.

215 Mogenson, 'October 1943', 39–43, 47–9; Lidegaard, *Countrymen*, 111–13.

216 Mogenson, 'October 1943', 52–7; Lidegaard, *Countrymen*, 147–57.

217 Mogenson, 'October 1943', 43–6; Lidegaard, *Countrymen*, 127–39, 173–89.

218 Mogenson, 'October 1943', 50–1.

219 Longerich, *Holocaust*, 399.

220 Fleming, *Auschwitz, the Allies and Censorship of the Holocaust*, 167–90; cf. Martin Gilbert, *Auschwitz and the Allies* (London: Michael Joseph, 1981), 73, 85–7, 105, 155, 161.

221 Harris, 'Broadcasting the Massacres. An analysis of the BBC's contemporary coverage of the Holocaust', 65–98; Fleming, *Auschwitz, the Allies and Censorship of the Holocaust*, 200–13; cf. Engel, *Facing a Holocaust*, 31–43, 71–4, 76–7, 172–8.

222 Fleming, *Auschwitz, the Allies and Censorship of the Holocaust*, 43–5; Tony Kushner, *The Persistence of Prejudice. Antisemitism in British Society during the*

Second World War (Manchester: Manchester University Press, 1989), 62–5, 82–5, 155–60; cf. Sompolinsky, *Britain and the Holocaust*, 119–41 and Shatzkes, *Holocaust and Rescue*, 134–43; Bolchover, *British Jewry and the Holocaust*, 83–143, on ideological differnces within the community.

223 Wyman, *The Abandonment of the Jews*, 143–56; Wyman and Medoff, *A Race Against Death*, 42–6; Breitman and Lichtman, *FDR and the Jews*, 228–32.

224 Wyman, *The Abandonment of the Jews*, 178–206; Wyman and Medoff, *A Race Against Death*, 46–9; Breitman and Lichtman, *FDR and the Jews*, 232–7.

225 Breitman and Lichtman, *FDR and the Jews*, 237; London, *Whitehall and the Jews*, 231–4; Wasserstein, *Britain and the Jews of Europe*, 291–7.

226 *McDonald Diaries*, II, 316–17; Ronald Zweig, 'The War Refugee Board and American Intelligence', in Cohen, Cochavi, Gelber eds, *The Shoah and the War*, 293–416; Richard Breitman, 'Other Responses to the Holocaust', in Richard Breitman et al. eds, *US Intelligence and the Nazis* (New York: Cambridge University Press, 2005), 45–64, esp. 58–64.

Eight – The Last Phase: 1944–1945

1 Kershaw, *Hitler 1936–1945*, 615, 624–5.
2 Gerhard Weinberg, 'German plans for victory, 1944–1945', in his *Germany, Hitler and World War II* (Cambridge: Cambridge University Press, 1995), 274–86; cf. Kershaw, *Hitler 1936–1945*, 609–15.
3 Hitler's 30 January 1944 speech at https://archive.org/stream/TheCompleteHitler-SpeechesAndProclamations-MaxDomarus/TheCompleteHitler-1932–1945-Vol1–4_djvu.txt
4 Weinberg, *A World At Arms*, 671–73; Kershaw, *Hitler 1936–1945*, 624–5; Vagi, Csosz and Kadar eds, *The Holocaust in Hungary*, 61–9; István Móscy, 'Hungary's Failed Strategic Surrender: Secret Wartime Negotiations with Britain', in Nándor Dreisziger ed., *Hungary in an Age of Total War (1938–1948)*, (New York: Columbia University Press, 1998), 86–106; Cesarani, *Eichmann*, 160–2.
5 Kershaw, *Hitler 1936–1945*, 636–7.
6 Kershaw, *Hitler 1936–1945*, 624–8; Braham, *The Politics of Genocide*, vol. 1, 381–9, 396–7, 421–6.
7 Dawidowicz, *The War Against the Jews*, 181–2, asserted that 'The Final Solution had top priority, even at a time of military exigencies.' Cf. Christian Gerlach, 'The decision making process for the deportation of Hungarian Jews', in Judit Molnár ed., *The Holocaust in Hungary in A European Perspective* (Budapest: Balassi Kiadó, 2005), 473–81, a summary of the thesis presented in Christian Gerlach and Götz Aly, *Das letze Kapitel: Realpolitik, Ideologie und der Mord an den ungarischen Juden 1944/45* (Stuttgart: dva, 2002).
8 Vagi, Csosz and Kadar eds, *The Holocaust in Hungary*, xli–xlii, 368–9.
9 Ibid, 1–22; László Karsai, 'Anti-Jewish laws and decrees in Hungary, 1920–1944' and László Csosz, 'Agrarian reform and race protection: the implementation of the Fourth Jewish Law', in Molnár ed., *The Holocaust in Hungary*, 143–66 and

180–97; Yehuda Don, 'Economic Implications of the Anti-Jewish Laws in Hungary', in Cesarani ed., *Genocide and Rescue. The Holocaust in Hungary 1944*, 47–76.

10 Robert Rozett, *Conscripted Slaves. Hungarian Jewish Forced Labourers on the Eastern Front during the Second World War* (Jerusalem: Yad Vashem, 2014), 44–9, 61–2, 72–88, 120–4, 143–50, and on massacres, 158–63.

11 Vagi, Csosz and Kadar eds, *The Holocaust in Hungary*, 36–46.

12 Cesarani, *Eichmann*, 159–63.

13 Braham, *The Politics of Genocide*, vol. 1, 406–18, 421–6, 558–60.

14 Ibid, 421–6.

15 Cesarani, *Eichmann*, 166.

16 Braham, *The Politics of Genocide*, vol. 1, 510–14, 515–28, 548–53; Vagi, Csosz and Kadar eds, *The Holocaust in Hungary*, 72–3; Ronald Zweig, *The Gold Train. The Destruction of the Jews and the Second World War's Most Terrible Robbery* (London: Penguin, 2000), 27–36, 51–61.

17 Cesarani, *Eichmann*, 164–6.

18 Braham, *The Politics of Genocide*, vol. 1, 527–8; Cesarani, *Eichmann*, 166–7.

19 Braham, *The Politics of Genocide*, vol. 1, 662–6; Safrian, *Eichmann's Men*, 196–204.

20 Vagi, Csosz and Kadar eds, *The Holocaust in Hungary*, 76–9; Braham, *The Politics of Genocide*, vol. 1, 583–652, 688–704, vol. 2, 711–33, 755–80.

21 Tim Cole, *Holocaust City. The Making of a Jewish Ghetto* (London: Routledge, 2002), 70–80, 81–91, 91–100.

22 Hedi Fried, *The Road to Auschwitz. Fragments of a Life*, trans. Michael Meyer (Lincoln: University of Nebraska Press, 1990), 56–7; Bela Zsolt, *Nine Suitcases*, trans. Ladislaus Löb (London: Jonathan Cape, 2004, first published in Hungarian 1946–7), 9–10.

23 Zsolt, *Nine Suitcases*, 31, 37.

24 Fried, *The Road to Auschwitz*, 72–3, 75–6.

25 Braham, *The Politics of Genocide*, vol. 1, 604–5, 664–8; Cesarani, *Eichmann*, 168–9.

26 Safrian, *Eichmann's Men*, 199–202; Cesarani, *Eichmann*, 171–2.

27 Vagi, Csosz and Kadar eds, *The Holocaust in Hungary*, 104–11; Cesarani, *Eichmann*, 170, 172.

28 Braham, *The Politics of Genocide*, vol. 1, 671–3, vol. 2, 773–4, 778–9.

29 Fried, *The Road to Auschwitz*, 75–6, 79; Simone Gigliotti, *The Train Journey. Transit, Captivity and Witnessing the Holocaust* (London: Berghahn, 2009), 78–85, 97–116. See also, Olga Lengyel, *Five Chimneys* (New York: Ziff-Davis Publishing, 1947), 15–19.

30 Fried, *The Road to Auschwitz*, 38; Zsolt, *Nine Suitcases*, ix; Vagi, Csosz and Kadar eds, *The Holocaust in Hungary*, 243–8, cf. Friedländer, *Nazi Germany and the Jews*, vol. 2, 613–15, on the vexed question of what Hungarian Jews knew and what they could have known.

31 Yehuda Bauer, *Jews for Sale? Nazi-Jewish Negotiations, 1933–1945* (New Haven: Yale University Press, 1994), 202–11; Cesarani, *Eichmann*, 180–2.

32 Bauer, *Jews for Sale?*, 67–101; Porat, *The Blue and the Yellow Stars of David*, 174–88.

33 Porat, *The Blue and the Yellow Stars of David*, 49–71, 111–26; Tuvia Friling, 'Istanbul 1942–1945: The Kollek–Avriel and Berman–Ofner networks', in Bankier ed., *Secret Intelligence and the Holocaust*, 105–56; Bauer, *Jews for Sale?*, 120–43.

34 Bauer, *Jews for Sale?*, 160–3; Cesarani, *Eichmann*, 173–5.

35 Longerich, *Himmler*, 707–11; Shlomo Aronson, *Hitler, the Allies, and the Jews* (Cambridge: Cambridge University Press, 2006), 227–89.

36 Bauer, *Jews for Sale?*, 162–71, 172–93; Porat, *The Blue and the Yellow Stars of David*, 188–211; Wasserstein, *Britain and the Jews of Europe*, 223–34; Shlomo Aronson, 'OSS X-2 and Rescue Efforts During the Holocaust', in Bankier ed., *Secret Intelligence and the Holocaust*, 65–104.

37 Ladislaus Löb, *Dealing with Satan. Kasztner's Daring Rescue Mission* (London: Jonathan Cape, 2008), 74–93, 96–120; Bauer, *Jews for Sale?*, 197–200.

38 Löb, *Dealing with Satan*, 93–6; Bauer, *Jews for Sale?*, 200–1.

39 Breitman and Lichtman, *FDR and the Jews*, 262–72; Ruth Gruber, *Haven. The Dramatic Story of 1,000 World War II Refugees and How They Came to America* (New York: Three Rivers Press, 2000 edn).

40 Breitman and Lichtman, *FDR and the Jews*, 272–5; Braham, *The Politics of Genocide*, vol. 2, 861–82; Bauer, *Jews for Sale?*, 232–8; Robert Rozett, 'International Interventions: The Role of Diplomats in Attempts to Rescue Jews in Hungary', in Randolph Braham and Scott Miller eds, *The Nazis' Last Victims. The Holocaust in Hungary* (Detroit: Wayne State University Press, 1998) 137–52; Paul A. Levine, *Raoul Wallenberg in Budapest. Myth, History and Holocaust* (London: Vallentine Mitchell, 2010), 101–249 and 133–4 on the dual role of the WRB representative in Stockholm as an OSS agent, a connection that may ultimately have compromised Wallenberg's status.

41 Weinberg, *A World at Arms*, 686–95, 703–16; Martin Blumenson, *The Duel for France, 1944* (New York: DaCapo Press, 1963), 1–166; Fritz, *Ostkrieg*, 405–21.

42 Vagi, Csosz and Kadar eds, *The Holocaust in Hungary*, 134–45; Cesarani, *Eichmann*, 184–5.

43 Wasserstein, *Britain and the Jews of Europe*, 234–41; Cesarani, *Eichmann*, 187–9.

44 Randolph Braham, 'Hungarian Jews', in Gutman and Berenbaum eds, *Anatomy of the Auschwitz Death Camp*, 456–68

45 Müller, *Eyewitness Auschwitz*, 123–33; van Pelt and Dwork, *Auschwitz*, 337–40; Vagi, Csosz and Kadar eds, *The Holocaust in Hungary*, 214–16, 219–20.

46 Fried, *Fragments of a Life*, 79–82.

47 Adelsberger, *Auschwitz. A Doctor's Story*, 63, 80–5; Menasche, *Birkenau*, 68–76.

48 Müller, *Eyewitness Auschwitz*, 133–43; Zywulska, *I came back*, 163–81; see also Alter Feinsilber deposition in Jadwiga Bezwínská and Danuta Czech eds, *Amidst a Nightmare of Crime. Manuscripts of Prisoners in Cremation Squads Found at Auschwitz*, trans. Krystyna Michalik (New York: Howard Fertig, 1973), 56.

49 Müller, *Eyewitness Auschwitz*, 138–9.

50 Fried, *Fragments of a Life*, 82–8, 102–15.

51 Pohl, 'The Holocaust and the concentration camps', in Caplan and Wachsmann eds, *Concentration Camps in Nazi Germany*, 158–9; Gutterman, *A Narrow Bridge to Life*, 29–37.

52 Wachsmann, *KL*, 444–61, 464–71 and summary in 'The dynamics of destruction', in Caplan and Wachsmann eds, *Concentration Camps in Nazi Germany*, 31–4; Fritz, *Ostkrieg*, 426; Tooze, *The Wages of Destruction*, 627–34.

53 Allen, *The Business of Genocide*, 208–32; Wachsmann, *KL*, 444–58; Gretchen Schaft and Gerhard Zeidler, *Commemorating Hell. The Public Memory of Mittlebau-Dora* (Urbana: University of Illinois Press, 2011), 19–34.

54 Gutterman, *A Narrow Bridge to Life*, 77–8, 97–9, 119–30.

55 Marrus and Paxton, *Vichy France and the Jews*, 332–5; Jackson, *France. The Dark Years*, 529–36; Longerich, *Holocaust*, 403–4.

56 Longerich, *Himmler*, 693–4; Zuccotti, *The Holocaust, the French, and the Jews*, 190–4, 199–202.

57 13 December 1943, 24 January, 1 February 1944, letter written 8 March 1944, *Berr Journal*, 228–31, 246, 252, 263–4 and 'Afterword' by Mariette Job, 271–3.

58 17, 20, 25 January 1943, *Berg Diary*, 208, 212–13.

59 Engelking and Leociak, *The Warsaw Ghetto*, 745–8; Yitzhak Katzenelson, *Vittel Diary [22.5.43–16.9.43]*, trans. Myer Cohen (Tel Aviv: Ghetto Fighters House, 1964), 25–31, 43–5; 1 March 1944, *Berg Diary*, 244. Two trainloads of passport holders from the Hotel Polski went to the exchange camp at Bergen-Belsen.

60 Poznanski, *Jews in France during World War II*, 443–6; Ryan, *The Holocaust and the Jews of Marseille*, 194–203; Zuccotti, *The Holocaust, the French, and the Jews*, 197–9; Safrian, *Eichmann's Men*, 178–9; for analysis of the final wave of killings in France and the leading role of Alois Brunner, see Tal Bruttmann, *La logique des bourreaux 1943–1944* (Paris: Hachette, 2006).

61 Zuccotti, *The Holocaust, the French, and the Jews*, 201–2.

62 3 February 1944, Koker, *Diary*, 331–2 and van Pelt 'Epilogue: The Final Year', 336–46; Gutterman, *A Narrow Bridge to Life*, 97–109.

63 Hesdörffer, *Twelve Years of Nazi Terror*, 85–100; 23 November, 10 December 1943, 16, 25 February 1944, Mechanicus, *Diary*, 195–6, 205, 255–6, 263–4 and Presser's 'Introduction', 12; Wasserstein, *The Ambiguity of Virtue,* 202–12.

64 Hesdörffer, *Twelve Years of Nazi Terror*, 85–100, 129–71; 4 October 1944, *Weiss Diary*, 117–33; Lederer, *Ghetto Theresienstadt*, 145–67.

65 Jean-Claude Favez, *The Red Cross and the Holocaust*, trans. John and Beryl Fletcher (Cambridge: Cambridge University Press, 1999), 22–43, 54–72, 83–91.

66 24 April, 23 May, June 1944 (all dates are approximate), *Manes Diary*, 144–5, 153–5, 170–6; *Weiss Diary*, 88, 94, 101–2; Favez, *The Red Cross and the Holocaust*, 43–4, 73–4; Rothkirchen, *The Jews of Bohemia and Moravia*, 256–7.

67 April, 30 September 1944 (approximate dates), *Manes Diary*, 233, 240–1; 17, 28 September 1944, *Weiss Diary*, 106–15.

68 Fritz, *Ostkrieg*, 429–33.

69 Arad, *The Holocaust in the Soviet Union*, 329–33; Daniel Blatman, *The Death Marches. The Final Phase of Nazi Genocide*, trans. Chaya Galai (Cambridge MA: Harvard University Press, 2011), 57–64; cf. Wachsmann, *KL*, 543–53, arguing that the evacuations were consistently brutal.

70 Katz, *One Who Came Back*, 132–54, 163–80.

71 9 January 1945, Tory, *Surviving the Holocaust*, 509–19; Angerick and Klein, *The 'Final Solution' in Riga*, 405–14.

72 Epstein, *Model Nazi*, 263–4.

73 8, 11, 14, 18, 28, February, 6, 7 March 1944, *Lodz Ghetto Chronicle*, 444–7, 448–9, 452, 454–6, 463, 468–70; Trunk, *Lodz Ghetto*, 250–4; Horowitz, *Ghettostadt*, 268–76.

74 16–19, 24, 26, 30 June, 8, 13 July 1944, *Lodz Ghetto Chronicle*, 503–11, 514–15, 515–17, 518, 522, 524–5; Montague, *Chelmno and the Holocaust*, 149–50.

75 17, 23, 25, 30 July 1944, *Lodz Ghetto Chronicle*, 527–8, 532, 534, 536; Rosenfeld, *In the Beginning was the Ghetto*, 280–1; Trunk, *Lodz Ghetto*, 394–9; Horowitz, *Ghettostadt*, 282–96.

76 Trunk, *Lodz Ghetto*, 261–9; Horowitz, *Ghettostadt*, 296–8.

77 Krakowski, *Chelmno*, 193–207.

78 Evans, *The Third Reich at War*, 630–46; Kershaw, *Hitler 1936–1945*, 698–705; Ian Kershaw, *The End. Hitler's Germany, 1944–45* (London: Allen Lane, 2011), 26–53, 144–5; Christof Dipper, '20 July and the "Jewish Question"' in Bankier ed., *Probing the Depths of German Antisemitism*, 463–78, but cf. Joachim Fest, *Plotting Hitler's Death. The German Resistance to Hitler 1939–1945*, trans. Bruce Little (London: Weidenfeld and Nicolson, 1996), 239–40, 326–7; Ulrich von Hassell was arrested on 28 July 1944 and executed on 8 September 1944, *Von Hassell Diaries*, 325–8; 21 July 1944, Reck-Malleczewen, *Diary of a Man in Despair*, 216–18.

79 Traudl Junge, *Until the Final Hour. Hitler's Last Secretary*, ed. Melissa Müller, trans. Anthea Bell (London: Weidenfeld and Nicolson, 2003), 134.

80 Field Post Inspection Office Army Group North, 'Report for September 1944', 5 October 1944, and SD Stuttgart Office Dept III C4, 'Report on the Leadership', 6 November 1944, *Secret Nazi Reports*, 652, 656; 20 August, 5 September 1944, 14 January 1945, *Klemperer Diary*, II, 321, 338, 375.

81 Weinberg, *A World at Arms*, 751–2, 755–7; Fritz, *Ostkrieg*, 422–9; Evans, *The Third Reich at War*, 65; Kershaw, *The End*, 60–75, 79–80; cf. Tooze, *The Wages of Destruction*, 627–40.

82 Weinberg, *A World at Arms*, 697–702, 760–5; Blumenson, *The Duel for France*, 367–408; Robin Neillands, *The Battle for the Rhine 1944* (London: Cassell, 2005) and Lloyd Clark, *Crossing the Rhine. Breaking Into Nazi Germany 1944 and 1945 – The Greatest Airborne Battles in History* (New York: Grove Press, 2008), 1–235, explain Allied misadventures.

83 Norman Davies, *Rising '44. 'The Battle for Warsaw'* (London: Pan, 2004), 403; Weinberg, *A World at Arms*, 703–13, 759–60; Zuckerman, *A Surplus of Memory*, 528–44; Willenberg, *Revolt in Treblinka*, 224–45; Paulsson, *Hidden City*, 165–83, 187–9, 189–96; Grabowski, *Hunt for the Jews*, 130–4.

84 Braham, *Politics of Genocide*, vol. 2, 947–56; Vagi, Csosz and Kadar eds, *The Holocaust in Hungary*, 147–60; Cesarani, *Eichmann*, 189–90.

85 Cole, *Holocaust City*, 201–4; Bauer, *Jews for Sale?*, 219–21; Cesarani, *Eichmann*, 190–5; Krisztián Ungváry, *The Battle for Budapest. 100 Days in World War II* (London: I. B. Tauris, 2003), 236–52.

86 László Karsai, 'The Last Phase of the Hungarian Holocaust: The Szálasi regime

and the Jews', in Braham and Miller eds, *The Nazis' Last Victims*, 103–16; on the dire conditions and the rescue efforts of diplomats, Levine, *Raoul Wallenberg in Budapest*, 290–368.

87 Longerich, *Holocaust*, 404–5; Blood, *Hitler's Bandit Hunters*, 269–70; Mawdsley, *Thunder in the East*, 352–5.

88 Yahil, *The Holocaust*, 523–4; Safrian, *Eichmann's Men*, 207–8.

89 Müller, *Eyewitness Auschwitz*, 110–23; Alfred Wetzler, *Escape from Hell. The True Story of the Auschwitz Protocol*, trans. Ewald Osers, ed. Péter Várnan (New York: Berghahn, 2007), 99–190 is a dramatized rendering of the escape.

90 Müller, *Eyewitness Auschwitz*, 110–23; the protocol is reproduced in Wetzler, *Escape from Hell*, 235–75; Fleming, *Auschwitz, the Allies and Censorship of the Holocaust*, 229–48; Miroslav Karny, 'The Vrba and Wetzler Report', in Gutman and Berenbaum eds, *Anatomy of the Auschwitz Death Camp*, 553–68.

91 Fleming, *Auschwitz, the Allies and Censorship of the Holocaust*, 248–51; Porat, *The Blue and the Yellow Stars of David*, 212–20; Cesarani, *Arthur Koestler*, 222–5.

92 Wasserstein, *Britain and the Jews of Europe*, 279–89; Overy, *The Bombing War*, 366–8, 583–5; see Michael J. Neufeld and Michael Berenbaum eds, *The Bombing of Auschwitz* (New York: St Martin's Press, 2000), for essays evaluating the contemporary evidence, assessing the conduct of the chief historical actors, and arriving at widely diverging conclusions.

93 Hermann Langbein, *Against All Hope. Resistance in the Nazi Concentration Camps 1938–1945* (New York: Continuum, 1994), 284–8; Swiebocki, *Auschwitz 1940–1945*, vol. IV, 245–52.

94 Müller, *Eyewitness Auschwitz*, 143–7, 152–60; testimony of Salman Lewental, in Bezwínská and Czech eds, *Amidst a Nightmare of Crime*, 162–70; Feinsilber deposition, 65–7.

95 Müller, *Eyewitness Auschwitz*, 160–3; Andrzej Strzelcki, 'The Liquidation of the Camp', in Danuta Czech et al. eds, *Auschwitz 1940–1945. Central Issues in the History of the Camp*, vol. V, *Epilogue*, trans. William Brand (Oswieçim: Auschwitz State Museum, 2000), 16–20; Wachsmann, *KL*, 537–41.

96 Van Pelt and Dwork, *Auschwitz*, 340; Piper, *Auschwitz 1940–1945*, vol. III, 205–31 and his essay 'The Number of Victims', in Gutman and Berenbaum eds, *Anatomy of the Auschwitz Death Camp*, 61–76.

97 Hitler's New Year message 1945 in Patrick Romane ed., *The Essential Hitler* (Wauconda, IL: Bolchazy-Carducci, 2007), 416–26; Kershaw, *Hitler 1936–1945*, 792–3; 5, 14 January 1945, *Klemperer Diary*, II, 373–4, 375.

98 Kershaw, *Hitler 1936–1945*, 756–61; Fritz, *Ostkreig*, 439–49, 459–69; Richard Bessel, *Germany 1945. From War to Peace* (London: Simon and Schuster, 2009), 15–47.

99 Blatman, *The Death Marches*, 51–7.

100 Ibid, 368–88.

101 Ibid, 250–61, 388–405, 407–27; Wachsmann, *KL*, 585–6, argues that the purpose of the forced marches was not annihilatory, that neither Jews nor other prisoners were intended to die in such vast numbers.

102 Gilbert, *Holocaust*, 769–77; cf. Yahil, *The Holocaust*, 526–7; Blatman, *The Death Marches*, 136–7.

103 Pohl, 'The Holocaust and the concentration camps', in Caplan and Wachsmann eds, *Concentration Camps in Nazi Germany*, 159–60; Schaft and Zeidler, *Commemorating Hell. The Public Memory of Mittlebau-Dora*, 25–38; Gutterman, *A Narrow Bridge to Life*, 77–8, 97–9, 119–30.

104 Müller, *Eyewitness Auschwitz*, 165–6; Adelsberger, *Auschwitz. A Doctor's Story*, 116–26; Daniel Blatman, 'The Death Marches, January–May 1945: Who Was Responsible for What?', *Yad Vashem Studies* 28 (2000), 155–202, esp. 161–74 on the evacuation of Auschwitz.

105 Müller, *Eyewitness Auschwitz*, 165–71.

106 Adelsberger, *Auschwitz. A Doctor's Story*, 126–9.

107 Nahon, *Birkenau. Camp of Death*, 109–16; Blatman, 'The Death Marches', 174–9 on the evacuation of Stutthof.

108 Katz, *One Who Came Back*, 195–210.

109 Hesdörffer, *Twelve Years of Nazi Terror*, 207–24.

110 Blatman, *The Death Marches*, 117–25.

111 Ibid, 272–342.

112 Longerich, *Holocaust*, 414–18; Wachsmann, *KL*, 576–95.

113 David Cesarani, 'A Brief History of Bergen-Belsen', in Suzanne Bardgett and David Cesarani eds, *Belsen 1945. New Historical Perspectives* (London: Vallentine Mitchell, 2006), 13–21; Christine Lattek, 'Bergen-Belsen: From "Privileged" Camp to Death Camp', in Jo Reilly et al. eds, *Belsen in History and Memory* (London: Frank Cass, 1997), 37–51, esp. 43–52; Ruth Zariz, 'Exchange of Populations as a Means of Jewish Salvation', in Cohen, Cochavi, Gelber eds, *The Shoah and the War*, 405–16.

114 14 August 1944, Abel J. Herzberg, *Between Two Streams. A Diary from Bergen-Belsen*, trans. Jack Santcross (London: Tauris Parke, 2008), 11; Habbo Knoch and Marlis Buchholz et al. eds, *Bergen-Belsen* (Göttingen: Wallstein Verlag, 2010).

115 Lattek, 'Bergen-Belsen', 52–5; Wachsmann, *KL*, 454–5.

116 18 August, 17, 23 September, 8 November 1944, Herzberg, *Between Two Streams*, 18–19, 100–1, 110, 160; Carol Ann Lee, *Roses from the Earth. The Biography of Anne Frank* (London: Viking, 1999), 179–84.

117 16 March 1945, Herzberg, *Between Two Streams*, 202; Lattek, 'Bergen-Belsen', 55–9; Wachsmann, *KL*, 565–8.

118 Fried, *The Road to Auschwitz*, 157–8.

119 Ibid, 160; Richard Breitman, 'Himmler and Bergen-Belsen', in Reilly et al. eds, *Belsen in History and Memory*, 72–84, esp. 80–81; Ben Shephard, *After Daybreak. The Liberation of Belsen, 1945* (London: Cape, 2005), 7–8.

120 Paul Kemp ed., *The Relief of Belsen, April 1945. Eyewitness Accounts* (London: Imperial War Museum, 1991), 10, 13–15.

121 Bauer, *Jews for Sale?*, 223–9; Longerich, *Himmler*, 708–11; Wachsmann, *KL*, 572–6.

122 Longerich, *Himmler*, 724–31; Sune Persson, *Escape from the Third Reich*, trans. Graham Long (Barnsley: Skyhorse, 2009), 28–30, 33–45, 58–62, 75–100.

123 Bauer, *Jews for Sale?*, 241–50; Persson, *Escape from the Third Reich*, 139–48, 174–81, 187–8, 206–15.

124 Longerich, *Himmler*, 728–31; Kershaw, *Hitler 1936–1945*, 817–18; Richard Breitman, 'Nazi Espionage: The Abwehr and SD Foreign Intelligence', in Breitman et al. eds, *US Intelligence and the Nazis*, 93–120, esp. 110–11; Persson, *Escape from the Third Reich*, 246–9.

125 Poznanski, *Jews in France during World War II*, 462–73; Zuckerman, *A Surplus of Memory*, 550–7.

126 Dan Stone, *The Liberation of the Camps: The End of the Holocaust and Its Aftermath* (London: Yale University Press, 2015), 18–21. For a rudimentary overview see John Bridgman, *The End of the Holocaust and the Liberation of the Camps* (London: Batsford, 1990).

127 Hart, *I shall survive*, 90–121.

128 Nahon, *Birkenau*, 109–17.

129 Adelsberger, *Auschwitz. A Doctor's Story*, 128–31.

130 October 1944–January 1945, 1–5 May 1944, *Weiss Dairy*, 143–63, 164–76.

131 19, 22–27 February, 28 April, 6 May 1945, *Klemperer Diary*, II, 389–96, 398–9, 452, 455.

Epilogue

1 *Documents on the Holocaust*, 162; Kershaw, *Hitler 1936–1945*, 821–3, 826–8; Friedländer, *Nazi Germany and the Jews*, vol. 2, 656. Translations vary between publications.

2 Kershaw, *The End*, 360–71. For the death throes of the Third Reich, see David Stafford, *Endgame 1945. Victory, Retribution, Liberation* (London: Little Brown, 2007) and Richard Bessel, *Germany 1945* (London: Simon and Schuster, 2009).

3 Stone, *Liberation*, 105–27; William I. Hitchcock, *Liberation. Europe 1945* (London: Faber and Faber, 2008), 215–80.

4 Alex Grobman, *Rekindling the Flame. American Chaplains and the Survivors of European Jewry, 1944–1945* (Detroit: Wayne State University Press, 1993), 55–61, 65–70, 89–110; Isaac Levy, *Witness to Evil. Bergen-Belsen 1945* (London: Peter Halban, 1995), 16–35, 44–63, for the activities of the Senior Jewish Chaplain to the British Liberation Army.

5 Jacques Vernant, *The Refugee in the Post-War World* (London: Allen and Unwin, 1953), 30–3; Leonard Dinnerstein, *America and the Survivors of the Holocaust* (New York: Columbia University Press, 1982), 5–8; London, *Whitehall and the Jews*, 255–63; David Cesarani, 'Great Britain', in David Wyman ed., *The World Reacts to the Holocaust* (Baltimore: Johns Hopkins University Press, 1996), 614–17. For an overview of the DP question in general see Mark Wyman, *Europe's Displaced Persons, 1945–1951* (Toronto: Associated University Presses, 1986).

6 Angelika Königseder and Juliane Wetzel, *Waiting for Hope. Jewish Displaced Persons in Post-World War II Germany*, trans. John Broadwin (Evanston, IL:

Northwestern University Press, 2001), 15–30; Dinnerstein, *America and the Survivors of the Holocaust*, 9–38; Stone, *Liberation*, 127–36.

7 Appendix B, Dinnerstein, *America and the Survivors of the Holocaust*, 291–305.

8 Königseder and Wetzel, *Waiting for Hope*, 61.

9 Margarete Myers Feinstein, 'Jewish Observance in Amalek's Shadow: Mourning, Marriage, and Birth Rituals among Displaced Persons in Germany', in Patt and Berkowitz eds, *'We Are Here'. New Approaches to Jewish Displaced Persons in Postwar Germany*, 257–88; Gabriel Finder and Judith Cohen, 'Memento Mori: Photographs from the Grave', in Gabriel Finder et al. eds, *Polin*, vol. 20, *Making Holocaust Memory* (Portland, OR: Littman Library, 2008), 3–54. For an overview of the Jewish DP experience, see Margarete Myers Feinstein, *Holocaust Survivors in Postwar Germany* (New York: Cambridge University Press, 2010).

10 Königseder and Wetzel, *Waiting for Hope*, 130–41; Feinstein, *Holocaust Survivors*, 238–48; Gabriel Finder and Laura Jockusch, 'Introduction', in Gabriel Finder and Laura Jockusch eds, *Jewish Honor Courts: Revenge, Retribution, and Reconciliation in Europe and Israel After the Holocaust* (Detroit: Wayne State University Press, 2014), 2–7 and in the same volume the separate studies by David Engel, 'Why Punish Collaborators?', 29–48; Laura Jockusch, 'Rehabilitating the Past. Jewish Honor Courts in Allied-Occupied Germany', 49–82; Gabriel Finder, 'Judenrat on Trial. Postwar Polish Jewry Sits in Judgment on its Wartime Leadership', 83–106; Simon Perego, 'Jurys d'honneur. The Stakes and Limits of Purges Among Jews in France After the Liberation', 137–64; Helga Embacher, 'Viennese Jewish Functionaries on Trial. Accusations, Defense Strategies and Hidden Agendas', 165–96; Katarzyna Person, 'Jews Accusing Jews. Denunciations of Alleged Collaborators in Jewish Honor Courts', 225–46.

11 Natalia Aleksiun, 'The Central Jewish Historical Commission in Poland, 1944–1947', in Finder et al. eds, *Polin*, vol. 20, 74–97; Laura Jockusch, *Collect and Record! Jewish Holocaust Documentation in Early Postwar Europe* (New York: Oxford University Press, 2012), 89–120.

12 Jockusch, *Collect and Record!*, 50–74, 121–59, 160–84. The early, and too often overlooked, research and documentation activity is captured in CDJC, *Les Juifs en Europe (1939–1945). Rapports Présentés à la Première Conférence Européenne des Commissions Historiques et des Centres de Documentation Juifs* (Paris: Éditions du Centre, 1949).

13 Hagit Lavsky, *New Beginnings. Holocaust Survivors in Bergen-Belsen and the British Zone in Germany, 1945–1950* (Detroit: Wayne State University Press, 2002), 51–60, 66–77; Königseder and Wetzel, *Waiting for Hope*, 161–210; Feinstein, *Holocaust Survivors*, 240–1.

14 Eva Kolinsky, *After the Holocaust: Jewish Survivors in Germany after 1945* (London: Pimlico, 2004), 151–69; Jay Geller, *Jews in Post-Holocaust Germany, 1945–1953* (New York: Cambridge University Press, 2005), 18–49; Michael Brenner, *After the Holocaust: Rebuilding Jewish Lives in Postwar Germany*, trans. Barbara Harshav (Princeton: Princeton University Press, 1999), 42–9, 52–4, 67–90.

15 Königseder and Wetzel, *Waiting for Hope*, 83–90; Alex Grobman, *Battling for*

Souls. The Vaad Hatzala Rescue Committee in Post-war Europe (Jersey City, NJ: Ktav, 2004), 68–202; Frank Stern, 'The Historic Triangle: Occupiers, Germans and Jews in Postwar Germany' and Constantin Goschler, 'The Attitude towards Jews in Bavaria after the Second World War', in Robert G. Moeller ed., *West Germany Under Construction. Politics, Society, and Culture in the Adenauer Era* (Ann Arbor: University of Michigan Press, 1997), 199–230 and 231–50.

16 Antony Polonsky, *The Jews in Poland and Russia*, vol. III, 603–8, 624–52; Monika Adamczyk-Garbowska, *Patterns of Return. Survivors' Postwar Journeys to Poland* (Washington, DC: US Holocaust Memorial Museum, 2007); Alina Skibinska, 'The Return of Jewish Holocaust Survivors and the Reaction of the Polish Population' and Andrzej Zbikowski, 'The Post-War Wave of Pogroms and Killings', in Feliks Tych and Monika Adamczyk-Garbowska eds, *Jewish Presence and Absence. The Aftermath of the Holocaust in Poland, 1944-2010*, trans. Grzegorz and Jessica Taylor Kucia (Jerusalem: Yad Vashem, 2014), 25–66 and 67–94. See also Gross with Gross, *Golden Harvest*, for continuities between wartime and post-war.

17 Bogner, *At the Mercy of Strangers*, 186–206, 216–18, 227–86; Gafny, *Dividing Hearts: The Removal of Jewish Children from Gentile Families in Poland in the Immediate Post Holocaust Years*, 81–272.

18 Jan Tomasz Gross, *Fear: Anti-Semitism in Poland after Auschwitz: An Essay in Historical Interpretation* (Princeton: Princeton University Press, 2006), 34–191; Zuckerman, *A Surplus of Memory*, 654–66; Natalia Aleksiun, 'The Polish Catholic Church and the Jewish Question in Poland, 1944–48', *Yad Vashem Studies*, 33, (2005), 143–70.

19 Zvi Mankowitz, *Life Between Memory and Hope: The Survivors of the Holocaust in Occupied Germany* (Cambridge: Cambridge University Press, 2002), 139–41; Zuckerman, *A Surplus of Memory*, 650; Zorach Warhaftig, *Uprooted: Jewish Refugees and Displaced Persons after Liberation* (New York: American Jewish Congress, 1946), 39.

20 Stone, *Liberation*, 180–7; Arieh J. Kochavi, *Post-Holocaust Politics: Britain, the United States, and Jewish Refugees, 1945-1948* (Chapel Hill and London: University of North Carolina Press, 2002), 60–72, 78–80.

21 For a personal account of the Cyprus camps by the leading AJJDC relief worker, see Morris Laub, *Last Barrier to Freedom: Internment of Jewish Holocaust Survivors on Cyprus, 1946-1949* (Berkeley, CA: Judah Magnes Museum, 1985).

22 For the conflict in Palestine, see David Cesarani, *Major Farran's Hat. Murder, Scandal and Britain's War against Jewish Terrorism, 1945-1948* (London: Heinemann, 2009); Tom Segev, *1949. The First Israelis* (New York: Henry Holt, 1998), 95–116. One in every three Jews in Israel in 1949 was born in Europe.

23 Dinnerstein, *America and the Survivors of the Holocaust*, 119–253.

24 Pieter Lagrou, 'Return to a Vanished World. European Societies and the Remnants of their Jewish Communities, 1945-1947', in David Bankier ed., *The Jews are Coming Back. The return of the Jews to their countries of origin after WW II* (Jerusalem: Yad Vashem, 2005), 1–24. See also, Pieter Lagrou, *The Legacy of Nazi Occupation: Patriotic Memory and National Recovery in Western Europe, 1945-1965* (Cambridge: Cambridge University Press, 1999), 251–87.

25 Poznanski, *Jews in France during World War II*, 462–73.

26 Renée Poznanski, 'French Apprehensions, Jewish Expectations: From a Social Imaginary to a Political Practice' and Patrick Weil, 'The return of the Jews in the nationality or in the territory of France (1943–1973)', in Bankier ed., *The Jews are Coming Back*, 25–57 and 57–71.

27 Jockusch, *Collect and Record!*, 46–74; Poznanski, 'French Apprehensions, Jewish Expectations'.

28 Frank Caestecker, 'The Reintegration of Jewish Survivors into Belgian Society, 1943–1947', in Bankier ed., *The Jews are Coming Back*, 72–107; Rudi van Doorslaer, 'The Expropriation of Jewish Property and Restitution in Belgium', in Dean, Goschler and Ther eds, *Robbery and Restitution. The Conflict over Jewish Property in Europe* (New York: Berghahn, 2007), 155–70.

29 Moore, *Victims and Survivors*, 238–44; Dienke Hondius, 'Bitter Homecoming. The Return and Reception of Dutch and Stateless Jews in the Netherlands', in Bankier ed., *The Jews are Coming Back*, 108–36, and *Return. Holocaust Survivors and Dutch Anti-Semitism*, trans. David Colmer (Westport, CT: Praeger, 2003), 45–112.

30 J. S. Fishman, 'The Reconstruction of the Dutch Jewish Community and its Implications for the Writing of Contemporary Jewish History', *Proceedings of the American Academy for Jewish Research*, 45 (1978), 67–101; Diane L. Wolf, *Beyond Anne Frank. Hidden Children and Postwar Families in Holland* (Berkeley: University of California Press, 2007), 111–21.

31 Moore, *Victims and Survivors*, 244–9; Ido de Haan, 'An Unresolved Controversy: The Jewish Honour Court in the Netherlands, 1946–50', in Jockusch and Finder eds, *Jewish Honor Courts*, 107–36; Presser, *Ashes in the Wind*, 264–77.

32 Revenge features in the early recordings made by David Boder. They can be accessed at the 'Voices of the Holocaust' project: http://voices.iit.edu/interviewee?doc=piskorzB. On Boder, see Alan Rosen, *The Wonder of Their Voices. The 1946 Holocaust Interviews of David Boder* (New York: Oxford University Press, 2010). Zuckerman, *A Surplus of Memory*, 630–4; Mankowitz, *Life Between Memory and Hope*, 235–42.

33 David Cesarani, 'The International Military Tribunal at Nuremberg: British Perspectives', in H. R. Reginbogin and C. J. M. Safferling eds, *Die Nürnburger Prozesse. Völkerstrafrecht seit 1945* (Munich: K. G. Saur, 2006), 31–8; Donald Bloxham, *Genocide on Trial. War Crimes, Trials and the Formation of Holocaust History and Memory* (Oxford: Oxford University Press, 2001), 97–101.

34 Arieh Kochavi, *Prelude to Nuremberg. Allied War Crimes Policy and the Question of Punishment* (Chapel Hill: University of North Carolina Press, 1998) narrates the tortured decision-making process from 1942 to 1945 and see also his 'The Role of Genocide in the Preparations for the Nuremberg Trials', in David Bankier and Dan Michman eds, *Holocaust and Justice. Representation and Historiography of the Holocaust in Post-War Trials* (Jerusalem: Yad Vashem, 2010), 59–80.

35 Boaz Cohen, 'Dr Jacob Robinson, the Insitute of Jewish Affairs and the Elusive Jewish Voice in Nuremberg', in Bankier and Michman eds, *Holocaust and Justice*, 81–100.

36 Michael Marrus, *The Nuremberg War Crimes Trial 1945–1946. A Documentary History* (New York: Bedford/St Martin's, 1997), 185–215; László Karsai and Judit Molnár eds, *The Kastzner Report. The Report of the Budapest Jewish Rescue Committee, 1943–1945* (Jerusalem: Yad Vashem, 2013), 55–322; Christian Delage, 'The Judicial Construction of the Genocide of the Jews at Nuremberg: Witnesses on the Stand and the Screen', in Bankier and Michman eds, *Holocaust and Justice*, 101–13; Bruce M. Stave and Michele Palmer with Leslie Frank Present, *Witnesses to Nuremberg. An Oral History of American Participants at the War Crimes Trials* (New York: Twayne, 1998), 22.

37 For the fate of the Jews in the IMT verdict see *The Judgment of Nuremberg 1946* (London: The Stationery Office, 1999, first published 1946), 123–31; Shirli Gilbert, '"We Long for a Home". Songs and Survival among Jewish Displaced Persons', in Patt and Berkowitz eds, '*We Are Here*', 289–307. For contrasting interpretations of the IMT's impact on how the public and historians came to understand the fate of the Jews, compare Bloxham, *Genocide on Trial* and Michael Marrus, 'The Holocaust at Nuremberg', *Yad Vashem Studies*, 26 (1998), 5–42.

38 Ludi, *Reparations for Nazi Victims in Postwar Europe*, 1–31; Ronald Zweig, *German Reparations and the Jewish World: A History of the Claims Conference* (Boulder, CO: Westview Press, 1987), 3–5; Nana Sagi, *German Reparations: A History of the Negotiations* (London: Macmillan, 1986), 14–38.

39 Geller, *Jews in Post-Holocaust Germany*, 55–9, 60–5.

40 Ilaria Pavan, 'Indifference and Forgetting: Italy and its Jewish Community, 1938–1970', in Dean, Goschler and Ther eds, *Robbery and Restitution*, 155–70; Guri Schwarz, *After Mussolini. Jewish Life and Jewish Memories in Post-Fascist Italy* (London: Vallentine Mitchell, 2012), 3–13 and 113–41, on the shaping of the historical record to meet contemporary political needs.

41 Stephen Wood and Ian Locke, '"Ex-Enemy Jews": the Fate of the Assets of Holocaust Victims and Survivors in Britain', in Avi Beker ed., *The Plunder of Jewish Property during the Holocaust* (New York: New York University Press, 2001), 209–26; David Cesarani, 'Jewish Victims of the Holocaust and Swiss Banks', *Dimensions*, 191 (1997), 3–6.

42 Stone, *Liberation*, 195–201; Regula Ludi, '"Why Switzerland?" Remarks on a Neutral's Role in the Nazi Program of Robbery and Allied Postwar Restitution Policy', in Dean, Goschler and Ther eds, *Robbery and Restitution*, 182–210. For the stuttering American effort at reparation, see Slany, *US and Allied Efforts to Recover and Restore*. The emerging Cold War is narrated with its impact on retribution in Tony Judt, *Postwar. A History of Europe Since 1945* (London: Heinemann, 2005), 41–62, 100–53,.

43 Jeffrey Herf, *Divided Memory. The Nazi Past in the Two Germanys* (Cambridge, MA: Harvard University Press, 1997), 69–105; Jeffrey M. Peck, 'Germany', in Wyman ed., *World Reacts to the Holocaust*, 447–72; Geller, *Jews in Post-Holocaust Germany*, 91–122; Laura Jockusch, '"Rehabilitating the Past?" Jewish Honor Courts in Allied-Occupied Germany' in Jockusch and Finder eds, *Jewish Honor Courts*, 49–82.

44 Livia Rothkirchen, 'Czechoslovakia', in Wyman ed., *World Reacts to the Holocaust*,

172–5; Yehoshua Büchler, 'Reconstruction Efforts in Hostile Surroundings – Slovaks and Jews after World War II', in Bankier ed., *The Jews Are Coming Back*, 257–76.

45 Kinga Fromjimovics, 'Different Interpretations of Reconstruction: The AJDC and the WJC in Hungary after the Holocaust', in Bankier ed., *The Jews Are Coming Back*, 277–92; Braham, *The Politics of Genocide*, vol. 2, 1301–17, 1317–32; Judit Molnár, 'Gendarmes Before the People's Court' and Agnes Peresztegi, 'Reparation and Compensation in Hungary, 1945–2003', in Molnár ed., *The Holocaust in Hungary*, 677–84 and 648–64.

46 Jean Ancel, '"The New Invasion" – The Return of Survivors from Transnistria', in Bankier ed., *The Jews Are Coming Back*, 231–56; Tuvia Friling, Radu Ioanid, Mihail E. Ionescu, eds, *Final Report of the International Commission on the Holocaust In Romania* (Iasi: Polirom, 2005), 313–32.

47 Yaacov Ro'i, 'The Reconstruction of Jewish Communities in the USSR, 1944–1947', in Bankier ed., *The Jews Are Coming Back*, 186–205; John Garrard and Carol Garrard, *The Bones of Berdichev. The Life and Fate of Vasily Grossman* (New York: Free Press, 1996), 177–92, 195–200; Ilya Altman, 'The History and Fate of *The Black Book* and *The Unknown Black Book*', in Rubenstein and Altman eds, *The Unknown Black Book*, xix–xxxix; Zvi Gittelman, 'Soviet Reactions to the Holocaust, 1945–1991', in Dobroscycki and Gurock eds, *The Holocaust in the Soviet Union*, 3–27.

INDEX

Permissions

The publishers gratefully acknowledge the following for permission to reproduce copyright material. © Ulrich Von Hassel, 2010, *The Ulrich Von Hassel Diaries: The Story of the Forces Against Hitler Inside Germany* and Pen and Sword Books. Lucjan Dobroszycki, *The Chronicle of the Lodz Ghetto*, © 1984 by Lucjan Dobroszycki, published by Yale University Press. Otto Dov Kulka and Eberhard Jäckel eds. William Templer trans. *Jews in the Secret Nazi Reports on Popular Opinion in Germany*, © 2010 by Yale University, published by Yale University Press. Kazimierz Sakowicz, *Ponary Diary, 1941–1943: A Bystander's Account of a Mass Murder*, © 2005 by Yad Vashem, published by Yale University Press. Herman Kruk, *The Last Days of the Jerusalem of Lithuania: Chronicles from the Vilna Ghetto and the Camps, 1939–1944*, © 2002 by YIVO Institute for Jewish Research, published by Yale University Pres. Kazik (Simha Rotem), *Memoirs of a Warsaw Ghetto Fighter*, © 1994, Yale University, published by Yale University Press. *Advocate for the Doomed: The Diaries and Papers of James G. McDonald, 1932–1935*, James G. McDonald, Richard Breitman, Barbara McDonald Stewart, and Severin Hochberg, Copyright © 2007, the United States Holocaust Memorial Museum, Reprinted with permission of Indiana University Press. McDonald, James G., Richard Breitman, Barbara McDonald Stewart, and Severin Hochberg, *Refugees and Rescue: The Diaries and Papers of James G. McDonald, 1935–1945*. Pp 10, 20, 29, 45, 62–64, 121, 270, 618, 622 © 2009, Reprinted with permission of Indiana University Press. *The Unknown Black Book: The Holocaust in the German-Occupied Soviet Territories*, Joshua Rubenstein and Ilya Altman eds, Copyright © 2010, the United States Holocaust Memorial Museum, Reprinted with permission of Indiana University Press. Gutman, Yisrael. *The Jews of Warsaw, 1939–1943: Ghetto, Underground, Revolt*. Pp 401–415, 427–8 © 1989, Reprinted with permission of Indiana University Press. By Christopher Isherwood, from *The Berlin Stories*, copyright © 1935 by Christopher Isherwood. Reprinted by permission of New Directions Publishing Corp. From *Ruth Maier's Diary* by Ruth Maier. Published by Harvill Secker. Reprinted by permission of The Random House Group Limited. Gaynor Johnson, *Our Man in Berlin: The Diary of Sir Eric Phipps, 1933–1937*, 2008, © Gaynor Johnson 2008, reproduced with permission of Palgrave Macmillan. © Martin Doerry, 2005, *My Wounded Heart* and Bloomsbury Publishing Plc. *Jewish Responses to Persecution: 1933–1938: Volume 1*, Jürgen Matthäus and Mark Roseman, © 2010 by AltaMira Press, published by Rowman & Littlefield. *Diary of a Witness, 1940–1943*, Raymond-Raoul Lambert, © 1985 by Librairie Arthème Fayard, published by Rowman & Littlefield. *The Warsaw Diary of Adam Czerniaków:*

Prelude to Doom, Adam Czerniaków, published by Rowman & Littlefield. *The Diary of Samuel Golfard and the Holocaust in Galicia,* Wendy Lower, © 2011 AltaMira Press, published by Rowman & Littlefield. *Germans No More: Accounts of Jewish Everyday Life, 1933–1938,* Margarete Limberg et al, © Margarete Limberg and Hubert Rubsaat, Reproduced by permission of Berghahn Books Inc. *Eyewitness Auschwitz: Three Years in the Gas Chambers,* Filip Muller, published by Ivan R. Dee, 1999. *The Jews & Germans of Hamburg,* J.A.S. Grenville, p.83, p.57, published by Routledge, 2012. *In the Beginning Was the Ghetto: Notebooks from Lodz,* Oskar Rosenfeld, published by Northwestern University Press. *At the Edge of the Abyss: A Concentration Camp Diary, 1943–1944,* David Koker, published by Northwestern University Press. *Your Loyal & Loving Son: Letters of Tank Gunner Karl Fuchs, 1937–41* by Horst Fuchs Richardson, published by Potomac Books, Inc and University of Nebraska Press. *Shanghai Refuge* by Ernest Heppner, published by Potomac Books, Inc and University of Nebraska Press. Reprinted from *The Road to Auschwitz: Fragments of a Life* by Heidi Fried, translated by Michael Meyer, by permission of the University of Nebraska Press, copyright 1990 by Heidi Fried. English translation by Michael Meyer. © 2009 *The Diary of Mary Berg* Ed. Susan Lee Pentlin, Oneworld Publications. Yosef Zelkovitsh and Josef Zelkowicz, *In Those Terrible Days: Writings from the Lodz Ghetto,* Yad Vashem Publications, 2003. Stanislaw Adler, *In the Warsaw Ghetto 1940–1943 an Account of a Witness the Memoirs of Stanislaw Adler,* Yad Vashem Publications, 1982. Israel Cymlich and Oscar Strawczynski, *Escaping Hell In Treblinka,* Yad Vashem Publications, 2007. Y. Arad, Israel Gutman and A. Margaliot eds, *Documents on the Holocaust: Selected Sources on the Destruction of Jews of Germany,* Yad Vashem Publications, 1987. Moty Stromer, *Memoirs of an Unfortunate Person: The Diary of Moty Stromer,* Yad Vashem, 2008. Michel Mazor, *The Vanished City: Everyday Life in the Warsaw Ghetto,* published by Marsilio, 1994. Hillel Seidman, *Warsaw Ghetto Diaries,* published by Targum, 1997. *Surviving the Holocaust: The Kovno Ghetto Diary* by Avraham Tory, edited by Martin Gilbert, translated by Jerzy Michalowicz, with textual and historical notes by Dina Porat, Copyright © 1990 by the President and Fellows of Harvard College. *Soldaten: On Fighting, Killing and Dying: The Secret Second World War Tapes of German POWs,* Sonke Neitzel, published by Simon & Schuster UK Ltd, 2013. Sonke Neitzel, *Tapping Hitler's Generals: Transcripts of Secret Conversations, 1942–1945,* 2007, Pen and Sword Books. Reprinted from *Lvov Ghetto Diary.* Copyright © 1990 by David Kahane and published by the University of Massachusetts Press. *Diary from the Years of Occupation,* Zygmunt Klukowski, published by University of Illinois Press, 1993. *The Wartime Diary of Edmund Kessler,* Edmund Kessler, published by Academic Studies Press, 2010. *The Complete Black Book of Russian Jewry,* Ilya Ehrenburg and Vasily Grossman, copyright © 2003 by Transaction Publishers. Reprinted by permission of the publisher. Excerpts from *A Community Under Siege, The Jews of Breslau under Nazism* by Abraham Ascher, Copyright © 2007 by the Board of Trustees of the Leland Stanford Jr. University, All rights reserved, Reprinted by permission of the publisher, Stanford University Press, sup.org. *Ashes in the Wind: The Destruction of Dutch Jewry,* Dr Jacob Presser, published by Souvenir Press Ltd, 2010. *Journal,* Hélène Berr, *Journal d'Hélène Berr* © Editions Tallandier, 2008, English Translation copyright © David Bellos, 2008, Reproduced by permission of Quercus Editions Limited. *Treblinka: A Survivor's Memory,* Chil Rajchman, © Chil Rajchman for